SCOTT FORESMAN

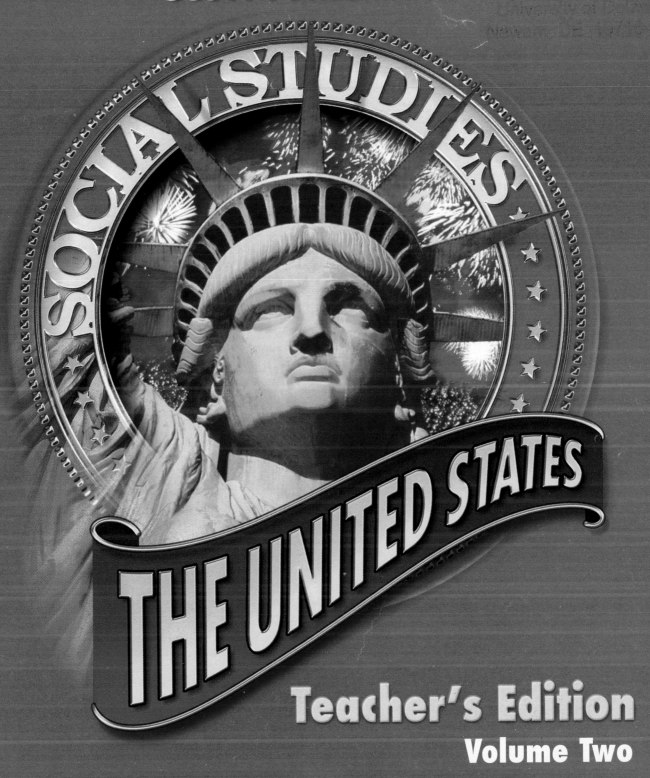

SOCIAL STUDIES

THE UNITED STATES

Teacher's Edition
Volume Two

Editorial Offices: Glenview, Illinois • Parsippany, New Jersey • New York, New York
Sales Offices: Boston, Massachusetts • Duluth, Georgia • Glenview, Illinois •
Coppell, Texas • Sacramento, California • Mesa, Arizona

ISBN: 0-328-23958-5

T 56372

★ ★ ★ **SCOTT FORESMAN** ★ ★ ★
SOCIAL STUDIES
GOLD EDITION

Freedom to read and learn

Reading is the #1 priority. (We understand.) Can you think of a social studies program as content-area reading? Absolutely. *Scott Foresman Social Studies* is designed to extend your reading curriculum. Explicit reading instruction and proven strategies are built into each unit. At Scott Foresman, reading is at the heart of everything we do.

Teach ····▸

Model ····▸

Practice····▸

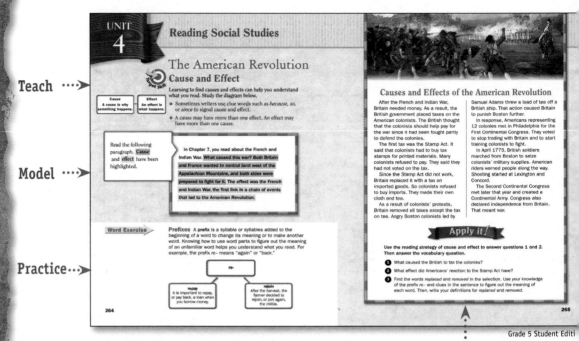

Grade 5 Student Editi

Direct, Explicit Reading Instruction

Only *Scott Foresman Social Studies* provides explicit, four-step reading instruction in every unit to improve students' comprehension.

Apply

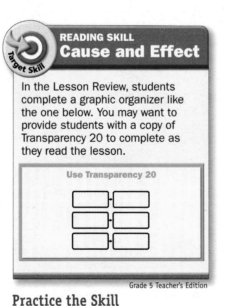

Grade 5 Teacher's Edition

Practice the Skill

Students practice the reading skill throughout each unit, so they can apply it independently.

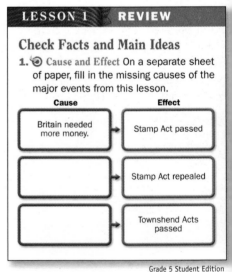

Grade 5 Student Edition

Review the Skill

The target reading skill is monitored continuously in Lesson, Chapter, and Unit Reviews.

Three Content Leveled
Readers—the Same Topic,
Vocabulary, and Skill!

Leveled readers for each unit of
Scott Foresman Social Studies help
all students access the same grade-
level skills and content. Compare
this with other social studies
programs. (There is no comparison!)

- The same topic at three
  reading levels

- The same key content vocabulary

- The same reading
  comprehension skill

Below-Level

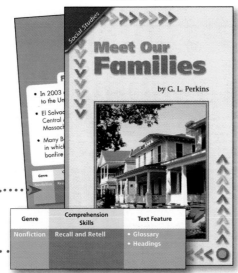

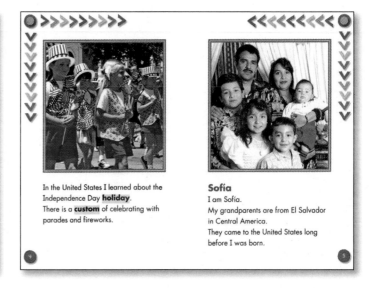

In the United States I learned about the
Independence Day **holiday**.
There is a **custom** of celebrating with
parades and fireworks.

Sofía
I am Sofía.
My grandparents are from El Salvador
in Central America.
They came to the United States long
before I was born.

On-Level

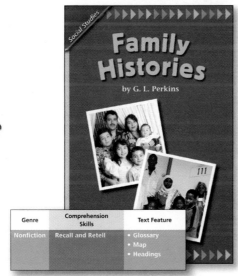

ONLINE
sfsuccessnet.com

Find the Books You Need
with Lightning Speed!

The Scott Foresman online Leveled
Reader Database helps you find
and manage the right books for
every student in your class.

**Select from over 1,000
leveled readers!**

- Search by the criteria you need
- Hear fluently read recordings
- Print out and e-mail assignments
- Teach lessons, use practice pages
- Read online at school or home

Sofía's Story
My name is Sofía. I was born in the
United States, but my grandparents are from
El Salvador. El Salvador is part of Central
America, between North America and South
America. El Salvador is a small country. It
has a tropical climate. El Salvador has several
volcanoes. Earthquakes also happen from time
to time.

My family is getting used to all of the new
things in the United States. The things that
were so different when we first came finally
seem familiar to us.

Advanced

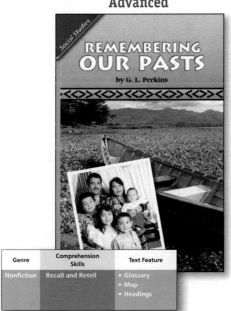

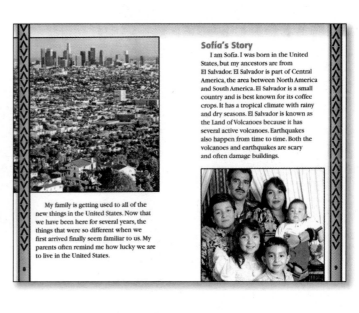

Sofía's Story
I am Sofía. I was born in the United
States, but my ancestors are from
El Salvador. El Salvador is part of Central
America, the area between North America
and South America. El Salvador is a small
country and is best known for its coffee
crops. It has a tropical climate with rainy
and dry seasons. El Salvador is known as
the Land of Volcanoes because it has
several active volcanoes. Earthquakes
also happen from time to time. Both the
volcanoes and earthquakes are scary
and often damage buildings.

My family is getting used to all of the
new things in the United States. Now that
we have been here for several years, the
things that were so different when we
first arrived finally seem familiar to us. My
parents often remind me how lucky we are
to live in the United States.

Freedom to act

You don't have to be a president, a soldier, or a famous celebrity to be a citizen hero. You just need to be responsible and caring. *Scott Foresman Social Studies* fosters the notion that every child can be a citizen hero. Good citizenship is about watching out for each other and lending a hand whenever possible.

CITIZEN HEROES

Racing to the Rescue

On a day of terrifying attacks, the heroic actions of New York City firefighters saved thousands of lives.

New York City's Ladder Company 21 has a long history of fighting fires and saving lives. When the company was first formed in 1890, firefighters rushed to fires on a truck pulled by three horses. Today Ladder Company 21 has computers and modern trucks. But some things have not changed. Firefighting is still a dangerous job that requires great courage. This is why New Yorkers have nicknamed the city's firefighters "New York's Bravest."

On the morning of September 11, 2001, terrorists crashed two planes into New York's World Trade Center. The call for help went out to fire stations all over the city. At Ladder Company 21, Benjamin Suarez was one many firefighters who were just finishing a 24-hour shift. But Suarez did not even think about leaving the job. He called his wife and said,

> *"I have to help the people."*

Then he and his fellow firefighters jumped on their trucks and raced to the scene of the attacks.

As firefighters arrived from around the city, they saw that the twin towers of the World Trade Center were on fire. They rushed into the buildings and up the stairs. "We saw them going up the stairs as we were going down," said a woman who escaped from one of the towers. The firefighters helped people who were injured or lost in the smoke. With the firefighters' help, thousands of people escaped to safety.

Not everyone survived, however. About 4,000 people were trapped in the buildings when they collapsed. More than 300 firefighters, including Benjamin Suarez, died while trying saving the lives of others. Like so many heroes on that terrible day, Suarez put the desire to help other people ahead of his own safety. "That's what Benny was about," said Captain Michael Farrell of Ladder Company 21.

In the days following the terrorist attacks, neighbors visited Ladder Company 21 to show their sympathy for the firefighters who had lost their lives. Many people left flowers and made donations to the firefighters' families. Children wrote letters in which they thanked firefighters for saving lives. Some children drew pictures showing firefighters performing brave actions. The firefighters hung these letters and pictures on the wall of the fire station. Similar scenes took place at fire stations all over the city.

Rudolph Giuliani, the mayor of New York City, thanked firefighters for their incredible courage:

> *"Without courage, nothing else can really happen. And there is no better example, none, than the courage of the Fire Department of the City of New York."*

New York's firefighters not only saved thousands of lives. Their actions inspired the entire nation. In a time of fear and danger, firefighters helped Americans have the courage to face the difficult times ahead.

BUILDING CITIZENSHIP
Caring
Respect
Responsibility
Fairness
Honesty
★ Courage

Courage in Action

Link to Current Events Every day, firefighters, police officers, and other rescue workers perform heroic acts in communities all over the nation. Read a newspaper from your community to find out about the recent actions of your ... ns did they take?

667

Grade 5 Student Editi

Citizen Heroes
Special lessons explore how everyday citizens and well-known Americans show good citizenship.

BUILDING CITIZENSHIP
Caring
Respect
Responsibility
Fairness
Honesty
★ **Courage**

Teach the Core Values of Freedom!
Students learn the important responsibilities of citizenship at every grade level.

Celebrate Freedom
This special resource helps you inspire patriotism through songs, symbols, and sayings of the United States.

Colonial Williamsburg

the nation's largest living history museum and an exclusive partner of Scott Foresman

Grade 3 Student Edition

Living History Lessons

Colonial Williamsburg makes history come alive with artifacts, reenactments, and thought-provoking activities.

Primary Sources CD-ROM

Help students think like historians. Produced in cooperation with Colonial Williamsburg, this award-winning multimedia program introduces primary source documents that spark interest in American history and the ideals of citizenship.

"Awards of Excellence"
Technology And Learning magazine

"Teachers' Choice Award"
Learning magazine

"To be engaged citizens, our children must understand their revolutionary heritage. They must understand that the future of the democracy depends on them."

Bill White, Director of Educational Development, Colonial Williamsburg Foundation

Freedom to explore

Freedom isn't free. People gave their lives for freedom. (And still do every day.) This is why you teach social studies. Students need to see they are the future defenders of America's freedoms. *Scott Foresman Social Studies* presents the story of our nation, the story of families and cultures, the story of our world.

The Revolution Begins

You Are There

It is late at night, April 18, 1775. The streets of Boston are quiet.

Most people are at home. You are outside gathering wood for the fire. Suddenly you hear the pounding feet of a young man as he races past you. He looks upset and seems intent on getting somewhere quickly.

You wonder, "Where is he going?" You don't know it at the time, but he carries important information. He is bringing it to Paul Revere. The young man has learned the British soldiers are on the move. Where are they going? What do they plan to do? How will all of this affect the colonists?

▶ Paul Revere warned colonists that the British were advancing.

PREVIEW

Focus on the Main Idea
The American Revolution began with the battles at Lexington and Concord.

PLACES
Concord, Massachusetts
Lexington, Massachusetts
Charlestown, Massachusetts

PEOPLE
John Hancock
William Dawes
Samuel Prescott
John Parker
William Prescott

VOCABULARY
American Revolution
Battle of Bunker Hill

Paul Revere's Ride

On the night of April 18, 1775, 700 British soldiers began to march from Boston. They were on their way to **Concord**, a town about 20 miles northwest of Boston. Over the past year, Patriot militias had been storing weapons in Concord. Now the British soldiers had orders to "seize and destroy" these military supplies.

There were rumors that the British had another goal as well—to arrest Samuel Adams and **John Hancock**. Like Adams, Hancock was an important Patriot leader in Boston. Both men were staying in Lexington, a town located between Boston and Concord.

The British wanted their march to be a secret. They did not want the militias in **Lexington** or Concord to know they were coming. So General Gage put extra guards on duty and gave them strict orders not to let any colonists leave Boston that night.

However, Paul Revere had learned of their secret plans. He set out to warn the militias in Lexington and Concord. "Two friends rowed me across Charles River," he later wrote. They passed dangerously close to a British warship. Then Revere rode west "upon a very good horse" shouting the news that the British were coming. "I alarmed almost every house, till I got to Lexington," he wrote. At the same time, a shoemaker n...

Revere reached Lexington first. He warned Adams and Hancock, who prepared their escape. When Dawes arrived, he and Revere set out for Concord together. They were joined by a young doctor named **Samuel Prescott**. British soldiers spotted the three riders on the road and ordered them to stop. Revere was captured. Dawes jumped from his horse and escaped into the woods. Prescott got away and rode on to Concord, where he warned the Concord militia to get ready.

REVIEW What was the effect of the ride of Revere, Dawes, and Prescott?
Cause and Effect

Literature and Social Studies

Paul Revere's Ride

In 1863 Henry Wadsworth Longfellow wrote about Paul Revere's midnight ride. Below are the first two stanzas from this famous poem.

*Listen my children and you shall hear
Of the midnight ride of Paul Revere,
On the eighteenth of April, in Seventy-five;
Hardly a man is now alive
Who remembers that famous day and year.*

*He said to his friend, "If the British march
By land or sea from the town to-night,
Hang a lantern aloft in the belfry arch
Of the North Church tower as a signal light,—
One if by land, and two if by sea:
And I on the opposite shore will be,
Ready to ride and spread the alarm
Through every ... village and farm,
... up to arm."*

You Are There
Feel the heart-pounding action! The "You Are There" writing style captivates young readers. Dramatic recordings add power and suspense.

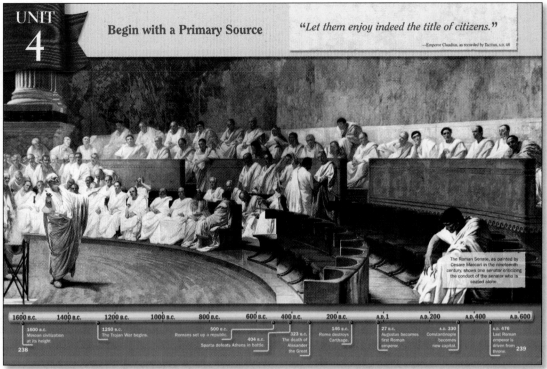

Grade 6 Student Edition

Stunning, Powerful, Gripping

Erase the notion that a social studies textbook has to be boring. *Scott Foresman Social Studies* is filled with rich, compelling visuals and content.

- Primary sources
- Museum-quality artwork
- Colorful maps and place locators
- Graphs, diagrams, time lines
- Brilliant photographs
- Full-page biographies

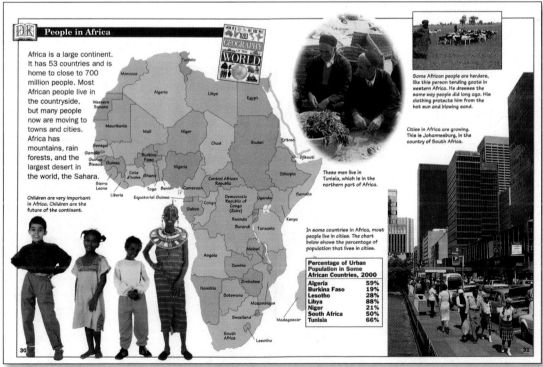

Grade 3 Student Edition

DK Eyewitness Reference Pages

The Eyewitness Book series has sold 50 million copies. Only Scott Foresman embeds richly illustrated, highly accessible DK Eyewitness reference pages into the text.

Freedom to teach

Do you feel you have to be a superhero just to teach reading and math? Who has time for social studies? You have time. Scott Foresman's Quick Teaching Plan and Quick Summary make social studies doable when time is short. Of course, Scott Foresman also provides all the tools you need to really dig into a topic. *Enjoy!*

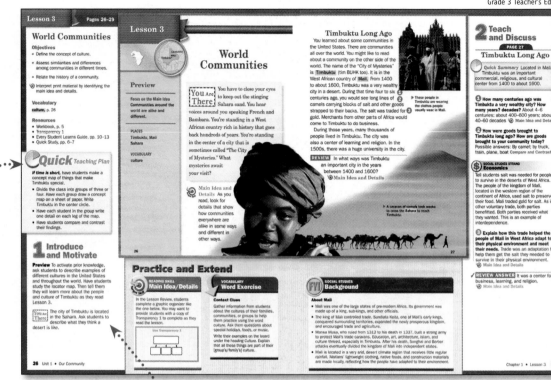

Quick Teaching Plan
Use the Quick Teaching Plan to make lessons a breeze.

Complete Lesson Plan
Dig into a topic with the three-step lesson plan.

Quick Summary
Focus on the key lesson content. It's a snap!

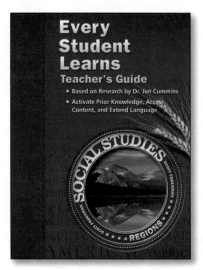

Every Student Learns
Here's quick help for your ESL/ELL students.

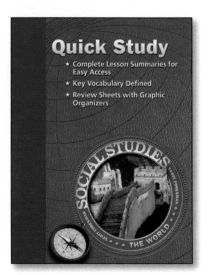

Quick Study
Here's quick access to content, vocabulary, and skills.

Components

Practice and Assessment

- Workbook
- Vocabulary Workbook
- Test Talk Practice Book
- Test Talk Transparencies
- Assessment Book

Leveled Readers

- Content Leveled Readers in English and Spanish
- Online Leveled Readers in English and Spanish

Map and Globe Skills

- Primary Atlas
- Student Atlas
- Big Book Atlas
- Outline Maps
- Laminated Desk Maps
- Map Sack
- Floor Map

Social Studies Activities

- Celebrate Freedom
- Social Studies Plus! A Hands-On Approach
- Read Alouds and Primary Sources
- Daily Activity Bank

Supplemental Resources

- Ancient Communities
- World Communities
- Our United States
- Latin America and Canada
- Native Americans
- Learning About Your State and Community

Reading Social Studies/ESL

- Quick Study
- Every Student Learns Teacher's Guide
- Vocabulary Cards
- Colorful Posters
- Transparencies
- Document-Based Questions
- Multi-Leveled Library
- Literature Library
- Literature Big Books

Technology

- Online Teacher's Edition
- Online Student Edition
- Digital Learning CD-ROM Powered by KnowledgeBox®
- Colonial Williamsburg Primary Sources CD-ROM
- MindPoint™ Quiz Show CD-ROM
- Video Field Trips Package

- Hand in Hand Video Package
- Songs and Music Audio CDs
- AudioText CDs
- Map Resources CD-ROM
- Teacher Resources CD-ROM
- ExamView® Test Bank CD-ROM
- sfsocialstudies.com

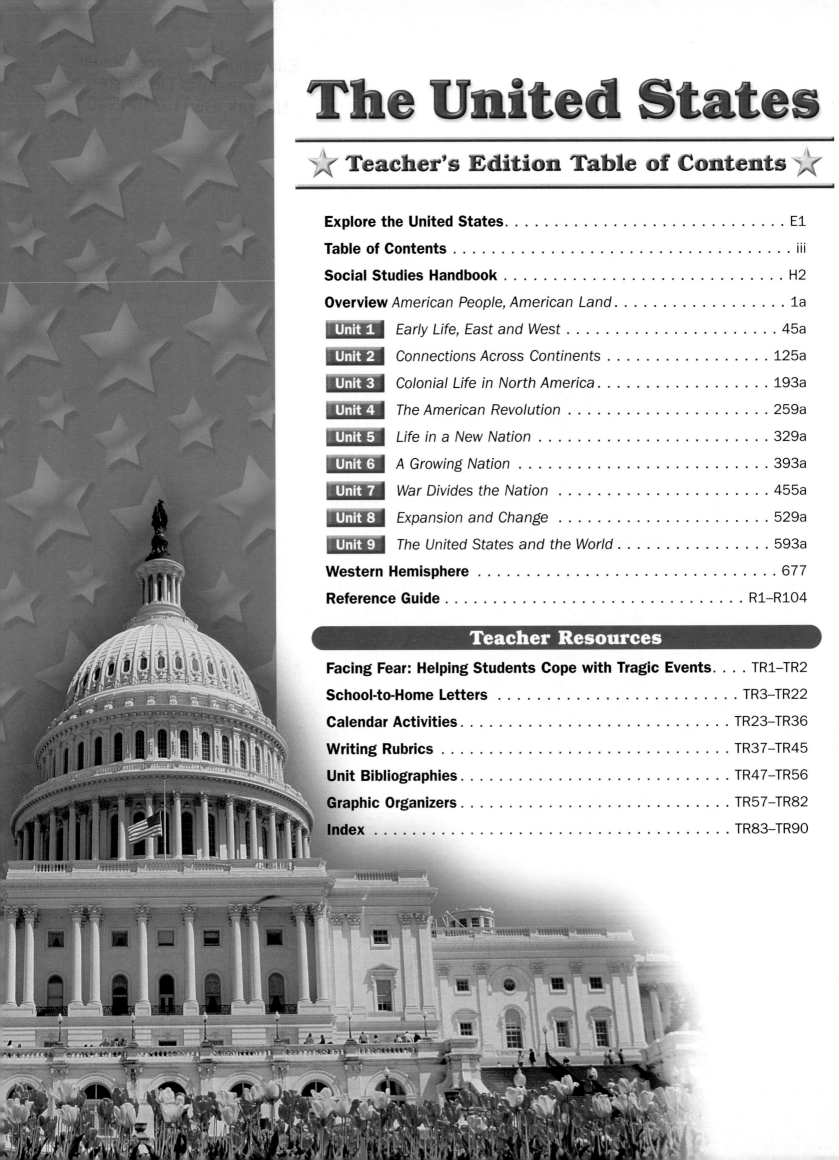

The United States

★ Teacher's Edition Table of Contents ★

Teacher Resources

SCOTT FORESMAN

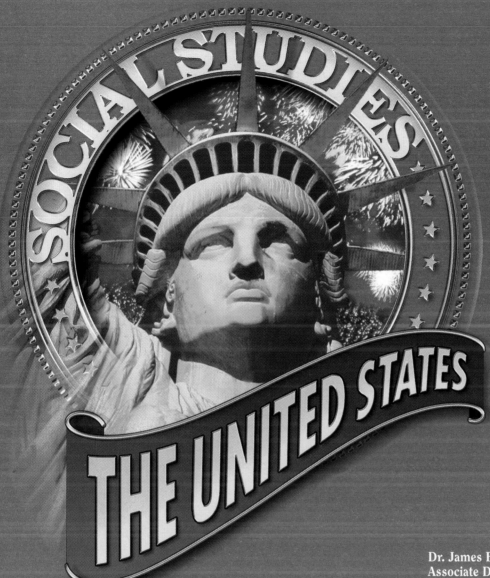

SOCIAL STUDIES

THE UNITED STATES

PROGRAM AUTHORS

Dr. Candy Dawson Boyd
Professor, School of Education
Director of Reading Programs
St. Mary's College
Moraga, California

Dr. Geneva Gay
Professor of Education
University of Washington
Seattle, Washington

Rita Geiger
Director of Social Studies and
Foreign Languages
Norman Public Schools
Norman, Oklahoma

Dr. James B. Kracht
Associate Dean for Undergraduate
Programs and Teacher Education
College of Education
Texas A&M University
College Station, Texas

Dr. Valerie Ooka Pang
Professor of Teacher Education
San Diego State University
San Diego, California

Dr. C. Frederick Risinger
Director, Professional Development
and Social Studies Education
Indiana University
Bloomington, Indiana

Sara Miranda Sanchez
Elementary and Early Childhood
Curriculum Coordinator
Albuquerque Public Schools
Albuquerque, New Mexico

CONTRIBUTING AUTHORS

Dr. Carol Berkin
Professor of History
Baruch College and the Graduate Center
The City University of New York
New York, New York

Lee A. Chase
Staff Development Specialist
Chesterfield County Public Schools
Chesterfield County, Virginia

Dr. Jim Cummins
Professor of Curriculum
Ontario Institute for Studies in Education
University of Toronto
Toronto, Canada

Dr. Allen D. Glenn
Professor and Dean Emeritus
Curriculum and Instruction
College of Education
University of Washington
Seattle, Washington

Dr. Carole L. Hahn
Professor, Educational Studies
Emory University
Atlanta, Georgia

Dr. M. Gail Hickey
Professor of Education
Indiana University-Purdue University
Fort Wayne, Indiana

Dr. Bonnie Meszaros
Associate Director
Center for Economic Education and
Entrepreneurship
University of Delaware
Newark, Delaware

CONTENT CONSULTANTS

Catherine Deans-Barrett
World History Specialist
Northbrook, Illinois

Dr. Michael Frassetto
Studies in Religions
Independent Scholar
Chicago, Illinois

Dr. Gerald Greenfield
Hispanic-Latino Studies
History Department
University of Wisconsin, Parkside
Kenosha, Wisconsin

Dr. Frederick Hoxie
Native American Studies
University of Illinois
Champaign, Illinois

Dr. Cheryl Johnson-Odim
Dean of Liberal Arts and Sciences and
Professor of History
African American History Specialist
Columbia College
Chicago, Illinois

Dr. Michael Khodarkovsky
Eastern European Studies
University of Chicago
Chicago, Illinois

Robert Moffet
U.S. History Specialist
Northbrook, Illinois

Dr. Ralph Nichols
East Asian History
University of Chicago
Chicago, Illinois

CLASSROOM REVIEWERS

Diana Vicknair Ard
Woodlake Elementary School
St. Tammany Parish
Mandeville, Louisiana

Sharon Berenson
Freehold Learning Center
Freehold, New Jersey

Betsy Blandford
Pocahontas Elementary School
Powhatan, Virginia

Nancy Neff Burgess
Upshur County Schools
Buckhannon-Upshur Middle School
Upshur County, West Virginia

Gloria Cantatore
Public School #5
West New York, New Jersey

Stephen Corsini
Content Specialist in Elementary Social Studies
School District 5 of Lexington
and Richland Counties
Ballentine, South Carolina

Deanna Crews
Millbrook Middle School
Elmore County
Millbrook, Alabama

Sally L. Costa
Hellen Caro Elementary School
Pensacola, Florida

LuAnn Curran
Westgate Elementary School
St. Petersburg, Florida

Kevin L. Curry
Social Studies Curriculum Chair
Hickory Flat Elementary School
Henry County, McDonough, Georgia

Sheila A. Czech
Sky Oaks Elementary School
Burnsville, Minnesota

Louis De Angelo
Office of Catholic Education
Archdiocese of Philadelphia
Philadelphia, Pennsylvania

Dr. Trish Dolasinski
Paradise Valley School District
Arrowhead Elementary School
Glendale, Arizona

Dr. John R. Doyle
Director of Social Studies Curriculum
Miami-Dade County Schools
Miami, Florida

Dr. Roceal Duke
District of Columbia Public Schools
Washington, D.C.

Peggy Flanagan
Roosevelt Elementary School
Community Consolidated School District #64
Park Ridge, Illinois

Sherill M. Farrell
Hillsborough County Schools
Valrico, Florida

Mary Flynn
Arrowhead Elementary School
Glendale, Arizona

Su Hickenbottom
Totem Falls Elementary School
Snohomish School District
Snohomish, Washington

Allan Jones
North Branch Public Schools
North Branch, Minnesota

Brandy Bowers Kerbow
Bettye Haun Elementary School
Plano ISD
Plano, Texas

Martha Sutton Maple
Shreve Island School
Shreveport, Louisiana

Lyn Metzger
Carpenter Elementary School
Community Consolidated School District #64
Park Ridge, Illinois

Marsha Munsey
Riverbend Elementary School
West Monroe, Louisiana

Christine Nixon
Warrington Elementary School
Escambia County School District
Pensacola, Florida

Cynthia K. Reneau
Muscogee County School District
Columbus, Georgia

Brandon Dale Rice
Secondary Education Social Science
Mobile County Public School System
Mobile, Alabama

Liz Salinas
Supervisor
Edgewood ISD
San Antonio, Texas

Beverly Scaling
Desert Hills Elementary
Las Cruces, New Mexico

Madeleine Schmitt
St. Louis Public Schools
St. Louis, Missouri

Barbara Schwartz
Central Square Intermediate School
Central Square, New York

Melody Stalker
Escambia County School District
Pensacola, Florida

Editorial Offices:
• Glenview, Illinois
• Parsippany, New Jersey
• New York, New York

Sales Offices:
• Boston, Massachusetts
• Duluth, Georgia
• Glenview, Illinois
• Coppell, Texas
• Sacramento, California
• Mesa, Arizona

www.sfsocialstudies.com

4 5 6 7 8 9 10 V057 15 14 13 12 11 10
09 08 07

Contents

UNIT 1

Early Life, East and West

UNIT 2

Connections Across Continents

UNIT 4

The American Revolution

UNIT 5

Life in a New Nation

UNIT 6

A Growing Nation

UNIT 7

War Divides the Nation

UNIT 8

Expansion and Change

UNIT 9

The United States and the World

Maps

Skills

Reading Social Studies

Map and Globe Skills

Thinking Skills

Research and Writing Skills

Chart and Graph Skills

Fact File

Citizen Heroes

Issues and Viewpoints

Then and Now

Here and There

Time Lines

Notes

Life in a New Nation

UNIT 5

Unit Planning Guide

Unit 5 • Life in a New Nation

Begin with a Primary Source pp. 330–331

Meet the People pp. 332–333

Reading Social Studies, Draw Conclusions pp. 334–335

Chapter Titles	Pacing	Main Ideas
Chapter 10 **Forming a New Government** pp. 336–357 ✓ **Chapter 10 Review** pp. 358–359	6 days	• The new nation struggled to govern itself under the Articles of Confederation. • At the Constitutional Convention, a group of leaders wrote the Constitution, a new plan for a stronger national government. • After a long debate, the states ratified the United States Constitution.
Chapter 11 **The Young United States** pp. 360–385 ✓ **Chapter 11 Review** pp. 386–387	7 days	• George Washington became the nation's first President and organized the new government. • The new nation doubled its size and expanded settlement westward. • The United States fought Britain in the War of 1812 to gain freedom of the seas and to end British interference with the westward expansion of the United States.

End with a Song pp. 388–389

✓ **Unit 5 Review** pp. 390–391

✓ **Unit 5 Project** p. 392

◀ This button honore
George Washingto
when he became t
first President of
United States.

✓ = Assessment Options

◀ **George Washington looks on as a delegate signs the new Constitution.**

Resources	Meeting Individual Needs
• Workbook, pp. 78–83	• ESL Support, TE pp. 340, 347, 354
• Every Student Learns Guide, pp. 142–153	• Leveled Practice, TE pp. 339, 346, 353
• Transparencies 23, 45	• Learning Styles, TE pp. 343, 357
• Quick Study, pp. 72–77	
• Workbook, p. 84	
✓ Chapter 10 Content Test, Assessment Book, pp. 57–59	✓ Chapter 10 Performance Assessment, TE p. 358
✓ Chapter 10 Skills Test, Assessment Book, pp. 59–60	

• Workbook, pp. 85–89	• ESL Support, TE pp. 364, 372, 383
• Every Student Learns Guide, pp. 154–165	• Leveled Practice, TE pp. 365, 373, 381
• Transparencies 6, 20, 23, 46, 47	• Learning Styles, TE pp. 367, 384
• Quick Study, pp. 78–83	
• Workbook, p. 90	
✓ Chapter 11 Content Test, Assessment Book, pp. 61–62	✓ Chapter 11 Performance Assessment, TE p. 386
✓ Chapter 11 Skills Test, Assessment Book, pp. 63–64	

Providing More Depth
Additional Resources

- Trade Books
- Family Activities
- Vocabulary Workbook and Cards
- Social Studies Plus! pp. 112–133
- Daily Activity Bank
- Read Alouds and Primary Sources pp. 84–99
- Big Book Atlas   • Student Atlas
- Outline Maps   • Desk Maps

 Technology

- AudioText
- Video Field Trips: Thomas Jefferson
- Songs and Music
- Digital Learning CD-ROM Powered by KnowledgeBox (Video clips and activities)
- MindPoint® Quiz Show CD-ROM
- ExamView® Test Bank CD-ROM
- Colonial Williamsburg Primary Sources CD-ROM
- Teacher Resources CD-ROM
- Map Resources CD-ROM
- SF SuccessNet: iText (Pupil Edition online), iTE (Teacher's Edition online), Online Planner
- **www.sfsocialstudies.com** (Biographies, news, references, maps, and activities)

 To establish guidelines for your students' safe and responsible use of the Internet, use the Scott Foresman Internet Guide.

Additional Internet Links

To find out more about:

- The United States Government, visit **http://bensguide.gpo.gov**
- The U.S. Presidency, visit **www.whitehousekids.gov**
- Lewis & Clark, click on *History* at **www.pbs.org**

Unit 5 Objectives

Beginning of Unit 5
- Use primary sources to acquire information. (p. 330)
- Identify the contributions of significant individuals during the period following the American Revolution. (p. 332)
- Analyze information by drawing conclusions. (p. 334)

Chapter 10

Lesson 1 A Weak Government
pp. 338–343
- List the main goals of the Articles of Confederation.
- Identify the weaknesses of the Articles of Confederation.
- Describe the causes of Shays' Rebellion.
- Explain the purpose of the Northwest Ordinance.

Lesson 2 Debate in Philadelphia
pp. 344–350
- Identify the purpose of the Constitutional Convention.
- Compare the competing plans for the Constitution.
- Describe the Great Compromise.
- List the goals of the Constitution.
- Identify the contributions of individuals who helped create the U.S. Constitution, including James Madison. (p. 351)

Lesson 3 Ratifying the Constitution
pp. 352–355
- Compare the views of Federalists with those of Antifederalists.
- Describe the Bill of Rights.
- Describe the government created by the Constitution.
- Use a research process to gather and report factual information. (p. 356)

Chapter 11

Lesson 1 Washington as President
pp. 362–366
- Describe how President Washington organized the Executive Branch around the Cabinet.
- Explain how political parties emerged in the American government system.
- Describe how the location and design of the nation's capital was decided upon.
- Describe the accomplishments of significant leaders of the United States, such as Benjamin Banneker. (p. 367)
- Evaluate the effects of the rise of political parties on government in the United States. (p. 368)

Lesson 2 Jefferson Looks West
pp. 370–376
- Explain why and how the United States expanded westward.
- Describe the Louisiana Purchase and tell what effect it had on the nation.
- Identify reasons for and findings of the Lewis and Clark Expedition.
- Use primary and secondary sources, such as visual information, to acquire information. (p. 377)
- Interpret information in visuals, including maps. (p. 378)

Lesson 3 Another War with Britain
pp. 380–384
- Identify reasons why the United States went to war a second time with Britain.
- Describe the main battles and the outcome of the War of 1812.
- Explain why and how "The Star-Spangled Banner" was written.
- Identify the challenges and contributions of people, including Tecumseh, from selected Native American groups. (p. 385)

End of Unit 5
- Sing or recite "The Star-Spangled Banner" and explain its history. (p. 388)
- Compare and contrast arguments for and against the Virginia Plan and the New Jersey Plan. (p. 392)

Assessment Options

✓ Formal Assessment

- **Lesson Reviews,** PE/TE pp. 343, 350, 355, 366, 376, 384
- **Chapter Reviews,** PE/TE pp. 358–359, 386–387
- **Chapter Tests,** Assessment Book, pp. 57–64
- **Unit Review,** PE/TE pp. 390–391
- **Unit Tests,** Assessment Book, pp. 65–68
- **ExamView® Test Bank CD-ROM**
  (test-generator software)

✓ Informal Assessment

- **Teacher's Edition Questions,** throughout Lessons and Features
- **Section Reviews,** PE/TE pp. 339–343, 345–348, 350, 353–355, 363–366, 371–373, 375–376, 381, 383–384
- **Close and Assess,** TE pp. 335, 343, 350, 351, 355, 357, 366, 367, 369, 376, 377, 379, 384, 385, 389

Ongoing Assessment

Ongoing Assessment is found throughout the Teacher's Edition lessons using an **If…then** model.

If = students' observable behavior,

then = reteaching and enrichment suggestions

✓ Portfolio Assessment

- **Portfolio Assessment,** TE pp. 329, 330, 391
- **Leveled Practice,** TE pp. 339, 346, 353, 365, 373, 381
- **Workbook Pages,** pp. 78–91
- **Chapter Review: Write About History,** PE/TE pp. 359, 387
- **Unit Review: Apply Skills,** PE/TE p. 390
- **Curriculum Connection: Writing,** PE/TE pp. 343, 384; TE pp. 351, 353, 356, 373, 381

✓ Performance Assessment

- **Hands-on Unit Project** (Unit 5 Performance Assessment), TE pp. 329, 359, 387, 392
- **Internet Activity,** PE p. 392
- **Chapter 10 Performance Assessment,** TE p. 358
- **Chapter 11 Performance Assessment,** TE p. 386
- **Unit Review: Write and Share,** PE/TE p. 391
- **Scoring Guides,** TE pp. 391–392

Test Talk

Test-Taking Strategies

Understand the Question
- **Locate Key Words in the Question,** TE pp. 345, 373
- **Locate Key Words in the Text,** TE pp. 339, 342

Understand the Answer
- **Choose the Right Answer,** Test Talk Practice Book
- **Use Information from the Text,** TE pp. 354, 375
- **Use Information from Graphics,** PE/TE p. 390; TE p. 349
- **Write Your Answer to Score High,** TE p. 377

For additional practice, use the Test Talk Practice Book.

Featured Strategy

Use Information from Graphics

Students will:

- Understand the question and form a statement that begins "I need to find out. . . ."
- Skim the graphics to find the right information to support their answer.

PE/TE p. 390; **TE** p. 349

Curriculum Connections

Integrating Your Day

The lessons, skills, and features of Unit 5 provide many opportunities to make connections between social studies and other areas of the elementary curriculum.

READING

Reading Skill–Draw Conclusions, PE/TE pp. 334–335, 338, 344, 352, 362

Lesson Review–Draw Conclusions, PE/TE pp. 343, 350, 355, 366

Use Reference Tools, TE p. 378

WRITING

Link to Writing, PE/TE pp. 343, 384

Write a Coded Message, TE p. 351

Write About an Issue, TE p. 353

Library References, TE p. 356

Summarize and Evaluate the Louisiana Purchase, TE p. 373

Consider War and Peace, TE p. 381

MATH

Calculate Area and Ratios, TE p. 342

Balance Equations, TE p. 348

Link to Mathematics, PE/TE pp. 350, 376

Calculate Mileage, TE p. 375

Social Studies

LITERATURE

Read Biographies, TE p. 332

The Constitution, TE p. 350

Learn More About Lewis and Clark, TE p. 374

SCIENCE

Mosquito Habitats, TE p. 366

ART

Interpret Fine Art, TE p. 330

Create a New Setting, TE p. 331

Create a Pamphlet, TE p. 348

Link to Art, PE/TE p. 355

MUSIC / DRAMA

Persuasive Viewpoints, TE p. 382

"The Star-Spangled Banner," TE p. 388

Write an Anthem, TE p. 389

 Look for this symbol throughout the Teacher's Edition to find **Curriculum Connections.**

Reading the Social Studies Textbook

by Candy Dawson Boyd, Ph.D.
St. Mary's College of California

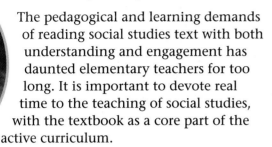

The pedagogical and learning demands of reading social studies text with both understanding and engagement has daunted elementary teachers for too long. It is important to devote real time to the teaching of social studies, with the textbook as a core part of the active curriculum.

A critical first step is for the teacher to carefully explore both the Teacher's Edition and Pupil Edition in the social studies textbook series. A perusal of the table of contents offers the structure of content in the form of units and chapters. Examining how individual components are structured at the lesson, chapter, special feature, unit, and overall textbook levels aids in assessing the reading strategies and skills readers need. Critical questions to ask include: How are lessons and chapters organized? Are there boldfaced subheadings to guide the reader through the text? Is vocabulary classified and labeled in clear ways that show relationships and important traits? Are illustrations, photographs, and primary source materials presented where they need to be to serve as support for the reader? Are visuals labeled in a way that informs the reader without being overwhelming? Are there a variety of clear, focused maps? The answers to these questions will impact how easily the reader will be able to engage text. Below are some ways Scott Foresman *Social Studies* structures its program to help students read with understanding and engagement.

- *Every unit has a **Reading Social Studies** feature that highlights a target reading skill. Students are then encouraged to apply that strategy throughout the unit.*

- *Every lesson ends with a **Lesson Review** that features a graphic organizer, which is often keyed to the reading skill for that unit.*

- ***Map Skill** features are found in many lessons. This allows students to connect visually to the content of the lesson while using map skills.*

- ***Primary Source** quotations are presented in the Pupil Edition in such a way that students can clearly separate expository text from quotations.*

ESL Support

by Jim Cummins, Ph.D.
University of Toronto

In Unit 5, you can use the following fundamental strategy to help ESL students expand their language abilities:

Extend Language

The development of academic language proficiency, for both ESL and non-ESL students, requires instructional strategies designed to enable students to harvest the language they encounter in the content areas. Students extend their command of academic language by reading extensively from texts that contain this form of language and by systematically studying how academic language is put together. Teachers play a crucial role both by providing opportunities and incentives for students to read academic texts and by demystifying how academic language works.

A systematic focus on and exploration of language is essential if students are to develop a curiosity about language and deepen their understanding of how words work. When students know some of the rules and conventions of how academic words are formed, it gives them an edge in extending their vocabulary. It helps them not only figure out the meanings of individual words but also how to form different parts of speech from these words.

The following examples in the Teacher's Edition will help you extend the language abilities of ESL students:

- ***Examine Word Meanings** on p. 340 deals with decoding words with endings and suffixes. Advanced ESL learners find words in the text that have endings and suffixes and learn strategies to determine their meanings.*

- ***Explore Multiple Meanings** on p. 364 asks English Language Learners to formulate different definitions for the word* party. *Intermediate learners extend language by making up sentences for the different meanings.*

Read Aloud

The Preamble to the Constitution of the United States

We the People of the United States, in Order to form a more perfect Union, establish Justice, insure domestic Tranquility, provide for the common defense, promote the general Welfare, and secure the Blessings of Liberty to ourselves and our Posterity, do ordain and establish this Constitution for the United States of America.

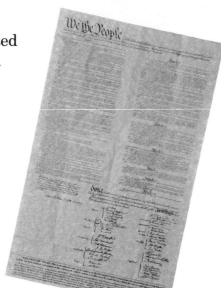

Build Background

- The Constitution of the United States was signed by 39 of 55 delegates on September 17, 1787.
- Ratification of the Constitution of the United States was completed on June 21, 1788.

Definitions

- *preamble:* introduction to a speech or a writing
- *justice:* lawfulness; fairness
- *tranquility:* peacefulness
- *posterity:* people's descendants

Read Alouds and Primary Sources

- *Read Alouds* and *Primary Sources* contain additional selections to be used with Unit 5.

Bibliography

The Inside-Out Book of Washington, D.C., by Roxie Munro (Seastar Publishing Co, ISBN 1-587-17078-7, 2001) **Easy**

The Star-Spangled Banner, by Francis Scott Key (Yearling Books, ISBN 0-440-40697-8, 1992) **Easy** *Children's Book of the Year*

The Voice of the People: American Democracy in Action, by Betsy Maestro (HarperTrophy, ISBN 0-688-16157-X, 1998) **Easy**

Francis Scott Key: Poet and Patriot (Discovery Biographies), by Lillie Patterson and Victor Dowd (Chelsea House Publishing, ISBN 0-791-01461-4, 1991) **On-Level**

More Perfect Union: The Story of Our Constitution, by Betsy Maestro (Econo-Clad Books, ISBN 0-833-56055-7, 1999) **On-Level** *ALA Notable Book*

The U.S. Constitution (Your Government: How It Works), by Joan Banks (Chelsea House Publishing, ISBN 0-791-05991-X, 2001) **On-Level**

A Kids' Guide to America's Bill of Rights: Curfews, Censorship, and the 100-Pound Giant, by Kathleen Krull (Avon Books, ISBN 0-380-97497-5, 1999) **Challenge**

Creating the Constitution: 1787 (Drama of American History), by Christopher Collier and James Lincoln Collier (Benchmark Books, ISBN 0-761-40776-6, 1998) **Challenge**

The Constitution of the United States (American Government in Action), by Karen Judson (Enslow Publishing, ISBN 0-894-90586-4, 1996) **Challenge**

Founding Fathers: Brief Lives of the Framers of the United States Constitution, by M. E. Bradford (University Press of Kansas, ISBN 0-700-60657-2, 2000) **Teacher reference**

The Debate on the Constitution, by Bernard Bailyn, ed. (Library of America, ISBN 0-940-45042-9, 1993) **Teacher reference**

Discovery Channel School Video *George Washington: The Unknown Years* Learn what prepared Washington to be a founding father. 26 minutes.

 Look for this symbol throughout the Teacher's Edition to find **Award-Winning Selections.** Additional book references are suggested throughout this unit.

Life in a
New Nation

UNIT
5

Why do people form governments?

Life in a
New Nation

Unit Overview

As a new nation the United States convened a Constitutional Convention in Philadelphia and wrote and adopted the U.S. Constitution. Political parties were born and westward expansion began. In 1812 Americans entered into another war with Britain.

Unit Outline

Chapter 10 *Forming a New Government,* pp. 336–359

Chapter 11 *The Young United States,* pp. 360–387

Unit Question

- Have students read the question under the picture.

- To activate prior knowledge, discuss students' ideas about government. Why do students think that people form governments? What purposes do governments have? How do governments accomplish their jobs or goals?

- Create a list of students' ideas about the reasons that people form governments.

- ✓**Portfolio Assessment** Keep this list to review with students at the end of the unit on p. 391.

Practice and Extend

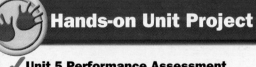

Hands-on Unit Project

✓ Unit 5 Performance Assessment

- The Unit Project, *Two Sides*, found on p. 392, is an ongoing performance assessment project to enrich students' learning throughout the unit.

- This project, which has students staging press coverage of opposing views about the ratification of the Constitution, may be started now or at any time during this unit of study.

- A performance assessment scoring guide is located on p. 392.

Begin with a Primary Source

Objective
- Use primary sources to acquire information.

Resource
- Poster 10

Interpret a Primary Source

- Tell students that this primary source is a quotation from the Preamble, or introduction, to the Constitution of the United States.

- The idea of a Union was an important concept. Before the Constitution, states were joined by the Articles of Confederation, which held the states together in a "league of friendship."

- ✓**Portfolio Assessment** Remind students of the lists they began that described reasons for forming governments. Have students continue their lists, adding the reasons why early Americans formed a government. You may want to read students the full text of the Preamble on p. 329h and p. 348. Review students' lists at the end of the unit on p. 391.

Interpret Fine Art

- This depiction of Washington's inauguration was painted in 1899.

- Remind students that this picture is based on the artist's impression of the event.

- Have students create "thought balloons" for figures in the painting. How might they have felt? What might they have been thinking?

1780 · · · · · 1790 · · ·

| 1781 Articles of Confederation approved by states | 1787 Constitutional Convention begins | 1788 Constitution is ratified | 1789 George Washington becomes the first president | 1791 Bill of Rights ratified |

330

1

Practice and Extend

FYI SOCIAL STUDIES
Background

About the Primary Source
- This phrase comes from the one-sentence Preamble to the U.S. Constitution.
- The delegates to the Constitutional Convention came from a variety of backgrounds. Most of the delegates were born in the colonies. Most had participated in the Revolution—at least 29 were in the Continental Army. Many had served in government positions.
- Tell students that the men who wrote the Constitution were especially concerned with limiting the power of the government, creating a system of checks and balances, and maintaining freedom for citizens.
- The U.S. Constitution is the oldest written national constitution operating in the world.

"...in order to form a more perfect Union..."

—From the Preamble to the United States Constitution

This painting of George Washington taking office as the first President of the United States was painted in 1899.

This time line at the bottom of the page covers a nearly forty-year period, starting shortly after the end of the American Revolution and ending after the conclusion of the War of 1812.

1 **How many years passed between the start of Washington's presidency and the moving of the federal government to Washington, D.C.?** About 11 years **Interpret Time Lines**

2 **Which event on the time line shows that the United States grew beyond its original borders?** Louisiana Purchase expands the size of the country **Draw Conclusions**

3 **How long did the War of 1812 last?** For about 3 years **Analyze Information**

1810   1820

800
ederal government
noves to
Washington, D.C.
1

1803
Louisiana Purchase
expands the size of
the country
2

1812
War of 1812
begins

1815
War of 1812
ends
3

331

 CURRICULUM CONNECTION
Art

Create a New Setting

• Have students select one or two of the people in the painting and draw them in a different setting.
• Students should include a caption.

Meet the People

Objective
- Identify the contributions of significant individuals during the period following the American Revolution.

Resource
- Poster 11

Research the People

Each of the people pictured on these pages played an important part during the time period that began shortly after the American Revolution and ended in 1820. Have students conduct research to find the answers to these questions.

- **Which of the people listed worked for a time as a compiler of almanacs?**
  Benjamin Banneker

- **Which coin has the likeness of Sacagawea on it?** One dollar

- **Besides serving as a political leader, what other contribution did Benjamin Rush make to further human rights?**
  He worked to ensure rights for people with mental illnesses.

- **Which of these people would you most like to meet? Explain why. What questions would you ask him or her?**
  Possible answer: Abigail Adams because she was interested in women's rights. I would ask her what it was like to be in a war with England.

Students may wish to write their own questions about other people on these pages for the rest of the class to answer.

Use the Time Line

Have students use the time line and biographies to answer the following questions.

1 Which person lived the longest? Which person had the shortest life?
James Madison lived the longest. Sacagawea had the shortest life.
Analyze Information

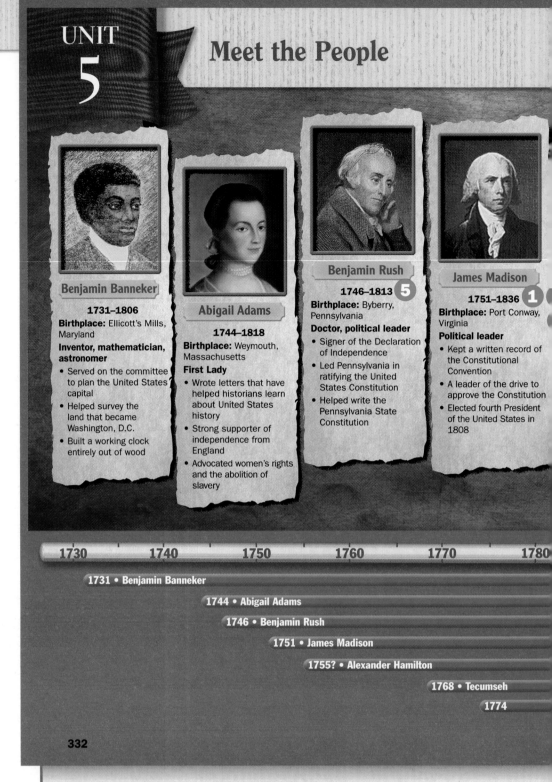

UNIT
5
Meet the People

Benjamin Banneker
1731–1806
Birthplace: Ellicott's Mills, Maryland
Inventor, mathematician, astronomer
- Served on the committee to plan the United States capital
- Helped survey the land that became Washington, D.C.
- Built a working clock entirely out of wood

Abigail Adams
1744–1818
Birthplace: Weymouth, Massachusetts
First Lady
- Wrote letters that have helped historians learn about United States history
- Strong supporter of independence from England
- Advocated women's rights and the abolition of slavery

Benjamin Rush
1746–1813 5
Birthplace: Byberry, Pennsylvania
Doctor, political leader
- Signer of the Declaration of Independence
- Led Pennsylvania in ratifying the United States Constitution
- Helped write the Pennsylvania State Constitution

James Madison
1751–1836 1
Birthplace: Port Conway, Virginia
Political leader
- Kept a written record of the Constitutional Convention
- A leader of the drive to approve the Constitution
- Elected fourth President of the United States in 1808

1730   1740   1750   1760   1770   1780

1731 • Benjamin Banneker
1744 • Abigail Adams
1746 • Benjamin Rush
1751 • James Madison
1755? • Alexander Hamilton
1768 • Tecumseh
1774

332

Practice and Extend

CURRICULUM CONNECTION
Literature

Read Biographies
Use the following biography selections to extend the content.

Dear Benjamin Banneker, by Andrea Davis Pinkney (Voyager, ISBN 0-152-01892-1, 1998) **Easy**

Across America: The Story of Lewis and Clark, by Jacqueline Morley and David Antram (Franklin Watts, ISBN 0-531-15342-8, 1999) **On-Level**

Woman of Independence: The Life of Abigail Adams, by Susan Provost Beller (iUniverse.com, ISBN 0-595-00789-9, 2000) **Challenge**

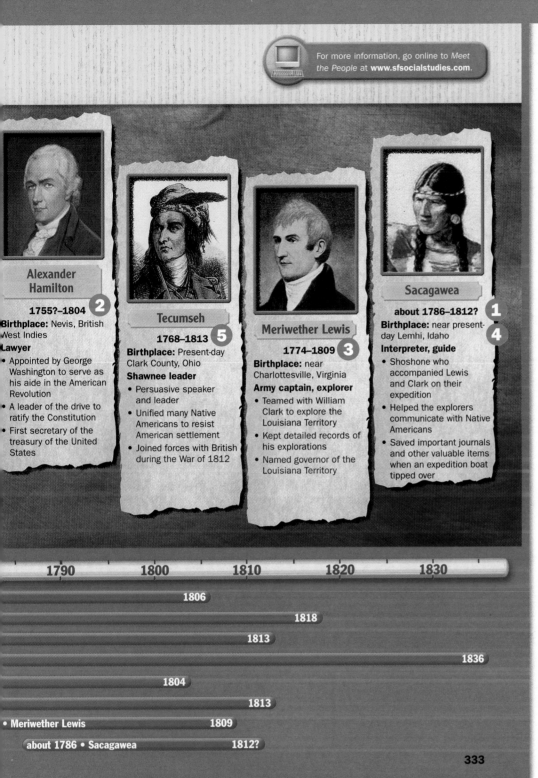

For more information, go online to *Meet the People* at **www.sfsocialstudies.com.**

Alexander Hamilton

1755?–1804 ②

Birthplace: Nevis, British West Indies

Lawyer

- Appointed by George Washington to serve as his aide in the American Revolution
- A leader of the drive to ratify the Constitution
- First secretary of the treasury of the United States

Tecumseh

1768–1813 ⑤

Birthplace: Present-day Clark County, Ohio

Shawnee leader

- Persuasive speaker and leader
- Unified many Native Americans to resist American settlement
- Joined forces with British during the War of 1812

Meriwether Lewis

1774–1809 ③

Birthplace: near Charlottesville, Virginia

Army captain, explorer

- Teamed with William Clark to explore the Louisiana Territory
- Kept detailed records of his explorations
- Named governor of the Louisiana Territory

Sacagawea

about 1786–1812? ①

Birthplace: near present-day Lemhi, Idaho ④

Interpreter, guide

- Shoshone who accompanied Lewis and Clark on their expedition
- Helped the explorers communicate with Native Americans
- Saved important journals and other valuable items when an expedition boat tipped over

1790   1800   1810   1820   1830

1806

1818

1813

1836

1804

1813

• Meriwether Lewis   1809

about 1786 • Sacagawea   1812?

333

② **How were James Madison and Alexander Hamilton alike?** Both were leaders of the drive to approve the Constitution. **Compare and Contrast**

③ **How were Meriwether Lewis and James Madison alike?** Possible answer: Both kept written records of events. **Compare and Contrast**

④ **Why is there a question mark on the year 1812 in Sacagawea's time line?** People are not sure of the exact date of her death. **Interpret Time Lines**

⑤ **Which two people died in the same year?** Benjamin Rush and Tecumseh **Interpret Time Lines**

Biographies

Three of the people shown here are discussed more extensively in the Biography pages in Unit 5.

- James Madison, p. 351
- Benjamin Banneker, p. 367
- Tecumseh, p. 385

Read About the People

The people shown here are discussed in the text on the following pages in Unit 5.

- Benjamin Banneker, pp. 365, 367
- Abigail Adams, p. 366
- Benjamin Rush, p. 354
- James Madison, pp. 345, 346, 351, 353, 382
- Alexander Hamilton, pp. 345, 353, 364, 368
- Tecumseh, pp. 381, 385
- Meriwether Lewis, pp. 374–375, 377
- Sacagawea, pp. 374–375

WEB SITE
Technology

Students can research the lives of the people on this page by clicking on *Meet the People* at **www.sfsocialstudies.com.**

Reading Social Studies

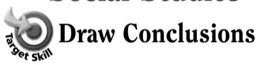

Draw Conclusions

Objective
- Analyze information by drawing conclusions.

Resource
- Workbook, p. 78

About the Unit Target Skill
- The target reading skill for this unit is Draw Conclusions.
- Students are introduced to the unit target skill here and are given an opportunity to practice it.
- Further opportunities to draw conclusions are found throughout Unit 5.

1 Introduce and Motivate

Preview Pose a scenario for students and help them draw conclusions. For example, you could describe a place without actually identifying it. Ask students to tell what place you are describing. Have them specify details that led them to draw that conclusion.

2 Teach and Discuss

- Explain that *drawing conclusions* is using facts to figure something out. A conclusion can be drawn using facts from a reading selection as well as by using personal knowledge and experiences.

- Have students read the paragraph on p. 334. Make sure they realize that the highlighting shows the facts and the conclusion that can be drawn from those facts.

Life in a New Nation

Draw Conclusions

Drawing conclusions about what you have read can help you better understand history. Sometimes a writer presents facts from which you can form an opinion, or conclusion. Writers may also present you with their own conclusions.

Identify **facts** and then **draw a conclusion** based on the facts.

- To draw conclusions, think logically. You can also use clues from what you have read and from your own knowledge and experience.

- Make sure you check your conclusion. Ask yourself if your conclusion makes sense or if there are any other possible conclusions.

In this paragraph, the **facts** and the **conclusion** that was drawn from them are highlighted.

> In Chapters 8 and 9, you read about the conflict between the colonies and Britain. Britain taxed the colonists without their consent. The colonists insisted that the British were violating their right to have a voice in government. The colonies declared independence from Britain and defended their right to govern themselves.

Word Exercise

Suffixes A **suffix** is a syllable or syllables put at the end of a word to change its meaning or to make another word. Knowing what a suffix means can help you figure out the meaning of an unfamiliar word. Sometimes a suffix can have multiple meanings. For example, the suffix *-ion* can mean "act of" and also "result of."

word	word parts	Meaning of *-ion*	Meaning of word
revolution	revolt + -ion	"act of"	"the act of revolting"
constitution	constitute (legally form) + -ion	"result of"	"the result of legally forming"

Practice and Extend

ACCESS CONTENT
ESL Support

Practice Drawing Conclusions Guide students to understand the process of drawing conclusions.

Beginning Act out a scenario that invites students to draw conclusions. For example, suppose that you are upset and protesting, like those who took part in Shays' Rebellion. Guide students to draw the conclusion that you are upset.

Intermediate Play a game with clues, similar to "Twenty Questions." Choose a term mentioned in the text, such as *the Cabinet,* and have students ask questions in order to conclude what the term is. Point out that drawing a conclusion involves using clues in a logical way.

Advanced Read or tell a simple story about George Washington, conveying his character traits. After you tell the story, ask students to draw conclusions about what he was like, using specific clues from the story.

Draw Conclusions About Life in a New Nation

During the American Revolution, the states had to determine a plan to govern themselves. In 1781, the 13 states approved the Articles of Confederation, which established a weak central government. Events such as the revolt of farmers in Shays' Rebellion made some people worry that the government was too weak.

In 1787, representatives of most of the states met to make the central government stronger. They ended up getting rid of the Articles of Confederation and writing the Constitution.

Not everyone liked the new document. Both those who wanted it adopted and those who did not, worked hard to convince others. Eventually, the Constitution was approved.

The country chose its first President, George Washington, in 1789. Washington established the practice of choosing a Cabinet, or group of advisors. He also directed the plan to move the site of the capital to what is now called Washington, D.C., and chose key members of the planning team.

The government would soon have a larger area to govern. Americans began moving west in greater numbers. They crossed the Appalachian Mountains in search of new hunting grounds, fresh farmlands, and a new home. In 1803, the United States purchased even more land—the Louisiana Territory. The country's territory now expanded all the way to the Rocky Mountains.

The United States went to war again with Britain in the War of 1812. The official song of the United States, "The Star-Spangled Banner," was written to celebrate an American victory during this war.

Use the reading strategy of drawing conclusions to answer questions 1 and 2. Then answer the vocabulary question.

1 What can you conclude about George Washington's role in early United States history?

2 What facts support the following conclusion: Americans moved west to look for new opportunities?

3 Look at the word *rebellion* in the passage. Which meaning does the suffix *-ion* have in *rebellion*? What does *rebellion* mean?

335

- Then have students read the longer practice sample on p. 335 and answer the questions that follow.

- Ask students why, when studying history, it is important to know how to draw conclusions. (To understand history, we need to consider the facts and decide what those facts mean to us. We can think about what historical figures said and did to understand what they were like and perhaps why they acted as they did.)

Suffixes

Word Exercise

Point out the word *confederation* to students. Explain that *confederate* means "to join together or ally for a special purpose." Ask students to figure out what meaning the suffix *-ion* has here and what *confederation* means. (The suffix *-ion* means "result of an act" here, and *confederation* means "something that is formed by people joining together for a special purpose.")

3 Close and Assess

Apply it!

1. George Washington was an important leader in early United States history.

2. Americans crossed the Appalachians in search of new hunting grounds, fresh farmland, and a new home; the United States purchased even more land—the Louisiana Territory.

3. The suffix *-ion* means "act or process of." *Rebellion* means "the act of rebelling."

Standardized Test Prep

Workbook, p. 78

- Use Workbook p. 78 to give students practice with standardized test format.

- Chapter and Unit Tests in the Assessment Book use standardized test format.

- Test-taking tips are contained in the front portion of the Assessment Book Teacher's Edition.

Also on Teacher Resources CD-ROM.

Chapter Planning Guide

Chapter 10 • Forming a New Government

Locating Time and Place pp. 336–337

Lesson Titles	Pacing	Main Ideas
Lesson 1 **A Weak Government** pp. 338–343	2 days	• The new nation struggled to govern itself under the Articles of Confederation.
Lesson 2 **Debate in Philadelphia** pp. 344–350	2 days	• At the Constitutional Convention, a group of leaders wrote the Constitution, a new plan for a stronger national government.
Biography: James Madison p. 351		• James Madison made his ideas heard and had a great influence on the early United States.
Lesson 3 **Ratifying the Constitution** pp. 352–355	2 days	• After a long debate, the states ratified the United States Constitution.
Research and Writing Skills: **Gather and Report Information** pp. 356–357		• Gathering information from reference sources and organizing that information are both important steps in the writing process.

✓ **Chapter 10 Review**
pp. 358–359

◄ **The first 10 amendments to the Constitution are known as the Bill of Rights.**

✓ = Assessment Options

Delegates to the Constitutional Convention met in the State House, later called Independence Hall.

Vocabulary	Resources	Meeting Individual Needs
Articles of Confederation ratify legislative branch executive branch judicial branch inflation Shays' Rebellion Northwest Ordinance	• Workbook, p. 80 • Transparencies 23, 45 • Every Student Learns Guide, pp. 142–145 • Quick Study, pp. 72–73	• Leveled Practice, TE p. 339 • ESL Support, TE p. 340 • Learning Styles, TE p. 343
delegate Constitutional Convention Virginia Plan New Jersey Plan compromise Great Compromise Three-Fifths Compromise Preamble reserved powers separation of powers checks and balances veto	• Workbook, p. 81 • Transparency 23 • Every Student Learns Guide, pp. 146–149 • Quick Study, pp. 74–75	• Leveled Practice, TE p. 346 • ESL Support, TE p. 347
Federalists federal Antifederalists the Federalist amendment Bill of Rights	• Workbook, p. 82 • Transparency 23 • Every Student Learns Guide, pp. 150–153 • Quick Study, pp. 76–77 • Workbook, p. 83	• Leveled Practice, TE p. 353 • ESL Support, TE p. 354 • Learning Styles, TE p. 357
	✓ Chapter 10 Content Test, Assessment Book, pp. 57–59 ✓ Chapter 10 Skills Test, Assessment Book, pp. 59–60	✓ Chapter 10 Performance Assessment, TE p. 358

Providing More Depth

Additional Resources

- Vocabulary Workbook and Cards
- Social Studies Plus! pp. 122–127
- Daily Activity Bank
- Big Book Atlas
- Student Atlas
- Outline Maps
- Desk Maps

 Technology

- AudioText
- MindPoint® Quiz Show CD-ROM
- ExamView® Test Bank CD-ROM
- Teacher Resources CD-ROM
- Map Resources CD-ROM
- SFSuccessNet: iText (Pupil Edition online), iTE (Teacher's Edition online), Online Planner
- **www.sfsocialstudies.com** (Biographies, news, references, maps, and activities)

 To establish guidelines for your students' safe and responsible use of the Internet, use the Scott Foresman Internet Guide.

Additional Internet Links

To find out more about:

- The U.S. Constitution, visit **www.nara.gov**
- The American Presidency, visit **www.americanhistory.si.edu**
- The Bill of Rights and other important documents in U.S. history, visit **www.nara.gov**

Key Internet Search Terms

- United States Constitution
- James Madison
- George Washington
- Articles of Confederation

Workbook Support

Use the following Workbook pages to support content and skills development as you teach Chapter 10. You can also view and print Workbook pages from the Teacher Resources CD-ROM.

Workbook, p. 78

Draw Conclusions

Use with Pages 334–335.

Directions: Read the information below. Then fill in the circle next to the correct answer.

The French Revolution took place at about the same time as the American Revolution. Both countries were trying to achieve a democratic form of government. One major difference, however, was that the French already had a government in place.

During the course of the French Revolution, the existing French government would be completely destroyed. The majority of French citizens were dissatisfied with it and would not rest until it was changed.

At that time, the French government was led by a king, and citizens belonged to different social classes. Benefits and privileges were given to some according to their social class. For instance, some classes did not have to pay taxes and were allowed to collect dues from the poorer classes.

Another factor leading to the French Revolution was a lack of money. France had just helped the United States battle Britain in the American Revolution, and now it needed money. France already taxed some of its people, but now the situation called for additional taxes. Representatives of the king decided to begin taxing *all* landowners. This unpopular action caused the people to rebel against their government and resist what they considered to be unfair treatment.

Violent protests took place throughout the country. Poorer citizens fought for their own rights and to keep the wealthy from receiving special privileges.

Before the end of the French Revolution, the existing social divisions were outlawed. However, France's problems were far from over.

1. Which statement supports the conclusion that the American Revolution helped spark the French Revolution?
   - Ⓐ The French government was ruled by a king.
   - Ⓑ French citizens belonged to different social classes.
   - ● France had just helped the Americans battle Britain in the American Revolution.
   - Ⓓ There was a great deal of civil unrest in France.

2. Which statement supports the conclusion that the majority of French people wanted a new form of government?
   - ● Poorer citizens fought for their rights and to keep the wealthy from receiving special privileges.
   - Ⓑ Money was one cause of the French Revolution.
   - Ⓒ Privileges were determined by social class.
   - Ⓓ France already taxed some of its people.

 Notes for Home: Your child learned how to draw conclusions about a historical event.
Home Activity: With your child, brainstorm a list of facts about the American Revolution and another list of facts about the French Revolution. Together, draw conclusions about how the Americans may have influenced the French citizenry to rebel against their government.

Use with Pupil Edition, p. 335

Workbook, p. 79

Vocabulary Preview

Use with Chapter 10.

Directions: Match each vocabulary term to its definition. Write the number of the term in the space provided. Not all terms will be used. You may use your glossary.

1. Articles of Confederation
2. ratify
3. legislative branch
4. executive branch
5. judicial branch
6. inflation
7. Shays' Rebellion
8. Northwest Ordinance
9. delegate
10. Constitutional Convention
11. Virginia Plan
12. New Jersey Plan
13. compromise
14. Great Compromise
15. Three-Fifths Compromise
16. Preamble
17. reserved powers
18. separation of powers
19. checks and balances
20. veto
21. Federalists
22. federal
23. Antifederalists
24. *The Federalist*
25. amendment
26. Bill of Rights

2 a. to approve something

19 b. system to guard against any one branch of the government becoming too powerful

7 c. movement by farmers to protest high taxes

9 d. a representative

12 e. plan that proposed that each state, regardless of size, would have the same number of representatives in Congress

25 f. an addition or change to the Constitution

6 g. happens when prices rise very quickly

13 h. each side gives up something to reach an agreement

15 i. three out of every five slaves would be counted for population and taxation

23 j. group of people who were not happy with the Constitution

10 k. assembly that replaced the Articles of Confederation

3 l. the part of the government that passes laws

21 m. formerly nationalist group that wanted a strong national government

11 n. plan that proposed that Congress should be given much greater power over the states

4 o. the part of the government that carries out laws

18 p. each branch of the government has different and separate powers

1 q. plan for national government where states would keep their freedom and independence

20 r. to refuse to sign into law

8 s. an order that commanded that the Northwest Territory be divided into smaller territories

22 t. refers to the national government

 Notes for Home: Your child learned about the formation of a new government for the United States.
Home Activity: Write each vocabulary word or its definition on a blank index card. Then read each card to your child, having him or her provide the missing word or definition.

Use with Pupil Edition, p. 336

Workbook, p. 80

Lesson 1: A Weak Government

Use with Pages 338–343.

Directions: Complete the following fact-and-conclusion chart. In each box at left, write one fact to support the conclusion. You may use your textbook.

Facts

- Congress could not pass laws to collect taxes to run the government.
- There were no branches of government to enforce or interpret laws.
- There was no uniform standard of currency.
- The government could not pass laws regarding foreign trade.
- Protests like Shays' Rebellion were occurring.

Conclusion

The Articles of Confederation created a weak form of government.

Directions: The United States needed money to repay the individuals and the countries who had loaned money for the American Revolution. The United States also needed to pay the soldiers who had fought in the war. Do you think Daniel Shays and others like him who fought in the war should have been taxed to pay the country's war debts? Explain.

Possible answers: No, because they had already done their part to support America's bid for independence; yes, because everyone's help was needed to keep America from losing its freedom

Notes for Home: Your child learned about problems in the government of the United States under the Articles of Confederation.
Home Activity: With your child, review this lesson and list facts and any conclusions that can be drawn.

Use with Pupil Edition, p. 343

Workbook Support

Workbook, p. 81

Use with Pages 344–350.

Lesson 2: Debate in Philadelphia

Directions: Describe each of the following three terms in your own words. Relate each term to at least one of the other terms. Finally, answer question 4. You may use your textbook.

1. Constitutional Convention

   A group of representatives met in Philadelphia with the goal of revising the Articles of Confederation. After a great deal of discussion, they ended up agreeing on the Great Compromise and other compromises and wrote a new constitution.

2. Virginia Plan

   During the Constitutional Convention, Southerners proposed that the Virginia Plan replace the Articles of Confederation. The plan called for a stronger central government with an executive and a judicial branch. It also stated that states with larger populations should have more congressional representatives than smaller states.

3. Great Compromise

   The Great Compromise was an agreement between the Virginia Plan and the New Jersey Plan. It would create two houses in Congress. Each state would have equal representation in the Senate but have representation based on population in the House of Representatives.

4. Why was a government with three branches considered to be a compromise?

   Possible answer: The three branches of government provide a system of checks and balances that does not allow any one branch to be all-powerful. It is a compromise because it is a strong form of government, yet the people still have control.

 Notes for Home: Your child learned about the creation of the United States Constitution.
Home Activity: With your child, talk about an event in your child's life when he or she had to compromise.

Use with Pupil Edition, p. 350

Workbook, p. 82

Use with Pages 352–355.

Lesson 3: Ratifying the Constitution

Directions: A flowchart is a diagram that shows, step by step, a process of how something works or happens. Complete the flowchart using the items in the box.

Antifederalists	*The Federalist* essays explained the weaknesses of Antifederalist arguments.
A Bill of Rights is promised.	All 13 states ratify the Constitution, making it the supreme law of the land.
Federalists	This group feared that the central government would pass laws that were not suitable for all parts of the country.

The Constitution is sent to the states for ratification.

Federalists

The Federalist essays explained the weaknesses of Antifederalist arguments.

Antifederalists

This group feared that the central government would pass laws that were not suitable for all parts of the country.

A Bill of Rights is promised.

All 13 states ratify the Constitution, making it the supreme law of the land.

 Notes for Home: Your child learned the sequence of events leading to the ratification of the Constitution.
Home Activity: With your child, discuss how history might have been different if one of the events in this flowchart had not occurred.

Use with Pupil Edition, p. 355

Workbook, p. 83

Use with Pages 356–357.

Gather and Report Information

Suppose you were going to write a report on the first Vice-President of the United States. Think of the information you would need to write your report.

Directions: Read the information about gathering and reporting information. Answer the questions that follow.

1. An encyclopedia has the following entries. Which one will you need?

   ● Adams, John (1735–1826) Second President of the United States
   Ⓑ Adams, John Couch (1819–1892) English astronomer
   Ⓒ Adams, John Quincy (1767–1848) Sixth President of the United States
   Ⓓ Adams, Samuel (1722–1803) Signer of the Declaration of Independence

2. Explain the reasoning behind your answer to question 1.

   Possible answer: It is very possible that the person who was the second President might have been the first Vice-President.

The Life of John Adams

Youth   Personal Life   Politics

3. What is the subject of the report outlined in the graphic organizer above? Explain your reasoning. **The Life of John Adams; this information is shown in the most important area of the organizer.**

4. An encyclopedia article on John Adams has the following subheadings. Which might be most useful for your report?

   Ⓐ Political Opponents
   Ⓑ U.S.S. John Adams
   ● Boyhood and Education
   Ⓓ The John Adams Institute

5. An Internet search reveals the following sources. Which one do you think is a primary source?

   ● Adams, John, *The Adams Papers*, 13 vols., ed. by Lyman H. Butterfield et al. (1961–77)
   Ⓑ Ferling, John, *John Adams: A Life* (1992)
   Ⓒ Kurtz, Stephen G., *The Presidency of John Adams* (1957)
   Ⓓ Shaw, Peter, *The Character of John Adams* (1976)

 Notes for Home: Your child learned how to gather and report information.
Home Activity: With your child, discuss where he or she might research information for a report. Together, analyze what types of information might be found in the library, in an encyclopedia, or on the Internet.

Use with Pupil Edition, p. 357

Workbook, p. 84

Use with Chapter 10.

Vocabulary Review

Directions: Circle the vocabulary term that best completes each sentence. Not all terms will be used.

Articles of Confederation	Constitutional Convention	checks and balances
ratify	Virginia Plan	veto
legislative branch	New Jersey Plan	Federalists
executive branch	compromise	federal
judicial branch	Great Compromise	Antifederalists
inflation	Three-Fifths Compromise	*The Federalist*
Shays' Rebellion	Preamble	amendment
Northwest Ordinance	reserved powers	Bill of Rights
delegate	separation of powers	

1. The (legislative branch, judicial branch) of government is responsible for the court system.

2. To approve a bill is to (veto, ratify) it.

3. The (compromise, delegate) from my state comes from my town.

4. The system of (checks and balances, separation of powers) guards against any one branch of the government becoming too powerful.

5. (Compromise, Inflation) happens when prices rise very quickly.

6. An addition or change is known as a(n) (amendment, veto).

7. The (Northwest Ordinance, Articles of Confederation) turned out to be a plan of government that was too weak in many people's opinions.

8. In a (compromise, constitution), each side gives up something to reach an agreement.

9. The (Three-Fifths Compromise, Bill of Rights) is a group of ten amendments to the Constitution.

10. The word (federal, inflation) refers to the national government.

11. (Reserved powers, Checks and balances) are powers left strictly to state governments.

12. The (Federalists, Antifederalists) were a group that wanted a strong national government.

Notes for Home: Your child learned how the United States struggled to find a suitable form of government.
Home Activity: With your child, study the vocabulary definitions by playing a question-and-answer game. First, read your child a definition. Then have him or her give the answer in question form, such as "What are the Articles of Confederation?"

Use with Pupil Edition, p. 359

Assessment Support

 Use these Assessment Book pages and the ExamView® Test Bank CD-ROM to assess content and skills in Chapter 10. You can also view and print Assessment Book pages from the Teacher Resources CD-ROM.

Assessment Book, p. 57

Chapter 10 Test
Part 1: Content Test

Directions: Fill in the circle next to the correct answer.

Lesson Objective (1:1)

1. What did the states hope to gain under the Articles of Confederation?
   - Ⓐ a strong central government
   - ● freedom, independence, and a firm league of friendship
   - Ⓒ a powerful government
   - Ⓓ a strong court system

Lesson Objective (1:2)

2. Which of the following BEST describes the government under the Articles of Confederation?
   - Ⓐ Congress collected enough money to run the government.
   - Ⓑ The judicial branch interpreted the laws.
   - ● Congress could not pass laws to collect taxes.
   - Ⓓ The legislative branch enforced the laws.

Lesson Objective (1:2)

3. What was one weakness of the Articles of Confederation?
   - ● The government had only one branch.
   - Ⓑ Each state paid taxes.
   - Ⓒ Laws could not be made.
   - Ⓓ Each state had one vote.

Lesson Objective (1:3)

4. What caused Shays' Rebellion?
   - Ⓐ Massachusetts had the power to tax its citizens.
   - Ⓑ Massachusetts needed to pay its debts.
   - Ⓒ Daniel Shays was an angry farmer.
   - ● Massachusetts property taxes were hard on farmers.

Lesson Objective (1:4)

5. Which of the following was ordered by the Northwest Ordinance of 1787?
   - ● divide the territory into smaller territories
   - Ⓑ make the territory into four states
   - Ⓒ make the territory into one state
   - Ⓓ make the entire territory equal to the other states

Lesson Objective (1:4)

6. Which of the following did NOT apply to the Northwest Ordinance of 1787?
   - Ⓐ The Northwest Territory had to be divided into smaller territories.
   - ● The Northwest Territory would automatically become a state.
   - Ⓒ A governor and judges were named to govern the territory.
   - Ⓓ Slavery was prohibited in the Northwest Territory.

Lesson Objective (2:1)

7. What was the original purpose of the Constitutional Convention?
   - Ⓐ make laws to stop dissenters
   - Ⓑ make a trade plan with Europe
   - ● revise the Articles of Confederation
   - Ⓓ elect a leader of the Confederation

Use with Pupil Edition, p. 358

Assessment Book, p. 58

Name _____ Date _____ | Chapter 10 Test |

Lesson Objective (2:2)

8. Which point in the Virginia Plan was objected to by supporters of the New Jersey Plan?
   - ● Larger states should have more representatives in Congress.
   - Ⓑ Congress requires greater power.
   - Ⓒ The government needs an executive branch.
   - Ⓓ The government needs a legislative branch.

Lesson Objective (2:3)

9. Which of the following does NOT describe the Great Compromise?
   - Ⓐ equal representation in the Senate
   - Ⓑ representation based on population in the House of Representatives
   - Ⓒ a Congress made up of two houses
   - ● enslaved people counted in state populations

Lesson Objective (2:1)

10. What was the outcome of the Constitutional Convention?
    - Ⓐ Compromises were proposed.
    - ● The Constitution replaced the Articles of Confederation.
    - Ⓒ The Articles of Confederation were amended.
    - Ⓓ Trade with Europe was established.

Lesson Objective (2:4)

11. Which of the following goals is stated in the Preamble to the Constitution?
    - ● to protect the people's liberty
    - Ⓑ to provide equality for all
    - Ⓒ to protect the people's health
    - Ⓓ to provide an education for all

Lesson Objective (2:4)

12. Which of the following is NOT a major goal of the Constitution?
    - Ⓐ to defend the nation
    - ● to control all laws in the states
    - Ⓒ to ensure peace
    - Ⓓ to establish justice

Lesson Objective (3:1)

13. Which group wanted a strong national government, like that set forth in the Constitution?
    - Ⓐ Antifederalists
    - Ⓑ Colonists
    - ● Federalists
    - Ⓓ Constitutionalists

Lesson Objective (3:1)

14. Which of the following BEST describes the Antifederalists?
    - Ⓐ people who were happy with the Constitution
    - Ⓑ people who wanted more power
    - Ⓒ people who wanted government to have more power
    - ● people who were unhappy with the Constitution

Lesson Objective (3:2)

15. Which of the following BEST describes the Bill of Rights?
    - Ⓐ list of the men who signed the Constitution
    - Ⓑ list of rights and wrongs as spelled out in the Constitution
    - ● ten Constitutional amendments specifying freedoms
    - Ⓓ list of laws governed by each state

Use with Pupil Edition, p. 358

Assessment Support

Lesson Objective (3:2)

16. What happened when Congress pledged to add the Bill of Rights to the Constitution?
   - Ⓐ Protests and uprisings occurred in many states.
   - Ⓑ Many states refused to sign the Constitution.
   - Ⓒ Many people moved away so it wouldn't affect them.
   - ● Many states signed the Constitution.

Lesson Objective (3:3)

17. How did Benjamin Franklin describe the government under the Constitution?
   - ● "A republic, if you can keep it."
   - Ⓑ "that precious depository of American happiness"
   - Ⓒ "First in war, first in peace."
   - Ⓓ "If men were angels, no government would be necessary."

Part 2: Skills Test

Directions: Use complete sentences to answer questions 1–8. Use a separate sheet of paper if you need more space.

1. How did the Articles of Confederation affect relations between the United States and European nations? **Summarize**

   The Articles of Confederation kept the United States from forming strong trading relationships with European nations because Congress could not pass laws making rules for trade. Some governments had little respect for the United States.

2. In what ways was the Northwest Ordinance of 1787 successful? **Summarize**

   The Northwest Ordinance of 1787 was successful because it was a plan for allowing a large piece of land to become states that were the equals of the original 13 states.

3. How did Shays' Rebellion and other protests affect the government? **Draw Conclusions**

   Shays' Rebellion and other protests caused concern among the nationalists. They believed a stronger national government was needed. Eventually the Articles of Confederation were replaced with the Constitution.

Use with Pupil Edition, p. 358

4. Why did the delegates draft a new plan instead of revising the Articles of Confederation? **Draw Conclusions**

   Some delegates thought that a revision would not make the national government strong enough. By proposing the Virginia and New Jersey Plans, delegates indicated that they were not happy with the Articles of Confederation and supported the idea of a new plan.

5. Why was it important for the delegates to be able to change their minds at the Constitutional Convention? **Draw Conclusions**

   The delegates had to compromise to come up with a plan with which most would agree. Sometimes a compromise means a person has to change his or her mind.

6. Who were the authors of *The Federalist* essays, and what were they trying to achieve? **Draw Conclusions**

   The Federalist essays were written by Federalists James Madison, Alexander Hamilton, and John Jay. They wanted to educate people on the weaknesses of the Antifederalists' arguments. They were hoping that once people were informed, they would see that the Antifederalists were incorrect in their opinions and vote for the Constitution.

7. What was the underlying reason that many states wanted the Bill of Rights to be part of the Constitution? **Main Idea and Details**

   The Bill of Rights places specific limits on government. Some people still feared that a strong government would become too powerful. The Bill of Rights took away this fear.

8. What do you think was meant when it was said that the Constitution provided a framework for a stronger central government? **Hypothesize**

   Possible answer: The Constitution provides the shell and not the details. The details can be added when necessary to make the Constitution relevant to the current society.

Use with Pupil Edition, p. 358

Forming a New Government

Chapter 10 Outline
- **Lesson 1, *A Weak Government,*** pp. 338–343
- **Lesson 2, *Debate in Philadelphia,*** pp. 344–350
- **Biography: *James Madison,*** p. 351
- **Lesson 3, *Ratifying the Constitution,*** pp. 352–355
- **Research and Writing Skills: *Gather and Report Information,*** pp. 356–357

Resources
- Workbook, p. 79: Vocabulary Preview
- Vocabulary Cards
- Social Studies Plus!

1786, Springfield, Massachusetts: Lesson 1

Share with students that this picture depicts a rebellion of farmers in Massachusetts who were angry about property taxes. Ask students to compare this picture with other pictures they may have seen as they studied the Revolutionary War.

1787, Philadelphia, Pennsylvania: Lesson 2

Explain to students that this picture shows George Washington leading a meeting to discuss creating a form of government for the United States. What do students think George Washington may be saying to the people gathered there? What kind of government might the people be discussing?

1787, New York City, New York: Lesson 3

Remind students that the United States has not always been governed by the Constitution. This picture is the title page of a document that tried to persuade people to support the Constitution. Ask students what problems early Americans may have had with the Constitution and the new government.

CHAPTER
10
Forming a
New Government

1786

Springfield, Massachusetts
Rebellion of farmers shows the weakness of the central government.
Lesson 1

1

1787

Philadelphia, Pennsylvania
Delegates meet to write the Constitution.
Lesson 2

2

1787

New York City, New York
Writings of *The Federalist* encourage the acceptance of the Constitution.
Lesson 3

THE

FEDERALIST:

A COLLECTION

OF

ESSAYS,

WRITTEN IN FAVOUR OF THE

NEW CONSTITUTION,

3

336

Practice and Extend

Vocabulary Preview

- Use Workbook p. 79 to help students preview the vocabulary words in this chapter.
- Use Vocabulary Cards to preview key concept words in this chapter.

 Also on Teacher Resources CD-ROM.

Workbook, p. 79

Vocabulary Preview

Directions: Match each vocabulary term to its definition. Write the number of the term in the space provided. Not all terms will be used. You may use your glossary.

1. Articles of Confederation	___ a. to approve something
2. ratify	___ b. system to guard against any one branch of the government becoming too powerful
3. legislative branch	___ c. movement by farmers to protest high taxes
4. executive branch	___ d. a representative
5. judicial branch	___ e. plan that proposed that each state, regardless of size, would have the same number of representatives in Congress
6. inflation	
7. Shays' Rebellion	___ f. an addition or change to the Constitution
8. Northwest Ordinance	___ g. happens when prices rise very quickly
9. delegate	___ h. each side gives up something to reach an agreement
10. Constitutional Convention	
11. Virginia Plan	___ i. three out of every five slaves would be counted for population and taxation
12. compromise	___ j. group of people who were not happy with the Constitution
13. New Jersey Plan	
14. Great Compromise	___ k. assembly that replaced the Articles of Confederation
15. Three-Fifths Compromise	___ l. the part of the government that passes laws
16. reserved powers	___ m. formerly nationalist group that wanted a strong national government
17. separation of powers	
18. checks and balances	___ n. plan that proposed that Congress should be given much greater power over the states
19. veto	
20. Federalist	___ o. the part of the government that carries out laws
21. federal	___ p. each branch of the government has different and separate powers
22. Antifederalists	
23. *The Federalist*	___ q. plan for national government where states would keep their freedom and independence
24. amendment	
25. ratification	___ r. to refuse to sign into law
26. Bill of Rights	___ s. an order that commanded that the Northwest Territory be divided into smaller territories
	___ t. refers to the national government

Notes for Home: Your child learned about the formation of a new government for the United States.
Home Activity: Write each vocabulary word or its definition on a blank index card. Then read each card to your child, having him or her provide the missing word or definition.

Locating Time and Place

Springfield

New York City
Philadelphia

UNITED STATES
1783

ATLANTIC
OCEAN

Why We Remember

In the summer of 1787, fifty-five people met in Philadelphia to write the Constitution. This document is the plan for a government that has lasted for more than 200 years. The Constitution created a lasting structure to govern the United States. The Constitution not only set up the plans for our representative democracy, it also protects our freedoms. Later changes, such as those giving greater numbers of people the right to vote, show that the Constitution continues to change through time.

337

- Have students examine the pictures shown on p. 336 for Lessons 1, 2, and 3.

- Remind students that each picture is coded with both a number and a color to link it to a place on the map on p. 337.

Why We Remember

Have students read the "Why We Remember" paragraph on p. 337, and ask them why events in this chapter might be important to them. Ask students what they know about the U.S. Constitution. How does it affect their daily lives? Have students imagine what it would be like if each of the states in the United States had its own separate government without a national government. How might life be different for ordinary citizens?

WEB SITE
Technology

You can learn more about Springfield, Massachusetts; Philadelphia, Pennsylvania; and New York City, New York by clicking on *Atlas* at **www.sfsocialstudies.com.**

SOCIAL STUDIES STRAND
Geography

Mental Mapping Have students draw the Appalachian Mountains, the Mississippi River, and a compass rose on an outline map of the United States. Ask students to recall what they know about the Treaty of Paris, and have them shade in the area of the United States in 1783. Discuss how the boundaries of the United States and those of the 13 Colonies changed.

A Weak Government

Objectives

- List the main goals of the Articles of Confederation.

- Identify the weaknesses of the Articles of Confederation.

- Describe the causes of Shays' Rebellion.

- Explain the purpose of the Northwest Ordinance.

Vocabulary

Articles of Confederation, p. 339;
ratify, p. 339; **legislative branch,** p. 339;
executive branch, p. 339;
judicial branch, p. 339; **inflation,** p. 340;
Shays' Rebellion, p. 341;
Northwest Ordinance, p. 342

Resources

- Workbook, p. 80
- Transparency 23, 45
- Every Student Learns Guide, pp. 142–145
- Quick Study, pp. 72–73

Quick Teaching Plan

If time is short, have students create a time line of the events in Lesson 1.

- Begin a time line on the board for students to copy. On the left end of the time line, write: *1776: The Declaration of Independence is adopted.*

- Have students read independently and add events in chronological order.

1 Introduce and Motivate

Preview To activate prior knowledge, ask students to tell about a time when they were in a group where the members disagreed on how it should be run and who should lead it. Tell students that, in Lesson 1, they will learn about the colonists' attempts to run the country after the American Revolution.

 Have students predict what kind of government Americans might want after they had been freed from British control.

LESSON 1

NORTHWEST TERRITORY   Springfield

1780			1790
1781 Articles of Confederation ratified by states	**1786-1787** Shays' Rebellion is fought in western Massachusetts	**1787** Northwest Ordinance organizes the Northwest Territory	

PREVIEW

Focus on the Main Idea
The new nation struggled to govern itself under the Articles of Confederation.

PLACES
Springfield, Massachusetts
Northwest Territory

PEOPLE
Daniel Shays

VOCABULARY
Articles of Confederation
ratify
legislative branch
executive branch
judicial branch
inflation
Shays' Rebellion
Northwest Ordinance of 1787

A Weak Government

You Are There You are tucked in bed, but voices coming from downstairs keep you awake. The Declaration of Independence has just been proclaimed. The adults in your family are excitedly discussing it and what it means.

"At last," says one, "we will be free of tyranny from the British government."

"But," says another, "what kind of government will we create to take its place? Will we simply replace British tyranny with American tyranny?"

Like many other Americans, members of your family have a deep distrust of government. They don't want a repeat of powerful governors and unfair laws. What they want is a government that is strong enough to protect citizens' rights. But they fear that government can just as easily threaten citizens' freedoms. How can a balance be found?

 Draw Conclusions As you read, decide how successful the Articles of Confederation were in setting up a strong government.

Practice and Extend

READING SKILL Draw Conclusions

In the Lesson Review, students complete a graphic organizer like the one below. You may want to provide students with a copy of Transparency 23 to complete as they read the lesson.

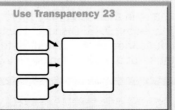

Use Transparency 23

VOCABULARY Word Exercise

Individual Word Study Ask students to think about the meaning of the verb *inflate*. Have them define it in their own words and use it in a sentence, such as *We needed air to inflate the balloon.* Remind them that the suffix *-ion* means "the act of doing something." Ask what *inflation* might mean. ("the act of making something larger") Discuss how this relates to the meaning of *inflation* as "when prices rise quickly."

The Articles of Confederation

With British rule removed, Americans had to create new plans of government for themselves. Leaders knew that they wanted their new nation to be a republic. But they did not want this government to have too much power over the people. Shortly after the members of the Continental Congress adopted the Declaration of Independence in 1776, they began debating a new plan for a national government. The plan was called the Articles of Confederation. A confederation is a group or league.

The **Articles of Confederation** stated that the states would keep their "freedom and independence." States would be joined in "a firm league of friendship," not a strong central government. The plan could not take effect until all 13 states ratified it. To **ratify** is to approve something. The Articles of Confederation were ratified in 1781.

Under the Articles of Confederation, Congress was the main governing body. It would make the laws for the new nation. But it could not pass laws to collect taxes to run the government. Congress could only ask each state to give taxes to pay for the expenses of Congress. However, it was difficult for Congress to collect enough money this way. Each state had one vote in Congress. To pass a law, at least 9 of the 13 states had to vote for it.

The Articles set up a central government with only one branch—a legislature, called Congress. A **legislative branch** is the part of government that passes laws. There was no executive branch to carry out the laws. An **executive branch** of government is headed by a leader such as a President. There was also no **judicial branch,** or court system, to interpret the laws.

REVIEW Why did the writers of the Articles of Confederation purposely create a weak central government? 🔵 **Draw Conclusions**

▶ The Articles of Confederation were adopted by the Second Continental Congress.

Painting by John Trumbull

339

Teach and Discuss

PAGE 339

The Articles of Confederation

🕐 *Quick Summary* The Articles of Confederation created a central government but allowed the states to have "freedom and independence."

1 **When did the Continental Congress meet to plan a new kind of government? When were their ideas approved?** After adopting the Declaration of Independence in 1776; the Articles of Confederation were ratified in 1781. **Sequence**

💲 **SOCIAL STUDIES STRAND Economics**

2 **Why was it important for the new government to be able to collect tax money?** Possible answer: The new government needed money to run the country. **Main Idea and Details**

🦉 **Test Talk**

Locate Key Words in the Text

3 **Compare the government created in the Articles to the government today.** Tell students to combine what they know about the government today with what the text tells about the government under the Articles. Both have a legislative branch. Today we also have a judicial and an executive branch. **Compare and Contrast**

✓ **REVIEW ANSWER** They wanted power to rest with individual states, not with a strong central government. 🔵 **Draw Conclusions**

❄️ **MEETING INDIVIDUAL NEEDS Leveled Practice**

Make a Speech Ask students to take on the roles of state officials in 1776. Have them craft arguments in favor of the creation of a weak national government.

Easy Students should give at least two reasons why a weak central government would be best for the states. **Reteach**

On-Level Students should list several reasons and support them with facts. Have students consider ending their presentations with their strongest arguments. **Extend**

Challenge Students can work in groups to create speeches with opposing viewpoints about the central government formed by the Articles of Confederation. Remind students that some speakers should oppose a weak central government and argue that the central government should be strong. **Enrich**

For a Lesson Summary, use Quick Study, p. 72.

A Government in Trouble

🕐 **Quick Summary** The Articles of Confederation led to problems with money and difficulty trading with other countries. The nationalists began to argue for a stronger government.

4 **What were the main weaknesses of the nation under the Articles of Confederation?** Inability to collect taxes, confusion with money from state to state, inflation, inability to trade with other countries, no executive or judicial branches **Main Idea and Details**

5 **Why do you think it was important for the United States to develop trade relationships with other countries?**
Possible answer: Many things that people needed could not be found or made in the United States.
Make Inferences

6 **What do you think might have happened if the United States had kept the Articles of Confederation?**
Possible answers: The country might have failed; each of the states may have become a separate country with its own government; the country might have fallen to a larger, stronger country in a war. **Predict**

✓ **Ongoing Assessment**

| **If...** students are unable to make reasonable predictions, | **then...** have them list the problems caused by the Articles of Confederation. Have students make predictions based on the problems they list. |

✓ **REVIEW ANSWER** The Articles of Confederation were making the nation weak, and a stronger government needed to be formed. 🔄 **Draw Conclusions**

A Government in Trouble

The weaknesses of the Articles of Confederation meant trouble for the new nation. Think about how difficult it would be for a government to operate without being able to pass laws to collect taxes. For example, Congress had to borrow large amounts of money to fight the American Revolution. It borrowed from both private people and foreign countries. Without the ability to collect taxes, it could not repay these debts. It also could not pay its soldiers.

The new nation also had other money problems. Today, we have coins and paper money that have the same value across the country. But then, both the Congress and the different states could make their own money. And each kind of money might have a different value. If you were alive then, you would have carried a jumble of money—paper bills printed by Congress, called "continentals," and perhaps some paper money printed by Vermont or by Pennsylvania. You might even have had a few foreign coins.

▶ Congress and the states printed paper money during and after the Revolution.

People had a hard time figuring out the value of these different kinds of money. Congress's paper money became almost worthless. This happened because of inflation that took place during the American Revolution. **Inflation** happens when prices rise very quickly. When this happens, money does not buy as much as it used to. The saying "not worth a continental" came to describe something of little or no value. How could businesses run well with such a jumble of money?

Under the Articles of Confederation, the national government was not only weak at home. It was also powerless in dealings with other countries. The new nation needed to develop strong trade with the nations of Europe. But because Congress could not pass laws making rules for such trade, some governments had little respect for the United States. Many of them hoped the new nation would fail.

By the middle 1780s, some Americans became alarmed about the nation's weakness. A group called the nationalists began arguing for a newer, stronger form of national government. The nationalists included leaders of the Revolution, such as George Washington and Ben Franklin. George Washington made this plea for change: "If the powers of Congress are inadequate [not strong enough], amend or alter [change] them."

REVIEW What conclusions did the nationalists draw about the Articles of Confederation? 🔄 **Draw Conclusions**

Practice and Extend

ESL **EXTEND LANGUAGE**
ESL Support

Examine Word Meanings Help students decode words with endings and suffixes.

Beginning Explain that the ending *-er* can be added to a word. Say "big" and "bigger" as you point to objects of different sizes. Point out *newer* and *stronger* on p. 340. Have students explain how these words differ from *new* and *strong*.

Intermediate Explain that the ending *-less* can be added to a word. Have students locate *powerless* on p. 340 and explain what it means.

Advanced Ask students to find words with endings and suffixes on p. 340. List the words on the board. Have students organize the words in a chart and add other words with the same ending or suffix. Have students tell the meaning of the words with and without the suffix or ending.

For additional ESL support, use Every Student Learns Guide, pp. 142–145.

Shays' Rebellion

An uprising of farmers in western Massachusetts in 1786 alarmed the nationalists even more than the nation's weakness. Like the other states, Massachusetts had borrowed money to fight the Revolutionary War. And like other states, it had the power to tax its citizens. One way to pay off its debt was to tax property. These taxes hit the farmers of the state especially hard.

Farmers found it harder and harder to pay property taxes and other debts. When they could not pay, state courts seized their farms. The courts also threw farmers who owed money into jail. The anger of the farmers grew. **Daniel Shays** was one of the angry farmers. A Revolutionary War veteran, he had fought at the battles of Bunker Hill, Ticonderoga, and Saratoga, rising to the rank of captain. The Marquis de Lafayette had presented Shays with a ceremonial sword to honor his service. But debts had forced Shays to sell this prized sword.

Shays became a leader in a movement that demanded lower taxes and the closing of courts that punished debtors. A debtor is a person who owes money. In September 1786, Captain Shays led a ragtag "army" of about 700 to close the court at **Springfield, Massachusetts.** Fewer than a quarter of them were armed with anything more than clubs. To keep **Shays' Rebellion** going, the farmers needed better weapons. So in January 1787, Shays led an attack on the federal arsenal at Springfield, where rifles and ammunition were stored.

Shays' attack was unsuccessful, and he fled to Vermont. But his rebellion gave the nationalists more ammunition in their battle to strengthen the national government.

REVIEW Why did Shays' Rebellion frighten the nationalists and other Americans? **Draw Conclusions**

Revolution in France

At the Same Time as the United States was struggling to create a government, France was having a revolution of its own. On July 14, 1789 in Paris, an angry crowd rose up against the king of France. Like the American Revolution, the French Revolution aimed at creating a representative government. France soon declared itself a republic. But it too faced many challenges before it could make a stable, representative government a reality.

341

🕐 ***Quick Summary*** Daniel Shays led a rebellion demanding lower property taxes and the closing of courts set up to punish debtors.

7 **What do you think motivated Daniel Shays to lead the rebellion?** Possible answers: He was angry about the property taxes; he had been forced to sell a prized possession in order to pay his debts. **Hypothesize**

Problem Solving

8 **What actions did Shays' "army" take? In what other ways might they have solved their problems?** They led an attack to close the courts and raided the weapons arsenal. They might have solved their problems in a less violent way, such as petitioning the governor or meeting with lawmakers. **Solve Problems**

✓ **REVIEW ANSWER** The rebellion showed that some citizens were not going to put up with new policies. **Draw Conclusions**

Revolution in France

Help students locate France on the map shown here and on a world map.

9 **Compare and contrast the American and French Revolutions.** Both were aimed at creating a new kind of government. The revolution in France took place within the country against its present king. The American Revolution was fought in colonies far away from the governing body. **Compare and Contrast**

FYI SOCIAL STUDIES Background

Daniel Shays' Military Career

Shays fought at key battles in the American Revolution, including Bunker Hill.

- After Shays retired from the military in 1780, he made his home in Pelham, Massachusetts, and held various town offices there.
- Shays was condemned to death for his part in the rebellion that bears his name. In 1788 he asked for a pardon, which he was granted.
- Later in his life, Shays received a pension for his service in the Revolution.

Noah Webster

- Noah Webster was an active member of the Federalist Party. He worked closely with George Washington and others.
- In 1785, Webster issued one of the first written calls for a Constitutional Convention.
- As an educator and the publisher of *American Dictionary of the English Language*, Webster was known as the "Schoolmaster to America."

The Northwest Ordinance of 1787

 Quick Summary The Northwest Ordinance provided for the conversion of lands gained by the Treaty of Paris into full-fledged states.

MAP SKILL The Northwest Territory, 1787

Point out that the area known as the Northwest Territory is now a portion of the United States known as the Midwest. Have students locate the area on a larger map of the United States.

10 **Why do you think that the Northwest Territory was such a desirable piece of land for the United States to own?** Possible answer: Being close to lakes and rivers provided for transportation and related industries, such as fishing. Evaluate

MAP SKILL Answer Mississippi River on the west; Ohio River on the south

11 **How did the United States acquire the land in the Northwest Territory?** The United States acquired the land from Great Britain by the Treaty of Paris. Cause and Effect

 Test Talk

Locate Key Words in the Text

12 **Based on the guidelines in the Northwest Ordinance, how do you think Congress might have defined a "state"?** Have students skim the text for words that match key words in the question, such as *Northwest Ordinance* and *Congress*. Possible answer: States needed a governor, at least 60,000 adult males, the rights of freedom of speech and religion, trial by jury, and public schools. ⟳ Draw Conclusions

✓ **REVIEW ANSWER** It provided a workable plan for converting new territories into states that became full partners in the nation. ⟳ Draw Conclusions

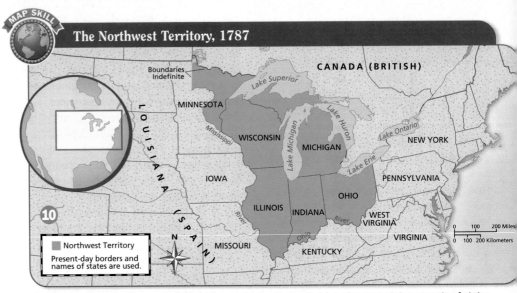

MAP SKILL The Northwest Territory, 1787

CANADA (BRITISH)

Northwest Territory

Present-day borders and names of states are used.

▶ The Northwest Territory was divided into smaller territories that later became states or parts of states.
MAP SKILL Location *What rivers bordered the Northwest Territory on the west and the south?*

The Northwest Ordinance of 1787

11 By the Treaty of Paris of 1783, the United States gained vast lands from the British. These new lands stretched to the Mississippi River in the west. How could these lands become states that were the equals of the original 13?

One part of these lands was called the **Northwest Territory.** Congress drew up a plan called the **Northwest Ordinance of 1787.** An ordinance is an official order. This ordinance commanded that the Northwest Territory be divided into smaller territories. The ordinance described the steps that all territories would follow to become states.

First, Congress would name a governor and three judges to govern the territory. Next, when the population of the territory reached 5,000 free adult males, the territory could elect a legislature. Then, when the population reached 60,000 adult males, the territory could petition, or ask, to become a state. **12** Finally, when Congress ratified the territory's petition, the new state would stand "on an equal footing with the original states."

Look at the map on this page. What states were formed from the Northwest Territory?

The Northwest Ordinance prohibited slavery in the Northwest Territory. It also promised the rights of freedom of speech and religion and trial by jury to settlers. And it stated that public schools would be established throughout the territory.

REVIEW Why can the Northwest Ordinance be considered a successful action by Congress under the Articles of Confederation? ⟳ Draw Conclusions

342

Practice and Extend

 CURRICULUM CONNECTION Math

Calculate Area and Ratios

- Have students use an almanac, atlas, or other reference to find the areas of the five states that were formed from the Northwest Territory.

- Have them calculate the total area of the territory.

- For an added challenge, have students find the population per square mile of each of the states today and write ratios to compare their average population densities.

 WEB SITE Technology

You can learn more about the Northwest Territory by clicking on *Atlas* at **www.sfsocialstudies.com.**

Growing Concerns

Despite the success of the Northwest Ordinance, nationalists were still alarmed by the weakness of the central government. Disorders like Shays' Rebellion increased their fears. Once again, George Washington expressed their concern:

"What stronger evidence can be given of the want of energy in our government than these disorders?...Thirteen [states] pulling against each other and all tugging at the...head [central government] will soon bring ruin on the whole."

Congress called on the states to send representatives to a meeting in Philadelphia in May 1787. This meeting was to be held for "the sole and express purpose of revising the Articles of Confederation."

REVIEW Why did George Washington conclude that greater unity among the states was necessary? 🔄 **Draw Conclusions**

Summarize the Lesson

1781 All 13 states ratified the Articles of Confederation, making it the framework for the national government.

1786 Western Massachusetts farmers led by Daniel Shays rebelled against taxes.

1787 Congress passed the Northwest Ordinance, which provided a model for how territories could be turned into new states.

LESSON 1 REVIEW

Check Facts and Main Ideas

1. 🔄 **Draw Conclusions** On a separate sheet of paper, fill in the missing facts that lead to the given conclusion.

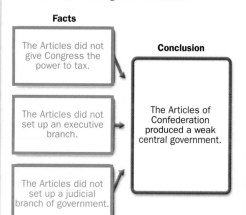

Facts

The Articles did not give Congress the power to tax.

The Articles did not set up an executive branch.

The Articles did not set up a judicial branch of government.

Conclusion

The Articles of Confederation produced a weak central government.

2. What were the goals of the **Articles of Confederation?**

3. What caused **Shays' Rebellion?**

4. **Critical Thinking:** *Cause and Effect* Identify the events that led to the **Northwest Ordinance** of 1787.

5. What led George Washington to say: "What stronger evidence can be given of the want of energy in our government?"

Link to ⟨∞⟩ **Writing**

Write a Letter to the Editor Suppose that you have just read about Shays' Rebellion in your local newspaper. Write a letter to the editor of your local newspaper in which you explain why you support or oppose the rebellion.

343

MEETING INDIVIDUAL NEEDS
Learning Styles

Describe the Concerns of the Nationalists
Using their individual learning styles, students review the concerns of the nationalists after the adoption of the Articles of Confederation.

Musical Learning Students may write a ballad depicting an event from the lesson. Have students present their work to the class.

Social Learning Students may convene a meeting, acting as nationalists discussing their concerns. Have them list their ideas for change and what their ideas could accomplish.

Workbook, p. 80

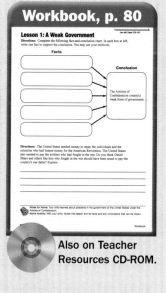

Lesson 1: A Weak Government

Directions: Complete the following fact-and-conclusion chart. In each box at left, write one fact to support the conclusion. You may use your textbook.

Facts

Conclusion

The Articles of Confederation created a weak form of government.

Also on Teacher Resources CD-ROM.

PAGE 343

Growing Concerns

🕐 *Quick Summary* Congress called a special meeting to revise the Articles of Confederation and create a stronger government.

Primary Source

A Letter to James Madison, Nov. 5, 1786 in the Papers of George Washington

⑬ **Why might pleas from George Washington have persuaded Congress to call a meeting?** Washington was well-respected for his role in the revolution.
🔄 **Draw Conclusions**

✓ **REVIEW ANSWER** Without unity, the democratic government might fail.
🔄 **Draw Conclusions**

3 Close and Assess

Summarize the Lesson

Compile a class outline. Small groups can each take one point and list related facts.

✓ **LESSON 1** **REVIEW**

1. 🔄 **Draw Conclusions** For possible answers, see the reduced pupil page.

2. To create a league of friendly states with a weak central government

3. Property taxes that forced many into debtors' prisons

4. **Critical Thinking:** *Cause and Effect* The nation had received land from Great Britain in the Treaty of Paris; a plan was needed to turn the territories into states.

5. Money problems, inflation, and Shays' Rebellion

Link to ⟨∞⟩ **Writing**

Students should give persuasive facts to support their opinions. Remind them to include facts from the lesson.

Debate in Philadelphia

Objectives

- Identify the purpose of the Constitutional Convention.

- Compare the competing plans for the Constitution.

- Describe the Great Compromise.

- List the goals of the Constitution.

Vocabulary

delegate, p. 345;
Constitutional Convention, p. 345;
Virginia Plan, p. 346;
New Jersey Plan, p. 346;
compromise, p. 347;
Great Compromise, p. 347;
Three-Fifths Compromise, p. 347;
Preamble, p. 348; **reserved powers,** p. 348;
separation of powers, p. 348;
checks and balances, p. 348; **veto,** p. 348

Resources

- Workbook, p. 81
- Transparency 23
- Every Student Learns Guide, pp. 146–149
- Quick Study, pp. 74–75

Quick Teaching Plan

If time is short, have students create a K-W-L chart to complete as they read.

- Students can write what they already know in the *K* column. They can record their questions in the *W* column and what they learn in the *L* column.

1 Introduce and Motivate

Preview Ask students what it means to debate. Tell students that they will learn more about the debates during the writing of the Constitution as they read Lesson 2.

You Are There As the convention began, many wondered whether or not it would succeed. Ask students to predict what problems the convention may encounter.

1785   1790

May 1787 Constitutional Convention begins

September 1787 Delegates to Constitutional Convention approve Constitution

●Philadelphia

PREVIEW

Focus on the Main Idea
At the Constitutional Convention, a group of leaders wrote the Constitution, a new plan for a stronger national government.

PLACES
Philadelphia, Pennsylvania

PEOPLE
James Madison
Alexander Hamilton

VOCABULARY
delegate
Constitutional Convention
Virginia Plan
New Jersey Plan
compromise
Great Compromise
Three-Fifths Compromise
Preamble
reserved powers
separation of powers
checks and balances
veto

344

Debate in Philadelphia

You Are There You are a reporter for a Philadelphia newspaper in 1787. You are about to cover your first big story.

Representatives from around the country are meeting in your city. The goal of the representatives? To strengthen the shaky national government.

Among the representatives is the beloved George Washington. On his arrival, he is greeted with an artillery salute and chiming bells. Hosting the convention is Pennsylvania's Benjamin Franklin. At 81, he is the oldest to take part.

Will the assembly succeed in its goal? You wonder what plan they can work out that will strengthen the nation's representative democracy.

Draw Conclusions As you read, see what conclusions you can draw about why the writers of the Constitution made the decisions they did.

Practice and Extend

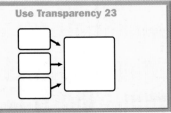

READING SKILL
Draw Conclusions

In the Lesson Review, students complete a graphic organizer like the one below. You may want to provide students with a copy of Transparency 23 to complete as they read the lesson.

Use Transparency 23

VOCABULARY
Word Exercise

Individual Word Study Some words may be used as different parts of speech. Write these sentences on the board: *They sent a delegate to the convention. We should delegate someone to go to the convention.* Discuss the meanings of *delegate* as a noun and verb. Ask students to read the sentences and tell you which part of speech *delegate* is in each sentence. Use a dictionary to show students that the part of speech can affect the pronunciation of *delegate.*

The Constitutional Convention

In late May 1787, 55 representatives, or **delegates,** began filing into the State House in **Philadelphia, Pennsylvania.** Some of them had been here many times before, as members of the Second Continental Congress. In this same hall, some had heard the Declaration of Independence proclaimed. Here some had faced the challenge of fighting the Revolution. Now they faced the challenge of strengthening the government in the new republic. The original goal of the delegates was to revise the Articles of Confederation. However, they would end up replacing the Articles with a new Constitution. Their meeting would become known as the **Constitutional Convention.**

One of the first delegates to arrive was **James Madison** of Virginia. Madison had been one of the youngest members of the Continental Congress. A leading nationalist, his day-to-day notes are the most complete record of the Constitutional Convention. The effort, he later admitted, "nearly killed me."

You will read more about Madison in the Biography on page 351.

From New York came **Alexander Hamilton.** He was barely out of his teens when he had become military aide to General Washington during the Revolutionary War. By now, he was a well-known lawyer and he had strong opinions of how government can and should work.

Like these men, the other delegates were among the smartest leaders in the country. More than half of them had fought in the Revolutionary War, and many had helped write their state constitutions. ②

To no one's surprise, the delegates unanimously elected George Washington to be the leader of the convention. They also decided ③ that they must work in secret. In his writings, Madison explained why. The delegates had to be able to speak freely and to change their minds. So guards were placed at the doors. Windows were nailed shut. Gravel was spread on the street outside to quiet street noises.

REVIEW Why did the delegates maintain secrecy about their work?
⊙ **Draw Conclusions**

▶ James Madison *(right)* was one of the leaders of the Constitutional Convention. Today the State House where the delegates met is called Independence Hall.

345

Meetings in Philadelphia

- Philadelphia was an important city during colonial times. Established in 1681, the city had a population of at least 30,000 by the 1770s, making it an important business center.

- One of Philadelphia's most famous residents was Benjamin Franklin, who was a member of the Second Continental Congress and served on the committee that assisted Thomas Jefferson in writing the Declaration of Independence. At the age of 81, Franklin was the oldest delegate to the Constitutional Convention.

- The city was chosen for the Continental Congress because of its location at the midpoint of the colonies. Philadelphia was to serve as the capital of the United States from 1790 to 1800.

2 Teach and Discuss

PAGE 345

The Constitutional Convention

🕐 *Quick Summary* In May 1787 delegates met in Philadelphia to revise the Articles of Confederation to form a stronger government.

 **Test Talk**

Locate Key Words in the Question

① **What was the goal of the delegates?** Have students use the key words *goal* and *delegates* to finish the statement "I need to find out. . . ." To revise the Articles; to strengthen the government **Main Idea and Details**

② **Do you think the delegates were qualified for their task? Why or why not?** Possible answer: Yes, some had worked on the Declaration of Independence, and many had helped write their state constitutions. ⊙ **Draw Conclusions**

③ *Unanimously* **means "in complete agreement." Why do you think George Washington was the unanimous choice to lead the convention?** Possible answer: He was well known and respected for his leadership skills. ⊙ **Draw Conclusions**

✓ **REVIEW ANSWER** They had to be able to speak freely and change their minds during debate.
⊙ **Draw Conclusions**

Competing Plans

 Quick Summary Delegates from Virginia and New Jersey proposed different plans for the new government.

Primary Source

Cited in *The Challenge of America,* by Stephen H. Bronz

④ Based on Mason's quotation, what did he consider important in government? Wisdom (wise) and justice (just) **Analyze Primary Sources**

H SOCIAL STUDIES STRAND
History

Remind students of the events that led up to the Constitutional Convention. The Articles of Confederation had resulted in a weak government and severe economic trouble for the nation.

⑤ Why was the Convention so important? What might have happened to the nation had it not been held? Possible answer: The nation needed a government that worked. The United States may have failed if a constitution had not been created.
Draw Conclusions

⑥ Summarize the main points of the Virginia Plan. Possible answer: Congress would have much greater power over the states. There would be three branches of government, and each state would have a number of representatives based on state population. **Summarize**

✓ Ongoing Assessment

If... students are unable to summarize the main points,	**then...** have students read the information about the Virginia Plan while you write the main ideas on the board. Volunteers can use your notes to create summaries.

✓ **REVIEW ANSWER** Both plans proposed a stronger national government, but they disagreed on how many representatives large and small states would have in Congress. **Compare and Contrast**

James Madison Alexander Hamilton George Washington

Ben Franklin

▶ The 55 delegates to the Constitutional Convention included many of the country's most important men. They elected George Washington as leader of the convention.

Competing Plans

Delegate George Mason of Virginia set the tone for the Constitutional Convention:

④ *"The eyes of the United States are turned upon this assembly... God grant that we may be able to satisfy them by establishing a wise and just government."*

⑤ Just about all the delegates agreed that the national government must be made stronger. Many believed that with a few changes the Articles of Confederation could do this. But James Madison and some other delegates thought differently. They wanted to throw out the Articles entirely and write a new constitution. So they made up their own plan. Virginia delegate Edmund Randolph presented it to the Convention.

The **Virginia Plan** proposed that Congress be given much greater power over the states. It also stated that the national government should have an executive branch to carry out laws created by Congress. In addition, the Virginia Plan stated that the national government should have a judicial branch to interpret the laws passed by Congress. This plan also said that states with larger populations, like Virginia, should have more representatives in Congress than should smaller states.

Smaller states had one major objection to the Virginia Plan. They did not believe that larger states should have more power than smaller states. So New Jersey delegate William Paterson proposed the **New Jersey Plan.** It stated that each state, large or small, would have the same number of representatives in Congress. In this way, all the states would have equal power.

Paterson argued for his plan this way: "There is no more reason that a great individual state, contributing much, should have more votes than a small one, contributing little, than a rich individual citizen should have more votes than a [poor] one."

Debate over the two competing plans continued into the hot summer.

REVIEW How would you compare and contrast the Virginia Plan and the New Jersey Plan? **Compare and Contrast**

Practice and Extend

 MEETING INDIVIDUAL NEEDS
Leveled Practice

The Virginia and New Jersey Plans Allow students to review the two plans.

Easy Make a T-chart on the board with the names of the two plans as column heads. Ask students to give details about each plan as you write their ideas in the appropriate columns. Alternatively, you can say the details aloud and ask students in which column those details belong. **Reteach**

On-Level Have students create Venn diagrams to compare and contrast the plans. Remind them that details describing both plans belong in the overlapping section. Students should share their work with the class. **Extend**

Challenge Students could act as Edmund Randolph and William Paterson and explain their proposals to classmates acting as delegates to the convention. You might prepare questions to ask the delegates. Encourage delegates to debate, supporting their opinions with sound reasons. **Enrich**

For a Lesson Summary, use Quick Study, p. 74.

A Compromise Plan

The only thing that could save the Convention from failure was compromise. In a **compromise,** each side gives up something to reach an agreement. Roger Sherman of Connecticut suggested that Congress should be made up of not just one part but of two parts, called houses. One of the houses would be a Senate and the other a House of Representatives. In the Senate, each and every state would be represented by two senators. The states would be equal in power in the Senate. But in the House of Representatives, population would determine the number of representatives each state had. Large states would have more representatives than small states.

After a month's discussion, the Convention finally agreed to Sherman's compromise. It came to be known as the **Great Compromise.**

At the same time, the delegates faced another difficult problem. States where slavery was practiced widely—Southern states— wanted enslaved people counted as part of their populations. This would give them more representation in Congress. But they did not want slaves counted when it came to being taxed. States without widespread slavery— Northern states—objected.

Finally the **Three-Fifths Compromise** was worked out. Enslaved people would be counted as part of a state's population for both representation in Congress and for taxes. However, only three-fifths of their number would count. This meant that only three out of every five slaves would be counted. If a state had 50,000 slaves, only 30,000 people would be added to the count of its population. **8**

Northern and Southern states also compromised about the slave trade. Northern delegates agreed that Congress would take no action against importing slaves for 20 years. Twenty years later, in 1808, Congress did outlaw the importing of enslaved people into the United States.

By September, the long, hot summer of debate finally ended in Philadelphia. Little did the delegates know that this Constitution would one day make the United States the world's oldest continuous republic. **9**

REVIEW Explain how Roger Sherman helped the Constitutional Convention succeed. **Summarize**

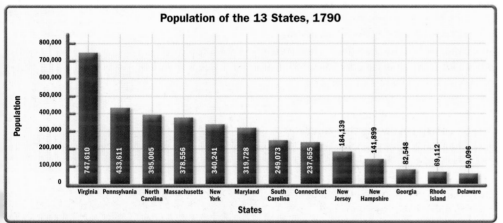

Population of the 13 States, 1790

State	Population
Virginia	747,610
Pennsylvania	433,611
North Carolina	395,005
Massachusetts	378,556
New York	340,241
Maryland	319,728
South Carolina	249,073
Connecticut	237,655
New Jersey	184,139
New Hampshire	141,899
Georgia	82,548
Rhode Island	69,112
Delaware	59,096

▶ The population of the states varied greatly in 1790.

GRAPH SKILL *Which states had the largest and smallest populations in 1790?*

347

A Compromise Plan

🕐 *Quick Summary* The Great Compromise and the Three-Fifths Compromise ended the convention.

7 **Explain the most important ideas of the Great Compromise.** Possible answer: Congress would have two houses, a Senate and a House of Representatives. Each state would have two senators and a number of representatives based on the state's population. **Main Idea and Details**

8 **Why do you think the Three-Fifths Compromise was accepted?** Possible answer: Because it held good and bad points for each side; counting enslaved people as part of the population would give Southern states more representation in Congress, but it would also enable the government to collect more tax money, which would benefit the Northern states. **Draw Conclusions**

9 **Tell, in time order, the main events of the Constitutional Convention.** Virginia Plan proposed; New Jersey Plan proposed; Great Compromise accepted; Three-Fifths Compromise worked out; convention ended **Sequence**

✓ **REVIEW ANSWER** Roger Sherman contributed to the Constitutional Convention and the creation of the U.S. Constitution by suggesting his "Great Compromise." This compromise helped determine the number of representatives each state would have in Congress. **Summarize**

GRAPH SKILL **Answer** Largest: Virginia; Smallest: Delaware

ESL **EXTEND LANGUAGE**
ESL Support

Examine Word Meanings Tell students that *compromise* means "to settle a dispute by giving up part of what each side demands."

Beginning Describe a recent situation in school or your community in which individuals or groups *compromised* in order to resolve an issue. Have students act out the situation to help them understand what took place.

Intermediate Pose a scenario to illustrate the meaning of *compromise*. You could, for example, point to one group of students and say, "They want to eat lunch at 12:00." Point to another group and say, "They want to eat lunch at 1:00. We can compromise and eat lunch at 12:30." Have students describe or pantomime other compromise scenarios.

Advanced Have students work in groups to create skits that show people compromising on an issue. Allow groups to present their work.
For additional ESL support, use Every Student Learns Guide, pp. 146–149.

Our Constitution

 **Quick Summary** The Constitution divides the government into three branches, identifies shared and reserved powers, and provides a system of checks and balances.

Primary Source

From the Constitution of the United States

10 **What goals for the nation are identified in the Preamble to the Constitution?** Union, justice, peace, defense, welfare, and liberty
Analyze Primary Sources

11 **What are reserved powers? Give an example.** Powers left for the states, such as managing education and elections Main Idea and Details

G SOCIAL STUDIES STRAND
Government

Tell students that the government of Great Britain is a constitutional monarchy and a parliamentary democracy. The head of state is a king or queen. A prime minister heads the government. The government has three branches, but their duties overlap.

12 **Compare the government set up by the Constitution to the government in England.** The U.S. government does not have a king, but an elected President. The U.S. government also has three branches. Compare and Contrast

13 **Explain what is meant by *separation of powers*.** Each branch of the government has different and separate powers.
Main Idea and Details

14 **Give one example of checks and balances in the U.S. government.** Possible answer: The President can veto an act that Congress has passed.
Apply Information

✓ **REVIEW ANSWER** The Legislative Branch makes laws, the Executive Branch puts laws into practice, and the Judicial Branch sees that laws are interpreted according to the Constitution. Main Idea and Details

Our Constitution

The Constitution begins with a **Preamble**, or introduction. It includes these ringing words:

> *"We the People of the United States, in Order to form a more perfect Union, establish Justice, insure domestic Tranquility, provide for the common defense, promote the general Welfare, and secure the Blessings of Liberty to ourselves and our Posterity, do ordain and establish this Constitution for the United States of America."*

The Preamble clearly set out the Constitution's major goals: to establish justice, to ensure peace, to defend the nation, and to **10** protect the people's well-being and liberty.

The Constitution then spelled out those powers that only the national government will have. For example, only the national government can make laws about trade with other countries. Only the national government may produce coins and paper money. The Constitution leaves many other powers strictly to state governments. These are called **reserved powers**, because they are "reserved," or left, for the states. Reserved powers include managing education and elections. The two levels of government share certain other powers, like passing **11** tax laws and managing roads.

The Constitution divides the national government into three branches. Congress makes up the Legislative Branch, which is charged with making laws. The job of putting the laws into practice and making sure they are obeyed falls to the Executive Branch,

348

headed by the President. The Judicial Branch, headed by the Supreme Court, sees that the laws are interpreted according to the Constitution. Look at the chart on the next page to study the powers of the three branches. This three-part government provides a **separation of powers**. In other words, each branch has different and separate powers.

To guard against any one branch becoming too powerful, the Constitution provides a system of **checks and balances**. As the chart shows, Congress has the right to pass laws. But the President can **veto**, or refuse to sign into law, an act that Congress wants. This is a check, or limit, that the President has on Congress. But Congress can overturn this veto if two-thirds of its members still want the law. This is a check Congress has on the President. Finally, the courts, or the Judicial Branch, can overturn what the Legislative or Executive Branch does if the courts find the actions to be against the Constitution.

One branch can check the power of another. So all branches can maintain a balance of power among them. Find more examples of checks and balances on the chart.

REVIEW Identify the role of each of the three branches of government.
Main Idea and Details

▶ The Preamble states the goals of the Constitution.

Practice and Extend

Create a Pamphlet

• Have students create an informational pamphlet explaining the branches of the U.S. government.

• Include both text and diagrams or other visuals that will help others understand the three branches, their duties, the system of checks and balances, the separation of powers, and how they promote the common good and protect individual rights.

Balance Equations

• Students may not realize that when they solve mathematical equations, they keep them in balance.

• Write the equation $75 \times n = 225$ on the chalkboard.

• As you explain the steps in solving the equation and isolating the variable, remind students that the equation must be kept *in balance*.

FACT FILE

The Three Branches of Government

The writers of the Constitution believed that government's powers should be limited. They created three separate branches with a system of checks and balances to limit the power of each branch. The people provide the final check over all three branches.

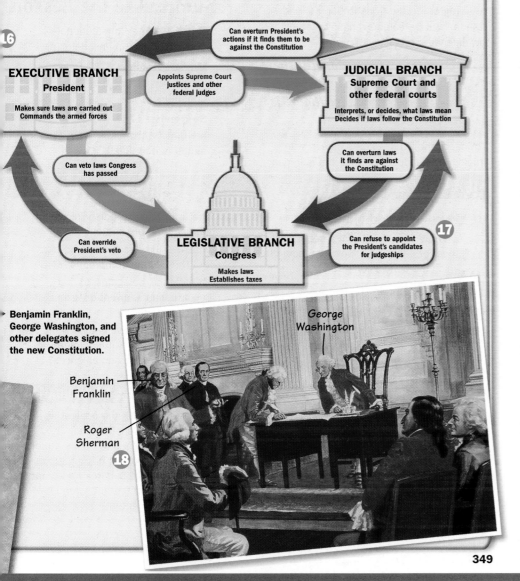

EXECUTIVE BRANCH
President
Makes sure laws are carried out
Commands the armed forces

Can overturn President's actions if it finds them to be against the Constitution

Appoints Supreme Court justices and other federal judges

JUDICIAL BRANCH
Supreme Court and other federal courts
Interprets, or decides, what laws mean
Decides if laws follow the Constitution

Can veto laws Congress has passed

Can overturn laws it finds are against the Constitution

Can override President's veto

LEGISLATIVE BRANCH
Congress
Makes laws
Establishes taxes

Can refuse to appoint the President's candidates for judgeships

Benjamin Franklin, George Washington, and other delegates signed the new Constitution.

George Washington

Benjamin Franklin

Roger Sherman

349

FACT FILE

The Three Branches of Government

15 **Why do you think that the writers of the Constitution believed that the government's powers should be limited?** Possible answer: They remembered the abuses of power that led to the American Revolution. Express Ideas

Test Talk

Use Information from Graphics

16 **Which branch is in charge of the U.S. armed forces?** Tell students to look at the chart to find the right answer. The Executive Branch Interpret Charts

G **SOCIAL STUDIES STRAND**
Government

Democratic Values The U.S. Constitution embodies some of our most important values and established key institutions. The U.S. Congress met for the first time on March 4, 1789, in New York.

Also inform students that their own state constitution expresses similar democratic values of those found in the U.S. Constitution. Discuss with students the democratic values that the constitutions share, as well as differences that may exist between the two documents.

17 **How does the Legislative Branch provide a "check" on the Judicial Branch?** It can refuse to appoint the President's candidates for judgeships. Interpret Charts

18 **Look at the picture of the delegates signing the Constitution. How do you think they may have felt?** Possible answer: They were happy, concerned, and relieved. Analyze Pictures

G **SOCIAL STUDIES STRAND**
Government

What the United States Government Does for Us

We depend on the national government to help us in our schools, communities, states, and country. The government makes and enforces laws that bring order to our lives and protect our basic rights. It provides defense of our country, regulates commerce and communication, and collects taxes to provide for the "general welfare" of all citizens. Tax money helps pay for Social Security, the armed forces, combating poverty, and even our interstate highway system and space program. The national government makes grants-in-aid to states and sometimes communities. On the state level this includes disaster relief, the preservation of resources, and the National Guard. In communities, help might come for housing projects or to prevent crime. Schools sometimes get aid to buy equipment or books or to establish reading programs. Have students discuss other ways the national government helps. Next, have them research the names of their representatives at the local, state, and national levels of government.

The Work Still Ahead

🕐 *Quick Summary* The Constitution was signed by a majority and then sent to the states to be ratified.

Primary Source

Cited in *A More Perfect Union,* by William Peters

19 **What idea did Franklin express before he signed the Constitution?** That the delegates could do no better and that this might be the best plan
Analyze Primary Sources

✓ **REVIEW ANSWER** The delegates needed to approve the Constitution. Nine of the 13 states needed to ratify the approved document. Sequence

3 Close and Assess

Summarize the Lesson

Ask students to create an acrostic using the word *Constitution.* Each letter should help form a word, fact, or idea about the Constitution.

✓ **LESSON 2** **REVIEW**

1. 🔄 **Draw Conclusions** For possible answers, see the reduced pupil page.

2. Madison was one of the leaders of the convention.

3. The plan to have two houses of Congress to account for differences in state populations; the plan for three-fifths of enslaved people to be counted

4. The original goal was to revise the Articles of Confederation.

5. **Critical Thinking:** *Evaluate* Possible answer: They believed that the government's powers should have limits.

About 71% signed it; about 69%

The Work Still Ahead

September 17, 1787, dawned as a cool, clear Monday. The time had come for the delegates to the Constitutional Convention to vote on the document they had created.

Weary of four months of disagreement and compromise, many had doubts about what they had created. One had even said, "I would sooner chop off my right hand than put it [agree] to the Constitution as it now stands." But Benjamin Franklin urged his fellow delegates to sign with him:

19 *"I consent...to this Constitution because I expect no better and because I am not sure that it is not the best."*

Most of the 55 delegates agreed with Franklin. One by one, 39 took the quill pen and signed. But the work had just begun. Nine of the states had to ratify the Constitution before it could become the supreme law of the land. And convincing them would not be easy.

REVIEW What was the sequence of events that had to take place for the Constitution to become the supreme law of the land? Sequence

Summarize the Lesson

- **May 1787** The Constitutional Convention met in Philadelphia.

- **May–September 1787** Delegates spent nearly four months creating a new Constitution.

- **September 1787** The delegates signed the Constitution and it went to the states to be ratified.

LESSON 2 **REVIEW**

Check Facts and Main Ideas

1. 🔄 Draw Conclusions On a separate sheet of paper, add two more facts on which the conclusion given below might be based.

Facts

| A legislative branch can concentrate on the work of making laws. |

Conclusion

| A separation of powers is a good way to divide the work of governing. |

| An executive branch can concentrate on carrying out the laws. |

| A judicial branch can concentrate on making sure the laws are interpreted according to the Constitution. |

2. What was James Madison's role in creating the Constitution?

3. What was the **Great Compromise?** The **Three-Fifths Compromise?**

4. What did the **delegates** to the **Constitutional Convention** expect to accomplish?

5. **Critical Thinking:** *Evaluate* Why did the writers of the Constitution create a system of **checks and balances?**

Link to ⌐○○⌐ **Mathematics**

Figure Percentage Of the original 55 delegates to the Constitutional Convention, 39 signed the Constitution. What percentage of the original group signed it? Nine of 13 states had to ratify the Constitution before it became law. What percentage is that?

350

Practice and Extend

CURRICULUM CONNECTION
Literature

The Constitution

The U.S. Constitution and You, by Syl Sobel (Barrons Juveniles, ISBN 0-764-11707-6, 2001) **Easy**

The U.S. Constitution: and Fascinating Facts About It, by Terry L. Jordan (Oak Hill Publishing, ISBN 1-891-74300-7, 1999) **On-Level**

The Dictionary of the U.S. Constitution, by Barbara Feinberg (Franklin Watts, ISBN 0-531-11570-4, 1999) **Challenge**

Workbook, p. 81

Lesson 2: Debate in Philadelphia

Directions: Describe each of the following three terms in your own words. Relate each term to at least one of the other terms. Finally, answer question 4. You may use your textbook.

1. Constitutional Convention

2. Virginia Plan

3. Great Compromise

4. Why was a government with three branches considered to be a compromise?

Notes for Home: Your child learned about the creation of the United States Constitution.
Home Activity: With your child, talk about an event in your child's life when he or she had to compromise.

Also on Teacher Resources CD-ROM

James Madison
1751–1836

As a child James Madison was small, shy, soft-spoken, and often sick. He did not have all of the obvious qualities of a leader. But he grew up to become the fourth President of the United States. He may have had a quiet voice, but he used it to speak out for what he believed.

One of the things he strongly believed in was religious freedom. In 1776, Madison attended the convention that met to create a constitution for the state of Virginia. He made sure the state's constitution guaranteed a person's "free exercise of religion." About ten years later Madison worked to pass the Virginia Statute of Religious Freedom, which was written by his lifelong friend, Thomas Jefferson. The statute prevented the state government from interfering with religion. This idea had also been supported in many other states and later became the law for all of the United States under an addition to the Constitution called the First Amendment.

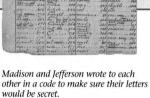

BIOFACT

Madison and Jefferson wrote to each other in a code to make sure their letters would be secret.

Madison also believed a strong central government was important to the success of the nation. He was an important leader at the Constitutional Convention in 1787 and many of his ideas became part of the Constitution. Later, his writings published in *The Federalist* papers helped convince people to ratify the Constitution. Madison became president in 1809. Under his leadership, the country fought another war with Britain. Shortly before his death, Madison expressed the importance of a country united under one central government:

> **"The advice nearest my heart and deepest in my convictions [belief] is that the Union of the States be cherished and perpetuated [made to last]."**

Learn from Biographies

Madison had a very quiet voice, but his ideas were heard and had great influence. How do you think Madison made himself heard?

For more information, go online to *Meet the People* at **www.sfsocialstudies.com.**

351

James Madison

Objective
- Identify the contributions of individuals who helped create the U.S. Constitution, including James Madison.

1 Introduce and Motivate

Preview Ask students what they learned about James Madison in Lesson 2. Tell them that they will read more about his contributions to the country.

2 Teach and Discuss

1 Summarize Madison's major contributions to the United States. Madison helped create a constitution for Virginia as well as the U.S. Constitution. He helped pass a statute on religious freedom and wrote articles to persuade others to ratify the Constitution. He also served as President of the United States. Summarize

3 Close and Assess

Learn from Biographies Answer
Possible answers: Madison probably thought carefully before he spoke; his writings and speeches may have been persuasive, with sound logic used to support his opinions.

WEB SITE
Technology

Students can find out more about James Madison by clicking on *Meet the People* at **www.sfsocialstudies.com.**

CURRICULUM CONNECTION
Writing

Write a Coded Message
- Madison and Jefferson wrote in code.
- Invite students to create codes of their own, along with answer keys.
- Encourage them to use their codes to write messages to classmates about the U.S. Constitution.

Ratifying the Constitution

Objectives

- Compare the views of Federalists with those of Antifederalists.

- Describe the Bill of Rights.

- Describe the government created by the Constitution.

Vocabulary

Federalists, p. 353; **federal,** p. 353;
Antifederalists, p. 353;
The Federalist, p. 353;
amendment, p. 354; **Bill of Rights,** p. 354

Resources

- Workbook, p. 82
- Transparency 23
- Every Student Learns Guide, pp. 150–153
- Quick Study, pp. 76–77

Quick Teaching Plan

If time is short, ask students to create outlines to show the main ideas and supporting details in this lesson.

- Write the three section titles on the board. Tell students to use these titles as the main points in their outlines.
- Students should write details about each of the main points as they read the lesson independently.

1 Introduce and Motivate

Preview To activate prior knowledge, review with students the debates that took place at the Constitutional Convention. Tell students that they will learn how the Constitution was ratified by the states as they read Lesson 3.

You Are There Remind students that George Mason set the tone for the Constitutional Convention. Ask students to predict whether ratification of the U.S. Constitution will go smoothly or prove difficult.

LESSON 3

New York City

1785			1790
	1787 Delaware is first state to ratify the Constitution	**1788** Constitution is ratified	**1** B is

PREVIEW

Focus on the Main Idea
After a long debate, the states ratified the United States Constitution.

PLACES
New York City, New York

PEOPLE
Benjamin Rush

VOCABULARY
Federalists
federal
Antifederalists
The Federalist
amendment
Bill of Rights

Ratifying the Constitution

You Are There It is June 4, 1788. You have just taken your seat as a delegate to the Virginia Constitutional Convention. George Mason rises to speak. He is the same man who expressed great hope for the Constitutional Convention in Philadelphia a year ago. But now he speaks out against the Constitution:

"The very idea of converting what was once a confederation to a consolidated [central] government is totally [against] every principle which…governed us….Will the people…submit to be individually taxed by two different and distinct powers? [the states and the national government]…These two…powers cannot exist long together. The one will destroy the other…"

Debates like this one have been raging across the 13 states. In each one, citizens of the state have met to decide whether or not that state will ratify the Constitution. It will be a close fight.

Draw Conclusions As you read, see what conclusions you can draw about why the Constitution was so hotly debated in the state conventions.

Practice and Extend

READING SKILL
Draw Conclusions

In the Lesson Review, students complete a graphic organizer like the one below. You may want to provide students with a copy of Transparency 23 to complete as they read the lesson.

Use Transparency 23

VOCABULARY
Word Exercise

Related Word Study Write *federal* on the board and discuss its meaning (p. 353). Then write *Federalists*. Ask what has been added (*-ist* and *-s*) and how these suffixes change the meaning of the word (a person who; plural). Then write *Antifederalists*. Explain that the prefix *anti-* means "opposite or against." So this group is against the Federalists. Point out that the last two words are capitalized because they were the names of political parties.

The Federalists and Antifederalists

The Constitution gave the nationalists the strong national government they had wanted. Now they became known as the **Federalists.** The word **federal** refers to the national government. But many people, like George Mason, were not happy with the Constitution. These people came to be known as the **Antifederalists.**

Many famous and powerful Americans were Antifederalists. In Virginia, along with Mason, there was Patrick Henry. In Massachusetts, Samuel Adams and John Hancock voiced opposition to the Constitution.

The Antifederalists strongly expressed their fears. One fear was that the Constitution would reduce the powers of the states. Patrick Henry expressed a second fear: "Your President may easily become king." The Antifederalists worried that the federal government would pass laws that were not suitable for one part of the country or another. It was "impossible," said some Antifederalists, to please all parts of the country with the same laws.

Antifederalists also argued that the Constitution did not truly protect important rights of Americans from the government. These rights included freedom of religion, freedom of the press, trial by jury, and others. Though not an Antifederalist, Thomas Jefferson, who was still in France, supported this argument. Jefferson believed that the people should be guaranteed certain rights. He

said that these rights could not be taken away by the government. Jefferson said: "A bill of rights is what the people are entitled to against every government on earth."

James Madison, Alexander Hamilton, and John Jay led the Federalist fight for the Constitution. They organized actions to educate the people about it. Madison, Hamilton, and John Jay of New York wrote a series of essays called **The Federalist.** The essays appeared at first in **New York City, New York** newspapers in 1787 and were read by many people. Each essay explained the weaknesses of an Antifederalist argument.

In *The Federalist: Number 51,* Madison defended the national government that the Constitution had created. Madison wrote:

> *"If men were angels, no government would be necessary. If angels were to govern men, [no]... controls on government would be necessary."* **4**

REVIEW How would you summarize arguments made against and for the Constitution? **Summarize**

▶ **Alexander Hamilton** wrote many of the essays that were printed in *The Federalist.*

THE
FEDERALIST:
A COLLECTION
OF
E S S A Y S,
WRITTEN IN FAVOUR OF THE

353

The Federalists and Antifederalists

🕐 *Quick Summary* Federalists supported a strong central government; Antifederalists opposed it.

① **What rights were important to Americans?** Freedom of religion and of the press; trial by jury and right to an attorney **Summarize**

② **Why might these rights not have been included in the Constitution?** Possible answer: The focus was on checks and balances not rights of individuals. **Hypothesize**

③ **How did the Federalists fight for approval of the Constitution?** They organized actions to educate people about it. **Generalize**

Primary Source
Cited in *The Federalist: Number 51,* by James Madison

④ **Why did James Madison believe that the government was necessary?** It makes sure that leaders acted lawfully. **Analyze Primary Sources**

✓ **REVIEW ANSWER** Against: loss of power by states; too much power invested in the President; individual rights not protected; For: strong central government; checks and balances and separation of powers **Summarize**

MEETING INDIVIDUAL NEEDS
Leveled Practice

Write About an Issue Work with students to review the methods used by the Federalists to promote the passage of the Constitution of the United States.

Easy Ask students to suppose that they are writing for *The Federalist.* Have them dictate sentences explaining why the Constitution should be ratified. **Reteach**

On-Level Have pairs of students write two newspaper editorials as if they were written in 1787—one in favor of the Constitution and one opposed. **Extend**

Challenge Have students consider the United States today. Challenge them to write what a Federalist and an Antifederalist might say about the Constitution and the effect that it has had on the country. **Enrich**

For a Lesson Summary, use Quick Study, p. 76.

The Bill of Rights

 **Quick Summary** The Bill of Rights pledged to guarantee personal freedoms by placing specific limits on government. This convinced some states to ratify the Constitution.

CHART SKILL Answer People have rights other than those found in the Constitution.

5 **Without the Bill of Rights, do you think the Constitution would have been ratified? Why or why not?** Possible answer: No, only five of the nine necessary states had ratified the Constitution when the offer was made to add a Bill of Rights. **Hypothesize**

Test Talk

Use Information from the Text

6 **What promise was made that led to Massachusetts's support of the Constitution?** Students should look back at the text to be sure they have the right information. The Federalists' promise to add a Bill of Rights to the Constitution **Cause and Effect**

7 **Which state ratified the Constitution first? Which state cast the deciding vote for the Constitution?** Delaware; New Hampshire **Sequence**

8 **Why were the first ten amendments to the Constitution called the Bill of Rights?** Each amendment guaranteed a certain right that was not specified in the Constitution. **Draw Conclusions**

✓ Ongoing Assessment

| If... students are unable to draw conclusions about the Bill of Rights, | then... have students read the text of the first ten amendments and ask them what rights each of the ten amendments addresses. |

✓ REVIEW ANSWER
It was added to guarantee freedoms by placing certain limits on government. Many states wanted it added. **Main Idea and Details**

Bill of Rights

Amendment	Subject
First	Protects freedom of religion, freedom of speech, freedom of the press, the right to assemble peacefully, and the right to voice complaints to the government.
Second	Protects the right to own and bear firearms.
Third	States that the government cannot force people to house soldiers during peacetime.
Fourth	Protects people from unfair searches and seizures of property.
Fifth	Guarantees that no one can be deprived of life, liberty, or property without the decision of a court of law.
Sixth	Guarantees the right to a trial by a jury and a lawyer in criminal cases.
Seventh	Guarantees the right to a trial by a jury in most civil cases.
Eighth	Prohibits very high bail, fines, and extreme punishments.
Ninth	Declares that the rights of the people are not limited to those in the Constitution.
Tenth	States that powers not granted to the federal government are left to the states or to the people.

▶ The first 10 amendments to the Constitution are known as the Bill of Rights.

CHART SKILL *What does the Ninth Amendment state?*

The Bill of Rights

A few states ratified the Constitution quickly. Delaware was the first, on December 7, 1787. Pennsylvania was the second state to ratify the Constitution, thanks in part to the efforts of Benjamin Rush. Rush was a prominent doctor and writer who had signed the Declaration of Independence. He wrote articles in Philadelphia newspapers urging Pennsylvania to accept the new Constitution. By January 1788, five of the necessary nine states had ratified the Constitution.

In Massachusetts, the Constitution's lack of a bill of rights helped Antifederalists. But the Federalists pledged that Congress would add a **5** Bill of Rights to the Constitution. An addition, or change, to the constitution is called an amendment . The Bill of Rights amendments would guarantee freedoms by placing specific limits on government. Because of the Federalists' pledge, in February 1788, a constitutional convention in Massachusetts voted for ratification.

This pledge of a Bill of Rights won over other states as well. In June 1788, New Hampshire became the ninth state to ratify the Constitution. Congress set March 4, 1789, as the date for the new government to begin work. By 1790, all 13 states had accepted the Constitution as the supreme law of the land.

When the first Congress under the Constitution met, one of its first acts was to pass the 10 amendments that would come to be called the Bill of Rights. The chart on this page summarizes the Bill of Rights. You can find the entire text of the Constitution and its amendments on pages R30–R60.

REVIEW Why was the Bill of Rights added to the Constitution? Main Idea and Details

354

Practice and Extend

 ESL ACTIVATE PRIOR KNOWLEDGE
ESL Support

Discuss Multiple Meaning Words

- Write the title of this section on the board: *The Bill of Rights*. Underline the words *Bill* and *Rights*.
- Ask students to brainstorm what they know about the meaning of the words *Bill* and *Rights*. Write suggested meanings on the board.
- Tell students that the underlined words have more than one meaning. Guide them as they look up both words in dictionaries, and help them determine which meaning of the word is used in the title.
- Ask students the best way to figure out which meaning of a multiple-meaning word is used in a particular sentence (by using context).
- Demonstrate the process and provide additional practice as necessary.

For additional ESL support, use Every Student Learns Guide, pp. 150–153.

A New Government

It had been about five years since the nationalists began pushing for a stronger central government. Now at last, the Constitution provided a framework for that government. George Washington called the Constitution "that precious depository [safe place] of American happiness."

Benjamin Franklin knew that the battle to create a fair and strong government was not over. According to Maryland delegate James McHenry, Franklin was approached at the end of the Convention and asked what type of government the country had. He replied,

"A republic, if you can keep it."

The American people would have much work ahead of them to keep the republic strong. **9**

REVIEW What do you think Washington meant when he called the Constitution "that precious depository of American happiness?
◆ Draw Conclusions

Summarize the Lesson

- **1787** Delaware was the first state to ratify the Constitution.
- **1788** The Constitution was ratified.
- **1791** The Bill of Rights was ratified.

LESSON 3 REVIEW

Check Facts and Main Ideas

1. ◆ Draw Conclusions On a separate sheet of paper, fill in the diagram with two more facts that support the conclusion.

Facts

| Antifederalists argued that the Constitution would reduce the power of the states. |
| Antifederalists argued that the central government would pass laws that may not be good for all the states |
| Antifederalists argued that the Constitution did not protect Americans' rights. |

Conclusion

Antifederalists did not want the Constitution to be ratified.

2. Who were the **Federalists?** The **Antifederalists?**

3. What was **The Federalists?**

4. Why is the **Bill of Rights** so important in American government?

5. Critical Thinking: *Express Ideas* Why do you think the Constitution is called a "living document"?

Link to ∞ Art

Create a Poster Using photographs cut out of newspapers or magazines, illustrate several of the first 10 amendments—the Bill of Rights—to the Constitution. Paste or tape the photographs on posterboard to make a poster. Label each photograph, telling which amendment it represents. Give your poster a title.

355

SOCIAL STUDIES Background

Future Amendments to the Constitution Future amendments to the Constitution would guarantee personal and state freedoms by placing specific limits on the central government. Because the Constitution can be changed through a legitimate constitutional amendment process, it is considered a "living document." Share with students some of the following amendments.

- 1865—Thirteenth Amendment: abolished slavery
- 1870—Fifteenth Amendment: guaranteed the right to vote regardless of race
- 1920—Nineteenth Amendment: gave women the right to vote

Workbook, p. 82

Lesson 3: Ratifying the Constitution

Directions: A flowchart is a diagram that shows, step by step, a process of how something works or happens. Complete the flowchart using the items in the box.

Antifederalism	*The Federalist* essays explained the weaknesses of Antifederalist arguments.
A Bill of Rights is promised.	All 13 states ratify the Constitution, making it the supreme law of the land.
Federalists	This group feared that the central government would pass laws that were not suitable for all parts of the country.

The Constitution is sent to the states for ratification.

Notes for Home: Your child learned the sequence of events leading to the ratification of the Constitution. *Home Activity:* With your child, discuss how history might have been different if one of the events in this flowchart had not occurred.

Also on Teacher Resources CD-ROM.

PAGE 355

A New Government

🕐 *Quick Summary* The Constitution provided a framework for a strong, fair central government.

9 **What do you think Franklin meant by his comment?** Keeping the United States a republic would require hard work. **Make Inferences**

✓**REVIEW ANSWER** Possible answer: The Constitution would help Americans protect their freedom and pursue their happiness. ◆ Draw Conclusions

3 Close and Assess

Summarize the Lesson

Have students create Venn diagrams to compare and contrast the views of the Federalists and the Antifederalists.

✓ **LESSON 3 REVIEW**

1. ◆ Draw Conclusions For possible answers, see the reduced pupil page.

2. Federalists wanted strong national government and supported the Constitution; Antifederalists did not.

3. A series of essays about the importance of ratifying the Constitution

4. It guarantees certain rights and personal freedoms to U.S. citizens.

5. **Critical Thinking: *Express Ideas*** Because the Constitution can undergo change

Link to ∞ Art

Ask students to explain how their pictures show the Bill of Rights.

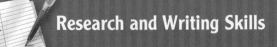

Research and Writing Skills

Gather and Report Information

Objective
- Use a research process to gather and report factual information.

Resource
- Workbook, p. 83

1 Introduce and Motivate

What does it mean to gather and organize information? Ask students why historians might consult reference sources as they conduct research about life in the past. Then have students read the **What?** section of text on p. 356 to help set the purpose of the lesson.

Why organize information gathered from research? Have students read the **Why?** section of text on p. 356. Ask them to summarize the research process (collect facts using various reference sources, organize the information, and write the report). Encourage them to explain the importance of each step.

2 Teach and Discuss

How is this skill used? Examine with students the pictures on p. 356.

- Tell students that it is usually a good idea to use multiple sources as they gather information.

- Work with students to list various reference sources they have used. Ask how these sources are used and what type of information can be found in each.

- Have students read the **How?** section of text on p. 357.

356 Unit 5 • Life in a New Nation

Research and Writing Skills

Gather and Report Information

What? To write a report, you will often have to find information beyond what is available in your textbook. Where can you find facts on topics you want to learn m about? The library and the Internet hold a vast amount of resources that provide information on almost any topic. But gathering a lot of information does not guara a good report. You must also know how to organize your report, including the mos important information, and how to write it clearly.

Why? In the previous lesson, you learned that the Federalists worked for the ratification of the Constitution and the Antifederalists worked against it. Suppose want to gather more information on the Federalists to write a report. First, you hav collect facts about the key Federalists and what they did to encourage the ratifica of the Constitution. You can use various reference sources, such as their own writings, encyclopedias, nonfiction books, and the Internet. Then you need to organize the information, and finally, write the report.

356

Practice and Extend

CURRICULUM CONNECTION
Writing

Library References
- Have students work in small groups to list and locate various primary and secondary reference sources about a historical event. Ask them to compare and contrast the accounts. For each source, students could list the type of information they would find there as well as basic steps for using the source. A visit to the library should help to spur ideas.

- Students may list resources such as encyclopedias, nonfiction books, and biographies, newspapers and magazines, artifacts, audiotapes of speeches and interviews, CD-ROMs, the Internet, and so on.

- Remind students always to cite the sources that they use. Also, tell students to put quotation marks around a writer's exact words. Warn students that copying another's words is called "plagiarism," and that writers should avoid plagiarizing when they report information.

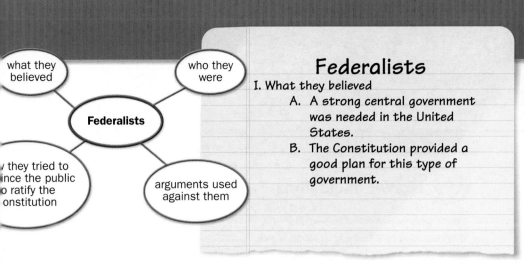

Federalists

I. What they believed
  A. A strong central government was needed in the United States.
  B. The Constitution provided a good plan for this type of government.

Graphic organizer nodes: what they believed · who they were · Federalists · how they tried to convince the public to ratify the constitution · arguments used against them

How? Before you begin your research, you should ask yourself: What do I want to know about the Federalists? You can use a graphic organizer like the one shown above to help you organize your thoughts. Notice how the subject of the report is in the middle and the branches are key subtopics. As you begin your research, you will be able to add branches to the subtopics that give more specific information on the subtopics. This will help you organize your report later on.

Once you have created a basic graphic organizer, you can begin your research. In the library, you will find the writings of many of the Federalists as well as encyclopedias that have information on almost any subject. These sources are organized alphabetically by topic. To find information on the Federalists, you might look up Federalists, the Constitution, or United States history. You can use the library's catalogue to find nonfiction books on the Federalists. A historical atlas, which contains maps and information about the past, might be a helpful resource as well. The Internet contains online encyclopedias and many Web sites with historical information. Remember to write down your sources for each piece of information you find.

Once you have gathered information on your topic and subtopics, it is time to organize and write the report. You can use your graphic organizer to help you make an outline for your report. Make sure you place your information in the correct order. Then write a rough draft. Read your rough draft to check for errors in spelling and grammar. Check to make sure you have expressed your ideas clearly. Have a classmate or teacher read your rough draft as well. Finally, write or type the final version of your report.

3

Think and Apply

1 Write the steps for gathering and reporting information in order.

2 What subjects might you look up in an encyclopedia if you needed to write a report on the Bill of Rights?

3 Why is it important to write a rough draft?

357

1 **What is the first step in conducting research?** Write a question or questions that you want to answer in order to determine your subject. You can use a graphic organizer to help organize your thoughts. Sequence

2 **In what cases might the Internet be a better reference source than a print encyclopedia?** Possible answer: When you need very current or up-to-date information ⟳ Draw Conclusions

3 **How will creating a graphic organizer help you draft your report?** The graphic can provide a framework for an outline, which can then help in writing a rough draft. Apply Information

3 Close and Assess

Think and Apply

1. Write a question or questions to guide research; identify appropriate sources and find those references; take notes and write down sources as you gather information; organize and write a draft of the report; edit the report and create a final version

2. Bill of Rights, U.S. Constitution

3. A rough draft helps a writer organize his or her thoughts. Editing the rough draft allows the writer to make ideas clearer and easier to read.

Workbook, p. 83

Gather and Report Information

Also on Teacher Resources CD-ROM.

Resources

- Assessment Book, pp. 57–60
- Workbook, p. 84: Vocabulary Review

Chapter Summary

For possible answers, see the reduced pupil page.

Vocabulary

Possible answers:

1. When a document is ratified, it is approved.

2. An amendment is an addition, or change, to the Constitution.

3. A delegate is a representative, or someone who speaks or acts for other people.

4. The New Jersey Plan for the Constitution stated that each state would have the same number of representatives in Congress.

5. Reserved powers are powers left to state governments.

6. The system of checks and balances prevents one branch of the government from becoming too powerful.

7. The Antifederalists were opposed to the Constitution and a strong central government.

8. The first ten amendments to the Constitution make up the Bill of Rights, which details the rights of citizens.

People and Places

1. Daniel Shays
2. Philadelphia
3. James Madison
4. Alexander Hamilton or John Jay or James Madison
5. Northwest Territory

Facts and Main Ideas

1. By having a governor, three judges, a legislature, and a population of at least 60,000 adult males

2. Legislative Branch: makes laws; Executive Branch: puts laws into practice; Judicial Branch: interprets laws

358 Unit 5 • Life in a New Nation

CHAPTER 10
REVIEW

1780

1781
Articles of Confederation ratified by states

Chapter Summary

Draw Conclusions

On a separate sheet of paper, fill in the diagram to supply three facts upon which the given conclusion could be based.

	Conclusion
Large and small states argued about how much power each should have.	
Northern and Southern states disagreed about how to count enslaved people.	The process of writing and ratifying the Constitution was marked by much struggle and debate.
At first, Antifederalists opposed ratification of the Constitution.	

Vocabulary

Write a sentence that explains the meaning of each vocabulary word. You may use two or more vocabulary words in a sentence.

1. ratify (p. 339)
2. amendment (p. 354)
3. delegate (p. 345)
4. New Jersey Plan (p. 346)
5. reserved powers (p. 348)
6. checks and balances (p. 348)
7. Antifederalists (p. 353)
8. Bill of Rights (p. 354)

People and Places

Fill in the blanks with the person or place that best completes the sentence.

1. _____ organized Massachusetts farmers in a rebellion against the state's government. (p. 341)
2. The Constitutional Convention took place in _____. (p. 345)
3. A record of the debates at the Constitutional Convention was kept by _____. (p. 345)
4. One contributor to The Federalist papers was _____ of New York. (p. 353)
5. In 1787, Congress decided how areas in the _____ could become states. (p. 342)

358

Practice and Extend

Assessment Options

✓ Chapter 10 Assessment

- Chapter 10 Content Test: Use Assessment Book, pp. 57–59.
- Chapter 10 Skills Test: Use Assessment Book, pp. 59–60.
- **Standardized Test Prep**
- Chapter 10 Tests contain standardized test format.

✓ Chapter 10 Performance Assessment

- Have students work in groups to list the main events and ideas surrounding one of the entries on the time line on pp. 358–359.
- Encourage students to use their lists to create questions for a quiz show about the creation of the U.S. Constitution and Bill of Rights.
- Gather the questions and use them to host a class quiz show. Assess students' understanding of the people, places, vocabulary, and events in Chapter 10.

1785

1786
Shays' Rebellion
begins

1787
Constitutional
Convention begins

1788
Constitution is
ratified

1790

1791
Bill of Rights
is ratified

Facts and Main Ideas

1. According to the Northwest Ordinance of 1787, how could a territory become a state?

2. Explain the purpose of each branch of government set up by the Constitution.

3. What rights does the First Amendment guarantee?

4. **Time Line** How many years were there between the Constitutional Convention and the ratification of the Constitution?

5. **Main Idea** Why was the national government so weak under the Articles of Confederation?

6. **Main Idea** Why was compromise important to the making of the Constitution? Give an example to support your answer.

7. **Main Idea** What two important things did the Federalists do to help get the Constitution passed in the states?

8. **Critical Thinking:** *Compare and Contrast* Compare and contrast the government set up by the Articles of Confederation and the government set up by the Constitution.

Write About History

1. **Write a pamphlet** as Daniel Shays, explaining the issues that farmers have about actions of the Massachusetts government. Use words and slogans to attract the legislature's attention.

2. **Write an editorial** for a newspaper explaining why you think states should or should not ratify the Constitution.

3. **Write a biography** on Alexander Hamilton. Use information from the text and from library resources to write a one-page biography. Include an illustration or photograph in your biography.

Apply Skills

Gather and Report Information

Use the graphic organizer below and the information on pages 356–357 to answer the questions below.

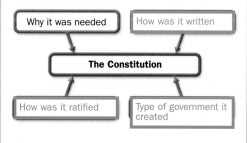

Why it was needed | How was it written

The Constitution

How was it ratified | Type of government it created

1. What steps would you follow to gather information for a report on the Constitution?

2. Complete the graphic organizer above with three more subtopics on the Constitution.

3. Using what you learned in Chapter 10, begin writing an outline using two of the subtopics from the Constitution graphic organizer.

Internet Activity

To get help with vocabulary, people, and terms, select dictionary or encyclopedia from *Social Studies Library* at **www.sfsocialstudies.com.**

359

Hands-on Unit Project

✓ Unit 5 Performance Assessment

- See p. 392 for information about using the Unit Project as a means of performance assessment.
- A scoring guide is provided on p. 392.

WEB SITE
Technology

For more information, students can select the dictionary or encyclopedia from *Social Studies Library* at **www.sfsocialstudies.com.**

Workbook, p. 84

Also on Teacher Resources CD-ROM.

---

3. Freedom of religion, speech, the press, peaceable assembly, and petitioning the government

4. One year

5. The Articles gave more powers to states, making the central government weak in many areas.

6. Compromise was needed because many different interests were represented. The Great Compromise provided a plan fair to both large and small states.

7. Educated potential voters; promised to add the Bill of Rights

8. Articles: Weak central government with only one branch; Constitution: Strong national government with three branches; In both, certain rights were given to states rather than to the federal government.

Write About History

1. Remind students to use persuasive language and to support opinions with facts.

2. Have students create lists to organize their writing. They can title the lists with their positions and then write details that support their positions.

3. Tell students to use at least three reference sources, reminding them to cite their sources and use quotation marks around authors' words.

Apply Skills

1. Write questions to answer through research; identify resources to find out about the Constitution

2. For possible answers, see the reduced pupil page.

3. Outlines should incorporate information from the chapter.

CHAPTER 1

Chapter Planning Guide

Chapter 11 • The Young United States

Locating Time and Place pp. 360–361

Lesson Titles	Pacing	Main Ideas
Lesson 1 **Washington as President** pp. 362–366	2 days	• George Washington became the nation's first President and organized the new government.
Biography: Benjamin Banneker p. 367 **Issues and Viewpoints:** **Forming Political Parties** pp. 368–369		• Benjamin Banneker re-created the plan for the new city, which became Washington, D.C. • Different ideas about government caused people to form political parties.
Lesson 2 **Jefferson Looks West** pp. 370–376	3 days	• The new nation doubled its size and expanded settlement westward.
Lewis and Clark p. 377 **Map and Globe Skills: Compare** **Population Density Maps** pp. 378–379		• Lewis and Clark traveled westward through the Louisiana Territory. • Population density maps can be used to learn how the population of an area changes over time.
Lesson 3 **Another War with Britain** pp. 380–384	2 days	• The United States fought Britain in the War of 1812 to gain freedom of the seas and to end British interference with the westward expansion of the United States.
Biography: Tecumseh p. 385		• Tecumseh, the leader of the Shawnee, battled to protect the lands he believed rightfully belonged to Native Americans.

✓**Chapter 11 Review**
pp. 386–387

◀ **Tecumseh was a Shawnee known for his bravery and speaking skills.**

✓ = Assessment Options

Jefferson invented this machine that he used to write a letter and make a copy at the same time.

Vocabulary	Resources	Meeting Individual Needs
electoral college inauguration Cabinet political party	• Workbook, p. 86 • Transparency 23 • Every Student Learns Guide, pp. 154–157 • Quick Study, pp. 78–79	• ESL Support, TE p. 364 • Leveled Practice, TE p. 365 • Learning Styles, TE p. 367
pioneer frontier Louisiana Purchase distribution map population density map	• Workbook, p. 87 • Transparencies 6, 46, 47 • Every Student Learns Guide, pp. 158–161 • Quick Study, pp. 80–81 • Workbook, p. 88	• ESL Support, TE p. 372 • Leveled Practice, TE p. 373
neutral Battle of Tippecanoe War Hawks War of 1812 national anthem Battle of New Orleans	• Workbook, p. 89 • Transparency 20 • Every Student Learns Guide, pp. 162–165 • Quick Study, pp. 82–83	• Leveled Practice, TE p. 381 • ESL Support, TE p. 383 • Learning Styles, TE p. 384
	✓ Chapter 11 Content Test, Assessment Book, pp. 61–62 ✓ Chapter 11 Skills Test, Assessment Book, pp. 63–64	✓ Chapter 11 Performance Assessment, TE p. 386

Providing More Depth

Additional Resources

- Vocabulary Workbook and Cards
- Social Studies Plus! pp. 128–133
- Daily Activity Bank
- Big Book Atlas
- Student Atlas
- Outline Maps
- Desk Maps

Technology

- AudioText
- MindPoint® Quiz Show CD-ROM
- ExamView® Test Bank CD-ROM
- Teacher Resources CD-ROM
- Map Resources CD-ROM
- SFSuccessNet: iText (Pupil Edition online), iTE (Teacher's Edition online), Online Planner
- **www.sfsocialstudies.com** (Biographies, news, references, maps, and activities)

 To establish guidelines for your students' safe and responsible use of the Internet, use the Scott Foresman Internet Guide.

Additional Internet Links

To find out more about:
- Thomas Jefferson, visit **www.whitehouse.gov**
- The Louisiana Purchase, visit **www.nara.gov**
- Tecumseh, visit **www.jmu.edu**

Key Internet Search Terms

- Thomas Jefferson
- Louisiana Purchase
- Tecumseh
- War of 1812

Workbook Support

 Use the following Workbook pages to support content and skills development as you teach Chapter 11. You can also view and print Workbook pages from the Teacher Resources CD-ROM.

Workbook, p. 85

Vocabulary Preview
Use with Chapter 11.

Directions: Choose the vocabulary term from the box that best completes each sentence. Not all terms will be used. Write the word on the line provided. You may use your glossary.

electoral college	pioneer	neutral	War of 1812
inauguration	frontier	Battle of Tippecanoe	national anthem
Cabinet	Louisiana Purchase	War Hawks	Battle of New Orleans
political party			

1. The **Louisiana Purchase** doubled the size of the United States.
2. "The Star-Spangled Banner" is the **national anthem** of the United States.
3. The **electoral college** is made up of people chosen by each state to vote for the President and Vice-President.
4. Daniel Boone was a **pioneer**, or person who pushed westward searching for land to settle.
5. To remain **neutral** is not to take sides.
6. A **political party** is an organized group of people who share a view of what government should be and do.
7. The **Battle of Tippecanoe** was fought in the present-day state of Indiana between United States forces and Tecumseh's soldiers.
8. **Battle of New Orleans** took place after the official end to the War of 1812 because the news had not yet arrived from Europe.
9. The **War of 1812** is remembered for dramatic battles at sea.
10. **Inauguration** is the ceremony when a newly elected President swears loyalty to the Constitution and takes office.
11. The **frontier** is the edge of settlement for early settlers who pushed westward.
12. Members of Congress who pressed for war against Britain were known as **War Hawks**.

 Notes for Home: Your child learned about the first struggles in our new nation.
Home Activity: With your child, practice spelling and defining the vocabulary words by creating a puzzle or writing each term in an original sentence.

Use with Pupil Edition, p. 360

Workbook, p. 86

Lesson 1: Washington as President
Use with Pages 362–366.

Directions: Match each name in the box to its description. Write the name on the line provided. Names may be used more than once.

George Washington	Thomas Jefferson	Benjamin Banneker
Alexander Hamilton	Pierre L'Enfant	John Adams

1. **Alexander Hamilton** He had plans to set up a national bank.
2. **George Washington** He was elected President by the electoral college in a unanimous vote.
3. **Thomas Jefferson** He was the secretary of state under Washington.
4. **Thomas Jefferson** He was a member of the Democratic-Republican party.
5. **Alexander Hamilton** He was the secretary of the treasury under Washington.
6. **Pierre L'Enfant** He designed the city of Washington, D.C.
7. **Thomas Jefferson** He opposed setting up a national bank.
8. **John Adams** He was the first President to live in the President's House.
9. **George Washington** Originally, he didn't want to become President.
10. **John Adams** He was the second President of the United States.
11. **Alexander Hamilton** He believed in a strong national government.
12. **Benjamin Banneker** He was an astronomer who helped survey the land where Washington, D.C., was built.
13. **Alexander Hamilton** He was a member of the Federalist political party.
14. **Thomas Jefferson** He wanted the country to remain a land of small farmers and skilled crafts workers.
15. **George Washington** He was "First in war, first in peace, and first in the hearts of his countrymen."

 Notes for Home: Your child learned about events that took place under President George Washington and Vice-President John Adams.
Home Activity: With your child, talk about how the U.S. government would be different today if two political parties had not developed.

Use with Pupil Edition, p. 366

Workbook, p. 87

Lesson 2: Jefferson Looks West
Use with Pages 370–376.

Directions: Complete each sentence with information from Lesson 2. You may use your textbook.

1. Thomas Jefferson was the **third** President of the United States.
2. Jefferson believed that the power of government belonged in the hands of the **people**.
3. In search of new lands to settle, Americans began moving **west** long before Jefferson became President.
4. Daniel Boone, an early pioneer, created the trail known as the **Wilderness Road**.
5. Boone led many pioneers through the **Cumberland Gap**, across the Appalachian Mountains.
6. Settlers along the Ohio and Mississippi Rivers used these waterways as **trade** routes to ship their products south.
7. Goods shipped along the Mississippi went to the Spanish-controlled port of **New Orleans** and then to the East Coast and Europe.
8. The United States doubled in size with the **Louisiana Purchase**, acquiring land that stretched from the Mississippi River to the Rocky Mountains.
9. Jefferson was interested in the lands to the west and chose **Lewis and Clark** to head an expedition to explore the unknown area.
10. The expedition to explore the West included the help of a French trapper and his Shoshone wife, **Sacagawea**, who served as a guide and interpreter for the expedition.

Notes for Home: Your child learned about changes in the nation under President Thomas Jefferson.
Home Activity: With your child, examine a map of the United States and list the present-day states that would not be part of the United States if not for the Louisiana Purchase and the Lewis and Clark expedition.

Use with Pupil Edition, p. 376

Workbook Support

Workbook, p. 88

Compare Population Density Maps

Use with Pages 378–379.

Population density maps show how many people live in an area. Comparing population density maps of the same area from different time periods can show how the population changed over time. In the maps below, each dot represents 200 enslaved persons.

Directions: Study the maps. Answer the questions that follow in the spaces provided.

Map A: 1790

Each dot represents 200 people. Present-day boundaries are shown.

Map B: 1830

Each dot represents 200 people. Present-day boundaries are shown.

1. According to Map A, which state had the greatest number of enslaved persons in 1790?

   Virginia

2. According to Map B, which two states had the greatest number of enslaved persons in 1830?

   Virginia and South Carolina

3. According to Map B, was the population of enslaved persons in 1830 more dense in Northern states or in Southern states?

   Southern states

4. According to Map A, which of the following states had the lowest population of enslaved persons in 1790? Circle the correct answer.

   Virginia   Maryland   (Pennsylvania)

5. According to the two maps, how did the population of enslaved persons in Kentucky change from 1790 to 1830?

   The population increased from 1790 to 1830. Kentucky went from lightly populated to densely populated.

 Notes for Home: Your child learned to read population density maps.
Home Activity: Using the maps on this page, discuss with your child possible reasons for the increase in the population of enslaved persons in the United States between 1790 and 1830.

Use with Pupil Edition, p. 379

Workbook, p. 89

Lesson 3: Another War with Britain

Use with Pages 380–384.

Directions: Read each pair of cause-and-effect statements. Label each statement *Cause* or *Effect* in the space provided. Draw an arrow from the cause to the effect.

1. Cause	Effect
France and Britain are at war. Neither wants the other to receive supplies from the United States.	Both France and Britain interfere with U.S. shipping.

2. Effect	Cause
U.S. trade with other countries is almost completely cut off.	The British Navy seizes U.S. sailors and cargo.

3. Effect	Cause
The Battle of Tippecanoe between U.S. forces and Native Americans is led by Shawnee leader Tecumseh.	Shawnee leader Tecumseh unites Native Americans to resist the settlement of pioneers.

4. Cause	Effect
The United States wants to end British-supported attacks against settlers on the frontier and to take Canada from the British.	America declares war on Britain. The War of 1812 lasts for two and one-half years.

5. Effect	Cause
The American warship *Constitution* receives the nickname "Old Ironsides."	In a battle between the United States and the British off the east coast of Canada, British cannonballs seem to bounce off the sides of the American warship *Constitution*.

Directions: Answer the following question in the space provided.

What is one unfulfilled American expectation of the War of 1812?

The United States never gained control of Canada.

 Notes for Home: Your child learned about why the United States went to war with Britain in 1812.
Home Activity: With your child, discuss how things might be different today if the United States still had an adversarial relationship with Britain. Ask whether he or she thinks the United States and Britain will ever declare war with each other in the future. Why or why not?

Use with Pupil Edition, p. 384

Workbook, p. 90

Vocabulary Review

Use with Chapter 11.

Directions: Complete the crossword puzzle using the clues below and the vocabulary words from Chapter 11.

Crossword with answers: PIONEER, POLITICAL, INAUGURATION, LOUISIANAPURCHASE, WAR, CABINET, NEWORLEANS, FEDERALIST, ANTHEM, ELECTORAL, TIPPECANOE, HAWKS

Across

1. An early settler who moved westward

4. A _____ party is an organized group of people who share a view of what government should be and do.

5. This ceremony is held when a newly elected President swears loyalty to the Constitution and takes office.

9. Agreement that doubled the size of the United States with land bought from the French

10. The _____ of 1812 is remembered for dramatic battles at sea.

11. The heads of certain government departments are known as this. These heads advise and help the President.

12. The official song of the United States is its national _____.

13. The _____ college is made up of people chosen by each state to vote for the President and Vice-President.

Down

2. The Battle of _____ took place after a treaty ending the war had been signed in Europe.

3. The edge of settlement for those who pushed westward

6. Not taking sides

7. The Battle of _____ was fought in the present-day state of Indiana between U.S. forces and Tecumseh's soldiers.

8. Members of Congress who pressed for war against Britain were known as War _____.

 Notes for Home: Your child learned about developments in the United States during the first presidency and thereafter.
Home Activity: With your child, create a word-search puzzle using the vocabulary terms. Create clues from the words' definitions.

Use with Pupil Edition, p. 387

Workbook, p. 91

5 Project   Two Sides

Directions: In a group, use your textbook and other references to research questions and answers for all roles. Then hold a press conference about the ratification of the Bill of Rights.

1. Questions a news reporter might ask a Federalist:

2. A Federalist's answers:

3. Questions a news reporter might ask an Antifederalist:

4. An Antifederalist's answers:

5. In the press conference, my role is (✔ one):

   ___ Federalist   ___ Antifederalist   ✔ News reporter

6. My argument (✔ one) for ___ or against ___ ratifying the Bill of Rights is _____

Most Antifederalists supported the Bill of Rights, which protected individual rights against government. Review students' roles to ensure they support arguments for or against ratification.

✔ Checklist for Students

___ I wrote my arguments for or against ratifying the Bill of Rights.

___ I wrote questions and answers on behalf of the news reporter, Federalists, and Antifederalists.

___ I chose a role to play in the press conference.

___ I helped stage the classroom press coverage.

 Notes for Home: Your child learned how Federalists and Antifederalists viewed the Bill of Rights.
Home Activity: With your child, discuss the importance of listening to opposing points of view. Give personal examples.

Use with Pupil Edition, p. 392

Assessment Support

Use these Assessment Book pages and the ExamView® Test Bank CD-ROM to assess content and skills in Chapter 11 and Unit 5. You can also view and print Assessment Book pages from the Teacher Resources CD-ROM.

Assessment Book, p. 61

Chapter 11 Test

Part 1: Content Test

Directions: Fill in the circle next to the correct answer.

Lesson Objective (1:1)

1. What was formed by the heads of the departments of the executive branch?
   - ● the Cabinet
   - Ⓑ the legislative branch
   - Ⓒ the judicial branch
   - Ⓓ the Senate

Lesson Objective (1:1)

2. What was the job of the Cabinet?
   - ● to advise the President
   - Ⓑ to run the government
   - Ⓒ to control the political parties
   - Ⓓ to inform the President of their decisions

Lesson Objective (1:2)

3. What caused political parties to emerge?
   - Ⓐ The Constitution created them.
   - Ⓑ Farmers wanted to represent themselves.
   - ● People had differences of opinion.
   - Ⓓ It was viewed as risky to have only one party.

Lesson Objective (1:2)

4. Whose ideas led to the development of two political parties?
   - Ⓐ Washington and Adams
   - Ⓑ Washington and Jefferson
   - Ⓒ Hamilton and Washington
   - ● Hamilton and Jefferson

Lesson Objective (1:3)

5. Who decided that the nation's capital would be moved to Washington, D.C.?
   - Ⓐ George Washington
   - ● Congress
   - Ⓒ Thomas Jefferson
   - Ⓓ voters

Lesson Objective (1:3)

6. What was the role of Pierre L'Enfant in the capital city?
   - Ⓐ He was hired to build homes.
   - Ⓑ He was hired to restore the city.
   - ● He was hired to design the city.
   - Ⓓ He was hired to bless the land.

Lesson Objective (2:2)

7. What did the United States wish to buy from the French when the Louisiana Purchase was made?
   - ● New Orleans
   - Ⓑ Mississippi River
   - Ⓒ Georgia
   - Ⓓ Missouri River

Lesson Objective (2:2)

8. What is one effect of the Louisiana Purchase on the United States?
   - Ⓐ The Mississippi River belonged to the French.
   - Ⓑ The port at New Orleans was closed.
   - ● The size of the country doubled.
   - Ⓓ A route to the Pacific was discovered.

Use with Pupil Edition, p. 386

Assessment Book, p. 62

Lesson Objective (2:1)

9. Which event took place because Jefferson wanted to find out about the West?
   - Ⓐ Spanish missions were built in California.
   - ● Lewis and Clark launched an expedition.
   - Ⓒ Settlers pushed the frontier.
   - Ⓓ Pioneers searched for land to settle.

Lesson Objective (2:3)

10. Which of the following was NOT a goal of the Lewis and Clark expedition?
    - Ⓐ to pay attention to the "soil and face of the country"
    - Ⓑ to establish relationships with the Native Americans
    - ● to reach the Gulf of Mexico
    - Ⓓ to find a water route to the Pacific Ocean

Lesson Objective (2:3)

11. Which of the following was NOT found by Lewis and Clark?
    - Ⓐ fabulous views
    - Ⓑ new plants and animals
    - Ⓒ a path over the Rocky Mountains
    - ● a water route to the Pacific Ocean

Lesson Objective (2:1)

12. Which of the following did NOT help the United States grow westward?
    - Ⓐ the Lewis and Clark expedition
    - Ⓑ the Louisiana Purchase
    - Ⓒ pioneers searching for new lands
    - ● the end of Jefferson's presidency

Lesson Objective (3:1)

13. What is the main reason the United States went to war with Britain for a second time?
    - Ⓐ to take over British lands
    - ● to gain freedom at sea
    - Ⓒ to stop British trade
    - Ⓓ to help France fight Britain

Lesson Objective (3:1)

14. Which of the following was NOT a factor in the United States' movement toward the War of 1812?
    - Ⓐ British alliance with Tecumseh to stop westward expansion
    - Ⓑ seizing of U.S. sailors by the British navy
    - ● British invasion of Washington, D.C.
    - Ⓓ seizing of U.S. cargo by the British navy

Lesson Objective (3:2)

15. For what is the War of 1812 best remembered?
    - Ⓐ the Battle at New York Harbor
    - Ⓑ American shrewdness
    - Ⓒ exchange of power from battle to battle
    - ● dramatic battles at sea

Lesson Objective (3:3)

16. What inspired Francis Scott Key to write "The Star-Spangled Banner"?
    - Ⓐ fireworks he saw from a ship
    - ● things he saw during the War of 1812
    - Ⓒ things he scribbled on an envelope
    - Ⓓ stories he collected from soldiers after the war

Lesson Objective (3:2)

17. What was the last battle associated with the War of 1812?
    - ● Battle of New Orleans
    - Ⓑ Battle of "Old Ironsides"
    - Ⓒ Battle at Montreal
    - Ⓓ Battle at Baltimore

Use with Pupil Edition, p. 386

Assessment Book, p. 63

Part 2: Skills Test

Directions: Use complete sentences to answer questions 1–6. Use a separate sheet of paper if you need more space.

1. What evidence is there that Washington supported the idea that the President should not be all-powerful? **Draw Conclusions**

   Possible answer: Washington set up his Cabinet to advise him on major decisions. This shows that he believed that decisions should not be made in isolation.

2. What message was Washington trying to convey when he warned against the destructive spirit of political parties? **Make Inferences**

   Possible answer: Washington wanted members of the government to work together. He believed that party divisions could weaken the government and create political enemies. Washington argued that everyone should work for the overall good of the country.

3. What facts support the conclusion that Jefferson was not a Federalist? **Draw Conclusions**

   Jefferson wanted the power to be in the hands of the people rather than the government. He felt that the Federalists had been too powerful when they were in control. To change things, he cut taxes and reduced the size of the armed forces.

4. What series of events led to the Louisiana Purchase? **Main Idea and Details**

   American pioneers used the Mississippi River and the port of New Orleans to ship goods to the East Coast and Europe. The Spanish closed the port to American trade, and the pioneers could not ship their products. Jefferson became interested in buying the port. The French gained control from the Spanish, and Jefferson made an agreement with the French to buy the Louisiana Territory.

Use with Pupil Edition, p. 386

Assessment Book, p. 64

5. What role did France play in causing the War of 1812? **Main Idea and Details**

   France and Britain were at war. Neither side wanted the other to receive goods from the United States, so they both interfered with U.S. shipping. The United States wanted to stop this interference and waged war on Britain to gain control of the seas.

Enslaved Persons: 1790   Enslaved Persons: 1830

6. Use the maps to answer the questions. **Compare Population Density Maps**

   a. What type of maps is shown?

   population density maps

   b. Compare the population of enslaved persons in Pennsylvania in 1790 and 1830.

   In 1790 the southern part of Pennsylvania had a few enslaved persons. By 1830, the state had none.

   c. In 1790 which two states had the densest population of enslaved persons?

   Maryland and Virginia

Use with Pupil Edition, p. 386

Assessment Support

Assessment Book, p. 65

Use with Pupil Edition, p. 390

Unit 5 Test

Part 1: Content Test

Directions: Fill in the circle next to the correct answer.

Lesson Objective (10–1:1)

1. What was a goal of the Articles of Confederation?
   - Ⓐ to have a strong court system
   - Ⓑ to have a central government that was all-powerful
   - Ⓒ to join the states in a weak government
   - ● to have a central government that kept the states strong

Lesson Objective (10–1:2)

2. Which of the following was NOT possible under the Articles of Confederation?
   - ● carry out laws
   - Ⓑ suggest new laws
   - Ⓒ one state, one vote
   - Ⓓ pass new laws

Lesson Objective (10–1:3)

3. Which of the following did NOT lead to Shays' Rebellion?
   - Ⓐ Farmers who didn't pay debts and taxes lost their farms.
   - Ⓑ Massachusetts farmers found it hard to pay debts and taxes.
   - ● Slaves were freed after the war.
   - Ⓓ Shays led a movement against taxes.

Lesson Objective (10–2:1)

4. Why did delegates meet at the Constitutional Convention?
   - Ⓐ to discuss dissenters
   - ● to revise the Articles of Confederation
   - Ⓒ to make plans for paying debts
   - Ⓓ to discuss making new money

Lesson Objective (10–2:2)

5. Which two plans presented different proposals for state representation?
   - Ⓐ New York and Georgia Plans
   - Ⓑ New Jersey and Georgia Plans
   - ● Virginia and New Jersey Plans
   - Ⓓ Virginia and New York Plans

Lesson Objective (10–2:3)

6. Which issue was the basis for the Great Compromise?
   - Ⓐ Supporters of the New Jersey Plan were against a stronger national government.
   - Ⓑ No one wanted to write a new plan.
   - Ⓒ Edmund Randolph wanted to lead the convention.
   - ● States with smaller populations wanted equal representation.

Lesson Objective (10–3:1)

7. Which BEST represents the viewpoint of the Federalists?
   - ● They wanted a strong national government.
   - Ⓑ They wanted the people to be in control, not the government.
   - Ⓒ They were unhappy with the Constitution.
   - Ⓓ They feared a strong central government.

Lesson Objective (10–3:2)

8. Which of the following describes the Bill of Rights?
   - Ⓐ ten changes to the Great Compromise
   - Ⓑ list of changes to the Articles of Confederation
   - Ⓒ list of freedoms granted by each state
   - ● ten freedoms added to the Constitution

Assessment Book, p. 66

Use with Pupil Edition, p. 390

Lesson Objective (10–3:3)

9. Which of the following is NOT a major goal of the Constitution of the United States?
   - Ⓐ establish justice
   - ● establish a national health care system
   - Ⓒ defend the nation
   - Ⓓ protect the people's well-being and liberty

Lesson Objective (11–1:1)

10. How did Washington organize his Cabinet?
    - Ⓐ He appointed a head of foreign affairs.
    - Ⓑ He used a representative from each state as an advisor.
    - ● He divided the work of the executive branch into departments and used the head of each department as an advisor.
    - Ⓓ He appointed his friends and family to make decisions.

Lesson Objective (11–1:2)

11. Why did two political parties emerge?
    - ● People had different ideas about how the government should be run.
    - Ⓑ People were unhappy with the President.
    - Ⓒ People didn't want to have a government.
    - Ⓓ People wanted to be told how to vote in presidential elections.

Lesson Objective (11–1:3)

12. Who was chosen to design the city of Washington, D.C.?
    - Ⓐ Benjamin Franklin
    - Ⓑ George Washington
    - Ⓒ Thomas Jefferson
    - ● Pierre L'Enfant

Lesson Objective (11–2:1)

13. Which of the following is NOT associated with westward expansion of the United States?
    - Ⓐ Daniel Boone
    - ● Washington, D.C.
    - Ⓒ Lewis and Clark
    - Ⓓ pioneers

Lesson Objective (11–2:2)

14. Which of the following BEST describes the effect of the Louisiana Purchase on the United States?
    - ● It doubled the size of the country.
    - Ⓑ It caused problems because the land was of no value.
    - Ⓒ It covered land from the Appalachians to the Atlantic coast.
    - Ⓓ It stretched to the Pacific Ocean.

Lesson Objective (11–2:3)

15. Which was NOT a reason the Lewis and Clark expedition took place?
    - Ⓐ to pay attention to the soil and the land
    - Ⓑ to establish relationships with the Native Americans
    - Ⓒ to bring information about the West to President Jefferson
    - ● to find a waterway to the Atlantic Ocean

Lesson Objective (11–3:1)

16. What did the United States hope to gain from the War of 1812?
    - Ⓐ control of the Pacific Ocean
    - ● freedom at sea
    - Ⓒ British ships
    - Ⓓ British shipping routes

Assessment Book, p. 67

Use with Pupil Edition, p. 390

Part 2: Skills Test

Directions: Use complete sentences to answer questions 1–6. Use a separate sheet of paper if you need more space.

1. How did the seizure of farms from Massachusetts farmers who could not pay property taxes affect the state's debt problem? **Draw Conclusions**

   It worsened the situation. Taking away the farmers' means of making money did nothing to help the state receive tax money to repay its debts.

2. How did the Northwest Ordinance of 1787 help the United States grow? **Make Inferences**

   The Northwest Ordinance dictated a set of conditions for the territory to become states. It also made the territory attractive to settlers by prohibiting slavery and promising freedom of speech, freedom of religion, and trial by jury.

3. Why is the Bill of Rights so important to the Constitution? **Main Idea and Details**

   The Constitution outlines guidelines for the nation as a whole. The Bill of Rights is a list of freedoms for individuals. Together they govern both the people and the nation, without the government being all-powerful.

4. What was the benefit of the President having a Cabinet? **Draw Conclusions**

   The President divided up the work so that he would not have to make decisions in isolation. This plan allowed him to focus on many things at once and be advised about his decisions from individuals who were experts in each area.

5. What effect did the Battle of New Orleans have on the War of 1812? **Main Idea and Details**

   It did not change the outcome of the war. The battle was fought after the war had been won by the United States but before news of a treaty reached New Orleans.

Assessment Book, p. 68

Use with Pupil Edition, p. 390

Population Density, 1790

Population Density, 1830

6. Use the maps to answer the questions. **Compare Population Density Maps**
   a. What can you learn by comparing the two maps?

   how population changed from 1790 to 1830

   b. Compare the population density of Georgia in 1790 and 1830.

   Possible answer: In 1790 few people lived in Georgia. The population of Georgia increased significantly by 1830.

The Young United States

Chapter 11 Outline

Resources

- Workbook, p. 85: Vocabulary Preview
- Vocabulary Cards
- Social Studies Plus!

1800, Washington, D.C.: Lesson 1

Ask students to share experiences or personal knowledge about the White House, such as where it is located and who lives there. (Washington, D.C.; the President)

1805, Near Present-Day Astoria, Oregon: Lesson 2

Ask students what they think the explorers pictured here—Lewis and Clark—might have seen during their exploration of the West. (Possible answers: Native American settlements, animals, vast prairies and mountains)

1814, Baltimore, Maryland: Lesson 3

This picture shows the inspiration for the U.S. national anthem. Ask students what the title of the anthem refers to. (It describes the flag as a banner with stars on it.)

CHAPTER
11
The Young United States

1800

Washington, D.C.
The federal government moves to the new capital city.

Lesson 1

1

1805

Near Present-Day Astoria, Oregon
Lewis and Clark reach the Pacific Ocean in their exploration of the West.

Lesson 2

2

1814

Baltimore, Maryland
Francis Scott Key writes The "Star-Spangled Banner" while watching the battle at Fort McHenry.

Lesson 3

3

360

Practice and Extend

Vocabulary Preview

- Use Workbook p. 85 to help students preview the vocabulary words in this chapter.
- Use Vocabulary Cards to preview key concept words in this chapter.

 Also on Teacher Resources CD-ROM.

Workbook, p. 85

Vocabulary Preview

Directions: Choose the vocabulary term from the box that best completes each sentence. Not all terms will be used. Write the word on the line provided. You may use your glossary.

electoral college	pioneer	neutral	War of 1812
inauguration	frontier	Battle of Tippecanoe	national anthem
Cabinet	Louisiana Purchase	War Hawks	Battle of New Orleans
political party			

1. The _____ doubled the size of the United States.
2. "The Star-Spangled Banner" is the _____ of the United States.
3. The _____ is made up of people chosen by each state to vote for the President and Vice-President.
4. Daniel Boone was a _____, or person who pushed westward searching for land to settle.
5. To remain _____ is not to take sides.
6. A _____ is an organized group of people who share a view of what government should be and do.
7. The _____ was fought in the present-day state of Indiana between United States forces and Tecumseh's soldiers.
8. The _____ took place after the official end to the War of 1812 because the news had not yet arrived from Europe.
9. The _____ is remembered for dramatic battles at sea.
10. _____ is the ceremony when a newly elected President swears loyalty to the Constitution and takes office.
11. The _____ is the edge of settlement for early settlers who pushed westward.
12. Members of Congress who pressed for war against Britain were known as _____

Notes for Home: Your child learned about the first struggles in our new nation.
Home Activity: With your child, practice spelling and defining the vocabulary words by creating a puzzle or writing each term in an original sentence.

Locating Time and Place

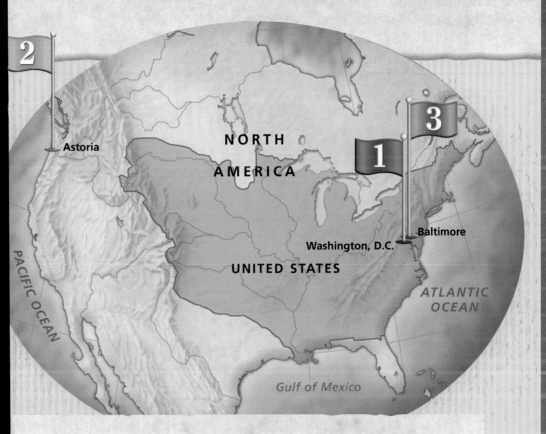

NORTH AMERICA

Astoria

UNITED STATES

Washington, D.C.

Baltimore

PACIFIC OCEAN

ATLANTIC OCEAN

Gulf of Mexico

Why We Remember

"...our flag was still there..."

As Francis Scott Key wrote down these words, which would become part of our national anthem, the United States was facing a serious threat. The year was 1814. British troops had invaded the nation's capital, burning the President's House and the Capitol Building. Key must have been wondering that day if the young republic could survive. But it did. In its early years the country faced many challenges. But after each, its flag was still waving. The young country was establishing itself as a strong nation filled with expanding opportunity.

361

- Have students examine the pictures shown on p. 360 for Lessons 1, 2, and 3.

- Remind students that each picture is coded with both a number and a color to link it to a place on the map on p. 361.

Why We Remember

Have students read the "Why We Remember" paragraph on p. 361, and ask them why events in this chapter might be important to them. Have students think about and discuss how the survival and establishment of the United States as a strong nation in the nineteenth century affected present-day life in the United States.

WEB SITE
Technology

You can learn more about Washington, D.C.; Astoria, Oregon; and Baltimore, Maryland by clicking on *Atlas* at **www.sfsocialstudies.com.**

SOCIAL STUDIES STRAND
Geography

Mental Mapping Have students draw a map of the United States from memory, including the Appalachian Mountains, the Mississippi River, the Rocky Mountains, and a compass rose. Have students work in pairs to plan a route from the Mississippi River to the Pacific Ocean, then discuss their route.

Washington as President

Objectives

- Describe how President Washington organized the Executive Branch around the Cabinet.

- Explain how political parties emerged in the American government system.

- Describe how the location and design of the nation's capital was decided upon.

Vocabulary

electoral college, p. 363;
inauguration, p. 363; **Cabinet,** p. 363;
political party, p. 364

Resources

- Workbook, p. 86
- Transparency 23
- Every Student Learns Guide, pp. 154–157
- Quick Study, pp. 78–79

Quick Teaching Plan

If time is short, have students write these names on a five-column chart: *George Washington, Alexander Hamilton, Thomas Jefferson, Pierre L'Enfant,* and *Benjamin Banneker.*

- Have students list the main contributions and points of view of each person in the appropriate column as they read the lesson independently.

1 Introduce and Motivate

Preview To activate prior knowledge, ask students to recall what they learned about the branches of government in Chapter 10. Tell students that they will learn how the provisions in the Constitution for electing a President were used in the first election in Lesson 1.

You Are There George Washington was sworn in as the first President of the United States on April 30, 1789. Have students describe what they might have seen and heard had they been at Washington's inauguration.

LESSON 1

New York
Washington, D.C.

1789
George Washington is elected first President of the United States

1796
John Adams is elected second President of the United States

1800
Federal governm[ent] moves to Washington, D.C.

PREVIEW

Focus on the Main Idea
George Washington became the nation's first President and organized the new government.

PLACES
New York City, New York
Washington, D.C.

PEOPLE
Pierre L'Enfant
Benjamin Banneker
Abigail Adams

VOCABULARY
electoral college
inauguration
Cabinet
political party

▶ This button was made in honor of George Washington becoming the first President of the United States. His swearing in was originally scheduled for "March the Fourth," as shown on the button.

Washington as President

You Are There It has been the most exciting time in your young life. You are part of the group accompanying George Washington on a 235-mile journey from Mount Vernon, his plantation in Virginia, to New York City, the nation's temporary capital. There, he is going to be sworn in as the first President of the United States.

All along the way, Americans pour out of their homes to cheer him. In Philadelphia, crowds pack the streets. Church bells ring. Fireworks streak across the sky.

Then, after you reach the New Jersey shore of the Hudson River, a satin-trimmed barge carries Washington on the final part of the trip. Colorfully decorated boats come out to welcome him. And the entire New York shoreline is packed with people. You can't wait to tell your friends back home all you have seen.

 Draw Conclusions As you read, see what conclusions you can draw about why George Washington was popular with the American people.

Practice and Extend

READING SKILL
Draw Conclusions

In the Lesson Review, students complete a graphic organizer like the one below. You may want to provide students with a copy of Transparency 23 to complete as they read the lesson.

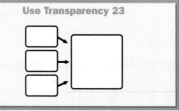

Use Transparency 23

VOCABULARY
Word Exercise

Context Clues The context of Washington becoming President makes it clear that *college* and *party* don't mean what most students think of when they see these words. Have students look these words up in the dictionary and choose the meaning that works best in the context in which each appears in the lesson. (college: organized association of persons having the same duties and purposes; party: group of people organized to influence government)

President Washington Takes Office

George Washington had said that he did not want to become President. At 56, he thought he was too old, and his health was not good. But Thomas Jefferson and Alexander Hamilton finally changed his mind. Hamilton convinced Washington that he was "indispensable"—absolutely needed—for the process of setting up the new government.

On February 4, 1789, Washington was elected President by the electoral college. The **electoral college** is made up of people chosen by each state who vote for President and Vice-President. The number of electors from each state equals the number of its senators plus the number of its representatives to the House of Representatives.

The vote for Washington was unanimous. In other words, all the members of the electoral college voted for him. No President since Washington has been elected unani-

▶ George Washington placed his hand on a Bible when he was inaugurated as President.

mously. He was later described by one of his generals as "First in war, first in peace, and first in the hearts of his countrymen." John Adams, a signer of the Declaration of Independence, was elected Vice-President.

April 30 was the date set for Washington's inauguration. An **inauguration** is the ceremony in which a newly elected President swears loyalty to the Constitution and takes office. At about noon, Washington stepped out on the balcony of the Federal Hall in **New York City, New York.** As the crowd below watched, he placed one hand on a Bible and raised his other hand in the air to take his oath as President of the United States. A cheer went up from the crowd: "Long live George Washington, President of the United States!"

Washington began dividing the work of the Executive Branch into different departments and choosing people to head them. Conducting foreign affairs, or relationships with other countries, became the job of the Department of State. Washington appointed Thomas Jefferson to become Secretary of State, the head of the Department of State. The Department of the Treasury would handle money matters. Alexander Hamilton was named its Secretary.

The heads of these and other departments became part of the President's **Cabinet.** Their job was to advise the President and help him to govern. The Constitution did not set up the Cabinet and its departments. That was Washington's idea. Washington made his decisions with great care. He was deeply aware that his actions would set examples for future leaders.

1
2

REVIEW Why did Washington's general say that Washington was first in war *and* peace?
 Draw Conclusions

 **SOCIAL STUDIES**
Background

About the Electoral College

- The establishment of the electoral college was suggested at the end of the Constitutional Convention by the Committee on Unfinished Parts.
- Under the original plan for the electoral college, states could decide how they would choose their electors.
- The number of electors for a state would be equal to the number of senators and representatives the state had.
- The electors would meet and vote for two people. The person with the greatest number of votes would be elected president, and the person with the second greatest number would become vice-president.
- In 1804 the adoption of the Twelfth Amendment to the U.S. Constitution provided for separate ballots for President and Vice-President.

 2 Teach and Discuss

PAGE 363

President Washington Takes Office

🕐 *Quick Summary* Washington was unanimously elected by the electoral college as the first President of the United States. He organized the new government by creating a Cabinet and its various departments to advise him.

⭐ **SOCIAL STUDIES STRAND**
Citizenship

Point out that one of George Washington's major contributions as a national leader was the establishment of a Cabinet and its departments.

1 What leadership qualities did Washington demonstrate by creating a Cabinet? Possible answer: The ability to delegate responsibilities to advisors and recognize essential leadership qualities in others **Make Inferences**

Decision Making

Washington had to make important decisions when naming the members of his Cabinet.

2 If you were advising President Washington, what qualities would you look for when recommending possible cabinet members? Possible answer: Qualities such as leadership, intelligence, diplomacy, loyalty, and honesty **Make Decisions**

✓ **REVIEW ANSWER** He led the nation's military forces during the American Revolution and later led the nation's government during peace.
 Draw Conclusions

Political Parties Are Born

Quick Summary The Federalists believed in a strong, active federal government, while the Democratic-Republicans favored a weaker, less active federal government.

3 **How did Jefferson feel about Hamilton's plans to set up a national bank? Why did he feel this way?** Jefferson did not want a national bank because he did not believe the government had that power according to the Constitution. Compare and Contrast

4 **How did Washington feel about the emergence of different political parties?** He believed their effects were destructive. Draw Conclusions

Ongoing Assessment

If... students cannot draw a reasonable conclusion about Washington's view of political parties,

then... reread Washington's warning and ask students to attempt to paraphrase it, e.g., Political parties cause people to oppose one another.

5 **Do you agree or disagree with Washington's view of political parties? Explain.** Possible answer: Disagree; because everyone should have the right to his or her own point of view and organized groups should be able to express these views Express Ideas

✓ **REVIEW ANSWER** Hamilton: for strong, active federal government; Jefferson: for less active federal government favoring small farmers and skilled workers Compare and Contrast

George Washington · Henry Knox · Alexander Hamilton · Thomas Jefferson · Edmund Randolph

Lithograph by Currier and Ives

▶ President Wa chose well-kn leaders to se his Cabinet.

Political Parties Are Born

Major decisions faced the new government, and key officials had very different ideas on how to make them. On one side stood Alexander Hamilton, the secretary of the treasury. His belief in a strong national government had not weakened. He believed that this strong government should be active in encouraging the growth of cities, trade, and factories. On the other side stood Thomas Jefferson, the secretary of state. He did not believe in a strong national government. He wanted the nation to remain a land of small farmers and skilled crafts workers. He believed that such a country would not need the strong government that Hamilton wanted.

Time and again, the two clashed in Cabinet meetings. When Hamilton announced plans to set up a national bank, Jefferson objected. He argued that the Constitution did not give **3** the national government that power.

Hamilton and Jefferson each had a large following among Americans. Eventually, the two sides organized themselves into two political parties. A **political party** is an organized group of people who share a view of what government should be and do. The political parties work to elect their members to government offices.

Hamilton's party continued under the name of Federalists. Federalists were generally in favor of a strong, active federal government. Jefferson's party came to be known as the Democratic-Republicans. This political party favored a weaker, less active federal government.

In 1796, in his Farewell Address as President, Washington warned against "the baneful [destructive] effects of the spirit of party." You can read more about the beginning of political parties in Issues and Viewpoints on pages 368–369. **5**

REVIEW How would you compare and contrast Hamilton's and Jefferson's ideas of government? Compare and Contrast

Practice and Extend

EXTEND LANGUAGE
ESL Support

Explore Multiple Meanings Explain that some words in English have more than one meaning. Use the word *party* to demonstrate this concept.

Beginning Write the word *party* on the board and read it. Have students share what they know about the meaning of *party*. As a group, formulate two different definitions for the word.

Intermediate Discuss two definitions of the word *party*. Have students make up sentences using each definition and share them with the class.

Advanced Have students look up definitions of the word *party* in a dictionary or thesaurus and discuss with them the different noun and verb meanings that they find. Students can then create a graphic organizer (e.g., semantic web) to display the meanings of *party* and present these meanings to the rest of the class.

For additional ESL support, use Every Student Learns Guide, pp. 154–157.

A New City

For 10 years, Congress had argued about a permanent site for the nation's capital. In 1790, a decision settled the matter.

The District of Columbia was selected as the nation's capital. It was a 10-square-mile area along the Potomac River not far from Washington's Virginia home. After Washington's death in 1799, it was renamed **Washington, D.C.** The D.C. stands for District of Columbia.

To design the city, Washington chose **Pierre L'Enfant** (lahn FAHNT), a French artist and engineer who had come to fight in the Revolution. An astronomer was needed to use latitude and longitude to survey the land. **Benjamin Banneker,** an inventor, mathematician, as well as astronomer, and the son of a freed slave, was asked to help with this task. You can read more about Banneker on page 367. The Map Adventure below gives you a chance to investigate the work of L'Enfant and Banneker.

REVIEW Why was an astronomer needed to help build the new capital city? **Summarize**

Map Adventure

Designing Washington, D.C.

You are looking at a present-day map of Washington, D.C. Can you identify the location of some of the capital city's major landmarks?

1. L'Enfant wanted the Capitol Building, where Congress meets, to go on a hill. Broad diagonal streets fan out from it. It faces toward the west. What letter marks this site?

2. They wanted to place a 12,000-foot-long grassy area in front of the Capitol Building. It is now called the Mall. What letter marks this site?

3. They placed the President's House, now known as the White House, at the end of a street that runs northwest from the Capitol. This street is now known as Pennsylvania Avenue. What letter marks the White House?

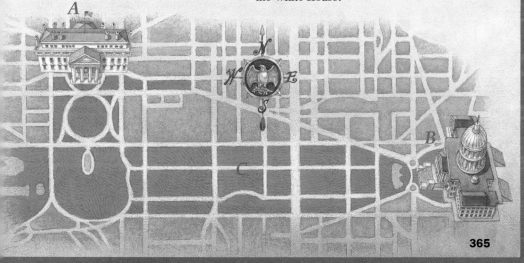

365

A New City

Quick Summary In 1790 the decision was made to make the District of Columbia the permanent site of the nation's capital. The city would be designed by Pierre L'Enfant and Benjamin Banneker.

6 **What site was chosen as the nation's capital? Why?** The District of Columbia; it was along the Potomac River, not far from Washington's home. Main Idea and Details

7 **Why did Washington choose Pierre L'Enfant and Benjamin Banneker to design the nation's capital?** L'Enfant had fought in the American Revolution and was an artist and engineer. Banneker was an astronomer who could help determine latitude and longitude. Analyze Information

✓ **REVIEW ANSWER** An astronomer was needed to help determine latitude and longitude, for the purpose of surveying. Summarize

Map Adventure Answers
1. B, **2.** C, **3.** A

MEETING INDIVIDUAL NEEDS
Leveled Practice

Plan a Tour Ask students to suppose they are visiting Washington, D.C., and want to plan a tour of the city.

Easy Have students use a map of Washington, D.C., to list three places to visit and tell why they want to visit each place. **Reteach**

On-Level Students should choose three places to visit and tell why they want to visit each place. Ask students to write directions to go from one place to the next. **Extend**

Challenge Have students research specific attractions in Washington, D.C., such as the Smithsonian Institution, the White House, or the Lincoln Memorial. Information about the Smithsonian Institution is available at **www.si.edu.** Ask students to present an oral report on one of the attractions. **Enrich**

For a Lesson Summary, use Quick Study, p. 78

Living in the President's House

🕐 *Quick Summary* When the federal government moved to Washington, D.C., in 1800, few of the buildings and streets had been completed.

Primary Source

Cited in *The American Reader*, by Paul M. Angle

8 **What do you visualize when you read Abigail Adams's letter?** Possible answer: Rooms with unpainted walls, little furniture, and a yard full of tall weeds **Analyze Primary Sources**

✓ **REVIEW ANSWER** Living there was difficult. 🔄 Draw Conclusions

3 Close and Assess

Summarize the Lesson

Have students write questions and answers about the events of Lesson 1 on separate index cards. Place ten question and matching answer cards facedown. Have students match cards.

✓ | **LESSON 1** | **REVIEW** |

1. 🔄 **Draw Conclusions** For possible answers, see the reduced pupil page.

2. To divide the work and get good advice

3. **Critical Thinking:** *Draw Conclusions* Different groups, or parties, had opposing ideas about how government should operate, and each group wanted the government to operate according to its ideas.

4. Federalist: Hamilton; Democratic-Republican: Jefferson

5. Banneker was asked to help because he had the skills and background needed to help with the task.

Link to ⬡—⬡ **Geography**

Student should include locations from the map on p. 365, a compass rose, and clear labels.

Living in the President's House

In 1800, when John Adams was President, the federal government moved to Washington, D.C., but few of its buildings were finished and its few streets were muddy paths. Congress met there for the first time in November. Its members had to crowd into the limited housing available. President John Adams, who had become the second President of the United States in 1796, and his wife Abigail moved into the President's House. Later, the building would be called the White House. The President's House was so new that the plaster on

▶ **Abigail Adams was the first "first lady" to live in the White House.**

Painting by Gilbert Stuart

its walls was still wet. **Abigail Adams** described it in a letter to a friend:

> *"There is not a single apartment [room] in it finished...We have not the least fence, yard, or other convenience."*

Even worse, the house was built in what was then a marshy area full of mosquitoes.

REVIEW What can you conclude about conditions in and around the President's House when John and Abigail Adams moved into it? 🔄 Draw Conclusions

Summarize the Lesson

— **1789** George Washington became the first President and organized the Executive Branch around a Cabinet.

— **1796** John Adams was elected second President of the United States.

— **1800** The federal government moved to Washington, D.C.

| **LESSON 1** | **REVIEW** |

Check Facts and Main Ideas

1. 🔄 **Draw Conclusions** On a separate sheet of paper, fill in the missing facts.

Facts

| He was elected President unanimously. |

| The capital city was named for him. |

| Important leaders like Jefferson and Hamilton requested that he run for President |

Conclusion

| George Washington was extremely popular with the American people. |

2. Explain Washington's purpose in naming people to his **Cabinet.**

3. **Critical Thinking:** *Draw Conclusions* Why did different **political parties** emerge in American government?

4. Who were the leaders of the Federalist and Democratic-Republican parties?

5. Why was Benjamin Banneker asked to help design the new capital?

Link to ⬡—⬡ **Geography**

Draw a Map Look back at the map of Washington, D.C., on page 365. How might you have laid out the area differently from L'Enfant? Draw a map showing how you might have designed the nation's capital.

Practice and Extend

CURRICULUM CONNECTION
Science

Mosquito Habitats

• Have students research the life cycle of mosquitos (adult lays eggs in water; eggs hatch into larvae; larvae become pupae; pupae mature into adults).

• Students can present their findings in a drawing with captions for each stage.

• Ask students to write a paragraph explaining why mosquitos live in wet areas.

Workbook, p. 86

Lesson 1: Washington as President

Directions: Match each name in the box to the description. Write the name on the line provided. Names may be used more than once.

| George Washington | Thomas Jefferson | Benjamin Banneker |
| Alexander Hamilton | Pierre L'Enfant | John Adams |

1. _____ He had plans to set up a national bank.
2. _____ He was elected President by the electoral college in a unanimous vote.
3. _____ He was the secretary of state under Washington.
4. _____ He was a member of the Democratic-Republican party.
5. _____ He was the secretary of the treasury under Washington.
6. _____ He designed the city of Washington, D.C.
7. _____ He opposed setting up a national bank.
8. _____ He was the first President to live in the President's House.
9. _____ Originally, he didn't want to become President.
10. _____ He was the second President of the United States.
11. _____ He believed in a strong national government.
12. _____ He was an astronomer who helped survey the land where Washington, D.C., was built.
13. _____ He was a member of the Federalist political party.
14. _____ He wanted the country to remain a land of small farmers and skilled crafts workers.
15. _____ He was "First in war, first in peace, and first in the hearts of his countrymen."

Notes for Home: Your child learned about events that took place under President George Washington and Vice-President John Adams.
Home Activity: With your child, talk about how the U.S. government would be different today if it had not developed.

💿 **Also on Teacher Resources CD-ROM**

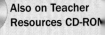

Benjamin Banneker
1731–1806

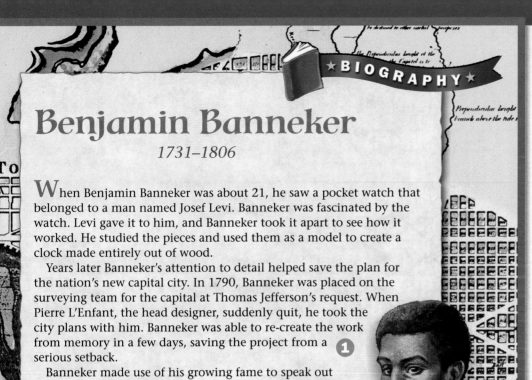

When Benjamin Banneker was about 21, he saw a pocket watch that belonged to a man named Josef Levi. Banneker was fascinated by the watch. Levi gave it to him, and Banneker took it apart to see how it worked. He studied the pieces and used them as a model to create a clock made entirely out of wood.

Years later Banneker's attention to detail helped save the plan for the nation's new capital city. In 1790, Banneker was placed on the surveying team for the capital at Thomas Jefferson's request. When Pierre L'Enfant, the head designer, suddenly quit, he took the city plans with him. Banneker was able to re-create the work from memory in a few days, saving the project from a serious setback. **1**

Banneker made use of his growing fame to speak out against slavery. Although Banneker grew up free on his family's farm in Maryland, his father had been a slave and he knew the effects of slavery. When Banneker completed his first book, he sent it to Secretary of State Thomas Jefferson and included a note asking Jefferson to help improve the treatment of African Americans. He wrote: **2**

"However variable [different] we may be in society or religion, however diversified in situation or color, we are all in the same family and stand in the same relation to [God]."

BIOFACT
Banneker's clock was recognized as the first to be made in colonial America and was said to strike every hour for over 40 years.

Learn from Biographies
In what ways did Banneker's desire to understand the world around him influence his own life and that of others?

For more information, go online to *Meet the People* at **www.sfsocialstudies.com.**

367

Benjamin Banneker

Objective
- Describe the accomplishments of significant leaders of the United States, such as Benjamin Banneker.

1 Introduce and Motivate

Preview To activate prior knowledge, ask students to share what they remember about Benjamin Banneker from p. 365. They will read about how his skills helped him succeed.

2 Teach and Discuss

1 How did Banneker's re-creation of the city plans save the project from a serious setback? If he had not been able to re-create the plans he would have had to design the city again, from the beginning. **Cause and Effect**

2 What was the purpose of the note Banneker sent to Jefferson? To point out that all people were equal and to encourage fair treatment of African Americans **Analyze Primary Sources**

3 Close and Assess

Learn from Biographies Answer
It led him to become an inventor and astronomer. He used his fame to try to improve the lives of others.

MEETING INDIVIDUAL NEEDS
Learning Styles

Benjamin Banneker Using their individual learning styles, students review the contributions of Benjamin Banneker.

Verbal Learning Have students reread the biography, do additional research, and take notes listing the contributions of Mr. Banneker. They can prepare a speech describing his accomplishments.

Kinesthetic Learning Have students write a script and act out a short scene from Banneker's life.

WEB SITE
Technology

Students can find out more about Benjamin Banneker by clicking on *Meet the People* at **www.sfsocialstudies.com.**

Forming Political Parties

Objective

- Evaluate the effects of the rise of political parties on government in the United States.

1 Introduce and Motivate

Preview To activate prior knowledge, ask students to describe the views of candidates or political parties they have read about, seen, or heard either in national, state, local, or their own school elections. To introduce the issue of forming political parties, remind students that Jefferson and Hamilton had different views about the role of the federal government. Point out that although their views differed, they both were members of George Washington's Cabinet.

2 Teach and Discuss

1 What is the main reason Washington was not in favor of political parties? He believed their disagreements would have destructive effects on the government.
Main Idea and Details

2 What did Dolley Madison like about political parties? What did she dislike about them? She liked to know about the different points of view and plans, but did not like the arguments.
Analyze Information

3 Jefferson and his followers became known as "Democratic-Republicans." Which of the parties he describes are the Democratic-Republicans? What other party does he describe? Jefferson's first description is of the Federalists; his second description is of the Democratic-Republicans.
Main Idea and Details

Forming Political Parties

Different ideas about government continue to exist in the United States today, just as they did more than 200 years ago.

"… Mr. Jefferson is at the head of a faction [group] decidedly hostile [unfriendly] to me…" Alexander Hamilton wrote these words to a friend in May 1792. Hamilton and Thomas Jefferson were two of President George Washington's most valued advisors. Yet, they had very different views, and the groups that formed around them became the nation's first political parties.

Political parties formed when George Washington was President because people had different ideas about government. Alexander Hamilton and his followers became known as the "Federalists." They favored a strong national government. Thomas Jefferson and his followers became known as the "Democratic-Republicans." They opposed a strong national government.

President Washington wanted members of his government to work together. As you have read, in his Farewell Address, he warned against "the baneful [destructive] effects of the spirit of party."

> **"[The spirit of party] serves always to distract the public councils and enfeeble [weaken] the public administration. It agitates the community with ill-founded jealousies and false alarms; kindles [starts up] the animosity [dislike] of one part against another; foments [stirs up] occasionally riot and insurrection [revolt]."**
>
> —George Washington, *1796*

Yet Washington realized that parties reflected "the strongest passions of the human mind." After he left office, political parties became even stronger. Today, more than 200 years later, political parties continue to debate different visions of government.

▶ George Washington *(left)* meets with two members of his Cabinet—Thomas Jefferson *(center)* and Alexander Hamilton *(right)*.

368

Practice and Extend

Decision Making

Use a Decision-Making Process

- Have students consider the following decision-making scenario: **Suppose you are an advisor to George Washington. You have listened to Hamilton's and Jefferson's different views about the role of the federal government. You can see advantages and disadvantages of both points of view.**

- Students should use the following decision-making process to decide whether to advise Washington to support Hamilton's or Jefferson's point of view. For each step in the process, have students discuss and write about what must be considered as they make their decision. Write these steps on the board or read them aloud.

1. Identify a situation that requires a decision.
2. Gather information.
3. Identify options.
4. Predict consequences.
5. Take action to implement a decision.

"I do not admire the contentions [battles] of parties...tho' on my own... I am anxious to know all the maneuverings [plans] of both, the one and the other...."

—**Dolley Madison**
1768–1849

t is true, there has some agitation of s [disturbance] een existing parties; loubtless the prudence tion] of the inhabitants e United States will r this to evaporate se this to go away]."

—**Mercy Otis Warren,**
1728–1814

"Men...are naturally divided into two parties: 1. Those who fear and distrust the people, and wish to draw all powers from them into the hands of the higher classes. 2. Those who identify themselves with the people, [and] have confidence in them....
In every country these two parties exist.

—**Thomas Jefferson,**
1743–1826

Issues and You

In the late 1700s and early 1800s many people feared that political parties would destroy the new republic. Do you think that rivalry between political parties is good or bad for the United States? Write an argument either for or against political parties. Find examples from newspapers, magazines, or the Internet to support your position.

369

 SOCIAL STUDIES STRAND
Government

Democratic Values and Institutions
Identify the political parties of some present-day national leaders for students. Discuss their viewpoints on national issues, and help students see how these views fit into either the Federalist or Democratic-Republican tradition.

4 How are the views of Dolley Madison and George Washington alike? How are they different? Alike: Neither likes the arguments inherent in political parties; Different: Dolley Madison is interested in learning about the opposing plans of parties. Compare and Contrast

3 Close and Assess

- Be sure students understand that they are not choosing which political party they support, but rather arguing for or against the existence of political parties in general.

- Have students brainstorm a list of keywords they can use to find information about the historic rivalry between political parties in the United States.

- Have students choose a form for presenting their arguments from among the following: oral report, videotape, written report, or debate.

SOCIAL STUDIES STRAND
Citizenship

Tell students that individuals can participate in political parties and civic affairs at the national level.

- **Political Parties** People who share the general views of a national political party may help elect candidates of the party.

- **Civic Affairs** Individuals may also volunteer for the American Red Cross, AmeriCorps, or similar organizations, which may sponsor projects in the areas of education or public safety.

WEB SITE
Technology

You can learn more about the people discussed on these pages by clicking on *Meet the People* at **www.sfsocialstudies.com.**

Jefferson Looks West

Objectives

- Explain why and how the United States expanded westward.

- Describe the Louisiana Purchase, and tell what effect it had on the nation.

- Identify reasons for and findings of the Lewis and Clark Expedition.

Vocabulary

pioneer, p. 372; **frontier,** p. 372; **Louisiana Purchase,** p. 373

Resources

- Workbook, p. 87
- Transparency 6, 46
- Every Student Learns Guide, pp. 158–161
- Quick Study, pp. 80–81

Quick Teaching Plan

If time is short, have students draw a time line to show the important events in this lesson.

- Have students write the following years on their time lines: 1775, 1800, 1801, 1802, 1803, 1804, 1809.

- As they read, have students summarize the important events that occurred during each year on their time line.

1 Introduce and Motivate

Preview To activate prior knowledge, ask students to recall Jefferson's view of the role of the federal government. Tell students that they will learn how the United States changed and grew during Jefferson's administration as they read Lesson 2.

You Are There As in all elections, the opposing political parties in the election campaign of 1800 felt strongly about their positions and worked hard to win voters to their sides. Have students discuss both points of view described on this page and then tell which party they might vote for and why.

370 Unit 5 • Life in a New Nation

LESSON 2

1800			1805
1800 Thomas Jefferson is elected third President of the United States	**1803** Louisiana Purchase expands the size of the country	**1804** Lewis and Clark set out to explore the Louisiana Territory	

PREVIEW

Focus on the Main Idea
The new nation doubled its size and expanded settlement westward.

PLACES
Wilderness Road
Cumberland Gap
Mississippi River
New Orleans
Louisiana Territory
St. Louis, Missouri
Missouri River

PEOPLE
Daniel Boone
James Monroe
Meriwether Lewis
William Clark
York
Sacagawea

VOCABULARY
pioneer
frontier
Louisiana Purchase

Jefferson Looks West

You Are There The Presidential election campaign of 1800 is in full swing. It is a bitter and nasty campaign. The Democratic-Republicans and their candidate, Thoma Jefferson, hurl charge after charge at the Federalists and their candidate, President John Adams. The Federalists hurl charges right back. You don't know which charges to believe.

The Federalists are the party of the rich, say the Democratic-Republicans. *Federalist officials have pu banks first and the people second.*

The Federalists reply, *The Democratic-Republican are troublemakers. They are trying to turn the nation's citizens against one another.*

Which side is right? Americans are going to cast vote soon. They have a lot to think about before they do.

Summarize As you read, note ideas that will help you summarize how federal government actions helped the new nation grow and develop.

370

Practice and Extend

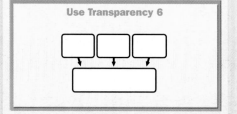

READING SKILL
Summarize

In the Lesson Review, students complete a graphic organizer like the one below. You may want to provide students with a copy of Transparency 6 to complete as they read the lesson.

> Use Transparency 6

VOCABULARY
Word Exercise

Individual Word Study Have students read the definition of *frontier* on p. 372. An *edge* is sometimes called a border. A frontier can be on the border between settled country and wild places, but it can also be the border between two countries. Ask students how understanding the meaning of frontier as "the edge of settlements" can help them understand what the word means in a phrase such as "the frontiers of science." (It is at the edge of what we know.)

Jefferson Wins Election of 1800

On the morning of March 4, 1801, Thomas Jefferson left his rooming house and walked up the hill to the Capitol Building, to be inaugurated as the third President of the United States. He had won a bitter election. However, he hoped that he and those who had opposed him could work together. In his inaugural speech, he said, "Every difference of opinion is not a difference of principle….We are all Republicans, we are all Federalists."

The new President had a wide range of interests and talents. He was a good writer, as the Declaration of Independence shows. He was a skilled violinist, a lifelong student of nature and science, and a talented architect. Among the buildings he designed was his own beautiful house called Monticello.

▶ Today visitors can tour Monticello to see how Jefferson lived. A man of many interests, he used a machine *(top right)* to write a letter and make a copy at the same time, and a tool *(bottom right)* for surveying.

As President, Jefferson wanted to "give government back to the people." He believed that the only way to guarantee the liberties of all citizens was to keep power in their hands. He got Congress to lower taxes it had passed under the Federalists. He reduced the size of the government and of the armed forces. "I am not among those that fear the people," he said. "They, and not the rich, are our dependence for continued freedom."

After Jefferson left office, he summed up his philosophy of government:

> **"The care of human life and happiness, not their destruction, is the first and only legitimate [true] object of good government."** ❷

REVIEW According to Jefferson, who should have the power of government?
🔁 **Draw Conclusions**

371

❷ Teach and Discuss

PAGE 371

Jefferson Wins Election of 1800

🕐 *Quick Summary* As the newly elected President, Jefferson wanted to bring the nation together under his philosophy that the people's happiness is the true purpose of good government.

❶ **How would you summarize Jefferson's message to the people in his inaugural address?** Possible answer: Even though we may have different opinions, we should now work together for the good of the country. Summarize

Primary Source
Cited in *Bartlett Familiar Quotations*, by Justin Kaplan, ed.

Explain that Jefferson's opinions about what makes good government were evident throughout his political career.

❷ **What does Jefferson suggest might be the effects of bad government?** The destruction of human life and happiness
🔁 **Draw Conclusions**

✔ **REVIEW ANSWER** Jefferson believed government power should be left in the hands of the people.
🔁 **Draw Conclusions**

FAST FACTS

Quotes from Jefferson What was Jefferson like? He had definite opinions about a wide variety of subjects. Here are a few quotations from Jefferson:

- **About music:** "Music is invaluable where a person has an ear. Where they have not, it should not be attempted."
- **About education:** "Whenever the people are well-informed, they can be trusted with their own government."
- **About reading:** "I cannot live without books."
- **About farmers:** "Cultivators of the earth are the most valuable citizens. They are the most vigorous, the most independent, the most virtuous, and they are tied to their country and wedded to its liberty and interests by the most lasting bonds."

A Nation Moving West

 Quick Summary Americans began moving westward across the Appalachian Mountains. Pioneers like Daniel Boone overcame hardships and built new towns along the western frontier.

❸ What do you think caused clashes between pioneers and Native Americans? Possible answer: The pioneers were moving onto land that Native Americans believed was the traditional home of their people.
⤴ Draw Conclusions

Ongoing Assessment

If... students cannot draw a reasonable conclusion about what caused clashes, **then...** have students explain how the pioneers' farms, roads, and towns might have affected the lives of Native Americans.

SOCIAL STUDIES STRAND
Geography

Before the creation of the Wilderness Road, only Native Americans used the Cumberland Gap to cross the Appalachian Mountains.

❹ How did the geographic factors of the Cumberland Gap affect the pattern of westward movement? Pioneers and Native Americans before them chose this route going west because the gap was a valley that made it easier to cross the mountains. **Cause and Effect**

✓ **REVIEW ANSWER** Possible answer: Crude housing, unending toil, and possible clashes with Native Americans
⤴ Draw Conclusions

372 Unit 5 • Life in a New Nation

Mildred Lane Kemper Art Museum, Washington University in St. Louis.

▶ Daniel Boone pioneers acros the Appalachia Mountains on Wilderness Ro

A Nation Moving West

Long before Thomas Jefferson became President, Americans had begun moving west. By the time the Revolution broke out, some people had already crossed the Appalachian Mountains in search of fertile land. Today, we call these early settlers **pioneers.**

Of course, other people already lived on these lands. Several different groups of Native Americans claimed these lands. Clashes between pioneers and these American Indians ❸ continued for some time. But settlement went on. The pioneers kept pushing the edge of their settlements farther and farther west. This edge of settlement became known as the **frontier.**

Daniel Boone was probably the best known of the early pioneers. He was a skilled woodsman who led many pioneers to the land west of the Appalachian Mountains.

In 1775, Boone created a trail, which came to be called the **Wilderness Road,** through the Appalachians from Virginia to Kentucky. The trail cuts through the **Cumberland Gap,**

a small valley that Native Americans had long used to cross the Appalachian Mountains. Soon thousands of pioneers were taking their wagons westward along the Wilderness Road.

Life was hard for pioneers on the frontier. Everything had to be done by hand, from cutting down trees, to building homes, to weaving cloth. Pioneer life could also be lonely. Often, the nearest neighbors lived miles away. Yet the pioneers overcame these hardships and built farms, homes, roads, and towns along the frontier.

Like many other pioneers, Daniel Boone kept moving farther west. By the end of his life he had reached Missouri, west of the Mississippi River. Boone described the lands to the east from which he had come as: "Too many people! Too crowded! Too crowded! I want more elbow room!"

REVIEW Provide three details that support the following main idea: Pioneer life was hard. ⤴ Draw Conclusions

372

Practice and Extend

 ACTIVATE PRIOR KNOWLEDGE
ESL Support

Identify Geographical Terms Help students understand the meaning of *mountain, valley,* and *trail.*

Beginning Display pictures of various landforms, such as *mountain, hill,* and *valley.* Have students point to and say the ones they have seen. Then ask them to draw a picture or an outline map with at least three geographical features displayed.

Intermediate Have students use phrases or brief sentences to tell about physical land features they have seen, such as mountains, valleys, or trails. You might want to display pictures of various landforms to prompt their thinking.

Advanced Help students recall the names of various landforms. Then have students describe a place they would like to visit and tell about a physical land feature they could see there.

For additional ESL support, use Every Student Learns Guide, pp. 158–161.

The Louisiana Purchase

Moving westward, the pioneers soon created settlements along or near the Ohio River and the **Mississippi River.** In a short time, the pioneers began to use these waterways as trade routes. The settlers used the rivers to ship products, like wheat and pigs, south to the port of **New Orleans.** From there, goods were shipped to the cities of the east coast and beyond to Europe. Without the growth of river routes and bustling ports, the pioneers would have had great trouble getting their products to distant markets.

At the end of the 1700s, Spain claimed a vast area of land west of the Mississippi River known as Louisiana. This land included New Orleans. In October 1802, Spain closed the port of New Orleans to American trade. The pioneers' products could not leave the port. Spain reopened the port a few months later. But the closing of the port concerned President Jefferson. He believed that something had to be done to make sure New Orleans would stay open for American trade.

Jefferson concluded that the United States had to buy the port.

In 1803 France had taken control of Louisiana from Spain. So Jefferson sent **James Monroe** to Paris to try to buy New Orleans and some land around it from the French. Monroe offered France $2 million.

At first, the French leader Napoleon did not want to sell the land. He hoped to settle all of Louisiana with French colonists. But he also needed money to fight a war against Britain. So Napoleon made a surprising offer. **6** He would sell, but not just New Orleans. He offered to sell the United States the entire Louisiana Territory for $15 million! Monroe agreed.

In 1803, the United States completed the **Louisiana Purchase.** With it, the nation doubled its size, adding 828,000 square miles, from the Mississippi River to the Rocky Mountains. And it did so at the cost of less than three cents an acre! Today, much of that land costs thousands of dollars an acre.

REVIEW Place the events leading up to the Louisiana Purchase in sequence. **Sequence**

► **The Louisiana Purchase expanded the United States west to the Rocky Mountains.**

The Louisiana Purchase

Quick Summary Jefferson purchased the Louisiana Territory from France to ensure that the port of New Orleans would remain open for American trade.

Test Talk

Locate Key Words in the Question

5 **What situation involving New Orleans did Jefferson want to avoid? How did he solve the problem?** Help students locate key words in the question such as *situation, New Orleans,* and *avoid.* He wanted to avoid having the port of New Orleans closed to American trade. He solved this problem by buying New Orleans and the land around it. **Summarize**

6 **Why did Napoleon sell the Louisiana Territory to the United States even though he did not want to?** He needed money to help fund a war France was fighting with Britain. **Cause and Effect**

✓ **REVIEW ANSWER** Closing of New Orleans to American shipping; France controls New Orleans; Americans offer to buy it for $2 million; Napoleon offers to sell all of Louisiana Territory for $15 million; the United States buys it **Sequence**

MEETING INDIVIDUAL NEEDS
Leveled Practice

Summarize and Evaluate the Louisiana Purchase Have students summarize the steps leading to the Louisiana Purchase and share what they think about Jefferson's actions.

Easy List the following actions by President Jefferson on the board. Ask students to tell whether they agree or disagree with each and why. **Reteach**

- Offer $2 million for New Orleans
- Pay $15 million for the Louisiana Territory

On-Level Have students write opinions in which they both agree and disagree with each of Jefferson's actions listed above. **Extend**

Challenge Have students write a one-page description telling what might have happened if Jefferson had not made the Louisiana Purchase. **Enrich**

For a Lesson Summary, use Quick Study, p. 80.

Lewis and Clark

🕐 **Quick Summary** Jefferson sent an expedition led by Lewis and Clark to explore the Louisiana Territory. They explored and mapped a vast area, opening the territory to future explorations and settlements.

7 What three goals did Jefferson set for Lewis and Clark's expedition? Search for a water route to the Pacific Ocean, establish relationships with the Native Americans, and record observations about the region **Summarize**

8 Jefferson wanted America to remain a land of small farmers and skilled craftsmen. Is this philosophy supported in any of the goals he set for Lewis and Clark? Explain. Yes; he asked Lewis and Clark to keep records of the soil, plants, animals, minerals, and climate of the land they explored. 🔵 **Draw Conclusions**

Literature and Social Studies

9 What does Lewis's account suggest about conditions on the expedition? Possible answer: You could not predict when conditions would become so poor that you would not be able to continue; conditions were often very uncomfortable. **Make Inferences**

Lewis and Clark

Long before the Louisiana Purchase, Thomas Jefferson had been fascinated by lands in the West. Who lived there, he wondered? What was the land like? Could the Missouri River possibly lead to a water route to the Pacific Ocean? Jefferson wanted to know the answers to these questions.

To find the answers, Jefferson sent an expedition to the newly acquired land, now called the **Louisiana Territory.** Jefferson chose **Meriwether Lewis,** who was an army captain, to lead the expedition. Lewis chose a fellow army captain, his friend **William Clark,** to share command.

7 Jefferson told the two captains they had three goals. One was to search for a water route to the Pacific Ocean. The second was to establish relationships with the Native Americans they met. Jefferson wanted the Indians to know his "wish to be neighborly, friendly, and useful to them." The third goal **8** was to pay close attention to "the soil and face of the country," to its plants, animals, minerals, climate, and to keep careful, written records of their findings. Today, the journals of Lewis and Clark are the main source of information about their expedition.

In May 1804, Lewis and Clark and other members of the expedition set out westward from **St. Louis, Missouri,** along the **Missouri River.** Follow their route on the map on the next page. The expedition included soldiers, river boatmen, hunters, and **York,** Clark's slave and childhood friend. During the expedition, York worked at Clark's side much of the time, and had shown he was ready to sacrifice his life to save Clark's. Nevertheless, when York later asked to be freed as a reward for his contributions to the expedition, Clark refused.

Three boats carried expedition members, equipment, and supplies. They did not know it then, but they would not return for another 28 months.

During their first winter, they hired a French Canadian fur trapper and his Shoshone wife, **Sacagawea** (sah KAH gah way ah), to act as

Literature and Social Studies

In his journal, Captain Meriwether Lewis wrote the following account of a sandstorm.

April 24th, 1805
The wind blew so hard during the whole of this day, that we were unable to move.... Sore eyes is a common complaint among the [people]. I believe it [comes] from the immense quantities of sand which is driven by the wind from the sandbars of the river in such clouds that you are unable to discover the opposite bank of the river...." **9**

▶ Sacagawea was a guide for Lewis and Clark.

Practice and Extend

CURRICULUM CONNECTION
Literature

Learn More About Lewis and Clark
- Have students read a book about Lewis and Clark, such as **The Captain's Dog: My Journey with Lewis and Clark,** by Roland Smith (Harcourt Brace, ISBN 0-152-02696-7, 2000).
- Students can present an oral report, video, audio recording, or storyboard that summarizes what they read.

FYI SOCIAL STUDIES
Background

Sacagawea
- Sacagawea's Shoshone name was *Boinaiv.* It means "grass maiden."
- The name "Sacagawea" may have been derived from the Hidatsa words for *bird* and *woman.*
- She gave birth to a baby boy, Jean-Baptiste, on February 11, 1805, and carried him on her back when the expedition set out on April 7.
- In addition to translating for the explorers, she identified plants and edible fruits and vegetables for them.
- When a boat tipped over, it was Sacagawea who saved the journals, medicines, and other valuables from being washed away.

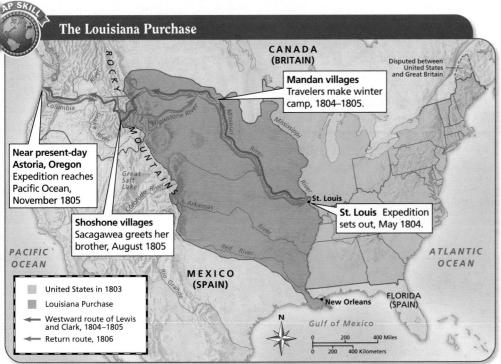

The Louisiana Purchase

Mandan villages Travelers make winter camp, 1804–1805.

Near present-day Astoria, Oregon Expedition reaches Pacific Ocean, November 1805

Shoshone villages Sacagawea greets her brother, August 1805

St. Louis Expedition sets out, May 1804.

CANADA (BRITAIN)

Disputed between United States and Great Britain

St. Louis

PACIFIC OCEAN

MEXICO (SPAIN)

ATLANTIC OCEAN

FLORIDA (SPAIN)

New Orleans

Gulf of Mexico

- United States in 1803
- Louisiana Purchase
- ← Westward route of Lewis and Clark, 1804–1805
- ← Return route, 1806

N

0   200   400 Miles
0   200   400 Kilometers

▶ The Lewis and Clark Expedition explored the Louisiana Territory and traveled on to the Pacific Ocean.

MAP SKILL Use Map Scale *About how many miles did the expedition travel from the Shoshone villages to the Pacific Ocean?*

interpreters and guides. Sacagawea helped Lewis and Clark establish good relations with Native Americans along the way. She helped translate Indian languages for the expedition. The baby she carried on her back signaled the peaceful purposes of the expedition.

Throughout the expedition, its members faced many hardships. They had to paddle their boats against strong river currents. Every now and then, a boat would turn over, sending equipment splashing into the water. And there was always the danger of being attacked by dangerous animals, like 900-pound grizzly bears.

But Lewis and Clark were rewarded with some fabulous views. They saw a herd of 20,000 bison stretching across the plain and

fast deerlike animals called pronghorns racing by. They crossed the tall, spectacular Rocky Mountains. Finally their eyes were filled with the sight of the great Pacific Ocean—"Ocean in view! O! the joy!" wrote Clark.

The explorers finally returned to St. Louis in September 1806. They had not found a water route to the Pacific. But they had recorded and described thousands of varieties of plants and animals, and even brought some back for Jefferson to examine. They had also mapped a vast area, opening it to future exploration and new settlers from the United States. ⑫

REVIEW Compare what the people of the United States knew about the Louisiana Territory before and after the Lewis and Clark Expedition. **Compare and Contrast**

375

CURRICULUM CONNECTION
Math

Calculate Mileage

- Tell students that Lewis and Clark's 28-month journey covered about 8,000 miles, more than double the straight-line distance from St. Louis to Astoria and back to St. Louis. Eight of those months the explorers stayed in camps.
- Have students estimate how many miles per traveling month the expedition averaged. (8,000 miles ÷ 20 months = about 400 miles per month)
- Ask students to use this figure to estimate how many miles per traveling day the expedition averaged. (400 ÷ 30 = about 13.3 miles per traveling day)

Point out that the Lewis and Clark Expedition is shown both going to and coming from the Pacific Ocean.

⑩ In which direction did Lewis and Clark travel when going toward the Pacific Ocean? Northwest **Interpret Maps**

MAP SKILL **Answer** about 500 miles

SOCIAL STUDIES STRAND
History

Other explorers followed in the wake of Lewis and Clark, such as Zebulon Pike. In 1805 he and his men trekked by boat and on foot from St. Louis to northern Minnesota, searching for the source of the Mississippi River. In 1806 he led an expedition to explore the Arkansas and Red Rivers. He is credited with being the first white man to view the mountain in Colorado known today as Pike's Peak.

Test Talk

Use Information from the Text

⑪ What characteristics do you think the members of the Lewis and Clark expedition possessed? Why? Have students note details that help them identify personal characteristics of the explorers. Possible answer: They were resourceful, strong, determined, and courageous. **Make Inferences**

⑫ Why do you think it was so important to try to find water routes rather than traveling across land? Possible answer: It is easier to move people and goods along water than to travel over rocky and mountainous land. **Make Inferences**

✓ **REVIEW ANSWER** Possible answer: Before: They knew about the port of New Orleans and that Native Americans lived in the territory. After: They knew about many different plants and animals. **Compare and Contrast**

A Growing Nation

🕐 **Quick Summary** America's population grew rapidly while the frontier moved farther west and nine new states joined the Union.

13 **What changes do you think took place in territories that became states and joined the Union?** Possible answer: The population continued to increase, towns were created, and homes and farms were built. 🔄 Draw Conclusions

✓ **REVIEW ANSWER** Possible answers: Kentucky, Tennessee, Indiana, Louisiana, Mississippi, Ohio, Illinois, and Alabama all had large enough populations to become states. Pioneers ventured west of the Mississippi River. **Main Idea and Details**

3 Close and Assess

Summarize the Lesson

Ask students to summarize the lesson by telling an effect of each event in the lesson summary. Students can then write causes and effects in a graphic organizer.

✓ | LESSON 2 | REVIEW |

1. **Summarize** For possible answers, see the reduced pupil page.

2. Jefferson believed in giving government "back to the people," lowering taxes, and reducing the size of government and the armed forces.

3. Boone marked the Wilderness Road through the Appalachian Mountains, making a path that pioneers could follow to settle the West.

4. **Critical Thinking: Evaluate** Possible answer: The Louisiana Purchase was a good deal, since it doubled the size of the country at a moderate cost.

5. The Lewis and Clark Expedition found out that a water route to the Pacific did not exist; it tried to foster good relations with the Native Americans; and it kept records of the geography and nature it encountered.

Link to 🔗 Mathematics

About $18 per square mile

376 Unit 5 • Life in a New Nation

A Growing Nation

From the time that Daniel Boone started marking the Wilderness Road to the end of Jefferson's second term as President in 1809, the American population almost tripled. It grew from about two and a half million to about seven million. New states joined the Union. Vermont became the fourteenth state in 1791. Kentucky, whose settlement had been led by Daniel Boone, followed in 1792. Then came Tennessee, in 1796.

Some states carved out of the Northwest Territory—Ohio, Indiana, and Illinois—would soon follow. So would the southern states of Louisiana, Mississippi, and Alabama. The nation was on the move, with pioneers venturing even beyond the Mississippi River. As the frontier moved farther west, new states continued to join the nation.

REVIEW What details can you supply to support the main idea that the nation was expanding to the west? **Main Idea and Details**

Summarize the Lesson

1800 Thomas Jefferson became the third President of the United States.

1803 The Louisiana Purchase doubled the size of the country.

1804 Lewis and Clark set out to explore the Louisiana Territory.

▶ Pioneers began moving into the Northwest Territory in the late 1700s.

LESSON 2 ⟩ REVIEW

Check Facts and Main Ideas

1. **Summarize** On a separate sheet of paper, fill in the events that are summarized.

| Louisiana Purchase | Lewis and Clark Expedition | Creation of Wilderness Road |

These events opened up new lands, allowing the United States to expand.

2. In your own words, summarize Jefferson's ideas about government.

3. How did Daniel Boone help the pioneers move westward?

4. **Critical Thinking: Evaluate** Was the Louisiana Purchase a good deal for the United States? Explain your answer.

5. In what ways did the Lewis and Clark Expedition fulfill its mission?

Link to 🔗 Mathematics

Calculate a Price You read that the Louisiana Territory covered 828,000 square miles and that the United States paid $15 million for it. Calculate the price per square mile.

Practice and Extend

FYI **SOCIAL STUDIES Background**

Daniel Boone

- As a child growing up on the North Carolina frontier, Daniel Boone enjoyed hunting and trapping.

- Even though the British prohibited western migration, Boone ignored the ban and explored the Appalachian Mountains.

- Together with 28 associates from the Transylvania Company, Boone built the Wilderness Road through the Cumberland Gap in the Appalachians.

- The first Anglo-American women to settle Kentucky were Daniel Boone's wife and daughter.

Workbook, p. 87

Lesson 2: Jefferson Looks West

Directions: Complete each sentence with information from Lesson 2. You may use your textbook.

1. Thomas Jefferson was the _____ President of the United States.

2. Jefferson believed that the power of government belonged in the hands of the _____

3. In search of new lands to settle, Americans began moving _____ long before Jefferson became President.

4. Daniel Boone, an early pioneer, created the trail known as the _____

5. Boone led many pioneers through the _____ across the Appalachian Mountains.

6. Settlers along the Ohio and Mississippi Rivers used these waterways as _____ routes to ship their products south.

7. Goods shipped along the Mississippi went to the Spanish-controlled port of _____ and then to the East Coast and Europe.

8. The United States doubled in size with the _____ requiring land that stretched from the Mississippi River to the Rocky Mountains.

9. Jefferson was interested in the lands to the west and chose _____ to lead an expedition to explore the unknown area.

10. The expedition to explore the West included the help of a French trapper and his Shoshone wife, _____ who served as a guide and interpreter for the expedition.

Notes for Home: Your child learned about changes in the nation under President Thomas Jefferson. Home Activity: With your child, examine a map of the United States and list the present-day states that would not be part of the United States if not for the Louisiana Purchase and the Lewis and Clark.

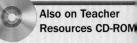

Also on Teacher Resources CD-ROM

Lewis and Clark

The Lewis and Clark expedition set out from St. Louis in 1804 to learn about the lands and peoples of the Louisiana Territory. Meriwether Lewis organized the expedition and chose William Clark to help lead it. Clark was responsible for mapping the landforms and bodies of water.

Detailed Diary
Lewis and Clark kept careful notes in the journal above of everything they saw.

Buffalo Robe
This robe, collected by Lewis and Clark during their expedition, is painted with a scene of Mandan and Minnetaree Native Americans fighting the Sioux and Arikara.

❶

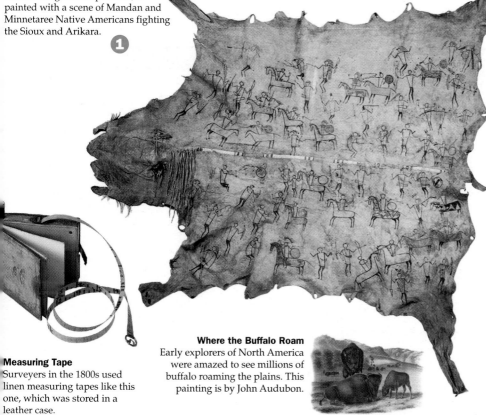

Measuring Tape
Surveyors in the 1800s used linen measuring tapes like this one, which was stored in a leather case.

Where the Buffalo Roam
Early explorers of North America were amazed to see millions of buffalo roaming the plains. This painting is by John Audubon.

377

Dorling Kindersley

Lewis and Clark

Objective

- Use primary and secondary sources, such as visual information, to acquire information.

1 Introduce and Motivate

- Have students write a journal entry to describe one scene a member of the expedition might have witnessed.

- Students will add to their journal entries later as part of the assessment for this page.

2 Teach and Discuss

❶ **What conclusion can you draw from the scene shown on the buffalo robe?**
Possible answer: The Sioux and the Arikara were allies to each other but enemies to the Mandan and Minnetaree.
⤵ **Draw Conclusions**

3 Close and Assess

Test Talk

Write Your Answer to Score High

Have students add to the journal entries they began earlier, using details from the text to describe events that could have happened. Discuss what new information they learned.

Problem Solving

Use a Problem-Solving Process

- Have students consider the following scenario: **Suppose you are a member of the Lewis and Clark Expedition. Another member of the expedition has disobeyed orders. Should Lewis and Clark dismiss this person?**

- Students should use the following problem-solving process to arrive at a solution. For each step in the process, have students discuss and write about what must be considered as they solve the problem. Write these steps on the board or read them aloud.

1. **Identify a problem.**
2. **Gather information.**
3. **List and consider options.**
4. **Consider advantages and disadvantages.**
5. **Choose and implement a solution.**
6. **Evaluate the effectiveness of the solution.**

Compare Population Density Maps

Objective

- Interpret information in visuals, including maps.

Vocabulary

distribution map, p. 378;
population density map, p. 378

Resource

- Workbook, p. 88
- Transparency 47

1 Introduce and Motivate

What is a population density map?
Ask students how a population map might help historians study changes in different regions. Then have students read the **What?** section of text on p. 378 to help set the purpose of the lesson.

Why use a population density map? Have students read the **Why?** section of text on p. 378. Ask them how a population density map of their town might have changed over the last ten years.

2 Teach and Discuss

How is this skill used? Examine with students the maps on pp. 378 and 379.

- Read the map legend with students and explain that the number of inhabitants per square mile is an average, and not the actual number of people.

- Point out that in order to compare populations using density maps, the region in both maps should be the same, but the time periods and populations should be different.

- Have students read the **How?** section on p. 379.

Compare Population Density Maps

What? Distribution Maps show the pattern of how things such as population and natural resources are spread out over an area. One type of map that shows the distribution of population is called a population density map. An area where a lot of people live is densely populated. If the area has few people living in it, it is lightly populated.

Why? In Lesson 2 you learned about the westward movement of people from the original 13 states after the Revolution. Later, more and more people continued moving west. Comparing population density maps from different time periods can show how population in an area has changed.

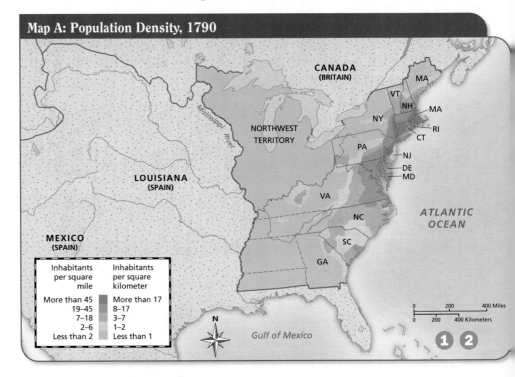

Map A: Population Density, 1790

378

Practice and Extend

CURRICULUM CONNECTION
Reading

Use Reference Tools

- Have students visit the school library to find reference tools containing maps, such as an atlas or an encyclopedia.

- Students should try to find population density maps. If students locate different population density maps for the same region, they can compare the maps.

- Ask students to share the maps they found.

SOCIAL STUDIES STRAND
Geography

The following map resources are available:

- Big Book Atlas
- Student Atlas
- Outline Maps
- Desk Maps
- Map Resources CD-ROM

Map B: Population Density, 1830

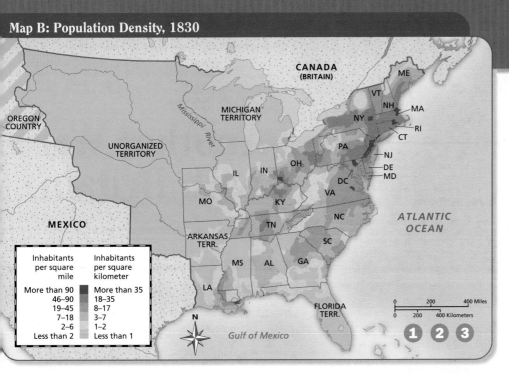

Inhabitants per square mile	Inhabitants per square kilometer
More than 90	More than 35
46–90	18–35
19–45	8–17
7–18	3–7
2–6	1–2
Less than 2	Less than 1

How? Map A shows the population density of the United States in 1790, based on the nation's first census. The census did not count Native Americans, so these maps do not show Native American population density. Each color on the map represents a number of people living in one square mile. To understand a square mile, picture a large square drawn on land in which each side measures one mile. According to Map A, the most densely populated areas are those in which more than 45 people lived within one square mile of land. What color represents these areas on the map? Notice that the population is most dense along the coast in the 13 original states. Few Americans lived outside these areas in 1790.

Map B shows United States population density in 1830. You can see that areas such as Kentucky had become more populated by

this time, about 50 years after Daniel Boone settled there. Lands that were part of the Louisiana Purchase, such as Missouri and Louisiana, were becoming more populated as well.

Think and Apply

1 What is a **distribution map?** What is a **population density map?**

2 How did the population of Virginia change from 1790 to 1830?

3 Which part of the Mississippi was most densely populated in 1830? Why was this area densely populated?

Internet Activity

For more information, go online to the *Atlas* at **www.sfsocialstudies.com**.

379

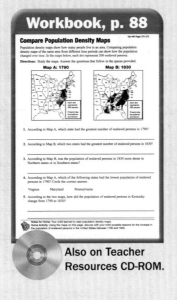

Workbook, p. 88

Compare Population Density Maps

Also on Teacher Resources CD-ROM.

---

1 **What was the population density of the area on the maps that is the present-day state of Ohio?** Answers should match the data shown on the maps. Possible answer: Fewer than 2 people per square mile in 1790 and from fewer than 2 to more than 90 people per square mile in 1830. Interpret Maps

SOCIAL STUDIES STRAND
Geography

Tell students that these population density maps show clusters of settlement in the United States. Have students look at Map A. Explain that early settlements of newcomers to America were near the eastern coast. Later settlements, as illustrated by Map B, were farther inland. Point out on Map B the sparse population in parts of the Appalachian Mountains and the dense population near the mouth of the Mississippi River.

2 **How is population density symbolized on these maps?** By color Interpret Maps

3 **How might a population density map for the United States today differ from the one shown for 1830?** Possible answer: The entire United States would be shown and many of the areas would have a much greater population density. Draw Conclusions

3 Close and Assess

Think and Apply

1. A distribution map shows the pattern of how things such as population and natural resources are spread out over an area. A population density map is a type of distribution map.

2. Virginia became more densely populated, especially in the western half of the state.

3. The area between Louisiana and the state of Mississippi; Possible answer: Because it was an important transportation route

Another War with Britain

Objectives

- Identify reasons why the United States went to war a second time with Britain.

- Describe the main battles and the outcome of the War of 1812.

- Explain why and how "The Star-Spangled Banner" was written.

Vocabulary

neutral, p. 381;
Battle of Tippecanoe, p. 381;
War Hawks, p. 382; **War of 1812,** p. 382;
national anthem, p. 383;
Battle of New Orleans, p. 384

Resources

- Workbook, p. 89
- Transparency 20
- Every Student Learns Guide, pp. 162–165
- Quick Study, pp. 82–83

Quick Teaching Plan

If time is short, have students write *The War of 1812* at the top of their paper and the following headings down the side of their paper: *Main Events, Causes,* and *Effects.*

- Have students read the lesson independently and record details under the appropriate heading.

1 Introduce and Motivate

Preview To activate prior knowledge, ask students to recall details about the American Revolution. Tell students that in Lesson 3 they will learn about another war with Britain—the War of 1812.

You Are There In 1807 Britain still considered some of the sailors who fought on the side of the colonies during the American Revolution to be deserters from the British Navy. Ask students if they agree or disagree with Britain's decision to capture sailors they thought were deserters.

LESSON 3

1805			1815

1808
James Madison is elected the fourth President of the United States

1812
The United States declares war on Britain

1815
The War of 1812 ends

PREVIEW

Focus on the Main Idea
The United States fought Britain in the War of 1812 to gain freedom of the seas and to end British interference with United States expansion westward.

PLACES
Baltimore, Maryland
Fort McHenry
New Orleans, Louisiana

PEOPLE
Tecumseh
James Madison
Henry Clay
Oliver Hazard Perry
Francis Scott Key
Dolley Madison
Andrew Jackson

VOCABULARY
neutral
Battle of Tippecanoe
War Hawks
War of 1812
national anthem
Battle of New Orleans

Another War with Britain

You Are There
The date is June 1807, and you are a sailor aboard the American Navy ship *Chesapeake.* When you sailed from Virginia, you thought you were on a peaceful mission. But now suddenly the British frigate *Leopard* looms up and its crew demands to board your ship. "We're looking for deserters from the British Navy," the British captain shouts.

Your captain refuses to let the British board the *Chesapeake.* The British respond with thundering cannon fire, killing three of your fellow sailors. To avoid further bloodshed, your captain allows the British to board. The British sailors pick out four of your crew, claim they are British deserters, and take them aboard the *Leopard.*

You don't know it at the time, but you have been part of an event that will help push the United States back into war with Britain.

Cause and Effect As you read, identify the causes and effects of major events described in the lesson.

380

Practice and Extend

READING SKILL
Cause and Effect

In the Lesson Review, students complete a graphic organizer like the one below. You may want to provide students with a copy of Transparency 20 to complete as they read the lesson.

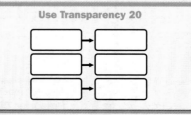

Use Transparency 20

VOCABULARY
Word Exercise

Individual Word Study Remind students that they can often determine the meaning of compound words by breaking them into parts. Read the definition of *anthem* to students: a song of praise, devotion, or patriotism. Ask what the word "national" tells them about the anthem. (it is about the nation, related to the country) Explain that the national anthem of any country is a song of praise or patriotism about that country.

Moving Toward War

In the early 1800s, events like the one you just read about happened again and again to ships of the United States. American ships were stopped not only by the British, but also by the French. During that time, Britain and France were at war. Neither country wanted the other to receive any supplies from the United States. So both interfered with United States shipping.

The actions by the British particularly angered the United States. The British often seized United States' sailors, claiming they were deserters from the British Navy. The British forced these sailors to work on British ships. Often, the men they seized were not British deserters at all but citizens of the United States. In addition, the British seized the cargoes, or goods, carried by the ships. Because of these actions by the British, trade between the United States and countries across the seas had nearly stopped by 1808.

This situation caused great tension between the United States and Britain. But President Jefferson did not want the United States to take the side of either the French or the British

in their war. He wanted the nation to remain **neutral,** or to not take sides. "Peace is our passion," he wrote.

In the Northwest Territory, there was another major source of tension with the British. The Shawnee leader **Tecumseh** (tih KUHM suh) ② was uniting Native Americans to resist pioneer settlement. Speaking of the tribes that had once lived in the territory, he said: "They have vanished before the [greed] and oppression of the white man as snow before a summer sun." The United States suspected, correctly, that the British were supporting Tecumseh.

In 1811, United States forces and Tecumseh's soldiers fought each other in what is now Indiana. Known as the **Battle of Tippecanoe** (tip ee kuh NEW), this fight was seen as a victory for the United States. This weakened Tecumseh's standing among the Native Americans, who had expected a great victory. You will read more about Tecumseh ③ on page 385.

REVIEW What can you conclude about Britain's attitude toward the United States during the early 1800s? 🔄 **Draw Conclusions**

Although neither side won the Battle of Tippecanoe, it was seen as a United States victory.

381

---

② Teach and Discuss

PAGE 381

Moving Toward War

⏱️ *Quick Summary* Tension between Britain and the United States increased. Trade almost came to a halt. The United States believed Britain was supporting Tecumseh in his attempt to hinder westward expansion.

❶ What effect did the war between Britain and France have on the United States during the early 1800s? Both countries interfered with U.S. shipping. **Cause and Effect**

C SOCIAL STUDIES STRAND Culture

Point out that Native Americans experienced many challenges as the United States changed and grew.

❷ How did Tecumseh feel about the pioneers who settled in the Northwest Territory? Possible answer: He resented them because he felt they had taken land that did not belong to them and that they had oppressed his people. 🔄 **Draw Conclusions**

❸ Why was the Battle of Tippecanoe a greater loss to Tecumseh? His standing among Native Americans was weakened because the fight was seen as a victory for the United States. **Cause and Effect**

✓ **REVIEW ANSWER** Britain continued to deal with the United States as an enemy, as it had during the American Revolution. 🔄 **Draw Conclusions**

The War of 1812

 Quick Summary Pressed by a group called the War Hawks, President Madison asked Congress to declare war on Britain in June of 1812.

4 **What did Henry Clay mean by "you had better abandon the ocean"?** If the United States did not fight the British, then they would not be able to sail on the Atlantic Ocean to trade.
Make Inferences

Decision Making

President Madison did not want to go to war with Britain, but in the end he decided to ask Congress to declare war.

5 **Why did President Madison decide to declare war against Britain? What other decisions might he have made?** He declared war because of Britain's attacks on American shipping, British support of attacks on settlers in the Northwestern frontier, and the hope of making Canada part of the United States. Possible answer: Madison might also have tried to negotiate a treaty with the British to end the incidents.
Make Decisions

6 **Why was the American warship Constitution nicknamed "Old Ironsides"?** In battle, cannonballs seemed to bounce off the ship, as if its sides were made of iron. **Cause and Effect**

(H) SOCIAL STUDIES STRAND
History

The Library of Congress is the nation's oldest federal cultural institution, begun as a legislative library in 1800. When the British burned the Capitol the 3,000 volumes were destroyed. Thomas Jefferson sold his personal collection of 6,487 volumes to the government to start a new library. Today it is the largest library in the world with more than 120 million items stored on more than 500 miles of bookshelves. Noah Webster also boosted the national culture with the first truly American dictionary in 1806. He stressed American pronunciation and usage, and listed unique American words such as *skunk* and *chowder*. He also used American spellings like *center* instead of *centre*.

► The USS *Constitution*, also called "Old Ironsides," defeated the British *Guerrière*.

The War of 1812

In 1809, **James Madison** became President. Like Jefferson, he wanted to keep the nation out of war with Britain. But British actions on the seas caused a wave of anger to sweep the country. In Congress, a group called the **War Hawks** pressed for war against Britain. These members of Congress protested Britain's attacks on American shipping. One of their leaders, **Henry Clay** of Kentucky, said that the United States had to go to war or "you had better abandon the ocean."

The War Hawks also wanted war for other reasons. First, they hoped to end British-supported attacks against settlers on the Northwestern frontier. Second, they wanted to drive the British out of Canada. Finally, in June 1812, President Madison asked Congress to declare war on Britain.

The **War of 1812** is remembered for dramatic battles at sea. In the waters of the Atlantic Ocean east of Canada, the American warship *Constitution* defeated the British warship *Guerrière* (gair YAIR). British cannonballs just seemed to bounce off the *Constitution*. "Her sides are made of iron!" shouted an American sailor. Actually, the sides of the *Constitution* were built of oak. Today, you can visit that ship, nicknamed "Old Ironsides," in Boston harbor. It is still part of the United States Navy and is the navy's oldest ship.

In 1813, the *Chesapeake*, which you read about in "You Are There," battled the British ship *Shannon* off Boston harbor. The *Chesapeake's* captain, James Lawrence, was badly wounded. His last words were, "Don't give up the ship!" Unfortunately, his crew had to give up. But his words became the navy's rallying cry.

That same year, Americans fought another famous naval battle, this time in the Great Lakes, on Lake Erie. For more than three hours, a United States fleet commanded by **Oliver Hazard Perry** fought a British fleet in one of the war's fiercest battles. After winning the battle, Perry sent the following

382

Practice and Extend

(FYI) SOCIAL STUDIES
Background

War Hawks

- This group of men was primarily made up of representatives elected to Congress in 1810.
- The War Hawks hoped to go to war to end British-supported attacks against settlers on the Northwestern frontier.
- They included political leaders Henry Clay and John C. Calhoun.
- Some War Hawks hoped to use a war with Britain to take Florida from Spain.

CURRICULUM CONNECTION
Drama

Persuasive Viewpoints

- Have partners create a short skit showing a conversation between Henry Clay and President Madison discussing their viewpoints about going to war with Britain.
- Make sure that students use persuasive language when describing the views of Henry Clay, a War Hawk.
- Have partners perform their skits for the class.

message: "We have met the enemy and they are ours."

Probably the lowest point for the United States in the war came in August 1814. A British force marched into Washington, D.C. and took control of the city. President Madison and other government officials barely got out in time. Important historical documents, like the Declaration of Independence, were hastily bundled up and carried off to safety. British troops set fire to the Capitol. They also broke into the President's House, which they burned.

The same British force then moved on to invade **Baltimore, Maryland.** But this time United States defenders were better prepared. **Fort McHenry,** defended by 1,000 United States troops, stood in the harbor. The British fleet had to sail past its guns to reach Baltimore. On the morning of

September 13, 1814, the British ships began bombarding the fort with cannon fire.

A young Washington lawyer, **Francis Scott Key,** watched as the bombardment continued into the night. He wondered how long the fort could hold out. As dawn broke on September 14, he had his answer. The United States flag still flew over the fort!

The British invaders finally gave up their attempt to capture Baltimore. Key scribbled a few verses on the back of an envelope describing what he had seen. His poem was later set to music and became known as "The Star-Spangled Banner." In 1931, this became the official song of the United States, its **national anthem.** You can read its words and music on pages 388–389.

REVIEW How would you sequence the important events in the British invasion of the United States? **Sequence**

Dolley Madison Saves a Painting

⑨

As British forces neared Washington, D.C., *Dolley Madison,* wife of the President, was told she had to leave the President's House quickly. She refused, saying that she must first make sure that Gilbert Stuart's "precious portrait" of George Washington was removed to safety. But the painting's frame was firmly screwed to the wall. "I have ordered the frame to be broken," she later wrote, "and the canvas taken out" and brought to safety. Only then did Dolley Madison leave the President's House. Today, you can visit the White House and see that famous painting on a wall in the East Room.

383

⑦ **Why was the march into Washington, D.C., by a British force probably the lowest point for the United States in the war?** The British troops took control of the city, set fire to the Capitol, and burned the President's House. This disrupted the nation's government. ⟳ **Draw Conclusions**

✓ Ongoing Assessment

| **If...** students do not understand why the British invasion of Washington, D.C., was a low point in the war, | **then...** remind them that Washington is the nation's capital, where the business of government is conducted. Discuss how the destruction of the city would affect government operations. |

⑧ **Why were the British able to take over Washington, D.C., but not able to capture Baltimore?** The United States was unprepared to defend Washington, D.C.; the Baltimore harbor had a fort, and defenders were better prepared. ⟳ **Main Idea and Details**

✓ REVIEW ANSWER Invaded Washington, D.C., and burned it; moved on toward Baltimore; tried to get past Fort McHenry; abandoned the invasion of Baltimore and sailed away **Sequence**

Dolley Madison Saves a Painting

⑨ **What conclusion can you draw about Dolley Madison based on her actions?** Possible answer: She was patriotic and considered the painting to be very important. ⟳ **Draw Conclusions**

Battle of New Orleans

Quick Summary Andrew Jackson and his troops defeated the British in the Battle of New Orleans. A treaty was signed ending the war.

10 **Do you think the War of 1812 had any positive effects on the United States? Why or why not?** Possible answer: Yes, by putting up such a strong fight, the United States showed the world that it was capable of defending itself on land and at sea.
Cause and Effect

✓ **REVIEW ANSWER** Possible answers: British interference with U.S. shipping might have ended anyway; the United States did not gain control of Canada.
Main Idea and Details

3 Close and Assess

Summarize the Lesson

Tell students to read the lesson summary, choose one main idea, and give a brief oral presentation about it.

✓ | LESSON 3 | REVIEW |

1. **Cause and Effect** For possible answers, see the reduced pupil page.

2. British sailors boarded American ships and captured crew and cargoes.

3. **Critical Thinking: Make Decisions** Go to war: Protect American shipping, end British-supported attacks against settlers, drive British out of Canada; Against War: Keep peace; Make sure students use the steps of decision–making in their answers.

4. Francis Scott Key wrote the words for "The Star-Spangled Banner."

5. A treaty had been signed two weeks earlier ending the war.

Link to ━━ **Writing**

Encourage students to include in their song information they have learned about the battle.

384 Unit 5 • Life in a New Nation

Battle of New Orleans

Another British fighting force set its sights on the port city of **New Orleans, Louisiana.** There the American general **Andrew Jackson** waited with an army of Kentucky and Tennessee militiamen.

On January 8, 1815, the British marched through the morning mist to attack Jackson's men. Jackson's forces killed thousands of British soldiers. Said one Kentucky soldier, "The field, it looked…like a sea of blood."

The victory turned Jackson into a national hero. However, the **Battle of New Orleans** would not have happened if a certain bit of news had arrived in New Orleans before January 8, 1815. A treaty ending the war had been signed in Europe two weeks earlier. But by January 8, news of the treaty had not yet crossed the Atlantic.

The War of 1812 turned out to have fewer effects than those who fought it had

expected. Since Britain and France had stopped fighting each other in 1814, they no longer interfered with United States ships. The United States never gained control of Canada. But the United States did show the world that it intended to defend itself at sea or on land.

REVIEW Identify a detail that supports the main idea that the War of 1812 had fewer effects than those who fought it expected.
Main Idea and Details

Summarize the Lesson

- **1808** James Madison was elected the fourth President of the United States.

- **1812** The War of 1812 between the United States and Britain began.

- **1815** The War of 1812 ended.

| LESSON 3 | REVIEW |

Check Facts and Main Ideas

1. **Cause and Effect** On a separate sheet of paper, fill in each missing cause or effect.

Cause	Effect
Britain attacks United States ships.	The United States trade with foreign countries is severely cut.
Tecumseh's forces do not win the Battle of Tippecanoe.	Tecumseh's standing weakens among fellow Native Americans.
Francis Scott Key watches British attack on Fort McHenry.	He is inspired to write the words for "The Star-Spangled Banner."

2. In what ways did Britain interfere with American shipping on the high seas?

3. **Critical Thinking: Make Decisions** If you had been President, would you have gone to war with Britain in 1812? Use the decision-making steps on page H3 to explain why or why not.

4. What was produced during the battle of Fort McHenry other than a United States victory?

5. If known, what fact would have prevented the **Battle of New Orleans?**

Link to ━━ **Writing**

Write a Song Suppose that you had witnessed a battle in the War of 1812. Write the words to a song about the battle as Francis Scott Key did after the battle of Fort McHenry.

384

Practice and Extend

MEETING INDIVIDUAL NEEDS
Learning Styles

Review the War of 1812 Using their individual learning styles, students review important events in the War of 1812.

Verbal Learning Have partners take turns telling each other about important events in the War of 1812. One partner can identify an event and the other can tell what he or she knows about it. Partners then switch roles and repeat until they have discussed major events.

Social Learning Have students play the roles of members of Congress in 1812 as they debate whether or not to declare war against Britain. Be sure that they give reasons to support their opinions.

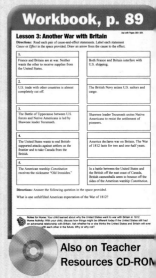

Workbook, p. 89

Lesson 3: Another War with Britain

Also on Teacher Resources CD-ROM

Tecumseh 1768–1813

Tecumseh grew up during a time of struggle. The Shawnee people were beginning a long struggle to defend their land in the Ohio River valley from the new American settlers. Fierce battles took place all around the young boy, resulting in the deaths of many Shawnee, including Tecumseh's father. As an adult, Tecumseh would lead the Shawnee in their efforts to keep their land.

Tecumseh fought his first battle at the side of his older brother when he was only 14 years old. Tecumseh earned respect for his bravery and also came to be known as a powerful speaker. After some Native American leaders signed a treaty giving up some Indian lands in Ohio, Tecumseh explained to a United States governor why the land should be returned:

"The white people have no right to take the land from the Indians, because they had it first; it is theirs."

BIOFACT

British General Isaac Brock gave this compass to Tecumseh before the Battle of Detroit in the War of 1812.

The Native Americans did not get their land back, but Tecumseh did not get discouraged. He believed that all Indian groups needed to unite. He traveled **①** for miles and miles, urging members of other groups to unite to protect Native American lands. His fiery speeches won over hundreds of followers.

Tecumseh decided to make his force an ally of the British army during the War of 1812. His soldiers helped the British win the Battle of Detroit. He was **②** determined to keep fighting for the American Indians. In one powerful speech, Tecumseh said:

"Our lives are in the hands of the Great Spirit. We are determined to defend our lands, and if it is His will, we wish to leave our bones upon them."

Tecumseh's speech turned out to be a prediction of his own future. He was killed at the Battle of the Thames in 1813.

Learn from Biographies

How did Tecumseh use his ability to speak clearly and passionately to help him achieve his goals?

For more information, go online to *Meet the People* at **www.sfsocialstudies.com.**

385

Tecumseh

Objective
- Identify the challenges and contributions of people, including Tecumseh, from selected Native American groups.

1 Introduce and Motivate

Preview Ask students to share what they remember about Tecumseh's role leading to the War of 1812. Tell students that they will read about the goals Tecumseh set for himself and other Native Americans.

2 Teach and Discuss

① **What character traits do you think Tecumseh possessed?** Possible answers: Bravery, courage, intelligence, determination, loyalty
⟳ Draw Conclusions

② **Why did Tecumseh decide to fight for the British during the War of 1812?** He was fighting against the United States in an attempt to defend Native American lands. Analyze Information

3 Close and Assess

Learn from Biographies Answer

Possible answer: He convinced many Native American groups to fight with him against the American settlers.

WEB SITE
Technology

Students can find out more about Tecumseh by clicking on *Meet the People* at **www.sfsocialstudies.com.**

SOCIAL STUDIES
Background

More About Tecumseh
- Tecumseh means "shooting star," or "meteor."
- After the loss at the battle of Tippecanoe in 1811, Tecumseh joined the British and served with them in the War of 1812, during which he was killed.
- After Tecumseh's death, Native American attempts to reclaim their lands resurfaced at different times, under different leaders, in different parts of the country.

CHAPTER 11 REVIEW

Resources

- Assessment Book, pp. 61–64
- Workbook, p. 90: Vocabulary Review

Chapter Summary

For possible answers, see the reduced pupil page.

Vocabulary

1. Cabinet, **2.** Battle of New Orleans, **3.** Louisiana Purchase, **4.** Battle of Tippecanoe, **5.** electoral college

People and Places

1. c, **2.** d, **3.** b, **4.** f, **5.** a, **6.** e

Facts and Main Ideas

1. She guided them through the Louisiana Territory and translated when they spoke to the Native Americans there. Her presence reassured the Native Americans that the expedition was peaceful.

2. British ships tried to capture Fort McHenry so they could invade Baltimore. They bombed the fort, but it held out. The British had to give up their attempt to take the city.

3. About one year

4. Washington introduced and appointed the first Cabinet. The site for the new capital was selected in what is now Washington, D.C. Political parties began to form.

5. The Wilderness Road allowed settlers to cross the Appalachians from Virginia to Kentucky more easily. The Louisiana Purchase gave Americans more land in the west to settle.

6. The United States wanted Britain to stop interfering both with U.S. trade on the seas and the expansion of the United States.

7. Good: It was in the geographic center of the original states. Bad: It was a marshy, unhealthy location. Today: It would be too costly to move the capital to a new location. It is no longer centrally located.

386 Unit 5 • Life in a New Nation

CHAPTER 11 REVIEW

1785

1789
George Washington elected first President of the United States

Chapter Summary

 Draw Conclusions

On a separate sheet of paper, fill in the three facts upon which the given conclusion could be based.

| The British had already stopped interfering with American ships. | | **Conclusion** |

The United States was not able to gain control of Canada.

The War of 1812 did not affect the United States as the country had expected, but it did benefit the country in other ways.

The United States demonstrated its strength to the world.

Vocabulary

Fill in the blanks with the vocabulary word that best completes the sentence.

1 The _____ is chosen by the President to advise the President and help govern. (p. 363)

2 The _____ mistakenly took place after a treaty ending the War of 1812 had already been signed. (p. 384)

3 Thomas Jefferson chose James Monroe to help complete the _____ in 1803. (p. 373)

4 Tecumseh's soldiers fought the Americans in the _____. (p. 381)

5 Members of the _____ are chosen by people in each state to elect the President. (p. 363)

People and Places

Match each person or place with the correct description.

1 New York City (p. 363)

2 Benjamin Banneker (p. 365)

3 William Clark (p. 374)

4 Cumberland Gap (p. 372)

5 Oliver Hazard Perry (p. 382)

6 Baltimore (p. 383)

a. United States fleet commander

b. explored Louisiana Territory

c. temporary capital where George Washington was inaugurated

d. surveyed the site of the nation's new capital

e. British failed to capture this city in the War of 1812

f. part of the Wilderness Road

386

Practice and Extend

Assessment Options

✓ Chapter 11 Assessment

- Chapter 11 Content Test: Use Assessment Book, pp. 61–62.
- Chapter 11 Skills Test: Use Assessment Book, pp. 63–64.

TEST PREP Standardized Test Prep

- Chapter 11 Tests contain standardized test format.

✓ Chapter 11 Performance Assessment

- Have students suppose they are journalists during the War of 1812. Have them write short news articles describing what is happening during the war.
- Remind students to find details in the chapter that tell who, what, where, when, why, and how.
- Assess students' understanding of the events of the War of 1812 that they write about in their speech or news articles.

1800

1800
Federal government moves to Washington, D.C.

1803
Louisiana Purchase expands the size of the country

1804
Lewis and Clark begin to explore the Louisiana Territory

1812
The United States declares war on Britain

1815

1815
The War of 1812 ends

Facts and Main Ideas

1 How did Sacagawea help Lewis and Clark on their expedition?

2 Describe the battle Francis Scott Key witnessed as he wrote the words for "The Star-Spangled Banner."

3 **Time Line** How many years were there between the Louisiana Purchase and its exploration?

4 **Main Idea** What changes in government took place under President George Washington?

5 **Main Idea** How did the efforts of Daniel Boone and the Louisiana Purchase encourage people to move westward?

6 **Main Idea** Why did the United States declare war on Britain in 1812?

7 **Critical Thinking:** *Evaluate* Do you think Washington, D.C., was a good location for the capital in 1800? Is it a good location today? Explain your answer.

Write About History

1 **Write a letter** to the United States government as a person living in 1812 explaining why you think the country should or should not enter into a war with Britain.

2 **Write an advertisement** encouraging Americans to settle in the new western lands of the United States. Include catchy phrases and photographs or illustrations.

3 **Write a journal entry** as Tecumseh. Explain why you think Native American groups should unite and how you plan to encourage them to do so.

Apply Skills

Compare Population Density Maps

The map below shows population density for each county of Virginia. Use the map to answer the questions that follow.

1 What color represents the counties with the lowest population density?

2 What is the population density of the county in which Roanoke is located?

3 How many counties have the highest level of population density? How do you know?

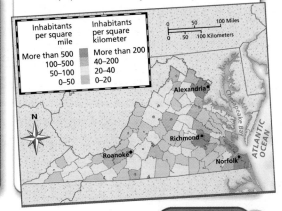

Inhabitants per square mile | Inhabitants per square kilometer
More than 500 | More than 200
100–500 | 40–200
50–100 | 20–40
0–50 | 0–20

0   50   100 Miles
0   50   100 Kilometers

Alexandria

Richmond

Roanoke

Norfolk

Chesapeake Bay

ATLANTIC OCEAN

Internet Activity

To get help with vocabulary, people, and terms, select dictionary or encyclopedia from *Social Studies Library* at **www.sfsocialstudies.com.**

Write About History

1. Have students support their opinions with facts from the chapter.

2. Suggest that students include a map in their ads to show where they would like Americans to settle.

3. Have students share their journal entries and compare reasons.

Apply Skills

1. Green

2. From 100–500 people per square mile; or 40–200 people per square kilometer.

3. Three; three counties are shown in the color representing "More than 500" people per square mile or "More than 200" people per square kilometer.

Hands-on Unit Project

✓ **Unit 5 Performance Assessment**

- See p. 392 for information about using the Unit Project as a means of performance assessment.
- A scoring guide is provided on p. 392.

WEB SITE
Technology

For more information, students can select the dictionary or encyclopedia from *Social Studies Library* at **www.socialstudies.com.**

Workbook, p. 90

Vocabulary Review

Directions: Complete the crossword puzzle using the clues below and the vocabulary words from Chapter 11.

Across

1. An early settler who moved westward
4. A _____ party is an organized group of people who share a view of what government should be and do.
5. This ceremony is held when a newly elected President swears loyalty to the Constitution and takes office.
9. Agreement that doubled the size of the United States with land bought from the French
10. The _____ of 1812 is remembered for dramatic battles at sea.
11. The heads of certain government departments are known as this. These heads advise and help the President.
12. The official song of the United States is its national _____.

Down

2. The Battle of _____ took place after a treaty ending the war had been signed in Europe.
3. The edge of settlement for those who pushed westward
6. Not taking sides
7. The Battle of _____ was fought in the present-day state of Indiana between U.S. forces and Tecumseh's soldiers.
8. Members of Congress who pressed for war against Britain were known as War _____.
13. The _____ college is made up of people chosen by each state to vote for the President and Vice-President.

Notes for Home: Your child learned about developments in the United States during the first presidency and thereafter.
Home Activity: With your child, create a word-search puzzle using the vocabulary terms. Create clues and definitions.

Also on Teacher Resources CD-ROM.

The Star-Spangled Banner

Objective

- Sing or recite "The Star-Spangled Banner" and explain its history.

1 Introduce and Motivate

Preview To activate prior knowledge, ask students on what occasion the lyrics to "The Star-Spangled Banner" were written and by whom.

Ask students what a "star-spangled banner" refers to. (The American flag, which seems to shine with stars)

2 Teach and Discuss

1 Which verse do we typically sing? Why might we only sing this verse?
Verse 1; Possible answer: So that we always sing the same words when we sing the anthem ⟳ Draw Conclusions

UNIT
5

End with a Song

The Star-Spangled Banner

By Francis Scott Key

As you read on page 383, Francis Scott Key wrote the words of what would become our national anthem during a key battle of the War of 1812. It quickly became popular across the nation. Read the verses of "The Star-Spangled Banner" below. What emotion did the sight of the American flag inspire in Key? Why do you think the song was chosen as our national anthem?

1
Oh, __ say! can you see, by the dawn's ear-ly light,
On the shore, dim-ly seen through the mists of the deep,
Oh, __ thus be it ever when __ free men shall stand

What so proud-ly we hailed at the twi-light's last gleam-ing
Where the foe's haugh-ty host in dread si-lence re-pos-es,
Be-tween their loved homes and the war's des-o-la-tion

Whose broad stripes and bright stars, through the per-il-ous fight,
What is that which the breeze, o'er the tow-er-ing steep,
Blest with vict-'ry and peace, may the heav'n-res-cued land

O'er the ram-parts we watched were so gal-lant-ly stream-ing
As it fit-ful-ly blows, half con-ceals, half dis-clos-es?
Praise the Pow'r that hath made and pre-served us a na-tion

388

Practice and Extend

 SOCIAL STUDIES
Background

"The Star-Spangled Banner"

- The melody for "The Star-Spangled Banner" was taken from "To Anacreon in Heaven," written by the British composer John Stafford Smith.
- The words were first published in 1814 in a broadside titled "Defence of Fort M'Henry."
- The title was changed to "The Star-Spangled Banner" in 1814 when it appeared as sheet music.
- The song was officially adopted as the U.S. national anthem in 1931 by an act of Congress.

 AUDIO CD
Technology

Play the CD, *Songs and Music,* to listen to "The Star-Spangled Banner."

And the rock-ets' red glare, the bombs burst-ing in air,
Now it catch-es the gleam of the morn-ing's first beam,
Then _ con-quer we must, for our cause it is just,

Gave proof through the night that our flag was still there.
In full glo-ry re-flected now _ shines on the stream;
And this be our motto: "In _ God is our trust!"

Oh, say, does that _ Star-Span-gled Ban-ner _ yet _ wave _
'Tis the Star-Span-gled _ Ban-ner, oh, long may _ it _ wave _
And the Star-Span-gled _ Ban-ner in tri-umph _ shall _ wave _

O'er the land _ of the free and the home of the brave?
O'er the land _ of the free and the home of the brave!
O'er the land _ of the free and the home of the brave!

389

2 Which words suggest that these events take place in the morning?
"by the dawn's early light. . . ."
Draw Conclusions

3 At the end of each verse, how does Francis Scott Key refer to the United States? "The land of the free and the home of the brave" Analyze Information

3 Close and Assess

- Have students work in groups to practice singing or reciting all of the verses and then sing or recite the complete national anthem for the class. Make sure that students stand and are respectful during the singing or recital of the anthem.

- Ask students why they think this song was chosen as the U.S. national anthem. (Possible answer: It points out the determination of the United States to fight for and retain its freedom and independence.)

- There are four verses to *The Star Spangled Banner.* The entire lyrics can be found at **http://www.loc.gov**

CURRICULUM CONNECTION
Music

Write an Anthem

Have students work in small groups to write a class, school, or community anthem.

- Students can first choose a familiar tune they will use for their anthem.
- Students should then work together to write the words and perform their anthems for the class.
- Make sure that students show proper respect for their class, school, and community as they compose and perform their anthems.

Resource
- Assessment Book, pp. 65–68

Main Ideas and Vocabulary TEST PREP

1. c, **2.** a, **3.** b, **4.** c

People and Vocabulary

1. b, **2.** c, **3.** d, **4.** f, **5.** e, **6.** a

Apply Skills

- Encourage students to suggest reasons that a certain table might have a higher population density than another table.

Test Talk

Use Information from Graphics
Use Apply Skills to model the Test Talk strategy.

Make sure that you understand the question.
Have students identify the map in the question. Students should finish the statement "I need to find out. . . ."

Make sure that you get information from the graphics.
Ask students to skim the map to find the right information to support their answer.

Main Ideas and Vocabulary TEST PREP

Read the passage below and use it to answer the questions that follow.

In 1781, the states adopted the Articles of Confederation. This plan established a weak central government, but the individual state governments were very strong. Rebellions and widespread inflation throughout the 13 states led many people to believe that a new plan of government was needed.

In 1787 delegates from many of the states met in Philadelphia to rewrite the Articles of Confederation. Instead, they created a new Constitution, which outlined a plan for a strong central government but also gave individual states the ability to govern themselves.

The backers of the Constitution faced a challenge in convincing the states to <u>ratify</u> it. Some people approved of the new plan for government, but others did not. In 1788 the Constitution was approved. The following year George Washington was elected as the country's first President.

During this time, Americans had begun moving west across the Appalachian Mountains. These <u>pioneers</u> wanted to build new homes and farm the land. In 1803 the United States purchased the Louisiana Territory from France, which expanded the country's territory all the way to the Rocky Mountains. President Thomas Jefferson sent Meriwether Lewis and William Clark to explore this land.

As the country expanded westward, conflicts broke out with Native Americans and the British. In June 1812, the United States declared war on Britain. Neither the British nor the Americans won the War of 1812, but the Americans proved they would fight to defend their country.

1 According to the passage, what was the main problem with the plan of government created by the Articles of Confederation?
A It created a strong central government and weak state governments.
B It caused wars between the states.
C It created a weak central government and strong state governments.
D It made the leaders of the country too powerful.

2 In the passage, the word <u>ratify</u> means—
A approve
B disapprove
C help
D allow

3 In the passage, the word <u>pioneers</u> means—
A explorers
B settlers
C business people
D politicians

4 What is the main idea of the passage?
A George Washington was the country's first President.
B The United States fought another war with Britain in 1812.
C The United States created a new plan for government and expanded its territory after the Revolution.
D The Articles of Confederation were not an effective plan of government for the United States.

390

Practice and Extend

Assessment Options

 Unit 5 Assessment
- Unit 5 Content Test:
  Use Assessment Book, pp. 65–66.
- Unit 5 Skills Test:
  Use Assessment Book, pp. 67–68.

TEST PREP Standardized Test Prep
- Unit 5 Tests contain standardized test format.

Unit 5 Performance Assessment
- See p. 392 for information about using the Unit Project as a means of Performance Assessment.
- A scoring guide for the Unit 5 Project is provided in the teacher's notes on p. 392.

 Test Talk
- Test Talk Practice Book

WEB SITE Technology

For more information, you can select the dictionary or encyclopedia from *Social Studies Library* at **www.sfsocialstudies.com**.

Test Talk

Use the diagram to help you find the answer.

People and Vocabulary

Match each person and vocabulary word to its definition.

1. **Northwest Ordinance** (p. 342)

2. **Great Compromise** (p. 347)

3. *The Federalist* (p. 353)

4. **Pierre L'Enfant** (p. 365)

5. **York** (p. 374)

6. **Tecumseh** (p. 381)

a. Shawnee leader

b. described how new states would be created

c. said Congress would be made up of two houses

d. essays that appeared in New York newspapers in support of the Constitution

e. took part in the Lewis and Clark expedition

f. helped design Washington, D.C.

Apply Skills

Create a **Distribution Map** Create a population density map of your school cafeteria. First record the number of people sitting at each table. Then draw a map showing the population of each table in the room. Be sure to create a key to show the number of people each color represents. Which table has the highest population density?

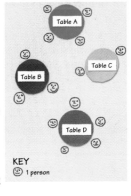

Write and Share

Have a Debate Think back to 1787, when the Constitution was first written. Not everyone was in favor of it. Divide into two groups. One group will represent the Federalists, the other will represent the Antifederalists. The groups will debate whether or not the 13 states should ratify the Constitution. Each member of each group should write an argument for or against ratification, and then present it in a formal debate in your classroom.

Read On Your Own

Look for books like these in the library.

391

Write and Share

- Have each member of the debate team prepare his or her argument and reasons to support it in written form.

- Students who will be watching the debate can write the headings *Before* and *After* on a sheet of paper. Have them write their opinions about ratifying the Constitution before they watch the debate, and then write it again after watching the debate.

- Use the following scoring guide.

✓**Assessment Scoring Guide**

	Have a Debate
6	Supports all ideas with detailed facts and logical reasons. Speaks clearly and uses appropriate expression.
5	Supports ideas with facts. Speaks clearly and appropriately.
4	Supports most ideas with facts. Speaks clearly.
3	Supports some ideas with facts.
2	Is uncertain of some ideas. Does not support ideas with facts or logical reasons.
1	Is unable to articulate ideas.

If you prefer a 4-point rubric, adjust accordingly.

Read on Your Own

Have students prepare oral reports using the following books.

Shh! We're Writing the Constitution, by Jean Fritz (Penguin Putnam Books for Young Readers, ISBN 0-698-11624-0, 1998) **Easy**

Off the Map: The Journals of Lewis and Clark, by Connie Roop and Peter Geiger Roop, eds. (Walker and Co., ISBN 0-802-77546-2, 1998) **On-Level**

How the U.S. Government Works, by Syl Sobel and Pam Tanzey (Barrons Juvenile, ISBN 0-764-11111-6, 1999) **Challenge**

Revisit the Unit Question

✓**Portfolio Assessment**

- Have students look at the list of ideas that they compiled at the beginning of the chapter about the reasons that people form governments.

- Have students look at the additions to their list: reasons that the early Americans had for forming the governments detailed in the Articles of Confederation and in the U.S. Constitution.

- Ask students to compare and contrast the ideas on their original list with the reasons they added as they read the chapter.

- Have students think again about the reasons why people form governments and write a one-paragraph summary on the topic.

- Have students add these lists and summaries to their Social Studies Portfolio.

Two Sides

Objective

• Compare and contrast arguments for and against the Virginia Plan and the New Jersey Plan.

Resource

• Workbook, p. 91

Materials

paper, pencils, poster board or large sheets of bulletin board paper, paints, crayons, or other coloring materials, reference materials

Follow This Procedure

• Tell students they will be holding a town meeting. They will present arguments for and against the Virginia Plan and the New Jersey Plan.

• Divide students into groups. Have them assign roles of moderator, one representative from Virginia and one representative from New Jersey.

• Have all students research and write both sides of the issue and prepare a list of questions for the town meeting.

• Set up two tables with signs that say "Virginia Plan" and "New Jersey Plan."

• Have classmates ask questions throughout the town meeting.

✓ Assessment Scoring Guide

Two Sides	
6	Clearly describes opposing sides using elaborate details, accurate information, and logical arguments.
5	Describes opposing sides using many details, mostly accurate information, and logical arguments.
4	Describes opposing sides using several details, mostly accurate information, and mostly logical arguments.
3	Describes opposing sides using few details, some inaccurate information, and illogical arguments.
2	Describes with difficulty opposing sides using few or no details, inaccurate information, and illogical arguments.
1	Cannot describe opposing sides.

If you prefer a 4-point rubric, adjust accordingly.

392 Unit 5 • Life in a New Nation

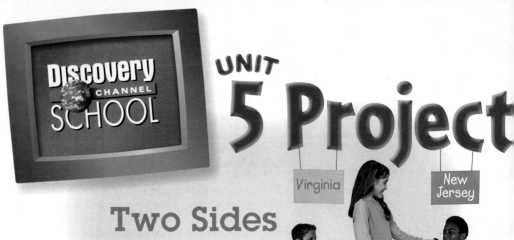

Two Sides

Tune in to the past for a special town meeting.

1 Prepare to hold a town meeting to present arguments for and against the Virginia Plan and the New Jersey Plan.

2 Assign roles. Include roles for reporters, spokespersons for each plan, and audience members to ask questions.

3 Research the arguments for and against each plan. Write questions to ask each spokesperson. The spokespersons of each plan will respond to audience questions and comments.

4 Stage the town meeting. Take turns asking questions and giving responses.

Internet Activity

Learn more about the United States and its growth as a nation. Go to www.sfsocialstudies.com/activities and select your grade and unit.

392

Practice and Extend

Hands-on Unit Project

✓ Performance Assessment

• The Unit Project can also be used as a performance assessment activity.

• Use the scoring guide to assess each group's work.

WEB SITE Technology

Students can launch the Internet Activity by clicking on *Grade 5, Unit 5* at **www.sfsocialstudies.com/activities.**

Workbook, p. 91

5 Project Two Sides

Directions: In a group, use your textbook and other references to research questions and answers for all roles. Then hold a press conference about the ratification of the Bill of Rights.

1. Questions a news reporter might ask a Federalist:

2. A Federalist's answers:

3. Questions a news reporter might ask an Antifederalist:

4. An Antifederalist's answers:

5. In the press conference, my role is (✔ one):
____ Federalist ____ Antifederalist ____ News reporter

6. My argument (✔ one) for ____ or against ____ ratifying the Bill of Rights is ____:

✔ Checklist for Students
____ I wrote my arguments for or against ratifying the Bill of Rights.
____ I wrote questions and answers on behalf of the news reporter, Federalists, and Antifederalists.
____ I chose a role to play in the press conference.
____ I helped stage the classroom press coverage.

Notes for Home: Your child learned how Federalists and Antifederalists viewed the Bill of Rights.
Home Activity: With your child, discuss the importance of listening to opposing points of view. Give personal examples.

Also on Teacher Resources CD-ROM

A Growing Nation

UNIT 6

Unit Planning Guide

Unit 6 • A Growing Nation

Begin with a Primary Source pp. 394–395

Meet the People pp. 396–397

Reading Social Studies, Compare and Contrast pp. 398–399

Chapter Titles	Pacing	Main Ideas
Chapter 12 **Times of Change** pp. 400–425	7 days	• In the 1820s and 1830s, the United States expanded its territory in North America and its power in the Western Hemisphere. • The Industrial Revolution dramatically changed the way Americans lived and worked. • Beginning in the 1830s, a spirit of reform changed life in the United States.
✓ **Chapter 12 Review** pp. 426–427		
Chapter 13 **People Moving South and West** pp. 428–447	5 days	• The United States expanded as Americans settled the South, revolted in Texas, and fought a war with Mexico. • Using a network of trails, people moved west to make better lives for themselves. • The discovery of gold in California led to rapid settlement of the region.
✓ **Chapter 13 Review** pp. 448–449		

End with Literature pp. 450–451

✓ **Unit 6 Review** pp. 452–453

✓ **Unit 6 Project** p. 454

✓ = Assessment Options

Elizabeth Cady Stanton spoke at the first women's rights convention ever held in the United States.

Resources	Meeting Individual Needs
• Workbook, pp. 93–98	• ESL Support, TE pp. 398, 403, 412, 417
• Every Student Learns Guide, pp. 166–177	• Leveled Practice, TE pp. 405, 409, 419
• Transparencies 14, 48	• Learning Styles, TE p. 410
• Quick Study, pp. 84–89	
• Workbook, p. 99	
✓ Chapter 12 Content Test, Assessment Book, pp. 69–70	✓ Chapter 12 Performance Assessment, TE p. 426
✓ Chapter 12 Skills Test, Assessment Book, pp. 71–72	

• Workbook, pp. 100–104	• Leveled Practice, TE pp. 433, 441, 444
• Every Student Learns Guide, pp. 178–189	• ESL Support, TE pp. 436, 439, 443
• Transparencies 6, 13, 14, 49	
• Quick Study, pp. 90–95	
• Workbook, p. 105	
✓ Chapter 13 Content Test, Assessment Book, pp. 73–74	✓ Chapter 13 Performance Assessment, TE p. 448
✓ Chapter 13 Skills Test, Assessment Book, pp. 75–76	

Families used covered wagons to move west.

Providing More Depth
Additional Resources
- Trade Books
- Family Activities
- Vocabulary Workbook and Cards
- Social Studies Plus! pp. 134–135
- Daily Activity Bank
- Read Alouds and Primary Sources pp. 100–115
- Big Book Atlas
- Student Atlas
- Outline Maps
- Desk Maps

 ## Technology

- AudioText
- Video Field Trips: Discovering California's Gold Country
- Songs and Music
- Digital Learning CD-ROM Powered by KnowledgeBox (Video clips and activities)
- MindPoint® Quiz Show CD-ROM
- ExamView® Test Bank CD-ROM
- Colonial Williamsburg Primary Sources CD-ROM
- Teacher Resources CD-ROM
- Map Resources CD-ROM
- SF SuccessNet: iText (Pupil Edition online), iTE (Teacher's Edition online), Online Planner
- **www.sfsocialstudies.com** (Biographies, news, references, maps, and activities)

 To establish guidelines for your students' safe and responsible use of the Internet, use the Scott Foresman Internet Guide.

Additional Internet Links

To find out more about:
- The Cherokee Nation, visit **www.cherokee.org**
- American Inventors and Inventions, visit **www.si.edu**
- The California Gold Rush, visit **www.sfmuseum.org**

Unit 6 Objectives

Beginning of Unit 6
- Use primary sources to acquire information. (p. 394)
- Identify the contributions of significant individuals to change and expansion in the United States in the early 1800s. (p. 396)
- Analyze information by comparing and contrasting. (p. 398)

In 1776 the Liberty Bell rang to celebrate the Declaration of Independence. Fifty years later, it rang in memory of Jefferson and Adams.

Assessment Options

✓ Formal Assessment

- **Lesson Reviews,** PE/TE pp. 406, 413, 420, 436, 441, 445
- **Chapter Reviews,** PE/TE pp. 426–427, 448–449
- **Chapter Tests,** Assessment Book, pp. 69–76
- **Unit Review,** PE/TE pp. 452–453
- **Unit Tests,** Assessment Book, pp. 77–80
- **ExamView® Test Bank CD-ROM** (test-generator software)

✓ Informal Assessment

- **Teacher's Edition Questions,** throughout Lessons and Features
- **Section Reviews,** PE/TE pp. 403–406, 409–413, 417–420, 431–432, 433–436, 439–441, 443–445
- **Close and Assess,** TE pp. 399, 406–407, 413, 415, 420–421, 423, 425, 436–437, 441, 445, 447, 451

Ongoing Assessment

Ongoing Assessment is found throughout the Teacher's Edition lessons using an **If…then** model.

If = students' observable behavior,	**then** = reteaching and enrichment suggestions

✓ Portfolio Assessment

- **Portfolio Assessment,** TE pp. 393, 394, 453
- **Leveled Practice,** TE pp. 405, 409, 419, 433, 441, 444
- **Workbook Pages,** pp. 92–106
- **Chapter Review: Write About History,** PE/TE pp. 427, 449
- **Unit Review: Apply Skills,** PE/TE p. 452
- **Curriculum Connection: Writing,** PE/TE pp. 406, 441; TE pp. 405, 413, 419, 432, 451

✓ Performance Assessment

- **Hands-on Unit Project** (Unit 6 Performance Assessment), TE pp. 393, 427, 449, 454
- **Internet Activity,** PE p. 454
- **Chapter 12 Performance Assessment,** TE p. 426
- **Chapter 13 Performance Assessment,** TE p. 448
- **Unit Review: Write and Share,** PE/TE p. 453
- **Scoring Guides,** TE pp. 452, 454

Test Talk

Test-Taking Strategies

Understand the Question
- **Locate Key Words in the Question,** TE p. 435
- **Locate Key Words in the Text,** TE p. 409

Understand the Answer
- **Choose the Right Answer,** Test Talk Practice Book
- **Use Information from the Text,** TE p. 432
- **Use Information from Graphics,** TE p. 440
- **Write Your Answer to Score High,** PE/TE p. 453

For additional practice, use the Test Talk Practice Book.

Featured Strategy

Write Your Answer to Score High

Students will:

- Make sure their answer is correct.
- Make sure their answer is complete.
- Make sure their answer is focused.

PE/TE p. 453

Curriculum Connections

Integrating Your Day

The lessons, skills, and features of Unit 6 provide many opportunities to make connections between social studies and other areas of the elementary curriculum.

READING

Reading Skill—Compare and Contrast, PE/TE pp. 398–399, 402, 408, 416, 430, 442

Lesson Review—Compare and Contrast, PE/TE pp. 406, 413, 420, 436, 445

WRITING

Write a Persuasive Letter, TE p. 405

Link to Writing, PE/TE pp. 406, 441

Inventions and Change, TE p. 413

Interpret a Document, TE p. 419

Write a Speech, TE p. 432

Write a Travel Article, TE p. 451

MATH

Multiply Fractions and Whole Numbers, TE p. 406

Calculate Miles per Hour, TE p. 411

Link to Mathematics, PE/TE pp. 413, 445

Social Studies

LITERATURE

Read Biographies, TE pp. 396, 407, 421

Frederick Douglass, TE p. 423

End with Literature, TE p. 450

SCIENCE

Gold Mining—Then and Now, TE p. 445

MUSIC / DRAMA

Interpret Lyrics, TE p. 420

Evaluate a Jingle, TE p. 447

ART

Interpret Fine Art, TE pp. 394–395

Create a Time Line, TE p. 395

Make a Cross-Section Diagram, TE p. 414

Link to Art, PE/TE p. 420

 Look for this symbol throughout the Teacher's Edition to find **Curriculum Connections.**

Professional Development

Women in History

by Carol Berkin, Ph.D.
The City University of New York

There has been an explosion of research and writing over the past three decades in the field of women's history. Gone are the days when historians could shake their heads and say they would love to include women in their books if only they had sources to quote. Women now speak to us through the diaries, letters, speeches, books, poems, songs, built structures, inventions, and human legacies they have left behind and that we have found and analyzed. The effort to make history a mirror in which to discover women's pasts as well as men's has been mounted by educators across the country, as well as by authors and publishers of texts.

We can trace the impact of major events on the lives of everyday citizens through women's experiences as effectively as we can through men's. And we do not have to stand history on its head to place women squarely in the flow of events.

When women are portrayed as people who shape the society around them, the past becomes much richer and more complex. Below are several ways *Scott Foresman Social Studies* incorporates the roles of women in history.

- *The You Are There feature on p. 416 allows students to suppose they are actually at the Seneca Falls Convention when Elizabeth Cady Stanton is speaking about women's rights. Important resolutions from the convention are shown on p. 419.*

- *The Biography feature on p. 421 highlights the life of Sojourner Truth, an African American woman who was a major historical figure in the development of the United States.*

- *The Colonial Williamsburg section on pp. 424–425 includes the quest for women's rights as a desire to fulfill the promise of the ideals of the Declaration of Independence.*

ESL Support

by Jim Cummins, Ph.D.
University of Toronto

In Unit 6, you can use the following fundamental strategy to help activate prior knowledge and build background for ESL students:

Activate Prior Knowledge/ Build Background

In social studies, the more a student already knows about a particular topic in the text, the more of the text she or he is likely to understand. Teachers can use a variety of strategies to activate students' prior knowledge. Discussion, visual stimuli, direct experience, writing, and dramatization can all be highly effective. Graphic organizers can be used to capture the results of brainstorming and discussion, and students can use them to record and organize prior knowledge.

Dramatization and role-play are effective ways to express students' prior knowledge or intuitions about various concepts or events in social studies.

The following examples in the Teacher's Edition will help you activate prior knowledge of ESL students:

- ***Explore Teamwork*** *on p. 403 invites beginning learners to act out a situation in which people have to work together. The understanding of the concept of teamwork will ultimately help students understand the meaning of* nationalism.

- ***Develop an Understanding of Early Transportation*** *on p. 439 helps students to acquire information about wagon trains. Intermediate learners record information on a K-W-L chart, and advanced learners create a Venn diagram to compare two vehicles.*

Read Aloud

from Andrew Jackson's First Annual Message to Congress (1829)

. . . I suggest for your consideration, the propriety of setting apart an ample district west of the Mississippi, and without the limits of any state or territory now formed, to be guaranteed to the Indian tribes as long as they shall occupy it, each tribe having a distinct control over the portion designated for its use. There they may be secured in the enjoyment of governments of their own choice, subject to no other control from the United States than such as may be necessary to preserve peace on the frontier and between the several tribes.

Build Background

- Andrew Jackson suggested to Congress that the United States set aside land for Native Americans outside the states or territories that had already been formed.

- Jackson went on to suggest that the migration of the tribes should be voluntary.

Definitions

- *propriety*: proper or suitable behavior
- *ample*: more than enough
- *designated*: named, indicated
- *preserve*: keep, maintain

Read Alouds and Primary Sources

- *Read Alouds and Primary Sources* contain additional selections to be used with Unit 6.

Bibliography

Eli Whitney: Great Inventor, by Jean Lee Latham (Chelsea House, ISBN 0-791-01453-3, 1991) **Easy**

Kids During the Industrial Revolution, by Lisa A. Wroble (Rosen Publishing Group, ISBN 0-823-95254-1, 1999) **Easy**

Only Passing Through: The Story of Sojourner Truth, by Anne Rockwell (Alfred A. Knopf, ISBN 0-679-99186-7, 2000) **Easy Coretta Scott King Honor Book**

Railroad, by Bobbie Kalman (Crabtree Publishing Co., ISBN 0-778-70108-5, 1999) **On-Level**

The Amazing Impossible Erie Canal, by Cheryl Harness (Aladdin, ISBN 0-689-82584-6, 1999) **On-Level**

They Shall Be Heard: Susan B. Anthony and Elizabeth Cady Stanton, by Kate Connell (Raintree, ISBN 0-811-48068-2, 1992) **On-Level**

Frederick Douglass & The Fight For Freedom, by Douglas Miller (Facts on File, ISBN 0-816-02996-2, 1993) **Challenge**

Industrial Revolution, by Mary Collins (Children's Press, ISBN 0-516-27036-2, 2000) **Challenge**

Trail of Tears: The Cherokee Journey From Home, by Marlene Targ Brill (Millbrook Press, ISBN 1-562-94486-X, 1995) **Challenge**

Let it Shine: Stories of Black Women Freedom Fighters, by Andrea Davis Pinkney (Harcourt Brace, ISBN 0-152-01005-X, 2000) **Teacher reference Coretta Scott King Honor Book**

Pushing the Bear: A Novel of the Trail of Tears, by Diane Glancy (Harvest Books, ISBN 0-156-00544-1, 1998) **Teacher reference**

The Industrial Revolution, by William Dudley, ed. (Greenhaven Press, Inc., ISBN 1-565-10706-3, 1998) **Teacher reference**

Discovery Channel School Videos The Battle of the Alamo. Watch a handful of Americans defend the Alamo mission in this re-creation of the famous battle; 51 minutes.

 Look for this symbol throughout the Teacher's Edition to find **Award-Winning Selections.** Additional book references are suggested throughout this unit.

A Growing Nation

Why do people move in search of new homes?

UNIT 6

A Growing Nation

Unit Overview

In the early 1800s, the United States experienced a variety of changes in areas such as government, technology, and civil rights. Another change was the expansion and movement of people to the southern frontier, Texas, and throughout the West.

Unit Outline

Chapter 12 *Times of Change*
pp. 400–427

Chapter 13 *People Moving South and West*
pp. 428–449

Unit Question

- Have students read the question under the painting.

- To activate prior knowledge, ask students if they have ever moved to a new home or if they know someone else who has. Discuss the reasons for these moves.

- Create a graphic organizer or a web that shows a variety of reasons why people move to new places and homes.

- ✓ **Portfolio Assessment** Keep this graphic organizer or web to review with students at the end of the unit on p. 453.

Practice and Extend

Hands-on Unit Project

✓ Unit 6 Performance Assessment

- The Unit Project, *Lure of the Land,* found on p. 454, is an ongoing performance assessment project to enrich students' learning throughout the unit.

- This project, which has students preparing and presenting a travel program about settlers in the West, may be started now or at any time during this unit of study.

- A performance assessment scoring guide is located on p. 454.

Begin with a Primary Source

Objective
- Use primary sources to acquire information.

Resource
- Poster 12

Interpret a Primary Source

- Tell students that this primary source is a quotation from a woman who traveled west to find a new home.

- Sarah Smith made this statement in 1838 after she made the long journey from the East to Oregon Country.

✓ **Portfolio Assessment** Remind students of the web they made showing different reasons for moving to a new home (see p. 393). As they read the unit, ask students to make a web of the reasons people in the United States moved west. Review students' webs at the end of the unit on p. 453.

Interpret Fine Art

- Tell students that this picture, which shows a western U.S. landscape in the nineteenth century, is called *The Rocky Mountains, Emigrants Crossing the Plains* and was printed by Currier and Ives.

- Ask students to describe the land and wagon trail shown in the picture and to imagine what life might have been like for the pioneers who traveled along this route.

- Ask students to examine the Native Americans in this picture. How are the Native Americans reacting to the pioneers, and why might the artist have posed them this way?

1820		1830

1823
Monroe Doctrine is issued

1825
The Erie Canal is completed

1828
Andrew Jackson is elected seventh President of the United States

394

Practice and Extend

SOCIAL STUDIES
Background

About the Primary Source
- The primary source above—the quotation by Sarah Smith—describes her feelings about the long journey she took to her new home in Oregon Country.
- In the early 1800s, the regions of Oregon Country and California contained few white settlers.
- Thousands of people, among them trappers and farmers, made the long journey west to claim and settle these lands.
- Settlers traveled along the Oregon Trail by packhorse and wagon train in search of the riches the West had to offer.

"I could hardly believe that the long journey was accomplished and I had found a home."

—Sarah Smith, settler in Oregon Country, 1838

This 1886 print by Currier and Ives shows pioneers crossing the Rocky Mountains.

Meet the Artist

- The firm of Nathaniel Currier and James Merritt Ives made lithographs, or pictures printed from crayon drawings on stove plates. Before cameras, people relied on lithographs for pictures of far away places, new inventions, or recent events.

- Currier began his career drawing disaster scenes. Once Ives became his partner in 1857, their new firm offered other subjects, such as pictures of trains and ships or of city and country life.

- Artists such as Currier's brother Lorenzo traveled west for the firm to sketch details about frontier life to be used in prints such as this one.

- Currier and Ives called themselves "Publishers of Cheap and Popular Prints." They intended for their art to be bought by everyone.

Use the Time Line

The time line at the bottom of the page shows the dates for some major events that led to the growth of the United States in the first half of the 1800s and to the westward movement of many settlers.

① How many years after the Monroe Doctrine was issued did Texas become an independent country? About 13 years Interpret Information

② What event on the time line probably had a big influence on westward movement? Gold is discovered in California. Draw Conclusions

③ What three western states are mentioned on the time line? Texas, Utah, and California Main Idea and Details

1840   1850

36
as becomes an
ependent country
1 **3**

1838 Frederick Douglass escapes slavery and becomes a leader in the movement to abolish it

1846 Mexican War begins

1847 Mormons settle in Utah
3

1848 Gold is discovered in California
2 **3** 395

CURRICULUM CONNECTION
Art

Create a Time Line

- Have students make a list of important events in their lives. Events could include siblings' births, family trips, or accomplishments such as learning to swim.
- Help students figure out during which year each event occurred.
- Write on the board the names and dates of three historical events (e.g. *January 2001, George W. Bush becomes President*).
- Have students create a time line that combines their personal events with historic ones. Each event should be clearly labeled and illustrated with a small picture.

Meet the People

Objective

- Identify the contributions of significant individuals to change and expansion in the United States in the early 1800s.

Resource

- Poster 13

Research the People

Each of the people pictured on these pages played an important part in changes that occurred in the United States during the early 1800s. Have students do research to find out the answers to the following questions.

- **What job did Andrew Jackson hold in the western district of North Carolina, which is now the state of Tennessee?** Prosecuting attorney

- **What nationality was John Ross's father?** Scottish

- **What woman worked closely with Elizabeth Cady Stanton in the fight for women's rights?** Susan B. Anthony

- **Where was James K. Polk educated?** University of North Carolina

Students may wish to write their own questions about other people on these pages for the rest of the class to answer.

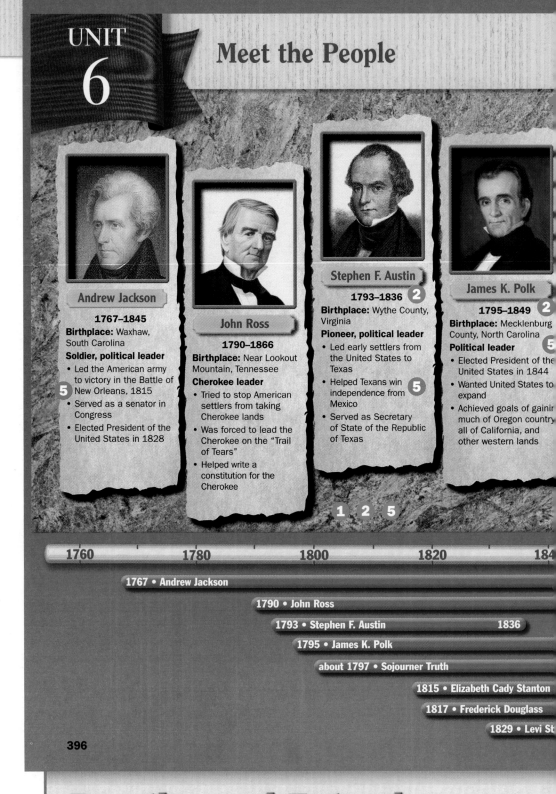

UNIT
6
Meet the People

Andrew Jackson

1767–1845
Birthplace: Waxhaw, South Carolina
Soldier, political leader
- Led the American army to victory in the Battle of New Orleans, 1815
- Served as a senator in Congress
- Elected President of the United States in 1828

John Ross

1790–1866
Birthplace: Near Lookout Mountain, Tennessee
Cherokee leader
- Tried to stop American settlers from taking Cherokee lands
- Was forced to lead the Cherokee on the "Trail of Tears"
- Helped write a constitution for the Cherokee

Stephen F. Austin

1793–1836
Birthplace: Wythe County, Virginia
Pioneer, political leader
- Led early settlers from the United States to Texas
- Helped Texans win independence from Mexico
- Served as Secretary of State of the Republic of Texas

James K. Polk

1795–1849
Birthplace: Mecklenburg County, North Carolina
Political leader
- Elected President of the United States in 1844
- Wanted United States to expand
- Achieved goals of gaining much of Oregon country, all of California, and other western lands

1760	1780	1800	1820	184

1767 • Andrew Jackson

1790 • John Ross

1793 • Stephen F. Austin   1836

1795 • James K. Polk

about 1797 • Sojourner Truth

1815 • Elizabeth Cady Stanton

1817 • Frederick Douglass

1829 • Levi St

Practice and Extend

CURRICULUM CONNECTION
Literature

Read Biographies

Use the following biography selections to extend the content.

Andrew Jackson, by Anne Welsbacher (ABDO Publishing, ISBN 1-562-39811-3, 1998) **On-Level**

Sojourner Truth and the Struggle for Freedom, by Edward Beecher Claflin (Barron's Educational Series, ISBN 0-812-03919-X, 1987) **On-Level**

Mr. Blue Jeans: A Story About Levi Strauss, by Maryann Weidt (Carolrhoda, ISBN 0-876-14588-8, 1992) **Challenge**

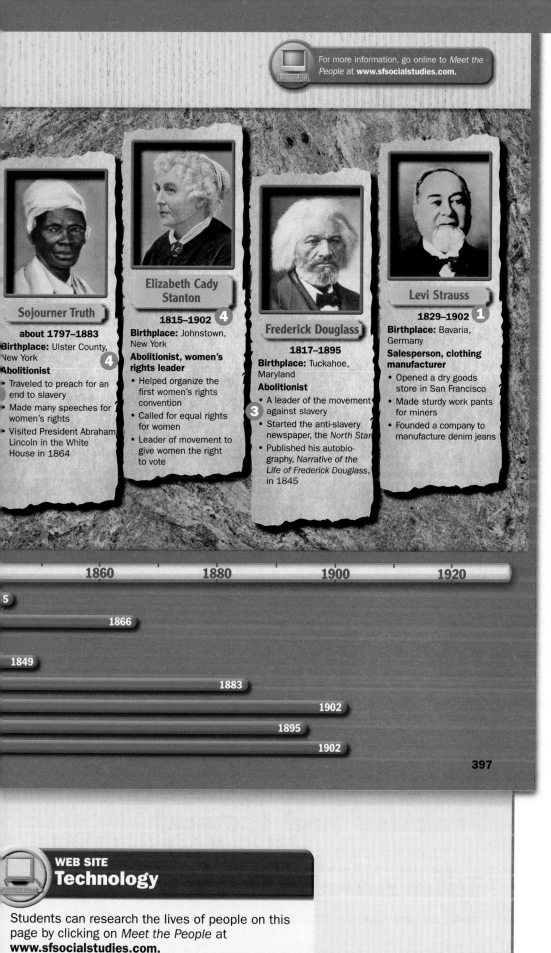

For more information, go online to *Meet the People* at **www.sfsocialstudies.com**.

Sojourner Truth

about 1797–1883

Birthplace: Ulster County, New York

Abolitionist

- Traveled to preach for an end to slavery
- Made many speeches for women's rights
- Visited President Abraham Lincoln in the White House in 1864

Elizabeth Cady Stanton

1815–1902

Birthplace: Johnstown, New York

Abolitionist, women's rights leader

- Helped organize the first women's rights convention
- Called for equal rights for women
- Leader of movement to give women the right to vote

Frederick Douglass

1817–1895

Birthplace: Tuckahoe, Maryland

Abolitionist

- A leader of the movement against slavery
- Started the anti-slavery newspaper, the *North Star*
- Published his autobiography, *Narrative of the Life of Frederick Douglass,* in 1845

Levi Strauss

1829–1902

Birthplace: Bavaria, Germany

Salesperson, clothing manufacturer

- Opened a dry goods store in San Francisco
- Made sturdy work pants for miners
- Founded a company to manufacture denim jeans

1860   1880   1900   1920

5
1866
1849
1883
1902
1895
1902

397

WEB SITE Technology

Students can research the lives of people on this page by clicking on *Meet the People* at **www.sfsocialstudies.com**.

Use the Time Line

Have students use the time line and biographies to answer the following questions.

1 **Which person was not born in the United States?** Levi Strauss
Analyze Information

2 **Which two people died before reaching the age of 60?** Stephen F. Austin and James K. Polk
Interpret Time Lines

3 **Describe one similarity between the accomplishments of Sojourner Truth and Frederick Douglass.** They both fought against slavery.
Compare and Contrast

4 **Which two people lived to be more than 80 years old?** Sojourner Truth and Elizabeth Cady Stanton
Interpret Time Lines

5 **What did Andrew Jackson, Stephen F. Austin, and James K. Polk have in common?** They were all political leaders.
Compare and Contrast

Biographies

Three of the people shown here are discussed more extensively in the Biography pages in Unit 6.

- Andrew Jackson, p. 407
- Sojourner Truth, p. 421
- James K. Polk, p. 437

Read About the People

The people shown here are discussed in the text on the following pages in Unit 6.

- Andrew Jackson, pp. 400, 403–405, 407, 431
- John Ross, p. 405
- Stephen F. Austin, p. 432
- James K. Polk, pp. 433–435, 437
- Sojourner Truth, pp. 418, 421
- Elizabeth Cady Stanton, p. 419
- Frederick Douglass, pp. 418, 422–423
- Levi Strauss, p. 444

Reading Social Studies

Compare and Contrast

Objective
Analyze information by comparing and contrasting.

Resource
• Workbook, p. 92

About the Unit Target Skill
• The target reading skill for this unit is Compare and Contrast.
• Students are introduced to the unit target skill here and are given an opportunity to practice it.
• Further opportunities to use compare and contrast are found throughout Unit 6.

1 Introduce and Motivate

Preview To activate prior knowledge, ask students to compare and contrast two people or events from previous units. (Possible answer: Similar—The Townshend Acts and the Stamp Act were both actions taken by the British to tax colonists and caused protests; Different—The Stamp Act called for a tax on printed goods; the Townshend Acts placed a tariff on all goods imported from Britain.)

2 Teach and Discuss

• Explain that comparing two items means telling how they are alike. Sometimes comparisons include words such as *both, as,* or *like.* Tell students that to contrast means to tell how two items are different. Writers might use clue words or phrases such as *unlike, in contrast,* or *different,* but often the reader has to read and look for the similarities and differences.

398 Unit 6 • A Growing Nation

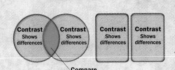

A Growing Nation
Compare and Contrast

You can use graphic organizers to help you compare and contrast as you read. A Venn diagram, shown below at left, helps you show how two things or events are similar or different. The other graphic organizer shows just differences.

• To compare, writers may use clue words or phrases such as <u>both, as,</u> or <u>like.</u> To contrast, writers may use clue words or phrases such as <u>unlike, in contrast,</u> <u>different.</u>

Read the following paragraph. **Comparisons** and **contrasts** have been highlighted.

> In Chapter 11, you read about how the Louisiana Purchase helped the United States gain territory to the west. Several years later, the United States began gaining territory from Spain and Mexico. Wars in Florida and Texas resulted in land gains for the United States. The country gained Florida from Spain and Texas and California from Mexico.

Word Exercise

Antonyms This passage compares and contrasts changes in the growing United States. When writers contrast two things, they often use **antonyms**, which are words that are opposite in meaning. Below is a chart that shows some antonyms from the passage.

farms	cities
factory made	made by hand
men	women

398

Practice and Extend

ESL   ACCESS CONTENT
ESL Support

Make a Chart Have students make charts to compare and contrast life in the United States before and after the War of 1812.

Beginning Make a T-chart labeled *Transportation Before War of 1812* and *Transportation After War of 1812.* Read the text with students. Ask students to tell about transportation before and after the war. Record ideas in the chart.

Intermediate Read the selection with students. Suggest that they listen for clue words, such as *before, after,* and *once,* to isolate ideas that relate to life before and after the war. Have students create a Venn diagram that compares and contrasts life in the United States at that time.

Advanced Have students read the selection and create a chart or Venn diagram as described above. Students can present the information from their charts and explain how life was similar and different before and after the war.

Compare and Contrast Events in a Growing Nation

After the War of 1812, the United States began changing greatly. Significant changes occurred in the ways that goods were produced and shipped.

Water power ran factories to make thread and cloth. People once made these goods by hand. Young people moved from farms to cities to work in factories. New inventions, such as the steel plow and mechanical reaper, speeded farm work.

The transportation system also grew. The country built canals, a national road, and railroads. These cut travel time for people and goods.

More people gained the right to vote. Before, in most places, only white male property holders could vote. By 1828 almost all white men could vote. But most non-white men and all women were denied the right to vote.

The United States grew in land and in power. In 1819, after a series of battles between United States and American Indian forces in Florida, Spain agreed to sell Florida to the United States. At about the same time, Mexico began allowing United States citizens to settle in Texas. In the 1840s, Mexico and the United States fought a war over Texas. Mexico lost that war and in 1848 sold much of its land to the United States. This land included California as well as part of the Southwest region.

Use the reading strategy of compare and contrast to answer questions 1 and 2. Then answer the vocabulary question.

1 Who gained the right to vote during this time and who did not?

2 Compare and contrast the ways that Florida and California became part of the United States. How were they similar? How were they different?

3 The passage talks about people who were denied the right to vote. What is another word in the passage that acts as an antonym for *denied*?

399

Workbook, p. 92

Compare and Contrast

Learning how to compare and contrast information will help you better understand similarities and differences. To compare, writers often use clue words such as *both, as,* or *like*. To contrast, words such as *unlike, in contrast,* or *different* may be used.

Directions: Fill in the circle next to the correct answer.

The role of women and women's rights have changed dramatically over the course of many years. In the early 1800s, women had few rights in contrast to men. Women and men were not considered equals.

Unlike men, women were not allowed to vote, and any property owned by a single woman became the property of her husband as soon as they were married.

During the American Revolution both men and women supported the war in the name of liberty and equality. Although the end of the war did not bring a change to women's rights, the idea of equality grew stronger.

The Industrial Revolution affected the role of women in society and women's

rights in general. One difference resulting from the Industrial Revolution was that women had the chance to work away from home. Working-class women also now had the opportunity to earn a wage, which belonged to the husband if she was married.

In 1848 the Seneca Falls Convention was held in honor of women's rights. It declared that women and men should be considered as equals. Other changes to women's rights also took place around the same time. Some states enacted laws allowing married women, like men, to own property; to control their own earnings; and to have joint custody of their children.

1. Which of the following was a right shared by both men and women as a result of the Industrial Revolution?
   (A) Men and women worked away from home.
   (B) Men and women owned property.
   (C) Men and women voted.
   (D) Men and women had equal custody of their children.

2. What right had women gained by the 1850s?
   (A) the right to full custody of their children
   (B) the right to vote
   (C) the right to own property
   (D) the right to fight in battle

Notes for Home: Your child learned how to compare and contrast written information.
Home Activity: With your child, draw a chart comparing and contrasting information in a newspaper article of interest.

- Have students read the sample paragraph on p. 398. Make sure they can explain why the first highlighted sentence *compares* Florida and Texas while the second highlighted sentence *contrasts* the two places.

- Then have students read the longer practice sample on p. 399 and answer the questions that follow.

- Ask students why it is helpful to compare and contrast when reading about history. (If you can tell how specific people and events in history are similar and different, it can help you make generalizations about certain times in history.)

Antonyms

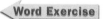

Write the following sentences on the board and have students think of antonyms for the underlined words. Help them brainstorm or use thesauruses. Discuss how antonyms help show contrast between ideas.

- <u>Significant</u> changes occurred in the ways that goods were produced and shipped. (*insignificant, minor*)

- New inventions, such as the steel plow and mechanical reaper, <u>speeded</u> farm work. (*slowed, delayed*)

- This land <u>included</u> California, as well as part of the Southwest region. (*excluded, left out*)

3 Close and Assess

Apply it!

1. White men without property gained the right to vote, and women and non-whites did not.

2. Both areas were sold to the United States by countries defeated in wars. However, the war in Florida was between the United States and Native Americans, while the war in the Southwest was with Mexico.

3. *Gained*

Chapter Planning Guide

Chapter 12 • Times of Change

Locating Time and Place pp. 400–401

Lesson Titles	Pacing	Main Ideas
Lesson 1 **The United States Turns Fifty** pp. 402–406	2 days	• In the 1820s and 1830s, the United States expanded its territory in North America and its power in the Western Hemisphere.
Biography: Andrew Jackson p. 407		• Andrew Jackson educated himself and tried to create laws that would protect all people, especially the poor.
Lesson 2 **A New Kind of Revolution** pp. 408–413	2 days	• The Industrial Revolution dramatically changed the way Americans lived and worked.
Chart and Graph Skills: Read a Cross-Section Diagram pp. 414–415		• A cross-section diagram can be used to view the inside of an object to see how it works.
Lesson 3 **The Struggle for Reforms** pp. 416–420	3 days	• Beginning in the 1830s, a spirit of reform changed life in the United States.
Biography: Sojourner Truth p. 421		• Sojourner Truth dedicated her life to telling people about the injustices of slavery.
Citizen Heroes: Fairness **Exposing Slavery's Evils** pp. 422–423		• Frederick Douglass led the fight for an end to slavery.
Colonial Williamsburg: Nineteenth-Century Reform Movements pp. 424–425		• Many people worked for reforms to make the ideals of the Declaration of Independence a reality for all Americans.

✓ **Chapter 12 Review**
pp. 426–427

▶ **Sojourner Truth published her story to speak out against slavery.**

✓ = Assessment Options

◀ Andrew Jackson, "the People's President," came from a poor family.

Vocabulary	Resources	Meeting Individual Needs
nationalism Era of Good Feelings Monroe Doctrine suffrage Indian Removal Act Trail of Tears	• Workbook, p. 94 • Transparency 14 • Every Student Learns Guide, pp. 166–169 • Quick Study, pp. 84–85	• ESL Support, TE p. 403 • Leveled Practice, TE p. 405
Industrial Revolution manufacture technology cotton gin mechanical reaper canal cross-section diagram	• Workbook, p. 95 • Transparencies 14, 18 • Every Student Learns Guide, pp. 170–173 • Quick Study, pp. 86–87 • Workbook, p. 96	• Leveled Practice, TE p. 409 • Learning Styles, TE p. 410 • ESL Support, TE p. 412
reform revival temperance abolitionist Seneca Falls Convention	• Workbook, p. 97 • Transparency 14 • Every Student Learns Guide, pp. 174–177 • Quick Study, pp. 88–89 • Workbook, p. 98	• ESL Support, TE p. 417 • Leveled Practice, TE p. 419
	✓ Chapter 12 Content Test, Assessment Book, pp. 69–70 ✓ Chapter 12 Skills Test, Assessment Book, pp. 71–72	✓ Chapter 12 Performance Assessment, TE p. 426

Providing More Depth

Additional Resources
- Vocabulary Workbook and Cards
- Social Studies Plus! pp. 144–149
- Daily Activity Bank
- Big Book Atlas
- Student Atlas
- Outline Maps
- Desk Maps

 Technology

- AudioText
- MindPoint® Quiz Show CD-ROM
- ExamView® Test Bank CD-ROM
- Teacher Resources CD-ROM
- Map Resources CD-ROM
- SFSuccessNet: iText (Pupil Edition online), iTE (Teacher's Edition online), Online Planner
- **www.sfsocialstudies.com** (biographies, news, references, maps, and activities)

 To establish guidelines for your students' safe and responsible use of the Internet, use the Scott Foresman Internet Guide.

Additional Internet Links
To find out more about:
- Andrew Jackson, visit **www.whitehouse.gov**
- Cherokee Trail of Tears Park, visit **www.trailoftears.org**
- Declaration of Sentiments, visit **www.nps.gov**

Key Internet Search Terms
- Andrew Jackson
- Indian Removal Act
- Industrial Revolution
- slavery
- women's rights

Workbook Support

 Use the following Workbook pages to support content and skills development as you teach Chapter 12. You can also view and print Workbook pages from the Teacher Resources CD-ROM.

Workbook, p. 92

Use with Pages 398–399.

Compare and Contrast

Learning how to compare and contrast information will help you better understand similarities and differences. To compare, writers often use clue words such as *both*, *as*, or *like*. To contrast, words such as *unlike*, *in contrast*, or *different* may be used.

Directions: Fill in the circle next to the correct answer.

The role of women and women's rights have changed dramatically over the course of many years. In the early 1800s, women had few rights in contrast to men. Women and men were not considered equals.

Unlike men, women were not allowed to vote, and any property owned by a single woman became the property of her husband as soon as they were married.

During the American Revolution both men and women supported the war in the name of liberty and equality. Although the end of the war did not bring a change to women's rights, the idea of equality grew stronger.

The Industrial Revolution affected the role of women in society and women's rights in general. One difference resulting from the Industrial Revolution was that women had the chance to work away from home. Working-class women also now had the opportunity to earn a wage, which belonged to the husband if she was married.

In 1848 the Seneca Falls Convention was held in honor of women's rights. It declared that women and men should be considered as equals. Other changes to women's rights also took place around the same time. Some states enacted laws allowing married women, like men, to own property; to control their own earnings; and to have joint custody of their children.

1. Which of the following was a right shared by both men and women as a result of the Industrial Revolution?
   ● Men and women worked away from home.
   Ⓑ Men and women owned property.
   Ⓒ Men and women voted.
   Ⓓ Men and women had equal custody of their children.

2. What right had women gained by the 1850s?
   Ⓐ the right to full custody of their children
   Ⓑ the right to vote
   ● the right to own property
   Ⓓ the right to fight in battle

 Notes for Home: Your child learned how to compare and contrast written information.
Home Activity: With your child, draw a chart comparing and contrasting information in a newspaper article of interest.

Use with Pupil Edition, p. 399

Workbook, p. 93

Use with Chapter 12.

Vocabulary Preview

Directions: Match each vocabulary term to its definition. Write the term in the space provided. Not all words will be used.

nationalism	Industrial Revolution	reform
Era of Good Feelings	manufacture	revival
Monroe Doctrine	technology	temperance
suffrage	cotton gin	abolitionist
Indian Removal Act	mechanical reaper	Seneca Falls Convention
Trail of Tears	canal	

1. **Seneca Falls Convention** — A convention called to take a stand for women's rights
2. **Trail of Tears** — The terrible journey forced upon the Cherokee to move to Indian Territory
3. **Monroe Doctrine** — A statement that warned European nations against considering the American continents for future colonization
4. **cotton gin** — A machine invented to clean the seeds out of cotton
5. **abolitionist** — A reformer who attacked slavery
6. **Industrial Revolution** — A time when people began producing goods by machine rather than by hand
7. **Indian Removal Act** — Act that ordered Native Americans of the southern United States to be moved west of the Mississippi River
8. **Era of Good Feelings** — A time when disagreements about national issues grew quiet
9. **suffrage** — The right to vote
10. **nationalism** — The idea that all people should pull together with a sense of strong pride in their country
11. **temperance** — Moderation
12. **reform** — Change

 Notes for Home: Your child learned vocabulary dealing with the mid-1800s, a time of growth and change in the United States.
Home Activity: Ask your child to use these terms to summarize the turbulent events in the United States during this time.

Use with Pupil Edition, p. 400

Workbook, p. 94

Use with Pages 402–406.

Lesson 1: The United States Turns Fifty

Directions: Match the events and descriptions in the box below with the President who was in office when they took place. Write each event in the space provided.

Issued warning to European nations not to consider the American continents as subject for future colonization

Headed a new political party, the Democrats

Era of Good Feelings enjoyed

Florida purchased from Spain for $5 million

Native Americans in the southern states forced to move west of the Mississippi

Known as "the man of the people"

Military leader and self-taught lawyer

Encouraged nationalism

President James Monroe	President Andrew Jackson
Encouraged nationalism	Military leader and self-taught lawyer
Era of Good Feelings enjoyed	Headed a new political party, the Democrats
Florida purchased from Spain for $5 million	Known as "the man of the people"
Issued warning to European nations not to consider the American continents as subject for future colonization	Native Americans living in the southern states forced to move west of the Mississippi

Critical Thinking: Compare and contrast how the United States expanded its borders under Presidents Monroe and Jackson.

Under Monroe, the United States purchased Florida from Spain.

Under Jackson, Native American lands were taken to make way for settlers, and Native Americans were forced to move.

Notes for Home: Your child learned about the early expansion of the United States.
Home Activity: Review the lesson with your child, and make a time line of the key events of the United States first 50 years.

Use with Pupil Edition, p. 406

Workbook, p. 95

Use with Pages 408–413.

Lesson 2: A New Kind of Revolution

Directions: Complete the chart by filling in the last column with one benefit of the following inventions. You may use your textbook.

Before the Invention	Invention	Benefit
There were no factories to spin cotton in the United States.	Samuel Slater built the first cotton-spinning mill in the United States.	The United States could produce its own cloth.
Cleaning seeds out of cotton was slow and difficult work.	Eli Whitney invented the cotton gin.	Production increased by 50 times.
Crops were harvested by hand.	Cyrus McCormick built the mechanical reaper.	It made harvesting wheat easier.
Iron plows were used to clear land.	John Deere developed the steel plow.	Steel plows cut through soil more easily than older plows.
Boats powered by sails or oars had difficulties traveling upstream, against the current.	Robert Fulton invented a riverboat powered by a steam engine.	Travel upstream, against the current, was faster.
Water transportation was cheaper than land transportation, but water routes did not flow in all parts of the country.	The Erie Canal was constructed.	The Erie Canal linked the Great Lakes and the Atlantic Ocean.
Horse-drawn wagons pulled heavy loads on rough roads.	Peter Cooper built a steam-powered locomotive.	Locomotives soon replaced horses carrying heavy loads.

Notes for Home: Your child learned about inventions of the Industrial Revolution.
Home Activity: Discuss inventions that help people work more quickly, more cheaply, and with less effort. What new inventions might help us in the near future?

Use with Pupil Edition, p. 413

Workbook Support

Workbook, p. 96

Read a Cross-Section Diagram
Use with Pages 414–415.

A cross-section diagram is a drawing that shows a view of something as if you could slice through it. Cross-section diagrams can show you how something works. This cross-section diagram shows you how the cotton gin worked.

Directions: Study the diagram and answer the questions that follow.

Eli Whitney's Cotton Gin

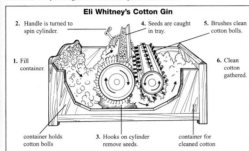

2. Handle is turned to spin cylinder.
4. Seeds are caught in tray.
5. Brushes clean cotton bolls.
1. Fill container.
6. Clean cotton gathered.
container holds cotton bolls
3. Hooks on cylinder remove seeds.
container for cleaned cotton

1. What do the hooks do?

   They latch onto the seeds on the cotton bolls and remove them.

2. What is the first step in using a cotton gin?

   Fill container with cotton bolls to be cleaned.

3. At what step and how are cotton bolls cleaned?

   Step 5: Brushes clean cotton bolls after the seeds are removed.

 Notes for Home: Your child learned how to read a cross-section diagram.
Home Activity: With your child, create a cross-section of a household appliance to show how it works. Use reference materials as necessary.

Use with Pupil Edition, p. 415

Workbook, p. 97

Lesson 3: The Struggle for Reforms
Use with Pages 416–420.

Directions: Complete the organizer with terms from the box. Write a brief description on the lines provided.

Abolitionists	Revivals
Attack on Bad Behavior	Seneca Falls Convention
Fight Against Slavery	Temperance
Religion	Women's Rights

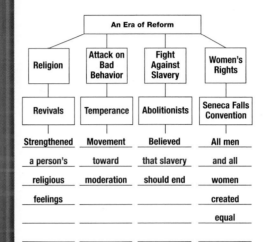

An Era of Reform

Religion	Attack on Bad Behavior	Fight Against Slavery	Women's Rights
Revivals	Temperance	Abolitionists	Seneca Falls Convention
Strengthened	Movement	Believed	All men
a person's	toward	that slavery	and all
religious	moderation	should end	women
feelings			created
			equal

 Notes for Home: Your child learned about the spirit of reform in the United States in the 1830s.
Home Activity: With your child, discuss government's attempts to make political and social reforms in the United States today. What are the goals of these efforts to enact change?

Use with Pupil Edition, p. 420

Workbook, p. 98

Writing Prompt: Making Changes

Throughout the nineteenth century, reformers worked to stop child labor. Finally, in 1938 Congress passed the Fair Labor Standards Act. It set 18 as the youngest age for factory workers. Do you think children should be allowed to work? Write about reasons you agree or disagree with the reformers.

Answers will vary.

Notes for Home: Your child learned about different reform movements.
Home Activity: With your child, discuss how life might be different today for women and African Americans if people had not worked to gain equal rights.

Use with Pupil Edition, p. 425

Workbook, p. 99

Vocabulary Review
Use with Chapter 12.

Directions: Circle the term that best completes each sentence.

1. Thousands of people were forced to relocate following the terms of the (Seneca Falls Convention, Indian Removal Act).

2. A peaceful atmosphere existed in the United States during the (Era of Good Feelings, Monroe Doctrine).

3. The (cotton gin, revival) increased workers' daily production tremendously.

4. Modern (technology, reform) has created many jobs.

5. Goods were sent on the (Trail of Tears, canal) to get to market.

6. The (Monroe Doctrine, Indian Removal Act) showed foreign powers that the United States was willing to fight for its land.

7. A Wednesday evening (revival, reform) was a popular function at many houses of worship.

8. The Second Great Awakening movement supported social (temperance, reform).

9. The (Seneca Falls Convention, Industrial Revolution) introduced an era of machine-made goods.

10. Many women who supported (temperance, technology) tried to stop the drinking of alcohol.

11. The invention of machines helped businesses (manufacture, reform) goods on a wide scale.

12. Frederick Douglass, a former slave, was an outspoken (mechanical reaper, abolitionist).

13. Many people died along the (Trail of Tears, Industrial Revolution).

14. The (revival, Seneca Falls Convention) in New York supported women's rights.

15. Women and minorities had to fight for (suffrage, temperance).

16. Independence Day celebrations reflect a spirit of (reform, nationalism) in the United States.

17. The (Era of Good Feelings, mechanical reaper) made it easier for farm workers to harvest wheat.

 Notes for Home: Your child learned about changes that Americans wanted to make to improve their lives.
Home Activity: Review with your child how changes in the 1800s affect our life today.

Use with Pupil Edition, p. 427

Assessment Support

 Use these Assessment Book pages and the ExamView® Test Bank CD-ROM to assess content and skills in Chapter 12. You can also view and print Assessment Book pages from the Teacher Resources CD-ROM.

Assessment Book, p. 69

Chapter 12 Test

Part 1: Content Test

Directions: Fill in the circle next to the correct answer.

Lesson Objective (1:1)

1. How did President Monroe react to European interest in the Americas?
   - ● He issued the Monroe Doctrine.
   - Ⓑ He supported peaceful expansion.
   - Ⓒ He urged people to work together.
   - Ⓓ He supported nationalism.

Lesson Objective (1:1)

2. Which of the following describes the purpose of the Monroe Doctrine?
   - Ⓐ to invite additional European colonization in the Americas
   - ● to protect American lands from future European colonization
   - Ⓒ to unite the Seminole and American settlers in Spanish Florida
   - Ⓓ to avoid war with European nations

Lesson Objective (1:2)

3. In what way was Andrew Jackson different from the previous six Presidents?
   - Ⓐ He was from a wealthy family from California.
   - ● He was the son of poor pioneers who had moved west.
   - Ⓒ His wealthy family was from Massachusetts or Virginia.
   - Ⓓ His poor family immigrated from Spain to the United States.

Lesson Objective (1:2)

4. What did Jackson's political party encourage?
   - Ⓐ people to move west where land was cheap
   - Ⓑ wealthy landowners to vote
   - Ⓒ people to buy land so they could have special privileges
   - ● the "common people" to vote

Lesson Objective (1:3)

5. What happened as settlers began to claim Indian lands in the Southeast?
   - Ⓐ Spain allowed the settlers to live in their colonies.
   - Ⓑ Land in the Southeast became expensive to purchase.
   - ● The Indian Removal Act was passed.
   - Ⓓ The United States continued to expand its borders peacefully.

Lesson Objective (1:3)

6. Which of the following was an effect of the Indian Removal Act?
   - ● Many Indians in the South were forced off their lands.
   - Ⓑ Settlers and Indians lived together peacefully.
   - Ⓒ The Cherokee formed a constitutional government.
   - Ⓓ Chief Justice John Marshall was elected to the Supreme Court.

Lesson Objective (2:1)

7. How were tools, cloth, and most other goods made before the Industrial Revolution?
   - Ⓐ by machine
   - Ⓑ by teams of workers
   - Ⓒ by millgirls in Lowell
   - ● by hand

Lesson Objective (2:1)

8. What effect did the Industrial Revolution have on the supply of goods?
   - Ⓐ No change was evident.
   - Ⓑ Only as much as was needed was made.
   - ● More goods were made.
   - Ⓓ Fewer goods were made.

Use with Pupil Edition, p. 426

Assessment Book, p. 70

Lesson Objective (2:2)

9. Which of the following did NOT lead to increased crop production?
   - Ⓐ mechanical reaper
   - Ⓑ cotton gin
   - ● thread-spinning mill
   - Ⓓ more slaves

Lesson Objective (2:2)

10. What effect did new machines have on Americans?
    - Ⓐ The demand for farm workers decreased.
    - Ⓑ The demand for slave labor decreased.
    - Ⓒ Goods made by machine were more costly.
    - ● Goods were produced more quickly and more cheaply.

Lesson Objective (2:3)

11. Which of the following was NOT a common way to transport manufactured goods to markets on the western frontier?
    - Ⓐ by road
    - ● by horse
    - Ⓒ by boat
    - Ⓓ by railroad

Lesson Objective (2:3)

12. Which of the following advances in technology improved land travel?
    - Ⓐ steamboats
    - Ⓑ airplanes
    - ● railroads
    - Ⓓ wagon trains

Lesson Objective (3:1)

13. Which of the following best describes the Second Great Awakening?
    - ● revival of religious beliefs
    - Ⓑ crusade to stop drinking alcohol
    - Ⓒ push for more education
    - Ⓓ crusade to end slavery

Lesson Objective (3:2)

14. Who were the reformers who moved to end slavery?
    - Ⓐ nationalists
    - ● abolitionists
    - Ⓒ leaders
    - Ⓓ revivalists

Lesson Objective (3:3)

15. Which was NOT a way the abolitionists spread their word?
    - Ⓐ preaching
    - Ⓑ speeches
    - ● riots
    - Ⓓ printed newspapers

Lesson Objective (3:3)

16. Which of the following was a goal of the women's rights movement?
    - Ⓐ separate duties
    - ● equality
    - Ⓒ temperance
    - Ⓓ publicity

Lesson Objective (3:4)

17. Which of the following was NOT a focus of the reform movement of the 1850s?
    - ● health
    - Ⓑ slavery
    - Ⓒ education
    - Ⓓ prisons

Use with Pupil Edition, p. 426

Assessment Support

Assessment Book, p. 71

Part 2: Skills Test

Directions: Use complete sentences to answer questions 1–7. Use a separate sheet of paper if you need more space.

1. What led President James Monroe to issue the Monroe Doctrine? **Cause and Effect**

   President Monroe wanted to prevent Russia, Britain, and other nations from colonizing the American continents.

2. Compare and contrast suffrage in the eastern and western states in the early 1800s. **Compare and Contrast**

   The eastern states granted suffrage only to white men who owned property. States farther west granted suffrage to all men, whether or not they were property owners.

3. What was the purpose of the Indian Removal Act? **Draw Conclusions**

   The United States wanted to open lands in the southern United States to white settlers for farming, trading, hunting, and herding, even if it had to ignore the rights of Indian groups to do so.

4. Why were more slaves needed to grow and pick cotton after the cotton gin was invented? **Analyze Information**

   The factories needed more raw cotton to make into cloth. More slaves were needed to grow and pick cotton because the demand for cotton increased.

5. Why did railroads replace water routes as the preferred way to travel? **Draw Conclusions**

   Train travel was faster, cheaper, and more comfortable. People also could get to more places by train than they could by water routes.

Use with Pupil Edition, p. 426

Assessment Book, p. 72

6. Who benefited from the Industrial Revolution? **Main Idea and Details**

   Everyone involved in making goods by machine benefited. Machines helped businesses make more goods at a cheaper cost. This allowed the businesses to make more products, earn more money, and hire more people, who then could buy the goods with money they earned. Also, consumers were able to buy cheaper goods.

7. What similar methods did antislavery reformers and supporters of women's rights use to share their message? **Compare and Contrast**

   Many supporters gave speeches, printed newspaper articles, and preached in support of the rights of slaves and women.

Apply Skills

Read a Cross-Section Diagram
Study the cross-section diagram of a modern locomotive. Then answer the questions.

1. How do you know this is a cross-section diagram?
2. What information does it give you?
3. What is the generator connected to?

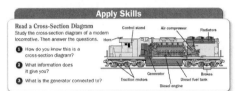

Modern Locomotive

8. Use the diagram to answer the questions. **Read a Cross-Section Diagram**
   a. What is the purpose of this diagram?

   to show the inside parts of a modern locomotive

   b. Where is the air compressor located?

   behind the engine and under the radiators

   c. How can this diagram help you understand how a locomotive works?

   Possible answer: The diagram helps me see what parts are inside a locomotive and where they are located.

Use with Pupil Edition, p. 426

Times of Change

Chapter 12 Outline

- **Lesson 1, *The United States Turns Fifty,*** pp. 402–406
- **Biography: *Andrew Jackson,*** p. 407
- **Lesson 2, *A New Kind of Revolution,*** pp. 408–413
- **Chart and Graph Skills: *Read a Cross-Section Diagram,*** pp. 414–415
- **Lesson 3, *The Struggle for Reforms,*** pp. 416–420
- **Biography: *Sojourner Truth,*** p. 421
- **Citizen Heroes: *Exposing Slavery's Evils,*** pp. 422–423
- **Colonial Williamsburg: *Nineteenth-Century Reform Movements,*** pp. 424–425

Resources

- Workbook, p. 93: Vocabulary Preview
- Vocabulary Cards
- Social Studies Plus!

1829, Washington, D.C.: Lesson 1

Tell students that Andrew Jackson was known as "the People's President." Have them study the picture and suggest what this name means. (Andrew Jackson was the first President that did not come from a wealthy family. He grew up poor and fought for the rights of all people, including the poor.)

1830, Baltimore, Maryland: Lesson 2

This picture shows *Tom Thumb,* a steam-powered locomotive—one of the many machines invented in the early 1830s. Ask students how this locomotive might have helped the United States grow. (Trains could move people and goods over longer distances more quickly.)

1848, Seneca Falls, New York: Lesson 3

Tell students that in the early 1800s women did not have the same rights as men. Ask students what they think the Seneca Falls Convention was about. (It was about getting women the right to vote.)

CHAPTER
12
Times of Change

1829

Washington, D.C.
Andrew Jackson becomes the seventh President of the United States.

Lesson 1

1830

Baltimore, Maryland
Tom Thumb, a steam-powered locomotive, races a horse.

Lesson 2

1

1848

Seneca Falls, New York
The Seneca Falls Convention issues a call for women's rights.

Lesson 3

2

3

400

Practice and Extend

Vocabulary Preview

- Use Workbook p. 93 to help students preview the vocabulary words in this chapter.
- Use Vocabulary Cards to preview key concept words in this chapter.

 Also on Teacher Resources CD-ROM.

Workbook, p. 93

Vocabulary Preview

Directions: Match each vocabulary term to its definition. Write the term in the space provided. Not all words will be used.

nationalism	Industrial Revolution	reform
Era of Good Feelings	manufacture	revival
Monroe Doctrine	technology	temperance
suffrage	cotton gin	abolitionist
Indian Removal Act	mechanical reaper	Seneca Falls Convention
Trail of Tears	canal	

1. _____ A convention called to take a stand for women's rights
2. _____ The terrible journey forced upon the Cherokee to move to Indian Territory
3. _____ A statement that warned European nations against considering the American continents for future colonization
4. _____ A machine invented to clean the seeds out of cotton
5. _____ A reformer who attacked slavery
6. _____ A time when people began producing goods by machine rather than by hand
7. _____ Act that ordered Native Americans of the southern United States be moved west of the Mississippi River
8. _____ A time when disagreements about national issues grew quiet
9. _____ The right to vote
10. _____ The idea that all people should pull together with a sense of strong pride in their country
11. _____ Moderation
12. _____ Change

Notes for Home: Your child learned vocabulary dealing with the mid-1800s, a time of growth and change in the United States.
Home Activity: Ask your child to use these terms to summarize the turbulent events in the United States during this time.

Locating Time and Place

UNITED STATES in 1829

PACIFIC OCEAN

Seneca Falls

Baltimore

Washington, D.C.

ATLANTIC OCEAN

Gulf of Mexico

Why We Remember

Today the majority of people in the United States live in cities and suburbs. In the early 1800s, the majority of Americans were farmers living in rural areas. It was the Industrial Revolution that began this huge change. People began leaving farms and moving to cities to work in the new factories. Inventions in transportation also came about during the Industrial Revolution. The steam engine, the steamboat, and the digging of canals meant that people and goods could travel farther and faster. The United States was growing, and very quickly. With that growth would also come conflict and struggles for change.

401

- Have students examine the pictures shown on p. 400 for Lessons 1, 2, and 3.

- Remind students that each picture is coded with both a number and a color to link it to a place on the map on p. 401.

Why We Remember

Have students read the "Why We Remember" paragraph on p. 401, and ask them why events in this chapter might be important to them. Have them consider what their lives would be like if they lived in the early 1800s, before much of the Industrial Revolution.

 WEB SITE
Technology

You can learn more about Washington, D.C.; Baltimore, Maryland; and Seneca Falls, New York by clicking on *Atlas* at **www.sfsocialstudies.com.**

 SOCIAL STUDIES STRAND
Geography

Mental Mapping Have students draw an outline map of the United States from memory, including the Great Lakes, and label New York City and Chicago. Tell students that they must find a route to ship goods between these two cities without using cars, trucks, or airplanes. Have students work in pairs to find routes. Remind them that goods can be shipped by water as well as over land.

The United States Turns Fifty

Objectives

- Describe the goal of the Monroe Doctrine.

- Explain how the United States changed politically in the 1820s.

- Describe the causes and effects of the Indian Removal Act of 1830.

Vocabulary

nationalism, p. 403;
Era of Good Feelings, p. 403;
Monroe Doctrine, p. 403; **suffrage,** p. 404;
Indian Removal Act, p. 405;
Trail of Tears, p. 406

Resources

- Workbook, p. 94
- Transparency 14
- Every Student Learns Guide, pp. 166–169
- Quick Study, pp. 84–85

Quick Teaching Plan

If time is short, write the vocabulary words and terms on the board.

- As students read the lesson, have them write definitions in their own words for each vocabulary word.

- Have students briefly describe the relevance of each term to events of the early 1800s.

1 Introduce and Motivate

Preview To activate prior knowledge, ask students to explain the significance of July 4. Tell students that they will learn about ways the United States continued to change and grow more than 50 years after gaining its independence as they read Lesson 1.

 Thomas Jefferson and John Adams fought hard to help create a nation. Have students describe the pride these men and other Americans might have felt as they celebrated the fiftieth birthday of the United States.

402 Unit 6 • A Growing Nation

INDIAN TERRITORY
FLORIDA

1820	1830	1840
1823 Monroe Doctrine is issued	**1828** Andrew Jackson is elected seventh President of the United States	**1838** Trail of Tears begins

PREVIEW

Focus on the Main Idea
In the 1820s and 1830s, the United States expanded its territory in North America and its power in the Western Hemisphere.

PLACES
Florida
Indian Territory

PEOPLE
James Monroe
Andrew Jackson
Sequoyah
John Ross

VOCABULARY
nationalism
Era of Good Feelings
Monroe Doctrine
suffrage
Indian Removal Act
Trail of Tears

▶ In 1776, the Liberty Bell rang to celebrate the Declaration of Independence. Fifty years later, it rang in memory of Jefferson and Adams.

402

The United States Turns Fifty

You Are There It is July 4, 1826—50 years from the day the Declaration of Independence was approved in Philadelphia. Americans hope that two founding fathers, although they are old and ill, can witness this celebration. Then something extraordinary happens! Thomas Jefferson, lying near death in Virginia, asks, "This is the Fourth?" Many miles to the north in Massachusetts—and a few hours later—John Adams murmurs his last words, "Thomas Jefferson survives." But Jefferson has already died. These two men have died on their nation's fiftieth birthday. But they lived to see the country they helped create grow strong and confident.

 Compare and Contrast As you read, compare and contrast the United States during President Monroe's presidency and after the presidency of Andrew Jackson.

Practice and Extend

READING SKILL
Compare/Contrast

In the Lesson Review, students complete a graphic organizer like the one below. You may want to provide students with a copy of Transparency 14 to complete as they read the lesson.

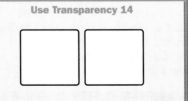

Use Transparency 14

VOCABULARY
Word Exercise

Related Word Study Tell students that, though the word *suffrage* resembles the word *suffer,* these words have different roots. The word *suffrage* comes from the Latin *suffragium,* or "supporting vote." In the late 1800s and early 1900s, women who worked to get the vote were known as *suffragettes.* A person who favors giving suffrage to more people, especially to women, is known as a *suffragist.*

The Monroe Doctrine

In 1817, a new President, **James Monroe,** took office. He was a believer in **nationalism,** the idea that all the people should pull together with a sense of strong pride in their country. At his inauguration speech, Monroe urged the American people to act as "one great family with a common interest."

Many Americans seemed to agree with Monroe. For a brief time, disagreements about national issues grew quiet. One Boston newspaper called the period an " **Era of Good Feelings.** "

However, Monroe faced major challenges from outside the country. Spain ruled **Florida** and a vast region from Texas to California. For years, slaves escaping from the southern United States had found safety in Florida. Some of the escaped people had found homes with the Seminole, a Florida American Indian tribe. The Seminole sometimes attacked American settlers in Georgia who had taken over American Indian lands. The Spanish did little to stop these attacks.

In 1817, Monroe sent General **Andrew Jackson,** the popular hero of the War of 1812, to stop the raids. Jackson attacked the Spanish in Florida and seized two of their forts. Troubled by uprisings in its other colonies, Spain found it hard to defend Florida. In a treaty in 1819, Spain agreed to sell Florida to the United States for $5 million.

Monroe was still concerned about other European nations. Both Russia and Britain were interested in taking over parts of Spain's weakened empire in the Americas. In 1823, Monroe issued a daring statement called the **Monroe Doctrine.** It warned European nations against interfering in the Western Hemisphere. "The American continents," Monroe said, "are…not to be considered as subject for future colonization by any European powers."

REVIEW How would you contrast the "Era of Good Feelings" with the period that came before it? Compare and Contrast

Revolutions in South America

At the Same Time… In 1819, Simón Bolívar [boh LEE vahr] led 2,500 soldiers through the cold mountain passes of Colombia and defeated a Spanish army. Bolívar's victory led to the establishment of Colombia. By the early 1820s, new independent nations had been created throughout the Americas.

403

The Monroe Doctrine

Quick Summary President James Monroe created the Monroe Doctrine in an effort to stop European nations from trying to control lands in the Western Hemisphere.

1 **Why do you think Spain decided to sell Florida to the United States?**
Andrew Jackson attacked the Spanish in Florida and seized two forts. Spain found it increasingly hard to defend Florida.
Draw Conclusions

✓ **REVIEW ANSWER** Possible answer: Before an "Era of Good Feelings," there were disagreements about national issues; during this time, disagreements about national issues grew quiet.
Compare and Contrast

Revolutions in South America

2 **Compare and contrast the revolutions in South America and the Revolutionary War in the United States.**
Similar: People were fighting for independence from European control. Different: The United States was forming one country while independent nations formed in South America.
Compare and Contrast

Ongoing Assessment

| **If…** students have difficulty comparing and contrasting the Revolutionary War in the United States and the revolutions in South America, | **then…** briefly review the unit on the Revolutionary War and create a chart on which to record similarities and differences. |

ACTIVATE PRIOR KNOWLEDGE
ESL Support

Explore Teamwork Children use what they know about teamwork to gain an understanding of *nationalism*. Explain that nationalism involves working together for a larger cause, not simply self-interest.

Beginning Have students work in pairs to draw a picture that conveys national pride.

Intermediate Have students describe a time when they have worked with a group to accomplish a goal. Students should describe the sequence of tasks they and the group completed.

Advanced Have students give an example of a situation involving teamwork that they have experienced or heard about. Ask them to first state the goal. They can then explain how the people worked together, what obstacles they faced, and how they finally achieved the goal.

For additional ESL support, use Every Student Learns Guide, pp. 166–169.

"The People's President"

🕐 **Quick Summary** Unlike the first six presidents, Andrew Jackson came from a poor family. In the election of 1828, he won a huge victory and was hailed as "the People's President."

3 **What are two examples of changes that took place in the early 1800s?**
Possible answer: People elected a President who was not from a wealthy family. White men who did not own property were given the right to vote.
Main Idea and Details

4 **Why do you think it was important to allow voting rights to more than just property owners?** Possible answer: The country was founded on the idea that all people were created equal, so it was unfair to let only a small group of people vote. **Express Ideas**

C **SOCIAL STUDIES STRAND**
Culture

5 **How did Jackson's campaign slogan demonstrate the different cultures in which each candidate was raised?**
Possible answer: Jackson grew up poor and had to fight for what he got. Adams was well-educated and wealthy and expressed his views in writing.
Analyze Information

6 **Compare and contrast Democrats and National Republicans.** Similar: Both parties claimed they were following the ideas of Thomas Jefferson. Different: The Democrats wanted all people, even the "common people," to vote.
🔄 Compare and Contrast

✓ **REVIEW ANSWER** John Quincy Adams was the highly educated and wealthy son of a former President. Andrew Jackson was the son of poor pioneers and he taught himself law.
🔄 Compare and Contrast

▶ Thousands of people went to the White House to celebrate Andrew Jackson's inauguration in 1829.

"The People's President"

Every one of the first six Presidents came from a wealthy Virginia or Massachusetts family. But the seventh was the son of poor pioneers. This was a sure sign that the country was changing.

In the early 1800s more people had moved west than ever before. With this movement came new ideas, some of which would spread back to the east. For example, the eastern states granted **suffrage**—the right to vote—mainly to white men who owned property. But the new states farther west granted suffrage **3** to all white men—property owners or not. The eastern states soon followed the western example. By the 1820s, a wider range of **4** white men could vote. Women, Native Americans, and most African Americans still were not allowed to vote.

In the election of 1828, Andrew Jackson ran against President John Quincy Adams. President Adams was the highly educated and wealthy son of the second President, John Adams. In contrast, Jackson had not gone to college, and he had taught himself law. He was also the military leader who won the Battle of New Orleans in the War of 1812. One of Jackson's election slogans declared that, "Adams…can write [but] Jackson…can fight."

Jackson headed a new political party, the Democrats. Adams's party was called the National Republicans. Both parties claimed they were following the ideas of Thomas Jefferson. Democrats urged everyone to vote, especially the "common people"—those with little property or wealth. Jackson's campaign promised "Equal rights for all; special privilege for none."

Jackson won a huge victory, sweeping both the western and the southern states. Many Americans praised him as "the man of the people." About 20,000 Jackson supporters poured into Washington, D.C., for his inauguration in 1829. In their enthusiasm, they rushed to the White House. One observer said, "…such a scene of confusion took place as is impossible to describe.…But it was the People's day, and the People's President and the People would rule." You will read more about Jackson in the Biography feature that follows this lesson.

REVIEW How would you contrast the backgrounds of John Quincy Adams and Andrew Jackson? 🔄 **Compare and Contrast**

404

Practice and Extend

 **SOCIAL STUDIES**
Background

Contact National Leaders

- So many of Jackson's supporters came to the White House after his inauguration that his friends had to help him leave through a side door.
- Tell students that today ordinary citizens are more likely to contact the President by letter, e-mail, or phone. The mailing address is The White House, 1600 Pennsylvania Avenue NW, Washington, DC 20500.
- To contact members of the House of Representatives, students can go to **www.house.gov** or call (202) 225-3121. Senators may be contacted at **www.senate.gov** or (202) 224-3121. Ask students to use these or other resources to find the political party of their representative.
- To contact appointed leaders, such as cabinet members, students may refer to an almanac or go to **www.whitehouse.gov** and search for cabinet.

American Indian Removal

In the 1820s and 1830s, many people were moving west. In the Southeast, settlers began moving into lands that belonged to five major American Indian groups—the Cherokee, Creek, Chickasaw, Choctaw, and Seminole.

The people of these Native American groups lived much as white settlers did—by farming, herding, hunting, and trading. A Cherokee named **Sequoyah** developed an alphabet for the Cherokee language. Using Sequoyah's alphabet, the Cherokee produced written materials, such as a newspaper called the *Phoenix*.

Life would soon change for the five Native American groups of the Southeast. In search of good farmland and gold, settlers continued moving onto the land of the five groups.

President Jackson supported the settlers. In 1830, Jackson encouraged Congress to pass the **Indian Removal Act**. This act gave the President the power to move Native Americans to land west of the Mississippi River. They would be moved to **Indian Territory,** land in what is now Oklahoma.

The five groups resisted. The Seminole fought for their land. After several years of battles, they were defeated by the United States army and forced to move west. Follow their route on the map below.

The Cherokee tried to keep their land by going to court. When the state of Georgia tried to take control of Cherokee land, Cherokee leader **John Ross** took his people's case to the Supreme Court. Chief Justice John Marshall agreed with Ross. The Court ruled that the Cherokee had the right to keep control of their traditional land.

When he heard of this ruling, President Jackson was reported to say, "John Marshall has made his decision, now let him enforce it." Without Jackson's support, the Supreme Court could not enforce its ruling.

REVIEW Contrast the views of John Marshall and Andrew Jackson on the rights of the Cherokee. 🔄 **Compare and Contrast**

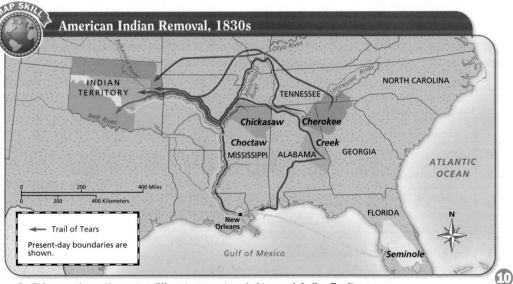

American Indian Removal, 1830s

← Trail of Tears

Present-day boundaries are shown.

▶ This map shows the routes different groups traveled to reach Indian Territory.

MAP SKILL Movement *Which Native American group crossed the Gulf of Mexico?*

405

PAGE 405

Indian Removal

🕐 *Quick Summary* In 1830, President Jackson urged Congress to pass the Indian Removal Act, which forced many Native Americans to move west of the Mississippi River.

7 **Why do you think the government wanted to force the Cherokee and other groups out of their homes?** Settlers wanted to make their homes where these groups lived. Cause and Effect

8 **How did the Cherokee react when the state of Georgia tried to take control of their land?** They brought their case to the Supreme Court. Main Idea and Details

9 **What did Jackson mean when he said "John Marshall has made his decision, now let him enforce it"?** He would not obey the decision and he knew John Marshall could not make him obey it. Make Inferences

✓ **REVIEW ANSWER** John Marshall: Cherokee could not be forced to leave their land; President Jackson: They could and should be forced to leave. 🔄 Compare and Contrast

🌐 **Indian Removal, 1830s**

10 **Which Native American group took the most northern route?** The Cherokee Interpret Maps

MAP SKILL Answer The Seminole

❄ MEETING INDIVIDUAL NEEDS
Leveled Practice

Write a Persuasive Letter Ask students to write about why the Cherokee should be allowed to stay on their lands.

Easy Ask students to describe good reasons for not forcing the Cherokee from their homes. Have different students write two or three sentences for each idea. Have students read their sentences together to form a "persuasive letter." **Reteach**

On-Level Have students write a persuasive letter with at least one paragraph that includes several details to support their argument. **Extend**

Challenge Students should write a persuasive letter to Andrew Jackson that challenges the Indian Removal Act. Ask them to try to influence the president to change his mind and allow the Native Americans to stay in their homes. **Enrich**

For a Lesson Summary, use Quick Study, p. 84.

The Trail of Tears

🕐 *Quick Summary* The Cherokee's 800-mile trip was so devastating that many did not survive.

Primary Source

Cited in *Cherokee Legends and the Trail of Tears,* by Thomas Bryan Underwood

⑪ **According to John Burnett, how were the Cherokee treated?** Possible answer: They were treated poorly.
Analyze Primary Sources

✓ **REVIEW ANSWER** Before: The Cherokee lived much like settlers; During: They lived as prisoners with no homes and few belongings.
🔄 Compare and Contrast

3 Close and Assess

Summarize the Lesson

After students examine the time line, have them summarize the causes and effects of changes in the United States during this period.

✓ **LESSON 1   REVIEW**

1. 🔄 **Compare and Contrast** For possible answers, see the reduced pupil page.

2. To warn European nations against interfering with the Western Hemisphere.

3. President Jackson did not come from a wealthy family in the East, but was the son of poor pioneers from the West.

4. White settlers wanted the land where these Native Americans lived. The Native Americans were forced to move and many died during the trip.

5. **Critical Thinking:** *Express Ideas* Democratic government involves people choosing elected representatives. To choose them, a citizen must have the right to vote.

Link to ⌘⌘ Writing

Students should consider the basic rights described in the U.S. Constitution.

406 Unit 6 • A Growing Nation

The Trail of Tears

In 1838, President Martin Van Buren ordered United States soldiers to force the Cherokee to leave their land. The 800-mile journey to Indian Territory was so terrible that it became known as the **Trail of Tears.**

A soldier named John Burnett never forgot what he saw on the Trail of Tears:

⑪ *"I saw the helpless Cherokees arrested and dragged from their homes… I saw them loaded like cattle or sheep into six hundred and forty-five wagons and started toward the west."*

By 1839, the Trail of Tears had ended. Of the 15,000 Cherokee who began the journey as many as one-fourth did not survive the trip. Many died from disease and bad weather.

REVIEW Compare the way the Cherokee people lived before the Trail of Tears with

▶ The route of the Cherokee became known as the Trail of Tears.

their experiences during the journey.
🔄 Compare and Contrast

Summarize the Lesson

— **1823** President James Monroe issued the Monroe Doctrine.

— **1828** Andrew Jackson was elected the seventh President of the United States.

— **1838** The long journey of the Cherokee on the Trail of Tears began.

LESSON 1   REVIEW

Check Facts and Main Ideas

1. 🔄 **Compare and Contrast** On a separate sheet of paper, fill in the "1830" box to show how conditions in the United States changed from 1817 to 1830.

1817
• James Monroe is President.
• Florida belongs to Spain.
• American Indians live on land in the southern states.

1830
• Andrew Jackson is President.
• Florida belongs to the United States.
• Law passed to remove Indians from southern states.

2. Why did President Monroe issue the **Monroe Doctrine?**

3. How did the election of Andrew Jackson as President show that the United States was changing?

4. Why did the United States pass the **Indian Removal Act,** and what was the result?

5. **Critical Thinking:** *Express Ideas* Why is the right to vote important in a democratic government?

Link to ⌘⌘   Writing

Write a Statement Put yourself in the place of a Cherokee leader. Write a statement to the Supreme Court giving reasons why your people have the right to stay on their land.

406

Practice and Extend

CURRICULUM CONNECTION
Math

Multiply Fractions and Whole Numbers

• About one-fourth of the approximately 15,000 Cherokee who began the journey did not survive. Have students calculate the number of people who did not survive the journey. (1/4 x 15,000 = 15,000/4 = about 3,750 Cherokee did not survive)

• Then have students calculate the approximate number of survivors. (15,000 – 3,750 = about 11,250)

Workbook, p. 94

Lesson 1: The United States Turns Fifty

Directions: Match the events and descriptions in the box below with the President who was in office when they took place. Write each event in the space provided.

Issued warning to European nations not to consider the American continents as subject for future colonization

Headed a new political party, the Democrats

Era of Good Feelings enjoyed

Florida purchased from Spain for $5 million

Native Americans in the southern states forced to move west of the Mississippi

Known as "the man of the people"

Military leader and self-taught lawyer

Encouraged nationalism

President James Monroe	President Andrew Jackson

Critical Thinking: Compare and contrast how the United States expanded its borders under Presidents Monroe and Jackson.

Notes for Home: Your child learned about the early expansion of the United States.
Home Activity: Review the lesson with your child, and make a time line of the key events of the United States first 50 years.

💿 **Also on Teacher Resources CD-ROM**

Andrew Jackson

1767–1845

Andrew Jackson was nine years old when the Declaration of Independence was signed in 1776. His mother and two brothers listened as he read it aloud. Andrew, like the rest of his family, was a strong supporter of the American Revolution.

When he was 13, he joined the militia, or volunteer army, of South Carolina. After a difficult battle, Andrew and his brother Robert went to a relative's home to rest and heal. But British troops soon found the brothers. A British officer ordered Andrew to clean his boots. When Andrew refused, the officer hit him with his sword.

Andrew and Robert were then taken to a prison camp, where both became ill with smallpox. During a prisoner exchange in 1781, Andrew and Robert were allowed to go home, but Robert had become too ill and soon died. Just after Andrew became healthy again, his mother died of illness while taking care of sick and wounded American soldiers. Andrew was alone.

The sacrifices of Andrew Jackson and his family during the American Revolution made him determined to protect people who, like him, grew up poor. He later said:

> *"In general, the great can protect themselves, but the poor and humble require the arm and shield [protection] of the law."*

Andrew Jackson became a teacher, lawyer, soldier, senator, and finally President of the United States.

Learn From Biographies

How did Jackson's experiences during the American Revolution affect his views about government?

For more information, go online to *Meet the People* at **www.sfsocialstudies.com.**

407

Andrew Jackson

Objectives
- Describe the historical movements that influenced the development of the United States.
- Name major historical figures, such as Andrew Jackson, and describe their involvement in the development of the United States.

1 Introduce and Motivate

Preview Tell students they will read about Andrew Jackson's early life and how it influenced the ideas he had during his presidency.

2 Teach and Discuss

1 **How would you describe Jackson based on his behavior with the British soldier?** Possible answers: Determined; stubborn **Express Ideas**

2 **Read the quote by Jackson. Restate the quote using your own words and explain whether this idea would still apply today.** Possible answer: Some people need more support and protection from the government. It still applies today. **Analyze Primary Sources**

3 Close and Assess

Learn from Biographies Answer

During the American Revolution, Jackson discovered that the poor had to make many sacrifices, so he decided that the government should try to protect them.

WEB SITE
Technology

Students can find out more about Andrew Jackson by clicking on *Meet the People* at **www.sfsocialstudies.com.**

CURRICULUM CONNECTION
Literature

Read Biographies

Andrew Jackson, by Steve Potts (Bridgestone Books, ISBN 1-560-65455-4, 1996) **Easy**

Andrew Jackson, by Anne Welsbacher (ABDO Publishing, ISBN 1-562-39811-3, 1998) **On-Level**

Andrew Jackson, by Alice Osinski (Children's Press, ISBN 0-516-41387-2, 1987) **Challenge**

A New Kind of Revolution

Objectives

- Explain how the Industrial Revolution changed the way goods were made.

- Describe how new inventions led to increased production of both manufactured and farm goods.

- Identify ways in which transportation changed in the United States in the early and middle 1800s.

Vocabulary

Industrial Revolution, p. 409; **manufacture,** p. 409; **technology,** p. 409; **cotton gin**, p. 410; **mechanical reaper,** p. 410; **canal,** p. 411

Resources

- Workbook, p. 95
- Transparency 14, 48
- Every Student Learns Guide, pp. 170–173
- Quick Study, pp. 86–87

Quick Teaching Plan

If time is short, have students make a list of each of the inventions or improvements mentioned in the lesson.

- As they read independently, have students write about how an invention or improvement changed the way Americans worked and lived.

1 Introduce and Motivate

Preview Ask students to describe different "high-tech" items that make modern life easier. Tell students they will learn more about inventions from the early 1800s as they read Lesson 2.

You Are There The "mill girls" worked long hours in crowded conditions for very little money. Ask students what they think it would be like to live in a small room with seven other people— many of them the same people with whom you work all day.

LESSON 2

1790			1830
1790 Samuel Slater builds the nation's first cotton-spinning factory	**1811** Construction begins on the National Road	**1825** The Erie Canal is completed	**1830** Peter Cooper develops the f[...] United States locomotive

Erie Canal — National Road — Lowell

PREVIEW

Focus on the Main Idea
The Industrial Revolution dramatically changed the way Americans lived and worked.

PLACES
Lowell
National Road
Erie Canal

PEOPLE
Samuel Slater
Francis Cabot Lowell
Eli Whitney
Robert Fulton

VOCABULARY
Industrial Revolution
manufacture
technology
cotton gin
mechanical reaper
canal

A New Kind of Revolution

You Are There

Bells startle you out of your sleep at 5:40 in the morning. It's time to get up. The seven other young women who share your room in the boardinghouse are getting up too. Just like you, they are from farm families and have recently moved to town.

You all go into the street to join the crowds of workers heading for the mills. At 6:00, the bells ring again. Hurry! The mills will start running in just 10 minutes.

The year is 1845 and you are a "mill girl" in the town of Lowell, Massachusetts. You earn 40 cents a day for a long day of hard work!

 Compare and Contrast
As you read, contrast ways of making and moving goods before the Industrial Revolution and after.

408

Practice and Extend

READING SKILL
Compare/Contrast

In the Lesson Review, students complete a graphic organizer like the one below. You may want to provide students with a copy of Transparency 14 to complete as they read the lesson.

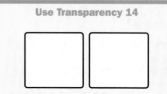
Use Transparency 14

VOCABULARY
Word Exercise

Related Word Study Have students read the definition of *technology* on p. 409. Point out that technology is not just computers. Very early technologies included starting fires and making metal. On the board, write *farm, home* and *transportation* at the heads of three columns. Ask students which items in the vocabulary list are technologies that would have been found on a farm. (cotton gin, mechanical reaper) Ask them to list other technologies under each of the three headings.

The Industrial Revolution

A time of change known as the Industrial Revolution caused the young women you just read about to leave their farm homes and move to town. The **Industrial Revolution** was a change in the way goods were produced, from handmade goods to goods made by machines. And businesses needed workers, like young farm women, to run the machines.

The invention of machines helped businesses manufacture goods much faster and more cheaply than before. To **manufacture** is to make goods, like cloth, from raw materials, like cotton fiber. The Industrial Revolution began in Britain in the middle 1700s. By the late 1700s, it had arrived in the United States. **Samuel Slater,** who began his career as a skilled worker in a cloth factory in Britain, helped bring the Industrial Revolution to the United States.

▶ Like Slater's cotton-spinning factory, this flour mill was powered by a rushing river.

Slater wanted to start a cloth factory in the United States. However, the British government wanted to keep its technology a secret. **Technology** is the way people use new ideas to make tools that improve people's lives. Britain had passed laws that made it illegal to take plans for the new technology out of the country.

Slater knew it was dangerous for him to try to take written plans with him. So he memorized the plans and then sailed for the United States. When Slater got to the United States, he used the plans he had memorized to build the first cotton-spinning mill, or factory, in the country. The mill was built in 1790 in Pawtucket, Rhode Island.

Slater used the flow of river waters to power his mill. The currents of river water turned giant water wheels, which were attached to belts and gears that set the machines in motion.

In 1812, **Francis Cabot Lowell,** a Boston merchant, decided to bring all the stages in cloth-making together. Spinning thread, weaving cloth, and dyeing it would all be done in one place. He put this idea into practice by building a large factory in **Lowell,** Massachusetts. Why in Lowell? There were two reasons: A river flowed through it, and there was a source of cheap and plentiful labor nearby.

The labor came from young women who lived on farms in the countryside. Because few of these young women had skills outside of farming and household tasks, they could not earn much money at home. In the 1830s and 1840s, thousands of these "mill girls," as they were called, came to work and live in Lowell and other New England factory towns.

REVIEW Explain why mill owners chose to build their factories near farms.
Cause and Effect

409

---

2 Teach and Discuss

PAGE 409

The Industrial Revolution

Quick Summary In the early 1800s, mills were built in the United States that allowed goods to be manufactured quickly and cheaply.

Test Talk

Locate Key Words in the Text

1 What were two effects caused by the invention of machines? Tell students that the answers to this question can be found in the second paragraph. Goods could be produced faster and many jobs were created. Cause and Effect

2 Why would Britain want to keep its technology a secret from the United States? So people in the United States would continue to buy goods produced in Britain Draw Conclusions

3 Why did the young farm women work for such low wages? They could not earn much money working at home. Main Idea and Details

✓ **REVIEW ANSWER** The mills needed many workers at low wages. Young people who lived on farms were a source of such workers. Cause and Effect

---

❄ **MEETING INDIVIDUAL NEEDS**
Leveled Practice

Compare and Contrast Have students compare and contrast life before and after the Industrial Revolution.

Easy Have students write about one difference in the way of life before and after the Industrial Revolution. **Reteach**

On-Level Have students compare and contrast how cloth may have been made prior to the Industrial Revolution with how it was made after the Industrial Revolution. **Extend**

Challenge Ask students to write two or three paragraphs comparing and contrasting life before and after the Industrial Revolution. Have them predict the effects this revolution might have on business and industry. **Enrich**

For a Lesson Summary, use Quick Study, p. 86.

Inventions Change Factories and Farms

🕐 **Quick Summary** Machines were invented that allowed factories to produce more goods, farmers to grow more food, and plantations to harvest more cotton.

④ Why did Eli Whitney invent the cotton gin? He heard planters complain about how hard it was to clean the seeds out of cotton. Cause and Effect

💲 SOCIAL STUDIES STRAND
Economics

Tell students that business and industry must pay close attention to the supply of and demand for the goods they produce. One effect of an increase or decrease in supply and demand is a change in price.

⑤ How did the construction of new mills in New England affect the demand for cotton? The demand for cotton increased. Cause and Effect

⑥ What inventions helped farmers grow and harvest more food? Possible answer: The mechanical reaper and steel plow Main Ideas and Details

✓ **REVIEW ANSWER** Before the invention of the cotton gin one worker could clean only about one pound of cotton a day. The machine could clean 50 times as much cotton a day as could be done by hand. 🔄 Compare and Contrast

⑦ Based on the graph, what can you conclude about cotton production in the early 1800s? It increased greatly each decade. Analyze Information

⑧ Between which two dates shown did cotton production increase by almost one million bales? 1840 and 1850 Interpret Graphs

GRAPH SKILL Answer Over 600,000 bales

Inventions Change Factories and Farms

The new mills of New England made cloth from cotton plants. The cotton was grown in the South on huge plantations, where most of the workers were enslaved people. Cotton was known as "King Cotton," because it ruled the South's economy.

The harvesting of cotton had been given a huge boost by the invention of a young New Englander, **Eli Whitney.** While visiting Georgia in 1792, he heard planters complain about how hard it was to clean the seeds out of cotton. This step was necessary before the cotton could be sold. Whitney learned that a worker could clean only about one pound of cotton a day. He later wrote:

> "I... struck on a plan, a machine with which one man will clean ten times as much cotton...."

Whitney's machine was called a **cotton gin.** The machine could clean 50 times as much cotton a day as could be done by hand. Mills needed the cotton, and plantations expanded to supply it. The increased demand for cotton led to the demand for more slaves to grow and pick it. The graph on this page shows how quickly cotton production increased.

Machines were helping with other kinds of farm work. Before the 1830s, farm workers harvested wheat by swinging a long blade. In 1831, Cyrus McCormick developed a horse-drawn **mechanical reaper** that could do the job more easily. Soon after, John Deere developed a plow made of steel rather than of iron. It could plow through thick soil more easily than older plows.

The new machines Americans were inventing meant that factories could produce more goods, often more cheaply. Farmers could grow more foods, and planters more cotton. More goods and more food meant more products for the people at home and for trade.

REVIEW Compare and contrast the cleaning of cotton before and after the invention of the cotton gin.
🔄 Compare and Contrast

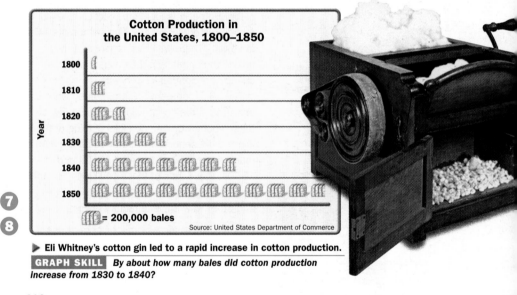

Cotton Production in the United States, 1800–1850

Year	
1800	▯
1810	▯▯▯
1820	▯▯▯ ▯▯▯
1830	▯▯▯ ▯▯▯ ▯▯▯ ▯
1840	▯▯▯ ▯▯▯ ▯▯▯ ▯▯▯ ▯▯▯ ▯▯
1850	▯▯▯ ▯▯▯ ▯▯▯ ▯▯▯ ▯▯▯ ▯▯▯ ▯▯▯ ▯▯▯ ▯▯

▯ = 200,000 bales

Source: United States Department of Commerce

▶ Eli Whitney's cotton gin led to a rapid increase in cotton production.

GRAPH SKILL *By about how many bales did cotton production increase from 1830 to 1840?*

Practice and Extend

❄ MEETING INDIVIDUAL NEEDS
Learning Styles

Interpret a Graph Using their individual learning styles, students analyze information in the graph on p. 410.

Logical Learning Give students counters or coins. Tell them that each counter stands for 100,000 bales of cotton. Have students round the numbers in the graph and make stacks to represent cotton production for each year.

Linguistic Learning Have students write a paragraph describing the information displayed in the graph.

Visual Learning Have students make a line graph using the data given in the pictograph. Ask them to study the slope of the lines to find where the least and greatest increases in cotton production occurred.

▶ Robert Fulton's *Clermont* could travel between New York City and Albany in 32 hours.

Moving Goods and People

Americans were producing more manufactured and farm goods than ever before. But people needed better ways to get their products to market. Settlers heading west also needed better methods of transportation. These needs led to major changes in transportation in the early 1800s.

In 1811, the federal government began building the **National Road.** Eventually it stretched from Cumberland, Maryland to Vandalia, Illinois. Settlers traveled west on the National Road while sheep, cattle, and hogs bound for eastern markets were sent along the road in the opposite direction.

Traveling the National Road—and all roads at the time—could be rough. Wagons got stuck in mud and in deep ruts left by other wagons. Rivers could provide smoother travel than roads. But boats powered by sails or oars had difficulty traveling upstream against a river's current.

Robert Fulton, an American engineer, set out to solve this problem. He developed a riverboat powered by a steam engine. On an early afternoon in August 1807, a crowd gathered to watch his boat, the *Clermont*, set off from New York City. An observer said, "Cheer after cheer went up from the vast throng." The *Clermont's*

destination was Albany, New York—150 miles upstream on the Hudson River. Thirty-two hours later, the *Clermont* arrived at Albany. It took four days for sailing ships to make the same trip. River travel took a giant leap forward.

Water transportation could carry both people and goods and was much cheaper than land transportation. But rivers did not flow in all parts of the country. Canals were one solution. A **canal** is a ditch dug through the land and filled with water. It is a narrow waterway that usually connects other bodies of water such as rivers, lakes, and seas.

One of the longest canals built in the early 1800s was the **Erie Canal.** In 1817, thousands of workers began digging a ditch that extended from Albany on the Hudson River to Buffalo on Lake Erie. In 1825, the Erie Canal opened. It linked the Great Lakes and the Atlantic Ocean. Thousands of people used the Erie Canal to travel from New York City to the Midwest. Manufactured goods could be shipped from eastern factories to the western frontier. Farm goods could be shipped in the opposite direction.

REVIEW How did Americans change their environment in order to improve transportation? Main Idea and Details

411

> PAGE 411

Moving Goods and People

🕐 *Quick Summary* Improved transportation enabled goods and people to be moved more easily.

9 **What led to transportation changes in the early 1800s?** People needed better ways to move products and to move themselves. Cause and Effect

10 **What was the National Road used for?** Moving people west and livestock east Main Idea and Details

11 **How was water transportation possible in places where rivers or lakes did not exist?** Workers dug canals to connect waterways. Main Idea and Details

12 **Why was the Erie Canal important to the growth and development of the United States?** People and goods could be moved faster and more cheaply between the East and the Midwest. Analyze Information

✓ Ongoing Assessment

If... students don't understand the importance of canals,

then... use a U.S. map to show how the Erie Canal connects natural waterways.

✓ **REVIEW ANSWER** New roads and canals were built. Main Idea and Details

---

 SOCIAL STUDIES
Background

The Erie Canal

- Governor DeWitt Clinton of New York proposed building a canal from the eastern shore of Lake Erie to the upper Hudson River.

- The state legislature allowed a budget of $7 million to build a canal about 363 miles long, 40 feet wide, and 4 feet deep.

- Before the canal was built, freight rates by land from Buffalo to New York City were $100 a ton. Rates on the canal were only $10 a ton.

 CURRICULUM CONNECTION
Math

Calculate Miles per Hour

- The steamboat traveled 150 miles in 32 hours. A sailboat made the trip in 4 days.

- Ask: What was the steamboat's rate in miles per hour? About how many hours quicker was the trip in the steamboat? (About 4.7 miles per hour; about 64 hours quicker)

Early Railroads

 Quick Summary With the development of the steam locomotive in 1830, the railroads soon became the cheapest and easiest way to travel in the United States.

13 Why do you think people decided to develop railroads? They were a faster means of transportation.
Draw Conclusions

Problem Solving

14 What problem was Peter Cooper trying to solve when he developed the steam engine locomotive? What might have been another solution to the problem? Which solution do you think would have been best? Possible answers: People needed ways to pull heavier loads faster than horses. Another way to move goods might have been to try to improve the roads. Since the *Tom Thumb* experiment went well, the railroad was probably the better solution to the problem. Improving the roads might have been time-consuming and expensive. **Solve Problems**

Map Adventure Answers

1. 20 miles per day; $375

2. The distance is about 360 miles. So 360 miles at 6 miles per hour = 60 hours. The cost is 2¢ a mile. So 2¢ per mile × 360 miles = 720¢, or $7.20

3. 360 miles at 40 miles per hour = 9 hours, or 51 hours shorter.

✓ **REVIEW ANSWER** The changes made travel faster and cheaper.
Cause and Effect

Early Railroads

Railroads began simply as rails laid down in a road. The rails were made of wood topped with iron. Horses pulled carts running along the rails. Since the rails were smoother than the roads, the horses could pull the carts **13** faster than they could pull wagons over roads.

Then Peter Cooper, one of the directors of the Baltimore & Ohio Railroad, got a better idea. Why not develop a steam engine, or locomotive, to pull the carts? He believed a locomotive would be able to pull heavier **14** loads faster than horses could.

In 1830, Cooper built a steam-powered locomotive. Because of its small size—weighing barely a ton—it became known as the Tom Thumb, after a tiny hero of old English stories. To let people know about his new

▶ The Tom Thumb lost its race against a horse, but s~~oon~~ locomotives were pulling many more goods than ho~~rses~~

machine, Cooper advertised "a race between a gray horse and the Tom Thumb." Which would win? A race horse or the "Iron Horse"?

On an August day that year, the locomotive and the gray horse lined up side by side.

Map Adventure

Getting Around a Growing Nation

You are in charge of arranging shipping and travel for a manufacturing company.

1. You have three tons of goods that you want to ship along the National Road from Baltimore to Wheeling, Virginia. A freight wagon will carry the goods 260 miles in about 13 days. If the wagon travels the same number of miles each day, how many miles per day will it travel? At $125 a ton, how much will the trip cost?

2. One of your clerks has to travel from Buffalo to Albany, a distance of about 360 miles. You decide to send him by boat over the Erie Canal. He will travel at 6 miles an hour and the cost will be 2 cents a mile. How many hours will the trip take? How much will it cost?

3. A few years later, you are able to send him on the same trip by railroad. The train travels at 40 miles per hour. How many hours shorter will the trip be by railroad than it was by boat?

Practice and Extend

ESL EXTEND LANGUAGE
ESL Support

Classify Types of Transportation Have students identify different methods of transportation.

Beginning Write these words on the board: *train, ferry, horse, plane, ship, truck.* Have students tell whether each word describes land, water, or air travel.

Intermediate Ask students to select one of the transportation methods above and write a paragraph to describe how it works.

Advanced Have students select two of the transportation methods and then write a paragraph to compare and contrast the items.

For additional ESL support use Every Student Learns Guide, pp. 170–173.

Cooper stood at the controls of the Tom Thumb. The race began. At first, the horse pulled ahead. But then the train picked up speed. Soon it was neck and neck with the horse, and then the Tom Thumb pulled ahead. A great cheer went up.

But suddenly, a safety valve broke in the engine. The locomotive slowed, and then fell behind the horse. The Tom Thumb lost this race. But locomotives would soon take over from horses.

Over the next 20 years, railroads replaced canals as the easiest and cheapest way to travel. By 1840, the United States had about 3,000 miles of railroad tracks, almost twice as much as Europe. A person could travel about 90 miles from New York City to Philadelphia by railroad in just a few hours instead of the day and a half the trip took by horse-drawn wagon.

REVIEW What effects did changes in transportation have on travel? *Cause and Effect*

Summarize the Lesson

— **1790** Samuel Slater built the nation's first cotton-spinning factory.

— **1811** Construction began on the National Road.

— **1825** The Erie Canal was completed.

— **1830** Peter Cooper developed a steam-powered locomotive.

LESSON 2	REVIEW

Check Facts and Main Ideas

1. **Compare and Contrast** On a separate sheet of paper, fill in the box to compare the way goods were produced and transported before and after the Industrial Revolution.

Before the Industrial Revolution	After the Industrial Revolution
• Goods were made by hand. • Cotton plants were cleaned by hand. • Wheat was harvested with a long blade. • Goods were moved by horse over rough road.	• Goods were made by machine. • Cotton gin cleaned cotton faster. • Wheat was harvested with a mechanical reaper. • Goods were moved by steam locomotives and steam boats.

2. How did the **Industrial Revolution** change the way Americans produced goods?

3. Why were New England factory towns built near rivers?

4. **Critical Thinking:** *Problem Solving* Suppose you were an inventor in the early 1830s. What problem would you have wanted to solve? Use the problem-solving steps on page H3.

5. What advantages did the locomotive have over carts pulled along rails by horses?

Link to **Mathematics**

Figure Hourly Wage In 1845, many mill girls earned 40 cents a day for working 12 hours. In 2001, the minimum, or lowest allowed, wage in the United States was $5.15 hour. About how much did mill girls earn an hour?

413

3 Close and Assess

Summarize the Lesson

Have students read the events listed in the summary. Ask them to write as many causes and effects as they can that relate to these events.

✓ | LESSON 2 | REVIEW |
|---|---|

1. **Compare and Contrast** For possible answers, see the reduced pupil page.

2. Making goods slowly by hand and with simple tools changed into making goods rapidly with machines.

3. The running water of the rivers was used to power the machines in the factories.

4. **Critical Thinking:** *Problem Solving* Accept all answers, but make sure that students support their answers.

5. The locomotive could pull heavier loads and could pull them faster than a horse could.

Link to **Mathematics**

About 3.3¢ per hour

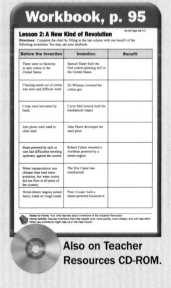

Workbook, p. 95

Also on Teacher Resources CD-ROM.

Read a Cross-Section Diagram

Objective
- Interpret and explain information from a cross-section diagram.

Vocabulary
cross-section diagram, p. 414

Resource
- Workbook, p. 96
- Transparency 48

1 Introduce and Motivate

What is a cross-section diagram?
Ask students how a cross-section diagram might be used by historians in the future to study inventions from earlier times. Then have students read the **What?** section of text on p. 414 to help set the purpose of the lesson.

Why use cross-section diagrams?
Have students read the **Why?** section of text on p. 414. Ask them what a cross-section diagram of a computer might look like.

2 Teach and Discuss

How is this skill used? Examine with students the cross-section diagrams on pp. 414 and 415.

- Point out that some cross-section diagrams are made up of one picture, but this one has two pictures that show how the canal works.

- Have students read the **How?** section of text on p. 415.

 **Chart and Graph Skills**

Read a Cross-Section Diagram

What? A cross-section diagram is a drawing that shows a view of something as if you could slice through it. Cross-section diagrams can be used to show you how something works.

Why? It is difficult to understand how a device works if you cannot see inside it. In a cross-section diagram, the artist "removes" part of the outside so that you can see how the inside

Gate   Gate

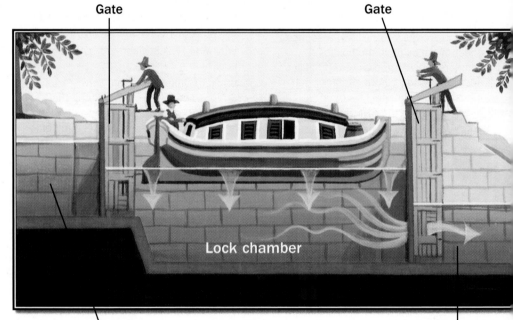

Lock chamber

Upstream water level

Downstream water level

414

Practice and Extend

 CURRICULUM CONNECTION
Art

Make a Cross-Section Diagram
- Have students select an object or machine that they are familiar with, such as an electric pencil sharpener.
- Ask students to make a cross-section diagram of this object or of a part of the object to show how it works.

FAST FACTS

Erie Canal
- The Erie Canal had to cross a rise in elevation of 500 feet.
- To do this, workers had to construct over 80 separate locks.

works. A cross-section diagram helps you see how canals like the Erie Canal work.

How? To use a cross-section diagram, you have to study the drawing carefully. Read the labels to identify each part of the diagram.

The diagram on this page shows how a boat moves from higher to lower water in the lock of a canal. A lock is a section of a canal that is closed off so that water can be removed or added. The water coming in or going out changes the level of the water in the lock so that a boat can be moved higher or lower.

Look at the cross-section diagram. Notice that the boat has to be moved to a lower water level. Locate the gates that will keep the boat in the lock while the water level is

being changed. Notice where the boat will go after the water level has been changed. ②③

Think and Apply

❶ What is the purpose of a canal lock?

❷ What do the lock gates do?

❸ This **cross-section diagram** shows how a boat is moved from a higher water level to a lower water level. How do you think a lock could be used to move a boat from a lower water level to a higher water level?

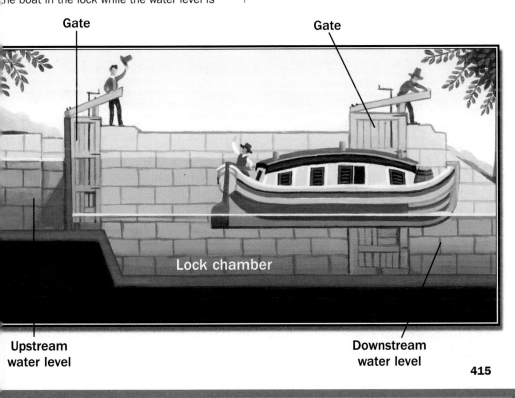

Gate   Gate

Lock chamber

Upstream water level   Downstream water level

415

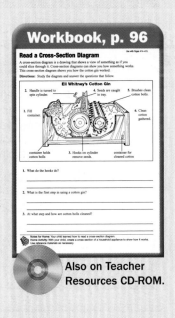

The Struggle for Reforms

Objectives

- Describe the historical movements that influenced the development of the United States.

- Identify and analyze groups in the United States that have influenced patterns of national behavior.

- Describe characteristics of groups that influenced the early development of the United States.

- Explain how groups, such as unions and political parties, have influenced the development of the United States.

Vocabulary

reform, p. 417; **revival,** p. 417; **temperance,** p. 417; **abolitionist,** p. 418; **Seneca Falls Convention,** p. 419

Resources

- Workbook, p. 97
- Transparency 14
- Every Student Learns Guide, pp. 174–177
- Quick Study, pp. 88–89

Quick *Teaching Plan*

If time is short, have students make a web with the word *reforms* in the middle.

- As they read, students add spokes to the web describing reforms that people from this period demanded.

1 Introduce and Motivate

Preview Ask students to name some of the rights that the founders of the United States felt were important. Tell students they will learn about some groups in this country whose rights had been denied.

 Elizabeth Cady Stanton was one of several women who spoke out about injustices against women. Ask students how it might have felt to live during a time when women did not have the right to vote.

LESSON 3

1830			1850
Early 1830s Second Great Awakening sweeps the country	**1838** Frederick Douglass escapes slavery and leads movement to abolish it	**1848** Seneca Falls Convention issues call for women's rights	

Seneca Falls NY

PREVIEW

Focus on the Main Idea
Beginning in the 1830s, a spirit of reform changed life in the United States.

PLACES
Seneca Falls

PEOPLE
Frederick Douglass
William Lloyd Garrison
Sojourner Truth
Lucretia Mott
Elizabeth Cady Stanton

VOCABULARY
reform
revival
temperance
abolitionist
Seneca Falls Convention

▶ Elizabeth Cady Stanton spoke at the first women's rights convention.

416

The Struggle for Reforms

You Are There It is the summer morning of Wednesday, July 19, 1848. You are part of a crowd heading for Wesleyan Chapel in Seneca Falls, New York. There you will witness the first women's rights convention ever held in the United States.

More than a hundred people—women and men—file into the rows of seats. A spirit of change fills the air here, and throughout the country.

One of the two women who called this convention, Elizabeth Cady Stanton, rises to speak. "We have met here today to…declare our right to be free…to be represented in the government…[to] demand our right to vote." These words will inspire people throughout the country.

 Compare and Contrast As you read, contrast conditions in the United States with the ways people wanted to change these conditions.

Practice and Extend

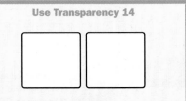

READING SKILL
Compare/Contrast

In the Lesson Review, students complete a graphic organizer like the one below. You may want to provide students with a copy of Transparency 14 to complete as they read the lesson.

Use Transparency 14	

VOCABULARY
Word Exercise

Related Word Study Write the word *revival* on the board. Tell students that this word literally means "bringing back to life." This word comes from the Latin *re-,* "again" and *vivere,* "to live." There are many words that come from *vivere,* including *vivacious, survive, convivial, vital,* and *vitamin.* Have students look up these words, then discuss how knowing the root *vivere* can help them remember what these words mean.

The Second Great Awakening

A spirit of **reform,** or change, began sweeping the country in the early 1800s. This movement grew out of a new awakening of religious feeling. The movement was called the Second Great Awakening. Like the first Great Awakening of a century earlier, this one stirred Americans to examine religion in their lives.

Camp meetings, like the one shown on this page, drew hundreds of people. The meetings were called **revivals,** because they revived, or brought back and strengthened, people's religious feelings. In the 1830s, Christian preachers like Charles G. Finney spoke to these gatherings for many hours. Finney demanded that his listeners accept "a new life of the spirit." His sermons were so fiery that the area where he preached, in central and western New York State, came to be called the "Burned-Over District."

Many became convinced that religion could make them better people. Once they became better people, they hoped to make life better for others too. In this way, they believed, they could create a better country.

The Second Great Awakening brought in the nation's first great era of reform. Some reformers attacked what they considered bad behavior, like gambling and drinking alcohol. Wives especially opposed alcohol, since husbands who drank heavily often treated their families badly. A major crusade to stop the drinking of alcohol began. It was called the **temperance** movement. Temperance means moderation. People in the temperance movement urged others to drink only small amounts of alcohol or none at all.

Reformers also had other causes. As you will see, bringing an end to slavery and gaining rights for women were important reform goals.

REVIEW How did the Second Great Awakening lead to the temperance movement? *Cause and Effect*

▶ Outdoor revivals often drew large crowds.

417

2 Teach and Discuss

PAGE 417

The Second Great Awakening

🕐 *Quick Summary* In the early 1800s, people attended religious gatherings to spread the idea that the country needed to consider reforms dealing with ideas such as how people behaved and how they treated others.

1 Why was the movement called an "awakening"? Possible answer: People were reviving or "awakening" ideas about religion that had not been thought about in a while. **Draw Conclusions**

2 What did Americans believe the focus on religion would do for them? They believed that religion would make them better people, and they hoped to make life better for others too. In this way they could create a better country. **Cause and Effect**

3 What changes did reformers want to make? Possible answers: They wanted to stop bad behavior, such as drinking and gambling, bring an end to slavery, and gain women's rights. **Main Idea and Details**

✓ **REVIEW ANSWER** In addition to other things, the Second Great Awakening focused on religion and correcting the bad behavior of some people, which included drinking too much alcohol. **Cause and Effect**

ESL EXTEND LANGUAGE ESL Support

Examine Prefixes *Reform* and *revival* are vocabulary words on p. 417. Help students understand meanings of words that contain the prefix *re-*.

Beginning Tell students that in many words the prefix *re-* means again. Write the following words on the board: *rebuild, recharge, reheat, rewrite, reuse, retell.* Help students figure out the meaning of each word.

Intermediate Have students give the definition orally for each word that you write on the board as part of the "Beginning" activity.

Advanced Ask students to brainstorm *re-* words. You may want to divide students into teams to brainstorm words. Teams can challenge each other as they list words. If challenged, teams must provide definitions for their words.

For additional ESL support, use Every Student Learns Guide, pp. 174–177.

Fighting Against Slavery

🕐 **Quick Summary** Reformers in the 1830s formed a movement to abolish, or eliminate, slavery.

4 **Why were some reformers called abolitionists?** They believed that slavery should be abolished, meaning erased or eliminated forever. Main Idea and Details

Primary Source

Cited in a speech by Frederick Douglass.

5 **What does Douglass mean when he says he stole his own body?** Possible answer: As a slave he was owned by another person. When he ran away, it was as if he was stealing himself from the slaveowner. Analyze Primary Sources

✓ Ongoing Assessment

If... students have difficulties understanding the quote as it relates to slavery,

then... focus on the idea of ownership and relate it to how people now have the freedom to move about as they please, but that in the time of slavery, they could not.

6 **What are two ideas or causes that Sojourner Truth spoke about?** Abolishing slavery and women's rights Main Idea and Details

✓ REVIEW ANSWER They formed anti-slavery groups, printed newspapers, and found speakers for speaking trips who had experienced slavery firsthand. Cause and Effect

Fighting Against Slavery

In the North, anti-slavery groups had formed as early as the Revolution. Colonial leaders such as Benjamin Franklin, Abigail Adams, and Benjamin Rush were members of such groups. Delegates to the Constitutional Convention had argued about ending slavery. Years later, John Quincy Adams, sixth President of the United States, wrote a poem that included these words: "nature's God commands the slave to rise…till not a slave shall on this earth be found."

In the 1830s, the movement to end slavery took on new life. Reformers attacked slavery as an evil that had to be erased, or abolished. Called **abolitionists,** these
4 reformers made speeches and printed newspapers to spread their message.

Frederick Douglass was a powerful and eloquent voice for the abolitionists. Born into slavery in Maryland, Douglass had escaped to New York City in 1838 by posing as a free sailor. Soon, he was traveling around the North on speaking trips for the Massachusetts Anti-Slavery Society. In one speech he said:

5 *"I appear before [you] this evening as a thief and a robber. I stole this head, these limbs, this body from my master and ran off with them."*

Douglass's stories of his own experiences as a slave—of merciless beatings and near starvation—won many supporters for the abolitionist movement. You will read more about Douglass in the Citizen Heroes feature on page 422.

In 1831 in Boston, **William Lloyd Garrison** started an abolitionist newspaper, *The*

▶ Abolitionist William Lloyd Garrison declared that his newspaper, *The Liberator*, would never stop fighting against slavery in the United States.

Liberator. Garrison condemned slavery loudly and clearly, writing: "I will be as harsh as truth and as uncompromising as justice. On this subject, I do not wish to think, or speak, or write, with moderation….and I will be heard!"

Another tireless abolitionist, **Sojourner Truth,** was born into slavery in New York State in the late 1700s. She escaped and became a preacher. She adopted the name Sojourner Truth to make clear her mission— to sojourn, or travel, spreading the truth. Though she could not read or write, Sojourner Truth could quote the Bible to convince listeners of the evils of slavery. She also preached in support of women's rights. You will read more about Sojourner Truth in the Biography feature following this lesson.

REVIEW How did abolitionists raise support for their movement? Cause and Effect

Practice and Extend

FYI **SOCIAL STUDIES** **Background**

More About William Lloyd Garrison

- William Lloyd Garrison believed in the principle called "immediate emancipation," which called for the immediate return of free blacks to Africa.
- Through his newspaper, *The Liberator*, Garrison became known as a radical supporter of the anti-slavery movement.
- Garrison helped establish the American Anti-Slavery Society, which began to support other reform efforts, such as women's rights.
- As Garrison's views became more radical, many of the conservative members of the Anti-Slavery Society left to form their own group. Part of their reason for leaving was their opposition to Garrison's allowing women to join the Anti-Slavery Society.

Women's Rights

Women in the early 1800s had few rights. For example, married women could not own property. Anything they owned when single immediately became the property of their husbands after marriage. Women were not allowed to vote, and most colleges did not accept women.

Many women of the time were active in reform movements. For example, **Lucretia Mott** and her friend **Elizabeth Cady Stanton** worked hard for both temperance and abolition. But when they went to London to attend an anti-slavery convention in 1840, they were forbidden to speak or to take any part in it. As women, all they could do was sit in the balcony and watch.

In 1848, Mott and Stanton decided to take a stand for women's rights by calling a convention in **Seneca Falls,** New York, which you read about in You Are There. At the **Seneca Falls Convention,** Stanton presented a Declaration of Sentiments based on the Declaration of Independence. In it she stated:

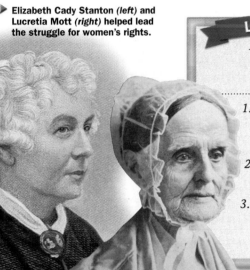

▶ Elizabeth Cady Stanton *(left)* and Lucretia Mott *(right)* helped lead the struggle for women's rights.

"We hold these truths to be self-evident: that all men and women are created equal..."

Both women and men at the convention went on to debate a series of resolutions, or statements, of the rights women should have. You can read some of these below. At the end, 68 women and 32 men signed the Declaration. Frederick Douglass was among the signers. Though Sojourner Truth did not attend, she soon began traveling to support women's rights.

Much of the press attacked the convention. One newspaper said, "A woman is a nobody." Many others claimed women were unfit for citizenship. But Stanton was pleased that the press at least reported on the convention. "Imagine the publicity given to our ideas," she said. "It will start women thinking, and men too."

REVIEW How would you summarize the rights that women lacked in the 1800s? *Summarize*

Literature and Social Studies

These are a few of the resolutions from the Seneca Falls Convention. What rights do they want?

1. All laws which...place [woman] in a position inferior to that of man...[have] no force or authority.

2. Woman is man's equal—was intended to be so by the Creator.

3. It is the duty of women in this country to secure to themselves their sacred right to elective franchise [the right to vote].

419

Women's Rights

🕐 *Quick Summary* Reformers in the mid-1800s took a stand for women's rights.

7 What event do you think influenced Mott and Stanton's decision to organize the Seneca Falls Convention? At the anti-slavery convention they attended in London, they were not allowed to speak or take part in any way. **Cause and Effect**

8 What happened at the Seneca Falls Convention? Stanton presented the Declaration of Sentiments. **Main Idea and Details**

9 Why do you think Frederick Douglass signed the Declaration? Possible answer: He knew what it was like to be denied rights and wanted to help the cause. **Draw Conclusions**

10 Why was Stanton pleased even though the newspapers printed negative things about the convention? Any publicity would help spread the convention's ideas and make people start thinking. **Main Idea and Details**

✓ **REVIEW ANSWER** They lacked the right to own property when married, to equal education, and to vote. **Summarize**

Literature and Social Studies

11 How are these resolutions like the ideas written in the Declaration of Independence? They talk about equality and the rights of people. **Compare and Contrast**

MEETING INDIVIDUAL NEEDS
Leveled Practice

Interpret a Document Have students summarize some of the ideas in the Declaration of Sentiments.

Easy Ask students to write a sentence that tells why women wrote the Declaration of Sentiments. **Reteach**

On-Level Have students write a brief summary of what some of the resolutions in the Declaration of Sentiments say. **Extend**

Challenge Ask students to rewrite some of the resolutions in their own words. **Enrich**

For a Lesson Summary, use Quick Study, p. 88.

The Spirit of Reform

Quick Summary Reformers focused on several social conditions that needed changing.

 **Why did Horace Mann fight for reforms in the educational system?** He believed that if people were educated they would not remain in poverty.
Main Idea and Details

How were prisoners like slaves? Both were treated poorly.
Compare and Contrast

✓ **REVIEW ANSWER** Possible answer: Public institutions must end cruel treatment of patients. **Draw Conclusions**

3 Close and Assess

Summarize the Lesson

Have students write sentences about facts they learned in the lesson, substituting a blank for a key word in each sentence. Have students take turns reading their sentences, while others write the word that completes the fact.

✓ **LESSON 3   REVIEW**

1. ⟳ **Compare and Contrast** For possible answers, see the reduced pupil page.

2. Movements to reduce the drinking of alcohol, to abolish slavery, to gain equal rights for women, to promote public education, to improve treatment of prisoners and the mentally ill

3. Both were African Americans, born into slavery, and fought to abolish slavery.

4. Unlike men, women could not vote or go to college. Also, married women could not own property.

5. **Critical Thinking:** *Make Inferences* Possible answer: They may have disagreed with any conditions or treatment that violated human rights.

Link to ⊶ Art

Posters should include a message that relates to the chosen cause.

The Spirit of Reform

In the first half of the 1800s, reformers identified a number of conditions in the United States that needed changing. In addition to slavery and the unequal treatment of women, these included a poor educational system, very bad living conditions in prisons, and the terrible treatment of mentally ill people.

In Massachusetts, Horace Mann believed that education was a way to fight poverty. Education, he said, could produce "intelligent and practical men" who would not remain poor. So Mann led the way in expanding public education. He got the school year in Massachusetts extended to at least six months. He also established more high schools and improved teacher training.

Also in Massachusetts, Dorothea Dix investigated the prisons and insane asylums of the state. Her findings exposed horrible conditions that needed reform. The mentally ill, Dix found, were "beaten with rods" and "lashed into obedience."

Few reforms came quickly. Many would take decades to accomplish. But the reformers carried on their work.

REVIEW What conclusions do you think readers of Dorothea Dix's reports drew from them? **Draw Conclusions**

Summarize the Lesson

— **1830s** The Second Great Awakening stirred a spirit of reform.

— **1838** The fight to end slavery gained a powerful speaker when Frederick Douglass escaped slavery and became a leader of the abolition movement.

— **1848** The movement for women's rights was launched at a convention in Seneca Falls, New York.

LESSON 3   REVIEW

Check Facts and Main Ideas

1. ⟳ **Compare and Contrast** On a separate sheet of paper, fill in the "Goals" box to compare problems in the United States with goals of reformers.

Problems		Goals
• Slavery • Women did not have equal rights with men.		• Abolitionists fought for the end of slavery. • The Seneca Falls Convention called for equal rights for women.

2. What **reform** movements were produced by the Second Great Awakening?

3. What did Frederick Douglass and Sojourner Truth have in common?

4. Compare the rights of men and women in the early 1800s.

5. **Critical Thinking:** *Make Inferences* Why might many reformers have worked for—or at least supported—several different reforms?

Link to ⊶ Art

Draw a Poster You are a supporter of one of the reforms you read about in this lesson. Choose a reform and draw a poster that you use to tell others about your cause.

Practice and Extend

 CURRICULUM CONNECTION Music

Interpret Lyrics

• Have students use library or online resources to research anti-slavery and abolitionist music that was created in the 1800s.

• If possible, students should locate some lyrics and interpret the meaning.

Workbook, p. 97

Lesson 3: The Struggle for Reforms

Directions: Complete the organizer with terms from the box. Write a brief description on the lines provided.

Abolitionists	Revivals
Attack on Bad Behavior	Seneca Falls Convention
Fight Against Slavery	Temperance
Religion	Women's Rights

An Era of Reform

Notes for Home: Your child learned about the spirit of reform in the United States in the 1800s. Home Activity: With your child, discuss government's attempts to make political and social reforms in the United States today. What are the goals of these efforts to enact change?

Also on Teacher Resources CD-ROM.

Sojourner Truth

about 1797–1883

Sojourner Truth was born into slavery in New York State with the name Isabella. When she was nine years old she was taken from her parents and sold to a new slaveowner. Later she said of this time, "Now the war began." (She meant that without her family, her life became even more difficult.)

She became hopeful when a new law in New York in 1817 said that enslaved people older than twenty-eight would be freed. Her owner, John Dumont, promised that if she worked especially hard, she would be freed in 1826, one year early. Sojourner Truth worked long hours, even when she cut her hand badly and it did not heal well. However, at the end of 1826 her owner broke his promise and refused to free her.

This was more than Sojourner Truth could take. At dawn, she left the farm where she had been enslaved and escaped to freedom.

In 1843, she changed her name to Sojourner Truth, because "sojourn" means "travel," and she believed that her purpose was to travel the country preaching about God and the injustices of slavery. To begin one of her most famous speeches, she sang a hymn that she had created. One of the verses said:

"I am pleading that my people
May have their rights restored;
For they have long been toiling,
And yet have no reward."

Learn from Biographies

Reread the hymn verse that Sojourner Truth sang. In your own words, what do you think she was trying to say?

For more information, go online to *Meet the People* at **www.sfsocialstudies.com.**

421

 ★ B I O G R A P H Y ★

Sojourner Truth

Objectives

- Describe the historical movements that influenced the development of the United States.

- Name major historical figures such as Sojourner Truth, and describe their involvement in the development of the United States.

- Analyze the diverse cultures that have contributed to the heritage of the United States.

1 Introduce and Motivate

Preview Ask students to recall what causes Sojourner Truth supported. Tell students they will read about her life and find out why she spoke out against injustices.

2 Teach and Discuss

1 Why did Truth work long, hard hours for John Dumont? He promised to free her if she did this. Main Idea and Details

2 What effect did Dumont's lie have on Truth? It caused her to escape from slavery. Cause and Effect

3 Close and Assess

Learn from Biographies Answer

Possible answer: It was wrong to force people to work so hard for nothing in return.

Exposing Slavery's Evils

Objectives

- Describe the historical movements that influenced the development of the United States.

- Name major historical figures, such as Frederick Douglass, and describe their involvement in the development of the United States.

- Analyze the diverse cultures that have contributed to the heritage of the United States.

1 Introduce and Motivate

Preview To activate prior knowledge, have students tell about people they have heard of who fought for fairness and justice.

2 Teach and Discuss

1 What made Frederick Douglass different from white abolitionists? He had been a slave and could speak about slavery from personal experience.
Compare and Contrast

2 Why did some people think Douglass was a fake? He spoke so well that some people could not believe he had been a slave. **Main Idea and Details**

CITIZEN HEROES

Exposing Slavery's Evils

He lived the first twenty years of his life in slavery. But Frederick Douglass escaped to tell his own story and to fight for fair treatment for all people and an end to slavery.

The speaker was a tall African American. His voice boomed out over the crowd as he held up his hands. "These hands—are they not mine?" he asked. "This body—is it not mine?" But, he said, "I'm still a slave and the bloodhound may chase me down." The hundreds of people attending the American Anti-Slavery Convention listened closely to his every word.

The speaker was Frederick Douglass. Three years before, in 1838, he had escaped slavery in Maryland and fled to the North. Like many abolitionists, Frederick Douglass believed deeply that slavery was wrong. Yet, unlike the white abolitionists, Douglass could speak about slavery from firsthand experience—and he spoke powerfully. In fact, Frederick Douglass spoke so well that some people began to accuse him of being a fake. "How could such an expressive man actually have been a slave?" some asked. Both to prove doubters wrong and expose the horrors of slavery, Frederick Douglass wrote his own story. His book, *Narrative of the Life of Frederick Douglass: An American Slave,* was published in 1845 and became an immediate success.

People were shocked to read about how slaves were treated. As a boy, Douglass said, he

422

Practice and Extend

**SOCIAL STUDIES
Background**

About Frederick Douglass

- Frederick Douglass, born into slavery as Frederick Bailey, lived with his grandmother on a plantation in Maryland. He was sent to the Auld family's house in Baltimore when he was 8 years old.

- Mrs. Auld taught Douglass to read, but she had to stop the lessons when Mr. Auld stated that learning would make Douglass unfit for slavery.

- After that Douglass continued learning with the help of schoolboys around the neighborhood and in the streets.

- When Douglass was 16, the plantation master died, and Douglass was sent back to the Maryland plantation to work as a field hand.

- Douglass first tried to escape in 1833, but the attempt failed. Five years later he ran away first to New York City and then to New Bedford, Massachusetts. He changed his name to Douglass to avoid slave hunters.

BUILDING
CITIZENSHIP
Caring
Respect
Responsibility
Fairness
Honesty
Courage

only had one shirt to wear throughout the cold winters and often did not have enough to eat. He saw his aunt beaten severely. When he was older, a cruel owner whipped him with tree branches until his back was bloody.

Some owners treated him better. A woman in Baltimore began to teach him how to read. But Douglass always hated being someone else's property. He told of looking at boats on the Chesapeake River and thinking:

> *"You move merrily before the gentle gale [wind], and I sadly before the bloody whip... O that I were free!... Why am I a slave?... I will not stand it.... God helping me...It cannot be that I shall live and die a slave."*

When he was twenty, Douglass escaped to New York. He gave thousands of speeches and wrote articles and three autobiographies. In 1847, he started his own anti-slavery newspaper, called *The North Star*. Frederick Douglass's fight against the unfairness of slavery inspired many people to join the fight to abolish it. Today his powerful words continue to inspire people seeking freedom and fairness around the world.

NARRATIVE
OF THE
LIFE
OF
FREDERICK DOUGLASS,
AN
AMERICAN SLAVE.

WRITTEN BY HIMSELF.

THE NORTH STAR

Fairness in Action

Research a situation in a part of the world today where people are treated unfairly because of their color or ethnic background. Write a short speech about the situation, making the speech as powerful as you can. Give facts to support your position.

423

③ **How did people react to Frederick Douglass's book?** They were shocked to learn that slaves were treated so badly.
Main Idea and Details

Primary Source

Cited in *Narrative of the Life of Frederick Douglass, An American Slave, Written by Himself,* by Frederick Douglass

④ **What does Douglass use as symbols of freedom and slavery in this quote?**
Freedom: ship moving in the wind;
Slavery: a bloody whip
Analyze Primary Sources

SOCIAL STUDIES STRAND
Citizenship

Prejudice Reduction Frederick Douglass dedicated his life to the emancipation of enslaved persons and obtaining voting rights and other civil liberties for African Americans and women.

⑤ **How was Frederick Douglass's life an example of fairness?** He fought for the fair treatment of all people.
Draw Conclusions

3 Close and Assess

Fairness in Action

- Encourage students to share the results of their research.

- Encourage students to explain why the treatment is unfair and to suggest what should be done about it.

CURRICULUM CONNECTION
Literature

Frederick Douglass

Frederick Douglass, by John Passaro (Child's World, ISBN 1-567-66621-3, 1999) **Easy**

Escape to Freedom: A Play About Young Frederick Douglass, by Ossie Davis (Penguin Putnam, ISBN 0-140-34355-5, 1990) **On-Level**

Frederick Douglass: Freedom's Force, by Melva Lawson Ware (Time-Life, ISBN 0-783-55437-0, 1999) **Challenge**

Nineteenth-Century Reform Movements

Objectives

- Use primary sources, such as visual materials, to learn about the past.

- Identify the ideals expressed in the Declaration of Independence.

- Identify groups of people excluded from the promise of the ideals of the Declaration of Independence and the nineteenth-century reform movements that worked to correct those omissions.

1 Introduce and Motivate

- Remind students that the Declaration of Independence was written in 1776. It proclaimed America's independence from Great Britain. It also established the idea in America that there was equality for all, but many Americans were neither free nor considered equal. Nineteenth-century reformers worked to correct those injustices.

- Review with students the wide variety of reform movements in the 1800s, including anti-slavery, temperance, women's suffrage, and education reform.

- Have students look back over pages 416–423 and make a list of groups that were denied freedom and/or equality at the time of the Declaration of Independence.

2 Teach and Discuss

H | SOCIAL STUDIES STRAND
History

- **The Declaration of Independence**
Explain to students that this founding document established the ideal of liberty and equality for all Americans, but it was nineteenth-century reformers—engaged citizens concerned about their country—who made the ideal a reality.

Ideals of the 19th-Century Reformers

The Declaration of Independence promised liberty and equality for all Americans. However, many people still were not treated equally after it was signed. Women did not have the same rights as men. Many African Americans were slaves. Most children did not go to school, and many worked in fields and shops. People of the nineteenth century reform movements worked to change these conditions.

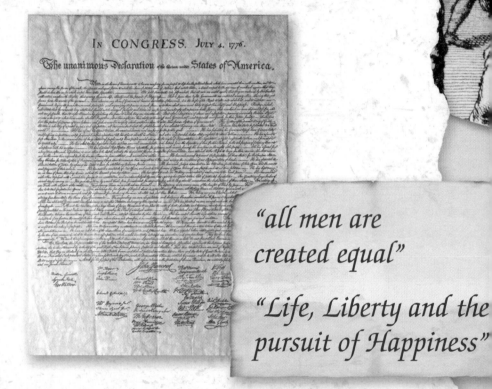

"all men are created equal"

"Life, Liberty and the pursuit of Happiness"

424

Practice and Extend

FYI | SOCIAL STUDIES
Background

Citizen Reformers *by Dr. William E. White, Colonial Williamsburg Historian*

- In early American society, many individuals were neither free nor equal. Reformers of the early nineteenth-century actively worked to correct some of these injustices.

- The U.S. Constitution was adopted in 1789. The first ten amendments, the Bill of Rights, were designed to guarantee basic rights and privileges for every citizen.

- Throughout our history, individuals and groups of citizens have influenced our lawmakers to amend the Constitution and craft new laws that extend freedom and equality to all Americans.

- Citizens have always been this country's reformers. As Supreme Court Justice Felix Frankfurter said, "In a democracy, the highest office is the office of citizen." By working in our communities and taking part in our government, we help extend the promise of freedom and equality to all.

dren who were not from wealthy
[fami]lies often did not get a formal
[edu]cation. Reformers worked to give all
[Ame]ricans the right to an education. The
[cha]nges these reformers started grew
[into] our modern public-school system.
[The] first law requiring children
[to at]tend school was passed in
[Mas]sachusetts in 1852. That
[was] 76 years after the Declaration
[of In]dependence. ▶

It was legal for African Americans to be
enslaved from the time they first arrived in
North America in the 1600s. The Declaration
of Independence did not change this. African
American reformers made speeches and
printed newspapers to protest slavery and
unfair treatment. In 1865, the Thirteenth
Amendment to the Constitution ended slavery
in the United States. That was 89 years after
the Declaration of Independence. ▼

[Chil]dren as young as seven had to work in early
[Am]erica. They worked on farms and in factories.
[Ref]ormers worked throughout the nineteenth century
[to s]top child labor. Finally, in 1938 Congress passed
[the] Fair Labor Standards Act. It set eighteen as the
[you]ngest age for factory workers. That was 162 years
[afte]r the Declaration of Independence.

▲

Women's rights were not the same as men's. They could not
vote. Married women could not own property. Women became
more active in politics as the reform movement began. They
helped create groups against slavery. They acted in support of
the temperance movement. Women also wanted to vote, but
their right to vote was not granted until 1920. That was 144
years after the Declaration of Independence.

The Declaration of Independence promised liberty and equality for all
Americans. We still work today to make sure this promise is kept.
Think of a group that you feel is not treated equally today. In a
well-organized paragraph, identify the problem and the things you or
others could do to change it.

425

CURRICULUM CONNECTION
Art

- Medallions, like the Anti-Slavery Medallion, were worn and displayed by people to show their opinion on certain issues.
- Help students review the list they created of groups of people who may not be treated equally today.
- Have students create their own reformer's medallion in support of an issue they believe would advance the freedom and equality of Americans.

Workbook, p. 98

Writing Prompt: Making Changes
Throughout the nineteenth century, reformers worked to stop child labor. Finally, in 1938 Congress passed the Fair Labor Standards Act. It set 18 as the youngest age for factory workers. Do you think children should be allowed to work? Write about reasons you agree or disagree with the reformers.

Notes for Home: Your child learned about different reform movements.
Home Activity: With your child, discuss how life might be different today for women and African Americans if people had not worked to gain equal rights.

Also on Teacher Resources CD-ROM.

- **Children's Book:** *Entertaining Fables for the Instruction of Children* This book was published in Scotland in 1789. Early Americans believed education was essential in a democratic society. Ask students to discuss why reformers believed education was important.

- **Anti-Slavery Medallion: "Am I Not a Man and a Brother?"** This ceramic medallion, manufactured by Josiah Wedgewood in Staffordshire, England, in 1787, was worn by Englishmen and Americans who opposed the slave trade. It depicts a slave in chains pleading for his freedom. Ask students how medallions, pins, and buttons are used today to show opinions.

- **Engraving: "Keep Within Compass..."** This engraving, published by Robert Dighton, in London, England in 1785, urges women to remain as homemakers. Ask students how nineteenth-century women worked to change their roles in society.

- **Engraving of a Blacksmith's Shop** This illustration appeared in Diderot's *Encyclopédie,* published in France in 1751. Have students use the engraving to interpret the demands of blacksmithing. Ask them why reformers wanted to stop child labor.

3 Close and Assess

- Have students review the reform movements about which they have learned. Discuss the characteristics of the leaders and methods they used that made those movements successful.

- Help students make a list of groups of people who may not be treated equally today. Have them select one and write a paragraph describing what steps they, or others, might take to make equality a reality for that group.

Resources

- Assessment Book, pp. 69–72
- Workbook, p. 99: Vocabulary Review

Chapter Summary

For possible answers, see the reduced pupil page.

Vocabulary

1. b, **2.** d, **3.** e, **4.** c, **5.** a

People and Events

Possible answers:

1. An Era of Good Feelings describes the time when there was little disagreement over national issues.

2. The Monroe Doctrine was a warning to European nations against interfering with countries in the Western Hemisphere.

3. Sequoyah was a Cherokee leader who developed an alphabet for the Cherokee language.

4. The Indian Removal Act ordered that all Native Americans of the southeastern states had to be moved west of the Mississippi River into Indian Territory.

5. The Industrial Revolution was a time when the invention of machines helped produce goods much faster and more cheaply than before.

6. Eli Whitney created a cotton gin, a machine that could clean 50 times as much cotton than by hand.

7. Robert Fulton designed the *Clermont*, the first riverboat that was powered by a steam engine.

8. The Erie Canal, opened in 1825, connected the Great Lakes to the Hudson River and the Atlantic Ocean, providing a water route between New York City and the Midwest.

9. Lucretia Mott, an abolitionist and a fighter for women's rights, helped organize the Seneca Falls Convention.

10. The Seneca Falls Convention was the first women's rights convention held in the United States.

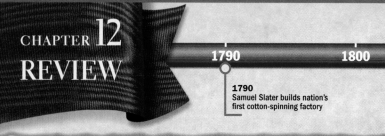

1790	1800	1810

1790 Samuel Slater builds nation's first cotton-spinning factory

1811 Construction begins on National Road

Chapter Summary

Target Skill

Compare and Contrast

On a separate sheet of paper, copy the graphic organizer to compare and contrast the United States before and after the 1820s. Include information about these two topics: suffrage and technology.

Before 1820s	After 1820s
· Suffrage was granted mainly to white men who owned property. · Goods were made by hand and moved by horses.	· Most white men could vote, whether they owned property or not. · Goods were made by machine and moved by steamboats and locomotives.

Vocabulary

Match each word with the correct definition or description.

1 nationalism (p. 403)

2 suffrage (p. 404)

3 cotton gin (p. 410)

4 mechanical reaper (p. 410)

5 abolitionist (p. 418)

a. reformer who fought against slavery

b. people pulling together with a sense of pride in their country

c. machine to harvest grain

d. the right to vote

e. machine to clean cotton

People and Events

Write a sentence explaining why each of the following people or events was important in the development of a growing nation. You may use two or more in a single sentence.

1 Era of Good Feelings (p. 403)

2 Monroe Doctrine (p. 403)

3 Sequoyah (p. 405)

4 Indian Removal Act (p. 405)

5 Industrial Revolution (p. 409)

6 Eli Whitney (p. 410)

7 Robert Fulton (p. 411)

8 Erie Canal (p. 411)

9 Lucretia Mott (p. 419)

10 Seneca Falls Convention (p. 419)

Practice and Extend

Assessment Options

✓ Chapter 12 Assessment

- Chapter 12 Content Test: Use Assessment Book, pp. 69–70.
- Chapter 12 Skills Test: Use Assessment Book, pp. 71–72.

Standardized Test Prep

- Chapter 12 Tests contain standardized test format.

✓ Chapter 12 Performance Assessment

- Have students present the beliefs of the people highlighted in the chapter.
- Each student can play the role of one of these people: Andrew Jackson, John Ross, Samuel Slater, Eli Whitney, Robert Fulton, Peter Cooper, Elizabeth Cady Stanton, Frederick Douglass, Sojourner Truth, and Lucretia Mott. Students should mention their roles in the changes of the early 1800s.
- Assess students' understanding of the people and their effects on life in the early 1800s.

1820	1830	1840	1850

1823
Monroe
Doctrine is
claimed

1825
The Erie
Canal is
completed

1828
Andrew
Jackson is
elected
President

1830
Peter Cooper develops
first United States
locomotive

1838
Trail of Tears
begins

1848
Seneca Falls
Convention issues call
for women's rights

Apply Skills

Read a Cross-Section Diagram

Study the cross-section diagram of a modern locomotive. Then answer the questions.

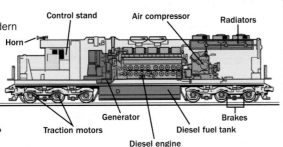

1 How do you know this is a cross-section diagram?

2 What information does it give you?

3 What is the generator connected to?

Facts and Main Ideas

Why did the United States send Andrew Jackson to Florida in 1817?

What invention led to the increase in cotton production?

Time Line How many years were there between the beginning of the National Road and the completion of the Erie Canal?

Main Idea In what ways did the United States expand its territory and power during the 1820s and 1830s?

Main Idea What important changes in the ways Americans lived and worked occurred as a result of the Industrial Revolution?

Main Idea Name three important movements started by reformers in the 1800s and describe their goals.

Critical Thinking: *Draw Conclusions* Why do you think Jackson was called "the People's President"?

Write About History

1 **Write a letter** that a soldier witnessing the Trail of Tears might have written to his family.

2 **Write a journal entry** of a young factory worker describing the activities of the day.

3 **Write a newspaper article** reporting on the events that took place at the Seneca Falls Convention.

Internet Activity

To get help with vocabulary, people, and terms, select dictionary or encyclopedia from *Social Studies Library* at www.sfsocialstudies.com.

427

Hands-on Unit Project

✓ **Unit 6 Performance Assessment**

- See p. 454 for information about using the Unit Project as a means of performance assessment.
- A scoring guide is provided on p. 454.

WEB SITE
Technology

For more information, students can select the dictionary or encyclopedia from *Social Studies Library* at www.sfsocialstudies.com.

Workbook, p. 99

Vocabulary Review

Directions: Circle the term that best completes each sentence.

1. Thousands of people were forced to relocate following the terms of the (Seneca Falls Convention, Indian Removal Act).
2. A peaceful atmosphere existed in the United States during the (Era of Good Feelings, Monroe Doctrine).
3. The (cotton gin, revival) increased workers' daily production tremendously.
4. Modern (technology, reform) has created many jobs.
5. Goods were sent on the (Trail of Tears, canal) to get to market.
6. The (Monroe Doctrine, Indian Removal Act) showed foreign powers that the United States was willing to fight for its land.
7. A Wednesday evening (revival, reform) was a popular function at many houses of worship.
8. The Second Great Awakening movement supported social (temperance, reform).
9. The (Seneca Falls Convention, Industrial Revolution) introduced an era of machine-made goods.
10. Many women who supported (temperance, technology) tried to stop the drinking of alcohol.
11. The invention of machines helped businesses (manufacture, reform) goods on a wide scale.
12. Frederick Douglass, a former slave, was an outspoken (mechanical reaper, abolitionist).
13. Many people died along the (Trail of Tears, Industrial Revolution).
14. The (revival, Seneca Falls Convention) in New York supported women's rights.
15. Women and minorities had to fight for (suffrage, temperance).
16. Independence Day celebrations reflect a spirit of (reform, nationalism) in the United States.
17. The (Era of Good Feelings, mechanical reaper) made it easier for farm workers to harvest wheat.

Notes for Home: Your child learned about changes that Americans wanted to make to improve their lives.
Home Activity: Review with your child how changes in the 1800s affect our life today.

**Also on Teacher
Resources CD-ROM.**

Apply Skills

1. Possible answer: It shows a train as if it has been cut in half.

2. It shows the location of certain parts of a modern locomotive.

3. The diesel engine

Facts and Main Ideas

1. To stop the Seminole raids from Florida into Georgia; to stop enslaved people from escaping to freedom by joining the Seminoles in Florida

2. The cotton gin

3. 14 years

4. The United States acquired Florida and encouraged people to move onto Native American lands; it increased its power by defeating Spanish forces and issuing the Monroe Doctrine.

5. People were using more machines to increase production on farms and in factories, many people were moving into cities to work in factories, and new ways developed to move people and goods on roads, waterways, and railroads.

6. Possible answer: The temperance movement to decrease alcohol consumption; the abolitionist movement to end slavery; the women's rights movement to gain equal rights for women

7. Unlike the first six Presidents, Jackson was from a poor pioneer family. He won the support of many white voters without much money or property.

Write About History

1. Students should consider the feelings of the Native Americans and the conditions under which they were forced to live.

2. Students might describe the crowded conditions in which the people lived and worked and the low compensation they received.

3. Students should accurately describe the events at the convention.

Chapter 12 • Review **427**

Chapter Planning Guide

Chapter 13 • People Moving South and West

Locating Time and Place pp. 428–429

Lesson Titles	Pacing	Main Ideas
Lesson 1 **Settling the South and Texas** pp. 430–436	2 days	• American settlers pushed south and west, while a revolution in Texas and a war with Mexico expanded the borders of the United States.
Biography: James K. Polk p. 437		• James K. Polk was an expansionist president who supported annexing Texas, settled Oregon's border with Britain, and gained land from Mexico.
Lesson 2 **Trails to the West** pp. 438–441	1 day	• Using a network of trails, people moved west to make better lives for themselves.
Lesson 3 **The Golden State** pp. 442–445	2 days	• The discovery of gold in California led to rapid settlement of the region.
Thinking Skills: **Evaluate Advertisements** pp. 446–447		• It is important to evaluate advertisements to make good decisions about the products or ideas they promote.

✓ **Chapter 13 Review**
pp. 448–449

◀ **Thousands of people came west to California in search of gold nuggets like these.**

✓ **= Assessment Options**

The Alamo in San Antonio ▶ played an important role in the history of Texas.

Vocabulary	Resources	Meeting Individual Needs
Texas Revolution annex manifest destiny Mexican War Bear Flag Revolt Treaty of Guadalupe Hidalgo	• Workbook, p. 101 • Transparencies 13, 49 • Every Student Learns Guide, pp. 178–181 • Quick Study, pp. 90–91	• Leveled Practice, TE p. 433 • ESL Support, TE p. 436
mountain men wagon train	• Workbook, p. 102 • Transparency 6 • Every Student Learns Guide, pp. 182–185 • Quick Study, pp. 92–93	• ESL Support, TE p. 439 • Leveled Practice, TE p. 441
gold rush forty-niners discrimination advertisement evaluate	• Workbook, p. 103 • Transparency 14 • Every Student Learns Guide, pp. 186–189 • Quick Study, pp. 94–95 • Workbook, p. 104	• ESL Support, TE p. 443 • Leveled Practice, TE p. 444
	✓ Chapter 13 Content Test, Assessment Book, pp. 73–74 ✓ Chapter 13 Skills Test, Assessment Book, pp. 75–76	✓ Chapter 13 Performance Assessment, TE p. 448

Providing More Depth

Additional Resources

• Vocabulary Workbook and Cards
• Social Studies Plus! pp. 150–155
• Daily Activity Bank
• Big Book Atlas
• Student Atlas
• Outline Maps
• Desk Maps

 Technology

• AudioText
• MindPoint® Quiz Show CD-ROM
• ExamView® Test Bank CD-ROM
• Teacher Resources CD-ROM
• Map Resources CD-ROM
• SFSuccessNet: iText (Pupil Edition online), iTE (Teacher's Edition online), Online Planner
• **www.sfsocialstudies.com** (Biographies, news, references, maps, and activities)

 To establish guidelines for your students' safe and responsible use of the Internet, use the Scott Foresman Internet Guide.

Additional Internet Links

To find out more about:

• The Alamo, visit **www.thealamo.org**
• Oregon Country and the Oregon Trail, visit **www.isu.edu**
• The California Gold Rush, visit **www.museumca.org**

Key Internet Search Terms

• James K. Polk
• Mexican War
• Oregon Trail
• California Trail

Workbook Support

 Use the following Workbook pages to support content and skills development as you teach Chapter 13. You can also view and print Workbook pages from the Teacher Resources CD-ROM.

Workbook, p. 100

Vocabulary Preview   Use with Chapter 13.

Directions: Define each term on the lines provided. You may use your glossary.

Texas Revolution ___ **Texas settlers' fight for their independence from Mexico**

annex ___ **To add**

manifest destiny ___ **The belief that the United States should expand west to the Pacific Ocean**

Mexican War ___ **War declared with Mexico in 1846 over the United States annexation of Texas**

Bear Flag Revolt ___ **American settlers in California revolted against Mexico and declared themselves independent.**

Treaty of Guadalupe Hidalgo ___ **Officially ended the Mexican War, in February 1848**

mountain man ___ **Fur trapper in the West**

wagon train ___ **A long line of covered wagons that transported settlers to the West**

gold rush ___ **A time when people left their jobs, farms, and homes in search of riches in California**

forty-niner ___ **A person who went to California during the gold rush of 1849**

discrimination ___ **Unfair treatment**

 Notes for Home: Your child learned terms related to the expansion of United States borders around 1850.
Home Activity: Have your child use these terms to tell how westward expansion helped the United States expand its borders.

Use with Pupil Edition, p. 428

Workbook, p. 101

Lesson 1: Settling the South and Texas   Use with Pages 430–436.

Directions: Sequence the events in the order in which they took place by numbering them from 1 to 12. You may use your textbook.

5 Texas settlers decide to fight for their independence from Mexico, and in 1835 the Texas Revolution begins.

1 Spain sells Florida to the United States.

12 The Treaty of Guadalupe Hidalgo is signed, officially ending the war with Mexico.

4 Fearing a rebellion, Mexican leaders pass a law in 1830 forbidding new settlers from the United States.

2 Stephen F. Austin brings settlers to Texas, which is part of Mexico, under a land grant.

10 Mexico still thinks of Texas as part of Mexico and disagrees on the border between the United States and Mexico.

6 Texas leaders form the Republic of Texas on March 2, 1836.

8 Many Americans are against annexing Texas because it would expand slavery in the United States and could lead to war with Mexico.

9 Texas is annexed and becomes a state in 1845.

7 As an independent country, Texas faces problems such as defending itself and having no money. Many Texans want to be annexed to the United States.

3 Tensions grow between Mexico and the settlers from the United States because the settlers bring enslaved people with them to Texas.

11 Efforts to find a peaceful solution fail, and the Mexican War begins on May 13, 1846.

 Notes for Home: Your child learned about the settlement of the South and how Texas became part of the United States.
Home Activity: With your child, review the sequence of events in Lesson 1, culminating in Texas becoming a state.

Use with Pupil Edition, p. 436

Workbook, p. 102

Lesson 2: Trails to the West   Use with Pages 438–441.

Directions: Write the number from each item in Column A on the line next to its example in Column B.

Column A	Column B
1. Period between 1840–1860 when more than 350,000 people moved to Oregon Country	**7** a. wagon train
2. First settlers to Oregon Country from the United States	**11** b. Salt Lake City
3. Fur trappers in the West	**2** c. fur trappers and missionaries
4. Reason missionaries wanted to move to Oregon Country	**5** d. Oregon Trail
5. The 2,000-mile route taken to Oregon Country by settlers	**9** e. Brigham Young
6. Treaty between the United States and Britain settling the border between Canada and Oregon caused this	**1** f. Oregon fever
7. A long line of covered wagons traveling to Oregon	**10** g. The Mormon Trail
8. Followers of the Church of Jesus Christ of Latter-day Saints	**6** h. More settlers headed to Oregon Country
9. Led the Mormons to found their own religious community	**3** i. mountain men
10. Route taken by the Mormons from Illinois across the Great Plains and the Rockies	**8** j. Mormons
11. Place founded by the Mormons in present-day Utah	**4** k. teach Christian religion to Native Americans

Notes for Home: Your child learned about people moving to the West along the Oregon and Mormon Trails.
Home Activity: With your child, discuss the difficulties families encounter as they move from one place to another.

Use with Pupil Edition, p. 441

Workbook Support

Workbook, p. 103

Use with Pages 442–445.

Lesson 3: The Golden State

Directions: Fill in each missing cause or effect. You may use your textbook.

Cause		Effect
1. **Cause** Gold was discovered at Sutter's Mill in California.	→	**Effect** **The gold rush started.**
2. **Cause** **The idea of finding gold led many people to California.**	→	**Effect** The number of people in San Francisco grew rapidly from 1848 to 1850.
3. **Cause** **Prices were high for food and supplies. Many miners couldn't find gold.**	→	**Effect** Many people left California, but some stayed to become merchants who served miners.
4. **Cause** Supplies and services were scarce but in high demand. Miners were willing to pay a lot of money for things.	→	**Effect** **Businesses prospered.**
5. **Cause** **Miners wanted sturdy pants.**	→	**Effect** Levi Strauss created sturdy pants out of canvas, and then denim, for the miners.
6. **Cause** People moved from many places, including other countries, to get wealthy in the gold rush.	→	**Effect** **The population in California grew quickly and was very varied.**

 Notes for Home: Your child learned how the gold rush affected California and the people who rushed to move there.
Home Activity: With your child, discuss how your community began. Learn what businesses attracted settlers to your area and when the population expanded.

Use with Pupil Edition, p. 445

Workbook, p. 104

Use with Pages 446–447.

Evaluate Advertisements

An advertisement tries to sell people goods, services, or ideas. The purpose of all advertisement is to interest people in what the advertiser is trying to sell. Ads for women's apparel were common in the 1800s.

Directions: Read this sample advertisement, and answer the questions that follow.

WHITE SILK BONNETS ARE ELEGANT ADDITIONS TO A FINE LADY'S WARDROBE. YOU CANNOT OWN TOO MANY!

This lovely ladies' bonnet is made of cool silk, covered with white spotted tulle. The edges of the front are gently pleated, so as to give it a graceful and delicate appearance.

1. What is this advertisement selling?
   Ladies' bonnets

2. Who might be interested in this ad?
   Women and/or merchants who sell women's apparel

3. What facts are stated about the product in the advertisement?
   The materials used to make the bonnet, the design of the bonnet, and why it is shaped that way

4. What words are used to encourage people to buy this item?
   Lovely, cool, graceful, delicate, elegant, fine

5. What, if anything, in the advertisement may be an exaggeration or inaccurate?
   Possible answers: The fabric is cool, only "fine ladies" may be interested, women cannot own enough of these hats.

 Notes for Home: Your child learned how to evaluate print advertisements.
Home Activity: Evaluate product advertisements in a magazine or on television. Identify the features of the product, then analyze the sales message for accuracy or exaggerated sales claims.

Use with Pupil Edition, p. 447

Workbook, p. 105

Use with Chapter 13.

Vocabulary Review

Directions: Use the vocabulary words from Chapter 13 to complete each item. Use the numbered letters to answer the clue that follows.

1. Suffering unfair treatment **d i s c r i m i n a t i o n**
2. People from all over the country rushed to California to find riches **g o l d   r u s h**
3. A line of covered wagons traveling west **w a g o n   t r a i n**
4. Fur trapper in the West **m o u n t a i n   m a n**
5. Texas settlers' fight for independence from Mexico **T e x a s   R e v o l u t i o n**
6. Officially ended the Mexican War **T r e a t y   o f   G u a d a l u p e   H i d a l g o**
7. Revolt by settlers leaves California independent from Mexico **B e a r   F l a g   R e v o l t**
8. To add a state to the Union **a n n e x**
9. Someone who went to California during the gold rush **f o r t y - n i n e r**
10. Mexico and the United States at war over Texas **M e x i c a n   W a r**

Clue: This policy expanded the nation from coast to coast.
m a n i f e s t   d e s t i n y

 **Notes for Home:** Your child learned how California and Texas became part of the United States.
Home Activity: With your child, locate Texas and California on a map of the United States. Use the scale to calculate how far settlers traveled from the East and Midwest to start a new life in these areas.

Use with Pupil Edition, p. 449

Workbook, p. 106

UNIT 6 Project   Lure of the Land

Directions: In a group, choose a trail that settlers might have taken. Then plan a travel program to share the settlers' experiences.

1. The trail our group chose is _____
2. Some reasons settlers chose this trail:
   _____
   _____
   _____
   _____

3. The (✔) shows some of the details shown on our map:
   ___ trail we chose   ___ mountains and other major landforms
   ___ other possible trails   ___ dangers or points of interest on the trail
   ___ cities or towns   ___ compass rose
   ___ state boundaries   ___ scale
   ___ rivers and other bodies of water   ___ key

4. Other materials we will use in our presentation:
   _____   _____   _____

Once groups select a westward trail to research, you may wish to help them locate and identify appropriate source maps from which to create their project maps.

✔ Checklist for Students
___ We chose a settlers' westward trail.
___ We researched reasons travelers used this trail to journey to the West.
___ We identified some reasons the settlers chose this trail.
___ We planned the features and details for our class.
___ We identified props, costumes, sound effects, and other materials.
___ We presented our travel program to the class.

 Notes for Home: Your child learned about trails settlers used to journey to the West.
Home Activity: With your child, research how early settlers traveled to your community. From what areas did most of your first settlers come?

Use with Pupil Edition, p. 454

Assessment Support

Use these Assessment Book pages and the ExamView® Test Bank CD-ROM to assess content and skills in Chapter 13. You can also view and print Assessment Book pages from the Teacher Resources CD-ROM.

Assessment Book, p. 73

Chapter 13 Test

Part 1: Content Test

Directions: Fill in the circle next to the correct answer.

Lesson Objective (1:1)

1. How did Mexico get settlers from the United States to build ranches and farms in Texas?
   - (A) American settlers conquered the people and took the land.
   - (B) Settlers from Spanish Florida colonized the land.
   - (C) Mexico traded the land for American-made goods.
   - ● Mexico gave Moses Austin a grant of land.

Lesson Objective (1:2)

2. Which of the following was a reason United States settlers in Texas wanted their independence?
   - (A) Settlers did not believe in slavery.
   - (B) Settlers wanted to become Catholic.
   - ● Settlers wanted more say in the government.
   - (D) Settlers wanted to bring in more settlers.

Lesson Objective (1:3)

3. Which of the following represents the opinion of some who were opposed to the annexation of Texas by the United States?
   - ● Annexing Texas could lead to war with Mexico.
   - (B) Annexing Texas could lead to war with Spain.
   - (C) Annexing Texas would mean more Catholics in the United States.
   - (D) Annexing Texas would decrease the number of slaves in the United States.

Lesson Objective (1:3)

4. Why did some citizens of the United States want to annex Texas?
   - (A) freedom of religion
   - (B) to expand the cattle range
   - (C) to go to war with Mexico
   - ● manifest destiny

Lesson Objective (1:4)

5. Which of the following battles was a United States victory during the Mexican War?
   - ● Bear Flag Revolt
   - (B) Battle of the Alamo
   - (C) Battle of San Jacinto
   - (D) Nueces River Battle

Lesson Objective (2:1)

6. What is one reason early settlers moved to Oregon Country?
   - (A) to have the right to vote
   - (B) to build on free land
   - ● to teach the Christian religion to Native Americans
   - (D) to be free from paying taxes to support the war

Lesson Objective (2:1)

7. Which of the following BEST describes Oregon fever?
   - ● people eagerly seeking a new life in the West
   - (B) people suffering from a deadly disease
   - (C) people eagerly seeking to become Christians
   - (D) people seeking to find the Pacific Ocean

Assessment Book   Unit 6, Chapter 13 Test **73**

Use with Pupil Edition, p. 448

Assessment Book, p. 74

Lesson Objective (2:2)

8. Which of the following BEST describes life along the Oregon Trail?
   - (A) peaceful journey to a new life
   - ● long and difficult journey
   - (C) short but dangerous journey to freedom
   - (D) easy journey across the land

Lesson Objective (2:2)

9. How did people travel along the Oregon Trail?
   - (A) by boat
   - ● by wagon train
   - (C) by railroad
   - (D) by canal

Lesson Objective (2:3)

10. Which of the following trails did NOT take people west?
    - (A) Mormon Trail
    - (B) Santa Fe Trail
    - ● Appalachian Trail
    - (D) Old Spanish Trail

Lesson Objective (2:4)

11. What caused the Mormons to choose to move west?
    - ● They had been mistreated because of their religious beliefs.
    - (B) They were interested in settling a new land.
    - (C) They wanted to get away from crowded areas.
    - (D) They wanted to build a church.

Lesson Objective (3:1)

12. How did the gold rush affect the population of California?
    - (A) The population stayed the same.
    - (B) The population grew slowly.
    - (C) The population was reduced.
    - ● The population grew rapidly.

Lesson Objective (3:2)

13. Which of the following trails did thousands of people use to go to California during the gold rush?
    - (A) Mormon Trail
    - ● California Trail
    - (C) Appalachian Trail
    - (D) Green Mountain Trail

Lesson Objective (3:2)

14. Which of the following BEST describes how people reached California during the gold rush?
    - ● all routes
    - (B) water routes
    - (C) land routes
    - (D) horseback

Lesson Objective (3:3)

15. Which of the following generalizations BEST describes gold miners?
    - (A) Few became sick.
    - (B) Life was easy in California.
    - ● Few found any gold at all.
    - (D) Many found gold mines.

Lesson Objective (3:4)

16. Which of the following BEST describes where forty-niners came from?
    - (A) China
    - ● many different places
    - (C) east coast of the United States
    - (D) farms in the United States

Lesson Objective (3:3)

17. Which of the following is NOT a hardship miners faced?
    - (A) lack of medicine
    - (B) no place to sleep
    - (C) high prices for goods
    - ● many places to look for gold

Use with Pupil Edition, p. 448

Assessment Book, p. 75

Part 2: Skills Test

Directions: Use complete sentences to answer questions 1–8. Use a separate sheet of paper if you need more space.

1. Why did American settlers in Texas rebel against the Mexican government? **Summarize**

   They were unhappy and unwilling to abide by some conditions, and they wanted more say in the government.

2. What effect did the Texans' defense of the Alamo have on Texas's fight for independence? **Cause and Effect**

   The Alamo defenders delayed Mexican troops long enough for Texas to sign up more soldiers. Sam Houston then was able to capture Santa Anna at San Jacinto, and Texas won its independence.

3. What was the opinion of Americans who opposed the Mexican War? **Main Idea and Details**

   Some Americans, including Abraham Lincoln, believed that the United States had unfairly started the war to gain more land from Mexico.

4. How did the first settlers' opinions of Oregon Country impact future movement in the 1840s? **Cause and Effect**

   The settlers sent letters home praising their new home. This encouraged others to move to Oregon Country as well.

Use with Pupil Edition, p. 448

Assessment Book, p. 76

5. What was the benefit of traveling in wagon trains on the 2,000-mile journey to Oregon Country? **Draw Conclusions**

   The journey to Oregon Country was dangerous. People traveling in a group helped each other out.

6. How did many entrepreneurs who moved to California during the gold rush become successful? **Main Idea and Details**

   The entrepreneurs supplied the miners with much-needed supplies and services. Because supplies and services were scarce and in great demand, the merchants could charge high prices and make large profits.

7. Compare and contrast miners' journeys to California with life in a mining camp. **Compare and Contrast**

   Compare: Both the journey to California and life in a mining camp were long, hard, and risky. Both the trip and mining were dangerous. Only a few miners struck it rich. Contrast: While on the journey, everyone was hopeful about finding gold. The rest were disappointed.

8. How did people who did not find gold in California contribute to the growth of the "Golden State"? **Draw Conclusions**

   Many began businesses that thrived because of the increased number of people who needed food, services, and supplies. Towns and cities grew up around the thriving businesses.

Use with Pupil Edition, p. 448

Assessment Support

Assessment Book, p. 77

Unit 6 Test

Part 1: Content Test

Directions: Fill in the circle next to the correct answer.

Lesson Objective (12–1:1)

1. Which of the following summarizes the Monroe Doctrine?
   - ● The United States will protect its interests in the Western Hemisphere.
   - Ⓑ Russia will expand its colonies to California.
   - Ⓒ Spain's colonies will change to British rule.
   - Ⓓ The United States will permit new European settlements in Spanish Florida.

Lesson Objective (12–1:2)

2. Which of the following describes President Andrew Jackson?
   - Ⓐ He resisted change.
   - Ⓑ He represented a select group.
   - ● He was a man of the people.
   - Ⓓ He was college educated.

Lesson Objective (12–1:3)

3. Which of the following BEST describes the Trail of Tears?
   - Ⓐ canal that led to the Pacific Ocean
   - Ⓑ trail leading across the Appalachian Mountains
   - Ⓒ long journey westward during which clothes were ripped
   - ● Native Americans in Southeast forced to move west

Lesson Objective (12–2:1)

4. What change took place during the Industrial Revolution?
   - ● More goods were made by machine.
   - Ⓑ More goods were made by hand.
   - Ⓒ Fewer women made goods.
   - Ⓓ Fewer goods were made.

Lesson Objective (12–2:2)

5. What effect did the mechanical reaper have on farming?
   - Ⓐ Animals were no longer needed.
   - ● It made harvesting crops easier.
   - Ⓒ More animals were needed.
   - Ⓓ It was more reliable than picking crops by hand.

Lesson Objective (12–3:4)

6. Which of the following is a movement to stop or reduce the use of alcohol?
   - ● temperance
   - Ⓑ abolition
   - Ⓒ revival
   - Ⓓ reform

Lesson Objective (12–3:2)

7. Which of the following people is NOT a known abolitionist?
   - Ⓐ Frederick Douglass
   - Ⓑ Sojourner Truth
   - Ⓒ William Lloyd Garrison
   - ● Horace Mann

Lesson Objective (12–3:3)

8. Which of the following BEST describes the goal of the women's rights movement?
   - Ⓐ Women should be allowed to vote.
   - ● Men and women should be treated as equals.
   - Ⓒ Women should be allowed to own land.
   - Ⓓ Women should be allowed to own property.

Use with Pupil Edition, p. 452

Assessment Book, p. 78

Lesson Objective (13–1:2)

9. What is one reason United States settlers in Texas wanted their independence from Mexico?
   - ● Slavery was illegal in Mexico and many settlers had slaves.
   - Ⓑ Most of the settlers were Catholic and wanted to change.
   - Ⓒ The settlers wanted the Mexican government to enforce its laws.
   - Ⓓ Mexico City was too far away for trade.

Lesson Objective (13–1:3)

10. Which of the following groups did NOT support the United States annexing Texas?
    - Ⓐ people who believed Catholicism would be forced upon them
    - ● people who believed it would expand slavery in the United States
    - Ⓒ people who believed in manifest destiny
    - Ⓓ people who wanted Texas to become a state

Lesson Objective (13–1:4)

11. Which of the following helped lead to a United States victory in the Mexican War?
    - Ⓐ Battle of San Jacinto
    - ● Battle of Buena Vista
    - Ⓒ Battle of the Rio Grande
    - Ⓓ Battle of the Alamo

Lesson Objective (13–2:1)

12. Which of the following is a reason people moved west?
    - Ⓐ to live in a large city
    - Ⓑ for the right to vote
    - Ⓒ to avoid taxes
    - ● for religious freedom

Lesson Objective (13–2:2)

13. Which of the following was NOT a danger along the Oregon Trail?
    - Ⓐ Wagons were swept away in fast-running river currents.
    - Ⓑ People died from sickness and accidents.
    - ● Missionaries taught the Christian religion to settlers.
    - Ⓓ Wagon trains were attacked.

Lesson Objective (13–2:4)

14. Why did the Mormons move west?
    - Ⓐ to settle in a Mexican colony
    - Ⓑ to learn Native American survival skills
    - Ⓒ to find gold
    - ● to worship as they pleased

Lesson Objective (13–3:2)

15. How did forty-niners reach California?
    - Ⓐ by wagon
    - ● by any means possible
    - Ⓒ by horseback
    - Ⓓ by ship

Lesson Objective (13–3:3)

16. Why did many miners have a difficult life?
    - ● Searching for gold was hard work, and gold was hard to find.
    - Ⓑ People came from all over, and California became overcrowded.
    - Ⓒ Many miners had to travel long distances to California.
    - Ⓓ Supplies were expensive and hard to buy.

Lesson Objective (13–3:4)

17. Which of the following BEST describes the population of California after the gold rush?
    - Ⓐ mostly Native American
    - Ⓑ mostly immigrant
    - Ⓒ mostly Mexican American
    - ● very diverse

Use with Pupil Edition, p. 452

Assessment Book, p. 79

Part 2: Skills Test

Directions: Use complete sentences to answer questions 1–6. Use a separate sheet of paper if you need more space.

1. Why was Andrew Jackson known as "the People's President"? **Analyze Information**

   > He was the son of poor pioneers who moved west, and he never attended college, as previous Presidents had. Jackson believed that "common people" should be in power. He encouraged all men, not just the privileged few, to vote, and his values supported all Americans.

2. Why do you think the speeches of abolitionist Frederick Douglass were so powerful? **Express Ideas**

   > Douglass's speeches drew upon his personal experiences as a slave. He was a powerful, well-spoken voice for freedom.

3. The Alamo is an important historical landmark in Texas and in the United States. For what is it remembered? **Interpret National Symbols**

   > Possible answers: The heroic defenders of the Alamo gave their lives for Texas's independence from Mexico. The quest for freedom led Texans to fight for their beliefs.

4. Which country gained more from the Treaty of Guadalupe Hidalgo—the United States or Mexico? Explain. **Point of View**

   > Points of view will vary. Mexico gained $15 million in exchange for some of its northern territory. The United States gained land that allowed it to stretch from coast to coast across North America.

Use with Pupil Edition, p. 452

Assessment Book, p. 80

5. What factors added to tensions between the Mexican government and United States settlers in Texas? To what did these tensions lead? **Summarize**

   > Many settlers from the United States took slaves with them to Texas, and slavery was illegal in Mexico. Settlers had agreed to become Catholics but once in Texas, they refused. The vast distance between Texas and the Mexican government in Mexico City made law enforcement difficult. Settlers wanted more say in the government of Texas; In 1830 Mexico banned more settlers from the United States from relocating to Texas.

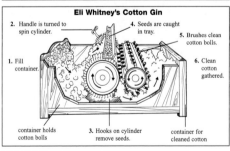

Eli Whitney's Cotton Gin

2. Handle is turned to spin cylinder.
4. Seeds are caught in tray.
5. Brushes clean cotton bolls.
1. Fill container.
6. Clean cotton gathered.
container holds cotton bolls
3. Hooks on cylinder remove seeds.
container for cleaned cotton

6. Use the diagram to answer the questions. **Read a Cross-Section Diagram**

   a. Why is reading the title and the labels of the diagram important?

   > so you know what the diagram is showing and what the parts are

   b. What is the purpose of this machine?

   > to remove seeds from the cotton bolls

   c. What is the purpose of the tray?

   > to catch the removed seeds

Use with Pupil Edition, p. 452

People Moving South and West

Chapter 13 Outline

Resources

- Workbook, p. 100: Vocabulary Preview
- Vocabulary Cards
- Social Studies Plus!

1836, San Antonio, Texas: Lesson 1

Ask students to use the title of the chapter and the caption next to the picture to predict why the people are fighting. (They are fighting over land in what is now Texas.)

1846, Oregon Country: Lesson 2

Have students note what the picture shows about how people traveled west. Ask students to suggest words that might describe these trips. *(difficult, slow, dirty, dangerous)*

1848, American River, California: Lesson 3

Ask students what the people in the picture are doing and to predict how this will affect California. (They are finding gold. Many people will flock to the area.)

1836

San Antonio, Texas
Texans fall at the Battle of the Alamo.

Lesson 1

1

1846

Oregon Country
The United States and Britain sign a treaty agreeing on the border between Oregon and Canada.

Lesson 2

2

1848

American River, California
Gold is discovered in California.

Lesson 3

3

428

Practice and Extend

Vocabulary Preview

- Use Workbook p. 100 to help students preview the vocabulary words in this chapter.
- Use Vocabulary Cards to preview key concept words in this chapter.

 Also on Teacher Resources CD-ROM.

Workbook, p. 100

Vocabulary Preview
Directions: Define each term on the lines provided. You may use your glossary.

Texas Revolution ____

annex ____

manifest destiny ____

Mexican War ____

Bear Flag Revolt ____

Treaty of Guadalupe Hidalgo ____

mountain man ____

wagon train ____

gold rush ____

forty-niner ____

discrimination ____

Notes for Home: Your child learned terms related to the expansion of United States borders around 1850.
Home Activity: Have your child use these terms to tell how westward expansion helped the United States expand its borders.

Locating Time and Place

 OREGON
COUNTRY

American River

PACIFIC OCEAN

UNITED STATES
1848

1

San
Antonio

ATLANTIC
OCEAN

Gulf of Mexico

Why We Remember

Think about the place where you live. Was it part of the United States when our country began? If you live west of the Mississippi River, the answer to that question is no. From 1819 to 1848—just less than 30 years—the United States expanded west to the Pacific Ocean. American settlers poured into these places and established homes and communities. Other people, such as Native Americans and Mexican Americans, lost their homes as the newcomers arrived. The story of how these areas—perhaps your own area—became part of this country is the story of Chapter 13.

429

Settling the South and Texas

Objectives

- Explain what brought settlers into the new southern frontier.
- Explain how the United States gained land from Mexico.
- Evaluate the reasons why United States settlers in Texas wanted independence from Mexico.
- Analyze the viewpoints of people in the United States who opposed annexation of Texas and who supported it.
- Relate the events that led to a United States victory in the Mexican War.

Vocabulary

Texas Revolution, p. 432; **annex,** p. 433; **manifest destiny,** p. 433; **Mexican War,** p. 434; **Bear Flag Revolt,** p. 434; **Treaty of Guadalupe Hidalgo,** p. 435

Resources

- Workbook, p. 101
- Transparency 13, 49
- Every Student Learns Guide, pp. 178–181
- Quick Study, pp. 90–91

Quick Teaching Plan

If time is short, have students make a Historical Story Map to outline the major concepts of the lesson.

1 Introduce and Motivate

Preview To activate prior knowledge, ask students to recall how the United States was changed by the Louisiana Purchase (Chapter 11, Lesson 2). Tell students that they will learn what happened when settlers from the United States moved into other areas added to the United States.

 Have students describe the hopes and fears for the future of the family in this scenario.

LESSON 1

1820		1840
1820s United States settlers begin moving to Texas and continue settling the South	**1836** Republic of Texas is formed	**1845** Texas and Florida become states

Settling the South and Texa

PREVIEW

Focus on the Main Idea
The United States expanded as Americans settled the South, revolted in Texas, and fought a war with Mexico.

PLACES
Florida
Texas
Mexico
San Antonio

PEOPLE
Osceola
Stephen F. Austin
Antonio López de Santa Anna
Juan Seguín
Sam Houston
James K. Polk

VOCABULARY
Texas Revolution
annex
manifest destiny
Mexican War
Bear Flag Revolt
Treaty of Guadalupe Hidalgo

You Are There

It's 1835 in Texas. Your family was one of the first 300 families from the United States to move to this Mexican-ruled territory. Your parents decided to leave your home in New Orleans in 1822 for the chance to buy cheap land for cattle ranching. Stephen F. Austin, who started a settlement along the Brazos River, led you and the other families to the area.

Your settlement has grown and thrived. But now tensions are growing with the Mexican government. The settlers from the United States are becoming increasingly unhappy being ruled by Mexico. Your family and others want Texas to be independent. Will there be a war between Texas and Mexico? ▶ **Stephen F. Austin**

Compare and Contrast
As you read, compare how the borders of the United States and Mexico changed over time.

430

Practice and Extend

READING SKILL Compare/Contrast

In the Lesson Review, students complete a graphic organizer like the one below. You may want to provide students with a copy of Transparency 13 to complete as they read the lesson.

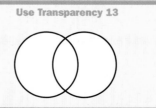

Use Transparency 13

VOCABULARY Word Exercise

Individual Word Study Explain that the word *annex* can be used as a noun or a verb. Write these sentences on the board: *The city is going to annex a nearby village. The school built an annex to house a new library.* Discuss the meanings of annex as a noun and a verb. Ask students to read the sentences and tell you which part of speech *annex* is in each sentence. Ask which form is used in the lesson. (verb) The pronunciation is the same whether it is used as a noun or a verb.

Moving South

Texas was not the only region attracting settlers in the early 1800s. (You will read about Texas on the next page). Treaties with Britain and Spain gave America control of the South. However, settlers did not come in great numbers until after 1814, when Andrew Jackson defeated the Native Americans at the Battle of Horseshoe Bend in present-day Alabama. You have read how Jackson's military role helped cause Spain to sell **Florida** in 1819, and he became the first military governor of this new American territory.

The great Seminole leader **Osceola** was captured in 1837, and Florida's Seminoles were finally defeated in 1842.

▶ Osceola fought to keep Seminole lands in Florida.

Settlers from Kentucky, Tennessee, and even New England began to move into the new southern frontier. But most settlers were farmers and planters from Georgia and the Carolinas, who brought enslaved people with them. The rich soil and warm climate of central Alabama and Mississippi were perfect for growing cotton, and the invention of the cotton gin made growing cotton even more profitable. In northern Alabama, settlers found rich deposits of iron. By 1817, enough people had moved to Mississippi for it to become a state. Alabama became a state in 1819. Florida had enough people for statehood by 1840, but was not admitted as a slave state until 1845 when the free state of Iowa could be admitted to keep a balance.

REVIEW What brought settlers into the new southern frontier? *Cause and effect*

Agriculture Expands in the South

Key:
- Tobacco
- Wheat
- Corn
- Cotton
- Rice
- Sheep
- Cattle
- Hogs

▶ This map shows animals and crops raised by settlers in the new southern frontier.

MAP SKILL Use a Key *What crop is not shown in any of the five states bordering the Gulf of Mexico?*

431

FAST FACTS

This page of Lesson 1 describes events in the South from the Battle of Horseshoe Bend in 1814 until Florida's statehood in 1845. Other events during this period include:

1823 Scottish chemist, Charles Macintosh, patented a waterproof fabric for raincoats by dissolving rubber in a tar and naphtha solution to join two layers of material. Raincoats are sometimes called macintoshes in his honor.

1824 Louis Braille, a Frenchman, developed the Braille reading system for people who cannot see. Braille lost his sight when he was three years old and created his system of raised dots when he was just 15 years old.

1833 On November 12 and 13, nearly every American community experienced one of the world's greatest meteor storms. Tens of thousands of meteors lit up the night sky. Many observers were fascinated or terrified because they did not understand what was happening.

---

2 Teach and Discuss

PAGE 431

Moving South

🕐 **Quick Summary** Settlers began to move in greater numbers into southern areas acquired by the United States or sparsely settled before the 1800s. The defeat of Native Americans, as well as the attraction of rich soil and a warm climate resulted in enough settlers to create several new states.

1 **What caused Florida to be opened to American settlers?** The area was purchased from Spain and the Seminole were defeated. **Cause and Effect**

2 **Why did planters bring enslaved people with them to the new southern frontier?** The enslaved people were needed to help grow and process the cotton. **Draw Conclusions**

3 **Why do you think keeping a balance of free states to slave states was important to some citizens?** Students may recall that each state elects two senators, and some citizens did not want one type of state to have more votes in the government. **Point of View**

✓ **REVIEW ANSWER** Gaining control of the areas, first from foreign powers and then from Native Americans, gave people the chance to settle the new frontier. The main attraction, especially in Alabama and Mississippi, was the rich soil and warm climate that were perfect for growing cotton. **Cause and Effect**

From Republic to State

⏱ **Quick Summary** After Texans won independence from Mexico, the Republic of Texas was annexed by the United States, increasing tensions between the United States and Mexico.

4 **What fact supports the opinion that the Texans who fought at the Alamo were determined to win their independence?** The fact that such a small group of settlers held off the Mexican army for 13 days shows their determination. Fact and Opinion

Test Talk

Use Information from the Text

5 **Give examples of how Tejanos participated in the Texas Revolution.** Tell students to skim the text to find the word *Tejano*. Tejanos joined the American settlers in Texas in making the decision to fight for independence from Mexico. Tejano soldiers died defending the Alamo. Juan Seguín was a Tejano leader who survived the Alamo battle because he was sent to get help. Main Idea and Details

Primary Source

Cited in *Texas: From the Frontier to Spindletop,* by James L. Haley

6 **Why did Houston want his soldiers to "remember the Alamo"?** He thought that remembering the sacrifices of the defenders of the Alamo would help the soldiers fight bravely. Analyze Primary Sources

7 **Summarize the major battles of the Texas Revolution.** Texans fought bravely at the Alamo but were outnumbered and lost to the Mexican army. Texans then surprised Santa Anna with an attack that caused the defeat of the Mexican army at San Jacinto. Summarize

▶ David Crockett fought in the Creek Indian War, served as a congressman from Tennessee, and died at the Alamo.

The Story of Texas

A project to settle people from the United States in **Texas** was pursued by **Stephen F. Austin** in the 1820s. Texas was then part of **Mexico,** and Mexico needed more settlers to build towns, farms, and ranches. By 1832 there were about 20,000 settlers from the United States in Texas. In some areas they outnumbered Mexican settlers—called *Tejanos* (tay HAH nohs)—ten to one.

Tensions grew between the Mexican government and the new settlers. Slavery was illegal in Mexico, but many settlers brought enslaved people with them from the United States. The Americans also refused to convert to the Catholic religion. They wanted more say in the government and resented being ruled from distant Mexico City. Fearing a rebellion, Mexico passed a law in 1830 forbidding additional American settlers.

By 1835, large numbers of Texas settlers, including Tejanos, decided to fight for their independence from Mexico. They began to

organize an army and a new government. The **Texas Revolution** began. In December 1835 the Mexican president **Antonio lopez de Santa Anna** led an army from Mexico City to put down the rebellion. The Texans declared independence and formed the Republic of Texas on March 2, 1836.

Santa Anna's forces had reached **San Antonio** in February, where he found Texans in a fortified Spanish mission called the Alamo. There were only 184 men in the Alamo facing thousands of Mexican soldiers. After a 13-day siege, the Mexicans attacked the walls on March 6. Almost all of the defenders were killed, including their leader, William Travis, and two famous frontiersmen, David Crockett and James Bowie. Tejano soldiers serving under **Juan Seguín** (say GEEN) also died defending the Alamo, but Seguín survived because he was sent to get help before the Alamo fell.

The Texans had been defeated, but they delayed the Mexican advance long enough for Texas to sign up more soldiers. **Sam Houston,** leader of the Texas army, decided to attack the Mexican army near the San Jacinto (hah SIN toh) River. Before the battle Houston encouraged the Texans,

> *"Some of us may be killed. . . . But soldiers, remember the Alamo! the Alamo! the Alamo! Victory is certain!"*

On April 21, Houston's forces surprised Santa Anna's army. Shouting "Remember the Alamo," they defeated the Mexican army and captured Santa Anna. In exchange for his freedom, Santa Anna agreed to withdraw his troops south of the Rio Grande.

432

Practice and Extend

CURRICULUM CONNECTION
Writing

Write a Speech

- Have students review the words Sam Houston used to urge on his troops as they prepared to attack the Mexican army. Ask students to compose other comments that Houston could have made in addressing his soldiers.

- Tell students to include in their speeches feelings and goals they predict Houston would have had as he faced the battle.

- Have students rehearse delivering their speeches expressively. Then have them present their talks to the class.

The Republic of Texas was now an independent country with Sam Houston as its elected president. It had its own flag with a single star, which is why Texas became known as the "Lone Star State." But it faced many problems. It needed to defend against raids from Mexico, and it was nearly broke. Many Texans wanted the United States to **annex,** or add, Texas as a state.

Sam Houston wrote a letter to President Andrew Jackson in 1836, asking him to "save us." Jackson refused, knowing that people in the United States disagreed about whether to annex Texas and make it a state. Many people in the United States believed in the idea of **manifest destiny,** or the belief that the United States should expand west to the Pacific Ocean. However, people opposed to slavery did not want Texas admitted because it would expand slavery in the United States.

Also, many feared that annexing Texas could lead to war with Mexico. The debate over Texas continued for almost ten years.

James K. Polk, who supported manifest destiny and annexing Texas, was elected President in 1844. The next year Congress voted to annex Texas and make it a state. You will read more about Polk in the Biography on page 437.

Tensions increased quickly between Mexico and the United States after Texas became a state. Although Mexico had signed a treaty granting Texas independence, it still thought of the area as part of Mexico. In addition, the United States and Mexico disagreed on the location of the Texas border.

REVIEW Why were people in the United States divided on the issue of Texas becoming a state? **Summarize**

8 How did Sam Houston want President Jackson to save Texans? He wanted Jackson to annex Texas and to help defend them against Mexican raids. **Make Inferences**

9 Describe three groups that would have disagreed with President Polk's decision to annex Texas. Possible answers: Groups against manifest destiny, groups against slavery, and groups afraid of war with Mexico **Draw Conclusions**

✓ **REVIEW ANSWER** Possible answer: Some people believed that annexing Texas would expand slavery and might lead to war with Mexico. Others believed in manifest destiny, that the United States should expand westward to the Pacific Ocean. **Summarize**

The Alamo

In 1905, the Alamo was made a historic monument. Today the Alamo still stands in downtown San Antonio. You can visit the place that played such an important role in the history of Texas and the United States.

433

The Alamo

Have students study the pictures of the Alamo.

10 How does the Alamo compare to the way it looked at the time of the battle? The building looks about the same now as it did then. **Compare and Contrast**

War with Mexico

🕐 **Quick Summary** The United States declared war on Mexico when Mexican troops crossed the Rio Grande. A month later, California declared its independence and joined the effort to drive the Mexican army south.

⑪ How long after the United States annexed Texas did war with Mexico break out? About one year
Main Idea and Details

⑫ How do you think those who believed in manifest destiny felt about the Bear Flag Revolt? They were pleased because it expanded the United States territory to the Pacific Ocean.
Make Inferences

⑬ Compare and contrast the Battle of Buena Vista with the battle at the Alamo. In both cases the Mexican army outnumbered its foe and soldiers refused to give up when the battle was difficult. Texans lost the battle at the Alamo, whereas the United States army won at Buena Vista.
↻ Compare and Contrast

✓ **REVIEW ANSWER** Some believed the war was an excuse to gain more land from Mexico. Main Idea and Details

War With Mexico

Attempts to find a peaceful solution to the conflict between the United States and Mexico broke down. To prepare for a possible war, President Polk sent troops led by General Zachary Taylor into the area between the Rio Grande and the Nueces River in January 1846. Fighting began when Mexican troops crossed the Rio Grande in April. Polk told the American people that Mexico "has invaded our territory, and shed American blood upon American soil." Congress declared war on May
⑪ 13, 1846—The Mexican War had begun.

Not all Americans supported the war. Abraham Lincoln, then a congressman from Illinois, believed that the United States had unfairly started the war to gain more land from Mexico. Mexico, he said, claimed the land where fighting began, just as the United States did. The writer, Henry David Thoreau, agreed and was put in jail when he refused to pay taxes to support the war.

▶ The Bear Flag Revolt got its name from the California flag. General Zachary Taylor led his troops to victory in Mexico.

CALIFORNIA REPUBLIC

Despite opposition to the war at home, United States troops were winning victories, especially in Mexico's northern territory. In June 1846 American settlers in California revolted, or rebelled, against the Mexican government. They captured the town of Sonoma and declared themselves independent. This became known as the Bear Flag Revolt because of the grizzly bear on the settlers' flag. The settlers joined with United States troops to drive the Mexican army south. By 1847, United States forces controlled all of New Mexico and California.

General Zachary Taylor had a more difficult time south of the Rio Grande. In the Battle of Buena Vista in February 1847, his troops were greatly outnumbered by those of Santa Anna. Before the battle began, Santa Anna sent a message to Taylor. "I wish to save you from a catastrophe," Santa Anna said. "You may surrender."

Taylor refused to give up. By the second day of fighting, the situation looked grim for the United States army. An American officer told Taylor, "General, we are whipped." But Taylor replied, "That is for me to determine." His troops went on to force Santa Anna to retreat. The victory made him a national hero.

REVIEW Why were some people opposed to the war with Mexico? *Main Idea and Details*

Practice and Extend

SOCIAL STUDIES
Background

Battle of Buena Vista
- General Taylor's army at Buena Vista consisted of about 5,000 men compared to the Mexican army that was 14,000 strong.
- In addition to being seriously outnumbered, the communication lines for Taylor's troops were cut by the Mexican army.
- The heavy fire of Taylor's army caused the Mexicans to retreat. They left their campfires burning so Taylor's troops would not realize that they were turning back.
- Taylor's victory against such great odds made him a national hero and helped him become President in 1848.

SOCIAL STUDIES
Background

California Bear Flag
- John Bidwell, one of the people who drew up California's resolution of independence, wrote in an 1891 magazine article that William Todd, nephew of Mary Todd Lincoln, created the Bear Flag.
- Supposedly, Todd used old paint that he found and drew a rough impression of a bear on a yard of cotton cloth.
- In 1911, the Bear Flag was adopted as California's official state flag. The bear represents courage or strength.

Expansion of the United States, 1783–1898

Expansion of the United States, 1783–1898

ALASKA PURCHASE 1867

CANADA

PACIFIC OCEAN

0 200 400 Miles
0 400 Kilometers

OREGON TERRITORY TREATY 1846

TREATY WITH BRITAIN 1818

TREATY WITH BRITAIN 1842

CANADA

L. Superior
L. Michigan
L. Huron
L. Ontario
L. Erie

LOUISIANA PURCHASE 1803

MEXICAN WAR TREATY 1848

UNITED STATES 1783

PACIFIC OCEAN

GADSDEN PURCHASE 1853

TEXAS 1845

ATLANTIC OCEAN

HAWAII 1898

PACIFIC OCEAN

0 100 Miles
0 100 Kilometers

Present-day boundaries are shown.

MEXICO

FLORIDA 1819

Gulf of Mexico

0 250 500 Miles
0 250 500 Kilometers

▶ As a result of the Mexican War, the territory of the United States extended to the Pacific Ocean.

MAP SKILL Place *What was the last state to become part of the United States?*

New Borders

President Polk ordered General Winfield Scott to invade Mexico by sea. Scott, like Taylor, was a veteran of the War of 1812. Scott's army captured the city of Veracruz on the eastern coast of Mexico and then marched to Mexico City. Scott captured Mexico City on September 14, 1847.

The Treaty of Guadalupe Hidalgo officially ended the Mexican War in February 1848. Mexico had to give up most of its northern territory to the United States. In return, the United States paid Mexico $15 million dollars. Look at the map to see the land that became part of the United States after the Mexican War. The states of California, Nevada, Utah, New Mexico,

and parts of Arizona, Colorado, and Wyoming were later created out of the territory gained from Mexico.

Five years later, the United States paid Mexico $10 million for more land in present-day southern Arizona and southwestern New Mexico. This was called the Gadsden Purchase.

The United States now stretched across the continent, from the Atlantic to the Pacific oceans. But, as you will read, the question of slavery in the new territories would soon begin to split the nation.

REVIEW How did the United States benefit from the Mexican War? Cause and Effect

435

SOCIAL STUDIES Background

Agreement with Mexico

- The treaty ending the Mexican War was named after the place where it was signed, Villa de Guadalupe Hidalgo in Mexico City.
- The agreement made the Rio Grande and the Gila River the boundary between the United States and Mexico.
- The United States received 525,000 square miles of land.

WEB SITE Technology

You can learn more about United States territories and the years they were acquired by clicking on *Atlas* at **www.sfsocialstudies.com**.

PAGE 435

New Borders

🕐 *Quick Summary* As a result of lands acquired in the Mexican War and through the Gadsden Purchase, the United States achieved its goal of expanding to the Pacific Ocean.

Expansion of the United States, 1783–1898

Test Talk

Locate Key Words in the Question

14 **What states were formed from Mexican territory gained in 1848?** Help students recognize that the date 1848 is key information in the question. Tell students to look at the map to find out which territory was gained that year. California, Nevada, Utah, and parts of Arizona, New Mexico, Colorado, and Wyoming **Interpret Maps**

MAP SKILL Answer Hawaii

15 **Predict how the issue of slavery in the new territories might further split the nation.** Possible answer: People might disagree about whether enslaved people should be permitted in the new territories. **Predict**

✓ **Ongoing Assessment**

If... students cannot predict how the issue of slavery will cause future problems,

then... discuss what would happen if representatives of slave states were voting on issues concerning slavery.

✓ **REVIEW ANSWER** The United States gained most of Mexico's northern territory, which would later be divided among seven states. **Cause and Effect**

Mexican Americans

 **Quick Summary** Many Mexican Americans stayed in Texas after the war. They shared their expertise and their culture with settlers.

16 **Why do you think settlers from the United States added Spanish words to their language?** To describe things that had not been part of their culture before **Make Inferences**

✓ **REVIEW ANSWER** Mexican Americans showed new settlers how to irrigate soil and raise cattle in the open-range system, and they contributed to the language. **Main Idea and Details**

3 Close and Assess

Summarize the Lesson

Have students create Sequence Chains. Ask students to write a significant date and event from the lesson in each box and an explanation of how one event led to the next.

✓ | **LESSON 1** | **REVIEW** |

1. ⟲ **Compare and Contrast** For possible answers, see the reduced pupil page.

2. The defeat of Native Americans, along with rich soil and a warm climate, perfect for growing cotton. Also, iron was found in Alabama.

3. **Critical Thinking: Summarize** The Texas army captured Santa Anna. In exchange for his release, he agreed to withdraw Mexican troops south of the Rio Grande.

4. He knew people did not agree on the issue of annexation.

5. Taylor won a key battle at Buena Vista in 1847. Scott captured Mexico City in September of 1847.

Link to ⟷ Geography
These states and dates should be included: California, 1850; Nevada, 1864; Colorado, 1876; Wyoming, 1890; Utah, 1896; Arizona and New Mexico, 1912

436 Unit 6 • A Growing Nation

Mexican Americans

About 75,000 Mexicans lived in the territory won by the United States. After the Mexican War they became United States citizens, and most decided to stay. However, even though the Treaty of Guadalupe Hidalgo guaranteed Mexican Americans the right to keep property, many were still pushed off their land. Despite these problems, Mexican Americans made important contributions to the United States. Many Spanish words became part of the English language, such as *patio, buffalo,* and *stampede.* Mexican Americans showed new settlers from the United States how to irrigate the soil and how to raise cattle. Mexicans had created the open-range system where cattle were allowed to roam freely over the land, rather than being fenced in. *Vaqueros,* or cowboys, herded the cattle, keeping them safe and bringing them to market.

16

REVIEW How did Mexican Americans contribute to the United States culture? **Main Idea and Details**

▶ A *vaquero* wore boot spurs like these when riding, to control the horse.

Summarize the Lesson

— **1819** United States buys Florida and settlers move into new southern frontier.

— **1836** United States settlers declared independence from Mexico and formed the Republic of Texas.

— **1846** The Mexican War began soon after Texas was annexed by the United States.

LESSON 1 REVIEW

Check Facts and Main Ideas

1. ⟲ **Compare and Contrast** On a separate sheet of paper, fill in the diagram comparing and contrasting United States boundaries in 1844 and 1854.

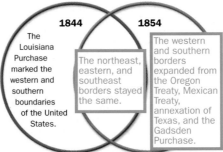

1844 — The Louisiana Purchase marked the western and southern boundaries of the United States.

The northeast, eastern, and southeast borders stayed the same.

1854 — The western and southern borders expanded from the Oregon Treaty, Mexican Treaty, annexation of Texas, and the Gadsden Purchase.

2. What factors attracted settlers to the new southern frontier?

3. **Critical Thinking: Summarize** How did Texas gain its independence from Mexico?

4. Why did President Andrew Jackson refuse Sam Houston's request for the United States to **annex** Texas?

5. How did Generals Winfield Scott and Zachary Taylor contribute to the United States victory in the **Mexican War**?

Link to ⟷ Geography

Make Tables of New States Look again at the map on page 435 that shows the land gained from Mexico. Make a table listing each new state created from this new United States territory and the year it became a state. Use the library or Internet for your research.

436

Practice and Extend

ESL **ACTIVATE PRIOR KNOWLEDGE**
ESL Support

Examine Spanish Words

- Ask students who know Spanish to work with students who do not to make a chart of Spanish words that have been incorporated into English—including ones mentioned in this section—and their English definitions.

- Have each group use books about Mexican culture to find other words borrowed from Mexican Americans.

- Have Spanish speakers pronounce the words on each chart so that the rest of the students can repeat the words after them.

For additional ESL support, use Every Student Learns Guide, pp. 178–181.

Workbook, p. 101

Lesson 1: Settling the South and Texas

Directions: Sequence the events in the order in which they took place by numbering them from 1 to 12. You may use your textbook.

___ Texas settlers decide to fight for their independence from Mexico, and in 1835 the Texas Revolution begins.

___ Spain sells Florida to the United States.

___ The Treaty of Guadalupe Hidalgo is signed, officially ending the war with Mexico.

___ Fearing a rebellion, Mexican leaders pass a law in 1830 forbidding new settlers from the United States.

___ Stephen F. Austin brings settlers to Texas, which is part of Mexico, under a land grant.

___ Mexico still thinks of Texas as part of Mexico and disagrees on the border between the United States and Mexico.

___ Many Americans are against annexing Texas because it would expand slavery in the United States and could lead to war with Mexico.

___ Texas is annexed and becomes a state in 1845.

___ As an independent country, Texas faces problems such as defending itself and having no money. Many Texans want to be annexed to the United States.

___ Tensions grow between Mexico and the settlers from the United States because the settlers bring enslaved people with them to Texas.

___ Efforts to find a peaceful solution fail, and the Mexican War begins on May 13, 1846.

Notes for Home: Your child learned about the settlement of the South and how Texas became part of the United States.
Home Activity: With your child, review the sequence of events in Lesson 1, culminating in Texas becoming...

 Also on Teacher Resources CD-ROM

James K. Polk
1795–1849

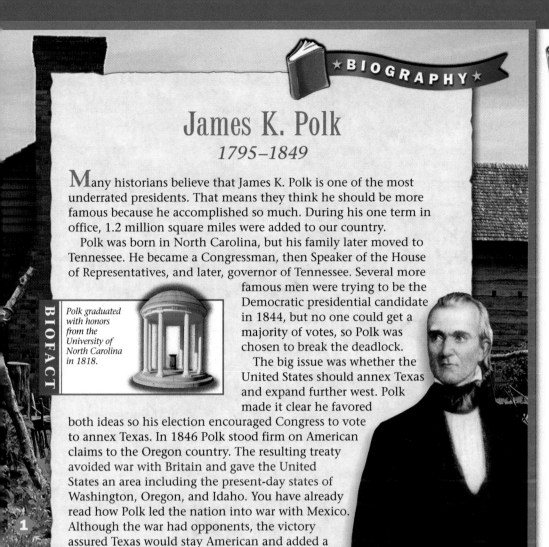

Many historians believe that James K. Polk is one of the most underrated presidents. That means they think he should be more famous because he accomplished so much. During his one term in office, 1.2 million square miles were added to our country.

Polk was born in North Carolina, but his family later moved to Tennessee. He became a Congressman, then Speaker of the House of Representatives, and later, governor of Tennessee. Several more famous men were trying to be the Democratic presidential candidate in 1844, but no one could get a majority of votes, so Polk was chosen to break the deadlock.

The big issue was whether the United States should annex Texas and expand further west. Polk made it clear he favored both ideas so his election encouraged Congress to vote to annex Texas. In 1846 Polk stood firm on American claims to the Oregon country. The resulting treaty avoided war with Britain and gave the United States an area including the present-day states of Washington, Oregon, and Idaho. You have already read how Polk led the nation into war with Mexico. Although the war had opponents, the victory assured Texas would stay American and added a vast area to the United States, including California. The idea of manifest destiny seemed fulfilled.

Polk was one of our hardest working presidents. He once said:

> "No president who performs his duties faithfully and conscientiously [with care] can have any leisure"

BIOFACT
Polk graduated with honors from the University of North Carolina in 1818.

Learn from Biographies
What did Polk do that makes some historians think he is underrated?

For more information, go online to *Meet the People* at **www.sfsocialstudies.com.**

437

James K. Polk

Objective
- Identify the contributions of significant individuals, such as James K. Polk.

1 Introduce and Motivate

Preview Ask students what they know about James K. Polk. Tell students they will learn how Polk's desire for expansion led to large areas being added to the United States.

2 Teach and Discuss

1 In what ways did Polk achieve his goals of expansion? He obtained a treaty with Britain gaining much of the Oregon country and the war with Mexico resulted in the addition of California and other areas. Main Idea and Details

2 How had Polk fulfilled the idea of manifest destiny? By gaining Oregon and California the United States had expanded west to the Pacific Ocean. Evaluate

3 Close and Assess

Learn from Biographies Answer
Possible answer: Even though he is not as famous as some presidents, in just one term in office he added vast areas to our country.

SOCIAL STUDIES Background

More About Polk
- The 1844 Democratic Party platform claimed the entire Oregon area, from the California border north to latitude 54°40'. Some Americans urged "Fifty four forty or fight," but Polk used diplomacy to gain a border at the 49th parallel.
- The United States gained important ports as a result of Polk's expansion. Besides San Francisco and San Diego, the waters around the future city of Seattle were obtained, aiding America's growing trade with Asia.
- Polk was unusually successful as President, achieving not only his expansionist goals, but also his domestic ones such as lowering the tariff. However, like most presidents, Polk has his critics. Some historians feel that he provoked war with Mexico, and the debate over slavery in the newly won lands contributed to the Civil War.

Trails to the West

Objectives

- Analyze the different reasons people moved west.

- Describe life on the Oregon Trail.

- Identify the main trails leading west.

- Explain the events that led to Mormons moving west.

Vocabulary

mountain men, p. 439; **wagon train,** p. 439

Resources

- Workbook, p. 102
- Transparency 6
- Every Student Learns Guide, pp. 182–185
- Quick Summary, pp. 92–93

Quick Teaching Plan

If time is short, have students make two-column Cause-and-Effect charts.

- As students read the lesson, ask them to list on the left side of the chart what caused people to travel to the West.

- On the right side of the chart, have students describe the effects of travel on settlers.

- Have pairs of students discuss the notes on their charts.

1 Introduce and Motivate

Preview Ask students who have moved or traveled a distance to share feelings they experienced about the event. Tell students that in Lesson 2 they will learn about the experiences of people who traveled west between 1840 and 1860.

 Trips such as the one experienced by the Todd family took about four to six months of travel over rugged terrain, including deserts and mountains. Ask students what they would have said or done if their family decided to move west in 1852.

1840			1850

1840s
Families begin moving west along the Oregon Trail

1846
Border is established between Oregon Country and Canada

1847
Mormons settle in Salt Lake City

OREGON COUNTRY
Salt Lake City
Mormon Trail
Oregon Trail

Trails to the West

PREVIEW

Focus on the Main Idea
Using a network of trails, people moved west to make better lives for themselves.

PLACES
Oregon Country
Oregon Trail
Mormon Trail
Salt Lake City

PEOPLE
Marcus Whitman
Narcissa Whitman
Joseph Smith
Brigham Young

VOCABULARY
mountain men
wagon train

You Are There   Teenager Mary Ellen Todd is learning to use a whip so that she can drive the team of oxen that is pulling her family's wagon west to Oregon. Since her parents decided to sell their farm in the east in 1852 and start over in Oregon, Mary Ellen says her life has been busy with "many things to be thought about and done."

Now they are finally on the westward trail with a group of other families and life has been very different from the routine on the farm. Just yesterday they had to cross a river, where one of the wagons was swept away in the fast-moving current. Despite the dangers of the trail, Mary Ellen looks forward to a new life in Oregon. From the news she has heard, she expects her new home to be a beautiful place where she can make a better life.

Summarize As you read, consider what opportunities moving west offered settlers.

438

Practice and Extend

READING SKILL
Summarize

In the Lesson Review, students complete a graphic organizer like the one below. You may want to provide students with a copy of Transparency 6 to complete as they read the lesson.

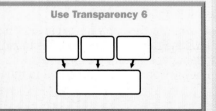

Use Transparency 6

VOCABULARY
Word Exercise

Context Clues Tell students to look at the words that make up the compound words *mountain men* and *wagon train*. Ask them to think about the meanings of the words based on their parts. Direct their attention to the picture on p. 439, and discuss what this suggests about the meaning of the term *wagon train*. Finally, have students look at the text's definition. Discuss what contributed to their ideas about the words and how that can help them remember the words' meaning.

"Oregon Fever"

Mary Ellen Todd was just one of the more than 350,000 people who moved to Oregon Country between 1840 and 1860. **Oregon Country** was the name given to the region that makes up the present-day northwestern United States. Before 1846, both the United States and Great Britain claimed it.

The first settlers to Oregon Country from the United States were fur trappers and missionaries. The fur trappers in the West were known as **mountain men.** They explored the area, often using survival skills taught to them by Native Americans.

Missionaries traveled to Oregon Country to teach the Christian religion to Native Americans. **Marcus Whitman** and his wife, **Narcissa,** left New York to live and work among the Cayuse Indians in 1836. Like other missionaries, they sent letters back east praising their new home.

The large movement of people to Oregon Country began in the 1840s. The 2,000-mile route they traveled became known as the **Oregon Trail.** In 1846, the United States and Great Britain signed a treaty agreeing on the border between Oregon and Canada. Settlement of the border question

encouraged even more settlers to head for Oregon. People eagerly seeking a new life in Oregon were said to have "Oregon fever."

This long and difficult journey was taken in covered wagons pulled by oxen or horses. People traveled in large groups, creating a long line of wagons called a **wagon train.** Life was hard and tiring for everyone. Rebecca Ketcham wrote in her journal:

> *"We can all, as soon as we stop, lie down on the grass or anywhere and be asleep in less than no time at all."*

There were many dangers on the trail. A fast-running river current could easily carry away a wagon trying to cross. Bad weather slowed the wagon trains. Many people died along the way from sickness and accidents.

Despite all the problems faced by the new settlers, they continued to pour into Oregon Country. One settler, Sarah Smith, wrote, "I could hardly believe that the long journey was accomplished and I had found a home."

REVIEW What kinds of difficulties did people on wagon trains face on the Oregon Trail? *Main Idea and Details*

▶ **Long wagon trains moved west on the Oregon Trail.**

439

Develop an Understanding of Early Transportation Help students acquire information about wagon trains.

Beginning Show a picture of a covered wagon. Have students point out details such as wooden wheels and canvas cover, where people sat, and where goods were stored.

Intermediate Guide students in a picture walk through a book such as *If You Traveled West in a Covered Wagon,* by Ellen Levine (Scholastic, ISBN 0-590-45158-8, 1992). Have students record details from the illustrations on a K-W-L chart.

Advanced Have students read additional information about the covered wagons that formed wagon trains. Have groups of students create a Venn diagram comparing a covered wagon to a pick-up truck, moving van, or mobile home.

For additional ESL support, use Every Student Learns Guide, pp. 182–185.

Teach and Discuss

PAGE 439

"Oregon Fever"

🕐 *Quick Summary* Thousands of people traveled west in the mid-1800s to start new lives in the Oregon Country.

1 **What were two reasons people headed west?** Possible answer: Some wanted to make a living as trappers; others went to teach their religion to Native Americans. **Main Idea and Details**

2 **What advantage would there have been to traveling in a wagon train?** Travelers could help and protect each other. **Make Inferences**

✓ **Ongoing Assessment**

If... students do not understand the benefit of settlers traveling in groups, | **then...** have them discuss illustrations that show the rough trails, the small wagons, and the dangers they faced.

Primary Source
Cited in *Women and Men on the Overland Trail,* by John Mack Faragher

3 **Rebecca Ketcham wrote that travelers could fall asleep anywhere. Why do you think this was so?** The hard work of traveling made them very tired. **Analyze Primary Sources**

✓ **REVIEW ANSWER** Bad weather, sickness, and accidents; hard work to pack and unpack camp, take care of the horses and oxen, find food and water, and make campfires **Main Idea and Details**

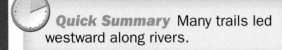

FACT FILE
On the Western Trails, 1840s

Quick Summary Many trails led westward along rivers.

Test Talk

Use Information from Graphics

4 **What was the most common starting point for the trails west?** Tell students to skim the boxes on the map to find starting points. Independence, Missouri Interpret Maps

5 **Which trail would many trappers choose to use?** Old Spanish Trail Interpret Maps

6 **What trail would people use to get to the Great Salt Lake area?** Mormon Trail Interpret Maps

The Mormon Trail

Quick Summary The Mormons headed west so they could live and worship without criticism.

7 **Why did Young want to move the Mormons further west?** So they could live and worship as they chose Draw Conclusions

✓ **REVIEW ANSWER** Smith killed by an anti-Mormon crowd; Young led Mormons west; Salt Lake City founded Sequence

SOCIAL STUDIES STRAND
History

John C. Frémont, 1813–1890, was nicknamed "The Pathfinder." Starting in 1838 he explored and surveyed much of the west between the Rockies and the Pacific, especially the Oregon Trail. His maps and accounts attracted many settlers. He also aided California in its fight for independence from Mexico, gained and then lost a fortune in gold, and was the new Republican Party's first ever candidate for president in 1856.

FACT FILE
On the Western Trails, 1840s

As you can see from this map, there were many trails westward. Notice that many of these trails followed the path of rivers, which provided travelers with water for drinking, cooking, and cleaning.

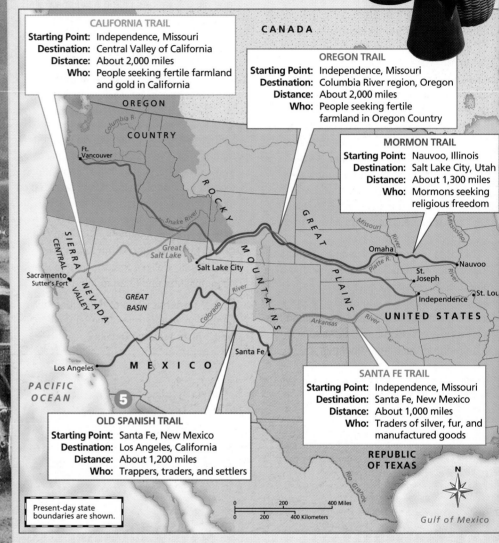

CALIFORNIA TRAIL
Starting Point: Independence, Missouri
Destination: Central Valley of California
Distance: About 2,000 miles
Who: People seeking fertile farmland and gold in California

OREGON TRAIL
Starting Point: Independence, Missouri
Destination: Columbia River region, Oregon
Distance: About 2,000 miles
Who: People seeking fertile farmland in Oregon Country

MORMON TRAIL
Starting Point: Nauvoo, Illinois
Destination: Salt Lake City, Utah
Distance: About 1,300 miles
Who: Mormons seeking religious freedom

OLD SPANISH TRAIL
Starting Point: Santa Fe, New Mexico
Destination: Los Angeles, California
Distance: About 1,200 miles
Who: Trappers, traders, and settlers

SANTA FE TRAIL
Starting Point: Independence, Missouri
Destination: Santa Fe, New Mexico
Distance: About 1,000 miles
Who: Traders of silver, fur, and manufactured goods

Present-day state boundaries are shown.

440

Practice and Extend

Problem Solving

Use a Problem-Solving Process

- Have students consider the following problem-solving scenario: **You are part of a family who has decided to move from your home in the East to a settlement in the West in 1845. Considering the small amount of space available in a wagon, what will your family pack for the journey?**

- Students should use the following problem-solving process to decide what to take on the trip. Ask students to work in small groups to discuss and write about what must be considered as they solve the problem. Then have groups compare and contrast their lists and discuss the rationales behind each item. Write the steps above on the board or read them aloud.

1. Identify a problem.
2. Gather information.
3. List and consider options.
4. Consider advantages and disadvantages.
5. Choose and implement a solution.
6. Evaluate the effectiveness of the solution.

The Mormon Trail

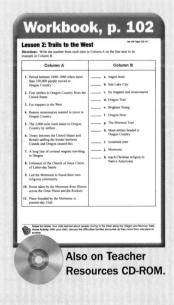

Some people moved west for religious freedom. **Joseph Smith** founded the Church of Jesus Christ of Latter-day Saints in Fayette, New York, in 1830. He and his followers, known as Mormons, were often treated badly because of their religious beliefs. After an angry anti-Mormon crowd in Illinois killed Smith, the new leader, **Brigham Young,** decided that church members should build their own community farther west to be able to live and worship as they chose.

Starting in 1846, Young led a large group of Mormons from Illinois across the Great Plains, and over the Rocky Mountains. Many others followed, and the path Young took came to be known as the **Mormon Trail.** In

► Joseph Smith *(above)* was 25 when he founded the Church of Jesus Christ of Latter-day Saints.

1847, Young and his followers reached the Great Salt Lake area, which then belonged to Mexico. The Mormons founded **Salt Lake City** in the present-day state of Utah. Their well-planned community grew rapidly.

As you will read in the next lesson, the possibility of finding gold also attracted many people to the West.

REVIEW What events led to the founding of Salt Lake City? **Sequence**

Summarize the Lesson

- **1840s** Families began to travel in wagon trains along the Oregon Trail.
- **1846** The United States and Great Britain agreed on a border in Oregon Country, encouraging more settlers to move to the area.
- **1847** Mormons settled in Salt Lake City after moving west in search of religious freedom.

LESSON 2 REVIEW

Check Facts and Main Ideas

1. **Summarize** On a separate sheet of paper, fill in the missing detail and summary of the lesson.

```
People moved          Missionaries          Mormons
to Oregon             moved west            moved west to
Country for           to teach the          find religious
fertile land.         Christian             freedom.
                      religion.
        │                  │                    │
        └──────────────────┼────────────────────┘
                           ▼
            People moved west to find
            opportunities for a better life.
```

2. What were the advantages and disadvantages of traveling west by **wagon train?**

3. Write a one-sentence summary describing each of the main trails leading west.

4. Explain the reasons different groups of people moved west.

5. **Critical Thinking:** *Draw Conclusions* Why do you think the 1846 treaty between the United States and Great Britain encouraged more settlement in Oregon Country?

Link to ⎯∞⎯ **Writing**

Write a Short Story Suppose you are a settler moving west in the 1840s. Which of the trails would you take and why? Write a short story describing your journey by wagon train.

441

Summarize the Lesson

Ask students to make predictions about the future of the settlement of the West (after 1847) and support their predictions with facts from the lesson.

✓ **LESSON 2 REVIEW**

1. **Summarize** For possible answers, see the reduced pupil page.

2. Disadvantage: The trip was dangerous. Advantage: Group travel meant protection.

3. The Oregon Trail led settlers northwest to Oregon Country; settlers seeking religious freedom took the Mormon Trail from Navoo, Illinois, to Salt Lake City, Utah; the California Trail was used by settlers who went from Missouri to California to find farmland; traders used the 1,000-mile-long Santa Fe Trail, which connected Independence, Missouri, and Santa Fe, New Mexico; the Old Spanish Trail connected Santa Fe, New Mexico, to Los Angeles, California.

4. Some moved for religious freedom or to do missionary work, and some to do fur trapping or farming.

5. **Critical Thinking:** *Draw Conclusions* People were more willing to settle in the West because the land was part of the United States.

Link to ⎯∞⎯ **Writing**

Students should include specific details.

Describe the Salt Lake Area Have students explore geographical features that affected settlers.

Easy Ask students to trace the Mormon Trail on p. 440, noting features such as mountains and lakes. **Reteach**

On-Level Have students research the features and climate of the Great Salt Lake area and discuss their impact on settlers. **Extend**

Challenge Ask students to use reference materials to research the geography of the Great Salt Lake area. Ask them to summarize what they find. **Enrich**

For a Lesson Summary, use Quick Study, p. 92.

Workbook, p. 102

Lesson 2: Trails to the West

Directions: Write the number from each item in Column A on the line next to its example in Column B.

Column A	Column B
1. Period between 1840–1860 when more than 350,000 people moved to Oregon Country	___ a. wagon train
2. First settlers to Oregon Country from the United States	___ b. Salt Lake City
3. Fur trappers in the West	___ c. fur trappers and missionaries
4. Reason missionaries wanted to move to Oregon Country	___ d. Oregon Trail
5. The 2,000-mile route taken to Oregon Country by settlers	___ e. Brigham Young
6. Treaty between the United States and Britain settling the border between Canada and Oregon caused this	___ f. Oregon fever
7. A long line of covered wagons traveling to Oregon	___ g. The Mormon Trail
8. Followers of the Church of Jesus Christ of Latter-day Saints	___ h. More settlers headed to Oregon Country
9. Led the Mormons to found their own religious community	___ i. mountain men
10. Route taken by the Mormons from Illinois across the Great Plains and the Rockies	___ j. Mormons
11. Place founded by the Mormons in present-day Utah	___ k. teach Christian religion to Native Americans

Notes for Home: Your child learned about people moving to the West along the Oregon and Mormon Trails.
Home Activity: With your child, discuss the difficulties families encounter as they move from one place to another.

💿 **Also on Teacher Resources CD-ROM.**

The Golden State

Objectives

- Identify the effects of the California gold rush on the population and development of California.

- Identify routes used by people to travel to California.

- Describe the successes, failures, and hardships of California's gold miners.

- Describe how the gold rush increased the size and diversity of the California population.

Vocabulary

gold rush, p. 443; **forty-niners,** p. 443; **discrimination,** p. 445

Resources

- Workbook, p. 103
- Transparency 14
- Every Student Learns Guide, pp. 186–189
- Quick Study, pp. 94–95

Quick Teaching Plan

If time is short, have students create Main Idea and Details charts to outline the important points of the lesson.

1 Introduce and Motivate

Preview Ask students to discuss the effects of a major change in their community or a nearby community, such as the building of a tourist attraction, factory, or large housing development. Tell them that they will read to find out how the discovery of gold changed California in the mid-1800s.

You Are There Many people were lured to California by advertising. Special edition newspaper accounts promised that gold was easy to find. Have students tell what effect they think the discovery of gold will have on California.

442 Unit 6 • A Growing Nation

1840		1850	

1848
Gold is discovered in California

1849
Miners rush to California from all over the world

1850
The new state of California has a fast-growing, varied population

PREVIEW

Focus on the Main Idea
The discovery of gold in California led to rapid settlement of the region.

PLACES
American River
California Trail
San Francisco

PEOPLE
James Marshall
John Sutter
Luzena Stanley Wilson
Levi Strauss

VOCABULARY
gold rush
forty-niners
discrimination

The Golden State

You Are There James Marshall is in charge of the construction of a sawmill near the banks of the American River in California. On January 24, 1848, Marshall is inspecting the water-filled ditch that leads back to the river. Suddenly he sees something shiny. He picks up the shiny speck and examines it. "It made my heart thump," he later says, "for I was certain it was gold."

James Marshall has discovered gold at Sutter's Mill. Soon the whole world will hear about the discovery and many people will head to California in search of riches.

▶ **The dream of finding gold nuggets like these drew thousands to California.**

 Compare and Contrast As you read, think about how California changed after the discovery of gold.

442

Practice and Extend

READING SKILL
Compare/Contrast

In the Lesson Review, students complete a graphic organizer like the one below. You may want to provide students with a copy of Transparency 14 to complete as they read the lesson.

Use Transparency 14

VOCABULARY
Word Exercise

Context Clues Explain that the word *discrimination* has multiple meanings. It can mean: "noticing a difference between things," "ability to make fine distinctions; good judgment," "a difference in attitude or treatment shown to a particular person, class, race, or gender." Tell students to use context to figure out which meaning *discrimination* has in the lesson. Discuss how the meanings are related and different.

The California Gold Rush

In 1848, carpenter James Marshall discovered gold while building a sawmill near California's American River. His employer was John Sutter, a pioneer and owner of the land where the gold was found. Sutter reported that his workers "got the gold fever like everybody else," and left to search for gold. Miners set up camps all over his land.

This was the gold rush—a time when people were leaving their jobs, farms, and homes to come to California in search of riches. Reports of the discovery of gold traveled by word of mouth and in newspapers and letters sent back east and all over the world. In 1849, more than 80,000 people arrived in California. People coming to California during the gold rush became known as forty-niners, after the year in which so many of them arrived there. Signs reading "Off to the Mines" went up in businesses around the United States.

Thousands of forty-niners came by wagon and horseback over the California Trail,

which climbed over the dangerous high slopes of the Sierra Nevada range. Pioneers followed trails established by guides such as James Beckwourth. Beckwourth Pass, high in the Sierra Nevada, is named after this guide, who made a trail through a gap in the high peaks.

Thousands of forty-niners also traveled by ship to San Francisco, which was near the gold fields. Some of the sea travelers sailed from the east coast of the United States, around the southern tip of South America and then north to California. This difficult 17,000-mile journey took from five to seven months to complete. Some forty-niners sailed to the east coast of Central America, made their way through thick forests to the Pacific Ocean, and there boarded ships bound for San Francisco. Still other forty-niners crossed the Pacific Ocean from China. As the table on this page shows, the small port village of San Francisco quickly grew into one of the major cities of the West.

REVIEW What caused the population of San Francisco to grow rapidly from 1848 to 1850? **Cause and Effect**

▶ The gold rush caused San Francisco to grow quickly from a small town to a busy city.

CHART SKILL *Between which two years on the chart did the population of San Francisco grow the most?*

Population of San Francisco, 1847-1860	
Year	**Population**
1847	800
1848	6,000
1850	25,000
1852	35,000
1856	50,000
1860	57,000

Source: U.S. Bureau of the Census

443

---

2 Teach and Discuss

PAGE 443
The California Gold Rush

⏱ **Quick Summary** People flocked to California after James Marshall found gold there in 1848.

1 **Why did people rush to California after James Marshall's discovery?** They hoped to become rich. **Draw Conclusions**

2 **How might John Sutter have felt about the results of the discovery?** Excited about finding gold on his land but distressed that workers left and people set up camps on his land. **Make Inferences**

3 **Summarize the ways people traveled to California.** By wagon and horseback, and by ship **Summarize**

4 **Predict the effects of people rushing to California.** It became more crowded, and there was a greater need for goods and services. **Hypothesize**

✓ **REVIEW ANSWER** San Francisco became the main port for people joining the California gold rush. **Cause and Effect**

5 **What was the population of San Francisco in 1856?** About 50,000 **Interpret Graphs**

CHART SKILL Answer 1848 and 1850

Ⓗ SOCIAL STUDIES STRAND
History

Following the California gold rush there were many mineral strikes and searches for ore attracting settlers to the west. Gold was discovered in the Colorado area in 1858, and the Comstock Lode of gold and silver was discovered in the Nevada area the next year. The first large numbers of Americans in Alaska came after gold was discovered in 1896.

ESL **ACTIVATE PRIOR KNOWLEDGE**
ESL Support

Access Background Information Have students discuss what they know about moving to a new place.

Beginning Have students draw a picture of their current home and then a picture of how a new home might look. Discuss the differences between the two.

Intermediate Have students make a list of all the things they would be sure to pack when moving.

Advanced Have students make a list of all the things that might change when moving and of all the things that would stay the same. Have students compare their lists.

For additional ESL support, use Every Student Learns Guide, pp. 186–189.

Mining for Gold

 Quick Summary Most forty-niners did not find the riches they had hoped for. Some left discouraged, but many stayed and set up profitable businesses.

6 **What facts support the opinion that gold mining was difficult?** The work was hard, and the miners did not have comfortable shelter, food, and medical attention. **Fact and Opinion**

Decision Making

7 **In 1849, would you have gone to California to search for gold? Explain.** Possible answers: Yes, because it would have been a chance for adventure and riches. No, because the trip and the work were too hard and the chance of finding gold was small. **Make Decisions**

✓ Ongoing Assessment

If... students have difficulty making a decision,	**then...** tell them to list advantages and disadvantages of the move. Ask them to review this data and use the information to make a decision.

 SOCIAL STUDIES STRAND
Economics

8 **Give examples of how entrepreneurs profited from the gold rush by meeting needs.** Miners paid Luzena Stanley Wilson for food and shelter, and they bought sturdy pants from Levi Strauss. **Main Idea and Details**

9 **What were other needs the forty-niners probably had in addition to those mentioned in this section?** Sample answers: tools, soap, groceries, cooking utensils, fuel **Hypothesize**

✓ REVIEW ANSWER
Supplies were limited and demand for goods was greater in California than in New York, so prices were higher in California. **Compare and Contrast**

▶ Hard-working gold miners *(above)* liked the tough denim pants made by Levi Strauss *(below)*.

Mining for Gold

For some, the dangers and hardships of the journey across land or sea were worth the goal of reaching California. For most, only disappointments waited for them. Most forty-niners found only small amounts of gold—if they found any at all. Searching for gold in streams and digging in gravel pits was hard work. When miners became sick, one wrote, they often had "no medicine, no bed but the ground."

Life was not easy in the mining camps. Because food and other supplies were scarce and demand was great, merchants could **6** charge high prices. William McSwain complained that miners **7** were paying one dollar for a pound of potatoes. In McSwain's home state of New York, potatoes cost only about one-half cent a pound. High prices and other challenges drove many to leave California. One miner declared "I have got enough of California and am coming home as fast as I can."

But others who came to California became successful selling supplies and services to the miners. Some entrepreneurs, such as **Luzena Stanley Wilson,** ran hotels and restau-

rants. Often these places were little more than shacks. "I bought two boards... (and) with my own hands I chopped stakes, drove them into the ground, and set up my (dining) table," Wilson reported. "Housekeeping was not difficult," she said, since there were "no windows to wash or carpets to take up." But the profits could be great. "Many a night have I shut my oven door on two milk pans filled high with bags of gold dust."

Shopkeeper **Levi Strauss,** an immigrant from Germany, moved to San Francisco in 1850. Strauss learned that miners wanted sturdy pants that would not easily fall apart. Together with a tailor, Strauss designed and made tough pants that were held together with rivets, or metal pins. At first the pants were made out of canvas, but later out of denim. Strauss's business prospered. Like many other newcomers to California, Strauss came to stay.

REVIEW Compare prices in California during the gold rush to those in New York. What accounts for the difference? **Compare and Contrast**

Practice and Extend

 **MEETING INDIVIDUAL NEEDS**
Leveled Practice

Create a Business Idea Have students identify a type of business that would have served the needs of the forty-niners.

Easy As entrepreneurs during the gold rush, have students create an ad for a business to meet the needs of forty-niners. **Reteach**

On-Level Ask students to write press releases for a new business that may have started during the gold rush. Tell students to discuss its purpose and how it will meet the customers' needs. **Extend**

Challenge A business plan explains its goals and how they will be reached. Tell students to act as entrepreneurs and create a business plan for a business to meet the needs of forty-niners. Have them describe resources they will need, their products or services, their customers, how they will advertise, and how to beat the competition. **Enrich**

For a Lesson Summary, use Quick Study, p. 94.

A Fast-Growing State

As a result of the gold rush, the population of California grew quickly. In 1845, about 15,000 people lived in Mexican-ruled California. In 1850, the year that California became a state, the United States census counted about 93,000 people there.

The new state's population was very varied. Tens of thousands were Native Americans—most not counted by the census. About 10,000 were Mexican Americans. They had become United States citizens after the Mexican War. Nearly one of every four Californians had immigrated from other countries.

Newcomers did find opportunities, but many also faced **discrimination**, or unfair treatment. In 1850, the state passed a law taxing immigrant miners $20 a month.

American-born miners did not have to pay the tax. Despite discrimination, however, many people continued to come to the "Golden State."

REVIEW Give details to support the main idea that California had a fast-growing population. Main Idea and Details

Summarize the Lesson

- **1848** Gold was discovered in California.
- **1849** Miners rushed to California from all over the world.
- **1850** Because of the gold rush, the population of California grew from 15,000 in 1845 to 93,000 in 1850, and became more varied.

LESSON 3 REVIEW

Check Facts and Main Idea

1. ↻ **Compare and Contrast** On a separate sheet of paper, fill in the box to describe what California was like before and after the discovery of gold.

Before 1848	After 1848
• Population of San Francisco is 800.	• Population of San Francisco soars to 57,000 in 12 years.
• California's population is about 17,000.	• California's population increases to about 93,000.
• California is not a state.	• California becomes a state.

2. Who were the **forty-niners** and why were they called this name?

3. Describe three routes people from the eastern part of the United States used to travel to California.

4. Do you think the gold-mining life was what the miners expected it to be? Explain.

5. **Critical Thinking:** *Analyze Information* What might lead you to conclude that there was **discrimination** against immigrants in California in 1850?

Link to ∞ **Mathematics**

Use a Chart Look at the chart on page 443. By how many people did San Francisco's population increase from 1847 to 1860?

445

Workbook, p. 103

Lesson 3: The Golden State

Directions: Fill in each missing cause or effect. You may use your textbook.

Cause	Effect
1. Gold was discovered at Sutter's Mill in California.	
2.	The number of people in San Francisco grew rapidly from 1848 to 1850.
3.	Many people left California, but some stayed to become merchants who served miners.
4. Supplies and services were scarce but in high demand. Miners were willing to pay a lot of money for things.	
5.	Levi Strauss created sturdy pants out of canvas, and then denim, for the miners.
6. People moved from many places, including other countries, to get wealthy in the gold rush.	

Also on Teacher Resources CD-ROM.

A Fast-Growing State

🕐 *Quick Summary* The population of California increased greatly as a result of the gold rush.

⑩ **Identify two groups that made up the diverse population of California around 1850.** Mexican Americans, Native Americans Main Idea and Details

✓ **REVIEW ANSWER** The population grew from about 15,000 in 1845 to about 93,000 in 1850. Main Idea and Details

③ Close and Assess

Summarize the Lesson

Ask students to tell how each event is related to the previous one.

✓ **LESSON 3 REVIEW**

1. ↻ **Compare and Contrast** For possible answers, see the reduced pupil page.

2. People who rushed to California for gold in 1849.

3. Over land by wagon; around South America by ship; to the east coast of Central America by ship, hike across Panama, and then by ship to California

4. No. Most miners found little or no gold and experienced hard times while mining.

5. **Critical Thinking:** *Analyze Information* California passed a law taxing only immigrant miners $20.

Link to ∞ **Mathematics**
By about 56,200 people

Evaluate Advertisements

Objectives
- Evaluate the statements in written advertisements.
- Identify facts, opinions, and exaggerations in written advertisements.

Vocabulary
advertisement, p. 446; **evaluate,** p. 447

Resource
- Workbook, p. 104

1 Introduce and Motivate

What are evaluations of advertisements? Ask students whether they have ever seen an advertisement for a product, such as a toy, and then been surprised when they saw the actual product. Then have students read the **What?** section of text on p. 446.

Why evaluate advertisements? Have students read the **Why?** section of text on p. 447. Ask them to describe ads that stick in their minds and express an opinion about whether these ads are accurate or exaggerated.

2 Teach and Discuss

How is this skill used? Examine the ad on p. 446 with students.

- Point out that both the pictures and words work together in ads to send messages and create moods.

- Ask students which words or lines in the ad get their attention first and why. (Possible response: *California Line for San Francisco* and *David Crockett* because the letters in these words are very large.)

- Have students read the **How?** section of text on p. 447.

Thinking Skills

Evaluate Advertisements

What? An **advertisement** tries to sell people goods, or services, or ideas. An advertisement, often called ad for short, may be printed, spoken, sung, or found on the Internet. The purpose is always the same—to interest people in what the advertiser is selling.

The advertiser may be selling any kind of goods, from toothbrushes, to clothing, to cars. Or the advertiser may be selling services, such as haircuts, cooking lessons, or a trip. Or the advertiser may even be selling an idea, such as urging people to vote for a person running for office.

The advertisement shown here was published in a newspaper in New York City during the early years of the gold rush.

Practice and Extend

SOCIAL STUDIES
Background

The Development of Advertising
- Advertising existed in the ancient world, but it was often by word of mouth.
- The invention of printing in the 1400s and 1500s had a major effect on advertising. The first newspaper ads appeared in the 1600s.
- The Industrial Revolution sparked even more interest in advertising. It was during this time that advertising agencies first appeared for the purpose of helping clients place ads in newspapers. Later, these agencies began to create the actual ads.

Orange juice is **GOOD** for you!

Drink Orange Juice

Get the vitamin C, fiber and potassium that you need!

How? When you look at an advertisement, you need to ask some questions in order to evaluate its accuracy.
- What is the advertiser selling?
- Who are the people the advertiser is trying to reach?
- What facts can be found in the advertisement?
- What words or illustrations are used to encourage people to buy something or to support an idea?
- How accurate is the advertisement? Is there anything in the advertisement that cannot possibly be true?

Why? It is important to **evaluate**, or make judgments about, advertisements in order to make good decisions about what goods or services to buy or what ideas to accept.

Advertisements can give you helpful information, such as facts about what is being sold. Advertisements can also exaggerate. They might say or suggest things that cannot possibly be accurate. Something that is accurate is true or correct. Whether accurate or misleading, ads often use names or pictures intended to catch people's interest.

Think and Apply

1 Look at the **advertisement** on page 446. What is it selling? Who might be interested in what is being sold?

2 What facts are given in the advertisement?

3 What does the picture show that cannot possibly be true?

447

---

1 **How is the use of David Crockett in this ad similar to some of today's ads?** Possible answer: Crockett was a hero to people of the time. His association with the company is similar to having sports heroes of today advertise athletic shoes or other products.
↪ Compare and Contrast

2 **What mood did the artist who drew the ad create? Why do you think that mood was chosen?** The mood is adventurous because the purpose of the ad was to make people want to experience the adventure of going west. **Make Inferences**

3 **Which part of the ad indicates that the ad was probably used only one time? Explain why.** "Is now rapidly loading at Pier 15, E.R. foot Wall St." and "over any other vessel now loading"; the word *now* and the specific location mean the ad might not be used again. **Analyze Primary Sources**

4 **Why do you think the ad mentions the ventilation system and the number of decks?** Possible answers: To highlight important features of the ship; to help people compare the *David Crockett* to another ship **Draw Conclusions**

3 Close and Assess

Think and Apply

1. The advertisement is selling passage to San Francisco on the ship *David Crockett*. It might interest people who want to make the voyage.

2. The ship loads at Pier 15 at the foot of Wall Street; it makes the passage to San Francisco in 115 days; it carries cargo; it has three decks; and it insures the cargo.

3. It shows David Crockett riding on the backs of two alligators and controlling them with reins.

CURRICULUM CONNECTION
Music

Evaluate a Jingle
- Have students tape-record an advertising jingle from radio or television.
- Ask students to answer the following questions about the ad: Who is the intended audience for the ad? What facts are included? How does the type of music convey the message? How accurate are the claims in the ad likely to be?
- Provide time for students to play their jingles and present their evaluations.

Workbook, p. 104

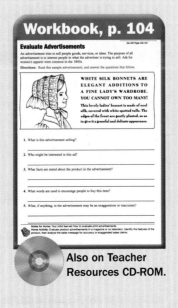

Evaluate Advertisements

An advertisement tries to sell people goods, services, or ideas. The purpose of all advertisement is to interest people in what the advertiser is trying to sell. Ads for women's apparel were common in the 1800s.

Directions: Read this sample advertisement, and answer the questions that follow.

WHITE SILK BONNETS ARE ELEGANT ADDITIONS TO A FINE LADY'S WARDROBE. YOU CANNOT OWN TOO MANY!

This lovely ladies' bonnet is made of cool silk, covered with white spotted tulle. The edges of the front are greatly pleated, so as to give it a graceful and delicate appearance.

1. What is this advertisement selling?

2. Who might be interested in this ad?

3. What facts are stated about the product in the advertisement?

4. What words are used to encourage people to buy this item?

5. What, if anything, in the advertisement may be an exaggeration or inaccurate?

Also on Teacher Resources CD-ROM.

Resources

- Assessment Book, pp. 73–76
- Workbook, p. 105: Vocabulary Review

Chapter Summary

For possible answers, see the reduced pupil page.

Vocabulary

1. d, **2.** e, **3.** b, **4.** c, **5.** a

People and Places

Possible answers:

1. Osceola was a Seminole leader who fought to keep land in Florida.

2. Stephen F. Austin led settlers from the United States into Texas in the 1820s.

3. Texans fought Mexicans at the Alamo, San Antonio.

4. Juan Seguín did not die at the Alamo because he was sent to get help.

5. The Oregon Trail was a major route pioneers took in the 1840s to reach the Oregon Country.

6. The Mormon Trail was a route members of the Church of Jesus Christ of Latter-day Saints took to Salt Lake City, where they hoped to find religious freedom.

7. Brigham Young led the Mormons to the Great Salt Lake region.

8. James Marshall discovered gold at a sawmill under construction in California in 1848, setting off the California gold rush.

9. San Francisco grew from a small town into a major city as a result of the gold rush.

10. Luzena Stanley Wilson ran a business to serve miners during the gold rush.

Facts and Main Ideas

1. The U.S. annexation of Texas and the dispute over the border with Mexico.

CHAPTER 13
REVIEW

1820	1830

1820s
United States settlers begin moving to Texas and continue settling the South

Chapter Summary

Compare and Contrast

Use the diagram to compare and contrast the reasons for population growth in Texas and California during the first half of the 1800s.

Texas — Newcomers wanted good farmland.

Both — Newcomers came from many states. Land was part of Mexico before it became part of the United States.

California — Newcomers hoped to find gold.

CALIFORNIA REPUBLIC

Vocabulary

Match each word with the correct definition or description.

1. **annex** (p. 433)
2. **manifest destiny** (p. 433)
3. **mountain men** (p. 439)
4. **gold rush** (p. 443)
5. **forty-niner** (p. 443)

a. person who went to California to look for gold

b. fur trappers and guides in the West

c. period when people went to California in search of riches

d. attach

e. belief that the United States should expand to the Pacific Ocean

People and Places

Write a sentence explaining why each of the following people or places was important in the growing nation. You may use two or more in a single sentence.

1. **Osceola** (p. 431)
2. **Stephen F. Austin** (p. 432)
3. **San Antonio** (p. 432)
4. **Juan Seguín** (p. 432)
5. **Oregon Trail** (p. 439)
6. **Mormon Trail** (p. 441)
7. **Brigham Young** (p. 441)
8. **James Marshall** (p. 443)
9. **San Francisco** (p. 443)
10. **Luzena Stanley Wilson** (p. 444)

Practice and Extend

Assessment Options

✓ Chapter 13 Assessment

- Chapter 13 Content Test: Use Assessment Book, pp. 73–74.
- Chapter 13 Skills Test: Use Assessment Book, pp. 75–76.

TEST PREP Standardized Test Prep

- Chapter 13 Tests contain standardized test format.

✓ Chapter 13 Performance Assessment

- Have small groups of students role-play settlers sitting around a campfire.
- Ask students to prepare a story about where they are going and why. Tell students to share what they know about the territory they are traveling to and the new life they will build.
- Assess students' understanding of the United States' acquisition of land in the West and their inclusion of accurate facts about the reasons people took this trip and the conditions they encountered.

36
public of
as is formed

1840s
Families begin
moving west along
the Oregon Trail

1845
Texas and
Florida
became
states

1846
Mexican
War
begins

1848
United States wins
Mexican War

1849
Gold-seekers rush
to California from
all over the world

1850
California
becomes a state

Facts and Main Ideas

Name two events that led to war between the United States and Mexico.

In what ways did people profit from the gold rush?

Time Line How many years was Texas a republic before it became a state?

Main Idea How did the Texas Revolution and the Mexican War expand the territory of the United States?

Main Idea Why were people willing to face the hardships of the trails to the West?

Main Idea What changes took place in California as a result of the discovery of gold?

Critical Thinking: *Understand Viewpoints* Would you have been in favor of the war with Mexico in 1846? Why or why not?

Write About History

Write a news story about the Battle of the Alamo.

Write a letter to a friend in the East about your travels along the Oregon Trail.

Write an advertisement for a product you are trying to sell to gold miners in 1849.

Apply Skills

Evaluate Advertisements

Read the advertisement below. Then answer the questions.

Merchants' Express Line of Clipper Ships
FOR
SAN FRANCISCO!
NONE BUT A 1 FAST SAILING CLIPPERS LOADED IN THIS LINE

THE EXTREME CLIPPER SHIP
OCEAN EXPRESS
WATSON, COMMANDER,
AT PIER **9**, EAST RIVER.

RANDOLPH M. COOLEY,
118 WATER ST., cor. Wall, Tontine Building.
Agents in San Francisco, De Witt, Kittle & Co.

1. What is this advertisement selling?

2. What does it show that cannot be true?

3. What words and phrases are used to suggest speed?

Internet Activity

To get help with vocabulary, people, and terms, select dictionary or encyclopedia from *Social Studies Library* at www.sfsocialstudies.com.

449

Hands-on Unit Project

✓ Unit 6 Performance Assessment

• See p. 454 for information about using the Unit Project as a means of performance assessment.

• A scoring guide is provided on p. 454.

WEB SITE
Technology

For more information, students can select the dictionary or encyclopedia from *Social Studies Library* at www.sfsocialstudies.com.

Workbook, p. 105

Vocabulary Review

Directions: Use the vocabulary words from Chapter 13 to complete each item. Use the numbered letters to answer the clue that follows.

1. Suffering unfair treatment

2. People from all over the country rushed to California to find riches

3. A line of covered wagons traveling west

4. Fur trapper in the West

5. Texas settlers' fight for independence from Mexico

6. Officially ended the Mexican War

7. Revolt by settlers leaves California independent from Mexico

8. To add a state to the Union

9. Someone who went to California during the gold rush

10. Mexico and the United States at war over Texas

Clue: This policy expanded the nation from coast to coast.

Also on Teacher
Resources CD-ROM.

2. Some made money from providing goods or services to miners.

3. Texas was a republic for nine years before becoming a state.

4. The Texas Revolution made Texas an independent nation, and then a state. The Mexican War forced Mexico to sell territory to the United States.

5. Some people sought better lives for themselves, while others sought new land, riches, or religious freedom.

6. The population increased rapidly; San Francisco grew quickly; the population became varied because of immigrants from many countries; prices rose on scarce items.

7. Possible answers: Those in favor might mention manifest destiny; those opposed might mention opposition to war or concern about the spread of slavery.

Write About History

1. The news story should present the reasons for the battle, the participants, and the outcome.

2. Students' letters should include details about the mode of transportation, the conditions of the trail, and the daily hardships.

3. Students' ads should show evidence of understanding forty-niners needs.

Apply Skills

1. Passage on the Ocean Express

2. A person riding on a flying fish

3. Possible answers: express, extreme, one of the fastest

Juan Seguín
A Hero of Texas

Objective
- Identify the accomplishments of notable individuals, such as Juan Seguín.

1 Introduce and Motivate

Preview To activate prior knowledge, ask students what they know about Juan Seguín. Tell students that they will learn more about Seguín's courage at the Alamo.

Ask students why it is useful to read a biography of a historical figure. (It explains the sacrifices the person made and the ideals in which he or she believed. It also provides models of admirable qualities, such as courage.)

2 Teach and Discuss

1 What facts support the opinion that the Texans were in a dangerous situation at the Alamo? Mexican troops surrounded the fort and continued firing their cannons while the Texans were running out of ammunition.
Fact and Opinion

2 What did Travis hope to accomplish by getting someone to sneak out of the fort? He wanted to send someone to get help for the Texans in the fort.
Main Idea and Details

Juan Seguín
A Hero of Texas
by Rita Kerr

This excerpt from a biography describes how Juan Seguín volunteered to try to escape from the Alamo and bring back additional Texan soldiers. Despite Seguín's efforts, help did not arrive in time to save the defenders of the Alamo.

With the first rays of light on February 24th, the Mexican cannons began their bombardment. The air grew thick with gunpowder and smoke. The shelling stopped to start again and stop.

Between attacks the Texans repaired the damage done to their defenses. Sentries watched toward the east for reinforcements. They did not come.

Inside the chapel were the wives and children. Captain Almeron Dickinson's wife, Susanna, and daughter were among the families. During the heavy bombardment the mothers knelt to pray and tried to soothe their frightened children. In the brief lulls between the fighting they cooked for the men.

With darkness, when the shooting died down, Davy Crockett and his men told stories and joked around the campfires. Often Davy played his fiddle and sang.

One day slipped into another as fighting continued but ammunition began to dwindle. In the black moonless nights, Santa Anna's army of thousands tightened its grasp like a giant vise until the Alamo was encircled on all four sides. There was no way to escape.

On the evening of February 29th, after six days of fighting, Colonel Travis called a meeting of his officers. One by one the men, including Juan Seguín, gathered around Travis's headquarters and waited. Their faces showed the strain of battle from the constant bombardment and lack of sleep.

450

Practice and Extend

 **SOCIAL STUDIES Background**

Colonel William Travis

- The man who inspired Juan Seguín to volunteer for his dangerous mission was called "the gallant Travis" and described as charming. He worked as a teacher and then as a lawyer before becoming a soldier.
- Initially, Travis and James Bowie were supposed to share the command of the assignment to defend the Alamo. However, Bowie became so ill that the 27-year-old Travis took full control.

"Men," Travis said, looking from one to another. "We must get help and reinforcements. There has been no answer to the dispatches sent to Fannin. I have written another. The question is, who will go?" He paused. "You realize, of course, the danger of crossing the enemy lines. We are surrounded. Anyone want to volunteer?" He looked from Crockett to Dickinson on around the room.

No one spoke.

Captain Juan Seguín stepped forward. All eyes rested on him. "Sir, I will go!" Travis protested, "But, Seguín, I need you."

"Sir, I think I am the only one who could get through those sentries. Being a Tejano, I could answer in Spanish if a soldier stopped me. I could pretend to be one of them." Travis shook his head. "I don't like it, but let's take a vote." The majority voted in favor of Juan Seguín being the messenger. Travis reluctantly agreed. "Besides, I'll be able to find my way in the dark, I know this country." "Colonel, I don't have a horse." Seguín paused to swallow the lump that formed in his throat with the thought of his Prince. "My horse was killed in one of their attacks. I'll ask Bowie if I can borrow his."

Travis nodded, rumpling his hair with his fingers. "Guess you are right, Seguín." He sighed. "Had hoped to use you if Santa Anna sent a message but this dispatch must get out of here. Better take one of your men with you." He handed Juan a paper from his desk. "Give this to Fannin. Tell him we must have help or—" He did not finish.

"Sir," Juan replied as he folded the message and put it in his pocket. "I'll take Antonio Oroche with me. But if we wait until it's dark and they've settled for the night, we'll have a better chance of getting through."

The Colonel sighed and agreed. "You're probably right. When you come back you'll hear a rifle shot every hour on the hour as a signal if we are still fighting. "Well," he paused, "good luck, Seguín. Our future rests on that message getting out so we can have reinforcements."

"I'll do my best, sir," Juan said and looked to his friends who shook his hand. "Good luck to you, amigos. Vaya usted con Dios." With a quick salute, Juan smashed his hat on his head and turned on his heels to walk out into the dusky evening. Drops of rain and a sharp north wind hit his face.

451

 What probably caused Seguín to volunteer to leave the fort? He wanted to help the other people who were trapped in the fort. **Cause and Effect**

4 **Summarize the reasons why Seguín had a better chance at getting out of the fort and getting help than the others.** He knew his way around if he was caught; because he was a Tejano, he could speak Spanish and pretend to be fighting on the Mexican side. **Summarize**

C **SOCIAL STUDIES STRAND**
Culture

Prejudice Reduction Heroes have come from many backgrounds and remind us of our strength through diversity. Tell students that many Hispanic citizens of Texas celebrate Seguín's heroism every year. Memorial celebrations of his life and accomplishments are held periodically in Seguín, Texas.

5 **Why do you think people today remember Seguín as a hero?** Even though he could not get help, he showed great courage in trying. **Make Inferences**

3 Close and Assess

- Have students dramatize the events told in the biography excerpt.

- Have students tell what additional information they learned about the battle at the Alamo from reading about Seguín. (Possible answers: Families supported the soldiers by praying and cooking for them. Colonel Travis had tried to send for help another time before he sent Seguín.)

CURRICULUM CONNECTION
Writing

Write a Travel Article

- Have students read portions of several Texas travel guides to find out what tourists at the Alamo would see today.

- Have them also read guidebooks and brochures about museums and other tourist attractions related to the Alamo.

- Tell students to write articles that could appear in a travel magazine or travel section of a newspaper to describe places a person could visit to learn more about the Alamo.

UNIT
6 Review

Resource
• Assessment Book, pp. 77–80

Main Ideas and Vocabulary | TEST PREP

1. b, **2.** c, **3.** b, **4.** a

People and Terms

1. d, **2.** f, **3.** e, **4.** c, **5.** a, **6.** b

Apply Skills

• Have students determine the audience and purpose for their ads.

• Have students use factual details from the unit in their ads.

• Use the following scoring guide.

✓ **Assessment Scoring Guide**

	Create Pioneer Advertisements
6	Establishes clear purpose with many factual details and exaggerated elements.
5	Establishes purpose with many factual details and exaggerated elements.
4	Establishes purpose with some factual details and exaggerated elements.
3	Establishes general purpose with few factual details and exaggerated elements.
2	Cannot establish clear purpose. Omits either factual details or exaggerated elements.
1	Is unable to create an ad with factual details and exaggeration.

If you prefer a 4-point rubric, adjust accordingly.

Main Ideas and Vocabulary | TEST PREP

Read the passage below and use it to answer the questions that follow.

After its fiftieth birthday in 1826, the United States grew in many ways. It gained land from Spain and Mexico and settled the Oregon border with Great Britain.

Canals, railroads, and better roads made travel faster. New routes such as the National Road and the Oregon Trail made it possible for people to move west.

During the Era of Good Feelings, a spirit of nationalism spread through the country. In the 1828 election of Andrew Jackson, more men voted than ever before. Jackson directed the forced removal of American Indians from the southeast to western lands.

Women began to work for suffrage and for other rights. People like Frederick Douglass and Sojourner Truth worked with others to try to end slavery.

Settlers from the United States moved to the new southern frontier and Texas. Mexico found it difficult to enforce its laws over the Texans, who fought the Texas Revolution to gain independence. The United States annexed Texas in 1845, setting off a war with Mexico. After winning the war, the United States bought new lands from Mexico in 1848.

People moved west to gain a better life in the Oregon Country. Many pioneers traveled in wagon trains. People poured into California after gold was discovered there in 1848.

1 According to the passage, what was one reason settlers moved west?
A The government said they should move.
B They went for a better life.
C There was no longer enough space to live in the East.
D They had to move because there were new forms of transportation.

2 In the passage, the word nationalism means—
A attacking other nations
B belief that the country had to grow
C pulling together with pride in one's country
D belief that all nations are equal

3 In the passage, the word suffrage means—
A suffering for one's beliefs
B the right to vote
C ending slavery
D property ownership

4 What is the main idea of the passage?
A The United States was growing.
B The United States was always at war.
C People in the United States did not like the nation's policies.
D California had a gold rush.

452

Practice and Extend

Assessment Options

✓ **Unit 6 Assessment**

• Unit 6 Content Test: Use Assessment Book, pp. 77–78.

• Unit 6 Skills Test: Use Assessment Book, pp. 79–80.

TEST PREP Standardized Test Prep

• Unit 6 Tests contain standardized test format.

✓ **Unit 6 Performance Assessment**

• See p. 454 for information about using the Unit Project as a means of Performance Assessment.

• A scoring guide for the Unit 6 Project is provided in the teacher's notes on p. 454.

 Test Talk

• Test Talk Practice Book

 WEB SITE Technology

For more information, you can select the dictionary or encyclopedia from *Social Studies Library* at **www.sfsocialstudies.com**.

People and Terms

Match each person and event to its definition.

1. **Monroe Doctrine** (p. 403)
2. **Elizabeth Cady Stanton** (p. 419)
3. **Sam Houston** (p. 432)
4. **Narcissa Whitman** (p. 439)
5. **John Sutter** (p. 443)
6. **forty-niner** (p. 443)

a. owned land where gold was discovered

b. person who went to California to find gold

c. missionary to the Oregon Country

d. warned Europeans to stay out of Western Hemisphere

e. first president of Republic of Texas

f. fighter for women's rights

Apply Skills

Create Pioneer Advertisements Create advertisements to attract newcomers to places described in this unit, such as the Great Salt Lake, Oregon Country, or gold fields of California. Try to include some exaggeration, as the ads of the time did. Use the style of the ad on pages 446–447 as a model. Afterwards, share your ad with classmates so that they can evaluate its accuracy.

GOLD! GOLD! GOLD!

All the gold you ever want just waiting to be picked up.

Write and Share

Present a Travel Talk Work in a group to present a talk about traveling to different parts of the country during the first half of the 1800s. Include different kinds of travel—railroads, roads, wagon trains, boats, combinations of travel—to different regions mentioned in this unit. Each student should write about his or her experiences and prepare maps or illustrations to show the routes taken. Each speaker should give a short talk and then answer questions about their reasons for travel and whether they found what they expected.

Read on Your Own

Look for books like these in the library.

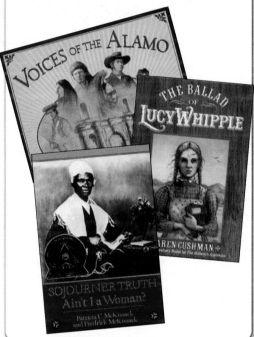

453

Write and Share

- Have students use webs to organize their ideas about their destination, mode of transportation, and route.

- Encourage students to be creative in planning their talks. Suggest that they use props and simple costumes.

- Before giving their talks, have students brainstorm questions they may be asked by their audience and prepare answers.

Test Talk

Write Your Answer to Score High

Use the Write and Share activity to model the Test Talk strategy.

Make sure the answer is correct. Students should make sure their written answer has only correct details.

Make sure the answer is complete. Have students include numerous details in their written answer.

Make sure the answer is focused. Students should make sure their written answer has only details that answer the question/complete the assignment.

Read on Your Own

Have students prepare oral reports using the following books.

Voices of the Alamo, by Sherry Garland (Scholastic Trade, ISBN 0-590-98833-6, 2000) **Easy**

The Ballad of Lucy Whipple, by Karen Cushman (HarperCollins Children's Books, ISBN 0-064-40684-9, 1998) **On-Level**

Sojourner Truth: Ain't I a Woman? by Patricia C. and Frederick McKissack (Scholastic, ISBN 0-590-44691-6, 1994) **Challenge** *Coretta Scott King Honor Book*

Revisit the Unit Question

✓ Portfolio Assessment

- Have students look at their web of reasons people move to new homes in modern times.

- Have students look at their web of reasons people in the United States moved west that they compiled throughout Unit 6.

- Ask students to compare and contrast their webs.

- Students should write one or two paragraphs about the reasons people move. Have students use examples to support these statements: *Some of the reasons people move depend on the time period. Some reasons are the same regardless of the time period.*

- Have students add these webs and paragraphs to their Social Studies Portfolio.

Lure of the Land

Objective
- Describe a westward migration route.

Resource
- Workbook, p. 106

Materials
paper, pencils, paints, markers, reference materials

Follow This Procedure
- Tell students they will present a travel program about settlers in the West. They will describe a trail or method of travel in this unit and present reasons settlers followed it. Students may also do additional research about ways settlers traveled west.

- Divide students into groups. Students may choose from these or other topics: method of transportation, climate, wildlife, geographical features (including distance traveled), or how settlers overcame dangers.

- Instruct students to make a poster or backdrop illustrating a trail or method of westward travel.

- Invite groups to present their posters and programs to the class.

- Use the following scoring guide.

✓ Assessment Scoring Guide

Lure of the Land	
6	Provides clear, detailed description using accurate information and elaborate details.
5	Provides good description using accurate information and details.
4	Provides fair description using mostly accurate information and few details.
3	Provides description using some inaccurate information and few details.
2	Provides poor description using inaccurate information and no details.
1	Cannot provide description of westward migration route.

If you prefer a 4-point rubric, adjust accordingly.

UNIT
6 Project

Lure of the Land

Tell about a trail that the settlers may have taken as they traveled west.

1 Form groups to prepare a travel program about settlers moving west. Choose a trail they may have taken.

2 Research and write the reasons travelers journeyed to the West on this trail.

3 Draw a map that illustrates the route of the trail. You may also want to combine groups to create a poster or backdrop for your program.

4 Present your program to the class.

Internet Activity

Explore westward movement on the Internet. Go to **www.sfsocialstudies.com/activities** and select your grade and unit.

454

Practice and Extend

Hands-on Unit Project

✓ Performance Assessment
- The Unit Project can also be used as a performance assessment activity.
- Use the scoring guide to assess each group's work.

WEB SITE Technology

Students can launch the Internet Activity by clicking on *Grade 5, Unit 6* at **www.sfsocialstudies.com/activities.**

Workbook, p. 106

6 Project Lure of the Land

Directions: In a group, choose a trail that settlers might have taken. Then plan a travel program to share the settlers' experiences.

1. The trail our group chose is _____
2. Some reasons settlers chose this trail: _____

3. The (✓) shows some of the details shown on our map:
   ___ trail we chose
   ___ other possible trails
   ___ cities or towns
   ___ state boundaries
   ___ rivers and other bodies of water
   ___ mountains and other major landforms
   ___ dangers or points of interest on the trail
   ___ compass rose
   ___ scale
   ___ key
4. Other materials we will use in our presentation: _____

✓ Checklist for Students
   ___ We chose a settlers' westward trail.
   ___ We researched reasons travelers used this trail to journey to the West.
   ___ We identified some reasons the settlers chose this trail.
   ___ We planned the features and details for our class.
   ___ We identified props, costumes, sound effects, and other materials.
   ___ We presented our travel program to the class.

Notes for Home: Your child learned about trails settlers used to journey to the West. Home Activity: With your child, research how early settlers traveled to your community. From what areas did most of your first settlers come?

Also on Teacher Resources CD-ROM.

War Divides the Nation

UNIT 7

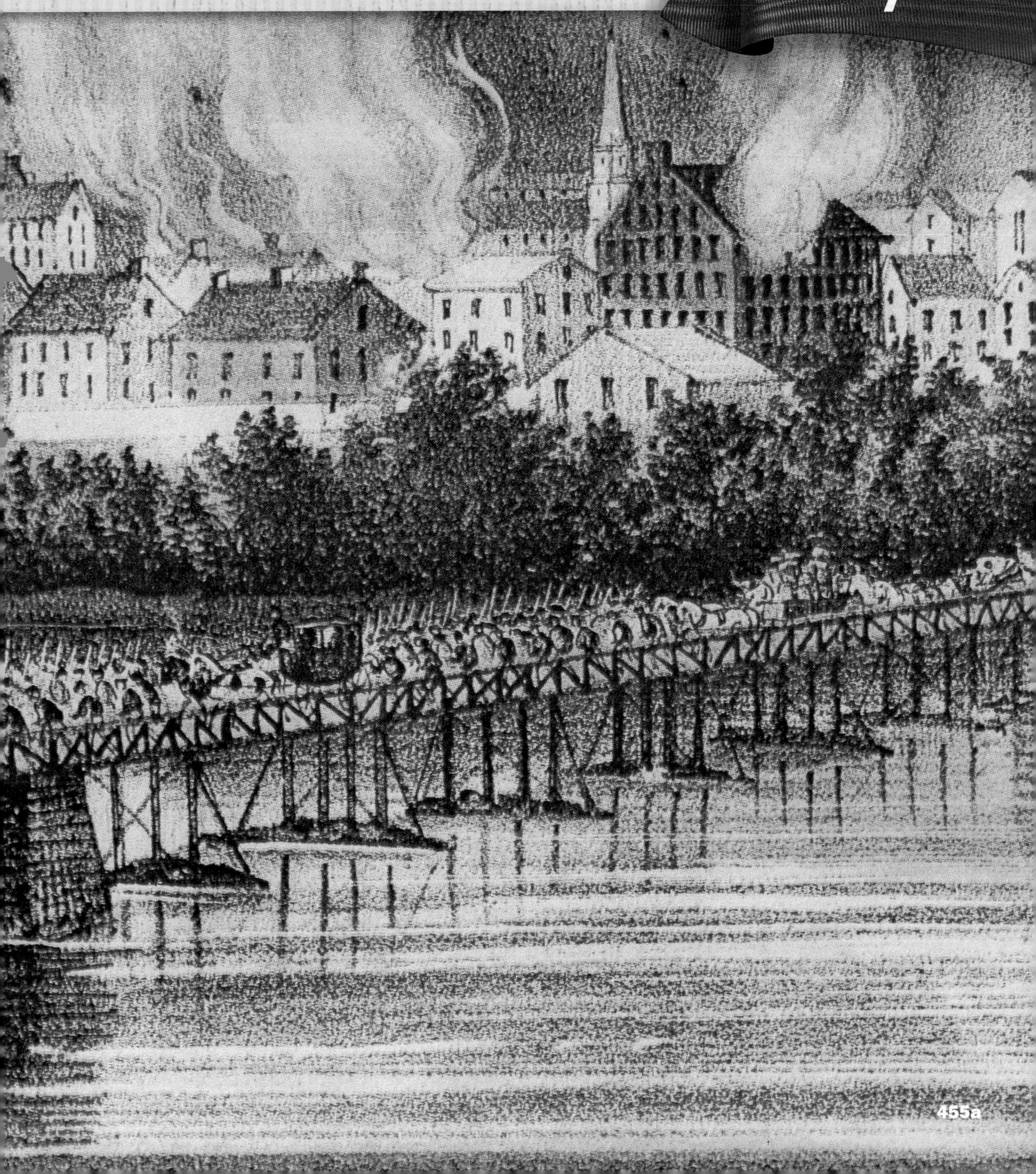

Unit Planning Guide

Unit 7 • War Divides the Nation

Begin with a Primary Source pp. 456–457

Meet the People pp. 458–459

Reading Social Studies, Main Idea and Details pp. 460–461

Chapter Titles	Pacing	Main Ideas
Chapter 14 **A Divided Nation** pp. 462–487	7 days	• Differences between North and South led to growing tensions between the two regions. • Enslaved African Americans resisted slavery in many different ways. • Despite attempts to compromise, the struggle over slavery threatened to tear the United States apart. • Eventually 11 Southern states seceded from the United States, leading to the outbreak of the Civil War.
✓ **Chapter 14 Review** pp. 488–489		
Chapter 15 **War and Reconstruction** pp. 490–521	9 days	• In the early years of the Civil War, the North and South formed strategies in hopes of gaining a quick victory. • As the Civil War continued, people in the North and the South suffered many hardships, including the growing loss of life. • A series of Northern victories led to the end of the Civil War by 1865. • The country faced many difficult challenges after the Civil War ended, including rebuilding the South and protecting the rights of newly freed African Americans.
✓ **Chapter 15 Review** pp. 522–523		

End with a Song pp. 524–525

✓ **Unit 7 Review** pp. 526–527

✓ **Unit 7 Project** p. 528

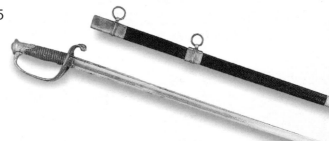

✓ = Assessment Options

This newspaper shares an opinion about the Fugitive Slave Law.

Resources	Meeting Individual Needs
• Workbook, pp. 108–114	• ESL Support, TE pp. 465, 471, 477, 487
• Every Student Learns Guide, pp. 190–205	
• Transparencies 1, 2, 4, 50, 51, 52, 53	• Leveled Practice, TE pp. 467, 474, 479, 482, 486
• Quick Study, pp. 96–103	• Learning Styles, TE pp. 473, 480
✓ Chapter 14 Content Test, Assessment Book, pp. 81–82	✓ Chapter 14 Performance Assessment, TE p. 488
✓ Chapter 14 Skills Test, Assessment Book, pp. 83–84	

• Workbook, pp. 115–121	• ESL Support, TE pp. 494, 502, 511, 519
• Every Student Learns Guide, pp. 206–221	
• Transparencies 1, 54, 55	• Leveled Practice, TE pp. 493, 499, 507, 512, 518
• Quick Study, pp. 104–111	• Learning Styles, TE p. 508
✓ Chapter 15 Content Test, Assessment Book, pp. 85–86	✓ Chapter 15 Performance Assessment, TE p. 522
✓ Chapter 15 Skills Test, Assessment Book, pp. 87–88	

These confederate swords were used in the Battle of Gettysburg.

Providing More Depth
Additional Resources

- Trade Books
- Family Activities
- Vocabulary Workbook and Cards
- Social Studies Plus! pp. 156–177
- Daily Activity Bank
- Read Alouds and Primary Sources pp. 116–132
- Big Book Atlas   • Student Atlas
- Outline Maps   • Desk Maps

Technology

- AudioText
- Video Field Trips: Abraham Lincoln
- Songs and Music
- Digital Learning CD-ROM Powered by KnowledgeBox (Video clips and activities)
- MindPoint® Quiz Show CD-ROM
- ExamView® Test Bank CD-ROM
- Colonial Williamsburg Primary Sources CD-ROM
- Teacher Resources CD-ROM
- Map Resources CD-ROM
- SF SuccessNet: iText (Pupil Edition online), iTE (Teacher's Edition online), Online Planner
- **www.sfsocialstudies.com** (Biographies, news, references, maps, and activities)

To establish guidelines for your students' safe and responsible use of the Internet, use the Scott Foresman Internet Guide.

Additional Internet Links

To find out more about:

- the Civil War, visit **www.gliah.uh.edu**
- Clara Barton, visit **www.greatwomen.org**
- abolitionists, visit **www.pbs.org**

Unit 7 Objectives

Beginning of Unit 7

- Use primary sources to acquire information. (p. 456)
- Identify the contributions of significant individuals during the time leading up to and including the U.S. Civil War. (p. 458)
- Analyze information by using supporting details to determine the main idea. (p. 460)

- Describe the differences between the economies and populations of the North and South.
- Identify the role that slavery played in the South in the mid-1800s.
- Explain how and why views about slavery differed in the North and South.
- Identify facts and opinions in writing. (p. 468)
- Consider the experiences of an individual writer and how those experiences may have shaped the writer's ideas. (p. 468)
- Describe a writer's point of view. (p. 468)

- Identify ways African Americans resisted slavery.
- Describe rebellions of African Americans against slavery.
- Explain how the Underground Railroad was used to free enslaved people.
- Describe the lives of free African Americans in the North and South.
- Identify the personal qualities that motivated Harriet Tubman to take risks in helping African Americans escape to freedom. (p. 475)

- Describe the causes and effects of the Missouri Compromise and the Compromise of 1850.
- Explain the causes of violence in Kansas in 1854.
- Draw conclusions about how Dred Scott and John Brown affected the split between the North and South.
- Compare the views on slavery of Abraham Lincoln and Stephen Douglas.
- Identify early influences in Abraham Lincoln's life that shaped his character and his deep feelings of patriotism. (p. 483)

- Describe the reasons why Southern states seceded from the Union.
- Identify the immediate cause of the start of the Civil War.
- Describe the goals the North and South hoped to achieve by fighting the Civil War.

- Identify the resources of the North and South.
- Compare the strategies of the North and South in the Civil War.
- Describe early battles in the Civil War.
- Explain how new military technology affected the way the war was fought.
- Identify the accomplishments of notable individuals, such as Robert E. Lee. (p. 497)

- Compare and contrast life for Northern and Southern soldiers.
- Analyze the effect of the Emancipation Proclamation on African Americans.
- Describe the contributions of African American soldiers to the Union war effort.
- Identify the different ways women contributed to the war effort in the North and South.
- Identify the accomplishments of notable individuals, such as Jody Williams. (p. 504)

- Describe the events of the Battle of Gettysburg.
- Analyze President Lincoln's Civil War goals as expressed in the Gettysburg Address.
- Identify the location and results of the major battles of the Civil War.
- Explain the reasons for the use of total war, and its consequences.
- Apply geographic skills to interpret legends and symbols on maps. (pp. 512–513)
- Identify and explain different forms of communications during the Civil War. (pp. 514–515)

- Explain why Congress disagreed with Johnson's plan for Reconstruction.
- Analyze the effect of the Reconstruction Acts.
- Evaluate the impact of the Thirteenth, Fourteenth, and Fifteenth Amendments.
- Describe life for African Americans after Reconstruction.

End of Unit 7

- Identify significant examples of music from various periods in U.S. history. (pp. 524–525)
- Describe the experiences of people living during the Civil War and Reconstruction. (p. 528)

◀ **Both Union and Confederate soldiers grew tired of war.**

Assessment Options

✓ Formal Assessment

- **Lesson Reviews,** PE/TE pp. 467, 474, 482, 487, 496, 503, 511, 521
- **Chapter Reviews,** PE/TE pp. 488–489, 522–523
- **Chapter Tests,** Assessment Book, pp. 81–88
- **Unit Review,** PE/TE pp. 526–527
- **Unit Tests,** Assessment Book, pp. 89–92
- **ExamView® Test Bank CD-ROM** (test-generator software)

✓ Informal Assessment

- **Teacher's Edition Questions,** throughout Lessons and Features
- **Section Reviews,** PE/TE pp. 465–467, 471–474, 477–482, 485–487, 493–496, 499–502, 507–510, 517–521
- **Close and Assess,** TE pp. 461, 467, 469, 474, 475, 482, 483, 487, 496, 497, 503, 505, 511, 513, 515, 521, 525

Ongoing Assessment

Ongoing Assessment is found throughout the Teacher's Edition lessons using an **If...then** model.

If = students' observable behavior,	**then** = reteaching and enrichment suggestions

✓ Portfolio Assessment

- **Portfolio Assessment,** TE pp. 455, 456, 527
- **Leveled Practice,** TE pp. 467, 474, 479, 482, 493, 499, 507, 512, 518
- **Workbook Pages,** pp. 107–122
- **Chapter Review: Write About History,** PE/TE pp. 489, 523
- **Unit Review: Apply Skills,** PE/TE p. 527
- **Curriculum Connection: Writing,** PE/TE pp. 482, 503, 521; TE pp. 457, 468, 472, 474, 475, 493, 499, 505, 509, 518

✓ Performance Assessment

- **Hands-on Unit Project** (Unit 7 Performance Assessment), TE pp. 455, 489, 523, 528
- **Internet Activity,** PE p. 528
- **Chapter 14 Performance Assessment,** TE p. 488
- **Chapter 15 Performance Assessment,** TE p. 522
- **Unit Review: Write and Share,** PE/TE p. 527
- **Scoring Guides,** TE pp. 527–528

Test Talk

Test-Taking Strategies

Understand the Question
- **Locate Key Words in the Question,** PE/TE p. 526; TE p. 495
- **Locate Key Words in the Text,** TE p. 500

Understand the Answer
- **Choose the Right Answer,** Test Talk Practice Book
- **Use Information from the Text,** TE p. 480
- **Use Information from Graphics,** TE p. 513
- **Write Your Answer to Score High,** TE p. 489

For additional practice, use the Test Talk Practice Book.

Featured Strategy

Locate Key Words in the Question
Students will:
- Find the key words in the question.
- Turn the key words into a statement that begins "I need to find out. . . ."

PE/TE p. 526; **TE** p. 495

Curriculum Connections

Integrating Your Day

The lessons, skills, and features of Unit 7 provide many opportunities to make connections between social studies and other areas of the elementary curriculum.

Social Studies

READING

Reading Skill—Main Idea and Details, TE pp. 460–461, 464, 470, 476, 484, 492, 498, 506, 516

Lesson Review—Main Idea and Details, TE pp. 467, 474, 482, 487, 496, 503, 511, 521

WRITING

Write a Speech, TE p. 457

Write an Editorial, TE p. 468

Create an Argument, TE p. 472

Write an Article, TE pp. 474, 518

Write Speeches, TE p. 475

Link to Writing, PE/TE pp. 482, 503, 521

Write a Summary, TE p. 493

Write a Letter, TE p. 499

Write an E-mail, TE p. 505

Write a Diary Entry, TE p. 509

Write a Short Story or Poem, TE p. 521

MATH

Disease Statistics, TE p. 496

Link to Mathematics, PE/TE pp. 496, 511

Calculate Totals, TE p. 501

Number Match, TE p. 507

LITERATURE

Read Biographies, TE pp. 458, 483

Read Books About Slavery, TE p. 469

SCIENCE

Link to Science, PE/TE p. 474

MUSIC / DRAMA

"When Johnny Comes Marching Home," PE/TE p. 524

Write a New Verse, TE p. 525

ART

Interpret Fine Art, TE p. 456

Link to Art, PE/TE p. 467

Create an Illustration, TE p. 468

Design Promotional Materials, TE p. 472

 Look for this symbol throughout the Teacher's Edition to find **Curriculum Connections.**

Professional Development

Making Social Studies Exciting

by Fred Risinger, Ph.D.
Indiana University

Elementary social studies is an essential subject. Understanding our society, its history and pluralistic culture, and the skills and processes of participatory citizenship are all taught through the social studies curriculum.

One need not choose between a teaching method that favors systematic information processing instructional strategies and a teaching method that involves a problem-solving, student-centered, project-oriented approach. Effective teaching uses elements of both methodologies.

One thing is certain—the most important person in the instructional process is you, the classroom teacher. When asked to name a best or favorite teacher, more students named a social studies teacher than any other. What does this say? I think it says that social studies—the dramatic, tragic, and uplifting story of men and women on this planet—is the most exciting part of the school curriculum. As a classroom teacher, you have the obligation, and the great opportunity, to bring that story to your students. Below are several ways the Scott Foresman program makes social studies come alive.

- *On p. 466 of the Teacher's Edition, students are told to suppose they are a plantation owner who does not believe in slavery. Students use a problem-solving process to decide how they would harvest their cotton before their crops are ruined.*

- *Students examine pictures on p. 490 of the Pupil's Edition that are springboards for discussion about important historical events.*

- *On p. 497 of the Teacher's Edition, students use a decision-making process to decide whether they should advise Robert E. Lee to accept or to reject the position as commander of the Virginia armed forces.*

ESL Support

by Jim Cummins, Ph.D.
University of Toronto

In Unit 7, you can use the following fundamental strategy to help ESL students access social studies content:

Access Content

Language is central to the teaching of virtually every school subject. When students learn social studies, they are learning a set of concepts related to the ways in which people have organized their communities and societies both historically and currently.

Social studies has its own specialized vocabulary that students must acquire if they are to be successful in learning the content. Examples of such vocabulary include *constitution, preamble, convention,* and many other words rarely heard on the playground.

Similarly, what linguists call *nominalization* is very common in the social studies text. Nominalization refers to the creation of abstract nouns from verbs and adjectives. These nouns, such as *immigrate/immigration* and *represent/representation,* express concepts that can be related to each other.

The following examples in the Teacher's Edition will help ESL students better understand the content of the unit:

- ***Examine Word Meaning*** *on p. 471 helps English Language Learners explore the meaning of the word* resist. *Advanced learners are led to understand that another form of* resist *is* resistance. *Students then discuss the word's meaning.*

- ***Demonstrate Concept Understanding*** *on p. 494 provides opportunities for students to show that they know the meaning of the word* retreat.

Read Aloud

from Abraham Lincoln's first inaugural address:

We are not enemies, but friends. We must not be enemies. Though passion may have strained it must not break our bonds of affection. The mystic chords of memory, stretching from every battlefield and patriot grave to every living heart and hearthstone all over this broad land, will yet swell the chorus of the Union, when again touched, as surely they will be, by the better angels of our nature.

Build Background

- These words are from President Abraham Lincoln's first inaugural address, which he delivered on Monday, March 4, 1861.
- Two weeks before Lincoln's inauguration, many of the states in the Southern part of the United States had left the Union to form a Confederacy, or association, of states. Jefferson Davis was its President.
- In his speech, Lincoln addressed the importance of uniting the country. The American Civil War had not yet begun.

Definitions

- *passion:* violent anger or rage
- *affection:* friendship or warmth

Read Alouds and Primary Sources

- *Read Alouds and Primary Sources* contains additional selections to be used with Unit 7.

Bibliography

A Freedom River, by Doreen Rappaport (Jump at the Sun Books, ISBN 0-786-80350-9, 2000) **Easy** **Coretta Scott King Honor Book**

Harriet and the Promised Land, by Jacob Lawrence (Aladdin Paperbacks, ISBN 0-689-80965-4, 1997) **Easy** **New York Times Best Illustrated Book**

Voice of Freedom: A Story About Frederick Douglass, by Maryann N. Weidt (Lerner Publishing Group, ISBN 1-575-05553-8, 2001) **Easy**

Lincoln: A Photobiography, by Russell Freedman (Clarion Books, ISBN 0-899-19380-3, 1987) **On-Level** **Newbery Medal**

Steal Away, by Jennifer Armstrong (Scholastic Paperbacks, ISBN 0-590-46921-5, 1993) **On-Level** **ALA Notable Book**

The World in the Time of Abraham Lincoln, by Fiona MacDonald (Chelsea House Publishers, ISBN 0-791-06028-4, 2000) **On-Level**

Anthony Burns: The Defeat and Triumph of a Fugitive Slave, by Virginia Hamilton (Laurel-Leaf, ISBN 0-679-83997-6, 1988) **Challenge** **ALA Notable Book, Boston Globe Horn Book Award, Jane Addams Book Award**

Dear Ellen Bee: A Civil War Scrapbook of Two Union Spies, by Mary E. Lyons and Muriel M. Branch (Atheneum, ISBN 0-689-82379-7, 2000) **Challenge**

House of Dies Drear, by Virginia Hamilton (Aladdin Paperbacks, ISBN 0-020-43520-7, 1984) **Challenge** **Edgar Allan Poe Juvenile Book**

Battle Cry of Freedom: The Civil War Era, by James M. McPherson (Oxford University Press, ISBN 0-19-516895-X, 2003) **Teacher reference**

With Malice Toward None: A Life of Abraham Lincoln, by Stephen B. Oates (HarperPerennial Library, ISBN 0-060-92471-3, 1994) **Teacher reference**

Discovery Channel School Video Slave Ship. Uncover shocking facts about the trans-Atlantic slave trade as African slaves take over the slave ship *Amistad;* 26 minutes.

Look for this symbol throughout the Teacher's Edition to find **Award-Winning Selections.** Additional book references are suggested throughout this unit.

War Divides the Nation

What might cause a nation to break apart?

War Divides the Nation

Unit Overview

Friction between the Northern and Southern states developed as the two regions differed more and more in their viewpoints on crucial issues. Conflicts between the regions resulted in the secession of the Southern states and, eventually, the U.S. Civil War.

Unit Outline

Chapter 14 A Divided Nation
pp. 462–489

Chapter 15 War and Reconstruction
pp. 490–523

Unit Question

- Have students read the question under the painting.

- To activate prior knowledge, ask students if they know of, or have heard of, nations that have collapsed or divided. What caused those problems? What kinds of differences of opinion or policy could lead to friction between different parts of a nation?

- Create a list of students' ideas about why nations may break apart. Encourage students to include factors they have heard or read about as well as additional factors that they think could contribute.

✓**Portfolio Assessment** Keep this list to review with students at the end of the unit on p. 527.

Practice and Extend

Hands-on Unit Project

✓**Unit 7 Performance Assessment**

- The Unit Project, *History Speaks,* found on p. 528, is an ongoing performance assessment project to enrich students' learning throughout the unit.

- This project, which has students prepare a talk about life during the Civil War and Reconstruction, may be started now or at any time during this unit of study.

- A performance assessment scoring guide is located on p. 528.

Begin with a Primary Source

Objective
• Use primary sources to acquire information.

Resource
• Poster 14

Interpret a Primary Source

• Tell students that this quotation is from the Gettysburg Address, which Lincoln gave at the dedication of the National Cemetery at this Civil War battlefield.

• The main speaker was Edward Everett, and he spoke for two hours. He later acknowledged that Lincoln's short address was brilliant.

• The full text of Lincoln's address is on p. 508.

✓ **Portfolio Assessment** Remind students of their lists of reasons that a nation might break apart. Have students continue their lists, adding the reasons that the United States began to break apart in the 1850s (see p. 455). As they read the unit, allow time for students to review and add to the list. Review students' lists at the end of the unit on p. 527.

Interpret Fine Art

• This picture shows the fall of Richmond, Virginia, and was printed by Currier and Ives in 1865. It shows Richmond, Virginia, which was the capital of the Confederate States of America.

• Spark discussion on the point of view of this piece. Do students think it was created by someone who was neutral about the outcome of the war?

• Have students discuss what this picture reveals about the costs of the Civil War to "ordinary" citizens.

1820		1850	1860		
1820 Congress passes Missouri Compromise	**1849** Harriet Tubman escapes slavery on the Underground Railroad		**1860** Abraham Lincoln is elected President	**April 1861** Southern forces fire on Fort Sumter, beginning the Civil War	January Emancip Proclam takes

456

Practice and Extend

FYI SOCIAL STUDIES
Background

About the Primary Source

• Many students will recognize the first words of the Gettysburg Address: *Four score and seven years ago our fathers brought forth on this continent a new nation. . . .* The phrase on p. 457 comes from the last sentence of the speech.

• Although Lincoln's speech was far shorter than that of the main speaker at the National Cemetery Dedication and was criticized by many of his opponents, his oration was quoted and praised by many.

• The Battle of Gettysburg, a defeat for Southern forces, took place from July 1 to 3, 1863. The losses in the battle were among the worst of the entire Civil War—more than 43,000 men were killed, wounded, missing, or captured.

• In 1895 the battlefield became a national military park.

> "...that these dead shall not have died in vain—that this nation, under God, shall have a new birth of freedom..."
>
> —Said by President Abraham Lincoln in the Gettysburg Address, November 19, 1863

This print by Currier and Ives shows the Fall of Richmond, Virginia, to Union forces in 1865.

Meet the Artist

- Nathaniel Currier and James Merritt Ives used lithography, a method of printing, to make black-and-white prints, which were then hand colored.

- Known as Currier and Ives from 1857, the company produced more than 7,500 different titles and a total of more than a million copies of these prints.

- Currier and Ives described themselves as "Publishers of Cheap and Popular Pictures."

- The lithographs were very popular. They helped people understand current events.

- Many of Currier and Ives's works showed daily life in the United States—scenes of family life, or of people at work or play. Today, these lithographs serve as a valuable record of what people's lives were like in an age before photography was widely available.

Use the Time Line

The time line at the bottom of the page covers a time period of nearly fifty years, starting with the Missouri Compromise and ending with the passage of the Reconstruction Act.

1 **How long did the Civil War last?** About four years **Interpret Time Lines**

2 **About how many years after Harriet Tubman's escape from slavery were all enslaved people legally freed by the 13th Amendment?** 16 years
Analyze Information

3 **Which event happened in March of 1867?** Congress passed the Reconstruction Act. **Interpret Time Lines**

1870

| ly 1863 attle of ettysburg fought | April 1865 Confederacy surrenders, ending the Civil War | December 1865 The 13th Amendment ends slavery | March 1867 Congress passes Reconstruction Act |

1 **2** **3**

457

CURRICULUM CONNECTION
Writing

Write a Speech

Have students suppose they have been asked to give speeches at the opening ceremonies for the National Park at the site of the Battle of Gettysburg. Provide ideas such as the following to spark students' thinking about speech topics:

- Tell why it is important to remember the sacrifices that were made during the Battle of Gettysburg. Explain why the Park Service decided to honor those who had fought there.
- Create a short "Hall of Fame" presentation about a person who was important during the time of the U.S. Civil War.
- Read Lincoln's Gettysburg Address. In your speech, explain Lincoln's thoughts in your own words and tell why you agree or disagree with his ideas.

Consider having students write and read their speeches with partners in preparation for presenting their work to the class.

UNIT 7

Meet the People

Objective
- Identify the contributions of significant individuals during the time leading up to and including the U.S. Civil War.

Resource
- Poster 15

Research the People

Each of the people pictured on these pages played an important role in the history of the United States between 1820 and 1867. Have students conduct research to find out the answers to the following questions.

- **What was surprising about Ulysses S. Grant's decision to attend the U.S. Military Academy?** Possible answer: He was not interested in the military, and many thought he was too "sloppy" to be a soldier.

- **What office did Henry Clay run for unsuccessfully?** He ran for President twice.

- **Describe some of the jobs that Clara Barton held.** She was a teacher, and she worked in the U.S. Patent Office.

- **What jobs did Harriet Tubman hold during her life after escaping from slavery?** Scout, spy, nurse, laundress, and founder of home for elderly people and orphans

Students may wish to write their own questions about other people on these pages for the rest of the class to answer.

Use the Time Line

Have students use the time line and biographies to answer the following questions.

1 Which person died before the Civil War began? Henry Clay
Analyze Information

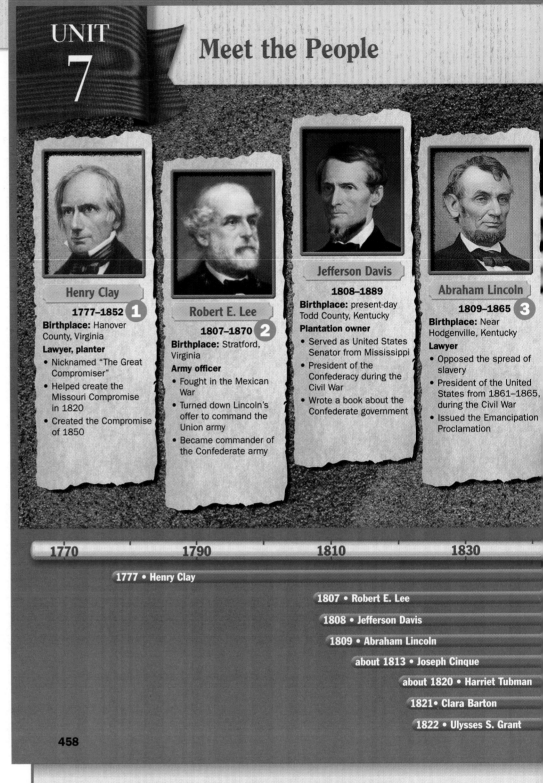

UNIT 7 — Meet the People

Henry Clay
1777–1852 ①
Birthplace: Hanover County, Virginia
Lawyer, planter
- Nicknamed "The Great Compromiser"
- Helped create the Missouri Compromise in 1820
- Created the Compromise of 1850

Robert E. Lee
1807–1870 ②
Birthplace: Stratford, Virginia
Army officer
- Fought in the Mexican War
- Turned down Lincoln's offer to command the Union army
- Became commander of the Confederate army

Jefferson Davis
1808–1889
Birthplace: present-day Todd County, Kentucky
Plantation owner
- Served as United States Senator from Mississippi
- President of the Confederacy during the Civil War
- Wrote a book about the Confederate government

Abraham Lincoln
1809–1865 ③
Birthplace: Near Hodgenville, Kentucky
Lawyer
- Opposed the spread of slavery
- President of the United States from 1861–1865, during the Civil War
- Issued the Emancipation Proclamation

1770   1790   1810   1830

1777 • Henry Clay
1807 • Robert E. Lee
1808 • Jefferson Davis
1809 • Abraham Lincoln
about 1813 • Joseph Cinque
about 1820 • Harriet Tubman
1821• Clara Barton
1822 • Ulysses S. Grant

458

Practice and Extend

CURRICULUM CONNECTION
Literature

Read Biographies
Use the following biography selections to extend the content.

Robert E. Lee, Brave Leader, by Rae Bains (Troll Associates, ISBN 0-816-70546-1, 1989) **Easy**

Harriet Tubman: Conductor on the Underground Railroad, by Ann Petry (Harper Trophy, ISBN 0-064-46181-5, 1996) **On-Level**

Clara Barton: Civil War Nurse, by Nancy Whitelaw (Enslow Publishers, ISBN 0-894-90778-6, 1997) **Challenge**

Joseph Cinque

about 1813–about 1879 **4**

Birthplace: present-day Sierra Leone, West Africa

Rice farmer, leader of slave ship rebellion

- African name was Sengbe Pieh, which was pronounced by the Spanish as "Cinque"
- Led African captives in a revolt aboard the slave ship *Amistad*
- Served as key witness during the *Amistad* trial

Harriet Tubman

about 1820–1913 **3**

Birthplace: Dorchester County, Maryland **5**

Conductor on the Underground Railroad, abolitionist

- Escaped from slavery in 1849 and settled in Philadelphia
- Made 19 trips to the South on the Underground Railroad and helped free over 300 slaves
- Spoke out against slavery and for women's rights

Clara Barton

1821–1912 **5**

Birthplace: Oxford, Massachusetts

Teacher, nurse

- Volunteered as a nurse during the Civil War
- Nicknamed the "Angel of the Battlefield"
- Founded the American Red Cross

Ulysses S. Grant

1822–1885 **2**

Birthplace: Point Pleasant, Ohio

Army officer

- Won the first major Union victory of the Civil War at Fort Donelson
- Appointed to command the Union armies by President Lincoln
- Elected President of the United States in 1868

1850	1870	1890	1910

1852

1870

1889

1865

about 1879

1913

1912

1885

459

2 **How were Robert E. Lee and Ulysses S. Grant similar?** Both were offered the opportunity to command the Union Army by Abraham Lincoln. Compare and Contrast

3 **Which person had the longest life? the shortest life?** Longest: Harriet Tubman; Shortest: Abraham Lincoln Analyze Information

4 **Why do you think that the date of death for Joseph Cinque is "about 1879"?** People are not sure of the exact date of his death; there may not have been records kept of his death. Analyze Information

5 **Which people were alive during the twentieth century?** Harriet Tubman and Clara Barton Interpret Time Lines

Biographies

Three of the people shown here are discussed more extensively in the Biography pages in Unit 7.

- Harriet Tubman, p. 475
- Abraham Lincoln, p. 483
- Robert E. Lee, p. 497

Read About the People

The people shown here are discussed in the text on the following pages in Unit 7.

- Henry Clay, pp. 477–478
- Robert E. Lee, pp. 495, 497, 507, 509–511
- Jefferson Davis, pp. 485–486
- Abraham Lincoln, pp. 481–483, 485–486, 500, 506, 508, 511, 516–517
- Joseph Cinque, p. 472
- Harriet Tubman, pp. 473, 475
- Clara Barton, p. 502
- Ulysses S. Grant, pp. 509–511

WEB SITE
Technology

Students can research the lives of people on this page by clicking on *Meet the People* at **www.sfsocialstudies.com.**

Reading Social Studies

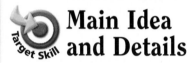

Main Idea and Details

Objective

Analyze information by using supporting details to determine the main idea.

Resource

• Workbook, p. 107

About the Unit Target Skill

• The target reading skill for this unit is Main Idea and Details.
• Students are introduced to the unit target skill here and are given an opportunity to practice it.
• Further opportunities to determine main ideas and details are found throughout Unit 7.

1 Introduce and Motivate

Preview Show students a short article from a newspaper. Ask what the headline does (tells what the article is about). Link the headline to the concept of main idea. It tells what the article is about, or the most important idea; and the article gives details that support that idea.

2 Teach and Discuss

• Explain that a main idea is the most important idea of a paragraph. Details are pieces of information that support (tell more about) the main idea.

• Have students read the paragraph on p. 460. Make sure they realize that the highlighting shows the main idea and the details that support the main idea. Each detail tells how the United States was growing and changing.

War Divides the Nation

Main Idea and Details

Look at the diagram to see how details support a main idea.
A main idea is the most important idea of a paragraph.
Details are information related to the main idea.
Each detail helps to support the main idea.

> Read the following paragraph. The **main idea** and **details** have been highlighted.

In Chapter 13, you read about how the United States was growing and changing. The development of roads, waterways, and the railroad allowed people to move west. The nation's land was expanding. The way people lived was also changing. In some places, cities were growing and attracting factory workers. In other parts of the country, people were still living on farms but changing the way they harvested their crops.

Word Exercise

Use Context Clues Sometimes you can use clues from the text to help you figure out the meaning of an unfamiliar word. Read the third paragraph of the passage. Here is how to figure out the meaning of *victorious*:

1. Reread the sentence before the sentence with *victorious*: What are *victories*? (wins)
2. Now reread the sentence that *victorious* is in. What does *surrendered* mean? (gave up)
3. Using *victories* and *surrendered*, what is the meaning of *victorious*? (winning)

460

Practice and Extend

ESL Support

Determine Main Ideas Guide students to understand how to determine the main idea of a paragraph.

Beginning Write a short paragraph on the board that consists of a main idea and several details. Read the first sentence aloud. As you underline this sentence, explain that it is the main idea. Then ask students to circle details.

Intermediate Make copies of a simple paragraph with a main idea sentence and several sentences with details. Cut each paragraph into sentence strips and give groups the strips for one paragraph. Students should put the sentences into an order that makes sense and identify the main idea.

Advanced Cut several paragraphs out of magazine or newspaper articles and distribute them to students. Students can work in pairs to underline the main idea and then use a colored pen to highlight supporting details.

Main Ideas and Details of War Divides a Nation

Differences between the Northern and Southern states led to many problems for the United States. The rural South depended on farming and slavery. The North had more factories and larger cities than the South.

Trouble grew when Abraham Lincoln became President in 1861. South Carolina broke away from the Union. Before long, eleven states in the South had done the same and formed the Confederate States of America. The country was divided and went to war. This war was called the Civil War.

Each side won some battles. In late 1863, Northern victories increased. In 1865, the North was victorious and the South surrendered.

Lincoln hoped to reunite the nation, but he was killed shortly after the Civil War. President Andrew Johnson and Congress fought over Reconstruction, or the plans for rebuilding the South. Amendments to the Constitution ended slavery and gave the vote to all male citizens, black and white.

Federal troops and Reconstruction laws governed Southern states. The Freedmen's Bureau, a federal agency, provided aid and set up schools for African Americans.

When Reconstruction ended in 1877, some Southerners tried to keep freed slaves from voting. Groups like the Ku Klux Klan burned black schools and terrified black men who tried to vote. Southern states also passed Jim Crow laws, which said African Americans could only use designated non-white areas in restaurants, trains, buses, hotels, and other public places.

Use the reading strategy of main idea and details to answer questions 1 and 2. Then answer the vocabulary question.

1 What is the main idea of the first paragraph?

2 What details support that main idea?

3 What clues can help you figure out the meaning of the word *rural* in the first paragraph of the passage? When you think you know what *rural* means, check a dictionary to see if you are correct.

461

Then have students read the longer practice sample on p. 461 and answer the questions that follow.

- Ask students why, when studying history, it is important to know how to figure out the main idea and identify details. (To understand history we need to figure out the most important ideas. Locating supporting details shows us whether or not our main ideas are accurate.)

Use Context Clues

Words and sentences that help students figure out meaning are called context clues. Discuss with students how to use context clues to figure out the meanings of the words *agency* and *designated* in the selection. After students reach a tentative conclusion about the meaning of each word, have them look it up in a dictionary, or read the definition to them. This will confirm whether or not they were correct and reinforce the word's meaning.

3 Close and Assess

Apply it!

1. Differences between the North and South led to many problems for the United States.

2. The South was rural and depended on farming and slavery, while the North had more factories and larger cities than the South.

3. Help students find context clues such as *farming, factories,* and *cities* and use them to figure out the meaning of *rural.* (in or of the country, as opposed to the city)

Standardized Test Prep

- Use Workbook p. 107 to give students practice with standardized test format.
- Chapter and Unit Tests in the Assessment Book use standardized test format.
- Test-taking tips are contained in the front portion of the Assessment Book Teacher's Edition.

Also on Teacher Resources CD-ROM.

Chapter Planning Guide

Chapter 14 • A Divided Nation

Locating Time and Place pp. 462–463

Lesson Titles	Pacing	Main Ideas
Lesson 1 **North and South Grow Apart** pp. 464–467	2 days	• Differences between North and South led to growing tensions between the two regions.
Thinking Skills: **Recognize Point of View** pp. 468–469		• Paying careful attention to descriptions and details can help you determine an author's point of view.
Lesson 2 **Resisting Slavery** pp. 470–474	2 days	• Enslaved African Americans resisted slavery in many different ways.
Biography: Harriet Tubman p. 475		• Harriet Tubman's courage helped her lead African Americans from slavery to freedom.
Lesson 3 **The Struggle Over Slavery** pp. 476–482	2 days	• Despite attempts to compromise, the struggle over slavery threatened to tear the United States apart.
Biography: Abraham Lincoln p. 483		• Reading about George Washington and Benjamin Franklin helped Abraham Lincoln develop his deep regard for the United States.
Lesson 4 **The First Shots Are Fired** pp. 484–487	1 day	• Eventually 11 Southern states seceded from the United States, leading to the outbreak of the Civil War.

✓ **Chapter 14 Review**
pp. 488–489

◄ **On April 12, 1861, Southern troops fired on Fort Sumter.**

✓ = Assessment Options

crop, was usually grown on large plantations.

Vocabulary	Resources	Meeting Individual Needs
sectionalism point of view	• Workbook, p. 109 • Transparency 4 • Every Student Learns Guide, pp. 190–193 • Quick Study, pp. 96–97 • Workbook, p. 110	• ESL Support, TE p. 465 • Leveled Practice, TE p. 467
slave codes Underground Railroad	• Workbook, p. 111 • Transparencies 2, 50 • Every Student Learns Guide, pp. 194–197 • Quick Study, pp. 98–99	• ESL Support, TE p. 471 • Learning Styles, TE p. 473 • Leveled Practice, TE p. 474
free state slave state states' rights Missouri Compromise Fugitive Slave Law Compromise of 1850 Kansas-Nebraska Law	• Workbook, p. 112 • Transparencies 2, 51, 52 • Every Student Learns Guide, pp. 198–201 • Quick Study, pp. 100–101	• ESL Support, TE p. 477 • Leveled Practice, TE pp. 479, 482 • Learning Styles, TE p. 480
secede Confederacy Union border state civil war	• Workbook, p. 113 • Transparencies 1, 53 • Every Student Learns Guide, pp. 202–205 • Quick Study, pp. 102–103	• Leveled Practice, TE p. 486 • ESL Support, TE p. 487
	✓ Chapter 14 Content Test, Assessment Book, pp. 81–82 ✓ Chapter 14 Skills Test, Assessment Book, pp. 83–84	✓ Chapter 14 Performance Assessment, TE p. 488

Additional Resources

- Vocabulary Workbook and Cards
- Social Studies Plus! pp. 166–171
- Daily Activity Bank
- Big Book Atlas
- Student Atlas
- Outline Maps
- Desk Maps

 Technology

- AudioText
- MindPoint® Quiz Show CD-ROM
- ExamView® Test Bank CD-ROM
- Teacher Resources CD-ROM
- Map Resources CD-ROM
- SFSuccessNet: iText (Pupil Edition online), iTE (Teacher's Edition online), Online Planner
- **www.sfsocialstudies.com** (Biographies, news, references, maps, and activities)

 To establish guidelines for your students' safe and responsible use of the Internet, use the Scott Foresman Internet Guide.

Additional Internet Links

To find out more about:

- Abraham Lincoln, visit **www.whitehouse.gov**
- Underground Railroad, visit **www.undergroundrailroad.org**
- Frederick Douglass, visit **www.frederickdouglass.org**

Key Internet Search Terms

- Abraham Lincoln
- Civil War
- Underground Railroad
- Harriet Tubman

the Teacher Resources CD-ROM.

Workbook, p. 107

Use with Pages 460-461.

Main Idea and Details

Directions: Fill in the circle next to the correct answer.

Many people believe slavery in the United States ended with the Emancipation Proclamation. This idea is not completely accurate. The Emancipation Proclamation did outlaw slavery, but slavery continued in some areas.

Only certain people were declared free by the Emancipation Proclamation. Those people were slaves who lived in Confederate states that were fighting against the Union. Slaves who lived in border states that were fighting for the Union were not granted freedom by the

proclamation. Also unaffected were those slaves living in Southern areas already under Union control.

Although the Emancipation Proclamation granted legal freedom to slaves living in Confederate states that were fighting against the Union, those states did not recognize Lincoln's laws. Therefore, the slaves saw no change.

All slavery in the United States officially ended in December of 1865 with the passage of the Thirteenth Amendment to the Constitution.

1. How did the Emancipation Proclamation affect slavery?
   - (A) It freed all slaves in all states.
   - (B) It freed slaves in Union territory.
   - ● It freed slaves in some states, but not in others.
   - (D) It did not free slaves.

2. Which slaves were not declared free by the Emancipation Proclamation?
   - (A) slaves who wanted to fight for the Union
   - (B) only African American women and children
   - ● those in border states and areas under Union control
   - (D) only male slaves in border states

3. Why did slavery continue in Confederate states fighting against the Union?
   - ● Those states did not recognize Lincoln's laws.
   - (B) The Union allowed it.
   - (C) The Thirteenth Amendment had not been passed.
   - (D) Those slaves did not want to move to the North.

4. What officially ended all slavery in the United States?
   - (A) the Emancipation Proclamation
   - ● the passage of the Thirteenth Amendment to the Constitution
   - (C) the Civil War
   - (D) the Confederate states

 Notes for Home: Your child learned about identifying the main idea and details of a passage.
Home Activity: With your child, choose a magazine or newspaper article of interest and work together to identify the article's main idea and details.

Use with Pupil Edition, p. 461

Workbook, p. 108

Use with Chapter 14.

Vocabulary Preview

Directions: Match each vocabulary word to its meaning. Write the vocabulary word on the line provided. Not all words will be used. You may use your glossary.

sectionalism	states' rights	secede
slave codes	Missouri Compromise	Confederacy
Underground Railroad	Fugitive Slave Law	Union
free state	Compromise of 1850	border state
slave state	Kansas-Nebraska Act	civil war

1. **secede** — to break away from
2. **border state** — state located between the Union and the Confederacy
3. **Compromise of 1850** — plan in which California entered the United States as a free state and the Fugitive Slave Law was passed
4. **Union** — states that remained loyal to the United States government
5. **free state** — state in which slavery was not allowed
6. **Fugitive Slave Law** — law which stated that escaped slaves had to be returned to their owners, even if they had reached Northern states where slavery was not allowed
7. **Kansas-Nebraska Act** — law allowing the people of Kansas and Nebraska to decide whether they would allow slavery in their territory
8. **Underground Railroad** — organized, secret system set up to help enslaved people escape from the South to freedom in the North or Canada
9. **sectionalism** — loyalty to a section or part of the country rather than to the whole country
10. **slave codes** — laws to control the behavior of slaves
11. **Confederacy** — government formed by the seven seceding states, also known as the Confederate States of America
12. **slave state** — state in which slavery was legally allowed

Notes for Home: Your child learned about problems between the North and the South and the compromises they developed.
Home Activity: Help your child learn the vocabulary terms by having him or her form comparisons between pairs of terms, such as *free state* and *slave state*, *Union* and *Confederacy*, and so on.

Use with Pupil Edition, p. 462

Workbook, p. 109

Use with Pages 464-467.

Lesson 1: North and South Grow Apart

Directions: Complete the compare-and-contrast table using information from Lesson 1. You may use your textbook.

Topic	In the North	In the South	Similar or Different?
The way of life in 1850	Most people still lived on farms, but more began working in factories and living in large towns and cities.	People lived a mostly rural way of life. People mostly lived and worked on farms and in small towns.	different
Point of view on tariffs on imported goods	They wanted higher tariffs on imported goods to increase U.S. companies' sales.	They wanted lower tariffs on imported goods to reduce the cost of buying those goods.	different
Point of view on the buying and selling of manufactured goods	They wanted to sell their goods to Americans.	They preferred to buy cheaper goods made in Great Britain.	different
Point of view on slavery	Most states outlawed slavery.	Slavery was profitable, so most states allowed it.	different

 Notes for Home: Your child learned about the different views of the North and the South during the mid-1800s.
Home Activity: With your child, discuss instances when your child's opinion or point of view might differ from that of a friend. Brainstorm positive ways to resolve or live with these differences.

Use with Pupil Edition, p. 467

Workbook, p. 110

Use with Pages 468-469.

Recognize Point of View

Point of view is the way a person looks at or thinks about a topic or situation and describes it. A person's point of view may be affected by his or her experiences and way of life.

Directions: Read the following poem. It was written by a Southern woman during the time when the South had to produce its own goods because it was blockaded by the North. Answer the questions that follow.

> My homespun dress is plain, I know;
> My hat's palmetto, too.
> But then it shows what Southern girls
> For Southern rights will do.
> We send the bravest of our land
> To battle with the foe,
> And we will lend a helping hand
> We love the South, you know.
> Hurrah! Hurrah!
> For the sunny South so dear.
> Three cheers for the homespun dress
> That Southern ladies wear.

1. What is the topic of the poem?
   The ladies of the South will sacrifice to help Southern soldiers.

2. What words does the writer use to show how she feels about Southern soldiers?
   The bravest of our land

3. What words does the writer use to show how she feels about the South?
   We love the South; the sunny South so dear

4. How do you think the writer feels about supporting the South in the war? How do you know?
   Possible answer: The writer is proud to support the South. Her homespun dress, although plain, shows that the South can survive on its own, without luxuries from Europe. This feeling is evident when the writer says "Three cheers for the homespun dress that Southern ladies wear."

 Notes for Home: Your child learned to identify the writer's point of view.
Home Activity: With your child, discuss a family situation or a situation at school in which two people had different points of view. Help your child recognize that different points of view can come from different goals or experiences.

Use with Pupil Edition, p. 469

Workbook Support

Workbook, p. 111

Lesson 2: Resisting Slavery

Use with Pages 470–474.

Directions: Categorize each term in the box by writing it in the column of the correct category below. You may use your textbook.

performed acts of cruelty	pretended to be sick
broke the tools they used	separated family members
learned to read	enforced slave codes
required permission to leave plantation	formed the Underground Railroad
used physical punishment	worked slowly

Methods of Controlling Slaves	Ways Slaves Resisted
performed acts of cruelty	broke the tools they used
required permission to leave plantation	learned to read
used physical punishment	pretended to be sick
separated family members	formed the Underground Railroad
enforced slave codes	worked slowly

Directions: Write the missing cause or effect on the line provided. You may use your textbook.

1. **Cause:** Slaves suffered cruel, harsh treatment.
   Effect: Slaves resisted.

2. **Cause:** Slaves led rebellions.
   Effect: Slave owners tried to prevent slaves from gathering and meeting with one another.

3. **Cause:** Captive Africans aboard the Spanish vessel *Amistad* seized the ship and ended up in the United States.
   Effect: The Supreme Court decided their fate and released them. All of the survivors returned to Africa that year.

 Notes for Home: Your child learned how slaves reacted to the treatment they received.
Home Activity: With your child, discuss how he or she feels when treated unfairly. Relate this feeling to how the slaves reacted when they were treated harshly and unfairly.

Use with Pupil Edition, p. 474

Workbook, p. 112

Lesson 3: The Struggle Over Slavery

Use with Pages 476–482.

Directions: Match each item in the first column to its clue or description in the second column. Write the number of the item on the line before its description.

1. Missouri Compromise
2. Fugitive Slave Law
3. Compromise of 1850
4. Kansas-Nebraska Act
5. *Uncle Tom's Cabin*
6. Dred Scott decision
7. John Brown's plan
8. Abraham Lincoln
9. Stephen Douglas

6 The Supreme Court ruled that slaves were not citizens of the United States and had no rights.

5 This book described the cruelties of slavery and won over many people to the abolitionist cause.

4 The people of each territory were allowed to decide whether it should be free or slave.

8 "If slavery is not wrong, then nothing is wrong. . . . [But I] would not do anything to bring about a war between the free and slave states."

2 Escaped slaves had to be returned to their owners, even if they had reached Northern states where slavery was not allowed.

7 A plan to attack pro-slavery people with weapons from the arsenal at Harper's Ferry further divided the North and the South in 1859.

1 The number of slave states and free states was kept balanced when Missouri was allowed into the Union as a slave state and Maine as a free state.

9 "Each state . . . has a right to do as it pleases on . . . slavery."

3 California became a free state, and the Fugitive Slave Law was passed.

Notes for Home: Your child learned about struggles over slavery that threatened to tear the United States apart.
Home Activity: With your child, choose a current controversial issue from the newspaper. Discuss citizens' opposing views and the divisions that can develop.

Use with Pupil Edition, p. 482

Workbook, p. 113

Lesson 4: The First Shots Are Fired

Use with Pages 484–487.

Directions: Sequence the events in the order in which they occurred by numbering them from 1 to 8. You may use your textbook.

7 Lincoln asks Union states for troops to put down the Confederate rebellion.

1 Abraham Lincoln is elected President of the United States.

8 Some states are angered by Lincoln's call for troops. Virginia, Arkansas, Tennessee, and North Carolina secede and join the Confederacy.

3 The Confederate States of America, or the Confederacy, is formed.

6 The Confederates attack Fort Sumter, which is surrendered two days later. The Civil War has started.

5 Jefferson Davis, president of the Confederacy, asks for the surrender of Union-held Fort Sumter in Charleston, South Carolina.

2 The Southern states of South Carolina, Alabama, Florida, Mississippi, Georgia, Louisiana, and Texas secede.

4 By Lincoln's inauguration on March 4, 1861, the Confederacy has control of most of the forts and military property in the South.

Directions: Explain each of the following points of view from the time of the American Civil War. You may use your textbook.

1. Explain the goal Lincoln and his supporters hoped to achieve by fighting the Civil War.
   Possible answer: Lincoln and his supporters wanted to preserve the Union.

2. Explain the goal Southerners hoped to achieve by fighting the Civil War.
   Southerners wanted to preserve states' rights and slavery.

3. Why do you think Northerners called Southerners "rebels"?
   Possible answer: Northerners thought the Southerners were rebelling against the established order of government and trying to get their own way.

 Notes for Home: Your child learned how differing points of view in the United States led to the Civil War.
Home Activity: With your child, discuss how differing viewpoints often can be perceived as threats or hostility. Brainstorm ways that better communication and compromise can be used to prevent these types of misunderstandings.

Use with Pupil Edition, p. 487

Workbook, p. 114

Vocabulary Review

Use with Chapter 14.

Directions: Choose the vocabulary word from the box that best completes each sentence. Write the word on the line provided. Not all words will be used.

sectionalism	states' rights	secede
slave codes	Missouri Compromise	Confederacy
Underground Railroad	Fugitive Slave Law	Union
free state	Compromise of 1850	border state
slave state	Kansas-Nebraska Act	civil war

1. The **Union** was made up of states that remained loyal to the United States government.

2. The **Compromise of 1850** allowed California to be admitted to the Union as a free state.

3. **States' rights** is the idea that people of a state can choose the laws that best fit their needs.

4. South Carolina was the first state to **secede** from the Union.

5. The **Missouri Compromise** preserved the balance between free and slave states.

6. The states that seceded from the Union formed the **Confederacy**.

7. The **Kansas-Nebraska Act** allowed people in certain areas to determine whether or not their territory would allow slavery.

8. Although some former slaves had reached the North and found freedom, the **Fugitive Slave Law** said they had to be returned to their owners.

9. **Slave codes** did not allow slaves to own land.

10. Slavery was illegal in California and any other **free state**.

11. Harriet Tubman became famous for helping slaves escape to freedom on the **Underground Railroad**.

Notes for Home: Your child learned about differences between the North and the South that divided the nation.
Home Activity: Have your child practice using the vocabulary terms in sentences of his or her own.

Use with Pupil Edition, p. 489

Assessment Support

Use these Assessment Book pages and the ExamView® Test Bank CD-ROM to assess content and skills in Chapter 14. You can also view and print Assessment Book pages from the Teacher Resources CD-ROM.

Assessment Book, p. 81

Chapter 14 Test
Part 1: Content Test
Directions: Fill in the circle next to the correct answer.

Lesson Objective (1:1)

1. Where did most Southerners live by the mid-1850s?
   - (A) cities and large towns
   - (B) cities and plantations
   - ● farms and small towns
   - (D) farms and plantations

Lesson Objective (1:1)

2. In what region of the United States were most of the nation's cities located by the 1850s?
   - ● North
   - (B) South
   - (C) East
   - (D) West

Lesson Objective (1:3)

3. What was the North's point of view on slavery by the 1850s?
   - ● Most Northern states had outlawed slavery.
   - (B) Most Northern states supported slavery.
   - (C) Most Northern factories hired slaves for workers.
   - (D) Slaves were found only on farms in the North.

Lesson Objective (1:2)

4. Which of the following describes slavery's role in the Southern economy?
   - (A) Slavery was expensive.
   - (B) Slavery was forbidden.
   - (C) Slavery was a luxury.
   - ● Slavery was profitable.

Lesson Objective (2:1)

5. Which of the following describes what slaves were doing when they resisted slavery?
   - (A) fighting their families
   - (B) fighting against rules
   - (C) being stubborn
   - ● fighting for their freedom

Lesson Objective (2:1)

6. Which of the following is one way in which slaves resisted slavery?
   - (A) telling family stories
   - (B) meeting with owners
   - (C) singing in the fields
   - ● holding back on work

Lesson Objective (2:2)

7. Which of the following was a slave rebellion that ended in the slaves returning to Africa?
   - (A) New Haven rebellion
   - ● *Amistad* rebellion
   - (C) slave rebellion
   - (D) abolitionists' rebellion

Lesson Objective (2:3)

8. What means did Harriet Tubman and others use to help slaves reach freedom in the North?
   - ● Underground Railroad
   - (B) churches
   - (C) schools
   - (D) *Amistad* rebellion

Use with Pupil Edition, p. 488

Assessment Book, p. 82

Lesson Objective (2:4)

9. Which of the following describes the lifestyle of free African Americans?
   - ● They lived in fear of losing their freedom.
   - (B) They lived the same as white citizens.
   - (C) They lived as paid slaves.
   - (D) They received many benefits.

Lesson Objective (3:1)

10. What problem did the Missouri Compromise solve?
    - (A) Southern states wanted to admit a free state.
    - ● Northerners did not want more slave states than free states.
    - (C) Missouri had to choose to be a free state or a slave state.
    - (D) Missouri wanted to join the United States as a free state.

Lesson Objective (3:2)

11. What led to violence in Kansas in 1854?
    - ● Northerners and Southerners disagreed over the results of the slavery vote.
    - (B) People voted for Kansas to be a slave state.
    - (C) People voted for Kansas to be a free state.
    - (D) Nebraska was split into Kansas and Nebraska.

Lesson Objective (3:3)

12. Why were people outraged at the Supreme Court's decision in the Dred Scott case?
    - (A) They believed it would solve many problems.
    - (B) They agreed with the decision.
    - ● The Court said African Americans had no rights.
    - (D) The Court ruled in favor of Scott.

Lesson Objective (3:3)

13. How did John Brown's raid at Harper's Ferry affect the nation?
    - (A) John Brown became a hero in the South.
    - (B) The North made John Brown a Union general.
    - ● It further divided the North and South.
    - (D) It drew the North and South together.

Lesson Objective (3:4)

14. Which statement represents Lincoln's and Douglas's views on slavery?
    - (A) They agreed on slavery.
    - (B) Neither one cared about slavery.
    - (C) Douglas opposed slavery, but Lincoln believed slavery had its place.
    - ● Lincoln opposed slavery, but Douglas thought slavery had its place.

Lesson Objective (4:1)

15. Which of the following is a reason Southern states seceded from the Union?
    - (A) They wanted to support the Union.
    - (B) They wanted to abolish slavery.
    - (C) They wanted their own flag.
    - ● They wanted to keep slavery.

Lesson Objective (4:2)

16. What officially started the Civil War?
    - ● battle at Fort Sumter
    - (B) disagreements between the North and the South
    - (C) disagreements between Lincoln and Davis
    - (D) disagreements between abolitionists and slave owners

Use with Pupil Edition, p. 488

Assessment Support

Assessment Book, p. 83

Lesson Objective (4:3)

17. What did the North hope to achieve by fighting the Civil War?
    - (A) preservation of states' rights
    - ● an end to slavery
    - (C) equality for all
    - (D) preservation of the slave system

Part 2: Skills Test

Directions: Use complete sentences to answer questions 1–8. Use a separate sheet of paper if you need more space.

1. Why did the Southern states prefer to buy manufactured goods from Britain rather than from the Northern states here at home? **Point of View**

   British goods were cheaper than Northern goods.

2. Why did Southern states fear the outlawing of slavery? **Main Idea and Details**

   Possible answers: Slavery was profitable to the Southern economy. The goods an enslaved person produced brought in at least twice as much money as the cost of owning a slave.

3. What details explain how the Underground Railroad was able to be so successful in its fight against slavery? **Main Idea and Details**

   The Underground Railroad was an organized, secret system. Both whites and African Americans helped slaves escape to the North or to Canada.

4. What is one similarity and one difference in the lifestyles of free African Americans in the North and slaves in the South? **Compare and Contrast**

   Possible answers: Different: Many free African Americans in the North found jobs and bought property. Slaves were not paid for their work. Alike: Both slaves and free African Americans struggled for their freedom.

Use with Pupil Edition, p. 488

Assessment Book, p. 84

5. What was the underlying issue the Missouri Compromise was intended to address? Was it successful or not? **Draw Conclusions**

   Possible answers: The Missouri Compromise was intended to address the issue of balance of power between free and slave states; it was successful for a while because it maintained the balance by allowing one free state and one slave state to join the Union at the same time.

6. Before the outbreak of the Civil War, how did President Lincoln balance his views on slavery and his goal for the nation? **Main Idea and Details**

   Lincoln put his goal of keeping the nation united above his goal to end slavery. He announced that he did not want to split the country and that he did not want the North and the South to be enemies.

7. Why do you think Jefferson Davis thought it was important to capture Fort Sumter? **Hypothesize**

   Possible answer: Jefferson Davis knew that the Northern forces would be a "powerful opposition" to the Confederacy. The Confederacy had already taken control of most forts and military property in the South, but Fort Sumter was still under Union control and could be used as a threat.

8. How did differing goals among people in the United States lead to the Civil War? **Main Idea and Details**

   Possible answer: People fought hoping to achieve different goals. In the Civil War some people were fighting to end slavery, some to preserve slavery, and some to preserve the Union.

Use with Pupil Edition, p. 488

A Divided Nation

Chapter 14 Outline

- **Lesson 1,** *North and South Grow Apart,* pp. 464–467
- **Thinking Skills:** *Recognize Point of View,* pp. 468–469
- **Lesson 2,** *Resisting Slavery,* pp. 470–474
- **Biography:** *Harriet Tubman,* p. 475
- **Lesson 3,** *The Struggle Over Slavery,* pp. 476–482
- **Biography:** *Abraham Lincoln,* p. 483
- **Lesson 4,** *The First Shots Are Fired,* pp. 484–487

Resources

- Workbook, p. 108: Vocabulary Preview
- Vocabulary Cards
- Social Studies Plus!

1820, United States: Lesson 1

Share with students that this picture shows enslaved African Americans working on a plantation in the southern United States. Ask students why some Americans owned slaves at that time.

1849, Philadelphia, Pennsylvania: Lesson 2

This picture shows Harriet Tubman, who escaped from slavery through the Underground Railroad. After her escape, she helped other enslaved people escape to freedom. Ask students to suggest words that describe her.

March 1861, Washington, D.C.: Lesson 3

Remind students that when Lincoln took office, the United States had "broken" into two separate groups of states. Ask students what they think Abraham Lincoln might have done to restore the union.

April 1861, Charleston, South Carolina: Lesson 4

This picture shows the battle at Fort Sumter, the first conflict in the Civil War. The bombardment of the fort resulted in victory for the Confederate forces. Ask students to calculate the length of time between Lincoln's taking office and the beginning of the war. (About one month)

CHAPTER
14

A Divided Nation

1820

United States
About 1.5 million enslaved people live in the United States, most in the Southern states.

Lesson 1

1849

Philadelphia, Pennsylvania
Harriet Tubman escapes to freedom in Philadelphia on the Underground Railroad.

Lesson 2

March 1861

Washington D.C.
Abraham Lincoln is inaugurated as President.

Lesson 3

April 1861

Charleston, South Carolina
Southern troops fire on Fort Sumter.

Lesson 4

462

Practice and Extend

Vocabulary Preview

- Use Workbook p. 108 to help students preview the vocabulary words in this chapter.
- Use Vocabulary Cards to preview key concept words in this chapter.

Also on Teacher Resources CD-ROM.

Workbook, p. 108

Vocabulary Preview
Directions: Match each vocabulary word to its meaning. Write the vocabulary word on the line provided. Not all words will be used. You may use your glossary.

sectionalism	states' rights	secede
slave codes	Missouri Compromise	Confederacy
Underground Railroad	Fugitive Slave Law	Union
free state	Compromise of 1850	border state
slave state	Kansas-Nebraska Act	civil war

1. _____ to break away from
2. _____ state located between the Union and the Confederacy
3. _____ plan in which California entered the United States as a free state and the Fugitive Slave Law was passed
4. _____ states that remained loyal to the United States government
5. _____ state in which slavery was not allowed
6. _____ Law which stated that escaped slaves had to be returned to their owners, even if they had reached Northern states where slavery was not allowed
7. _____ law allowing the people of Kansas and Nebraska to decide whether they would allow slavery in their territory
8. _____ organized, secret system set up to help enslaved people escape from the South to freedom in the North or Canada
9. _____ loyalty to a section or part of the country rather than to the whole country
10. _____ laws to control the behavior of slaves
11. _____ government formed by the seven seceding states, also known as the Confederate States of America
12. _____ state in which slavery was legally allowed

Notes for Home: Your child learned about problems between the North and the South and the compromises they developed.
Home Activity: Help your child learn the vocabulary terms by having him or her form comparisons between pairs of terms, such as free state and slave state, Union and Confederacy, and so on.

Locating Time and Place

UNITED STATES

PACIFIC OCEAN

Philadelphia

Washington, D.C.

Charleston

ATLANTIC OCEAN

Gulf of Mexico

Why We Remember

"…one nation under God, indivisible, with liberty and justice for all."
These words are part of the Pledge of Allegiance, which Americans have said for many years. But there was a time when the words were not true for all Americans. In the middle 1800s, the United States was one nation divided into two parts, the North and the South. In the South, enslaved people grew crops such as cotton on plantations. In the North, where slavery was illegal, many people worked in factories and lived in cities. Differences between the North and the South sparked serious conflicts, which in 1861 set off a terrible war. By the end of the war, Americans began the long task of rebuilding the country—"with liberty and justice for all."

463

- Have students examine the pictures shown on p. 462 for Lessons 1, 2, 3, and 4.

- Remind students that each picture is coded with both a number and a color to link it to a place on the map on p. 463.

Why We Remember

Have students read the "Why We Remember" paragraph on p. 463, and ask them why events in this chapter might be important to them. Ask students to imagine what it would be like to live in this country if it were still divided. What lessons do students think people may have learned from the Civil War? How do these lessons still affect us today?

WEB SITE
Technology

You can learn more about Philadelphia, Pennsylvania; Washington, D.C.; and Charleston, South Carolina by clicking on *Atlas* at **www.sfsocialstudies.com.**

FYI SOCIAL STUDIES
Background

Largest U.S. Cities in 1860

- In 1860 the ten largest cities in the United States were, in order from most to least populous: New York City, NY; Philadelphia, PA; Brooklyn City, NY; Baltimore, MD; Boston, MA; New Orleans, LA; Cincinnati, OH; St. Louis, MO; Chicago, IL; and Buffalo, NY.

- In 1860, New York City had over 800,000 residents.

North and South Grow Apart

Objectives

- Describe the differences between the economies and populations of the North and South.

- Identify the role that slavery played in the South in the mid-1800s.

- Explain how and why views about slavery differed in the North and South.

Vocabulary

sectionalism, p. 465

Resources

- Workbook, p. 109
- Transparency 4
- Every Student Learns Guide, pp. 190–193
- Quick Study, pp. 96–97

Quick Teaching Plan

If time is short, have students create a chart of the characteristics of the North and the South in the mid-1800s.

- Have students make a T-chart with the two headings *Northern United States* and *Southern United States*.

- Students can add details as they read. They should also include viewpoints from each place.

1 Introduce and Motivate

Preview Ask students to list reasons why the two regions might grow apart. Ask students to recall what life in the United States was like in the 1800s. Tell students that, in Lesson 1, they will learn more about the differences between these two regions.

You Are There The economy of the Southern United States depended upon cotton, while the Northern United States relied more on industry than on agriculture. Have students predict what effect the differences between the two regions might have on the country as a whole.

Unit 7 • War Divides the Nation

LESSON 1

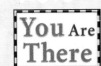

1840		1860
1846 Congress votes to lower tariffs on imports		**1860** The number of enslaved African Americans in the United States reaches four million

PREVIEW

Focus on the Main Idea
Differences between North and South led to growing tensions between the two regions.

PEOPLE
David Walker

VOCABULARY
sectionalism

464

North and South Grow Apart

You Are There The year is 1850, and you are a sailor on a ship that carries goods to and from ports on the East coast of the United States. Your ship glides into the port of Charleston, South Carolina, and ties up at a dock. You see hundreds of bundles of cotton waiting to be loaded onto your ship. The cotton has been grown on plantations across the South. You know that most of the work on those plantations is done by people who are enslaved.

You join the other sailors to unload your ship of its cargo of manufactured goods from Boston, Massachusetts. The cargo includes tools, machines, and cloth made by free workers in factories. You know that Charleston and Boston are part of the same country, the United States. Yet they are so different they might well be parts of different countries. Before long their differences will lead to war.

 Main Idea and Details As you read, focus on how the North and South differed and how each of the differences pushed the two regions apart.

Practice and Extend

READING SKILL
Main Idea/Details

In the Lesson Review, students complete a graphic organizer like the one below. You may want to provide students with a copy of Transparency 4 to complete as they read the lesson.

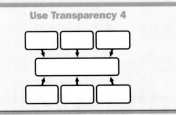

Use Transparency 4

VOCABULARY
Word Exercise

Individual Word Study Explain to students that more than one suffix can be added to a word. The suffix *-al* means "of, like, or having the nature of," so sectional means "of a section." Relate that *-ism* means "act, practice, quality of being, or system." So sectionalism is the practice of focusing on your section, rather than being part of a whole. Discuss other words with *-ism*, such as *heroism, criticism,* or *plagiarism.*

Two Regions

Many changes had taken place in the United States since the country was formed. The North and South had always been quite different geographically, but after the start of the Industrial Revolution, the differences between the two regions increased dramatically.

Southerners lived a mostly rural way of life. Most lived and worked on farms and in small towns. By the middle 1800s, few Southern cities had a population of over 15,000.

In contrast, many Northerners at that time lived an urban way of life. Although most Northerners still lived on farms, more and more people worked in factories and lived in large towns and cities. In 1860 nine of the ten largest cities in the United States were located in the North. The bar graph and circle graphs below show how the populations of the North and South differed in 1850.

Factory owners and factory workers in the North had different goals from those of planta-tion owners and farmers in the South. These different interests caused a strong disagree-ment in 1846. A law passed by Congress in that year caused the disagreement. The law lowered the tariffs the United States charged for goods imported from other countries. This made Northern factory owners angry.

The Northern states had wanted higher tar-iffs, or taxes on imported goods. Higher prices on imported goods would encourage Americans to buy manufactured goods from the North.

The Southern states, however, wanted lower tariffs. They preferred to buy the cheaper goods made in Great Britain. ❷

The way of life of one section of the United States was threatening the way of life in the other section of the United States. These differences caused sectionalism in our country. **Sectionalism** is a loyalty to a section or part of the country rather than to the whole country.

REVIEW Explain how differences between the North and South led to conflict between them. ⟳ Main Idea and Details

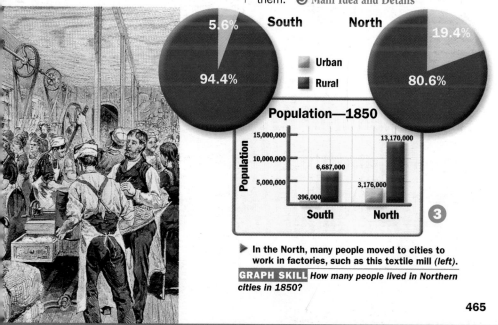

South
5.6%
94.4%

North
19.4%
80.6%

Urban
Rural

Population—1850

South 396,000 / 6,687,000
North 3,176,000 / 13,170,000

▶ In the North, many people moved to cities to work in factories, such as this textile mill *(left)*.

GRAPH SKILL *How many people lived in Northern cities in 1850?*

465

2 Teach and Discuss

PAGE 465

Two Regions

🕐 *Quick Summary* The rural way of life in the South and the industrial way of life in the North led to sectionalism, or intense loyalty to one part of the country.

❶ **Why were nine of the ten largest U.S. cities in 1860 in the North rather than in the South?** Many Northerners worked in factories and lived in cities. In the South, agriculture was the way of life, so more people lived on farms and in small towns. **Draw Conclusions**

$ **SOCIAL STUDIES STRAND**
Economics

❷ **How might the lower tariffs on foreign goods affect the wages of workers in the North?** Lower tariffs meant that people could buy goods made in foreign countries for less money. With less money coming in to American industry, factory owners might need to lower wages to keep their businesses running. **Cause and Effect**

✓ **REVIEW ANSWER** The way of life in the South was rural, while that of the North was more urban. The North wanted higher tariffs, while the South wanted lower tariffs. ⟳ Main Idea and Details

❸ **Which section of the country has the largest total population in 1850?** The North **Interpret Graphs**

GRAPH SKILL **Answer** 3,176,000

Slavery in the South

⏱ *Quick Summary* Slavery was profitable to the agricultural South, while the practice was outlawed in most Northern states. African Americans suffered from discrimination in all parts of the United States.

4 **Why do you think that most Northern states had outlawed slavery by 1850?** Possible answers: Enslaved workers were not as needed there because there were many people living in cities to do the work in factories. Students should recognize that the practice of slavery had previously existed in the North. **Draw Conclusions**

5 **What kinds of discrimination did free African Americans face in the United States in 1860?** They did not have the right to vote in many states. In New York, African Americans had to own land and live in the state for three years before they could vote.
↪ **Main Idea and Details**

✓ Ongoing Assessment

If... students are unable to support the main idea that African Americans faced discrimination,	**then...** ask students if they believe people are truly free when they are unable to vote in elections.

✓ REVIEW ANSWER The goods an enslaved person produced brought in at least twice as much money as the cost of owning a slave. ↪ **Main Idea and Details**

GRAPH SKILL **Answer** About 400,000

Different Views on Slavery

⏱ *Quick Summary* Abolitionists insisted that slavery should end, but many slave owners disagreed.

Slavery in the South

One very important difference between the North and the South was slavery. Slavery was allowed in the Southern states, where enslaved people grew such crops as cotton, tobacco, and rice. By 1850 most Northern states had outlawed slavery. Northern workers were free and were paid for their work. In many Northern **4** factories, however, workers put in long hours, under difficult conditions, for low pay.

Slavery was profitable to the economy of the South. The goods an enslaved person produced brought in at least twice as much money as the cost of owning the slave. In 1850 about six out of every ten slaves in the South worked in the cotton fields. Cotton was usually grown on large plantations. However, many slaves lived on small farms. On these smaller farms, the owner often worked in the fields alongside a small group of slaves. But only about one-third of Southern farmers owned slaves.

By 1860 enslaved African Americans in the United States totaled almost four million

people. In some states, they outnumbered the free whites. The line graph on this page shows how the number of enslaved people changed between 1820 and 1860. It also shows changes in the population of free African Americans during the same time. Most of the enslaved African Americans lived in the South, while most of the free African Americans lived in the North.

Even free African Americans did not always have the same voting rights as whites. In some states, only people who owned property could vote. However, in states where this requirement had been dropped for whites, such as in New York, blacks still had to own land before they could vote. Throughout the country African Americans suffered from discrimination. They did not have the rights of full citizenship.

REVIEW Identify the main reason why the South wanted to keep slavery.
↪ **Main Idea and Details**

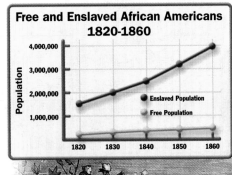

Free and Enslaved African Americans 1820–1860

Population: 4,000,000 / 3,000,000 / 2,000,000 / 1,000,000

- Enslaved Population
- Free Population

1820 1830 1840 1850 1860

The Granger Collection

466

▶ As Southern cotton plantations *(below)* grew, so did the number of enslaved African Americans.

GRAPH SKILL *About what was the population of free African Americans in 1840?*

Practice and Extend

Problem Solving

Use a Problem-Solving Process

- Have students consider the following problem-solving scenario: **Suppose you are a plantation owner with a large amount of cotton to harvest. You do not believe it is right to own another person, so you do not own slaves. Yet you need help on your farm and you live far from a city.**

- Students should use the following problem-solving process to decide how they will harvest their cotton before their crops are ruined. For each step in the process, have students work in small groups to discuss and write about what must be considered as they solve the problem. Write the steps above on the board or read them aloud.

1. Identify a problem.
2. Gather information.
3. List and consider options.
4. Consider advantages and disadvantages.
5. Choose and implement a solution.
6. Evaluate the effectiveness of the solution.

Different Views on Slavery

As you have read, abolitionists opposed the practice of slavery and fought to end slavery everywhere in the country. They insisted that slavery should be abolished because it was wrong for one human being to own another. One abolitionist, a free African American named David Walker, asked this about the Southern slave owners:

> *"How would they like us to make slaves of...them?"*

But Southern slave owners defended slavery. They pointed to the evils of factories in the North, where people worked long hours, in bad surroundings, for little pay.

Slave owners argued that slaves were better off than Northern factory workers.

Debate continued throughout the middle 1800s. But, as you will read, words were not the only weapons to be used against slavery.

REVIEW Identify one argument that supported the idea that slavery should be abolished. ⟳ **Main Idea and Details**

Summarize the Lesson

1846 Congress voted to lower the tariff on imports, which angered many Northerners.

1860 The number of enslaved African Americans in the United States reached almost four million.

Primary Source

Cited in *A Documentary History of the Negro People in the United States,* by Herbert Aptheker, ed.

6 **What feelings did David Walker express in his question?** Possible answers: Frustration, sadness, defiance
Analyze Primary Sources

✓ **REVIEW ANSWER** It is wrong for one human being to own another.
⟳ **Main Idea and Details**

3 Close and Assess

Summarize the Lesson

Review the time line with students. Then have them use the two main ideas on the time line to create outlines. Remind them that their outlines should include supporting details to explain each main idea. Allow time for students to share their outlines with the class.

✓ **LESSON 1** **REVIEW**

1. ⟳ **Main Idea and Details** For possible answers, see the reduced pupil page.

2. Different viewpoints on the tariff helped cause sectionalism, because each side began to show more loyalty to its own part of the country.

3. Enslaved; from the graph on p. 466

4. **Critical Thinking:** *Make Inferences* Possible answer: Factory workers in the North worked long hours for low pay.

5. It is wrong for one human being to own another.

 **Link to** **Art**

Students' art should be titled, detailed, clearly labeled, and perhaps focused on daily life, slavery, or tariffs.

LESSON 1 REVIEW

Check Facts and Main Ideas

1. ⟳ **Main Idea and Details** On a sheet of paper, complete the graphic organizer to show details supporting the main idea.

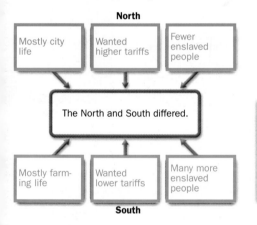

North

Mostly city life

Wanted higher tariffs

Fewer enslaved people

The North and South differed.

Mostly farming life

Wanted lower tariffs

Many more enslaved people

South

2. Describe how tariffs affected relations between North and South. Use the word **sectionalism** in your answer.

3. In 1860 were more African Americans enslaved or free? How do you know?

4. **Critical Thinking:** *Make Inferences* What conditions existed in the North that might lead to problems at a later date?

5. Describe the main argument of people opposed to slavery.

Link to **Art**

Create a Graph or Illustration Choose one topic from the lesson. Then show with a graph or a picture how the North and the South were growing apart.

467

Interpret a Graph Using the graph on p. 466, have students find and analyze data.

Easy Model how to find the answer to questions such as *What was the population of free African Americans in 1850?* Pose other questions for students to answer. **Reteach**

On-Level Ask students questions that call for interpretation: Which population grew more quickly? Explain your answers. **Extend**

Challenge Ask students to create questions and answers about the graph. Have students pose questions to each other. **Enrich**

For a Lesson Summary, use Quick Study, p. 96.

Workbook, p. 109

Lesson 1: North and South Grow Apart

Directions: Complete the compare-and-contrast table using information from Lesson 1. You may use your textbook.

Topic	In the North	In the South	Similar or Different?
The way of life in 1850			
Point of view on tariffs on imported goods			
Point of view on the buying and selling of manufactured goods			
Point of view on slavery			

Notes for Home: Your child learned about the different views of the North and the South during the mid-1800s.
Home Activity: With your child, discuss instances when your child's opinion or point of view might differ from a friend's. Brainstorm positive ways to resolve or live with these differences.

Also on Teacher Resources CD-ROM.

Recognize Point of View

Objectives

- Identify facts and opinions in writing.

- Consider the experiences of an individual writer and how those experiences may have shaped the writer's ideas.

- Describe a writer's point of view.

Vocabulary

point of view, p. 468

Resource

- Workbook, p. 110

1 Introduce and Motivate

What is point of view? Read aloud a recent editorial that expresses an opinion. Ask students if they could tell how the writer felt about the topic. After discussion, have students read the **What?** section of text on p. 468 to help set the purpose of the lesson.

Why identify the point of view? Have students read the **Why?** section of text on p. 468. Ask them what details they would use to support an editorial with the point of view that recess should be longer (e.g., need for exercise; a break helps people work better).

2 Teach and Discuss

How is this skill used? Examine with students the selections on p. 469.

- Point out that the two selections have very different points of view.

- Ask students to summarize the point of view of each of the selections. Help students identify words that indicate point of view.

- Have students read the **How?** section of text on p. 468.

Recognize Point of View

What? Point of view is the way a person looks at or thinks about a topic or situation. A person's point of view may be affected by his or her experiences and way of life. As you have read in Lesson 1, people had very different points of view about slavery.

In the selections on these pages, two writers expressed their points of view about slavery. The writers tried to support their points of view with descriptions and details.

Selection A was written by George Fitzhugh, a lawyer who was a supporter of slavery. His family had lived in the South for many years and had owned a 500-acre plantation.

Selection B was written by Frances Anne (Fanny) Kemble, a famous British actress married to Pierce Butler, an American. In 1836 Butler inherited two Southern plantations and became one of the largest slaveholders in the country. His wife became an opponent of slavery and moved back to Britain. Years later she wrote of her experiences in *Journal of a Residence on a Georgian Plantation.*

George Fitzhugh

Fanny Kemble

Why? As a reader, you need to be able to identify a writer's point of view so that you can understand the writer's choice of details. Writers may use their own feelings and beliefs when they decide what to include and how to tell their story.

How? To recognize a writer's point of view, you may follow these steps:

1. Identify the topic.

2. Determine which statements are fact and which are opinions.

3. Look for words or phrases that tell how a writer feels about the topic.

4. Consider the writer's experiences and way of life. How might these affect the writer's point of view?

5. Describe the writer's point of view.

Practice and Extend

CURRICULUM CONNECTION
Writing

Write an Editorial

- Ask students to write editorials for the school newspaper. They could focus on a school or community topic.

- Suggest that students begin with an opinion. They should include persuasive facts and opinions that would influence readers to have the same point of view about the topic.

CURRICULUM CONNECTION
Art

Create an Illustration

- Remind students that an illustration can reveal an artist's point of view.

- Ask students to make illustrations for the two selections on p. 469. Point out that the subject will be the same, but the details will reflect different points of view.

- Allow time for students to display their artwork. Classmates can try to determine which illustrations should accompany each piece.

Selection A

1 *"The negro slaves of the South are the happiest, and in some sense, the freest people in the world. The children and the aged and infirm [sick or weak] work not at all, and yet have all the comforts and necessaries [needs] of life provided for them. They enjoy liberty, because they are oppressed [weighed down] neither by care nor labor.*

2 *The women do little hard work, and are protected from ... their husbands by their masters [slave owners]. The negro men and ... boys work, on the average, in good weather, not more than nine hours a day. The balance of their time is spent in [relaxation]. Besides, they have their Sabbaths and holidays.... They can sleep at any hour.... We do not know whether free laborers [in the North] ever sleep."*

—George Fitzhugh

Selection B

"I have sometimes been haunted [worried] with the idea that it was ... [a] duty, knowing what I know, and having seen what I have seen, to do all that lies in my power to show the dangers and the evils of this frightful institution [slavery]...The handcuff, the lash—the tearing away of children from parents, of husbands from wives—the weary trudging [walking] ...along the common highways, the labor of body, the despair of mind [hopelessness], the sickness of heart—these are the realities which belong to the system, and form the rule, rather than the exception, in the slave's experience."

—Fanny Kemble

Think and Apply

1 What is the subject of both of these writers?

2 What details does each writer use to support his or her point of view?

3 What are the points of view each writer reveals?

4 How might the experiences and way of life of each writer affect his or her point of view?

469

CURRICULUM CONNECTION
Literature

Read Books About Slavery Have students identify points of view and supporting details in literature.

Sweet Clara and the Freedom Quilt, by Deborah Hopkinson (Random House, ISBN 0-679-87472-0, 1995) **Easy**

The Africans (We Came to North America), by Jen Green (Crabtree Publishing, ISBN 0-778-70198-0, 2000) **On-Level**

Nightjohn, by Gary Paulsen (Delacorte Press, ISBN 0-385-30838-8, 1993) **Challenge**

Workbook, p. 110

Recognize Point of View

Point of view is the way a person looks at or thinks about a topic or situation and describes it. A person's point of view may be affected by his or her experiences and way of life.

Directions: Read the following poem. It was written by a Southern woman during the time when the South had to produce its own goods because it was blockaded by the North. Answer the questions that follow.

> My homespun dress is plain, I know;
> My hat's palmetto, too.
> But then it shows what Southern girls
> For Southern rights will do.
> We send the bravest of our land
> To battle with the foe,
> And we will lend a helping hand
> We love the South, you know.
> Hurrah! Hurrah!
> For the sunny South so dear.
> Three cheers for the homespun dress
> That Southern ladies wear.

1. What is the topic of the poem?

2. What words does the writer use to show how she feels about Southern soldiers?

3. What words does the writer use to show how she feels about the South?

4. How do you think the writer feels about supporting the South in the war? How do you know?

Notes for Home: Your child learned to identify the writer's point of view.
Home Activity: With your child, discuss a family situation or a situation at school in which two people had different points of view. Help your child recognize that different points of view can come from different experiences.

Also on Teacher Resources CD-ROM.

---

1 Which words in the first sentence of Selection A reveal the writer's point of view? "happiest," "freest people" Point of View

2 Fitzhugh states in his article the point of view that slaves are "free." What does he think makes enslaved people free? Possible answer: Some of the slaves, such as the children and the aged, do not work, yet they are given necessities of life, such as food and shelter. Draw Conclusions

3 Why do you think Kemble believed it was her "duty" to show the dangers of slavery? Possible answer: She wanted other people to know about the suffering of enslaved people so that more people would pressure the government to end slavery. Hypothesize

3 Close and Assess

Think and Apply

1. The condition of the life of a slave

2. Fitzhugh says slaves work only nine hours a day and that children and old and sick people are taken care of; Kemble says slaves suffer from handcuffs, lashes, separation of families, hard labor, and despair.

3. Fitzhugh's point of view is that a slave's life is an easy life, and a slave is better off than a free worker. Kemble's point of view is that slaves are treated harshly and cruelly.

4. Fitzhugh was from an old Southern family that had probably owned slaves; after seeing the mistreatment of enslaved people, Kemble became an opponent of slavery.

Resisting Slavery

Objectives

- Identify ways African Americans resisted slavery.
- Describe rebellions of African Americans against slavery.
- Explain how the Underground Railroad was used to free enslaved people.
- Describe the lives of free African Americans in the North and South.

Vocabulary

slave codes, p. 471;
Underground Railroad, p. 473

Resources

- Workbook, p. 111
- Transparencies 2, 50
- Every Student Learns Guide, pp. 194–197
- Quick Study, pp. 98–99

Quick Teaching Plan

If time is short, have students create a word web about resisting slavery.

- Ask students to write the title of the lesson in the middle of a piece of paper and draw a circle around it.
- As students read, they can create detail webs by drawing spokes from the central circle and writing methods that were used to resist slavery.

1 Introduce and Motivate

Preview To activate prior knowledge, ask students what it means to *resist* (refuse to give in or go along). Tell students that, in Lesson 2, they will learn more about how enslaved African Americans resisted slavery.

You Are There Students may recognize Patrick Henry's words "liberty or . . . death." Ask students what meaning those words might have had for enslaved people and how those people may have tried to gain liberty.

LESSON 2

1830			1850
1831 Nat Turner leads a slave rebellion in Virginia	**1841** The Supreme Court frees the prisoners from the slave ship *Amistad*	**1849** Harriet Tubman esca from slavery on the Underground Railroa	

PREVIEW

Focus on the Main Idea
Enslaved African Americans resisted slavery in many different ways.

PLACES
Southampton County, Virginia
New Haven, Connecticut

PEOPLE
Nat Turner
Joseph Cinque
Harriet Tubman
Levi Coffin
Catherine Coffin

VOCABULARY
slave codes
Underground Railroad

Resisting Slavery

You Are There September 11, 1853, in Richmond, Virginia. In a house in the city, J.H. Hill, an escaped slave, waits for a message.

Later Hill wrote, "Nine months I was trying to get away. I was secreted [hidden] a long time in a kitchen of a merchant." And then the long awaited message arrives. He is to meet a guide who will try to lead him to freedom in the North. Early next morning, Hill leaves his hiding place and carefully makes his way to the guide. "I felt composed [calm]," Hill reports, "for I had started…that morning for liberty or for death." Hill reached the North where, at last, he found liberty.

Main Idea and Details As you read, note the details that support the main idea that African Americans resisted slavery.

470

Practice and Extend

READING SKILL
Main Idea/Details

In the Lesson Review, students complete a graphic organizer like the one below. You may want to provide students with a copy of Transparency 2 to complete as they read the lesson.

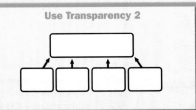

Use Transparency 2

VOCABULARY
Word Exercise

Individual Word Study Write *Underground Railroad* on the board and discuss its meaning. The Underground Railroad was neither underground nor a railroad. Ask students why they think it got its name. (Possible answer: underground, because it was secret; railroad, because it takes people somewhere) *Underground Railroad* is an example of figurative language, using ideas and images that are suggested by words but not the actual meanings of the words.

African Americans Resist Slavery

Some enslaved people, like J. H. Hill, resisted slavery by risking their lives in daring escapes. Other slaves found different ways to resist.

When enslaved people resisted slavery, they were fighting for their freedom. They were also fighting against a cruel system. They had no choices. They would be moved when they were sold, and they could not control who bought them. Many owners treated slaves well, but some beat or abused their slaves.

Another form of cruelty was the breaking up of families. Abream Scriven, a slave sold by his owner in 1858, was forced to leave his wife, father, and mother. He wrote these words to his wife:

> *"Give my love to my father and mother and tell them good bye for me, and if we shall not meet in this world I hope to meet in heaven."*

Slave owners had almost complete control over a slave's life. The owners told them when to start work and when to end work. Slaves could not leave the plantation without permission. Slave owners also decided whether slaves could marry and the age at which their children had to begin working.

Slave codes, or laws to control the behavior of slaves, also made life difficult for them. For example, most slave codes did not allow a slave to hit a white person, even in self-defense. Slaves were not allowed to own property, and few were allowed to buy and sell goods.

Resistance took many forms. Some slaves simply refused to obey the owner. Other slaves resisted by holding back the main thing they could control, their work. They worked more slowly, or pretended to be sick. Others broke the tools that were needed to do work.

Many enslaved people resisted by breaking rules that were meant to keep them ignorant. For example, slaves often were not allowed to learn to read or write. Some slaves learned in secret, risking punishment if they were found out.

REVIEW Describe some ways enslaved African Americans resisted slavery. *Main Idea and Details*

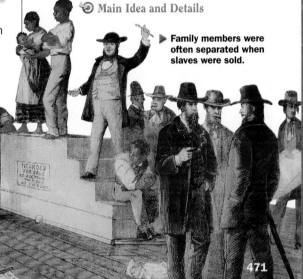

▶ Family members were often separated when slaves were sold.

471

ACCESS CONTENT
ESL Support

Examine Word Meaning Work with students to explore the meaning of *resist.*

Beginning Have students in pairs use a dictionary to look up *resist.* Talk through the meaning of the term with them. Then invite them to pantomime the meaning (e.g., fists raised in a fighting posture).

Intermediate Consider giving a sentence frame for students to complete: African Americans resisted slavery by _____. Students can work with partners to find examples in the text, insert the examples in the sentence, and share their sentences with the class.

Advanced Discuss other forms of *resist* with students: *resisted, resisting, resister, resistance.* Then have students identify the suffixes and discuss how the different suffixes change the form of the word (e.g., One form of *resistance* to slavery was _____.).

For additional ESL support, use Every Student Learns Guide, pp. 194–197.

Teach and Discuss

African Americans Resist Slavery

Quick Summary In order to gain their freedom, slaves resisted by refusing to obey, holding back in their work, or secretly breaking laws.

Primary Source
Cited in *A People's History of the United States,* by Howard Zinn

1 **Why do you think that some slaveholders broke up enslaved people's families?** Possible answers: To demonstrate power over enslaved people; to discourage plans for resisting or escaping **Draw Conclusions**

2 **How were some slaveholders cruel to enslaved people?** Possible answers: Subjected them to physical punishment, broke up families, controlled people's lives **Main Idea and Details**

Problem Solving

3 **Enslaved people resisted in several ways. Which solution to the problem do you think was the best? Explain.** Possible answer: Refusing to work because it would cause economic hardships for slaveholders **Solve Problems**

4 **Why do you think slave codes prohibited enslaved people from learning to read and write?** Possible answer: To prevent them from communicating effectively and planning a revolt **Draw Conclusions**

✓ **REVIEW ANSWER** Refused to obey owners, worked more slowly, pretended to be sick, broke tools, and learned to read and write **Main Idea and Details**

Slave Rebellions

🕐 *Quick Summary* Slave owners tried to prevent rebellions, but rebellions, such as the one led by Nat Turner, did occur.

⑤ Why did slave owners try to keep slaves from meeting with each other?
To prevent them from planning rebellions
Cause and Effect

⑥ Retell, in chronological order, the events surrounding the *Amistad*. A group of captive Africans seized control of the *Amistad*; they were tricked into sailing to the United States; the U.S. Navy captured and imprisoned the Africans; they were freed by the U.S. Supreme Court and returned to Africa. Sequence

✓ **Ongoing Assessment**

| If... students are unable to retell the events in order, | then... write the words *first, second, third, then,* and *finally* on the board. Ask volunteers to record the major events next to the words. |

⭐ **SOCIAL STUDIES STRAND**
Citizenship

- Remind students that because the Africans from the *Amistad* were not U.S. citizens, they had no right to an attorney or a trial by jury.

- Ask students what they know about due process rights.

✓ **REVIEW ANSWER** The Nat Turner rebellion was stopped and the rebels were executed. The *Amistad* rebellion was successful and led to the freeing of the captives. Compare and Contrast

The *Amistad*

⑦ Why do you think that people might want to visit the *Amistad*? Possible answer: Visitors may want to celebrate the bravery of the people involved.
Express Ideas

Slave Rebellions

⑤ To prevent enslaved people from planning rebellions, slave owners tried to keep slaves from gathering and meeting with one another. Still, rebellions did occur. One was planned and led by **Nat Turner** in Virginia.

In August 1831, Turner and his followers killed about 60 whites in **Southampton County, Virginia.** United States and Virginia troops were called in to stop them. The soldiers killed more than 100 African Americans before the rebellion was ended. Turner escaped but was later captured. He was hanged on November 11, 1831.

A later rebellion had a different ending. In 1839, a group of 53 captive Africans seized control of the *Amistad,* a Spanish slave ship carrying them from one port to another in Cuba. The Africans were led by a farmer from West Africa who became known as **Joseph Cinque** (SEEN kay). He told the Africans: "We may as well die in trying to be free."

After taking control of the ship, the Africans told a Spanish sailor to sail them back to Africa. But the Spaniard tricked them and instead sailed the *Amistad* north along the coast of the United States. The United States Navy captured the *Amistad* near Long Island, New York. The Africans were taken as prisoners to **New Haven, Connecticut.**

At first, the United States planned to return the ship and the Africans to the Spanish. Abolitionists and Northern newspapers printed articles against this plan and in support of the Africans. With their help, the Africans' fight for freedom eventually came before the Supreme Court. There, former President John Quincy Adams presented the Africans' case. He argued that the Africans were not property but human beings and should not be returned to Spain.

On March 9, 1841, the Supreme Court reached its decision. It agreed with Adams and freed the Africans. All 35 of the Africans who survived the rebellion sailed back to Africa later that year.

REVIEW Contrast the Nat Turner and *Amistad* rebellions. Compare and Contrast

The *Amistad*
In 2000, a full-size reproduction of the *Amistad* was launched at Mystic Seaport, a museum in Connecticut. People can visit the ship there, or at ports to which it sails, to hear the story of the *Amistad* rebellion.

⑦

472

▶ Joseph Cinque (*above*) le the rebellion that took control of the Spanish sl ship, *Amistad*. The pictu left shows the reproducti of the *Amistad*.

Practice and Extend

CURRICULUM CONNECTION
Art

Design Promotional Materials
- Have students suppose that they are promoting the launch of the *Amistad* reproduction.

- Invite them to design a poster or brochure to celebrate the launch. Their work should express the importance of the exhibit.

- Readers should have a good idea of what they will learn from visiting the ship and museum.

CURRICULUM CONNECTION
Writing

Create an Argument
- Ask students to consider the actions of John Quincy Adams and create arguments to present to the Supreme Court on behalf of the Africans on the *Amistad*.

- Their arguments should persuade the Justices to free the Africans.

- Tell students to use a formal tone and support their argument with facts.

Routes of the Underground Railroad

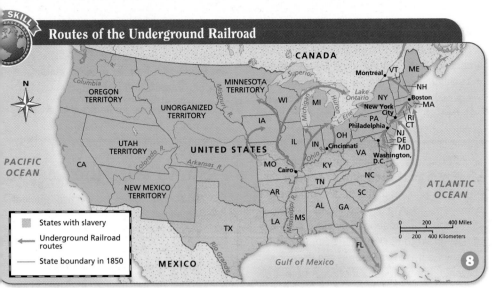

► This map shows the routes traveled by people escaping from slavery on the Underground Railroad.

MAP SKILL Use Routes *To what other country did many slaves escape?*

Underground Railroad

Thousands of enslaved African Americans resisted slavery by trying to escape. The Underground Railroad was an organized, secret system set up to help enslaved people escape from the South to freedom in the North or Canada. The map on this page shows its routes.

The Underground Railroad probably got its name when railroads became popular. The guides, or people who helped those escaping, were called "conductors." The houses, barns, and other places where runaways hid along their journey were known as "stations."

To find their way north, escaping slaves were guided by the North Star. On cloudy nights they felt for moss on tree trunks, because moss tends to grow on the north side of a tree. All along the journey, they faced the risk of capture, a severe beating, or death.

Between 40,000 and 100,000 slaves escaped using the Underground Railroad. Harriet Tubman was the most famous

"conductor." In about 1849, Tubman escaped from slavery herself and settled in Philadelphia. But before the Civil War she returned south 19 times to lead more than 300 people, including her mother and father, to freedom. Tubman later said, "On my underground railroad, I never ran my train off the track and I never lost a passenger." You can read more about Tubman in the Biography on page 475.

Not all "conductors" in the Underground Railroad were African Americans. Levi Coffin was a white teacher who had opened a school for slaves in North Carolina. After slave owners closed his school, Coffin moved to Indiana. There he became one of the leading "conductors" of the Underground Railroad. He and his wife Catherine Coffin helped more than 2,000 slaves escape to freedom.

REVIEW Write a brief summary of the way the Underground Railroad helped people escape slavery. Summarize

473

Underground Railroad

⏱ *Quick Summary* An organized, secret system, the Underground Railroad, helped enslaved people from the South escape to freedom in the North or Canada.

MAP SKILL
Routes of the Underground Railroad

⑧ **Which city is the origin of a route that led some enslaved people to the Minnesota Territory?** Cairo
Interpret Maps

MAP SKILL Answer Canada

⑨ **Compare and contrast the Underground Railroad with a "real" railroad.** Both railroads had set routes, moved people from one place to another, and had "conductors" and "stations." The Underground Railroad was not an actual rail system with tracks.
Compare and Contrast

⑩ **What risks did enslaved people face when using the Underground Railroad?** Possible answer: Capture, punishment, or even death 🔄 **Main Idea and Details**

⑪ **What personal characteristics does Harriet Tubman reveal in her quotation?** Courage, self-confidence, pride, and a sense of humor **Draw Conclusions**

✓ **REVIEW ANSWER** Guides, called "conductors," led escaped slaves from one hiding place, or "station," to another, until the enslaved people reached freedom in the North or in Canada. **Summarize**

MEETING INDIVIDUAL NEEDS
Learning Styles

The Underground Railroad Using their individual learning styles, students explore the Underground Railroad.

Musical Learning Have students work in small groups to compose songs that would help enslaved people remember a route on the railroad. Remind students to refer to the map as they write.

Individual Learning Ask students to write at least three journal entries that an enslaved person may have written while using the Underground Railroad to escape to freedom. Journal entries could include information about the route as well as the hopes and fears of the escaping slave.

Logical Learning Encourage students to use the map on this page as well as a map with a mileage scale to compute the distances of the routes of the Underground Railroad. Ask students to calculate how long it might take to follow several of the routes if escaping slaves could travel 25 miles in a day.

Free African Americans

 **Quick Summary** By 1860 only one out of nine African Americans in the United States was free.

12 **In 1860 where did most free African Americans in the United States live?**
In cities ⟲ Main Idea and Details

✓ **REVIEW ANSWER** Without a certificate of freedom, they could be sent back into slavery. Escaped slaves in the North could be kidnapped and returned to slavery in the South. ⟲ Main Idea and Details

3 Close and Assess

Summarize the Lesson

Have groups of students list details about or illustrate one of the main ideas. Students can combine their work to create a large class outline.

✓ **LESSON 2**   **REVIEW**

1. ⟲ **Main Idea and Details** For possible answers, see the reduced pupil page.

2. To control the behavior of slaves.

3. **Critical Thinking: *Cause and Effect*** To prevent enslaved people from planning rebellions.

4. Guides led escaped enslaved people from one hiding place to another.

5. Laws prevented them from holding some jobs; threats and violence from white workers made it difficult to find work; they feared being sent back into slavery.

Link to ⟋∞⟍ Science

Encourage students to draw pictures showing the North Star and the surrounding stars. Ask students which other groups of people may have used the North Star to find their way (e.g., sailors).

474 Unit 7 • War Divides the Nation

Free African Americans

By 1860 about 4.5 million African Americans lived in the United States. About 4.1 million lived in the South. Only one out of every nine African Americans in the country **12** was free. Most free African Americans lived in cities. But although they were free, they feared losing their freedom. Any white person could accuse a free black person of being a slave. Without a certificate of freedom, African Americans in the South could be sent back into slavery. Escaped slaves in the North could be kidnapped by slave catchers and returned to slavery in the South.

Many Southern states passed laws preventing free African Americans from holding certain jobs. In the North and the South, finding work was made more difficult by threats and violence from white workers.

Still, thousands of free blacks found jobs and bought property. In New Orleans, 650 African Americans owned land in 1850. This was by far the largest number of black landowners of any city in the United States.

REVIEW Why did free African Americans have much to fear about keeping their freedom? ⟲ Main Idea and Details

Summarize the Lesson

— **1831** Nat Turner led a slave rebellion in Virginia.

— **1841** Africans who had seized control of the slave ship *Amistad* gained their freedom in the Supreme Court.

— **1849** Harriet Tubman escaped slavery and began leading people to freedom on the Underground Railroad.

LESSON 2   **REVIEW**

Check Facts and Main Ideas

1. ⟲ **Main Idea and Details** On a separate sheet of paper, complete the graphic organizer to show the details that support the main idea that enslaved African Americans resisted slavery.

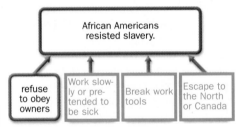

2. What was the purpose of the **slave codes** ?

3. **Critical Thinking: *Cause and Effect*** Why would slave owners want to keep slaves from gathering or meeting one another?

4. Describe how enslaved African Americans escaped to freedom on the **Underground Railroad** .

5. What challenges were faced by free African Americans in the North and South?

Link to ⟋∞⟍ Science

Locate the North Star Escaping African Americans used the North Star to help them find the direction north. Do research to locate the North Star. Then one evening, when it is dark enough, look for the star and determine north.

474

Practice and Extend

 **MEETING INDIVIDUAL NEEDS**
Leveled Practice

Write an Article Have students write an article as if they were a reporter in the 1860s. Students may need to do additional research.

Easy Have students write three or four sentences about the Nat Turner rebellion. They should answer *Who? What? Where? When? Why?* and *How?* **Reteach**

On-Level Have students write a newsletter article for Underground Railroad conductors to read. **Extend**

Challenge Students can write an article about the *Amistad* incident and speculate how it might affect the future slave trade. **Enrich**

For a Lesson Summary, use Quick Study p. 98.

Workbook, p. 111

Lesson 2: Resisting Slavery

Methods of Controlling Slaves	Ways Slaves Resisted

Also on Teacher Resources CD-RO

Harriet Tubman

1820(?)–1913

As a teenager in Maryland, Harriet Tubman had only known a life of slavery, yet she grew tougher by resisting or fighting back. She even survived a serious head injury that she suffered while helping another slave escape. As a result of the injury, for the rest of her life Harriet could not control falling asleep at odd times, suffered from bad headaches, and had a deep scar. Yet nothing could prevent her from seeking freedom.

When she was about 28 years old, Harriet Tubman escaped and made her way 90 miles on the Underground Railroad to Philadelphia. Although she was afraid, she later explained,

❶ *I had reasoned this out in my mind....I had a right to liberty or death; if I could not have one, I would have the other, for no man should take me alive.*

❷ Despite the dangers, before the Civil War Tubman returned again and again to the South to help lead other African Americans from slavery to freedom. No one in her care was ever caught.

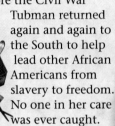

During the Civil War, Tubman served the United States army as a nurse and a scout, helping to free almost 800 slaves in one attempt.

BIOFACT

Learn from Biographies

How do you think Harriet Tubman's scar and trouble with sleeping could have made her escape more dangerous? Why do you think that she returned to the South so many times despite all of the dangers?

For more information, go online to *Meet the People* at **www.sfsocialstudies.com.**

475

Harriet Tubman

Objective

- Identify the personal qualities that motivated Harriet Tubman to take risks in helping African Americans escape to freedom.

1 Introduce and Motivate

Preview To activate prior knowledge, ask students to recall what they learned about Harriet Tubman in Lesson 2. Tell students they will read more about her courage.

2 Teach and Discuss

❶ **What two choices did Harriet Tubman say she had the right to choose between?** Liberty or death
Analyze Primary Sources

❷ **What did Tubman do during the Civil War?** Served the U.S. Army as a nurse and a scout; helped free almost 800 slaves at once ⟳ Main Idea and Details

3 Close and Assess

Learn from Biographies Answer

Possible answer: Her scar made her easy to recognize, and she might fall asleep at any time. She knew the value of freedom and wanted to help others achieve their goal of liberty.

WEB SITE
Technology

Students can find out more about Harriet Tubman by clicking on *Meet the People* at **www.sfsocialstudies.com.**

CURRICULUM CONNECTION
Writing

Write Speeches

- Tell students to suppose that Harriet Tubman is going to be honored with a museum display at a Heroes Hall of Fame.

- Invite students to write speeches that could be given at the opening of the display.

- Students' speeches should describe Tubman's life, explain why she is remembered today, and tell why she deserves the status of "hero."

The Struggle Over Slavery

Objectives

- Describe the causes and effects of the Missouri Compromise and the Compromise of 1850.

- Explain the causes of violence in Kansas in 1854.

- Draw conclusions about how Dred Scott and John Brown affected the split between the North and South.

- Compare the views on slavery of Abraham Lincoln and Stephen Douglas.

Vocabulary

free state, p. 477; **slave state,** p. 477; **states' rights,** p. 477; **Missouri Compromise,** p. 477; **Fugitive Slave Law,** p. 478; **Compromise of 1850,** p. 478; **Kansas-Nebraska Act,** p. 479

Resources

- Workbook, p. 112
- Transparencies 2, 51, 52
- Every Student Learns Guide, pp. 198–201
- Quick Study, pp. 100–101

Quick *Teaching Plan*

If time is short, ask students to create a time line as they read.

- Students can begin by recording main ideas about the Missouri Compromise.
- Remind students to add other dates and details from the lesson.

1 Introduce and Motivate

Preview To activate prior knowledge, have students summarize the conflicts over slavery. Tell students that they will find out more about the issue of slavery in Lesson 3.

You Are There — Remind students that in 1850, the United States was still acquiring territory and admitting new states. Ask them to predict how adding new states might cause problems.

476 Unit 7 • War Divides the Nation

LESSON 3

NEBRASKA TERR.
KANSAS TERR.
Harpers Ferry

1820				1860
1820 Missouri Compromise		1850 Fugitive Slave Law	1857 Dred Scott case	1860 Abraham Linc⸱ elected Presid⸱

PREVIEW

Focus on the Main Idea
Despite attempts to compromise, the struggle over slavery threatened to tear the United States apart.

PLACES
Nebraska Territory
Kansas Territory
Harpers Ferry, Virginia

PEOPLE
John C. Calhoun
Henry Clay
Daniel Webster
Stephen Douglas
Harriet Beecher Stowe
Dred Scott
John Brown
Abraham Lincoln

VOCABULARY
free state
slave state
states' rights
Missouri Compromise
Fugitive Slave Law
Compromise of 1850
Kansas-Nebraska Act

476

The Struggle over Slavery

 You Are There

Your old home in Ohio lies hundreds of miles behind you as you ride into the Kansas Territory. On this spring day in 1854, you meet a group of 650 settlers from New England. They tell you they have all pledged to keep Kansas free of slavery.

You have also met other people coming to Kansas who have different views. One group is from neighboring Missouri, a slave state. Their aim is to make the Kansas Territory a place where people can own slaves.

Wherever you go, you hear arguments about whether or not Kansas should allow slavery. You also hear stories of violence between people on both sides of this argument. The issue of slavery is splitting Kansas apart. Soon it will threaten to split apart the entire country.

 Main Idea and Details As you read, look for details that support the main idea that slavery was threatening to split the country apart in the middle 1800s.

Practice and Extend

READING SKILL
Main Idea/Details

In the Lesson Review, students complete a graphic organizer like the one below. You may want to provide students with a copy of Transparency 2 to complete as they read the lesson.

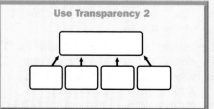
Use Transparency 2

VOCABULARY
Word Exercise

Individual Word Study Explain to students that the word *compromise* means "to settle by agreeing that each side will give up a part of what is wanted." Compromises are usually reached to settle disagreements. Compromise comes from the Latin *com-,* meaning "together," and *promittere,* "promise"—and the word *promise* can be seen in the English word. So both sides promise to give something up in order to settle the issue.

The Missouri Compromise, 1820

CANADA

OREGON COUNTRY

UNORGANIZED TERRITORY

PACIFIC OCEAN

UNITED STATES

MEXICO

VT ME
NH
NY MA
RI CT
PA NJ
OH DE
IN MD
IL VA
MO KY NC
ARKANSAS TERRITORY TN SC
MS AL GA
LA
FLORIDA TERRITORY

ATLANTIC OCEAN

Gulf of Mexico

MICHIGAN TERR.

N

0   200   400 Miles
0   200   400 Kilometers

Legend:
- Free states
- Free territories
- Line of Missouri Compromise
- Missouri Compromise
- Slave states
- Slave territories
- Boundaries in 1820

▶ The Missouri Compromise kept the balance between free states and slave states.

MAP SKILL Use a Map Key *Which two states were admitted as part of the Missouri Compromise?*

Missouri Compromise

In 1819, the United States was made up of 11 free states and 11 slave states. A **free state** was one in which slavery was not allowed. A **slave state** was one in which slavery was allowed. Since each state had two United States senators, the Senate was balanced evenly between senators that favored slavery and senators that opposed slavery.

In 1819 the people of Missouri asked for statehood as a slave state. Northern states did not want Missouri to be admitted as a slave state. Southern states took the opposite position.

John C. Calhoun from South Carolina was a leader of the Southerners in the Senate. Calhoun was a believer in **states' rights**—the idea that states have the right to make decisions about issues that concern them. According to Calhoun, slavery should be legal if a state's people wanted it to be.

Senator **Henry Clay** of Kentucky, who would become known as "The Great Compromiser," urged a solution called the **Missouri Compromise.** In 1820 Missouri was admitted as a slave state, and Maine was admitted as a free state. There were now 24 states, evenly balanced between free states and slave states.

What would happen when more new states were formed from land gained in the Louisiana Purchase? The Missouri Compromise tried to settle this question. Look at the map above and find the Missouri Compromise line. According to the Missouri Compromise, new states north of this line would be free states. New states south of this line could allow slavery.

REVIEW How did the Missouri Compromise affect the way future states would be admitted to the United States?
⟲ Main Idea and Details

477

---

2 Teach and Discuss

PAGE 477

Missouri Compromise

Quick Summary Henry Clay's Missouri Compromise kept the balance between free and slave states.

The Missouri Compromise, 1820

1 **Did the Missouri Compromise allow more free states or slave states?** Neither, the states were equally balanced **Interpret Maps**

MAP SKILL **Answer** Maine and Missouri

2 **How would the balance of the Senate be affected by new states that were admitted to the United States?** Two senators were elected from every state. If more slave states than free states were admitted to the United States, there would be more senators who represented the interests of slave states. Many wanted the Senate to be equal. **Cause and Effect**

SOCIAL STUDIES STRAND
Geography

The Mason-Dixon line is commonly used to describe the boundary between the slave states of the South and the free states of the North after the Missouri Compromise, although it was originally drawn in the 1760s to determine precise borders between Delaware, Maryland, and Pennsylvania.

✓ **REVIEW ANSWER** The Missouri Compromise established a line of latitude north of which (with the exception of Missouri) slavery would not be allowed and south of which slavery would be allowed. ⟲ Main Idea and Details

---

ESL
ACCESS CONTENT
ESL Support

Discuss Compromise Help students understand *compromise*.

Beginning Demonstrate the meaning of *compromise* with this scenario: "John wants to go to a ball game; his sister wants to go to a movie. They *compromise* by going to a movie about a ball game." Have students role play the scenario.

Intermediate Using the map above, point to the states that were part of the U.S. before Missouri and Maine were admitted. Have students count the number of slave states and free states. Ask what would happen if one new state was a slave state or a free state. Discuss how the compromise maintained a balance.

Advanced Have students work in groups of four to role-play a discussion that might have occurred between Henry Clay and John C. Calhoun. Two students can role-play Clay and Calhoun, and two students can listen and discuss. Then have students switch roles.

For additional ESL support, use Every Student Learns Guide, pp. 198–201.

The Compromise of 1850

 Quick Summary The Compromise of 1850 admitted California as a free state while enacting the Fugitive Slave Law.

SOCIAL STUDIES STRAND
Geography

Point out on a map California, Missouri, and the latitude line for the Missouri Compromise (36° 30´N). Show students that the line traverses California.

3 Why was the Missouri Compromise unable to settle the question of California being admitted as a free state? The latitude line dividing slave states and free states cuts through the middle of California; the balance between free and slave states was threatened.
Apply Information

Primary Source

Cited in *The Oxford History of the American People,* by Samuel Eliot Morison

4 What does John Calhoun's letter reveal about his attitude toward the North? He is angry and frustrated with it.
Analyze Primary Sources

5 What did the Fugitive Slave Law say? Slaves who escaped, even if they had reached the North, would be returned to their owners if caught.
Main Idea and Details

6 How did the Compromise of 1850 fit into the idea of states' rights? People living in the territories gained from Mexico could vote for whether or not they wanted to allow the practice of slavery.
Apply Information

7 At first Calhoun opposed admitting California as a free state, yet he supported the Compromise of 1850. What do you think may have changed his mind? The Compromise of 1850 led to passage of the Fugitive Slave Law. **Draw Conclusions**

✓ **REVIEW ANSWER** California would be admitted as a free state if a Fugitive Slave Law was passed. Slavery would be allowed in the territories acquired from Mexico if people in those territories voted for slavery. **Main Ideas and Details**

478 Unit 7 • War Divides the Nation

The Compromise of 1850

For a time, the Missouri Compromise settled the question about the balance of free and slave states. But in 1849, California—which was part of the lands the United States had gained from the Mexican War—applied for statehood as a free state. At that time the United States was made up of 15 free states and 15 slave states. Once again, the balance between free and slave states was threatened.

John Calhoun wrote to his daughter about the South's reaction to California's request:

> *"I trust we shall persist in our resistance [to California].... We have borne the wrongs and insults of the North long enough."*

Calhoun hoped that the Southern members of Congress would force the North to turn down California's request to enter as a free state.

Henry Clay again suggested a compromise. Clay proposed that the South accept California as a free state. In return, the North should agree to pass the **Fugitive Slave Law.** This law said that escaped slaves had to be returned to their owners, even if they had reached Northern states where slavery was not allowed. Clay's compromise also suggested a way to accept other new states from the territories gained from Mexico. He proposed that slavery be allowed in these territories if the people living there voted for it.

Daniel Webster, a senator from Massachusetts, spoke in favor of the compromise. Webster was an opponent of slavery. Yet like Clay, he wanted to keep the country together. Webster said, "We must view things as they are. Slavery does exist in the United States."

478

With the support of Calhoun and Webster, Congress passed Clay's plan. It was called the **Compromise of 1850.** California became a free state, and the Fugitive Slave Law was passed. But the battle over slavery was far from over.

The Compromise of 1850 was made to keep the North and the South from splitting apart over slavery. But as Senator Salmon P. Chase of Ohio said later, "The question of slavery in the territories has been avoided. It has not been settled." The truth of his words became clear in 1854, as huge numbers of settlers were entering the Nebraska Territory west of the Missouri River.

REVIEW What were the main proposals of the Compromise of 1850?
◑ Main Idea and Details

▶ Many newspapers printed opinions about the new Fugitive Slave Law.

Practice and Extend

SOCIAL STUDIES
Background

About Daniel Webster

- At the age of 15, Daniel Webster entered Dartmouth College, where he excelled at public speaking. When he graduated, he taught school and studied law. He soon became a prominent lawyer.
- After becoming a member of the House of Representatives, Webster became an influential and well-paid lawyer.
- Webster directly opposed John C. Calhoun's declarations of states' rights. As Webster defended the powers of the federal government, he said, "Liberty *and* Union, now and forever, one and inseparable!"
- Webster supported the Compromise of 1850 not because he defended the rights of states, but because he thought that the terrain in the West would not support plantations or farms, making slavery unnecessary.

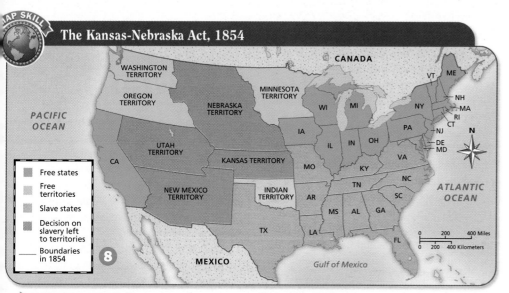

MAP SKILL
The Kansas-Nebraska Act, 1854

Free states

Free territories

Slave states

Decision on slavery left to territories

Boundaries in 1854

▶ This map shows how the Kansas-Nebraska Act affected the United States.

MAP SKILL Region *What was the only state in the West region in 1854?*

"Bleeding Kansas"

In 1854 Senator **Stephen Douglas** of Illinois proposed that Nebraska be split into two territories: the **Nebraska Territory** in the north and the **Kansas Territory** in the south. Because both territories were north of the Missouri Compromise line, both would be free territories. However, many Southerners insisted that slavery be allowed in both the Nebraska and the Kansas territories.

Congress again looked for a solution. Senator Douglas suggested a compromise: let the people of each territory decide whether it should be free or slave. Congress passed this law, which came to be known as the **Kansas-Nebraska Act.** Instead of solving the problem, the law created a new one in Kansas.

Because a majority vote would decide whether Kansas would be free or slave, people who favored one side or the other rushed to settle in Kansas. People against slavery came

from the North. People for slavery came from the South, especially from neighboring Missouri, a slave state.

The people of Kansas voted for slavery. But many who voted were not Kansans at all. They had crossed the border from Missouri just to vote for slavery. Northerners claimed the vote was illegal. Southerners disagreed. Within Kansas, though most people just wanted to establish homes and live in peace, there were leaders on both sides of the slavery issue who were trying to cause a fight. Violence broke out in many parts of the Kansas Territory. Because of the many acts of violence, Kansas became known as "bleeding Kansas." These would not be the last drops of blood spilled between those who favored and opposed slavery.

REVIEW In what way did the Kansas-Nebraska Act change a part of the Missouri Compromise? **Compare and Contrast**

479

"Bleeding Kansas"

🕐 **Quick Summary** Although the Kansas-Nebraska Act was created to solve the problem of whether slavery would be allowed in the two territories, it prompted violent disputes.

MAP SKILL
The Kansas-Nebraska Act, 1854

8 **According to the terms of the Missouri Compromise, would Kansas have been a free state or a slave state?** Free state **Apply Information**

MAP SKILL **Answer** California

9 **Why did people from neighboring states rush to Kansas to vote on the question of slavery?** A majority vote would decide the outcome, so people against slavery came from the North and those for slavery came from the South to vote. **Cause and Effect**

10 **Why do you think that the issue of slavery caused so much violence?** Possible answer: People had strong feelings about the way of life in their region of the country, and they did not want their way of life threatened by another region. **Express Ideas**

✓ **REVIEW ANSWER** The Missouri Compromise declared that states and territories north of a certain line of latitude should be free. The Kansas-Nebraska Act left the decision to the people of the two territories, even though they were north of this latitude. **Compare and Contrast**

❄ MEETING INDIVIDUAL NEEDS
Leveled Practice

Review Acts Have students review acts regarding new states (The Missouri Compromise, the Compromise of 1850, and the Kansas-Nebraska Act).

Easy Write *Missouri Compromise* on the board and say, "This act made Maine a free state." Students should show thumbs up because the statement is true. Continue with the other acts. Students show thumbs down for false. **Reteach**

On-Level Write the names of the acts on the board and have groups of students choose one. They should list the main features of the act. Allow time for students to share their lists. **Extend**

Challenge Students participate in panel discussions, acting as one of the people from the lesson. In character, students explain their viewpoints. Audience members can question the characters. **Enrich**

For a Lesson Summary, use Quick Study, p. 100.

A Divided Country

⏱ *Quick Summary* Events such as the publication of *Uncle Tom's Cabin* and the Dred Scott decision heightened emotions about the issue of slavery and further divided the United States.

Test Talk

Use Information from the Text

11 **How did the publication of *Uncle Tom's Cabin* affect people's feelings about slavery? Why did the book have that effect?** Students should skim the first paragraph to find out what the effect was. The book, which sold many copies, won some people over to the abolitionist cause because it described the cruelties of slavery. **Cause and Effect**

---

12 **Why did John Brown lead a raid on the arsenal at Harper's Ferry?** To steal weapons for attacking slave owners in Virginia ⊙ **Main Idea and Details**

✓ Ongoing Assessment

If... students do not understand Brown's importance to the abolitionist cause,

then... read them variants of the song "John Brown's Body" to illustrate how people later drew inspiration from his actions.

✓ **REVIEW ANSWER** Dred Scott sought to gain his freedom from slavery peacefully. John Brown sought to abolish slavery violently. **Compare and Contrast**

Literature and Social Studies

Read the passage aloud for students, asking them to listen for vivid words that provoke strong emotions.

13 **What does this passage reveal about slavery?** Possible answer: It shows the cruelty of the slave traders and the harsh and frightening conditions under which enslaved people lived. It shows how mothers and their children suffered. **Apply Information**

A Divided Country

In addition to the violence in "bleeding Kansas," other events deepened the split between the North and the South. One was the publication of *Uncle Tom's Cabin*, a novel by **Harriet Beecher Stowe**, in 1852 Stowe's novel described the cruelties of slavery. It sold about 300,000 copies in the first year after it was published, winning over many people to the abolitionist cause.

Another important event was the case of **Dred Scott**, an enslaved African American from Missouri. Scott's owner had taken him to Illinois, a free state, and to Wisconsin, a free territory, and then back to Missouri, a slave state. Then Scott's owner died. Scott went to court claiming he was a free man because he had lived in a free state.

Scott's case reached the United States Supreme Court. The 1857 decision written by Chief Justice Roger Taney said that Scott "had no rights" because African Americans were not citizens of the United States. Many Americans were outraged by the Supreme Court's decision. Frederick Douglass said that the decision would bring about events that would "overthrow...the whole slave system."

Another event that further divided the North and the South occurred in 1859. Abolitionist **John Brown**, who had led attacks on pro-slavery people in Kansas, made plans to attack slave owners in Virginia. To carry out his plan, Brown needed weapons. He planned to steal them from the army's arsenal at **Harpers Ferry, Virginia** (now West Virginia). An arsenal is a place where weapons are stored.

On October 16 Brown and 21 other men, black and white, started on their raid. But federal and state soldiers stopped them, killing some of the raiders. Brown was taken prisoner and, after being found guilty, was sentenced to death. He was hanged. But his actions showed that the struggle over slavery was growing. Compromise was becoming harder to find.

REVIEW Contrast the goals of Dred Scott and John Brown. **Compare and Contrast**

Literature and Social Studies

In this excerpt from *Uncle Tom's Cabin*, **13** Harriet Beecher Stowe describes the struggle of an enslaved mother named Eliza to keep her child from slave traders who wanted to take her child away from her.

"[Eliza's] room opened by a side door to the river. She caught her child, and sprang down the steps toward it. The [slave] trader caught a full glimpse of her, just as she was disappearing down the bank, and throwing himself from his horse...he was after her like a hound after a deer. In that dizzy moment her feet...[hardly] seemed to touch the ground, and a moment brought her to the water's edge....and, nerved with strength such as God gives only to the desperate,

480

with one wild cry and flying leap, she vaulted sheer [jumped clear] over the ...current by the shore, on to the raft of ice beyond. It was a desperate leap,—impossible to anything but madness and despair."

Practice and Extend

MEETING INDIVIDUAL NEEDS
Learning Styles

Review Events in the Struggle Over Slavery Using their individual learning styles, students review the different actions taken in response to conflicts about slavery.

Visual Learning Students can make illustrated time lines to show lesson events. Make certain they include specific dates, complete descriptions, and appropriate illustrations.

Linguistic Learning Ask students to suppose they are developing a documentary film about lesson events. Work with students to brainstorm a list of important events to include. Have them work independently or in small groups to write a script for a portion of the documentary, describing one of the events. If time allows, students can perform their scripts for the class.

15

Many people called him "The Rail Splitter," because when he was young he split logs with an axe to make the rails of fences. Lincoln was opposed to the spread of slavery and spoke of the "ultimate extinction," or final end, of slavery.

Lincoln's opponent was Democratic Senator Stephen Douglas. Douglas was known as the "Little Giant" because, although he was short, he was a giant when it came to making speeches that changed people's ideas. Douglas believed in states' rights. He said, "Each state...has a right to do as it pleases on...slavery."

16

The candidates made speeches and debated throughout Illinois about the spread of slavery. The Lincoln-Douglas debates became well known because both candidates were such good speakers. Lincoln said:

> *"If slavery is not wrong, then nothing is wrong....[But I] would not do anything to bring about a war between the free and slave states."*

17

Douglas stated:

> *"If each state will only agree to mind its own business... this republic can exist forever divided into free and slave states."*

Douglas won the election, but the debates made Lincoln the new leader of the Republican Party. Within two years, he would be the Republican candidate for President. You can read more about Lincoln in the Biography on page 483.

REVIEW Summarize the views on slavery held by Lincoln and Douglas. **Summarize**

The Granger Collection

▶ Abraham Lincoln spoke out against the spread of slavery while running for the Senate against Stephen Douglas.

A New Political Party

The issue of slavery led to the end of one political party and the beginning of another. The Whigs, split between a group against slavery and a group for it, ceased to exist. In 1854 some of its members who opposed slavery joined with other slavery opponents to form the Republican Party. Now, two major political parties, Republican and Democrat, battled over the issues of slavery and states' rights.

No election showed this conflict more clearly than the 1858 campaign for the United States Senate in Illinois. The Republicans chose **Abraham Lincoln** as their candidate. Lincoln was a lawyer from Springfield, Illinois.

481

A New Political Party

🕐 *Quick Summary* The Whig Party disbanded and the Republican Party was born. The Lincoln-Douglas debates set the stage for Abraham Lincoln's presidential candidacy.

14 **Explain what caused the end of the Whig Party.** Within the party, one group was against slavery, and another group was for it. **Cause and Effect**

15 **What do the details in the picture tell you about the Lincoln-Douglas debates?** Possible answer: The flag and the people's formal clothing show that the debates were important. **Analyze Pictures**

H **SOCIAL STUDIES STRAND**
History

Remind students that Illinois was a Northern state and that slavery had been outlawed in Illinois.

16 **What do you think Douglas thought about slavery? What did Douglas think was important?** Possible answer: It is not clear from the information here; states' right to choose **Evaluate**

Primary Source

Cited in *The Impending Crisis*, by David M. Potter

17 **Based on Lincoln's quotation, what do you think he considered the most important issue in the election?** Preserving the Union; keeping slave states and free states from fighting **Analyze Primary Sources**

✓ **REVIEW ANSWER** Lincoln believed that slavery was wrong. Douglas believed that each state should decide whether or not to allow slavery. **Summarize**

SOCIAL STUDIES
Background

About the Whig Party

• The Whig Party was organized in 1834 by people who opposed President Andrew Jackson.

• The Whig Party took its name from the British political party that opposed royal privileges.

About the Lincoln-Douglas Debates

• Democratic Senator Stephen Douglas and Republican challenger Abraham Lincoln had seven debates.

• Lincoln stressed the importance of unity: "A house divided against itself cannot stand."

Lincoln Is Elected President

🕐 *Quick Summary* Southerners feared that President Lincoln would try to end slavery and refuse to let the South have a voice in the government.

18 **Do you think Southerners were justified in their fears about Lincoln? Why or why not?** Possible answer: No, Lincoln had spoken out against slavery, but he also favored unity. **Evaluate**

✓ **REVIEW ANSWER** Lincoln feared that the United States might split up if the North and South became enemies. If possible, read the Read Aloud passage on p. 455h to students again. **Draw Conclusions**

 **Close and Assess**

Summarize the Lesson

Have students create a graphic organizer using one of the events on the time line and supporting it with details.

✓ **LESSON 3** **REVIEW**

1. 🔄 **Main Idea and Details** For possible answers, see the reduced pupil page.

2. Missouri became a slave state; Maine became a free state.

3. California was a free state. Territories were allowed to vote on whether or not they wanted to allow slavery.

4. Dred Scott was a slave who sought freedom through the courts; John Brown tried to overthrow slavery violently; caused a further split

5. **Critical Thinking:** *Make Inferences* Preserving the nation; he thought slavery was wrong, but he did not want a war between the states.

Link to 🔗 Writing

Remind students to use quotation marks for speakers' exact words.

Lincoln Is Elected President

In the election of 1860, the Democratic Party split. Northern Democrats chose Stephen Douglas to run for President. Southern Democrats chose John Breckinridge of Kentucky. The Republicans chose Abraham Lincoln.

Lincoln won the election, but without winning any Southern electoral votes. Southerners feared that Lincoln would attempt to end slavery not only in the western territories but in the Southern states as well. Southerners also worried that they would have no voice in the new government. Lincoln said to the South, "We must not be

18 enemies." However, many on both sides viewed the other side as their enemy. In the North and South, the time of compromise had passed.

REVIEW Why do you think Lincoln said, "We must not be enemies" after he became President? **Draw Conclusions**

Summarize the Lesson

— **1820** Congress passed the Missouri Compromise.

— **1850** The Fugitive Slave Law was passed as part of the Compromise of 1850.

— **1857** In the Dred Scott case, the Supreme Court ruled that slaves were not citizens and had no rights, even in free states.

— **1860** Abraham Lincoln was elected President without any Southern support.

LESSON 3 **REVIEW**

Check Facts and Main Ideas

1. 🔄 **Main Idea and Details** On a separate sheet of paper, complete the graphic organizer with details that support the main idea.

There were many attempts to compromise, but the struggle over slavery threatened to tear the United States apart.

The Missouri Compromise → The Fugitive Slave Law and the Compromise of 1850 → The Kansas-Nebraska Act → Dred Scott and John Brown

2. How did the **Missouri Compromise** keep the balance of **free and slave states**?

3. How did the **Compromise of 1850** affect slavery in California and the territories gained from Mexico?

4. Who were Dred Scott and John Brown? How did their actions affect the split between the North and South?

5. **Critical Thinking:** *Make Inferences* What was more important to Abraham Lincoln, abolishing slavery or preserving the nation? Explain.

Link to 🔗 Writing

Write a Conversation Write a conversation about the spread of slavery that might have occurred among Americans in the 1850s. You can base your conversation on the words of American leaders in this lesson, such as John C. Calhoun, Daniel Webster, Frederick Douglass, Harriet Beecher Stowe, Abraham Lincoln, and Stephen Douglas. Use the term **states' rights** in your conversation.

Practice and Extend

 MEETING INDIVIDUAL NEEDS
Leveled Practice

Give an Oral Presentation Have students draw from the lesson to present information orally.

Easy Ask students to discuss a person from the lesson whom they admire. They should give reasons. **Reteach**

On-Level Students should prepare and deliver a speech about states' rights and how they affected slavery and the conflict between the North and South. **Extend**

Challenge Students prepare and deliver persuasive speeches explaining which act they think had the greatest impact on the slavery issue. **Enrich**

For a Lesson Summary, use Quick Study, p. 100.

Workbook, p. 112

Lesson 3: The Struggle Over Slavery

Directions: Match each item in the first column to its clue or description in the second column. Write the number of the item on the line before its description.

1. Missouri Compromise
2. Fugitive Slave Law
3. Compromise of 1850
4. Kansas-Nebraska Act
5. *Uncle Tom's Cabin*
6. Dred Scott decision
7. John Brown's plan
8. Abraham Lincoln
9. Stephen Douglas

___ The Supreme Court ruled that slaves were not citizens of the United States and had no rights.

___ This book described the cruelties of slavery and won over many people to the abolitionist cause.

___ The people of each territory were allowed to decide whether it should be free or slave.

___ "If slavery is not wrong, then nothing is wrong.... [But I] would not do anything to bring about a war between the free and slave states."

___ Escaped slaves had to be returned to their owners, even if they had reached Northern states where slavery was not allowed.

___ A plan to attack pro-slavery people with weapons from the arsenal at Harpers Ferry further divided the North and South in 1859.

___ The number of slave states and free states was kept balanced when Missouri was allowed into the Union as a slave state and Maine as a free state.

___ "Each state ... has a right to do as it pleases on ... slavery."

___ California became a free state, and the Fugitive Slave Law was passed.

Notes for Home: Your child learned about struggles over slavery that threatened to tear the United States apart.
Home Activity: With your child, choose a current controversial issue from the newspaper. Discuss citizens' and the divisions that can develop.

🔵 **Also on Teacher Resources CD-ROM**

Abraham Lincoln 1809–1865

Young Abraham Lincoln had to help his father on the family farm and only attended school for a total of about one year during his life. Yet Abe read anything he could get his hands on. He once said, "My best friend is the man who'll get me a book." So when a neighboring farmer, Josiah Crawford, offered to lend him a biography of George Washington, Abe was thrilled. Unfortunately, one rainy night, the book was left near the leaky cabin walls and got soaked. Abe told the truth, and Crawford was not angry. Abe paid him back by working in his fields.

The book on Washington became one of Abe's favorites, along with the autobiography of Benjamin Franklin. From these, Abe learned about the men who founded the United States and why the dream of a free country was so important to them.

BIOFACT

Lincoln grew his beard in response to a suggestion from 11-year-old Grace Bedell, who wrote him a letter.

Throughout his life, Lincoln educated himself through reading. When he decided to become a lawyer, he taught himself by studying law books. Even when he was the President, Lincoln read books to learn how to lead the war effort. After the election of 1860, President Lincoln made a speech sharing his deep belief in the future of the United States that he had read about since his childhood. With tension rising between the North and South, he said:

> "If we do not make common cause to save the good old ship of the Union on this voyage, nobody will have a chance to pilot her on another voyage."

Learn from Biographies

How do you think Lincoln's reading of how Washington met the challenges of the American Revolution helped Lincoln meet the challenges of the Civil War?

For more information, go online to *Meet the People* at **www.sfsocialstudies.com.**

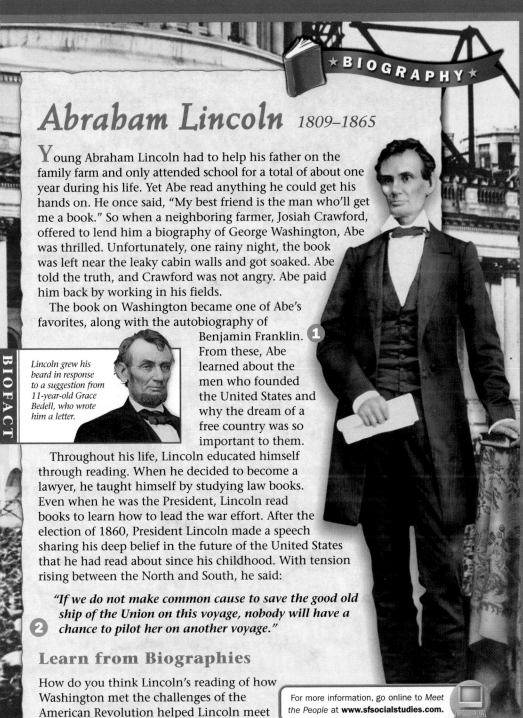

483

Read Biographies Encourage students to read about Abraham Lincoln. Have students create an annotated bibliography for future reference.

Abe Lincoln Remembers, by Ann Warren Turner (HarperCollins Juvenile Books, ISBN 0-060-27577-4, 2000) **Easy**

Abraham Lincoln the Writer: A Treasury of His Greatest Speeches and Letters, edited by Harold Holzer (Boyds Mills Press, ISBN 1-563-97772-9, 2000) **On-Level**

Lincoln: In His Own Words, by Milton Melzer, ed. (Harcourt, ISBN 0-152-45437-3, 1993) **Challenge**

Abraham Lincoln

Objective

- Identify early influences in Abraham Lincoln's life that shaped his character and his deep feelings of patriotism.

1 Introduce and Motivate

Preview To activate prior knowledge, ask students to list what they learned about Abraham Lincoln in Lesson 3. Tell students they will read more about Lincoln's early influences.

2 Teach and Discuss

1 Who were Lincoln's heroes? Why do you think he admired these people? George Washington and Benjamin Franklin; they helped found the United States and believed that the dream of a free country was very important.
Main Idea and Details

2 What did Lincoln mean by the "ship of the Union"? To what voyage was Lincoln referring? The ship was the United States, and the voyage was the attempt to preserve the Union.
Make Inferences

3 Close and Assess

Learn from Biographies Answer

Possible answer: He may have been inspired by Washington's courage, dedication, and dream of a free country.

The First Shots Are Fired

Objectives

- Describe the reasons why Southern states seceded from the Union.
- Identify the immediate cause of the start of the Civil War.
- Describe the goals the North and South hoped to achieve by fighting the Civil War.

Vocabulary

secede, p. 485; **Confederacy,** p. 485; **Union,** p. 485; **border state,** p. 486; **civil war,** p. 487

Resources

- Workbook, p. 113
- Transparencies 1, 53
- Every Student Learns Guide, pp. 202–205
- Quick Study, pp. 102–103

Quick Teaching Plan

If time is short, ask students to create a three-column chart with the headings *Causes, Events,* and *Effects.*

- Have students list important events as they read through the lesson independently.
- For each event, students should list either a cause for that event, and/or an effect that the event had on people and other events of the time.

1 Introduce and Motivate

Preview To activate prior knowledge, review the tensions that had arisen between the North and South. Tell students that, in Lesson 4, they will learn about what happened when attempts to reach a peaceful solution failed.

You Are There The bombing of Fort Sumter by Confederate forces rallied the North. Ask students what they think will happen now that the first shots have been fired.

LESSON 4

1860	1862

December 1860
South Carolina is the first state to break away from the United States

February 1861
Seven Southern states form the Confederate States of America

April 1861
Confederate forces fire on United States troops at Fort Sumter

Fort Sumter

PREVIEW

Focus on the Main Idea
Eventually 11 Southern states seceded from the United States, leading to the outbreak of the Civil War.

PLACES
Fort Sumter, South Carolina

PEOPLE
Jefferson Davis

VOCABULARY
secede
Confederacy
Union
border state
civil war

The First Shots Are Fired

You Are There

Dawn is about to break in Charleston, South Carolina. The date is April 12, 1861. Mary Boykin Chesnut, the wife of a Southern officer, is staying as a guest in a house near Charleston Harbor. Troops of the Southern states begin firing on Fort Sumter, a United States fort on an island in the harbor.

Chesnut describes the event in her diary:

"I do not pretend to go to sleep…How can I?" She is kept awake by the "heavy booming of a cannon." She springs out of bed and falls to her knees. "I prayed as I never prayed before." Chesnut then puts on her shawl and climbs to the top floor of the house to get a better view. "The shells were bursting." The roar of the cannons fills the air. "We watched up there, and everybody wondered that Fort Sumter did not fire a shot."

Sequence As you read, identify the events that led to the start of the Civil War.

Practice and Extend

READING SKILL
Sequence

In the Lesson Review, students complete a graphic organizer like the one below. You may want to provide students with a copy of Transparency 10 to complete as they read the lesson.

Use Transparency 10

VOCABULARY
Word Exercise

Individual Word Study Write the words *secede, Confederacy,* and *Union* on the board. Discuss their meanings. Using new words together in a written sentence (or paragraph) is a good way to remember how the words relate to one another. Ask students to suggest sentences that use *secede, Confederacy,* and *Union.* For example, *The Confederacy was made up of states that seceded from the Union.* Write all correct responses on the board.

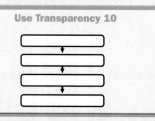

Southern States Secede

Many Southerners believed that the South should **secede,** or break away, from the United States. In December 1860, almost two months after Abraham Lincoln was elected President, South Carolina decided to secede.

By February 1, 1861, six more states—Alabama, Florida, Mississippi, Georgia, Louisiana, and Texas—had seceded. Representatives from the seven seceding states met in Montgomery, Alabama. On February 8, they formed their own government. It was called the Confederate States of America, or the **Confederacy.**

The Confederacy adopted a constitution that supported states' rights and slavery. The Confederate constitution said that its congress could not pass laws that denied "the right of property in…slaves."

The Confederacy also elected **Jefferson Davis,** a former United States senator from Mississippi, as its President. Like Abraham Lincoln, Jefferson Davis was born in

Kentucky, in a log cabin. But Davis grew up in Mississippi on a plantation owned by his family. Later he developed his own plantation on land given to him by his oldest brother.

After becoming president of the Confederacy, Davis said the Southern states should "look forward to success, to peace, and to prosperity." But in a letter to his wife Varina, he wrote that the Southern states were "threatened by a powerful opposition." That opposition came from the United States and its newly elected President, Abraham Lincoln.

Lincoln was inaugurated on March 4, 1861. By then the Confederacy had taken control of most of the forts and military property of the United States in the South. The states that remained loyal to the United States government were called the **Union.** One of the forts still under Union control was **Fort Sumter,** in the harbor of Charleston, South Carolina.

REVIEW Summarize the events that occurred as the Confederacy was formed. **Summarize**

▶ Jefferson Davis (below) was president of the Confederacy. The Confederate attack on Fort Sumter (left) was the start of the Civil War.

485

SOCIAL STUDIES
Background

About the Confederate States of America

- The Confederate States adopted symbols to show that they were an independent country. They designed their own postage stamps and created a flag known as the "Stars and Bars."

- The Confederates felt that their cotton industry would gain them formal recognition from the governments of foreign countries, but the Confederacy was unable to successfully establish relations with Great Britain, France, or any other power in Europe.

- Students may think that all the slave states were part of the Confederacy, but four of the slave states stayed in the Union. (Delaware, Maryland, Missouri, and Kentucky)

2 Teach and Discuss

PAGE 485

Southern States Secede

🕐 **Quick Summary** Shortly after Abraham Lincoln's election, seven Southern states seceded from the Union to form the Confederacy. Jefferson Davis became the President of the Confederate States of America.

1 Contrast the Confederate Constitution with the U.S. Constitution. U.S. Constitution: gave many powers to the federal government; Confederate Constitution: more power to the states; slavery was lawful **Compare and Contrast**

✓ Ongoing Assessment

| **If…** students have difficulty contrasting the two Constitutions, | **then…** have students reread the paragraph about the Confederate Constitution. Discuss how it might differ from the U.S. Constitution. |

2 How did President Jefferson Davis feel about the Confederacy? The Southern states could be peaceful and prosperous, but they were also threatened by opposition from the United States. **Main Idea and Details**

✓ REVIEW ANSWER Abraham Lincoln was elected President. South Carolina seceded from the United States, followed by six other states. The Confederate States of America was formed. A Confederate Constitution was adopted and Jefferson Davis was elected President of the Confederacy. **Summarize**

The War Begins

Quick Summary Confederate forces fired the first shots of the Civil War when they bombed Fort Sumter in the harbor of Charleston, South Carolina. Abraham Lincoln responded by asking Union states to supply soldiers to put down the rebellion.

MAP SKILL The Union and the Confederacy, 1861–1865

Guide students as they use the key to determine which states and territories were controlled by the Union and the Confederacy.

3 **Which states were border states?** Missouri, Kentucky, West Virginia, Maryland, and Delaware **Interpret Maps**

MAP SKILL Answer Texas

4 **Why did Confederate forces begin firing on Fort Sumter?** A Union officer agreed to surrender the fort, but asked for three days' wait. The Confederate commander gave orders to fire on the fort if it was not surrendered in one hour after the demand was made. When Union officers did not give up the fort within the demanded amount of time, Confederate forces began shelling it. **Cause and Effect**

5 **Why do you think the call for troops caused more states to secede?** Possible answer: These states may have been worried about the issue of states' rights. They may have felt that their right to own slaves was being threatened by the upcoming war. **Draw Conclusions**

6 **Why do you think that the border states stayed in the Union but would not provide soldiers to fight in the war?** Possible answer: These states may have believed it was important to remain part of the United States, but they did not want to fight against people who held some of the same beliefs that they did. **Evaluate**

486 Unit 7 • War Divides the Nation

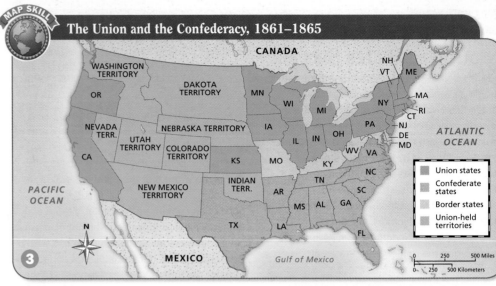

MAP SKILL The Union and the Confederacy, 1861–1865

Union states
Confederate states
Border states
Union-held territories

▶ This map shows the United States during the Civil War. Find West Virginia, which broke away from Virginia and voted to stay in the Union. West Virginia became a state in 1863.

MAP SKILL Place *Name the Confederate state that reached farthest to the west.*

The War Begins

On April 9, 1861, Jefferson Davis met with his advisers to discuss Fort Sumter. One adviser said that making the first strike against the Union would put the Confederacy "in the wrong." Davis disagreed and decided to send officers to ask for the surrender of the fort.

A Union officer, Robert Anderson, commanded Fort Sumter. He agreed to surrender if the Confederacy would wait three more days. But the Confederate commander, Pierre G.T. Beauregard (BOH ruh gard), had given orders to fire on Fort Sumter if Anderson did not surrender in one hour.

4 The Confederates began firing on Fort Sumter on Friday, April 12, at 4:30 A.M. The bombing continued into Saturday. With little food and water, Major Anderson was forced to surrender and left the fort on Sunday.

Lincoln responded to the attack on Fort Sumter and its surrender by asking Union states to supply 75,000 soldiers to put down

486

the Confederate rebellion. Lincoln believed this could be done quickly, and said the soldiers would only be needed for 90 days.

Lincoln's call for troops so angered the states of Virginia, Arkansas, Tennessee, and North Carolina, that they seceded and joined the Confederacy. There were now 11 states in the Confederacy and 23 in the Union. Four of the Union states—Delaware, Maryland, Missouri, and Kentucky—were slave states that seemed unsure of whether to stay in the Union or join the Confederacy. These were called the **border states** because, as you see on the map above, they were located between the Union and Confederacy. Three of these states—Delaware, Missouri, and Kentucky—said they would not provide soldiers. Maryland said it would, but only to defend Washington, D.C.

Lincoln believed it was important to keep these border states in the Union, even though they were slave states. That is why in 1861 he continued to say that his aim was to hold the United States together, not to

---

Practice and Extend

MEETING INDIVIDUAL NEEDS
Leveled Practice

Act as Reporters Have students act as on-the-scene reporters giving firsthand accounts of the shelling at Fort Sumter.

Easy Students can reread the account of the bombing, using tone and word emphasis to underscore important events. Each time a student reads, a volunteer can provide a "recap," summarizing what was said. **Reteach**

On-Level Have students paraphrase or summarize the lesson. They can add ideas about what these events may mean for the future of the Union and the Confederacy. Remind them to use vivid, colorful language that will help their listeners feel as if they are witnessing the events themselves. **Extend**

Challenge Building on the "On-Level" idea, groups of students can interview "bystanders" and important figures from history, such as the commander of Fort Sumter, Jefferson Davis, and Abraham Lincoln. **Enrich**

For a Lesson Summary, use Quick Study, p. 102.

abolish slavery. You will soon learn that neither goal would be quickly or easily achieved.

The conflict between the states arose for a number of reasons. For Lincoln and his supporters, the main reason for fighting the war was to preserve, or keep together, the Union. However, other supporters of the North believed they were fighting to end slavery. Southerners fought the war to preserve states' rights and slavery. They also believed they were defending their homeland and their way of life.

The battle at Fort Sumter began the American Civil War. A **civil war** is a war between people of the same country. Some Northerners described the war as a rebellion and the Confederacy as a group of rebels. Many Southerners accepted the name *rebel* with pride. To them the conflict was known as the War for Southern Independence. They

also called it the War of Northern Aggression. The title War Between the States is also commonly used. But no matter what it was called, the war would be longer and bloodier than anyone guessed in the spring of 1861.

REVIEW What were the main differences between the reasons the North and South fought the Civil War? **Compare and Contrast**

Summarize the Lesson

— **December 1860** South Carolina became the first state to secede from the United States.

— **February 1861** Seven Southern states formed the Confederate States of America.

— **April 1861** Confederate forces fired on United States troops at Fort Sumter, a battle that began the Civil War.

LESSON 4 REVIEW

Check Facts and Main Ideas

1. **Sequence** On a separate sheet of paper, complete the graphic organizer to show the events that led up to the start of the Civil War.

The Civil War began on April 12, 1861

↓

Seven Southern states secede from the United States and form the Confederate States of America.

↓

The Confederacy elects Jefferson Davis as its president.

↓

Jefferson Davis sent Confederate soldiers to make Fort Sumter surrender.

2. Why did the southern states **secede?**

3. **Critical Thinking:** *Draw Conclusions* What might have been Jefferson Davis's reason for attacking Fort Sumter?

4. Describe Abraham Lincoln's main reason for fighting the Civil War.

5. Why, at the beginning of the Civil War, did Lincoln not say that he was fighting the war to end slavery?

Link to  **Writing**

Write an Article Suppose you are part of the **Union** or **Confederacy** when the war began in 1861. Research the man who is your president and write a brief article explaining why he is qualified for his position.

487

---

7 **Compare and contrast Abraham Lincoln's reasons for involvement in the Civil War with reasons of other Northerners.** Although he thought that slavery was wrong, Lincoln's main reason for fighting was to preserve the Union. Other Northerners believed they were going to war to end slavery. **Compare and Contrast**

✓ **REVIEW ANSWER** Northerners fought the war to keep the Union together and to end slavery. Southerners fought the war to preserve states' rights and slavery and to defend their homeland and way of life. **Compare and Contrast**

3 Close and Assess

Summarize the Lesson

Have students create a cause and effect chart using two of the points on the time line.

✓ **LESSON 4** **REVIEW**

1. 🌀 **Main Idea and Details** For possible answers, see the reduced pupil page.

2. To preserve the rights of states and to uphold the practice of slavery

3. Possible answer: To show that the fort now belonged to the Confederacy.

4. To preserve the Union

5. **Critical Thinking:** *Express Ideas* The border states were still part of the Union, yet they allowed slavery. If Lincoln had said he was fighting the war to end slavery, the border states may have joined the Confederacy.

Link to **Writing**

Review with students the background of the two men before they begin their research.

ACCESS CONTENT
ESL Support

Review Sequence Help students order events.

Beginning Have groups of students choose one sentence from the lesson. Write the sentences on the board and have students sequence them.

Intermediate Write events from the lesson on strips of paper and give a set to each pair of students. Students should put the strips in order.

Advanced Have students write lesson events on index cards and arrange the cards in order. Students can use the cards to summarize the lesson, using transition words between events.

For additional ESL support, use Every Student Learns Guide, pp. 202–205.

Workbook, p. 113

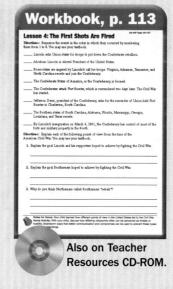

Lesson 4: The First Shots Are Fired

Directions: Sequence the events in the order in which they occurred by numbering them from 1 to 8. You may use your textbook.

___ Lincoln asks Union states for troops to put down the Confederate rebellion.

___ Abraham Lincoln is elected President of the United States.

___ Some states are angered by Lincoln's call for troops. Virginia, Arkansas, Tennessee, and North Carolina secede and join the Confederacy.

___ The Confederate States of America, or the Confederacy, is formed.

___ The Confederates attack Fort Sumter, which is surrendered two days later. The Civil War has started.

___ Jefferson Davis, president of the Confederacy, asks for the surrender of Union-held Fort Sumter in Charleston, South Carolina.

___ The Southern states of South Carolina, Alabama, Florida, Mississippi, Georgia, Louisiana, and Texas secede.

___ By Lincoln's inauguration on March 4, 1861, the Confederacy has control of most of the forts and military property in the South.

Directions: Explain each of the following points of view from the time of the American Civil War. You may use your textbook.

1. Explain the goal Lincoln and his supporters hoped to achieve by fighting the Civil War.

2. Explain the goal Southerners hoped to achieve by fighting the Civil War.

3. Why do you think Northerners called Southerners "rebels"?

Also on Teacher Resources CD-ROM.

Resources

- Assessment Book, pp. 81–84
- Workbook, p. 114: Vocabulary Review

Chapter Summary

For possible answers, see the reduced pupil page.

Vocabulary

1. b, **2.** d, **3.** a, **4.** e, **5.** c

People and Terms

1. David Walker was a free African American who spoke against slavery.
2. Nat Turner led an armed uprising of slaves in Virginia.
3. Southern states seceded from the Union and formed the Confederacy.
4. Harriet Tubman led many slaves from the South to freedom in the North.
5. John C. Calhoun was a U.S. senator from South Carolina who believed in a state's right to decide which laws best served its own needs.
6. The Fugitive Slave Law said that escaped slaves had to be returned.
7. Harriet Beecher Stowe wrote *Uncle Tom's Cabin*, which convinced many people to support abolition.
8. In the Dred Scott case, the Supreme Court ruled that slaves had no rights because they were not citizens.
9. Jefferson Davis became the President of the Confederate States.
10. The states loyal to the U.S. government were called the Union.

Facts and Main Ideas

1. When slaves worked, where they went, and whether they could marry
2. Anti-slavery members of the Whig Party formed the Republican Party.
3. About 26 years
4. Attitudes toward states' rights, tariffs, and slavery
5. Escapes, refusals to obey orders, and rebellions
6. It was difficult for people with differing opinions about slavery to get along.
7. The South worried that Lincoln would prohibit slavery. This belief led Southern states to secede and form their own government.
8. So that neither side would have more power in the United States Senate.

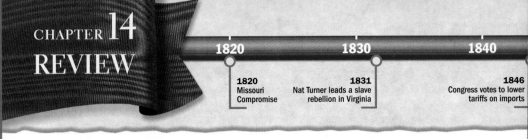

1820	1830	1840

1820
Missouri Compromise

1831
Nat Turner leads a slave rebellion in Virginia

1846
Congress votes to lower tariffs on imports

Chapter Summary

Main Idea and Details

On a separate sheet of paper, fill in the main compromises made in Congress before the Civil War.

Congress made several compromises to keep the North and South from splitting apart.

Missouri Compromise

Compromise of 1850

Kansas-Nebraska Act

▶ **Tattered flag from the battle at Fort Sumter**

Vocabulary

Match each word with the correct definition or description.

1. **sectionalism** (p. 465)
2. **slave codes** (p. 471)
3. **free state** (p. 477)
4. **secede** (p. 485)
5. **Underground Railroad** (p. 473)

a. state that does not permit slavery

b. loyalty to a part of a country, not to the whole country

c. secret system to help slaves escape to freedom

d. laws controlling behavior of slaves

e. break away

People and Terms

Write a sentence explaining why each of the following people or terms was important in the events that led to the start of the Civil War. You may use two or more in a single sentence.

1. **David Walker** (p. 467)
2. **Nat Turner** (p. 472)
3. **Confederacy** (p. 485)
4. **Harriet Tubman** (p. 473)
5. **John C. Calhoun** (p. 477)
6. **Fugitive Slave Law** (p. 478)
7. **Harriet Beecher Stowe** (p. 480)
8. **Dred Scott** (p. 480)
9. **Jefferson Davis** (p. 485)
10. **Union** (p. 485)

488

Practice and Extend

Assessment Options

✓Chapter 14 Assessment

- Chapter 14 Content Test: Use Assessment Book, pp. 81–82.
- Chapter 14 Skills Test: Use Assessment Book, pp. 83–84.

Standardized Test Prep

- Chapter 14 Tests contain standardized test format.

✓Chapter 14 Performance Assessment

- Have students work in small groups to create displays (or plan displays) for a museum that showcases U.S. history in the years leading up to the Civil War.
- Students might include drawings of important figures with short biographies, maps, excerpts from speeches, and descriptions of the compromises. Students should explain why these resources are important to understanding this period.
- As students present their work, assess their knowledge of key concepts in the chapter.

1849
Harriet Tubman escapes slavery on the Underground Railroad

1857
Dred Scott case

1860
Abraham Lincoln is elected President

February 1861
Confederate States of America formed

April 1861
Southern forces fire on U.S. troops at Fort Sumter

Facts and Main Ideas

1. What kinds of control did slave owners have over the lives of slaves?

2. How did the issue of slavery lead to a new political party?

3. **Time Line** How many years were there between the Nat Turner revolt and the Dred Scott case?

4. **Main Idea** What were some differences between the North and South that increased tensions between the two regions?

5. **Main Idea** How did many slaves resist slavery?

6. **Main Idea** How did the differences over slavery threaten the existence of the United States?

7. **Main Idea** What effect did Lincoln's election have on the South?

8. **Critical Thinking:** *Draw Conclusions* Why did people work to keep a balance between the number of slave states and free states?

Write About History

1. **Write a journal entry** as a person who observed the battle at Fort Sumter.

2. **Write a poem** about a person mentioned in this chapter whom you admire.

3. **Write a short speech** you might have given as a senator for or against the Missouri Compromise.

Apply Skills

Recognize Point of View
Read the two sections below from the Lincoln-Douglas debates. Then answer the questions.

"If slavery is not wrong, then nothing is wrong...[But I] would not do anything to bring about a war between the free and slave states."

—Abraham Lincoln

"If each state will only agree to mind its own business...this republic can exist forever divided into free and slave states."

—Stephen Douglas

1. What is the subject of each section?

2. What is Lincoln's viewpoint about slavery?

3. What is Douglas's viewpoint about slavery?

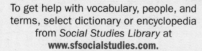

Internet Activity

To get help with vocabulary, people, and terms, select dictionary or encyclopedia from *Social Studies Library* at **www.sfsocialstudies.com.**

489

Write About History

Test Talk

Write Your Answer to Score High

1. Remind students that a journal entry should be written from the first-person point of view. Tell students to use details from the chapter to make their journal entries realistic.

2. Remind students that poems do not have to rhyme. Students should use words and images to "paint a picture" of the subject they choose.

3. Encourage students to list their opinions and persuasive facts supporting those opinions. Remind them that their speeches should have a formal and respectful tone.

Apply Skills

1. The subject is slavery and its effect on the relationship of free states and slave states.

2. Lincoln believes that slavery is wrong, but does not believe there should be a war between free states and slave states.

3. Douglas believes that the question of slavery should be left up to each state.

Hands-on Unit Project

✓ **Unit 7 Performance Assessment**

- See p. 528 for information about using the Unit Project as a means of performance assessment.
- A scoring guide is provided on p. 528.

WEB SITE
Technology

For more information, students can select the dictionary or encyclopedia from *Social Studies Library* at **www.sfsocialstudies.com.**

Workbook, p. 114

Vocabulary Review

Directions: Choose the vocabulary word from the box that best completes each sentence. Write the word on the line provided. Not all words will be used.

sectionalism	states' rights	secede
slave codes	Missouri Compromise	Confederacy
Underground Railroad	Fugitive Slave Law	Union
free state	Compromise of 1850	border state
slave state	Kansas-Nebraska Act	civil war

1. The _____ was made up of states that remained loyal to the United States government.

2. The _____ allowed California to be admitted to the Union as a free state.

3. _____ is the idea that people of a state can choose the laws that best fit their needs.

4. South Carolina was the first state to _____ from the Union.

5. The _____ preserved the balance between free and slave states.

6. The states that seceded from the Union formed the _____.

7. The _____ allowed people in certain areas to determine whether or not their territory would allow slavery.

8. Although some former slaves had reached the North and found freedom, the _____ said they had to be returned to their owners.

9. A _____ did not allow slaves to own land.

10. Slavery was illegal in California and any other _____.

11. Harriet Tubman became famous for helping slaves escape to freedom on the _____.

Notes for Home: Your child learned about differences between the North and the South that divided the nation.
Home Activity: Have your child practice using the vocabulary terms in sentences of his or her own.

Also on Teacher Resources CD-ROM.

CHAPTER 15

Chapter Planning Guide

Chapter 15 • War and Reconstruction

Locating Time and Place pp. 490–491

Lesson Titles	Pacing	Main Ideas
Lesson 1 **The Early Stages of the War** pp. 492–496		• In the early years of the Civil War, the North and South formed strategies in hopes of gaining a quick victory.
Biography: Robert E. Lee p. 497	2 days	• Robert E. Lee made the difficult decision to command the Virginia forces.
Lesson 2 **Life During the War** pp. 498–503		• As the Civil War continued, people in the North and the South suffered many hardships, including the growing loss of life.
⭐ **Citizen Heroes:** **Caring** **Working for Lasting Peace** pp. 504–505	2 days	• Jody Williams continues her efforts to rid the world of landmines.
Lesson 3 **How the North Won** pp. 506–511		• A series of Northern victories led to the end of the Civil War by 1865.
Map and Globe Skills: **Read a Road Map** pp. 512–513	3 days	• Road maps allow you to figure out how to get from one place to another.
📖 **Communications During the Civil War** pp. 514–515		• Both Union and Confederate armies used Morse code and secret military codes to communicate.
Lesson 4 **The End of Slavery** pp. 516–521		• The country faced many difficult challenges after the Civil War ended, including rebuilding the South and protecting the rights of newly freed African Americans.
	2 days	

✓ **Chapter 15 Review**
pp. 522–523

HARPER'S WEEKLY.
JOURNAL OF CIVILIZATION

◀ **African American men were granted the right to vote by the Fifteenth Amendment.**

✓ **= Assessment Options**

490a Unit 7 • War Divides the Nation

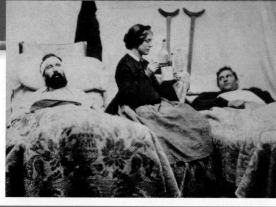

◄ **During the war some women cared for soldiers.**

Vocabulary	Resources	Meeting Individual Needs
blockade Anaconda Plan First Battle of Bull Run Battle of Antietam	• Workbook, p. 116 • Transparency 1 • Every Student Learns Guide, pp. 206–209 • Quick Study, pp. 104–105	• Leveled Practice, TE p. 493 • ESL Support, TE p. 494
draft Emancipation Proclamation	• Workbook, p. 117 • Transparency 1 • Every Student Learns Guide, pp. 210–213 • Quick Study, pp. 106–107	• Leveled Practice, TE p. 499 • ESL Support, TE p. 502
Battle of Gettysburg Gettysburg Address Battle of Vicksburg total war road map interstate highway	• Workbook, pp. 118–119 • Transparencies 1, 54, 55 • Every Student Learns Guide, pp. 214–217 • Quick Study, pp. 108–109	• Leveled Practice, TE p. 507, 512 • Learning Styles, TE p. 508 • ESL Support, TE p. 511
assassination, Reconstruction, Thirteenth Amendment, black codes, Freedmen's Bureau, Fourteenth Amendment, Fifteenth Amendment, impeachment, Jim Crow laws, segregation, sharecropping	• Workbook, p. 120 • Transparency 1 • Every Student Learns Guide, pp. 218–221 • Quick Study, pp. 110–111	• Leveled Practice, TE p. 518 • ESL Support, TE p. 519
	✓Chapter 15 Content Test, Assessment Book pp. 85–86 ✓Chapter 15 Skills Test, Assessment Book, pp. 87–88	✓Chapter 15 Performance Assessment, TE p. 522

Providing More Depth

Additional Resources

- Vocabulary Workbook and Cards
- Social Studies Plus! pp. 172–177
- Daily Activity Bank
- Big Book Atlas
- Student Atlas
- Outline Maps
- Desk Maps

 Technology

- AudioText
- MindPoint® Quiz Show CD-ROM
- ExamView® Test Bank CD-ROM
- Teacher Resources CD-ROM
- Map Resources CD-ROM
- SFSuccessNet: iText (Pupil Edition online), iTE (Teacher's Edition online), Online Planner
- **www.sfsocialstudies.com** (Biographies, news, references, maps, and activities)

 To establish guidelines for your students' safe and responsible use of the Internet, use the Scott Foresman Internet Guide.

Additional Internet Links

To find out more about:
- Women in the Civil War, visit **www.nara.gov**
- International Campaign to Ban Landmines, visit **www.icbl.org**
- Gettysburg National Military Park, visit **www.nps.gov**
- The Union ship *Monitor,* visit **www.oceanexplorer.noaa. gov**

Key Internet Search Terms
- Emancipation Proclamation
- Battle of Gettysburg

Workbook Support

Use the following Workbook pages to support content and skills development as you teach Chapter 15. You can also view and print Workbook pages from the Teacher Resources CD-ROM.

Workbook, p. 115

Vocabulary Preview

Use with Chapter 15.

Directions: Circle the vocabulary term that best completes each sentence.

1. The (Anaconda Plan, Reconstruction) was a three-part war strategy to crush the South during the Civil War.

2. Slavery was abolished by the (Thirteenth Amendment, Fourteenth Amendment) to the Constitution.

3. The (First Battle of Bull Run, Battle of Gettysburg) lasted three days and was one of the most important battles of the Civil War.

4. African Americans became U.S. citizens under the (Fourteenth Amendment, Thirteenth Amendment) to the Constitution.

5. At the (Battle of Antietam, Battle of Vicksburg), Union forces blockaded the city and bombarded it for 48 days.

6. (Segregation, Sharecropping) is the separation of blacks and whites.

7. Both the North and the South instituted the (blockade, draft) to get men to fight in the war.

8. The (Gettysburg Address, Emancipation Proclamation) granted freedom to slaves in any Confederate states that were still battling the Union.

9. The time after the war when the country was rebuilding and healing is known as (Reconstruction, segregation).

10. The (black codes, blockade) kept supplies from reaching Southern soldiers.

11. One of the early battles of the war was the (Battle of Gettysburg, First Battle of Bull Run).

12. People in many U.S. cities paid their respects to President Lincoln after his (assassination, impeachment).

13. The (Freedmen's Bureau, Emancipation Proclamation) was established to help former slaves after the war.

14. All male citizens received the right to vote with the ratification of the (Thirteenth Amendment, Fifteenth Amendment) to the Constitution.

15. The (Emancipation Proclamation, Jim Crow laws) enforced separation of blacks and whites.

16. Republicans in Congress called for the (total war, impeachment) of President Andrew Johnson.

 Notes for Home: Your child learned about events during and after the Civil War.
Home Activity: With your child, review each vocabulary term and its definition to make sure the term fits in the sentence. Then make your own sentences using the vocabulary terms.

Use with Pupil Edition, p. 490

Workbook, p. 116

Lesson 1: The Early Stages of the War

Use with Pages 492–496.

Directions: Complete each compare-and-contrast table with information about the Union and the Confederacy. You may use your textbook.

	Supporters of the North	Supporters of the South
Reason for fighting	to preserve the Union	to preserve their way of life

	Northerners	Southerners
Believed advantage over the opposition	Armies needed supplies, and the North produced more than 90 percent of the country's weapons, cloth, shoes, and iron.	The South's more rural way of life would better prepare soldiers for war. The South had a history of producing military leaders.

	Union	Confederacy
War strategies	Three-part plan of action: (1) set up a blockade of the Confederacy's Atlantic and Gulf coasts, (2) capture territory along the Mississippi to weaken the Confederacy by cutting the Southern states in two, (3) attack the Confederacy from both the east and the west.	Defend the Confederacy until the North grows tired and gives up. Northerners, who have nothing to gain, will not fight as fiercely as Southerners. Britain will assist in the war because English clothing mills depend on Southern cotton.

Notes for Home: Your child learned about different attitudes toward war and different strategies used by the North and South during the Civil War.
Home Activity: With your child, discuss possible problems the Union and the Confederacy might have had to consider when forming their war strategies. Ask your child what could have gone wrong in each case.

Use with Pupil Edition, p. 496

Workbook, p. 117

Lesson 2: Life During the War

Use with Pages 498–503.

Directions: For each main idea, write a supporting detail on the line provided. You may use your textbook.

1. **Main Idea:** News of the war spread in many ways.
   Detail: The news spread through letters, newspaper articles, and photographs.

2. **Main Idea:** As the war continued, both sides had trouble getting more soldiers.
   Detail: Possible answers: The number of volunteers decreased, so both sides passed draft laws; in the Union, men paid $300 to avoid fighting; in the Confederacy, some men paid substitutes to fight in their place.

3. **Main Idea:** Most of the soldiers who died in the Civil War did not die in battle.
   Detail: Possible answer: Disease was the most common cause of death in the Civil War.

4. **Main Idea:** The Civil War did not begin as a war against slavery.
   Detail: Lincoln's goal was to keep the nation united.

5. **Main Idea:** African Americans who wished to serve in the war were not treated the same as white soldiers.
   Detail: Possible answers: At first, African Americans were not allowed to join the Union army; African American soldiers were paid less than white soldiers at first.

6. **Main Idea:** Women contributed to the war effort in many ways.
   Detail: Possible answers: Women ran businesses and farms and became teachers and office workers; some women became spies; some women became nurses; some women gathered supplies for soldiers.

 Notes for Home: Your child learned about difficult conditions during the war.
Home Activity: With your child, make a list of the difficulties soldiers and civilians experienced during the Civil War. Discuss how these types of difficulties might have made your family feel about the war, the enemy, and the country.

Use with Pupil Edition, p. 503

Workbook, p. 118

Lesson 3: How the North Won

Use with Pages 506–511.

Directions: Match each term in the box with its clue. Write the term on the line provided.

Battle of Gettysburg	Ulysses S. Grant	total war
Gettysburg Address	Battle of Vicksburg	Robert E. Lee
Anaconda Plan	William Tecumseh Sherman	Appomattox Court House

1. Place where Generals Lee and Grant met to discuss the terms of the Confederates' surrender of the Civil War **Appomattox Court House**

2. "I would rather die a thousand deaths." **Robert E. Lee**

3. President Lincoln made a short speech at a ceremony to dedicate a national cemetery. In his speech, Lincoln inspired the Union to keep fighting for a united nation and the end of slavery. **Gettysburg Address**

4. A method of warfare designed to destroy the opposing army and the people's will to fight **total war**

5. This three-day battle began on July 1, 1863. It was one of the most important battles of the Civil War. It was an important victory for the North and a costly battle for both sides. **Battle of Gettysburg**

6. Head of the Union forces in the Battle of Vicksburg **Ulysses S. Grant**

7. The surrender of this battle by the Southerners cut the Confederacy in two. **Battle of Vicksburg**

8. The Union blockade at the Battle of Vicksburg was part of this strategy to gain control of the Mississippi River and weaken the Confederacy. **Anaconda Plan**

9. Led soldiers in a destructive "March to the Sea" **William Tecumseh Sherman**

 Notes for Home: Your child learned how the North used strategies to win the Civil War.
Home Activity: With your child, brainstorm strategies for winning a game such as checkers, chess, or cards. Discuss the advantages of using a strategy to defeat an opponent.

Use with Pupil Edition, p. 511

490c Unit 7 • War Divides the Nation

Workbook Support

Workbook, p. 119

Use with Pages 512–513.

Read a Road Map

A road map shows roads, cities, and places of interest. Drivers use road maps to figure out how to get from one place to another.

Directions: Use the road map to answer the following questions.

1. General Sherman's army probably walked and rode horses from Atlanta to Savannah, Georgia. What major roads might you take today to drive between these two cities?

   Possible answers: Interstate 75 and Interstate 16

2. What major city would you pass through when traveling along this route from Atlanta to Savannah? **Macon**

3. According to this map, what other roads might you take to travel from Atlanta to Savannah? **Possible answers: Hwy 23 and Hwy 80**

4. Examine the map. Why do you think General Sherman's march was known as the "March to the Sea"? **Possible answer: Savannah is located on the ocean, and the march from Atlanta to Savannah would go toward the sea.**

5. General Sherman's army left Savannah and went to South Carolina. If you were to drive from Savannah to South Carolina today, what major road might you take?

   Possible answer: Interstate 95

 Notes for Home: Your child learned how to read a road map.
Home Activity: With your child, look at a road map of your state. Together, determine the most direct route from your city to one of your state's borders. Next, find the most scenic route.

Use with Pupil Edition, p. 513

Workbook, p. 120

Use with Pages 516–521.

Lesson 4: The End of Slavery

Directions: Define each term or phrase. Use a separate sheet of paper if you need more room. You may use your textbook.

1. Reconstruction **The rebuilding and healing of the country after the Civil War**

2. Thirteenth Amendment **The amendment that abolished slavery in the United States**

3. black codes **Laws that denied African Americans many things, including the right to vote, to take part in jury trials, to own land or guns, or to take certain jobs; allowed unemployed African Americans to be fined or arrested**

4. Freedmen's Bureau **Bureau established to help the 4 million former slaves after the war**

5. Ku Klux Klan **Group formed to restore white control over African Americans after the war**

6. Fourteenth Amendment **Gave African Americans citizenship and equal protection of the law**

7. Jim Crow laws **Laws that enforced segregation**

8. sharecropping **The practice of renting land from landowners and then paying the rent with a portion of the crop produced on that land**

 Notes for Home: Your child learned about how the United States changed after the Civil War.
Home Activity: With your child, review the series of changes that took place during Reconstruction and discuss who benefited from each change.

Use with Pupil Edition, p. 521

Workbook, p. 121

Use with Chapter 15.

Vocabulary Review

Directions: Use the vocabulary words from Chapter 15 to complete the following sentences. Write the correct word in the space provided. You may use your textbook.

1. **Segregation** is the separation of blacks and whites.

2. The shutting off of an area by troops or ships to keep people and supplies from moving in or out is known as a **blockade**.

3. At the Battle of **Vicksburg**, Union forces blockaded the city and bombarded it with cannon fire by land and sea for 48 days.

4. **Sharecropping** is the practice of renting land from a landowner and paying rent with a portion of the crop produced on that land.

5. The murdering of a government or political leader is known as an **assassination**.

6. Laws that denied blacks the right to vote or take part in jury trials were known as **black codes**.

7. A method of warfare that destroys not only the opposing army but also the people's will to fight is known as **total war**.

8. In the Battle of **Antietam**, Union and Confederate forces clashed near the town of Sharpsburg in Maryland.

9. The First Battle of **Bull Run**, one of the early battles of the Civil War, was won by the Confederates.

10. The **Freedmen's Bureau** was established to help the more than 4 million former slaves after the war.

11. **Reconstruction** refers to the rebuilding of the country after the Civil War.

12. The Battle of **Gettysburg** lasted three days and was one of the most important battles of the Civil War.

13. **Jim Crow** laws enforced the separation of blacks and whites.

14. The **Anaconda** Plan was a war strategy designed to "squeeze" the Confederacy.

 Notes for Home: Your child learned about how the Civil War divided the nation and what steps were taken to heal and rebuild the country afterward.
Home Activity: With your child, analyze the relationships among the vocabulary terms for this unit. Begin by having your child place each term on a time line for the Civil War era.

Use with Pupil Edition, p. 523

Workbook, p. 122

UNIT 7 Project History Speaks

Directions: In a group, prepare a talk that might have been given by a famous person who lived during the Civil War or Reconstruction.

1. We considered the following people who lived during the Civil War or Reconstruction as subjects for our talk:

From the North	From the South
_____	_____
_____	_____
_____	_____

2. Our group chose _____ from the candidates we considered.

3. Details from this person's life include:

   _____

   _____

   _____

   _____

   _____

4. _____ will play the part of _____ for our class presentation.

5. The (✔) shows visuals we presented to the class:
   ___ drawings ___ pictures ___ artifacts ___ other: _____

You may wish to review the subjects chosen by each group to ensure that they reflect a variety of individuals and perspectives from the Civil War period.

✔ Checklist for Students

_____ We identified a famous person to talk about the time period.
_____ We researched details about the life and times of this person.
_____ We named a group member to present the talk to the class.
_____ We showed visuals of Civil War life to the class.

 Notes for Home: Your child helped prepare a first-person presentation on the Civil War period.
Home Activity: Ask your child to tell you about the historical figure his or her group selected. Encourage your child to share details about the life of this person.

Use with Pupil Edition, p. 528

Assessment Support

Use these Assessment Book pages and the ExamView® Test Bank CD-ROM to assess content and skills in Chapter 15. You can also view and print Assessment Book pages from the Teacher Resources CD-ROM.

Assessment Book, p. 85

Chapter 15 Test

Part 1: Content Test

Directions: Fill in the circle next to the correct answer.

Lesson Objective (1:1)

1. Which of the following did the South see as its advantage in the war?
   - Ⓐ The South had plenty of cotton for cloth.
   - Ⓑ The South produced more than half of the country's wheat.
   - Ⓒ The army needed supplies.
   - ● Southerners' rural lifestyles better prepared soldiers for war.

Lesson Objective (1:2)

2. Which of the following was a war strategy used by the Union?
   - Ⓐ stampede
   - ● blockade
   - Ⓒ bombing
   - Ⓓ air raid

Lesson Objective (1:2)

3. Which of the following did Confederates believe?
   - Ⓐ Northerners would fight a long time.
   - Ⓑ Britain would help the Union.
   - ● Northerners would grow tired of fighting and give up.
   - Ⓓ The Union would use the Anaconda Plan.

Lesson Objective (1:3)

4. Which of the following describes the early battles of the Civil War?
   - ● They were confusing because most of the troops were new to war.
   - Ⓑ They were well organized and efficient.
   - Ⓒ The Union always won because the North had better soldiers.
   - Ⓓ The Confederacy always won because the South had better soldiers.

Lesson Objective (1:4)

5. Which of the following describes the effect of new military technology on the Civil War?
   - Ⓐ More accurate weapons resulted in fewer casualties.
   - ● More accurate weapons resulted in huge casualties.
   - Ⓒ Stronger ships resulted in fewer sea battles.
   - Ⓓ New weapons reduced the need for blockades.

Lesson Objective (2:1)

6. Which of the following was NOT experienced by both Northern and Southern soldiers?
   - Ⓐ Soldiers were unhappy with the food.
   - Ⓑ Soldiers saw friends die.
   - ● Soldiers often had to fight in bare feet.
   - Ⓓ Soldiers were drafted.

Lesson Objective (2:2)

7. What was the Emancipation Proclamation?
   - Ⓐ a statement giving freedom to all women
   - Ⓑ a statement giving freedom to all people in the United States
   - Ⓒ a statement giving freedom to all Confederate states still at war with the Union
   - ● a statement giving freedom to slaves in all Confederate states still at war with the Union

Use with Pupil Edition, p. 522

Assessment Book, p. 86

Lesson Objective (2:3)

8. What is one way African Americans served the Union's war effort?
   - ● They engaged in combat.
   - Ⓑ They protested against slavery.
   - Ⓒ They supported freedom and went to Canada.
   - Ⓓ They staged demonstrations to end the war.

Lesson Objective (2:4)

9. Which is NOT one way women contributed to the war effort?
   - Ⓐ They cared for the soldiers.
   - ● They ran the government.
   - Ⓒ They ran businesses.
   - Ⓓ They were spies.

Lesson Objective (3:1)

10. Which of the following describes the Battle of Gettysburg?
    - Ⓐ Lee and Pickett battled against each other, and the North won.
    - Ⓑ Lee's retreat to Virginia won the battle for the South.
    - Ⓒ The Pennsylvania battle was won by the South.
    - ● The three-day struggle was won by the North.

Lesson Objective (3:3)

11. Which cut the Confederacy in two?
    - ● Battle of Vicksburg
    - Ⓑ Battle of Gettysburg
    - Ⓒ Battle of Savannah
    - Ⓓ Battle of Bull Run

Lesson Objective (3:4)

12. Which is a result of total war?
    - Ⓐ Everybody helps out any way they can.
    - Ⓑ An area is squeezed the way a snake would squeeze its prey.
    - Ⓒ Supplies are cut off.
    - ● The people's will to fight is destroyed.

Lesson Objective (4:1)

13. Why did Congress disagree with President Andrew Johnson's Reconstruction plan?
    - ● They thought it was too easy on the South.
    - Ⓑ They did not want to include all of the Southern states.
    - Ⓒ They did not want to allow all African Americans to be free.
    - Ⓓ They thought the plan was cruel to Southerners.

Lesson Objective (4:2)

14. Which of the following was an effect of the Reconstruction Acts?
    - Ⓐ All African Americans had the right to vote.
    - ● African American men had the right to vote.
    - Ⓒ African Americans could lobby Congress for the right to vote.
    - Ⓓ African Americans were not allowed to vote.

Lesson Objective (4:3)

15. What did the passage of the Thirteenth, Fourteenth, and Fifteenth Amendments mean for African Americans?
    - ● African Americans were free citizens, and the men could vote.
    - Ⓑ African Americans became citizens.
    - Ⓒ Slavery was abolished.
    - Ⓓ Equal protection could not be denied any citizen.

Use with Pupil Edition, p. 522

Assessment Book, p. 87

Part 2: Skills Test

Directions: Use complete sentences to answer questions 1–5. Use a separate sheet of paper if you need more space.

1. How did the South plan to win the war? **Summarize**

   Southerners planned to wear down the North because they believed that Northerners would quickly grow tired of fighting and give up. They also were hoping to get aid from Britain.

2. Do you think advances such as improved guns, railroads, and early hand grenades were more harmful or helpful during the Civil War? Explain. **Express Ideas**

   Accept all reasonable answers. Possible answer: These advances caused a huge increase in casualties on both sides and, therefore, may have done more harm than good.

3. How was life difficult for soldiers during the Civil War? **Main Idea and Details**

   Possible answer: Supplies were short, and soldiers had to make do with food they disliked. They had to walk long distances and often wore out their shoes before new ones arrived. They were exposed to harsh weather conditions with no protection. They suffered and died from disease and infection.

4. Why do you think General Grant allowed total war to be used to defeat Lee but then offered to feed Lee's men after their surrender? **Draw Conclusions**

   Possible answer: Grant did what was necessary to win the war. However, he realized that the Confederate soldiers were now his countrymen and that everyone would have to forgive each other for the nation to heal.

Use with Pupil Edition, p. 522

Assessment Book, p. 88

5. Why did Reconstruction include the Thirteenth, Fourteenth, and Fifteenth Amendments? **Make Inferences**

   Possible answer: The goal of Reconstruction was to rebuild and heal the nation. Abolishing slavery was the first step in recognizing African Americans as valuable people. Granting citizenship and the right to vote helped make all men equal.

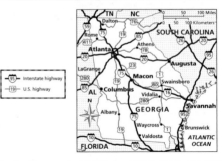

Road Map of Georgia

6. Use the map to answer the questions **Read a Road Map**
   a. What interstate highways run through Georgia?

   Highways 75, 95, 16, 85, 20, 59

   b. What route would you take to travel from Vadalia to Albany?

   U.S. highway 280 west to U.S. highway 19 south to Albany

   c. What distance in miles would you travel if you went from Atlanta to Macon?

   about 75 miles

Use with Pupil Edition, p. 522

Assessment Support

Assessment Book, p. 89

Use with Pupil Edition, p. 526

Unit 7 Test

Part 1: Content Test

Directions: Fill in the circle next to the correct answer.

Lesson Objective (14–1:1)

1. Which of the following was becoming more popular among people in the North during the 1850s?
   - (A) working on small farms
   - ● working in factories
   - (C) living on small farms
   - (D) living in small towns

Lesson Objective (14–1:3)

2. Why did Southerners want to preserve slavery?
   - (A) Slaves were their friends.
   - (B) Slaves obeyed them.
   - ● Slavery was profitable for them.
   - (D) Slavery made them feel important.

Lesson Objective (14–2:1)

3. Which of the following is a way slaves resisted slavery?
   - ● They pretended to be sick.
   - (B) They held prayer meetings.
   - (C) They told family stories.
   - (D) They sang while they worked.

Lesson Objective (14–2:3)

4. What was the purpose of the Underground Railroad?
   - (A) It was a secret railroad that ran only at night.
   - (B) It was a secret organization to turn in slaves.
   - (C) It carried people to other cities at night.
   - ● It helped slaves escape to freedom.

Lesson Objective (14–3:1)

5. What was the result of the Missouri Compromise?
   - (A) Missouri would be divided into two territories.
   - (B) Mississippi could be a slave state.
   - (C) Missouri could choose to be a free or a slave state.
   - ● The balance was kept between free and slave states.

Lesson Objective (14–3:3)

6. What was the effect of the Dred Scott decision?
   - (A) The North and South agreed on the decision.
   - (B) Many Northerners agreed with the decision.
   - ● The split between the North and the South worsened.
   - (D) Most Southerners disagreed with the decision.

Lesson Objective (14–3:4)

7. How did many Southerners feel about Lincoln's election to the presidency?
   - (A) Many were happy because Lincoln was a fair man.
   - ● Many were unhappy because Lincoln was against slavery.
   - (C) Many did not care because Lincoln promised to make no changes.
   - (D) Many were happy because they wanted to end slavery.

Assessment Book, p. 90

Use with Pupil Edition, p. 526

Lesson Objective (14–4:1)

8. Why did Southern states secede from the Union?
   - (A) Lincoln came from the North.
   - ● They wanted to keep slavery.
   - (C) They had not voted for Lincoln.
   - (D) They wanted to change slavery laws.

Lesson Objective (14–4:3)

9. What did the South hope to achieve by fighting the Civil War?
   - ● preservation of slavery
   - (B) an end to slavery
   - (C) equality for all
   - (D) preservation of the Union

Lesson Objective (15–1:1)

10. Which of the following was NOT an advantage held by the North during the Civil War?
    - (A) It produced most of the country's shoes and wheat.
    - (B) It had more railroads than the Confederacy.
    - (C) It produced more than 90 percent of the country's weapons.
    - ● It had a history of producing military leaders.

Lesson Objective (15–1:4)

11. How did new technology affect the war?
    - (A) Women could join the forces.
    - (B) Battles were less deadly.
    - (C) Soldiers healed more quickly.
    - ● Soldiers could use weapons more accurately.

Lesson Objective (15–2:1)

12. Which of the following describes life for both Northern and Southern soldiers?
    - (A) A blockade cut off their supplies.
    - ● They watched many of their friends die.
    - (C) Their forces were outnumbered by the opposition.
    - (D) Britain provided much-needed aid.

Lesson Objective (15–2:2)

13. How did African Americans respond to the Emancipation Proclamation?
    - (A) Many fled to Canada.
    - (B) Many chose to remain slaves.
    - ● Many joined the Union army.
    - (D) Many protested.

Lesson Objective (15–3:3)

14. Where did Sherman use a strategy of total war to defeat the South?
    - ● Georgia
    - (B) Pennsylvania
    - (C) Maryland
    - (D) Virginia

Lesson Objective (15–3:4)

15. Which of the following BEST describes total war?
    - (A) Destroy all buildings and farms that might help the enemy win.
    - (B) Destroy all weapons.
    - ● Destroy anything that might help the enemy win, including the people's will to fight.
    - (D) Destroy all military establishments in enemy territory.

Lesson Objective (15–4:1)

16. Why did Congress object to Johnson's Reconstruction plan?
    - (A) Congress wanted stricter laws for African Americans.
    - ● Congress objected to Johnson's efforts to limit African Americans' rights.
    - (C) Congress wanted to allow the South to do as it pleased.
    - (D) Congress wanted laws that were less harsh for the South.

Assessment Book, p. 91

Use with Pupil Edition, p. 526

Part 2: Skills Test

Directions: Use complete sentences to answer questions 1–5. Use a separate sheet of paper if you need more space.

1. How did lifestyles in the North and the South differ during the mid-1800s? **Compare and Contrast**

   Possible answer: In the South, most people had a rural lifestyle. They lived on farms and in small towns. Although most Northerners still lived on farms, more and more worked in factories and lived in large towns and cities. They had an urban lifestyle.

2. What do you think were two long-term effects of the Dred Scott decision? **Draw Conclusions**

   Accept all reasonable answers. Possible answers: It firmly divided the nation into antislavery and pro-slavery groups; it established that African Americans did not have legal rights that were equal to those of whites.

3. What steps led to the outbreak of the Civil War? **Sequence**

   Possible answer: North and South split over slavery, Lincoln is elected President, Southern states secede and form Confederacy, Jefferson Davis's forces capture Fort Sumter, Lincoln uses Union forces to put down Confederate rebellion.

4. Why do you think African Americans were only allowed to fight in the Union army once the war had been raging for many months? **Draw Conclusions**

   Possible answer: By that point, the Union desperately needed soldiers. White men were refusing to fight. The army decided to take all the help it could get, and after Lincoln issued the Emancipation Proclamation, African Americans were allowed to join the Union army to show their support.

Assessment Book, p. 92

Use with Pupil Edition, p. 526

5. How were African Americans' lives different at the end of Reconstruction? **Main Idea and Details**

   New laws were passed that placed African Americans under many restrictions. Life became very difficult for most. Work was scarce, and many became sharecroppers.

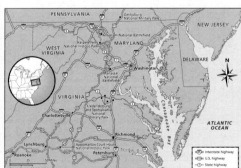

Road Map of Maryland and Eastern Virginia

6. Use the map to answer the questions. **Read a Road Map**
   a. What interstate highway would you use to travel from Charlottesville to Richmond?

      interstate highway 64

   b. How many miles along interstate highway 95 would you travel going from Richmond to Petersburg?

      25 miles

   c. How could you use this map to plan a trip to visit Civil War sites?

      Possible answer: The map shows me the location of some sites and helps me figure out how far apart they are.

War and Reconstruction

Chapter 15 Outline

- **Lesson 1,** *The Early Stages of the War,* pp. 492–496
- **Biography:** *Robert E. Lee,* p. 497
- **Lesson 2,** *Life During the War,* pp. 498–503
- **Citizen Heroes:** *Working for Lasting Peace,* pp. 504–505
- **Lesson 3,** *How the North Won,* pp. 506–511
- **Map and Globe Skills:** *Read a Road Map,* pp. 512–513
- **DK** *Communications During the Civil War,* pp. 514–515
- **Lesson 4,** *The End of Slavery,* pp. 516–521

Resources

- Workbook, p. 115: Vocabulary Preview
- Vocabulary Cards
- Social Studies Plus!

1861, Manassas Junction, Virginia: Lesson 1

This picture shows hand-to-hand combat in the Civil War. Ask students what dangers troops faced. (Possible answers: Being shot; being trampled)

1863, Charleston, South Carolina: Lesson 2

Tell students that this picture shows African American Union troops.

1865, Appomattox Court House, Virginia: Lesson 3

This picture shows General Robert E. Lee surrendering to Ulysses S. Grant at Appomattox Court House. Ask students about how long the Civil War lasted. (About 4 years, from 1861 to 1865)

1865, Washington, D.C.: Lesson 4

This picture shows John Wilkes Booth assassinating President Lincoln. Ask students what the President was doing when he was shot. (Watching a play)

War and Reconstruction

1861
Manassas Junction, Virginia
Confederate troops win the first major battle of the Civil War.
Lesson 1

1

1863
Charleston, South Carolina
African American troops of the Union army attack Fort Wagner.
Lesson 2

2

1865
Appomattox Court House, Virginia
The South surrenders.
Lesson 3

3

1865
Washington, D.C.
President Lincoln is assassinated.
Lesson 4

4

490

Practice and Extend

Vocabulary Preview

- Use Workbook p. 115 to help students preview the vocabulary words in this chapter.
- Use Vocabulary Cards to preview key concept words in this chapter.

 Also on Teacher Resources CD-ROM.

Workbook, p. 115

Vocabulary Preview

Directions: Circle the vocabulary term that best completes each sentence.

1. The (Anaconda Plan, Reconstruction) was a three-part war strategy to crush the South during the Civil War.

2. Slavery was abolished by the (Thirteenth Amendment, Fourteenth Amendment) to the Constitution.

3. The (First Battle of Bull Run, Battle of Gettysburg) lasted three days and was one of the most important battles of the Civil War.

4. African Americans became U.S. citizens under the (Fourteenth Amendment, Thirteenth Amendment) to the Constitution.

5. At the (Battle of Antietam, Battle of Vicksburg), Union forces blockaded the city and bombarded it for 48 days.

6. (Segregation, Sharecropping) is the separation of blacks and whites.

7. Both the North and the South motivated the (blockade, draft) to get men to fight in the war.

8. The (Gettysburg Address, Emancipation Proclamation) granted freedom to slaves in any Confederate states that were still battling the Union.

9. The time after the war when the country was rebuilding and healing is known as (Reconstruction, segregation).

10. The (black codes, blockade) kept supplies from reaching Southern soldiers.

11. One of the early battles of the war was the (Battle of Gettysburg, First Battle of Bull Run).

12. People in many U.S. cities paid their respects to President Lincoln after his (assassination, impeachment).

13. The (Freedmen's Bureau, Emancipation Proclamation) was established to help former slaves after the war.

14. All male citizens received the right to vote with the ratification of the (Thirteenth Amendment, Fifteenth Amendment) to the Constitution.

15. The (Emancipation Proclamation, Jim Crow laws) enforced separation of blacks and whites.

16. Republicans in Congress called for the (trial war, impeachment) of President Andrew Johnson.

Notes for Home: Your child learned about events during and after the Civil War.
Home Activity: With your child, review each vocabulary term and its definition to make sure the term fits in the sentence. Then make your own sentences using the vocabulary terms.

Locating Time and Place

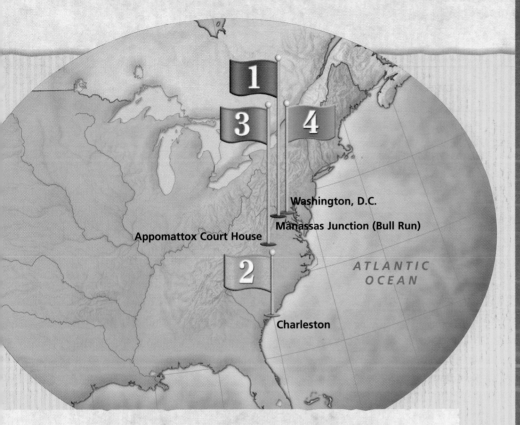

1

3   4

Washington, D.C.

Manassas Junction (Bull Run)

Appomattox Court House

2

ATLANTIC
OCEAN

Charleston

Why We Remember

*"…that government of the people, by the people, for the people,
shall not perish from the earth."*
In 1863, in the middle of the Civil War, these words rang out over a scarred battlefield where many Union and Confederate soldiers had died a few months before. The battlefield was at Gettysburg, Pennsylvania. The speaker was President Abraham Lincoln. At the time, no one was sure who would win the war. But Lincoln was sure of his goal—to preserve the nation that had been born only 87 years earlier.

491

- Have students examine the pictures shown on p. 490 for Lessons 1, 2, 3, and 4.

- Remind students that each picture is coded with both a number and a color to link it to a place on the map on p. 491.

Why We Remember

Have students read the "Why We Remember" paragraph on p. 491, and ask them why events in this chapter might be important to them. Ask students what "government of the people, by the people, and for the people" means and why it is so important to Americans.

WEB SITE
Technology

You can learn more about Manassas Junction, Virginia; Charleston, South Carolina; Appomattox Court House, Virginia; and Washington, D.C., by clicking on **www.sfsocialstudies.com.**

SOCIAL STUDIES STRAND
Geography

Mental Mapping On an outline map of the United States, have students draw and label the city of New Orleans, the Mississippi River, and the states of Virginia and Tennessee. These four locations were Union objectives during the Civil War. Have students decide which of these locations was most important to winning the war. Have them rank locations in order of importance. Discuss answers.

The Early Stages of the War

Objectives

- Identify the resources of the North and South.
- Compare the strategies of the North and South in the Civil War.
- Describe early battles in the Civil War.
- Explain how new military technology affected the way the war was fought.

Vocabulary

blockade, p. 494; **Anaconda Plan,** p. 494; **First Battle of Bull Run,** p. 495; **Battle of Antietam,** p. 495

Resources

- Workbook, p. 116
- Transparency 1
- Every Student Learns Guide, pp. 206–209
- Quick Study, pp. 104–105

Quick Teaching Plan

If time is short, have students read the lesson independently and copy and complete the following chart.

	NORTH	SOUTH
Advantages		
Strategies		
First Battle of Bull Run		
Battle of Antietam		
Ships		

1 Introduce and Motivate

Preview To activate prior knowledge, ask students what they remember about the causes of the Civil War. Tell students that they will learn about early battles in the Civil War in Lesson 1.

You Are There Soldiers in the Civil War often found themselves fighting against family members. Have students discuss their opinions about members of the same family joining armies on different sides.

LESSON 1

1861			1863
April 1861 Union begins blockade of Southern ports	July 1861 First Battle of Bull Run	September 1862 Battle of Antietam	

PREVIEW

Focus on the Main Idea
In the early years of the Civil War, the North and South formed strategies in hopes of gaining a quick victory.

PLACES
Richmond, Virginia
Manassas Junction, Virginia

PEOPLE
Winfield Scott
Thomas "Stonewall" Jackson
Robert E. Lee

VOCABULARY
blockade
Anaconda Plan
First Battle of Bull Run
Battle of Antietam

▶ This canteen was carried by a Confederate soldier in the Civil War.

The Early Stages of the War

You Are There

It is the summer of 1861. Dawn breaks over your Kentucky farm. You hear a rooster crowing. Below your attic bedroom, your mother lets out a cry. You peer down from your room and see her holding a sheet of paper. It is a letter from your oldest brother Joshua. He left last night to join the Union Army.

Joshua and your second-oldest brother William had been arguing about the war since spring. "The Union forever!" Joshua would say. "Down with Northern tyranny!" William would shout. You just hope the war ends soon.

You read in the newspaper that the Confederates have just won a victory in Virginia. Expecting a short war, many Southern men are rushing to join the army before the war ends. You wonder if William will leave to join the Confederate forces. If he does, could he and Joshua end up fighting against each other, brother against brother?

 Main Idea and Details As you read, note how the North and South prepared for war.

492

Practice and Extend

READING SKILL
Main Idea/Details

In the Lesson Review, students complete a graphic organizer like the one below. You may want to provide students with a copy of Transparency 1 to complete as they read the lesson.

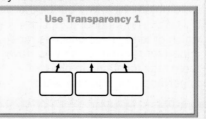

Use Transparency 1

VOCABULARY
Word Exercise

Related Word Study Point out that *blockade* has part of its own definition already visible—block. A *blockade* is when the military blocks an area. The suffix *-ade* means "act, action, or product." So *blockade* is the act of blocking. The "product" with which students are likely to be familiar is *lemonade,* which uses this same suffix.

Advantages and Disadvantages

Many supporters of the North believed they were fighting to preserve the Union. However, most Southern supporters thought that they were fighting to preserve their way of life. Sometimes these different opinions divided families. Some of President Lincoln's own family sided with the South. Four brothers of his wife Mary fought for the Confederacy.

Besides strong feelings, each side thought that it had an advantage over the other. Southerners believed that their more rural way of life would better prepare soldiers for war. Many Southerners hunted and were familiar with weapons. The South also had a history of producing military leaders. A larger share of the Mexican War veterans came from the South.

But an army needed supplies. In 1860 the Northern states produced more than 90 percent of the country's weapons, cloth, shoes, and iron. They also produced more than half of the country's corn and 80 percent of the wheat.

Moving supplies was also important to an army. The Union had far more railroads, canals, and roads than the Confederacy. In addition, the Union was able to raise far more money. By the end of the war, the Union had spent more than $2.6 billion. The Confederacy had spent only $1 billion.

REVIEW Why did each side believe that it would win the war? **Summarize**

FACT FILE

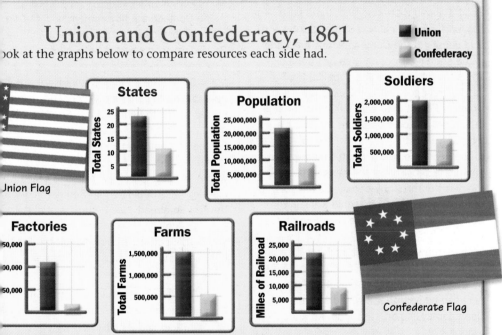

Union and Confederacy, 1861

Look at the graphs below to compare resources each side had.

■ Union
□ Confederacy

Union Flag

Confederate Flag

493

Write a Summary Ask students to summarize the information in the graphs.

Easy Have students work in pairs or small groups. Assign one resource to each group. Have each group write a sentence to summarize its resource, then share sentences. **Reteach**

On-Level Have groups of students write paragraphs to summarize the information for all of the resources in the graphs. **Extend**

Challenge Have students summarize the information on the graph by calculating, then reporting the difference in each resource between the North and South. Have them write a conclusion comparing and contrasting how these differences might have affected each side. **Enrich**

For a Lesson Summary, use Quick Study, p. 104.

---

2 Teach and Discuss

PAGE 493

Advantages and Disadvantages

🕐 *Quick Summary* The North had better access to supplies and transportation. The South felt its soldiers were better prepared to fight.

1 **How did the North's reason for fighting the war differ from the South's?** The North wanted to preserve the Union, whereas the South was fighting to preserve its way of life. **Compare and Contrast**

2 **What advantages did the various transportation systems give the North during the Civil War?** Possible answer: The North was better able to move supplies. **Make Inferences**

✓ **REVIEW ANSWER** South: More rural way of life would prepare them for war; had more Mexican War veterans; they were fighting for their homeland; North: More resources, including railroads, canals, roads, and money **Summarize**

FACT FILE
Union and Confederacy, 1861

3 **What was the difference in the number of factories between the North and South? What effect might this have had?** The North had over 90,000 more factories than the South and could produce more supplies. **Interpret Graphs**

Strategies

Quick Summary The North and South planned different strategies in hopes of quickly ending the war.

4 **What strategies did the Confederacy believe would bring them victory?** Defend territory until the North gave up; Southern soldiers would fight more fiercely for their land; Britain would help the South Main Idea and Details

✓ Ongoing Assessment

If... students do not understand the South's strategies, **then...** guide them to copy and complete this Main Idea and Details chart.

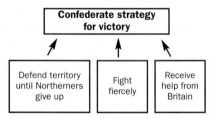

Confederate strategy for victory

Defend territory until Northerners give up | Fight fiercely | Receive help from Britain

Problem Solving

5 **What problem did Britain's cotton surplus cause for the South?** Britain no longer needed as much of the South's cotton, so there was little reason to assist the South in the war.
Solve Problems

✓ REVIEW ANSWER
First there would be a blockade of Southern ports to prevent supplies from reaching the Confederate states. Then the Union would gain control of the Mississippi River, cutting the Confederacy in half. Then the Union would invade the Confederacy from the east and west.
 Main Idea and Details

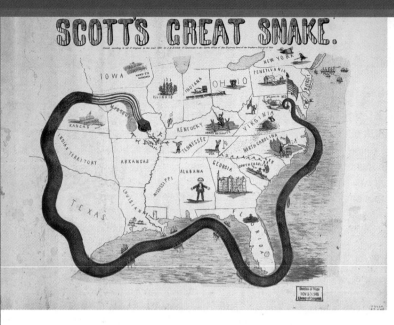

SCOTT'S GREAT SNAKE.

▶ This cartoon illustrated the Anaconda Plan by showing an anaconda snake surrounding the Confederacy.

Strategies

President Abraham Lincoln sought advice on how to win the war from General **Winfield Scott,** who had fought in the Mexican War. Scott planned a strategy with three parts. The first part was a blockade of the Atlantic and Gulf coasts of the Confederacy. A **blockade** is the shutting off of an area by troops or ships to keep people and supplies from moving in or out. With a blockade the South would not be able to ship its cotton for sale in Europe. Cotton sales were the South's main way of getting money to pay for the war.

The second stage of Scott's plan was to capture territory along the Mississippi River, the heart of the Confederacy. Gaining control of the Mississippi River would weaken the Confederacy by cutting the Southern states in two.

Third, the Union would attack the Confederacy from the east and west. Scott's strategy was called the **Anaconda Plan,** because he said that it would squeeze the Confederacy like an anaconda. An anaconda

is a huge snake that kills prey by wrapping itself around an animal and suffocating it. Lincoln liked the plan. He ordered the blockade on April 19, one week after the fall of Fort Sumter.

The Confederate government had its own strategy for victory. First, it believed that the Confederacy only had to defend its territory until the Northerners got tired and gave up. Many Southerners believed that Northerners had nothing to gain from victory and would not be willing to fight for long. Southerners assumed that their soldiers would fight more fiercely for their land and their way of life.

The Confederacy also believed that Britain would assist it in the war because British clothing mills depended on Southern cotton. But Britain already had a surplus of cotton and was looking to India and Egypt for new sources of cotton. Britain allowed the South to build several warships in its shipyards, but it did not send any soldiers.

REVIEW How did Winfield Scott's Anaconda Plan attempt to weaken the Southern states?
 Main Idea and Details

494

Practice and Extend

ESL ACCESS CONTENT
ESL Support

Demonstrate Concept Understanding After they read p. 495, have students demonstrate their understanding of the concept of "retreat" in a war.

Beginning Divide the class into two groups. Have one group carry a sign labeled "North" and the other group "South." At your prompting, have students act out the sequence of advances and retreats during the First Battle of Bull Run.

Intermediate Have students write journal entries as if they were retreating soldiers in the First Battle of Bull Run.

Advanced Have students write a speech for Robert E. Lee to raise the morale of Confederate troops after their defeat at Antietam.

For additional ESL support, use Every Student Learns Guide, pp. 206–209.

Early Battles

Early successes gave the Confederacy confidence. President Lincoln sent 35,000 troops to invade **Richmond, Virginia,** the capital of the Confederacy. On the way, on July 21, 1861, they met Confederate troops at a small stream called Bull Run near the town of **Manassas Junction, Virginia.**

The **First Battle of Bull Run** was a confusing event. Early on, the fighting went in the Union's favor. Some Confederate soldiers began to turn back, but one general from Virginia told his men to hold their place. Because the general and his men stood "like a stone wall," he became known as **Thomas "Stonewall" Jackson.**

More Confederates arrived, and soon the tide turned in their favor. The Union soldiers retreated. The casualties in the First Battle of Bull Run amounted to 3,000 for the Union and 2,000 for the Confederacy. Casualties include soldiers killed, wounded, captured, or missing. Many battles took place across the South.

Union forces won some, but the Confederates seemed to be winning the war. In May 1862, "Stonewall" Jackson defeated the Union army in Virginia, and some feared that he could take over Washington, D.C.

On September 17, 1862, Union and Confederate forces met near the town of Sharpsburg, Maryland, in the **Battle of Antietam** (an TEET um). The battle involved one of the Confederacy's most capable generals, **Robert E. Lee.** He had been asked to fight for the Union, but refused. Lee decided to serve the Confederacy after Virginia, the state of his birth, joined the other Southern states. You will read more about Robert E. Lee in the Biography on page 497.

The battle was an important victory for the Union. After Antietam, Britain ended its support for the Southern states. The Confederacy would have to fight alone.

REVIEW What effect did winning the Battle of Antietam have on the Union?
Cause and Effect

Lithograph by Kurz & Allison

▶ With more than 23,000 casualties, the massive Battle of Antietam was the single bloodiest day of the entire Civil War.

495

Early Battles

🕐 *Quick Summary* The Confederacy won the First Battle of Bull Run but lost the Battle of Antietam.

Test Talk

Locate Key Words in the Question

6 **About how much time passed between the First Battle of Bull Run and the Battle of Antietam?** Have students tell who or what in the questions are key words. About one year and two months **Sequence**

7 **Why do you think Robert E. Lee decided to fight for the Confederacy?** Possible answer: He was loyal to Virginia, the state of his birth. **Point of View**

✓ **REVIEW ANSWER** After the Battle of Antietam, the Union did not have to worry about Britain supporting the Confederacy. **Cause and Effect**

SOCIAL STUDIES
Background

About the Early Battles

- The First Battle of Bull Run is known in the South by a different name: "The First Battle of Manassas," or simply "First Manassas."
- During the beginning of the First Battle of Bull Run, people came out from Washington, D.C., in carriages to watch the battle as if it were a spectator sport. They made a hasty retreat when the tide turned against the Union.
- Antietam spurred Lincoln to issue the Emancipation Proclamation.
- The Battle of Antietam got its name from a creek near the site of the battle.
- Antietam was the bloodiest battle of the Civil War up to that point.

Technology and War

 Quick Summary The soldiers of the Civil War used new technologies to fight.

 SOCIAL STUDIES STRAND
Science • Technology

8 **What new technology did the _Virginia_ and the _Monitor_ have?** An iron covering **Draw Conclusions**

✓ **REVIEW ANSWER** Advantages: Soldiers could shoot farther and more accurately; Disadvantages: More casualties **Compare and Contrast**

3 Close and Assess

Summarize the Lesson

Tell students to write and answer one question about each event in the summary. Students can share their questions.

✓ | **LESSON 1** | **REVIEW** |

1. 🌎 **Main Idea and Details** For possible answers, see the reduced pupil page.

2. Union: Produced wheat, corn, weapons, clothes, and iron; had more railroads, canals, roads, and money; Confederacy: More Mexican War generals, familiarity with weapons

3. North: Blockade ports, control of the Mississippi; South: Defend land until North gives up and hope Britain will help

4. Union was winning; Jackson refused to retreat; more Confederate troops arrived; Union troops retreated

5. **Critical Thinking:** *Analyze Information* Allowed them to kill or wound more enemies; caused more death from disease and infection

Link to ⬡⬡ **Mathematics**

About 13 million more people; about 13,000 more miles; more people could serve in the army or produce supplies. More miles of railroad would improve transportation.

Technology and War

Recent technologies were used and new technologies were developed during the Civil War. Soldiers used rifles that could shoot farther and more accurately than guns used in previous wars. Railroads quickly moved troops and supplies to battlefronts. The Confederacy built several submarines—ships that could travel under the water's surface—to overcome the Union's blockade. Both sides used an early version of the hand grenade.

Another new weapon was the ironclad, or iron covered ship. The Confederates built an ironclad by taking an abandoned Union ship called the *Merrimack* and covering it with iron. They renamed it the *Virginia*. In March 1862, the *Virginia* easily sank several wooden Union ships. Union cannonballs simply bounced off the *Virginia's* iron sides. Then, on March 9, a **8** Union ironclad named the *Monitor* arrived to battle the *Virginia*. The two ships fired at each other for hours. But neither ship was able to seriously damage the other.

These new technologies made the war more deadly, resulting in huge numbers of casualties. Unfortunately, medical knowledge had not advanced as much as other technologies. Many soldiers died from disease and infection

REVIEW What were the advantages and disadvantages of new technology in the Civil War? **Compare and Contrast**

Summarize the Lesson

- **April 19, 1861** The Union began a blockade of Southern ports.
- **July 21, 1861** Confederate forces defeated Union troops in the First Battle of Bull Run in Manassas.
- **September 17, 1862** Union and Confederate troops fought a bloody battle at Antietam, an important Union victory.

| **LESSON 1** | **REVIEW** |

Check Facts and Main Ideas

1. 🌎 **Main Idea and Details** On a separate sheet of paper fill in the details of the **Anaconda Plan** .

General Winfield Scott's Anaconda Plan attempted to weaken the Confederate states.

| A Union block-ade of Southern ports would cut off supplies to the South. | The Union would gain control of the Mississippi River and cut the Confederacy in half. | Union armies would attack the Confederacy from east and west. |

2. Compare advantages the Union had at the beginning of the war to those of the Confederacy.

3. How did the strategies of the North and South differ?

4. Summarize the events of the **First Battle of Bull Run** .

5. **Critical Thinking:** *Analyze Information* What effect did military technology have on Civil War soldiers?

Link to ⬡⬡ **Mathematics**

Analyze Graphs Look again at the graphs on page 493. How many more people lived in the Northern states than in the Southern states? How many more miles of railroad did the North have compared to the South? Why would a larger population and more miles of railroad be an advantage?

496

Practice and Extend

 CURRICULUM CONNECTION
Math

Disease Statistics Display the following chart and have students draw conclusions about which diseases caused the most deaths for the Northern army during the Civil War. (Diarrhea/Dysentery and Typhoid)

Disease	Deaths
Diarrhea/Dysentery	44,558
Malaria	10,063
Typhoid	34,833
Typhus	958
Yellow Fever	436

Workbook, p. 116

Lesson 1: The Early Stages of the War

Directions: Complete each compare-and-contrast table with information about the Union and the Confederacy. You may use your textbook.

	Supporters of the North	Supporters of the South
Reason for fighting		

	Northerners	Southerners
Believed advantage over the opposition		

	Union	Confederacy
War strategy		

Notes for Home: Your child learned about different attitudes toward war and different strategies used by the North and South during the Civil War.
Home Activity: With your child, discuss possible problems the Union and the Confederacy might have had in forming their war strategies. Ask your child what could have gone wrong in each case.

💿 **Also on Teacher Resources CD-RO**

Robert E. Lee *1807–1870*

Robert E. Lee did not know his own father for a very long time. When Robert was six, his father, Harry Lee, visited a friend who published a newspaper that criticized the United States for going to war with Britain in 1812. Like his friend, Harry Lee opposed this war. A group of angry people attacked the newspaper offices while Harry Lee was inside, and he was badly beaten. Robert had to say goodbye as his father boarded a ship to Barbados, where he went to heal from his wounds. Harry Lee died before he could return home.

Many years later, at the beginning of the Civil War, Robert E. Lee was asked to make the most difficult decision of his life. Lee was a rising star in the United States Army. But Lee had been born and raised in Virginia, and, although he personally disapproved of slavery, he loved his home and his state. Perhaps he thought of his father, who had defended the things he loved at great cost to himself. Lee resigned from the United States Army, and wrote:

> *"I have not been able to make up my mind to raise my hand against my relatives, my children, my home."*

Lee hoped that Virginia would not take sides in the conflict, and he would not have to fight at all. But when Virginia seceded and joined the Confederacy, his path became clear to him. Lee accepted a position commanding Virginia's forces. Later, Lee's wife Mary remembered the night of his decision. She said that he had "wept tears of blood."

BIOFACT

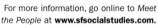

Lee rode his beloved horse Traveller throughout the Civil War. Traveller outlived Lee, walked behind Lee's coffin at his funeral, and is buried near Lee's grave in Lexington, Virginia.

Learn from Biographies

Why was Lee's decision so difficult to make? What do you think his wife meant when she said that he "wept tears of blood"?

For more information, go online to *Meet the People* at **www.sfsocialstudies.com.**

497

Robert E. Lee

Objective
- Identify the accomplishments of notable individuals, such as Robert E. Lee.

1 Introduce and Motivate

Preview To activate prior knowledge, ask students to share what they remember about Robert E. Lee from p. 495.

2 Teach and Discuss

1 What personal traits do you think Lee possessed? Possible answer: He was compassionate, brave, loyal, and conscientious. Draw Conclusions

2 What might have affected Lee's decision to resign from the U.S. Army? He thought of his father who had lost his life defending the things he loved. Cause and Effect

3 Close and Assess

Learn from Biographies Answer

He was doing well in the army but he was loyal to Virginia. She meant that he was very torn about his decision.

Decision Making

Use a Decision-Making Process

- Have students consider the following decision-making scenario: **Suppose you are an advisor to Robert E. Lee. You have just heard that he must decide whether or not to command the forces in Virginia. You understand he is against slavery, yet loyal to his state.**

- Students should use the following decision-making process to decide whether to advise Lee to accept or reject the position as commander of the Virginia armed forces. For each step in the process, have students discuss and write about what must be considered as they make their decision. Write these steps on the board or read them aloud.

1. Identify a situation that requires a decision.
2. Gather information.
3. Identify opinions.
4. Predict consequences.
5. Take action to implement a decision.

Life During the War

Objectives

- Compare and contrast life for Northern and Southern soldiers.
- Analyze the effect of the Emancipation Proclamation on African Americans.
- Describe the contributions of African American soldiers to the Union war effort.
- Identify the different ways women contributed to the war effort in the North and South.

Vocabulary

draft, p. 499;
Emancipation Proclamation, p. 500

Resources

- Workbook, p. 117
- Transparency 1
- Every Student Learns Guide, pp. 210–213
- Quick Study, pp. 106–107

Quick Teaching Plan

If time is short, have students create word webs for the lesson.

- Have students write *Soldiers,* *African Americans,* and *Women* in separate webs.
- As they read, students should add details to each web.

1 Introduce and Motivate

Preview Ask students to share any personal knowledge they may have about life in the armed forces. Tell students that in Lesson 2 they will learn about life in the armed forces during the Civil War.

You Are There Both soldiers and civilians are affected by war, no matter which side they are on. Have students discuss whether or not they believe being victorious in battle makes the war experience any easier.

LESSON 2

1863 | 1864

January 1863
Emancipation Proclamation takes effect

July 1863
African American troops attack Fort Wagner

June 1
Congress gives black white troops equal

Fort Wagner

PREVIEW

Focus on the Main Idea
As the Civil War continued, people in the North and the South suffered many hardships, including the growing loss of life.

PLACES
Fort Wagner, South Carolina

PEOPLE
Mathew Brady
William Carney
Belle Boyd
Clara Barton

VOCABULARY
draft
Emancipation Proclamation

Life During the War

You Are There These letters are from soldiers who fought in the Battle of Fredericksburg in Virginia on December 13, 1862. They were on opposing sides, but whether fighting for the Union or the Confederacy, soldiers were horrified by the loss of life.

December 16, 1862

Gone are the proud hopes, the high aspirations [goals] that swelled our bosoms [chests] a few days ago. Once more unsuccessful, and only a bloody record to show our men were brave.

Captain William T. Lusk, Union soldier

January 11, 1863

I can inform you that I have seen the Monkey Show [battle] at last, and I don't want to see it anymore. Martha I can't tell you how many dead I did see...one thing is sure, I don't want to see that sight anymore.

Private Thomas Warrick, Confederate soldier

 Main Idea and Details As you read, note the difficulties during the Civil War for both soldiers and civilians.

498

Practice and Extend

 **READING SKILL Main Idea/Details**

In the Lesson Review, students complete a graphic organizer like the one below. You may want to provide students with a copy of Transparency 1 to complete as they read the lesson.

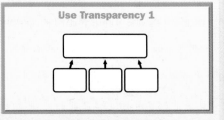

Use Transparency 1

VOCABULARY Word Exercise

Context Clues Point out that *draft* is a multiple-meaning word. Ask students to tell some meanings of *draft,* and write them on the board. (Students may need dictionaries.) These might include a light wind; required military service; an early version of a piece of writing; and something that pulls or is pulled, such as a draft horse. Tell students to use context as they read to figure out which meaning *draft* has in the lesson. (required military service)

Life for Soldiers

Families of soldiers like Captain Lusk and Private Warrick learned about the war from soldier's letters and newspaper articles. They could also see the horrors of war thanks to a new technology—photography. Civil War photographers like **Mathew Brady** took pictures of the countless dead on the battle-field. Photographs also showed soldiers warming themselves by the campfire or resting after a long day's march.

The soldiers Brady photographed were much like any young Americans of the mid 1800s. The average age of a Civil War soldier was about 25. However, drummer boys as young as twelve years old went to the battlefield.

A soldier's life was a hard one, even when he was not in battle. Soldiers might march as many as 25 miles a day while carrying about 50 pounds of supplies in knapsacks, or backpacks. They grew thirsty marching in summer's heat and shivered through winter's cold.

The marching was especially tough for Confederate soldiers. The Union blockade prevented many supplies from reaching Southern armies. Soldiers wore out their shoes, and often fought in bare feet until they could get another pair.

On both sides, soldiers were usually unhappy with the food. They were given beans, bacon, pickled beef, salt pork, and a tough flour-and-water biscuit called "hardtack." When they could, troops hunted for food in nearby forests, or even raided local farms.

As the war continued, volunteers for the war decreased. A volunteer is a person who chooses freely to join or do something. Both sides passed draft laws. A **draft** requires men of a certain age to serve in the military if they are called. However, Confederates who owned 20 or more slaves could pay substitutes to take their place. In the Union, men could pay $300 to avoid fighting in the war.

The draft was unpopular in the North and in the South, because it favored the wealthy. In July 1863, riots broke out in New York City to protest the draft. Many called the conflict "a rich man's war and a poor man's fight." **1**

Losses on each side were terrible. A total of about one million Union and Confederate soldiers were killed or wounded. In comparison, only about 10,600 Patriots were killed in the Revolutionary War. Disease was the most common cause of death in the Civil War. Of the more than 360,000 soldiers that died in the Union army, only about 110,000 died in battle. In the Confederate army, 258,000 soldiers died, but only about 94,000 died in battle. As you read in Lesson 1, disease and infections killed many soldiers. This is because no one knew about germs yet, so doctors did not know how to keep wounds from getting infected. **2**

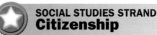

REVIEW What were some of the challenges faced by Civil War soldiers?
⟳ Main Idea and Details

▶ Life was difficult and dangerous for both Union soldiers *(left)* and Confederate soldiers *(right)*.

499

Life for Soldiers

🕐 *Quick Summary* Both the Union and Confederate soldiers suffered on and off the field.

1 **What was meant by the expression identifying the Civil War as "a rich man's war and a poor man's fight"?** Rich people could pay money or substitute others to avoid fighting in the war, leaving poor people to fight the battles.
Draw Conclusions

✓ **Ongoing Assessment**

| **If...** students do not understand the expression, "a rich man's war and a poor man's fight," | **then...** have them list the draft requirements for both the North and South. |

⭐ **SOCIAL STUDIES STRAND**
Citizenship

Joining the armed forces of a country is just one way individuals can participate in civic affairs at the national level.

2 **What contribution did soldiers in the Civil War make to their country?** Possible answer: They fought against the enemy and some gave their lives.
⟳ Main Idea and Details

✓ **REVIEW ANSWER** Soldiers had to deal with the threat of death or injury, difficult marches, lack of water and poor food, little protection from the elements, and shortages in supplies.
⟳ Main Idea and Details

MEETING INDIVIDUAL NEEDS
Leveled Practice

Write a Letter Have students write a letter as if they were soldiers in the Northern or Southern armies.

Easy Have students write a letter to their family telling about one aspect of their experiences, such as the food, the marches, or the living conditions. **Reteach**

On-Level Have students write a letter home describing a sequence of experiences over one week. **Extend**

Advanced After students read the text, have them write a letter to the editor of a newspaper, describing their experiences as a soldier and giving their opinion of the war and the draft rules. **Enrich**

For a Lesson Summary, use Quick Study, p. 106.

The Emancipation Proclamation

 **Quick Summary** The Emancipation Proclamation freed slaves in the Confederate states at war with the Union.

③ What was Lincoln's attitude toward slavery? How can you tell? He believed it should be abolished. He issued the Emancipation Proclamation. **Point of View**

Primary Source

Cited in *From Slavery to Freedom: A History of African Americans,* by John Hope Franklin and Alfred A. Moss, Jr.

Explain that the Emancipation Proclamation made it clear that one of Lincoln's goals was to end slavery.

Test Talk

Locate Key Words in the Text

④ Why did some slaves not gain their freedom after this proclamation? Have students locate key words in the text that match key words in the question, such as proclamation. Because it proclaimed freedom only for enslaved people who were in states that were at war with the Union **Analyze Primary Sources**

✔ **REVIEW ANSWER** The Emancipation Proclamation said that slaves in Confederate states not controlled by the Union were free, and it encouraged many African Americans to fight for the Union cause. **Cause and Effect**

 ## Slaves and Serfs

⑤ What conclusion can you draw about enslavement during the 1800s? Possible answer: Enslavement was a worldwide condition that began coming to an end during the late nineteenth century. **Draw Conclusions**

The Emancipation Proclamation

At first, the Civil War was not a war against slavery. Lincoln's goal was to preserve the Union, or keep the country together. By 1862, though, Lincoln began to believe that he could save the Union only by making the abolition of slavery a goal of the war.

Lincoln's advisers feared that ending slavery would hurt the war effort. Some said that it would unite the South and divide the North. But Lincoln explained, "Slavery must die that the nation might live."

On January 1, 1863, President Lincoln issued the **Emancipation Proclamation.** Emancipate means "to set free." A proclamation is a statement. The Emancipation Proclamation was a statement that freed all slaves in the Confederate states at war with the Union. Moments before signing the proclamation Lincoln said, "I never in my life ③ felt more certain that I was doing right." The

Proclamation said:

> "Slaves within any State . . . in rebellion against the United States, shall be then . . . and forever free."

The Emancipation Proclamation did not end slavery in the border states or in Confederate land that Union forces already controlled. It did declare an end to slavery in the rest of the Confederacy. But since Union forces did not control these areas, most African Americans remained enslaved.

Free African Americans like Frederick Douglass supported Lincoln's efforts. Douglass encouraged African Americans to assist the Union in the war. "Fly to arms," he wrote. Large numbers of African Americans responded by joining the Union army.

REVIEW What was a result of the Emancipation Proclamation? **Cause and Effect**

Slaves and Serfs

At About the Same Time that President Lincoln was issuing the Emancipation Proclamation, people in other areas of the world were gaining liberty. In 1861 leaders in Russia began freeing people called serfs. Serfs worked on an owner's land in exchange for protection and housing. Like slaves, serfs could not marry, change their occupation, or leave the land without the owner's permission.

⑤

EUROPE RUSSIA ASIA

500

Practice and Extend

 **SOCIAL STUDIES Background**

Serfdom

- Serfdom was a condition of tenant farmers in medieval Europe and Asia in which serfs were obligated to farm a plot of land belonging to their landlord.
- Serfs had to provide their own food and clothing, and also give a portion of their crops to the landlord.
- A serf could become free only through liberation by the landlord, being rescued, or escaping.
- In 1861 serfs in Russia were granted freedom and their own pieces of land under Alexander II's Edict of Emancipation.

The African American soldiers of the 54th Regiment gained fame for their brave attack on Fort Wagner.

The Granger Collection

Library of Congress

African Americans in the War

In the beginning of the war, African Americans were not allowed to join the army. But they did serve as cooks, servants, and other workers. They were first allowed to join the Union army in 1862.

African American soldiers were not treated the same as whites. They received less pay than white soldiers. They had to buy their own uniforms, while white soldiers did not.

The situation improved for African Americans before the end of the war. One reason for this change was the role played by the Massachusetts 54th Colored Regiment. A regiment is a group of 600 to 1,000 soldiers. The 54th was one of the first groups of black troops to be organized for combat in the Union army.

On July 18, 1863, the 54th Regiment led an attack on **Fort Wagner** in South Carolina.

Confederate fire was heavy, but the men of the 54th charged the fort before being forced back. The group lost more than four out of every ten men.

A sergeant in the battle, **William Carney,** was seriously wounded. Yet he never dropped the regiment's flag. Carney later said that he had fought "to serve my country and my oppressed brothers." He was one of 16 African Americans to win the Congressional Medal of Honor during the war.

The Union did not win the battle at Fort Wagner. But the bravery of the 54th Regiment changed the minds of many Northerners who had doubted the abilities of black soldiers to fight. Nearly 200,000 black soldiers fought for the Union in the Civil War, and 37,000 lost their lives. In June 1864, Congress voted to give black and white troops equal pay. **6**

REVIEW What conclusion can you draw about why African American troops fought in the Civil War? **Draw Conclusions**

501

African Americans in the War

🕐 *Quick Summary* The role of African Americans in the Civil War changed as they proved their ability and willingness to fight for their country and their freedom.

6 **Because of the 54th Regiment, how did the situation improve for African American soldiers?** They were recognized as heroes. Many Northerners no longer doubted the abilities of black soldiers to fight, and Congress voted to give black and white troops equal pay. **Cause and Effect**

✓ **REVIEW ANSWER** Many African Americans felt loyalty to the Union and wanted to fight for its cause. Some may have wanted to prove their abilities on the battlefield. **Draw Conclusions**

CURRICULUM CONNECTION
Math

Calculate Totals

- Have students calculate the approximate number of African American soldiers who survived the Civil War. (About 163,000)
- Have advanced students find the percentage of African American soldiers who died in the Civil War by completing the following calculation:

$37{,}000 \div 200{,}000 = 37 \div 200 = 0.185 = 18.5\%$

Women and the War

 Quick Summary Women contributed to the war effort by working on farms, in offices, schools, and hospitals, by spying, and by caring for soldiers on the battlefield.

$ SOCIAL STUDIES STRAND
Economics

Explain that prices typically rise when the supply of a good is limited and/or demand increases.

7 How did supply and demand affect consumers in the South during the Civil War? Because there was a shortage of much-needed supplies for the war effort in the South, consumers had to pay higher prices for whatever supplies they could get. **Cause and Effect**

8 Compare and contrast the contributions made by women in the North and South. Both helped by working, caring for the wounded, and sending food for armies; Women in the South protested the rise in cost of supplies, which were in short supply in the South. **Compare and Contrast**

✓ **REVIEW ANSWER** Possible answers: Women ran farms and businesses, and became teachers, office workers, spies, soldiers, and nurses. They also sewed clothing for the soldiers and sent them any food they could spare.
Cause and Effect

The War Goes On

 Quick Summary Both the North and South were tired of the ravages of war and wanted it to end.

9 What do you think was the most difficult thing soldiers had to endure? Possible answer: Watching family and friends die **Express Ideas**

✓ **REVIEW ANSWER** In both places, they were tired of it.
Compare and Contrast

▶ Belle Boyd *(below)* worked as a spy. Other women cared for soldiers in hospitals *(right)*.

Women and the War

Women contributed to the war effort in many ways. They ran farms and businesses while their husbands were fighting. They became teachers and office workers. Some even became involved in the war more directly. Frances Clalin, for example, disguised herself as a man so that she could fight in the Union army.

Some women became spies. Women were less likely to be suspected as spies and were punished less severely if they were caught. They often hid weapons and documents under their large hoop skirts to avoid being caught. **Belle Boyd**, nicknamed "La Belle Rebelle," was one of the most famous Confederate spies. She continued spying even after six arrests. She once communicated to a Confederate by hiding messages inside rubber balls and throwing them out of her cell window.

Women in the North and the South worked in hospitals as nurses and other caregivers. Sojourner Truth gathered supplies for black regiments. One Northern woman, **Clara Barton,** explained why she cared for soldiers, "While our soldiers stand and fight, I can stand and feed and nurse them." Barton earned the nickname "Angel of the Battlefield" as she cared for wounded soldiers during the First Battle of Bull Run. In 1881 Barton organized the American Association of the Red Cross to help victims of wars and natural disasters.

Women in the South also had to deal with shortages in supplies. Because demand was greater than supply, prices rose dramatically. The average Southern family's monthly food bill rose from $6.65 just before the war to $68 in 1863. In April of that year, hundreds of women rioted in Richmond to protest the rise in prices. Similar bread riots occurred in other Southern cities as well.

Despite their own difficulties, women in the North and South did all they could for the soldiers. They sewed clothing, rolled bandages, sold personal possessions, and sent any food they could spare to the armies.

REVIEW How did women help the war effort? **Main Idea and Details**

Practice and Extend

ESL EXTEND LANGUAGE
ESL Support

Examine Word Meanings A *bandage* is a strip of fabric, usually gauze, which is used to wrap wounds. Women rolled bandages to make them easy to use when needed.

Beginning Show students examples of different kinds of bandages, which you can most likely obtain from the school nurse. Have students take turns "bandaging" by following your verbal directions.

Intermediate Have students write a paragraph from the point of view of a Civil War nurse. Students should use the word *bandage* in their paragraph.

Advanced Have students work in pairs to create a dialogue between a Civil War doctor or nurse and a patient. Students should use the word *bandage* as both a noun and a verb.

For additional ESL support, use Every Student Learns Guide, pp. 210–213.

The War Goes On

In 1863 the Vice President of the Confederacy, Alexander Stephens, said "A large majority on both sides are tired of the war." And it was true. Union and Confederate soldiers alike were singing a song called "When This Cruel War Is Over." The lack of supplies, delays in pay, sleeping uncovered in the rain, and the terrible death of friends and family members were taking their toll. **9**

By 1863 some soldiers were refusing to go to war. Thousands of Union and Confederate men deserted, or left their military duty without permission. Explained one Union soldier, "I'm tired of the war anyhow, and my time's up soon."

▶ **Soldiers on both sides were tired of war.**

But, as you will read, Union victories would soon lead to the war's end.

REVIEW Compare how people in the North and the South felt about the war after the first two years. **Compare and Contrast**

Summarize the Lesson

- **January 1863** President Abraham Lincoln formally issued the Emancipation Proclamation, freeing slaves in territories still fighting Union forces.
- **July 1863** The Massachusetts 54th, one of the first African American regiments to fight for the Union, attacked Fort Wagner in South Carolina.
- **June 1864** Congress gave black soldiers the same pay as white soldiers.

LESSON 2   REVIEW

Check Facts and Main Ideas

1. **Main Idea and Details** On a separate sheet of paper, fill in the details that support the main idea.

> Soldiers and civilians faced many difficulties during the Civil War.

| Soldiers faced lack of supplies, poor shelter, difficult marches, and threats of death and injury. | African American soldiers faced unequal pay and the doubts of citizens in their abilities to fight. | Women in the North and South faced shortages and inflation, and the possibility of losing a loved one in the war. |

2. Why was the Civil War called a "rich man's war and a poor man's fight?"

3. **Critical Thinking: Problem-Solving** Suppose you had to help President Lincoln decide when to issue the **Emancipation Proclamation**. How would you solve this problem?

4. How did the Massachusetts 54th help change people's minds?

5. What role did women play in the Civil War?

Link to Writing

Write Letters Letters written by soldiers and their families often described conditions on the battlefield or at home. Write a letter detailing life as a Civil War soldier. Write another letter in response relating the situation at home in the city or on a farm. Use the word **draft** in your answer.

503

Close and Assess

Summarize the Lesson

Tell students to examine the vertical time line. Ask them to summarize the lesson by reviewing how the events are related.

✓ LESSON 2   REVIEW

1. **Main Idea and Details** For possible answers, see the reduced pupil page.

2. South: A man could pay for a substitute if he owned 20 or more slaves; North: A man could pay $300 to avoid fighting.

3. **Critical Thinking: Problem Solving** Possible answer: First I would analyze how the war was going for both sides. Then I would advise President Lincoln of his options, weighing the advantages and disadvantages.

4. Many Northerners no longer doubted the ability and bravery of black soldiers.

5. Possible answers: Took over the jobs their husbands held before the Civil War; became soldiers, spies, nurses, or made clothing and sent food

Link to Writing

Consider having students deliver their letters as soldiers to another classmate who then responds as a family member at home.

SOCIAL STUDIES Background

Civil War Anesthesia

- Explain how scientific discoveries and technological innovations have benefited individuals in the United States.
- William Thomas Morton, an American, was among the first to use a general anesthetic on surgical patients. He used an inhaler that he had devised to administer ether to a patient before surgery on October 16, 1846. This made surgery painless.
- Doctors began using this technique routinely on wounded Civil War soldiers before performing surgery.

Workbook, p. 117

Lesson 2: Life During the War

Directions: For each main idea, write a supporting detail on the line provided. You may use your textbook.

1. **Main Idea:** News of the war spread in many ways.
   Detail: _____

2. **Main Idea:** As the war continued, both sides had trouble getting more soldiers.
   Detail: _____

3. **Main Idea:** Most of the soldiers who died in the Civil War did not die in battle.
   Detail: _____

4. **Main Idea:** The Civil War did not begin as a war against slavery.
   Detail: _____

5. **Main Idea:** African Americans who worked to serve in the war were not treated the same as white soldiers.
   Detail: _____

6. **Main Idea:** Women contributed to the war effort in many ways.
   Detail: _____

Notes for Home: Your child learned about difficult conditions during the war.
Home Activity: With your child, make a list of the difficulties soldiers and civilians experienced during the Civil War. Discuss how these types of difficulties might have made your family feel about the war, the country.

Also on Teacher Resources CD-ROM.

Working for Lasting Peace

Objective

- Identify the accomplishments of notable individuals, such as Jody Williams.

1 Introduce and Motivate

Preview To activate prior knowledge, have students describe a time when they or another person were treated unfairly. Ask them if they took any action to stop this mistreatment, and if so, have them describe it.

2 Teach and Discuss

Primary Source

Cited in a CNN report on 1997 Nobel Prize winners: "Jody Williams: The Woman Who Waged War on Land Mines"

1 **What point was Jody Williams trying to make in this quote?** Landmines continue to kill innocent people even after a war has ended.
Analyze Primary Sources

CITIZEN HEROES

Working for Lasting Peace

Many years after the terrible bloodshed of the Civil War, new kinds of weapons such as landmines pose a threat to the lives of innocent people.

When Jody Williams heard schoolchildren pick on her brother, Stephen, she got angry. "I couldn't understand why people would be mean to him because he was deaf," says Williams. From that early experience of cruelty in Poultney, Vermont, came Williams's fierce desire to "stop bullies [from] being mean to...people, just because they are weak."

Today defending innocent people against landmines is Jody Williams's life work. Landmines have been used since the late 1800s. They are hidden in the ground and are intended to harm enemy soldiers during war by exploding when people walk over them. When the wars end, however, many landmines remain. Today millions and millions of landmines are in the ground in about 70 countries—mainly poor ones like Angola, Afghanistan, and Cambodia. Williams says:

"The landmine cannot tell the difference between a soldier or a civilian [a person who is not soldier]....Once peace is declared, the landmi[ne] does not recognize tha[t] peace.

The landmine is eterna[l] [always] prepared to take victims."

▶ Jody Williams shared the 1997 Nobel Peace Prize with Tun Channareth, a victim of a landmine in Cambodia.

504

Practice and Extend

SOCIAL STUDIES
Background

More About Jody Williams

- Williams was born on October 9, 1950.
- Williams was awarded degrees at the University of Vermont and Johns Hopkins School of Advanced International Studies.
- Williams has held jobs as Deputy Director of Medical Aid for El Salvador and has taught in Mexico, the United Kingdom, and Washington, D.C.

BUILDING
CITIZENSHIP
Caring

Respect
Responsibility
Fairness
Honesty
Courage

In the 1980s Jody Williams learned of the dangers of landmines while working for human rights in war-torn Central America. There she saw children who had lost legs or arms after stepping on buried landmines. She met families who could not farm land because there were so many landmines buried there.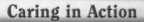

In 1991 Jody Williams and others started the International Campaign to Ban Landmines (ICBL). Their goal is a landmine-free planet. Williams works tirelessly for a ban on landmines, visiting affected countries and sending e-mails and faxes to tell people around the world about the dangers of these buried killers.

In recognition of their efforts, Jody Williams and ICBL were awarded the Nobel Peace Prize in December 1997. At the end of 1997, leaders from 121 countries signed a treaty to outlaw landmine production and destroy existing landmines.

Caring in Action

Link to Current Events "When we began we were just three people sitting in a room," says Williams about ICBL's beginnings. "It's breathtaking what you can do when you set a goal and put all your energy into it." Get together with two other classmates. What caring action can you plan for your school or community? What are some steps your group could take to carry it out?

CAMPAIGN BAN LANDMINES

505

2 Why did landmines prevent farmers from farming their land in Central America? If they tried to plant crops, they might dig up or step on a landmine and be injured or killed. Cause and Effect

 Problem Solving

Democratic Values and Institutions
Discuss with students how responsible members of a democratic society can use democratic processes to solve problems.

3 How does the ICBL propose to solve the problem of landmines around the world? They hope all countries will agree to ban landmines, outlaw landmine production in the future, and destroy existing landmines. Solve Problems

3 Close and Assess

Caring in Action

Link to Current Events

- Have students research the problem they want to solve in their community and present information to others.

- Point out that solving problems in the community involves citizenship skills, such as mobilizing information, people, and other resources.

CURRICULUM CONNECTION
Writing

Write an E-mail

- Have students pretend they are working with Williams in the ICBL.

- Have them write an e-mail they would send to leaders of countries around the world to make them aware of the dangers of the buried landmines.

- Students should include ideas about how the leaders could help eliminate landmines now and in the future.

How the North Won

Objectives

- Describe the events of the Battle of Gettysburg.
- Analyze President Lincoln's Civil War goals as expressed in the Gettysburg Address.
- Identify the location and results of the major battles of the Civil War.
- Explain the reasons for the use of total war and its consequences.

Vocabulary

Battle of Gettysburg, p. 507;
Gettysburg Address, p. 508;
Battle of Vicksburg, p. 509;
total war, p. 510

Resources

- Workbook, p. 118
- Transparencies 1, 54
- Every Student Learns Guide, pp. 214–217
- Quick Study, pp. 108–109

Quick Teaching Plan

If time is short, have students copy and complete the following diagram as they read the lesson independently. Have students add more boxes using the *Places* from Lesson 3.

Where: Gettysburg		Where:
When: 1863	→	When:
What Happened:		What Happened:

1 Introduce and Motivate

Preview Ask students to recall how the North and South were affected by the Civil War. Tell students they will learn about how the Civil War finally ended in Lesson 3.

 The Gettysburg Address was one of Lincoln's most famous speeches. It honored soldiers who died in the Battle of Gettysburg. Ask students what they think Lincoln might have said in the speech.

LESSON 3

1863			1865
July 1863 The Union gains control of the Mississippi River	**November 1863** President Lincoln delivers the Gettysburg Address		**April 1865** The Confederacy surrenders to the Union

PREVIEW

Focus on the Main Idea
A series of Northern victories led to the end of the Civil War by 1865.

PLACES
Gettysburg, Pennsylvania
Vicksburg, Mississippi
Atlanta, Georgia
Savannah, Georgia
Appomattox Court House, Virginia

PEOPLE
Ulysses S. Grant
William Tecumseh Sherman

VOCABULARY
Battle of Gettysburg
Gettysburg Address
Battle of Vicksburg
total war

506

How the North Won

You Are There
The date is November 19, 1863. About 15,000 people have gathered at Gettysburg, Pennsylvania. They are here for a ceremony to honor the soldiers who died in the Battle of Gettysburg just four months earlier. President Lincoln has been asked to speak.

The main speaker at the event is former Massachusetts governor, Edward Everett. He delivers a speech that lasts almost two hours. Finally President Lincoln rises and addresses the crowd for about three minutes. The speech is so short that no one realizes that Lincoln is finished. The crowd is silent for a moment. Then a few people begin to clap. Lincoln sits down before the photographer can take his picture.

One newspaper calls his speech "silly." Lincoln calls it "a flat failure." But his speech, the Gettysburg Address, will become known as one of the greatest speeches in United States history.

Main Idea and Details As you read, keep in mind the goals of the North as the war reached an end.

Practice and Extend

READING SKILL
Main Idea/Details

In the Lesson Review, students complete a graphic organizer like the one below. You may want to provide students with a copy of Transparency 1 to complete as they read the lesson.

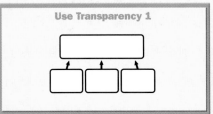

Use Transparency 1

VOCABULARY
Word Exercise

Context Clues The word *address* has a different meaning in this lesson than the most common meaning. Preview page 508 with students. Ask: **What does *address* mean in the lesson?** (a speech) **What clues did you use to figure out the meaning?** ("speak"; "speech") Explain that *address* with this meaning can also be used as a verb. Give an example, such as "President Lincoln was asked to **address** the audience."

The Battle of Gettysburg

One of the most important battles of the Civil War was a three-day struggle fought in Gettysburg, Pennsylvania. This was the farthest north that Confederate forces had advanced into Union territory.

The Battle of Gettysburg began on July 1, 1863. The Confederates, led by Robert E. Lee, pushed the Union soldiers back, but missed an opportunity to pursue the Northerners and follow up their attack.

By the second day of fighting, more Union soldiers had arrived. The Confederates attacked again, but the Union troops held their ground. One Confederate from Texas remembered "the balls [bullets] were whizzing so thick that it looked like a man could hold out a hat and catch it full."

On July 3 more than 150 Confederate cannons fired at Union troops. The Northerners responded with their cannons. The noise was so loud, it was heard 140 miles away in Pittsburgh. Southern troops, including those commanded by General George Pickett, made an attack called "Pickett's Charge." Thousands of Confederates marched through open space toward the well-protected Union troops. The attack was a disaster. More than 5,000 Confederates were killed or wounded.

The Battle of Gettysburg was an important victory for the North. Lee's advance into the North was stopped, and he retreated back into Virginia. It was also a costly battle for both sides. There were more than 23,000 Union casualties. The South suffered more than 28,000 casualties.

REVIEW Describe the events of each day in the Battle of Gettysburg. **Sequence**

Map Adventure

Battle of Gettysburg, 1863

Suppose you are visiting the battle site where the fighting at Gettysburg took place. Today it is a national military park. Answer the questions about the battle site.

1. Describe the location of the Union and Confederate headquarters.
2. In which direction was Pickett's Charge made?
3. What advantage did the location of Little Round Top give the Union forces?

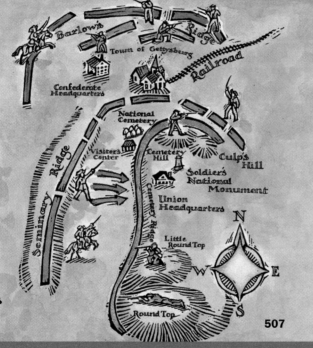

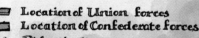
▬ Location of Union forces
▬ Location of Confederate forces
⇨ Pickett's Charge

507

MEETING INDIVIDUAL NEEDS
Leveled Practice

Number Match Have students match estimates with facts.

Easy Reorder the facts in Column B. Have students match the numbers in Column A with a fact in Column B. (Correct facts are shown.) **Reteach**

On-Level List the numbers in Column A. Have students find and write the fact in Column B. **Extend**

Challenge Have students choose one fact to research and write about for a class presentation. **Enrich**

Battle of Gettysburg	
Column A	**Column B**
About 140	Number of miles to Pittsburgh
More than 5,000	Number of Confederates killed or wounded in "Pickett's Charge"
More than 23,000	Number of Union casualties
More than 28,000	Number of Confederate casualties

For a Lesson Summary, use Quick Study, p. 108.

2 Teach and Discuss

PAGE 507

The Battle of Gettysburg

🕐 **Quick Summary** The well-protected Union troops won the Battle of Gettysburg, causing the Confederates to retreat to Virginia.

1 **What mistake did the Confederate soldiers make that caused them to lose the battle?** They did not follow up on their first attack quickly enough. By the next day more Union soldiers had arrived. **Cause and Effect**

✓ **Ongoing Assessment**

If... students cannot identify the mistake that caused the Confederate loss,	then... ask what might have happened if the Confederates had pursued the Northerners and followed up their attack at the end of the first day of fighting.

✓ **REVIEW ANSWER** During the first day Confederate soldiers pushed Union soldiers back but failed to follow up their attack. By the second day, more Union soldiers had arrived. The Confederates attacked again, but Union soldiers held their ground. "Pickett's Charge" occurred during the third day. The attack was a disaster for the Confederates. **Sequence**

Map Adventure Answers

1. The Union headquarters was located just east of Cemetery Ridge. The Confederate headquarters was located just north of Seminary Ridge. **2.** East **3.** It helped protect them because the Confederates had to attack uphill.

The Gettysburg Address

 Quick Summary President Lincoln gave the Gettysburg Address at the dedication of the Gettysburg cemetery in November, 1863.

⭐ SOCIAL STUDIES STRAND
Citizenship

Point out that Lincoln's leadership qualities were evident in his Gettysburg Address.

② **In what ways was the message of the Gettysburg Address consistent with Lincoln's wish to preserve the Union before the Civil War began?** In the Gettysburg Address, Lincoln urged people to remain together to support the cause of preserving the Union.
🔄 **Main Idea and Details**

✓ **REVIEW ANSWER** Lincoln said that the soldiers had given their lives so that the nation might live. He believed their bravery would be long remembered.
🔄 **Main Idea and Details**

Primary Source

Cited in *The Annals of America*, Volume 9, published by Encyclopædia Britannica, Inc.

Explain that the Gettysburg Address honored the soldiers who died at Gettysburg and inspired the Union.

③ **In the Gettysburg Address, how did Lincoln suggest that people honor the soldiers who died at the Battle of Gettysburg?** By increasing their devotion to support the cause of saving the Union
Analyze Primary Sources

The Gettysburg Address

In November 1863, the Gettysburg battlefield was made into a national cemetery to honor the men who died there. As you have read, President Lincoln was one of the people asked to speak at the ceremony. Read his speech, known as the **Gettysburg Address.**

The Gettysburg Address inspired the Union to keep fighting. The speech made it clear that a united nation and the end of slavery were worth fighting for.

REVIEW How did President Lincoln express his admiration for the soldiers who had died at Gettysburg? 🔄 **Main Idea and Details**

The Gettysburg Address

Four score [80] and seven years ago our fathers brought forth on this continent a new nation, conceived [formed] in Liberty, and dedicated [devoted] to the proposition [idea] that all men are created equal.

Now we are engaged in a great civil war, testing whether that nation, or any nation so conceived and so dedicated, can long endure. We are met on a great battlefield of that war. We have come to dedicate a portion of that field, as a final resting place for those who here gave their lives that that nation might live. It is altogether fitting and proper that we should do this.

But, in a larger sense, we cannot dedicate—we cannot consecrate [make worthy of respect]—we cannot hallow [make holy]—this ground. The brave men, living and dead, who struggled here, have consecrated it, far above our poor power to add or detract [take away]. The world will little note, nor long remember what we say here, but it can never forget what they did here. It is for us the living, rather, to be dedicated here to the unfinished work which they who fought here have thus far so nobly advanced. It is rather for us to be here dedicated to the great task remaining before us—that from these honored dead we take increased devotion to that cause for which they gave the last full measure of devotion—that we here highly resolve [are determined] that these dead shall not have died in vain—that this nation, under God, shall have a new birth of freedom—and that government of the people, by the people, for the people, shall not perish [die out] from the earth.

Painting by J. L. G. Ferris

508

Practice and Extend

✳ MEETING INDIVIDUAL NEEDS
Learning Styles

Review the Gettysburg Address Using their individual learning styles, students review the contents of the Gettysburg Address.

Verbal Learning Have a group of students present a choral reading of the Gettysburg Address with proper tone and expression.

Auditory Learning Have students listen to the choral reading to find the main idea of the speech. (To honor the soldiers who died at the Battle of Gettysburg by continuing to support the Union)

The Tide Turns

The Battle of Gettysburg was one of a series of battles that turned the tide of the war in favor of the Union. As you read in Lesson 1, one part of the Anaconda Plan called for Union troops to gain control of the Mississippi River to weaken the Confederacy. Capturing **Vicksburg, Mississippi,** which lay on the east bank of the river, would achieve this goal.

General **Ulysses S. Grant,** who had served with General Robert E. Lee in the Mexican War, headed the Union forces in the **Battle of Vicksburg.** In May 1863, Union forces began a blockade of the city. They bombarded Vicksburg with cannon fire by land and water for 48 days. Many people in the town dug caves in the hillside for protection.

Confederate civilians and soldiers in Vicksburg faced starvation under the Union blockade. Butcher shops sold rats, and soldiers received one biscuit and one piece of bacon a day.

Finally, on July 4, 1863, one day after the Battle of Gettysburg ended, the Southerners surrendered Vicksburg. The Confederacy was cut in two. Study the map below to see where Vicksburg and other major battles of the Civil War took place.

REVIEW Why do you think it took so long for the Confederates to surrender at Vicksburg? Draw Conclusions

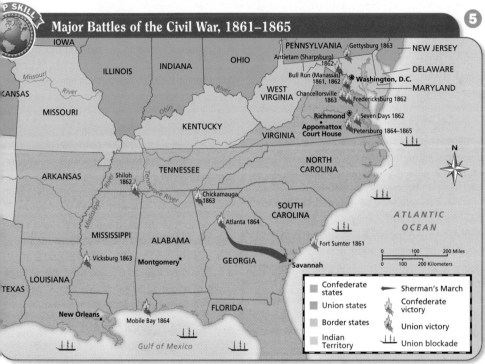

MAP SKILL Major Battles of the Civil War, 1861–1865

In July 1863, Union victories at Gettysburg and Vicksburg turned the tide of the war.

MAP SKILL Use a Map Scale *How many miles apart were the battles of Gettysburg and Vicksburg?*

509

The War Ends

🕐 **Quick Summary** Sherman's march through Georgia ended with the North linking with Grant's army and the fall of Richmond. Lee then surrendered and ended the war.

6 **Why did the Confederate army not fight when Sherman marched on Savannah?** Possible answer: They realized it was of no use since Sherman had just destroyed Atlanta and had so many Union soldiers. Make Inferences

Primary Source

Cited in *The Civil War: A Narrative–Red River to Appomattox,* by Shelby Foote

7 **What do Lee's words suggest about him?** Possible answer: He was a proud man, but sensible. He realized his soldiers could not achieve victory and more would die if he did not surrender. Analyze Primary Sources

8 **What can you conclude about Grant's characteristics, based on his actions in Appomattox Court House? Explain.** Possible answer: He was a fair and considerate person who did not take advantage of those whom he had defeated. He gave food to the Confederate soldiers and allowed them to keep their horses and weapons. Draw Conclusions

Primary Source

Cited in *The Oxford History of the American People,* by Samuel Eliot Morison

9 **To whom was Grant referring with the term "rebels"?** Confederate soldiers Analyze Primary Sources

✓ **REVIEW ANSWER** Possible answer: In addition to winning battles and capturing territory, Sherman wanted to break the Confederacy's will to fight. Cause and Effect

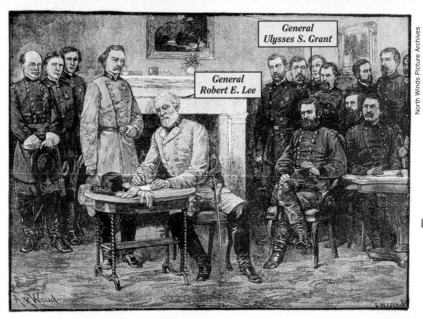

General Ulysses S. Grant

General Robert E. Lee

► After four years of fighting, General Lee agreed to surrender his army to General Grant.

The War Ends

General Grant was given control of all Union forces in March 1864. Grant continued to wear down the Confederate army with the help of Union General **William Tecumseh Sherman.**

Sherman moved his army toward **Atlanta, Georgia,** a vital industrial and railway center. The opposing Confederate army could not defend the city and retreated. Atlanta fell to the Union on September 2, 1864.

General Sherman used a method of warfare called **total war.** The aim of total war is to destroy not just the opposing army, but the people's will to fight. Sherman's men ordered everyone to leave Atlanta, and burned almost the entire city.

Starting in November, his army moved southeast toward **Savannah, Georgia.** The Union soldiers marched 300 miles in a 60-mile wide path. As they went, they destroyed anything that might help the South keep fighting, including houses, railroads, barns, and fields. Soldiers caused $100 million dollars worth of damage in Sherman's "March to the Sea."

Savannah fell without a fight on December 21, 1864. Sherman wrote to Lincoln, "I…present you as a Christmas gift the city of Savannah." Sherman's men then moved to South Carolina, causing even more destruction in the state where the war began.

Sherman's army moved north to link with Grant's army. The Northerners were closing in on Lee's army in Virginia. In April 1865, Confederate soldiers left Richmond, and Union troops entered on April 3. President Lincoln arrived to tour the captured Confederate capital. The city's former slaves cheered him.

Lee's army of 55,000 was tired and starving. The men tried to escape west, but Grant's force of about 113,000 outnumbered and trapped them. Lee admitted to his men,

> *"There is nothing left for me to do but go and see General Grant, and I would rather die a thousand deaths."*

510

Practice and Extend

FYI **SOCIAL STUDIES** **Background**

The Beginning and End of the War

- In 1861, Wilmer McLean was making a stew for Confederate General P. G. T. Beauregard in his home on the Bull Run in Northern Virginia. During the action at the First Battle of Bull Run, an artillery shell fell down the chimney and into the stew.
- McLean decided to find a safer place to live and bought a farmhouse in Appomattox County.
- It was in this farmhouse that Lee and Grant would meet for the surrender.
- It could be said that the Civil War began in the kitchen of McLean's first home and ended in the parlor of his second home.

Generals Lee and Grant met in a farmhouse **Appomattox Court House, Virginia,** on April , 1865 to discuss the terms of surrender. rant allowed Lee's men to go free. The outherners were allowed to keep their personal weapons and any horses they had. rant also offered to give Lee's men food from nion supplies. Lee accepted. As Lee returned his men, the Union soldiers began to cheer. rant silenced them, explaining,

> *"The war is over; the rebels are our countrymen again."*

The Civil War was the most destructive ar in United States history. About 620,000 oldiers died. Towns, farms, and industries— ostly in the South—were ruined. Families ad been torn apart by the struggle.

Even so, Lincoln expressed sympathy for e South. After news of the Confederate urrender reached Washington, D.C., he ppeared before a crowd and asked a band play the song "Dixie," one of the battle songs of the Confederacy. "I have always thought 'Dixie' one of the best tunes I ever heard," he told the people.

Lincoln wanted the country to be rebuilt. He had a plan to heal the nation's deep divisions. But he would never see his plans carried out.

REVIEW What were the results of General Sherman's strategy of total war?
Cause and Effect

Summarize the Lesson

- **July 4, 1863** Union soldiers led by General Grant cut the Confederacy in two by capturing Vicksburg, Mississippi.

- **November 19, 1863** President Abraham Lincoln gave the Gettysburg Address honoring the men who died in battle there.

- **April 9, 1865** General Robert E. Lee surrendered to General Ulysses S. Grant at Appomattox Court House, Virginia, ending the Civil War.

LESSON 3   REVIEW

Check Facts and Main Ideas

1. **Main Idea and Details** On a separate sheet of paper, fill in the missing details to the main idea.

> The Union used several strategies to achieve decisive victories in the last years of the Civil War.

| nion held a high n during the of Gettysburg, ting them from acking derates. | The Union blockaded Vicksburg, forcing them to surrender when they faced starvation. | General Sherman used total war, destroying any resources that the South might use to keep fighting. |

2. What circumstances led the Union to victory on the third day in the **Battle of Gettysburg**?

3. What were Lincoln's goals as expressed in the **Gettysburg Address**?

4. **Critical Thinking: *Interpret Maps*** Look at the map on page 509. In what state did most of the major battles occur in the Civil War? Give a reason you think this would be so.

5. What was the purpose of **total war** and Sherman's "March to the Sea"?

Link to [chain] Mathematics

Analyze a Speech Reread President Lincoln's Gettysburg Address on page 508. What year was he referring to in the speech when he said "Four score and seven years ago"? Why would he have referred to that year?

511

3 Close and Assess

Summarize the Lesson

Have pairs of students share details about each event.

✓ **LESSON 3   REVIEW**

1. **Main Idea and Details** For possible answers, see the reduced pupil page.

2. Possible answer: The Union army was well protected while the Confederates marched toward them in the open.

3. Lincoln wanted to honor the soldiers who had died and to rally the people to preserve the Union.

4. **Critical Thinking: *Interpret Maps***
   Virginia; The Union army might have concentrated its forces in this area in an attempt to capture the Confederate capital, Richmond, and to defend Washington, D.C.

5. To capture Savannah; the Union destroyed almost everything in its path because Sherman wanted to weaken the Confederacy.

Link to [chain] **Mathematics**

Explain that a score means 20 years and that students first have to calculate how many years four score and seven are. He believed the Civil War soldiers were fighting to preserve the nation the Patriots had fought to create in 1776.

ESL **EXTEND LANGUAGE**
ESL Support

Explore Words About the South Help students identify and explore words about people and places.

Beginning Have students look at the map on p. 486. Name states and have students say *yes* or *no* to indicate whether they were in the Confederacy.

Intermediate Have students use words such as *Confederacy, rebels,* and *Dixie* in a paragraph. Then have students read their paragraphs to partners.

Advanced Have students create and share a dialogue between Lincoln and Grant or Lee discussing how the country might be rebuilt.

For additional ESL support, use Every Student Learns Guide, pp. 214–217.

Workbook, p. 118

Lesson 3: How the North Won

Directions: Match each term in the box with its clue. Write the term on the line provided.

Battle of Gettysburg	Ulysses S. Grant	total war
Gettysburg Address	Battle of Vicksburg	Robert E. Lee
Anaconda Plan	William Tecumseh Sherman	Appomattox Court House

1. Place where Generals Lee and Grant met to discuss the terms of the Confederates' surrender of the Civil War

2. "I would rather die a thousand deaths."

3. President Lincoln made a short speech at a ceremony to dedicate a national cemetery. In his speech, Lincoln inspired the Union to keep fighting for a united nation and the end of slavery.

4. A method of warfare designed to destroy the opposing army and the people's will to fight

5. This three-day battle began on July 1, 1863. It was one of the most important battles of the Civil War. It was an important victory for the North and a costly battle for both sides.

6. Head of the Union forces in the Battle of Vicksburg

7. The surrender of this battle by the Southerners cut the Confederacy in two.

8. The Union blockade at the Battle of Vicksburg was part of their strategy to gain control of the Mississippi River and weaken the Confederacy.

9. Led soldiers in a destructive "March to the Sea"

Also on Teacher Resources CD-ROM.

Read a Road Map

Objective

- Apply geographic skills to interpret legends and symbols on maps.

Vocabulary

road map, p. 512;
interstate highway, p. 512

Resource

- Workbook, p. 119

1 Introduce and Motivate

What is a road map? Ask students how people might use a road map. What information can be found on a road map? Then have students read the **What?** section of text on p. 512 to help set the purpose of the lesson.

Why use a road map? Have students read the **Why?** section of text on p. 512. Ask them how using a road map might make it easier to locate and visit places of interest.

2 Teach and Discuss

How is this skill used? Examine the map on p. 513 with students.

- Point out that interstate highways are identified by a shield with a black top and the number of the highway. These are usually three- or four-lane highways.

- Explain that cities are marked with small circles and points of interest, such as battlefields, are marked with small squares.

- Have students read the **How?** section of text on p. 513.

Read a Road Map

What? A **road map** is a map that shows roads, cities, and places of interest. Different types of lines show large and small highways and even smaller roads. Symbols show if a road is a major **interstate highway**, a large road that connects cities in different states. Other symbols show state roads, and still others show smaller roads.

Different sizes of color areas and dots are used to show cities and towns of various sizes. Many road maps use special symbols to show places of interest. Some road maps also show distances from one place to another.

Why? People often have to drive to places they do not know. They may be traveling for business, vacation, or other reasons. Drivers use road maps to figure out how to get from one place to another.

Many people are interested in the history of the Civil War. Some visit Civil War sites. Our nation keeps many Civil War sites as parks or monuments. Tourists may go from one site to another during a vacation. Often they visit places they have never been before, and they find their way with road maps.

▶ **Today the Gettysburg battlefield is a national military park.**

512

Practice and Extend

 **MEETING INDIVIDUAL NEEDS**
Leveled Practice

Give Directions Ask students to use the road map on p. 513 to give directions from one city to another.

Easy Have students complete sentence frames similar to the following by telling the direction and road to travel: To go from Richmond to Washington, D.C., travel north on highway 95. **Reteach**

On-Level Have students choose two cities shown on the map and write directions telling the road, direction, and distance to travel to go from one city to the other. **Extend**

Challenge Have students choose three cities on the map and write sets of directions to go from the first city to the second and the second city to the third. **Enrich**

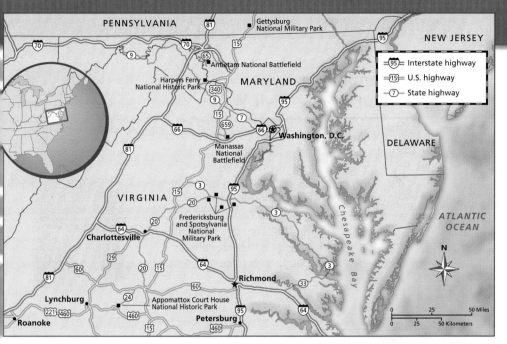

95	Interstate highway
15	U.S. highway
7	State highway

How? To use a road map, you need to know where you are and where you want to go. Then you find these places on the map. You also have to understand what kinds of roads are shown and how they are marked on the map.

Say that you are starting at Richmond, Virginia, and want to get to Gettysburg, Pennsylvania. Look at the road map on this page, which shows many Civil War sites in Pennsylvania, Maryland, and Virginia. You notice that Gettysburg is about 180 miles north of Richmond. You see that Route 64 goes northwest from Richmond to Route 15. From there, Route 15 goes north all the way to Gettysburg.

① ② ③

Think and Apply

❶ How would you travel from Gettysburg National Military Park to Manassas National Battlefield?

❷ What interstate highway is part of the shortest route from Manassas National Battlefield Park to Washington, D.C.?

❸ How would you travel from Washington, D.C. to the Fredericksburg and Spotsylvania National Military Park?

Internet Activity

For more information, go online to the *Atlas* at
www.sfsocialstudies.com.

513

SOCIAL STUDIES STRAND
Geography

Use the map to help students identify geographic factors that influence present patterns of settlement and population distribution in the United States.

- A significant percentage of the populations of Maryland, Delaware, and northeastern Virginia work for the government rather than for private companies.

- Ask students why they think this is true.

❶ Could you use a road map to find the population of a region? Why or why not? No, population is usually shown on population density maps. Interpret Maps

❷ What is the most direct way to get from Petersburg to Appomattox Court House Park by car? Take Route 460 west to Route 24. Interpret Maps

Test Talk

Use Information from Graphics

❸ What symbol is used to mark Washington, D.C., the capital of the United States? Have students find the place on the map to help them answer the question. A star inside a circle Interpret Maps

3 Close and Assess

Think and Apply

1. Take Route 15 south to Interstate 66. Follow Interstate 66 east to Manassas National Battlefield.

2. Interstate 66

3. Take Interstate 66 to 95 south. Two of the park's four locations are just south of the intersection of 95 and Route 3. The other two are west of there, where Routes 3 and 20 meet.

SOCIAL STUDIES STRAND
Geography

The following map resources are available:

- Big Book Atlas
- Student Atlas
- Outline Maps
- Desk Maps
- Map Resources CD-ROM

Workbook, p. 119

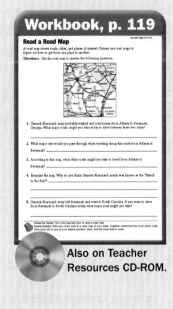

Read a Road Map

A road map shows roads, cities, and places of interest. Drivers use road maps to figure out how to get from one place to another.

Directions: Use the road map to answer the following questions.

1. General Sherman's army probably walked and rode home from Atlanta to Savannah, Georgia. What major roads might you take today to drive between these two cities?

2. What major city would you pass through when traveling along this route from Atlanta to Savannah?

3. According to this map, what other roads might you take to travel from Atlanta to Savannah?

4. Examine the map. Why do you think General Sherman's march was known as the "March to the Sea"?

5. General Sherman's army left Savannah and went to South Carolina. If you were to drive from Savannah to South Carolina today, what major road might you take?

Also on Teacher Resources CD-ROM.

Dorling Kindersley

Communications During the Civil War

Objective

- Identify and explain different forms of communications during the Civil War.

1 Introduce and Motivate

- Tell students that the quality of communication during a war can lead to victory or defeat.

- Before students read this page ask them to brainstorm a list of facts they know about telegraphs. Have them include parts of a telegraph, items needed to operate telegraphs, and codes used. Tell students they will learn more about telegraphs as they read these pages.

- Students will add to their lists later as part of the assessment for this page.

2 Teach and Discuss

1 What limitation did signal drums have that telegraphs did not? They could only be heard short distances. Telegraph signals could be sent across many miles. Compare and Contrast

2 What important capability did the army field telegrapher's wagon have? It could move from place to place, so telegraphs could be sent and received wherever the troops might have to move to during battle. Draw Conclusions

Communications During the Civil War

The Civil War was one of the first large conflicts in which armies could communicate instantly using the telegraph, which sent messages along wires. By 1861 every state east of the Mississippi River was linked by telegraph wires. That April, when the Confederacy attacked Fort Sumter in South Carolina, word went out immediately: "Fort Sumter is fired upon." Both Union and Confederate armies used Morse Code and secret military codes to communicate.

Signal Drum
Drums and bugles were played on the field, signaling instructions for firing and troop movements. This drum was found on the Gettysburg battlefield.

Animal hide drum head

Handpainted eagle and crest

Strapping to keep drum head taut

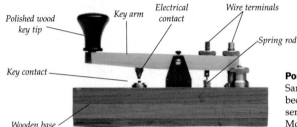

Polished wood key tip

Key arm

Electrical contact

Wire terminals

Spring rod

Key contact

Wooden base

Portable Telegraph Key ❹
Samuel Morse, an American artist who became an inventor, developed a way to send telegraph messages using a code called Morse Code.

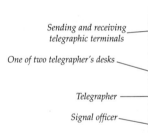

Rolled canvas window blind

Sending and receiving telegraphic terminals

One of two telegrapher's desks

Telegrapher

Signal officer

❷ **Army Field Telegrapher's Wagon**
This portable telegrapher's office had sending and receiving sets.

514

Practice and Extend

 SOCIAL STUDIES Background

Morse Code

- Students may enjoy writing out messages using Morse Code.
- Display the following symbols or have students find them in a reference source in the library or on the Internet.

Morse Code Alphabet

A ·—	I ··	Q ——·—	X —··—
B —···	J ·———	R ·—·	Y —·——
C —·—·	K —·—	S ···	Z ——··
D —··	L ·—··	T —	comma — ——··——
E ·	M ——	U ··—	period ·—·—·—
F ··—·	N —·	V ···—	question mark ··——··
G ——·	O ———	W ·——	
H ····	P ·——·		

Hanging Military Telegraph Wires
As armies moved, telegraph wires had to be strung to areas that might not have been wired yet. Army telegraph poles were often trees from which bark and limbs had been removed.

Insulated wire hook

Bamboo field poles for temporary hook-ups to existing heavy lines

Wire spool

Field telegrapher's wagon

③

④

Beardslee Telegraph
Most soldiers could not read Morse Code, so the Union army adopted the Beardslee telegraph. Electric signals sent or received over the Beardslee system moved a metal arrow around a large brass wheel with the letters of the alphabet stamped on it. These letters spelled out messages in English or secret code. The Beardslee's range was limited to five miles.

Sending and receiving key and letter indicator

Brass wheel with stamped letters

Receiving terminals

Sending terminals

Letter wheel gear mechanism

Wire wrapping

Service door

Carrying strap

Brass fittings

515

③ Why were telegraph wires necessary? So electrical signals could travel from one place to another
Draw Conclusions

④ How were Beardslee's telegraph and Samuel Morse's telegraph alike? How were they different? Alike: Both transmitted electrical signals; Different: Beardslee's telegraph spelled out messages using letters while Morse's used a code. **Compare and Contrast**

③ Close and Assess

- Encourage students to learn more about other means of communication in encyclopedias or history books.

- Ask students to add to their lists that they began earlier. Have students discuss what new information they learned from the pictures on these pages.

FYI SOCIAL STUDIES
Background

Communicating by Flag
- In 1856 Albert J. Myer developed a way to communicate on the battlefield by using flags.
- The system, which used only one flag, was called wigwag. It was effective for communications between troops miles apart.

The End of Slavery

Objectives

- Explain why Congress disagreed with Johnson's plan for Reconstruction.
- Analyze the effect of the Reconstruction Acts.
- Evaluate the impact of the Thirteenth, Fourteenth, and Fifteenth Amendments.
- Describe life for African Americans after Reconstruction.

Vocabulary

assassination, p. 517; **Reconstruction,** p. 517; **Thirteenth Amendment,** p. 517; **black codes**, p. 517; **Freedmen's Bureau,** p. 518; **Fourteenth Amendment,** p. 519; **Fifteenth Amendment,** p. 519; **impeachment,** p. 519; **Jim Crow laws,** p. 520; **segregation,** p. 520; **sharecropping,** p. 520

Resources

- Workbook, p. 120
- Transparency 1
- Every Student Learns Guide, pp. 218–221
- Quick Study, pp. 110–111

Quick Teaching Plan

If time is short, have students work in pairs to copy and complete this chart:

Effects of Reconstruction on African Americans	
Reconstruction under Congress	End of Reconstruction

1 Introduce and Motivate

Preview To activate prior knowledge, ask students to recall Lincoln's goals in fighting the Civil War. Tell students that in Lesson 4 they will learn whether or not Lincoln's goals were realized.

You Are There Not everyone was happy with the way the Civil War ended. Ask students to predict how Lincoln's assassination might affect relations between the North and South.

516 Unit 7 • War Divides the Nation

LESSON 4

1865		1867
April 1865 President Lincoln is killed	**December 1865** Thirteenth Amendment ends slavery	**March 1867** Congress passes the first Reconstruction Act

Washington, D.C.

PREVIEW

Focus on the Main Idea
The country faced many difficult challenges after the Civil War ended, including rebuilding the South and protecting the rights of newly freed African Americans.

PLACES
Washington, D.C.

PEOPLE
Andrew Johnson
Hiram R. Revels
Blanche K. Bruce

VOCABULARY
assassination
Reconstruction
Thirteenth Amendment
black codes
Freedmen's Bureau
Fourteenth Amendment
Fifteenth Amendment
impeachment
Jim Crow laws
segregation
sharecropping

516

The End of Slavery

You Are There It is Friday, some time after 10:00 P.M. President Abraham Lincoln and his wife, Mary, are enjoying a play. The President and his guests are seated in a box above the stage of Ford's Theater.

Suddenly, the audience hears something like an explosion. Blue-colored smoke comes from the box where the President is seated. Mary Lincoln screams. President Lincoln has been shot. The bullet has entered the back of his head near his left ear. Lincoln is still breathing, but is unconscious.

A young doctor comes forward to aid the President. After checking his wound, he says, "It is impossible for him to recover."

 Main Idea and Details
As you read, look for details about rebuilding the nation after the Civil War.

▶ Poster for the play President Lincoln was seeing when he was shot.

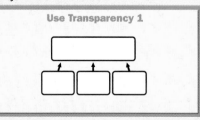

Practice and Extend

READING SKILL
Main Idea/Details

In the Lesson Review, students complete a graphic organizer like the one below. You may want to provide students with a copy of Transparency 1 to complete as they read the lesson.

Use Transparency 1

VOCABULARY
Word Exercise

Related Word Study Write *assassination, assassinate,* and *assassin* on the board. Have students read the definition of *assassination* in the text (p. 517). Ask students to think about what *assassinate* and *assassin* mean, based on the definition of *assassination.* (to murder a leader, a murderer of a leader) Confirm correct definitions, and discuss how students reached their conclusions.

A New President

After being shot, President Abraham Lincoln died in the early morning of April 15, 1865, in **Washington, D.C.** Until that time, no United States President had ever been assassinated. **Assassination** is the murder of a government or political leader.

Lincoln's killer was John Wilkes Booth, a 26-year-old actor who supported the Confederacy. Federal troops found Booth in a Virginia barn where he was shot and killed after he refused to surrender. Others who took part in the assassination plan were also caught and later hanged.

A funeral train carried President Lincoln's body to his hometown of Springfield, Illinois, where he was buried. People in New York City, Philadelphia, Cleveland, Chicago, and other cities paid their respects as the train passed through their communities.

▶ **People lined the streets when Lincoln's funeral train passed through New York City.**

THE NATION MOURNS

Collection of the New York Historical Society

Vice President **Andrew Johnson** became the new President. The former senator from Tennessee intended to carry out Lincoln's plan for **Reconstruction** —the rebuilding and healing of the country after the war.

One of the first steps toward reconstruction was ending slavery throughout the nation. The **Thirteenth Amendment,** which abolished slavery in the United States, took effect on December 18, 1865.

Johnson also had a plan to readmit the former Confederate states into the Union. Each state had to form a new state government. It had to pledge to obey all federal laws and deal fairly with newly freed African Americans. By the end of 1865, President Johnson believed that Reconstruction was complete.

Under Johnson's plan, though, Southern states were free to pass laws called **black codes.** These laws denied African American men the right to vote or act as jurors in a trial. Black people also could not own guns, take certain jobs, or own land. African Americans who were out of work might be fined or arrested. The laws had the effect of making an African American's life much the same as it had been under slavery. **1**

Many in Congress were angered by the black codes. They thought Johnson's Reconstruction plan was too easy on the South. The Republicans, who had won a majority in both houses of Congress, did not trust Johnson, who was a Southerner and had been a Democrat before becoming Lincoln's Vice President. Members of Congress began developing a new plan of Reconstruction. **2**

REVIEW What effect did black codes have on African Americans? *Cause and Effect*

517

SOCIAL STUDIES
Background

After the Assassination

- After John Wilkes Booth shot Lincoln, he jumped down onto the stage and broke his leg. He and a co-conspirator, David Herold, escaped and fled.
- Dr. Samuel Mudd set and splinted Booth's broken leg.
- Booth and Herold were caught near Bowling Green, Virginia, on April 26. Herold surrendered, but Booth was shot and killed.
- Within days Booth's co-conspirators were arrested, including Dr. Mudd. He was found guilty and sentenced to life imprisonment. He was imprisoned for a time in the Dry Tortugas Islands west of Key West, Florida.
- Dr. Mudd was later pardoned by President Andrew Johnson.

A New President

🕐 *Quick Summary* Although the Thirteenth Amendment prohibited slavery, Southern states passed black codes that made conditions for African Americans similar to those under slavery.

1 Why do you think the Southern states passed black codes? Possible answer: To prevent African Americans from gaining freedom even though slavery had been abolished *Make Inferences*

✓ Ongoing Assessment

If... students cannot make an inference about the purpose of black codes,	**then...** ask the following questions and discuss students' responses. What did the Thirteenth Amendment do? (End slavery) How did the Southern states feel about slavery? (They were in favor of slavery.) What did the black codes do? (Allowed the Southern states to treat African Americans in a way similar to when they were enslaved)

2 How did Lincoln and Johnson differ in their policies? Possible answer: Lincoln was less sympathetic toward the South. *Compare and Contrast*

✓ **REVIEW ANSWER** Black codes tried to place limitations on African Americans similar to those they faced under slavery. Under black codes, African Americans could not vote, participate in jury trials, own guns or land, or hold certain jobs. *Cause and Effect*

Reconstruction Under Congress

Quick Summary The Reconstruction Acts gave many freedoms to African Americans. White Southerners resisted these changes.

Problem Solving

3 **What problems did people in the war-torn South face? How did Congress attempt to solve them?** Possible answer: People needed greater access to hospitals and schools. The Freedmen's Bureau built hospitals and schools for blacks in the South. **Solve Problems**

C SOCIAL STUDIES STRAND
Culture

- Tell students that the Freedmen's Bureau maintained extensive records of the births, marriages, and deaths of many former slaves.

- These documents have been preserved by many local organizations, and have helped African Americans in researching their family histories.

- The publication of *Roots,* by Alex Haley, introduced new possibilities in researching African American genealogy and focused new interest in family reunions.

- At such joyous occasions, extended families of African Americans meet to exchange traditions and family lore.

4 **Who were carpetbaggers?** Northerners who moved south to start businesses; they often carried suitcases made of carpet. **Main Idea and Details**

5 **What was the main method the Ku Klux Klan used to restore white control in the South?** Terror and violence
Main Idea and Details

✓ **REVIEW ANSWER** Under Congress's Reconstruction plan, Southern states had to draft new constitutions giving African American men the right to vote. African Americans were allowed to hold public office, and former Confederate leaders could not vote or hold office. Buildings, roads, and bridges were repaired. New railroads were built, and a system of free education was established.
Main Idea and Details

518 Unit 7 • War Divides the Nation

Reconstruction Under Congress

Congress passed the first Reconstruction Act in 1867. The former Confederate states were divided into five military districts, and about 20,000 federal troops were sent to the South. The troops, led by military governors, were responsible for maintaining order, supervising elections, and preventing discrimination against African Americans.

The Reconstruction Acts required Southern states to write new state constitutions giving African American men the right to vote. The Acts also prevented former Confederate leaders and military officers from voting or holding elected office.

The **Freedmen's Bureau** was established to help the 4 million freedmen, or former slaves, after the war. The Freedmen's Bureau built hospitals and schools for blacks in the South. The Bureau hired black and white teachers from the North and the South.

For the first time in United States history, African Americans became elected officials. In Mississippi, two African Americans were elected United States senators. In 1870 Republican **Hiram R. Revels,** a minister and teacher, was elected to the Senate seat that Jefferson Davis held before the Civil War. In 1874 **Blanche K. Bruce,** a former slave, was elected to the Senate. Twenty other African Americans from the South were also elected to the House of Representatives.

▶ During Reconstruction, African American children studied at new schools in the South.

Many white Southerners did not like the changes brought by Reconstruction. Some resented the new state governments, which they felt were forced on them by outsiders. Some were angered by Northerners who moved south to start businesses. These new arrivals were called carpetbaggers, because they often arrived carrying their belongings in suitcases made of carpet. Southerners who supported Reconstruction were called scalawags. Carpetbaggers and scalawags were accused of trying to profit from the hardships of the South.

New leaders raised taxes to help rebuild roads, construct railroads, and establish a free education system. Many Southerners had a hard time paying these taxes. They were trying to rebuild their own farms and businesses.

Some white Southerners also objected to the rights gained by African Americans. After the new state governments repealed black codes, a small group of white Southerners formed the Ku Klux Klan. The Klan's goal was to restore white control over the lives of African Americans. Members of the Klan burned African American schools and homes, and attacked blacks for trying to vote.

REVIEW What changes did Congress bring about in the South during Reconstruction?
Main Idea and Details

▶ Hiram R. Revels was elected to the Senate.

518

Practice and Extend

MEETING INDIVIDUAL NEEDS
Leveled Practice

Write an Article Ask students to write a newspaper article about Reconstruction.

Easy Have students write headlines for an article announcing the passage of the Reconstruction Acts. **Reteach**

On-Level Have students write a newspaper article describing the new rights and resources African Americans will have as part of the Reconstruction Act. **Extend**

Challenge Have students write a newspaper article that contains an interview with an African American who experienced life in the South before and after the Civil War. **Enrich**

For a Lesson Summary, use Quick Study, p. 110.

New Amendments

Before being readmitted into the Union, former Confederate states had to accept two new amendments. The **Fourteenth Amendment,** ratified in July 1868, gave African Americans citizenship and said that no state could deny the equal protection of the law to all citizens.

The **Fifteenth Amendment,** ratified in March 1870, gave all male citizens the right to vote. It stated,

> *"the right of citizens of the United States to vote shall not be denied...on account of race, color, or previous condition of servitude [slavery]."*

Sojourner Truth pointed out that a woman had "a right to have just as much as a man." But the Fifteenth Amendment did not give voting rights to women. This angered many women who had fought for abolition and thought women as well as African Americans should have the right to vote.

President Johnson opposed the Fourteenth Amendment and other Reconstruction laws. He believed that the Reconstruction Acts were unlawful because they were passed without the representation of Southern states in Congress. He tried to block the passage of several laws that granted further rights to African Americans.

Angry about Johnson's actions, the Republicans in Congress tried to remove him from office by **impeachment.** Impeachment is the bringing of charges of wrongdoing against an elected official by the House of Representatives. If found guilty in a Senate trial, an impeached President is removed from office. Johnson avoided being removed from office by one vote in May 1868, but his ability to lead the nation was weakened.

REVIEW Why did Congress want to impeach President Johnson? **Summarize**

▶ After the Fifteenth Amendment became law, African American men were able to vote.

CHART SKILL *Describe the rights provided by the Thirteenth, Fourteenth, and Fifteenth Amendments.*

Reconstruction Amendments, 1865–1870

Amendment	Ratified	Description
Thirteenth	December 1865	Declares slavery illegal
Fourteenth	July 1868	Declares former slaves to be citizens and guarantees equal protection of the law to all citizens
Fifteenth	February 1870	Prevents the denial of the right to vote based on race or previous condition of enslavement

7

519

New Amendments

🕐 *Quick Summary* The Fourteenth and Fifteenth Amendments were passed during Reconstruction. President Johnson tried to block the passage of laws that granted rights to African Americans.

Primary Source
Cited in *The World Almanac 2001*

6 **How did the Fifteenth Amendment both expand and continue to limit which citizens had the right to vote?** It stated that citizens could not be denied the right to vote based on race, color, or previous condition of servitude; it did not give voting rights to women.
Analyze Primary Sources

✓ **REVIEW ANSWER** Because Johnson tried to block the passage of several laws that granted further rights to African Americans **Summarize**

7 **What was the main purpose of the Thirteenth, Fourteenth, and Fifteenth Amendments?** To provide more rights for people who were formerly enslaved
↻ **Main Idea and Details**

CHART SKILL **Answer** Thirteenth Amendment: right to freedom; Fourteenth Amendment: rights of citizenship and equal protection; Fifteenth Amendment: right to vote

Reconstruction Ends

🕐 *Quick Summary* By 1877 white Southern Democrats had regained their power in state governments and restricted most of the rights African Americans won during Reconstruction.

8 **Why were African Americans in the South unable to vote even though the Constitution gave them the right to vote?** Possible answer: Southern Democrats passed new laws in state constitutions that included a "grandfather clause" that prevented them from voting. Cause and Effect

9 **What were the Jim Crow laws?** Jim Crow laws enforced segregation of blacks and whites. 🔄 Main Idea and Details

✓ **REVIEW ANSWER** After Reconstruction ended, the way of life for African Americans in the South became much like it had been during slavery. Southern lawmakers set up policies, including poll taxes, reading tests, and "grandfather clauses," to prevent African Americans from voting. Jim Crow laws segregated blacks and whites. Many African Americans also became indebted in the system of sharecropping. Draw Conclusions

After Reconstruction

🕐 *Quick Summary* Although it had some successes, after Reconstruction, African Americans lost many rights they had won, and the South remained the poorest section of the country.

10 **How did the North contribute to African Americans losing their rights?** Many whites in the North lost interest in the problems of African Americans. Cause and Effect

Library of Congress

▶ Federal troops left the South in 1877, marking the end of Reconstruction.

Reconstruction Ends

By 1870, all of the former Confederate states had met the requirements of Reconstruction and were readmitted to the Union. In 1877, the remaining federal troops were withdrawn from the South.

White Southern Democrats regained their power in state governments. Almost immediately, new laws were passed that again restricted the rights of African Americans. Whites tried to prevent blacks from voting in several ways. They set up voting booths far from African American communities, or changed the location of the booths without informing blacks. Some states required a poll tax, or a payment, in order to vote. Many African Americans could not afford the poll tax.

In some places blacks were forced to take a reading test before voting. Under slavery, many people had not been allowed to learn to read or write, and so they failed the test. A "grandfather clause" was added to some state constitutions. It said that men could only vote if their father or grandfather had voted before 1867. The "grandfather clause" kept most African Americans from voting because they had not gained the right to vote until 1870.

8

Jim Crow laws were also passed. These laws enforced **segregation,** or separation of

blacks and whites. Under Jim Crow laws, blacks could not sit with whites on trains, or stay in certain hotels. They also could not ea in certain restaurants or attend certain theaters, schools, or parks.

During Reconstruction, Congressman Thaddeus Stevens said that every African American adult should be given "40 acres and a mule." His purpose was to help former slaves begin new lives. However, no land was ever distributed to former slaves.

Many African Americans were forced to return to the plantations where they had worked as slaves because they could not find jobs elsewhere. Many blacks as well as whites became trapped in a system called **sharecropping.** Sharecroppers rented land from landowners. They paid for their rent with a portion of their crop. Sharecroppers then used the rest of their crop to pay for food, clothing, and the equipment they needed to farm.

Usually, the costs of sharecropping were higher than the pay they received. Share-cropper John Mosley explained, "When our crop was gathered we would still be in debt."

REVIEW What conclusions can you draw about how life changed in the South after Reconstruction ended? Draw Conclusions

---

Practice and Extend

 **SOCIAL STUDIES Background**

More About the End of Reconstruction

- Only African Americans were required to pass reading tests before voting. Many whites were illiterate as well, but they were not compelled to take literacy tests and therefore did not lose their right to vote.

- Some whites were also entrapped in the sharecropping system, although it was more widespread among blacks.

 SOCIAL STUDIES STRAND Government

Participation in Government

- Remind students that one way people in a republic participate in government is through voting.

- For example, in a national election, registered voters vote for the President. Votes are counted state by state. In many states the candidate with the most votes gets all of that state's electoral votes.

- Explain that preventing African Americans from voting meant that they did not participate in the government.

After Reconstruction

Reconstruction had some successes in the South. A public school system was established and many industries were expanded. However, many of Reconstruction's goals failed to have a lasting impact.

After Reconstruction, the South remained the poorest section of the country. In addition, African Americans lost the political power they had gained during Reconstruction. Most blacks continued to perform the same labor they had done as slaves.

Many whites in the North lost interest in the problems faced by Southern blacks. The nation soon turned its attention to other issues. It would be many years before African Americans would gain the freedoms Reconstruction had hoped to guarantee.

REVIEW What were some of the successes and failures of Reconstruction?
Draw Conclusions

Summarize the Lesson

April 1865 President Abraham Lincoln was assassinated.

December 1865 The Thirteenth Amendment was adopted, abolishing slavery in the United States.

March 1867 Congress passed the Reconstruction Acts, sending military forces to the former Confederate states.

LESSON 4 REVIEW

Check Facts and Main Ideas

1. **Main Idea and Details** On a separate sheet of paper, fill in the details to the main idea.

The nation faced many challenges after the Civil War.

The assassination of Lincoln.

Carrying out the plan of Reconstruction to rebuild after the war.

Need to protect rights of African Americans, including amendments ending slavery and giving them the vote.

2. Why did Republicans in Congress dislike Johnson's **Reconstruction** plan?

3. **Critical Thinking: *Cause and Effect*** How did the Reconstruction Acts affect the South?

4. Why were three amendments added to the Constitution during Reconstruction?

5. How were the lives of African Americans made more difficult after the end of Reconstruction? Use the word **segregation** in your answer.

Link to Writing

Research Biographies Many African Americans became government leaders for the first time during Reconstruction. Research Hiram R. Revels, Blanche K. Bruce, or another African American member of Congress elected during Reconstruction. Were they enslaved or free before the Civil War? How did they become involved in politics? How did the end of Reconstruction affect them? Write a summary of what you learn.

521

✓**REVIEW ANSWER** Possible answer: Reconstruction had laid the foundation for a public school system and an expansion of Southern industries, but it had failed to permanently guarantee the rights of African Americans. **Draw Conclusions**

3 Close and Assess

Summarize the Lesson

Tell students to read the lesson summary. Then have them write about the dates 1868, 1870, and 1877, describing events for each.

✓ **LESSON 4 REVIEW**

1. **Main Idea and Details** For possible answers, see the reduced pupil page.

2. Southern states were still free to pass black codes, limiting the rights of African Americans.

3. **Critical Thinking: *Cause and Effect*** It expanded the rights of African Americans, but white Southerners resented this intrusion, and many of these policies did not last.

4. Possible answer: To insure the basic rights of all African Americans

5. Jim Crow laws enforced segregation and restricted where African Americans could go; poll taxes and reading tests limited their right to vote; sharecropping trapped them in debt.

Link to Writing

Give students the option of presenting their findings as an oral report, visual presentation, audio report, or written report.

CURRICULUM CONNECTION
Writing

Write a Short Story or Poem

- Have student work in pairs to write a short story or poem on one of the following topics: Life as a Sharecropper, The African American Experience During Reconstruction, The African American Experience After Reconstruction.

- Encourage students to use literary devices, such as dialogue and figurative language.

- Students may wish to do further research to learn more about the topic they choose.

Workbook, p. 120

Lesson 4: The End of Slavery

Directions: Define each term or phrase. Use a separate sheet of paper if you need more room. You may use your textbook.

1. Reconstruction

2. Thirteenth Amendment

3. black codes

4. Freedmen's Bureau

5. Ku Klux Klan

6. Fourteenth Amendment

7. Jim Crow laws

8. sharecropping

Notes for Home: Your child learned about how the United States changed after the Civil War.
Home Activity: With your child, review the series of changes that took place during Reconstruction and discuss who benefited from each change.

Also on Teacher Resources CD-ROM.

Resources

- Assessment Book, pp. 85–88
- Workbook, p. 121: Vocabulary Review

Chapter Summary

For possible answers, see the reduced pupil page.

Vocabulary

1. a, **2.** e, **3.** d, **4.** b, **5.** c

People and Terms

Possible answers:

1. The Anaconda Plan called for blockading Confederate ports, capturing land along the Mississippi River, and attacking from the east and west.

2. Thomas "Stonewall" Jackson helped the Confederates win the First Battle of Bull Run by refusing to retreat.

3. Mathew Brady's photographs showed civilians the realities of war.

4. The Emancipation Proclamation, issued by Lincoln on Jan. 1, 1863, freed slaves in all areas of the Confederacy not under Union control.

5. Clara Barton cared for wounded Union soldiers during the Civil War.

6. The Battle of Gettysburg turned the tide of the Civil War for the North.

7. William Tecumseh Sherman's men used the strategy of "total war" to destroy the South's will to fight.

8. The Freedmen's Bureau helped freed slaves after the Civil War by building hospitals and schools for them.

9. Hiram R. Revels became one of the first African Americans elected to Congress during Reconstruction.

10. Jim Crow laws enforced racial segregation.

Facts and Main Ideas

1. Rifles that shot farther and more accurately, railroads, submarines, ironclad ships, and hand grenades

2. It proved to many that black soldiers were capable of fighting just as effectively as white soldiers.

CHAPTER **15**
REVIEW

1861	1862	1863

April 1861
Union blockade of Southern ports begins

January 1863
Emancipation Proclamation takes effect

Chapter Summary

Main Idea and Details

On a separate sheet of paper, fill in other details that support the main idea. Find at least one detail for each lesson of the chapter.

> The Civil War and Reconstruction had many effects on the nation.

> Often during the Civil War, members of the same family supported different sides.

> Soldiers had faced shortages in food, weapons, clothing, and shelter, and the possibility of injury or death.

> About 620,000 soldiers died in the Civil War fighting for the North and the South.

> The Rec Acts poss Afric Ame serv Cong the 1

Vocabulary

Match each word with the correct definition or description.

1. **blockade** (p. 494)
2. **draft** (p. 499)
3. **total war** (p. 510)
4. **black codes** (p. 517)
5. **impeachment** (p. 519)

a. preventing supplies from moving in or out

b. laws denying rights to African Americans

c. charging an official with unlawful action

d. destroying an enemy's will to fight

e. law requiring people to serve in the military

People and Terms

Write a sentence explaining why each of the following people or terms was important. You may use two or more in a single sentence.

1. **Anaconda Plan** (p. 494)
2. **Thomas "Stonewall" Jackson** (p. 495)
3. **Mathew Brady** (p. 499)
4. **Emancipation Proclamation** (p. 500)
5. **Clara Barton** (p. 502)
6. **Battle of Gettysburg** (p. 507)
7. **William Tecumseh Sherman** (p. 510)
8. **Freedmen's Bureau** (p. 518)
9. **Hiram R. Revels** (p. 518)
10. **Jim Crow laws** (p. 520)

Practice and Extend

Assessment Options

✓ Chapter 15 Assessment

- Chapter 15 Content Test: Use Assessment Book, pp. 85–86.
- Chapter 15 Skills Test: Use Assessment Book, pp. 87–88.

Standardized Test Prep

- Chapter 15 Tests contain standardized test format.

✓ Chapter 15 Performance Assessment

- Have students think about what it was like to be a Northern or Southern soldier during the Civil War. Have them draw a picture and write a one- or two-sentence summary about their living conditions.

- Have partners act out a conversation between a Northerner and a Southerner who are discussing their opinions about Reconstruction in the South.

- Assess students' understanding of the Civil War and Reconstruction experiences by means of their drawings and conversations.

1863
e of Gettysburg is a
y for Union forces

November 1863
President Lincoln delivers
Gettysburg Address

April 1865
Confederacy surrenders
President Lincoln is killed

December 1865
Thirteenth Amendment
abolishes slavery

Facts and Main Ideas

What kinds of new technology were used during the Civil War?

Describe the significance of the attack on Fort Wagner.

Time Line How long did the Civil War last?

Main Idea What early strategies did each side plan for quick victories?

Main Idea What hardships did people on each side suffer during the Civil War?

Main Idea How did the Union army gain key victories in the final years of the war?

Main Idea What were the goals of Reconstruction?

Critical Thinking: *Compare and Contrast* Compare the lives of African Americans living in the South before the Civil War and after Reconstruction.

Write About History

Write a newspaper story about one of the battles discussed in your text.

Write a journal entry as a soldier describing General Robert E. Lee's surrender to General Grant.

Write a letter telling a friend about the *Monitor* or the *Virginia,* how these ironclads worked, and what they were like.

Apply Skills

Use Road Maps
Study the road map below. Then answer the questions.

1. Which three interstate highways lead into and out of Atlanta?

2. How would you travel from Atlanta to Savannah?

3. Andersonville National Historic Site is the location of a Civil War prisoner of war camp. How would you travel to Andersonville from Kennesaw Mountain National Battlefield?

Internet Activity

To get help with vocabulary, people, and terms, select dictionary or encyclopedia from *Social Studies Library* at **www.sfsocialstudies.com.**

523

Hands-on Unit Project

✓ **Unit 7 Performance Assessment**
- See p. 528 for information about using the Unit Project as a means of performance assessment.
- A scoring guide is provided on p. 528.

WEB SITE
Technology

For more information, students can select the dictionary or encyclopedia from *Social Studies Library* at **www.sfsocialstudies.com.**

Workbook, p. 121

Vocabulary Review

Directions: Use the vocabulary words from Chapter 15 to complete the following sentences. Write the correct word in the space provided. You may use your textbook.

1. _____ is the separation of blacks and whites.

2. The shutting off of an area by troops or ships to keep people and supplies from moving in or out is known as a _____.

3. At the Battle of _____ Union forces blockaded the city and bombarded it with cannon fire by land and sea for 48 days.

4. _____ is the practice of renting land from a landowner and paying rent with a portion of the crop produced on that land.

5. The murdering of a government or political leader is known as an _____.

6. Laws that denied blacks the right to vote or take part in jury trials were known as _____.

7. A method of warfare that destroys not only the opposing army but also the people's will to fight is known as _____.

8. In the Battle of _____ Union and Confederate forces clashed near the town of Sharpsburg in Maryland.

9. The First Battle of _____, one of the early battles of the Civil War, was won by the Confederates.

10. The _____ was established to help the more than 4 million former slaves after the war.

11. _____ refers to the rebuilding of the country after the Civil War.

12. The Battle of _____ lasted three days and was one of the most important battles of the Civil War.

13. _____ laws enforced the separation of blacks and whites.

14. The _____ Plan was a war strategy designed to "squeeze" the Confederacy.

Notes for Home: Your child learned about how the Civil War divided the nation and what steps were taken to heal and rebuild the country afterward.
Home Activity: With your child, analyze the relationships among the vocabulary terms for this unit. Begin by placing each term on a time line for the Civil War.

Also on Teacher Resources CD-ROM.

---

3. About four years, from April 1861 to April 1865

4. North: Blockade Southern ports, gain control of the Mississippi River, and attack from the east and west; South: Defend land until North gave up and hope Britain would help

5. Soldiers: death, disease, injury; Civilians: not enough food or clothing; loss of family and friends

6. Gettysburg: Confederates did not follow up attack on first day and the Union troops had well-protected positions the next two days; Vicksburg: Surrounded city to cut off supplies; Atlanta to Savannah: destroyed nearly everything

7. To guarantee rights to African Americans, reunite the country, rebuild the war-torn South, and, to some, punish the South for seceding from the Union

8. Similar to the lives of enslaved people before the Civil War; Jim Crow laws, poll taxes, reading tests, grandfather clauses, and sharecropping denied rights and equal opportunities to African Americans.

Write About History

1. Suggest that students include *Who, What, When, Where,* and *Why* in their stories.

2. Students can suppose they are an eyewitness to the surrender.

3. The letters might provide clues as to whether the author is from the North or the South.

Apply Skills

1. Interstate highways 75, 85, and 20

2. One route is to go southeast on Highway 75 and then take Highway 16 to Savannah.

3. One route is to take Highway 75 to Route 19 and then take local road 49 to the site.

When Johnny Comes Marching Home

Objective

- Identify significant examples of music from various periods in U.S. history.

1 Introduce and Motivate

Preview To activate prior knowledge, ask students about the conditions both Northern and Southern soldiers endured during the Civil War. Discuss how they probably felt about the end of the war. Ask how students think the families of the soldiers felt.

2 Teach and Discuss

1 **For about how long did the war go on after this song was written?** About two more years **Analyze Information**

2 **How did this song attempt to raise the morale of soldiers?** It suggested that those back home supported them and were anxious for their return. **Draw Conclusions**

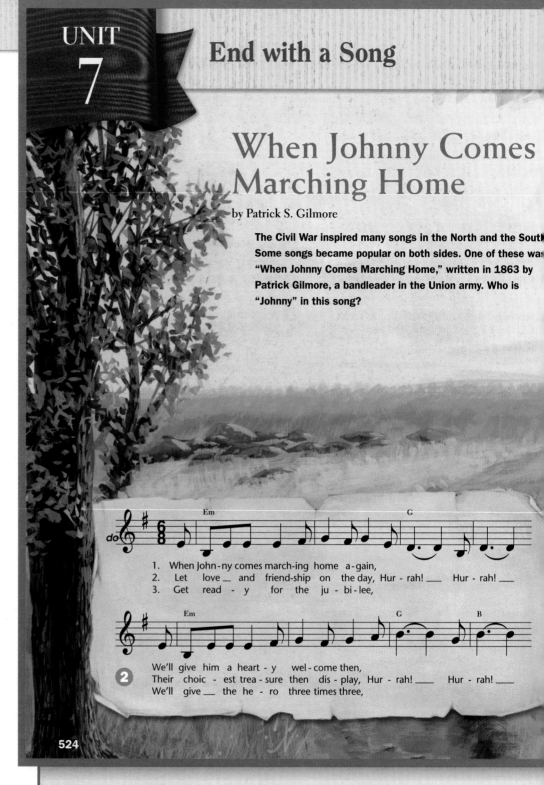

UNIT
7

End with a Song

When Johnny Comes Marching Home

by Patrick S. Gilmore

The Civil War inspired many songs in the North and the South. Some songs became popular on both sides. One of these was "When Johnny Comes Marching Home," written in 1863 by Patrick Gilmore, a bandleader in the Union army. Who is "Johnny" in this song?

1. When John-ny comes march-ing home a-gain,
2. Let love _ and friend-ship on the day, Hur - rah! ___ Hur - rah! ___
3. Get read - y for the ju - bi - lee,

We'll give him a heart - y wel - come then,
Their choic - est trea - sure then dis - play, Hur - rah! ___ Hur - rah! ___
We'll give _ the he - ro three times three,

524

Practice and Extend

 **SOCIAL STUDIES Background**

"When Johnny Comes Marching Home"

- Patrick S. Gilmore was a bandmaster of the Union army.
- Soldiers in both armies sang this song and identified with "Johnny."
- People waiting at home sang with hope and joy about the day "When Johnny Comes Marching Home."

AUDIO CD Technology

Play the CD, *Songs and Music*, to listen to "When Johnny Comes Marching Home."

③ Close and Assess

- Have one group of students practice singing the first verse, another practice the second, and another practice the third. Have each group perform its verse.

- Ask students why they think this song was popular both in the North and South. (Possible answer: Both sides were tired of the war and wanted their families reunited.)

③
The men will cheer, the boys will shout, The la-dies they will all turn out,
And let each one per-form some part, To fill with joy the war-rior's heart,
The laur-el wreath is read-y now To place up-on his roy-al brow,

And we'll shout "Hur - rah" when John-ny comes march-ing home! __

525

CURRICULUM CONNECTION
Music

Write a New Verse
- Have students work in pairs or groups to write another verse to the song.
- Students can use the first verse as a model.
- Students may wish to write a new verse from the perspective of a soldier arriving home.

Resource
- Assessment Book, pp. 89–92

Main Ideas and Vocabulary TEST PREP

1. b, **2.** d, **3.** b, **4.** c

Test Talk

Locate Key Words in the Question
Use Main Ideas and Vocabulary, Question 3, to model the Test Talk strategy.

Make sure that you understand the question.
Have students ask themselves, "Who or what is this question about?" The words that tell *who* or *what* the question is about are key words.

Find key words in the question.
Students should use the key word *seceded* in a sentence that begins "I need to find out. . . ."

People and Terms

1. e, **2.** a, **3.** f, **4.** c, **5.** d, **6.** b

Apply Skills

- Students can use newspapers and magazines to find articles and copy them for their scrapbooks.

- Encourage students to use a variety of sources for each point of view.

Test Talk
Look for the key words in the question.

Main Ideas and Vocabulary TEST PREP

Read the passage below and use it to answer the questions that follow.

The growing nation faced problems of sectionalism. Northerners and Southerners disagreed about whether slavery should be allowed in new states. Northern and Southern states also had different ways of life. Many Northerners and Southerners were loyal to their region of the country.

Abraham Lincoln joined the Republican Party, which opposed the spread of slavery. After he was elected President in 1860, South Carolina seceded from the Union. Other Southern states followed and formed the Confederacy. Confederate troops attacked Union-held Fort Sumter in April 1861, beginning the Civil War.

The Civil War dragged on for four years. New weapons of war left many soldiers dead or wounded. A lack of knowledge of disease killed many more. In the spring of 1865, the Confederacy surrendered. President Lincoln was killed shortly afterwards by a Confederate supporter.

Congress passed the Reconstruction Acts to rebuild the country and readmit the Southern states to the Union. Federal troops were sent to the South to maintain order and regulate elections. During this period, much of the damage from the war was repaired. African American men were granted the right to vote and some became members of Congress. The Freedmen's Bureau built hospitals and schools to help freed slaves.

When Reconstruction ended in 1877, many laws were passed to again restrict the rights of African Americans. Jim Crow laws segregated blacks and whites.

1 According to the passage, what was one difference between the North and South?
A Northerners and Southerners had similar ways of life.
B Northerners and Southerners disagreed about slavery in new states.
C The South had more resources.
D The North had more resources.

2 In the passage, the word sectionalism means—
A wanting to divide the country in half
B ending slavery in part of the country
C loyalty to one's country
D loyalty to one's region

3 In the passage, the word seceded means—
A joined with others
B broke away from a group
C objected to something
D formed a new government

4 What is the main idea of the passage?
A The North won the Civil War.
B The Civil War ended slavery.
C Differences between North and South led to the Civil War.
D War destroys people and places.

526

Practice and Extend

Assessment Options

✓ **Unit 7 Assessment**
- Unit 7 Content Test:
  Use Assessment Book, pp. 89–90.
- Unit 7 Skills Test:
  Use Assessment Book, pp. 91–92.

Standardized Test Prep
- Unit 7 Tests contain standardized test format.

✓ **Unit 7 Performance Assessment**
- See p. 528 for information about using the Unit Project as a means of Performance Assessment.
- A scoring guide for the Unit 7 Project is provided in the teacher's notes on p. 528.

Test Talk
- Test Talk Practice Book

WEB SITE
Technology

For more information, students can select the dictionary or encyclopedia from *Social Studies Library* at **www.sfsocialstudies.com.**

People and Terms

:ch each person and term to its definition.

- Joseph Cinque (p. 472)
- John Brown (p. 480)
- border state (p. 486)
- Catherine Coffin (p. 473)
- Ulysses S. Grant (p. 509)
- segregation (p. 520)

a. abolitionist who attacked an arsenal at Harpers Ferry

b. separating people

c. helped slaves escape to freedom

d. leader of Union forces at the Battle of Vicksburg

e. leader of *Amistad* rebellion

f. allowed slavery but did not secede

Write and Share

Create a Quiz Show Work with a group of students to create a quiz show about some of the main events and people in the period just before, during, and after the Civil War. Select a quiz show host and assistants to write the questions and answers. Then select contestants and develop a scoring system. Decide on a prize for the winner, and present the show to your class.

Read on Your Own

Look for these books in the library.

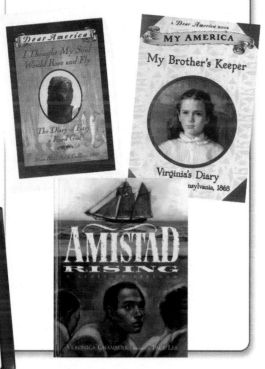

527

Apply Skills

epare a scrapbook about different points of ew on a current subject. First, choose the topic. en clip articles that present opposing points of ew about the topic. Paste the articles into a rapbook. Under each article, write a sentence at summarizes the writer's point of view.

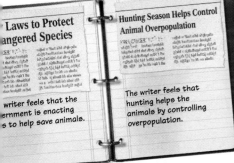

Revisit the Unit Question

✓**Portfolio Assessment**

- Have students look at the lists they compiled throughout Unit 7 of ideas about why nations may break apart.
- Have students compare and contrast their lists.

- Direct students to write a one-paragraph summary of these ideas from the lists. After each idea, suggest that students write a way to prevent the action from causing a nation to break apart.
- Have students add these lists and summaries to their Social Studies Portfolio.

Write and Share

- Have students use the People, Places, and Vocabulary of each lesson as the subject for some of their questions.
- Students can also change section headings into questions.
- Use the following scoring guide.

✓**Assessment Scoring Guide**

Create a Quiz Show	
6	Writes many questions and accurate answers. Covers all main topics. Accurate scoring system.
5	Writes a number of questions with accurate answers. Covers many main topics. Accurate scoring system.
4	Write some questions with some correct answers. Covers some main topics. Accurate scoring system.
3	Writes few questions, with many incorrect answers. Covers some main topics. Inaccurate scoring system.
2	Writes few questions and most answers are incorrect. Covers few main topics. Inaccurate scoring system.
1	Student is unable to create a quiz show.

If you prefer a 4-point rubric, adjust accordingly.

Read on Your Own

Have students prepare oral reports using the following books.

I Thought My Soul Would Rise and Fly: The Diary of Patsy, a Freed Girl, by Joyce Hansen (Scholastic, Inc., ISBN 0-590-84913-1, 1997) **Easy**

My Brother's Keeper: Virginia's Diary—Gettysburg, Pennsylvania, by Mary Pope Osborne (Scholastic, ISBN 0-439-15307-7, 2000) **On-Level**

Amistad Rising: A Story of Freedom, by Veronica Chambers (Harcourt Brace, ISBN 0-152-01803-4, 1998) **Challenge**

History Speaks

Objective
- Describe the experiences of people living during the Civil War and Reconstruction.

Resource
- Workbook, p. 122

Materials
paper, pens, pencils, reference materials

Follow This Procedure
- Tell students they will present an oral history documentary by preparing interviews for people who lived during the Civil War and Reconstruction. Explain that oral history might be tape-recorded historical information obtained during interviews about personal experiences and recollections.

- Help students brainstorm people who could provide eyewitness accounts: soldiers, slaves, people freed from slavery, children, plantation owners, and so on. Have them choose people representing the North and South.

- Divide students into groups. Students will write questions and answers and choose who will play historic roles and who will interview.

- Invite each group to present their oral history documentary to the class.

- Use the following scoring guide.

✓ Assessment Scoring Guide

History Speaks	
6	Presents well-written script with elaborate details and accurate information.
5	Presents well-written script with clear details and accurate information.
4	Presents script with several details and accurate information.
3	Presents script with several details and some inaccurate information.
2	Presents script with few details and some inaccurate information.
1	Presents poorly written script with no details and inaccurate information.

If you prefer a 4-point rubric, adjust accordingly.

UNIT 7 Project

History Speaks

Present the history of people from the time of the Civil War.

1 Form a group and choose a famous person who lived during the Civil War or Reconstruction.

2 Write a talk for the person to give to the class. Include details of what life was like during this time period.

3 Choose a person in your group to play the part of the famous person.

4 Present the talk to the class. You may want to include drawings of Civil War life to show to the class.

5 Have other students ask questions after the talk.

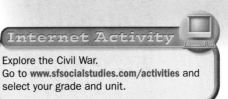

Internet Activity

Explore the Civil War.
Go to www.sfsocialstudies.com/activities and select your grade and unit.

528

Practice and Extend

Hands-on Unit Project

✓ Performance Assessment
- The Unit Project can also be used as a performance assessment activity.
- Use the scoring guide to assess each group's work.

WEB SITE Technology

Students can launch the Internet Activity by clicking on *Grade 5, Unit 7* at **www.sfsocialstudies.com/activities**.

Workbook, p. 122

Also on Teacher Resources CD-ROM

Expansion and Change

Unit Planning Guide

Unit 8 • Expansion and Change

Begin with a Primary Source pp. 530–531

Meet the People pp. 532–533

Reading Social Studies, Sequence pp. 534–535

Chapter Titles	Pacing	Main Ideas
Chapter 16 **Crossing the Continent** pp. 536–557	5 days	• After years of hard work, the first railroad across the United States was completed in 1869. • Following the Civil War, farmers and cowboys helped the Great Plains become an important farming and ranching region. • In the 1860s and 1870s, many Native American groups fought to maintain control of their traditional lands.
✓ **Chapter 16 Review** pp. 558–559		
Chapter 17 **Industry and Immigration** pp. 560–585	7 days	• In the late 1800s, new inventions powered the growth of American industry and changed the way people lived. • During the late 1800s and early 1900s, millions of immigrants moved to American cities, and workers struggled for better conditions. • By the end of the 1800s, the United States had gained new territory and become a world power.
✓ **Chapter 17 Review** pp. 586–587		

End with a Song pp. 588–589

✓ **Unit 8 Review** pp. 590–591

✓ **Unit 8 Project** p. 592

✓ = Assessment Options

◀ **A golden spike symbolized the completion of the first transcontinental railroad.**

Resources	Meeting Individual Needs
• Workbook, pp. 124–129	• ESL Support, TE pp. 539, 548, 555
• Every Student Learns Guide, pp. 222–233	• Leveled Practice, TE pp. 540, 551, 556
• Transparencies 10, 11, 56, 57, 58	• Learning Styles, TE p. 550
• Quick Study, pp. 112–117	
• Workbook, p. 130	
✓ Chapter 16 Content Test, Assessment Book, pp. 93–94	✓ Chapter 16 Performance Assessment, TE p. 558
✓ Chapter 16 Skills Test, Assessment Book, pp. 95–96	

• Workbook, pp. 131–135	• Leveled Practice, TE pp. 564, 570, 581
• Every Student Learns Guide, pp. 234–245	• ESL Support, TE pp. 566, 574, 579
• Transparencies 1, 11, 21	• Learning Styles, TE p. 567
• Quick Study, pp. 118–123	
• Workbook, p. 136	
✓ Chapter 17 Content Test, Assessment Book, pp. 97–98	✓ Chapter 17 Performance Assessment, TE p. 586
✓ Chapter 17 Skills Test, Assessment Book, pp. 99–100	

taly's Guglielmo Marconi nvented the radio at the age of 20.

Providing More Depth

Additional Resources

- Trade Books
- Family Activities
- Vocabulary Workbook and Cards
- Social Studies Plus! pp. 178–199
- Daily Activity Bank
- Read Alouds and Primary Sources pp. 133–149
- Big Book Atlas   • Student Atlas
- Outline Maps   • Desk Maps

 Technology

- AudioText
- Video Field Trips: The Expanding Railroad
- Songs and Music
- Digital Learning CD-ROM Powered by KnowledgeBox (Video clips and activities)
- MindPoint® Quiz Show CD-ROM
- ExamView® Test Bank CD-ROM
- Colonial Williamsburg Primary Sources CD-ROM
- Teacher Resources CD-ROM
- Map Resources CD-ROM
- SF SuccessNet: iText (Pupil Edition online), iTE (Teacher's Edition online), Online Planner
- **www.sfsocialstudies.com** (Biographies, news, references, maps, and activities)

⚠ *To establish guidelines for your students' safe and responsible use of the Internet, use the Scott Foresman Internet Guide.*

Additional Internet Links

To find out more about:

- The Battle of Little Bighorn, visit **www.custerslaststand.org**
- Jane Addams, visit **www.greatwomen.org**
- Immigrants coming to the United States in the late 1800s and early 1900s, visit **www.ellisisland.org**

Unit 8 Objectives

▲ **Orville and Wilbur Wright built *Flyer*, the world's first successful airplane.**

Assessment Options

✓ Formal Assessment

- **Lesson Reviews,** PE/TE pp. 541, 552, 557, 567, 574, 582
- **Chapter Reviews,** PE/TE pp. 558–559, 586–587
- **Chapter Tests,** Assessment Book, pp. 93–100
- **Unit Review,** PE/TE pp. 590–591
- **Unit Tests,** Assessment Book, pp. 101–104
- **ExamView® Test Bank CD-ROM** (test-generator software)

✓ Informal Assessment

- **Teacher's Edition Questions,** throughout Lessons and Features
- **Section Reviews,** PE/TE pp. 539–540, 547–552, 555–556, 563–567, 569–574, 579–582
- **Close and Assess,** PE/TE pp. 535, 541, 543, 545, 552–553, 557, 567, 574–575, 577, 582–583, 585, 589

Ongoing Assessment

Ongoing Assessment is found throughout the Teacher's Edition lessons using an **If...then** model.

If = students' observable behavior,	**then =** reteaching and enrichment suggestions

✓ Portfolio Assessment

- **Portfolio Assessment,** TE pp. 529, 530, 591
- **Leveled Practice,** TE pp. 540, 551, 556, 564, 570, 581
- **Workbook Pages,** pp. 123–137
- **Chapter Review: Write About History,** PE/TE pp. 559, 587
- **Unit Review: Apply Skills,** PE/TE p. 590
- **Curriculum Connection: Writing,** PE/TE pp. 552, 574; TE pp. 531, 577

✓ Performance Assessment

- **Hands-on Unit Project** (Unit 8 Performance Assessment), PE/TE pp. 529, 559, 587, 592
- **Internet Activity,** PE p. 592
- **Chapter 16 Performance Assessment,** PE/TE p. 558
- **Chapter 17 Performance Assessment,** PE/TE p. 586
- **Unit Review: Write and Share,** PE/TE p. 591
- **Scoring Guides,** TE pp. 591–592

Test Talk

Test-Taking Strategies

Understand the Question
- **Locate Key Words in the Question,** TE p. 570
- **Locate Key Words in the Text,** PE/TE p. 590, TE p. 580

Understand the Answer
- **Choose the Right Answer,** Test Talk Practice Book
- **Use Information from the Text,** TE p. 564
- **Use Information from Graphics,** TE p. 543
- **Write Your Answer to Score High,** TE p. 557

For additional practice, use the Test Talk Practice Book.

Featured Strategy

Locate Key Words in the Text

Students will:
- Make sure that they understand the key words in the question.
- Find key words in the text that match the key words in the question.

PE/TE p. 590, **TE** p. 580

Curriculum Connections

Integrating Your Day

The lessons, skills, and features of Unit 8 provide many opportunities to make connections between social studies and other areas of the elementary curriculum.

READING

Reading Skill–Sequence, PE/TE pp. 534–535, 538, 546, 554, 562

Lesson Review–Sequence, PE/TE pp. 541, 552, 557, 567

MATH

Link to Mathematics, PE/TE p. 541

Solve Time Word Problems, TE p. 543

Calculate Travel Time TE p. 545

Calculate Profits, TE p. 550

WRITING

Write a Letter, TE pp. 531, 551, 577

Link to Writing, PE/TE pp. 552, 574

Social Studies

LITERATURE

Read Biographies, TE pp. 532, 575

Read About Thomas Edison, TE p. 563

Read About Immigrants, TE p. 571

Mary Antin's Book, TE p. 575

Read About Theodore Roosevelt, TE p. 582

SCIENCE

Research Crops of the Great Plains, TE p. 552

Link to Science, PE/TE p. 567

ART

Interpret Fine Art, TE pp. 530–531

Create a Mural, TE p. 564

Paint a Setting, TE p. 589

MUSIC / DRAMA

Red River Valley, PE/TE p. 588

 Look for this symbol throughout the Teacher's Edition to find **Curriculum Connections.**

Professional Development

Curriculum, Instruction, and Assessment

by James B. Kracht, Ph.D.
Texas A & M University

One of the most important principles of an effective teaching-learning system is that curriculum, instruction, and assessment must be tightly joined and fully aligned. If instruction is not focused on the curriculum or if assessment does not match the curriculum, students will not be able to demonstrate their mastery of what was to be learned, either because they were not taught the content or the content has not been assessed. Careful alignment of curriculum, instruction, and assessment, however, can reveal areas of student mastery and areas in which additional instruction is necessary.

Assessment is co-equal in importance to curriculum and instruction in an effective teaching-learning system. Both teachers and students benefit from the process of assessment, and their experiences can be positive if assessment receives as much attention as curriculum and instruction, especially at higher cognitive levels. Below are ways *Scott Foresman Social Studies* incorporates assessment into this program:

- *Each unit includes Formal and Informal Assessments. The Ongoing Assessments, which are found throughout the units, provide reteaching and enrichment suggestions.*

- *Portfolio Assessments include a Link to Current Events as well as Curriculum Connections.*

- *The Performance Assessment evaluates students' mastery through a Hands-on Unit Project.*

- *Test Talk helps you prepare your students for high-stakes testing. Questions throughout the Teacher's Edition focus on different test-taking strategies.*

ESL Support

by Jim Cummins, Ph.D.
University of Toronto

In Unit 8, you can use the following fundamental strategy to help ESL students expand their language abilities:

Extend Language

Many ESL students who have acquired fluent conversational skills are still a long way from grade-level performance in academic language proficiency (e.g., reading comprehension). Similarly, ESL (and native-speaking) students who can "read" English fluently may have only a very limited understanding of the words they can decode.

In short, academic language proficiency does not automatically develop on the basis of either students' conversational fluency in English or their knowledge of discrete language skills. Learning academic language requires specific instructional strategies.

The following examples in the Teacher's Edition will help you to extend the language abilities of ESL students:

- ***Examine Compound Words*** *on p. 539 helps students understand meanings of words by studying the two words that make up a compound word.*

- ***Multiple-Meaning Words*** *on p. 555 asks students to examine words with more than one meaning. Students act out word meanings, write them in sentences, or discuss their meanings.*

Read Aloud

from *The Promised Land* by Mary Antin

. . . I am only one of many whose fate has been to live a page of modern history. We are the strands of the cable that binds the Old World to the New. As the ships that brought us link the shores of Europe and America, so our lives span the bitter sea of racial differences and misunderstandings. Before we came, the New World knew not the Old; but since we have begun to come, the Young World has taken the Old by the hand, and the two are learning to march side by side, seeking a common destiny . . . .

Build Background

- Mary Antin immigrated to the United States from Russia in 1894. She learned firsthand of the difficulties immigrants faced in the New World.

- This text is from the Introduction of Antin's autobiography *The Promised Land.* She saw herself as two different people—the young woman who grew up in Russia, and the person who struggled for success in the United States.

- Another quotation from Mary Antin can be found on p. 531. Her biography is on p. 575.

Definition

- *destiny:* events that are certain to happen to a person

Read Alouds and Primary Sources

- *Read Alouds and Primary Sources* contains additional selections to be used with Unit 8.

Bibliography

New Land: A First Year on the Prairie, by Marilynn Reynolds (Orca Books, ISBN 1-551-43071-1, 1999) **Easy**

Pony Express!, by Steven Kroll (Scholastic Incorporated, ISBN 0-590-20240-5, 2000) **Easy**

Ten Mile Day: The Building of the Transcontinental Railroad, by Mary Ann Fraser (Henry Holt & Co., ISBN 0-805-04703-4, 1996) **Easy**

Andrew Carnegie: Builder of Libraries, by Charnan Simon (Children's Press, ISBN 0-516-20289-8, 1997) **On-Level**

Ellis Island: A True Book, by Patricia R. Quiri (Children's Press, ISBN 0-516-20622-2, 1998) **On-Level**

Industry & Business (Life in America 100 Years Ago Series), by Linda Leuzzi (Chelsea House Publishers, ISBN 0-791-02846-1, 1997) **On-Level**

Legendary Labor Leaders, by Thomas Streissguth (Oliver Press, ISBN 1-881-50844-7, 1998) **Challenge**

Sitting Bull and His World, by Albert Marrin (Dutton, ISBN 0-525-45944-8, 2000) **Challenge NCSS Notable Book**

Soldier Boy, by Brian Burks (Harcourt Brace, ISBN 0-152-01219-2, 1997) **Challenge**

The Great Migrations: 1880s–1912, by William L. Katz (Steck-Vaughn Company, ISBN 0-811-42915-6, 1996) **Teacher reference**

Nothing Like It in the World: The Men Who Built the Transcontinental Railroad, 1863–1869, by Stephen E. Ambrose (Simon & Schuster, ISBN 0-684-84609-8, 2000) **Teacher reference**

The Prairies & Their People, by David Flint (Raintree, ISBN 0-817-24673-8, 1994) **Teacher reference**

Discovery Channel School Video *The Real American Cowboy* Learn about the real life of the American cowboy: It was tough and lonely. 26 minutes.

Look for this symbol throughout the Teacher's Edition to find **Award-Winning Selections.** Additional book references are suggested throughout this unit.

Expansion and Change

UNIT 8

Why do immigrants come to the United States?

Expansion and Change

Unit Overview

In the late 1800s a transcontinental railroad influenced settlement of the Western United States, and friction developed between Native Americans and the settlers. Technology brought many changes, and immigrants from all over the world came to the United States.

Unit Outline

Chapter 16 *Crossing the Continent*
pp. 536–559

Chapter 17 *Industry and Immigration*
pp. 560–587

Unit Question

- Have students read the question under the painting.

- To activate prior knowledge, ask students what rights we have as U.S. citizens.

- Create a list of reasons why people today decide to move from other countries to the United States.

- ✓**Portfolio Assessment** Keep this list to review with students at the end of the unit on p. 591.

Practice and Extend

Hands-on Unit Project

The First Telephone

✓ **Unit 8 Performance Assessment**

- The Unit Project, *Invention Conventions,* found on p. 592, is an ongoing performance assessment project to enrich students' learning throughout the unit.

- This project, which has students creating advertisements of an invention's features and benefits, may be started now or at any time during this unit of study.

- A performance assessment scoring guide is located on p. 592.

Begin with a Primary Source

Objective
• Use primary sources to acquire information.

Resource
• Poster 16

Interpret a Primary Source

• Tell students that this primary source is a quotation from the autobiography of Mary Antin, a Russian immigrant.

• **Why did many immigrants look upon the United States as a land of promise?** Many immigrants came to the United States seeking a better life for themselves and their families.

• Tell students that the Read Aloud from p. 529h was also from Mary Antin's autobiography *The Promised Land.*

• ✓**Portfolio Assessment** Remind students of the list they created of reasons why people today decide to move to the United States (see p. 529). Have students keep a list of the reasons people immigrated to the United States in the late 1800s and at the turn of the century as they read the unit. Review students' lists at the end of the unit on p. 591.

Interpret Fine Art

• Point out that *First View of the Lady* is based on painter Mort Künstler's idea of what a group of immigrants looked like as they saw the Statue of Liberty for the very first time.

• Have students discuss what they think the immigrants might have been thinking as the statue came into view.

• Have students look at the people's faces and explain what the expressions tell about their first impression of the New World.

530 Unit 8 • Expansion and Change

1860			1870			
	1862 Congress passes Homestead Act	1867 United States buys Alaska from Russia	1869 Transcontinental railroad completed	March 1876 Alexander Graham Bell invents the telephone	June 1876 Lakota defeat Custer at Battle of Little Bighorn	
530		①	②	③		

Practice and Extend

FYI SOCIAL STUDIES **Background**

About the Primary Source

• The primary source above—the quotation from *The Promised Land*—tells what Mary Antin and other immigrants thought and felt when they first caught a glimpse of the United States.

• Antin wrote books about the experiences and dreams she and other immigrants had when they came to the United States.

• Antin also gave lectures about immigration and fought against proposals to impose restrictions on immigration into the United States.

"Our eyes beheld the Promised Land"

—Written by Mary Antin in *The Promised Land*, published in 1912

Artist Mort Künstler's painting "First View of the Lady" shows new immigrants seeing the Statue of Liberty for the first time.

1890 1900

American
rs establish town
demus, Kansas

1889
Jane Addams opens
Hull House in Chicago

1898
Spanish American
War ends with United
States victory

531

Meet the Artist

- Mort Künstler's body of work includes numerous paintings of historic subjects. Künstler often focuses on Civil War subject matter.

- *First View of the Lady* is part of the artist's Ellis Island series, which also includes the paintings *Freedom* and *Ellis Island—Main Hall*.

- Künstler has exhibited his work in New York, Virginia, and in galleries and museums across the United States.

Use the Time Line

The time line at the bottom of the page shows the dates for some major events that led to changes and expansion of the United States in the late 1800s.

1 **Which event resulted in a large expansion of the United States territories?** United States buys Alaska from Russia Main Idea and Details

2 **How many years after the Homestead Act was passed was the transcontinental railroad completed?** About seven years Analyze Information

3 **What event on the time line do you think helped increase communication capabilities around the country?** Alexander Graham Bell invents the telephone Draw Conclusions

---

CURRICULUM CONNECTION
Writing

Write a Letter

- Have students suppose that they are one of the immigrants aboard the ship in the painting *First View of the Lady*.

- Ask students to write a letter to a friend who still lives in their homeland. They should describe what they see and what they believe might happen when they arrive on land.

Meet the People

Objective

- Identify the contributions of significant individuals in the United States during the late 1800s.

Resource

- Poster 17

Research the People

Each of the people pictured on these pages played an important part in changes that occurred in the United States during the late 1800s. Have students do research to find out the answers to the following questions.

- **What were some of the causes to which Andrew Carnegie donated money?** Possible answer: Improvement of universities; building libraries, theaters, and child-welfare centers; scientific research

- **What was the name of the movement against annexation of the Hawaiian islands and headed by Liliuokalani?** "Oni pa'a" or "Stand Firm" movement

- **What was the name of the man who helped Bell in experiments for transmitting sound by electricity?** Thomas Watson

- **What colleges did Theodore Roosevelt attend?** Harvard and Columbia Law School

Students may wish to write their own questions about other people on these pages for the rest of the class to answer.

Use the Time Line

Have students use the time line and biographies to answer the following questions.

1 **Which two people were born in the Northeast?** Lewis Latimer and Theodore Roosevelt Analyze Information

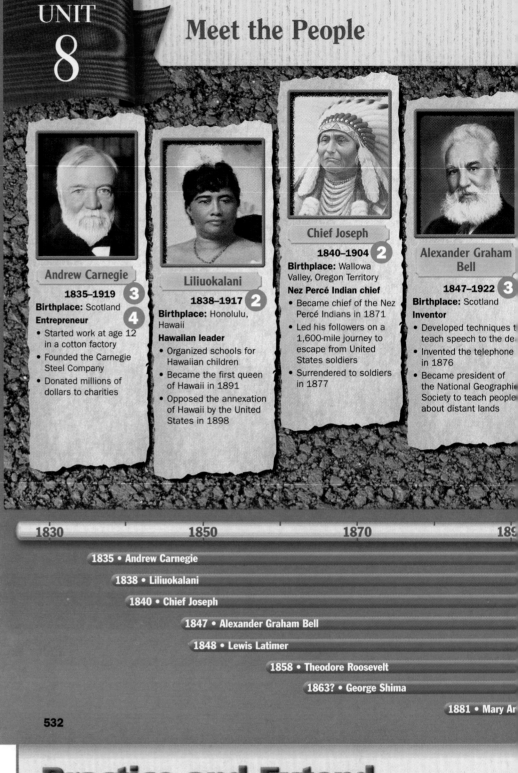

UNIT

8

Meet the People

Andrew Carnegie

1835–1919 **3**

Birthplace: Scotland

Entrepreneur **4**

- Started work at age 12 in a cotton factory
- Founded the Carnegie Steel Company
- Donated millions of dollars to charities

Liliuokalani

1838–1917 **2**

Birthplace: Honolulu, Hawaii

Hawaiian leader

- Organized schools for Hawaiian children
- Became the first queen of Hawaii in 1891
- Opposed the annexation of Hawaii by the United States in 1898

Chief Joseph

1840–1904 **2**

Birthplace: Wallowa Valley, Oregon Territory

Nez Percé Indian chief

- Became chief of the Nez Percé Indians in 1871
- Led his followers on a 1,600-mile journey to escape from United States soldiers
- Surrendered to soldiers in 1877

Alexander Graham Bell

1847–1922 **3**

Birthplace: Scotland

Inventor

- Developed techniques t teach speech to the de
- Invented the telephone in 1876
- Became president of the National Geographic Society to teach people about distant lands

1830   1850   1870   189

1835 • Andrew Carnegie

1838 • Liliuokalani

1840 • Chief Joseph

1847 • Alexander Graham Bell

1848 • Lewis Latimer

1858 • Theodore Roosevelt

1863? • George Shima

1881 • Mary Ar

532

Practice and Extend

CURRICULUM CONNECTION
Literature

Read Biographies Use the following biography selections to extend the content.

Teddy Roosevelt: Young Rough Rider, by Edd Winfield Parks (Aladdin, ISBN 0-689-71349-5, 1989) **Easy**

The Story of Alexander Graham Bell: Inventor of the Telephone, by Margaret Davidson (Gareth Stevens Publishing, ISBN 0-836-81483-5, 1997) **On-Level**

Chief Joseph: Nez Perce Leader, by Marian W. Taylor (Chelsea House, ISBN 0-791-01708-7, 1993) **Challenge**

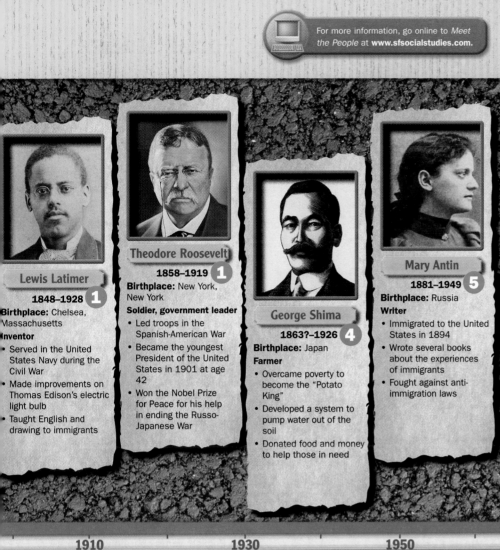

For more information, go online to *Meet the People* at **www.sfsocialstudies.com**.

Lewis Latimer
1848–1928 1
Birthplace: Chelsea, Massachusetts
Inventor
- Served in the United States Navy during the Civil War
- Made improvements on Thomas Edison's electric light bulb
- Taught English and drawing to immigrants

Theodore Roosevelt
1858–1919 1
Birthplace: New York, New York
Soldier, government leader
- Led troops in the Spanish-American War
- Became the youngest President of the United States in 1901 at age 42
- Won the Nobel Prize for Peace for his help in ending the Russo-Japanese War

George Shima
1863?–1926 4
Birthplace: Japan
Farmer
- Overcame poverty to become the "Potato King"
- Developed a system to pump water out of the soil
- Donated food and money to help those in need

Mary Antin
1881–1949 5
Birthplace: Russia
Writer
- Immigrated to the United States in 1894
- Wrote several books about the experiences of immigrants
- Fought against anti-immigration laws

2 **What is one thing that Liliuokalani and Chief Joseph have in common?** They were both leaders of their people. Compare and Contrast

3 **Describe one similarity between Andrew Carnegie and Alexander Graham Bell.** Both were born in Scotland. Compare and Contrast

4 **Which two people donated food or money to others?** Andrew Carnegie and George Shima Analyze Information

5 **Which person lived until approximately the middle of the twentieth century?** Mary Antin Interpret Time Lines

Biographies

Three of the people shown here are discussed more extensively in the Biography pages in Unit 8.

- George Shima, p. 553
- Mary Antin, p. 575
- Theodore Roosevelt, p. 583

Read About the People

The people shown here are discussed in the text on the following pages in Unit 8.

- Andrew Carnegie, p. 564
- Liliuokalani, p. 579
- Chief Joseph, p. 556
- Alexander Graham Bell, p. 563
- Lewis Latimer, p. 563
- Theodore Roosevelt, pp. PE 580, 582, 583
- George Shima, pp. PE 552, 553
- Mary Antin, pp. PE 569, 575

WEB SITE
Technology

Students can research the lives of people on this page by clicking on *Meet the People* at **www.sfsocialstudies.com**.

Objective

Analyze information by sequencing events.

Resource

- Workbook, p. 123

About the Unit Target Skill

- The target reading skill for this unit is Sequence.
- Students are introduced to the unit target skill here and are given an opportunity to practice it.
- Further opportunities to use sequence are found throughout Unit 8.

1 Introduce and Motivate

Preview To activate prior knowledge, ask students to sequence a series of events from previous units in the textbook. (For example, Britain imposed the Stamp Tax in 1765; colonists protested, and Britain had it repealed in 1766; in 1767 the Parliament passed the Townshend Acts, placing a tariff on British goods; colonists boycotted British goods; in 1770 the Townshend Acts were repealed.)

2 Teach and Discuss

- Explain that a sequence is a logical order of events. In history, events take place in a particular order. As students read about these events, suggest that they look for clues such as dates and words that indicate order (e.g., *first, then, after*).

Expansion and Change
Sequence

When you read about history, it is important to understand the sequence, or order, in which events took place.

- Dates can be used to establish sequence.
- Clue words such as *first* or *before* can also indicate sequence.
- If there are no dates or clue words, you can figure out sequence by reading closely to determine the writer's intention.

Dates and clue phrases are highlighted in **yellow.** Sequences without clue phrases are highlighted in **blue.**

Even before the Civil War ended, the United States began to build railroads across the country. The first cross-country railroad was started in 1862. It was completed in 1869, when the eastern and western branches met at Promontory Point, Utah. Railroad travel began to replace travel by ship and by wagon or stagecoach.

Word Exercise

Word Roots Some English words contain word roots borrowed from other languages. A word root has the same meaning in every word it is part of. Knowing the meanings of word roots can help you figure out the meanings of the words they are in. The word *telegraph* contains the word roots *tele* and *graph*.

| tele "far" | + | graph "writing" | = | **telegraph** "system for sending written messages over long distances" |

534

Practice and Extend

 ACCESS CONTENT
ESL Support

Write a Sequence Have students write a sequence to describe how to do or make something.

Beginning Have students tell with words and gestures how to do something they are familiar with, such as play a game or solve a math problem. Ask them to emphasize what comes first, second, next, last, and so on.

Intermediate Ask students to write a sequence of directions about the activity above as a numbered list.

Advanced Have students write a paragraph that describes how to do or make something. Tell them to make sure the paragraph follows a logical sequence and uses clue words to describe the order.

Expansion and Change: A Sequence of Events

Before the Civil War ended, the nation began to build a railroad across the land. One company built tracks west from Omaha, Nebraska. Another company built tracks east from Sacramento, California. The two met at Promontory Point, Utah Territory, on May 10, 1869.

At the same time, people were working to speed communications. In 1860, the Pony Express shortened time for mail to cross the country. Telegraph lines were built the following year and replaced the Pony Express. In time, the telephone would replace the telegraph.

The government provided land on the Great Plains to people who would farm. American Indians worried about the

changes. Non-natives killed buffalo and moved onto Indian Territory.

Immigrants arrived from many countries. Earlier immigrants came mainly from northern and western Europe. Newer immigrants came from eastern and southern Europe.

Some immigrants farmed land or worked in coal mines. Others settled in cities and worked at jobs such as steel-making and sewing clothing. Many worked long hours for little pay. Workers joined labor unions to demand better working conditions. After many years of struggle, workers won shorter hours and safer workplaces.

The nation also gained territory. It bought Alaska in 1867. In 1898, it gained Hawaii.

Use the reading strategy of sequence to answer questions 1 and 2. Then answer the vocabulary question.

1 In what sequence did the following appear: the telegraph, telephone, Pony Express?

2 Was Alaska acquired before or after Hawaii?

3 Find another word in the selection that starts with *tele*. Use a graphic organizer like the one on page 534 to show the word roots and their meanings, along with the meaning of the word. Look up the word in a dictionary to check your work.

535

- Have students read the sample paragraph on p. 534. Make sure they can recognize that the phrases highlighted in yellow contain clues and the blue highlighted phrases are sequences without clues.

- Then have students read the longer practice sample on p. 535 and answer the questions that follow.

- Ask students why it is important to understand the sequence of events when reading about history. (Understanding the order in which events took place can help you understand how they are related.)

Word Roots

Ask students if they can think of other words that begin with *tele. (telegram, television)* Have them chart these words the way *telegraph* is charted on p. 534. Ask them to consider what *phonograph* means, based on what they learned about telephone and telegraph ("sound writing"). Have students think of other words they know that use the roots *graph* or *phono.* (graphics, phonics, autograph, and so on)

3 Close and Assess

Apply it!

1. The Pony Express came first, then the telegraph, and later the telephone.

2. Alaska was acquired before Hawaii.

3. *Telephone* is a word combining *tele* or "far" with *phono* or "sound." It is a machine that can send sound over long distances

---

Standardized Test Prep

- Use Workbook p. 123 to give students practice with standardized test format.

- Chapter and Unit Tests in the Assessment Book use standardized test format.

- Test-taking tips are contained in the front portion of the Assessment Book Teacher's Edition.

Also on Teacher Resources CD-ROM.

Workbook, p. 123

Chapter Planning Guide

Chapter 16 • Crossing the Continent

Locating Time and Place pp. 536–537

Lesson Titles	Pacing	Main Ideas
Lesson 1 **Rails Across the Nation** pp. 538–541	2 days	• After years of hard work, the first railroad across the United States was completed in 1869.
Map and Globe Skills: Read a Time Zone Map pp. 542–543 **Colonial Williamsburg: Westward Growth of America, 1607–1862** pp. 544–545		• A time zone map shows the different times in the time zones on Earth. • Overcoming physical constraints and using technological advances, people moved west and the nation expanded.
Lesson 2 **Farmers and Cowboys** pp. 546–552	2 days	• Following the Civil War, farmers and cowboys helped the Great Plains become an important farming and ranching region.
Biography: George Shima p. 553		• A Japanese immigrant named George Shima came to the United States a poor man and became wealthy by creating a successful potato-farming empire.
Lesson 3 **War in the West** pp. 554–557	1 day	• In the 1860s and 1870s, many Native American groups fought to maintain control of their traditional lands.

✓ **Chapter 16 Review**
pp. 558–559

◀ **Nat Love became a cowboy when he was only fifteen.**

✓ = Assessment Options

◄ In 1860, the Pony Express was the fastest way to send mail.

Vocabulary	Resources	Meeting Individual Needs
Pony Express Telegraph Transcontinental railroad Time zone Standard time	• Workbook, p. 125 • Transparencies 10, 56, 57 • Every Student Learns Guide, pp. 222–225 • Quick Study, pp. 112–113 • Workbook, p. 126 • Workbook, p. 127	• ESL Support, TE p. 539 • Leveled Practice, TE p. 540
Homestead Act Homesteaders Sodbusters Exodusters Cattle drives Barbed wire	• Workbook, p. 128 • Transparency 11 • Every Student Learns Guide, pp. 226–229 • Quick Study, pp. 114–115	• ESL Support, TE p. 548 • Learning Styles, TE p. 550 • Leveled Practice, TE p. 551
Reservation Battle of Little Bighorn	• Workbook, p. 129 • Transparencies 10, 58 • Every Student Learns Guide, pp. 230–233 • Quick Study, pp. 116–117	• ESL Support, TE p. 555 • Leveled Practice, TE p. 556
	✓ Chapter 16 Content Test, Assessment Book, pp. 93–94 ✓ Chapter 16 Skills Test, Assessment Book, pp. 95–96	✓ Chapter 16 Performance Assessment, TE p. 558

Providing More Depth

Additional Resources
- Vocabulary Workbook and Cards
- Social Studies Plus! pp. 188–193
- Daily Activity Bank
- Big Book Atlas
- Student Atlas
- Outline Maps
- Desk Maps

- AudioText
- MindPoint® Quiz Show CD-ROM
- ExamView® Test Bank CD-ROM
- Teacher Resources CD-ROM
- Map Resources CD-ROM
- SFSuccessNet: iText (Pupil Edition online), iTE (Teacher's Edition online), Online Planner
- **www.sfsocialstudies.com** (Biographies, news, references, maps, and activities)

 To establish guidelines for your students' safe and responsible use of the Internet, use the Scott Foresman Internet Guide.

Additional Internet Links

To find out more about:
- The transcontinental railroad, visit **www.pbs.org**
- African American homesteaders, visit **www.loc.gov**
- Lakota Indians, visit **www.lakotastory.org**

Key Internet Search Terms
- transcontinental railroad
- homesteader
- cattle drive
- American West
- Great Plains

Workbook Support

Use the following Workbook pages to support content and skills development as you teach Chapter 16. You can also view and print Workbook pages from the Teacher Resources CD-ROM.

Workbook, p. 123

Sequence

Use with Pages 534–535.

Directions: Fill in the circle next to the correct answer.

The United States began expanding westward during the 1800s. This expansion brought change to many people and parts of the nation.

As an increasing number of settlers moved west, the need for cross-country transportation and communication grew. Settlers on the frontier did not want to be isolated from friends and family back East.

Several new services were created to meet this need. First was the Pony Express. It lasted about a year until the first cross-country telegraph line was completed. A year later, in 1862, construction of the transcontinental railroad began.

At the same time the nation was laying railroad ties to link the East and West, the Homestead Act was encouraging people to settle the Midwest. The Homestead Act

gave land to settlers. In 1877 many African American pioneers took advantage of the Homestead Act and settled Nicodemus, Kansas. Nicodemus became a bustling town and still lives on today as a symbol of freedom and opportunity.

In the Great Plains, Native Americans found their lives changing. In 1868 the U.S. government moved the Lakota people to the Great Lakota Reservation, an area that included the Black Hills. Just six years later, gold was found in the Black Hills, and the U.S. government again tried to move the Lakota. The Lakota refused to leave and defeated the United States in 1876 at the Battle of Little Bighorn, also known as Custer's Last Stand. One year later, the Lakota were defeated and moved to a new reservation.

1. Which of the following happened first?
● Lakota moved to the Great Lakota Reservation
Ⓑ Nicodemus founded
Ⓒ gold discovered in Black Hills
Ⓓ Lakota defeated U.S. military

2. Which of the following shows the correct sequence of events?
Ⓐ Nicodemus founded, Lakota Reservation created
Ⓑ Battle of Little Bighorn, Pony Express established
Ⓒ Lakota move to new lands, railroad construction begins
● Custer's Last Stand, African American pioneers found Nicodemus

Notes for Home: Your child learned how to sequence events that took place during the expansion of the United States.
Home Activity: Ask your child whether he or she would have liked to have lived during the time when the country was growing and technology was developing. Discuss why or why not.

Use with Pupil Edition, p. 535

Workbook, p. 124

Vocabulary Preview

Use with Chapter 16.

Directions: Match each word with its meaning. Write the vocabulary word on the line next to its meaning. You may use your glossary.

Pony Express	Homestead Act	exoduster	reservation
telegraph	homesteader	cattle drive	Battle of Little Bighorn
transcontinental railroad	sodbuster	barbed wire	

1. __Pony Express__ business in which mail was delivered by express riders on horseback

2. __barbed wire__ twisted wire with sharp points used by homesteaders to keep cattle off their farmland

3. __Homestead Act__ government plan that offered free land to pioneers willing to start new farms on the Great Plains

4. __Battle of Little Bighorn__ Lakota defeat of General George Custer's U.S. troops

5. __cattle drive__ cowboys moving herds of cattle north to the railroad lines that extended across the Great Plains

6. __exoduster__ an African American pioneer who started a new life in Kansas or Nebraska

7. __homesteader__ a settler who claimed land through the Homestead Act

8. __reservation__ an area of land set aside for Native Americans

9. __sodbuster__ a Great Plains farmer who had to dig through the tough sod before planting crops

10. __telegraph__ replaced the Pony Express and sent messages along wires using electricity

11. __transcontinental railroad__ railroad that crossed the continent

Notes for Home: Your child learned about changes that occurred as the United States expanded.
Home Activity: Have your child practice the vocabulary words by using them in sentences of his or her own.

Use with Pupil Edition, p. 536

Workbook, p. 125

Lesson 1: Rails Across the Nation

Use with Pages 538–541.

Directions: Circle the answer that best completes each sentence.

1. In the 1850s thousands of miles of (railroad tracks, paved highways) crisscrossed the East.

2. The journey to the West by wagon or by ship could take (two weeks, months).

3. (Stagecoach, Pony Express) riders traveled in a horse-drawn wagon that traveled in stages, or short sections.

4. The (wagon train, Pony Express) delivered mail faster than was possible by stagecoach.

5. The (telegraph, stagecoach) put the Pony Express out of business.

6. Messages were sent along electrical wires in the form of (Navajo Code, Morse Code).

7. People were interested in building the (transcontinental railroad, stagecoach) to move people and goods across the nation.

8. Central Pacific workers began building tracks heading (east, west).

9. Both the Central Pacific and the Union Pacific had difficulties finding enough (workers, machines) for the huge project.

10. Union Pacific workers were challenged by (Native Americans, buffalo) when the tracks crossed hunting areas.

11. The railroad was completed when the tracks laid by Central Pacific and Union Pacific workers met at (Promontory Point, Salt Lake City) in Utah Territory.

Directions: Sequence the events below by drawing a line from each date in the first column to an event from that year in the second column.

1858	a. transcontinental railroad construction begins
1860	b. stagecoach travel begins
1861	c. transcontinental railroad is completed
1862	d. Pony Express delivery begins
1869	e. transcontinental telegraph communication begins

Notes for Home: Your child learned about early travel to the West and the building of the transcontinental railroad.
Home Activity: With your child, sequence the events involved in building the transcontinental railroad.

Use with Pupil Edition, p. 541

Workbook, p. 126

Time Zone Map

Use with Pages 542–543.

A time zone map tells you in what time zone a place is located. With this information you can figure out the time in other places across the country. Regardless of where you live, zones to the east of you are later than the zone in which you are located. Zones to the west of you are earlier.

Directions: Use the time zone map below to answer the questions that follow.

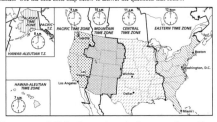

1. Suppose you were in Wichita, Kansas, and wanted to share some good news with your brother in Boston, Massachusetts. He gets home from work at 5:30 P.M. At what time might you place a call from your time zone to reach him at home after work?

Ⓐ 2:30 P.M.   Ⓑ 2:45 P.M.   Ⓒ 3:45 P.M.   ● 4:45 P.M.

2. Bus, train, and airplane schedules list departure and arrival times according to the city in which each action takes place. Suppose you live in Dallas, Texas, and a relative is visiting from Los Angeles, California. The plane is scheduled to land in Dallas at 3:00 P.M. What time will it be in Los Angeles, when the plane lands in Dallas?

Ⓐ 12:00 P.M.   ● 1:00 P.M.   Ⓒ 4:00 P.M.   Ⓓ 5:00 P.M.

3. Suppose you live in Las Vegas, Nevada, and you want to watch a live TV broadcast from Washington, D.C., scheduled to begin at 7:00 P.M. D.C. time. At what time should you tune in to the broadcast?

● 4:00 P.M.   Ⓑ 6:00 P.M.   Ⓒ 9:00 P.M.   Ⓓ 10:00 P.M.

4. Suppose you used an overnight delivery service to send a package from your home in Seattle, Washington, to a friend in Miami, Florida. The service promises to deliver the package by 10:00 A.M. Florida time. At what time can you call from Seattle to make sure your friend has received the package?

Ⓐ 1:00 A.M.   ● 7:00 A.M.   Ⓒ 12:00 P.M.   Ⓓ 1:00 P.M.

Notes for Home: Your child learned about time zones.
Home Activity: With your child, practice calculating time in other time zones. You may wish to use TV shows, travel schedules, or phone calls as examples.

Use with Pupil Edition, p. 543

Workbook Support

Workbook, p. 127

Writing Prompt: Leaving Home

Long ago, the United States grew as Americans traveled westward. Many people left home for the first time to settle in a new place. Think about your first time away from home. How did you feel? What did you see? Write a paragraph to tell about it.

Answers will vary.

_____

_____

_____

_____

_____

_____

_____

_____

_____

_____

_____

_____

_____

_____

_____

_____

 Notes for Home: Your child learned about transportation changes and westward expansion.
Home Activity: With your child, discuss some of the reasons people move. Compare and contrast reasons for moving today and long ago.

Use with Pupil Edition, p. 545

Workbook, p. 128

Lesson 2: Farmers and Cowboys

Use with Pages 546–552.

Directions: Answer the clues below. Then find and circle the answers in the puzzle. Answers may appear horizontally, vertically, or diagonally in the puzzle.

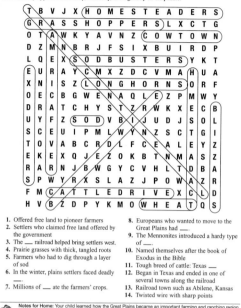

1. Offered free land to pioneer farmers
2. Settlers who claimed free land offered by the government
3. The ___ railroad helped bring settlers west.
4. Prairie grasses with thick, tangled roots
5. Farmers who had to dig through a layer of sod
6. In the winter, plains settlers faced deadly ___.
7. Millions of ___ ate the farmers' crops.
8. Europeans who wanted to move to the Great Plains had ___.
9. The Mennonites introduced a hardy type of ___.
10. Named themselves after the book of Exodus in the Bible
11. Tough breed of cattle: Texas ___
12. Began in Texas and ended in one of several towns along the railroad
13. Railroad town such as Abilene, Kansas
14. Twisted wire with sharp points

 Notes for Home: Your child learned how the Great Plains became an important farming and ranching region.
Home Activity: Discuss with your child that people had to weigh the pros and cons of leaving their homes and moving west. Together, create a chart listing the pros and cons of moving to the Great Plains during the mid-1800s.

Use with Pupil Edition, p. 552

Workbook, p. 129

Lesson 3: War in the West

Use with Pages 554–557.

Directions: Sequence the events in the order in which they occurred. Number the events from 1 (earliest) to 10 (most recent). You may use your textbook.

7 United States soldiers march into the Black Hills hoping to defeat the Lakota and move them onto a new reservation.

3 Government leaders want to move Native Americans onto reservations to make room for expanding railroad lines and new farms, ranches, and mines.

1 Railroads bring many settlers to the Great Plains. Farmers and ranchers begin fencing their land, and herds of buffalo begin to disappear.

4 The United States and the Lakota sign a treaty creating the Great Lakota Reservation, which includes the Black Hills.

6 The United States offers to buy land from the Lakota, but the Lakota refuse to sell.

10 Native American writers and filmmakers continue to tell stories about their people's history and way of life.

8 General Custer and his troops attack the Lakota, and all are killed in a battle known as the Battle of Little Bighorn.

2 Native Americans see that their traditional way of life is being threatened.

9 The Nez Percé surrender to the United States after being chased for 1,600 miles.

5 Gold is found in the Black Hills, and miners illegally rush onto Lakota land.

Directions: Complete the cause-and-effect chart below.

Cause	Effect
Buffalo were hunted for their hides, for sport, and to feed railroad workers.	**Possible answer: The buffalo herds began to disappear, threatening the Native Americans' way of life.**
Possible answer: United States soldiers were sent to capture the Nez Percé and take them to a reservation.	The Nez Percé fled and were pursued for three months by United States soldiers.

 **Notes for Home:** Your child learned about struggles between Native Americans and the United States government as the West was settled.
Home Activity: With your child, discuss the causes and effects of the wars between the Native Americans and the U.S. government. Discuss what major changes were forced on Native Americans.

Use with Pupil Edition, p. 557

Workbook, p. 130

Vocabulary Review

Use with Chapter 16.

Directions: Choose the vocabulary word below that best completes each sentence. Write the word on the line provided.

Pony Express	homesteader	barbed wire
telegraph	sodbuster	reservation
transcontinental railroad	exoduster	Battle of Little Bighorn
Homestead Act	cattle drive	

1. Two companies built the **transcontinental railroad** to connect the country by rail.

2. An African American pioneer who started a new life in Kansas or Nebraska was an **exoduster**.

3. **Barbed wire** is used by farmers to create inexpensive fences to keep cattle off their farmland.

4. The government offered the **Homestead Act**, granting free land to pioneers willing to start new farms on the Great Plains.

5. Native Americans were moved to a **reservation**, or land set aside by the government.

6. The **Pony Express** made mail delivery faster than by stagecoach.

7. U.S. General George Custer was killed in the **Battle of Little Bighorn**.

8. A farmer on the Great Plains was known as a **sodbuster** because of the tough soil in that area.

9. Cowboys participated in a **cattle drive** to get their cattle north to the railroad lines.

10. A **homesteader** was someone who took advantage of the government plan to grant land to settlers who would farm the Great Plains.

11. With the invention of the **telegraph**, messages were sent along wires using electricity.

Notes for Home: Your child learned about changes that occurred as the nation expanded.
Home Activity: Practice the vocabulary words by having a spelling bee or a definition bee involving several friends or family members.

Use with Pupil Edition, p. 559

Assessment Support

 Use these Assessment Book pages and the ExamView® Test Bank CD-ROM to assess content and skills in Chapter 16. You can also view and print Assessment Book pages from the Teacher Resources CD-ROM.

Assessment Book, p. 93

Chapter 16 Test

Part 1: Content Test

Directions: Fill in the circle next to the correct answer.

Lesson Objective (1:2)

1. Why did people prefer the telegraph to the Pony Express?
   - Ⓐ It lasted longer.
   - Ⓑ Messages were safer.
   - Ⓒ Fewer people were needed.
   - ● It was faster.

Lesson Objective (1:1)

2. What did the transcontinental railroad do that the telegraph could not?
   - Ⓐ carry messages across the country
   - ● carry people and goods across the country
   - Ⓒ allow communication
   - Ⓓ use electric lines

Lesson Objective (1:1)

3. Why were people eager to build the transcontinental railroad?
   - ● It would link the East and West.
   - Ⓑ It would carry goods to the East.
   - Ⓒ It was faster than the telegraph.
   - Ⓓ It was cheaper than horses.

Lesson Objective (1:3)

4. What problem did Central Pacific workers face while building the railroad?
   - Ⓐ There were too many people who wanted to work.
   - ● They had to blast tunnels through the mountains.
   - Ⓒ Native American villages were in the way.
   - Ⓓ The buffalo refused to move.

Lesson Objective (1:3)

5. Which of the following BEST describes problems faced by Union Pacific workers?
   - ● They came into conflict with Native Americans.
   - Ⓑ The mountains were difficult to cross.
   - Ⓒ It was hard to get the buffalo to move out of the way.
   - Ⓓ The Lakota were poor workers.

Lesson Objective (1:4)

6. How did the transcontinental railroad change life in the United States?
   - Ⓐ People stopped settling new lands.
   - Ⓑ The Pony Express was no longer needed.
   - ● People and goods could travel across the country in just a few days.
   - Ⓓ People no longer traveled by stagecoach.

Lesson Objective (2:1)

7. Why was the Homestead Act necessary?
   - Ⓐ The government had too much land.
   - ● Few settlers had moved to the Great Plains.
   - Ⓒ Native Americans on the plains wanted neighbors.
   - Ⓓ There were too many buffalo.

Lesson Objective (2:2)

8. Which of the following does NOT describe the hardships of farming on the Great Plains?
   - Ⓐ The sod had to be broken to prepare fields for crops.
   - Ⓑ Shelters had to be built.
   - ● There was a lot of wheat to cut down.
   - Ⓓ The weather could be harsh.

Use with Pupil Edition, p. 558

Assessment Book, p. 94

Lesson Objective (2:3)

9. Why did many Europeans move to the Great Plains?
   - Ⓐ The land had run out at home.
   - Ⓑ They were fleeing from a war.
   - Ⓒ They wanted to sell the land later.
   - ● The promise of good land was attractive.

Lesson Objective (2:3)

10. Why did the exodusters go to the Great Plains?
    - ● They were making a journey to freedom.
    - Ⓑ They wanted to hunt buffalo.
    - Ⓒ They wanted to build a city.
    - Ⓓ They wanted to spread their religion.

Lesson Objective (2:4)

11. Why did cattle drives begin?
    - Ⓐ Ranchers began moving to the East.
    - Ⓑ There were too many cattle in Texas.
    - ● Ranchers wanted to get their cattle to the East.
    - Ⓓ Cowboys wanted to practice moving cattle.

Lesson Objective (2:4)

12. Which of the following helped bring an end to cattle drives?
    - Ⓐ Farmers in the East started to raise more cattle.
    - Ⓑ The cattle wouldn't eat the wheat grown on the Great Plains.
    - Ⓒ Cattle rustlers stole entire herds.
    - ● The railroad expanded to Texas.

Lesson Objective (3:1)

13. Which of the following describes how farmers and ranchers changed the Great Plains?
    - Ⓐ The land became difficult to farm.
    - ● Farmers and ranchers began fencing the land.
    - Ⓒ The area turned into a desert.
    - Ⓓ The area became an important buffalo preserve.

Lesson Objective (3:1)

14. Which of the following is NOT a way the transcontinental railroad changed the Great Plains?
    - Ⓐ Thousands of settlers moved there.
    - Ⓑ Settlers began fencing the land.
    - ● Many Native Americans took jobs with the railroad.
    - Ⓓ The buffalo began to disappear.

Lesson Objective (3:2)

15. How did many Native Americans react to changes to their homeland?
    - Ⓐ They helped the pioneers settle the land.
    - Ⓑ They chose to move away to new places.
    - Ⓒ They were eager to change and grow.
    - ● They fought for their land and way of life.

Lesson Objective (3:3)

16. What happened to both the Lakota and the Nez Percé during the 1870s?
    - Ⓐ Both became great friends of the U.S. government.
    - Ⓑ The U.S. government lost wars to both.
    - ● Both were forced to leave their homelands.
    - Ⓓ The U.S. government bought land from both.

Use with Pupil Edition, p. 558

Assessment Support

Part 2: Skills Test

Directions: Use complete sentences to answer questions 1–6. Use a separate sheet of paper if you need more space.

1. Describe in detail three methods of sending messages across the country during the 1860s. Sequence them in the order in which they were developed. **Sequence**

   Possible answers (in this order): Stagecoach—traveled in stages, carried people, goods, and messages; Pony Express— mail delivery system, young riders traveled 75 miles each; telegraph—sent Morse Code messages across electrical lines; transcontinental railroad—carried people, goods, and messages quickly across the country

2. Why did the Union Pacific and the Central Pacific race against each other while building the transcontinental railroad? How do you think the race affected workers' attitudes about the obstacles they faced? **Cause and Effect**

   Possible answers: Both companies were paid in land and money for every mile of track they completed, so both wanted to complete the most miles; Workers did not want anything to slow them down, so they overcame obstacles.

3. Why do you think the Great Plains region was known as the "Great American Desert"? **Draw Conclusions**

   Possible answer: It was a vast region of dry grassland that looked too harsh to settle.

4. What conditions made life difficult for homesteaders? What helped homesteaders survive? Give examples. **Compare and Contrast**

   Possible answers: Difficulties: Tough soil; harsh weather, including floods, droughts, prairie fires, blizzards, and grasshoppers; Aids to survival: Steel plow to cut sod, windmills to pump water, homesteaders' own determination

Use with Pupil Edition, p. 558

---

5. Why do you think Lakota leader Sitting Bull said "I do not want to sell any land to the government"? Explain. **Make Inferences**

   Possible answer: Sitting Bull probably did not trust or like the U.S. government because it had forced his people off their homeland and now wanted to take their new land from them.

6. What role did the buffalo play in the conflict between Native Americans and the United States government? **Main Idea and Details**

   Possible answer: The U.S. government helped kill off the buffalo that the Native Americans depended upon for survival. This created conflict between the two groups.

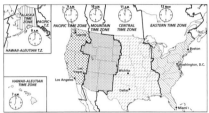

United States Time Zones

7. Use the map to answer the questions. **Read a Time Zone Map**

   a. How many times zones does the United States have? __**six**__

   b. What is the name of the time zone in which Seattle is located?

   Pacific time zone

   c. What time is it in Los Angeles and in Hawaii when it is 6:00 p.m. in Boston?

   9:00 p.m. in Los Angeles and 1:00 p.m. in Hawaii

Use with Pupil Edition, p. 558

Crossing the Continent

Chapter 16 Outline

Resources

- Workbook, p. 124: Vocabulary Preview
- Vocabulary Cards
- Social Studies Plus!

1869, Promontory Point, Utah Territory: Lesson 1

Tell students that a golden spike was hammered into the track to show that the transcontinental railroad was completed. Have them study the picture and suggest why this was such an important event. (Now people could travel much more quickly and easily from the East to the West, and goods could be shipped more efficiently.)

1877, Nicodemus, Kansas: Lesson 2

This picture shows a town that was established by African American pioneers. Ask students why this would not have been possible just fifteen years prior to 1877. (Fifteen years earlier slavery was still in effect and Kansas was a slave state.)

1877, Bear Paw Mountains, Montana Territory: Lesson 3

Tell students that the government forced Chief Joseph and the Nez Percé to give up their land after a long fight. Ask students to suggest why the Nez Percé may have chosen to surrender. (Possible answer: They were tired of fleeing and fighting.)

536 Unit 8 • Expansion and Change

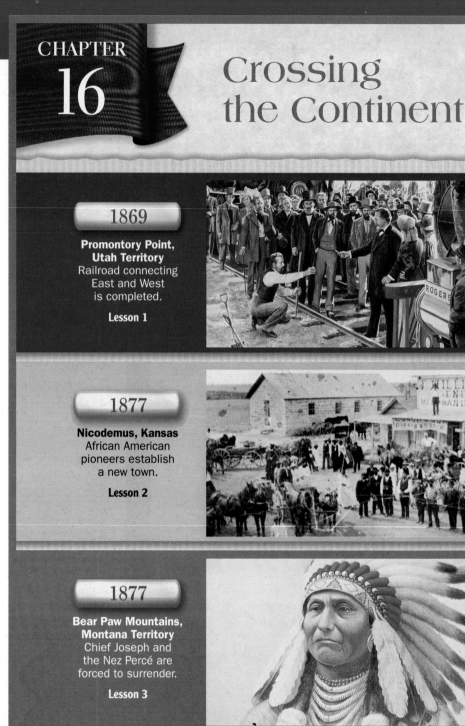

CHAPTER
16

Crossing the Continent

1869
Promontory Point, Utah Territory
Railroad connecting East and West is completed.
Lesson 1

1877
Nicodemus, Kansas
African American pioneers establish a new town.
Lesson 2

1877
Bear Paw Mountains, Montana Territory
Chief Joseph and the Nez Percé are forced to surrender.
Lesson 3

536

Practice and Extend

Vocabulary Preview

- Use Workbook p. 124 to help students preview the vocabulary words in this chapter.
- Use Vocabulary Cards to preview key concept words in this chapter.

 Also on Teacher Resources CD-ROM.

Workbook, p. 124

Locating Time and Place

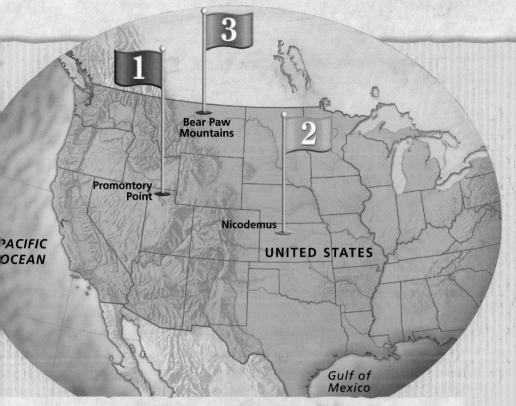

Locating Time and Place

- Have students examine the pictures shown on p. 536 for Lessons 1, 2, and 3.

- Remind students that each picture is coded with both a number and a color to link it to a place on the map on p. 537.

Why We Remember

Have students read the "Why We Remember" paragraph on p. 537, and ask them why events in this chapter might be important to them. Have them consider how the settlement of the United States might have differed if the railroad had not linked the two coasts.

Why We Remember

By the late 1860s, the map of the United States would have looked pretty familiar to you. Old and new states crowded the middle and eastern parts of the country from Canada to the Gulf of Mexico. Two new states, Oregon and California, formed a ribbon of land in the far west. The nation was coming together from East and West. Telegraph wires and railroad tracks were built across the open plains and mountains, linking the two parts of the growing country. Soon pioneers began to settle on this land. At the same time, Native Americans were being forced from their homes. The way of life of all Americans was being changed in ways no one could have predicted.

537

WEB SITE
Technology

You can learn more about Promontory Point, Utah Territory; Nicodemus, Kansas; and the Bear Paw Mountains, Montana Territory, by clicking on *Atlas* at **www.sfsocialstudies.com.**

SOCIAL STUDIES STRAND
Geography

Mental Mapping Have students draw an outline map of the United States from memory and label New York City, Chicago, St. Louis, and San Francisco. Have students work in pairs to plan a railroad across the continent that links all four cities. Remind students that they must take major landforms, such as rivers and mountain ranges, into account as they plan their routes.

Rails Across the Nation

Objectives

- Analyze the developments that helped link the East and the West.

- Explain why the telegraph replaced the Pony Express.

- Describe the difficulties faced in building the transcontinental railroad.

- Predict how the transcontinental railroad might change the United States.

Vocabulary

Pony Express, p. 539; **telegraph,** p. 539; **transcontinental railroad,** p. 539

Resources

- Workbook, p. 125
- Transparency 10
- Every Student Learns Guide, pp. 222–225
- Quick Study, pp. 112–113

Quick Teaching Plan

If time is short, have students make a three-column chart labeled *Before the Railroad, During Construction,* and *After Completion.*

- Have students fill in the first two columns with facts and events about the United States before and during the construction of the transcontinental railroad.

- In the third column, have students predict how the United States changed after the railroad was completed.

1 Introduce and Motivate

Preview To activate prior knowledge, ask students to tell about a long trip they have taken. Tell students that they will learn about changes in travel and communication in the United States as they read Lesson 1.

You Are There Before the transcontinental railroad was built, travel across the country was difficult. Ask students to predict changes the railroad might bring.

538 Unit 8 • Expansion and Change

LESSON 1

1860		1870

1861 First telegraph line crosses the nation

1862 Construction of transcontinental railroad begins

1869 Transcontinental railroad completed

Promontory Point
Sacramento • Omaha

PREVIEW

Focus on the Main Idea
After years of hard work, the first railroad across the United States was completed in 1869.

PLACES
Omaha, Nebraska
Sacramento, California
Promontory Point,
   Utah Territory

PEOPLE
Samuel Morse

VOCABULARY
Pony Express
telegraph
transcontinental railroad

WILLIAMSVILLE & EAST DOVER.

U.S. MAIL

538

Rails Across the Nation

You Are There

It is a burning hot July day in 1859. You are crammed into the back of a horse-drawn wagon, rattling across an endless prairie. You feel a little sick from the constant bouncing and swaying of the seat. And you are covered with dust and itching all over from some kind of bug bites. "It's the sand gnats," the man next to you says when he sees you scratching.

This journey began three days ago in Missouri. Now you are in either Kansas or Nebraska, you are not exactly sure. But you know you are heading west toward California. And you know the trip will take at least three weeks.

So do you regret your decision to cross the country by stagecoach? Not really. This is your first chance to see huge herds of buffalo and snow-covered mountains. It is going to be an adventure.

Sequence As you read, pay attention to the order of events that helped link the East and West.

Practice and Extend

READING SKILL
Sequence

In the Lesson Review, students complete a graphic organizer like the one below. You may want to provide students with a copy of Transparency 10 to complete as they read the lesson.

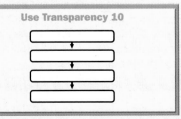

Use Transparency 10

VOCABULARY
Word Exercise

Related Word Study Remind students that *tele* is Greek for "far." Tell them that *scope* is from the Greek word *skopein,* meaning "to see." Have them chart *telescope* the way *telegraph* is charted on p. 534. Help students to think of other words containing *scope.* (microscope, periscope, stethoscope) Have them use dictionaries to check on the meanings of these words and how they relate to *scope.*

Linking East and West

It was not easy to get across the United States in the 1850s. There were thousands of miles of railroad tracks, but they were mostly in the eastern part of the country. To reach the West, people traveled in wagons pulled by oxen or horses. The only other way to get from the east coast to the west coast was by ship. Either way, the journey could take months. And since mail traveled the same routes as people, it took months to send news across the country. People began looking for faster ways to move people and mail across the United States.

In 1858, travelers were offered a new way to cross the country—the stagecoach. Stagecoaches were horse-drawn wagons that traveled in stages, or short sections. If the weather was good, stagecoaches could bring people and bags of mail from Missouri to California in only 25 days.

In 1860, a new business called the **Pony Express** began delivering mail from Missouri to California in just 10 days. How was this possible? The Pony Express was like a 2,000-mile relay race. Each express rider rode about 75 miles, then handed his bags of mail on to a new rider. The riders were mostly teenagers, some as young as 13.

The Pony Express was soon put out of business by an invention called the telegraph. The **telegraph** sent messages along wires using electricity. An American inventor named **Samuel Morse** developed a way to send telegraph messages using a code called Morse Code. The first telegraph line across the country was completed in October 1861. Morse Code messages could now be sent from coast to coast in just a few minutes!

The telegraph allowed news to travel quickly, but it did not help people or goods cross the country. Many people believed that the best way to link East and West would be to build a **transcontinental railroad**—a railroad across the continent. President Abraham Lincoln agreed. In 1862, during the Civil War, the United States government gave two companies the right to start building the transcontinental railroad. The Union Pacific began building track west from **Omaha, Nebraska.** The Central Pacific began building east from **Sacramento, California.**

REVIEW What event in 1861 brought the Pony Express to an end? ↻ Sequence

▶ By changing horses every 10 or 15 miles, Pony Express riders were able to deliver mail more quickly.

539

---

2 Teach and Discuss

PAGE 539

Linking East and West

Quick Summary New ways of linking East and West improved travel and communication in the mid-1800s.

1 What influenced people to develop the stagecoach, the Pony Express, and the telegraph? They were looking for faster ways to travel and to send news from East to West. **Cause and Effect**

2 Why do you think that most Pony Express riders were young? The conditions were tough, so the riders needed to be strong and healthy. **Draw Conclusions**

✓ **Ongoing Assessment**

If... students have difficulty understanding the routes and distances mentioned in the text,

then... display a map of the United States comparing the distance one rider traveled (about 75 miles) with the total distance from Missouri to California (about 2,000 miles).

$ SOCIAL STUDIES STRAND Economics

Tell students that inventions such as the telegraph had a great impact on the economy.

3 What jobs were created and eliminated by the telegraph? Created: Telegraph operators and people who installed the systems; Eliminated: Express riders and others who worked for the Pony Express **Make Inferences**

✓ **REVIEW ANSWER** The completion of a transcontinental telegraph line
↻ Sequence

Building the Railroad

🕐 *Quick Summary* Workers for the Central Pacific and Union Pacific Railroads had to overcome many obstacles as they built a railroad to connect the East and the West.

④ Where did many of the railroad workers come from? They were Irish, German, and Chinese immigrants, as well as former soldiers and former slaves. Main Idea and Details

⑤ What caused the railroad companies to work so hard? They were competing against each other because they were paid in land and money for each mile of track they completed. Cause and Effect

⑥ What caused conflict between Union Pacific workers and Native Americans? The track began to cross traditional Native American hunting grounds. Cause and Effect

✓ **REVIEW ANSWER** The Central Pacific had to build track over the Sierra Nevada. The Union Pacific came into conflict with Native Americans. Cause and Effect

 **Transcontinental Railroads, 1869–1893**

⑦ Which railroads connected Omaha and San Francisco? Central Pacific and Union Pacific Interpret Maps

MAP SKILL Answer Southern Pacific

The Golden Spike

🕐 *Quick Summary* A golden spike was pounded into the track where the Central Pacific and Union Pacific tracks met in Utah Territory.

⑧ What was the significance of the golden spike? It marked the completion of the transcontinental railroad. Main Idea and Details

✓ **REVIEW ANSWER** About seven years
Sequence

Building the Railroad

Both railroad companies faced serious difficulties. One problem was finding enough workers for this huge construction project. The Union Pacific hired former Civil War soldiers, former slaves, and Irish and German immigrants. The Central Pacific's work force ④ was also diverse, including thousands of Chinese immigrants.

The two railroad companies raced against each other. Each company was paid in land and money for every mile of track it completed. But ⑤ the landforms of the West did not always allow work to move quickly. Central Pacific workers had the seemingly impossible job of building tracks over the steep slopes of the Sierra Nevada mountain range. Chinese workers did much of the difficult and daring work of blasting tunnels through the mountain's solid rock. Many Chinese workers were killed in dynamite accidents.

On the Great Plains, Union Pacific workers came into conflict with Native Americans. As the railroad moved west, the tracks began to

▶ **Chinese immigrants helped build tracks through the mountains of the West.**

540

cross the traditional hunting grounds of groups such as the Lakota and Cheyenne. Many Native American leaders did not want the railroad to cross this land. "We do not want you here," a Lakota chief named Red Cloud told Union Pacific workers. "You are scaring away the buffalo."

The Union Pacific was determined to continue building, however. Soldiers began guarding the railroad workers. The track continued moving west.

REVIEW Describe the difficulties each transcontinental railroad company faced after 1862. Cause and Effect

MAP SKILL Transcontinental Railroads, 1869–1893

▶ **By 1893, several transcontinental railroad lines had been completed.**

MAP SKILL Use Routes *Which railroad line served the city of New Orleans?*

Practice and Extend

 ISSUES AND VIEWPOINTS Critical Thinking

Analyze Different Viewpoints Write on the board the list shown here. Have students use details to analyze differing viewpoints.

Easy Help students think of one example for each of the benefits and problems listed. **Reteach**

On-Level Ask students to identify other benefits and problems and then decide whether the benefits outweigh the problems. Have students suggest how some of the problems might be solved. **Extend**

Challenge Have students take a stand either for or against the construction of a transcontinental railroad and write an essay that includes reasons for their choice. **Enrich**

For a Lesson Summary, use Quick Study, p. 112.

Transcontinental Railroad	
Benefits	**Problems**
• faster travel	• getting workers
• better communication	• crossing mountains and rivers
	• conflicts with Native Americans

The Golden Spike

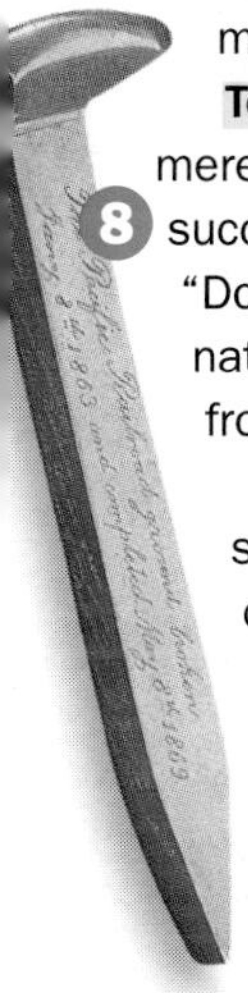

On May 10, 1869, the tracks of the Union Pacific and Central Pacific finally met at **Promontory Point, Utah Territory.** A golden spike was hammered into the track to symbolize the success of the project. The message "Done" was telegraphed around the nation. There were celebrations from New York to San Francisco.

8

As the map on page 540 shows, several other railroad lines soon crossed the West. People could now travel from coast to coast in under 10 days. As you will read, these new railroads brought change and conflict to the United States.

REVIEW How many years did it take to complete the transcontinental railroad? Sequence

Summarize the Lesson

1861 The first telegraph line across the United States was completed.

1862 The Union Pacific and Central Pacific began construction of the transcontinental railroad.

1869 The transcontinental railroad was completed at Promontory Point, Utah Territory

LESSON 1 REVIEW

Check Facts and Main Ideas

1. Sequence On a separate sheet of paper, fill in the missing dates from this diagram.

   - Pony Express begins delivering mail across the West—1860
   - First telegraph line stretches across the United States 1861
   - Work on transcontinental railroad begins 1862
   - Union Pacific and Central Pacific railroads meet in Utah 1869

2. What caused the **Pony Express** to go out of business?
3. Describe the different kinds of problems faced by the Union Pacific and Central Pacific railroads.
4. According to his quote on page 540, why did Red Cloud oppose railroad construction across the Great Plains?
5. **Critical Thinking: *Predict*** What kinds of changes do you think the **transcontinental railroad** brought to the United States?

Link to Mathematics

Plan the Pony Express Suppose you were planning the Pony Express. You know the route is 2,000 miles. And you know each rider will ride 75 miles. What is the minimum number of riders you will need to hire?

541

3 Close and Assess

Summarize the Lesson

Have students read the events listed on the time line and provide one cause or effect for each.

✓ LESSON 1 REVIEW

1. **Sequence** For possible answers, see the reduced pupil page.
2. A new invention, the telegraph, made it possible to send messages across the country in just minutes.
3. Union Pacific workers came into conflict with Native Americans who did not want the railroad to cross their hunting grounds. Central Pacific workers had to build over the Sierra Nevada. Chinese workers did much of the dangerous work of blasting tunnels through the mountains.
4. Red Cloud said that the construction was scaring away the buffalo.
5. **Critical Thinking: *Predict*** Possible answer: Increased settlement, conflict with Native Americans, and faster travel

Link to Mathematics

2,000 ÷ 75 = 26.66; 27 riders would be needed to ride 2,000 miles

SOCIAL STUDIES STRAND
Economics

About the Railroads

- Describe the impact of specialization and division of labor on the economic growth of the United States.
- Tell students that the railroad allowed farmers and ranchers in the West to specialize in producing goods for a national market, rather than just a local market.
- More people could be hired to work in the fields or herd cattle. The world of the cowboy was created by the railroad, as ranchers hired men to herd their cattle to railroad stations.

Workbook, p. 125

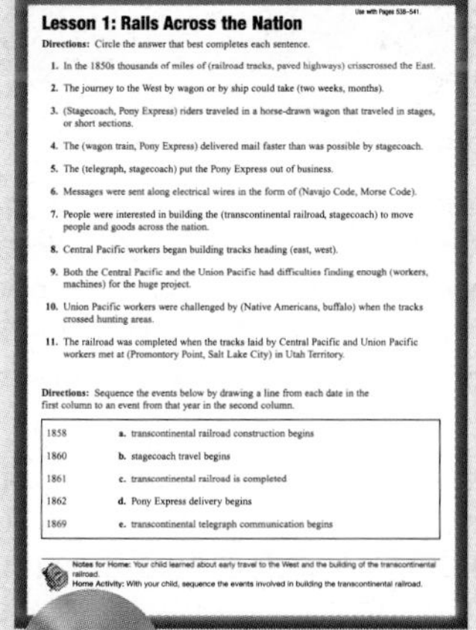

Lesson 1: Rails Across the Nation Use with Pages 538–541.

Directions: Circle the answer that best completes each sentence.

1. In the 1850s thousands of miles of (railroad tracks, paved highways) crisscrossed the East.
2. The journey to the West by wagon or by ship could take (two weeks, months).
3. (Stagecoach, Pony Express) riders traveled in a horse-drawn wagon that traveled in stages, or short sections.
4. The (wagon train, Pony Express) delivered mail faster than was possible by stagecoach.
5. The (telegraph, stagecoach) put the Pony Express out of business.
6. Messages were sent along electrical wires in the form of (Navajo Code, Morse Code).
7. People were interested in building the (transcontinental railroad, stagecoach) to move people and goods across the nation.
8. Central Pacific workers began building tracks heading (east, west).
9. Both the Central Pacific and the Union Pacific had difficulties finding enough (workers, machines) for the huge project.
10. Union Pacific workers were challenged by (Native Americans, buffalo) when the tracks crossed hunting areas.
11. The railroad was completed when the tracks laid by Central Pacific and Union Pacific workers met at (Promontory Point, Salt Lake City) in Utah Territory.

Directions: Sequence the events below by drawing a line from each date in the first column to an event from that year in the second column.

1858	a. transcontinental railroad construction begins
1860	b. stagecoach travel begins
1861	c. transcontinental railroad is completed
1862	d. Pony Express delivery begins
1869	e. transcontinental telegraph communication begins

Notes for Home: Your child learned about early travel to the West and the building of the transcontinental railroad.
Home Activity: With your child, sequence the events involved in building the transcontinental railroad.

Also on Teacher Resources CD-ROM.

Read a Time Zone Map

Objective

- Interpret information in maps.

Vocabulary

time zone, p. 542; **standard time,** p. 542

Resource

- Workbook, p. 126

 Introduce and Motivate

What is a time zone map? Ask students how people might use time zone maps to plan different events. Then have students read the **What?** section of text on p. 542 to help set the purpose of the lesson.

Why use time zone maps? Have students read the **Why?** section of text on p. 542. Ask them to describe problems that might occur today if there was no standard time.

2 Teach and Discuss

How is this skill used? Examine with students the time zone map on p. 542.

Map and Globe Skills

Read a Time Zone Map

Hawaii–Aleutian time

What? A time zone is an area on Earth that runs north and south in which all places have the same time. Earth is divided into 24 different time zones. Standard time is the time set by law for all the places in a time zone.

Why? At one time, each community decided its own time. Because of this, two communities that were close to each other might have different times. This could be confusing and was not practical. Problems increased when trains started to cross the country in the 1870s. Think of how confusing train schedules would have been if each town on a railroad line decided its own time. People needed ① a time system they could depend on.

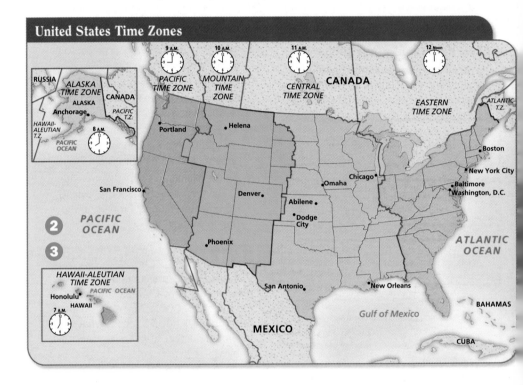

United States Time Zones

542

Practice and Extend

SOCIAL STUDIES STRAND
Geography

The following map resources are available:

- Big Book Atlas
- Student Atlas
- Outline Maps
- Desk Maps
- Map Resources CD-ROM

Decision Making

Use a Decision-Making Process

- Have students consider the following scenario: **You live in Massachusetts. You want to call your cousin who lives in Alaska. Your cousin goes to sleep at 9:00 P.M. and wakes up at 7:00 A.M. When should you call so that you do not wake her up?**

- Students should use the following process to decide what time to call. For each step, have students discuss and write about what must be considered as they make their decision. Write the steps above on the board or read them aloud.

1. **Identify a situation that requires a decision.**
2. **Gather information.**
3. **Identify options.**
4. **Predict consequences.**
5. **Take action to implement a decision.**

| Alaska Time | Pacific Time | Mountain Time | Central Time | Eastern Time |

To solve this problem, in the late 1870s, Canadian railway engineer Sandford Fleming worked out a plan for the 24 worldwide time zones that are used today.

If you drive from New York to California, you go through four of these time zones. It is important for you to know when the time changes and what time it is in the new zone. You would also need to have this information if you have promised to telephone someone at a particular time in a part of the country that is in a different time zone.

How? The map shows the six time zones of the United States. Standard time in each is one hour different from the time in the zone on either side. To help you understand how this works, look at the clocks shown with each time zone. Notice that each time zone has a name. Standard time is the same throughout each time zone.

To use a time zone map, you need to know whether you are east or west of another time zone. The time in a zone that is east of you is later than the time in your zone. The time in a zone that is west of you is earlier than the time in your zone.

If you were to travel east, you would move your watch ahead one hour for each time zone you entered. If you were to travel west, you would move your watch back one hour for each time zone you entered.

For example, say you live in San Antonio, and your watch shows that the time is 3:00 P.M. What is the time in New York City and in San Francisco? Find all three cities on the map and note the time zone of each. San Antonio is in the Central Time Zone. In which time zone is New York City? San Francisco? New York City is one time zone to the east of San Antonio. So the time there is one hour later than your time, or 4:00 P.M. San Francisco is two time zones to the west, so the time there is two hours earlier than your time, or 1:00 P.M.

Think and Apply

1. What **time zone** do you live in?

2. In what time zones are Denver and Boston? What time is it in Denver when it is 12 noon in Boston?

3. If you are in Baltimore and want to watch a ballgame that starts at 2:00 P.M. in Chicago, what time should you turn on your television set?

Internet Activity

For more information, go online to the *Atlas* at www.sfsocialstudies.com.

543

1 **Why were time zones developed?** Possible answer: A dependable time system made train travel practical and less confusing. Main Idea and Details

2 **What happens to time as you go from east to west in the United States?** The time gets earlier. Analyze Information

Test Talk

Use Information from Graphics

3 **What is the time difference between Washington, D.C., and New Orleans?** Tell students to use details from the map to support their answer. 1 hour
Interpret Maps

3 Close and Assess

Think and Apply

1. Answers will vary; help students use the map to find their time zone.

2. Denver is in the Mountain Time Zone, and Boston is in the Eastern Time Zone. It is 10:00 A.M. in Denver when it is 12 noon in Boston.

3. 3:00 P.M.

CURRICULUM CONNECTION
Math

Solve Time Word Problems

• Suppose you are in Georgia. At 6:32 P.M. you phone a friend in Texas. If the conversation lasts for 42 minutes, what time is it in Texas when the call ends?
(6:14 P.M. Central Time)

• You are in Portland, Oregon, and must make a 15-minute call to a company in Baltimore. If the company closes at 5:00 P.M. Eastern Time, what is the latest time that you could place the call?
(1:45 P.M. Pacific Time)

Workbook, p. 126

Time Zone Map

A time zone map tells you in what time zone a place is located. With this information you can figure out the time in other places across the country. Regardless of where you live, zones to the east of you are later than the zone in which you are located. Zones to the west of you are earlier.

Directions: Use the time zone map below to answer the questions that follow.

1. Suppose you were in Wichita, Kansas, and wanted to share some good news with your brother in Boston, Massachusetts. He gets home from work at 5:30 P.M. At what time might you place a call from your time zone to reach him at home after work?
   Ⓐ 2:30 P.M.   Ⓑ 2:45 P.M.   Ⓒ 3:45 P.M.   Ⓓ 4:45 P.M.

2. Bus, train, and airplane schedules list departure and arrival times according to the city in which each action takes place. Suppose you live in Dallas, Texas, and a relative is visiting from Los Angeles, California. The plane is scheduled to land in Dallas at 3:00 P.M. What time will it be in Los Angeles, when the plane lands in Dallas?
   Ⓐ 12:00 P.M.   Ⓑ 1:00 P.M.   Ⓒ 4:00 P.M.   Ⓓ 5:00 P.M.

3. Suppose you live in Las Vegas, Nevada, and you want to watch a live TV broadcast from Washington, D.C., scheduled to begin at 7:00 P.M. D.C. time. At what time should you tune in to the broadcast?
   Ⓐ 4:00 P.M.   Ⓑ 6:00 P.M.   Ⓒ 9:00 P.M.   Ⓓ 10:00 P.M.

4. Suppose you used an overnight delivery service to send a package from your home in Seattle, Washington, to a friend in Miami, Florida. The service promises to deliver the package by 10:00 A.M. Florida time. At what time can you call from Seattle to make sure your friend has received the package?
   Ⓐ 1:00 A.M.   Ⓑ 7:00 A.M.   Ⓒ 12:00 P.M.   Ⓓ 1:00 P.M.

Notes for Home: Your child learned about time zones.
Home Activity: With your child, practice calculating time in other time zones. You may wish to use TV shows, travel schedules, or phone calls as examples.

Also on Teacher Resources CD-ROM.

Westward Growth of America, 1607–1862

Objectives

- Identify key events involved in and reasons for Americans' movement westward.

- Identify the physical constraints and technological advances that challenged and aided Americans' movement westward, including natural terrain and advances in modes of transportation.

1 Introduce and Motivate

- Review with students the location of the original 13 colonies. Explain that before the year 1800, most Americans lived east of the Mississippi River.

- Have students point out on the map the natural physical barriers that may have made travel west difficult. Include major landforms, such as the Appalachian Mountains, Mississippi River, and Rocky Mountains, as well as terrain obstacles (dense forests, vegetation, etc.).

- Have students list the reasons they think many Americans wanted to move west. Reasons should include land ownership, farmland, economic opportunity, and religious freedom.

2 Teach and Discuss

SOCIAL STUDIES STRAND
History

"A Map of the British and French Dominions in North America."
This map was created by John Mitchell, a mapmaker in London, England, in 1755. Mitchell never traveled to America. He constructed this map using drawings, maps, and surveys created by others. The boundary lines stretching westward show that Americans were looking toward the west from the very beginning.

Living History from
Colonial Williamsburg
www.history.org

Westward Growth of America, 1607-1862

John Mitchell published this map of North America in 1775. You can see from the map that Americans were looking west very early in our history. Over time, people moved west and the nation expanded. Here are some key events in the westward growth of our nation.

Omaha, NE

Independence, MO

St. Louis, MO

Practice and Extend

SOCIAL STUDIES
Background

Looking to the West by Dr. William E. White, Colonial Williamsburg Historian

- During the eighteenth and nineteenth centuries, Americans moved westward. Some people sought the freedom and adventure of living on the frontier. Some people wanted to find land of their own to farm. Some people set up new businesses. Some people harvested the natural resources of the wilderness.

- According to James Madison, by 1803 America had "fixed its destiny westward and secured room to grow in freedom for generations to come."

- Over time, technology made travel west much faster. Canals created smooth travel, without challenges in terrain. Wagon trains made cross-country travel possible for pioneer families. Steamboats turned rivers into major travel routes.

- As people moved west, travel became faster and more efficient. Pioneers took months to reach the Pacific from the Midwest. When the Union Pacific opened in 1870, a person could go from Omaha to San Francisco in just four days.

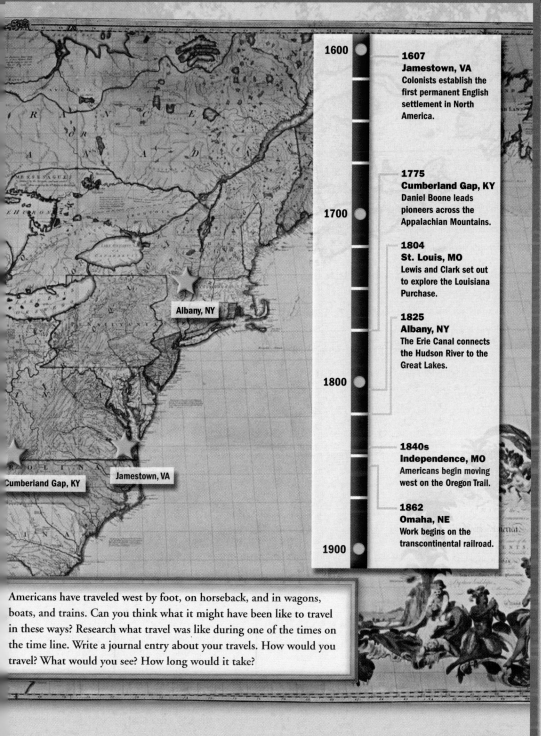

1600

1607
Jamestown, VA
Colonists establish the first permanent English settlement in North America.

1700

1775
Cumberland Gap, KY
Daniel Boone leads pioneers across the Appalachian Mountains.

1804
St. Louis, MO
Lewis and Clark set out to explore the Louisiana Purchase.

1825
Albany, NY
The Erie Canal connects the Hudson River to the Great Lakes.

1800

1840s
Independence, MO
Americans begin moving west on the Oregon Trail.

1862
Omaha, NE
Work begins on the transcontinental railroad.

1900

Albany, NY

Cumberland Gap, KY   Jamestown, VA

Americans have traveled west by foot, on horseback, and in wagons, boats, and trains. Can you think what it might have been like to travel in these ways? Research what travel was like during one of the times on the time line. Write a journal entry about your travels. How would you travel? What would you see? How long would it take?

545

- **1607** It took English settlers 144 days to travel to Jamestown. Ask students what difficulties they might encounter traveling on a boat for such a long time.

- **1775** Pioneers traveled on foot and horseback along the Wilderness Road through the Cumberland Gap. The road was widened in the 1790s to allow for Conestoga wagons.

- **1804–1806** The Lewis and Clark expedition traveled by boat, on foot, and on horseback, against river currents and over the Rocky Mountains. Ask students what supplies they think Lewis and Clark needed to bring.

- **1825** The Erie Canal connected Albany, New York, on the Hudson River, to Lake Erie. Goods could be shipped by boat through New York. Ask students how they think life changed because of the canal.

- **1840s** Pioneers traveled along the Oregon Trail by covered wagons, horseback, and on foot. The trip, which covered rugged terrain and Indian territory, took about four to six months.

- **1862** The transcontinental railroad allowed for travel across the entire continent by steam locomotive in ten days. Have students discuss why this encouraged westward movement.

3 Close and Assess

- Have each student choose one method of travel from the time line. Brainstorm with students what details they might include in a travel journal.

- Have students research their mode of travel. Encourage students to look for things such as how travelers prepared and what obstacles they encountered. Have students write a journal entry from a pioneer traveler's perspective.

CURRICULUM CONNECTION
Math

Calculate Travel Time

- Mention that St. Louis, Missouri, is about 562 miles from Pittsburgh, Pennsylvania.

- Ask students to calculate how long it would take a person to travel from Pittsburgh to St. Louis in each of the following ways (for each, divide 562 by the number of miles per hour):

    1. On foot, at 3 miles per hour. *187.3 hours, or almost 8 days*

    2. On horseback, at 5 miles per hour. *112.4 hours, or about 4 and a half days*

    3. By steam locomotive, at 30 miles per hour. *18.7 hours*

Workbook, p. 127

Writing Prompt: Leaving Home

Long ago, the United States grew as Americans traveled westward. Many people left home for the first time to settle in a new place. Think about your first time away from home. How did you feel? What did you see? Write a paragraph to tell about it.

Notes for Home: Your child learned about transportation changes and westward expansion.
Home Activity: With your child, discuss some of the reasons people move. Compare and contrast reasons for moving today and long ago.

Also on Teacher Resources CD-ROM.

Farmers and Cowboys

Objectives

- Explain how the Homestead Act worked.

- Describe the hardships of farming on the Great Plains.

- Analyze the reasons why different groups came to the Great Plains.

- Evaluate the causes of the rise and fall of cattle drives.

Vocabulary

Homestead Act, p. 547;
homesteaders, p. 547; **sodbusters,** p. 547;
exodusters, p. 549; **cattle drives,** p. 550;
barbed wire, p. 551

Resources

- Workbook, p. 128
- Transparency 11
- Every Student Learns Guide, pp. 226–229
- Quick Study, pp. 114–115

Quick Teaching Plan

If time is short, have students read the lesson independently, looking for similarities and differences between the lifestyles of farmers and ranchers.

- Have students create a Venn diagram that compares and contrasts the lifestyles of farmers and ranchers.

1 Introduce and Motivate

Preview To activate prior knowledge, ask students to tell about a friend or relative who has moved far away from them. Tell students they will learn about people who left their homes to settle in the Great Plains.

You Are There Pioneers built homes on land that the government was giving away. Ask students why they think the home described on p. 546 was dug into the ground.

LESSON 2

GREAT PLAINS
Nicodemus • Abilene

1860			1880

1862 Congress passes the Homestead Act

1866 Goodnight-Loving Trail is established

1877 African American pioneers town of Nicodemus, Kansas

PREVIEW

Focus on the Main Idea
Following the Civil War, farmers and cowboys helped the Great Plains become an important farming and ranching region.

PLACES
Great Plains
Nicodemus, Kansas
Abilene, Kansas

PEOPLE
Charles Goodnight
Nat Love
George Shima

VOCABULARY
Homestead Act
homesteaders
sodbusters
exodusters
cattle drives
barbed wire

Farmers and Cowboys

You Are There Howard Ruede (roo day) has just finished building his new home— if you can call it a home. Actually, it is a large opening dug into the ground with a roof of wood. But it will keep out the wind, and at least some of the rain.

It is the summer of 1877, and this 23-year-old pioneer has just moved west to the Kansas prairie. He brought his entire life savings of about $50. Luckily, the house only cost him $10 to build.

Sitting on a homemade chair in his dark, damp home, Howard writes a letter to his family back in Pennsylvania. He describes his land, and the farm he dreams of building. Howard has years of hard work ahead of him. And he is looking forward to it.

 Sequence As you read, list the sequence of events that brought change to the Great Plains.

546

Practice and Extend

READING SKILL
Sequence

In the Lesson Review, students complete a graphic organizer like the one below. You may want to provide students with a copy of Transparency 11 to complete as they read the lesson.

Use Transparency 11

VOCABULARY
Word Exercise

Related Word Study Explain that *stead* means place. Something that is *instead of* is in place of. A homestead was a place you could have a home. In fact, a homestead came to mean a house with its buildings and grounds or a parcel of land given to a settler for building a home. Remembering that a homestead is a place to have a home can help students remember that the Homestead Act provided land for building homes. Homesteaders were simply people who built homesteads.

The Homestead Act

As you have read, many Americans were eager to go west in the middle 1800s. Oregon farmland and California gold lured thousands of settlers to the West. On their way, pioneers crossed the **Great Plains** as quickly as they could. This vast region of dry grassland was often called the "Great American Desert." People did not think it would ever make good farmland. As a result, the Great Plains attracted very few pioneers.

The United States government decided to try to encourage people to move to the Great Plains. In 1862, Congress passed the **Homestead Act,** which offered free land to pioneers willing to start new farms. If you were a man over the age of 21, a woman whose husband had died, or the head of a family, you could claim 160 acres of land. You had to pay a small registration fee— usually about $10—and farm your land and live on it for five years. Then the land was yours. Settlers who claimed land through this law were called **homesteaders.**

New transcontinental railroad lines helped homesteaders move west. Like many homesteaders, Howard Ruede traveled by train to his new home. After claiming his plot of land and digging an underground shelter, he began trying to establish a farm. This was not easy. The grasses of the Great Plains had thick, tangled roots that reached several inches down into the soil. Before planting crops, Ruede had to dig through this "sod." Great Plains farmers like Ruede soon became known as **sodbusters.**

After ripping up the sod from his land, Ruede did what most homesteaders did—he used it to build a new house. In a region with few trees or rocks, sod proved to be a useful building material. Houses built from blocks of sod stayed cool in summer, warm in winter, and were fireproof. Unfortunately for the homesteaders, the sod walls were often home to bugs, mice, and snakes. **3**

REVIEW In correct order, list four things Howard Ruede did after arriving in Kansas in 1877. ⟳ Sequence

▶ This pioneer family built a sod house in Nebraska.

547

FAST FACTS

Students may enjoy learning these facts about the Homestead Act.

- The Homestead Act was debated for 20 years before it was finally passed in 1862. Northern business owners feared that property values would decrease and the labor supply would be reduced if people could move west and obtain free land. Southerners were afraid that homesteaders would oppose slavery.

- By the beginning of the 1900s, the government had given away more than 80 million acres of land in the Midwest, the Great Plains, and the West to about 600,000 farmers.

- Homesteading continued in Alaska until 1986.

---

2 Teach and Discuss

PAGE 547

The Homestead Act

🕐 *Quick Summary* To attract settlers to the Great Plains, the government in 1862 created the Homestead Act, which offered free land to pioneers willing to start new farms.

1 **Why did few pioneers want to settle in the Great Plains?** They thought the land would not be suitable for farming. **Cause and Effect**

2 **What did the government do to encourage settlers to live in the Great Plains?** Possible answer: Give land away to settlers who would use it for farming **Cause and Effect**

3 **What were the advantages and disadvantages of using sod for housing?** Advantages: It was free; sod houses were cool in summer, warm in winter, and fireproof. Disadvantages: Sod was home to bugs, mice, and snakes. **Analyze Information**

✓ **REVIEW ANSWER** He claimed a plot of land, dug an underground shelter, dug up sod, and used it to build a house. ⟳ Sequence

Life on the Plains

🕐 *Quick Summary* Although new technology helped homesteaders with farming efforts, pioneers faced many difficulties caused by weather and natural disasters.

S|T SOCIAL STUDIES STRAND
Science • Technology

Tell students that one problem in using the iron plow was that the prairie soil would stick to it, making the plowing process more difficult and time-consuming. Steel plows were more effective—not as much soil would stick to them.

4 How did new technology help farmers? The steel plows made plowing easier and faster and windmills pumped water from deep beneath the ground.
Main Idea and Details

5 Why were fires frequent events in the fall? The grass was dry after summer droughts. **Cause and Effect**

Primary Source
Cited in *Reader's Digest Story of the Great American West,* by Edward S. Barnard, ed.

6 Why do you think the author used the expression "sea of fire" to describe prairie fires? The prairie is a large, open area where you can see for miles. A large prairie fire would be visible from far away.
Analyze Primary Sources

7 Compare and contrast summers and winters in the plains. Both seasons could have extreme conditions that caused problems. Summers were very hot and dry. Winters were bitter cold with blizzards and ice storms.
Compare and Contrast

✓ **REVIEW ANSWER** The homesteaders had to face tornados, hailstorms, floods, droughts, fires, blizzards, ice storms, and swarms of grasshoppers. **Summarize**

Life on the Plains

New technology helped homesteaders survive on the Great Plains. An inventor from Indiana named James Oliver designed a new kind of steel plow that could cut through the tough prairie sod. Special windmills were designed to pump water from deep beneath the ground. Mostly, however, homesteaders had to rely on their own determination and muscle. A pioneer from England named Percy Ebbutt put it simply: "You must make up your mind to rough it."

Roughing it included facing the harsh weather conditions and deadly natural disasters of the Great Plains. Spring often brought tornados, hailstorms, and flooding. Summers could mean scorching heat and frequent droughts. In fall, the prairie grass dried, and settlers had to watch for prairie fires. An immigrant from Norway named Gro Svendsen described these fires in a letter to his family in 1863.

> *"It is a strange and terrible sight to see all the fields a sea of fire. Quite often the scorching flames sweep everything along in their path—people, cattle, hay, fences."*

Winters brought bitter cold, along with ice storms and blizzards. An especially deadly

▶ A farmer hopes for rain on the Great Plains.

blizzard hit the Dakota Territory and Nebraska in January 1888. It was called the "school-children's storm" because it struck in the afternoon, while many children were walking home from school.

If the weather was not enough to worry about, farmers also faced the dreaded grasshopper. In the mid-1870s, millions of grasshoppers swarmed across the Great Plains. They darkened the sky and covered the ground in layers up to six inches high. The insects ate everything in their path—crops, grass, even fences and axe handles. "Nebraska would have had a splendid crop if the grasshoppers had stayed away a while," wrote homesteader Mattie Oblinger in 1876.

REVIEW What obstacles faced the homesteaders? **Summarize**

▶ Windmills are still used on Great Plains farms.

548

Practice and Extend

ESL BUILD BACKGROUND
ESL Support

Understand Cause and Effect Students use what they know about weather to discuss the effects it can have.

Beginning Have students work in pairs to construct a web of words describing one of the weather situations described in the text.

Intermediate Ask students to describe the typical weather problems that occur each season and how this weather can affect the plains farmers.

Advanced Have students write a report about how weather might impact a homesteader's ability to harvest and sell crops. Students should share their reports with classmates.

For additional ESL support, use Every Student Learns Guide, pp. 226–229.

"America Fever"

The harsh environment of the Great Plains drove many farmers back to eastern towns and cities. But the promise of good land continued to attract new settlers. In Europe, the desire to move to the Great Plains was so great it became known as "America fever." Hundreds of thousands of people from Germany, Sweden, Norway, Russia, and other European nations crossed the Atlantic Ocean to begin new lives on the Great Plains.

Many of these immigrants brought valuable farming skills to the United States. For example, members of a religious group called the Mennonites began arriving in Kansas in the early 1870s. Mennonite farmers brought seeds for a hardy type of wheat that they had grown in Europe. Until this time, American farmers were having a hard time finding a type of wheat that could survive the weather on the Great Plains. The wheat brought by the Mennonites grew well in Kansas. The Great Plains soon became one of the world's most productive wheat-growing regions—and it still is today.

The Homestead Act also provided opportunities for African American homesteaders. As you have read, African Americans continued to face discrimination after the end of slavery. In the 1870s, a carpenter from Tennessee named Benjamin Singleton began urging his fellow African Americans to move west. "We needed land for our children," he later said.

Calling themselves **exodusters,** thousands of African American pioneers started new lives in Kansas and Nebraska. The name "exodusters" came from a book of the Bible called Exodus. This book tells the story of Moses leading the Israelites out of slavery. Many southern African Americans felt that their story was similar—they too were making a journey to freedom.

REVIEW How did Mennonites contribute to the success of farming on the Great Plains? **Draw Conclusions**

Nicodemus, Kansas

The town of **Nicodemus** (nik e DEE muhs), Kansas, was founded by African American pioneers in 1877. By the end of the 1880s, Nicodemus had grown into a bustling town, with stores, churches, newspapers, a school, and a baseball team. Today, Nicodemus lives on as a symbol of freedom and opportunity. Visitors come from all over the country to see the town's historic buildings and celebrate the important contributions of African American pioneers.

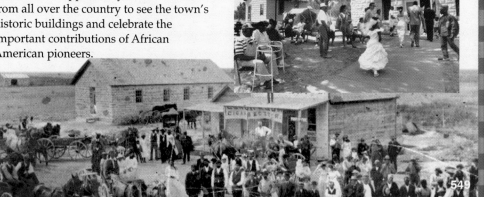

549

PAGE 549

"America Fever"

Quick Summary The Homestead Act provided opportunities for African Americans and immigrants and helped bring about important developments in farming.

8 Why do you think immigrants came to settle on the Great Plains? They could get good land for free and perhaps make a better life for themselves. Make Inferences

9 Why had American farmers experienced difficulties in growing wheat? They had a hard time finding wheat that could survive in the extreme weather. Main Idea and Details

10 What effect did the Homestead Act have on African Americans? It allowed them to own land and build new communities. Cause and Effect

---

✓ **REVIEW ANSWER** The Mennonites brought seeds for a type of wheat that grew well on the Great Plains. Draw Conclusions

Nicodemus, Kansas

Have students compare and contrast the photographs of Nicodemus, Kansas, as it appeared in the 1800s and as it looks today.

11 What does the town of Nicodemus symbolize? Possible answer: It symbolizes freedom and opportunity. Main Idea and Details

The Rise of Cattle Drives

🕐 **Quick Summary** Cattle were herded from Texas to the new railroad lines on the Great Plains and shipped to eastern cities.

12 **Why did ranchers want to sell their cattle in the East?** Beef was scarce there and the ranchers could make huge profits. **Main Ideas and Details**

✓ Ongoing Assessment

| **If...** students have difficulty understanding the reasons for the cattle drives, | **then...** have them calculate the profit on longhorns that were purchased for $4 each in Texas and sold for about $40 each in the East. |

🗺 Problem Solving

13 **What were the problems cattle ranchers faced? How did they solve them? Do you think their solutions were successful?** Possible answer: Ranchers needed to get their cattle to eastern cities. Cowboys drove herds to a railroad line and the cattle were shipped east by train. The solution was successful—thousands of cattle passed through cowtowns such as Abilene. **Solve Problems**

14 **Why were some towns known as cowtowns?** So many cattle were moved through the towns. **Draw Conclusions**

✓ REVIEW ANSWER
Cattle sold for about $4 each in Texas and for about $40 in eastern cities—a difference of $36. This is because beef was scarce in the East and plentiful in Texas. **Compare and Contrast**

Map Adventure Answers

1. Chisholm Trail

2. About 60 days

3. Cattle trails led to railroad lines. These lines came together in Chicago, making it a logical center for the beef industry.

The Rise of Cattle Drives

While farmers were struggling to survive on the Great Plains, the cattle ranching industry was developing farther south. The first cows were brought to North America by the Spanish in the early 1600s. By the end of the Civil War, there were about 5 million cattle in Texas. They were a tough breed known as Texas longhorns.

In the 1860s, longhorns sold for about $4 each in Texas. But they were worth about $40 each in the growing cities of the East, where beef was scarce. Cattle ranchers realized they could make huge profits, but only if **12** they could figure out a way to get their cattle across the country.

The solution was the cattle drive. On **cattle drives,** cowboys drove, or moved, huge herds of cattle north to the new railroad lines extending across the Great Plains. The cattle drives began in Texas and ended in towns along the railroad. From these towns, cattle were shipped by train to eastern cities. Some of these towns, like **Abilene, Kansas,** became known as cowtowns. In 1871 alone, about 700,000 longhorns trampled through the dirt streets of Abilene.

REVIEW By how much did the price of cattle in Texas and eastern cities differ? Why? **Compare and Contrast**

Map Adventure

The Long Cattle Drives
Starting from Texas, there are several routes you can take to drive your cattle to the railroad.

1. Which trail would you follow if you wanted to drive your cattle to Abilene, Kansas?

2. Traveling 10 miles a day, how long would it take to drive your cattle from San Antonio to Dodge City?

3. By the 1880s, the city of Chicago had become the nation's leading supplier of fresh beef. How does the map help explain this?

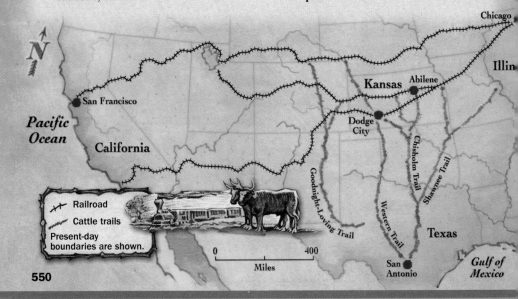

Practice and Extend

MEETING INDIVIDUAL NEEDS
Learning Styles

Discuss Cattle Drives Using their individual learning styles, students describe cattle drives.

Verbal Learning Have students persuade a partner to take one of the routes on the map, naming cities or states that it goes through.

Social Learning Students can work in groups and take turns explaining the route they might take if they were on a cattle drive and why.

CURRICULUM CONNECTION
Math

Calculate Profits

- The selling price of longhorns in the East is how many times greater than in Texas? (40 ÷ 4 = 10 times greater)

- Suppose that after paying expenses to move the cattle, a rancher makes a profit of $32 for each longhorn sold. How much profit would the rancher make on 525 cattle? 1,200 cattle? 2,500 cattle? ($16,800; $38,400; $80,000)

Painting by Frederick Remington

▶ Working long days on horseback, cowboys earned about $30 a month.

Cowboy Life

In 1866, Charles Goodnight and his partner Oliver Loving drove their herd of 2,000 longhorns north from Texas to Colorado. This route soon became known as the Goodnight-Loving Trail. "There were many hardships and dangers," wrote Charles Goodnight. But overall, he remembered his days on the trail as the happiest time of his life.

> *"Most of the time we were solitary adventurers in a great land as fresh and new as a spring morning."*

Cowboys were a diverse group. About a third of all cowboys were Mexican American or African American. Many were very young. An African American cowboy named Nat Love began working on cattle drives when he was just 15. Love later became famous for his cowboy skills. He wrote a book about his adventures on the cattle trail. Cowboys like Nat Love lived a hard, dangerous, and lonely life

▶ Nat Love was a famous cowboy.

on the long cattle drives. They worked 16-hour days on horseback, seven days a week. At night, they took turns watching the herd.

Cattle drives usually covered about 10 miles a day. The large herds moved along slowly, grazing as they walked. But longhorns were nervous animals, and there was the constant danger of a stampede. In a stampede, entire herds of longhorns took off running wildly. They could trample horses and people, or charge into rivers and drown. To try to keep the animals calm, cowboys would sing to them. You can read the words to one of these songs on page 589.

By the late 1880s, the cattle drives came to an end. One cause was the growing conflict between cattle ranchers and farmers on the Great Plains. To keep cattle off their farmland, homesteaders began fencing in their land. They used a new type of fence made of barbed wire, or twisted wire with sharp points. Barbed wire fences, which were cheap and easy to build, began enclosing the vast open plains. Expanding railroad lines also helped end the cattle drives. As new railroad lines reached into Texas, it was no longer necessary for ranchers to drive their cattle north.

REVIEW What brought the age of cattle drives to an end? Cause and Effect

551

Cowboy Life

🕐 *Quick Summary* Cowboys worked long, hard days and faced many dangers as they drove herds of cattle north from Texas.

15 **Where was the Goodnight-Loving Trail?** It went from Texas to Colorado. Main Ideas and Details

Primary Source
Cited in *The West: An Illustrated History*, by Geoffrey C. Ward

16 **What do you think Charles Goodnight meant by "solitary adventurers"? How do you think he felt about cowboy life?** Possible answer: The cowboy life was lonely, but exciting. Goodnight liked being outdoors and having different experiences each day. Analyze Primary Sources

17 **What are two details that support the idea that a cowboy's life was hard and dangerous?** 16-hour work days, 7-day work weeks, constant danger of a stampede Main Idea and Details

18 **What caused farmers to fence in their land?** Possible answer: The cattle grazed on and walked over the farmland. Cause and Effect

✓ **REVIEW ANSWER** Farmers began fencing in their land and new railroad lines reached into Texas. Cause and Effect

---

Growth in the West

Quick Summary In the late 1800s some western towns grew into important cities. The West also attracted farmers from other countries.

19 **What brought so many people to the West Coast?** New railroad lines
Cause and Effect

✓ **REVIEW ANSWER** Many towns at the western end of the railroad lines grew into important cities. Summarize

3 Close and Assess

Summarize the Lesson

✓ **LESSON 2**   **REVIEW**

Have students examine the vertical time line. Then ask them to give several examples of expansion and change.

1. ⟳ **Sequence** For possible answers, see the reduced pupil page.

2. Farmers had to pay a small registration fee and then farm and live on their land for five years.

3. Possible answers: Hot summers, cold winters, droughts, prairie fires, blizzards, grasshoppers

4. **Critical Thinking:** *Decision-Making* Accept all answers, but make sure students can support their answers.

5. Cattle drives began because ranchers wanted to find a way to get their cattle to eastern cities, where the price of beef was high.

Link to ⟨◯◯⟩ **Writing**

Students' letters should express a point of view about the lifestyle they describe. They might describe the advantages and disadvantages of this lifestyle and give reasons for wanting or not wanting to stay in Kansas.

552 Unit 8 • Expansion and Change

Growth in the West

19 Throughout the late 1800s, new railroad lines brought thousands of people to the West. Towns at the western end of railroad lines, such as Los Angeles, California, and Seattle, Washington, soon grew into important cities. Many of the new settlers established farms in the West.

The West also attracted farmers from other countries. In the late 1800s, thousands of Japanese immigrants began arriving in California. Many Japanese families built successful farms in the West. You will read about one successful Japanese farmer, **George Shima,** (SHEE mah) in the Biography on the next page.

REVIEW How did railroads help the West to grow? Summarize

Summarize the Lesson

- **1862** The Homestead Act was passed, giving Americans access to free land in the Great Plains.

- **1866** The Goodnight-Loving Trail became the first of several cattle trails out of Texas.

- **1870s** African American pioneers founded many new towns, including Nicodemus, Kansas.

LESSON 2 ⟩ **REVIEW**

Check Facts and Main Ideas

1. ⟳ **Sequence** Redraw this diagram on a separate sheet of paper, putting the events in their correct order. Include the year of each event.

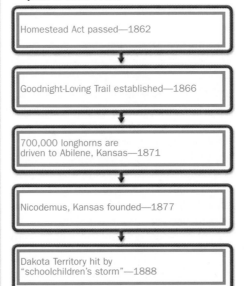

Homestead Act passed—1862

↓

Goodnight-Loving Trail established—1866

↓

700,000 longhorns are driven to Abilene, Kansas—1871

↓

Nicodemus, Kansas founded—1877

↓

Dakota Territory hit by "schoolchildren's storm"—1888

2. What did people have to do to get land through the **Homestead Act?**

3. Describe three hardships faced by farmers on the Great Plains.

4. **Critical Thinking:** *Decision-Making* You know about the difficulties of living and farming on the Great Plains. Would you have wanted to move there? Use the Decision-Making steps on page H3.

5. What led to the rise of **cattle drives?**

Link to ⟨◯◯⟩ **Writing**

Write a Letter Suppose you are a young homesteader in Kansas. Write a letter to your family in the East describing your new life. What have you accomplished? What challenges do you face? Do you expect to stay in Kansas for a long time? Why or why not?

552

Practice and Extend

CURRICULUM CONNECTION
Science

Research Crops of the Great Plains

- Have students use library or online resources to gather information about different kinds of crops that are grown in the Great Plains.

- Students should try to find out what kind of conditions (e.g., soil, weather) are suitable for different crops and why they are grown in particular areas.

- If possible, ask students to research other facts about crops, such as the length of time from planting until harvest, special care needed during growth, or how the crop is used once it is harvested.

Workbook, p. 128

Lesson 2: Farmers and Cowboys

Directions: Answer the clues below. Then find and circle the answers in the puzzle. Answers may appear horizontally, vertically, or diagonally in the puzzle.

```
T B V J X H O M E S T E A D E R S
G R A S S H O P P E R S L X C T G
O T A W K Y A V N Z C O W T O W N
D Z M N B R J F S I X B U I R D P
L Q E X S O D B U S T E R S Y K T
E U R A Y C M X Z D C V M A U U A
X N I S Z L O N G H O R N S O R F
O E C B G W E N A N O L L Z Z F M Y
D R A T C H Y S T Z R W K X E C B
U Y F Z S O D V B I J U D J S O L
S C E U I P M L W Y N Z S C T G I
T O V A B C R D L F C E A L E Y Z
E K E X Q J E Z O K B T N M A S Z
R A R N J B W G Y C V H L T D B A
S P W Y R X S L A Z J P O W A Z R
F M C A T T L E D R I V E X C L D
H V B Z D P Y K M O W H E A T Q S
```

1. Offered free land to pioneer farmers
2. Settlers who claimed free land offered by the government
3. The ___ railroad helped bring settlers west
4. Prairie grasses with thick, tangled roots
5. Farmers who had to dig through a layer of sod
6. In the winter, plains settlers faced deadly ___
7. Millions of ___ ate the farmers' crops

8. Europeans who wanted to move to the Great Plains had ___
9. The Mennonites introduced a hardy type of ___
10. Named themselves after the book of Exodus in the Bible
11. Tough breed of cattle: Texas ___
12. Began in Texas and ended in one of several towns along the railroad
13. Railroad town such as Abilene, Kansas
14. Twisted wire with sharp points

Notes for Home: Your child learned how the Great Plains became an important farming and ranching region.
Home Activity: Discuss with your child that people had to weigh the pros and cons of leaving their homes and moving west. Together, create a chart listing the pros and cons of moving to the Great Plains during this time.

⊙ **Also on Teacher Resources CD-ROM**

George Shima

about 1863–1926

George Shima, who was born in Japan, arrived in California in 1888. He was so poor that he had nothing to eat. He soon got a job harvesting potatoes and pulling up tree stumps on a farm in the San Joaquin (wah KEEN) Valley. Shima did whatever he could to learn about farming. He later remembered:

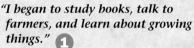

Shima was the first grower to wash and classify potatoes before selling them, so that the best of his crop could be sold for more money.

BIOFACT

"I began to study books, talk to farmers, and learn about growing things." ➊

Soon, Shima had made enough money to rent ten acres of land, where he experimented with growing potatoes. He made farmland on the many small, marshy islands in the San Joaquin River by pumping water out of the soil, creating ideal conditions for growing potatoes. Over time, he bought and drained more land, planting potatoes everywhere. Soon, he had a quickly-expanding business that made him wealthy. Shima became known as the "Potato King."

But things were not always easy. Despite his success, Shima sometimes met discrimination. When he bought a new home near a university, some white people protested. But Shima would not move. The United States was his home, he said, and his family would stay. ➋

Shima became an important leader in his community. He was president of the Japanese Association of California for many years. Shima also donated food to those in need and paid for college educations for poor students.

Learn from Biographies

Like many immigrants, George Shima made contributions to the United States. What were some of his contributions?

For more information, go online to *Meet the People* at **www.sfsocialstudies.com.**

553

George Shima

Objective

- Identify the contributions of people from selected immigrant groups.

➊ Introduce and Motivate

Preview To activate prior knowledge, ask students what they know about growing plants. Tell students they will read about a Japanese immigrant who faced challenges and developed a successful method for growing potatoes.

➋ Teach and Discuss

➊ **How do you think George Shima got the idea of pumping water out of the land?** He learned about the conditions needed for growing potatoes by working on farms, reading, and talking to farmers. Draw Conclusions

➋ **What is one detail that supports the idea the Shima experienced discrimination?** Some white people did not want him to live in their neighborhood. Main Idea and Details

➌ Close and Assess

Learn from Biographies Answer

Shima was an important leader in his community. He donated food to those in need and paid for college educations for some poor students.

SOCIAL STUDIES STRAND
Economics

Staple Crops Tell students that some countries' economies depend heavily on the success of a particular crop.

- In the early 1800s, potatoes were the principal food eaten by about half of the population of Ireland.
- In 1845, and for four years following, diseased potato crops rotted in the fields in Ireland.
- More than one million Irish died of starvation or other diseases. Many others immigrated to North America and to Britain.

WEB SITE
Technology

Students can find out more about George Shima by clicking on *Meet the People* at **www.sfsocialstudies.com.**

War in the West

Objectives

- Describe the ways that transcontinental railroads, farmers, and ranchers changed the Great Plains.

- Evaluate the reaction of Plains Indians to changes on the Great Plains.

- Compare the struggles of the Lakota and the Nez Percé in the 1870s.

- Explain ways in which Native Americans are keeping their traditions alive today.

Vocabulary

reservation, p. 555;
Battle of Little Bighorn, p. 556

Resources

- Workbook, p. 129
- Transparency 10
- Every Student Learns Guide, pp. 230–233
- Quick Study, pp. 116–117

Quick Teaching Plan

If time is short, have students make a compare and contrast chart, using the headings *U.S. Government* and *Native Americans.*

- Have students look for details that explain why these groups experienced conflicts in the 1860s and 1870s.

- Suggest that students compare and contrast what these groups wanted, as well as what they did not want.

1 Introduce and Motivate

Preview To activate prior knowledge, ask students if they have ever been forced to give up something they wanted to keep. Tell students they will learn about battles that occurred when the U.S. government wanted to take Native American land in the West.

You Are There Sitting Bull did not intend to sell any land to the government. Ask students to predict what might happen as a result of his refusal to sell land.

LESSON 3

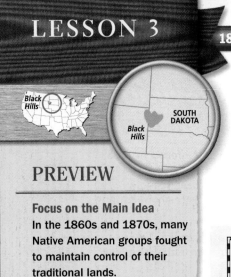

1870			1880

1874
Gold found on Lakota land in Black Hills

1876
Lakota defeat Custer at Battle of Little Bighorn

1877
Nez Percé are defeated in Montana

PREVIEW

Focus on the Main Idea
In the 1860s and 1870s, many Native American groups fought to maintain control of their traditional lands.

PLACES
Black Hills

PEOPLE
Sitting Bull
George Custer
Chief Joseph

VOCABULARY
reservation
Battle of Little Bighorn

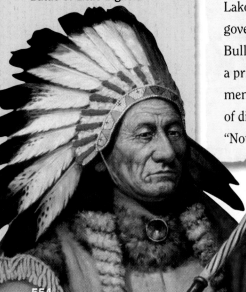

554

War in the West

You Are There The Lakota call this land *Paha Sapa*, meaning the Black Hills. This region of rugged cliffs, forested hills, and dark green valleys is sacred to the Lakota people. According to a treaty signed in 1868, the Black Hills are to belong to the Lakota people forever. But things have changed since then. It is now 1875. Gold has been found in the Black Hills.

The United States government hopes that the Lakota will be willing to sell the Black Hills. The government asks a Lakota leader named Sitting Bull to come to a meeting, where they can discuss a price. "I do not want to sell any land to the government," Sitting Bull replies. He picks up a tiny bit of dirt between his thumb and forefinger, and adds, "Not even as much as this."

Sequence As you read, pay attention to the order of events that led to the defeat of Native Americans on the Great Plains.

▶ **Lakota leader Sitting Bull**

Practice and Extend

READING SKILL
Sequence

In the Lesson Review, students complete a graphic organizer like the one below. You may want to provide students with a copy of Transparency 10 to complete as they read the lesson.

Use Transparency 10

VOCABULARY
Word Exercise

Individual Word Study Tell students that *reservation* is a multiple meaning word. In the text, it means "land set aside for Native Americans." It can also mean "an arrangement to have a room or seat held in advance for your use later" and "a hesitancy or keeping back." As previously noted (p. 34), reserve has to do with keeping back. Discuss how all the definitions have some element of keeping something back or setting it aside. In the text, what has been set aside? (land)

Conflict on the Plains

The Lakota chief **Sitting Bull** saw that the Great Plains were changing. New railroad lines were bringing thousands of settlers to the plains. Farmers and ranchers were fencing in the land. And the vast herds of buffalo were beginning to disappear. Buffalo were killed to feed railroad workers. They were also hunted for their hides, or for sport. There had once been about 30 million buffalo on the Great Plains. By the late 1880s, there were fewer than 1,000.

Native Americans on the Great Plains saw that their way of life was threatened. They relied on the buffalo for food, clothing, and shelter. Their traditional way of life included hunting buffalo, and moving freely across the open plains. As Sitting Bull explained, most Lakota wanted to continue living in this way.

> *"The life my people want is a life of freedom. I have seen nothing that a white man has, houses or railways or clothing or food, that is as good as the right to move in the open country, and live in our fashion [way]."*

The United States government encouraged the killing of buffalo to help defeat the Native Americans by wiping out one of their major resources. Government leaders wanted to move Native Americans onto reservations. A **reservation** is an area of land set aside for Native Americans.

In 1868, United States government and Lakota leaders signed a treaty creating the Great Lakota Reservation. This large reservation included the **Black Hills** and other land in what is now North Dakota, Wyoming, and Montana. Then, in 1874, gold was found in the Black Hills. About 15,000 gold miners illegally rushed onto Lakota land. The United States offered Lakota leaders $6 million for the land, but the Lakota were not interested in selling.

In 1876, United States soldiers marched into the Black Hills. They hoped to defeat the Lakota and force them onto a new reservation. But the Lakota were ready to fight for their land. **③**

REVIEW What key events took place after gold was found in the Black Hills?
◎ Sequence

▶ **Trains often slowed down to allow railroad workers and passengers to shoot buffalo.**

555

PAGE 555

② Teach and Discuss

Conflict on the Plains

🕐 ***Quick Summary*** Native Americans realized that changes on the Great Plains threatened their way of life.

① What caused the decline of the buffalo population? They were killed to feed railroad workers; people hunted buffalo for their hides or for sport.
Cause and Effect

Primary Source
Cited in *The West: An Illustrated History,* by Geoffrey C. Ward

Ask a volunteer to read aloud the quote by Sitting Bull.

② What did freedom mean to the Lakota? The right to move around the open plains and hunt buffalo
Analyze Primary Sources

③ What do you think happened when soldiers marched into the Black Hills? They ended up in a battle with the Lakota. **Make Predictions**

✓ **REVIEW ANSWER** Thousands of gold miners rushed onto Lakota land. The U.S. government offered to buy the land, but the Lakota did not want to sell. Soldiers entered the Black Hills to take the land by force. ◎ Sequence

EXTEND LANGUAGE
ESL Support

Multiple-Meaning Words Help students understand words that have different meanings.

Beginning Give students two meanings for *reservation* (land set aside for Native Americans; an agreement to set aside a seat in a restaurant or a room in a hotel) and *sport* (fun or play; an organized form of physical activity, such as soccer or baseball). Ask students to act out each meaning.

Intermediate Have students work in pairs to write sentences using each of the two meanings of *reservation* and *sport*.

Advanced Ask students to find the words *reservation, sport,* and *fashion* in this lesson. Lead students in a discussion of the different meanings of each word. Encourage them to brainstorm other words they know with more than one meaning.

For additional ESL support, use Every Student Learns Guide, pp. 230–233.

End of the Wars

 Quick Summary Sitting Bull of the Lakota and Chief Joseph of the Nez Percé led their people in battles against the U.S. government, which wanted to take away their land.

4 **What was the Battle of Little Bighorn?** A battle in Montana between American soldiers, led by George Custer, and the Lakota, led by Crazy Horse
Summarize

5 **Why do you think the government wanted the Nez Percé to leave their land?** The government and settlers wanted the land and its resources.
Draw Conclusions

✓ Ongoing Assessment

| **If…** students have difficulty understanding the government's reason for wanting these lands, | **then…** explain that the discovery of gold in the Black Hills made the reservation land much more valuable. |

Primary Source
Cited in *Bury My Heart at Wounded Knee*, by Dee Brown

6 **How do you think Chief Joseph felt as he spoke these words?** Possible answers: Tired, sad, angry, defeated
Analyze Primary Sources

Major Native American Reservations, 1890

Point out that some groups live on more than one reservation.

7 **Which groups lived just south of the border between Canada and the United States?** Blackfoot, Spokane

MAP SKILL **Answer** Ute, Hopi

8 **What was the result of the wars between the government and the Native Americans?** By the end of the 1800s, most Native Americans had been forced onto reservations.
Cause and Effect

✓ REVIEW ANSWER About 1.25 million
Main Idea and Details

End of the Wars

In June 1876, Sitting Bull and several thousand Lakota were camped near the Little Bighorn River in Montana. On June 25, **George Custer** led an attack on the Lakota camp. A Lakota leader named Crazy Horse helped lead the fight against Custer. The American soldiers were badly outnumbered, and they were quickly surrounded. Custer was killed, along with his entire force of over 200 men. This became known as the **4** **Battle of Little Bighorn.**

After the Battle of Little Bighorn, the United States sent more soldiers to defeat the Lakota. By 1877, most Lakota people had been forced onto reservations.

At this time, other Native American people were also fighting for their land. The Nez Percé (NEZ PERS) lived in the Wallowa Valley of Oregon. The government wanted to move the Nez Percé to a reservation in Idaho Territory. **5** But the Nez Percé did not want to leave their land. "It has always belonged to my people," said Nez Percé leader **Chief Joseph.**

In June 1877, United States soldiers were sent to capture the Nez Percé and take them to a reservation. But the Nez Percé refused to be taken. For the next three months, the army chased the Nez Percé 1,600 miles across Oregon, Idaho, and Montana. Several fierce battles were fought along the way.

Running short on food and supplies, the Nez Percé tried to escape into Canada. They were just 40 miles from the border when they were surrounded by American soldiers. Chief Joseph agreed to surrender, saying,

> *"I am tired of fighting. Our chiefs are killed…. The little children are freezing to death…. I am tired; my heart is sick and sad. From where the sun now stands I will fight no more forever."* **6**

MAP SKILL **Major Native American Reservations, 1890**

▶ By 1890, Native Americans were forced to live on reservations throughout the West.

MAP SKILL **Location** *Which two groups lived near the Navajo reservation?*

556

Practice and Extend

MEETING INDIVIDUAL NEEDS
Leveled Practice

Participate in a Dialogue or Debate Have groups of students create dialogues or debates centered around the conflicts between the U.S. government and Native Americans in the 1800s.

Easy Guide groups in creating a list of discussion points that might be part of a dialogue between the leaders of the Lakota and U.S. government officials following the Battle of Little Bighorn. **Reteach**

On-Level Ask groups to create and present a dialogue that might have taken place between Chief Joseph and the U.S. soldiers during his surrender. **Extend**

Advanced Have groups prepare and present a debate between officials in the U.S. government and leaders of the Native Americans at the end of the 1800s. Suggest that they include a discussion of government policies and Native American sentiments. **Enrich**

For a Lesson Summary, use Quick Study, p. 116.

The Lakota and Nez Percé were just two of many Native American groups that fought for their land. By the end of the 1800s, however, these wars came to an end. Most Native Americans had been forced onto reservations.

Look at the map of Native American reservations on page 556. Of the 2.5 million Native Americans in the United States today, about half live on or near reservations.

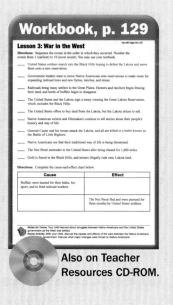

Both on and off reservations, a wide variety of Native American groups are trying to maintain their traditional cultures. Young people are learning the languages of their

▶ Chief Joseph tried to lead the Nez Percé to Canada.

ancestors, and about 200 tribal languages are still spoken today. Native American writers and filmmakers continue to tell stories about their people's history and way of life.

REVIEW About how many Native Americans live on reservations today? **Main Idea and Details**

Summarize the Lesson

1874 Thousands of miners illegally entered Lakota land after gold was discovered in the Black Hills.

1876 The Lakota defeated Custer's army at the Battle of Little Bighorn.

1877 After a 1,600-mile chase, the Nez Percé were captured in Montana.

LESSON 3 · REVIEW

Check Facts and Main Ideas

1. ⟳ Sequence On a separate sheet of paper, create a time line of the Lakota people's struggle for their land. Fill in one key event for each year shown.

> 1868—U.S. and Lakota sign treaty giving Black Hills to Lakota

> 1874—Gold discovered in Black Hills

> 1876—Battle of Little Bighorn

> 1877—Lakota forced onto reservations

2. How did railroads, farmers, and ranchers affect buffalo on the Great Plains?

3. How did the falling buffalo population affect the Plains Indians?

4. **Critical Thinking:** *Make Inferences* How do you think many Native Americans felt about living on **reservations?** What evidence can you find in the lesson to support this inference?

5. What are some ways in which Native Americans are keeping their traditions alive today?

Link to ⟨○-○⟩ Language Arts

Tell a Story One of the ways that Native American people keep their traditions alive is by telling stories. In the library, find a book of Native American stories. Read a story and write a summary of it. Then read the summary to your class.

557

---

3 Close and Assess

Summarize the Lesson

Have students read the events described on the vertical time line. Ask them to list at least one effect of each event.

✓ **LESSON 3** **REVIEW**

1. ⟳ **Sequence** For possible answers, see the reduced pupil page.

2. They caused the buffalo to begin disappearing from the plains.

3. The Plains Indians lost one of their major resources, and they could no longer live their traditional way of life.

4. **Critical Thinking:** *Make Inferences* Possible answers: They were used to living freely and did not want to live in a new place. The lesson uses the word "forced," which implies that Native Americans were not happy about moving to reservations.

Test Talk

Write Your Answer to Score High

5. Tell students to use details from the text to support their written answer. Young people are learning Native American languages, and Native American writers and filmmakers continue to tell stories about their people's history and way of life.

Link to ⟨○-○⟩ Language Arts

Students' summaries may include elements of setting, character, conflict, and solution.

FYI SOCIAL STUDIES Background

Sitting Bull

• Skirmishing between Sitting Bull and the government began in 1863.

• In May 1877, Sitting Bull escaped to Canada. Canadian law prohibited the government from aiding Sitting Bull and his people. He was forced to surrender due to lack of food.

Chief Joseph

• Though outnumbered by the U.S. Army, Chief Joseph's warriors outwitted the soldiers.

• Tired and sick, the Nez Percé eventually surrendered without having lost a single battle.

Workbook, p. 129

Lesson 3: War in the West

Directions: Sequence the events in the order in which they occurred. Number the events from 1 (earliest) to 10 (most recent). You may use your textbook.

___ United States soldiers march into the Black Hills hoping to defeat the Lakota and move them onto a new reservation.

___ Government leaders want to move Native Americans onto reservations to make room for expanding railroad lines and new farms, ranches, and mines.

___ Railroads bring many settlers to the Great Plains. Farmers and ranchers begin fencing their land, and herds of buffalo begin to disappear.

___ The United States and the Lakota sign a treaty creating the Great Lakota Reservation, which includes the Black Hills.

___ The United States offers to buy land from the Lakota, but the Lakota refuse to sell.

___ Native American writers and filmmakers continue to tell stories about their people's history and way of life.

___ General Custer and his troops attack the Lakota, and all are killed in a battle known as the Battle of Little Bighorn.

___ Native Americans see that their traditional way of life is being threatened.

___ The Nez Percé surrender to the United States after being chased for 1,600 miles.

___ Gold is found in the Black Hills, and miners illegally rush onto Lakota land.

Directions: Complete the cause-and-effect chart below.

Cause	Effect
Buffalo were hunted for their hides, for sport, and to feed railroad workers.	
	The Nez Percé fled and were pursued for three months by United States soldiers.

Also on Teacher Resources CD-ROM.

Resources

- Assessment Book, pp. 93–96
- Workbook, p. 130: Vocabulary Review

Chapter Summary

For possible answers, see the reduced pupil page.

Vocabulary

1. c, **2.** a, **3.** d, **4.** b, **5.** e

People and Terms

Possible answers:

1. Samuel Morse developed telegraph messages using a code called the Morse code.

2. The Pony Express was a group of riders that delivered mail between Missouri and the West Coast.

3. The Homestead Act offered free land to pioneers if they lived on it and farmed it for five years.

4. Cattle drives moved cattle from the Southwest to railroad lines with connections to eastern cities.

5. George Shima was a Japanese immigrant who moved to California and raised potatoes.

6. Sitting Bull was a Lakota leader who fought against soldiers trying to take over Native American lands in the Black Hills.

7. At the Battle of Little Bighorn, the Lakota defeated General Custer and more than 200 soldiers.

8. Chief Joseph led the Nez Percé people against soldiers who were sent to force them off their land.

Facts and Main Ideas

1. The stagecoach cut the time needed to travel from Missouri to California from months to 25 days.

2. The railroad lines crossed the traditional Native American hunting grounds and settlers farmed or fenced in some of this land. Many buffalo—which some Native Americans depended on for survival—were killed.

3. About two years

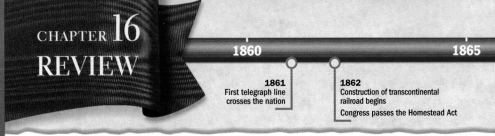

1860   1865

1861
First telegraph line crosses the nation

1862
Construction of transcontinental railroad begins
Congress passes the Homestead Act

Chapter Summary

Sequence

Copy the diagram onto a separate sheet of paper. Put the events in correct time order with their dates.

| 1861—First telegraph line crosses the nation |
| 1862—Congress passes Homestead Act |
| 1869—Transcontinental railroad completed |
| 1877—Nez Percé defeated |

Vocabulary

Match each word with the correct definition or description.

1 telegraph (p. 539)

2 homesteader (p. 547)

3 sodbuster (p. 547)

4 exoduster (p. 549)

5 reservation (p. 555)

a. settler who received land through the Homestead Act

b. African American pioneer farmer

c. invention that sends messages over electrical wires

d. Great Plains farmer

e. area of land set aside for Native Americans

People and Terms

Write a sentence explaining why each of the following people or terms was important in the expansion of the West. You may use two or more in a single sentence.

1 Samuel Morse (p. 539)

2 Pony Express (p. 539)

3 Homestead Act (p. 547)

4 cattle drives (p. 550)

5 George Shima (p. 552)

6 Sitting Bull (p. 555)

7 Battle of Little Bighorn (p. 556)

8 Chief Joseph (p. 556)

558

Practice and Extend

Assessment Options

✓Chapter 16 Assessment

- Chapter 16 Content Test: Use Assessment Book, pp. 93–94.
- Chapter 16 Skills Test: Use Assessment Book, pp. 95–96.

Standardized Test Prep

- Chapter 16 Tests contain standardized test format.

✓Chapter 19 Performance Assessment

- Have students work in groups to present a play about life on the plains. Some students may play the role of homesteaders, while others portray the Native American way of life.

- Ask different groups of students to play different scenes. Some students can perform actions and others can narrate.

- Assess students' understanding of the sequence of events and their effects on lifestyles.

1869
Transcontinental railroad completed

1874
Gold found on Lakota land in Black Hills

1876
Lakota defeat Custer at Battle of Little Bighorn

1877
African American pioneers establish town of Nicodemus, Kansas

Nez Percé are defeated in Montana

Facts and Main Ideas

- How did the stagecoach improve on earlier means of travel?

- How did railroad lines and new settlers affect Native Americans?

- **Time Line** How many years passed between the discovery of gold in the Black Hills and the Battle of Little Bighorn?

- **Main Idea** What different challenges made the work of the Union Pacific and Central Pacific railroads so difficult?

- **Main Idea** How did the Homestead Act help people get land?

- **Main Idea** How and why were Native American lands threatened by newcomers?

- **Critical Thinking:** *Compare and Contrast* Compare the points of view held by Native Americans and the United States government about American Indian lands.

Write About History

- **Write a brief news message** describing events at Promontory Point, Utah Territory, on May 10, 1869.

- **Write a letter home** about your experience as a homesteader.

- **Write a help wanted ad** for a cowboy. Explain the responsibilities and benefits of the job.

Apply Skills

Use Time Zone Maps
Study the United States time zone map on page 542. Then answer the questions,

1. How many time zones share a border with Mexico? Which ones are they?

2. How many time zones apart are Omaha and Denver? What time is it in Denver when it is 8:00 A.M. in Omaha?

3. How many time zones apart are Portland and Boston? What time would a person in Portland make a call to reach a friend in Boston at 1:00 P.M. Boston time?

Internet Activity
To get help with vocabulary, people, and terms, select dictionary or encyclopedia from *Social Studies Library* at www.sfsocialstudies.com.

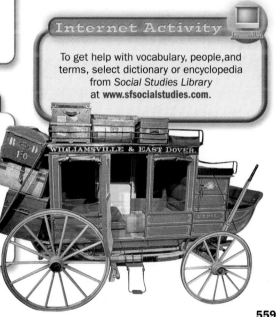

WILLIAMSVILLE & EAST DOVER.

559

4. Railroad workers had to lay track across the steep slopes of the Sierra Nevada mountain range.

5. The Homestead Act gave settlers land on the plains for a small registration fee as long as they farmed it and lived on it for five years.

6. Railroads, which made travel easier for settlers, scared off the buffalo. Also, buffalo were killed to feed railroad workers and hunted for their hides, or for sport. The government forced Native Americans off much of their land.

7. Possible answer: The government wanted to buy the lands and relocate Native Americans onto reservations. The Native Americans wanted to keep their land and continue their traditional lifestyle of traveling over the open plains.

Write About History

1. Students should consider the enormity of the transcontinental project and its importance to the development of the United States.

2. Suggest that students include both the difficulties of this lifestyle and the opportunities it provides.

3. Students should use persuasive language and present a logical argument in their ads.

Apply Skills

1. Three; Central, Mountain, and Pacific

2. One time zone; 7:00 A.M.

3. Three time zones; 10:00 A.M.

Hands-on Unit Project

✓ Unit 8 Performance Assessment

- See p. 592 for information about using the Unit Project as a means of performance assessment.

- A scoring guide is provided on p. 592.

WEB SITE
Technology

For more information, students can select the dictionary or encyclopedia from *Social Studies Library* at www.sfsocialstudies.com.

Workbook, p. 130

Vocabulary Review

Directions: Choose the vocabulary word below that best completes each sentence. Write the word on the line provided.

Pony Express	homesteader	barbed wire
telegraph	sodbuster	reservation
transcontinental railroad	exoduster	Battle of Little Bighorn
Homestead Act	cattle drive	

1. Two companies built the _____ to connect the country by rail.

2. An African American pioneer who started a new life in Kansas or Nebraska was an _____.

3. _____ is used by farmers to create inexpensive fences to keep cattle off their farmland.

4. The government offered the _____ granting free land to pioneers willing to start new farms on the Great Plains.

5. Native Americans were moved to a _____, or land set aside by the government.

6. The _____ made mail delivery faster than by stagecoach.

7. U.S. General George Custer was killed in the _____.

8. A farmer on the Great Plains was known as a _____ because of the tough sod of that area.

9. Cowboys participated in a _____ to get their cattle north to the railroad lines.

10. A _____ was someone who took advantage of the government plan to grant land to settlers who would farm the Great Plains.

11. With the invention of the _____, messages were sent along wires using electricity.

Notes for Home: Your child learned about changes that occurred as the nation expanded.
Home Activity: Practice the vocabulary words by having a spelling bee or a definition bee involving several friends or family members.

Also on Teacher Resources CD-ROM.

Chapter Planning Guide

Chapter 17 • Industry and Immigration

Locating Time and Place pp. 560–561

Lesson Titles	Pacing	Main Ideas
Lesson 1 **Inventions and Big Business** pp. 562–567	2 days	• In the late 1800s, new inventions powered the growth of American industry and changed the way people lived.
Lesson 2 **New Americans** pp. 568–574	3 days	• During the late 1800s and early 1900s, millions of immigrants moved to American cities, and workers struggled for better conditions.
Biography: Mary Antin p. 575 **Issues and Viewpoints: Working Against Child Labor** pp. 576–577		• Mary Antin's ability to write allowed her to share the experience of her immigrant family's journey to the United States. • From the 1800s through today, people have worked to end child labor.
Lesson 3 **Expansion Overseas** pp. 578–582	2 days	• By the end of the 1800s, the United States had gained new territory and become a world power.
Biography: Theodore Roosevelt p. 583 **Thinking Skills: Credibility of a Source** pp. 584–585		• Theodore Roosevelt used his role as governor and later as President to preserve the environment and to help people who could not protect themselves. • It is important to evaluate the credibility of information by considering the author's background and purpose.

✔ **Chapter 17 Review**
pp. 586–587

▶ **Teddy Roosevelt inspired a new name for toy bears.**

✔ = Assessment Options

◀ **The first telephone**

Vocabulary	Resources	Meeting Individual Needs
onopoly orporation	• Workbook, p. 132 • Transparency 11 • Every Student Learns Guide, pp. 234–237 • Quick Study, pp. 118–119	• Leveled Practice, TE p. 564 • ESL Support, TE p. 566 • Learning Styles, TE p. 567
enement rejudice ettlement house bor union rike	• Workbook, p. 133 • Transparency 1 • Every Student Learns Guide, pp. 238–241 • Quick Study, pp. 120–121	• Leveled Practice, TE p. 570 • ESL Support, TE p. 574
panish-American War ough Riders uffalo Soldiers urce	• Workbook, p. 134 • Transparency 21 • Every Student Learns Guide, pp. 242–245 • Quick Study, pp. 122–123 • Workbook, p. 135	• ESL Support, TE p. 579 • Leveled Practice, TE p. 581
	✓ Chapter 17 Content Test, Assessment Book, pp. 97–98 ✓ Chapter 17 Skills Test, Assessment Book, pp. 99–100	✓ Chapter 17 Performance Assessment, TE p. 586

Providing More Depth

Additional Resources

• Vocabulary Workbook and Cards
• Social Studies Plus! pp. 194–199
• Daily Activity Bank
• Big Book Atlas
• Student Atlas
• Outline Maps
• Desk Maps

 **Technology**

• AudioText
• MindPoint® Quiz Show CD-ROM
• ExamView® Test Bank CD-ROM
• Teacher Resources CD-ROM
• Map Resources CD-ROM
• SFSuccessNet: iText (Pupil Edition online), iTE (Teacher's Edition online), Online Planner
• **www.sfsocialstudies.com** (Biographies, news, references, maps, and activities)

 To establish guidelines for your students' safe and responsible use of the Internet, use the Scott Foresman Internet Guide.

Additional Internet Links

To find out more about:

• Inventions of the nineteenth and twentieth centuries, visit **www.moah.org**
• Theodore Roosevelt, visit **www.whitehouse.gov**
• The Spanish-American War, visit **www.pbs.org**

Key Internet Search Terms

• immigrants
• inventors
• child labor
• U.S.S. *Maine*

Workbook Support

Use the following Workbook pages to support content and skills development as you teach Chapter 17. You can also view and print Workbook pages from the Teacher Resources CD-ROM.

Workbook, p. 131

Use with Chapter 17.

Vocabulary Preview

Directions: Write the definition of each term on the lines provided. You may use your glossary.

1. monopoly __A company that has control over an entire industry and stops competition__

2. corporation __A business that is owned by investors__

3. tenement __A building that is divided into small apartments__

4. prejudice __An unfair negative opinion about a group of people__

5. settlement house __A center that provides help for those who have little money__

6. labor union __A group of workers who have joined together to fight for improved working conditions and better wages__

7. strike __Workers' refusal to work until business owners meet their demands__

8. Spanish-American War __The war between Spain and the United States that started when the USS *Maine* exploded in Cuba's Havana harbor__

9. Rough Rider __A volunteer in Theodore Roosevelt's group of soldiers who fought in the Spanish-American War__

10. Buffalo Soldier __Experienced African American soldier who fought against Native Americans on the Great Plains and alongside the Rough Riders in the Spanish-American War__

Notes for Home: Your child learned about life in the United States in the late 1800s.
Home Activity: Have your child write each vocabulary term in an original sentence. If he or she has difficulty, find the term in the text and explore how it is used.

Use with Pupil Edition, p. 560

Workbook, p. 132

Lesson 1: Inventions and Big Business

Use with Pages 562–567.

Directions: Match each person listed in the box below to an invention or accomplishment listed in the chart. Some answers will be used more than once. You may use your textbook.

| John D. Rockefeller | Lewis Latimer | Andrew Carnegie |
| Alexander Graham Bell | Thomas Edison | Henry Bessemer |

Invention/Accomplishment	Person Responsible
1. telephone	Alexander Graham Bell
2. phonograph	Thomas Edison
3. helped make steel a major industry in the United States	Andrew Carnegie
4. movie camera	Thomas Edison
5. light bulb	Thomas Edison
6. long-lasting light bulb	Lewis Latimer
7. gave away more than $300 million to help build universities, libraries, museums, and theaters	Andrew Carnegie
8. founded Standard Oil	John D. Rockefeller
9. new process for making steel	Henry Bessemer

Notes for Home: Your child learned about American entrepreneurs and inventors of the late 1800s.
Home Activity: With your child, brainstorm a list of benefits we enjoy today because of the accomplishments of the people listed in the chart.

Use with Pupil Edition, p. 567

Workbook, p. 133

Lesson 2: New Americans

Use with Pages 568–574.

Directions: Complete each sentence using terms and concepts from Lesson 2. Use an additional sheet of paper if you need more space. You may use your textbook.

1. During the late 1800s, many immigrants came to the United States from __northern and western Europe__

2. During the early 1900s, many immigrants came to the United States from __southern and eastern Europe__

3. Many Europeans left their homes to escape __hardships__ such as hunger, poverty, lack jobs, lack of freedom, and religious persecution.

4. For millions of European immigrants, __Ellis Island__ was their first stop in the United State

5. Many Asian immigrants first came to __Angel Island__ and waited there for permission to enter the United States.

6. Upon arriving in the United States, two things most immigrants did first were __find a place to stay__ and __and find a job__

7. Most immigrants settled in cities where there were busy __factories__ and many jobs.

8. Many immigrants and people from towns and farms moved into cities, causing a __shortage of housing__

9. __Tenements__ often provided unhealthy living conditions.

10. Although many immigrants faced __prejudice__, many received help in improving their live

11. Some people took jobs in crowded workshops known as __sweatshops__, where conditions often were very dangerous.

12. To fight for better working conditions and better wages, many workers joined __labor unions__

13. Samuel Gompers founded the __American Federation of Labor, or AFL,__ to give unions more power.

Notes for Home: Your child learned about the lives of new immigrants to the United States during the la 1800s and early 1900s.
Home Activity: With your child, discuss the difficulties a new student at school might face and what you child might do to help that person with the adjustment. Compare this to the difficulties immigrants faced

Use with Pupil Edition, p. 574

Workbook Support

Workbook, p. 134

Lesson 3: Expansion Overseas

Use with Pages 578–582.

Directions: Complete the cause-and-effect chart with information from Lesson 3. You may use your textbook.

Cause	Effect
1. Russia offers to sell Alaska for 2 cents an acre. U.S. Secretary of State William Seward insists Alaska is worth buying.	**The U.S. Senate votes to approve the purchase of Alaska for $7.2 million.**
2. **Gold is found in Alaska.**	Thousands of miners rush north in search of wealth and adventure.
3. American planters discover that the Hawaiian climate is good for growing sugarcane and pineapples.	**American planters establish several large plantations in Hawaii.**
4. Queen Liliuokalani of Hawaii wants native-born Hawaiians to remain in control of the islands.	**American planters revolt against Queen Liliuokalani, and U.S. soldiers support the planters.**
5. Queen Liliuokalani yields her authority to the United States to avoid bloodshed.	**Hawaii becomes part of the United States.**
6. **In 1895 the Cuban people revolt against Spanish rule.**	Spanish soldiers imprison hundreds of thousands of Cubans to keep people from joining the revolution.
7. People in the United States are angered by Spain's treatment of the Cuban people. American-owned businesses in Cuba begin feeling the effects of the war.	**U.S. President McKinley sends the battleship USS *Maine* to Cuba's Havana harbor to protect the lives and property of Americans in Cuba.**
8. **An explosion destroys the battleship USS *Maine*, killing 260 Americans.**	Americans blame Spain for the explosion. Congress declares war on April 25, 1898, and the Spanish-American War begins.
9. **The United States defeats Spain in the Spanish-American War.**	The United States emerges as a world power.

Notes for Home: Your child learned how the United States expanded and became a world power.
Home Activity: With your child, make a chart comparing and contrasting the ways the United States gained control of Alaska, Hawaii, Puerto Rico, the Philippines, and Guam.

Use with Pupil Edition, p. 582

Workbook, p. 135

Credibility of a Source

Use with Pages 584–585.

Some sources of information are more believable than others. This is due, in part, to who is presenting the information.

Directions: Read the two passages about General George Armstrong Custer and answer the questions that follow.

Passage A comes from a historical novel. The story is presented as a part-fact, part-fiction presentation of Custer's journal. As you read the words, imagine them to be directly from Custer, himself.

> *Perhaps I have worshiped my superiors too well with not enough thought of myself. [My wife,] Libbie, says that I have always been too hasty in putting the needs of others ahead of my own.*

Passage B comes from a biography. It is based on fact. At times the author includes a personal point of view or conclusion, as well as reports from others who were involved in the actual situation.

> *What [Custer] did was perfectly in keeping with his nature. He did what he had always done: push ahead, disregard orders, start a fight. . . .*
> *So he marched his men most of the night and flung them into battle when—as a number of Native Americans noted—they were so tired their legs shook when they dismounted.*

1. According to Passage A, how did Custer treat his superiors? According to Passage B?

   Passage A says Custer worshiped his superiors. Passage B states that he disregarded orders.

2. According to Passage A, how did Custer treat others, in general? According to Passage B?

   Passage A says Custer put the needs of others ahead of his own. Passage B states that he marched his men into battle when they were too tired to fight.

3. Which passage has more credibility? Why?

   Possible answer: Passage B is more credible because it is based on fact and contains information from actual participants in the events. Passage A is based only partially on fact.

Notes for Home: Your child learned how to determine the credibility of a source.
Home Activity: With your child, brainstorm various sources of information and discuss the credibility of each.

Use with Pupil Edition, p. 585

Workbook, p. 136

Vocabulary Review

Use with Chapter 17.

Directions: Read the following statements. Then write *T* (True) or *F* (False) on the line before each statement. If the answer is false, correct the statement to make it true. You may use your textbook. Not all words will be used.

F 1. A monopoly is any business that is owned by investors.

   A corporation is any business that is owned by investors.

T 2. In some cities, poor people received help at a settlement house.

F 3. The workers decided to stage a monopoly until the owners met their demands.

   The workers decided to stage a strike until the owners met their demands.

F 4. The African American soldiers who defended Americans and American property in Cuba were known as Rough Riders.

   The African American soldiers who defended Americans and American property in Cuba were known as Buffalo Soldiers.

T 5. A volunteer soldier under Theodore Roosevelt who defended Americans in Cuba was known as a Rough Rider.

F 6. When a single company controls an entire industry and stops competition, it is called a corporation.

   When a single company controls an entire industry and stops competition, it is called a monopoly.

F 7. A settlement house is a building that is divided into small apartments.

   A tenement is a building that is divided into small apartments.

Notes for Home: Your child learned how industry and immigration affected the United States during the mid-1800s to late 1800s.
Home Activity: With your child, take turns role-playing a situation for each vocabulary term. You may wish to use real-life situations from the text as models.

Use with Pupil Edition, p. 587

Workbook, p. 137

UNIT 8 Project Invention Conventions

Directions: Make a poster or advertisement for an invention from the late 1800s.

1. The invention we chose is _____

2. The name of the inventor is _____

3. The purpose of the invention is _____

4. Special features of this invention include _____

5. The (✔) shows the benefits of this invention:
   ____ helping people ____ saving money ____ saving time ____ other: _____

6. Reasons people should use this invention are _____

7. This invention changed the world because _____

8. This is what the invention looked like.

Encourage students to ask questions of each "inventor" as if they are potential customers. Have students respond with details from their research.

✔ Checklist for Students
____ We chose an invention from the late 1800s.
____ We identified the inventor, and we described the invention's purpose, features, and benefits.
____ We made a poster or advertisement for the invention.
____ We included a picture of the invention on the poster.
____ We presented our poster or advertisement to the class.

Notes for Home: Your child researched an invention from the 1800s and advertised its features to the class.
Home Activity: With your child, identify a modern invention you both agree has changed the world. Discuss how it has impacted your life.

Use with Pupil Edition, p. 592

Assessment Support

Use these Assessment Book pages and the ExamView® Test Bank CD-ROM to assess content and skills in Chapter 17 and Unit 8. You can also view and print Assessment Book pages from the Teacher Resources CD-ROM.

Assessment Book, p. 97

Chapter 17 Test

Part 1: Content Test

Directions: Fill in the circle next to the correct answer.

Lesson Objective (1:1)

1. Who invented the telephone?
   - ● Alexander Graham Bell
   - Ⓑ Thomas Edison
   - Ⓒ Andrew Carnegie
   - Ⓓ Lewis Latimer

Lesson Objective (1:1)

2. Thomas Edison is known for the successful development of which of the following?
   - Ⓐ the electric motor
   - Ⓑ the telegraph
   - Ⓒ the telephone
   - ● the electric light bulb

Lesson Objective (1:2)

3. Why was the development of the Bessemer process important?
   - Ⓐ It made steel that was weak enough to bend by hand.
   - Ⓑ It produced strong but expensive steel.
   - ● It produced strong steel at affordable prices.
   - Ⓓ It reduced people's need for steel.

Lesson Objective (1:3)

4. Which of the following people helped steel become a major industry in the United States?
   - Ⓐ Thomas Edison
   - ● Andrew Carnegie
   - Ⓒ Alexander Graham Bell
   - Ⓓ Lewis Latimer

Lesson Objective (1:3)

5. Why did Andrew Carnegie donate millions of dollars to build universities, libraries, museums, and theaters?
   - Ⓐ He wanted to win young people's votes.
   - Ⓑ He wanted to own those places one day.
   - Ⓒ He needed places for his employees to go in their spare time.
   - ● He felt it was important to use his wealth to help others.

Lesson Objective (1:4)

6. By the early 1900s, the automobile had created a demand for products made from which of the following?
   - Ⓐ steel
   - Ⓑ iron
   - ● oil
   - Ⓓ gold

Lesson Objective (1:5)

7. What is one way industry changed people's lifestyles in the United States?
   - Ⓐ More Americans found jobs on farms.
   - Ⓑ More people began working from their homes.
   - Ⓒ People moved away from the city.
   - ● More women began working outside the home.

Use with Pupil Edition, p. 586

Assessment Book, p. 98

Lesson Objective (2:1)

8. Which of the following is NOT a reason why immigrants came to the United States?
   - Ⓐ They wanted to escape religious persecution.
   - ● They were homesick.
   - Ⓒ They wanted to escape poverty.
   - Ⓓ They wanted to be free.

Lesson Objective (2:2)

9. What was one hardship faced by many immigrants to the United States?
   - Ⓐ Many jobs were available.
   - Ⓑ Others from their own country lived here.
   - ● Many Americans were prejudiced against them.
   - Ⓓ There was much opportunity.

Lesson Objective (2:3)

10. Why were labor unions formed?
    - ● for better working conditions and better pay
    - Ⓑ to get equal pay for men and women
    - Ⓒ to help create monopolies
    - Ⓓ to receive paid holidays

Lesson Objective (2:4)

11. What did the American Federation of Labor help unions accomplish?
    - ● Unions were able to join together and be stronger.
    - Ⓑ Unions were able to create laws.
    - Ⓒ Unions were able to draft new members.
    - Ⓓ Unions never again had an unsuccessful strike.

Lesson Objective (2:4)

12. Which of the following is NOT an accomplishment of labor unions?
    - Ⓐ shorter hours
    - Ⓑ improved safety
    - Ⓒ better working conditions
    - ● the right to quit

Lesson Objective (3:1)

13. Why did William Seward want the United States to purchase Alaska?
    - Ⓐ He knew there was gold there.
    - Ⓑ He wanted to be close to Russia.
    - Ⓒ He believed it was worth buying.
    - ● He wanted a place where the United States could hold the Winter Olympics.

Lesson Objective (3:2)

14. Who were the first Americans to become powerful in Hawaii?
    - Ⓐ ranchers
    - ● planters
    - Ⓒ fishers
    - Ⓓ miners

Lesson Objective (3:2)

15. Why did the queen of Hawaii yield her authority to the United States?
    - Ⓐ The people asked her to.
    - Ⓑ She wanted her people to be Americans.
    - Ⓒ She was promised a seat in the U.S. Congress.
    - ● She wanted to avoid bloodshed.

Use with Pupil Edition, p. 586

Assessment Book, p. 99

Lesson Objective (3:3)

16. Which of the following events started the Spanish-American War?
    - ● The USS *Maine* exploded in Cuba's Havana harbor.
    - Ⓑ The USS *Maine* was sent to Cuba to protect Americans.
    - Ⓒ Spanish soldiers imprisoned many Cubans.
    - Ⓓ U.S. businesses in Cuba declared war.

Lesson Objective (3:4)

17. How was the United States viewed by the world as a result of the Spanish-American War?
    - Ⓐ as a weak nation
    - ● as a world power
    - Ⓒ as a desirable place to live
    - Ⓓ as a warlike dictatorship

Part 2: Skills Test

Directions: Use complete sentences to answer questions 1–8. Use a separate sheet of paper if you need more space.

1. Why do you think the telephone became so successful so quickly? **Draw Conclusions**

   Possible answer: The telephone allowed people to talk to each other over long distances, changing the way people communicated.

2. How did the work of Lewis Latimer help make Edison's light bulb practical for everyday use? **Main Idea and Details**

   Possible answer: Edison's light bulb did not last long enough to be practical. Latimer invented a bulb that lasted longer.

3. How did Andrew Carnegie go from being a poor immigrant to one of the wealthiest people in the world? **Summarize**

   Possible answer: Carnegie used the Bessemer process to make strong, affordable steel. He also controlled the whole steel-making process, so he was able to keep most of the profits earned.

Use with Pupil Edition, p. 586

Assessment Book, p. 100

4. Why do you think some immigrants left their homeland to move to a place where their future was uncertain? **Make Inferences**

   Possible answer: Although life in the United States was uncertain, many people faced such poor conditions in their homeland that they were willing to take the risk.

5. What hardships did some immigrants to the United States face in the late 1800s and early 1900s? Why do you think they tolerated these conditions? **Draw Conclusions**

   Possible answers: Life in crowded tenements, prejudice, long work hours, unsafe conditions, low pay; This still was a better life than the one they had left behind.

6. What event helped lead to the formation of labor unions? How do you think labor unions affected the availability of jobs? Explain. **Make Inferences**

   In March 1911 a fire at the Triangle Shirtwaist Company killed 146 workers. Possible answer: Unions may have reduced the number of jobs because companies had to spend more money improving working conditions and wages.

7. What events, in order, led to Alaska and Hawaii becoming part of the United States? **Sequence**

   Alaska: Russia offers to sell Alaska for 2 cents an acre. United States accepts the offer. Hawaii: American planters establish large plantations in Hawaii. U.S. planters lead a revolt against the queen of Hawaii. U.S. soldiers support the planters. The Hawaiian queen yields her power.

8. Describe two ways you think things might be different today if Spain had not been accused of destroying the battleship USS *Maine.* **Make Inferences**

   Possible answers: No Spanish-American War; more Cubans killed by Spanish soldiers; Theodore Roosevelt not a war hero and then President; Puerto Rico, Philippines, and Guam not U.S. territories; United States not recognized as a world power as soon as it was

Use with Pupil Edition, p. 586

Assessment Support

Unit 8 Test

Part 1: Content Test

Directions: Fill in the circle next to the correct answer.

Lesson Objective (16–1:2)

1. Why did the telegraph replace the Pony Express?
   - A It was a safer journey.
   - B Messages only took a few days.
   - ● It was faster.
   - D Messages were shorter.

Lesson Objective (16–1:1)

2. Why did people want the transcontinental railroad?
   - ● People and goods would travel faster between the East and West.
   - B It would carry goods and people across the East.
   - C It was safer than the Pony Express.
   - D It was faster than the telegraph.

Lesson Objective (16–1:4)

3. Which of the following was NOT an effect of the transcontinental railroad?
   - A People in the West could stay in touch with relatives in the East.
   - B More people visited different parts of the country.
   - C People in the East could get fresh beef from Texas.
   - ● People could commute each day between the East and West.

Lesson Objective (16–2:1)

4. Why did many pioneers become homesteaders?
   - ● The government gave them free land to farm.
   - B They would not have to farm the land.
   - C They wanted to build great cities and factories.
   - D There was a lot of wheat growing on the land.

Lesson Objective (16–2:3)

5. What attracted many people to the Great Plains?
   - A There was a train stop there.
   - B They could not make it to the West Coast.
   - ● They were seeking a better life.
   - D They were seeking jobs in factories.

Lesson Objective (16–2:4)

6. What effect did the homesteaders' fences have on cattle drives?
   - A More cattle needed to be moved to the East.
   - B The cattle could roam freely inside the fences.
   - C They made cattle drives more important.
   - ● They helped bring an end to cattle drives.

Lesson Objective (16–3:1)

7. Which of the following was NOT a change brought to the Great Plains by U.S. expansion?
   - A Farmers fenced in the land.
   - ● People left the Great Plains to move east.
   - C Native Americans were forced to change their lifestyles.
   - D The buffalo began to disappear.

Lesson Objective (16–3:2)

8. How did Native Americans react to changes caused by U.S. expansion?
   - A They moved the buffalo to new lands.
   - B They helped build the railroad.
   - C They willingly helped the settlers.
   - ● They fought to keep their lands and maintain their way of life.

Lesson Objective (16–3:3)

9. What is one difference between the way the Lakota and the Nez Percé reacted to the U.S. government's demands?
   - A The Lakota fought, and the Nez Percé left peacefully.
   - B Only the Lakota became U.S. soldiers.
   - ● The Lakota moved peacefully to a new reservation, and the Nez Percé resisted.
   - D The Nez Percé escaped to Canada, and the Lakota stayed on their homeland.

Lesson Objective (17–1:1)

10. Which of the following is Alexander Graham Bell famous for inventing?
    - A light bulb
    - ● telephone
    - C phonograph
    - D automobile

Lesson Objective (17–1:2)

11. Which of the following people invented the process that made steel strong and affordable?
    - A Thomas Edison
    - B Alexander Graham Bell
    - C Lewis Latimer
    - ● Henry Bessemer

Lesson Objective (17–1:5)

12. Which of the following was NOT a way industry changed the American way of life?
    - ● Settlers began moving west.
    - B More people moved from farms to the cities.
    - C More women found work outside of the home.
    - D There were millions of new jobs.

Lesson Objective (17–2:1)

13. Which of the following is a reason why immigrants came to the United States?
    - A to live in a tenement
    - B to experience prejudice
    - C to protest the opening of Hull House
    - ● to improve their lives

Lesson Objective (17–2:3)

14. Which of the following is a goal of labor unions?
    - ● to improve working conditions
    - B to pay factory workers
    - C to receive equal work
    - D to close down all factories

Lesson Objective (17–2:4)

15. Which of the following is an accomplishment of labor unions?
    - A increased hours of work
    - ● improved safety on the job
    - C locked doors surrounding all work rooms
    - D lower minimum age of workers

Lesson Objective (17–3:1)

16. Which of the following indicates that the purchase of Alaska was a good decision?
    - ● Gold was discovered in Alaska.
    - B People laughed and called it Seward's Icebox.
    - C Hawaii became a state.
    - D Alaska was considered a vast, useless land of snow and ice.

Lesson Objective (17–3:4)

17. Which of the following did NOT become part of the United States as a result of the Spanish-American War?
    - A Guam
    - B the Philippines
    - C Puerto Rico
    - ● Cuba

Part 2: Skills Test

Directions: Use complete sentences to answer questions 1–5. Use a separate sheet of paper if you need more space.

1. If you were a pioneer moving westward in the 1800s, what circumstances or events might convince you to stay in the Great Plains? What might convince you to continue on to the West Coast? **Express Ideas**

   Accept all reasonable answers. Possible answers: Free land and remaining relatively close to friends and family in the East might have made the Great Plains attractive; Land that was difficult to farm, harsh weather, and conflicts with Native Americans might have caused settlers to move on to the West Coast.

2. How do you think farmers in the Great Plains felt about cattle drives? How do you know? **Draw Conclusions**

   Farmers in the Great Plains did not like cattle drives. The farmers put barbed-wire fences around their fields to protect their crops from the cattle that came through on cattle drives.

3. What actions by the U.S. government and by Native Americans showed how each group viewed the buffalo? **Compare and Contrast**

   The government felt the buffalo were unimportant and had them killed. Native Americans felt the buffalo were very important and tried to protect them by working to keep the railroad and settlers away.

4. Why was the development of strong, affordable steel important? **Summarize**

   Possible answer: Steel is much stronger than iron, but was much more expensive. The Bessemer process made steel more affordable to use for a wider variety of products.

5. What series of events caused the United States to send the battleship USS *Maine* to Cuba? **Sequence**

   Cuban people revolted against Spanish rule; Spain imprisoned many, and thousands died; Americans wanted to protect Cuban people and American-owned businesses in Cuba; United States sent USS *Maine* to Cuba's Havana harbor

United States Time Zones

6. Suppose it were 10:00 A.M. in Wichita. What time would it be in each of the other cities shown in the table? Use the map to complete the chart. **Read a Time Zone Map**

City	Time	Time Zone
Wichita	10:00 A.M.	Central
Boston	11:00 A.M.	Eastern
Helena	9:00 A.M.	Mountain
Las Vegas	8:00 A.M.	Pacific
Miami	11:00 A.M.	Eastern
Anchorage	7:00 A.M.	Hawaii-Aleutian

Industry and Immigration

Resources

- Workbook, p. 131: Vocabulary Preview
- Vocabulary Cards
- Social Studies Plus!

1876, Boston, Massachusetts: Lesson 1

Ask students to describe the impact that the invention of the telephone had on communication. (People could communicate faster and farther.)

1889, Chicago, Illinois: Lesson 2

This picture shows a settlement house, or place where poor people could go for educational and personal services. Ask students what help the poor might need. (Possible answer: child care, medical treatment, reading classes)

1898, Havana, Cuba: Lesson 3

Ask students how the event pictured could lead to a war. (Blaming another country could lead to war between the United States and that country.)

1876

Boston, Massachusetts
Alexander Graham Bell invents the telephone.

Lesson 1

1889

Chicago, Illinois
Jane Addams opens a settlement house to help the poor.

Lesson 2

1898

Havana, Cuba
United States battleship *Maine* explodes, leading to the Spanish-American War.

Lesson 3

560

Practice and Extend

Vocabulary Preview

- Use Workbook p. 131 to help students preview the vocabulary words in this chapter.
- Use Vocabulary Cards to preview key concept words in this chapter.

 Also on Teacher Resources CD-ROM.

Workbook, p. 131

Vocabulary Preview
Directions: Write the definition of each term on the lines provided. You may use your glossary.

1. monopoly _____
2. corporation _____
3. tenement _____
4. prejudice _____
5. settlement house _____

6. labor union _____

7. strike _____

8. Spanish-American War _____

9. Rough Rider _____

10. Buffalo Soldier _____

Notes for Home: Your child learned about life in the United States in the late 1800s.
Home Activity: Have your child write each vocabulary term in an original sentence. If he or she has difficulty, find the term in the text and explore how it is used.

Locating Time and Place

2 · Chicago · UNITED STATES

1 · Boston

ATLANTIC OCEAN

3

Gulf of Mexico

Havana

CUBA

Why We Remember

"Give me your tired, your poor,
Your huddled masses yearning to breathe free…"

These words are part of a poem by Emma Lazarus that was written for the Statue of Liberty in New York Harbor. "Lady Liberty" has been a symbol of hope and freedom for the millions of immigrants who have come to the United States from all over the world. In this unit you will see how Americans—both newcomers and those born here—contributed to the remarkable growth and changes that altered our nation forever.

561

- Have students examine the pictures shown on p. 560 for Lessons 1, 2, and 3.

- Remind students that each picture is coded with a number and a color to link it to a place on the map on p. 561.

Why We Remember

Have students read the "Why We Remember" paragraph on p. 561, and ask them why events in this chapter might be important to them. Have students discuss neighborhoods, groups, or individuals in their community who keep alive the memory of other countries.

WEB SITE Technology

You can learn more about Boston, Massachusetts; Chicago, Illinois; and Havana, Cuba by clicking on *Atlas* at **www.sfsocialstudies.com**.

FYI SOCIAL STUDIES Background

The Statue of Liberty Ask students to share experiences or personal knowledge about the Statue of Liberty.

- France gave her to the U.S. as a sign of international friendship.

- One of her engineers, Gustave-Eiffel, also designed the Eiffel Tower.

- The seven spikes of her crown stand for the seven seas and the seven continents of the world.

- She holds a tablet in her left hand, inscribed "July 4, 1776."

Inventions and Big Business

Objectives

- Identify important inventions of Alexander Graham Bell and Thomas Edison.

- Explain the significance of the Bessemer steel-making process.

- Evaluate the accomplishments of Andrew Carnegie.

- Describe the rise of the oil industry in the United States.

- Explain how industry changed the American way of life.

Vocabulary

monopoly, p. 566; **corporation,** p. 566

Resources

- Workbook, p. 132
- Transparency 11
- Every Student Learns Guide, pp. 234–237
- Quick Study, pp. 118–119

Quick Teaching Plan

If time is short, have students write a "5 W's Summary" about one or more of the inventions in Lesson 1.

- As students read the lesson, have them take notes to answer the questions *Who? What? When? Where? Why?* about each invention.

- Have students use their notes to write their summary.

1 Introduce and Motivate

Preview Ask students to recall developments in communication from Chapter 16. Tell students that they will learn about another development in communication as they read Lesson 1.

You Are There The Bells' "talking-machine" paved the way for an invention that changed communication forever. Ask students to predict what invention the experiment led to.

1855   1880

| 1859 | 1876 | 1879 |
| Oil is discovered in Pennsylvania | Alexander Graham Bell invents the telephone | Thomas Edison d the electric light |

Cleveland   Menlo Park
       Pittsburgh

PREVIEW

Focus on the Main Idea
In the late 1800s, new inventions powered the growth of American industry and changed the way people lived.

PLACES
Menlo Park, New Jersey
Pittsburgh, Pennsylvania
Cleveland, Ohio

PEOPLE
Alexander Graham Bell
Thomas Edison
Lewis Latimer
Andrew Carnegie
John D. Rockefeller

VOCABULARY
monopoly
corporation

▶ **The world's first telephone**

Inventions and Big Business

You Are There The year is 1863. The place is Edinburgh, Scotland. A 16-year-old boy named Alexander has just finished building a very strange machine out of tin, rubber, and wood. He calls it a "talking-machine" because it is designed to imitate the human voice. He built it with the help of his brother Melville, who is 18

The brothers have set up their machine to say the word "Mamma." But will anyone think it sounds like a real person? They decide to find out. They bring the machine out into the street. The brothers hide while the machine calls out, "Mamma, mamma." And sure enough, people come outside to see who is calling. "Good gracious," says one neighbor, "what can be the matter with that baby?"

The brothers congratulate each other on a successful experiment.

 Sequence As you read, keep track of the sequence of important events that changed the way Americans lived.

562

Practice and Extend

READING SKILL
Sequence

In the Lesson Review, students complete a graphic organizer like the one below. You may want to provide students with a copy of Transparency 11 to complete as they read the lesson.

```
Use Transparency 11
```

VOCABULARY
Word Exercise

Related Word Study Write on the board *corporation, incorporate,* and *corporate.* Have students read the definition of *corporation* on p. 566. *Corporate* comes from the Latin *corporatum,* which means "formed into a body." Explain that *body* can mean a group of people that form a unit. Discuss how making a single business out of many investors is forming them into a body. Show how adding *in-* (meaning "into") and *–ion* ("the act of doing something") alter the meaning of *corporate.*

Inventors Change the Country

Alexander Graham Bell was always interested in sound and speech. As you just read, he built a talking-machine when he was 16. By the time he was in his twenties, he had a new idea. He believed it was possible to make a machine that would allow people to talk to each other across wires. He called this idea the "talking telegraph."

In 1871, Bell moved to Boston, Massachusetts. He worked at the Boston School for the Deaf, teaching deaf students to speak. At night, Bell continued working on his talking telegraph, or telephone. He hired Thomas Watson to help him build models of his inventions. On March 10, 1876, Bell was ready to test his invention. Bell and Watson stood in separate rooms, with the doors closed. Into one end of the telephone, Bell shouted,

"Mr. Watson, come here, I want to see you."

Watson raced into Bell's room and announced that he had heard the sentence clearly.

The telephone quickly changed the way people communicated with each other. By the time Bell died in 1922, there were over 13 million telephones in use in the United States and Canada.

Another inventor who helped change the country was **Thomas Edison.** In his workshop in **Menlo Park, New Jersey,** Edison developed hundreds of inventions, including the phonograph and the movie camera. Of all his inventions, however, the most difficult was the electric light bulb. All the bulbs he built burned out quickly or exploded. "I've tried everything," Edison wrote. "I have not failed. I've just found 10,000 ways that won't work."

In 1879 Edison solved the problem. He built a bulb that glowed for two days. In 1882 **Lewis Latimer,** whose father had escaped slavery, invented a bulb that lasted much longer. The work of both Edison and Latimer helped make electric lights practical for everyday use.

REVIEW Which was invented first, the telephone or the light bulb? ↻ Sequence

▶ Alexander Graham Bell *(far left)* and Lewis Latimer *(left)* helped change the way Americans lived.

563

2 Teach and Discuss

PAGE 563

Inventors Change the Country

🕐 *Quick Summary* American inventors created products that changed the way people lived.

Primary Source

Cited in *The Importance of Alexander Graham Bell,* by Robyn M. Weaver

1 **Why was Bell's simple request to Mr. Watson so important?** It represented the beginning of the telephone. Analyze Primary Sources

2 **What effect would the invention of the telephone have on communication?** People would be able to communicate with others without making personal visits or waiting for mail to be delivered. Cause and Effect

3 **What were some of Thomas Edison's accomplishments?** He invented the phonograph, movie camera, and electric light bulb. Summarize

4 **What was Lewis Latimer's accomplishment?** He invented a bulb that lasted much longer than two days and helped make electric lights practical for everyday use. Summarize

✓ **REVIEW ANSWER** The telephone ↻ Sequence

 CURRICULUM CONNECTION Literature

Read About Thomas Edison

Thomas A. Edison: Young Inventor, by Sue Guthridge (Alladin, ISBN 0-020-41850-7, 1986) **Easy**

Thomas Edison & Electricity, by Steve Parker (Chelsea House, ISBN 0-791-03012-1, 1995) **On-Level**

The Story of Thomas Alva Edison, by Margaret Cousins (Random House, ISBN 0-394-84883-7, 1998) **Challenge**

 SOCIAL STUDIES Background

Primary and Secondary Sources

- Review with students how to differentiate between, locate, and use primary and secondary sources to acquire information about Texas.
- Students can use the Library of Congress's American Memory website at **memory.loc.gov** to locate primary and secondary source material.
- They can view film footage taken by Thomas Edison in 1900 of a hurricane in Galveston, Texas.

The Rise of Steel

 Quick Summary Andrew Carnegie's entrepreneurial spirit led to the United States becoming a world leader in steel production.

 SOCIAL STUDIES STRAND
Science • Technology

5 **What effect did the Bessemer furnace have on the production of steel?** It produced strong steel at affordable prices. Cause and Effect

Test Talk

Use Information from the Text

6 **Summarize what Andrew Carnegie did to help steel-making become a major industry in the United States.** Have students make notes about details from the text that answer the question. Ask them to check their notes. He bought mines to furnish the resources needed, bought ships and railroads to transport the resources, and used the Bessemer furnace to make the steel. Summarize

7 **Explain Andrew Carnegie's statement about using wealth.** Rich people should use their money to help others. Evaluate

✓ **REVIEW ANSWER** Steel was too expensive to use for big projects like railroads. Summarize

The Rise of Steel

In the early days of the Industrial Revolution, iron was used for major construction projects such as railroads and bridges. People knew that steel was stronger than iron. For example, steel railroad tracks lasted 20 times longer than tracks made from iron. But steel was very expensive to produce, so it could not be used for huge projects like railroad building. That changed in 1856, when an English inventor named Henry Bessemer developed the Bessemer process, a new way of making steel. Bessemer's specially-designed furnaces produced strong **5** steel at affordable prices. It was now possible to produce steel in massive quantities.

An entrepreneur named **Andrew Carnegie** saw that there could be a huge market for steel in the rapidly growing United States. In the 1870s, Carnegie began using the Bessemer process to make steel in **Pittsburgh, Pennsylvania.** His goal was to produce steel at the lowest possible price. He bought mines to provide his steel mills with necessary resources, such as iron and coal. He bought ships and railroads to bring the resources to his mills, and to deliver the finished steel all over the country.

Carnegie helped steel-making become a major industry in the United States. By 1900, the United States was producing more steel than any other country in the world. Steel was used to build new railroads, buildings, and bridges all over the country.

In the year 1900 alone, Andrew Carnegie's personal profits topped $25 million. He had come to the United States as a poor immigrant from Scotland at the age of 13. Now he was one of the world's richest people. He believed that it was his responsibility to use his wealth to help others. "The man who dies rich dies disgraced," he often said. Carnegie gave away over $300 million to build universities, libraries, museums, and theaters.

REVIEW Why were early railroads built from iron instead of steel? Summarize

► Andrew Carnegie produced steel for a rapidly growing nation.

564

Practice and Extend

 MEETING INDIVIDUAL NEEDS
Leveled Practice

Write About a New Product Have students write about the benefits of steel.

Easy Have students create a newspaper ad that might have appeared in the 1870s to persuade builders of the advantages of using steel. **Reteach**

On-Level Have students work in pairs to plan a sales call that they might make to an 1870s builder who is planning to construct a new bridge. Remind them to include facts and examples that will persuade the builder to use steel. **Extend**

Challenge Have students write a brief article comparing and contrasting the use of steel with wood or some other building material common in the 1870s. They may use print or electronic resources to obtain additional information. **Enrich**

For a Lesson Summary, use Quick Study, p. 118.

 CURRICULUM CONNECTION
Art

Create a Mural

• Have students search local newspapers for information about entrepreneurs in their city or state who are contributing in some way to the community.

• Ask each student to create a captioned illustration to show the contribution of one entrepreneur.

• Attach all the illustrations to a large piece of paper to form a patchwork mural. Title it *Entrepreneurs Giving to the Community*. Display the work in a place where others in the school may see it.

FACT FILE

Invention Time Line

Here are some of the inventions that changed life in the United States and around the world. Can you picture what life would be like today without some of these inventions?

1856 Bessemer process for steel-making
Steel makes it possible to construct skyscrapers in the late 1800s.

1873 Typewriter
American inventor Christopher Latham Sholes builds the first typewriter.

1876 Telephone
In 1887, the first long distance phone line connects New York and Philadelphia.

1879 Electric light bulb
Electric lights begin lighting city streets in 1880.

1885 Automobile
The earliest cars can only go 8 miles per hour.

1895 Radio
Italy's Guglielmo Marconi invents the radio at the age of 20.

1903 Airplane
Orville and Wilbur Wright build *Flyer,* the world's first successful airplane.

565

FACT FILE
Invention Time Line

 SOCIAL STUDIES STRAND
Economics

Have students recall how the free enterprise system works in the United States. Discuss with them ways that inventions contributed to the development of the system.

8 What is one way the communication inventions of the late 1800s eventually affected the way people bought and sold goods? Possible answer: Radio made it possible to influence consumer choices by advertising goods for sale; the telephone may have helped business owners to manage stock and keep track of supply and demand. **Make Inferences**

9 About how many years after the invention of the automobile was the airplane invented? About 18 years
Sequence

 Decision Making

10 Which of the inventions on the time line do you think was most important? Defend your answer. Possible answer: The telephone was most important because it connected people, and it helped lead to modern technologies such as the Internet. **Make Decisions**

 SOCIAL STUDIES STRAND
History

Horatio Alger, Jr. wrote more than 100 "rags-to-riches" books about young heroes who began life as penniless urchins or orphans, but achieved great success and wealth through their self-reliance and perseverance. Andrew Carnegie appeared to some readers as a real-life Horatio Alger story. Others saw men like Carnegie and Rockefeller as "robber barons" who had made their fortunes in an unfair and ruthless manner. Supporters celebrated them as "captains of industry" who brought efficiency and order to business.

Problem Solving

Use a Problem-Solving Process

- Have students consider the following problem-solving scenario: **Choose a school-related or household chore that you do regularly or have done before. Think of an invention that could be used to make this task easier or more fun.**

- Students should use the following problem-solving process to decide on an invention to do the task they have identified. Ask students to work in small groups to discuss and write about what must be considered as they solve the problem. Then have groups compare and contrast their plans to select the invention that is most creative and the one that is the most practical. Write the steps above on the board or read them aloud.

1. Identify a problem.
2. Gather information.
3. List and consider options.
4. Consider advantages and disadvantages.
5. Choose and implement a solution.
6. Evaluate the effectiveness of the solution.

Rockefeller and the Oil Industry

Quick Summary The discovery of oil by Edwin Drake and the efforts of John D. Rockefeller led to the development of the U.S. oil industry.

11 **Why was oil called "black gold"?**
People rushed to try to make their fortunes as they had during the gold rush in California. Also, oil is a valuable resource, just as gold is. **Make Inferences**

$ SOCIAL STUDIES STRAND
Economics

Remind students that the free enterprise system allows people to set up any business they choose. Have students describe why Carnegie and Rockefeller might have chosen to organize and manage the steel and oil industries. (They realized there could be a huge demand for these products in the future.) Discuss mergers and monopolies and how they affect competition.

12 **Compare and contrast Andrew Carnegie with John D. Rockefeller.**
Both were very successful in starting industries in the United States. Carnegie worked with steel, but Rockefeller was involved with oil. **Compare and Contrast**

13 **Why was oil so important to society?**
It was turned into many useful products, such as kerosene for lighting and gasoline and motor oil for automobiles.
Main Idea and Details

14 **How can both businesses and individuals profit from corporations?** A corporation profits when people buy its stock. Individuals profit when the value of the stock rises. **Main Idea and Details**

✓ Ongoing Assessment

If... students have difficulty explaining the relationship between investors and corporations,

then... explain that half of Americans own stocks. The money they pay for the stock allows businesses to grow. Corporations share profits with the stockholders.

✓ REVIEW ANSWER Automobiles increased the demand for products made from oil. **Cause and Effect**

566 Unit 8 • Expansion and Change

Rockefeller and the Oil Industry

On August 27, 1859, a former railroad conductor named Edwin Drake drilled a hole in the ground in western Pennsylvania. When he reached a depth of 69 feet, thick, black liquid came up from the ground. This was oil—exactly what Drake had been hoping to find. People rushed to the region to drill for oil, or "black gold" as people starting calling it. A new industry was born.

Oil pumped from the ground is called crude oil. Crude oil was shipped to oil refineries, where it was turned into useful products such as kerosene. Kerosene lamps were the main source of lighting in the United States. This was before Edison had invented the light bulb.

John D. Rockefeller saw an opportunity to make a fortune. He built his first oil refinery in **Cleveland, Ohio,** in 1863. Using the profits from this business, he bought other refineries. By the early 1880s, Standard Oil controlled about 90 percent of the oil business in the United States. Standard Oil had become a monopoly. A **monopoly** is a company that has control of an entire industry and stops competition.

By the early 1900s, a new invention—the automobile—was creating a growing demand for products made from oil. Automobiles needed gasoline and motor oil. Refineries began turning crude oil into these valuable products. With a growing public demand for these products, people searched for oil all over the country. Major oil discoveries were made in Texas, Oklahoma, and California. The oil industry continued to grow, and it remains one of the biggest and most important industries in the country today.

Big businesses were important in other industries as well, such as railroad building and coal mining. Many of these businesses were corporations. A **corporation** is a business that is owned by investors. People can invest in a corporation by buying shares of the company, called stocks. People buy stock in a corporation, hoping the price of the stock will go up. Today, many of the nation's biggest businesses are corporations.

REVIEW What effect did automobiles have on the oil industry? **Cause and Effect**

▶ The 1901 Spindletop gusher in Texas (*left*) was the biggest oil strike so far in the country. John D. Rockefeller (*right*) built refineries to make oil into useful products.

566

Practice and Extend

ESL **BUILD BACKGROUND**
ESL Support

Explore Word Meanings Have students learn more about the oil industry. Inform students that some detergents, plastics, paints, antiseptics, and cosmetics are made from oil.

Beginning Have students discuss in pairs different uses of the word *oil*. After they have generated ideas, have them confirm or extend their understanding by looking up the word in a dictionary.

Intermediate Have students cut out newspaper ads showing the price of some items made from oil. Help them analyze why the prices will get higher or lower if the price of oil rises or falls.

Advanced Have groups research more uses for oil. Students can then share their findings with the class, using visuals if possible.

For additional ESL support, use Every Student Learns Guide, pp. 234–237.

A Time of Growth

The late 1800s was a time of rapid change in the United States. Inventions and growing industries created millions of new jobs. More women began working outside the home than ever before. Some women found jobs in offices and as telephone operators.

Before the Civil War, most Americans had lived and worked on farms. By 1900, more Americans worked in industries than on farms. And as growing industries continued creating new jobs in cities, people moved to cities by the thousands. Chicago, for example, had been a town of 30,000 people in 1850. By 1900, Chicago was home to nearly 2 million people. Many of these new arrivals were immigrants. Immigrants came from all over the world to find jobs in the United States. You will read their story in the next lesson.

REVIEW How did growing businesses lead to the growth of cities? **Main Idea and Details**

Summarize the Lesson

1859 Oil was discovered in Pennsylvania, leading to the rise of the oil industry.

1876 Alexander Graham Bell invented the telephone.

1879 Thomas Edison developed the first working electric light bulb.

LESSON 1 REVIEW

Check Facts and Main Ideas

1. **Sequence** Redraw this chart on a separate sheet of paper, putting the events in their correct order. Include the year of each event.

> Henry Bessemer develops the Bessemer process—1856
> ↓
> John D. Rockefeller builds his first oil refinery—1863
> ↓
> Alexander Graham Bell moves to Boston—1871
> ↓
> Christopher Latham Sholes builds the first typewriter—1873
> ↓
> The first automobile is built—1885

2. How did Alexander Graham Bell's invention affect communication in the United States?

3. What important invention was made by Henry Bessemer? Why was this invention important?

4. **Critical Thinking:** *Draw Conclusions* Why do you think Andrew Carnegie bought iron mines and coal mines?

5. Why was Rockefeller's Standard Oil Company considered a **monopoly?**

Link to ⚭ **Science**

Study Inventors For hundreds of years, inventors have changed the way people live. Choose one inventor and find out more about him or her. Write a one-page report about the inventor. Explain how the inventor's work changed the way people lived.

567

A Time of Growth

🕐 *Quick Summary* Business growth affected how and where people lived.

15 **List three jobs created by inventions and discoveries in this lesson.** Possible answers: Gas station owner, telephone operator, radio announcer **Make Inferences**

✓ **REVIEW ANSWER** They created jobs in cities, so people came to cities. **Main Idea and Details**

3 Close and Assess

Summarize the Lesson

Have students list several ways that each development on the time line would have affected people in the late 1800s.

✓ **LESSON 1 REVIEW**

1. **Sequence** For possible answers, see the reduced pupil page.

2. Communication became easier and quicker.

3. The Bessemer process; made steel at affordable prices.

4. **Critical Thinking:** *Draw Conclusions* To provide resources for making steel at the lowest price

5. It had control of an entire industry.

Link to ⚭ **Science**

Students' reports should focus on the inventor's impact on society.

❄ **MEETING INDIVIDUAL NEEDS**
Learning Styles

Present an Invention Have students use their individual learning styles to research and present one of the inventions described in this lesson.

Verbal Learning Have students discuss with the class the need the invention fills, how people met the need before the invention, and how the inventor created the device or process.

Musical Learning Have students create a song describing the discovery and uses of the invention.

Auditory Learning Have groups audiotape reenactments of the first public demonstration of one of the inventions.

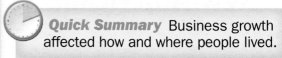

Workbook, p. 132

Lesson 1: Inventions and Big Business

Directions: Match each person listed in the box below to an invention or accomplishment listed in the chart. Some answers will be used more than once. You may use your textbook.

| John D. Rockefeller | Lewis Latimer | Andrew Carnegie |
| Alexander Graham Bell | Thomas Edison | Henry Bessemer |

Invention/Accomplishment	Person Responsible
1. telephone	
2. phonograph	
3. helped make steel a major industry in the United States	
4. movie camera	
5. light bulb	
6. long-lasting light bulb	
7. gave away more than $300 million to help build universities, libraries, museums, and theaters	
8. founded Standard Oil	
9. new process for making steel	

Notes for Home: Your child learned about American entrepreneurs and inventors of the late 1800s. Home Activity: With your child, brainstorm a list of benefits we enjoy today because of the accomplishments of the people listed in the chart.

Also on Teacher Resources CD-ROM.

New Americans

Objectives

- Describe several reasons why immigrants came to the United States.

- Identify the hardships immigrants faced in American cities.

- Explain the reasons labor unions were formed.

- Analyze the accomplishments of labor unions in the United States.

Vocabulary

tenement, p. 571; **prejudice,** p. 571; **settlement house,** p. 571; **labor union,** p. 572; **strike,** p. 573

Resources

- Workbook, p. 133
- Transparency 1
- Every Student Learns Guide, pp. 238–241
- Quick Study, pp. 120–121

Quick Teaching Plan

If time is short, have students create Plus/Minus Charts.

- Tell students to make two-column charts. Have them label the columns *Plus* and *Minus.*

- Ask students to read the lesson independently. Have them take notes in the *Plus* and *Minus* columns about benefits and difficulties immigrants faced in the United States.

1 Introduce and Motivate

Preview Ask students to summarize any stories about immigrants that they have heard or read. Tell students that they will learn more about people who moved to the United States from other countries in the late 1800s and early 1900s as they read Lesson 2.

You Are There Point out that many immigrants stepped off their ships into a whole new world. Ask students to list sights, sounds, smells, and tastes they think Nathan may have encountered as he walked along the street.

568 Unit 8 • Expansion and Change

LESSON 2

Angel Island • • Ellis Island

1885   1895

1886 Samuel Gompers forms the American Federation of Labor

1889 Jane Addams opens Hull House in Chicago

1894 Mary Antin arrives in the United States

PREVIEW

Focus on the Main Idea
During the late 1800s and early 1900s, millions of immigrants moved to American cities and workers struggled for better conditions.

PLACES
Ellis Island
Angel Island

PEOPLE
Mary Antin
Jane Addams
Samuel Gompers
Mary Harris Jones

VOCABULARY
tenement
prejudice
settlement house
labor union
strike

568

New Americans

You Are There Newcomer Nathan Nussenbaum (NUSS en bowm) stands on a crowded New York City street with his trunk. He stares at the tall buildings and rushing crowds of people.

The year is 1896. Nathan, a Jewish teenager from Austria, has just arrived in the United States. He has a total of nine dollars in his pocket. He speaks German and Yiddish—a language spoken by many Jews in Europe—but almost no English. He knows no one in this country.

He walks through the busy streets. Every time he hears the word "listen" he turns around. He thinks people are saying "Nisn" which is how you say the name Nathan in Yiddish. He soon realizes that people are not talking to him.

Nathan knows that it will be difficult to adjust to life in the United States. But he is not discouraged. "I was determined to try my luck in this country," he later said.

Main Idea and Details As you read, pay attention to the different ways in which the United States changed during the late 1800s and early 1900s.

Practice and Extend

READING SKILL
Main Idea and Details

In the Lesson Review, students complete a graphic organizer like the one below. You may want to provide students with a copy of Transparency 1 to complete as they read the lesson.

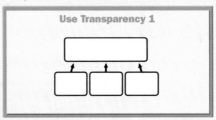

Use Transparency 1

VOCABULARY
Word Exercise

Related Word Study Have students read the definition for *tenement* on p. 571. Tell students that a closely related word is *tenant,* a person who rents a room, building, or land. These words come from the Latin *tenere,* "to hold." The person who is paying the rent is the person who "holds" or occupies the building. Other words from *tenere* are retention, detention, lieutenant, and sustenance. Have students look up these words and discuss how they are related to the idea of "hold."

New Immigrants

Nathan Nussenbaum was one of over 23 million immigrants who arrived in the United States between 1880 and 1920. During the late 1800s, the largest numbers of immigrants came from the countries of northern and western Europe, including Ireland, Great Britain, Germany, and Sweden. In the early 1900s, the greatest numbers came from southern and eastern European countries, such as Italy, Austria-Hungary, and Russia.

Why did so many people leave their homelands? Many were escaping hardships at home, such as poverty, hunger, lack of jobs, or lack of freedom. Many Jewish immigrants left Europe to escape religious persecution. A young immigrant from Russia named **Mary Antin** remembered that she had not been allowed to attend school in Russia. You will read her story in the Biography following this lesson.

For millions of immigrants from Europe, the first stop in the United States was **Ellis Island,** a small island in New York Harbor. At Ellis Island, immigrants were checked for diseases and asked questions about where they planned to live and work.

For immigrants from Asia in the early 1900s, the first stop was **Angel Island** in San Francisco Bay. Many Asian immigrants spent weeks or months on Angel Island, waiting for permission to enter the United States. Some expressed their frustration by writing poems. One person wrote:

> *"Counting on my fingers, several months have elapsed [passed]. Still I am at the beginning of the road."*

REVIEW What were some reasons that immigrants left their homes to come to the United States? **Main Idea and Details**

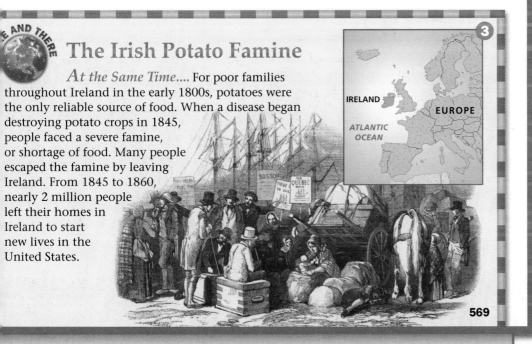

The Irish Potato Famine

At the Same Time.... For poor families throughout Ireland in the early 1800s, potatoes were the only reliable source of food. When a disease began destroying potato crops in 1845, people faced a severe famine, or shortage of food. Many people escaped the famine by leaving Ireland. From 1845 to 1860, nearly 2 million people left their homes in Ireland to start new lives in the United States.

IRELAND
EUROPE
ATLANTIC OCEAN

569

2 Teach and Discuss

PAGE 569

New Immigrants

🕐 *Quick Summary* During the late 1800s and early 1900s, millions of immigrants came to the United States from Europe and Asia.

❶ Why were immigrants checked for diseases and asked where they planned to live and work? To be sure that they did not spread illness and that they would not be homeless and jobless **Make Inferences**

Primary Source

Cited in *Island: Poetry and History of Chinese Immigrants on Angel Island, 1910 to 1949,* by Him Mark Lai, Genny Lim, and Judy Yung, eds.

❷ What did the person mean who wrote "Still I am at the beginning of the road"? The writer was still waiting to begin a new life in the United States. **Analyze Primary Sources**

✓ **REVIEW ANSWER** People hoped to find freedom, jobs, and a better life. **Main Idea and Details**

The Irish Potato Famine

❸ Why did many immigrants come from Ireland in the mid-1800s? To escape the potato famine **Cause and Effect**

FYI **SOCIAL STUDIES**
Background

Ellis Island

- Ellis Island was named for Samuel Ellis, who owned it in the late 1700s.
- The area is a landfill formed by dumping ballast, a heavy material used to stabilize ships. Ellis Island was used as a fort before becoming a processing station for immigrants.
- Approximately 17 million immigrants arrived at Ellis Island between 1892 and 1924.
- The Ellis Island Immigration Museum was opened in 1990.

Cost of Immigration

- Steamship tickets for the journey from Europe to the United States cost between $25 and $35 per person.
- Some families had to sell their houses and many of their belongings in their homeland to buy tickets and to get established in the United States.

Arriving and Settling

Quick Summary As they struggled to establish themselves in the United States, immigrants coped with language differences and ways of life that were very different from those in their homelands.

Test Talk

Locate Key Words in the Question

4 Why would subways and electric streetcars have been important for immigrants? Have students turn the question into a statement: *I need to find out. . . .* Few people would have had money for their own cars. Subways and streetcars allowed them to go to work and other places. **Make Inferences**

5 Where did Walter Mrozowski likely go to get help getting settled? Why? Since he was alone, he probably went to a neighborhood where other people of Polish descent had settled. The people in the neighborhood would have spoken his language and may have helped him find the things he needed. **Draw Conclusions**

✓ **REVIEW ANSWER** He wanted to find a place to stay and to find a job.
 Sequence

6 From what places did the largest numbers of immigrants come in the early 1900s? Where did most come from in the late 1900s? In the early 1900s, the largest number came from Europe; in the late 1900s, the largest number came from Latin America. **Compare and Contrast**

GRAPH SKILL Answer About 8 million

SOCIAL STUDIES STRAND
Citizenship

Jacob Riis was an immigrant from Denmark. In 1890 he published a book called *How the Other Half Lives*. In words and photographs he revealed the terrible conditions faced by poor people in New York City. Some readers were moved by the book and donated money to help, and city officials began to take action.

570 Unit 8 • Expansion and Change

Arriving and Settling

What was it like for immigrants to arrive in a big American city in the late 1800s or early 1900s? For many, it was like stepping into a different world. This was a time when American cities were growing and changing. Cities like New York and Chicago were beginning to build skyscrapers. Boston built the nation's first underground train, or subway, in 1897. In many cities, passengers rode electric streetcars to and from work. And in the early 1900s, automobiles began competing for space on the crowded city streets.

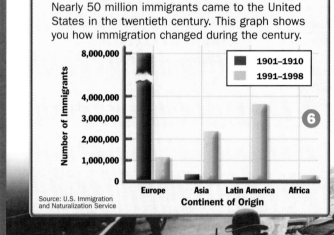

Immigration in the Twentieth Century
Nearly 50 million immigrants came to the United States in the twentieth century. This graph shows you how immigration changed during the century.

Legend:
- 1901–1910
- 1991–1998

Y-axis: Number of Immigrants — 0, 1,000,000, 2,000,000, 3,000,000, 4,000,000, 8,000,000

X-axis: Continent of Origin — Europe, Asia, Latin America, Africa

Source: U.S. Immigration and Naturalization Service

An immigrant from Poland named Walter Mrozowski (mroh ZOW skee) never forgot how he felt during his first few minutes in New York. "I was in a new world," he remembered. "I kept my courage up. I had to. There was no one to help me."

Like many recent arrivals, Mrozowski needed to do two things right away—find a place to stay and find a job. Some immigrants had friends or relatives whom they could go to for help. Those who did not know anyone usually headed to a neighborhood where there were other people from their homeland. Living in a community where the language and traditions were familiar made it a little easier for immigrants to adjust to life in a new country.

REVIEW After arriving in New York, what two things did Walter Mrozowski want to do right away? Sequence

GRAPH SKILL *About how many Europeans came to the United States between 1901 and 1910?*

▶ Busy street markets were common in immigrant neighborhoods.

Practice and Extend

MEETING INDIVIDUAL NEEDS
Leveled Practice

Read About Immigrants Have students use literature to research the lives of various immigrants. Have them identify similarities and differences within and among racial, ethnic, and religious groups. Some books are suggested on pp. 529h and 571.

Easy Have students review pictures, headings, and captions in a book about immigrants. Have them tell what they learned about immigrants. **Reteach**

On-Level Ask students to read a book about immigrants. Have them write a journal entry from the point of view of a person in the book. **Extend**

Challenge Have pairs of students research and present what people and immigrant groups have made a contribution to your state. Make sure students include people from different backgrounds. **Enrich**

For a Lesson Summary, use Quick Study, p. 120.

Life in the Cities

Most immigrants settled in cities, where there were busy factories and many jobs. People were also moving to the cities from small towns and farms all over the United States. With so many people moving to cities, there was soon a shortage of housing. New arrivals crowded into **tenements,** or buildings that are divided into small apartments. In tenements, families of eight or more often lived together in one tiny apartment. Some apartments lacked heat. Others had no windows, making it hard to get enough fresh air. Diseases spread quickly in such unhealthy living conditions.

When looking for work, immigrants sometimes faced the added hardship of prejudice. **Prejudice** is an unfair negative opinion about a group of people. For example, job advertisements sometimes included phrases like "No Irish need apply." Immigrants from many different countries faced similar kinds of prejudice.

At the same time, many Americans across the country worked to help immigrants improve their lives. Christian and Jewish organizations started schools, gave aid, and worked for change, and groups of successful immigrants aided struggling newcomers. In

▶ Jane Addams opened Hull House in 1889.

1889, **Jane Addams** rented an old house in a poor neighborhood in Chicago. She fixed it up and opened it as a settlement house called Hull House. A **settlement house** is a center that provides help for those who have little money. At Hull House, immigrants could take free English classes and get help finding work. There was a daycare center for the children of families where both parents worked. Hundreds of settlement houses soon opened in cities around the country.

REVIEW Summarize living conditions for immigrants in tenements. **Summarize**

▶ Many immigrant families lived and worked in small tenement apartments like this one in New York City.

571

Life in the Cities

Quick Summary Immigrants dealt with housing shortages, uncomfortable and unhealthy living conditions, and prejudice. Settlement houses were established to assist immigrants.

7 **Why did many immigrants settle in crowded cities rather than in rural areas where they would have had more space?** They had a better chance of finding jobs in the cities. Main Idea and Details

8 **What might have caused some people who had been living in the United States to be prejudiced against immigrant workers?** Possible answer: They did not want immigrants to get the jobs they desired for themselves. **Make Inferences**

Prejudice Reduction Remind students of our nation's motto: *E Pluribus Unum* (out of many, one). Discuss the importance of immigration in our nation's past and how immigrants continue to bring strength, talent, and diversity to the United States.

9 **How might a settlement house have been useful to Walter Mrozowski?** Possible answer: He could have learned English and received help finding a job. **Main Idea and Details**

✓ **REVIEW ANSWER** Immigrants lived in small, cramped apartments that often lacked heat and fresh air. **Summarize**

ST **SOCIAL STUDIES STRAND**
Science

- Inform students that illness and death from tuberculosis was common among tenement dwellers.

- When Selman A. Waksman isolated the antibiotic streptomycin in 1943, tuberculosis was effectively eradicated in the United States.

CURRICULUM CONNECTION
Literature

Read About Immigrants

When Jesse Came Across the Sea, by Amy Hest (Candlewick, ISBN 0-763-60094-6, 1997) **Easy**

Yang the Second and Her Secret Admirers, by Lensey Namioka (Bantam Doubleday Books, ISBN 0-440-41641-8, 2000) **On-Level**

The Orphan of Ellis Island: A Time-Travel Adventure, by Elvira Woodruff (Scholastic, ISBN 0-590-48245-9, 1997) **Challenge**

FYI **SOCIAL STUDIES**
Background

Progress in Education

- In parts of the U.S., students attended one-room schools—one teacher taught all grades and subjects in a single classroom.

- Horace Mann helped to increase support for schools. He founded the first public normal school, a teacher-training school, in the United States.

- In 1925 Tennessee Governor Austin Peay helped his state with an education law that increased school construction and raised educational standards.

Workers and Unions

🕐 **Quick Summary** Men, women, and children worked long hours in poor conditions and earned low wages. Labor unions were established to help workers improve their situations.

⑩ Why do you think people put up with poor working conditions and low pay in factories? Possible answer: Many did not have the training to do anything other than factory work, and they badly needed their salaries. **Point of View**

Primary Source

Cited in *Out of the Sweatshop: The Struggle for Industrial Democracy,* by Leon Stein

⑪ What does Sadie Frowne's description tell about her work? She was under so much pressure to work quickly that she sometimes got hurt. **Analyze Primary Sources**

⑫ Why would it be better for workers to try to change working conditions through a labor union rather than on their own? By joining with others, workers have a better chance of being taken seriously. Also, a business owner may fire one person, but is less likely to fire a large group. **Draw Conclusions**

⑬ How would working as a child have affected a person's future? When children worked, they could not go to school. They could not learn new skills that would enable them to get better jobs as adults. **Make Inferences**

✓ **REVIEW ANSWER** Dangerous working conditions, low pay, and long working hours caused many people to join labor unions. **Cause and Effect**

Workers and Unions

As you have read, industry created millions of new jobs. Both immigrants and people born in the United States found work in factories and mines. But it was a difficult time for workers.

You know about the success of Andrew Carnegie's steel mills. Many workers at Carnegie's mills, however, barely earned enough money to survive. At Carnegie's Homestead Steel Works in Homestead, Pennsylvania, steelworkers put in 12-hour days, seven days a week. They got two vacation days ⑩ a year—Independence Day and Christmas. The average salary was $10 a week.

Many women worked in clothing factories, where they earned even less. Women operated sewing machines in hot, cramped workshops known as sweatshops. A teenager named Sadie Frowne talked about what it was like to work in a sweatshop in New York City.

> ⑪ *"The machines go like mad all day because the faster you work the more money you get. Sometimes in my haste I get my finger caught and the needle goes right through it.... I bind the finger up with a piece of cotton and go on working."*

Sweatshops could be very dangerous places to work. At a sweatshop run by the Triangle Shirtwaist Company in New York, workers worried about fires. They asked the owners to build fire escapes and keep the workshop doors unlocked. The owners refused. On a Saturday afternoon in March, 1911, a fire started. Workers were trapped inside. The fire killed 146 people, mostly young women.

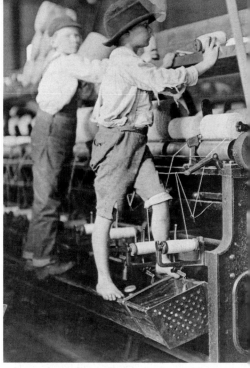

▶ In cotton mills like this one, children climbed onto the machines to keep them running.

Low wages, long workdays, and disasters like the Triangle Shirtwaist Company fire encouraged many workers to join labor unions. In **labor unions,** workers join together to fight for improved working conditions and better wages.

Unions along with others also worked to end child labor. In 1910, nearly 2 million children were working in the United States. Children performed dangerous jobs in places like cotton mills and coal mines, earning just 10 to 20 cents a day. You will read more about the struggle to end child labor in Issues and Viewpoints following this lesson.

REVIEW What caused people to join labor unions? **Cause and Effect**

Practice and Extend

 **SOCIAL STUDIES Background**

Sweatshops

- In England, people who made their employees work long hours for poor wages were called *sweaters*, and from this term came the word *sweatshops*.
- Sweatshops consisted of families or other groups who worked in their homes or in small factories.
- Sweatshops generally produced goods such as clothing, shoes, soap, and artificial flowers. People did *piecework*, meaning that they were paid for the number of items they produced, not for the number of hours they worked.
- Although sweatshop wages were poor, the cost of common items was also lower. For example, in 1897 a bar of soap might have cost a nickel, a toothbrush could have been bought for a dime, and a dress for one dollar.

Going on Strike

One of the first union leaders in the United States was **Samuel Gompers.** As a teenager, Gompers worked in a cigar factory in New York City. He helped form a union of cigar factory workers. When owners cut cigar makers' wages in 1877, Gompers helped lead his union on a strike. In a **strike,** workers refuse to work until business owners meet their demands.

This strike did not work. Factory owners ignored the union's demand for better wages. Gompers realized that unions would have more power if they joined together. In 1886, Gompers brought many workers' unions together to form the American Federation of Labor, or AFL. The AFL fought for better wages, an 8-hour work day, safer working conditions, and an end to child labor.

At times, tensions between striking union workers and business owners erupted into violence. This happened at Carnegie's Homestead Steel Works in 1892. Workers went on strike for higher wages, but the factory manager refused to bargain with the striking workers. Instead, he hired armed guards to break up the strike. The guards clashed with workers, and people on both sides were killed. The Homestead Strike lasted several months, but the workers were not able to win higher wages.

Coal miners were also struggling to improve their working conditions. A woman named **Mary Harris Jones** helped lead this effort. When she was in her 50s, Jones began traveling to mining towns in the Appalachian Mountains. "Join the union, boys," she urged the miners. Miners began calling her "Mother Jones." Mine owners threatened Jones, but she refused to stop her work. Well into her 90s, she continued organizing unions and speaking out in support of better treatment for workers.

REVIEW Why did Samuel Gompers want many labor unions to join together? **Draw Conclusions**

▶ **Mary Harris Jones (***above***) continued working for unions into her 90s. A 1913 strike (***below***) included workers from many nations.**

`573`

Going on Strike

🕐 **Quick Summary** Strikes were used as a means of forcing owners to listen to workers' demands.

14 Why did Samuel Gompers think that workers could get more money by going on strike? He hoped that the factory owners would be upset that no cigars were being made, and, therefore, listen to the workers' concerns. **Make Inferences**

15 What might have caused owners to refuse to bargain with workers? Possible answer: They did not want to pay higher wages. Also, they may have feared that if they gave their workers what they wanted once, they might have to do it again and again. **Cause and Effect**

✓ **Ongoing Assessment**

If... students have difficulty understanding the refusal by owners to bargain,	**then...** explain that a business's profits depend on sales, cost of materials, number of workers, and pay rate. Discuss what happens to profits when wages increase and other factors stay the same. (profits fall)

16 What did Samuel Gompers and Mary Harris Jones have in common? Both tried to help workers get better pay and working conditions. **Compare and Contrast**

✓ **REVIEW ANSWER** He believed unions would have more power if they joined together. **Draw Conclusions**

FAST FACTS

This page describes historical events in the United States between 1877 and 1892. Other events that occurred during this time period include:

1879 James Ritty invented the first **cash register** to keep his workers from stealing his profits. John Patterson improved the design in 1884 and sold the new device to business owners.

1880 *Ben-Hur*, by Major-General Lew Wallace, was published. It was one of the best-selling books of the nineteenth century.

1886 The **Statue of Liberty** was dedicated on October 28 by President Grover Cleveland. The statue was a gift from France and represented the friendship between France and the United States. The statue rests on Liberty Island near Ellis Island.

Improving Conditions

Quick Summary Working conditions improved somewhat as labor unions, some business owners, and religious and political leaders worked together.

17 **What examples of the benefits and disadvantages of the free enterprise system in the United States might most immigrants have given? Explain.**
Possible answer: Pay was low, but higher than in their homelands; working conditions were often poor, but were improving slowly. **Draw Conclusions**

✓ **REVIEW ANSWER** Working hours were shortened and the workplace became safer. **Main Idea and Details**

3 Close and Assess

Summarize the Lesson

Ask students to identify character traits of each of the people noted on the time line and explain how the people's activities demonstrated those traits.

✓ **LESSON 2   REVIEW**

1. **Main Idea and Details** For possible answers, see the reduced pupil page.

2. Possible answer: To find work and escape poverty, famine, and persecution

3. Many immigrants were forced to live in crowded, unsafe tenements.

4. **Critical Thinking: *Evaluate*** Workers realized that they had to join together to fight for safer working conditions.

5. To honor the contributions of workers in the United States

Link to ⌒⌒ Writing

Students' letters might also describe the immigrants' struggle for improved living and working conditions.

Improving Conditions

Along with labor unions, some business owners, religious organizations, and political leaders also helped to improve life for workers. Slowly, conditions began to improve. New laws shortened hours and improved safety in the workplace.

People from all over the world continued coming to the United States in search of work. Even if the pay was not high, it was more than most immigrants could have hoped to earn in their native country.

A new holiday was created to honor the contribution of workers in the United States. The first Labor Day celebration was held in New York City in September 1882. Within a few years, workers were holding Labor Day celebrations in many cities. In 1894, Congress declared Labor Day a national holiday.

REVIEW How did working conditions improve? **Main Idea and Details**

▶ **The first Labor Day celebration was held in New York City in 1882.**

Summarize the Lesson

- **1886** Samuel Gompers brought many unions together to form the American Federation of Labor.
- **1889** Jane Addams opened Hull House in Chicago to help the city's poor.
- **1894** Mary Antin arrived in the United States, one of millions of immigrants who came in search of a better life.

LESSON 2   REVIEW

Check Facts and Main Ideas

1. **Main Idea and Details** Complete the chart below by filling in three details that tell how the United States changed in the late 1800s and early 1900s.

The United States changed in the late 1800s and early 1900s.

| millions of immigrants arrived in the United States | labor unions helped improve life for workers | new inventions changed life for many people |

2. What are three different reasons that immigrants came to the United States?

3. How did the shortage of housing affect immigrants in American cities?

4. **Critical Thinking: *Evaluate*** Why do you think the Triangle Shirtwaist Company fire might have encouraged people to join **labor unions?**

5. What is the purpose of Labor Day?

Link to ⌒⌒ Writing

Write a Letter Suppose the year is 1896 and you are a new immigrant in the United States. Write a letter home explaining why you decided to come to the United States. Describe what you have seen so far and what you think about it. Explain what your plans are for the future.

574

Practice and Extend

ESL **BUILD BACKGROUND**
ESL Support

Labor Day Explain that this holiday honors those who have struggled for fair labor practices.

Beginning Explain that *labor* is another word for work. Have students role-play ways to do labor.

Intermediate Have students create a Venn diagram to show similarities and differences in workers' lives in the past and present.

Advanced Have students research the meaning of Labor Day and how it is celebrated.

For additional ESL support, use Every Student Learns Guide, pp. 238–241.

Workbook, p. 133

Also on Teacher Resources CD-RO

Mary Antin
1881–1949

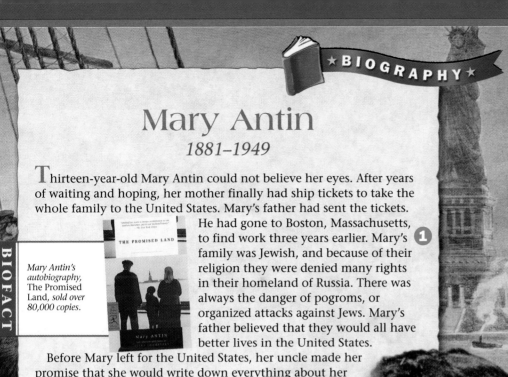

Thirteen-year-old Mary Antin could not believe her eyes. After years of waiting and hoping, her mother finally had ship tickets to take the whole family to the United States. Mary's father had sent the tickets. He had gone to Boston, Massachusetts, to find work three years earlier. Mary's family was Jewish, and because of their religion they were denied many rights in their homeland of Russia. There was always the danger of pogroms, or organized attacks against Jews. Mary's father believed that they would all have better lives in the United States.

Mary Antin's autobiography, The Promised Land, *sold over 80,000 copies.*

Before Mary left for the United States, her uncle made her promise that she would write down everything about her journey. Just to reach the ship was difficult, and Mary was often scared. She sometimes traveled in trains so crowded that there was no room to move.

Finally, Mary boarded a ship to cross the Atlantic Ocean. She later described the end of her journey:

> *"And so suffering, fearing, brooding, rejoicing, we crept nearer and nearer to the coveted [desired] shore, until, on a glorious May morning, six weeks after our departure from [Russia], our eyes beheld the Promised Land, and my father received us in his arms."*

Mary kept her promise to her uncle and wrote a long letter about the trip that brought her to a new land. Later, she would use a copy of this letter as a basis for several successful books about her experiences.

Learn from Biographies

What did Mary mean when she said, "Our eyes beheld the Promised Land"?

For more information, go online to *Meet the People* at **www.sfsocialstudies.com.**

575

★ BIOGRAPHY ★

Mary Antin

Objective

- Analyze the experiences of immigrants, such as Mary Antin.

1 Introduce and Motivate

Preview Ask students what they know about immigrants who came to the United States. Tell students that they will learn about Mary Antin, whose family left Russia in the late 1800s.

Ask why it is important to know about people who came to the United States. (Their stories can help us learn what it was like to come to the U.S.)

2 Teach and Discuss

1 Why do you think Mary's father sent for his family when he did? He found a job and a place to live. **Draw Conclusions**

2 Why do you think Mary's uncle asked her to write down her experiences? Possible answer: To share her experiences with family members who stayed in Russia; writing could help her deal with the changes that she faced **Hypothesize**

3 Close and Assess

Learn from Biographies Answer

She believed that the United States held the promise of a better life for her family.

 **SOCIAL STUDIES Background**

Religious Holidays

- Tell students that among the rights denied to Jews in Russia was the right to celebrate religious holidays.
- Have students describe religious celebrations they may know about in the United States, such as Hanukkah, Christmas, or Ramadan.
- Have students discuss what is similar and different about these celebrations.

 SOCIAL STUDIES Background

Mary Antin's Book

- Mary Antin's book, ***The Promised Land*** (Modern Library, ISBN 0-375-75739-2, 2001), was published in 1912 and is still in print today.
- A picture book titled ***Streets of Gold*** (Dial Books for Young Readers, ISBN 0-803-72149-8, 1999), by Rosemary Wells, is based on Mary Antin's memoir.

Working Against Child Labor

Objectives

- Explain how the Industrial Revolution caused changes in society that led to clashes between certain groups of Americans.

- Explain how industry changed many Americans' way of life.

- Explain how an individual is able to take part in civic affairs at the national level.

1 Introduce and Motivate

Preview To activate prior knowledge, ask students what they know about working conditions in the late 1800s and early 1900s. Ask how these conditions might affect a child. Tell students that they will learn about child labor and what people did about it.

2 Teach and Discuss

1 **At the age of twelve, what did Florence Kelley observe at a glassmaking factory?** Boys about her size were doing hard, dangerous work. Main Idea and Details

2 **Summarize what Kelley did about her observation and tell the results.** She wrote reports and encouraged people not to buy products made with child labor. The result was that laws were passed forbidding child labor. Summarize

3 **Why did Kelley use the word *robbed* when she said that not going to school was a result of child labor?** The word *robbed* has a strong meaning, which shows that Kelley believed children were being denied their rights when they were working in factories rather than attending school. Analyze Primary Sources

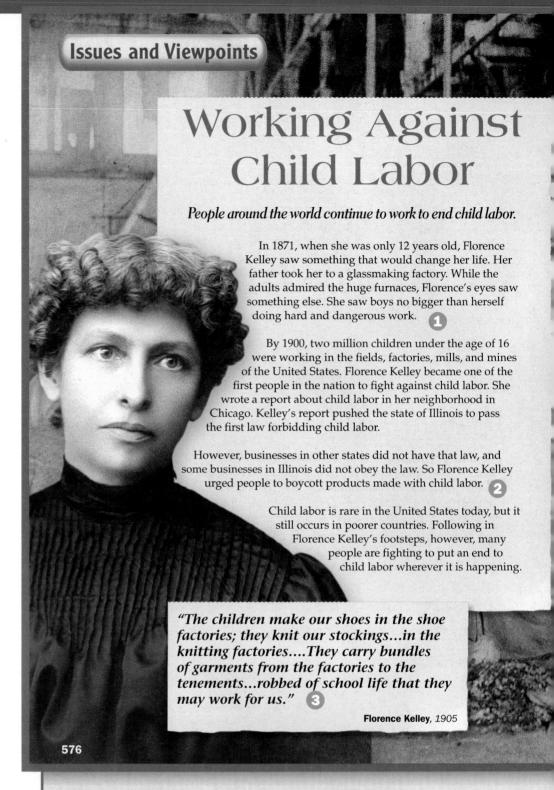

Issues and Viewpoints

Working Against Child Labor

People around the world continue to work to end child labor.

In 1871, when she was only 12 years old, Florence Kelley saw something that would change her life. Her father took her to a glassmaking factory. While the adults admired the huge furnaces, Florence's eyes saw something else. She saw boys no bigger than herself doing hard and dangerous work. **1**

By 1900, two million children under the age of 16 were working in the fields, factories, mills, and mines of the United States. Florence Kelley became one of the first people in the nation to fight against child labor. She wrote a report about child labor in her neighborhood in Chicago. Kelley's report pushed the state of Illinois to pass the first law forbidding child labor.

However, businesses in other states did not have that law, and some businesses in Illinois did not obey the law. So Florence Kelley urged people to boycott products made with child labor. **2**

Child labor is rare in the United States today, but it still occurs in poorer countries. Following in Florence Kelley's footsteps, however, many people are fighting to put an end to child labor wherever it is happening.

"The children make our shoes in the shoe factories; they knit our stockings...in the knitting factories....They carry bundles of garments from the factories to the tenements...robbed of school life that they may work for us." **3**

Florence Kelley, *1905*

576

Practice and Extend

FYI SOCIAL STUDIES
Background

Fighting Against Child Labor

- Librarian Helen Marot used her research and writing skills to speak out against child labor. She wrote a report that led to the New York legislature passing the Compulsory Education Act in 1903.
- Teacher Grace Abbott worked at Hull House and wrote articles and books to inspire people to address the issue of child labor. In 1917 she became the director of the United States Children's Bureau, which was formed to protect children.

Social Reform

- The creed of the Social Gospel movement of the late 1800s included abolition of child labor, better wages for workers, and better working conditions for women.
- Dwight L. Moody gave up a prosperous business to do missionary work in poor Chicago neighborhoods. An enthusiastic preacher, he founded the Moody Church and worked in urban areas across the country to provide recreation and education for youth.

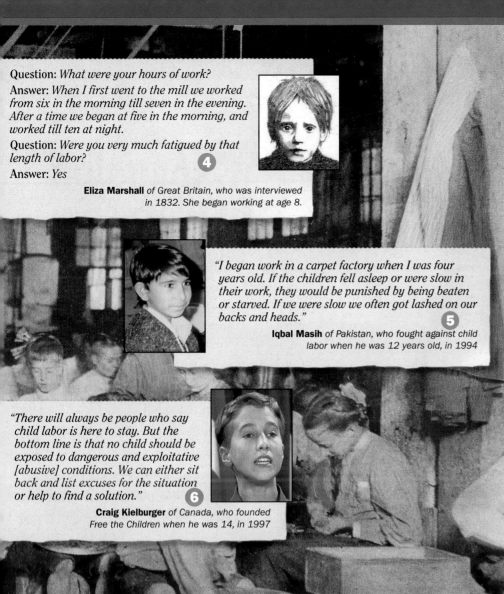

Question: *What were your hours of work?*

Answer: *When I first went to the mill we worked from six in the morning till seven in the evening. After a time we began at five in the morning, and worked till ten at night.*

Question: *Were you very much fatigued by that length of labor?*

Answer: *Yes*

Eliza Marshall *of Great Britain, who was interviewed in 1832. She began working at age 8.*

"I began work in a carpet factory when I was four years old. If the children fell asleep or were slow in their work, they would be punished by being beaten or starved. If we were slow we often got lashed on our backs and heads."

Iqbal Masih *of Pakistan, who fought against child labor when he was 12 years old, in 1994*

"There will always be people who say child labor is here to stay. But the bottom line is that no child should be exposed to dangerous and exploitative [abusive] conditions. We can either sit back and list excuses for the situation or help to find a solution."

Craig Kielburger *of Canada, who founded Free the Children when he was 14, in 1997*

Issues and You

The struggle against child labor continues today. Do research in newspapers and on the Internet to learn what people are doing to fight against child labor around the world.

577

---

4 Why do you think some parents permitted children to work the kinds of hours Eliza Marshall worked? Possible answer: They may have felt their children had to work in order to make enough money for the family. Cause and Effect

5 Compare Iqbal Masih's situation with that of children in the late 1800s and early 1900s. In Masih's situation, as in the past, a young child was forced to work hard under difficult or dangerous conditions. Compare and Contrast

6 What is Craig Kielburger's view about child labor? He believes we should not tolerate it and should work to stop it. Main Idea and Details

3 Close and Assess

Issues and You

- After reviewing several reports about groups battling child labor, have each student focus on one group or activity.

- In conducting their research, have students search for answers to the following questions: How might perceptions about child labor vary in different regions, such as urban compared to rural? What is the current situation involving child labor? Where is it taking place? Who is trying to help? What is the individual or group doing? What have been the results so far?

- Have students use a web with one of the questions on each branch for note taking. Have students use these notes as the basis for oral reports.

FYI SOCIAL STUDIES
Background

Craig Kielburger

- Craig Kielburger grew up in a suburb of Toronto, Canada, with his parents and his older brother Marc.

- Kielburger visits working children all over the world and speaks in defense of children's rights.

- Kielburger and his friends founded Free the Children, a worldwide network of children helping children. Their organization has more than 100,000 active members in more than 25 countries.

CURRICULUM CONNECTION
Writing

Write a Letter

- Have students discuss what questions they might ask Craig Kielburger and his friends about their organization and their efforts to improve children's lives.

- Direct students to write a letter to Craig Kielburger asking him about his life and his causes.

Expansion Overseas

Objectives

- Evaluate the American decision to purchase Alaska.

- Explain how the United States acquired Hawaii.

- Describe the events leading up to the Spanish-American War.

- Analyze the effects of the Spanish-American War.

Vocabulary

Spanish-American War, p. 580;
Rough Riders, p. 580;
Buffalo Soldiers, p. 581

Resources

- Workbook, p. 134
- Transparency 21
- Every Student Learns Guide, pp. 242–245
- Quick Study, pp. 122–123

Quick Teaching Plan

If time is short, have students create annotated maps.

- Provide each student with an outline map of the United States.

- As students read the lesson independently, have them color or shade the lands that were acquired by the United States in 1867 and 1898.

- Have students write key facts about how each area was acquired.

1 Introduce and Motivate

Preview Ask students to describe the expanding boundaries of the United States during the mid-1800s. Tell them that they will learn how the United States expanded even further in the late 1800s as they read Lesson 3.

You Are There Consider Russia's offer to sell Alaska to the United States. Explain whether or not this is a wise purchase.

LESSON 3

1860   1900

1867
United States buys Alaska from Russia

July 1898
Hawaii is annexed by the United States

August 1898
Spanish-American War ends with United States victory

PREVIEW

Focus on the Main Idea
By the end of the 1800s, the United States had gained new territory and become a world power.

PLACES
Puerto Rico
Cuba

PEOPLE
Liliuokalani
Theodore Roosevelt

VOCABULARY
Spanish-American War
Rough Riders
Buffalo Soldiers

▶ Alaska is huge—bigger than Texas, California, and Montana put together.

Expansion Overseas

You Are There It is March 1867. Russia has offered to sell Alaska to the United States. But does the United States want to buy? As a United States senator, you will help decide this question. No one seems to know very much about Alaska, but here is what you have found out:

- Russia has offered to sell Alaska for $7.2 million, which works out to about 2 cents an acre.

- Several thousand people live in Alaska—most are native Inuit people, some are Russian.

- There are reports that the land is rich in resources such as timber and coal—and maybe even gold.

Have you made up your mind yet? How will you vote on this important issue?

Cause and Effect As you read, pay attention to the events that led to American expansion overseas.

578

Practice and Extend

Cause and Effect

In the Lesson Review, students complete a graphic organizer like the one below. You may want to provide students with a copy of Transparency 21 to complete as they read the lesson.

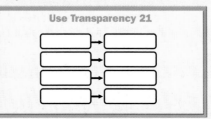

Use Transparency 21

Word Exercise

Context Clues Write *Spanish-American War* in the center of a word web, then have students find clues in the text that help establish context and assist them in remembering the significance of the war and why it had this name. (Possible context clues might include Spain's treatment of Cubans, belief that Spain attacked a U.S. ship, Americans volunteered to fight, Americans defeated Spanish.)

Alaska and Hawaii

It is not often that you get a chance to buy land for 2 cents an acre. Still, when the Russian government offered to sell the Alaska territory to the United States, many Americans opposed the deal. They pictured Alaska as a vast, useless land of snow and ice. But William Seward, the United States secretary of state, insisted that Alaska was worth buying. And in April 1867, the Senate voted to approve the purchase of Alaska for $7.2 million.

At first, newspapers joked about Alaska, calling it "Seward's Icebox." The laughing stopped, however, when gold was discovered in Alaska. Thousands of miners rushed north in search of wealth and adventure. **1**

Thousands of miles southwest of Alaska lies Hawaii, a group of islands in the Pacific Ocean. During the 1800s, American planters began moving to Hawaii. They found that the islands' warm climate was perfect for growing sugarcane and pineapples. By the late 1800s, Americans had established several large plantations in Hawaii.

At this time, Hawaii was ruled by Queen **Liliuokalani** (li lee uh woh kuh LAH nee). She felt that American planters were becoming too powerful in Hawaii. She wanted native-born Hawaiians to remain in control of the islands. In 1893, American planters led a revolt against the queen. United States soldiers arrived to support the planters. Queen Liliuokalani realized she could not win this battle. "I yielded [gave up] my authority to the forces of the United States in order to avoid bloodshed," she wrote. Hawaii was annexed by the United States in July 1898. **2**

> **REVIEW** How did Hawaii become part of the United States? *Cause and Effect*

▶ **Queen Liliuokalani (above) wrote many songs about Hawaii that are still sung today.**

Literature and Social Studies

To Build a Fire

A young American writer named Jack London traveled to Alaska in 1897. In a story called "To Build a Fire," a gold miner falls into a stream on a bitter cold Alaska day. He must build a fire quickly, or he will freeze to death.

....

"He worked slowly and carefully, keenly aware of his danger. Gradually, as the flame grew stronger, he increased the size of the twigs with which he fed it. He squatted in the snow, pulling the twigs out from their entanglement in the brush and feeding directly to the flame. He knew there must be no failure. When it is seventy-five below zero, a man must not fail in his first attempt to build a fire...." **3**

---

2 Teach and Discuss

PAGE 579

Alaska and Hawaii

🕐 *Quick Summary* Between 1867 and 1898 the United States expanded by acquiring both Alaska and Hawaii.

1 **At first Alaska was called "Seward's Icebox." Make up a nickname that could have been used after the discovery of gold in Alaska.** Possible answer: "Seward's Gold Chest" **Express Ideas**

G **SOCIAL STUDIES STRAND**
Government

Point out that Hawaii was annexed, or added on as a minor part, by the United States in 1898 and became an American territory in 1900.

2 **What did Queen Liliuokalani mean by saying that she gave up her authority to avoid bloodshed?** She decided not to fight the United States to prevent having her people hurt in a war. **Analyze Primary Sources**

✓ **REVIEW ANSWER** American planters led a revolt against the Queen who ruled Hawaii. The United States annexed Hawaii in 1898. **Cause and Effect**

Literature and Social Studies

Have students read the introduction and excerpt from "To Build a Fire."

3 **Why is the man in the story working slowly and carefully?** He probably has few resources for building a fire so he wants to do it right the first time. Without the fire, he will freeze to death. **Cause and Effect**

The Spanish-American War

🕐 **Quick Summary** When an explosion in 1898 destroyed the battleship *Maine*, the United States blamed Spain and declared war. As a result of this war, the United States gained control of Puerto Rico, the Philippines, and Guam.

Test Talk

Locate Key Words in the Text

4 **What were two reasons the United States became involved in the Cuban revolt?** Tell students to find key words in the text—such as *Cuba* and *United States*—to find the right answer. The United States was concerned about the way the Spanish were treating Cubans, and about the safety of U.S. businesses in Cuba. **Cause and Effect**

5 **Tell the sequence of events described on p. 580.** In 1895 Cubans revolted. In 1898 President McKinley decided the United States should get involved. In February 1898, the battleship USS *Maine* was destroyed. In April 1898, the Spanish-American War began. The United States Navy destroyed the Spanish fleet in the Philippines. 🔄 **Sequence**

✓ Ongoing Assessment

If... students cannot construct the sequence of events from reading the text,	**then...** have them make a sequence chain or time line to illustrate what happened and when each event occurred.

6 **What do you think might have happened if the United States had known that the *Maine* probably exploded because of an accident?** Possible answer: The United States may not have declared war at that time but may have fought Spain later due to concerns it had. **Hypothesize**

▶ The explosion of the *Maine* shocked Americans.

The Spanish-American War

You know that Spain once had a huge empire in North and South America. By the late 1800s, however, Spain had just two colonies in the Western Hemisphere—the Caribbean islands of **Puerto Rico** and **Cuba.** In 1895, the Cuban people revolted against Spanish rule. The Spanish army reacted harshly. To keep people from joining the revolution, Spanish soldiers imprisoned hundreds of thousands of Cubans.

Many people in the United States were angered by Spain's treatment of the Cuban people. The war was also causing the destruction of United States-owned businesses in Cuba. The United States government decided to act. In 1898, President McKinley sent the battleship USS *Maine* to Cuba's Havana harbor. The *Maine's* goal was to protect the lives and property of Americans in Cuba.

On the night of February 15, a huge explosion destroyed the *Maine*, killing 260 Americans. Several United States newspapers reported that Spain was responsible for the deadly explosion. In fact, there was no evidence of this. In the years since, studies have shown that an accident aboard the *Maine* probably caused the explosion. But at the time, Americans blamed Spain. People called for action, crying "Remember the *Maine!*" Congress declared war on April 25, 1898, and the **Spanish-American War** began.

The United States Navy's first goal was to destroy the Spanish fleet in the Philippines, a Spanish colony in the Pacific Ocean. United States battleships sailed to the Philippines under the command of Commodore George Dewey. When Dewey spotted the Spanish ships in Manila Bay, he told Captain Charles Gridley, "You may fire when you are ready, Gridley." The Spanish fleet was completely destroyed. **6**

Nearly one million Americans volunteered to fight in the Spanish-American War. **Theodore Roosevelt,** the assistant secretary of the navy, left his job to organize a group of volunteer soldiers. He put together a diverse fighting force of cowboys, Native Americans, and college athletes. Newspapers began calling Roosevelt's soldiers the **Rough Riders.**

On July 1, 1898, the Rough Riders charged at the Spanish on Cuba's San Juan Hill.

580

Practice and Extend

SOCIAL STUDIES Background

Destruction of the Spanish Fleet

• When the Spanish-American War broke out, Spain's navy was not ready to do battle with the well-prepared United States.

• Commodore Dewey had anticipated a possible battle in the Philippines, which belonged to Spain at the time, and had studied the area. Once the United States had declared war on Spain, Dewey quickly destroyed the Spanish fleet without losing the life of a single American sailor.

▶ Theodore Roosevelt led the Rough Riders up San Juan Hill.

Charging alongside Roosevelt and his troops were several units of experienced African American soldiers. These soldiers were known as **Buffalo Soldiers,** a nickname they got while serving in the wars against Native Americans on the Great Plains.

The Americans defeated the Spanish in the Battle of San Juan Hill. Two days later, American ships destroyed the Spanish fleet in Cuba. In August, the United States and Spain agreed to a treaty ending the war.

On the map below, you can see some of the effects of the United States victory in the Spanish-American War. The United States gained control of several Spanish territories, including Puerto Rico, the Philippines, and Guam. Cuba gained independence from Spain.

The Philippines remained an American territory until 1946, when it became an independent nation. Puerto Rico and Guam are still part of the United States and their people are United States citizens.

REVIEW What territories did the United States gain by winning the Spanish-American War? *Main Idea and Details*

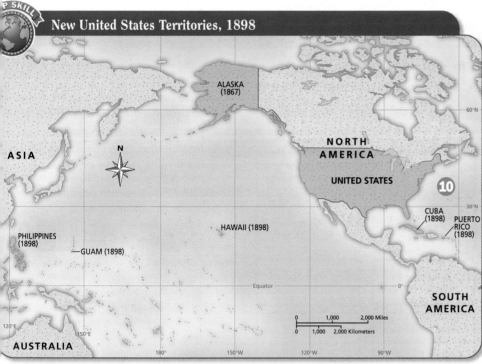

New United States Territories, 1898

ALASKA (1867)

ASIA

NORTH AMERICA

UNITED STATES

CUBA (1898)

PUERTO RICO (1898)

HAWAII (1898)

PHILIPPINES (1898)

GUAM (1898)

Equator

SOUTH AMERICA

AUSTRALIA

▶ By 1898, the United States controlled territories throughout the Pacific Ocean.

MAP SKILL Use Latitude and Longitude *Estimate the location of Guam using latitude and longitude.*

581

⑦ What are two facts to support the opinion that Americans backed the Spanish-American War? Possible answer: Almost one million Americans joined the fight; Theodore Roosevelt left his job to organize fighting troops. Fact and Opinion

⑧ Compare and contrast the Rough Riders with the Buffalo Soldiers. Both groups fought bravely at the Battle of San Juan Hill. The Rough Riders were mainly cowboys, Native Americans, and athletes organized to fight in the Spanish-American War. The Buffalo Soldiers were African American soldiers who had fought in wars against Native Americans. Compare and Contrast

⑨ For how many months did the Spanish-American War last? About four months Sequence

✓ **REVIEW ANSWER** Puerto Rico, the Philippines, and Guam
Main Idea and Details

New United States Territories, 1898

Have students note the year each territory was acquired.

⑩ How many years after the purchase of Alaska did Hawaii become a territory of the United States? About 31 years
Sequence

MAP SKILL Answer 13°N, 145°E

ℍ SOCIAL STUDIES STRAND
History

Heroes of past wars, as well as leaders in future conflicts, saw action in the Spanish-American War. Former Confederate general "Fighting Joe" Wheeler commanded troops in Cuba and the Philippines. The 9th and 10th Cavalry units of Buffalo Soldiers, veterans of the Great Plains wars, served courageously. One of their quartermasters, a white soldier named John J. Pershing, served bravely in Cuba and later commanded African American soldiers fighting in Mexico. Pershing became supreme commander of American forces during World War I.

A New World Power

 **Quick Summary** The United States emerged from the Spanish-American War as a world power.

11 **Why was Theodore Roosevelt considered a hero?** He had shown leadership and dedication by successfully leading the Rough Riders in battle. **Draw Conclusions**

✓ **REVIEW ANSWER** After the war, the United States was viewed by other countries as a world power. **Cause and Effect**

3 Close and Assess

Summarize the Lesson

Tell students to examine the vertical time line. Ask them to make three concept webs, using each bulleted point as a central idea surrounded by several details.

✓ **LESSON 3** **REVIEW**

1. **Cause and Effect** For possible answers, see the reduced pupil page.

2. Seward supported the purchase of what many thought was a frozen wasteland.

3. The American military supported a revolt by American planters. Queen Liliuokalani gave up her power. Later, the United States annexed Hawaii.

4. African American soldiers who fought in the wars against Native Americans and in the Spanish-American War.

5. **Critical Thinking:** *Draw Conclusions* In the late 1800s, the United States gained territory around the world and defeated Spain in the Spanish-American War.

Link to ○-○ **Geography**

Students' reports should include facts about the landforms, resources, plant and animal life, and people of the area they choose. Remind students to use standard grammar, spelling, sentence structure, and punctuation.

582 Unit 8 • Expansion and Change

A New World Power

With its swift victory over Spain, the United States showed that it had become a powerful nation. The United States was now a world power, or one of the most powerful nations in the world.

Theodore Roosevelt became a national hero. As he stepped off the boat from Cuba, a crowd of people shouted, "Hurrah for Teddy **11** and the Rough Riders!" Roosevelt was soon elected governor of New York and later became President of the United States. In the Biography on the next page, you will find out how childhood experiences helped prepare Roosevelt for leadership.

Victory in the Spanish-American War, however, was costly. Over 5,000 American soldiers died during the war. Of these, fewer than 400 were killed in battle. The rest died from diseases such as malaria and yellow fever.

REVIEW How did the Spanish-American War change the role of the United States in the world? **Cause and Effect**

Summarize the Lesson

- **1867** The United States purchased Alaska from Russia for $7.2 million.

- **July 1898** Hawaii was annexed by the United States.

- **August 1898** With victory in the Spanish-American War, the United States gained new territory and became a world power.

LESSON 3 **REVIEW**

Check Facts and Main Ideas

1. **Cause and Effect** Complete this chart by filling in one effect for each event listed below.

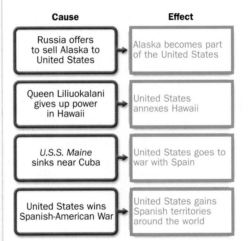

Cause	Effect
Russia offers to sell Alaska to United States	Alaska becomes part of the United States
Queen Liliuokalani gives up power in Hawaii	United States annexes Hawaii
U.S.S. Maine sinks near Cuba	United States goes to war with Spain
United States wins Spanish-American War	United States gains Spanish territories around the world

2. Why did newspapers call Alaska "Seward's Icebox"?

3. How did the American military help Hawaii become part of the United States?

4. Who were the **Buffalo Soldiers?**

5. **Critical Thinking:** *Draw Conclusions* By 1900, the United States was seen as a world power. How do you think the events described in this lesson helped the United States become a world power?

Link to ○-○ **Geography**

Write a Report Look back at the map of new United States territories on page 581. Choose one of these places and find out more about it. Write a short report describing the land and people of this place.

Practice and Extend

 CURRICULUM CONNECTION
Literature

Read About Theodore Roosevelt

Theodore Roosevelt, by Michael A. Schuman (Enslow, ISBN 0-894-90836-7, 1997) **Easy**

Bully for You, Teddy Roosevelt, by Jean Fritz (PaperStar, ISBN 0-698-11609-7, 1997) **On-Level** *ALA Notable Book*

James K. Polk, Abraham Lincoln, Theodore Roosevelt (Presidents Who Dared), by Edmund Lindop (Twenty-First Century, ISBN 0-805-03402-1, 1995) **Challenge**

Workbook, p. 134

Lesson 3: Expansion Overseas

Directions: Complete the cause-and-effect chart with information from Lesson 3. You may use your textbook.

Cause	Effect
1. Russia offers to sell Alaska for 2 cents an acre. U.S. Secretary of State William Seward insists Alaska is worth buying.	
2.	Thousands of miners rush north in search of wealth and adventure.
3. American planters discover that the Hawaii climate is good for growing sugarcane and pineapples.	
4. Queen Liliuokalani of Hawaii wants native-born Hawaiians to remain in control of the islands.	
5. Queen Liliuokalani yields her authority to the United States to avoid bloodshed.	
6.	Spanish soldiers imprison hundreds of thousands of Cubans to keep people from joining the revolution.
7. People in the United States are angered by Spain's treatment of the Cuban people. American-owned businesses in Cuba begin feeling the effects of the war.	
8.	Americans blame Spain for the attack. Congress declares war on April 25, 1898, and the Spanish-American War begins.
9.	The United States emerges as a world power.

Notes for Home: Your child learned how the United States expanded and became a world power.
Home Activity: With your child, make a chart comparing and contrasting the ways the United States gained control of Alaska, Hawaii, Puerto Rico, the Philippines, and Guam.

Also on Teacher Resources CD-ROM

Theodore Roosevelt
1858–1919

As a child, Teddy Roosevelt was often sick, and this left him very weak. One day when he was 13, Teddy was alone on a train when two boys started to tease him. They made fun of his glasses, his clothes, and his skinniness. Right then and there Teddy decided that he would build up his body so no one would ever tease him again.

Back at home, he started exercising with weights and taking boxing lessons. Soon he was winning track and field events such as foot races and the broad jump. In his twenties, Roosevelt went out west to the Dakota Territory. There he became an expert horseback rider, roping cattle and building fences as well as most cowboys. But he never forgot the lesson he had learned as a child. Roosevelt **❶** was determined that he would do everything he could to protect the weak.

Between 1898 and 1900, as governor of New York, Roosevelt backed laws to protect women and children from unhealthy conditions where they worked and from long hours of work. Roosevelt became known as a person who stood up for the poor.

Roosevelt also loved nature and fought to protect it. As President, he told Congress that, **❷**

"To waste, to destroy, our natural resources, to skin and exhaust [use up] the land instead of using it so as to increase its usefulness, will result in undermining [weakening]...the very prosperity [good life]...which we ought...to hand down to [our children]..." **❸**

Learn from Biographies

Describe how Roosevelt's experience with childhood illness affected his ideas as an adult.

BIOFACT
Named in honor of Teddy Roosevelt, the teddy bear became a popular toy in the early 1900s.

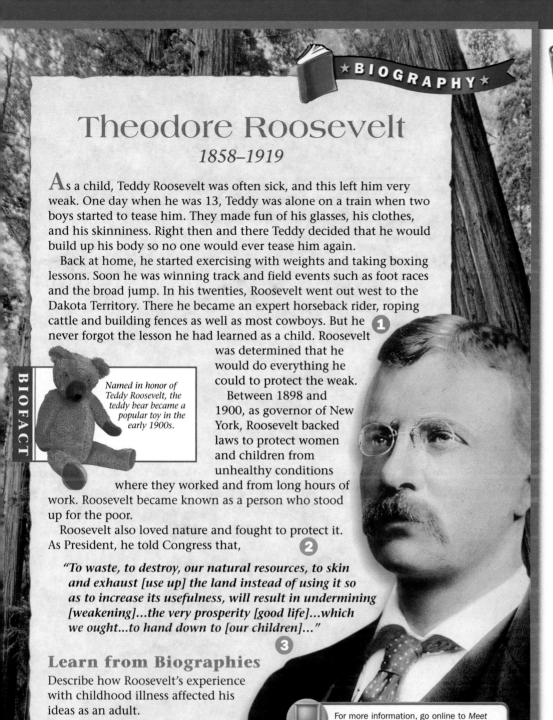

For more information, go online to *Meet the People* at **www.sfsocialstudies.com**.

583

Theodore Roosevelt

Objective
- Identify the achievements of people who have made contributions to society.

1 Introduce and Motivate

Preview To activate prior knowledge, ask students what they know about Theodore Roosevelt. Tell them that they will read more about his life.

2 Teach and Discuss

❶ Summarize the actions Roosevelt took to build up his body. Possible answer: He lifted weights, boxed, ran races, and rode horses. Summarize

❷ What fact supports the opinion that Roosevelt built a strong character and a strong body? He stood up for what he believed in. Fact and Opinion

❸ What did Roosevelt fear might happen to our natural resources? People would destroy them without thought. Analyze Primary Sources

3 Close and Assess

Learn from Biographies Answer

As a child, he was teased about his weakness, so as an adult, he wanted to protect the weak.

WEB SITE Technology

Students can find out more about Theodore Roosevelt by clicking on *Meet the People* at **www.sfsocialstudies.com**.

FYI SOCIAL STUDIES Background

Theodore Roosevelt
- Roosevelt had asthma and poor eyesight.
- Roosevelt was committed to developing his mind and his body. Due to his health, he was tutored at home. He went on to graduate from Harvard University.
- He used his time in the Dakota Territory to strengthen his body and to recover from the grief he felt when both his mother and wife died on the same day—February 14, 1884.

Thinking Skills

Credibility of a Source

Objective
- Identify credible sources of information.

Vocabulary
source, p. 584

Resource
- Workbook, p. 135

1 Introduce and Motivate

What is "credibility of a source"?
Ask students to share any prior knowledge about the meaning of *credibility* and its relationship to sources of information. Then have students read the **What?** section of text on p. 584.

Why determine the credibility of a source? Have students read the **Why?** section of text on p. 584. Ask them to give examples of sources of information they find that they think are likely to be credible and ones they think are not.

2 Teach and Discuss

How is this skill used? Examine with students Source A and Source B. Have students determine which is the primary source and which is the secondary source and compare and contrast them.

- Discuss the term *motivation* with students. Have them discuss the probable motivations of the writers of Source A and Source B.

- Point out that word choice can be a clue to credibility. Have students identify examples of objective (giving facts without bias) and subjective (influenced by personal feelings) ways to describe an event.

- Have students read the **How?** section of text on p. 585.

Thinking Skills

Credibility of a Source

What? A source is any written or oral account that may provide information. Some sources are credible, or reliable. Other sources are not credible, or not reliable. When you decide if a source is credible or not credible, you are determining whether or not to believe the information the source is giving you.

Why? Do you sometimes read or hear about things you find difficult to believe? Perhaps you should believe them.

▶ This painting shows one artist's view of the explosion of the *Maine.*

Source A

I was...so quiet that Lieutenant J. Hood came up and asked laughingly if I was asleep. I said "No, I am on watch." Scarcely had I spoken when there came a dull, sullen roar. Would to God that I could blot out the sound and the scenes that followed. Then came a sharp explosion—some say numerous detonations [blasts]. I remember only one....I have no theories as to the cause of the explosion. I cannot form any. I, with others, had heard the Havana harbor was full of torpedoes [mines], but the officers whose duty it was to examine into that reported that they found no signs of any. Personally, I do not believe that the Spanish had anything to do with the disaster.

1 **2**

—Lieutenant John J. Blandin

584

Practice and Extend

 SOCIAL STUDIES Background

Yellow Journalism
- Sensationalized news is often called *yellow journalism*.
- The term was first used in the 1890s to describe the methods that two New York City newspapers used to compete with each other for readers.
- The practice of using extreme sensationalism by city papers died out around 1900. Some techniques such as banner headlines, colored comics, and widespread use of illustrations continue today.

Or perhaps you should not. You need to know how to determine the credibility of any source of information.

In 1898, the United States battleship *Maine* exploded in Havana Harbor. Americans and others wondered what caused the explosion. The ship's officers and sailors who survived wrote reports.

At the same time, some newspaper publishers decided that they could sell many newspapers if they printed sensational stories, or stories that would make people excited or interested. This kind of writing is called "yellow journalism."

Source A is from a report by Lieutenant John J. Blandin, who was on board the *Maine* when it exploded. Source B is from a front-page article published in the *New York Journal* on February 17, 1898.

How? To determine whether a source is credible, the first step is to consider the author of the source. Decide whether the author has first-hand or expert knowledge about the event. Decide whether the author has any reason to exaggerate, change the facts, or describe events in a particular way. It also helps to find out whether the author does or does not have a reputation for being truthful and accurate.

Source B

Think and Apply

1 Where is **Source** A from? Where is Source B from?

2 What did Lieutenant Blandin say about the probable cause of the explosion? What did the newspaper say about the probable cause of the explosion?

3 Which report do you think has more credibility? Why?

585

1 **What is one fact and one opinion in Lieutenant Blandin's report?** Possible answers: It is a fact that he heard an explosion. It is his opinion that the Spanish were not responsible. Fact and Opinion

2 **What could have caused parts of the lieutenant's report to be incorrect even though he was there?** The terror of the situation might have caused him to remember incorrectly. Analyze Information

3 **What are examples of strong words and phrases the *Journal* reporter used to try to convince people the explosion was Spain's fault?** Possible answers: Naval officers think the *Maine* was destroyed by a Spanish mine; Spanish officials protest too much. Recognize Bias

Close and Assess

Think and Apply

1. Source A is a report by an officer who was on the *Maine* when it exploded. Source B is a newspaper.

2. Lieutenant Blandin says he does not know what caused the explosion, but he does not think the Spanish had anything to do with it. The *Journal* suggests that the explosion was not an accident and reports that officers on the *Maine* think it was caused by a Spanish mine.

3. Most students will say that the lieutenant's report is more credible because he was there, and he cites the reports of investigating officers. He does not appear to have a personal reason for holding one opinion or another, and he admits to uncertainty. In contrast, the *Journal* draws a conclusion without offering any firsthand evidence. The *Journal* may have decided that it could sell more newspapers by whipping up public anger and excitement.

FYI **SOCIAL STUDIES Background**

Reporting on the USS *Maine*

- The newspapers of the late 1800s did not generally include photographs. Therefore, people who wanted to see a portrayal of the event sought out stereographs—pictures mounted on cardboard that were placed in a viewer.

- In 1976, Admiral Hyman Rickover of the U.S. Navy undertook another study of the sinking of the *Maine*. The resulting book, **How the Battleship Maine Was Destroyed**, asserted that the Spanish were not responsible.

Workbook, p. 135

Also on Teacher Resources CD-ROM.

Resources

- Assessment Book, pp. 97–100
- Workbook, p. 136: Vocabulary Review

Chapter Summary

For possible answers, see the reduced pupil page.

Vocabulary

1. T, **2.** F; A corporation is a business owned by investors, **3.** T, **4.** F; Workers organized labor unions to improve their working conditions, **5.** T

People and Terms

Possible answers:

1. Lewis Latimer invented a light bulb that lasted longer than Edison's.

2. Andrew Carnegie created a huge steel industry in the United States and became one of the wealthiest people in the world. He donated money to build libraries, universities, and museums.

3. John D. Rockefeller built oil refineries and soon controlled a monopoly of the U.S. oil business.

4. Jane Addams opened Hull House, which offered services, such as free English classes and daycare, to poor immigrants.

5. Samuel Gompers formed the American Federation of Labor (AFL) to fight for shorter workdays and safer working conditions.

6. Mary Harris Jones, also called Mother Jones, urged coal miners to join unions to improve their working conditions.

7. Queen Liliuokalani ruled Hawaii at the time American planters revolted. The United States later annexed Hawaii.

8. Buffalo Soldiers fought alongside Theodore Roosevelt in the Spanish-American War.

Facts and Main Ideas

1. Carnegie bought coal and iron mines, ships, and railroads.

1860	1865	1870

1859 Oil is discovered in Pennsylvania

1867 United States buys Alaska from Russia

Chapter Summary

Sequence

On a separate sheet of paper, copy the chart and place the following events in the sequence in which they happened. Include the date for each one.

- 1863—John D. Rockefeller builds his first oil refinery
- 1873—Christopher Latham Sholes builds the first typewriter
- 1882—First Labor Day celebration
- 1895—Cuban people revolt against Spanish rule
- 1897—The nation's first subway is built in Boston
- 1898—The Spanish American War begins

Vocabulary

On a separate sheet of paper, write **T** for each sentence that correctly defines the underlined word and **F** for each definition that is false. If false, rewrite the definition so it is correct.

1. A monopoly is a company that controls an entire industry. (p. 566)

2. A corporation is a business owned by one person. (p. 566)

3. A building divided into small apartments is called a tenement. (p. 571)

4. Employers organized labor unions to improve their working conditions. (p. 572)

5. Soldiers who fought with Theodore Roosevelt were called Rough Riders. (p. 580)

People and Terms

Write a sentence explaining the role of each of the following people or terms in the changing United States of the late 1800s. You may use two or more in a single sentence.

1. Lewis Latimer (p. 563)
2. Andrew Carnegie (p. 564)
3. John D. Rockefeller (p. 566)
4. Jane Addams (p. 571)
5. Samuel Gompers (p. 573)
6. Mary Harris Jones (p. 573)
7. Liliuokalani (p. 579)
8. Buffalo Soldier (p. 581)

586

Practice and Extend

Assessment Options

✓ Chapter 17 Assessment

- Chapter 17 Content Test: Use Assessment Book, pp. 97–98.
- Chapter 17 Skills Test: Use Assessment Book, pp. 99–100.

Standardized Test Prep

- Chapter 17 Tests contain standardized test format.

✓ Chapter 17 Performance Assessment

- Assign small groups the name of a person discussed in the chapter. Have students act out a significant event related to that person's life.

- Have the class watch each re-enactment and then explain what has been depicted and how it changed life in the United States.

- Assess students' understanding of significant inventions, discoveries, and events of the late 1800s and early 1900s.

1876
Alexander Graham Bell invents the telephone

1879
Thomas Edison develops the electric light bulb

1889
Jane Addams opens Hull House in Chicago

July 1898
Hawaii is annexed by the United States
August 1898
Spanish-American War ends with United States victory

Facts and Main Ideas

- What businesses did Andrew Carnegie buy in order to produce and transport steel?

- How did immigration in the early 1900s differ from immigration in the late 1800s?

- What territories did the United States gain as a result of the Spanish–American War?

- **Time Line** How many years were there between the time the United States took over Alaska and Hawaii?

- **Main Idea** What were some inventions that brought about major changes in the way people lived in the late 1800s?

- **Main Idea** What problems did many immigrants face?

- **Main Idea** What events made the United States a world power by the end of the 1800s?

- **Critical Thinking:** *Draw Conclusions* Life was difficult for an immigrant in the late 1800s and early 1900s. Why do you think people continued to come to the United States?

Write About History

- **Write a letter** to a friend describing a new invention from the late 1800s. Explain how it will change the way people live.

- **Write an editorial** trying to convince workers either to join or not to join a labor union.

- **Write a newspaper article** giving the benefits and problems of the United States purchasing Alaska from Russia.

Apply Skills

Evaluate the Credibility of a Source
Read the newspaper article below. Then answer the questions.

HAWAIIANS CALL FOR INDEPENDENCE

Thousands Gather in Palace Square

Honolulu, October 8, 1897—Thousands of Hawaiians gathered in Honolulu's Palace Square today to show support for Hawaiian independence. Hawaiian leaders made patriotic speeches and the crowd responded with cries of "Independence now and forever!" The protesters hoped to send a strong message to Washington, D.C., where leaders are now considering a treaty to annex Hawaii. This would make Hawaii part of the United States.

Protesters are not the only ones being heard in this debate, however. United States Senator John Tyler Morgan is here in Hawaii to try to convince the Hawaiian people to support annexation. In public speeches and interviews, Morgan has argued that Hawaiians will enjoy increased opportunities as citizens of the United States.

1. What information does the newspaper article give?

2. Whose views are given?

3. How credible is this newspaper article?

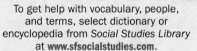

To get help with vocabulary, people, and terms, select dictionary or encyclopedia from *Social Studies Library* at **www.sfsocialstudies.com**.

587

Hands-on Unit Project

✓ **Unit 8 Performance Assessment**

- See p. 592 for information about using the Unit Project as a means of performance assessment.

- A scoring guide is provided on p. 592.

WEB SITE
Technology

For more information, students can select the dictionary or encyclopedia from *Social Studies Library* at **www.sfsocialstudies.com**.

Workbook, p. 136

Vocabulary Review

Directions: Read the following statement. Then write *T* (True) or *F* (False) on the line before each statement. If the answer is false, correct the statement to make it true. You may use your textbook. Not all words will be used.

____ 1. A monopoly is any business that is owned by investors.

____ 2. In some cities, poor people received help at a settlement house.

____ 3. The workers decided to stage a monopoly until the owners met their demands.

____ 4. The African American soldiers who defended Americans and American property in Cuba were known as Rough Riders.

____ 5. A volunteer soldier under Theodore Roosevelt who defended Americans in Cuba was known as a Rough Rider.

____ 6. When a single company controls an entire industry and stops competition, it is called a corporation.

____ 7. A settlement house is a building that is divided into small apartments.

Also on Teacher Resources CD-ROM.

---

2. Late 1800s: immigrants came mainly from northern and western Europe; early 1900s: most came from southern and eastern Europe.

3. Puerto Rico, the Philippines, and Guam

4. About 31 years

5. The telephone, electric light bulb, typewriter, and radio

6. Living in crowded tenements and taking jobs with low wages, long hours, little vacation time, and dangerous working conditions

7. The acquisition of Alaska and Hawaii as well as the defeat of Spain

8. Possible answer: Many immigrants faced persecution, famines, poverty, or few job opportunities in their native homelands.

Write About History

1. Students' letters should clearly identify the purpose and significance of an invention and tell who was responsible for its creation.

2. Students' editorials should clearly identify their position and include reasons and facts to support it.

3. Students' articles should explain pros and cons for the purchase of Alaska.

Apply Skills

1. Thousands of protesters gathered to support Hawaiian independence. Senator Morgan argued in favor of the annexation of Hawaii.

2. Both those for Hawaiian independence and for annexation

3. Possible answer: It is credible because the reporter tells about both sides of the argument.

Red River Valley

Objectives

- Identify pieces of music from different periods in U.S. history.

- Explain how pieces of music reflect the times in which they were written.

1 Introduce and Motivate

Preview Ask students if they know the history of the song "Red River Valley." Tell students that they will learn more about this song and what it means.

Ask students how studying a song from a certain time can be useful. (It can provide another means to understand the people and the times.)

2 Teach and Discuss

1 **How is the singer of the song feeling? Why?** Sad because a friend is leaving the Red River Valley
Cause and Effect

Red River Valley

If you had worked on the cattle drives of the 1800s you would probably have known lots of cowboy songs. Cowboys sang these songs to keep their cattle calm. And they sang to pass the time during the long, lonely days and nights on the trail. What does the cowboy song "Red River Valley" tell you about what life was like for cowboys?

588

Practice and Extend

 SOCIAL STUDIES
Background

"Red River Valley"

- The song was originally named "In the Bright Mohawk Valley" and was popular in New York.
- Later the song spread throughout the South and became a cowboy tune focused on the Red River Valley.

 AUDIO CD
Technology

Play the CD, *Songs and Music*, to listen to "Red River Valley."

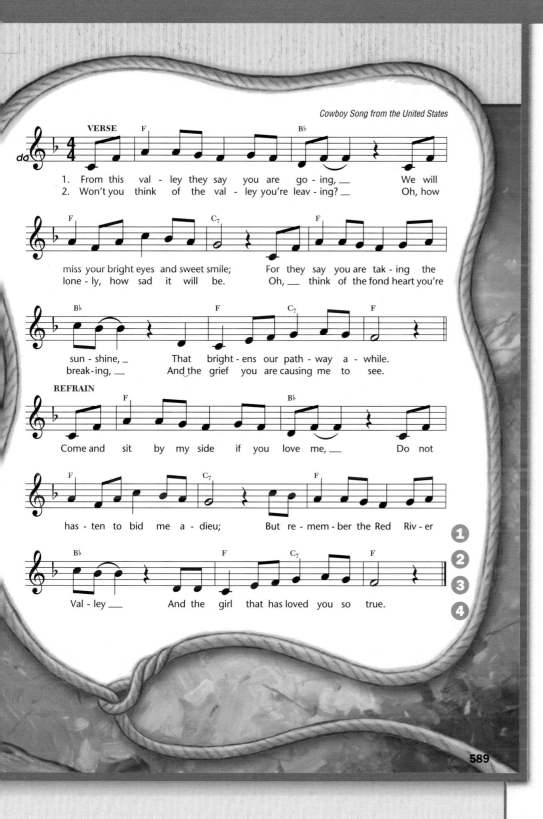

Cowboy Song from the United States

VERSE

1. From this val-ley they say you are go-ing, __ We will miss your bright eyes and sweet smile; For they say you are tak-ing the sun-shine, __ That bright-ens our path-way a-while.

2. Won't you think of the val-ley you're leav-ing? __ Oh, how lone-ly, how sad it will be. Oh, __ think of the fond heart you're break-ing, __ And the grief you are caus-ing me to see.

REFRAIN

Come and sit by my side if you love me, __ Do not has-ten to bid me a-dieu; But re-mem-ber the Red Riv-er Val-ley __ And the girl that has loved you so true.

589

2 **What is another way of saying, "Do not hasten to bid me adieu"?** Possible answer: Do not be in such a hurry to say goodbye. Express Ideas

3 **What might the line "For they say you are taking the sunshine" mean?** Possible answer: It will seem like the sun will never shine again once the person leaves the valley. Make Inferences

4 **Why might the person be leaving the Red River Valley?** Possible answers: To begin a cattle drive, find a new job, or to go east. Hypothesize

3 Close and Assess

- Have students gather simple props such as cowboy hats, guitars, and harmonicas to use in singing the song. Videotape the performance.

- Direct students to think of this song as a poem that tells a story. Have students discuss the events and characters in the "story." Point out the line "For they say you are taking the sunshine." Tell students to ask themselves if this is a logical action. They should ask themselves "Would this character really take the sunshine?" Then ask students to write a summary of the events and feelings described in the song.

CURRICULUM CONNECTION
Art

Paint a Setting

- Have students use watercolors or tempera paints to create an illustration of the setting of the song.
- Have students look at pictures of the area where the Red River flows to get ideas of how to depict the valley.

Resource
- Assessment Book, pp. 101–104

Main Ideas and Vocabulary TEST PREP

1. b, **2.** d, **3.** c, **4.** b

Test Talk

Locate Key Words in the Text
Use Main Ideas and Vocabulary, Question 3, to model the Test Talk Strategy.

Make sure that you understand the question.
Have students find the key word in the question. Students should finish the statement "I need to find out. . . ."

Find key words in the text.
Have students reread or skim the text to look for key words that will help them answer the question.

People and Terms

1. e, **2.** b, **3.** a, **4.** f, **5.** c, **6.** d

Apply Skills

- Encourage students to select sites that are spread across the United States rather than clustered in one area.

- Suggest that students use a main idea sentence for their explanation and follow up with at least one supporting statement or example.

Test Talk

Find keywords in the text.

Main Ideas and Vocabulary TEST PREP

Read the passage below and use it to answer the questions that follow.

After the Civil War, the United States expanded in many ways. It developed new industries and gained more territory. The population grew larger and more varied.

Improvements in transportation and communication linked together the different parts of the country. The transcontinental railroad shortened travel time. The telegraph made it possible to send messages almost immediately using Morse Code.

A new process made it possible to produce steel in great quantities. The electric light bulb was soon lighting streets and homes.

Immigrants came from Europe, Asia, and Latin America. They often faced <u>prejudice</u>. Yet they made up a large part of the work force in mines and factories and on farms.

Some workers organized labor unions to demand better pay and working conditions. When factory owners refused, workers sometimes organized <u>strikes</u>. After many years, the government passed laws regulating work hours and safety.

In 1867, the United States bought Alaska from Russia. More territory was added when the nation annexed Hawaii in 1898.

1 According to the passage, what helped link different parts of the United States?
- **A** People wrote letters to relatives.
- **B** Improvements in transportation and communication shortened the time it took to travel and send messages.
- **C** Farmers spread the news when they took their crops to market.
- **D** Labor leaders kept union members informed.

2 In the passage, the word <u>prejudice</u> means—
- **A** hard work
- **B** language difficulties
- **C** new inventions
- **D** unfair opinions

3 In the passage, the word <u>strike</u> means—
- **A** writing a letter to ask for better conditions
- **B** joining together to damage equipment
- **C** refusal to work unless demands are met
- **D** searching for a new job

4 What is the main idea of the passage?
- **A** New inventions changed farming.
- **B** The country expanded in industry, population, and territory.
- **C** Immigrants went on strikes.
- **D** The country bought Alaska.

590

Practice and Extend

Assessment Options

✓ **Unit 8 Assessment**
- Unit 8 Content Test: Use Assessment Book, pp. 101–102.
- Unit 8 Skills Test: Use Assessment Book, pp. 103–104.

TEST PREP **Standardized Test Prep**
- Unit 8 Tests contain standardized test format.

✓ **Unit 8 Performance Assessment**
- See p. 592 for information about using the Unit Project as a means of Performance Assessment.
- A scoring guide for the Unit 8 Project is provided in the teacher's notes on p. 592.

Test Talk
- Test Talk Practice Book

WEB SITE
Technology

For more information, students can select the dictionary or encyclopedia from *Social Studies Library* at **www.sfsocialstudies.com**.

People and Terms

[M]atch each person and term to its definition.

1. **transcontinental railroad** (p. 539)
2. **barbed wire** (p. 551)
3. **George Custer** (p. 556)
4. **corporation** (p. 566)
5. **Mary Antin** (p. 569)
6. **Theodore Roosevelt** (p. 580)

a. killed at the Battle of Little Bighorn

b. twisted wire used as a fence

c. author who wrote about her experiences as an immigrant

d. fought with Rough Riders in the Spanish-American War

e. train running across the country

f. business owned by investors

Apply Skills

[C]reate a Time Zone Exhibit Take a large map of [th]e United States and select at least ten places, [in]cluding one near where you live. Choose [pl]aces that you would like to visit. Make sure [s]ome places are in different time zones from [y]our own. Mark each place with the correct time [w]hen it is 12:00 noon in your town. Explain why [it] is important to know the time in other [lo]cations.

Write and Share

Present an Immigrant History Display Have all the students in the class identify at least one country or region from which their families or a person they know emigrated. Using a large world map, place pushpins in each place from which a person came. Research some of those locations and present your findings to the class.

Read on Your Own

Look for books like these in the library.

591

Revisit the Unit Question

✓ Portfolio Assessment

- Have students review the list of reasons why people today decide to move from other countries to the United States.
- Have students list the reasons earlier immigrants came to the United States.
- Ask students to compare and contrast their lists and write a brief paragraph.
- Have students add these lists and paragraphs to their Social Studies Portfolio.

Write and Share

- Provide atlases, encyclopedias, and nonfiction books for students to use in conducting their research.

- Encourage students to use Main Idea Tables to organize the information for their displays.

- Encourage students to find or create illustrations to include in their displays.

- Use the following scoring guide.

✓ Assessment Scoring Guide

Immigrant History Display	
6	Presents well-organized, accurate information clearly focused on specific area. Includes elaborate details and relevant illustrations.
5	Presents accurate information and details and some illustrations related to area.
4	Presents some accurate information and details and at least one illustration related to area.
3	Presents general information with few details.
2	Presents inaccurate information and no details.
1	Is unable to provide an adequate presentation.

If you prefer a 4-point rubric, adjust accordingly.

Read on Your Own

Have students prepare oral reports using the following books.

Eyewitness: Cowboy, by David H. Murdoch (Dorling Kindersley Publishing, ISBN 0-789-45854-3, 2000) **Easy**

Immigrant Kids, by Russell Freedman (Puffin, ISBN 0-140-37594-5, 1995) **On-Level**

Alexander Graham Bell: An Inventive Life, by Elizabeth MacLeod (Kids Can Press, ISBN 1-550-74456-9, 1999) **Challenge**

Invention Conventions

Objective
- Describe a historic invention's features and benefits.

Resource
- Workbook, p. 137

Materials
poster board or large sheets of paper, paints, markers, pencils, reference materials

Follow This Procedure
- Tell students they will advertise inventions from the late 1800s. Give examples of some inventions from this era: automobiles, telephones, motion pictures, lightbulbs, and phonographs.

- Discuss how inventions have changed the world. For example, automobiles allowed people to live farther from their work places.

- Divide students into groups. Have them research benefits and results of the invention, as well as the inventor's goals. Students may portray the inventor in their advertisement. Invite students to present to the class.

- Use the following scoring guide.

✓ Assessment Scoring Guide

Invention Convention	
6	Describes invention using elaborate details, accurate content, and precise word choices.
5	Presents time line with many significant dates, important details, and relevant illustrations.
4	Describes invention using some details, accurate content, some vague word choices.
3	Describes invention using few details, some inaccurate content, and incorrect word choices.
2	Describes invention using no details, inaccurate content, and incorrect word choices.
1	Is unable to describe an invention.

If you prefer a 4-point rubric, adjust accordingly.

UNIT
8 Project

Invention Conventions

Advertise a product from the past.

1 Form a group and choose an invention from the late 1800s.

2 Research the invention and describe what made the invention popular or revolutionary. Write who invented it and why, how it helped people, if it saved time or money, and if it changed the world.

3 Make a poster or large advertisement for this invention. Include a picture of the product.

4 Present your advertisement to the class. You may pretend to be the inventor.

The First Telephone

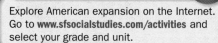

Internet Activity

Explore American expansion on the Internet. Go to **www.sfsocialstudies.com/activities** and select your grade and unit.

592

Practice and Extend

Hands-on Unit Project

✓ Performance Assessment
- The Unit Project can also be used as a performance assessment activity.
- Use the scoring guide to assess each group's work.

WEB SITE Technology

Students can launch the Internet Activity by clicking on *Grade 5, Unit 8* at **www.sfsocialstudies.com/activities.**

Workbook, p. 137

8 Project · Invention Conventions

Directions: Make a poster or advertisement for an invention from the late 1800s.

1. The invention we chose is ___
2. The name of the inventor is ___
3. The purpose of the invention is ___
4. Special features of this invention include ___
5. The (✓) shows the benefits of this invention:
   ___ helping people ___ saving money ___ saving time ___ other: ___
6. Reasons people should use this invention are ___
7. This invention changed the world because ___
8. This is what the invention looked like.

Checklist for Students
___ We chose an invention from the late 1800s.
___ We identified the inventor, and we described the invention's purpose, features, and benefits.
___ We made a poster or advertisement for the invention.
___ We included a picture of the invention on the poster.
___ We presented our poster or advertisement to the class.

Notes for Home: Your child researched an invention from the 1800s and advertised its features to the class.
Home Activity: With your child, identify a modern invention you both agree has changed the world. Discuss how it has impacted your life.

Also on Teacher Resources CD-ROM.

The United States and the World

UNIT 9

Unit Planning Guide

Unit 9 • The United States and the World

Begin with a Primary Source pp. 594–595

Meet the People pp. 596–597

Reading Social Studies, Summarize pp. 598–599

Chapter Titles	Pacing	Main Ideas
Chapter 18 **Becoming a World Power** pp. 600–631 ✓ **Chapter 18 Review** pp. 632–633	8 days	• As President, Theodore Roosevelt prompted reform at home and expanded United States power overseas. • The United States fought in World War I, leading to important and long-lasting changes in American life. • After World War I, the United States went through the boom of the 1920s and the Great Depression of the 1930s. • The United States and its allies fought and won World War II, the most widespread and costliest war in human history.
Chapter 19 **Into the Twenty-first Century** pp. 634–669 ✓ **Chapter 19 Review** pp. 670–671	8 days	• The Cold War was a worldwide struggle between the United States and the Soviet Union. • In the 1950s and 1960s, African Americans, women, and other groups struggled to gain civil rights and equal opportunities. • The United States continued to oppose the spread of communism and Soviet power in the 1960s and 1970s. • The Cold War finally ended in the late 1980s, leaving the United States as the world's only superpower.

End with a Song pp. 672–673

✓ **Unit 9 Review** pp. 674–675

✓ **Unit 9 Project** p. 676

✓ = Assessment Options

◀ **Many Americans learned about World War II by listening to the radio.**

Resources	Meeting Individual Needs
• Workbook, pp. 139–145	• ESL Support, TE pp. 604, 610, 617, 619, 626
• Every Student Learns Guide, pp. 246–261	
• Transparencies 6, 7, 59, 60	• Leveled Practice, TE pp. 605, 613, 622, 627
• Quick Study, pp. 124–131	• Learning Styles, TE pp. 618
• Workbook, p. 146	
✓ Chapter 18 Content Test, Assessment Book, pp. 105–106	✓ Chapter 18 Performance Assessment, TE p. 632
✓ Chapter 18 Skills Test, Assessment Book, pp. 107–108	

• Workbook, pp. 147–152	• ESL Support, TE pp. 638, 644, 653, 660
• Every Student Learns Guide, pp. 262–277	
• Transparencies 1, 6, 20, 61, 62	• Leveled Practice, TE pp. 641, 646, 654, 666
• Quick Study, pp. 132–139	• Learning Styles, TE p. 667
• Workbook, p. 153	
✓ Chapter 19 Content Test, Assessment Book, pp. 109–110	✓ Chapter 19 Performance Assessment, TE p. 670
✓ Chapter 19 Skills Test, Assessment Book, pp. 111–112	

Martin Luther King, Jr., was a leader of the civil rights movement. He favored nonviolent demonstrations, including marches.

Providing More Depth
Additional Resources
- Trade Books
- Family Activities
- Vocabulary Workbook and Cards
- Social Studies Plus! pp. 200–221
- Daily Activity Bank
- Read Alouds and Primary Sources pp. 150–166
- Big Book Atlas   • Student Atlas
- Outline Maps   • Desk Maps

 Technology

- AudioText
- Video Field Trips: The Great Depression
- Songs and Music
- Digital Learning CD-ROM Powered by KnowledgeBox (Video clips and activities)
- MindPoint® Quiz Show CD-ROM
- ExamView® Test Bank CD-ROM
- Colonial Williamsburg Primary Sources CD-ROM
- Teacher Resources CD-ROM
- Map Resources CD-ROM
- SF SuccessNet: iText (Pupil Edition online), iTE (Teacher's Edition online), Online Planner
- **www.sfsocialstudies.com** (Biographies, news, references, maps, and activities)

 To establish guidelines for your students' safe and responsible use of the Internet, use the Scott Foresman Internet Guide.

Additional Internet Links

To find out more about:
- World War II, visit **www.wrightmuseum.org**
- D-Day, visit **www.ddaymuseum.org**
- The Holocaust, visit **www.ushmm.org**

Unit 9 Objectives

Beginning of Unit 9

- Use primary sources to acquire information. (p. 594)
- Identify the accomplishments of notable individuals who have made contributions to society in civil rights, women's rights, military actions, and politics. (p. 596)
- Analyze information by summarizing. (p. 598)

Chapter 18

Lesson 1 A Time of Reforms
pp. 602–605

- Define who the muckrakers were and explain what they wanted to do.
- Identify major reforms that Theodore Roosevelt spearheaded as President.
- Explain how and why the United States built the Panama Canal.
- Interpret information in political cartoons. (p. 606)

Lesson 2 World War I
pp. 608–614

- Describe why and how World War I was fought.
- Explain the role of the United States in World War I.
- Explain how and when women got the right to vote.
- Identify the causes and effects of the Great Migration.
- Use primary sources, such as visual information, to acquire information about airplanes of World War I. (p. 615)

Lesson 3 Times of Plenty, Times of Hardship pp. 616–622

- Identify the effects of new industrial developments on the nation's economy.
- Describe major developments in American culture during the 1920s.
- Explain how the New Deal was created to respond to the Great Depression.
- Relate what life was like in the United States during the Great Depression.
- Identify leaders in the national government, including President Franklin Delano Roosevelt. (p. 623)

Lesson 4 World War II
pp. 624–630

- Identify the causes of World War II.
- Explain how the United States was drawn into World War II and how it prepared to fight the war.
- Describe how the Allies won victory in both Europe and Asia.
- Analyze the costs of World War II.
- Describe the accident that almost ended Dwight David Eisenhower's military career. (p. 631)
- Identify Dwight David Eisenhower's major achievements. (p. 631)

Chapter 19

Lesson 1 A Dangerous World
pp. 636–641

- Describe the beginning of the Cold War.
- Analyze the American decision to fight in the Korean War.
- Explain how Cold War conflicts led to the Cuban Missile Crisis.
- Evaluate the causes of the arms race.

Lesson 2 Struggle for Equal Rights
pp. 642–648

- Evaluate the importance of *Brown* v. *Board of Education.*
- Explain the major events of the Montgomery bus boycott.
- Describe the efforts of Martin Luther King, Jr., in the Civil Rights Movement.
- Identify the goals of the women's rights movement.
- Identify the civil rights goals of Martin Luther King, Jr. (p. 645)
- Describe the strategy King used to achieve his goals. (p. 645)
- Describe the group of people Dolores Huerta helped. (p. 649)
- Identify the organization Dolores Huerta helped form. (p. 649)

Lesson 3 The Cold War Continues
pp. 650–655

- Identify some of the major events of the space race.
- Analyze major causes and effects of the Vietnam War.
- Evaluate President Richard Nixon's trips to China and the Soviet Union.
- Describe the level of Cold War tensions at the beginning of the 1980s.
- Interpret information from map projections. (p. 656)

Lesson 4 Looking Toward the Future
pp. 658–667

- Describe how relations between the United States and the Soviet Union changed during the 1980s.
- Explain how the Cold War ended.
- Identify key post-Cold War events, including the Persian Gulf War, the Clinton impeachment, the rise of the Internet, and the struggle against terrorism.
- Evaluate a variety of questions about the future of the United States.
- Identify accomplishments of individuals who made significant contributions in the area of public safety. (p. 668)

End of Unit 9

- Identify significant examples of music from various periods in U.S. history. (p. 672)
- Explain how examples of music reflect the times during which they were written. (p. 672)
- Describe historic events, technological advances, and everyday life during a decade in the 1900s. (p. 676)

Destruction of the Berlin Wall ▶
was one sign that the Cold
War was ending.

Assessment Options

✓ Formal Assessment

- **Lesson Reviews,** PE/TE pp. 605, 614, 622, 630, 641, 648, 655, 667
- **Chapter Reviews,** PE/TE pp. 632–633, 670–671
- **Chapter Tests,** Assessment Book, pp. 105–112
- **Unit Review,** PE/TE pp. 674–675
- **Unit Tests,** Assessment Book, pp. 113–116
- **ExamView® Test Bank CD-ROM** (test-generator software)

✓ Informal Assessment

- **Teacher's Edition Questions,** throughout Lessons and Features
- **Section Reviews,** PE/TE pp. 603–605, 609–614, 617–622, 625–630, 637–641, 643–644, 646–648, 651–655, 659–667
- **Close and Assess,** PE/TE pp. 599, 605, 607, 614–615, 622–623, 630–631, 641, 645, 648–649, 655, 657, 667, 669, 673

Ongoing Assessment

Ongoing Assessment is found throughout the Teacher's Edition lessons using an **If...then** model.

If = students' observable behavior,	**then** = reteaching and enrichment suggestions

✓ Portfolio Assessment

- **Portfolio Assessment,** TE pp. 593, 594, 675
- **Leveled Practice,** TE pp. 605, 613, 622, 627, 641, 646, 654, 666
- **Workbook Pages,** pp. 138–154
- **Chapter Review: Write About History,** PE/TE pp. 633, 671
- **Unit Review: Apply Skills,** PE/TE pp. 674–675
- **Curriculum Connection: Writing,** PE/TE pp. 614, 665; TE pp. 605, 613, 627, 640, 641, 652, 668

✓ Performance Assessment

- **Hands-on Unit Project** (Unit 9 Performance Assessment), PE/TE pp. 593, 633, 671, 676
- **Internet Activity,** PE/TE p. 676
- **Chapter 18 Performance Assessment,** TE p. 632
- **Chapter 19 Performance Assessment,** TE p. 670
- **Unit Review: Write and Share,** PE/TE p. 675
- **Scoring Guide,** TE pp. 675–676

Test Talk

Test-Taking Strategies

Understand the Question
- **Locate Key Words in the Question,** TE p. 610
- **Locate Key Words in the Text,** TE p. 652

Understand the Answer
- **Choose the Right Answer,** PE p. 675, TE p. 674
- **Use Information from the Text,** TE p. 669
- **Use Information from Graphics,** TE p. 629
- **Write Your Answer to Score High,** TE p. 633

For additional practice, use the Test Talk Practice Book.

Featured Strategy

Choose the Right Answer
Students will:
- Narrow the answer choices and rule out choices they know are wrong.
- Choose the best answer.

PE p. 675, **TE** p. 674

Curriculum Connections

Integrating Your Day

The lessons, skills, and features of Unit 9 provide many opportunities to make connections between social studies and other areas of the elementary curriculum.

Social Studies

READING

Reading Skill—Summarize, PE/TE pp. 598–599, 602, 608, 616, 624, 636, 650

Lesson Review—Summarize, PE/TE pp. 605, 614, 622, 630, 641, 655

MATH

Panama Canal Calculations, TE p. 604

Link to Mathematics, PE/TE p. 605

Find and Compare Ratios, TE p. 611

Compare a Sphere with a Plane, TE p. 656

WRITING

Write a Speech, TE p. 605

Write a Job Description, TE p. 613

Link to Writing, PE/TE pp. 614, 667

Write a Journal Entry or Letter, TE p. 627

Write a Biography, TE p. 640

Write a Biography Picture Book, TE p. 652

Write a Poem, TE p. 668

LITERATURE

Read Biographies, TE pp. 596, 614, 623, 645, 651

Read and Interpret Poetry, TE p. 618

Learn More About World War II, TE p. 630

Read About Vietnam, TE p. 652

Read About Firefighting, TE p. 669

SCIENCE

The Atomic Bomb, TE p. 629

Link to Science, PE/TE p. 655

MUSIC / DRAMA

Read King's Speech, TE p. 595

You're a Grand Old Flag, PE/TE pp. 672–673

Write a Patriotic Song, TE p. 672

Compare and Contrast Songs, TE p. 673

ART

Interpret Fine Art, TE p. 594

Create a Political Cartoon, TE p. 606

 Look for this symbol throughout the Teacher's Edition to find **Curriculum Connections.**

Professional Development

Economics in a Crowded Curriculum

by Bonnie Meszaros, Ph.D.
University of Delaware

Elementary teachers are faced with the daunting task of figuring out how to fit social studies, particularly economics, into a crowded curriculum. After teaching reading, language arts, and math each day, just how much time is left? There just never seems to be enough time to teach all that needs to be taught.

Teachers often question why it is necessary to introduce economics in the elementary grades, arguing that the discipline is more relevant to older students. But research shows that even young students can learn economics. Studies also show that ethnic and income backgrounds and gender of students matter very little. The most important variable explaining students' learning is the extent to which economic concepts are taught.

Students live in an economic world and bring economic knowledge and experience into the classroom. At an early age, they make consumer choices involving spending, saving, and even borrowing. They are exposed through the media to an array of economic problems facing their community and the world. But even with articulated national and state standards, economics continues to be underrepresented in the elementary grades. Below are several ways *Scott Foresman Social Studies* incorporates the study of economics into its program.

- *Chapter 18 explores the economic aftermath of the Roaring Twenties, the Great Depression, and the Dust Bowl.*
- *The graph on p. 647 of the Pupil's Edition compares the salaries of women and men between 1950 and 1999. Students learn about women's struggles for fair pay and equal opportunities in the workplace.*

ESL Support

by Jim Cummins, Ph.D.
University of Toronto

In Unit 9, you can use the following fundamental strategy to activate students' prior knowledge and build background.

Activate Prior Knowledge/ Build Background

Allowing students to relate what they already know to the abstract content of a unit is important for all students, but especially for English Language Learners. Gaps in students' prior knowledge will either be filled by contributions from other students, as in group brainstorming, or become evident to the teacher who can then build the necessary background knowledge.

Discussion and dramatization are both effective strategies that help build background and activate prior knowledge. When teachers activate students' prior knowledge, it communicates a sense of respect for what students already know and an interest in their cultural background.

The following examples in the Teacher's Edition will help you activate prior knowledge and build background for ESL students:

- *Apply the Concept of Surplus on p. 619 presents the scenario of a factory that produces more T-shirts than it can sell to demonstrate the concept of surplus.*
- *Understand Symbolism on p. 653 invites students to discuss and research the behaviors of a hawk and a dove to help students understand why these particular birds symbolize war and peace.*

Read Aloud

"In Flanders Fields"
by John McCrae

In Flanders fields the poppies blow
Between the crosses, row on row,
That mark our place; and in the sky
The larks, still bravely singing, fly
Scarce heard amid the guns below.

We are the Dead. Short days ago
We lived, felt dawn, saw sunset glow,
Loved, and were loved, and now we lie
In Flanders fields.

Take up our quarrel with the foe:
To you from failing hands we throw
The torch; be yours to hold it high.
If ye break faith with us who die
We shall not sleep, though poppies grow
In Flanders fields.

Build Background

- Major John McCrae was a Canadian surgeon who served in Belgium in 1915 treating wounded soldiers during World War I. He wrote this poem while serving at the second Battle of Ypres, in memory of his friend Lt. Alexis Helmer, who was killed by a shell burst.
- Poppies will blossom only in soil that has been disturbed. Much of the soil on the battlefield at Ypres had been disturbed, so poppies had bloomed everywhere.
- This poem appeared in *Punch*, a British magazine, on December 8, 1915.

Definitions

- *Flanders:* region in northern Belgium
- *crosses:* grave markers

Read Alouds and Primary Sources

- *Read Alouds and Primary Sources* contains additional selections to be used with Unit 9.

Bibliography

Free At Last: The Story of Martin Luther King, Jr., by Angela Bull (Dorling Kindersley, ISBN 0-789-45717-2, 2000) **Easy**

Pearl Harbor Is Burning: A Story of World War II, by Kathleen V. Kudlinski (Penguin Putnam Books for Young Readers, ISBN 0-140-34509-4, 1993) **Easy**

Rose Blanche, by Roberto Innocenti (Stewart, Tabori & Chang, ISBN 1-556-70207-8, 1990) **Easy**

Airplanes of World War II, by Nancy Robinson Masters (Capstone, ISBN 1-560-65531-3, 1998) **On-Level**

Attack on Pearl Harbor: The True Story of the Day America Entered World War II, by Shelley Tanaka (Hyperion Books for Children, ISBN 0-786-80736-9, 2001) **On-Level**

The Fall of the Soviet Union, by Miles Harvey (Scholastic Library Publishing, ISBN 0-516-46694-1, 1995) **On-Level**

Great Depression in American History, by David K. Fremon (Enslow Publishers, ISBN 0-894-90881-2, 1997) **Challenge**

Rosie the Riveter: Women Working on the Home Front in World War II, by Penny Colman (Crown Publishers, Inc., ISBN 0-517-88567-0, 1998) **Challenge ALA Notable Book**

The Good Fight: How World War II Was Won, by Stephen Ambrose (Atheneum Books for Young Readers, ISBN 0-689-84361-5, 2001) **Challenge**

Cold War: The American Crusade Against the Soviet Union and World Communism, 1945–1990, by James A. Warren (HarperCollins Children's, ISBN 0-688-10596-3, 1996) **Teacher reference**

The Great Society to the Reagan Era: 1964–1993, by William Loren Katz (Raintree, ISBN 0-811-42919-9, 1993) **Teacher reference**

The Last Days of Innocence: America at War, 1917–1918, by Meirion and Susie Harries (Vintage Books, ISBN 0-679-74376-6, 1998) **Teacher reference**

Discovery Channel School Video Free At Last Meet the heroic men and women who were killed in the fight against racism and for equality. 54 minutes.

 Look for this symbol throughout the Teacher's Edition to find **Award-Winning Selections.** Additional book references are suggested throughout this unit.

The United States and the World

What is your dream for our country's future?

593

The United States and the World

Unit Overview

In the 1900s the United States became involved in events happening around the world. It fought in both World War I and World War II and led the campaign against communism.

Unit Outline

Chapter 18 *Becoming a World Power* pp. 600–633

Chapter 19 *Into the Twenty-first Century* pp. 634–671

Unit Question

- Have students read the question under the picture.

- To activate prior knowledge, ask students what hopes and dreams our country's founding fathers had when they created the Constitution.

- Create a list of hopes and dreams that students have for the future of our country.

- ✓**Portfolio Assessment** Keep this list to review with students at the end of the unit on p. 675.

Practice and Extend

Hands-on Unit Project

✓ **Unit 9 Performance Assessment**

- The Unit Project, *Then and Now,* found on p. 676, is an ongoing performance assessment project to enrich students' learning throughout the unit.

- This project, a documentary about a decade from the 1900s, may be started now or at any time during this unit of study.

- A performance assessment scoring guide is located on p. 676.

Begin with a Primary Source

Objective

- Use primary sources to acquire information.

Resource

- Poster 18

Interpret a Primary Source

- Tell students that this primary source is a quotation from a speech delivered by Martin Luther King, Jr., in 1963.

- King was a civil rights leader who had a dream. Ask students to name some things that King might have dreamed of. (Possible answer: Everyone would be treated fairly; all people would have an opportunity to get an education, hold a good job, and participate in community life.)

✓**Portfolio Assessment** Remind students of the list they created of hopes and dreams for our country's future (see p. 593). Have students keep a list of the ideas that people fought for in the 1900s as they read the unit. Review students' lists at the end of the unit on p. 675.

Interpret Fine Art

- Point out to students that this is a computer image.

- Have students discuss what they think the image shows. (The idea of all for one and one for all.)

- Ask students how the image relates to the quote from Martin Luther King, Jr.'s speech. (He dreamed that one day all people would live together in harmony.)

1910	①		1930		②	1950	③
1914 Panama Canal opens		1917 United States enters World War I	1929 The stock market crashes		1941 United States enters World War II		1954 Segregation in public schools is declared illegal

594

Practice and Extend

 **SOCIAL STUDIES**
Background

About the Primary Source

- The primary source above—the quotation from Martin Luther King, Jr.'s speech—is a phrase that he repeated to tell what his hopes were for this country. He dreamed that one day all people, regardless of color or background, would truly be treated equally and would live together in harmony.

- King delivered this speech from the steps of the Lincoln Memorial in Washington, D.C., during the Civil Rights March on August 28, 1963.

- In 1964 Congress passed the Civil Rights Act, which prohibited many acts of discrimination.

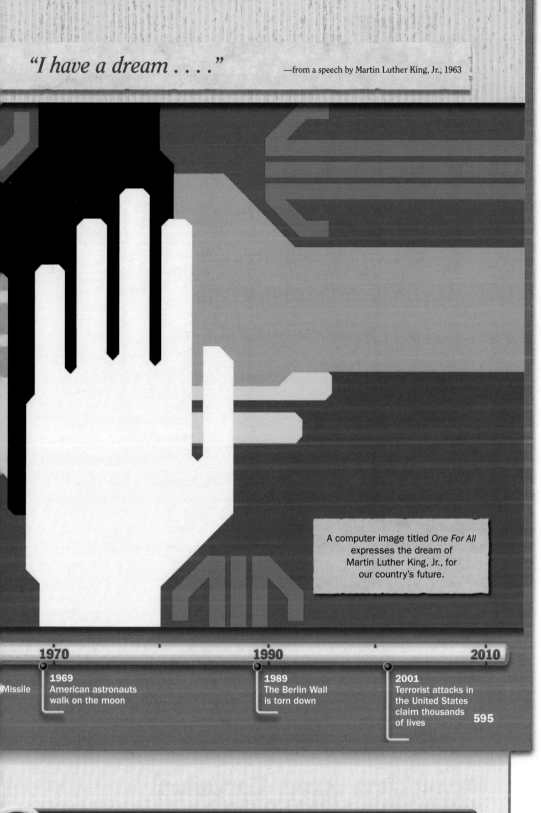

"I have a dream . . . ."   —from a speech by Martin Luther King, Jr., 1963

A computer image titled *One For All* expresses the dream of Martin Luther King, Jr., for our country's future.

1970

1990

2010

Missile

1969
American astronauts
walk on the moon

1989
The Berlin Wall
is torn down

2001
Terrorist attacks in
the United States
claim thousands
of lives

595

Use the Time Line

The time line at the bottom of the page shows the dates for some major national and global events in which the United States was involved during the 1900s.

1 **What event on the time line do you think had an important effect on travel between the east and west coasts of the United States?** The opening of the Panama Canal Draw Conclusions

2 **How many years after the United States entered World War I did it enter World War II?** About 24 years
Analyze Information

3 **What important event occurred in 1954?** Segregation in public schools was declared illegal.
Main Idea and Details

CURRICULUM CONNECTION
Drama

Read King's Speech

- Read aloud excerpts from Martin Luther King, Jr.'s speech, the complete text of which you may find on the Internet.
- Provide pairs of students with a sentence or two from the speech to paraphrase.
- Allow time for students to read aloud the sentence from the speech and their paraphrased sentence.

UNIT 9

Meet the People

Objective
- Identify the accomplishments of notable individuals who have made contributions to society in civil rights, women's rights, military actions, and politics.

Resource
- Poster 19

Research the People

Each of the people pictured on these pages influenced changes in society that occurred in the United States during the 1900s. Have students do research to find out the answers to the following questions.

- **What was the name of the periodical for which Susan B. Anthony was publisher from 1868 to 1870?** *The Revolution*

- **Why did Ida Wells-Barnett bring a lawsuit against the Chesapeake & Ohio Railroad?** She had been forced to give up her train seat when she refused to move to the "colored only" car.

- **What was the purpose of the Atlantic Charter, which Franklin D. Roosevelt and Winston Churchill created together in 1941?** It promised that the United States and Britain would work to end Nazi rule.

- **What nickname was used for Ronald Reagan as a result of his notable speaking ability?** The Great Communicator

Students may wish to write their own questions about other people on these pages for the rest of the class to answer.

Use the Time Line

Have students use the time line and biographies to answer the following questions.

① **Which President had a background as an army officer?** Dwight D. Eisenhower
Analyze Information

596 Unit 9 • The United States and the World

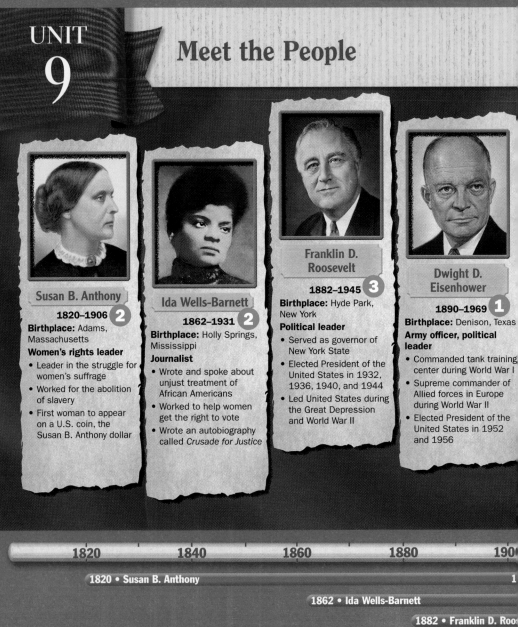

UNIT 9   Meet the People

Susan B. Anthony
1820–1906 ②
Birthplace: Adams, Massachusetts
Women's rights leader
- Leader in the struggle for women's suffrage
- Worked for the abolition of slavery
- First woman to appear on a U.S. coin, the Susan B. Anthony dollar

Ida Wells-Barnett
1862–1931 ②
Birthplace: Holly Springs, Mississippi
Journalist
- Wrote and spoke about unjust treatment of African Americans
- Worked to help women get the right to vote
- Wrote an autobiography called *Crusade for Justice*

Franklin D. Roosevelt
1882–1945 ③
Birthplace: Hyde Park, New York
Political leader
- Served as governor of New York State
- Elected President of the United States in 1932, 1936, 1940, and 1944
- Led United States during the Great Depression and World War II

Dwight D. Eisenhower
1890–1969 ①
Birthplace: Denison, Texas
Army officer, political leader
- Commanded tank training center during World War I
- Supreme commander of Allied forces in Europe during World War II
- Elected President of the United States in 1952 and 1956

| 1820 | 1840 | 1860 | 1880 | 190 |

1820 • Susan B. Anthony
1862 • Ida Wells-Barnett
1882 • Franklin D. Roos
1890

596

Practice and Extend

 CURRICULUM CONNECTION
Literature

Read Biographies Use the following biography selections to extend the content.

Young Martin's Promise, by Walter Dean Myers (Raintree, ISBN 0-811-48050-X, 1993) **Easy**

Dwight D. Eisenhower, by Paul Joseph (ABDO Publishing, ISBN 1-562-39744-3, 1999) **On-Level**

Franklin D. Roosevelt, by Karen Bornemann Spies (Enslow Publishers, ISBN 0-766-01038-4, 1999) **Challenge**

For more information, go online to *Meet the People* at **www.sfsocialstudies.com**.

Ronald Reagan

1911–2004 ③

Birthplace: Tampico, Illinois

Political leader, actor

- Became a movie actor in his twenties
- Served as governor of California for eight years
- Elected President of the United States in 1980 and 1984

Martin Luther King, Jr.

1929–1968 ④

Birthplace: Atlanta, Georgia

Minister, civil rights leader

- Gained fame as a civil rights leader who believed in nonviolent protest
- Delivered "I Have a Dream" speech before more than 200,000 people in Washington, D.C., in 1963
- Awarded Nobel Peace Prize in 1964

Dolores Huerta

1930– ⑤

Birthplace: Dawson, New Mexico

Labor union leader

- Worked to improve life for migrant farm workers
- Joined with César Chávez to form the United Farm Workers labor union
- Began a radio station to speak for farm workers and immigrants

Maya Ying Lin

1959– ⑤

Birthplace: Athens, Ohio

Architect, artist

- Designed the Vietnam Veterans Memorial in Washington, D.C.
- Designed the Civil Rights Memorial in Montgomery, Alabama
- Wrote *Boundaries*, a book about her life and work

| 1920 | 1940 | 1960 | 1980 | 2000 |

1931

1945

- Dwight D. Eisenhower — 1969

1911 • Ronald Reagan — 2004

1929 • Martin Luther King, Jr. — 1968

1930 • Dolores Huerta

1959 • Maya Ying Lin

597

② What did Susan B. Anthony and Ida Wells-Barnett have in common? They both worked to help African Americans and to promote women's rights. Compare and Contrast

③ What do Franklin D. Roosevelt and Ronald Reagan have in common? They both were governors and served more than one term as President. Compare and Contrast

④ How old was Martin Luther King, Jr., when he died? 39 Analyze Information

⑤ Which two women shown here were alive at the turn of the twenty-first century? Dolores Huerta and Maya Ying Lin Interpret Time Lines

Biographies

Four of the people shown here are discussed more extensively in the Biography pages in Unit 9.

- Franklin D. Roosevelt, p. 623
- Dwight D. Eisenhower, p. 631
- Martin Luther King, Jr., p. 645
- Dolores Huerta, p. 649

Read About the People

The people shown here are discussed in the text on the following pages in Unit 9.

- Susan B. Anthony, p. 612
- Ida Wells-Barnett, p. 614
- Franklin D. Roosevelt, pp. 620, 622–627
- Dwight D. Eisenhower, pp. 628, 631
- Ronald Reagan, p. 659
- Martin Luther King, Jr., pp. 644–646
- Dolores Huerta, pp. 648–649
- Maya Ying Lin, p. 653

**WEB SITE
Technology**

Students can research the lives of people on this page by clicking on *Meet the People* at **www.sfsocialstudies.com.**

Reading Social Studies

Summarize

Target Skill

Objective

Analyze information by summarizing.

Resource

- Workbook, p. 138

About the Unit Target Skill

- The target reading skill for this unit is Summarize.
- Students are introduced to the unit target skill here and are given an opportunity to practice it.
- Further opportunities to use summarizing are found throughout Unit 9.

1 Introduce and Motivate

Preview To activate prior knowledge, ask students to summarize an important event from a previous unit in the textbook. (Example: The transcontinental railroad was completed on May 10, 1869. The Union Pacific Railroad began building tracks west from Nebraska, while the Central Pacific Railroad started building east from California. Both companies faced labor problems, tough terrain, and conflicts with Native Americans. Despite the difficulties, the railroad was completed and celebrations took place across the country.)

2 Teach and Discuss

- Explain that a summary is a brief statement that tells the most important ideas of a paragraph or story. A summary should include a few key words or sentences. As they read, students should look for key words that describe the most important ideas.

The United States and the World

Summarize

Target Skill

Understanding how to write a summary will help you to find the main idea of what you read.

- Summarizing is describing the main idea of a passage, paragraph, or story in a few words.
- A good summary is short and includes key words.

Summarize

| Information with Details | Information with Details | Information with Details |

Sometimes a paragraph's **summary** appears after **details** are removed.

In Chapters 18 and 19, you will read that the United States took part in activities outside its borders. In the 1900s, the United States took an even greater part in world affairs. It sent troops to fight alongside its allies in World War I and World War II. It joined the United Nations. It led the fight against the spread of communism. By the end of the 1900s, it became the greatest power in the world.

Word Exercise

Multiple Meanings The word *depression* has many different meanings. The word web below shows three of them.

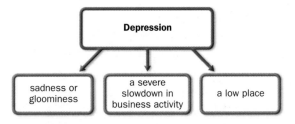

Depression

| sadness or gloominess | a severe slowdown in business activity | a low place |

598

Practice and Extend

ESL ACCESS CONTENT
ESL Support

Summarize Events Have students summarize a real-life event.

Beginning Have students use words and gestures to summarize an event, such as the cause of the Irish potato famine (p. 569).

Intermediate Ask students to summarize a situation that involved more than one event, such as the expansion of the United States in the late 1800s (p. 579).

Advanced Have students summarize a series of complicated events, such as how inventions changed many people's daily lives in the United States (p. 565).

Summarizing the United States and the World

The United States became a world power at the end of the 1800s. As the 1900s began, it became even more powerful.

In 1914, the United States completed the Panama Canal. The canal became an important short cut for international shipping between the Pacific and Atlantic Oceans.

Also in 1914, war broke out in Europe. The United States tried to stay out of the war. But after Germany sank United States ships, the United States declared war on Germany. The United States helped its allies win World War I.

A depression hit the United States and Europe in the 1930s. Bad times aided the rise of German, Japanese, and Italian dictators who wanted to conquer other nations. Once again the United States tried to keep out of war. Then Japan bombed United States ships at Pearl Harbor in Hawaii. The United States declared war on Japan. Germany and Italy declared war on the United States. Again Americans fought overseas.

After winning World War II, the United States faced a Cold War against the Soviet Union and communism. Although the two nations never directly fought each other, wars broke out several times in which the United States fought communism and Soviet allies. Americans fought in the Korean War and the Vietnam War to keep communism from spreading.

In 1991, the Soviet Union broke up into fifteen countries. The United States found itself as the world's only superpower.

Use the reading strategy of summarizing to answer questions 1 and 2. Then answer the vocabulary question.

1. What events led the United States to get involved in two world wars?

2. What are some ways that the United States fought the spread of communism?

3. In the passage, which meaning does the word *depression* have?

599

Multiple Meanings

Write the following sentences on the board. Ask students which meaning depression has in each sentence.

- Some people suffer from **depression** in the winter. (sadness)

- The rabbit was hiding in a small **depression** near the fence. (a low place)

- High prices and too few jobs can lead to **depression.** (a severe slowdown in business)

3 Close and Assess

Apply it!

1. Other countries attacked, threatened, or declared war on the United States.

2. Americans fought in the Korean War and the Vietnam War.

3. It means "a severe slowdown in business."

Standardized Test Prep

Workbook, p. 138

- Use Workbook p. 138 to give students practice with standardized test format.

- Chapter and Unit Tests in the Assessment Book use standardized test format.

- Test-taking tips are contained in the front portion of the Assessment Book Teacher's Edition.

Also on Teacher Resources CD-ROM.

Chapter Planning Guide

Chapter 18 • Becoming a World Power

Locating Time and Place pp. 600–601

Lesson Titles	Pacing	Main Ideas
Lesson 1 **A Time of Reforms** pp. 602–605	2 days	• As President, Theodore Roosevelt prompted reform at home and expanded United States power overseas.
Research and Writing Skills: Interpret Political Cartoons pp. 606–607		• A political cartoon is a drawing of people or news events, designed to make people laugh but also to make them think about the person or event.
Lesson 2 **World War I** pp. 608–614	2 days	• The United States fought in World War I, leading to important and long-lasting changes in American life.
War in the Air p. 615		• Although airplanes were a new invention when World War I began, people soon discovered many uses for them.
Lesson 3 **Times of Plenty, Times of Hardship** pp. 616–622	2 days	• After World War I, the United States went through the boom of the 1920s and the Great Depression of the 1930s.
Biography: Franklin Delano Roosevelt p. 623		• Franklin D. Roosevelt had polio and could not walk, but his determination kept his political career going.
Lesson 4 **World War II** pp. 624–630	2 days	• The United States and its allies fought and won World War II, the most widespread and costliest war in human history.
Biography: Dwight David Eisenhower p. 631		• After an exceptional military career, Dwight Eisenhower was elected President in 1953.

✔ **Chapter 18 Review** pp. 632–633

✔ = Assessment Options

◀ **Charles Lindbergh flew non-stop from New York to Paris, France, and won $25,000.**

◀ During World War II many women in the United States worked in factories.

Vocabulary	Resources	Meeting Individual Needs
Progressives muckraker isthmus political cartoon	• Workbook, p. 140 • Transparencies 7, 59, 60 • Every Student Learns Guide, pp. 246–249 • Quick Study, pp. 124–125 • Workbook, p. 141	• ESL Support, TE p. 604 • Leveled Practice, TE p. 605
World War I alliance League of Nations Treaty of Versailles isolationism Nineteenth Amendment Great Migration	• Workbook, p. 142 • Transparency 6 • Every Student Learns Guide, pp. 250–253 • Quick Study, pp. 126–127 • Workbook, p. 143	• ESL Support, TE p. 610 • Leveled Practice, TE p. 613
assembly line Harlem Renaissance unemployment stock market Great Depression New Deal Dust Bowl	• Workbook, p. 144 • Transparencies 6, 61, 62 • Every Student Learns Guide, pp. 254–257 • Quick Study, pp. 128–129	• ESL Support, TE pp. 617, 619 • Learning Styles, p. 618 • Leveled Practice, TE p. 622
dictator World War II concentration camp Holocaust atomic bomb	• Workbook, p. 145 • Transparency 6 • Every Student Learns Guide, pp. 258–261 • Quick Study, pp. 130–131	• ESL Support, TE p. 626 • Leveled Practice, TE p. 627
	✓ Chapter 18 Content Test, Assessment Book, pp. 105–106 ✓ Chapter 18 Skills Test, Assessment Book, pp. 107–108	✓ Chapter 18 Performance Assessment, TE p. 632

Providing More Depth

Additional Resources
• Vocabulary Workbook and Cards
• Social Studies Plus! pp. 210–215
• Daily Activity Bank
• Big Book Atlas
• Student Atlas
• Outline Maps
• Desk Maps

 Technology

• AudioText
• MindPoint® Quiz Show CD-ROM
• ExamView® Test Bank CD-ROM
• Teacher Resources CD-ROM
• Map Resources CD-ROM
• SFSuccessNet: iText (Pupil Edition online), iTE (Teacher's Edition online), Online Planner
• **www.sfsocialstudies.com** (Biographies, news, references, maps, and activities)

 To establish guidelines for your students' safe and responsible use of the Internet, use the Scott Foresman Internet Guide.

Additional Internet Links
To find out more about:
• Theodore Roosevelt and Reforms, visit **www.theodoreroosevelt.org**
• World War I and World War II, visit **www.nara.gov**
• The Great Depression, visit **newdeal.feri.org**

Key Internet Search Terms
• Panama Canal
• Theodore Roosevelt
• Great Migration
• Great Depression

Workbook Support

Use the following Workbook pages to support content and skills development as you teach Chapter 18. You can also view and print Workbook pages from the Teacher Resources CD-ROM.

Workbook, p. 138

Summarize
Use with Pages 596–599.

Directions: Read the passage. Then fill in the circle next to the correct answer.

In the United States, civil rights are guaranteed to all citizens. However, this was not always true. African Americans and other minorities have long struggled for their civil rights in this country.

In 1892, the Supreme Court allowed segregation and "separate but equal" services for blacks and whites. Many African Americans felt that separate services, even in name, were unequal.

Change came about slowly. In 1950, during the Korean War, African American soldiers and white soldiers fought side by side. Four years later, the Supreme Court ruled that the segregation of public schools was illegal. One year later, an African American woman named Rosa Parks inspired the Montgomery bus boycott. In 1956, the Supreme Court ruled that segregation on

public buses also was illegal.

Civil rights leaders such as Martin Luther King, Jr., and Malcolm X, and groups such as the NAACP emerged to support desegregation on all levels. Over time, this period became known as the Civil Rights Movement.

President John F. Kennedy added to the effort by proposing a new civil rights bill to better protect the rights of all citizens. The bill became law in 1964, after Kennedy's assassination.

The Civil Rights Act of 1964 banned segregation in all public places. The Voting Rights Act of 1965 protected all Americans' rights to vote. African Americans could no longer be prevented from voting. This finally gave them the power to change laws that they felt were unfair.

1. What was the direct result of the Montgomery bus boycott?
   Ⓐ Segregation in the military ceased to exist.
   ● Segregation on public buses was ruled illegal.
   Ⓒ Segregation of public schools ended.
   Ⓓ Segregation in all public places was ruled illegal.

2. How have civil rights changed in the United States since 1890?
   Ⓐ Separate but equal is considered fair for everybody.
   Ⓑ A civil rights bill now protects the rights of some citizens.
   ● Segregation is illegal and all citizens can vote.
   Ⓓ Segregation in the military is legal.

 Notes for Home: Your child learned how to summarize a passage.
Home Activity: Ask your child to summarize a favorite story or event. Remind him or her that a summary has few details. Challenge your child to eliminate as many words as possible from his or her summary without making it ineffective.

Use with Pupil Edition, p. 599

Workbook, p. 139

Vocabulary Preview
Use with Chapter 18.

Directions: Write the definition of each vocabulary term on the line provided. Use a separate sheet of paper if necessary. You may use your glossary.

1. Progressives — Reformers who worked to improve government
2. muckraker — Writer who exposed shameful conditions in U.S.
3. isthmus — Narrow strip of land that connects two larger areas
4. World War I — War between Allies and Central Powers, 1914–1918
5. alliance — Agreement among nations to defend one another
6. League of Nations — Organization of nations formed after WWI
7. Treaty of Versailles — Treaty signed in 1919 that ended WWI
8. Nineteenth Amendment — Gave women the right to vote
9. Great Migration — 1915–1940s, African Americans moved to North
10. assembly line — Method of mass production past a line of workers
11. Harlem Renaissance — Cultural movement centered in Harlem, NY
12. unemployment — The number of workers without jobs
13. stock market — Organized market where stocks are bought and sold
14. Great Depression — Severe economic depression begun in 1929
15. New Deal — FDR's programs for recovery from Great Depression
16. Dust Bowl — 1930s drought in Great Plains destroyed farms
17. dictator — Leader in complete control of a country
18. World War II — War between Allies and Axis Powers, 1939–1945
19. concentration camp — WWII prison in which Nazis murdered millions
20. Holocaust — The murder of 6 million Jews during World War II
21. atomic bomb — Powerful bomb with great destructive force

 **Notes for Home:** Your child learned about events in the early to mid-1900s.
Home Activity: Ask your child to use each vocabulary term in an original sentence.

Use with Pupil Edition, p. 600

Workbook, p. 140

Lesson 1: A Time of Reforms
Use with Pages 602–605.

Directions: Complete the chart by filling in the second column with the specific reform or reformer's main purpose or goal. You may use your textbook.

Reform/Reformer	Reform Goal
Theodore Roosevelt	Possible answer: To conserve more land and natural resources
Progressives	To stop unfair business practices and to improve the way government worked
Muckrakers	To uncover shameful conditions in business and other areas of American life
Sherman Antitrust Act	To improve competition by attacking trusts and forcing them to break up into smaller companies
Meat Inspection Act	To allow government inspectors to examine meat to make sure it would not make people sick
Pure Food and Drug Act	To make food and medicine safer by requiring companies to tell the truth about their products
Army doctors Walter Reed and W. C. Gorgas	To drain areas of standing water to decrease the mosquito population and the incidence of yellow fever and malaria

Notes for Home: Your child learned about reforms during Theodore Roosevelt's term of office.
Home Activity: With your child, read the label from any food package and discuss the importance of knowing which ingredients were used in preparing the food. Encourage your child to consider people's food allergies and other health issues.

Use with Pupil Edition, p. 605

Workbook Support

Use with Pages 606–607.

Interpret Political Cartoons

A political cartoon is a drawing that shows people or events in the news in a way that makes you smile or laugh. The goal of political cartoons is to make you think about events.

Directions: Use this cartoon about women's rights to answer the questions below.

"MAKE WAY!"

1. Where do the women appear in this cartoon? What are they doing? Why do you think the cartoonist portrayed these characters as she did?

On top of the world; Fighting together; Possible answer: To show that women have gained power and now are in control of the world

2. What do you think the signs in the cartoon represent?

Possible answer: The causes for which the women are fighting

3. In this cartoon, men are being pushed off the world. What do you think this means?

Possible answer: Women have gained power and no longer need men.

4. A woman named Laura Foster drew this political cartoon. How do you think she felt about women's rights? Explain.

Possible answer: I think she supported women's rights because her cartoon shows women on top of the world and in control.

Notes for Home: Your child learned how to interpret political cartoons.
Home Activity: With your child, look through recent newspapers or magazines to find a political cartoon. Discuss the cartoon's message and the cartoonist's point of view.

Use with Pupil Edition, p. 607

Use with Pages 608–614.

Lesson 2: World War I

Directions: Read each cause below and write its effect on the line provided.

1. **Cause:** European nations compete with one another for land, trade, and military power.
   Effect: **World War I begins.**

2. **Cause:** In a telegram, Germany asks Mexico to enter the war on the side of the Central Powers. If Mexico agrees, Germany promises to help Mexico get back lands it had lost to the United States in the Mexican War. Soon after, Germany sinks American-owned trade ships.
   Effect: **The United States joins the Allied Powers in World War I.**

3. **Cause:** As U.S. men enter World War I, U.S. women replace them in the workforce. Women argue that, since they can do the same jobs as men, they should be given the same right to vote.
   Effect: **The Nineteenth Amendment is passed.**

4. **Cause:** The North promises better-paying jobs and less discrimination to Southern African Americans.
   Effect: **The Great Migration occurs.**

Directions: Circle the term that does not belong in each group. On the line, write why the term does not belong.

5. Britain, France, Russia, (Switzerland)
   Switzerland was not part of the Allied Powers.

6. (Australia,) Austria-Hungary, Germany, Turkey
   Australia was not part of the Central Powers.

7. League of Nations, President Wilson, (Red Cross,) Treaty of Versailles
   President Wilson helped organize the Treaty of Versailles, which created the League of Nations.

8. Nineteenth Amendment, Carrie Chapman Catt, Susan B. Anthony, (W.E.B. DuBois)
   DuBois was not known for fighting for women's suffrage.

9. Ida Wells Barnett, W.E.B. DuBois, (John Muir,) Booker T. Washington
   Muir was not known for fighting against discrimination.

Notes for Home: Your child learned how World War I affected life in the United States.
Home Activity: With your child, make a list of jobs traditionally held by men and jobs traditionally held by women. Discuss how women's actions during World War I broke these traditional stereotypes. Ask your child how it might be unproductive to limit people to certain jobs simply because of their gender.

Use with Pupil Edition, p. 614

Use with Pages 615.

Writing Prompt: New Inventions

The invention of the airplane had a major impact on the way in which World War I was fought. New inventions continue to be developed that change the way we live every day. What could you invent to change your life? Draw a picture of your invention. Write a paragraph to tell about it.

Drawings will vary.

Answers will vary.

Notes for Home: Your child learned about the early planes used during World War I.
Home Activity: With your child, compare and contrast the technology used in World War I to the technology available to the military today. How might technological advances affect the ways in which a war is fought today?

Use with Pupil Edition, p. 615

Use with Pages 616–622.

Lesson 3: Times of Plenty, Times of Hardship

Directions: The chart contains important events in the postwar history of the United States. Complete the chart by matching each name or term from the box to one of the statements below. Not all words will be used.

Henry Ford	stock market crash	Charles Lindbergh	radio
Harlem Renaissance	severe drought	Eleanor Roosevelt	Amelia Earhart
Zora Neale Hurston	Social Security Act	Model T	Dust Bowl
bread lines	the Wright Brothers	Langston Hughes	high unemployment
Franklin D. Roosevelt	movies	CCC	cardboard shacks

Advances in Travel	The Roaring Twenties	The Great Depression	The New Deal
The Wright Brothers made the first successful powered airplane flight.	**Movies** moved from "silents" to "talkies," becoming a popular form of entertainment.	Farmers and factories produced more goods than consumers could buy, causing **high unemployment**	**Franklin D. Roosevelt** worked to help the jobless and the poor and rebuild the economy.
Amelia Earhart was the first woman to fly solo across the Atlantic Ocean.	**Radio** brought music, comedy, drama, sports, and news into people's homes.	As a result of the **stock market crash** the economy went from boom to bust.	More than 2 million unemployed young men went to work for the **CCC**
Henry Ford developed the assembly line and produced the **Model T**	A period of cultural growth that produced many famous African American artists was the **Harlem Renaissance**	A **severe drought** hit the Great Plains, earning the area the nickname the **Dust Bowl**	Passed in 1935, the **Social Security Act** provided payments to the unemployed and the elderly

Notes for Home: Your child learned about good times and difficult times in postwar America.
Home Activity: With your child, make a chart comparing life during the Roaring Twenties and the Great Depression. Discuss how today's economic situation is similar to and different from these two eras.

Use with Pupil Edition, p. 622

Use with Pages 624–630.

Lesson 4: World War II

Directions: Complete each summary chart below with information from Lesson 4. You may use your textbook.

Summary

Possible answer: Hard economic times in Europe cause many people to wish they had a leader who could make their troubles disappear. Some people are willing to sacrifice their own freedom to obtain such a leader.

In Italy, Benito Mussolini becomes dictator in 1922.	In Germany, Adolf Hitler becomes dictator in 1933.	In Japan, a group of military leaders come to power.

Events

Summary

Important alliances are formed throughout Europe as dictators and military leaders begin trying to conquer and control more nations. The result is World War II.

Italy, Germany, and Japan begin invading other nations.	Britain and France join forces against Germany and Italy.	Germany invades Poland, a nation Britain and France have agreed to protect.

Events

Notes for Home: Your child learned about World War II, its cause, and some of its effects.
Home Activity: With your child, discuss some of the reasons why countries declare war. Discuss whether war is ever justified and, if so, when. Examine with your child some of the far-reaching effects of war.

Use with Pupil Edition, p. 630

Use with Chapter 18.

Vocabulary Review

Directions: Classify the vocabulary terms from Chapter 18 by listing each term in one of the categories below. On the lines below each box, write a sentence summarizing how the terms in that category are related.

The United States

Progressives	unemployment	Harlem Renaissance
Great Migration	stock market	muckraker
Nineteenth Amendment	Great Depression	assembly line
Dust Bowl	New Deal	

Possible answer: During the first half of the twentieth century, the United States went through many changes. Some changes were positive, but others brought difficult times.

Countries Other than the United States

dictator	concentration camp	Holocaust

Possible answer: Some dictators who rose to power in Europe harmed millions of people.

Both the United States and Other Countries

alliance	isthmus
League of Nations	World War II
Treaty of Versailles	atomic bomb
World War I	

Possible answer: The United States and other countries made alliances, developed defense strategies, and fought in wars.

Notes for Home: Your child learned about important events in the first half of the 1900s.
Home Activity: With your child, develop a one-minute oral summary of the first half of the twentieth century. Encourage your child to use as many of the vocabulary terms as possible in the summary.

Use with Pupil Edition, p. 633

Assessment Support

Use these Assessment Book pages and the ExamView® Test Bank CD-ROM to assess content and skills in Chapter 18. You can also view and print Assessment Book pages from the Teacher Resources CD-ROM.

Assessment Book, p. 105

Chapter 18 Test

Part 1: Content Test

Directions: Fill in the circle next to the correct answer.

Lesson Objective (1:1)

1. Which of the following describes muckrakers?
   ● writers and journalists who were reformers
   Ⓑ lawmakers who were reformers
   Ⓒ political leaders who were reformers
   Ⓓ lawmakers who were not reformers

Lesson Objective (1:2)

2. Which of the following was NOT one of the reforms led by President Theodore Roosevelt?
   Ⓐ the breakup of large companies
   Ⓑ cleanliness in food processing
   ● desegregation in public places
   Ⓓ truthful product advertising

Lesson Objective (1:3)

3. Which of the following was a major reason for building the Panama Canal?
   Ⓐ It allowed easy access to South America.
   Ⓑ It allowed the United States to trade more weapons with Panama.
   Ⓒ It allowed negotiations between the U.S. and Colombia.
   ● It allowed fast travel between the Atlantic and Pacific Oceans.

Lesson Objective (1:3)

4. What country did the United States back for independence in order to build the Panama Canal?
   ● Panama
   Ⓑ Colombia
   Ⓒ Peru
   Ⓓ Venezuela

Lesson Objective (2:1)

5. Which of the following BEST describes the cause of World War I?
   ● European nations competed for land, trade, and military power.
   Ⓑ European and Asian nations fought for control of land.
   Ⓒ European and American nations fought over control of the seas.
   Ⓓ European nations competed over advanced weaponry.

Lesson Objective (2:1)

6. How did technology affect World War I?
   Ⓐ It had no effect because the war was fought on the ground.
   Ⓑ The use of tanks and other vehicles shortened the war.
   Ⓒ Fewer people died because of new methods of protection.
   ● It provided more powerful and deadly weapons.

Lesson Objective (2:2)

7. Which BEST describes the role of the United States in World War I?
   Ⓐ joined Central Powers against Allies
   ● joined Allies against Central Powers
   Ⓒ joined Mexico against Germany
   Ⓓ joined Britain against France

Use with Pupil Edition, p. 632

Assessment Book, p. 106

Lesson Objective (2:3)

8. What argument did women use to win the right to vote?
   Ⓐ Women were as educated as men and deserved the right to vote.
   ● Women could do a man's job and deserved the right to vote.
   Ⓒ Women outnumbered men and deserved the right to vote.
   Ⓓ Women were stronger than men and deserved the right to vote.

Lesson Objective (2:4)

9. Which was a major reason why millions of African Americans moved to the North during the Great Migration?
   Ⓐ better weather conditions
   Ⓑ lower cost of living
   Ⓒ segregation in the North
   ● high-paying factory jobs

Lesson Objective (3:1)

10. Which of the following was NOT an effect of the Model T?
    Ⓐ People took more trips for vacation.
    ● People saved more money.
    Ⓒ People could live farther from work.
    Ⓓ Farmers were less isolated.

Lesson Objective (3:2)

11. Which of the following BEST describes the Harlem Renaissance?
    Ⓐ period of time when Harlem was rebuilt
    Ⓑ famous hotel during the 1920s
    Ⓒ night club where many jazz musicians became famous
    ● period of cultural growth during the 1920s

Lesson Objective (3:4)

12. Which of the following does NOT describe life during the Great Depression?
    ● People took more trips for vacation.
    Ⓑ People lost their homes and lived in shacks.
    Ⓒ People lost their jobs, causing high unemployment.
    Ⓓ People lost money in the stock market crash.

Lesson Objective (3:3)

13. Which of the following BEST describes the main purpose of the New Deal?
    Ⓐ stimulate growth in culture and the arts
    Ⓑ help children learn to read
    Ⓒ offer more farmland at low prices
    ● help the nation recover from the Great Depression

Lesson Objective (4:1)

14. How did dictators start World War II?
    Ⓐ They showed other dictators how to rule effectively.
    Ⓑ Each dictator ruled with an iron fist.
    ● They tried to take over other countries.
    Ⓓ They formed a peaceful alliance to support each other.

Lesson Objective (4:2)

15. What action drew the United States into World War II?
    Ⓐ The Soviet Union joined the Allies.
    ● The Japanese bombed Pearl Harbor, Hawaii.
    Ⓒ Britain asked for help in defeating the Germans.
    Ⓓ France surrendered to the Germans.

Use with Pupil Edition, p. 632

Assessment Support

Assessment Book, p. 107

Lesson Objective (4:3)

16. What strategy did the Allies use to defeat the Germans in World War II?
● They squeezed Germany from two directions.
Ⓑ They pushed the Germans into France.
Ⓒ They pushed the Germans into the Soviet Union.
Ⓓ They allowed the Germans to take Poland.

Lesson Objective (4:4)

17. Which of the following is NOT an accurate description of World War II?
Ⓐ It was the most widespread war in human history.
Ⓑ It had the most advanced weapons in human history.
● It was the longest war in human history.
Ⓓ It was the bloodiest war in human history.

Part 2: Skills Test

Directions: Use complete sentences to answer questions 1–8. Use a separate sheet of paper if you need more space.

1. Why might some people think of Theodore Roosevelt as a reform President? **Main Idea and Details**

   Theodore Roosevelt promoted many reforms, including protecting more of the nation's lands, passing antitrust laws, cleaning up the meatpacking industry, and requiring food and drug companies to tell the truth about their products.

2. Why did the United States want to construct the Panama Canal? **Summarize**

   The United States wanted to shorten the time it took to travel between the Atlantic and Pacific Oceans for trade and military purposes.

3. Why do you think the United States entered World War I? **Draw Conclusions**

   Possible answer: The United States joined the war for reasons of self-preservation. The telegram from Germany to Mexico suggested a future war between Mexico and the United States. Also, when the Germans sank American ships, the United States knew it could no longer stay out of the war.

Use with Pupil Edition, p. 632

Assessment Book, p. 108

4. How did World War I lead to the right to vote for U.S. women? **Cause and Effect**

   When U.S. men left to fight in the war, women took over their jobs and kept the country running. For the first time, women began doing jobs traditionally held by men. After the war, women argued that if they could do men's work, they deserved the same right to vote.

5. How did the airplane and the automobile change the lives of many Americans in the early 1900s? **Main Idea and Details**

   Possible answer: The airplane and the automobile gave Americans a new freedom to travel and see more of the world. They also could live farther from work, town, and their families without becoming isolated.

6. What did Dust Bowl farmers hope to accomplish by moving west? Were they successful? Explain. **Summarize**

   They hoped to find work and new lives in California. However, few jobs were available in California, and those that did exist paid low wages.

7. What series of events led the Soviet Union to join the side of the Allies during World War II? **Sequence**

   Before World War II, Germany's Hitler and the Soviet Union's Stalin signed an agreement saying that their nations would not attack each other. Two years later, Hitler broke the agreement. Stalin then joined the Allies.

8. How were Japanese Americans treated during World War II? Why did some Americans feel this was necessary? Were their fears justified? **Summarize**

   Thousands were mistreated, and many were forced to spend the rest of the war in relocation camps. Some Americans felt this was necessary to protect the country. Possible answer: No. In fact, thousands of Japanese Americans fought for the United States in World War II.

Use with Pupil Edition, p. 632

Becoming a World Power

Chapter 18 Outline

- **Lesson 1, *A Time of Reforms,*** pp. 602–605
- **Research and Writing Skills: *Interpret Political Cartoons,*** pp. 606–607
- **Lesson 2, *World War I,*** pp. 608–614
- **📖 *War in the Air,*** p. 615
- **Lesson 3, *Times of Plenty, Times of Hardship,*** pp. 616–622
- **Biography: *Franklin Delano Roosevelt,*** p. 623
- **Lesson 4, *World War II,*** pp. 624–630
- **Biography: *Dwight David Eisenhower,*** p. 631

Resources

- Workbook, p. 139: Vocabulary Preview
- Vocabulary Cards
- Social Studies Plus!

1914, Panama: Lesson 1

Tell students that the Panama Canal is a waterway through which ships travel between the Atlantic and Pacific Oceans. Ask students why the United States built this canal. (It is a quicker, shorter shipping route than traveling around the southernmost tip of South America.)

1920, United States: Lesson 2

Ask students what the women in the picture are doing and why this was such an important event. (Voting; before 1920 in most places in the United States, women could not vote.)

1929, New York City, New York: Lesson 3

Tell students that the stock market crash marked the start of hard times for many people. Ask students why the people in the picture were standing in a line to get food. (They had no money since there were few jobs.)

1941, Pearl Harbor, Hawaii: Lesson 4

This picture shows the Japanese bombing U.S. ships. Have students compare the Lesson 1 picture with this picture. (The Lesson 1 picture shows a ship in a canal. This picture shows a sinking ship.)

CHAPTER
18

Becoming a World Power

1914
Panama
The Panama Canal opens.

Lesson 1

1

1920
United States
Women gain the right to vote.

Lesson 2

2

1929
New York City, New York
The stock market crashes and the Great Depression begins.

Lesson 3

3

1941
Pearl Harbor, Hawaii
After Japan attacks Pearl Harbor, the United States enters World War II.

Lesson 4

4

600

Vocabulary Preview

- Use Workbook p. 139 to help students preview the vocabulary words in this chapter.
- Use Vocabulary Cards to preview key concept words in this chapter.

 Also on Teacher Resources CD-ROM.

Workbook, p. 139

Vocabulary Preview

Directions: Write the definition of each vocabulary term on the line provided. Use a separate sheet of paper if necessary. You may use your glossary.

1. Progressives _____
2. muckraker _____
3. isthmus _____
4. World War I _____
5. alliance _____
6. League of Nations _____
7. Treaty of Versailles _____
8. Nineteenth Amendment _____
9. Great Migration _____
10. assembly line _____
11. Harlem Renaissance _____
12. unemployment _____
13. stock market _____
14. Great Depression _____
15. New Deal _____
16. Dust Bowl _____
17. dictator _____
18. World War II _____
19. concentration camp _____
20. Holocaust _____
21. atomic bomb _____

Notes for Home: Your child learned about events in the early to mid-1900s.
Home Activity: Ask your child to use each vocabulary term in an original sentence.

Locating Time and Place

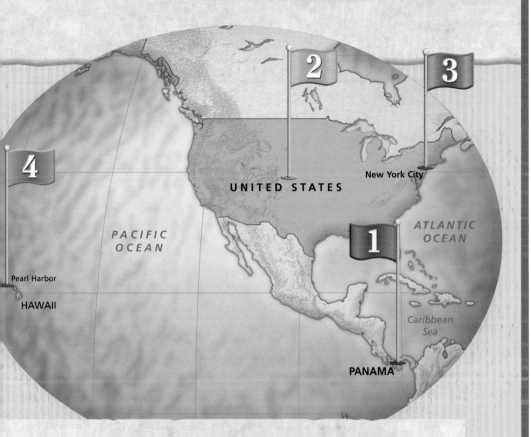

Why We Remember

In 1936, President Franklin D. Roosevelt declared, "This generation of Americans has a rendezvous with destiny" [meeting with its future]. Although he was speaking about Americans of the 1930s, his words could have described all Americans who lived in the first half of the 1900s. During those years, the United States faced great challenges. It fought in two terrible world wars, which involved many nations of the world, and struggled through serious economic problems at home. But the United States met each challenge and became one of the most powerful nations in the world.

601

- Have students examine the pictures shown on p. 600 for Lessons 1, 2, 3, and 4.

- Remind students that each picture is coded with both a number and a color to link it to a place on the map on p. 601.

Why We Remember

Have students read the "Why We Remember" paragraph on p. 601, and ask them why events in this chapter might be important to them. Have them consider how their lives might be different if the United States had not become the superpower it is today.

WEB SITE
Technology

You can learn more about Panama; the United States; New York City, New York; and Pearl Harbor, Hawaii, by clicking on *Atlas* at **www.sfsocialstudies.com.**

SOCIAL STUDIES STRAND
Geography

Mental Mapping Have students draw an outline map of the seven continents from memory. Have them label the continents and oceans. They should include a compass rose, the equator, and the prime meridian.

A Time of Reforms

Objectives

- Define who the muckrakers were and explain what they wanted to do.

- Identify major reforms that Theodore Roosevelt spearheaded as President.

- Explain how and why the United States built the Panama Canal.

Vocabulary

Progressives, p. 603; **muckraker,** p. 603; **isthmus,** p. 604

Resources

- Workbook, p. 140
- Transparency 7
- Every Student Learns Guide, pp. 246–249
- Quick Study, pp. 124–125

Quick Teaching Plan

If time is short, have students write *Reforms* and *Panama Canal* on separate index cards.

- Ask students to read the lesson independently.

- Have them write a summary of the reforms Theodore Roosevelt made when he was President. Then ask students to summarize how and why the Panama Canal was built.

- Have students share their summaries with the class.

1 Introduce and Motivate

Preview Ask students to describe what changes they might make if they were in charge of their school or their town. Tell students they will learn about reforms Theodore Roosevelt made when he was in charge of the United States.

You Are There Remind students that as the United States grew during the 1700s, 1800s, and 1900s, people developed land that was once wilderness. Ask students what Roosevelt could do to help conserve natural resources.

602 Unit 9 • The United States and the World

LESSON 1

1900			1915
1901 Theodore Roosevelt becomes President	**1906** Upton Sinclair writes *The Jungle*		**1914** Panama Canal opens

PREVIEW

Focus on the Main Idea
As President, Theodore Roosevelt promoted reform at home and expanded United States power overseas.

PLACES
Panama Canal

PEOPLE
Ida Tarbell
Upton Sinclair

VOCABULARY
Progressives
muckraker
isthmus

▶ President Theodore Roosevelt

602

A Time of Reforms

You Are There "I want to drop politics absolutely for four days and just be in the open with you," writes young President Theodore Roosevelt to his friend John Muir in 1903. Soon, Roosevelt escapes the White House and joins Muir on a camping trip in Yosemite National Park in California.

For the next three days, the two men ride Yosemite's trails on horseback. They rest at its cool, rushing streams and stare in wonder at its majestic mountains. They marvel at the variety of wildlife. The trip convinces Roosevelt that he must do more to conserve our natural resources. Of the sights he has seen, he says, "It would be a shame to our civilization to let them disappear…. We are not building this country of ours for a day. It is to last through the ages."

 Summarize As you read, list the changes that Theodore Roosevelt and other reformers supported and then summarize them.

Practice and Extend

READING SKILL Summarize

In the Lesson Review, students complete a graphic organizer like the one below. You may want to provide students with a copy of Transparency 7 to complete as they read the lesson.

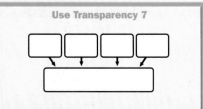

Use Transparency 7

VOCABULARY Word Exercise

Individual Word Study Write *muckraker* on the board, then direct students' attention to p. 603. Ask how the use of the rake in the cartoon helps show what muck is. Have a volunteer read the definition of *muck* from the dictionary. Discuss why this is a good word to describe scandal. Explain the meaning of *muckraker* as used in the lesson and ask students how they think this group of writers got its name.

Reforms at Home

The Spanish-American War had made Theodore Roosevelt a national hero. In 1900, he was elected Vice President under Republican President William McKinley. But within a year, McKinley was assassinated. In 1901, at age 42, Roosevelt became the youngest man ever to be President. In 1904, he was elected to a full term as President.

One of Roosevelt's goals was greater conservation of land and natural resources. By the time he left the White House in 1909, Roosevelt had helped add several national parks to the nation's protected land. He also agreed with the goals of a group of reformers known as Progressives. **Progressives** worked to stop unfair practices by businesses and improve the way government worked.

Writers made up another group of Progressives. They were called **muckrakers** because they uncovered what some people saw as "muck"— shameful conditions in business and other areas of American life.

In 1902 muckraker **Ida Tarbell** wrote a series of magazine articles about Standard Oil, the company founded by John D. Rockefeller. She wrote about how several companies might join to control a whole industry, such as the oil industry. These large companies, often called trusts, had the power to drive out any competition. Corporations usually compete with each other by trying to make the best product for the lowest price. But without competition, a trust could charge higher prices for its products.

Tarbell's work helped convince Roosevelt that he should be an active

"trust-buster." He used the Sherman Antitrust Act, passed in 1890, to attack trusts. This law allowed the government to force trusts to break up into smaller companies. **4**

In 1906, muckraker **Upton Sinclair** wrote a novel called *The Jungle*. In this book, Sinclair told about unsafe conditions in the meatpacking plants of Chicago. Roosevelt had barely finished reading the book when he told his secretary of agriculture, James Wilson, to investigate the lack of cleanliness in food processing.

Soon, Roosevelt supported and signed two reform acts—the Meat Inspection Act and the Pure Food and Drug Act. The Meat Inspection Act allowed government inspectors to examine meat to make sure it would not make people sick. The Pure Food and Drug Act helped make food and medicine safer by requiring companies to tell the truth about their products.

REVIEW How would you summarize the reforms that Theodore Roosevelt promoted?
➤ Summarize

This famous political cartoon showed President Roosevelt's response to problems in the meat industry.

North Wind Picture Archives

603

FYI **SOCIAL STUDIES**
Background

The Origin of the Teddy Bear

- This popular stuffed animal was named for President Theodore Roosevelt.
- Roosevelt was on a rather unsuccessful hunting trip, but his guides finally located a bear that he could shoot.
- When Roosevelt saw the bear, which was very tired from being chased by guides and dogs, he did not want to shoot him for sport.
- A shopkeeper heard the story and asked Roosevelt's permission to use the name *Teddy's bears* for the toy bears in his store window. The President agreed, and later the name was changed to Teddy bear.

Teach and Discuss

Reforms at Home

🕐 *Quick Summary* Progressives, including President Theodore Roosevelt, favored conservation, encouraged business competition, and promoted cleanliness in meatpacking plants.

1 **After being elected President in 1904, what was one of Roosevelt's goals?** Greater conservation of land and natural resources **Main Idea and Details**

2 **What causes companies to try to make the best product for the lowest price?** Competition **Cause and Effect**

3 **What is one effect several large companies can have when they control an entire industry?** Possible answer: The companies can charge higher prices for their products. **Cause and Effect**

4 **What did the Sherman Antitrust Act allow the government to do?** Force trusts to break up into smaller companies **Main Idea and Details**

✓ **REVIEW ANSWER** Roosevelt conserved natural resources by creating national parks, stopped unfair business practices with antitrust laws, and signed laws to improve food and drug safety.
➤ Summarize

The Panama Canal

🕐 **Quick Summary** The Panama Canal was completed in 1914, allowing ships to travel between the Atlantic and Pacific Oceans quickly.

5 **Why was the canal built?** To create a faster route for ships and military vessels **Main Idea and Details**

✓ **Ongoing Assessment**

If... students do not understand the purpose for building the Panama Canal,	**then...** use a map to compare the route around the tip of South America with the trip through Panama.

6 **Why do you think Panama agreed to let the United States build a canal through its country?** Possible answer: Panama probably received money for agreeing to let the United States build a canal through its land, and the canal may have promised trade opportunities. **Make Inferences**

7 **What did the United States do to get rid of some of the mosquitoes in the area?** Drained standing water so mosquitoes could not lay eggs **Cause and Effect**

Map Adventure Answers

1. Southeast
2. Colon; Panama City
3. Gatun, Pedro Miguel, Miraflores

The Panama Canal

From his days as assistant secretary of the navy, Theodore Roosevelt supported increasing American naval power. Like many others, he wanted United States ships to be able to travel between the Atlantic and Pacific Oceans quickly, both for trading and military purposes. Yet such a trip could easily take more than two months! To sail from the east coast of the United States to the west coast, a ship had to sail around Cape Horn at the **5** southern tip of South America.

That same trip could be shortened from months to days if a canal could be cut across the Isthmus of Panama. An `isthmus` is a narrow strip of land that connects two larger areas. The Isthmus of Panama connects North and South America. Roosevelt set out to build such a canal. But first, he had to solve a number of problems.

For one thing, the United States had to get control of the land. Panama at that time was part of the South American nation of Colombia. Colombia refused to give up Panama. But backed by the United States, leaders in Panama declared independence in 1903. Panama then agreed to let the United States build a canal through its land.

Second, disease-carrying mosquitoes lived in the dense rain forest through which the canal would be built. They carried the deadly diseases yellow fever and malaria. The United States could not hope to succeed until it controlled the mosquitoes that carried these diseases. Army doctors Walter Reed and W. C. Gorgas led the effort to drain the areas of standing water where mosquitoes laid their eggs. The mosquito population shrank and so did the number of cases of yellow fever and malaria.

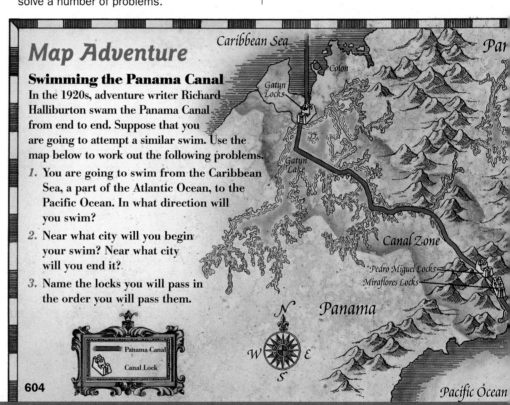

Map Adventure

Swimming the Panama Canal
In the 1920s, adventure writer Richard Halliburton swam the Panama Canal from end to end. Suppose that you are going to attempt a similar swim. Use the map below to work out the following problems.

1. You are going to swim from the Caribbean Sea, a part of the Atlantic Ocean, to the Pacific Ocean. In what direction will you swim?
2. Near what city will you begin your swim? Near what city will you end it?
3. Name the locks you will pass in the order you will pass them.

604

Practice and Extend

CURRICULUM CONNECTION
Math

Panama Canal Calculations

- What speed would a steamship travel to go 50 miles in 9 hours? (A little more than 5.5 miles per hour)
- What is the ratio of the workforce to the number of miles in the canal? (About 40,000 workers to 50 miles, or about 800 workers for every 1 mile)

ACCESS CONTENT
ESL Support

Discuss Canals Students use visuals to understand why and how the Panama Canal was built.

Beginning Have students label the United States, the Atlantic and Pacific Oceans, Cape Horn, and the Panama Canal on an outline map of the Western Hemisphere. Have students draw both routes between the two oceans.

Intermediate Have students write, as two column heads, *Reasons for the Canal* and *Problems*. Students should add labeled drawings to each column.

Advanced Have students make a flowchart for each problem encountered when building the canal, e.g., Panama belonged to Colombia ⟶ Panama declared independence ⟶ Panama agreed to the canal.

For additional ESL support, use Every Student Learns Guide, pp. 246–249.

greatest engineering feat of the ages." Now a steamship could move from one end of the canal to the other in just nine hours!

REVIEW How would you summarize the obstacles the United States had to overcome to complete the Panama Canal? 🔁 **Summarize**

President Roosevelt took a turn at the controls of a steam shovel in Panama.

Third, the mountains, swamps, and mud made the job of digging a canal very difficult. But in 1904, over 40,000 people and lines of steam shovels set to work. On August 15, 1914, the 50-mile long **Panama Canal** was opened for shipping. Roosevelt called it "the

Summarize the Lesson

1901 Theodore Roosevelt became President after President McKinley was assassinated.

1906 Upton Sinclair wrote *The Jungle,* describing unhealthy conditions in Chicago's meatpacking plants.

1914 The Panama Canal opened, allowing ships to make the journey between the east and west coasts of the United States much more quickly.

LESSON 1 REVIEW

Check Facts and Main Ideas

1. 🔁 **Summarize** On a separate sheet of paper, complete the chart to summarize the major events of the presidency of Theodore Roosevelt.

Details or Events

- Roosevelt helps create new national parks.
- Roosevelt becomes a "trust buster."
- Roosevelt supports the Pure Food and Drug Act.
- Roosevelt begins the building of the Panama Canal.

Summary

Theodore Roosevelt wanted to protect consumers, conserve resources, and improve national naval power and trade with other countries.

2. **Critical Thinking:** *Evaluate* Do you think "muckraker" is a good term to describe writers like Ida Tarbell and Upton Sinclair? Explain.

3. Describe three reforms supported by Theodore Roosevelt.

4. Why did the United States want to build a canal across Panama?

5. Describe the problems the United States faced in building the Panama Canal.

Link to 🔗 Mathematics

Calculate Cost Ships going through the Panama Canal must pay a toll based on their cargo space. The swimmer Richard Halliburton also had to pay a toll—36 cents. The Panama Canal measures about 50 miles from end to end. About how much did Halliburton pay per mile of his trip?

605

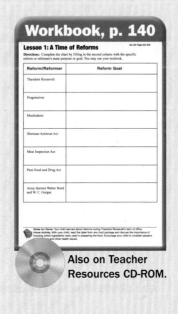

Workbook, p. 140

Lesson 1: A Time of Reforms

Directions: Complete the chart by filling in the second column with the specific reform or reformer's main purpose or goal. You may use your textbook.

Reform/Reformer	Reform Goal
Theodore Roosevelt	
Progressives	
Muckrakers	
Sherman Antitrust Act	
Meat Inspection Act	
Pure Food and Drug Act	
Army doctors Walter Reed and W. C. Gorgas	

Also on Teacher Resources CD-ROM.

✓ **REVIEW ANSWER** To build the Panama Canal, the United States had to help Panama become independent, find ways to control disease-carrying mosquitoes, and dig through mountains and swamps. 🔁 **Summarize**

3 Close and Assess

Summarize the Lesson

Ask students to list three major accomplishments of Theodore Roosevelt's presidency and explain how these achievements benefited the United States.

✓ **LESSON 1 REVIEW**

1. 🔁 **Summarize** For possible answers, see the reduced pupil page.

2. **Critical Thinking:** *Evaluate* Possible answer: Yes; Tarbell and Sinclair dug up muck, or dirt, about the practices of certain corporations and about unsanitary conditions in meatpacking plants.

3. Possible answers: Limiting the power of trusts, inspecting food and drugs, and protecting the country's natural resources

4. So military and trade ships could move more quickly between the Atlantic and Pacific Oceans

5. Getting control of the land; losing workers to diseases such as malaria and yellow fever; digging through mountains, swamps, and mud

Link to 🔗 Mathematics

36 cents ÷ 50 miles = $0.0072/mile, or less than one cent per mile

Interpret Political Cartoons

Objective
- Interpret information in political cartoons.

Vocabulary
political cartoon, p. 606

Resource
- Workbook, p. 141

1 Introduce and Motivate

What is a political cartoon? Ask students how a political cartoon might be used by historians in the future to study our time. Then have students read the **What?** section of text on p. 606 to help set the purpose of the lesson.

Why use political cartoons? Have students read the **Why?** section of text on p. 606. Ask them what a cartoon for current people or events might look like.

2 Teach and Discuss

How is this skill used? Examine the political cartoons on p. 606 with students.

- Tell students that political cartoonists use symbols to represent different ideas in their messages.

- Explain that the symbols along with other illustrations take the place of written words. Some cartoons may have words as labels, but to understand the message a person has to examine the drawings and symbols.

- Have students read the **How?** section of text on p. 606.

Research and Writing Skills

Interpret Political Cartoons

What? A political cartoon is a drawing that shows people or events in the news in a way that makes you smile or laugh. The goal of political cartoons is to make you think about events. Political cartoons often have a point of view.

Why? You can find political cartoons in newspapers and magazines. Often the cartoonist wants to express an opinion about people or events. You may or may not agree with the opinion, but a good political cartoon should make you think about the issue.

How? To understand a political cartoon, you need to understand the symbols that the cartoonist uses. For example, a drawing of a character called Uncle Sam is often a symbol for the United States. A drawing of a donkey is a symbol for the Democratic Party, and a drawing of an elephant is a symbol for the Republican Party. Political cartoonists first created these symbols.

Republican Party

Democratic P

Uncle Sam

606

Practice and Extend

SOCIAL STUDIES STRAND
Government

CURRICULUM CONNECTION
Art

Analyze Different Viewpoints
- Have students look at the political cartoon on p. 270.
- Ask students to identify the point of view that Benjamin Franklin expressed in this cartoon. (He strongly favored uniting.)
- Have students identify an opposing point of view. (Staying separated)
- Lead a discussion of how the idea of staying separate might be shown in a political cartoon.

Create a Political Cartoon
- Ask students to think about an issue or topic that is important at the local, state, or national level, and which relates to a person, place, or event.
- Have students decide what they think about the issue or topic and then design and draw a cartoon to show their feelings.
- Encourage students to look at others' cartoons and try to interpret the message.

In Lesson 1, you read about President Theodore Roosevelt's reforms. Look at the political cartoon on this page. Do you recognize the lion tamer? He is President Roosevelt. The cartoonist made the face look like Roosevelt. Just in case you did not recognize the face, he wrote "San Juan" on the chest medal to show that the lion tamer is the hero of the Battle of San Juan Hill during the Spanish-American War.

In the cartoon, Roosevelt is holding a whip to tame the lions. Each lion has a label to show what it stands for. For example, the lion closest to the reader is labeled "BEEF TRUST." The lions are walking out of a door labeled "WALL ST." The stocks of many large companies are traded in the New York Stock Exchange, located on Wall Street in New York City.

The cartoonist is saying something about Theodore Roosevelt and the trusts. If you have ever seen a lion tamer, you probably can figure out what the cartoonist intended.

Think and Apply

1. What labels are shown on the lions in the **political cartoon?**

2. What is the label on the door from which another lion appears? Why do you think the door has that label?

3. What do you think the cartoonist intends to say about Theodore Roosevelt and the trusts?

607

---

1 Why did the cartoonist include the words "San Juan" on the lion tamer's chest? So people would know the lion tamer is the hero of the Battle of San Juan Hill, Theodore Roosevelt
Main Idea and Details

2 Why would the cartoonist use lions to represent the trusts? Possible answer: Lions are strong and fierce.
Make Inferences

3 What do you notice about Roosevelt's arms in the cartoon? What does this tell you about the cartoonist's opinion of Roosevelt? They are muscular. The cartoonist probably thinks Roosevelt is strong and tough.
Analyze Primary Sources

3 Close and Assess

Think and Apply

1. Oil trust, steel trust, beef trust, coffee trust, sugar trust, railroad trust

2. The label is Wall Street, and it probably means that some of these trusts are part of Wall Street where the New York Stock Exchange is located.

3. The cartoonist probably means to say that Roosevelt is taming the trusts with the antitrust laws.

Workbook, p. 141

Interpret Political Cartoons

Also on Teacher Resources CD-ROM.

World War I

Objectives

- Describe why and how World War I was fought.

- Explain the role of the United States in World War I.

- Explain how and when women got the right to vote.

- Identify the causes and effects of the Great Migration.

Vocabulary

World War I, p. 609; **alliance,** p. 609;
League of Nations, p. 611;
Treaty of Versailles, p. 611;
isolationism, p. 611;
Nineteenth Amendment, p. 612;
Great Migration, p. 613

Resources

- Workbook, p. 142
- Transparency 6
- Every Student Learns Guide, pp. 250–253
- Quick Study, pp. 126–127

Quick Teaching Plan

If time is short, have students make a two-column cause-and-effect chart.

- Students should write the causes of World War I in the *Cause* column.
- In the *Effect* column, students describe the various effects of the war.
- Have students draw arrows to connect causes with effects.

1 Introduce and Motivate

Preview To activate prior knowledge, ask students why the United States fought wars during the 1700s and 1800s. Tell students they will learn about World War I, which involved many different countries around the world.

You Are There By 1916, the United States had become one of the world's powers. Ask students to predict what will happen after the United States enters World War I.

608 Unit 9 • The United States and the World

1910				1920

1914 World War I begins in Europe

1915 Great Migration of African Americans begins

1917 United States enters World War I

1920 American women gain the right to vote

World War I

PREVIEW

Focus on the Main Idea
The United States fought in World War I, leading to important and long-lasting changes in American life.

PLACES
Versailles, France

PEOPLE
Woodrow Wilson
Susan B. Anthony
Carrie Chapman Catt
W. E. B. Du Bois
Booker T. Washington
Ida Wells-Barnett

VOCABULARY
World War I
alliance
League of Nations
Treaty of Versailles
isolationism
Nineteenth Amendment
Great Migration

You Are There It is 1916. One of the bloodiest battles in history has just ended at Verdun in France. A young American, Samuel Benson, is there to help wounded French soldiers. Benson is a volunteer in the American Ambulance Service. For months he has been transporting wounded soldiers to medical aid stations. Now he sits down to write himself a letter:

"My dear sir, self:…You may sometimes think you have it pretty hard staying out here in France away from home and loved ones…laboring without pay, and often getting little rest or sleep. But listen…you are at this hour in the midst of the biggest crisis of history. The world has never seen such a moment… and [you are] living for others."

That "moment" is World War I. It is being fought mainly in Europe but also in Africa and Asia. Soon the United States will enter the war.

Summarize As you read, summarize major events of World War I and how they changed American life.

608

Practice and Extend

READING SKILL
Summarize

In the Lesson Review, students complete a graphic organizer like the one below. You may want to provide students with a copy of Transparency 6 to complete as they read the lesson.

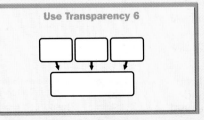

Use Transparency 6

VOCABULARY
Word Exercise

Related Word Study Write the words *migration, migrate, immigrant,* and *emigrant* on the board. Tell students that the word *migrate* means "to move." Talk about how the prefix *in-* means "into" and the prefix *e-* means "out of." Therefore, an *immigrant* is someone who moves into a country, and an *emigrant* is someone who leaves one country for another. Discuss how *migration* means "the act of moving from one area to another."

Fighting Begins in Europe

What had brought on this world war, which would one day be called **World War I**? Fierce rivalries had developed among European nations. They competed with one another for land, for trade, and for military power.

Fearing attack from their rivals, several nations formed alliances. An **alliance** is an agreement among nations to defend one another. If one member of an alliance is attacked, the other members promise to come to its aid. The two major alliances were the Allied Powers, which included Britain, France, and Russia, and the Central Powers led by Germany, Austria-Hungary, and Turkey.

In August 1914, the system of alliances drew most of Europe into a long and hard-fought war. When you read about the American Civil War, you learned that technology had changed the way that war was fought. Nearly 60 years later, new technology had once again created weapons that were far more powerful and deadly than older ones. For example, both sides used poison gases that blistered skin, burned lungs, and blinded eyes.

Engineers turned the airplane, developed just a few years earlier, into a weapon of war. Airplanes dropped bombs on enemy targets and fired machine guns at troops on the ground. Airplanes also fought each other in the air.

Most of the fighting, however, took place on the ground. Soldiers on each side dug a system of trenches that faced each other and could extend hundreds of miles. Barbed-wire fences protected the front of each trench. A "no-man's land" spread out between the opposing armies. Soldiers ate, drank, and slept in the dark trenches, which were often flooded and filled with rats.

Each side shot at the other's trenches, or sent gases into them. Occasionally, troops on one side would go "over the top." They climbed out of their trenches, crawled through the barbed wire, and raced across no-man's land to attack the enemy. As casualties climbed month after month, it seemed that the killing would never end.

REVIEW Why was World War I so much deadlier than earlier wars?
Draw Conclusions

▶ Soldiers fought in trenches *(below)* and were taught how to use gas masks *(left)* to protect themselves during poison gas attacks.

609

SOCIAL STUDIES STRAND
Science • Technology

The Influence of Technology on War

- Technology efforts may include offensive arms, defensive weapons, transportation, communication, and sensors.
- New technological advances in World War I included field telephones and switchboards, radios, wireless telegraph sets, and hand-held rocket launchers.
- Airplanes and airships were another type of new technology used during the war. Airships, or zeppelins, contained hydrogen gas.
- Airplanes flew missions over enemy territory to gain information about troop movements. Pilots who shot down many enemy planes were called aces.
- At the start of the war, Germany had 13 airships. Because hydrogen exploded so easily, the Germans lost many airships and decided to eliminate them.

 Teach and Discuss

PAGE 609

Fighting Begins in Europe

🕐 *Quick Summary* The system of alliances drew most of Europe into a long and deadly war in which new and powerful weapons were used.

① **What caused European countries to form alliances?** Many countries were competing for land, trade, and military power. Fearing attack from their rivals, they wanted to protect themselves. **Cause and Effect**

✓ **Ongoing Assessment**

If... students have difficulty understanding why European countries had conflicts,

then... display a map of Europe and discuss the varying sizes of different countries, the location of ports, and so on. Point out the Allied Powers and the Central Powers.

② **What were some of the effects of poison gas used in the war?** Blistered skin, burned lungs, blinded eyes **Cause and Effect**

③ **Why do you think the area between the opposing armies' trenches was called "no-man's land"?** Possible answer: The trenches were each army's territory, but no one was able to claim the land between the trenches, and no man wanted to go there. **Draw Conclusions**

✓ **REVIEW ANSWER** New technologies created weapons that could kill in much greater numbers than earlier weapons. **Draw Conclusions**

The United States Enters the War

Quick Summary The United States remained out of the war until it learned that Germany had promised to return to Mexico the lands it lost from the United States and that German submarines had sunk three American-owned trade ships.

Test Talk

Locate Key Words in the Question

4 The Central Powers tried to influence which country to enter the war? Have students find the key words in the question (*Central Powers, enter*). Mexico **Main Idea and Details**

5 Why do you think the United States did not want Mexico to join the Central Powers? Possible answers: Mexico is located close to the United States; through Mexico, the Central Powers could more easily attack the United States. The Central Powers promised to get back land Mexico had lost to the United States. **Draw Conclusions**

Primary Source

Cited in Woodrow Wilson's address to Congress on April 2, 1917

6 What do you think Wilson meant by "the right"? Possible answers: That which is right; things that are good or just; doing the right thing **Analyze Primary Sources**

✓ **REVIEW ANSWER** The United States learned of a telegram from Germany to Mexico that promised Mexico help in getting back land it had lost to the United States if Mexico entered the war on the side of the Central Powers. German submarines sank three American-owned trade ships, killing American sailors. **Summarize**

The United States Enters the War

At first, the United States stayed out of World War I. President **Woodrow Wilson** urged Americans to remain "impartial [neutral] in thought as well as in action."

But in early 1917, certain events caused Americans to turn firmly against the Central Powers. One event involved a telegram. In January, the United States learned about a telegram that had been sent from Germany to Mexico. In the telegram Germany asked Mexico to enter the war on the side of the Central Powers. In return, Germany promised to help Mexico to get back lands it had lost to the United States in the Mexican War.

A second event occurred in February. Germany ordered its submarines to attack any ships suspected of carrying weapons to the Allied Powers. German submarines sank three American-owned trade ships in March. The deaths of American sailors angered many in the United States.

▶ President Wilson asked Congress to declare war in 1917.

610

Poster by James Montgomery Flagg, 1918

▶ This poster used the symbol of Uncle Sam to encourage young men to volunteer for the army.

On April 2, President Wilson asked Congress to declare war on the Central Powers. He stated,

"It is a fearful thing to lead this great peaceful people into war, into the most terrible and disastrous of all wars.... But the right is more precious than the peace."

President Wilson hoped that by entering the war, the United States would make the world "safe for democracy." On April 6, 1917 Congress declared war on Germany.

REVIEW Summarize the reasons that led the United States to enter World War I. **Summarize**

Practice and Extend

ACCESS CONTENT
ESL Support

Make a Time Line Students make a time line of events leading up to the United States declaring war on Germany.

Beginning Identify symbols for events leading to war. Sketch and label a submarine and ship on the board. Point out the soldiers pictured on p. 609. Explain that a telegram is like a note. Help students act out passing a note and getting caught. Have students use these symbols for their time line.

Intermediate Students' captions for each event on their time line should be a complete sentence.

Advanced Students should write a sentence describing each event on their time line and another sentence explaining how the event affected the United States.

For additional ESL support, use Every Student Learns Guide, pp. 250–253.

The War Ends

The arrival of American troops in Europe increased the fighting strength of the war-weary Allied Powers. Gradually, the Americans helped drive back the equally tired troops of the Central Powers. More than 4 million American soldiers, sailors, and marines fought in World War I.

In September 1918, more than one million United States troops fought in a huge battle in the Meuse-Argonne (MUZ ahr GOHN), a region of northeastern France. More Americans fought in this battle than in any other single battle in United States history. The Allied Powers won the battle, which led to the final defeat of the Central Powers.

On November 11, 1918, the Central Powers surrendered. Today, November 11 is celebrated as Veterans Day to remember the Americans who fought in World War I and in our nation's other wars.

In World War I, losses were huge for both sides. The Central Powers lost more than 3 million soldiers and nearly 3.5 million civilians. The Allied Powers lost nearly 5 million soldiers and more than 3 million civilians. The United States alone lost about 120,000 troops, and many more were wounded.

In December 1918, the French welcomed President Wilson to France. In January 1919, he and the other Allied leaders met in **Versailles, France** (vair SIGH), outside Paris, to draw up a peace treaty. Wilson hoped for a treaty that would not punish the Central Powers and one that would make sure of a lasting peace. He proposed creating an international organization to prevent wars—a **League of Nations.** ⑩

The **Treaty of Versailles** officially ended World War I. But against Wilson's wishes, the treaty punished the Central Powers. It demanded that Germany pay heavy fines and not rebuild its armed forces. However, the treaty also created the League of Nations, which Wilson had wanted.

The United States Senate refused to approve the Treaty of Versailles or join the League. Many Americans feared that the League might force the United States into future wars. They hoped to once more avoid overseas political involvement, which became known as **isolationism.** The lasting peace Wilson had wanted so badly would last only about 20 years.

REVIEW List in order the major events that brought World War I to an end and led to a peace treaty. *Sequence*

► This painting, called *Armistice Night*, shows Americans celebrating the end of World War I.

611

PAGE 611

The War Ends

Quick Summary Once American troops entered the war, they helped the Allied Powers defeat the Central Powers. In January 1919 world leaders signed the Treaty of Versailles and created an organization to prevent wars.

⑦ **Why do you think the Allied Powers were able to win the war with America's help?** Possible answer: Both sides had been fighting for a long time and were war-weary. Large numbers of fresh U.S. troops entered the war, increasing the fighting strength of the Allied Powers. **Make Inferences**

⑧ **Which battle led to the defeat of the Central Powers?** A huge battle in the Meuse-Argonne region **Cause and Effect**

⑨ **Which side lost more soldiers?** Allied Powers **Analyze Information**

G SOCIAL STUDIES STRAND
Government

Republican senator Henry Cabot Lodge led the Senate's opposition to America's adoption of the League of Nations covenant in the Treaty of Versailles. He feared that doing so would limit America's ability to act as it wished in times of crisis.

⑩ **Summarize Woodrow Wilson's hopes for a treaty that would end the war.** Possible answer: He did not want the Central Powers to be punished, and he wanted to create an organization that would prevent future wars. **Summarize**

✓ **REVIEW ANSWER** The United States sent troops to Europe; Allied Powers won a battle in the Meuse-Argonne region; the Treaty of Versailles officially ended the war. **Sequence**

Women Get the Right to Vote

🕐 **Quick Summary** Shortly after the end of the war, Congress passed the Nineteenth Amendment to the Constitution, which gave women the right to vote.

Primary Source

Cited in *The Quotable Woman: An Encyclopedia of Useful Quotations,* by Elaine Partnow, ed.

Remind students that women had been fighting for equal rights for many years, but they still were not allowed to vote.

⑪ Read the quote by Susan B. Anthony, and restate it in your own words. Possible answer: For women to have equal rights, they must have a say in making laws and helping elect those who make laws they follow.
Analyze Primary Sources

⑫ What did Carrie Chapman Catt do to help women get the right to vote? She worked to persuade Congress and states to pass an amendment to the Constitution, and she was convinced she would succeed. Main Idea and Details

⑬ What effects did World War I have on women's causes? Women became more powerful as they joined the workforce and the military. This gave them a stronger argument for the right to vote.
Cause and Effect

Primary Source

Cited in the Nineteenth Amendment of the United States Constitution

⑭ Why do you think the Nineteenth Amendment includes the words "denied or abridged," and not just "denied"? Possible answer: To prevent states from allowing women to vote but limiting (abridging) their power in some other way Analyze Primary Sources

✓ **REVIEW ANSWER** Catt worked to get Congress and the states to pass an amendment to the Constitution giving women the right to vote. In 1919 the Nineteenth Amendment was passed.
Main Idea and Details

Women Get the Right to Vote

The year World War I ended was the 70th anniversary of the first convention for women's rights, the Seneca Falls Convention. Its leaders, Lucretia Mott and Elizabeth Cady Stanton, had been dead for many years. But their struggle for a woman's right to vote had continued.

Susan B. Anthony, another leader in the struggle for suffrage, had said:

⑪ *"There will never be complete equality until women themselves help to make laws and elect lawmakers."*

Shortly before her death in 1906, Anthony said of the struggle for women's suffrage, "Failure is impossible."

Another leader of the suffrage movement, Carrie Chapman Catt, worked to get Congress and the states to pass an amendment to the constitution giving women the right to vote. Like Anthony, she was certain of victory. "When a just cause reaches its flood tide…whatever stands in its way must fall ⑫ before its overwhelming power."

World War I helped strengthen the cause of women's suffrage. As men went into the armed forces, women replaced them in the workforce. They worked in jobs they had never held before, such as repairing automobiles and driving buses. Women worked in

factories producing weapons. And about 11,000 joined the women's branch of the United States Navy, which had never before allowed women to serve in its ranks. If women could do all this, they argued, surely they should be allowed to vote! ⑬

In 1919, Congress agreed and passed the Nineteenth Amendment to the Constitution. It stated that:

▶ Posters like this suppo[rt] women's right to vote.

"The right of citizens to vote shall not be denied or abridged [limited] by the United States or by any state on account of [the] sex [of a person]."

In August 1920, the states ratified the amendment and it became the law of the land. Later that year, 91-year-old Charlotte Woodward, the last survivor of the Seneca Falls Convention, proudly cast her first vote.

REVIEW How did Carrie Chapman Catt help women get the right to vote?
Main Idea and Details

▶ Women lined up to vote after passage of the Nineteenth Amendment.

Practice and Extend

FAST FACTS

- Due largely to the efforts of suffragist Jeannette Rankin, women who lived in Montana obtained the right to vote in 1914, six years prior to the ratification of the Nineteenth Amendment.
- Anne Dallas Dudley served as national director for the campaign to pass the Nineteenth Amendment and helped her home state of Tennessee become the final state to support women's suffrage.

FYI SOCIAL STUDIES Background

About Carrie Chapman Catt

- Catt was a longtime member of the National American Woman Suffrage Association (NAWSA), which led the movement for women's right to vote.
- Catt helped reorganize NAWSA to allow it to gain support at both state and federal levels.
- After the Nineteenth Amendment was passed, Catt reorganized NAWSA again, creating the League of Women Voters.

Artist Jacob Lawrence told the story of the Great Migration in 1940–1941 with a famous series of 60 paintings. This painting, titled *The Migrants Arrived in Great Numbers*, shows families on the move north.

The Museum of Modern Art, New York. Gift of Mrs. David M. Levy. Tempera on gesso on composition board, 12" x 18".

The Great Migration

World War I helped begin the movement of millions of African Americans from the South to the North. The United States armed forces needed tons of military equipment, such as tanks, trucks, ships, weapons, and ammunition. Suddenly there was an increased demand for people to work in the factories that produced these goods. And many of these factories were located in Northern cities.

Many African Americans in the South were poor sharecroppers. Discrimination held them back from a good education, job opportunities, and many of their basic rights as citizens. The North now offered higher-paying jobs in war industries. African Americans also hoped that there would be less discrimination in the North.

Between 1915 and the 1940s, about 5 million African Americans moved north in what came to be called the **Great Migration.** Unfortunately, conditions in the North were not as welcoming as many African Americans hoped. In Northern cities, they still faced discrimination and segregation. They could only live in certain neighborhoods and attend certain schools. When World War I ended, many lost their jobs or found that only low-paying jobs were open to them.

African American leaders worked to end such discrimination. In the early 1900s, **W. E. B. Du Bois** (BOYZ) helped to start the National Association for the Advancement of Colored People, or the NAACP. The main goal of Du Bois and the NAACP was to bring an immediate end to racial discrimination against African Americans.

Booker T. Washington also worked for the rights of African Americans, but he believed in a more gradual end to discrimination. Born into slavery, Washington was a founder of Tuskegee Institute, a college for African Americans. To Washington, education and training for jobs were keys to equality. With education, he believed, African Americans would gradually overcome racial discrimination in both the South and the North.

REVIEW Compare and contrast what African Americans hoped for in the North and what they found. **Compare and Contrast**

613

The Great Migration

Quick Summary The war created many jobs in factories located in Northern cities. Millions of African Americans moved from the South to the North, hoping for better jobs and education and less discrimination.

15 What was one cause of the Great Migration? Possible answers: More plentiful, higher paying jobs; better educational opportunities; the promise of less discrimination Cause and Effect

16 For about how many years did the Great Migration last? About 25 years Analyze Information

17 What was the goal of the NAACP? To bring an immediate end to racial discrimination against African Americans Main Idea and Details

Problem Solving

18 What did Booker T. Washington think was a solution to the problem of discrimination? Possible answer: He believed that education and job training were keys to equality. The result would be a gradual overcoming of racial discrimination. Solve Problems

✓ **REVIEW ANSWER** African Americans hoped for higher-paying jobs, better education, and an end to racial discrimination. They found that they still faced discrimination in the North; after the war many lost their jobs or only found low-paying jobs open to them. Compare and Contrast

Fighting Discrimination

Quick Summary Ida Wells-Barnett started the first suffrage organization for African American women and worked to fight discrimination against African Americans.

19 **Why do you think Wells-Barnett decided to start a newspaper?** Possible answer: To express her views on discrimination **Draw Conclusions**

✓ **REVIEW ANSWER** She fought segregation in transportation and started one of the first African American women's suffrage organizations.
Main Idea and Details

3 Close and Assess

Summarize the Lesson

After students read about the events on the timeline, have them write several multiple-choice questions about the material in the lesson. Students should exchange their questions with classmates.

✓ | LESSON 2 | REVIEW |

1. 🔄 **Summarize** For possible answers, see the reduced pupil page.

2. Allied Powers and Central Powers

3. In 1917 the United States entered the war on the side of the Allied Powers and provided additional military power to help the Allied Powers defeat the Central Powers.

4. **Critical Thinking:** *Problem Solving* Accept reasonable responses that indicate use of the problem-solving steps.

5. In the Great Migration, many African Americans moved from farms in the South to cities and factory jobs in the North, where they continued to encounter discrimination.

Link to ⟨―⟩ **Writing**

Students' letters should express how they feel about the war and what they experience day to day. Suggest that they tell what they hope the outcome of the war will be.

614 Unit 9 • The United States and the World

Fighting Discrimination

The daughter of slaves, **Ida Wells-Barnett** was born in 1862 in Mississippi. Wells-Barnett went to Chicago in 1893. There she helped start and wrote for an African American newspaper. She started one of the first suffrage organizations for African American women. She fought—and won—a battle against the passage of a state law that would have

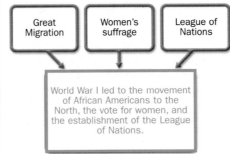

▶ Ida Wells-Barnett told her story in an autobiography called *Crusade for Justice.*

segregated blacks and whites on trains and buses in Illinois.

REVIEW What actions taken by Ida Wells-Barnett support the main idea that she was a fighter against discrimination?
Main Idea and Details

Summarize the Lesson

- **1914** World War I began in Europe between the Allied Powers and Central Powers.

- **1915** The need for factory workers helped cause the Great Migration of African Americans from the South to the North.

- **1917** The United States entered World War I on the side of the Allied Powers.

- **1920** The Nineteenth Amendment to the Constitution was ratified, giving American women the right to vote.

LESSON 2 **REVIEW**

Check Facts and Main Ideas

1. 🔄 **Summarize** On a separate sheet of paper, complete the chart to summarize the changes brought about by World War I.

Events

| Great Migration | Women's suffrage | League of Nations |

World War I led to the movement of African Americans to the North, the vote for women, and the establishment of the League of Nations.

Summary

2. Identify the two **alliances** that fought each other in **World War I.**

3. What role did the United States play in World War I?

4. **Critical Thinking:** *Problem Solving* Identify a problem in the news today and suggest a possible solution. Use the problem-solving steps on page H5.

5. What was the effect of the **Great Migration** on African Americans in the United States?

Link to ⟨―⟩ **Writing**

Write a Letter Put yourself in the place of an American soldier or nurse in France in World War I. Write a letter home telling about your experience. Describe what you are seeing, how you are living, and what you hope for the future.

614

Practice and Extend

CURRICULUM CONNECTION
Literature

Read Biographies

- Have students search on the Internet or in the local library for books about Ida Wells-Barnett, such as *Princess of the Press: The Story of Ida B. Wells-Barnett,* by Angela Shelf Medearis (Penguin Putnam, ISBN 0-525-67493-4, 1997).

- Have students give a brief report using the information they found. If students read a book, their report might be in the form of a book review.

Workbook, p. 142

Lesson 2: World War I

Directions: Read each cause below and write its effect on the line provided.

1. **Cause:** European nations compete with one another for land, trade, and military power.
   Effect:

2. **Cause:** In a telegram, Germany asks Mexico to enter the war on the side of the Central Powers. If Mexico agrees, Germany promises to help Mexico get back lands it had lost to the United States in the Mexican War. Soon after, Germany sinks American-owned trade ships.
   Effect:

3. **Cause:** As U.S. men enter World War I, U.S. women replace them in the workforce. Women argue that, since they can do the same jobs as men, they should be given the same right to vote.
   Effect:

4. **Cause:** The North promises better-paying jobs and less discrimination to Southern African Americans.
   Effect:

Directions: Circle the term that does not belong in each group. On the line, write why the term does not belong.

5. Britain, France, Russia, Switzerland

6. Australia, Austria-Hungary, Germany, Turkey

7. League of Nations, President Wilson, Red Cross, Treaty of Versailles

8. Nineteenth Amendment, Carrie Chapman Catt, Susan B. Anthony, W.E.B. DuBois

9. Ida Wells Barnett, W.E.B. DuBois, John Muir, Booker T. Washington

Notes for Home: Your child learned how World War I affected life in the United States.
Home Activity: With your child, make a list of jobs traditionally held by men and jobs traditionally held by women. Discuss how women's suffrage during World War I made these traditional stereotypes. Ask what jobs might be unproductive to limit people to certain jobs simply because of their gender.

💿 **Also on Teacher Resources CD-ROM**

War in the Air

When World War I started in 1914, the history of powered flight was barely 10 years old. The first warplanes flew as observation craft. They scouted enemy lines from the air and helped direct artillery fire. Soon planes were carrying bombs to drop on enemy targets. By the end of the war, the role of military aircraft had changed from being a minor help to a major force in their own right. ❶

Leather hood and mask

Leather face mask and anti-splinter glass goggles

Raised collar to keep neck warm

Sheepskin lined leather gloves to protect against frostbite

Flying Gear
Pilots flew in open cockpits, so they wore special clothing to keep out the cold.

Sheepskin boots

Thick sole to give a good grip

Air "Aces"
To qualify as an air "ace", a pilot had to bring down at least five enemy aircraft. Captain Eddie Rickenbacker, an American "ace" and war hero, had 24 1/3 hits.

Wooden box-structure wings covered with canvas

wooden struts

26 ft. 11 in. wingspan

Symbol of British Royal Flying Corps, later the Royal Air Force

Sopwith Camel
The Sopwith F1 Camel first flew in battle in June 1917. It became the most successful Allied fighter in shooting down German aircraft. Pilots enjoyed flying the Camel because it was easy to steer and could make sharp turns at high speed.

615

Dorling Kindersley

War in the Air

Objective
• Use primary sources, such as visual information, to acquire information about airplanes of World War I.

Resource
• Workbook, p. 143

1 Introduce and Motivate

• Tell students that new technologies, such as aircraft, changed the ways that wars were fought.

• Have students list ways airplanes were used in World War I. Tell students they will learn more as they read this page.

• Students will add to their lists later.

2 Teach and Discuss

❶ **For what sorts of actions were airplanes used in World War I?** Scouting enemy lines, directing artillery fire, and bombing. **Main Idea and Details**

3 Close and Assess

• Ask students to add to their lists of the uses of airplanes that they began earlier. Have students discuss what uses they learned about from the pictures and text on this page.

Workbook, p. 143

Writing Prompt: The invention of the airplane had a major impact on the way in which World War I was fought. New inventions continue to be developed that change the way we live every day. What could you invent to change your life? Draw a picture of your invention. Write a paragraph to tell about it.

Notes for Home: Your child learned about the early planes used during World War I.
Home Activity: With your child, compare and contrast the technology used in World War I to the technology available to the military today. How might technological advances affect the ways in which a war is fought today?

Also on Teacher Resources CD-ROM.

Times of Plenty, Times of Hardship

Objectives

- Identify the effects of new industrial developments on the nation's economy.
- Describe major developments in American culture during the 1920s.
- Explain how the New Deal was created to respond to the Great Depression.
- Relate what life was like in the United States during the Great Depression.

Vocabulary

assembly line, p. 617; **Harlem Renaissance,** p. 618; **unemployment,** p. 619; **stock market,** p. 619; **Great Depression,** p. 619; **New Deal,** p. 620; **Dust Bowl,** p. 621

Resources

- Workbook, p. 144
- Transparency 6, 59
- Every Student Learns Guide, pp. 254–257
- Quick Study, pp. 128–129

Quick Teaching Plan

If time is short, have students make a compare-and-contrast chart headed *Times of Plenty* and *Times of Hardship*.

- Have students read for facts and events that go under each heading.
- Have students write a brief summary of the times of plenty and of hardship in the 1920s and 1930s.

1 Introduce and Motivate

Preview Have students list different forms of transportation on which they have traveled. Tell students that they will learn about the new ways of traveling that were developed in the early 1900s.

You Are There Charles Lindbergh was the first pilot to fly nonstop from New York to Paris. Ask students to describe what this long journey alone in a small plane might have been like.

LESSON 3

1925

1927 Charles Lindbergh flies across the Atlantic Ocean

1929 The stock market crashes

1933 Franklin D. Roosevelt becomes President

1935

Kitty Hawk

PREVIEW

Focus on the Main Idea
After World War I, the United States went through the boom of the 1920s and the Great Depression of the 1930s.

PLACES
Kitty Hawk, North Carolina

PEOPLE
Charles Lindbergh
Wilbur Wright
Orville Wright
Amelia Earhart
Henry Ford
F. Scott Fitzgerald
Ernest Hemingway
Langston Hughes
Zora Neale Hurston
Franklin D. Roosevelt
Eleanor Roosevelt

VOCABULARY
assembly line
Harlem Renaissance
unemployment
stock market
Great Depression
New Deal
Dust Bowl

► Charles Lindbergh after his famous flight

616

Times of Plenty, Times of Hardship

You Are There The race is on! Since 1919, a prize of $25,000 has been waiting for the first person who can fly nonstop from New York to Paris, France. On this gray, drizzly morning of May 20, 1927, a 25-year-old airmail pilot settles in at the controls of his plane, the *Spirit of St. Louis.* Space is tight because tanks of fuel fill every spare inch. Two canteens of water and five cans of food are all he has to drink and eat.

At 8:00 A.M., the pilot switches on his engine and starts down the field. The plane lifts off the ground. Telephone wires loom ahead. Clearing them by barely 20 feet, the pilot is on his way. For nearly 34 hours, he will head east, fighting to stay awake. But Charles Lindbergh will succeed. He will reach Paris and become a world hero known as the "Lone Eagle."

Summarize As you read, identify and summarize the major events of the 1920s and 1930s.

Practice and Extend

READING SKILL Summarize

In the Lesson Review, students complete a graphic organizer like the one below. You may want to provide students with a copy of Transparency 6 to complete as they read the lesson.

Use Transparency 6

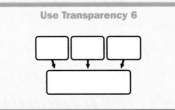

VOCABULARY Word Exercise

Individual Word Study Write *Harlem Renaissance* on the board. Have students turn back to p. 112 in their texts to review what *Renaissance* means. Then ask students to turn to p. 618 and read what the Harlem Renaissance was. Ask what Harlem is, then discuss how the rise of arts in this location led to the naming of this period of cultural growth.

New Ways to Travel

The daring flight of **Charles Lindbergh** was made possible by an event that had happened nearly 25 years earlier on a beach in **Kitty Hawk, North Carolina.** There on December 17, 1903, **Wilbur Wright** and **Orville Wright**—bicycle mechanics from Dayton, Ohio—made the world's first successful powered airplane flight. A new era of travel had begun.

Gradually, an airplane industry developed in the United States. Pilots like **Amelia Earhart** promoted the growth of the airplane industry. In 1932 Earhart became the first woman to fly solo across the Atlantic Ocean. In 1937, she attempted to make the first flight around the world, but her plane vanished and she was never found.

At the same time, another new industry—the automobile industry—was changing American life. Beginning in the late 1800s, American companies built cars by hand. They were very expensive and were sometimes called "rich men's toys." But **Henry Ford,** an entrepreneur and inventor from Michigan, found a way to make cars that cost less.

Ford used an **assembly line,** a way of making a car in which the product was moved past groups of workers. Each group did a specific task. This is specialization, or the process of focusing on one part of production. First, a car frame was put on the assembly line. As it moved along, workers attached parts to it. When it reached the end of the assembly line, the car was completed. **②**

In 1908, Ford began selling a new car, the Model T. It was an enormous success. It was simple and boxy, and workers could assemble it in an hour and a half. The car sold for less than $500—a price that many people could afford. No longer were automobiles just for the wealthy.

Cars gave Americans a kind of freedom they never had before. People could live farther from their jobs and still get to them quickly. Farmers were less isolated in rural areas. And families could more easily take trips for vacation. **③**

REVIEW Summarize changes in transportation in the early 1900s and the effects of these changes. ⟳ **Summarize**

▶ **Ford's Model T** *(above)* and the Wright Brothers's airplane *Flyer (below)* changed the way people traveled.

617

The Roaring Twenties

 Quick Summary During the 1920s the U.S. economy had an economic boom, and people lived better than they had before. Movies, radio, literature, and music became extremely popular.

**$ SOCIAL STUDIES STRAND
Economics**

Remind students how the free enterprise system works in the United States (see p. 19). Tell them that business owners can choose which products to make or sell and at what price to sell them. Consumers are free to choose what products to buy and whether to buy them.

Explain to students that due to the economic boom of the 1920s, many people bought on credit with money they did not have. With this system, known as installment buying, people could make a weekly, monthly, or yearly payment on a purchased item.

4 What effects did the economic boom have? People made higher wages and worked fewer hours. Times were good and many people were living better than they had before. Cause and Effect

5 How do you think the radio helped change the way people lived? Possible answer: People could listen to music and programs and get the latest news in their own homes. They did not have to go out to do these things. Draw Conclusions

✓ **REVIEW ANSWER** Movies drew ever-growing audiences. Many Americans bought radios to hear music, comedy, drama, sports, and the news. More people were interested in new forms of music like jazz. Main Idea and Details

Literature and Social Studies

6 What message is Langston Hughes sending in this poem? He is saying that soon African Americans will be treated the same as white Americans. Make Inferences

The Roaring Twenties

The 1920s was a period of strong economic growth—a boom. Boom times gave people higher wages and shorter work weeks to enjoy themselves. People called this period the "Roaring Twenties." This was a way of saying that times were good and many people were **4** living better than they had before.

Movies drew ever-growing audiences. The first movies were called "silents" because they had no sound. "Talkies," or movies with sound, began to be released in the late 1920s. Another new invention, radio, also entertained American families. The radio brought music, comedy, drama, sports, and **5** news into people's homes.

Young American writers wrote popular books. **F. Scott Fitzgerald** wrote about life during the Roaring Twenties. **Ernest Hemingway** based some of his most famous books on his experiences in World War I.

In Harlem, a section of New York City where many African Americans lived, there was a period of cultural growth called the **Harlem Renaissance.** It produced many famous African American artists, including the writers **Langston Hughes** and **Zora Neale Hurston.** Harlem also became a center for a new musical form that had grown out of the black American experience—jazz. The popularity of this music gave the 1920s yet another nickname—the "Jazz Age."

REVIEW What details support the main idea that the 1920s was a time when new forms of entertainment became popular? **Main Idea and Details**

▶ Baseball star Babe Ruth *(right)* helped make his sport popular around the country. Langston Hughes *(far right)* wrote poems and plays about the African American experience.

618

Literature and Social Studies

Langston Hughes wrote this poem, *I, Too,* in 1925. What did he mean when he wrote, "I, too, am America"?

I, too, sing America.

I am the darker brother.
They send me to eat in the kitchen
When company comes,
But I laugh,
And eat well,
And grow strong.

Tomorrow,
I'll be at the table
When company comes.
Nobody'll dare
Say to me,
"Eat in the kitchen,"
Then.

Besides,
They'll see how beautiful I am
And be ashamed—

I, too, am America. **6**

Practice and Extend

**✳ MEETING INDIVIDUAL NEEDS
Learning Styles**

Read and Interpret Poetry Using their individual learning styles, students read and interpret Langston Hughes's poem *I, Too.*

Musical Learning Encourage students to sing the poem to one of their favorite tunes or to a tune of their own invention. Ask students to explain why the tune they sing fits the purpose of the poem.

Verbal Learning Students can read the poem aloud with a partner and discuss the significance of each stanza to identify the purpose of the poem.

Kinesthetic Learning Students can give a dramatic reading of the poem and act it out with emotion. Ask students to explain why the emotions they use to act out the poem fit the purpose of the poem.

► This headline announced the 1929 stock market crash that helped lead to the Great Depression. Long bread lines were soon a common sight in many cities and towns.

The Great Crash

Weaknesses soon began to appear in the booming economy of the Roaring Twenties. To help feed the Allied Powers in World War I, farmers had borrowed money to buy additional land and tools to produce more food. After the war, they had a surplus of crops. As supply increased, food prices fell. Farmers had difficulty paying off their debts.

Factories, too, produced more goods than they could sell. With not enough buyers for their products, factories began laying off workers. **Unemployment,** or the number of workers without jobs, began to grow. Rising unemployment meant fewer people could afford to buy new products.

Meanwhile, many Americans tried to make money in the **stock market,** an organized market where stocks are bought and sold. Investors, or people who buy stocks, hoped that stock prices would rise so they could sell their stocks and make a profit. Stock prices kept rising in the late 1920s.

But prices began to fall slowly in 1929. On October 29, Black Tuesday, a crash occurred and stock prices fell quickly. For example, the stock price of a radio company plunged from over $100 to $28. As the stock market fell, billions of dollars were lost. Many people lost all their savings.

The economy went from boom to bust. Farmers in debt began losing their farms. By 1932, unemployment grew to one out of four people. Homeowners who were out of work could not keep up loan payments and lost their homes. Some banks went broke when money they had lent could not be repaid.

The United States entered a period known as the **Great Depression,** which lasted from 1929 to about 1939. It was not the nation's first depression, or period of economic hardship, but it was the worst.

Some people who lost their homes moved into makeshift villages of tents and shacks that became known as Hoovervilles. Some people without jobs stood in long bread lines, waiting for a cup of soup and a piece of bread. "Everyone in America was looking for work," said Langston Hughes.

REVIEW What were some of the causes and effects of the Great Depression? *Cause and Effect*

619

The Great Crash

🕐 *Quick Summary* At the end of the 1920s, a surplus of goods, higher unemployment, widespread debt, and other factors caused stock prices to fall and finally crash.

7 Why did farmers have difficulty paying off their debts? They had borrowed money to buy land and tools to produce more food, but the profits they received for their crops were not enough to pay their debts. **Analyze Information**

8 What was one cause of rising unemployment? Possible answer: Factories could not sell all of the products they manufactured, and they began laying off workers. **Cause and Effect**

9 Why did the stock market crash have such an enormous effect on the economy? Many consumers lost money because they had invested in the stock market. Consumers could not buy goods, so companies also lost money. **Cause and Effect**

10 What groups of Americans lost money after the stock market crash? Just about everyone—factory workers, farmers, bankers **Main Idea and Details**

✓ **REVIEW ANSWER** Causes: Surplus of food and other goods; investors bought too much stock. Effects: Widespread unemployment; sharp fall in stock values; homeowners and farmers could not pay loans; people lost money in some failed banks; many people did not have enough to eat. **Cause and Effect**

The New Deal

Quick Summary Franklin Delano Roosevelt and Congress put programs into place to help people and the economy recover, and to change conditions that had caused the Great Depression.

Primary Source

Cited in Franklin Delano Roosevelt's Inaugural Address in 1933

11 What do you think Americans feared? Not having work; being homeless and hungry; not knowing what to expect of the future **Analyze Primary Sources**

12 What did Roosevelt expect to accomplish with the New Deal? To help the jobless and poor; help the nation's economy recover; reform conditions that had brought on the Great Depression **Main Idea and Details**

Problem Solving

13 What solutions did New Deal programs offer to solve the problems caused by the Great Depression? CCC set up work camps to give young men wages, housing, and food for working to conserve forestlands; other programs created jobs and helped the banking system; Social Security Act gave payments to the unemployed and elderly. **Solve Problems**

✓ Ongoing Assessment

If... students have difficulty understanding the relationship between the problems of the Great Depression and the solutions offered by the New Deal,

then... organize the answer to the question into a chart listing the different problems as headings.

14 How did Eleanor Roosevelt help her husband? She traveled the country to see if conditions were improving. **Main Idea and Details**

✓ **REVIEW ANSWER** Possible answer: Fear of the Great Depression might prevent the nation from overcoming it. **Draw Conclusions**

The New Deal

"I pledge you, I pledge myself to a new deal for the American people." This was the promise made by **Franklin D. Roosevelt** as he campaigned for President in 1932. Roosevelt, a distant cousin of Theodore Roosevelt, won an easy victory and entered the White House in 1933. At his inauguration, he urged the worried nation to become more hopeful about the future. He said:

11 *"The only thing we have to fear is fear itself."*

Roosevelt had three goals. The first was to help the jobless and poor. The second was to help the nation's economy recover. Finally, Roosevelt wanted to reform conditions that had brought on the Great Depression. Working with Congress, he soon began putting a series of programs in place. These programs came to **12** be called the **New Deal.**

Congress passed many New Deal programs during the first 100 days of Roosevelt's term. One was the Civilian Conservation Corps, or CCC. It set up work camps for more than 2 million unemployed young men, and gave them wages, housing, and food. The men worked to conserve forests and other natural resources. Several New Deal programs created jobs or encouraged private companies to create more jobs. Others aimed to help the banking system get back on its feet. The Social Security Act, passed in 1935, provided payments to the unemployed and the elderly. These payments were paid for by the taxes of employers and employees.

As you will read in the Biography on page 623, Roosevelt had been crippled by polio. He spent much of his time in a wheelchair. But he received help from his wife, **Eleanor Roosevelt.** She traveled the country to see if conditions were improving.

Eleanor Roosevelt said, "These trips gave me a wonderful opportunity to visit all kinds of places and to see and get to know a good cross section of people. Always during my free time I visited as many government projects as possible, often managing to arrive without advance notice so that they could not be polished up for my inspection." She was especially concerned about whether children, women, and African Americans were being fairly treated.

REVIEW What do you think President Roosevelt meant when he said, "The only thing we have to fear is fear itself"? **Draw Conclusions**

▶ Franklin and Eleanor Roosevelt greeted supporters in 1941, on the day Franklin Roosevelt began his third term as President.

620

Practice and Extend

ISSUES AND VIEWPOINTS
Critical Thinking

Analyze Different Viewpoints Write these lists on the board and read them aloud. Ask students to compare and contrast solutions posed by the government and private sectors.

Government
- CCC offered wages, housing, and food
- Programs created jobs
- FDIC insured bank deposits
- Social Security paid money to widows, elderly, unemployed

Private Sector
- Private charities set up soup kitchens
- Red Cross distributed food and seeds
- Workers organized unions to support better work conditions

▶ This photograph of a family moving west from the Dust Bowl was taken by Dorothea Lange. Her pictures showed the hardships of life during the Great Depression.

Photograph by Dorothea Lange

The Dust Bowl

New Deal programs brought changes to people living in rural areas. The Tennessee Valley Authority, or TVA, built dams along rivers in the South. Dams were built to prevent flooding, provide electricity to the area, and make transportation on the rivers easier. TVA construction created thousands of jobs and improved the land and living conditions for farmers.

Farther west, extremely dry weather in the Great Plains caused what became known as the **Dust Bowl**. A severe drought hit the area in the 1930s. Farmers helplessly watched their soil turn to dust in the hot sun. High winds scattered the soil, leaving some farms unusable. One Texas farmer said:

> *"If the wind blew one way, here came the dark dust from Oklahoma. Another way and it was the gray dust from Kansas.... Little farms were buried. The town was blackened."*

Many people in the Dust Bowl left their useless farms. They packed all their belongings and headed west, hoping to find work and new lives in California. One traveler asked, "Do you reckon I'd be out on the highway if I had it good at home?"

Disappointment lay ahead for many of those who went west. In California few jobs were available and most of those jobs paid low wages.

REVIEW What were the effects of the Dust Bowl? *Cause and Effect*

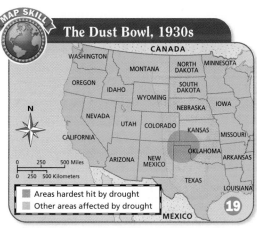

The Dust Bowl, 1930s

Areas hardest hit by drought
Other areas affected by drought

▶ **Drought turned parts of the Great Plains into a "Dust Bowl."**

MAP SKILL Place *Which states were hardest hit by drought?*

621

The Dust Bowl

🕐 ***Quick Summary*** Partly due to a serious drought in the Great Plains, some farmlands became useless. Many farmers headed to California to look for work.

15 **Why did the Tennessee Valley Authority build dams along rivers in the South?** To prevent flooding, provide electricity, improve river transportation **Main Idea and Details**

16 **What was one cause of the Dust Bowl?** Drought **Cause and Effect**

Primary Source

Cited in *This Fabulous Century: Volume IV, 1930–1940,* by Maitland A. Edey, ed.

17 **How do you think the farmers felt about the Dust Bowl?** Possible answers: Helpless, discouraged, fearful **Analyze Primary Sources**

Decision Making

18 **What decision did many farmers make as a result of the Dust Bowl? Was it wise? Explain.** Possible answers: Left their farms; Yes; some land was unusable. **Make Decisions**

✓ **REVIEW ANSWER** Farmlands became useless. Many farmers left their land and went west for work. **Cause and Effect**

The Dust Bowl, 1930s

19 **What was the southernmost state affected by the drought?** Texas **Interpret Maps**

MAP SKILL Answer parts of Colorado, Kansas, Oklahoma, Texas, New Mexico

About the Dust Bowl

- The Great Plains region is generally dry in the summer. Before the plains were used for farming, the area was covered with prairie grasses. The roots of this grass retained water and held the soil in place so it could withstand dry conditions.

- Another cause of the Dust Bowl was poor land management. Farmers had continuously plowed the ground and pulled up deeply rooted prairie grasses to prepare the ground for crops. When the drought hit, nothing else could grow to replace the prairie grass root system that had been holding the soil in place. The high winds blew away much of the uncovered soil.

Hard Times Continue

Quick Summary Although the New Deal helped some people, the Great Depression continued for many years.

Primary Source

Cited in *Bartlett's Familiar Quotations,* compiled by John Bartlett

20 **According to Roosevelt's quote, what did many Americans still need?** Homes, clothes, and food **Analyze Primary Sources**

✓ **REVIEW ANSWER** They helped people live through the Great Depression until the economy recovered. They also expanded the government's role in people's lives. **Draw Conclusions**

3 Close and Assess

Summarize the Lesson

Have students write a brief description for each bulleted item on the vertical time line.

✓ **LESSON 3   REVIEW**

1. For possible answers, see the reduced pupil page. 🔄 **Summarize**

2. Assembly line; inexpensively manufactured cars could be bought by Americans who then could move more freely.

3. **Critical Thinking: *Compare and Contrast*** The 1920s had a booming economy and new entertainment such as "talkie" movies and radio shows. During the 1930s many lost their jobs and all of their savings.

4. Possible answers: The CCC set up work camps for young men, giving them wages, housing, and food in return for working to conserve natural resources. Social Security gave money to the elderly and the unemployed.

5. After a severe drought made Dust Bowl farmers' lands useless, they moved to California to find work.

Link to ⭕─⭕ Language Arts

Suggest that students skim the table of contents and the index in the biography to find topics.

Hard Times Continue

Despite all of the New Deal programs, the Great Depression continued. Unemployment remained high. By 1935, only about 12 percent of those unemployed in 1932 had found jobs. In 1937, President Roosevelt recognized that times were still hard. He said,

20
> *"I see one-third of a nation ill-housed, ill-clad, ill-nourished [poorly fed]."*

▶ Unemployment remained high during the Great Depression.

However, the New Deal and many private groups did help many people survive the Great Depression until the economy improved. Some programs, like Social Security, are still in effect today.

With Roosevelt's reforms, the government became larger and more powerful. Many people today disagree about how big a role the government should play in people's lives.

REVIEW Describe the results of President Roosevelt's New Deal programs. **Draw Conclusions**

Summarize the Lesson

• **1927** Pilot Charles Lindbergh became the first person to make a solo flight across the Atlantic Ocean.

• **1929** The stock market crashed and the Great Depression began.

• **1933** Franklin D. Roosevelt became President and started the New Deal.

LESSON 3   REVIEW

Check Facts and Main Ideas

1. 🔄 **Summarize** On a separate sheet of paper, write details for the following summary.

1920s was a boom time for the economy.	President Roosevelt's New Deal attempted to help the nation during the Great Depression.	Drought and winds destroyed many farms in the Great Plains during the 1930s.

From the 1920s to the 1930s, the United States went from economic boom to severe depression.

2. What system of making products did Henry Ford develop, and how did it affect the nation?

3. **Critical Thinking: *Compare and Contrast*** Compare American life in the "Roaring Twenties" with American life in the **Great Depression** of the 1930s.

4. Describe two **New Deal** programs.

5. Why did **Dust Bowl** farmers move to California?

Link to ⭕─⭕ Language Arts

Read a Biography Choose a person from the Roaring Twenties or Great Depression, and read a biography about that person. Then write a short book report explaining the role this person played during this period.

622

Practice and Extend

MEETING INDIVIDUAL NEEDS
Leveled Practice

Find Out About Frances Perkins Have students research a person important to the implementation of the Social Security Act.

Easy Have students use an encyclopedia or the Internet to find the dates when Perkins lived (1882–1965). **Reteach**

On-Level Ask students to find out about Perkins's service in the Cabinet (Secretary of Labor 1933–1945; first woman cabinet member). **Extend**

Challenge Have students research Perkins's life and then write a paragraph about her. **Enrich**

For a Lesson Summary, use Quick Study, p. 128.

Workbook, p. 144

Lesson 3: Times of Plenty, Times of Hardship

Also on Teacher Resources CD-R

Franklin Delano Roosevelt
1882–1945

As a young man, most things came easily to Franklin D. Roosevelt. Born into a wealthy family, he had the best of everything. So when Roosevelt went on vacation with his wife and children in 1921, he could not imagine that anything would go wrong. But one morning, when Roosevelt tried to get up, his legs did not work. He had a disease called polio, and for the rest of his life, he would not be able to walk without help.

Franklin Roosevelt never gave up. When he was allowed out of bed, he pulled himself up staircases and tried to go farther each day using crutches. Three years later, Roosevelt was asked to make a speech in support of the Democratic candidate for President. On the night of the speech, wearing heavy braces on his legs, Roosevelt leaned one arm on a cane and the other on his son, James. Breathing hard and straining with each step, Roosevelt made it to the podium. He leaned there to catch his breath, then looked up and smiled. The crowd cheered.

The Franklin Delano Roosevelt Memorial was dedicated on May 1, 1997, in Washington, D.C.

In 1932, during the Great Depression, Roosevelt was elected President. He worked to help others facing difficult situations. Roosevelt was usually photographed sitting behind his desk, and many Americans did not realize that he could not walk. After his illness, he began to see the world differently. He once said,

"If you have spent two years in bed trying to wiggle your big toe, everything else seems easy."

Learn From Biographies

One of Roosevelt's close friends said that after he got polio, he "began to see the other fellow's point of view." Why should leaders be able to see more than one point of view?

For more information, go online to *Meet the People* at **www.sfsocialstudies.com.**

623

CURRICULUM CONNECTION
Literature

Read Biographies

Franklin D. Roosevelt, by Steve Potts (Capstone, ISBN 1-560-65453-8, 1996) **Easy**

Franklin D. Roosevelt, by Paul Joseph (ABDO Publishing, ISBN 1-562-39813-X, 2002) **On-Level**

Franklin D. Roosevelt: The Four-Term President, by Michael A. Schuman (Enslow Publishers, ISBN 0-894-90696-8, 1996) **Challenge**

Franklin Delano Roosevelt

Objective

• Identify leaders in the national government, including President Franklin Delano Roosevelt.

1 Introduce and Motivate

Preview To activate prior knowledge, ask students what they know about the accomplishments Franklin Delano Roosevelt made during his presidency. Tell students they will read about obstacles that Roosevelt had to overcome.

2 Teach and Discuss

1 What caused Roosevelt to lose the ability to walk without help? The disease polio Cause and Effect

2 How do you think Roosevelt's disease affected his outlook on life? Possible answer: It may have made him more determined to overcome obstacles facing him and made him appreciate life more. Draw Conclusions

3 Close and Assess

Learn from Biographies Answer

Leaders need to be able to see many points of view in order to understand the differing views of the people they represent.

World War II

Objectives

- Identify the causes of World War II.

- Explain how the United States was drawn into World War II and how it prepared to fight the war.

- Describe how the Allies won victory in both Europe and Asia.

- Analyze the costs of World War II.

Vocabulary

dictator, p. 625; **World War II,** p. 625; **concentration camp,** p. 628; **Holocaust,** p. 628; **atomic bomb,** p. 629

Resources

- Workbook, p. 145
- Transparency 6, 60
- Every Student Learns Guide, pp. 258–261
- Quick Study, pp. 130–131

Quick Teaching Plan

If time is short, have students make a cause-and-effect chart.

- As they read, have students look for causes and effects of World War II.

- Suggest that students consider the causes of the war and its effects on the United States and on the other countries involved.

1 Introduce and Motivate

Preview To activate prior knowledge, ask students why the United States fought in World War I. Tell students that, in Lesson 4, they will learn about the causes and effects of involvement by the United States in World War II.

You Are There In this speech Roosevelt said he wanted peace, but he warned that the United States might become involved in the war. Ask students what war might mean for the United States.

624 Unit 9 • The United States and the World

1940   1945

1941
Japanese bomb
Pearl Harbor

1944
Normandy
invasion

May 1945
Germans sur
August 19
Japanese su

Normandy
Hiroshima
Pearl Harbor

PREVIEW

Focus on the Main Idea
The United States and its allies fought and won World War II, the most widespread and costliest war in human history.

PLACES
Pearl Harbor, Hawaii
Normandy, France
Hiroshima, Japan

PEOPLE
Benito Mussolini
Adolf Hitler
Joseph Stalin
Dwight D. Eisenhower
Harry S. Truman

VOCABULARY
dictator
World War II
concentration camp
Holocaust
atomic bomb

▶ People listened to news on radios like this one in the 1930s.

624

World War II

You Are There
It is the evening of October 5, 1937. You turn on your radio to listen to your favorite program. But instead, you hear President Franklin Roosevelt giving a speech "The peace, the freedom, and the security of 90 percent of the population of the world is being jeopardized [risked] by the remaining 10 percent....It seems to be unfortunately true that the epidemic of world lawlessness is spreading....We are determined to keep out of war, yet we cannot insure [defend] ourselves against the disastrous effects of war and the dangers of involvement."

What war is President Roosevelt talking about? How will it affect your life and that of your fellow Americans? You listen to the rest of the speech and wonder about the future.

Summarize As you read, summarize major reasons why World War II began and ended as it did.

Practice and Extend

READING SKILL
Summarize

In the Lesson Review, students complete a graphic organizer like the one below. You may want to provide students with a copy of Transparency 6 to complete as they read the lesson.

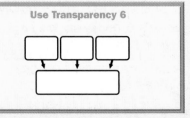

Use Transparency 6

VOCABULARY
Word Exercise

Related Word Study The suffix *-ic* can mean "of or having to do with," having the nature of," or "made up of." So in *atomic bomb,* the word *atomic* means "of or having to do with atoms." Ask students if they know what atoms are. Have students brainstorm for other words that have the *-ic* suffix, and discuss how it helps them understand what the word means. (heroic, geometric, volcanic, and so on) Most dictionaries offer other examples under *-ic*.

World War II Begins

President Roosevelt was talking about a growing problem in Europe. Economic hard times had struck there as well. In Europe, many people longed for leaders who they thought could make their troubles disappear. Some people were so desperate they were willing to sacrifice their own freedom. The stage was set for the rise of ambitious leaders who gained complete control of their countries and their people. These leaders were known as **dictators.**

In Italy, the dictator **Benito Mussolini** came to power in 1922. In 1933 a dictator came to power in Germany. **Adolf Hitler** was the head of Germany's Nazi Party, and believed that Germans were superior to other people. He also spoke of hatred for the Jews, who had lived in Germany for more than one thousand years. Throughout the 1930s, Hitler's power grew stronger, and mistreatment of Jews increased. He spoke of using force to expand the country's borders. Hitler said, "Some day, when I order war, I shall not…hesitate because of the ten million young men I shall be sending to their death."

In Japan, a group of military leaders came to power. Like Mussolini and Hitler, these leaders

▶ Adolf Hitler watched German troops march through Poland in 1939.

spoke of conquering other countries. They wanted Japan to dominate east Asia.

Before long, these three nations—Italy, Germany, and Japan—were on the march into other people's lands. In 1935 Mussolini attacked the African nation of Ethiopia in order to make it an Italian colony. In 1937 Japan invaded China. In the late 1930s, Hitler gained control of Austria and Czechoslovakia. In 1936 Germany and Italy signed a pact, or treaty, agreeing to support each other. Later they were joined by Japan. Their alliance became known as the Axis.

In Western Europe, Britain and France opposed Germany and Italy. They became known as the Allies. On September 1, 1939, Hitler sent his troops into Poland, which the Allies had promised to protect. Britain and France declared war on Germany. For the second time in 25 years, a major war had begun. It was called **World War II.**

> **REVIEW** How would you summarize the beginning of World War II? ⟳ Summarize

625

---

2 Teach and Discuss

PAGE 625

World War II Begins

🕐 ***Quick Summary*** Hard times overseas led to the rise of dictators who wanted to conquer other countries. European countries began forming alliances, and much of the world became involved in another major war.

1 **Why were people in Europe willing to let dictators gain control?** They were looking for leaders who they thought could make their problems disappear. **Main Idea and Details**

2 **What did Japan, Italy, and Germany have in common?** Possible answer: They all had leaders who wanted to conquer other countries. **Compare and Contrast**

3 **What countries formed the Axis? the Allies?** Axis: Germany, Italy, Japan; Allies: Britain and France **Main Idea and Details**

✓ **REVIEW ANSWER** Dictators in Germany, Italy, and Japan joined together as the Axis. When Germany invaded Poland in September 1939, Britain and France, having pledged to defend Poland, responded by declaring war on Germany. ⟳ Summarize

---

🌐 **SOCIAL STUDIES STRAND**
Geography

Countries Involved in World War II

- Many students may be unfamiliar with some of the countries in the lesson. Help students locate these countries and former countries on a large wall map: Italy, Germany, Japan, Ethiopia, China, Austria, Czechoslovakia, Britain, France, Poland, and the Soviet Union.

- Tell students that the present-day Czech Republic and Slovakia used to be Czechoslovakia. Explain that the Soviet Union (also called the Union of Soviet Socialist Republics) is now many different countries, the largest of which is Russia.

- Call on volunteers to point out these places on the map.

- Throughout the lesson as you discuss countries' involvement in the events of World War II, remind students of their location.

Americans at War

Quick Summary By June 1941 German forces had attacked France and the Soviet Union. The United States stayed out of the war until the Japanese bombed Hawaii.

4 **What caused the Soviet Union to join the Allies?** Germany broke its pact with the Soviet Union. **Cause and Effect**

5 **How did Roosevelt feel about the war in 1940?** He did not want America to be involved. **Analyze Information**

6 **What changed Roosevelt's mind about American involvement in the War?** Japan launched a surprise attack on Pearl Harbor. **Cause and Effect**

Primary Source
Cited in Franklin Roosevelt's address to Congress on December 8, 1941

7 **Why do you think Roosevelt used the words *suddenly* and *deliberately*?** Possible answer: To show that there was no mistake and that Japan meant to harm U.S. Navy ships **Analyze Primary Sources**

 **Pearl Harbor, Hawaii**

8 **Why was the attack on Pearl Harbor such an important event in history?** It was the reason why the United States entered World War II. **Evaluate**

Americans at War

Germany's armies were very successful in the war's early years. German soldiers moved west, and in a matter of months, France surrendered. Britain fought off a huge air attack by the German air force and battled German forces in North Africa.

In June 1941, Germany invaded the Soviet Union, a huge country in Eastern Europe and Northern Asia. The Soviet Union was also led by a dictator, **Joseph Stalin.** A few days before World War II began, Stalin and Hitler had signed a pact agreeing that their nations would not attack each other. Two years later, Hitler broke the agreement by attacking the **4** Soviet Union. Stalin then joined the Allies.

The United States watched as German forces charged east and west, north and south. Mothers urged President Roosevelt not to send their sons to Europe yet again. In 1940 he promised, "Your boys are not **5** going to be sent into any foreign wars."

Then early one Sunday morning—December 7, 1941—the United States was forced into the war. In a surprise attack, Japanese planes bombed United States Navy ships anchored at **Pearl Harbor, Hawaii.** More than 2,000 American sailors, soldiers, and civilians were killed. The next day, President Roosevelt addressed Congress:

"Yesterday, December 7, 1941—a date which will live in infamy—the United States of America was suddenly and deliberately attacked by naval and air forces of the Empire of Japan."

At Roosevelt's request, Congress declared war on Japan. On December 11, Germany and Italy declared war on the United States. The United States now joined the Allies.

Car makers switched over to producing war planes and tanks. Clothing makers poured out millions of military uniforms. By 1942,

Pearl Harbor, Hawaii
One of the American ships sunk in the attack on Pearl Harbor was the USS *Arizona*. Many of the more than 1,100 sailors who died on the *Arizona* went down with the ship. Today, you can see the remains of the ship under the harbor. A floating memorial above the ship honors the Americans killed at Pearl Harbor.

Pearl Harbor, HAWAII

626

Practice and Extend

 SOCIAL STUDIES STRAND
History

Surprise Attacks The attack on Pearl Harbor in 1941 may trigger a discussion about the attacks on the World Trade Center and the Pentagon on September 11, 2001. Students may want to share memories and ask questions about these attacks.

- Mention that America responded with great patriotism and humanity. Many people volunteered their time and resources.
- For suggestions about how to help children deal with fear and loss, see pages TR1–TR2 of this Teacher's Edition.

 **ACCESS CONTENT**
ESL Support

Explore World War II Help students understand key events in World War II by using a map or a time line.

Beginning Provide students with half a sheet of acetate and an erasable marker. Have them place the acetate over the map on p. 629. They should draw an arrow from Germany to the Soviet Union and label it *June 1941*. They can draw an arrow from Japan to Pearl Harbor and label it *December 7, 1941*.

Intermediate Have students make a time line of events on this page. Students should write a sentence for each event.

Advanced Students should write a paragraph explaining why the United States did not enter the war until December 1941.

For additional ESL support, use Every Student Learns Guide, pp. 258–261.

▶ "Rosie the Riveter" (*right*) became a symbol of the women who kept American factories running during World War II.

The Granger Collection

one-third of American production went toward the war effort. All this spending by the government and companies created more jobs. As men joined the armed services by the millions, women took men's places on factory assembly lines. By 1944, 3.5 million women were working in factories making weapons.

Feelings of patriotism were strong at home. Fears of enemies living in the country also were high. Within a week of the attack on Pearl Harbor, over 2,000 German, Italian, and Japanese people in the United States had been arrested for suspicion of working against the United States war effort.

Japanese Americans soon faced more mistreatment. President Roosevelt signed Executive Order #9066, which allowed the military to remove from the West Coast anyone seen as a threat. The Supreme Court upheld the order. By the summer of 1942, over 110,000 Japanese Americans were forced to leave their homes on the West Coast. Although none were convicted of treason, Japanese Americans were sent to

relocation camps around the country. Yoshiko Uchida described the day the military came to take her community away:

"Before long, we were told to board the buses that lined the street outside, and the people living nearby came out of their houses to watch." ⑫

Many Japanese Americans were forced to spend the rest of the war at relocation camps.

Still, many Japanese Americans wanted to serve the United States. One man, Henry Ebihara, wrote to the secretary of war, "I only ask that I be given a chance to fight to preserve the principles that I have been brought up on." Eventually Japanese Americans who had been born in the United States were allowed to join the army. Thousands served the nation in World War II. ⑬

REVIEW How did events at Pearl Harbor change the American position on World War II? **Cause and Effect**

627

---

⑨ What effect did the U.S.'s entrance into the war have on industry? Production of planes, tanks, and military uniforms increased; this created new jobs, many taken by women as men joined the armed services. **Cause and Effect**

Tell students that the supply of many consumer goods was limited during the war. Many important items, such as food, clothing, and gasoline, were rationed. Remind students that scarcity of resources requires careful choices and responsible citizenship.

⑩ What were some of the advantages and disadvantages of production for the war effort? Advantages: More jobs; opportunities for women to work; Disadvantages: Even though workers had money, there was a shortage of goods. **Compare and Contrast**

⑪ Why were many Japanese Americans sent to relocation camps? Many Americans feared that some Japanese Americans were working against the U.S. war effort. **Main Idea and Details**

Primary Source
Cited in *Life in a Japanese American Internment Camp*, by Diane Yancey

⑫ Compare and contrast the situations of Uchida and of the people who watched her be taken away. Uchida and the watching people lived in the same area, but she was forced to leave while they stayed. **Compare and Contrast**

⑬ How did many Japanese Americans show their support for the United States? They joined and served in the army. **Apply Information**

✓ **REVIEW ANSWER** The United States could no longer stay out of the war. They joined the Allies to fight against the Axis. **Cause and Effect**

Write a Journal Entry or Letter Ask students to think about what it would have been like to be a woman working in a factory making products needed in the war.

Easy Ask students to write a statement about the difference between working in the home and working in a factory. **Reteach**

On-Level Ask students to choose a product, such as uniforms, canned food, or weapons, and have students write about how making the product will help American soldiers. **Extend**

Challenge Tell students to suppose that they are a factory worker with a family member who is fighting in the war. Have students write a letter from the factory worker to the family member. **Enrich**

For a Lesson Summary, use Quick Study, p. 130.

Victory in Europe

14 **How did the Americans help Britain and the Soviet Union?** Possible answer: They supplied equipment, food, and soldiers. Main Idea and Details

15 **What is one detail that supports the idea that the invasion in Normandy was a success?** Possible answer: Within one month after D-Day, one million Allied troops had landed in France and began their fight east toward Germany, driving the Germans out of Western Europe. Main Idea and Details

✓ **Ongoing Assessment**

| **If...** students have difficulties understanding how the Allies squeezed the Germans, | **then...** display a map of Europe showing the route of the Allied troops moving eastward through France into Germany and west from the former Soviet Union toward Germany. |

16 **How many months were there from D-Day to Germany's surrender on V-E Day?** About 11 months
Analyze Information

Primary Source

Cited in a letter by First Lt. William Cowling, written in May 1945

17 **What does this statement tell you about how the Nazis treated prisoners?** Possible answer: They treated the prisoners very poorly. They were given little to eat or wear. Draw Conclusions

⭐ **SOCIAL STUDIES STRAND**
Citizenship

Prejudice Reduction Remind students that since the Holocaust many people have said: "Never again." Ask them what they can do as responsible citizens to recognize and resist the kinds of prejudice that caused the Holocaust. How can they help promote cultural differences as a positive force in the United States and the world?

✓ **REVIEW ANSWER** The Allies found concentration camps in which the Nazis murdered Jews and other people they blamed for Germany's problems.
 Summarize

Victory in Europe

Britain and the Soviet Union needed help to keep fighting Germany. American ships delivered millions of tons of equipment and food to the Allies. American soldiers went too. More than 16 million Americans served in the military during World War II.

The Allies planned to attack German-held Europe by launching the greatest sea invasion in history. Five thousand ships carried Allied soldiers from Britain to the beaches of **Normandy,** in northern France. The leader of the invasion was American Army General **Dwight D. Eisenhower.** D-Day, or the day of the attack, began on June 6, 1944. At 6:30 in the morning, 150,000 Allied troops landed on the beaches of Normandy as Germans fired weapons at the invading Allied soldiers. About 11,000 Allied aircraft joined the fight.

Though the Allies suffered heavy losses, the invasion was successful. Within a month, one million Allied troops had come ashore in France. For the next eight months, they fought their way east toward Germany, driving the Germans out of Western Europe. At the same time, troops from the Soviet Union

▶ Jews throughout Nazi-controlled Europe were forced to wear patches identifying them as Jews *(above)*. Allied troops faced enemy guns as they waded ashore at Normandy *(below)*.

628

moved west. The Allies squeezed Germany from two directions. Finally, on May 8, 1945, Germany surrendered. The Allies greeted the victory with joy and named May 8th V-E Day—Victory in Europe.

As the Allies freed Europe, they found horrors along the way. Hitler and the Nazis had built **concentration camps.** In these camps they imprisoned Jews and other people they unfairly blamed for Germany's problems. About 12 million men, women, and children—6 million of them Jews—were murdered in concentration camps. Hitler's goal was to destroy the Jewish people. Historians call the murder of 6 million Jews the **Holocaust** (HAHL uh cawst), a word meaning "widespread destruction."

An American army officer named William Cowling helped free one of the concentration camps. He wrote this about the prisoners there:

> *"They were dirty, starved skeletons with torn tattered clothes....It is unbelievable how any human can treat others as they were treated. "*

REVIEW What did the Allies find as they freed Europe? 🔄 Summarize

Practice and Extend

FYI **SOCIAL STUDIES**
Background

About the Holocaust

- Adolf Hitler began persecuting German Jews soon after becoming the chancellor of Germany in January 1933.
- Courts, universities, and the government fired Jewish workers. Jewish businesses were boycotted and then destroyed.
- The Nürnberg Laws (1935) prohibited Jews from marrying other Germans and took away their citizenship. Attacks took place on November 9

and 10, 1938, which demolished almost all synagogues and other Jewish establishments in Germany.
- At the time the war began in 1939, German Jews had lost their rights to education, property, and freedom of movement. They were forced to live in Jewish ghettos.
- During the war, Jews were put into concentration camps where they were either murdered or forced to join labor groups. Many died from extreme work and lack of food.

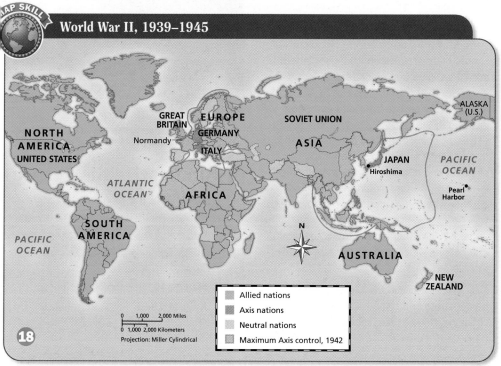

World War II, 1939–1945

Allied nations

Axis nations

Neutral nations

Maximum Axis control, 1942

0 1,000 2,000 Miles

0 1,000 2,000 Kilometers

Projection: Miller Cylindrical

18

▶ By 1942, German armies had captured nearly all of Europe and North Africa.

MAP SKILL Location *Which major Axis nation was in Asia?*

Victory in Asia

Meanwhile, battles had been raging in Asia. The Allies fought to free islands in the Pacific from Japanese rule. By early 1945, the United States was closing in on Japan. The Military made plans to invade Japan, but they feared that such an attack could cost as many as one million American lives.

In April 1945, President Roosevelt suddenly died. Vice President **Harry S. Truman** took the oath as President. He later said, "I felt like the moon, the stars and all the planets had fallen on me."

Truman soon learned that American scientists had developed the most deadly weapon yet—the **atomic bomb.** One such "super bomb" dropped on an enemy could create more destruction than 20,000 tons of ordinary explosives. Truman decided to use the atomic bomb against Japan. He hoped it would force Japan to surrender. This would make an invasion unnecessary and save many American lives.

On August 6, 1945, the United States Air Force dropped an atomic bomb on the Japanese city of **Hiroshima.** With a blinding flash, it destroyed the city and killed nearly 80,000 people in just a few moments. Three days later, the United States dropped a second atomic bomb on the city of Nagasaki, killing another 40,000 Japanese. On August 14, Japan surrendered. World War II had ended at last.

20

21

REVIEW Why did President Truman decide to use the atomic bomb?

Main Idea and Details

629

Victory in Asia

🕐 *Quick Summary* While fighting was ongoing in Europe, battles raged on in Asia. Fearing that an invasion of Japan would cost many American lives, President Harry Truman decided to drop the atomic bomb on Japan to force Japan to surrender.

World War II, 1939–1945

🦉 **Test Talk**

Use Information from Graphics

18 **What four Allied nations are named on the map?** Have students skim the map to find the names of the Allied countries. United States, Great Britain, Soviet Union, and Australia Interpret Maps

MAP SKILL Answer Japan

19 **Why were military officials hesitant to invade Japan?** They feared that such an attack could cost as many as one million lives. Main Idea and Details

20 **On what two cities was the atomic bomb used?** Hiroshima and Nagasaki Main Idea and Details

21 **About how many people were killed in these two cities?** About 120,000 people Main Idea and Details

✓ **REVIEW ANSWER** President Truman believed that using the atomic bomb would force Japan to surrender, preventing an invasion of Japan and saving many American lives. Main Idea and Details

CURRICULUM CONNECTION
Science

The Atomic Bomb

- An atom is a tiny particle that is the basic unit of matter. At the center of an atom is the nucleus, which has a positive charge. The nucleus of an atom contains protons (positive charge) and neutrons (no charge).

- When the nuclei of certain kinds of atoms are split apart, large quantities of thermal energy, gamma rays, and neutrons are released. When these neutrons hit the nuclei of nearby atoms, they cause those nuclei to split also. This reaction can cause a chain reaction. This can be used to cause an enormous explosion, like that of an atomic bomb.

- The atomic bomb that was dropped on Hiroshima used uranium and had the force of more than 15,000 tons of TNT. The Nagasaki bomb, which used plutonium, created about the same amount of energy as 21,000 tons of TNT.

The Costs of War

⏱ *Quick Summary* World War II left behind record high casualties and deadly new weapons.

22 **What challenges do you think the United States had to deal with in regard to the new weapons?** Possible answer: Ensuring that other countries did not develop or steal the technology for building these weapons **Draw Conclusions**

✓ **REVIEW ANSWER** That it was becoming much more dangerous **Draw Conclusions**

3 Close and Assess

Summarize the Lesson

Have students read the events listed on the time line. Ask them to add two or three events to the time line using the information from this lesson.

✓ | LESSON 4 | REVIEW |

1. 🔄 **Summarize** For possible answers, see the reduced pupil page.

2. Germany, Italy, and Japan, led by the dictators who wanted to gain control of other lands, formed the Axis. Great Britain, France, the Soviet Union, and the United States formed the Allies to combat Axis aggression.

3. Declared war on Japan; became suspicious of certain people living in the United States

4. Invaded Normandy, France; squeezed Germany from two sides; dropped atomic bombs on Japan

5. **Critical Thinking:** *Make Generalizations* Many died in military battles; millions killed in Nazi concentration camps; Japanese Americans sent to relocation camps

Link to 🔗 **Language Arts**

Students' paragraphs should include facts and be well organized.

The Costs of War

World War II was by far the bloodiest war in human history. Between 40 million and 50 million civilians and soldiers died in the conflict. Over 400,000 of those were Americans. Almost every part of the world had been involved in the war.

The dropping of atomic bombs had shown that people could now create weapons more powerful and deadly than anyone dreamed of in the past. Nations could threaten one another with terrors not known before. In the years to come, the United States would play a major role in helping to rebuild the world and dealing with the challenges of these **22** terrible new weapons.

REVIEW What did the atomic bomb demonstrate about the way the world was changing? **Draw Conclusions**

The Granger Collection

▶ This atomic explosion destroyed Hiroshima and introduced the world to a terrible new weapon.

Summarize the Lesson

- **1941** After the Japanese bombed Pearl Harbor, the United States entered World War II on the side of the Allies.
- **1944** The Allies invaded Normandy, France, on June 6.
- **May 1945** Germany surrendered.
- **August 1945** Japan surrendered.

| LESSON 4 | REVIEW |

Check Facts and Main Ideas

1. 🔄 **Summarize** On a separate sheet of paper, write a sentence that summarizes the details below.

Events

| Thousands of Americans died in the Japanese attack on Pearl Harbor. | Millions were imprisoned and killed in Nazi concentration camps during World War II. | Nearly 80,000 Japanese died when the U.S. dropped an atomic bomb on Hiroshima. |

World War II was the bloodiest war in history.

Summary

2. What major nations fought in **World War II** and why?

3. How did the United States government react to the bombing of Pearl Harbor?

4. What strategies did the Allies use in Europe and the Pacific?

5. **Critical Thinking:** *Make Generalizations* Describe some of the terrible effects of World War II on civilians.

Link to 🔗 **Language Arts**

Research Advertisements There were many shortages during World War II, and people were asked to conserve and contribute what they could. Research different ways advertisements in the United States encouraged people to get involved. Write a paragraph summarizing your findings.

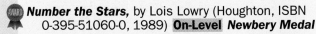

Practice and Extend

⬡ **CURRICULUM CONNECTION**
Literature

Learn More About World War II

Extend the content with the following selections:

The Little Ships: The Heroic Rescue at Dunkirk in World War II, by Louise Borden (Simon & Schuster Children's, ISBN 0-689-80827-5, 1997) **Easy**

🏅 ***Number the Stars,*** by Lois Lowry (Houghton, ISBN 0-395-51060-0, 1989) **On-Level** *Newbery Medal*

A Garden of Thorns: My Memoir of Surviving World War II in France, by Roger De Anfrasio (Silk City Press, ISBN 0-965-44522-4, 2000) **Challenge**

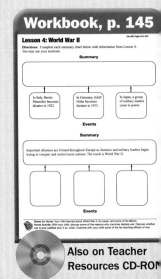

Workbook, p. 145

Lesson 4: World War II

Directions: Complete each summary chart below with information from Lesson 4. You may use your textbook.

Summary

| In Italy, Benito Mussolini becomes dictator in 1922. | In Germany, Adolf Hitler becomes dictator in 1933. | In Japan, a group of military leaders come to power. |

Events

Summary

Important alliances are formed throughout Europe as dictators and military leaders begin trying to conquer and control more nations. The result is World War II.

Events

🔵 **Also on Teacher Resources CD-ROM**

Dwight David Eisenhower
1890–1969

Dwight David Eisenhower, nicknamed "Ike," was where he most loved to be—on the football field. Ike had the ball on a running play in the next-to-last game of the season. As he rushed past his opponents, someone grabbed his foot. Ike finished the play, but he knew something was wrong. His knee had been severely injured. A few days later, doctors told Ike the bad news: he would never play football again.

The injury saddened Ike. At first, he thought about leaving West Point Military Academy. But he stayed on. Soon he started exercising again, adjusting to a weak knee by concentrating on strengthening his arms.

Right before he graduated, a doctor at West Point told Ike that his damaged knee might prevent him from being a good soldier and that he should consider giving up his army career. But Ike succeeded in becoming an officer in the United States Army.

In 1943, Eisenhower helped design a short jacket for United States Army troops. The jacket came to be known as the "Eisenhower Jacket," or "Ike Jacket."

It was a good thing, too. Eisenhower went on to become a very successful army officer. **(1)** During World War II, he commanded the Allied troops that landed in Europe on D-Day, the 6th of June 1944.

This was the greatest invasion from the sea in history. It began the drive that would help defeat Germany. In 1953, Eisenhower became President of the United States. In his first speech as President, he said: **(2)**

"We must be willing, individually and as a nation, to accept whatever sacrifices may be required of us. A people that values its privileges above its principles soon loses both." **(3)**

Learn from Biographies

Why do you think Eisenhower did not quit West Point after his injury? How do you think this experience affected his later decisions as a soldier, and as President?

For more information, go online to *Meet the People* at **www.sfsocialstudies.com.**

631

Dwight David Eisenhower

Objectives

- Describe the accident that almost ended Dwight David Eisenhower's military career.

- Identify Dwight David Eisenhower's major achievements.

1 Introduce and Motivate

Preview To activate prior knowledge, ask students what major campaign Eisenhower commanded in World War II. Tell students they will read about an injury that Eisenhower overcame.

2 Teach and Discuss

(1) Identify a detail that supports the idea that Eisenhower was determined. Possible answer: He overcame his injury to become a successful army officer. Main Idea and Details

(2) What was one of Eisenhower's greatest military accomplishments? Possible answer: Commanded troops that landed on D-Day Analyze Information

(3) What message was Eisenhower sending in his speech? Possible answer: All citizens must make an effort to protect the nation's founding principles. Analyze Primary Sources

3 Close and Assess

Learn from Biographies Answer

Possible answer: He was determined to have an army career. Determination helped him face hard situations.

WEB SITE
Technology

Students can find out more about Dwight David Eisenhower by clicking on *Meet the People* at **www.sfsocialstudies.com.**

SOCIAL STUDIES
Background

Audie Murphy

- Audie Murphy, the most decorated American combat soldier of World War II, had a successful army career.

- He was part of the Allied troops who attacked the Germans in France.

- During this invasion, about 150,000 soldiers landed on the beaches and about 11,000 aircraft attacked from the sky.

CHAPTER 18
REVIEW

Chapter Summary

For possible answers, see the reduced pupil page.

Vocabulary

1. d, **2.** a, **3.** e, **4.** b, **5.** c

People and Terms

Possible answers:

1. Ida Tarbell wrote about attempts by trusts to control the oil industry.
2. Upton Sinclair's novel *The Jungle* revealed the filthy conditions in meatpacking plants.
3. The Treaty of Versailles ended World War I, imposed severe punishments on the Central Powers, and created the League of Nations.
4. Susan B. Anthony helped women gain the right to vote.
5. During the Great Migration many African Americans moved from the South to the North for higher paying jobs.
6. Charles Lindbergh was the first pilot to fly nonstop from New York to Paris.
7. During the Great Depression many people lost their jobs and homes.
8. The Dust Bowl was an area of the Great Plains hit by severe drought.
9. General Dwight David Eisenhower led the attack at Normandy, France, on D-Day in World War II.
10. The two atomic bombs dropped by the United States on Japan in 1945 killed more than 120,000 people, causing Japan to surrender.

Facts and Main Ideas

1. Writers and journalists who wrote about conditions in business and other areas; their work led to some reforms.
2. Built dams along rivers in the South to prevent flooding, provide electricity, and make transportation easier
3. About 24 years

632 Unit 9 • The United States and the World

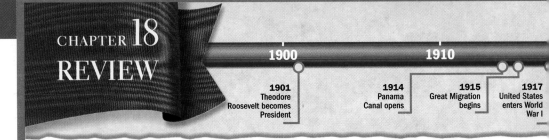

CHAPTER 18
REVIEW

1900			1910		
1901 Theodore Roosevelt becomes President		**1914** Panama Canal opens	**1915** Great Migration begins		**1917** United States enters World War I

Chapter Summary

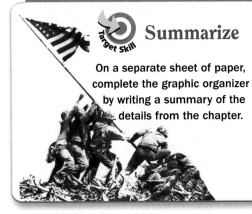

Summarize

On a separate sheet of paper, complete the graphic organizer by writing a summary of the details from the chapter.

Details

| The United States finished building the Panama Canal in 1914. | The United States helped the Allied Powers win World War I. | The Allies, including the United States, were victors in World War II. |

→ The United States became a world power in the early 20th century. ←

Summary

Vocabulary

Match each word with the correct definition.

1. **isthmus** (p. 604)
2. **alliance** (p. 609)
3. **assembly line** (p. 617)
4. **unemployment** (p. 619)
5. **dictator** (p. 625)

a. agreement among nations to defend one another

b. number of workers looking for jobs

c. leader with complete control of a country and its people

d. strip of land connecting two larger areas

e. method of manufacturing in which the product moves past groups of workers

People and Terms

Write a sentence explaining why each of the following people or terms was important in the first half of the 1900s. You may use two or more in a single sentence.

1. **Ida Tarbell** (p. 603)
2. **Upton Sinclair** (p. 603)
3. **Treaty of Versailles** (p. 611)
4. **Susan B. Anthony** (p. 612)
5. **Great Migration** (p. 613)
6. **Charles Lindbergh** (p. 617)
7. **Great Depression** (p. 619)
8. **Dust Bowl** (p. 621)
9. **Dwight D. Eisenhower** (p. 628)
10. **atomic bomb** (p. 629)

632

Practice and Extend

Assessment Options

☑ Chapter 18 Assessment

- Chapter 18 Content Test: Use Assessment Book, pp. 105–106.
- Chapter 18 Skills Test: Use Assessment Book, pp. 107–108.

Standardized Test Prep

- Chapter 18 Tests contain standardized test format.

☑ Chapter 18 Performance Assessment

- Have students work in groups to create a sequence of important events from the turn of the century to the end of World War II.
- As a group, students should plan events to be highlighted. Have each student be responsible for presenting one of the important events.
- Have students give a brief summary of when and where the event took place and explain its causes and effects as well as its importance. Encourage students to use visuals or props.
- Assess students' understanding of the sequence of events and their effects.

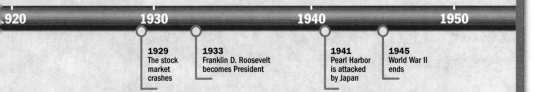

1929
The stock market crashes

1933
Franklin D. Roosevelt becomes President

1941
Pearl Harbor is attacked by Japan

1945
World War II ends

Facts and Main Ideas

- Who were the muckrakers? What did they accomplish?

- What did the Tennessee Valley Authority do?

- **Time Line** How many years were there between the time that the United States entered World War I and the Japanese attack of Pearl Harbor?

- **Main Idea** How did Theodore Roosevelt promote reform at home and expand the nation's power abroad?

- **Main Idea** What major, long-lasting changes came about in American life as a result of fighting in World War I?

- **Main Idea** How did the United States economy of the 1920s differ from the economy of the 1930s?

- **Main Idea** How did World War II affect civilians and soldiers?

- **Critical Thinking:** *Make Generalizations* The United States wanted to stay out of both World War I and World War II. What caused it to enter each war?

Write About History

- **Write a biography** of one of the people in this chapter.

- **Write a short report** about advances made in transportation in the 1900s.

- **Draw a political cartoon** about a current event and write a caption for it.

Apply Skills

Interpret Political Cartoons
Answer the questions about this cartoon.

1 What is this cartoon about?

2 What is the man throwing? What does it stand for?

3 What do you think is the cartoonist's point of view?

Internet Activity

To get help with vocabulary, people, and terms, select dictionary or encyclopedia from *Social Studies Library* at www.sfsocialstudies.com.

633

---

4. By helping to create national parks, working to end trusts, and supporting laws to guarantee safe food; by increasing U.S. naval power and starting the Panama Canal.

5. New jobs and the right for women to vote; many African Americans went North for better jobs.

6. The 1920s economy boomed, while the 1930s were a time of severe economic hardship.

7. It was the bloodiest war in history, with about 40 to 50 million civilians and soldiers killed, including about 6 million Jews killed in the Holocaust.

8. Entered World War I because Germany asked Mexico to enter the war against the United States and its submarines sank U.S. ships; entered World War II after Japan bombed Pearl Harbor.

Write About History

Test Talk

Write Your Answer to Score High

1. Students should describe the accomplishments of the person they choose and consider how he or she affected the United States and the world. Students should make sure that their answer has correct details.

2. Remind students to include an explanation of how the advances in transportation affected people.

3. Students might consider a local, state, or national event or issue.

Apply Skills

1. The importance of recycling and how people can be lazy about doing it

2. A globe; destroying the environment

3. If we do not make recycling a way of life, the earth will be damaged.

Hands-on Unit Project

✓ Unit 9 Performance Assessment

- See p. 674 for information about using the Unit Project as a means of performance assessment.
- A scoring guide is provided on p. 674.

WEB SITE
Technology

For more information, students can select the dictionary or encyclopedia from *Social Studies Library* at **www.sfsocialstudies.com**.

Workbook, p. 146

Vocabulary Review

Directions: Classify the vocabulary terms from Chapter 18 by listing each term in one of the categories below. On the lines below each box, write a sentence summarizing the terms in that category are related.

The United States

Countries Other than the United States

Both the United States and Other Countries

Notes for Home: Your child learned about important events in the first half of the 1900s. Home Activity: With your child, develop a one-minute oral summary of the first half of the twentieth century. Encourage your child to use as many of the vocabulary terms as possible in the summary.

Also on Teacher Resources CD-ROM.

Chapter Planning Guide

Chapter 19 • Into the Twenty-first Century

Locating Time and Place pp. 634–635

Lesson Titles	Pacing	Main Ideas
Lesson 1 **A Dangerous World** pp. 636–641	2 days	• The Cold War was a worldwide struggle between the United States and the Soviet Union.
Lesson 2 **Struggle for Equal Rights** pp. 642–648 **Biography: Martin Luther King, Jr.** p. 645 **Biography: Dolores Huerta** p. 649	2 days	• In the 1950s and 1960s, African Americans, women and other groups struggled to gain civil rights and equal opportunities. • The values Martin Luther King, Jr., developed early in his life led to his lifelong leadership role in nonviolen efforts for equal rights. • Based on prejudice she experienced as a young Mexic American, Dolores Huerta helped to create the first union dedicated to protecting the rights of farm worker
Lesson 3 **The Cold War Continues** pp. 650–655 **Map and Globe Skills:** **Understand Map Projections** pp. 656–657	2 days	• The United States continued to oppose the spread o communism and Soviet power in the 1960s and 1970 • Map projections attempt to show Earth's round surfac on a flat page, which causes some degree of distortio
Lesson 4 **Looking Toward the Future** pp. 658–667 ⭐ **Citizen Heroes:** ⬤Courage⬤ **Racing to the Rescue** pp. 668–669	2 days	• The Cold War finally ended in the late 1980s, leaving the United States as the world's only superpower. • Benjamin Suarez and other firefighters rescued thousands of people before being killed in the collapse of the World Trade Center towers.

✓ **Chapter 19 Review**
pp. 670–671

◀ **Martin Luther King, Jr., was awarded the Nobel Peace Prize in 1964.**

✓ = Assessment Options

In 1957 the Soviet Union launched *Sputnik I*, the first artificial satellite to orbit Earth. ▶

Vocabulary	Resources	Meeting Individual Needs
United Nations communism Cold War Iron Curtain Korean War Cuban Missile Crisis arms race	• Workbook, p. 148 • Transparency 6 • Every Student Learns Guide, pp. 262–265 • Quick Study, pp. 132–133	• ESL Support, TE p. 638 • Leveled Practice, TE p. 641
civil rights	• Workbook, p. 149 • Transparency 20 • Every Student Learns Guide, pp. 266–269 • Quick Study, pp. 134–135	• ESL Support, TE p. 644 • Leveled Practice, TE p. 646
space race Vietnam War arms control Watergate Scandal map projection	• Workbook, p. 150 • Transparency 6 • Every Student Learns Guide, pp. 270–273 • Quick Study, pp. 136–137 • Workbook, p. 151	• ESL Support, TE p. 653 • Critical Thinking, TE p. 654
Persian Gulf War Internet	• Workbook, p. 152 • Transparency 1 • Every Student Learns Guide, pp. 274–277 • Quick Study, pp. 138–139	• ESL Support, TE p. 660 • Leveled Practice, TE p. 666 • Learning Styles, TE p. 667
	✓ Chapter 19 Content Test, Assessment Book, pp. 109–110 ✓ Chapter 19 Skills Test, Assessment Book, pp. 111–112	✓ Chapter 19 Performance Assessment, TE p. 670

Providing More Depth

Additional Resources

- Vocabulary Workbook and Cards
- Social Studies Plus! pp. 216–221
- Daily Activity Bank
- Big Book Atlas
- Student Atlas
- Outline Maps
- Desk Maps

 Technology

- AudioText
- MindPoint® Quiz Show CD-ROM
- ExamView® Test Bank CD-ROM
- Teacher Resources CD-ROM
- Map Resources CD-ROM
- SFSuccessNet: iText (Pupil Edition online), iTE (Teacher's Edition online), Online Planner
- **www.sfsocialstudies.com** (Biographies, news, references, maps, and activities)

 To establish guidelines for your students' safe and responsible use of the Internet, use the Scott Foresman Internet Guide.

Additional Internet Links

To find out more about:
- The United Nations, visit **www.un.org**
- The Vietnam Veterans Memorial, visit **www.nps.gov**
- The International Space Station, visit **www.spaceflight.nasa.gov**

Key Internet Search Terms
- Cold War
- Apollo Missions
- Sandra Day O'Connor
- Colin Powell

Workbook Support

 Use the following Workbook pages to support content and skills development as you teach Chapter 19. You can also view and print Workbook pages from the Teacher Resources CD-ROM.

Workbook, p. 147

Vocabulary Preview

Use with Chapter 19.

Directions: Circle the term that best matches the definition or description.

1. Cold War   (arms control)
   A deal between the United States and the Soviet Union to limit the production of weapons

2. (United Nations)   civil rights
   An organization formed in 1945 consisting of 50 nations dedicated to finding peaceful solutions to international problems

3. (Cold War)   communism
   The long, bitter struggle between the United States and the Soviet Union

4. (Internet)   Iron Curtain
   A worldwide network of computers developed in the 1960s as a communication system that would continue working even after a nuclear attack

5. Vietnam War   (Persian Gulf War)
   War that began in 1990 when Iraq invaded its neighbor Kuwait, hoping to get Kuwait's rich oil supply

6. (civil rights)   legal rights
   The rights guaranteed to all citizens by the U.S. Constitution

7. (communism)   Iron Curtain
   A political and economic system in which the government owns all the businesses and land, and individuals have little personal freedom

8. space race   (arms race)
   The race between the United States and the Soviet Union to build more powerful weapons

9. (Korean War)   Persian Gulf War
   War that began in 1950 when communist North Korean forces invaded South Korea

10. (Iron Curtain)   Cuban Missile Crisis
    The line dividing the continent of Europe into communist and noncommunist countries

11. Cold War   (Vietnam War)
    War that began when communist North Vietnam attacked South Vietnam in an effort to unify all of Vietnam under communist rule

12. (Watergate Scandal)   Internet
    Scandal that forced President Richard Nixon to resign from office in 1974

Notes for Home: Your child learned about U.S. conflicts and compromises in the years after World War II.
Home Activity: With your child, write each vocabulary term on an index card and each definition on a separate card. Shuffle the cards and turn them all face down. Then have your child turn cards over one at a time in an attempt to match each term with its definition. Be sure to turn the unmatched cards face down again.

Use with Pupil Edition, p. 634

Workbook, p. 148

Lesson 1: A Dangerous World

Use with Pages 636–641.

Directions: Complete each sentence with information from Lesson 1. Write the answer on the line provided. You may use your textbook.

1. The **United Nations** is an organization formed in 1945 that promised that its 50 member nations would work to find peaceful solutions to international problems.

2. **The United States** and **the Soviet Union** were the world's two superpowers after World War II.

3. In 1945 the Soviet Union had a **communist** government.

4. The United States and the Soviet Union had different views on communism, which resulted in the **Cold War**.

5. At the end of World War II, the nations in **Eastern Europe** were under Soviet control and established communist governments loyal to the Soviet Union.

6. The **Iron Curtain** divided the continent of Europe into communist and noncommunist countries.

7. The **Marshall Plan** was a program launched by U.S. President Harry S. Truman to help the nations of Western Europe recover from World War II.

8. The post-World War II military alliance formed by the United States and the nations of Western Europe was called the **North Atlantic Treaty Organization**.

9. Through the Korean War, the United States was able to keep communism from spreading into **South Korea**.

10. In 1959, under leader Fidel Castro, Cuba became the first communist nation in the **Western** Hemisphere.

11. In 1962 the United States took action to keep the Soviets from setting up nuclear missiles in Cuba. This was called the **Cuban Missile Crisis**.

12. The **hydrogen bomb**, developed by the United States and the Soviet Union, is 1,000 times more powerful than the atomic bomb used in Hiroshima.

Notes for Home: Your child learned about the United States' determination to keep communism from spreading.
Home Activity: With your child, discuss why it might be important to keep communism from spreading in other parts of the world. Ask your child what causes he or she thinks might justify getting involved in a war.

Use with Pupil Edition, p. 641

Workbook, p. 149

Lesson 2: Struggle for Equal Rights

Use with Pages 642–648.

Directions: Match each term in the box to its description. Write the answer on the line provided.

Harry S. Truman	Rosa Parks	Sandra Day O'Connor
separate but equal	Martin Luther King, Jr.	NOW
Thurgood Marshall	Civil Rights Act of 1964	Shirley Chisholm
civil rights	Malcolm X	Dolores Huerta

1. **civil rights** — The rights that are guaranteed to all citizens by the Constitution

2. **Thurgood Marshall** — Tried to convince the Supreme Court to declare that segregation is illegal under the Constitution

3. **Rosa Parks** — Was the inspiration for the Montgomery bus boycott

4. **Malcolm X** — Civil rights leader who urged African Americans to rely on themselves to bring change

5. **Harry S. Truman** — Ordered an end to segregation in the military in 1948

6. **separate but equal** — Supreme Court language that allowed segregated public services and schools for African Americans

7. **NOW** — Women's rights organization formed in 1966 to fight for fair pay and equal opportunities for women

8. **Shirley Chisholm** — First African American woman elected to Congress

9. **Dolores Huerta** — Helped create a union to improve the lives of migrant farm workers

10. **Civil Rights Act of 1964** — Law banning segregation in all public places in the United States

11. **Sandra Day O'Connor** — In 1981 became the first woman named to the Supreme Court

12. **Martin Luther King, Jr.** — Organized a march in Washington, D.C., in August 1963, calling for an end to prejudice

Notes for Home: Your child learned about women's and African Americans' struggles for equal rights.
Home Activity: Discuss with your child how he or she likes to be treated when playing with other children. Ask him or her to explain the idea of fairness and then work together to brainstorm examples of fair and unfair treatment.

Use with Pupil Edition, p. 648

Workbook, p. 150

Lesson 3: The Cold War Continues

Use with Pages 650–655.

Directions: Write the letter of the effect on the line beside each cause. You may use your textbook.

	Cause		Effect
b	1. Soviets launch Sputnik.	a.	Vietnam is united under communist rule.
g	2. Soviets send the first man to orbit Earth.	b.	U.S. leaders fear that the Soviets will use their new knowledge about space exploration to attack the United States.
k	3. Vietnam gains independence from France.	c.	Each side agrees to limit nuclear weapons, and tensions are eased.
d	4. North Vietnam tries to unite all of Vietnam under communist rule.	d.	South Vietnam resists communism and the Vietnam War begins.
h	5. U.S. armed forces go to Vietnam.	e.	President Jimmy Carter objects to the Soviets' attempt to expand their power and refuses to send U.S. athletes to the 1980 Olympics in Moscow.
a	6. In April 1975, South Vietnam surrenders to North Vietnam.		
i	7. U.S. President Nixon tries to change the Cold War relationship between the United States and China.	f.	Nixon becomes the only President to resign from office.
c	8. Nixon and Soviet leaders sign an arms control agreement.	g.	In an effort to win the space race, the U.S. works toward being the first country to send a person to the moon.
f	9. Nixon is involved in the Watergate scandal.	h.	Americans are divided on the issue of U.S. involvement in the Vietnam War.
j	10. U.S. President Jimmy Carter tries to bring peace to Israel and Egypt.	i.	Nixon is successful in trying to improve relations and, in 1972, becomes the first U.S. President to visit China.
e	11. Cold War tensions increase when Soviet troops invade Afghanistan in December 1979.	j.	Leaders of Israel and Egypt visit the United States and sign a peace treaty in March 1979.
		k.	Vietnam is split into North Vietnam and South Korea.

Notes for Home: Your child learned about Cold War tensions between the United States and the Soviet Union.
Home Activity: With your child, discuss the positive and negative effects of the Cold War on the United States and the world. Ask your child how the space race and the arms race might have had different results if the United States and the Soviet Union had worked together rather than against each other.

Use with Pupil Edition, p. 655

Workbook Support

Workbook, p. 151

Understand Map Projections
Use With Pages 656-657.

A map projection is a way to show the round Earth on a flat surface. Because Earth is a sphere, all map projections have errors in size, shape, distance, or direction.

Directions: Use the maps on this page to answer the questions below. Use a separate sheet of paper if you need more space.

Map A

Map B

Projection: **Mercator**

Projection: **equal-area**

1. Of the two maps shown here, which is the Mercator projection? Which is an equal-area projection? Label the maps accordingly. **Map A: Mercator projection map; Map B: equal-area projection map**

2. What types of distortion are found on a Mercator projection? **The shapes and sizes of the land are more accurate near the equator and more distorted farther away from the equator.**

3. Compare the continent of South America on the two map projections above. What difference, if any, do you see? **On the equal-area projection, South America appears larger and closer to its actual size.**

4. Which map projection should you use to accurately compare the sizes of Greenland and South America? Why? **The equal-area projection; because the size and shape of Greenland would be less distorted**

 Notes for Home: Your child learned about map projections and their distortions.
Home Activity: Using the maps on this page or in the textbook, work with your child to compare the distances between lines of latitude on each map. Explain that uneven distances are a clue to one type of map distortion.

Use with Pupil Edition, p. 657

Workbook, p. 152

Lesson 4: Looking Toward the Future
Use with Pages 658-665.

Directions: Sequence the events in the order in which they occurred. Number them from 1 (earliest) to 10 (most recent). You may use your textbook.

4 The Berlin Wall is destroyed, and several communist governments in Eastern Europe are replaced with elected governments.

1 Newly elected U.S. President Ronald Reagan believes the United States should strengthen its military to block Soviet efforts to expand communism around the world.

7 The United States leads a group of more than 20 nations in Operation Desert Storm, an attack on Iraqi forces in Kuwait.

10 The 2000 U.S. presidential election is one of the closest races in history. George W. Bush wins the electoral college vote, and Al Gore wins the popular vote. George W. Bush is declared President.

3 The Soviet Union and the United States sign an arms control agreement in which both countries agree to destroy some of their nuclear weapons.

5 The Soviet Union breaks up into 15 independent republics, and Gorbachev announces that the Cold War is over.

9 During his second term in office, President Clinton faces a scandal and is impeached.

6 The Middle Eastern nation of Iraq invades Kuwait in an effort to take control of Kuwait's rich oil supply. This begins the Persian Gulf War. The United States must decide whether to help end the conflict.

2 Soviet leader Mikhail Gorbachev begins reforming the country by allowing people more political and economic freedom.

8 U.S. President William Clinton appoints Madeleine Albright as secretary of state. She is the first woman to hold this position.

Directions: In recent decades, many changes have occurred in politics, science, technology, and culture. What is one change that you think will occur in the next 50 years? Why?

Possible answers: Advances in the Internet, virtual reality, other forms of technology, or in other arenas.

 Notes for Home: Your child learned about changes in politics and technology that will affect the future.
Home Activity: With your child, discuss inventions and other changes that might take place during this century. Ask whether your child thinks each potential change will have positive or negative effects on the world and why.

Use with Pupil Edition, p. 665

Workbook, p. 153

Vocabulary Review
Use with Chapter 19.

Directions: Use the vocabulary words from Chapter 19 to complete the crossword puzzle.

Across

4. Iraq invaded Kuwait, sparking the _____ _____ War.

7. Fifty nations dedicated to finding peaceful solutions to international problems

9. A political and economic system in which the government owns all the businesses and land

12. The line dividing the continent of Europe into communist and noncommunist countries

13. The war that started when North Vietnam tried to unify all of Vietnam under communist rule

14. Worldwide network of computers

Down

1. The _____ War started when the North Koreans invaded South Korea.

2. The long, bitter struggle between the United States and the Soviet Union was called the _____ War.

3. The contest to be first to explore outer space was known as the _____ race.

5. The _____ _____ Crisis happened when the Soviets sent nuclear weapons to Cuba.

6. The U.S. Constitution guarantees these to all citizens.

8. The U.S. and Soviet Union's competition to build more weapons was known as the _____ race.

10. Because of an arms _____ agreement, the United States and the Soviet Union limited the number of weapons they produced.

11. President Nixon resigned for his involvement in the _____ scandal.

 Notes for Home: Your child learned about events in the second half of the 1900s.
Home Activity: With your child, play a game of "Name That War," in which you supply details and your child supplies the name of the specific war from this chapter.

Use with Pupil Edition, p. 671

Workbook, p. 154

UNIT 9 Project   Then and Now

DISCOVERY SCHOOL

Directions: In a group, plan a documentary about historic events and advances in technology during a decade from the 1900s.

1. We chose the decade 19___–19___.

2. The (✔) shows which topics we researched:

___ historic events   ___ technological advances   ___ transportation   ___ entertainment
___ clothing   ___ home life   ___ education   ___ occupations
___ other: _____

3. The following people from the decade will speak for the documentary:

Name: _____   Role: _____
Name: _____   Role: _____
Name: _____   Role: _____

4. My role in the documentary is _____

5. Questions about living in the 19___s:

_____
_____
_____

6. Answers to questions about the 19___s:

_____
_____
_____

Have group members confirm that answers to the questions they write are supported by the research they conducted.

✔ Checklist for Students

___ The group chose a decade from the 1900s.
___ The group researched topics about living in the 19__s.
___ Roles were assigned for the documentary.
___ The group wrote questions and answers about the decade.
___ The group presented its documentary to the class.

 **Notes for Home:** Your child participated in a group presentation on a decade from the 1900s.
Home Activity: Discuss with your child your favorite decade of the twentieth century. Describe the clothing, home life, transportation, and important events of this time period.

Use with Pupil Edition, p. 674

Assessment Support

Use these Assessment Book pages and the ExamView® Test Bank CD-ROM to assess content and skills in Chapter 19. You can also view and print Assessment Book pages from the Teacher Resources CD-ROM.

Assessment Book, p. 109

Chapter 19 Test

Part 1: Content Test

Directions: Fill in the circle next to the correct answer.

Lesson Objective (1:1)

1. Which two superpowers were involved in the Cold War?
   - ● the United States and the Soviet Union
   - Ⓑ Britain and the Soviet Union
   - Ⓒ France and Germany
   - Ⓓ Japan and the Soviet Union

Lesson Objective (1:1)

2. Which of the following symbolized the early days of the Cold War?
   - Ⓐ communism
   - ● the Iron Curtain
   - Ⓒ democracy
   - Ⓓ nuclear attacks

Lesson Objective (1:2)

3. Why did the United States enter the Korean War?
   - ● It did not want another country to fall to the communists.
   - Ⓑ It did not want another country to be split.
   - Ⓒ It wanted to attack North Korea.
   - Ⓓ It wanted to sell more weapons to its allies.

Lesson Objective (1:3)

4. Why did the United States want the Soviet Union to remove its nuclear weapons from Cuba?
   - Ⓐ It wanted to protect Cuba from communism.
   - ● Cuba is close to the United States border.
   - Ⓒ It was protecting nearby countries in Central America.
   - Ⓓ The United States did not have any missiles of its own.

Lesson Objective (1:4)

5. What was one cause of the arms race between the United States and the Soviet Union?
   - Ⓐ to provide jobs
   - Ⓑ the H-bomb
   - ● a fear of attack
   - Ⓓ a new U.S. President

Lesson Objective (2:1)

6. What was the result of the Supreme Court's ruling that segregation in public schools was illegal?
   - Ⓐ All children could not attend the same schools.
   - ● All children could attend the same schools.
   - Ⓒ Public schools were separated by race.
   - Ⓓ Only white students could attend public schools.

Lesson Objective (2:2)

7. Whose actions started the Montgomery bus boycott?
   - Ⓐ Sandra Day O'Connor
   - Ⓑ Martin Luther King, Jr.
   - Ⓒ John F. Kennedy
   - ● Rosa Parks

Lesson Objective (2:3)

8. Who planned a nonviolent march in Washington, D.C., to help convince Congress to pass the civil rights bill?
   - Ⓐ Sandra Day O'Connor
   - Ⓑ Thurgood Marshall
   - ● Martin Luther King, Jr.
   - Ⓓ John F. Kennedy

Use with Pupil Edition, p. 668

Assessment Book, p. 110

Lesson Objective (2:4)

9. Which of the following was most important to women in the 1950s?
   - Ⓐ equal education opportunities
   - Ⓑ equal credit opportunities
   - Ⓒ equal health-care opportunities
   - ● equal employment opportunities

Lesson Objective (3:1)

10. Which of the following BEST describes the Soviet satellite *Sputnik*?
    - ● the first satellite launched into space
    - Ⓑ the first satellite to reach the moon
    - Ⓒ the first satellite to carry a person into space
    - Ⓓ the first satellite to carry a laboratory rat into space

Lesson Objective (3:2)

11. Which of the following caused the Vietnam War?
    - Ⓐ Japan attacked South Vietnam.
    - ● North Vietnam wanted all of Vietnam to be communist.
    - Ⓒ South Vietnam wanted to remain communist.
    - Ⓓ The Soviet Union attacked South Vietnam.

Lesson Objective (3:3)

12. What was one result of President Nixon's trip to the Soviet Union?
    - Ⓐ Watergate
    - Ⓑ improved relations with China
    - Ⓒ Vietnam Veterans Memorial
    - ● arms control agreement

Lesson Objective (3:4)

13. Which of the following BEST describes Cold War tensions in the early 1980s?
    - Ⓐ Tensions were gone.
    - Ⓑ Tensions were about the same.
    - Ⓒ Tensions were decreasing.
    - ● Tensions were on the rise.

Lesson Objective (4:1)

14. How did Soviet leader Mikhail Gorbachev improve U.S.-Soviet relations during the 1980s?
    - Ⓐ He restricted the Soviet people more than ever before.
    - Ⓑ He urged the Soviet people to strengthen their communist ideals.
    - ● He gave the Soviet people more political and economic freedom.
    - Ⓓ He worked hard to build more nuclear weapons.

Lesson Objective (4:2)

15. Which of the following symbolizes the end of the Cold War?
    - Ⓐ U.S. President Bush worked toward easing tensions.
    - ● The Soviet Union broke up into 15 independent republics.
    - Ⓒ People in Eastern Europe were gaining more freedom.
    - Ⓓ The Berlin Wall was built.

Lesson Objective (4:3)

16. In which war was the United States involved in the early 1990s?
    - Ⓐ Korean War
    - Ⓑ Iraqi War
    - ● Persian Gulf War
    - Ⓓ Vietnam War

Lesson Objective (4:4)

17. Which of the following is a logical prediction about the future of the United States?
    - ● The United States will make new advances in Internet technology.
    - Ⓑ The United States will take over all former Soviet republics.
    - Ⓒ The United States will become a communist nation.
    - Ⓓ The United States will rebuild the Berlin Wall.

Use with Pupil Edition, p. 668

Assessment Book, p. 111

Part 2: Skills Test

Directions: Use complete sentences to answer questions 1–5. Use a separate sheet of paper if you need more space.

1. After World War II, Joseph Stalin insisted that the nations of Eastern Europe establish communist governments. How did the rest of the world react to this action? **Summarize**

   Possible answer: The United States and other nations set up programs such as the Marshall Plan and the North Atlantic Treaty Organization to keep Western Europe strong and to keep communism from spreading.

2. During the Cold War, why did the United States continue to develop nuclear weapons if it hoped to never use them? **Draw Conclusions**

   Possible answer: The United States believed that if it had more powerful weapons than the Soviets, the Soviets would be afraid to attack.

3. What did the Supreme Court mean by "separate but equal"? Why did many people feel this idea was faulty? **Main Idea and Details**

   States could legally provide segregated services for blacks and whites, as long as the services were of equal quality; Because many states spent much less money on teachers, schools, and books for African American children, segregated schools almost never were of equal quality.

4. Why was the 1969 voyage of the *Apollo 11* so important to the United States? **Draw Conclusions**

   Possible answer: The United States had fallen behind the Soviet Union in the space race and feared that the Soviets would use this advantage to attack the United States. When the U.S. spaceship *Apollo 11* put the first person on the moon, the United States took the lead in the race.

Use with Pupil Edition, p. 668

Assessment Book, p. 112

5. What do you think might have happened if the United States had not decided to try to keep communism from spreading through Europe? **Hypothesize**

   Possible answer: Nations in Western Europe and elsewhere might have established communist governments and eventually become powerful enough to force the United States to become communist.

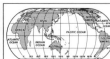

Map A

Map B

6. Use the map to answer the questions. **Understand Map Projections**
   a. What type of map is Map A? What type is Map B?

   Map A: an equal-area projection map; Map B: a Mercator map

   b. How do Map A and Map B differ?

   On Map A, the lines of longitude curve. On Map B, the lines are straight.

   c. Which map would be better for comparing the actual sizes of Greenland and Africa?

   Map A

Use with Pupil Edition, p. 668

Assessment Support

Assessment Book, p. 113

Unit 9 Test

Part 1: Content Test

Directions: Fill in the circle next to the correct answer.

Lesson Objective (18–1:1)

1. What was the name for writers and journalists who wanted reforms?
   - Ⓐ scouts
   - ● muckrakers
   - Ⓒ scourers
   - Ⓓ muskrats

Lesson Objective (18–1:3)

2. Which of the following was the main reason for building the Panama Canal?
   - Ⓐ Panama wanted its independence from Colombia.
   - Ⓑ The United States got rid of disease-carrying mosquitoes.
   - ● The canal made the trip between the Atlantic and Pacific Oceans quicker.
   - Ⓓ The United States controlled the Isthmus of Panama.

Lesson Objective (18–2:2)

3. With the United States help, which side won World War I?
   - Ⓐ Central Powers
   - Ⓑ Alliance of Nations
   - ● Allied Powers
   - Ⓓ League of Nations

Lesson Objective (18–2:3)

4. When did women get the right to vote?
   - Ⓐ during World War I
   - Ⓑ during World War II
   - ● in 1920, with the ratification of the Nineteenth Amendment
   - Ⓓ in 1918, with the signing of the Treaty of Versailles

Lesson Objective (18–2:4)

5. Which of the following BEST describes the Great Migration?
   - ● Many African Americans moved to the North for better jobs.
   - Ⓑ Many Americans left their useless lands and moved west.
   - Ⓒ Many Canadians moved to the northern United States.
   - Ⓓ Many Europeans moved to the United States for better jobs.

Lesson Objective (18–3:2)

6. Which of the following did NOT have a major effect on culture in the 1920s?
   - Ⓐ radio
   - ● television
   - Ⓒ movies
   - Ⓓ jazz

Lesson Objective (18–3:4)

7. Which of the following does NOT describe life during the Great Depression?
   - Ⓐ Many farmers lost their farms.
   - Ⓑ Many people were homeless.
   - Ⓒ Many people were unemployed.
   - ● Many people bought cars.

Lesson Objective (18–4:2)

8. How did the United States prepare to fight in World War II?
   - Ⓐ Many jobs were eliminated.
   - Ⓑ The government reduced its spending.
   - ● U.S. factories produced planes, tanks, and uniforms.
   - Ⓓ It cleared areas on the East coast to serve as battlefields.

Use with Pupil Edition, p. 672

Assessment Book, p. 114

Lesson Objective (18–4:3)

9. What weapon stopped the fighting in Asia and ended World War II?
   - Ⓐ modern grenades, which gave U.S. soldiers an advantage
   - Ⓑ airplanes, which allowed U.S. air raids on Japan
   - Ⓒ modern tanks, which fired on Japanese soldiers
   - ● the atomic bomb, which destroyed Hiroshima and Nagasaki

Lesson Objective (19–1:1)

10. Which superpower struggled against the Soviet Union in the Cold War?
    - Ⓐ Great Britain
    - ● United States
    - Ⓒ Germany
    - Ⓓ Japan

Lesson Objective (19–1:4)

11. Why did the United States and the Soviet Union have an arms race?
    - Ⓐ Together, they wanted to be the strongest nations in the world.
    - Ⓑ They wanted to join forces against other nations.
    - Ⓒ They wanted superior weapons to fight other nations.
    - ● They wanted to be prepared for war against each other.

Lesson Objective (19–2:1)

12. What did Thurgood Marshall convince the Supreme Court to do in 1954?
    - Ⓐ rule that women deserved the same rights as men
    - Ⓑ rule that all men deserved to be treated equally
    - ● rule that segregation in public schools was illegal
    - Ⓓ rule that segregation was legal only in public places

Lesson Objective (19–2:4)

13. Which of the following opportunities was made possible by the women's rights movement?
    - Ⓐ Linda Brown was able to attend school near her home.
    - Ⓑ Women worked in factories during the war.
    - Ⓒ Women were not allowed to vote.
    - ● Sandra Day O'Connor was named to the Supreme Court.

Lesson Objective (19–3:1)

14. Why is Neil Armstrong an important figure in the space race?
    - Ⓐ He was the first person to be launched into space.
    - Ⓑ He was the first person to orbit Earth.
    - ● He was the first person to walk on the moon.
    - Ⓓ He was the first American to fly in a Soviet rocket.

Lesson Objective (19–3:2)

15. How did the Vietnam War affect American society?
    - Ⓐ Most Americans wanted U.S. soldiers to fight in Vietnam.
    - ● Americans were divided on the issue of fighting in Vietnam.
    - Ⓒ Most Americans did not want U.S. soldiers to fight in Vietnam.
    - Ⓓ Most Americans wanted the United States to take over Vietnam.

Lesson Objective (19–4:2)

16. What was the result of the Soviet Union splitting into independent republics?
    - ● The Cold War ended.
    - Ⓑ Democracy became weaker.
    - Ⓒ Communism became stronger.
    - Ⓓ Cold War tensions increased.

Use with Pupil Edition, p. 672

Assessment Book, p. 115

Part 2: Skills Test

Directions: Use complete sentences to answer questions 1–6. Use a separate sheet of paper if you need more space.

1. What was the Great Migration, and why did it take place? **Main Idea and Details**

   Between 1915 and the 1940s, about 5 million African Americans moved from the South to the North; The North offered higher-paying jobs than the South. African Americans moved north hoping to find a better way of life and less discrimination.

2. Compare the causes of the Great Depression and the Dust Bowl. **Compare and Contrast**

   Alike: many people lost their jobs and everything they had; Different: the Great Depression was caused by the stock market crash in 1929, which led businesses to close and many people to lose their jobs and their life's savings. The Dust Bowl was caused by a severe drought that turned the soil to dust, which farmers could not use for growing crops.

3. In the years before World War II, why did some dictators believe they could take over Europe and other parts of the world? **Draw Conclusions**

   The economy was so poor, many Europeans turned to dictators who promised to make their troubles disappear. These dictators then joined forces and attempted to take over Europe and other parts of the world.

4. What series of events led to the Cuban Missile Crisis? What was its outcome? **Sequence**

   Soviets began setting up nuclear missiles in Cuba, President John F. Kennedy insisted that the Soviets remove the missiles, and Kennedy threatened to block Soviet weapons ships; the Soviets agreed to remove the weapons, and the crisis ended.

Use with Pupil Edition, p. 672

Assessment Book, p. 116

5. What events changed relations between the United States and the Soviet Union during the 1980s? **Summarize**

   Gorbachev gave the people more political and economic freedom. Then he and U.S. President Ronald Reagan signed an arms control agreement. Later, several Eastern European countries overthrew their communist governments.

Map A

Map B

6. Use the map to answer the questions. **Understand Map Projections**

   a. Which map is an equal-area projection map?

   Map A

   b. How are Map A and Map B similar? Different?

   Both maps show the continents, the oceans, and the lines of longitude and latitude. On Map A, the lines of longitude are curved, not straight as in Map B.

   c. Which map would you use to compare the actual distances between two continents?

   Map A

Use with Pupil Edition, p. 672

Into the Twenty-first Century

Chapter 19 Outline

Resources

- Workbook, p. 147: Vocabulary Preview
- Vocabulary Cards
- Social Studies Plus!

1945, San Francisco, California: Lesson 1

Tell students that this picture shows the meeting that formed the United Nations. Ask why nations of the world might meet together. (To solve problems and to promote world peace)

1963, Washington, D.C.: Lesson 2

Explain that this picture shows a civil rights march. Ask students what kinds of rights the marchers might be seeking. (Equal opportunities for jobs, education, and voting)

1969, South Vietnam: Lesson 3

Ask students to describe the setting of this scene from the Vietnam War. Have them look at a map and identify the location of Vietnam. (It is in Southeast Asia on the China Sea.)

1989, Berlin, Germany: Lesson 4

Ask students to describe what is happening in the picture. Have them describe what pulling down a wall symbolizes. (It symbolizes being ready to communicate and work with others.)

CHAPTER
19

Into the Twenty-first Century

1945

San Francisco, California
The United Nations is formed.

Lesson 1

1963

Washington, D.C.
Martin Luther King, Jr., leads a large civil rights march.

Lesson 2

1969

South Vietnam
Thousands of American soldiers fight in the Vietnam War.

Lesson 3

1989

Berlin, Germany
The Berlin Wall is pulled down.

Lesson 4

634

Practice and Extend

Vocabulary Preview

- Use Workbook p. 147 to help students preview the vocabulary words in this chapter.
- Use Vocabulary Cards to preview key concept words in this chapter.

 Also on Teacher Resources CD-ROM.

Workbook, p. 147

Vocabulary Preview

Directions: Circle the term that best matches the definition or description.

1. Cold War .... arms control
   A deal between the United States and the Soviet Union to limit the production of weapons
2. United Nations .... civil rights
   An organization formed in 1945 consisting of 50 nations dedicated to finding peaceful solutions to international problems
3. Cold War .... communism
   The long, bitter struggle between United States and the Soviet Union
4. Internet .... Iron Curtain
   A worldwide network of computers developed in the 1900s as a communication system that would continue working even after a nuclear attack
5. Vietnam War .... Persian Gulf War
   War that began in 1990 when Iraq invaded its neighbor Kuwait, hoping to get Kuwait's rich oil supply
6. civil rights .... legal rights
   The rights guaranteed to all citizens by the U.S. Constitution
7. communism .... Iron Curtain
   A political and economic system in which the government owns all the businesses and land, and individuals have little personal freedom
8. space race .... arms race
   The race between the United States and the Soviet Union to build more powerful weapons
9. Korean War .... Persian Gulf War
   War that began in 1950 when communist North Korean forces invaded South Korea
10. Iron Curtain .... Cuban Missile Crisis
    The line dividing the continent of Europe into communist and noncommunist countries
11. Cold War .... Vietnam War
    War that began when communist North Vietnam attacked South Vietnam in an effort to unify all of Vietnam under communist rule
12. Watergate Scandal .... Internet
    Scandal that forced President Richard Nixon to resign from office in 1974

    Notes for Home: Your child learned about U.S. conflicts and compromises in the years after World War II.
    Home Activity: With your child, write each vocabulary term on an index card and each definition on a separate card. Shuffle the cards and turn them all face down. Then have your child turn cards over one at a time in an attempt to match each term with its definition. Have her or him turn the unmatched cards face down again.

Locating Time and Place

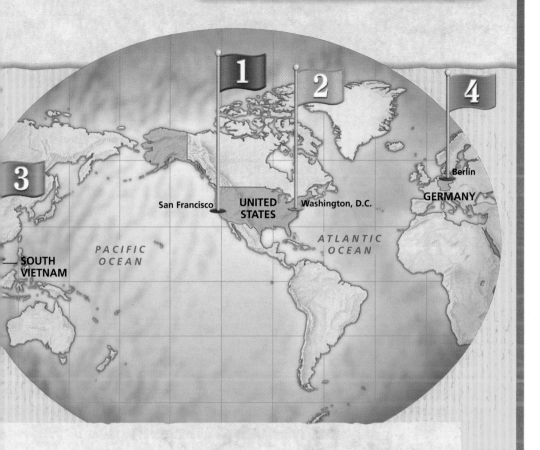

Why We Remember

The late 1900s were a time of remarkable changes both in the United States and around the world. By the time the 20th century ended, most Americans were treated more fairly than ever before. Some countries, like the Soviet Union, were broken up into smaller countries. The United States and the world faced new challenges, many of which continue today. But they are working to settle problems peacefully and use new technology and medical discoveries to improve conditions for all people.

635

- Have students examine the pictures shown on p. 634 for Lessons 1, 2, 3, and 4.

- Remind students that each picture is coded with a number and a color to link it to a place on the map on p. 635.

Why We Remember

Have students read the "Why We Remember" paragraph on p. 635, and ask them why events in this chapter might be important to them. Have them consider how science, technology, politics, and family life have changed since their parents and grandparents were children.

WEB SITE
Technology

You can learn more about San Francisco, California; Washington, D.C.; South Vietnam; and Berlin, Germany, by clicking on *Atlas* at **www.sfsocialstudies.com.**

SOCIAL STUDIES STRAND
Geography

Mental Mapping Have students draw an outline map of the seven continents from memory. Have students work together in small groups with their maps to choose and label four countries that they think will be most important to the history of the twenty-first century. Then have each group share their choices and the reasons for their choices with the class.

A Dangerous World

Objectives

- Describe the beginning of the Cold War.
- Analyze the American decision to fight in the Korean War.
- Explain how Cold War conflicts led to the Cuban Missile Crisis.
- Evaluate the causes of the arms race.

Vocabulary

United Nations, p. 637;
communism, p. 637; **Cold War,** p. 637;
Iron Curtain, p. 638; **Korean War,** p. 639;
Cuban Missile Crisis, p. 640;
arms race, p. 641

Resources

- Workbook, p. 148
- Transparency 6, 61
- Every Student Learns Guide, pp. 262–265
- Quick Study, pp. 132–133

Quick Teaching Plan

If time is short, have students read *Focus on the Main Idea* and write at least three questions pertaining to that information.

- As students read independently, have them record relevant information under each of their questions.
- After reading, have students write several sentences answering each of their questions.

1 Introduce and Motivate

Preview Ask students what current issues cause them concern. Tell students they will learn more about the concerns of people in the mid-1900s as they read Lesson 1.

You Are There In the 1950s, people in the United States were worried about a possible nuclear attack from the Soviet Union. Ask students what it would be like to live underground with a few other people for several months.

LESSON 1

1945			1965
1945 The United Nations is formed	**1950** The Korean War begins		**1962** Cuban Missile Crisis

A Dangerous World

PREVIEW

Focus on the Main Idea
The Cold War was a worldwide struggle between the United States and the Soviet Union.

PLACES
North Korea
South Korea

PEOPLE
Harry S. Truman
Douglas MacArthur
Dwight D. Eisenhower
John F. Kennedy
Lyndon B. Johnson

VOCABULARY
United Nations
communism
Cold War
Iron Curtain
Korean War
Cuban Missile Crisis
arms race

▶ Signs like this marked public bomb shelters.

FALLOUT SHELTER

636

You Are There You are walking home from school on a spring day in 1954. You notice that your neighbor is digging in his backyard. Curious, you walk up and ask him what he is doing.

"Building a bomb shelter," he says.

"What for?" you ask.

"In case the Soviet Union attacks us with atomic bombs," he explains.

"You would hide in there?" you wonder.

"My whole family would," he says. "I am going to stock this underground shelter with enough food and water for months."

He goes back to his digging. You continue toward home. You have been hearing a lot about nuclear bombs lately. At school, your teacher showed the class how to duck under their desks in case of a nuclear attack. What is everyone so worried about? Is there really a chance that there will be a nuclear war?

Summarize As you read, pay attention to the key events that led to rising tensions between the United States and Soviet Union

---

Practice and Extend

READING SKILL
Summarize

In the Lesson Review, students complete a graphic organizer like the one below. You may want to provide students with a copy of Transparency 6 to complete as they read the lesson.

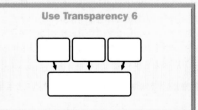

Use Transparency 6

VOCABULARY
Word Exercise

Related Word Study Write *Cold War* and *Iron Curtain* on the board and discuss their meanings. Explain that these names are examples of figurative language, which uses ideas and images that are suggested by words but not the actual meanings of the words. Have students read the definitions of these terms, then discuss what ideas and images these names borrow from the literal meanings of the words.

A New Kind of War

In April 1945, as World War II was coming to an end, representatives of 50 different nations met in San Francisco, California. They formed a new organization called the **United Nations,** or U.N. The U.N. members promised to work together to find peaceful solutions to international problems.

The United States and the Soviet Union both joined the United Nations. These were the world's two "superpowers," or most powerful nations on Earth. Besides being powerful, however, the United States and the Soviet Union had very little in common. A communist government controlled the Soviet Union. **Communism** is a political and economic system in which the government owns all the businesses and land. Individuals have little personal freedom under communism.

The Soviet leader, Joseph Stalin, wanted to help other communist governments come to power all over the world. In contrast, the United States supported elected governments and free enterprise. American leaders were committed to stopping the spread of communism. This commitment led to the Cold War. The **Cold War** was a long, bitter struggle between the United States and the Soviet Union, and their different ways of life. The Cold War was fought all over the world—sometimes with words and money, and sometimes with weapons.

Both the United States and the Soviet Union built thousands of atomic bombs during the Cold War. These bombs, also known as nuclear weapons, caused people all over the world to live in fear. In American schools, children were taught to get under their desks in case of a nuclear attack. And businesses began selling a new item—underground bomb shelters. For $5,000, families could buy the fanciest shelter. It came with a telephone and bathroom.

REVIEW What two nations struggled with each other in the Cold War? Why?

⮎ Summarize

▶ The United Nations flag *(above)* began flying in 1945. During the 1950s schools held "duck and cover" drills *(left)* and some families built backyard bomb shelters *(below).*

637

SOCIAL STUDIES
Economic Systems

The Free Enterprise System

- Mostly a market economy in which individuals and businesses make economic decisions.
- Individuals and privately owned businesses decide how to conserve resources and to use them to produce goods and services.
- Privately owned businesses control the economy.
- A good response to consumer needs and wants.

Communism

- Mainly a command economy in which government makes many economic decisions.
- Government decides how to conserve resources and to use them to produce goods and services.
- Government owns all resources, land, and businesses.
- A slow response to consumer needs and wants.

---

② Teach and Discuss

PAGE 637

A New Kind of War

🕐 *Quick Summary* The United States and the Soviet Union joined the United Nations, an organization dedicated to world peace, even though they were involved in the Cold War.

💲 SOCIAL STUDIES STRAND
Economics

Despite the fears of the Cold War, the post World War II era was a time of economic prosperity. The return of veterans and a general confidence in America's strength led to an economic boom that secured the role of the United States as a world superpower.

❶ Why do you think people around the world were interested in forming the United Nations in 1945? They had just suffered through World War II and did not want another major war to occur. **Cause and Effect**

❷ Compare and contrast the United States and the Soviet Union in 1945. Similarities: Both were superpowers. Differences: The United States supported elected governments and free enterprise; the Soviet Union had a communist government that controlled businesses and land. Individuals had little personal freedom. **Compare and Contrast**

❸ What was the cause of the Cold War? The Soviet Union supported communism throughout the world, while the United States was committed to stopping the spread of communism. **Cause and Effect**

❹ Why did the United States and the Soviet Union build thousands of atomic bombs during the Cold War? They feared that the Cold War would develop into an actual war, and they wanted to defend themselves. **Make Inferences**

✓ **REVIEW ANSWER** The United States and the Soviet Union; each nation supported a different way of life.
⮎ Summarize

The Iron Curtain Falls

 Quick Summary The Marshall Plan and NATO were formed in response to the "Iron Curtain" that divided Europe into communist and noncommunist countries.

MAP SKILL The Iron Curtain in Europe, 1945–1989

Have students examine the map's legend to note how communist and capitalist territories are designated.

5 **What was Germany's involvement in communism?** The country was divided: East Germany was communist and West Germany was capitalist. **Interpret Maps**

MAP SKILL Answer West Germany, Austria, Italy, and Greece

6 **Why were the United States and other nations alarmed about Stalin's actions?** The Soviet Union imposed communist governments on the nations of Eastern Europe and wanted to establish a communist hold on other nations. **Make Inferences**

Primary Source

Cited in *Grand Expectations: The United States, 1945–1974,* by James T. Patterson

7 **What term did Churchill use to describe the political division in Europe in 1946? Why do you think he used that phrase?** An iron curtain; Possible answer: Because iron is heavy, rigid, and stops communication **Analyze Primary Sources**

8 **Why did President Truman work to strengthen the nations of Western Europe?** To prevent communism from spreading to these countries **Make Inferences**

9 **What is NATO, and what is its purpose?** NATO, the North Atlantic Treaty Organization, is a military alliance between the United States and Western Europe; to protect the United States and the nations of Europe **Summarize**

✓ **REVIEW ANSWER** To help Western Europe recover from the damage caused by World War II **Main Idea and Details**

MAP SKILL The Iron Curtain in Europe, 1945–1989

Legend:
— "Iron Curtain"
☐ Communist nations
☐ Capitalist nations

► An Iron Curtain divided Eastern and Western Europe. President Truman (*right*) worked to help Western Europe recover from World War II.

MAP SKILL Place *Which four capitalist countries bordered the Iron Curtain?*

The Iron Curtain Falls

The Cold War began as World War II ended. When the war ended in 1945, Soviet troops had control of the nations of Eastern Europe. Stalin made sure that each country established a communist government that was loyal to the Soviet Union.

6 The Soviet actions alarmed leaders in the United States and other nations. Winston Churchill, who had led Great Britain during World War II, declared in 1946,

7 *"An iron curtain has descended [fallen] across the continent."*

Look at the map on this page and you will see what Churchill meant. The **Iron Curtain** was the line dividing the continent of Europe into communist and noncommunist countries. In response to the Soviet control of Eastern Europe, President **Harry S. Truman** worked to strengthen the nations of Western Europe.

Under a program called the Marshall Plan, the United States spent billions of dollars to help Western Europe recover from the damage caused by World War II. The United States also formed a military alliance with the nations of Western Europe. This alliance was called the North Atlantic Treaty Organization, or NATO.

REVIEW What was the goal of the Marshall Plan? **Main Idea and Details**

638

Practice and Extend

 **ACCESS CONTENT**
ESL Support

Analyze a Primary Source Help students understand the meaning of *Iron Curtain.* Explain that the Iron Curtain was figurative. Review the meanings of *communist* and *capitalist.*

Beginning Have students form a human "iron curtain." Ask a student to hold a sign labeled *Communist* and to stand on one side of the line. Have another student stand on the other side and hold a *Capitalist* sign.

Intermediate Have students say what the Iron Curtain represented. (It was a line. It divided Europe. Some countries were communist. Others were capitalist.)

Advanced Have students explain the Iron Curtain and how communist and capitalist countries differed.

For additional ESL support, use Every Student Learns Guide, pp. 262–265.

Cold War Conflicts

The Cold War turned violent in Korea in 1950. Following World War II, Korea had been divided into **North Korea** and **South Korea.** North Korea established a communist government with the support of the Soviet Union. On the night of June 25, North Korean forces invaded South Korea. They hoped to unify the country under a communist government.

The United Nations called for North Korean troops to return to North Korea. But the invasion continued. President Truman decided to send United States forces to protect South Korea. He did not want another country to fall under Soviet control. "There's no telling what they'll do, if we don't put up a fight right now," he said. The **Korean War** had begun.

In the Korean War, soldiers from 15 other countries in the United Nations joined American soldiers. Under the command of famous World War II General **Douglas MacArthur,** U.N. forces drove the North Koreans back. Then, in October, Chinese soldiers joined the North Koreans. China had become a communist nation in 1949. Fierce fighting continued for over two years, but neither side was able to take control of the country.

In 1952, **Dwight D. Eisenhower** was elected President. He worked to end the Korean War. The fighting ended in 1953, with Korea still divided into two nations. The United States had helped stop communist forces from taking over South Korea. This achievement had a price, however. Over 33,000 American soldiers died in the Korean War.

Cold War conflicts affected life in the United States as well. In 1950, Wisconsin Senator Joseph McCarthy shocked the nation when he claimed that there were communists working inside the United States government and military. Both the House of Representatives and the Senate formed committees to investigate communists in the United States. Many people were called before these committees, and asked questions about their political beliefs and their loyalty to the United States. Many who refused to answer questions were put in jail. Others lost their jobs, even when there was no evidence that they supported communism. **13**

REVIEW What events led to the beginning of the Korean War? *Sequence*

▶ **Dwight D. Eisenhower visited American troops in Korea in December 1952, soon after he won the presidential election.**

639

PAGE 639

Cold War Conflicts

Quick Summary In a continued effort to stop the spread of communism, the United States became involved in the Korean War.

10 **What was the cause of the Korean War?** North Korea invaded South Korea in an attempt to unify the two countries under a communist government. **Cause and Effect**

11 **How did the United Nations play a role in the Korean War?** They sided with South Korea in resisting aggression. Sixteen countries from the United Nations, led by the United States, sent troops to South Korea to protect them from Soviet control. **Summarize**

12 **How did the Korean War end?** It ended with Korea still divided into two nations. **Main Idea and Details**

13 **Why were some Americans alarmed about having communist supporters in the United States?** Some Americans may have been concerned about a communist takeover and the possible loss of personal freedom. **Analyze Information**

✓ **REVIEW ANSWER** North Korea established a communist government with the support of the Soviet Union. North Korean forces invaded South Korea with the goal of uniting the countries under one communist government. The United States and the United Nations decided to send troops to protect South Korea. **Sequence**

SOCIAL STUDIES
Background

Korean War

- After North Korean troops invaded South Korea, the UN met in an emergency session and decided to help South Korea.
- The Soviet delegate, who was protesting another decision made by the UN, was not present to veto the group's decision.
- The commander of the UN forces, General Douglas MacArthur, was also one of the most important generals in World War II.

McCarthyism

- Joseph McCarthy was a relatively unknown senator until he charged that 205 communists were within the State Department. He was unable to provide factual evidence to support his allegations.
- The hysteria that resulted from the senator's charges became known as *McCarthyism*.
- At one point, he even accused President Eisenhower of communist sympathies.

The Cuban Missile Crisis

🕐 **Quick Summary** When the Soviet Union set up nuclear missiles in communist Cuba, President John F. Kennedy demanded that they be removed. The Soviets eventually complied.

14 Compare and contrast President Kennedy to Presidents Truman and Eisenhower. Similar: All three were concerned about the spread of communism. Different: Kennedy was younger and he was Roman Catholic. Compare and Contrast

15 Why was it so dangerous to have Soviet missiles in Cuba? The Soviets could easily launch an attack on the United States from Cuba. Make Inferences

16 Summarize the events in the Cold War that led to the Cuban Missile Crisis. With the support of the Soviet Union, Cuba became a communist nation. In October 1962, American spy planes discovered that the Soviets were setting up nuclear missiles in Cuba. President Kennedy insisted that the Soviets remove their missiles from Cuba. 🔄 Summarize

✓ Ongoing Assessment

If... students have difficulty recalling the sequence of events,

then... have them draw a series of boxes connected with arrows. Ask them to fill in key events related to the Cuban Missile Crisis.

Primary Source

Cited in *John F. Kennedy: Commander in Chief: A Profile in Leadership*, by Pierre Salinger

17 What did Kennedy believe about the importance of working toward peace? Possible answer: All people share some interests and goals, so they should work toward peace. Analyze Primary Sources

✓ REVIEW ANSWER People were afraid that the Missile Crisis might lead to a nuclear war between the United States and the Soviet Union.

Main Idea and Details

▶ President Kennedy went on television to tell the nation about the Cuban Missile Crisis.

The Cuban Missile Crisis

In 1959, Fidel Castro led a successful revolution in Cuba. With the support of the Soviet Union, Castro formed a communist government. Cuba became the first communist nation in the Western Hemisphere. This alarmed many Americans, including **John F. Kennedy,** who was elected President in 1960.

Kennedy was the first Roman Catholic President in American history. At age 43, he was also the youngest person ever elected President. Like Truman and Eisenhower, Kennedy spent much of his time dealing with **14** Cold War conflicts.

The most dangerous of these conflicts was the **Cuban Missile Crisis.** In October 1962, American spy planes discovered that the Soviets were setting up nuclear missiles in **15** Cuba—just 90 miles from the coast of Florida.

On the night of October 22, Kennedy went on television to tell Americans the frightening news. He insisted that the Soviets must **16** remove their missiles from Cuba. He declared that the United States Navy was going to block Soviet ships from bringing any more weapons to Cuba.

For the next few days, people all over the world watched the news with increasing fear. As Soviet ships approached Cuba, it looked like the world's two most powerful nations were moving closer and closer to nuclear

war. Finally, the Soviet ships turned back. The Soviets agreed to remove their missiles from Cuba.

The crisis was over, but both American and Soviet leaders realized how close they had come to fighting a disastrous war. In a speech in Washington, D.C., Kennedy spoke of the importance of working toward peace. He said that the people of the United States and the Soviet Union shared many of the same interests and goals.

> *"Our most basic common link is that we all inhabit this small planet. We all breathe the same air. We all cherish our children's future."*

On November 22, 1963, President Kennedy was in Dallas, Texas. He and his wife, Jacqueline Kennedy, rode in an open car, waving to supporters. Suddenly, gunshots were fired. President Kennedy was assassinated. Hours later, Vice-President **Lyndon B. Johnson** was sworn in as the new President. In his first address to Congress, Johnson expressed the grief of millions of Americans saying, "All I have I would gladly have given not to be standing here today."

REVIEW Why did people watch the news with fear during the Cuban Missile Crisis?
Main Idea and Details

Practice and Extend

 **SOCIAL STUDIES Background**

The Peace Corps

- In 1961, Kennedy initiated the Peace Corps as a volunteer organization to assist countries worldwide.

- Through the Peace Corps, skilled volunteers are sent to developing countries to assist with education, agriculture, health, technology, and other community services.

- Today the Peace Corps serves in about 90 countries, including those of Eastern Europe.

 CURRICULUM CONNECTION Writing

Write a Biography

- Have small groups of students use online resources or their local library to research the life of President John F. Kennedy.

- Ask students to concentrate on Kennedy's handling of Cold War conflicts.

- Have students use a Main Idea graphic organizer to record facts they find in their research.

- Ask each group to produce a short biography.

The Arms Race Continues

The Cold War continued, and so did the arms race between the United States and the Soviet Union. An **arms race** is a race to build more powerful weapons.

The Soviet Union had exploded its first nuclear weapon in 1949. Then, in the 1950s, scientists in both countries developed hydrogen bombs, or H-bombs. Each H-bomb was 1,000 times more powerful than the atomic bombs that had destroyed Hiroshima and Nagasaki in World War II.

Many Americans worried about the race to build such powerful weapons. "Where will it lead us?" asked President Eisenhower. Still, American leaders felt that it was important to stay ahead of the Soviet Union in the arms race. The strategy was simple—if the United States had more powerful weapons than the Soviets, the Soviets would be afraid to attack. Therefore, the United States continued building nuclear weapons, hoping they would never be used. (18)

REVIEW Why did the United States want to stay ahead in the arms race? 🔄 **Summarize**

Summarize the Lesson

1945 The United Nations was formed to allow nations to work together to find peaceful solutions to problems.

1950 The Korean War began after North Korea invaded South Korea.

1962 The Soviet Union put nuclear missiles in Cuba, leading to the Cuban Missile Crisis.

LESSON 1 REVIEW

Check Facts and Main Ideas

1. 🔄 **Summarize** On a separate sheet of paper, complete the chart below by summarizing three key **Cold War** events.

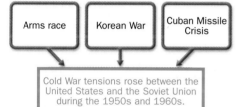

Cold War tensions rose between the United States and the Soviet Union during the 1950s and 1960s.

2. What differences between the United States and the Soviet Union led to the beginning of the Cold War?

3. Why did Truman believe the United States should fight in the **Korean War?**

4. What actions did Kennedy take after Soviet missiles were discovered in Cuba?

5. **Critical Thinking:** *Express Ideas* Do you believe it was important for the United States to stay ahead of the Soviet Union in the **arms race?** Explain.

Link to 🔗 **Geography**

Work with Maps Look at the map on page 638. Of the communist nations, which is farthest south? Among the capitalist nations, which is the farthest south?

641

The Arms Race Continues

🕐 *Quick Summary* The United States and the Soviet Union focused on building their defenses, including nuclear weapons.

(18) **Do you think the arms race was justified?** Possible answers: Yes; it kept both countries equal in power. No; there were other ways to solve the problems between the United States and the Soviet Union. **Make Decisions**

✓ **REVIEW ANSWER** To make the Soviets afraid to attack 🔄 **Summarize**

3 Close and Assess

Summarize the Lesson

Have students create a cause-and-effect chart to summarize the time line.

✓ **LESSON 1 REVIEW**

1. 🔄 **Summarize** For possible answers, see the reduced pupil page.

2. The United States supported democracy and free enterprise. The Soviet Union supported communism.

3. To stop the spread of communism

4. Kennedy told Americans about the missiles, demanded they be removed, and declared that the United States would block any more weapons shipments to Cuba.

5. **Critical Thinking:** *Express Ideas* Students should support their answers with logical explanations.

Link to 🔗 **Geography**
Albania; Greece

Workbook, p. 148

Lesson 1: A Dangerous World

Directions: Complete each sentence with information from Lesson 1. Write the answer on the line provided. You may use your textbook.

1. The _____ is an organization formed in 1945 that promised that its 50 member nations would work to find peaceful solutions to international problems.

2. _____ and _____ were the world's two superpowers after World War II.

3. In 1945 the Soviet Union had a _____ government.

4. The United States and the Soviet Union had different views on communism, which resulted in the _____.

5. At the end of World War II, the nations in _____ were under Soviet control and established communist governments loyal to the Soviet Union.

6. The _____ divided the continent of Europe into communist and noncommunist countries.

7. The _____ was a program launched by U.S. President Harry S. Truman to help the nations of Western Europe recover from World War II.

8. The post-World War II military alliance formed by the United States and the nations of Western Europe was called the _____.

9. Through the Korean War, the United States was able to keep communism from spreading into _____.

10. In 1959, under leader Fidel Castro, Cuba became the first communist nation in the _____ Hemisphere.

11. In 1962 the United States took action to keep the Soviets from setting up nuclear missiles in Cuba. This was called the _____.

12. The _____, developed by the United States and the Soviet Union, in 1,000 times more powerful than the atomic bomb used in Hiroshima.

Notes for Home: Your child learned about the United States' determination to keep communism from spreading.
Home Activity: With your child, discuss why it might be important to keep communism from spreading in the world. Ask your child what causes he or she thinks might justify getting involved in a war.

Also on Teacher Resources CD-ROM.

Struggle for Equal Rights

Objectives

- Evaluate the importance of *Brown* v. *Board of Education*.

- Explain the major events of the Montgomery bus boycott.

- Describe the efforts of Martin Luther King, Jr., in the Civil Rights Movement.

- Identify the goals of the women's rights movement.

Vocabulary

civil rights, p. 643

Resources

- Workbook, p. 149
- Transparency 20
- Every Student Learns Guide, pp. 266–269
- Quick Study, pp. 134–135

Quick Teaching Plan

If time is short, have students make an annotated time line.

- Have students record important dates and details as they read the lesson independently.

- After students finish reading the lesson, have them use their notes to make a time line with annotations about the important events.

- Display students' time lines.

1 Introduce and Motivate

Preview Ask students to explain the meaning of the phrase "equal rights for all." Tell students they will learn more about the struggle for equal rights in the United States after World War II as they read Lesson 2.

 Have students predict how the Court ruled on this case about segregation and how Americans reacted to the decision.

LESSON 2

1950   1980

1954
Supreme Court declares segregation in public schools illegal

1963
Martin Luther King, Jr., leads civil rights march in Washington, D.C.

1981
Sandra Day O'Connor is first woman named to Supreme Court

PREVIEW

Focus on the Main Idea
In the 1950s and 1960s, African Americans, women, and other groups struggled to gain civil rights and equal opportunities.

PLACES
Montgomery, Alabama
Washington, D.C.

PEOPLE
Thurgood Marshall
Rosa Parks
Martin Luther King, Jr.
Malcolm X
Sandra Day O'Connor
César Chávez
Dolores Huerta

VOCABULARY
civil rights

▶ Thurgood Marshall

642

Struggle for Equal Rights

You Are There It is December 9, 1952. At the Supreme Court in Washington, D.C., one of the most important cases in American history is about to begin. The courtroom is packed with people. Hundreds more wait outside, hoping for a chance to get in.

A lawyer named Thurgood Marshall stands to speak. Marshall has already argued 15 cases before the Supreme Court. He has won 13 of them.

This case is about segregation in public schools. Many states have laws declaring that black and white children must attend separate schools. Marshall argues that these laws are wrong. He insists that segregation takes away rights guaranteed to African American children by the Constitution.

The arguments continue for three days. And then the nation waits for the decision of the Court.

Cause and Effect As you read, pay attention to the causes and effects of the civil rights movement.

Practice and Extend

READING SKILL
Cause and Effect

In the Lesson Review, students complete a graphic organizer like the one below. You may want to provide students with a copy of Transparency 20 to complete as they read the lesson.

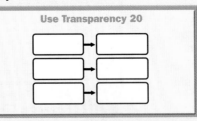

Use Transparency 20

VOCABULARY
Word Exercise

Individual Word Study Write *civil rights* on the board. Explain that the word *civil* means "having to do with citizens or with society." Ask students what civil rights are, based on this definition of civil. (Civil rights are rights that people have as citizens of a country or members of a society.) Ask students to give examples of civil rights that they enjoy in the United States, such as the right to free speech and equal treatment under the law. List examples on the board.

Struggle to End Segregation

The struggle against segregation gained an important victory after World War II. In 1948, President Truman ordered an end to segregation in the United States military. Since before the Civil War, white and black Americans had fought in separate units. Beginning with the Korean War in 1950, this segregation finally came to an end.

Segregation in many public places continued, however, especially in the South. At this time, segregation was legal. In 1892, the Supreme Court had ruled that services for white and black citizens could be "separate but equal." In other words, a state could separate white and black children into different schools, as long as the schools were of equal quality. In reality, segregated schools were almost never of equal quality. Many states spent much less money on schools, teachers, and books for African American children.

The NAACP decided to try to end school segregation. The organization's head lawyer, **Thurgood Marshall,** knew that he would have to get the Supreme Court to declare that segregation was illegal under the Constitution.

Marshall got his chance with a case based on the experience of a seven-year-old African American girl named Linda Brown. Linda Brown was not allowed to attend the public school a few blocks from her home

in Topeka, Kansas. It was for white children only. She had to take a bus to a school for African American children. Linda's parents insisted that this school was of lower quality than the school near their home. The Browns took their case to court.

On May 17, 1954, the Supreme Court announced its decision in this case. The Court ruled that segregation of public schools was illegal under the Constitution. A newspaper called the *Chicago Defender* declared the Court's ruling a "second emancipation proclamation." The growing Civil Rights Movement had won a major victory. **Civil rights** are the rights that are guaranteed to all citizens by the Constitution.

REVIEW Why did Linda Brown's parents go to court?
Cause and Effect

▶ Segregated schools *(below)* were declared illegal in the Supreme Court case based on the experience of Linda Brown *(right)*.

643

 Teach and Discuss

PAGE 643

Struggle to End Segregation

Quick Summary In a landmark case in 1954, the Supreme Court declared that segregation of public schools was illegal.

① **Why do you think President Truman decided to end segregation in the military?** Both black and white soldiers were doing the same jobs and facing the same dangers. **Make Inferences**

② **Which details support the opinion that African American schools were unsatisfactory despite the "separate but equal" rule?** Possible answer: Many states spent much less money on schools, teachers, and books for African American children. **Fact and Opinion**

③ **How did attorney Thurgood Marshall help end segregation in public schools?** He took on the case of Linda Brown and persuaded the Supreme Court to declare segregation illegal under the Constitution. **Summarize**

④ **What did the *Chicago Defender* mean by calling the Court's ruling a "second emancipation proclamation"?** The first emancipation proclamation freed African Americans from slavery. The Supreme Court's decision freed them from school segregation. **Analyze Information**

✓ **REVIEW ANSWER** They wanted Linda to be allowed to go to the public school that was closest to their home and that they believed was of higher quality than the school for African Americans. **Cause and Effect**

The Montgomery Bus Boycott

 Quick Summary Rosa Parks's refusal to obey a segregation law on a public bus in 1955 led to boycotts and protests for equal rights.

5 **What can you tell about Rosa Parks from her actions and words?** Possible answer: She was not afraid to stand up for her beliefs. Make Inferences

$ **SOCIAL STUDIES STRAND**
Economics

6 **How did the Montgomery bus boycott affect the bus service and the rest of the community?** Possible answer: Because many bus riders refused to ride the buses, the bus service lost money. Over the course of the year, the bus service may have reduced the number of buses and laid off employees to reduce expenses, which would have affected people still using the service. Cause and Effect

✓ Ongoing Assessment

If... students have difficulty understanding the effects of the boycott,

then... have students compare the amount of money earned from a bus loaded with passengers to a sparsely filled bus. Have them calculate the amount of money lost over a week, month, and year.

Primary Source

Cited in *Eyes on the Prize: America's Civil Rights Years, 1954–1965,* by Juan Williams

7 **What do King's words mean?** Possible answer: People fought against unfair situations and won the fight. Analyze Primary Sources

✓ REVIEW ANSWER
She refused to move when the bus driver told her to do so. Main Idea and Details

The Montgomery Bus Boycott

On December 1, 1955, **Rosa Parks,** an African American woman, got on a bus in **Montgomery, Alabama.** She sat down in a seat in the middle of the bus. Under state law, African Americans were supposed to sit in the back of the bus. African Americans could sit in the middle of the bus only if no white passengers wanted these seats.

As the bus continued its route, more people got on. The bus driver told Parks to move back so that a white passenger could have her seat. Parks refused. "Well, if you don't stand up, I'm going to have to call the police and have you arrested," the driver threatened. **5** "You may do that," Parks replied. She was arrested and taken to jail.

News of the arrest angered many African Americans in Montgomery. "People were fed up," explained a local leader named

▶ Civil rights leader Rosa Parks sat in the front of the bus after the successful end of the Montgomery bus boycott.

644

Jo Ann Robinson. Robinson and other leaders decided to organize a bus boycott.

The Montgomery bus boycott began the following Monday. Refusing to ride the buses, African Americans carpooled or walked to work. A 26-year-old minister named **Martin Luther King, Jr.,** watched with excitement as empty buses passed by his home. "I could hardly believe what I saw," he said. King was one of the leaders of the bus boycott.

The boycott continued for more than a year. Meanwhile, the case of Rosa Parks and bus segregation went all the way to the Supreme Court. In November 1956, the Court declared that segregation on public buses was illegal. The long boycott ended with victory. King gave credit to all the African Americans who had walked until,

> *"the walls of segregation were finally battered by the forces of justice."*

King gained national attention as a powerful speaker and an important civil rights leader. During the late 1950s and early 1960s, he led protests and marches in many parts of the country. As you will read in the Biography on the next page, King believed that nonviolent protest was the best way to bring change.

The work of thousands of people in the Civil Rights Movement convinced President Kennedy that the federal government should do more to protect the rights of all American citizens. In 1963, Kennedy proposed a new civil rights bill that would end segregation everywhere in the United States.

REVIEW Why was Rosa Parks arrested in 1955? Main Idea and Details

Practice and Extend

 EXTEND LANGUAGE
ESL Support

Develop a Concept Help students explore the concept of segregation.

Beginning Explain that *segregation* means *separate* or *divide.* Have students use toys to act out segregation.

Intermediate Have students brainstorm in English and in their home languages synonyms for *segregate.* Have them discuss why segregation of people on the basis of race or religion was bad.

Advanced Tell students that the word *segregate* comes from the Latin roots meaning "apart" and "flock." Help students connect this meaning to the practice of setting individuals apart from society based on race. Discuss how segregation might affect the people who are left out.

For additional ESL support, use Every Student Learns Guide, pp. 266–269.

Martin Luther King, Jr. *1929–1968*

Fourteen-year-old Martin Luther King, Jr., was having an exciting night. He and his teacher had traveled from their hometown of Atlanta, Georgia, to Dublin, a town farther south. Martin was competing in a speech-making contest. In his speech, he stated that under the United States Constitution, black people should have the same rights as whites. Martin said: **1**

> *"Today thirteen million black sons and daughters of our forefathers [ancestors] continue the fight....We believe with them that if freedom is good for any it is good for all."* **2**

In 1964, in honor of his nonviolent work for equal rights, Martin Luther King, Jr., was awarded the Nobel Peace Prize.

BIOFACT

Martin won the contest and left feeling great. He and his teacher got on a bus back to Atlanta and settled into their seats. A few stops further on, white travelers came onto the crowded bus. The driver told Martin and his teacher that they would have to stand up so that the whites could sit—this was the law. Martin did not want to move, and the driver got angry. Martin's teacher finally convinced Martin to stand. The trip back to Atlanta was ninety miles. Martin later said that standing during that trip made him angrier than he would ever be again. **3**

The ideals Martin Luther King, Jr., spoke of as a teenager became the foundation of his life's work. He became a minister and a leader in the Civil Rights Movement. He spent his adult years speaking and organizing for the right of African Americans to vote, to go to good schools, to get decent jobs, and to have all the opportunities and freedoms enjoyed by other Americans. King preached nonviolence, which means resisting peacefully. He helped to accomplish enormous changes in the United States. In 1968, he was assassinated at the age of 39.

Learn from Biographies

How did the speech young Martin gave at the contest contrast with his experience later that same night?

For more information, go online to *Meet the People* at **www.sfsocialstudies.com.**

645

Martin Luther King, Jr.

Objectives
- Identify the civil rights goals of Martin Luther King, Jr.
- Describe the strategy King used to achieve his goals.

1 Introduce and Motivate

Preview Ask students what they know about Martin Luther King, Jr. Tell them they will learn how his early experiences and beliefs led to his later deeds.

2 Teach and Discuss

- Ask students how King inspired people throughout his life.

1 What event supports the opinion that King was a serious thinker even as a young person? His teenage speech about equality Fact and Opinion

2 What did King mean by "... if freedom is good for any it is good for all"? Possible answer: All people have the same rights. Analyze Primary Sources

3 What experience did both King and Rosa Parks undergo? Both were forced to give up bus seats to whites. Analyze Information

3 Close and Assess

Learn from Biographies Answer

He had spoken about equal rights guaranteed by the Constitution, but then he experienced the results of an unfair law.

Gains and Losses

🕐 **Quick Summary** Martin Luther King, Jr., President John F. Kennedy, and Malcolm X worked for equal rights, but assassinations cut their work short.

Primary Source

Cited in *I Have a Dream: Writings and Speeches that Changed the World,* by James Melvin Washington, ed.

8 **What was King's hope?** People would be judged by their character, not race **Analyze Primary Sources**

9 **Contrast Congress's 1964 action with the Supreme Court's 1954 action.** The Court outlawed segregation in public schools. Congress outlawed it in any public place. **Analyze Information**

Primary Source

Cited in *The Autobiography of Malcolm X,* by Malcolm X and Alex Haley

10 **Compare and contrast Malcolm X's words with Kennedy's words on p. 640.** Both: All people can live and work together. Kennedy's focus: different countries; Malcolm X's focus: different races **Compare and Contrast**

11 **Why was there an increase in the number of African Americans in Congress after 1965?** More African Americans were able to vote, and they voted for people they felt would represent them well. **Cause and Effect**

12 **Why is this section titled "Gains and Losses"?** African Americans gained rights in the 1960s, but lost civil rights leaders. **Draw Conclusions**

SOCIAL STUDIES STRAND
Citizenship

Prejudice Reduction Ask students what they can do as responsible and respectful citizens to help make sure that Dr. King's dream continues to come true.

✓ **REVIEW ANSWER** Many African Americans were able to vote for the first time. **Cause and Effect**

Gains and Losses

King and other civil rights leaders planned a massive march in Washington, D.C. They hoped the March on Washington might convince Congress to pass President Kennedy's civil rights bill. On August 28, 1963, over 200,000 Americans gathered in the nation's capital to show their support for civil rights. Standing before the Lincoln Memorial, King called for an end to prejudice in United States. He spoke of his hopes for the future, saying,

8 *"I have a dream my four little children will one day live in a nation where they will not be judged by the color of their skin but by the content of their character...."*

As you have read, President Kennedy was killed in November 1963. President Johnson urged Congress to "honor President Kennedy's memory" by passing the civil rights bill. The following year, Congress passed the Civil **9** Rights Act of 1964. This law banned segregation in all public places in the United States. A year later, Congress passed the Voting Rights Act of 1965. African Americans already had the right to vote, but they were often prevented from voting in some parts of the South. The Voting Rights Act protected the right of all Americans to vote. As a result, hundreds of thousands of African Americans were able to vote for the first time.

One civil rights leader, Malcolm X, felt that new civil rights laws would not bring change quickly enough.

▶ Martin Luther King, Jr., and his wife Coretta Scott King *(far right)* led many marches in support of civil rights.

646

He believed that white Americans would never fully support equal rights for black citizens. Malcolm X urged African Americans to rely on themselves. He said, "The American black man should be focusing his every effort toward building his own businesses and decent homes for himself." Later in his life, Malcolm X talked more of blacks and whites working together to bring change.

"Black men and white men truly could be brothers."

By the end of the 1960s, the number of African Americans winning elections to Congress and other government offices was growing quickly. But neither Malcolm X nor Martin Luther King, Jr., lived to see these historic changes. Malcolm X was shot and killed while speaking in New York City in February 1965. Then, in April 1968, Martin Luther King, Jr., was assassinated in Memphis, Tennessee.

REVIEW What was one effect of the Voting Rights Act of 1965? **Cause and Effect**

Practice and Extend

MEETING INDIVIDUAL NEEDS
Leveled Practice

Honoring Martin Luther King, Jr. Have students help plan for Martin Luther King, Jr., Day—a holiday that honors the work of the civil rights leader.

Easy Ask students to draw and label a picture showing one activity to do in honor of King. Provide time for students to share and explain their ideas. **Reteach**

On-Level Have students read an informational article to add to their knowledge of King. Then have them prepare speeches that could be delivered on the holiday to point out his accomplishments. **Extend**

Challenge Ask students to research King's role in the 1963 civil rights protests in Birmingham, Alabama. **Enrich**

For a Lesson Summary, use Quick Study, p. 134.

▶ Ruth Bader Ginsburg *(back row)* joined Sandra Day O'Connor *(front row)* on the Supreme Court in 1993.

Equal Rights for Women

You know that many women began working outside the home during World War I and World War II. During the 1950s, the number of women in the workplace continued to grow. As the chart below shows, however, women usually earned less than men. When it came to choosing a type of job, women did not always have the same opportunities as men.

A young woman named **Sandra Day O'Connor** graduated from Stanford Law School in 1952. She was one of the top students in her class. But when she began looking for work as a lawyer, she found that many law firms did not want to hire female lawyers. She remembered,

> *"I interviewed with law firms in Los Angeles and San Francisco, but none had ever hired a woman before as a lawyer, and they were not prepared to do so."*

As O'Connor discovered, some jobs were seen as men's work.

In 1966, Betty Friedan helped form the National Organization for Women, or NOW. NOW became a leader in the women's rights movement, a struggle for fair pay and equal opportunities for women. Not all women agreed with all the goals of the women's rights movement. Phyllis Schlafly wrote books and articles supporting women who wanted to focus on their traditional role of working in the home.

During the 1960s and 1970s, women began gaining new opportunities in a wide variety of areas. In 1968, Shirley Chisholm became the first African American woman elected to the United States Congress. And in 1981, Sandra Day O'Connor became the first woman named to the Supreme Court. She announced her retirement in 2005.

REVIEW Did opportunities for women change from the 1950s to the 1970s? Explain. **Compare and Contrast**

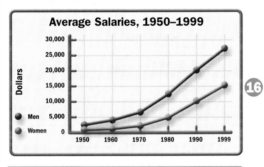

Average Salaries, 1950–1999

- ● Men
- ● Women

GRAPH SKILL *About how much higher was the average salary for men than for women in 1999?*

647

PAGE 647

Equal Rights for Women

🕐 *Quick Summary* In the mid-1900s, women struggled for fair pay and equal opportunities.

Primary Source

Cited in *Sandra Day O'Connor: Supreme Court Justice* from the *Women of Achievement series,* by Peter Huber

13 How did Sandra Day O'Connor probably feel when she said these words? Explain. Frustrated that she had worked hard to prepare herself to be a lawyer, but then had problems getting a job **Analyze Primary Sources**

14 Summarize the changes that the women's rights movement was trying to make. It was trying to help women receive fair pay and equal opportunities in the workplace. **Summarize**

15 What did O'Connor prove by becoming a successful lawyer and judge? Persistence pays off; women should be afforded equal opportunities in the workforce. **Point of View**

✓ **REVIEW ANSWER** Yes; women gained new opportunities in the struggle for fair pay and equal opportunities. **Compare and Contrast**

16 How did the salaries of women compare to those of men between 1950 and 1999? Traditionally women's salaries were lower than those of men. **Interpret Graphs**

GRAPH SKILL Answer About $12–13,000 higher a year

SOCIAL STUDIES
Background

Malcolm X

- Malcolm Little changed his name to Malcolm X for religious reasons.
- At first Malcolm X rejected both integration and racial equality, striving instead for black separatism and self-dependence.
- A 1964 religious pilgrimage to Mecca changed some of Malcolm X's views, and he began to work for peace between black and white people.
- In 1965, Malcolm X was killed by assassins at a rally in Harlem, New York.

Sandra Day O'Connor

- Sandra Day O'Connor, born in Arizona in 1930, grew up on a ranch without electricity or plumbing.
- Her parents sent her to live with her grandmother in El Paso, Texas, so she could get a good education.
- At one point she turned down an offer to be a legal secretary and worked as a deputy county attorney.
- Eventually she started a law office to launch her successful career.

Working for Change

🕐 **Quick Summary** The Civil Rights Movement inspired Native Americans, Mexican Americans, people with disabilities, and other groups to push for equal rights.

17 **In addition to African Americans and women, what other groups struggled to gain equal rights during the latter half of the 1900s?** Native Americans, Mexican Americans, and people with disabilities
🔄 Summarize

✓ **REVIEW ANSWER** To protect the rights of people with disabilities 🔄 Summarize

3 Close and Assess

Summarize the Lesson

List important people and events from Lesson 2 in random order. Have students describe their significance and put them in chronological order.

✓ | LESSON 2 | REVIEW |

1. **Cause and Effect** For possible answers, see the reduced pupil page.

2. Thurgood Marshall

3. Parks sparked the boycott by getting arrested for refusing to move to the back of a public bus. Robinson helped organize the boycott. King was a leader of the boycott.

4. Women wanted fair pay and equal opportunities in the workplace.

5. **Critical Thinking: Compare and Contrast** King believed that nonviolent protest should be used to change laws. Malcolm X felt that changing the law would not bring change fast enough. He urged African Americans to rely on themselves.

| Link to ∞ Language Arts |

Thurgood Marshall was the first African American named to the Supreme Court.

Working for Change

The Civil Rights Movement inspired many groups to work for change. Native American leaders worked to improve life and increase opportunities for Native Americans. Two Mexican American leaders, **César Chávez** and **Dolores Huerta** (HWAIR tah), formed a union for migrant farm workers. Migrant workers move from farm to farm, putting in long days of exhausting work for very low pay. You will read more about this struggle on page 649. Laws were also passed to assure freedom from discrimination in housing, employment, and other areas.

▶ **César Chávez worked for the rights of farm workers.**

The Americans with Disabilities Act was another step toward equal rights for all Americans. Passed in 1990, this law made illegal for businesses to refuse to hire some one because that person has a disability.

REVIEW What is the goal of the Americans with Disabilities Act? 🔄 Summarize

Summarize the Lesson

— **1954** The Supreme Court declared that segregation in public schools was illegal

— **1963** Martin Luther King, Jr., led 250,000 people in a civil rights march in Washington, D.C.

— **1981** Sandra Day O'Connor became the first woman named to the Supreme Court.

| LESSON 2 | REVIEW |

Check Facts and Main Ideas

1. **Cause and Effect** On a separate sheet of paper, complete the chart below by filling in the effects of several major events of the **Civil Rights** Movement.

Cause		Effect
NAACP challenges school segregation	→	Supreme Court rules that segregation of public schools is illegal under the Constitution.
Montgomery bus boycott	→	Supreme Court rules that segregation of public buses is illegal.
Voting Rights Act of 1965	→	Hundreds of thousands of African Americans are able to vote for the first time.

2. What civil rights lawyer won the case that outlawed segregation in schools?

3. Describe the roles of Rosa Parks, Jo Ann Robinson, and Martin Luther King, Jr., in the Montgomery bus boycott.

4. What were some goals of the women's rights movement of the 1960s and 1970s?

5. **Critical Thinking: Compare and Contrast** How did the views of Malcolm X differ from those of Martin Luther King, Jr.?

| Link to ∞ Language Arts |

Find Information You read that Sandra Day O'Connor was the first woman named to the Supreme Court. In 1967, another person from this lesson became the first African American named to the Supreme Court. Who was this person? Find the answer in a book or on the Internet.

Practice and Extend

Ⓗ SOCIAL STUDIES STRAND
History

American Indian Civil Rights The American Indian Movement (AIM) is a civil rights group founded in 1968. Its purpose is to help improve living conditions for and protect the rights of American Indians. AIM has been associated with some controversial activities. It is active today as a group that inspires American Indian culture renewal and protests the use of American Indians as sports team mascots.

Workbook, p. 149

Lesson 2: Struggle for Equal Rights

Directions: Match each term in the box to its description. Write the answer on the line provided.

Harry S. Truman	Rosa Parks	Sandra Day O'Connor
separate but equal	Martin Luther King, Jr.	NOW
Thurgood Marshall	Civil Rights Act of 1964	Shirley Chisholm
civil rights	Malcolm X	Dolores Huerta

1. _____ The rights that are guaranteed to all citizens by the Constitution
2. _____ Tried to convince the Supreme Court to declare that segregation is illegal under the Constitution
3. _____ Was the inspiration for the Montgomery bus boycott
4. _____ Civil rights leader who urged African Americans to rely on themselves to bring change
5. _____ Ordered an end to segregation in the military in 1948
6. _____ Supreme Court language that allowed segregated public services and schools for African Americans
7. _____ Women's rights organization formed in 1966 to fight for fair pay and equal opportunities for women
8. _____ First African American woman elected to Congress
9. _____ Helped create a union to improve the lives of migrant farm workers
10. _____ Law banning segregation in all public places in the United States
11. _____ In 1981 became the first woman named to the Supreme Court
12. _____ Organized a march in Washington, D.C., in August 1963, calling for an end to prejudice

Notes for Home: Your child learned about women's and African Americans' struggles for equal rights.
Home Activity: Discuss with your child how he or she likes to be treated when playing with other children. Then ask him or her to explain the idea of fairness and then work together to brainstorm examples of fair play.

💿 **Also on Teacher Resources CD-RO**

Dolores Huerta
1930–

As a child, Dolores Huerta had watched her father try to earn a living as a migrant worker—moving from farm to farm, looking for enough work to feed his family. Migrant workers, many of whom were Mexican Americans, were usually paid very little, and often had no idea when or where they would find their next job.

In high school, Dolores was known as a girl who liked to talk a lot and always did well in class. In one class she received an A for every paper she wrote and every test she took. Yet she was very surprised when she saw her final grade, a C. The teacher did not believe that Dolores, a Mexican American, could do such good work on her own. Dolores later remembered this time in her life as a difficult one. She said:

BIOFACT

To support a farm worker's strike, Dolores Huerta helped organize a boycott of table grapes in the 1960s.

"I started noticing racism as a teenager and it took a long time to get over the feelings." ❶

After college, Huerta became an elementary school teacher but soon decided that she wanted to work to improve the lives of migrant workers. "I couldn't stand seeing kids come to class hungry and needing shoes," she said. ❷

Along with César Chávez, Huerta helped to create the first union for farm workers in the United States. The union, the National Farm Workers Association, successfully fought for such benefits as better pay, health insurance, and safer working conditions for farm workers. Today they also fight to reduce the exposure of farm workers to dangerous chemicals.

Learn from Biographies

How do you think Dolores Huerta's experiences as a child affected her choice of work? What caused her to change careers from teaching to union organizing?

For more information, go online to *Meet the People* at **www.sfsocialstudies.com.**

649

★BIOGRAPHY★

Dolores Huerta

Objectives

- Describe the group of people Dolores Huerta helped.

- Identify the organization Dolores Huerta helped form.

1 Introduce and Motivate

Preview To activate prior knowledge, ask students what they know about Dolores Huerta.

2 Teach and Discuss

❶ **How do Huerta's and Martin Luther King, Jr.'s experiences as young people correspond?** They both noticed racism as teenagers and experienced its effects. **Compare and Contrast**

❷ **How did Huerta's negative experiences help her make some positive changes?** They spurred her efforts to improve the lives of migrant workers. **Analyze Information**

3 Close and Assess

Learn from Biographies Answer

Possible answer: Her father's struggles as a migrant worker and the conditions of workers' children made her want to address the problems of farm workers. She stopped teaching because she "couldn't stand seeing kids come to class hungry and needing shoes."

FYI SOCIAL STUDIES
Background

Hispanic Americans

- Hispanic Americans are Americans of Spanish-speaking descent.

- Some are descendants of Mexicans who were living in the Southwest when it became part of the United States. Most of the other Hispanic Americans or their ancestors emigrated from Latin America.

- The mid-1900s saw a rise in Hispanic immigration. For example, many Puerto Ricans moved to New York City and many Cubans came to Florida.

- According to the 2000 census, more than 35 million people of Hispanic descent live in our country, making it the largest minority group. Here are Hispanic American percentages for a sampling of states: 42.1% of New Mexico, 32.4 % of California, 32% of Texas, 16.8% of Florida, and 15.1% of New York.

The Cold War Continues

Objectives

- Identify some of the major events of the space race.

- Analyze major causes and effects of the Vietnam War.

- Evaluate President Richard Nixon's trips to China and the Soviet Union.

- Describe the level of Cold War tensions at the beginning of the 1980s.

Vocabulary

space race, p. 651; **Vietnam War,** p. 653; **arms control,** p. 654; **Watergate Scandal,** p. 654

Resources

- Workbook, p. 150
- Transparency 6, 62
- Every Student Learns Guide, pp. 270–273
- Quick Study, pp. 136–137

Quick Teaching Plan

If time is short, have students create journal entries by drawing a vertical line down the center of a sheet of paper and labeling the left side *Summary* and the right side *Response.*

- Have students read the lesson independently, summarize the major events on the left side of the page, and write their response on the right.

1 Introduce and Motivate

Preview Have students brainstorm words that describe the relationship between the United States and the Soviet Union during the Cold War. Tell students they will learn more about this conflict as they read Lesson 3.

You Are There Neil Armstrong did something no other human had done before. Have students write interview questions they would have asked him after his walk on the moon.

the United States and the World

LESSON 3

1968 Over 500,000 American soldiers are in Vietnam

1969 American astronauts walk on the moon

1972 President Nixon travels to China and the Soviet Union

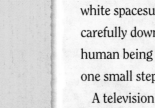

NORTH VIETNAM

SOUTH VIETNAM

PREVIEW

Focus on the Main Idea
The United States continued to oppose the spread of communism and Soviet power in the 1960s and 1970s.

PLACES
North Vietnam
South Vietnam

PEOPLE
John Glenn
Richard Nixon
Maya Ying Lin
Gerald Ford
Jimmy Carter

VOCABULARY
space race
Vietnam War
arms control
Watergate Scandal

► The Eagle was specially designed to land on the moon.

650

The Cold War Continues

You Are There The date is July 20, 1969. The American spacecraft *Eagle* drifts down toward the surface of the moon.

Inside are American astronauts Neil Armstrong and Edwin Aldrin. They set the craft down gently on the moon's gray, dusty surface. "The *Eagle* has landed," Armstrong reports.

A small hatch in the craft opens. Wearing a puffy white spacesuit and a giant helmet, Armstrong backs carefully down a ladder. As he becomes the first human being to step on the moon, he says, "That's one small step for man…one giant leap for mankind."

A television camera on *Eagle* beams these incredible images back to Earth. All over the world, millions of people stare with wonder at their television screens. No one has ever seen anything like this on TV before.

Summarize As you read, summarize key Cold War events of the 1960s and 1970s.

Practice and Extend

READING SKILL
Summarize

In the Lesson Review, students complete a graphic organizer like the one below. You may want to provide students with a copy of Transparency 6 to complete as they read the lesson.

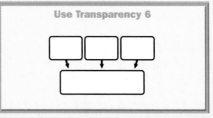

Use Transparency 6

VOCABULARY
Word Exercise

Related Word Study *Arms* is a homonym. Homonyms are words that are spelled and pronounced the same, but that have different meanings and different word origins. *Arms* can mean "the part of the human body between the shoulder and the hand" or "weapons." Ask students which meaning *arms* has in *arms control.* Have students check the definition on p. 654 to see if they are correct. Have students practice making sentences using these two meanings.

The Space Race

On October 4, 1957, the Soviet Union launched a basketball-sized satellite named *Sputnik* into space. A satellite is an object that is sent into space and circles Earth. *Sputnik* was the first satellite ever launched into space.

Americans were shocked. The United States was clearly behind in the space race—a race to explore outer space. Many Americans felt that it would be dangerous to lose this race. Americans worried that if the Soviets knew more about exploring space, they might use this advantage to attack the United States.

▶ *Sputnik* made history in 1957.

The Soviets took another step forward in 1961 when a Soviet astronaut became the first person to orbit, or circle, Earth in space.

Then the United States began to catch up. In 1962, John Glenn became the first American to orbit Earth. On July 16, 1969, the American spaceship *Apollo 11* blasted off and headed toward the moon.

The spaceship reached the moon four days later. Astronauts Neil Armstrong and Edwin "Buzz" Aldrin got into *Eagle*, a small spacecraft that was specially designed to land on the moon. They guided *Eagle* down to the moon's surface. As the world watched on television, Armstrong and Aldrin became the first people ever to walk on the moon. They collected rocks and did some experiments. They also spoke to President Richard Nixon. He told them: ❷

> *"Neil and Buzz, I am talking to you by telephone from the Oval Office at the White House, and this certainly has to be the most historic telephone call ever made."* ❸

Before leaving the moon, Armstrong and Aldrin planted an American flag and a plaque stating, "We came in peace." With the success of *Apollo 11*, the United States had clearly taken the lead in the space race.

REVIEW What are four things that Armstrong and Aldrin did while they were on the moon in 1969? ⟳ Summarize

▶ The world watched American astronauts walk on the moon in 1969.

---

2 Teach and Discuss

PAGE 651

The Space Race

🕐 ***Quick Summary*** In the 1950s and 1960s, the United States and the Soviet Union raced to explore outer space.

❶ **What details support the idea that in 1961 the Soviet Union was ahead in the space race?** By 1961, the Soviet Union had sent the first satellite and the first astronaut into space. **Main Idea and Details**

🧩 Decision Making

❷ **Would you have wanted to be the first person to walk on the moon? Explain.** Possible answers: Yes; it would have been a chance to do something historic and helpful for mankind. No; the experience would have been too dangerous. **Make Decisions**

Primary Source

Cited in *Apollo: Expeditions to the Moon,* by Edgar M. Cortright

❸ **Do you agree or disagree with Nixon's statement? Explain.** Possible answers: I agree because the astronauts did something that no one else had ever done; I disagree because the first time a telephone was used was more historic. **Analyze Primary Sources**

✓ **REVIEW ANSWER** Possible answers: They conducted experiments, collected rocks, spoke to Nixon, planted an American flag, and left a plaque. ⟳ Summarize

---

CURRICULUM CONNECTION
Literature

Read Biographies

John Glenn: A Space Biography, by Barbara Kramer (Enslow Publishers, Inc., ISBN 0-894-90964-9, 1998) **Easy**

Mae Jemison, by Sonia W. Black (Mondo Publishers, ISBN 1-572-55801-6, 2000) **On-Level** *NCSS Notable Book*

Sally Ride: Shooting for the Stars, by Jane Hurwitz (Ballantine Books, ISBN 0-449-90394-0, 1989) **Challenge**

FYI SOCIAL STUDIES
Background

Senator John Glenn

- Identify leaders in the national government, such as John Glenn.

- In 1974, Glenn ran for office as a Democratic Party candidate for U.S. Senate. He was elected, and served until 1998 as a senator representing the state of Ohio.

- In that same year, he founded the Glenn Institute for Public Service and Public Policy, which researches public policy issues and trains future American Leaders.

The Vietnam War

 Quick Summary North Vietnam established a communist government and attempted to take over South Vietnam, which resulted in a war involving the United States. The Vietnam War ended when Vietnam was united under a communist government.

North and South Vietnam

4 **What country is located to the north of North Vietnam?** China **Interpret Maps**

MAP SKILL **Answer** Laos

5 **How and when did Vietnam become a divided country?** When Vietnam won its independence from the French in 1954, the country became divided, and North Vietnam established a communist government. **Sequence**

6 **Why do you think the North Vietnamese believed they could unite all of Vietnam under one communist government?** They had the support of the Soviet Union and China. **Draw Conclusions**

Test Talk

Locate Key Words in the Text

7 **Why did the United States get involved in the Vietnam War?** Have students find details and key words from the text to support their answers. The United States was committed to stopping the spread of communism. American leaders sent money, weapons, and American soldiers to help the South Vietnamese resist the communists and establish a democratic republic. **Cause and Effect**

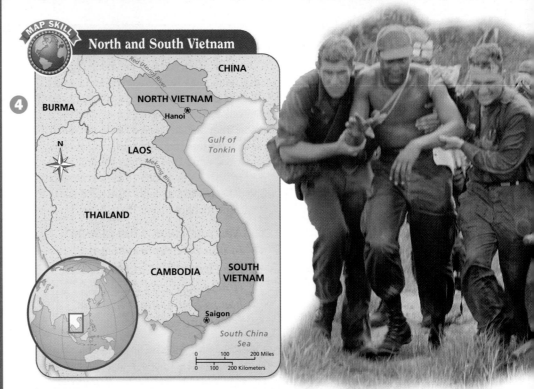

North and South Vietnam

4 BURMA • CHINA • NORTH VIETNAM • Hanoi • Gulf of Tonkin • LAOS • Mekong River • Red (Hong) River • THAILAND • CAMBODIA • SOUTH VIETNAM • Saigon • South China Sea • N • 0 100 200 Miles • 0 100 200 Kilometers

▶ Vietnam was divided in 1954. American soldiers fought to keep South Vietnam independent from North Vietnam.

MAP SKILL Location *Which country bordered both North Vietnam and South Vietnam?*

The Vietnam War

Since the late 1800s, Vietnam had been a colony of France. Following World War II, the Vietnamese fought to gain independence from France. The French were defeated in 1954. One war had ended, but another war was about to begin.

The treaty that ended fighting between Vietnam and France divided Vietnam into **5** **North Vietnam** and **South Vietnam.** You can see this region of Asia on the map above.

North Vietnam established a communist government. With the support of the Soviet Union and China, North Vietnam began working to unite all of Vietnam under one **6** communist government. South Vietnamese leaders resisted the communists, and a long war began.

The United States was committed to stopping the spread of communism. American leaders hoped to help make South Vietnam a democratic republic. Presidents Eisenhower and Kennedy sent money and weapons to the government of South Vietnam. American soldiers were sent to help train the South Vietnamese army.

In spite of this aid, the communists were winning the war. Lyndon Johnson, who became President in 1963, was determined not to allow the communist forces to win. "I'm not going to lose Vietnam," he said. In 1964, Johnson sent more American soldiers to Vietnam. Over the next few years, the

652

Practice and Extend

CURRICULUM CONNECTION
Literature

Read About Vietnam

The Wall, by Eve Bunting (Houghton Mifflin, ISBN 0-395-62977-2, 1992) **Easy**

A Place Called Heartbreak: A Story of Vietnam, by Walter Dean Myers (Raintree Steck-Vaughn, ISBN 0-811-48077-1, 1992) **On-Level**

The Valiant Women of the Vietnam War, by Karen Zeinert (Millbrook Press, ISBN 0-761-31268-4, 2000) **Challenge** *NCSS Notable Book*

CURRICULUM CONNECTION
Writing

Write a Biography Picture Book

- Have students conduct further research on the life of one of the U.S. Presidents mentioned in this lesson.

- Have students create a picture book about the President's life before, during, and after his presidency.

- Display students' books in the classroom or school library.

American involvement in the **Vietnam War** grew quickly. By 1968, there were over 500,000 American soldiers in Vietnam.

American soldiers often fought in small groups in Vietnam. They cut their way through thick jungles and waded through flooded rice fields in search of communist forces. Surprise attacks could come from any direction at any time, day or night.

In the United States, people watched film of the fighting on television. This was the first time that Americans could watch scenes from a war on the evening news.

Should the United States continue fighting in Vietnam? In the late 1960s, this question began to divide Americans. People who supported the war were known as "hawks." They believed that the war was necessary to stop the spread of communism. People who opposed the war were called "doves." They believed the conflict in Vietnam was a civil war that should be settled by the Vietnamese people.

Richard Nixon was elected President in 1968. He wanted to remove American soldiers from Vietnam, but he did not want to allow the communists to win the war. From 1969 to 1972, the number of American soldiers in Vietnam fell from 540,000 to 50,000. At the same time, American planes increased their bombing of North Vietnam. Nixon hoped this would convince the North Vietnamese to stop fighting. The fighting continued, however.

In January 1973, the United States signed a cease-fire, or an agreement to stop fighting, with North Vietnam. In March, the last American troops left Vietnam. South Vietnam and North Vietnam continued fighting. In April 1975, South Vietnam surrendered to North Vietnam. The war was over, and Vietnam was united under a communist government.

About 2 million Vietnamese had been killed during the fighting. Over 57,000 Americans had been killed, and nearly 2,000 **10** were still missing. In 1980, a competition was held to design a memorial to the American men and women who served in Vietnam. It was won by a 21-year-old college student named **Maya Ying Lin.** Today, you can see her design if you visit the Vietnam Veterans Memorial in Washington, D.C.

REVIEW How did hawks and doves differ in their views on the Vietnam War?
Compare and Contrast

▶ The names of American soldiers killed in Vietnam are carved in the black granite of the Vietnam Veterans Memorial.

653

8 **What made fighting in Vietnam particularly difficult?** Thick jungles and surprise attacks Cause and Effect

9 **How do you think seeing scenes of the fighting on television affected Americans?** It probably made them more aware of the casualties and hardships of war. Hypothesize

10 **Compare and contrast the Korean War and the Vietnam War.** Both Korea and Vietnam were divided countries with the north being communist. In both cases, the Soviet Union and China supported the efforts of the north to unify the country under a communist government. The United States tried to help the south resist in both cases. The number of Americans who lost their lives in Korea was about 33,000, whereas about 57,000 died in Vietnam. South Korea was able to resist communism; South Vietnam was not.
Compare and Contrast

Ongoing Assessment

If... students have difficulty identifying the similarities and differences between the two wars,

then... have them revisit Lesson 1 and use that information along with information in this lesson to create a Venn diagram.

✓ **REVIEW ANSWER** The hawks supported the war, and the doves opposed it. Compare and Contrast

Nixon Visits China

🕐 **Quick Summary** President Nixon succeeded in improving U.S. relations with China and the Soviet Union, which included getting Soviet leaders to agree to arms control. Nixon's successes were overshadowed by the Watergate Scandal, which resulted in his resignation.

11 **What historic event is shown in the photograph?** The first time an American President visited China **Analyze Pictures**

12 **Why was China's invitation to Nixon significant?** It showed that the country was open to a friendlier relationship with the United States. **Make Inferences**

13 **Compare and contrast the arms race and the arms control agreement.** Both involved the production of nuclear weapons and both were intended to prevent war. The arms race resulted in the production of more nuclear weapons, whereas the arms control agreement limited the number of nuclear weapons each side could have. **Compare and Contrast**

14 **Summarize Nixon's accomplishments in China and Russia.** He met with Chinese and Soviet leaders to improve the relationship between those countries and the United States. Together with Soviet leaders, he signed an arms control agreement. 🔄 **Summarize**

15 **Why did Nixon resign?** He faced the likelihood of being impeached for illegal activities. **Main Idea and Details**

✓ **REVIEW ANSWER** It helped ease tensions between the two countries. **Cause and Effect**

11 ▶ President Nixon walked along the Great Wall of China during his historic visit in 1972.

Nixon Visits China

Since a communist government came to power in China in 1949, the United States and China had been bitter Cold War rivals. President Nixon wanted to change this. He began working to improve relations with China. "If there is anything I want to do before I die, it is to go to China," Nixon said. No American president had ever been to China.

Nixon's work paid off in 1972, when the Chinese government invited him to visit. Nixon went to China and met with Mao Zedong (MOW ze DOONG), the Chinese leader. This was an important step toward more friendly **12** relations with China.

Later that year, Nixon traveled to the Soviet Union. He met with Soviet leaders and signed an **arms control** agreement—a deal to limit **13** the production of weapons. This agreement limited the number of nuclear weapons each side could have and helped ease tensions between **14** the United States and Soviet Union.

Nixon's success in China and the Soviet Union helped him win reelection in November

1972. But the **Watergate Scandal** soon brought an end to his second term. A scandal is an action that leads to shame or disgrace.

Why was the scandal named Watergate? While Nixon was running for reelection, five men were caught breaking into an office in the Watergate building in Washington, D.C. The office belonged to the Democratic party. Nixon was a Republican. The men who broke into the office had been looking for information on Nixon's political opponents.

Nixon insisted he had not helped plan the break-in. Over the next year, however, evidence showed that Nixon had taken some illegal actions to hide information about the Watergate break-in.

Congress prepared to impeach Nixon, or accuse him of crimes. On August 9, 1974, Nixon resigned. He was the only President ever to resign from office. Vice President **Gerald Ford** became the new President.

REVIEW What was one effect of the arms control agreement between the United States and the Soviet Union? **Cause and Effect**

Practice and Extend

ISSUES AND VIEWPOINTS
Critical Thinking

Analyze Different Viewpoints Write the following quotations on the board or read them aloud. Have students examine each speaker's viewpoint about Richard Nixon.

Easy Have students compare and contrast the speakers' viewpoints. **Reteach**

On-Level Ask students to identify a supporting reason or detail for each speaker's viewpoint. **Extend**

Challenge Ask students to do further reading about Nixon and identify several reasons for each viewpoint. **Enrich**

For a Lesson Summary, use Quick Study, p. 136.

" . . . Richard Nixon . . . has been excessively maligned (spoken ill of) for his faults and inadequately recognized for his virtues."

—Jonathan Aitken
Nixon: A Life

" . . . Richard Nixon's abuses and deceptions may have led many citizens not to trust their leaders at all."

—Anthony Summers
The Arrogance of Power

Tensions Rise Again

Jimmy Carter was elected President in 1976. One of President Carter's main goals was to try to help bring peace between Egypt and Israel. These two nations border each other in Southwest Asia—a region also known as the Middle East. Egypt and Israel had been enemies for a long time and had fought several wars. Carter invited the leaders of both nations to the United States. They worked out a peace treaty, which was signed in March 1979.

Carter also hoped to continue lowering Cold War tensions with the Soviet Union. These hopes were crushed in December 1979, when Soviet troops invaded Afghanistan, a nation in Asia bordering the Soviet Union. Carter spoke out against this attempt to expand Soviet power. The United States refused to send athletes to the 1980 Summer Olympics, held in the Soviet capital of Moscow. As the 1980s began, Cold War tensions were on the rise again.

REVIEW Carter helped which two Middle Eastern nations reach a peace agreement in 1979?
Main Idea and Details

Summarize the Lesson

- **1968** The number of American soldiers serving in the Vietnam War topped 500,000.
- **1969** American astronaut Neil Armstrong became the first person ever to walk on the moon.
- **1972** President Nixon's trips to China and the Soviet Union helped to ease Cold War tensions.

▶ **President Jimmy Carter** *(above)*

LESSON 3   REVIEW

Check Facts and Main Ideas

1. **Summarize** On a separate sheet of paper, complete the chart below by summarizing these key Cold War events.

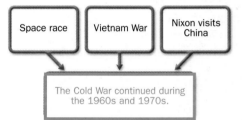

2. How did the success of *Sputnik* affect the **space race?**

3. **Critical Thinking:** *Point of View* Was President Johnson a hawk or a dove? Explain how you reached your answer.

4. How did Nixon's trip to China affect relations between the United States and China?

5. Were Cold War tensions rising or falling as the 1980s began? Explain.

Link to [⚭] Science

Research Space Today the United States and Russia work together on the International Space Station. Do some research in books or on the Internet. Write a one-page paper about the space station. What kinds of experiments are being done on the space station today?

655

Tensions Rise Again

Quick Summary President Carter succeeded in establishing a peace treaty between Egypt and Israel, but Cold War tensions increased after Soviet troops invaded Afghanistan.

16 **Why did Carter invite Egyptian and Israeli leaders to the United States?** To help them establish peaceful relations
Main Idea and Details

✓ **REVIEW ANSWER** Egypt and Israel
Main Idea and Details

3 Close and Assess

Summarize the Lesson

Have students examine the vertical time line and write newspaper headlines pertaining to the key events listed.

✓ **LESSON 3   REVIEW**

1. **Summarize** For possible answers, see the reduced pupil page.

2. The United States saw that it was behind in the space race, and needed to catch up with the Soviet Union.

3. **Critical Thinking:** *Point of View* A hawk because he supported sending American troops to Vietnam

4. It led to improved relations between the United States and China.

5. Cold War tensions were rising following the Soviet invasion of Afghanistan in 1979.

Link to [⚭] Science

Students' reports should identify specific examples of scientific and environmental studies.

H **SOCIAL STUDIES STRAND**
History

Conflicts with Afghanistan The discussion of Afghanistan and the Soviet Union may incite questions about the more recent conflict between the United States and Afghanistan.

- Students may have questions about past and current events relating to the United States and Afghanistan.

- Students may also want to share their thoughts and memories about the tragedies of September 11, 2001.

- For suggestions about how to help children deal with conflict, fear, and loss, see pages TR1–TR2 of this Teacher's Edition.

Workbook, p. 150

Lesson 3: The Cold War Continues

Directions: Write the letter of the effect on the line beside each cause. You may use your textbook.

Cause	Effect
___ 1. Soviets launch Sputnik.	a. Vietnam is united under communist rule.
___ 2. Soviets send the first man to orbit Earth.	b. U.S. leaders fear that the Soviets will use their new knowledge about space exploration to attack the United States.
___ 3. Vietnam gains independence from France.	c. Each side agrees to limit nuclear weapons, and tensions are eased.
___ 4. North Vietnam tries to unite all of Vietnam under communist rule.	d. South Vietnam resists communism and the Vietnam War begins.
___ 5. U.S. armed forces go to Vietnam.	e. President Jimmy Carter objects to the Soviets' attempt to expand their power and refuses to send U.S. athletes to the 1980 Olympics in Moscow.
___ 6. In April 1975, South Vietnam surrenders to North Vietnam.	
___ 7. U.S. President Nixon tries to change the Cold War relationship between the United States and China.	f. Nixon becomes the only President to resign from office.
___ 8. Nixon and Soviet leaders sign an arms control agreement.	g. In an effort to win the space race, the U.S. works toward being the first country to send a person to the moon.
___ 9. Nixon is involved in the Watergate scandal.	h. Americans are divided on the issue of U.S. involvement in the Vietnam War.
___ 10. U.S. President Jimmy Carter tries to bring peace to Israel and Egypt.	i. Nixon is successful in trying to improve relations and, in 1972, becomes the first U.S. President to visit China.
___ 11. Cold War tensions increase when Soviet troops invade Afghanistan in December 1979.	j. Leaders of Israel and Egypt visit the United States and Egypt sign a peace treaty in March 1979.
	k. Vietnam is split into North Vietnam and South Vietnam.

Notes for Home: Your child learned about Cold War tensions between the United States and the Soviet Union. **Home Activity:** With your child, discuss the positive and negative effects of the Cold War on the United States and the world. Ask your child how the space race and the arms race might have had different effects on the United States and the Soviet Union had worked together rather than against each other.

Also on Teacher Resources CD-ROM.

Understand Map Projections

Objective

- Interpret information from map projections.

Vocabulary

map projection, p. 656

Resource

- Workbook, p. 151

1 Introduce and Motivate

What is a map projection? Show students a sphere, such as a beach ball or an orange, and ask how they would show the entire surface on a sheet of paper. Then have students read the **What?** section of text on p. 656 to help set the purpose of the lesson.

Why use a map projection? Have students read the **Why?** section of text on p. 656. Ask them why people do not take globes when they travel.

Understand Map Projections

What? You have seen many maps of the world in this book, including the map on page 629. Each map is really a map projection. A **map projection** is a way of showing the round Earth on a flat surface, such as a piece of paper.

A globe is a sphere like Earth and therefore can show places accurately in size and shape. Globes also show accurate distances between places. But all flat maps, or map projections, have errors in size, shape, distance, or direction. These errors are called distortions. They occur because it is not possible to show a round Earth as a flat surface without changing something. Each map projection has advantages and disadvantages.

Why? A globe is the most accurate way of showing the world, but no one takes globes along when they travel. We use maps. It is important to understand the kind of map we see and the kind of distortion it has. Then we understand what features may be accurate on the map and what may be distorted.

Map A

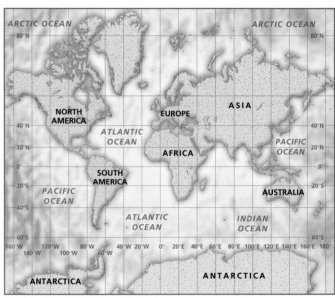

656

Practice and Extend

CURRICULUM CONNECTION
Math

Compare a Sphere with a Plane

- Help students explore the problem of converting a spherical shape to a flat surface.
- Divide the class into groups. Give each group a grapefruit or orange. Have students try to take the skin off the fruit in one piece and lay it flat.
- Have groups present their approaches and discuss the distortion between the spherical and the flat version.

SOCIAL STUDIES STRAND
Geography

The following map resources are available:

- Big Book Atlas
- Student Atlas
- Outline Maps
- Desk Maps
- Map Resources CD-ROM

WEB SITE
Technology

Students can find out more by clicking on *Atlas* at **www.sfsocialstudies.com.** Help students identify key search terms.

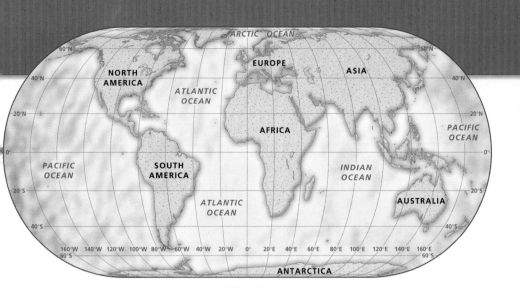

Map B

How? Look at Map A. It uses a Mercator (mer KAY ter) projection. Gerardus Mercator first introduced this kind of map in 1569. If you study the map, you will see that the lines of latitude are all parallel to one another, as they are on a globe. But the lines of longitude are also shown parallel. On a globe, lines of longitude all meet at the North and South poles.

On a Mercator projection, the distances and the shapes and sizes of the land are fairly accurate near the equator. But places farther north and south on the map appear larger and farther apart than they really are. For example, Greenland seems to be larger than Africa, but Africa is really fourteen times larger than Greenland.

This kind of map was useful for sailors who sailed east or west from Europe. They were interested in locating places by latitude.

Another type of projection is the equal-area projection, seen in Map B. It tries to correct the distortions by showing the lines of longitude—except for the prime meridian—

curving in toward the poles. As a result, the sizes of land are closer to their actual sizes than they are on a Mercator projection. Compare the sizes of Africa and Greenland on this map. Compare the shapes of the continents on the two maps.

1. What is a **map projection?**

2. On which map do the continents of South America and Africa appear more equal in size?

3. Which map would you use to compare the actual sizes of North and South America?

Internet Activity

For more information, go online to the Atlas at
www.sfsocialstudies.com.

657

SOCIAL STUDIES Background

Gerardus Mercator

- Gerardus Mercator was born in 1512 in Rupelmonde, Belgium. His travels as a young man inspired him to study geography, mathematics, and astronomy, during which time he learned the art of mapmaking.

- By the time he was 24, Mercator had earned a widespread reputation for being an expert geographer.

- In 1552, Mercator moved to Germany, where he continued to develop his skills and perfect the Mercator projection.

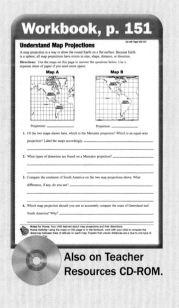

Also on Teacher Resources CD-ROM.

---

2 Teach and Discuss

How is this skill used? Examine with students the maps on pp. 656 and 657.

- Have groups of students use overhead transparencies and marking pens to trace land masses from Map A and compare them to Map B.

- Point out that the use of mathematical calculations, aerial photography, satellites, and computers has increased the accuracy of maps.

- Have students read the **How?** section of text on p. 657.

1 What is the best tool for a teacher wishing to show students the accurate size and shape of continents? Why? A globe; it is the most accurate because it is a sphere like Earth. **Main Idea and Details**

2 What is a main difference between a Mercator projection and an equal-area projection? Possible answer: On a Mercator projection, the lines of longitude are parallel, which is not accurate. On an equal-area projection, the lines of longitude are curved toward the poles. **Compare and Contrast**

3 Close and Assess

Think and Apply

1. A map projection is a way of showing a round object, such as a globe, on a flat surface.

2. They appear more equal in size on the equal-area projection.

3. Map B

Looking Toward the Future

Objectives

- Describe how relations between the United States and the Soviet Union changed during the 1980s.

- Explain how the Cold War ended.

- Identify key post-Cold War events, including the Persian Gulf War, the Clinton impeachment, the rise of the Internet, and the struggle against terrorism.

- Evaluate a variety of questions about the future of the United States.

Vocabulary

Persian Gulf War, p. 660; **Internet,** p. 661

Resources

- Workbook, p. 152
- Transparency 1
- Every Student Learns Guide, pp. 274–277
- Quick Study, pp. 138–139

Quick Teaching Plan

If time is short, have students make a two-column chart with the headings *Accomplishments* and *Challenges.*

- As students read the lesson independently, have them list world and national accomplishments and chart current and potential future challenges.

- Have them code the challenges as primarily U.S. (US) or world (W) challenges and discuss possible solutions.

1 Introduce and Motivate

Preview Ask students to summarize the relationship between the United States and communist countries in the early 1980s. Tell students they will learn about the end of the Cold War.

You Are There When the Berlin Wall fell, East and West Germans felt many emotions. Ask students why they may have felt joy and fear.

658 Unit 9 • The United States and the World

LESSON 4

1985				2000

1989
The Berlin Wall is torn down.

1991
Iraq is defeated in the Persian Gulf War.

2001
Terrorist attacks in the United States kill thousands of people.

PREVIEW

Focus on the Main Idea
The Cold War finally ended in the late 1980s, leaving the United States as the world's only superpower.

PLACES
Iraq
Afghanistan

PEOPLE
Ronald Reagan
Mikhail Gorbachev
George Bush
Colin Powell
Bill Clinton
Madeleine Albright
George W. Bush

VOCABULARY
Persian Gulf War
Internet

▶ **A piece of the Berlin Wall.**

658

Looking Toward the Future

You Are There
The date is November 9, 1989, and something shocking is happening in the German city of Berlin. Since 1961, the Berlin Wall has divided this city. East Berlin is part of communist East Germany. West Berlin is part of West Germany and has a free government and a free market economy.

But all that is now changing. Crowds of people from both East and West Berlin have jumped onto the Berlin Wall. On top of the wall, people are dancing and singing. Some take hammers or axes and smash off pieces of the hated wall.

People all over the world have good reason to celebrate. For 28 years, the Berlin Wall has stood as a reminder of the Cold War. And now the wall is coming down. The Cold War is finally coming to an end.

Main Idea and Details As you read, think about how the world has changed since the end of the Cold War.

Practice and Extend

READING SKILL
Main Idea and Details

In the Lesson Review, students complete a graphic organizer like the one below. You may want to provide students with a copy of Transparency 1 to complete as they read the lesson.

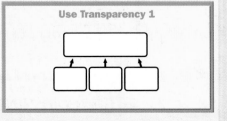

Use Transparency 1

VOCABULARY
Word Exercise

Individual Word Study Ask students if they are familiar with the word *Internet*. When the Internet was invented, it had to be named. Ask students if they remember what the prefix *inter-* means. ("with" or "between or among") Have students guess how this relates to the Internet. (there is a connection among computers) The word *Internet* was coined, or invented, by combining *interconnected* and *networks*. The Internet is a system of interconnected networks.

The Cold War Ends

When the 1980s began, the end of the Cold War seemed far away. The new American President, **Ronald Reagan,** called the Soviet Union an "evil empire." He believed the United States needed to strengthen its military in order to block Soviet efforts to expand communism around the world. The United States increased spending on new and more powerful weapons.

The Soviet Union was also spending large amounts of money on weapons. But the Soviet economy was not nearly as strong as the American economy. The high cost of the arms race was weakening the Soviet Union.

In 1985, a new leader named **Mikhail Gorbachev** (mi KAYL GOR bah chahv) came to power in the Soviet Union. Gorbachev began reforming the country by allowing people more political and economic freedom. He also allowed more freedom to the people of Eastern Europe.

Relations between the Soviet Union and the United States began to improve. In 1987, Reagan and Gorbachev signed a new arms control agreement. For the first time, the United States and the Soviet Union agreed to destroy some of their nuclear weapons.

After serving as Reagan's Vice President for eight years, **George Bush** became President in 1989. Bush continued working with Gorbachev to ease Cold War tensions.

Meanwhile, as people in Eastern Europe gained more freedom, they began working to overthrow their communist governments. In 1989, Communist governments fell in Poland, Hungary, and several other nations. All over Eastern Europe people were replacing communist governments with elected governments and free enterprise economies. The Berlin Wall was destroyed. Then, in 1991, the Soviet Union itself broke up into 15 independent republics. "The Cold War is now behind us," Gorbachev announced.

The Cold War was finally over. President Bush said:

> *"The end of the Cold War was clearly a victory for the forces of freedom and democracy."*

REVIEW What reforms did Mikhail Gorbachev make in the Soviet Union?
Main Idea and Details

In 1987 President Reagan stood at the Berlin Wall and challenged: "Mr. Gorbachev, tear down this wall!" Three years later, Reagan himself helped destroy the wall.

North Sea   Baltic Sea

Berlin

EUROPE

Former East Germany
Former West Germany

659

SOCIAL STUDIES
Background

New Governments After the fall of communism, Eastern European countries established different forms of elected governments with free enterprise systems.

- Germany and Russia are federal republics.
- Hungary and Bulgaria are parliamentary democracies.
- Czechoslovakia split into the Czech and Slovak Republics. Both are ruled by parliamentary democracies.

Teach and Discuss

The Cold War Ends

Quick Summary During the administrations of President Reagan and President Bush, tensions between the United States and the Soviet Union began to ease, and the Cold War ended.

1 **What was Reagan's plan for stopping the spread of communism?** To strengthen the U.S. military and build new and more powerful weapons **Main Idea and Details**

2 **How did the arms control of 1972 differ from that of 1987?** In 1972, the United States and the Soviet Union agreed to limit production of arms. In 1987, they agreed to destroy some weapons. **Compare and Contrast**

3 **What sequence of events caused the end of the Cold War?** Eastern Europeans overthrew their communist governments. East and West Germany were united, and the Soviet Union broke into independent republics. **Sequence**

Primary Source
From an interview for the CNN series *Cold War*

4 **How was the end of the Cold War a victory for freedom and democracy?** As Eastern Europeans gained more freedom, elected governments replaced communist governments. **Analyze Primary Sources**

✓ **REVIEW ANSWER** Gorbachev allowed more political and economic freedom. **Main Idea and Details**

A New Role in the World

 Quick Summary After the breakup of the Soviet Union in 1991, the United States faced difficult decisions about its role as the world's only superpower.

5 **Give examples of how a country's power can be used for positive or negative purposes.** Possible answers: Positive purpose: a country that uses its wealth to help other countries; Negative purpose: a country that uses its strength to take over another country **Apply Information**

$ **SOCIAL STUDIES STRAND**
Economics

Point out that governments might sometimes harm other countries by making decisions for their own economic gain.

6 **What did Iraq hope to accomplish by invading Kuwait?** Iraq hoped to receive the financial benefits of Kuwait's oil resources. **Draw Conclusions**

Primary Source
From a speech at the U.S. Naval Academy on April 15, 1997

7 **What was Madeleine Albright's viewpoint on relations between countries?** She believed that nations must work together to prevent war and bring peace. **Analyze Primary Sources**

8 **What facts support the opinion that there was progress in equal rights by the turn of the century?** Albright was the first female secretary of state, and then Colin Powell became the first African American secretary of state. **Fact and Opinion**

✓ **REVIEW ANSWER** The war was caused by Iraq invading Kuwait. It ended with Iraq being driven out of Kuwait. **Sequence**

▶ **Colin Powell met with American troops in Saudi Arabia before Operation Desert Storm.**

A New Role in the World

The United States was now the world's only superpower. This position brought many new challenges. For example, how should the United States use its power? Should the American government and military play a leading role in trying to end conflicts around **5** the world?

The United States faced these questions in the **Persian Gulf War.** In 1990, the Middle Eastern nation of **Iraq** invaded its neighbor, Kuwait. Iraq's dictator, Saddam Hussein, (sah DAHM hoo SAYN) wanted to take con- **6** trol of Kuwait's rich oil supply.

President Bush decided to work with other nations to force Iraq out of Kuwait. The United Nations demanded that Iraq leave Kuwait, but Hussein refused. In January 1991, the United States led an alliance of over 20 nations in Operation Desert Storm, an attack on Iraqi forces in Kuwait. General **Colin Powell,** the highest-ranking officer in the United States

armed forces, was one of the planners of Desert Storm. The fighting lasted only six weeks. Iraq was driven out of Kuwait.

Elected in 1992, President **Bill Clinton** continued working with other nations to settle conflicts around the world. One of the people who helped President Clinton make decisions was **Madeleine Albright,** who became secretary of state in 1997. Albright was the first woman to be secretary of state. She believed that cooperation between nations was the key to peace. She said,

> *"We must maintain strong alliances, for there is no better way to prevent war."*

Albright served until 2001, when Colin Powell became the new secretary of state. He was the first African American to head the State Department.

REVIEW What caused the Persian Gulf War and how did it end? **Sequence**

660

Practice and Extend

 EXTEND LANGUAGE
ESL Support

Interpret a Quotation Help students understand the meaning of Madeleine Albright's words.

Beginning Have students dramatize a situation where they cooperate with others to achieve a goal.

Intermediate Tell students to use a thesaurus to find synonyms for the key words in the quotation. Have them use the synonyms to paraphrase the quotation.

Advanced Ask students to paraphrase the quotation, using a dictionary to look up any unfamiliar words. Then have them give another example of its application.

For additional ESL support, use Every Student Learns Guide, pp. 274–277.

Turn of the Century

President Clinton was reelected in 1996. Then, like President Nixon, Clinton faced a serious scandal during his second term. During an investigation of his actions, Clinton lied while under oath. In 1998, the House of Representatives voted to impeach Clinton. He was only the second President to be impeached. After a trial in the Senate, senators voted not to remove Clinton from office.

The presidential election of 2000 was one of the closest in American history. **George W. Bush,** the son of President George Bush, faced Al Gore, who had served as Bill Clinton's Vice President for eight years. Gore received 50.9 million votes and Bush received 50.4 million. Bush, however, won the vote in the electoral college 271–266. Bush became the forty-third President in 2001. In 2004, Bush was reelected to a second term when he defeated John Kerry.

One important development of the 1990s was the rise of the Internet. You may know that the **Internet** is a worldwide network of computers. But did you know that the Internet started as a result of the Cold War? During the 1960s, the United States government wanted to build a communication system that would continue working even after a nuclear attack. American scientists came up with the idea of linking computers together. Today, millions of people use the Internet every day.

REVIEW Who were the two main candidates in the presidential election of 2004?
Main Idea and Details

▶ President George W. Bush (above).

South Africa

At the Same Time . . . Another major development of the 1990s was the end of apartheid, or racial segregation, in South Africa. Under apartheid, black South Africans were not allowed to vote and had few rights. Apartheid finally came to an end in the early 1990s. In 1994, black and white South Africans elected Nelson Mandela as their President. Mandela had spent 28 years in prison for leading opposition to apartheid. Now he was the leader of a changing nation.

SOUTH AFRICA

661

Turn of the Century

🕐 *Quick Summary* At the turn of the century, several important events occurred, including the impeachment of President Clinton and the closest presidential election in American history.

9 Why was Clinton not removed from office after he was impeached? Although Clinton was impeached, or formally charged with wrongful conduct while in office, senators voted not to remove him from office. **Main Idea and Details**

Ongoing Assessment ✓

If... students are confused about the impeachment proceedings involving Clinton,	**then...** explain that if the House votes for impeachment, a trial is held in the Senate. If the Senate finds the President guilty of the charges, then he is removed from office.

10 What are some ways the Internet changed the world? Possible answers: It helped people communicate in new and easier ways. It makes great quantities of information easily available. **Cause and Effect**

✓ **REVIEW ANSWER** George W. Bush and John Kerry **Main Idea and Details**

South Africa

11 Why might South Africans have wanted Nelson Mandela to be President? He had shown his commitment to the rights of all South Africans. **Draw Conclusions**

Americans United

Quick Summary Americans came together to help each other during and after the terrorist attacks on September 11, 2001. People around the world also gave their support and help to fight terrorist groups.

12 Summarize what terrorists did on September 11, 2001, in the United States. They hijacked planes and crashed them into the World Trade Center, the Pentagon, and a field in Pennsylvania. ↻ Summarize

H SOCIAL STUDIES STRAND
History

Point out the Empire State Building, which is visible in the center of the After picture. From 1931 to 1972, this 102-story building was the tallest building in the world. After the attack it became the tallest building in the city.

13 How were the World Trade Center towers similar to and different from other tall buildings in New York City?
Possible answer: The buildings are similar because they are all built very close together, and most of them look like rectangles from the side. They are different because the World Trade Center towers look much taller than the other buildings. Analyze Pictures

Primary Source
From a speech to the American people on September 20, 2001

14 How did President George W. Bush describe the current times? As an age of liberty everywhere
Analyze Primary Sources

Americans United

You might think of history as something that happened long ago. But one of the most shocking events in American history took place on September 11, 2001. On this day, terrorists carried out a massive attack against the United States. Terrorists are people who use violence and fear to try to achieve their goals.

Americans will never forget the morning of September 11, 2001. A group of terrorists hijacked, or took over by force, four airplanes, carrying a total of 226 people. The terrorists crashed two of the planes into the twin towers of the World Trade Center in New York City. These two 110-story buildings were completely destroyed. The terrorists crashed a third plane into the Pentagon, the headquarters of the Department of Defense, located near Washington, D.C. A fourth plane crashed in a **12** field in Pennsylvania. About 3,000 people were killed in these terrible attacks.

The American people showed courage and caring in the face of this frightening challenge. Firefighters, police officers, and rescue workers rushed to the scenes of the crashes, risking their own lives to save the lives of others. In cities and towns all over the country, people lined up to give blood to help those injured in the attacks. Millions of people of all ages donated food, clothing, and money.

The United States government and military immediately began working on additional ways to fight terrorism and prevent future attacks. In a speech to the American people on September 20, President George W. Bush told the country to prepare for a long and difficult war against terrorist groups worldwide. He also praised the American people for pulling together and expressed hope for the future:

"As long as the United States of America is determined and strong, this will not be an age of terror. This will be an age of liberty here and across the world."

▶ Before the terrorist attacks *(top)*, the twin towers of the World Trade Center rose high above New York City. After the attacks *(bottom)*, the city's skyline was changed forever. New York City firefighters *(far right)* showed that their spirit was still strong by raising the American flag at the site of the attacks.

Before

After

13

662

Practice and Extend

G SOCIAL STUDIES STRAND
Government

Leaders in America

- Have students identify and compare the leadership qualities of national leaders. Discuss with students the leadership qualities national leaders displayed after the terrorist attacks.

- Tell students that some leaders, including President George W. Bush and New York City Mayor Rudolph Guiliani, spoke to citizens often. Their public appearances gave people confidence that the government was working smoothly.

- Explain that in the first few weeks after the attacks, other leaders, including Vice President Dick Cheney and Secretary of State Colin Powell, worked more behind the scenes. They talked to leaders in other countries and participated in the decision-making process.

Our shared belief in ideals such as freedom, justice, and equality helped Americans pull together to face the challenges ahead. The United States government determined that the September 11 attacks were planned by a terrorist group called al Qaeda (al KEYE dah), led by a terrorist named Osama bin Laden. Military action against the terrorists was planned.

Another unfortunate event brought Americans together to help those in need. On December 26, 2004, an undersea earthquake in the Indian Ocean created a tsunami that devastated several countries in Southeast Asia. In response, the American people gave more than one billion dollars to help victims and their families.

Americans also helped victims of Hurricanes Katrina and Rita, which devastated the Gulf Coast from Alabama to Louisiana in 2005. The hurricanes caused extensive flooding and property damage and forced many people to leave the area. Many Americans helped rebuild the area after the storm.

REVIEW How did Americans respond to the terrorist attacks of September 11, 2001?
Main Idea and Details

FACT FILE

Heroes Help Others

After the events of September 11, 2001, the Asian tsunami disaster, and Hurricanes Katrina and Rita, Americans showed their concern by helping those in need.

Rescue workers carried people injured by Hurricane Katrina to nearby hospitals and treatment facilities for help.

This search dog, named Porkchop, needed medical care after helping find victims at the World Trade Center.

These students performed at the Kids of Hope Tsunami Relief Gala on April 21, 2005, in California. The event helped raise money for tsunami victims. **16**

663

---

15 **What ideals unite Americans?**
Freedom, justice, and equality
Main Idea and Details

✓ **REVIEW ANSWER** Firefighters, police officers, and rescue workers risked their lives to save the lives of others. Throughout the country, people lined up to give blood, and they donated food, clothing, and money. Main Idea and Details

FACT FILE

Heroes Help Others

16 **Why do you think students performed at the Relief Gala in California?** Possible answer: They were far away from the victims of the tsunami, and it was one way they could help. They wanted to raise money for the tsunami victims to help those who were injured or lost their homes. Make Inferences

$ **SOCIAL STUDIES STRAND**
Economics

Within five weeks of the attack, a total of one billion dollars had been donated. Citizens, celebrities, and businesses all participated in raising these funds for various relief organizations.

17 **Who are heroes of the September 11, 2001, attack?** Possible answer: Many people, including firefighters, police officers, rescue workers, people who gave blood, and search dogs and the people who took care of them.
Make Inferences

FYI **SOCIAL STUDIES**
Background

Terrorism

- Terrorism is deliberate and unpredictable violence. Because it involves surprise attacks, its victims are not prepared to defend themselves.
- Terrorism is different from a declared war, in which nations openly fight other nations in battles.
- Terrorism is conducted for a specific reason. The purpose may be to gain publicity for the terrorists' ideas, to retaliate for a real or imagined wrong, or to hurt a group or government that the terrorists regard as an enemy.
- Some terrorists may say they are attacking for religious reasons, but other followers of that religion would probably disagree.
- Terrorism has existed for many years. It was used during the Greek and Roman Empires and during the French Revolution. After the Civil War in the United States, the Ku Klux Klan emerged as a terrorist group.

The Struggle Against Terrorism

Quick Summary America used military force to attack terrorist bases in Afghanistan and to remove the leader of Iraq. A long rebuilding process began in both countries.

18 **What did American troops accomplish in Afghanistan?** The Taliban government surrendered, some terrorists were captured, and rebuilding began. **Summarize**

19 **What sequence of events caused Saddam Hussein to lose power?** After the 1991 Persian Gulf War he promised to destroy weapons of mass destruction. He did not cooperate with the United Nations inspectors, so the United States and other nations invaded Iraq and forced him from power. **Sequence**

20 **Why do you think the United States worked to rebuild Afghanistan and Iraq?** Possible answer: To show the people of these countries that the United States wanted to help make their lives better and bring democratic government to them. **Make Inferences**

✓ **REVIEW ANSWER** After the Taliban government in Afghanistan refused to help capture terrorists in their country, the United States attacked to capture terrorists and destroy their bases. In Iraq, the fighting resulted from Saddam Hussein's failure to cooperate with United Nations inspectors who were checking to see if he had destroyed weapons of mass destruction as promised. **Compare and Contrast**

The Struggle Against Terrorism

The al Qaeda terrorists opposed American influence in Western and Central Asia. Al Qaeda had made deadly attacks against American targets even before September 11. Since 1997 the group had been based in the Central Asian nation of Afghanistan. The United States demanded that the government of Afghanistan capture bin Laden and other al Qaeda leaders. But the group controlling the government, the Taliban (TAH le bahn), refused. President Bush and Congress decided to take military action.

On October 7, 2001, United States forces began attacking Taliban troops and al Qaeda training bases. Some Afghans who opposed the Taliban joined the fight. In December 2001, the Taliban government surrendered. **18** Some al Qaeda terrorists were captured. Others, including Osama bin Laden, escaped. Working with the United Nations, the United States began helping Afghanistan rebuild and establish a new, democratic government.

President Bush told the American people that the fighting in Afghanistan was just the beginning of a long, difficult war against

terrorists around the world. The United States led a global search for terrorists.

President Bush also considered taking military action against Saddam Hussein, the dictator of Iraq. As part of the agreement that ended the 1991 Persian Gulf War, Hussein had promised to destroy Iraq's weapons of mass destruction. Those are nuclear weapons or weapons that spread poison chemicals or deadly diseases. He agreed to let experts from the United Nations inspect Iraq to make sure these weapons were destroyed. However, Hussein did not cooperate with the United Nations, and the inspectors could not determine if Iraq had destroyed the weapons.

Leaders in the Bush administration argued that military force should be used to remove Hussein from power. Leaders of some countries did not believe war was necessary, but 30 countries agreed to help the United States remove Hussein. On March 20, 2003, American forces began bombing Baghdad, the capital of Iraq. The United States and Great Britain led a coalition force, or united group of military forces from various countries, into Iraq. Coalition forces quickly defeated the Iraqi army and Hussein lost power. As in Afghanistan, a long rebuilding process began.

REVIEW Describe the reasons for fighting in Afganistan and Iraq. **Compare and Contrast**

▶ **American troops attacked Iraq in March 2003.**

Practice and Extend

SOCIAL STUDIES STRAND
Economics

Stocks and Bonds

- Stocks and bonds are two ways people increase the value of their money. Other ways are bank savings accounts and investing in real estate or valuable goods.
- Stocks are the money value of companies divided into shares that people buy as an investment. A stockholder is usually paid a dividend when profits occur, and money can also be made when the stock increases in value. When most stock prices are increasing steadily over a period of time it is called a *bull market,* and the opposite trend is called a *bear market.*
- A bond is a printed promise by a government or company to repay the amount of money borrowed at a certain interest rate at a certain time.
- Have students research how events like the September 11 attacks can affect the stock market. Have them find out if the current market is *bear* or *bull.*

Rebuilding at Home

After September 11, 2001, New York City Mayor Rudolph Giuliani said, "This massive attack was intended to break our spirit. It has not done that. It has made us stronger, more determined, and more resolved." Americans immediately began to repair the damage done by the attacks. Within a year the destroyed section of the Pentagon had been repaired. At the World Trade Center, workers removed more than 100,000 truckloads of broken steel and concrete. A design for new buildings and a memorial park for the site was approved in 2003.

The United States government also changed in response to September 11. In 2003 Tom Ridge became the first head of a new government department called the Department of Homeland Security. One of the department's main jobs is to protect the United States from terrorism.

REVIEW What steps did Americans take to rebuild the damage done by the September 11 attacks? **Summarize**

Western and Central Asia

Map labels: EUROPE, Black Sea, RUSSIA, KAZAKHSTAN, UZBEKISTAN, KYRGYZSTAN, GEORGIA, ARMENIA, Caspian Sea, TURKMENISTAN, CHINA, TURKEY, TAJIKISTAN, ASIA, AZERBAIJAN, Kabul, CYPRUS, SYRIA, AFGHANISTAN, Mediterranean Sea, LEBANON, Baghdad, IRAN, ISRAEL, IRAQ, PAKISTAN, LIBYA, WEST BANK, JORDAN, • City, EGYPT, KUWAIT, INDIA, BAHRAIN, Persian Gulf, QATAR, Gulf of Oman, AFRICA, SAUDI ARABIA, UNITED ARAB EMIRATES, OMAN, Arabian Sea, Red Sea, SUDAN, ERITREA, YEMEN, ETHIOPIA, Gulf of Aden, INDIAN OCEAN

0 250 500 Miles
0 250 500 Kilometers

► The United States military became involved in conflicts in Iraq and Afghanistan in the early 2000s.

MAP SKILL Location *What country lies between Iraq and Afghanistan?*

665

Rebuilding at Home

Quick Summary After the September 11 attacks the spirit of Americans became stronger as the Pentagon was rebuilt and new plans for the World Trade Center site were approved. The government added a new department to protect the United States from terrorism.

Primary Source

From a speech to the United Nations special session on terrorism on October 1, 2001

21 Mayor Giuliani said; "This massive attack was intended to break our spirit. It has not done that." What did he mean? Possible answer: Instead of making Americans feel defeated, it caused them to feel stronger and more united as they helped each other and repaired the damage.
Analyze Primary Sources

✓ **REVIEW ANSWER** The Pentagon was repaired, the World Trade Center site was cleaned up, and plans were made to rebuild on the site. **Summarize**

22 How did the government change in response to the September 11 attacks? The Department of Homeland Security was begun in order to protect the United States from terrorism.

Western and Central Asia

23 Which country has direct access to a body of water leading to the Indian Ocean, Iraq or Afghanistan? Iraq
Interpret Maps

MAP SKILL Answer Iran

Looking Ahead

🕐 *Quick Summary* Today's students will use their problem-solving skills to improve society.

㉔ How do you think our society will change in the future? Answer one of the questions in the last paragraph on p. 666 and defend your prediction. Possible answer: New medicines will allow people to live longer. **Predict**

FACT FILE
Challenges of the Twenty-first Century

㉕ Do you think countries will become more cooperative or more isolated in the future? Why? Possible answer: They will cooperate more as they work together on projects such as the International Space Station, fight against terrorist groups, and use new technologies to communicate. **Express Ideas**

㉖ How might the use of computers by students affect the future of the United States? Possible answer: Because students are learning about computers when they are young, they might gain skills that will allow them to think about world problems in new ways and find new solutions. **Predict**

㉗ How might new inventions protect the environment? Possible answer: We might find ways to make greater use of solar, wind, or tidal power so that natural resources can be conserved. **Hypothesize**

㉘ Give an example of how countries use modern technology to work together and solve world challenges. Possible answer: Scientists from around the world use the Internet to share information about medicines that cure diseases. **Apply Information**

㉙ Think about a future career. How might it help you contribute to solving a world problem? Possible answer: Scientist; work to find new medicines to help sick people **Express Ideas**

Looking Ahead

Think about some of the major events you have read about in this book. You know that in the late 1700s, Americans battled for independence from Britain and struggled to form a new country. In the 1800s, the nation was nearly split apart in the Civil War. In the 1900s, the United States fought in two world wars, while citizens at home continued the struggle for equal rights. Today Americans face the challenge of terrorism in the United States and around the world. As Americans look to the future, we see many new challenges, as well as many new opportunities.

Look at the Fact File below, which asks you to think about the challenges and opportunities ahead. Do you have any predictions for the future? For example, will we succeed in ending terrorism? What do you think will be the most important invention of the twenty-first century? Will new medicines allow most people to live to be over 100? Will we find new ways to conserve natural resources and protect our environment?

FACT FILE
Challenges of the Twenty-first Century

You have read about many of the challenges the United States has faced in its history. What challenges will Americans face in the future?

The United States and Russia were enemies during the Cold War, but now we cooperate in exploring space. What discoveries will be made in outer space?

㉕ Computers have made it easier to share information and keep in touch with people all over the world. How will computers and the Internet continue to change our lives?

As the world changes, the United States and its allies prepare to face new kinds of threats. Do you think nations will fight different kinds of wars than they have in the past?

Scientists have given new hope to people with serious injuries or life-threatening diseases. What medical discoveries will improve lives in the future?

666

Practice and Extend

❄ **MEETING INDIVIDUAL NEEDS**
Leveled Practice

Research New Technology Have students use print and online resources to find out more about space, computers and the Internet, environment, and health.

Easy Have students locate and read a brief article about a current event in one of the areas. Have them write a prediction for a possible next step or discovery. **Reteach**

On-Level Ask students to locate and read two articles about one of the areas and then predict a development in the future. Have them write a brief blurb for a magazine of the future on the invention or discovery they have predicted. **Extend**

Challenge Tell students to read several sources concerning a current event in one of the areas. Have them describe an invention or discovery that could further this work. Ask them to present their ideas to the class. **Enrich**

For a Lesson Summary, use Quick Study, p. 138.

It is not just fascinating to think about questions like these. It is also important. That is because in the future you will do more than think about these questions. You and your classmates will be the ones who will help answer them. The 29

answers you and others find may well be in the history books studied by your children and grandchildren.

REVIEW What is one question you have about the future? Add a question of your own to the questions on this page.
Main Idea and Details

Summarize the Lesson

- **1989** The Berlin Wall, a symbol of the Cold War, was torn down.
- **1991** The United States and its allies drove Iraq out of Kuwait in the Persian Gulf War.
- **2001** Thousands died in terrorist attacks on the United States.
- **2003** A design for rebuilding the World Trade Center site is approved.

LESSON 4 **REVIEW**

Check Facts and Main Ideas

1. **Main Idea and Details** On a separate sheet of paper, complete the chart below by listing three major changes that have taken place since the early 1980s.

```
┌─────────────────────────────────┐
│  The world has changed since    │
│       the early 1980s.          │
└─────────────────────────────────┘
      ↑            ↑            ↑
┌──────────┐ ┌──────────┐ ┌──────────┐
│The Internet│ │The Cold War│ │Terrorists│
│ became   │ │ ended.   │ │attacked the│
│ popular. │ │          │ │   U.S.   │
└──────────┘ └──────────┘ └──────────┘
```

2. Did relations between the United States and the Soviet Union improve during the 1980s? Explain.

3. How did the Cold War help lead to the development of the **Internet?**

4. Following the terrorist attacks of September 11, 2001, did the United States act alone in battling terrorism? Explain.

5. **Critical Thinking:** *Predict* Reread the list of questions on this page. Pick one of these questions, or write a question of your own about the future. Then write a one-page paper, answering the question with your predictions for the future.

Link to ∞ **Writing**

Look Toward the Future Write a one-page paper describing what you think is the most important challenge facing the United States today. Explain what you can do to help meet this challenge.

667

✓ **REVIEW ANSWER** Students can ask any question about the future, such as *How can nations work together for peace?*
Main Idea and Details

3 Close and Assess

Summarize the Lesson

Have students list items they could put in a time capsule to remember important events from this time. Have them write a sentence to explain the reason for including each item.

✓ **LESSON 4** **REVIEW**

1. **Main Idea and Details** For possible answers, see the reduced pupil page.

2. Yes; Gorbachev's reforms helped lead to improved relations. In 1987, the two nations signed an arms control agreement.

3. In the 1960s, the U.S. government linked computers together, and this system developed into the Internet.

4. No; people from all over the world supported the United States, and national leaders, including the Prime Minister of Great Britain, joined the fight.

5. **Critical Thinking:** *Predict* Answers should include a question about the future and a one-page answer on the student's predictions.

Link to ∞ **Writing**

Students should identify a specific challenge and present logical suggestions for addressing it.

Workbook, p. 152

Lesson 4: Looking Toward the Future

Directions: Sequence the events in the order in which they occurred. Number them from 1 (earliest) to 10 (most recent). You may use your textbook.

___ The Berlin Wall is destroyed, and several communist governments in Eastern Europe are replaced with elected governments.

___ Newly elected U.S. President Ronald Reagan believes the United States should strengthen its military to block Soviet efforts to expand communism around the world.

___ The United States leads a group of more than 20 nations in Operation Desert Storm, an attack on Iraqi forces in Kuwait.

___ The 2000 U.S. presidential election is one of the closest races in history. George W. Bush wins the electoral college vote, and Al Gore wins the popular vote. George W. Bush is declared President.

___ The Soviet Union and the United States sign an arms control agreement in which both countries agree to destroy some of their nuclear weapons.

___ The Soviet Union breaks up into 15 independent republics, and Gorbachev announces that the Cold War is over.

___ During his second term in office, President Clinton faces a scandal and is impeached.

___ The Middle Eastern nation of Iraq invades Kuwait in an effort to take control of Kuwait's rich oil supply. This begins the Persian Gulf War. The United States must decide whether to help end the conflict.

___ Soviet leader Mikhail Gorbachev begins reforming the country by allowing people more political and economic freedom.

___ U.S. President William Clinton appoints Madeleine Albright as secretary of state. She is the first woman to hold this position.

Directions: In recent decades, many changes have occurred in politics, science, technology, and culture. What is one change that you think will occur in the next 50 years? Why?

_____

_____

_____

Also on Teacher Resources CD-ROM.

Racing to the Rescue

Objective

- Identify accomplishments of individuals who made significant contributions to society in the area of public safety.

1 Introduce and Motivate

Preview To activate prior knowledge, have students describe someone's difficult or dangerous action that helped at least one other person.

2 Teach and Discuss

Primary Source

Cited in *The New York Times*, October 3, 2001

1 Why do you think Suarez kept working even after his 24-hour shift was over? Possible answer: He may have been tired, but he knew people needed his help. The World Trade Center was such a big building that many firefighters were needed.
Make Inferences

CITIZEN HEROES

Racing to the Rescue

On a day of terrifying attacks, the heroic actions of New York City firefighters saved thousands of lives.

New York City's Ladder Company 21 has a long history of fighting fires and saving lives. When the company was first formed in 1890, firefighters rushed to fires on a truck pulled by three horses. Today Ladder Company 21 uses computers and modern trucks. But some things have not changed. Firefighting is still a dangerous job that requires great courage. This is why New Yorkers have nicknamed the city's firefighters "New York's Bravest."

On the morning of September 11, 2001, terrorists crashed two planes into New York's World Trade Center. The call for help went out to fire stations all over the city. At Ladder Company 21, Benjamin Suarez was one of many firefighters who were just finishing a 24-hour shift. But Suarez did not even think about leaving the job. He called his wife and said,

1 *"I have to help the people."*

Then he and his fellow firefighters jumped on their trucks and raced to the scene of the attacks.

As firefighters arrived from around the city, they saw that the twin towers of the World Trade Center were on fire. They rushed into the buildings and up the stairs. "We saw them going up the stairs as we were going down," said a woman who escaped from one of the towers. The firefighters helped people who were injured or lost in the smoke. With **2** the firefighters' help, thousands of people escaped to safety.

668

Practice and Extend

CURRICULUM CONNECTION
Writing

Write a Poem

- Have students provide examples of courageous actions as you list them on the board.
- Ask students to write a poem about courage. Explain that students may refer to the list on the board or use their own ideas.
- Students may write about courage in general or about a specific courageous act.
- Remind students that not all poems rhyme.
- Allow students to share their poems in a poetry reading or by posting their poems in a display. Some students may want to create illustrations to accompany their displayed poems.

SOCIAL STUDIES
Background

World Trade Center

- The World Trade Center was a complex of buildings covering sixteen acres on Manhattan Island. The two main towers in the complex each had 110 floors.
- Each tower had 97 passenger elevators. The fastest elevators traveled 27 feet per second, making the trip to the top in 4.8 minutes.
- The complex had its own zip code: 10048.
- When the buildings were built, more than 1.2 million cubic yards of earth were removed. That excavated earth became the land on which Battery City Park was constructed.

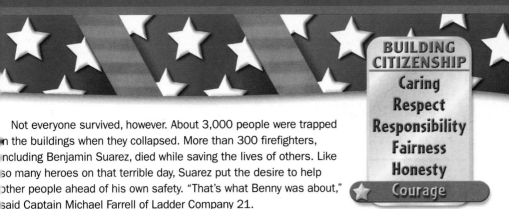

Not everyone survived, however. About 3,000 people were trapped in the buildings when they collapsed. More than 300 firefighters, including Benjamin Suarez, died while saving the lives of others. Like so many heroes on that terrible day, Suarez put the desire to help other people ahead of his own safety. "That's what Benny was about," said Captain Michael Farrell of Ladder Company 21.

In the days following the terrorist attacks, neighbors visited Ladder Company 21 to show their sympathy for the firefighters who had lost their lives. Many people left flowers and made donations to the firefighters' families. Children wrote letters in which they thanked firefighters for saving lives. Some children drew pictures showing firefighters performing brave actions. The firefighters hung these letters and pictures on the wall of the fire station. Similar scenes took place at fire stations all ③ over the city.

Rudolph Giuliani, the mayor of New York City, thanked firefighters for their incredible courage:

> *"Without courage, nothing else can really happen. And there is no better example, none, than the courage of the Fire Department of the City of New York."* ④

New York's firefighters not only saved thousands of lives, their actions inspired the entire nation. In a time of fear and danger, firefighters helped Americans have the courage to face the difficult times ahead.

Courage in Action

Link to Current Events Every day, firefighters, police officers, and other rescue workers perform heroic acts in communities all over the nation. Read a newspaper from your community to find out about the recent actions of your local firefighters or other emergency workers. What actions did they take? How did these actions show courage?

669

---

② **What would have happened if Suarez and other firefighters had not rushed into the buildings?** Thousands of people would not have escaped to safety. **Draw Conclusions**

Test Talk

Use Information from the Text

③ **How did people show their appreciation for the firefighters' courage?** Have students skim the text to find details describing what people did to show their appreciation. They left flowers, made donations to firefighters' families, wrote letters, drew pictures, and praised firefighters in speeches. **Main Idea and Details**

Primary Source

From Remarks at the Fire Department Promotions Ceremony, September 16, 2001

④ **What did Rudolph Giuliani say was the best example of courage?** The New York City Fire Department **Analyze Primary Sources**

③ Close and Assess

Courage in Action

Link to Current Events

- You may want to provide additional newspaper clippings about firefighters, emergency medical personnel, or police officers.

- Have students summarize the newspaper article, identifying the dangers the workers faced.

CURRICULUM CONNECTION
Literature

Read About Firefighting The following selections provide additional information about firefighters' work.

Fire! by Joy Masoff (Scholastic, Inc., ISBN 0-590-97872-1, 1998) **Easy**

Firefighting: Behind the Scenes, by Maria Mudd-Ruth (Houghton Mifflin, ISBN 0-395-70129-5, 1998) **On-Level**

Fire in Their Eyes: Wildfires and the People Who Fight Them, by Karen Magnuson Beil (Harcourt, ISBN 0-152-01042-4, 1999) **Challenge**

Resources

- Assessment Book, pp. 109–112
- Workbook, p. 153: Vocabulary Review

Chapter Summary

For possible answers, see the reduced pupil page.

Vocabulary

1. c, **2.** b, **3.** e, **4.** a, **5.** d

People and Terms

Possible answers:

1. The Iron Curtain separated Europe into communist and noncommunist countries after World War II.

2. UN forces fought the Korean War to defend South Korea against the invading army from North Korea.

3. The Cuban Missile Crisis occurred when the United States learned that the Soviet Union was setting up nuclear missiles in Cuba.

4. Thurgood Marshall was the NAACP's lawyer in the Supreme Court case that declared segregation in public schools illegal.

5. After Rosa Parks was arrested for refusing to give up her seat on the bus, Martin Luther King, Jr., led the Montgomery bus boycott.

6. John Glenn was the first American to orbit Earth.

7. The United States fought in the Vietnam War to prevent communist North Vietnam from taking over noncommunist South Vietnam.

8. The United States led an alliance of nations in the Persian Gulf War in order to drive Iraq out of Kuwait.

9. Colin Powell helped plan the operation that succeeded in driving Iraq out of Kuwait.

10. Madeleine Albright was the first female secretary of state.

Facts and Main Ideas

1. To find peaceful solutions to international problems

2. It protected African Americans' right to vote.

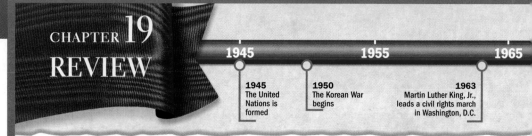

CHAPTER 19
REVIEW

1945	1955	1965

1945 The United Nations is formed

1950 The Korean War begins

1963 Martin Luther King, Jr., leads a civil rights march in Washington, D.C.

Chapter Summary

 **Summarizing**

On a separate sheet of paper, complete this graphic organizer by filling in four details from this chapter.

▶ A rock from the moon

Details

| After the Cuban Missile Crisis, the Soviet Union removed missiles from Cuba. | Neil Armstrong and Buzz Aldrin became the first people to land on the moon. | Over 57,000 Americans were killed in the Vietnam War. | Terrorist attacks in the United States kill thousands of people. |

Since the end of World War II there have been major changes in the United States and around the world.

Summary

Vocabulary

Match each word with the correct definition or description.

1 communism (p. 637)

2 arms race (p. 641)

3 space race (p. 651)

4 arms control (p. 654)

5 Internet (p. 661)

a. agreement to limit the production of weapons

b. competition to build more powerful weapons

c. political and economic system in which the government owns all businesses and land

d. worldwide network of computers

e. competition to explore outer space

People and Terms

Write a sentence explaining why each of the following people or terms was important to the United States in the 1900s. You may use two more in a single sentence.

1 Iron Curtain (p. 638)

2 Korean War (p. 639)

3 Cuban Missile Crisis (p. 640)

4 Thurgood Marshall (p. 643)

5 Rosa Parks (p. 644)

6 John Glenn (p. 651)

7 Vietnam War (p. 653)

8 Persian Gulf War (p. 660)

9 Colin Powell (p. 660)

10 Madeleine Albright (p. 660)

670

Practice and Extend

Assessment Options

✓ **Chapter 19 Assessment**

- Chapter 19 Content Test: Use Assessment Book, pp. 109–110.
- Chapter 19 Skills Test: Use Assessment Book, pp. 111–112.

Standardized Test Prep

- Chapter 19 Tests contain standardized test format.

✓ **Chapter 19 Performance Assessment**

- Have students work in groups to create albums that contain six to ten simulated photographs of significant events covered in this chapter. Have students draw the simulated photographs and write captions.
- Ask students from each group to role-play grandparents and grandchildren. Have the "grandparents" show the album and tell about the events. Have the "grandchildren" ask follow-up questions.
- Assess students' understanding of key events that took place after World War II.

1969 American astronauts walk on the moon

1972 President Nixon travels to China

1981 Sandra Day O'Connor is the first woman named to the Supreme Court

1989 The Berlin Wall is torn down

2001 Terrorist attacks in the United States kill thousands

Facts and Main Ideas

1. Why was the United Nations established?

2. What did the Voting Rights Act of 1965 accomplish?

3. How has the Internet changed people's lives?

4. **Time Line** How many years after the United Nations was formed did the Korean War begin?

5. **Main Idea** What was the Cold War and which countries were involved?

6. **Main Idea** What were some key events in the African American struggle to gain civil rights and equal opportunity?

7. **Main Idea** How did the United States continue to oppose the spread of communism in the 1960s and 1970s?

8. **Main Idea** What have been some of the challenges the United States faced after the Cold War ended?

9. **Critical Thinking:** *Evaluate* How might meetings like the one between President Nixon and China's Mao Zedong help the United States?

Write About History

1. **Write a list of hopes** for the future of the United States.

2. **Write a TV news story** about the Cuban Missile Crisis.

3. **Write a short story** about Rosa Parks and the Montgomery bus boycott.

Apply Skills

Understand Map Projections

Study the map below. Then answer the questions.

1. Is this a Mercator projection or an equal-area projection? Explain.

2. Compare this map with Map B on page 657. How are they similar? How are they different?

3. Which map do you think is better for measuring the distance between North America and Asia? Why?

Internet Activity

To get help with vocabulary, people, and terms, select dictionary or encyclopedia from *Social Studies Library* at www.sfsocialstudies.com.

671

3. Millions of people use it every day to communicate and share information.

4. Five years

5. A struggle between the United States and the Soviet Union involving their different ways of life

6. The *Brown* v. *Board of Education* case, the Montgomery bus boycott, the March on Washington, the Civil Rights Act of 1964, and the Voting Rights Act of 1965

7. By fighting in Vietnam and trying to improve relations with China and the Soviet Union

8. Deciding how to use its power and what role to play in world conflicts

9. They might help ease tensions and build friendly relations.

Write About History

1. Students' lists should relate to current issues and include logical predictions about future issues.

2. Students' stories should include key figures in the crisis, an explanation of its causes, and a summary of its resolution.

3. Students' stories should include main ideas and details about the Montgomery bus boycott.

Apply Skills

1. This is an equal-area projection because the sizes, shapes, and distances are fairly accurate.

2. Similar: Both are equal-area projections; Different: This map is centered on the Pacific Ocean, and the map on p. 657 is centered on the Atlantic Ocean.

3. This map; it shows the distance between the United States and Asia.

Hands-on Unit Project

✓ Unit 9 Performance Assessment

- See p. 676 for information about using the Unit Project as a means of performance assessment.
- A scoring guide is provided on p. 676.

WEB SITE
Technology

For more information, students can select the dictionary or encyclopedia from *Social Studies Library* at **www.sfsocialstudies.com**.

Workbook, p. 153

Vocabulary Review

Directions: Use the vocabulary words from Chapter 19 to complete the crossword puzzle.

Across
4. Iraq invaded Kuwait, sparking the _____ War.
7. Fifty nations dedicated to finding peaceful solutions to international problems
9. A political and economic system in which the government owns all the businesses and land
12. The line dividing the continent of Europe into communist and noncommunist countries
13. The war that started when North Vietnam tried to unify all of Vietnam under communist rule
14. Worldwide network of computers

Down
1. The _____ War started when the North Koreans invaded South Korea.
2. The long, bitter struggle between the United States and the Soviet Union was called the _____ War.
3. The contest to be first to explore outer space was known as the _____ race.
5. The _____ Crisis happened when the Soviets sent nuclear weapons to Cuba.
6. The U.S. Constitution guarantees these to all citizens.
8. The U.S. and Soviet Union's competition to build more weapons was known as the _____ race.
10. Because of an arms _____ agreement, the United States and the Soviet Union limited the number of weapons they produced.
11. President Nixon resigned for his involvement in the _____ scandal.

Also on Teacher Resources CD-ROM.

"You're a Grand Old Flag"

Objectives

- Identify significant examples of music from various periods in U.S. history.

- Explain how examples of music reflect the times during which they were written.

1 Introduce and Motivate

Preview To activate prior knowledge, ask students if they know the song "You're a Grand Old Flag." Tell them that it conveys some ideas about the U.S. flag.

Ask students how studying a song about the flag can be helpful. If necessary, remind students of the words from the Pledge of Allegiance (See p. 11) ". . . to the Flag . . . and to the Republic for which it stands . . ." and explain that the flag stands for the United States. (You can learn about what the country stands for, such as freedom.)

2 Teach and Discuss

1 How does the songwriter feel about our country? He loves it.
Main Idea and Details

The American flag has inspired artists and writers for more than two hundred years. In the early 1900s, American song-writer George M. Cohan wrote his own tribute to the flag. Read the words to "You're a Grand Old Flag." What was Cohan saying about the American flag and the nation it represents?

672

Practice and Extend

CURRICULUM CONNECTION
Music

Write a Patriotic Song

- Have students brainstorm words and phrases that tell about the United States—what it stands for, who its citizens are, and what students appreciate about it.

- Allow students to work individually or in groups to write the lyrics or compose music for their own patriotic song.

- Give students time to practice their songs and then schedule a performance. You may want to invite students from other classrooms or family members.

AUDIO CD
Technology

Play the CD *Songs and Music* to listen to "You're a Grand Old Flag."

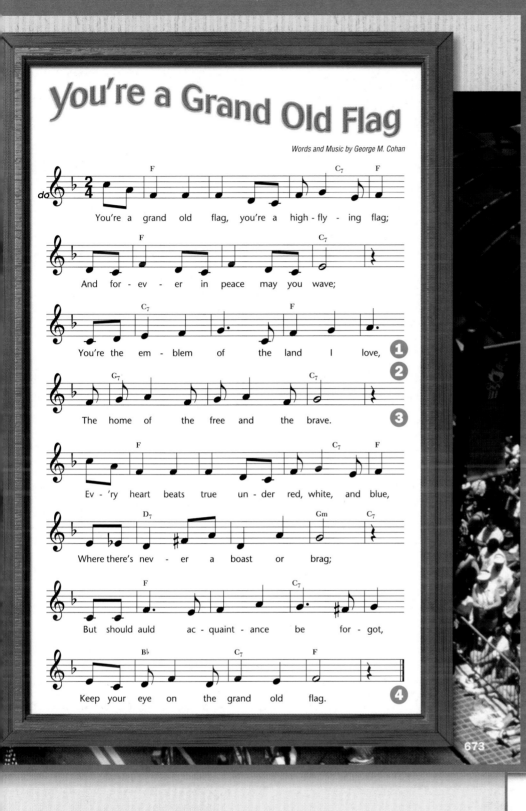

You're a Grand Old Flag

Words and Music by George M. Cohan

You're a grand old flag, you're a high-fly-ing flag;

And for-ev-er in peace may you wave;

You're the em-blem of the land I love, **1** **2**

The home of the free and the brave. **3**

Ev-'ry heart beats true un-der red, white, and blue,

Where there's nev-er a boast or brag;

But should auld ac-quaint-ance be for-got,

Keep your eye on the grand old flag. **4**

673

2 **Which lines in the song say that the flag is a symbol of the United States?**
"You're the emblem of / the land I love.
Analyze Information

3 **Which phrase in the song is similar to one in "The Star-Spangled Banner"?**
Home of the free and the brave (*land of the free and home of the brave* in "The Star-Spangled Banner")
Compare and Contrast

4 **What do the last two lines of the song mean?** Possible answer: People may forget some of their friends, but they will always remember the flag and the United States. **Make Inferences**

3 Close and Assess

- Have students discuss ways to perform this song. Students may be interested in using hand gestures to emphasize the lyrics or using musical instruments to play the melody.

- Ask students to suggest additional stanzas that could be added to the song.

SOCIAL STUDIES STRAND
Citizenship

American Flag Etiquette

To close the lesson, remind students of these simple rules of flag etiquette.

- Do not let the flag touch the ground when it is flying or when you are raising and lowering it.

- You can fly the flag day and night. If you display it at night, you should spotlight the flag.

- If you hang a flag vertically on a window or a building, you should hang it so that the blue union is on the top left when viewed from outside.

- You should display the American flag to the right of any other flags you display.

- To salute the flag, stand and put your hand over your heart. You can also give a hand salute.

SOCIAL STUDIES
Culture

Compare and Contrast Songs

- Make available recordings and lyrics of several other patriotic songs, including "America the Beautiful" (see p. 1h) and "The Star-Spangled Banner" (see pp. 388–389).

- Ask students to discuss similarities and differences in the sentiments and the tone of the songs.

Resource

- Assessment Book, pp. 113–116

Main Ideas and Vocabulary · TEST PREP

1. a, 2. c, 3. b, 4. b

People and Places

1. e, 2. a, 3. f, 4. b, 5. c, 6. d

Test Talk

Choose the Right Answer

Use People and Places, Question 3, to model the Test Talk strategy.

Narrow the answer choices.

Tell students to read each answer choice carefully. Students should rule out any choice that they know is wrong.

Compare chosen answer with the text.

After students mark their answer choice, tell them to check their answer by comparing it with the text.

Apply Skills

- Political cartoons from local newspapers may be easier for students to understand since they may deal with familiar issues.

- Provide guided practice in deciphering the symbolism, irony, and exaggeration of political cartoons before starting.

Main Ideas and Vocabulary · TEST PREP

Read the passage below and use it to answer the questions that follow.

In the early 1900s, changes in the United States happened as a result of activities at home and overseas. Reformers urged the conservation of natural resources. The muckrakers exposed shameful conditions in businesses like food processing.

In 1917 the United States began fighting with the Allied Powers against the Central Powers in World War I. The war brought many women and African Americans into factory jobs. After the war, women got the right to vote.

The 1920s provided a better life for many. Movies, radio, and automobiles changed entertainment and transportation.

In 1929, the stock market crashed, and the Great Depression began. Many people were out of work. New Deal programs tried to help the nation recover.

World War II helped pull the United States out of the Great Depression. One third of all production went toward the war effort, and many new jobs were created.

After the war, the United States and the Soviet Union faced each other in the Cold War. During this time, the two nations raced to develop more powerful weapons and make advances in space exploration.

Life for Americans was very different at the end of the 1900s than it was at the beginning. The Cold War had ended, leaving the United States as the only remaining superpower. Many people enjoyed more opportunities than in the past. And different technologies like the Internet were increasing communication.

1 According to the passage, why did women and African Americas find new jobs during World War I?
- **A** Factories needed workers.
- **B** New laws made people hire them.
- **C** Reformers insisted on hiring women and African Americans.
- **D** The Nineteenth Amendment demanded better jobs.

2 In the passage the word muckrakers means—
- **A** inventors
- **B** soldiers
- **C** writers who expose bad conditions
- **D** civil rights activists

3 In the passage the term stock market means—
- **A** market where cattle are bought and sold
- **B** market where shares of companies are bought and sold
- **C** market where land is bought and sold
- **D** market where jobs are offered

4 What is the main idea of the passage?
- **A** Reformers exposed shameful conditions.
- **B** The 1900s brought changes in the way Americans lived.
- **C** The United States fought in several wars.
- **D** New inventions changed America.

674

Practice and Extend

Assessment Options

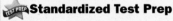 **Unit 9 Assessment**

- Unit 9 Content Test:
  Use Assessment Book,
  pp. 113–114.
- Unit 9 Skills Test:
  Use Assessment Book,
  pp. 115–116.

Standardized Test Prep

- Unit 9 Tests contain standardized test format.

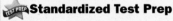 **Unit 9 Performance Assessment**

- See p. 676 for information about using the Unit Project as a means of Performance Assessment.
- A scoring guide for the Unit 9 Project is provided in the teacher's notes on p. 676.

Test Talk

- Test Talk Practice Book

WEB SITE Technology

For more information, students can select the dictionary or encyclopedia from *Social Studies Library* at **www.sfsocialstudies.com.**

Test Talk

Narrow the answer choices. Rule out answers you know are wrong.

People and Places

Match each person and place to its definition.

1. **Panama Canal** (p. 605)

2. **Versailles, France** (p. 611)

3. **Kitty Hawk** (p. 617)

4. **George W. Bush** (p. 661)

5. **César Chávez** (p. 648)

6. **Maya Ying Lin** (p. 653)

a. where the World War I peace treaty was signed

b. became President in 2001

c. worked to improve conditions for migrant farm workers

d. designer of the Vietnam Veterans Memorial

e. built by the United States to connect the Atlantic and Pacific Oceans

f. site of first airplane flight

Apply Skills

Create a **Political Cartoon Display** Make a poster of political cartoons you have found in newspapers or magazines. You can add cartoons that you draw yourself. Under each cartoon, write a sentence or two explaining what the cartoon is about and what point of view it has about the subject.

Write and Share

Present a Time Line Your teacher will divide the class into groups. Each group will prepare a time line showing some of the main events from one decade of the 1900s: 1901–1910, 1911–1920, and so on. Use your textbook and other resources to identify important events from the decade. Then prepare illustrations about the selected events. Finally, each group will give a short presentation about the events selected, showing the illustrations as they speak.

Read on Your Own

Look for books like these in the library.

675

Revisit the Unit Question

✓ **Portfolio Assessment**

- Have students look at the list they created at the beginning of Unit 9 of the hopes and dreams they have for the future of our country.
- Have students look at the list they created throughout Unit 9 of the ideas that people fought for during the 1900s.
- Ask students to compare and contrast their lists.
- Have students write a summary expressing how their own ideas about what the United States stands for may have changed.
- Have students add these lists and summaries to their Social Studies Portfolio.

Write and Share

- Provide students with rulers and construction paper to make time lines. Remind them to focus on the main events of the decade.
- Students may want to refer to the time lines in the unit and use them as a starting point for creating more detailed graphics.
- Encourage students to discuss and plan their illustrations before drawing them.

✓ **Assessment Scoring Guide**

	Present a Time Line
6	Presents time line with most important events of the decade; concise, accurate details; many relevant illustrations.
5	Many significant dates, important details, and relevant illustrations.
4	Includes many significant dates; some details and illustrations.
3	Few appropriate dates, details, and relevant illustrations.
2	Very few appropriate dates, details, and illustrations.
1	Is unable to create appropriate time line.

If you prefer a 4-point rubric, adjust accordingly.

Read on Your Own

Have students prepare oral reports using the following books.

Footprints on the Moon, by Alexandra Siy (Charlesbridge Publishing, ISBN 1-570-91408-7, 2001) **Easy**

Fighting for Honor: Japanese Americans and World War II, by Michael L. Cooper (Houghton Mifflin, ISBN 0-395-91375-6, 2000) **On-Level**

Eleanor Roosevelt: A Life of Discovery, by Russell Freedman (Houghton Mifflin, ISBN 0-395-84520-3, 1997) **Challenge**

Unit Project

Then and Now

Objective
- Describe historic events, technological advances, and everyday life during a decade in the 1900s.

Resource
- Workbook, p. 154

Materials
paper, pencils, pens, reference materials

Follow This Procedure
- Tell students they will prepare documentaries about different decades in the 20th century. Divide the class into groups, trying to have each decade represented.

- Explain to students that they will present their research in question-and-answer interviews. Help students select roles they will play of people living during their decade.

- Students should include details about major historic events and advances in technology, as well as transportation, clothing, home life, and so on.

- Invite students to present their documentaries to the class. If possible, they may want to videotape them.

- Use the following scoring guide.

✓ Assessment Scoring Guide

Present a Documentary	
6	Provides well-organized, detailed description; accurate, relevant information; precise word choices.
5	Provides detailed description, accurate information, and precise word choices.
4	Provides some details in description, mostly accurate information, and clear world choices.
3	Provides few details in description, some inaccurate information, and vague word choices.
2	Provides few or no details in description, inaccurate information, and incorrect word choices.
1	Cannot describe decade in the 1900s.

If you prefer a 4-point rubric, adjust accordingly.

Then and Now

Bring the past to life in a documentary.

1 Form a group and choose a decade from the 1900s.

2 Research historic events, advances in technology, and changes in everyday life that occurred during the decade.

3 Have each person in the group take on the role of a person living in the decade. Write what each person would say as if he or she were speaking for a documentary. Decide who will speak first, second, and so on.

4 Give your presentation to the class. If a video camera is available, film the presentation.

Internet Activity

Explore the 1900s on the Internet. Go to **www.sfsocialstudies.com/activities** and select your grade and unit.

676

Practice and Extend

Hands-on Unit Project

✓ Performance Assessment
- The Unit Project can also be used as a performance assessment activity.
- Use the scoring guide to assess each group's work.

WEB SITE
Technology

Students can launch the Internet Activity by clicking on *Grade 5, Unit 9* at **www.sfsocialstudies.com/activities**.

Workbook, p. 154

9 Project Then and Now

Directions: In a group, plan a documentary about historic events and advances in technology during a decade from the 1900s.

1. We chose the decade 19___–19___.
2. The (✓) shows which topics we researched.
   ___ historic events ___ technological advances ___ transportation ___ entertainment
   ___ clothing ___ home life ___ education ___ occupations
   ___ other _____
3. The following people from the decade will speak for the documentary:
   Name: _____ Role: _____
   Name: _____ Role: _____
   Name: _____ Role: _____
4. My role in the documentary is _____
5. Questions about living in the 19___s:

6. Answers to questions about the 19___s:

Checklist for Students
___ The group chose a decade from the 1900s.
___ The group researched topics about living in the 19___s.
___ Roles were assigned for the documentary.
___ The group wrote questions and answers about the decade.
___ The group presented its documentary to the class.

Notes for Home: Your child participated in a group presentation on a decade from the 1900s.
Home Activity: Discuss with your child your family's decade of the twentieth century. Describe the clothing, home life, transportation, and important events of this time period.

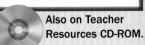

Also on Teacher Resources CD-ROM.

Western Hemisphere

A Visual Introduction

CANADA

UNITED STATES

MEXICO   CARIBBEAN REGION

CENTRAL AMERICA   SOUTH AMERICA

Who are our neighbors in the Western Hemisphere?

677

A Visual Introduction

Overview

The Western Hemisphere includes the continents of North America and South America. The landscape, climate, people, and lifestyles of the Western Hemisphere vary greatly from country to country in North, Central, and South America.

Outline

- **Canada,** pp. 678–681
- **Mexico,** pp. 682–685
- **The Countries of Central America,** pp. 686–687
- **The Countries of the Caribbean Region,** pp. 688–689
- **The Countries of South America,** pp. 690–691

Question

- Have students read the question under the picture.

- To activate prior knowledge, have students name countries in the Western Hemisphere. Record their answers.

- Have the class create a list of questions about the Western Hemisphere.

- After completing their study of the Western Hemisphere, ask students to attempt to answer the questions they listed.

SOCIAL STUDIES
Background

Organization of American States

- The OAS was formed to promote peaceful cooperation among the nations in the Americas. The OAS includes most of the independent nations in the Western Hemisphere.

- The OAS has sent missions to oversee fair elections and support initiatives for peace and civil rights in many nations, including Nicaragua, Suriname, Haiti, and Guatemala.

- Regular meetings of the General Assembly are held every year, and special meetings are called as necessary. Approval of two-thirds of the representatives present is required for member states to act as a whole.

Canada

1 Introduce and Motivate

Preview To introduce students to Canada, have a volunteer point out the country on a large world map. Ask students to identify its location relative to the United States. (North)

To activate prior knowledge, invite students to share what they know about the climate, landscape, regions, and people of Canada. Have them consider how Canada and the United States are similar and different.

2 Teach and Discuss

1 **What does this map show about the physical features of Canada?** Possible answer: Canada has many mountains and bodies of water. Interpret Maps

2 **What do the lines on the map of Canada suggest?** That the country is composed of parts (provinces or territories) just as the United States is composed of states Make Inferences

Capital
Ottawa

Population
31,278,097

Area
3,851,800
square miles

Official languages
English, French

▶ The Canadian Shield occupies about half of Canada's land and includes some of the most ancient rocks in North America. **4**

Map labels: ARCTIC OCEAN, Beaufort Sea, Klondike R., MACKENZIE MOUNTAINS, Mackenzie R., Great Bear Lake, YUKON TERRITORY, Whitehorse, NORTHWEST TERRITO..., Great Slave Lake, Yellow..., ROCKY MOUNTAINS, PACIFIC RANGES AND, COAST, INTERIOR, BRITISH COLUMBIA, MOUNTAINS AND LOWLANDS, MOUNTAINS, ALBERTA, SAS..., GREA..., PLAINS, Edmonton, PACIFIC OCEAN, Victoria

Legend:
⊛ National capital
★ Province and territory capital
--- Province border
-·-· International border

678

Practice and Extend

CURRICULUM CONNECTION
Math

Compare Data Have students use data from p. 678 and a current encyclopedia to compare Canada and the United States. Write the following math problems on the board:

- Which country has a greater area, Canada or the United States? Calculate the difference. (Canada; 3,851,800 sq. mi. – 3,679,192 sq. mi. = 172,608 sq. mi. larger)

- Compare the average monthly temperatures of a city in Canada to a city in the United States. Draw a double bar graph or a line graph to compare the two sets of data. Then write three questions about your graph for classmates to answer. Provide the answers on the back of your paper.

CURRICULUM CONNECTION
Science

Mining for Minerals

- Canada is one of the world's leading producers of minerals, including gold, copper, iron, and uranium. The Canadian Shield is a major source of these valuable minerals.

- Have students research Canada's minerals and mineral products (petroleum and natural gas).

- Have them make a chart listing the names and locations of the minerals and mineral products. You may also have them make a map of the locations.

- Challenge students to explain how the minerals are mined, processed, and used.

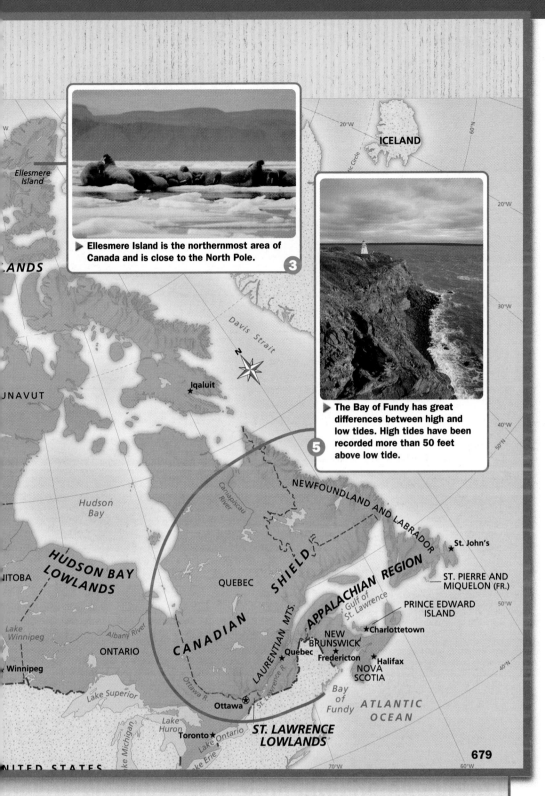

ICELAND

Ellesmere Island

Davis Strait

Iqaluit

NUNAVUT

Hudson Bay

HUDSON BAY LOWLANDS

MANITOBA

Lake Winnipeg

Winnipeg

Albany River

ONTARIO

Lake Superior

Lake Michigan

Lake Huron

Toronto

Lake Ontario

Lake Erie

UNITED STATES

Caniapiscau River

QUEBEC

CANADIAN SHIELD

NEWFOUNDLAND AND LABRADOR

St. John's

ST. PIERRE AND MIQUELON (FR.)

LAURENTIAN MTS.

APPALACHIAN REGION

Gulf of St. Lawrence

PRINCE EDWARD ISLAND

Charlottetown

NEW BRUNSWICK

Quebec

Fredericton

Halifax

NOVA SCOTIA

Ottawa R.

Ottawa

St. Lawrence R.

Bay of Fundy

ATLANTIC OCEAN

ST. LAWRENCE LOWLANDS

▶ Ellesmere Island is the northernmost area of Canada and is close to the North Pole. **3**

▶ The Bay of Fundy has great differences between high and low tides. High tides have been recorded more than 50 feet above low tide. **5**

679

3 **Which part of Canada do you think gets the coldest? Why do you think so?** Possible answer: Ellesmere Island; it is the northernmost area of Canada and is close to the North Pole. Draw Conclusions

4 **Where in Canada would you find some of the most ancient rocks in North America?** In land that is part of the Canadian Shield Main Idea and Details

5 **Where is the Bay of Fundy located?** Along the southeast coast of Canada Interpret Maps

 SOCIAL STUDIES
Background

About the Canadian Shield

- The Canadian Shield is a massive, rocky region shaped like a giant horseshoe. It covers about 1,864,000 square miles.
- It curves around Hudson Bay, from the Arctic coast of the Northwest Territories to the Labrador coast of Newfoundland. It also extends slightly into the United States, forming part of the Adirondack Mountains and the Superior Uplands.
- Geologists estimate that most of the Canadian Shield was formed about 600 million to 5 billion years ago.
- Due to weathering and erosion, the Canadian Shield now consists mostly of low hills as well as large forests and thousands of lakes.

Canada History

6 **What two events in the 1800s most likely caused a great increase in the population of western Canada?** The completion of the transcontinental railroad (1885) and the discovery of gold near the Klondike River in the present-day Yukon Territory (1896). **Cause and Effect**

7 **How long has Canada been self-governing within the British Empire?** Students should subtract 1931 from the present year to determine the answer. **Interpret Time Lines**

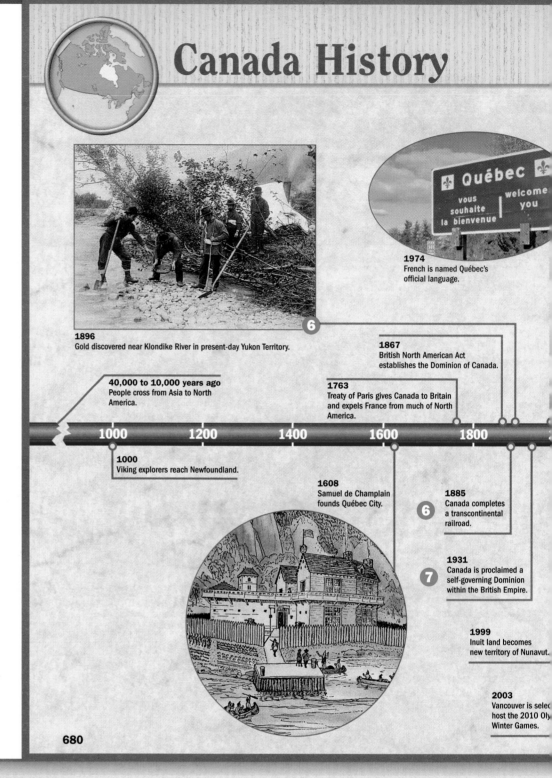

Canada History

1974
French is named Québec's official language.

1896
Gold discovered near Klondike River in present-day Yukon Territory.

1867
British North American Act establishes the Dominion of Canada.

40,000 to 10,000 years ago
People cross from Asia to North America.

1763
Treaty of Paris gives Canada to Britain and expels France from much of North America.

1000 | **1200** | **1400** | **1600** | **1800**

1000
Viking explorers reach Newfoundland.

1608
Samuel de Champlain founds Québec City.

1885
Canada completes a transcontinental railroad.

1931
Canada is proclaimed a self-governing Dominion within the British Empire.

1999
Inuit land becomes new territory of Nunavut.

2003
Vancouver is selec[ted] host the 2010 Oly[mpic] Winter Games.

680

Practice and Extend

anada Today

anada's natural beauty makes it a favorite place for
acations.

▶ Iqaluit (ih cah LOO it) is the capital and
largest community in the newly created
territory of Nunavut (NOO nuh voot). **8**

8 9

▶ Toronto is Canada's
largest city.

d on Your Own

books like these in the library.

681

8 **How does Iqaluit, the largest
community in Nunavut, differ from
Toronto, the largest city in Canada?**
Possible answer: In Iqaluit, there are
mostly small houses, and the area
seems fairly uncluttered. In Toronto,
lots of tall buildings crowd together.
Analyze Pictures

9 **Why do you think people enjoy
visiting and living in Canada?** Possible
answer: They probably enjoy the variety
Canada offers, with its natural beauty
and exciting cities. Evaluate

3 Close and Assess

Read On Your Own

Have students prepare written or oral
reports using the following books. Have
them include maps in their presentation.

*Wow Canada!: Exploring This Land from Coast
to Coast to Coast,* by Vivien Bowers and
Daniel C. Hobbs (Owl Communications,
ISBN 1-895-68894-9, 2000) **Easy**

Québec (Hello Canada Series), by Janice
Hamilton (Fitzhenry & Whiteside, Ltd., ISBN
1-550-41275-2, 1999) **On-Level**

*Yukon Gold: The Story of the Klondike Gold
Rush,* by Charlotte Foltz Jones (Holiday
House, ISBN 0-823-41403-5, 1998)
Challenge

CURRICULUM CONNECTION
Reading

Create a Bulletin-Board Display

- Place a map of Canada in the center of a large bulletin board.
- Divide the class into groups and assign a Canadian province or territory to
  each group. (Provinces: Alberta, British Columbia, Manitoba, New Brunswick,
  Newfoundland, Nova Scotia, Ontario, Prince Edward Island, Quebec,
  Saskatchewan; Territories: Yukon Territory, Northwest Territories, Nunavut)
- Have each group prepare a fact sheet about their province or territory.
- Have each group use yarn and staples to connect their fact sheet to the
  matching section of the map.
- Have students find or draw related pictures to add to the display.
- Review and discuss the completed display with the class.

Mexico

1 Introduce and Motivate

Preview To introduce students to Mexico, have a volunteer point out the country on a large world map and identify its location relative to the United States. (South) Then have students name the U.S. states that are on the United States–Mexico border. (California, Arizona, New Mexico, Texas)

To activate prior knowledge, invite students to share their experiences visiting or living in Mexico. Prompt them to share details about the people, places, crafts, and other aspects of culture in Mexico.

2 Teach and Discuss

1 What does the map show about the landscape of Mexico? Possible answer: Mexico has many mountain ranges and a long coastline. **Interpret Maps**

G SOCIAL STUDIES STRAND
Geography

Review with students that a peninsula is land that has water on three sides.

2 Mexico has two large peninsulas. In which parts of the country are they located? One is in the west (Baja California) and the other, the Yucatán Peninsula, is in the east. **Interpret Maps**

3 What do you notice about the vegetation in the Sonoran Desert? Why do you think those kinds of plants grow there? The vegetation consists primarily of tall cacti and short shrubs; those kinds of plants can survive in a desert climate. **Analyze Pictures**

Mexico

Capital
Mexico City

Population
100,349,766

Area
761,600
square miles

Official language
Spanish

▶ The Sonoran Desert is the hottest desert in North America. It is home to many plants including the huge saguaro (suh GWAR oh) cactus.

682

Practice and Extend

CURRICULUM CONNECTION
Math

Write Number Sentences

- Refer students to p. 682 and write on the board:
  United States: 3,679,192 sq. mi.
  Texas: 261,914 sq. mi.
- Have students write number sentences comparing the areas of Mexico, the United States, and Texas. Tell them to use the symbols >, <, or =.

CURRICULUM CONNECTION
Music

The National Anthem of Mexico

- Go online to find a copy of the Mexican national anthem.
- Distribute copies of the anthem to the class. Have students who might be familiar with the anthem help to teach it to classmates.
- After students learn the national anthem, have them listen to a variety of Mexican music, including *corridos* (folk songs) and *mariachi*.

The volcano Orizaba (oh ree SAH bah) is the highest point in Mexico, at over 18,400 feet. **④**

Legend	
⊛	National capital
★	State capital
- - -	State border
-•-•-	International border
——	Pan American Highway

The rain forests of the Yucatán (YOO cah tahn) Peninsula are home to many people and a variety of animals and plants. **⑤**

④ By looking at the picture, how do you know that the Orizaba volcano reaches an extremely high altitude? Possible answer: The picture shows snow at the top of the volcano. Analyze Pictures

⑤ Compare and contrast the climate in the Sonoran Desert with the climate in the Yucatán Peninsula. The Sonoran Desert is usually very dry, and the Yucatán Peninsula is home to rain forests. Compare and Contrast

 SOCIAL STUDIES
Background

More About the Geography of Mexico

- Mexico has one of the most diverse landscapes in the world. The climate, land formations, and plant life can vary greatly within a short distance.
- The Rio Grande (or *Río Bravo*, as it is known in Mexico) forms about two-thirds (1,240 miles) of the international boundary between the United States and Mexico.
- Northern Mexico consists mostly of deserts and semideserts.

- The Plateau of Central Mexico varies from elevated plateaus to a series of mountain ranges and volcanoes.
- Southern Mexico also has a diverse landscape, from the rocky Pacific coastlines of the Southern Uplands to the tropical rain forests at the southern end of the Yucatán Peninsula. A wide variety of wildlife, including hundreds of kinds of birds, is found in this region.

Mexico History

6 Which Spanish conquistador established Mexico City? Hernando Cortés **Main Idea and Details**

7 Which two countries did Mexico fight after it won its independence from Spain? The United States and France **Sequence**

8 Why do Mexicans today celebrate Cinco de Mayo? To celebrate Mexico's defeat of the French in 1862 **Main Idea and Details**

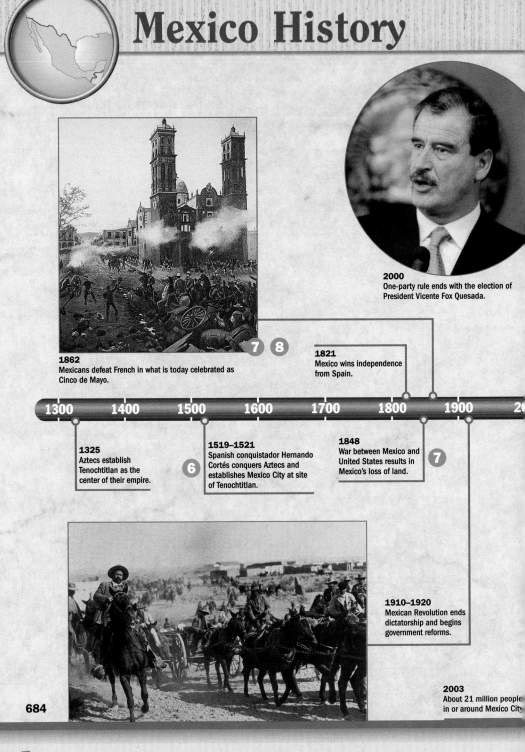

Mexico History

2000
One-party rule ends with the election of President Vicente Fox Quesada.

1862
Mexicans defeat French in what is today celebrated as Cinco de Mayo.

1821
Mexico wins independence from Spain.

| 1300 | 1400 | 1500 | 1600 | 1700 | 1800 | 1900 | 2(|

1325
Aztecs establish Tenochtitlan as the center of their empire.

1519–1521
Spanish conquistador Hernando Cortés conquers Aztecs and establishes Mexico City at site of Tenochtitlan.

1848
War between Mexico and United States results in Mexico's loss of land.

1910–1920
Mexican Revolution ends dictatorship and begins government reforms.

2003
About 21 million people in or around Mexico City

684

Practice and Extend

CURRICULUM CONNECTION
Writing

Create a Travel Brochure

- Have students create a brochure about Mexico.
- Students should include facts and illustrations that will persuade tourists to travel to Mexico.
- Students may use encyclopedias, books, or the Internet to do their research. Remind students to use reliable sources and to verify facts.
- You may want to contact a travel agent and ask for a few brochures students could use for reference.

MEETING INDIVIDUAL NEEDS
Leveled Practice

Interpret the Time Line Help students interpret the time line on p. 684. Be sure students understand that a time line is arranged in chronological order.

Easy Have students create and display a simpler version of the time line. Students may copy pictures for several of these events from other parts of the textbook. **Reteach**

On-Level Explain to students the connection between centuries and years. For example, tell students that the twentieth century includes events that occurred in the 1900s. Help students make oral sentences about the centuries in which events on the time line occurred. **Extend**

Challenge Give students an envelope containing the time-line facts on slips of paper. Have students use the slips to recreate the time line. Encourage students to write and illustrate additional facts about Mexico's history. **Enrich**

exico Today

ely populated Mexico City, the country's capital, is one of
rgest cities in the world.
9

▶ Almost every city, town, and village in Mexico
has a market, like this one in Chiapas, where
farmers sell or trade their goods.
10

ient Mayan ruins
v many tourists to
s such as this
ple in Palenque in
state of Chiapas.
11

Read on Your Own

Look for books like these in the library.

685

Mexico Today

9 **What do the picture and caption tell about Mexico City? How do you know?** Possible answer: The population is dense, as shown by the many people. **Analyze Pictures**

10 **Compare and contrast the market in Mexico that is pictured and a store in the United States.** Both have food or other goods for people to buy. In stores, goods may be in packages or on shelves. In a market, goods are in large containers, and the market appears to be outside. **Compare and Contrast**

H SOCIAL STUDIES STRAND
History

Remind students that the Maya were Native Americans who lived in Mexico. The Mayan civilization peaked between about A.D. 250 and 900.

11 **What are Mayan ruins?** The remains of structures built by the Maya long ago **Draw Conclusions**

3 Close and Assess

Read On Your Own

Have students create trivia cards using the following books.

Mexico: The Land, by Bobbie Kalman (Crabtree Publishing, ISBN 0-865-05214-X, 1993) **Easy**

Daily Life in Ancient and Modern Mexico City, by Steve Cory (Runestone Press, ISBN 0-822-53212-3, 1999) **On-Level**

Fiesta! Mexico's Great Celebrations, by Elizabeth Silverthorne (Millbrook Press, ISBN 1-562-94055-4, 1992) **Challenge**

The Countries of Central America

The Countries of Central America

1 Introduce and Motivate

Preview To introduce students to Central America, have students predict the location of the region just by its name. Then point out the location on a world map. Have students refer to the map on pp. 686 and 687 as you point out the locations of the different countries in Central America.

To activate prior knowledge, ask students what they know about the Panama Canal. Point out the country of Panama and explain that the Panama Canal links the Atlantic Ocean to the Pacific Ocean.

2 Teach and Discuss

❶ **How are the flags of Central America similar? How are they different?** Possible answers: Five of the seven flags have blue and white stripes; Guatemala's flag is the only one with vertical stripes; two of the flags have stars, and the other flags have a different symbol or emblem in the center. Compare and Contrast

❷ **Which country in Central America has the largest area? Which country has the most people?** Nicaragua has the largest area; Guatemala has the most people. Compare and Contrast

❸ **What do you notice about the languages of Central America?** Spanish is spoken in all of the countries except Belize, in which the official language is English. Generalize

❹ **Off the coast of which country is the second-largest coral reef in the world?** Belize Main Idea and Details

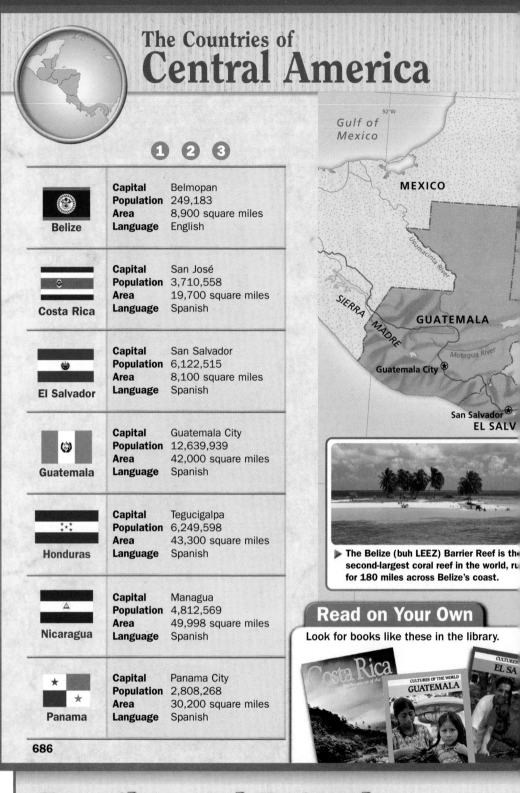

❶ ❷ ❸

Belize	Capital	Belmopan
	Population	249,183
	Area	8,900 square miles
	Language	English
Costa Rica	Capital	San José
	Population	3,710,558
	Area	19,700 square miles
	Language	Spanish
El Salvador	Capital	San Salvador
	Population	6,122,515
	Area	8,100 square miles
	Language	Spanish
Guatemala	Capital	Guatemala City
	Population	12,639,939
	Area	42,000 square miles
	Language	Spanish
Honduras	Capital	Tegucigalpa
	Population	6,249,598
	Area	43,300 square miles
	Language	Spanish
Nicaragua	Capital	Managua
	Population	4,812,569
	Area	49,998 square miles
	Language	Spanish
Panama	Capital	Panama City
	Population	2,808,268
	Area	30,200 square miles
	Language	Spanish

Gulf of Mexico

MEXICO

GUATEMALA

Guatemala City

San Salvador
EL SALV

► The Belize (buh LEEZ) Barrier Reef is the second-largest coral reef in the world, ru for 180 miles across Belize's coast.

Read on Your Own
Look for books like these in the library.

686

Practice and Extend

MEETING INDIVIDUAL NEEDS
Leveled Practice

Make Flag Cards Have students make flag cards to review facts and figures about countries in Central America, Mexico, and Canada. As the class learns about other countries in the Western Hemisphere, have them make more flag cards to add to their deck.

Easy Students should draw each flag on a separate index card. On the back of each card, have them write the name of the country. **Reteach**

On-Level Students should draw each flag on a separate index card. On the back of each card, have them write the name of the country and facts from this book. **Extend**

Challenge Students should draw each flag on a separate index card. On the back of each card, have them write the name of the country, facts from this book, and facts they discover from other resources, such as an almanac or an encyclopedia. **Enrich**

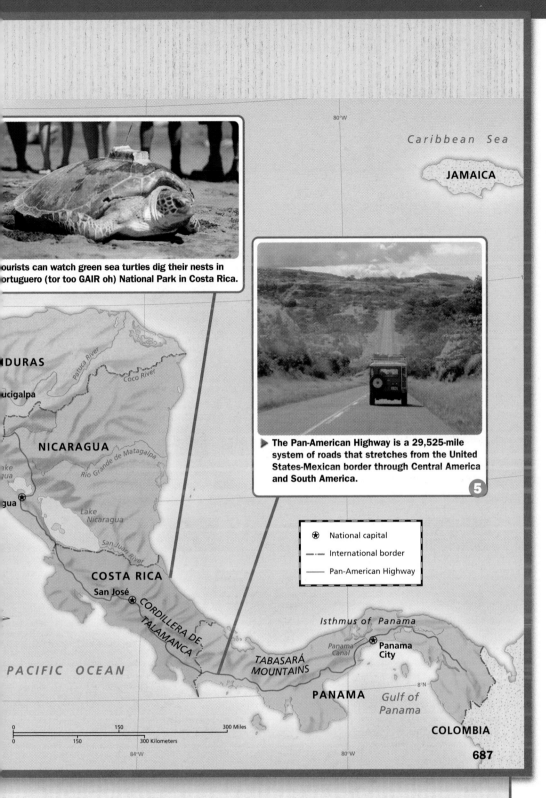

Tourists can watch green sea turtles dig their nests in Tortuguero (tor too GAIR oh) National Park in Costa Rica.

▶ The Pan-American Highway is a 29,525-mile system of roads that stretches from the United States-Mexican border through Central America and South America.

5

National capital
International border
Pan-American Highway

687

5 Why do you think the Pan-American Highway was built? To make it easier to transport goods and travel through the Central American countries
Make Inferences

3 Close and Assess

Read On Your Own

Have students prepare oral or written reports using the following books. Encourage them to record important facts on note cards as they read the books.

Costa Rica (Enchantment of the World, Second Series), by Marion Morrison (Children's Press, ISBN 0-516-20469-6, 1998) **On-Level**

Guatemala (Cultures of the World), by Sean Sheehan (Marshall Cavendish, ISBN 0-761-40812-6, 1998) **Challenge**

El Salvador (Cultures of the World), by Erin Foley (Marshall Cavendish, ISBN 1-854-35696-8, 1995) **Challenge**

SOCIAL STUDIES Background

More About Central America

- Central America covers about 202,000 square miles and supports over 35 million people.
- Most of the people live in the highlands of the mountainous regions.
- The rugged mountains that crisscross the region make transportation and economic development difficult.
- The Pan-American Highway links six Central American countries to eleven other American countries. It extends from Mexico through Guatemala, El Salvador, Honduras, Nicaragua, Costa Rica, and into Panama. The Darien Gap, a stretch of about 70 miles of jungle, blocks the highway at Yaviza, Panama. Motorists can ship their cars to Colombia or Venezuela in South America and then continue along the highway, which ends in southern Chile.

The Countries of the Caribbean Region

The Countries of the Caribbean Region

Antigua and Barbuda 1	**Capital** Saint John's **Population** 66,464 **Area** 170 square miles **Language** English	
The Bahamas	**Capital** Nassau **Population** 294,982 **Area** 5,400 square miles **Language** English	
Barbados 1	**Capital** Bridgetown **Population** 274,059 **Area** 170 square miles **Language** English	
Cuba 2	**Capital** Havana **Population** 11,141,997 **Area** 42,800 square miles **Language** Spanish	
Dominica	**Capital** Roseau **Population** 71,540 **Area** 300 square miles **Language** English	
Dominican Republic 2	**Capital** Santo Domingo **Population** 8,442,533 **Area** 18,800 square miles **Language** Spanish	
Grenada 1	**Capital** Saint George's **Population** 89,312 **Area** 130 square miles **Language** English	
Haiti	**Capital** Port-au-Prince **Population** 6,867,995 **Area** 10,700 square **Languages** Haitian Creole, F
Jamaica	**Capital** Kingston **Population** 2,652,689 **Area** 4,200 square m **Language** English
Puerto Rico (U.S.A.) 2	**Capital** San Juan **Population** 3,889,507 **Area** 3,508 square m **Languages** Spanish, English
St. Kitts and Nevis 3	**Capital** Basseterre **Population** 38,819 **Area** 104 square mile **Language** English
St. Lucia	**Capital** Castries **Population** 156,260 **Area** 240 square mile **Language** English
St. Vincent and the Grenadines 1	**Capital** Kingstown **Population** 115,461 **Area** 130 square mile **Language** English
Trinidad and Tobago	**Capital** Port-of-Spain **Population** 1,175,523 **Area** 2,000 square m **Language** English

688

---

1 Introduce and Motivate

Preview To introduce students to the Caribbean region (also known as the West Indies), show students the group of islands on a large world map and have them identify their location relative to the United States. (Southeast) Point out that there are many islands in the Caribbean Sea.

To activate prior knowledge, have students imagine what it would be like to live on an island in the Caribbean Sea. Invite students to share their ideas.

2 Teach and Discuss

1 Which countries in the Caribbean have the same area? Antigua/Barbuda and Barbados (170 square miles); Grenada and St. Vincent/the Grenadines (130 square miles) Categorize

2 Which national flags use the same colors as the United States flag? Cuba, Dominican Republic, and Puerto Rico Categorize

---

Practice and Extend

CURRICULUM CONNECTION
Math

Create and Use a Database Have students make a database from the facts about the Caribbean countries and sort the data by category.

- Students may use spreadsheets or another software program if one is available. Alternately, students may write facts on index cards.
- If students use index cards, suggest that they color-code population, area, and language by writing each type of fact in a different color. They may also choose to write each of these types of facts in a different corner of the index card.
- Ask students to figure out different ways to sort, group, and sequence the countries of the Caribbean region, such as by alphabetical order, numerical order by area, and numerical order by population. Have partners identify the sorting method.

MEETING INDIVIDUAL NEEDS
Learning Styles

Review the Caribbean Region Using their individual learning styles, students review information about the Caribbean countries.

Verbal Learning Assign a Caribbean country to each student. Have students research facts about that country and then give an oral report to the class.

Social Learning Have teams play "Where Am I?" using information from the chart on p. 688. Give clues about a country in the Caribbean. Have the teams guess the place. Each team gets only one guess per clue. The team that guesses correctly earns a point.

688 Western Hemisphere

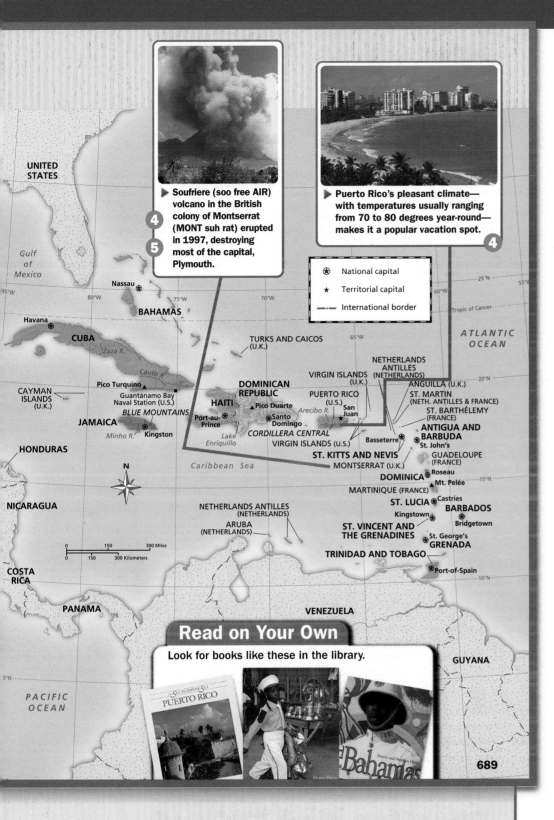

▶ Soufriere (soo free AIR) volcano in the British colony of Montserrat (MONT suh rat) erupted in 1997, destroying most of the capital, Plymouth.

▶ Puerto Rico's pleasant climate—with temperatures usually ranging from 70 to 80 degrees year-round—makes it a popular vacation spot.

⊛ National capital
★ Territorial capital
—·— International border

UNITED STATES

Gulf of Mexico

Nassau

BAHAMAS

Havana
CUBA
Zaza R.
Pico Turquino ▲

CAYMAN ISLANDS (U.K.)
Guantánamo Bay Naval Station (U.S.)
Cauto R.

JAMAICA
BLUE MOUNTAINS
Minho R. Kingston

HONDURAS

HAITI
Port-au-Prince ⊛
▲Pico Duarte
⊛Santo Domingo
Lake Enriquillo
CORDILLERA CENTRAL
VIRGIN ISLANDS (U.S.)

DOMINICAN REPUBLIC

PUERTO RICO (U.S.)
Arecibo R. San Juan ★

VIRGIN ISLANDS (U.K.)

TURKS AND CAICOS (U.K.)

NETHERLANDS ANTILLES (NETHERLANDS)

ANGUILLA (U.K.)
ST. MARTIN (NETH. ANTILLES & FRANCE)
ST. BARTHÉLEMY (FRANCE)

ANTIGUA AND BARBUDA
St. John's ⊛
Basseterre ⊛
ST. KITTS AND NEVIS
MONTSERRAT (U.K.)
GUADELOUPE (FRANCE)

DOMINICA ⊛ Roseau
▲ Mt. Pelée
MARTINIQUE (FRANCE)

ST. LUCIA ⊛ Castries
Kingstown ⊛
BARBADOS
Bridgetown ⊛

NETHERLANDS ANTILLES (NETHERLANDS)
ARUBA (NETHERLANDS)

ST. VINCENT AND THE GRENADINES
St. George's ⊛ GRENADA

TRINIDAD AND TOBAGO
⊛Port-of-Spain

NICARAGUA

Caribbean Sea

N

0   150   300 Miles
0   150   300 Kilometers

COSTA RICA

PANAMA

VENEZUELA

GUYANA

PACIFIC OCEAN

ATLANTIC OCEAN

Tropic of Cancer

Read on Your Own

Look for books like these in the library.

PUERTO RICO
Haiti
the Bahamas

689

③ **The smallest U.S. state (Rhode Island) has an area of about 1,212 square miles. What is the smallest country in the Caribbean? How much larger is Rhode Island than this country?** St. Kitts and Nevis (104 square miles); Rhode Island is 1,108 square miles larger, or more than eleven times larger than St. Kitts and Nevis. **Compare and Contrast**

④ **What features of the Caribbean region are shown in the pictures and described in the captions on this page?** Warm tropical beaches and volcanoes **Analyze Pictures**

⑤ **What caused massive destruction in Montserrat in 1997?** The eruption of the Soufrière volcano **Cause and Effect**

Close and Assess

Read On Your Own

Have students prepare oral reports using the following books. Encourage them to create posters for their presentation.

Puerto Rico (From Sea to Shining Sea Series), by Dennis Brindell Fradin (Children's Press, ISBN 0-516-03856-7, 1998) **On-Level**

Haiti (Enchantment of the World, Second Series), by Martin Hintz (Children's Press, ISBN 0-516-20603-6, 1998) **Challenge**

The Bahamas (Enchantment of the World, Second Series), by Martin Hintz (Children's Press, ISBN 0-516-20583-8, 1997) **Challenge**

FYI SOCIAL STUDIES
Background

More About the Caribbean Region

- There are three main groups of islands in the Caribbean region: the Bahamas, consisting of about 700 small islands; the Greater Antilles, which includes the large islands of Cuba, Jamaica, Haiti, Puerto Rico, and the Dominican Republic; and the Lesser Antilles, which encompasses the smaller islands southeast of Puerto Rico.
- The chain of Caribbean islands extends for more than 2,000 miles. Many of the islands were formed by volcanoes.
- Christopher Columbus was the first European to reach the islands, which were later named the West Indies.
- Soon after the islands were discovered, European countries claimed them. Today many of the islands are independent nations.

The Countries of South America

The Countries of
South America

1 Introduce and Motivate

Preview To introduce students to South America, have a volunteer point out the continent on a large world map and compare its size with that of North America. (South America is smaller.) Point out that the equator runs through South America.

To activate prior knowledge, have students share what they know about the land, people, and wildlife of South America. Prompt them by naming some of the countries and mentioning the Amazon rain forest.

2 Teach and Discuss

① How many different official languages are spoken in South America? What are they? Seven: Spanish, Quechua, Aymara, Portuguese, French, English, and Dutch
Interpret Charts

② About 281 million people live in the United States, and about 31 million people live in Canada. Which South American countries have more people than Canada but fewer people than the United States? Argentina, Brazil, and Colombia *Compare and Contrast*

③ Which country's capital has a name that is similar to the name of the country? Brazil (capital: Brasilia)
Compare and Contrast

---

①

② Argentina	**Capital** Buenos Aires **Population** 36,955,182 **Area** 1,068,300 square miles **Language** Spanish	
Bolivia	**Capital** La Paz and Sucre **Population** 8,152,620 **Area** 424,200 square miles **Languages** Spanish, Quechua, Aymara	
② ③ Brazil	**Capital** Brasília **Population** 172,860,370 **Area** 3,286,478 square miles **Language** Portuguese	
Chile	**Capital** Santiago **Population** 15,153,797 **Area** 292,300 square miles **Language** Spanish	
② Colombia	**Capital** Bogotá **Population** 39,685,655 **Area** 439,700 square miles **Language** Spanish	
Ecuador	**Capital** Quito **Population** 12,920,092 **Area** 109,500 square miles **Language** Spanish	
French Guiana (France)	**Capital** Cayenne **Population** 172,605 **Area** 33,399 square miles **Language** French	

Guyana	**Capital** Georgetown **Population** 697,286 **Area** 83,000 square r **Language** English
Paraguay	**Capital** Asunción **Population** 5,585,828 **Area** 157,000 square **Language** Spanish
Peru	**Capital** Lima **Population** 27,012,899 **Area** 496,200 square **Languages** Spanish, Quechu
Suriname	**Capital** Paramaribo **Population** 431,303 **Area** 63,000 square **Language** Dutch
Uruguay	**Capital** Montevideo **Population** 3,334,074 **Area** 68,000 square r **Language** Spanish
Venezuela	**Capital** Caracas **Population** 23,542,649 **Area** 352,100 square **Language** Spanish

690

Practice and Extend

MEETING INDIVIDUAL NEEDS
Leveled Practice

Make a Map Have students make a tactile map of South America.

Easy Have students draw and label an outline map of South America on foam board and make toothpick flags for the countries on the map. **Reteach**

On-Level Have students make a puzzle of South America using cardboard or poster board. Tell them to write the name of the country on the front of the puzzle piece and write the name of the capital on the back. Challenge students to reassemble the puzzle and recall the capitals correctly. **Extend**

Challenge Have students use clay or papier-mâché to make a three-dimensional map of South America. Remind them to include a color-coded map key. You might also have students write fact cards to display around their map. Encourage students to refer to a variety of resources, including printed and online atlases. **Enrich**

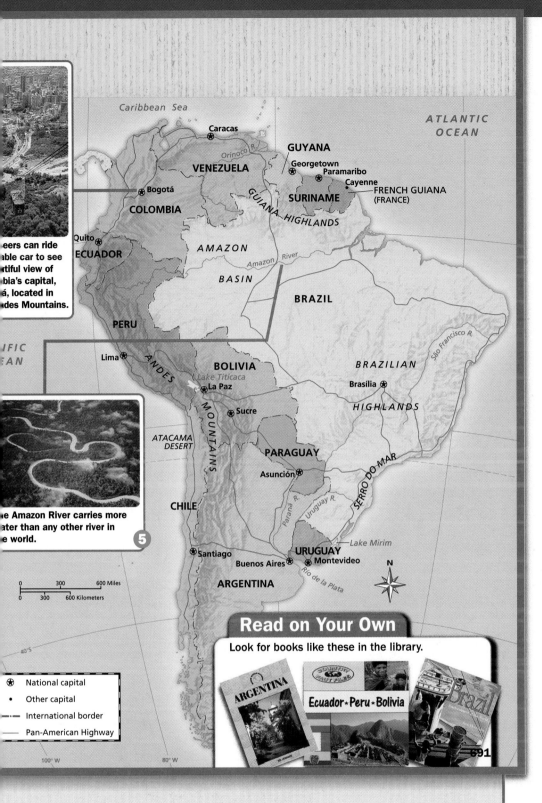

eers can ride
ble car to see
tiful view of
bia's capital,
á, located in
des Mountains.

Caribbean Sea

ATLANTIC
OCEAN

Caracas

GUYANA

Orinoco R.

VENEZUELA

Georgetown
Paramaribo

Bogotá

Cayenne
FRENCH GUIANA
(FRANCE)

GUIANA

SURINAME

COLOMBIA

HIGHLANDS

Quito

ECUADOR

AMAZON

Amazon River

BASIN

BRAZIL

São Francisco R.

PERU

BRAZILIAN

IFIC
EAN

Lima

ANDES

BOLIVIA

Lake Titicaca

HIGHLANDS

La Paz

Brasília

Sucre

ATACAMA
DESERT

MOUNTAINS

PARAGUAY

SERRO DO MAR

Asunción

e Amazon River carries more
ater than any other river in
e world.

⑤

CHILE

Paraná R.

Uruguay R.

Lake Mirim

Santiago

URUGUAY

Buenos Aires

Montevideo

N

300   600 Miles

ARGENTINA

Río de la Plata

0   300   600 Kilometers

40°S

Read on Your Own

Look for books like these in the library.

✷   National capital

•   Other capital

–·–   International border

——   Pan-American Highway

ARGENTINA

Ecuador•Peru•Bolivia

Brazil

100° W   80° W

691

④ **What chain of mountains extends along the western coast of South America?** The Andes Mountains
Main Idea and Details

⑤ **What do you notice about the route of the Amazon River, as shown on the map?** Possible answers: It runs across the continent and into the Atlantic Ocean; it crosses the northern part of the continent. Interpret Maps

③ Close and Assess

Have students prepare oral reports using the following books. Have classmates take notes and answer questions after each oral report.

Argentina: (Major World Nations), by Sol Liebowitz (Chelsea House, ISBN 0-791-04730-X, 1998) **Easy**

Ecuador, Peru, and Bolivia (Country Fact Files Series), by Edward Parker (Raintree/Steck Vaughn, ISBN 0-817-25403-X, 1998) **On-Level**

Brazil (Enchantment of the World, Second Series), by Ann Heinrichs (Children's Press, ISBN 0-516-20602-8, 1997) **Challenge**

Ⓖ SOCIAL STUDIES STRAND
Geography

Create a Board Game

- Have small groups of students create a board game about South America. For example, students can create a game about traveling down the Amazon River or on the Pan American Highway.

- Have students research facts to include in their game. Encourage them to include facts about the people, climate, landscape, natural resources, wildlife, and cities of various South American countries.

- Provide time for students to play one another's games.

Notes

Reference Guide

Table of Contents

Atlas
Photograph of the Continents

Atlas
Map of the World: Political

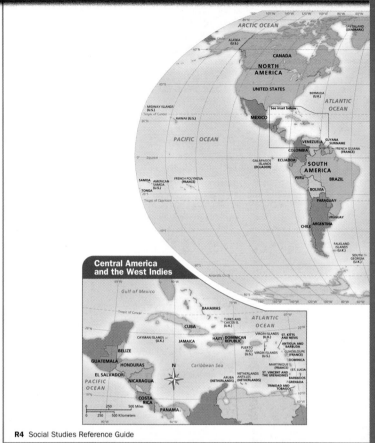

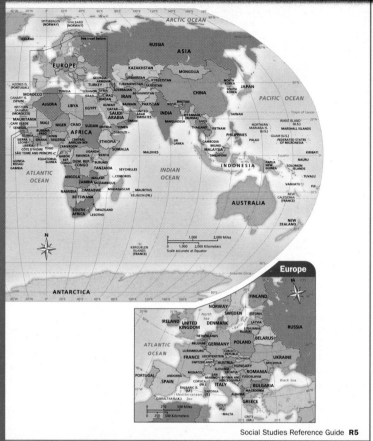

Atlas
Map of the Western Hemisphere: Political

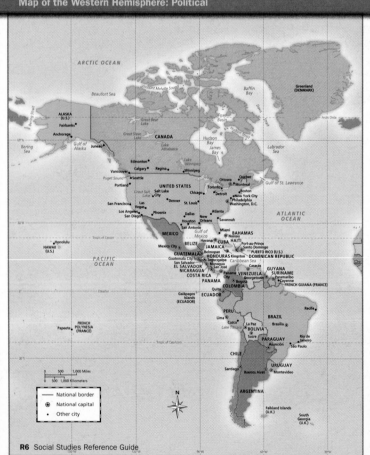

National border
National capital
Other city

Map of the Western Hemisphere: Physical

▲ Mountain peak
National border

Atlas
Map of North America: Political

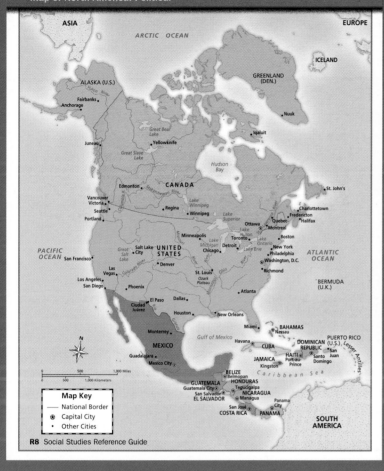

ASIA
ARCTIC OCEAN
EUROPE
ICELAND

GREENLAND (DEN.)

ALASKA (U.S.)
Fairbanks
Anchorage
Juneau

Nuuk

Iqaluit

Yellowknife
Great Bear Lake
Great Slave Lake

Hudson Bay

CANADA
Edmonton
Vancouver
Victoria
Seattle
Portland
Regina
Winnipeg
Lake Winnipeg
Lake Superior
Ottawa
Montreal
Quebec
Fredericton
Charlottetown
Halifax

St. John's

PACIFIC OCEAN

San Francisco
Great Salt Lake
Salt Lake City
UNITED STATES
Minneapolis
Lake Michigan
Detroit
Chicago
Lake Huron
Lake Erie
Lake Ontario
Toronto
Boston
New York
Philadelphia
Washington, D.C.
Richmond

ATLANTIC OCEAN

Las Vegas
Denver
St. Louis
Ozark Plateau
Los Angeles
San Diego
Phoenix
El Paso
Dallas
Atlanta

BERMUDA (U.K.)

Ciudad Juárez
Houston
New Orleans
Miami

Monterrey
Gulf of Mexico
BAHAMAS
Nassau

Guadalajara
MEXICO
Havana
CUBA
PUERTO RICO (U.S.)
San Juan
Mexico City
HAITI
Port-au-Prince
Santo Domingo
DOMINICAN REPUBLIC
Lesser Antilles
Kingston
JAMAICA
Caribbean Sea
BELIZE
Belmopan
GUATEMALA
HONDURAS
Guatemala City
Tegucigalpa
San Salvador
NICARAGUA
EL SALVADOR
Managua
SOUTH AMERICA
San José
Panama City
COSTA RICA
PANAMA

N

0 500 1,000 Miles
0 500 1,000 Kilometers

Map Key
— National Border
⊛ Capital City
• Other Cities

Map of North America: Physical

ASIA
ARCTIC OCEAN
EUROPE

Chukchi Sea
Bering Sea
Bering Strait
Beaufort Sea
Queen Elizabeth Islands
Ellesmere Island
Iceland
Greenland

Aleutian Islands
Bristol Bay
Brooks Range
Yukon River
Banks Island
Victoria Island
Parry Islands
Baffin Bay

Kodiak Island
Gulf of Alaska
Alaska Peninsula
Mt. McKinley 20,320 ft. (6,194 m)
Mackenzie Mts.
Great Bear Lake
Mackenzie River
Baffin Island
Foxe Basin

Queen Charlotte Islands
Great Slave Lake
Lake Athabasca
Hudson Strait
Labrador Sea

Vancouver Island
Saskatchewan River
CANADIAN SHIELD
Hudson Bay
James Bay
Labrador
Newfoundland
Gulf of St. Lawrence

PACIFIC OCEAN
NORTH AMERICA
ROCKY MOUNTAINS
GREAT PLAINS
Columbia Plateau
Snake River
Black Hills
Lake Manitoba
Lake Winnipeg
Lake Superior
Lake Huron
Lake Michigan
INTERIOR PLAINS
Lake Erie
Lake Ontario
APPALACHIAN MTS.
Cape Cod
Long Island
Chesapeake Bay
Cape Hatteras
ATLANTIC OCEAN
BERMUDA

Mt. Whitney 14,495 ft. (4,418 m)
GREAT BASIN
Death Valley (lowest point in N.A.) -282 ft. (-86 m)
Mojave Desert
Colorado River
Colorado Plateau
Platte R.
Arkansas River
Ozark Plateau
Ohio
Tennessee River
Red River

Sierra Madre Occidental
Gulf of California
Sierra Madre Oriental
Citlaltépetl 18,701 ft. (5,700 m)
COASTAL PLAIN
Gulf of Mexico
Straits of Florida
Bahamas
WEST INDIES
Cuba
Hispaniola
Puerto Rico
Lesser Antilles

Bay of Campeche
Yucatán Peninsula
Greater Antilles
Jamaica
Caribbean Sea

Lake Nicaragua
Isthmus of Panama
Gulf of Panama
SOUTH AMERICA

N

0 500 1,000 Miles
0 500 1,000 Kilometers

Map Key
▲ Mountain peak
— National border

Atlas
Map of the United States of America

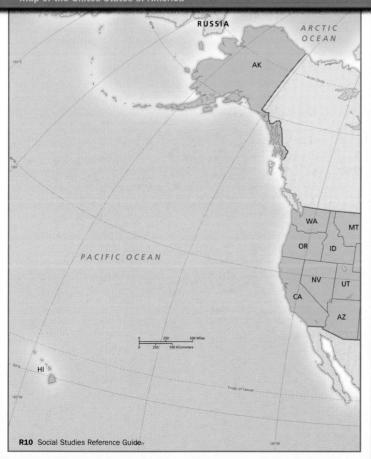

RUSSIA
ARCTIC OCEAN

AK
Arctic Circle

PACIFIC OCEAN

WA MT
OR ID
NV UT
CA AZ

0 250 500 Miles
0 250 500 Kilometers

HI
Tropic of Cancer

Greenland (DENMARK)

CANADA

ND MN ME
SD WI VT NH
WY IA MI NY MA CT RI
NE IL IN OH PA NJ
CO KS MO KY WV VA DE MD DC
NM OK AR TN NC
MS AL GA SC
TX LA FL
ATLANTIC OCEAN

MEXICO
Gulf of Mexico
BAHAMAS
CUBA
HAITI DOM. REP.
JAMAICA

N

State or area	Abbreviation
Alabama	AL
Alaska	AK
Arizona	AZ
Arkansas	AR
California	CA
Colorado	CO
Connecticut	CT
Delaware	DE
District of Columbia	DC
Florida	FL
Georgia	GA
Hawaii	HI
Idaho	ID
Illinois	IL
Indiana	IN
Iowa	IA
Kansas	KS
Kentucky	KY
Louisiana	LA
Maine	ME
Maryland	MD
Massachusetts	MA
Michigan	MI
Minnesota	MN
Mississippi	MS
Missouri	MO
Montana	MT
Nebraska	NE
Nevada	NV
New Hampshire	NH
New Jersey	NJ
New Mexico	NM
New York	NY
North Carolina	NC
North Dakota	ND
Ohio	OH
Oklahoma	OK
Oregon	OR
Pennsylvania	PA
Rhode Island	RI
South Carolina	SC
South Dakota	SD
Tennessee	TN
Texas	TX
Utah	UT
Vermont	VT
Virginia	VA
Washington	WA
West Virginia	WV
Wisconsin	WI
Wyoming	WY

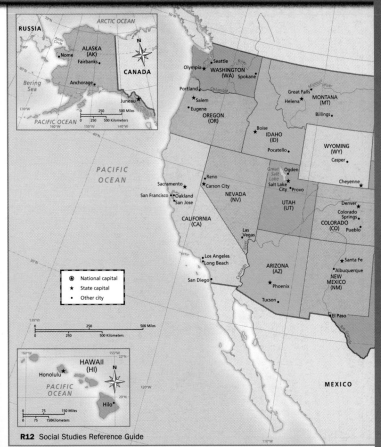

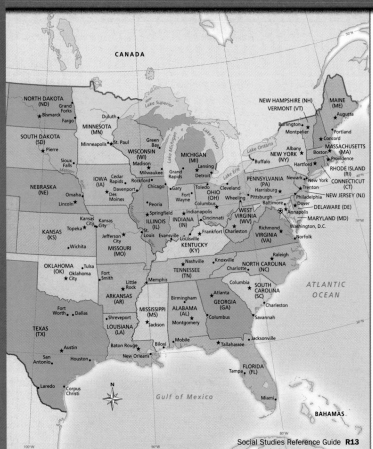

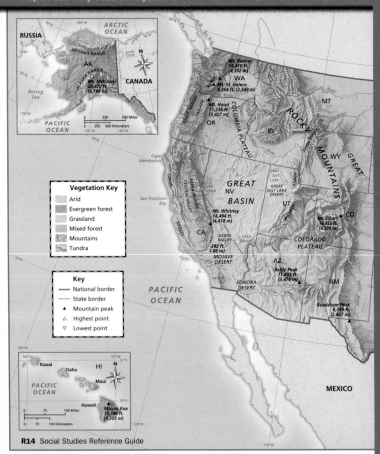

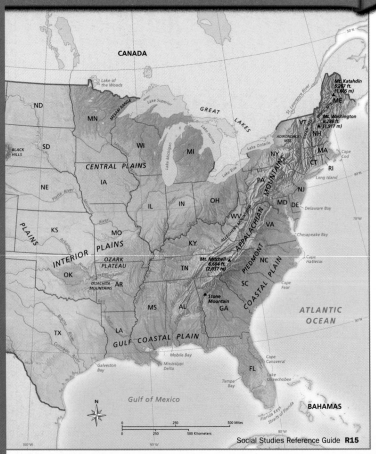

Geography Terms

basin bowl-shaped area of land surrounded by higher land

bay narrower part of an ocean or lake that cuts into land

canal narrow waterway dug across land mainly for ship travel

canyon steep, narrow valley with high sides

cliff steep wall of rock or earth, sometimes called a bluff

coast land at the edge of a large body of water such as an ocean

coastal plain area of flat land along an ocean or sea

delta triangle-shaped area of land at the mouth of a river

desert very dry land

fall line area along which rivers form waterfalls or rapids as the rivers drop to lower land

floodplain flat land, near a river, that is formed by dirt left by floods

foothills hilly land at the bottom of a mountain

glacier giant sheet of ice that moves very slowly across land

gulf body of water, larger than most bays, with land around part of it

harbor sheltered body of water where ships safely tie up to land

hill rounded land higher than the land around it

inlet narrow strip of water running from a large body of water either into land or between islands

island land with water all around it

lake large body of water with land all or nearly all around it

mesa flat-topped hill, with steep sides

mountain a very tall hill; highest land on Earth

mountain pass narrow channel or path through a mountain range

mountain range long row of mountains

mouth place where a river empties into another body of water

ocean any of four largest bodies of water on Earth

peak pointed top of a mountain

peninsula land with water on three sides

plain very large area of flat land

plateau high, wide area of flat land, with steep sides

prairie large area of flat land, with few or no trees, similar to a plain

river large stream of water leading to a lake, other river, or ocean

riverbank land at a river's edge

sea large body of water somewhat smaller than an ocean

sea level an ocean's surface, compared to which land can be measured either above or below

source place where a river begins

swamp very shallow water covering low land filled with trees and other plants

tributary stream or river that runs into a larger river

valley low land between mountains or hills

volcano mountain with opening at the top formed by violent bursts of steam and hot rock

waterfall steep falling of water from a high to a lower place

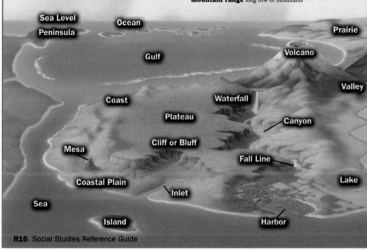

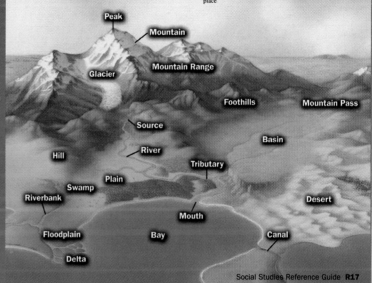

Facts About Our Fifty States

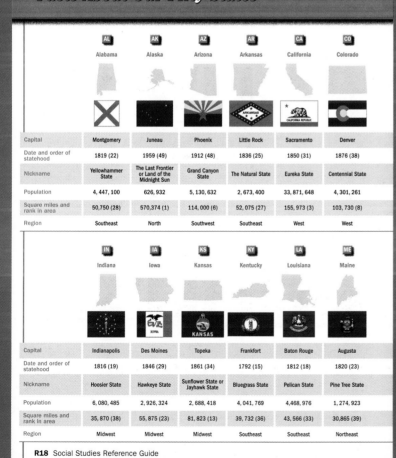

	Alabama	Alaska	Arizona	Arkansas	California	Colorado
Capital	Montgomery	Juneau	Phoenix	Little Rock	Sacramento	Denver
Date and order of statehood	1819 (22)	1959 (49)	1912 (48)	1836 (25)	1850 (31)	1876 (38)
Nickname	Yellowhammer State	The Last Frontier or Land of the Midnight Sun	Grand Canyon State	The Natural State	Eureka State	Centennial State
Population	4,447,100	626,932	5,130,632	2,673,400	33,871,648	4,301,261
Square miles and rank in area	50,750 (28)	570,374 (1)	114,000 (6)	52,075 (27)	155,973 (3)	103,730 (8)
Region	Southeast	North	Southwest	Southeast	West	West

	Indiana	Iowa	Kansas	Kentucky	Louisiana	Maine
Capital	Indianapolis	Des Moines	Topeka	Frankfort	Baton Rouge	Augusta
Date and order of statehood	1816 (19)	1846 (29)	1861 (34)	1792 (15)	1812 (18)	1820 (23)
Nickname	Hoosier State	Hawkeye State	Sunflower State or Jayhawk State	Bluegrass State	Pelican State	Pine Tree State
Population	6,080,485	2,926,324	2,688,418	4,041,769	4,468,976	1,274,923
Square miles and rank in area	35,870 (38)	55,875 (23)	81,823 (13)	39,732 (36)	43,566 (33)	30,865 (39)
Region	Midwest	Midwest	Midwest	Southeast	Southeast	Northeast

	Connecticut	Delaware	Florida	Georgia	Hawaii	Idaho	Illinois
Capital	Hartford	Dover	Tallahassee	Atlanta	Honolulu	Boise	Springfield
Date and order of statehood	1788 (5)	1787 (1)	1845 (27)	1788 (4)	1959 (50)	1890 (43)	1818 (21)
Nickname	Constitution State	Diamond State; First State	Sunshine State	Peach State	Aloha State	Gem State	Land of Lincoln
Population	3,405,565	783,600	15,982,378	8,186,453	1,211,537	1,293,953	12,419,293
Square miles and rank in area	4,845 (48)	1,955 (49)	53,997 (26)	57,919 (21)	6,423 (47)	82,751 (11)	55,593 (24)
Region	Northeast	Northeast	Southeast	Southeast	West	West	Midwest

	Maryland	Massachusetts	Michigan	Minnesota	Mississippi	Missouri	Montana
Capital	Annapolis	Boston	Lansing	St. Paul	Jackson	Jefferson City	Helena
Date and order of statehood	1788 (7)	1788 (6)	1837 (26)	1858 (32)	1817 (20)	1821 (24)	1889 (41)
Nickname	Free State	Bay State	Wolverine State	North Star State	Magnolia State	Show Me State	Treasure State
Population	5,296,486	6,349,097	9,938,444	4,919,479	2,844,658	5,595,211	902,195
Square miles and rank in area	9,775 (42)	7,838 (45)	56,809 (22)	79,617 (14)	46,914 (31)	68,898 (18)	145,556 (4)
Region	Northeast	Northeast	Midwest	Midwest	Southeast	Midwest	West

Facts About Our Fifty States

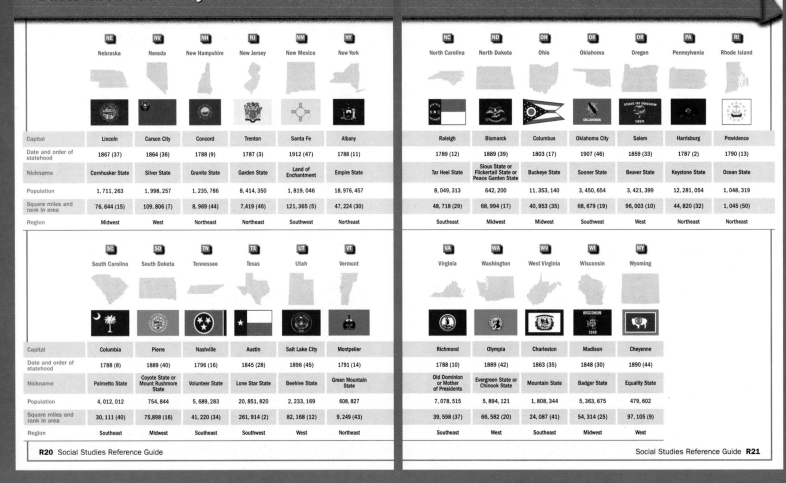

	NE Nebraska	NV Nevada	NH New Hampshire	NJ New Jersey	NM New Mexico	NY New York
Capital	Lincoln	Carson City	Concord	Trenton	Santa Fe	Albany
Date and order of statehood	1867 (37)	1864 (36)	1788 (9)	1787 (3)	1912 (47)	1788 (11)
Nickname	Cornhusker State	Silver State	Granite State	Garden State	Land of Enchantment	Empire State
Population	1,711,263	1,998,257	1,235,786	8,414,350	1,819,046	18,976,457
Square miles and rank in area	76,644 (15)	109,806 (7)	8,969 (44)	7,419 (46)	121,365 (5)	47,224 (30)
Region	Midwest	West	Northeast	Northeast	Southwest	Northeast

	SC South Carolina	SD South Dakota	TN Tennessee	TX Texas	UT Utah	VT Vermont
Capital	Columbia	Pierre	Nashville	Austin	Salt Lake City	Montpelier
Date and order of statehood	1788 (8)	1889 (40)	1796 (16)	1845 (28)	1896 (45)	1791 (14)
Nickname	Palmetto State	Coyote State or Mount Rushmore State	Volunteer State	Lone Star State	Beehive State	Green Mountain State
Population	4,012,012	754,844	5,689,283	20,851,820	2,233,169	608,827
Square miles and rank in area	30,111 (40)	75,898 (16)	41,220 (34)	261,914 (2)	82,168 (12)	9,249 (43)
Region	Southeast	Midwest	Southeast	Southwest	West	Northeast

	NC North Carolina	ND North Dakota	OH Ohio	OK Oklahoma	OR Oregon	PA Pennsylvania	RI Rhode Island
Capital	Raleigh	Bismarck	Columbus	Oklahoma City	Salem	Harrisburg	Providence
Date and order of statehood	1789 (12)	1889 (39)	1803 (17)	1907 (46)	1859 (33)	1787 (2)	1790 (13)
Nickname	Tar Heel State	Sioux State or Flickertail State or Peace Garden State	Buckeye State	Sooner State	Beaver State	Keystone State	Ocean State
Population	8,049,313	642,200	11,353,140	3,450,654	3,421,399	12,281,054	1,048,319
Square miles and rank in area	48,718 (29)	68,994 (17)	40,953 (35)	68,679 (19)	96,003 (10)	44,820 (32)	1,045 (50)
Region	Southeast	Midwest	Midwest	Southwest	West	Northeast	Northeast

	VA Virginia	WA Washington	WV West Virginia	WI Wisconsin	WY Wyoming
Capital	Richmond	Olympia	Charleston	Madison	Cheyenne
Date and order of statehood	1788 (10)	1889 (42)	1863 (35)	1848 (30)	1890 (44)
Nickname	Old Dominion or Mother of Presidents	Evergreen State or Chinook State	Mountain State	Badger State	Equality State
Population	7,078,515	5,894,121	1,808,344	5,363,675	479,602
Square miles and rank in area	39,598 (37)	66,582 (20)	24,087 (41)	54,314 (25)	97,105 (9)
Region	Southeast	West	Southeast	Midwest	West

Facts About Our Presidents

	1 George Washington	2 John Adams	3 Thomas Jefferson	4 James Madison	5 James Monroe
Years in Office	1789-1797	1797-1801	1801-1809	1809-1817	1817-1825
Life Span	1732-1799	1735-1826	1743-1826	1751-1836	1758-1831
Birthplace	Westmoreland County, Virginia	Braintree County, Massachusetts	Abemarle County, Virginia	Port Conway, Virginia	Westmoreland County, Virginia
Home State	Virginia	Massachusetts	Virginia	Virginia	Virginia
Political Party	none	Federalist	Democratic-Republican	Democratic-Republican	Democratic-Republican
First Lady	Martha Dandridge Washington	Abigail Smith Adams	Martha Skelton Jefferson	Dolley Payne Madison	Elizabeth Kortright Monroe
Religion	Episcopalian	Unitarian	Deist	Episcopalian	Episcopalian

	12 Zachary Taylor	13 Millard Fillmore	14 Franklin Pierce	15 James Buchanan	16 Abraham Lincoln
Years in Office	1849-1850	1850-1853	1853-1857	1857-1861	1861-1865
Life Span	1784-1850	1800-1874	1804-1869	1791-1868	1809-1865
Birthplace	Orange County, Virginia	Cayuga County, New York	Hillsboro, New Hampshire	Mercersburg, Pennsylvania	Harden County, Kentucky
Home State	Virginia	New York	New Hampshire	Pennsylvania	Illinois
Political Party	Whig	Whig	Democratic	Democratic	Republican
First Lady	Margaret Smith Taylor	Abigail Powers Filmore	Jane Appleton Pierce	None	Mary Todd Lincoln
Religion	Episcopalian	Unitarian	Episcopalian	Presbyterian	Attended Presbyterian services

	6 John Quincy Adams	7 Andrew Jackson	8 Martin Van Buren	9 William H. Harrison	10 John Tyler	11 James K. Polk
Years in Office	1825-1829	1829-1837	1837-1841	1841	1841-1845	1845-1849
Life Span	1767-1848	1767-1845	1782-1862	1773-1841	1790-1862	1795-1849
Birthplace	Braintree, Massachusetts	Waxhaw, South Carolina	Kinderhook, New York	Charles City County, Virginia	Charles City County, Virginia	Mecklenburg County, North Carolina
Home State	Massachusetts	Tennessee	New York	Ohio	Virginia	Tennessee
Political Party	Democratic-Republican	Democratic	Democratic	Whig	Whig	Democratic
First Lady	Louisa Johnson Adams	None	None	Anna Symmes Harrison	Letitia Christian Tyler; Julia Gardiner Tyler	Sarah Childress Polk
Religion	Unitarian	Presbyterian	Dutch Reformed	Episcopalian	Episcopalian	Methodist

	17 Andrew Johnson	18 Ulysses S. Grant	19 Rutherford B. Hayes	20 James A. Garfield	21 Chester A. Arthur	22 24 Grover Cleveland
Years in Office	1865-1869	1869-1877	1877-1881	1881	1881-1885	1885-1889; 1893-1897
Life Span	1808-1875	1822-1885	1822-1893	1831-1881	1829-1886	1837-1908
Birthplace	Raleigh, North Carolina	Point Pleasant, Ohio	Delaware, Ohio	Orange, Ohio	Fairfield, Vermont	Caldwell, New Jersey
Home State	Tennessee	Illinois	Ohio	Ohio	New York	New York
Political Party	National Union	Republican	Republican	Republican	Republican	Democratic
First Lady	Eliza McCardle Johnson	Julia Dent Grant	Lucy Webb Hayes	Lucretia Randolph Garfield	None	Frances Folsom Cleveland
Religion	Attended Methodist services	Methodist	Methodist	Disciples of Christ	Episcopalian	Presbyterian

Facts About Our Presidents

	23 Benjamin Harrison	25 William McKinley	26 Theodore Roosevelt	27 William H. Taft	28 Woodrow Wilson
Years in Office	1889–1893	1897–1901	1901–1909	1909–1913	1913–1921
Life Span	1833–1901	1843–1901	1858–1919	1857–1930	1856–1924
Birthplace	North Bend, Ohio	Niles, Ohio	New York, New York	Cincinnati, Ohio	Staunton, Virginia
Home State	Indiana	Ohio	New York	Ohio	New Jersey
Political Party	Republican	Republican	Republican	Republican	Democratic
First Lady	Caroline Scott Harrison	Ida Saxton McKinley	Edith Carow Roosevelt	Helen Herron Taft	Ellen Axson Wilson; Edith Galt Wilson
Religion	Presbyterian	Methodist	Dutch Reformed	Unitarian	Presbyterian

	29 Warren G. Harding	30 Calvin Coolidge	31 Herbert Hoover	32 Franklin D. Roosevelt	33 Harry S. Truman	34 Dwight D. Eisenhower
Years in Office	1921–1923	1923–1929	1929–1933	1933–1945	1945–1953	1953–1961
Life Span	1865–1923	1872–1933	1874–1964	1882–1945	1884–1972	1890–1969
Birthplace	Morrow County, Ohio	Plymouth, Vermont	West Branch, Iowa	Hyde Park, New York	Lamar, Missouri	Denison, Texas
Home State	Ohio	Massachusetts	California	New York	Missouri	Kansas
Political Party	Republican	Republican	Republican	Democratic	Democratic	Republican
First Lady	Florence DeWolfe Harding	Grace Goodhue Coolidge	Lou Henry Hoover	Anna Eleanor Roosevelt	Bess Wallace Truman	Marie "Mamie" Doud Eisenhower
Religion	Baptist	Congregational	Quaker	Episcopalian	Baptist	Presbyterian

	35 John F. Kennedy	36 Lyndon B. Johnson	37 Richard M. Nixon	38 Gerald R. Ford	39 James E. Carter
Years in Office	1961–1963	1963–1969	1969–1974	1974–1977	1977–1981
Life Span	1917–1963	1908–1973	1913–1994	1913–2006	1924–
Birthplace	Brookline, Massachusetts	Stonewall, Texas	Yorba Linda, California	Omaha, Nebraska	Plains, Georgia
Home State	Massachusetts	Texas	California	Michigan	Georgia
Political Party	Democratic	Democratic	Republican	Republican	Democratic
First Lady	Jacqueline Bouvier Kennedy	Claudia "Lady Bird" Taylor Johnson	Thelma "Pat" Ryan Nixon	Elizabeth (Betty) Warren Ford	Rosalynn Smith Carter
Religion	Roman Catholic	Disciples of Christ	Quaker	Episcopalian	Southern Baptist

	40 Ronald Reagan	41 George H. W. Bush	42 William J. Clinton	43 George W. Bush
Years in Office	1981–1989	1989–1993	1993–2001	2001–
Life Span	1911–2004	1924–	1946–	1946–
Birthplace	Tampico, Illinois	Milton, Massachusetts	Hope, Arkansas	New Haven, Connecticut
Home State	California	Texas	Arkansas	Texas
Political Party	Republican	Republican	Democratic	Republican
First Lady	Anne "Nancy" Davis Reagan	Barbara Pierce Bush	Hillary Rodham Clinton	Laura Welch Bush
Religion	Disciples of Christ	Episcopalian	Baptist	Methodist

United States Documents
The Declaration of Independence

Sometimes in history it becomes necessary for a group of people to break political ties with the country that rules it. When this happens, it is proper to explain the reasons for the need to separate.

We believe that all men are created equal and given by their Creator certain rights that cannot be taken away. People have the right to live, be free, and seek happiness.

Governments are established to protect these rights. The government gets its power from the support of the people it governs. If any form of government tries to take away the basic rights, it is the right of the people to change or end the government and to establish a new government that seems most likely to result in their safety and happiness.

Wise judgment will require that long-existing governments should not be changed for unimportant or temporary reasons. History has shown that people are more willing to suffer under a bad government than to get rid of the government they are used to. But when there are so many abuses and misuses of power by the government, it is the right and duty of the people to throw off such government and form a new government to protect their basic rights.

The colonies have suffered patiently, and now it is necessary for them to change the government. The king of Great Britain has repeatedly abused his power over these states. To prove this, the following facts are given.

In Congress, July 4, 1776
The unanimous Declaration of the thirteen United States of America

When, in the course of human events, it becomes necessary for one people to dissolve the political bands which have connected them with another, and to assume, among the powers of the earth, the separate and equal station to which the laws of nature and nature's God entitle them, a decent respect to the opinions of mankind requires that they should declare the causes which impel them to the separation.

We hold these truths to be self-evident, that all men are created equal, that they are endowed by their Creator with certain unalienable rights, that among these are life, liberty, and the pursuit of happiness.

That to secure these rights, governments are instituted among men, deriving their just powers from the consent of the governed; that whenever any form of government becomes destructive of these ends, it is the right of the people to alter or to abolish it, and to institute new government, laying its foundation on such principles and organizing its powers in such form, as to them shall seem most likely to effect their safety and happiness.

Prudence, indeed, will dictate that governments long established should not be changed for light and transient causes; and accordingly all experience hath shown that mankind are more disposed to suffer, while evils are sufferable, than to right themselves by abolishing the forms to which they are accustomed. But when a long train of abuses and usurpations, pursuing invariably the same object, evinces a design to reduce them under absolute despotism, it is their right, it is their duty, to throw off such government, and to provide new guards for their future security.

Such has been the patient sufferance of these colonies; and such is now the necessity which constrains them to alter their former systems of government. The history of the present king of Great Britain is a history of repeated injuries and usurpations, all having in direct object the establishment of an absolute tyranny over these states. To prove this, let facts be submitted to a candid world.

He has refused his assent to laws the most wholesome and necessary for the public good. He has forbidden his governors to pass laws of immediate and pressing importance, unless suspended in their operation till his assent should be obtained; and when so suspended, he has utterly neglected to attend to them.

He has refused to pass other laws for the accommodation of large districts of people, unless those people would relinquish the right of representation in the legislature, a right inestimable to them, and formidable to tyrants only.

He has called together legislative bodies at places unusual, uncomfortable, and distant from the depository of their public records, for the sole purpose of fatiguing them into compliance with his measures.

He has dissolved representative houses repeatedly, for opposing, with manly firmness, his invasions on the rights of the people.

He has refused, for a long time after such dissolutions, to cause others to be elected; whereby the legislative powers, incapable of annihilation, have returned to the people at large for their exercise; the state remaining, in the meantime, exposed to all the dangers of invasion from without and convulsions within.

He has endeavored to prevent the population of these states; for that purpose obstructing the laws for the naturalization of foreigners, refusing to pass others to encourage their migrations hither, and raising the conditions of new appropriations of lands.

He has obstructed the administration of justice, by refusing his assent to laws for establishing judiciary powers.

He has made judges dependent on his will alone for the tenure of their offices, and the amount and payment of their salaries.

He has erected a multitude of new offices, and sent hither swarms of officers to harass our people and eat out their substance.

He has kept among us, in times of peace, standing armies, without the consent of our legislatures.

He has affected to render the military independent of, and superior to, the civil power.

He has combined with others to subject us to a jurisdiction foreign to our constitution and unacknowledged by our laws, giving his assent to their acts of pretended legislation:

The king has not given his approval to needed laws. He has not allowed his governors to pass laws needed immediately. The king has made the governors delay laws until they can get his permission and then he has ignored the laws.

He has refused to pass other laws for the help of large districts of people, unless those people would give up the right of representation in the legislature, a right priceless to them, and threatening only to tyrants.

He has called together legislative bodies at unusual places, uncomfortable, and distant from where they store their public records, and only for the purpose of tiring them into obeying his measures.

He has repeatedly done away with legislative groups that firmly opposed him for taking away the rights of the people.

After he has dissolved these representative meetings, he has refused to allow new elections. Because of this lack of legislative power, the people are exposed to the dangers of invasion from without and within.

He has tried to prevent people from immigrating to these states by blocking the process for foreigners to become citizens; refusing to pass laws to encourage people to travel to America, and making it harder to move to and own new lands.

He has interfered with the administration of justice, by refusing to approve laws for establishing courts.

He has made judges do what he wants by controlling how long they serve and how much they are paid.

He has created many new government offices, and sent many officials to torment our people and live off of our hard work.

In times of peace, he has kept soldiers among us, without the consent of our legislatures.

He has tried to make the military separate from, and superior to, the civil government.

He and others have made us live under laws that are different from our laws. He has given his approval to these unfair laws that parliament has adopted:

United States Documents

The Declaration of Independence

For forcing us to feed and house many British soldiers;

For using pretend trials to protect British soldiers from punishment for murdering people in America;

For cutting off our trade with the world;

For taxing us without our consent;

For taking away, in many cases, the benefits of trial by jury;

For taking us to Britain, to be tried for made-up offenses;

For doing away with the free system of English laws in a neighboring province, and establishing a harsh government there, and enlarging its boundaries, as a way to introduce the same absolute rule into these colonies;

For taking away our governing documents, doing away with our most valuable laws, and changing our governments completely;

For setting aside our own legislatures, and declaring that Great Britain has power to make laws for us in all cases whatsoever.

He has deserted government here, by not protecting us and waging war against us.

He has robbed our ships on the seas, destroyed our coasts, burned our towns, and destroyed the lives of our people.

He is at this time sending large armies of foreign hired soldiers to complete the works of death, destruction, and injustice. These deeds are among the cruelest ever seen in history, and are totally unworthy of the head of a civilized nation.

He has forced our fellow citizens, who were captured on the high seas, to fight against America, to kill their friends and family, or to be killed themselves.

He has stirred up civil disorder among us, and has tried to cause the merciless killing of the people living on the frontiers by the Indians, whose rule of warfare includes the deliberate killing of people regardless of age, sex, or conditions.

In every stage of these mistreatments we have asked for a solution in the most humble terms; our repeated requests have been answered only by repeated injury. A prince who is so unfair and acts like a dictator is unfit to be the ruler of a free people.

For quartering large bodies of armed troops among us;

For protecting them, by a mock trial, from punishment for any murders which they should commit on the inhabitants of these states;

For cutting off our trade with all parts of the world;

For imposing taxes on us without our consent;

For depriving us, in many cases, of the benefits of trial by jury;

For transporting us beyond seas, to be tried for pretended offenses;

For abolishing the free system of English laws in a neighboring province, establishing therein an arbitrary government, and enlarging its boundaries, so as to render it at once an example and fit instrument for introducing the same absolute rule into these colonies;

For taking away our charters, abolishing our most valuable laws, and altering fundamentally the forms of our governments;

For suspending our own legislatures, and declaring themselves invested with power to legislate for us in all cases whatsoever.

He has abdicated government here, by declaring us out of his protection and waging war against us.

He has plundered our seas, ravaged our coasts, burned our towns, and destroyed the lives of our people.

He is at this time transporting large armies of foreign mercenaries to complete the works of death, desolation, and tyranny already begun with circumstances of cruelty and perfidy scarcely paralleled in the most barbarous ages, and totally unworthy the head of a civilized nation.

He has constrained our fellow citizens, taken captive on the high seas, to bear arms against their country, to become the executioners of their friends and brethren, or to fall themselves by their hands.

He has excited domestic insurrection among us, and has endeavored to bring on the inhabitants of our frontiers, the merciless Indian savages, whose known rule of warfare is an undistinguished destruction of all ages, sexes, and conditions.

In every stage of these oppressions we have petitioned for redress in the most humble terms; our repeated petitions have been answered only by repeated injury. A prince, whose character is thus marked by every act which may define a tyrant, is unfit to be the ruler of a free people.

Nor have we been wanting in attentions to our British brethren. We have warned them, from time to time, of attempts by their legislature to extend an unwarrantable jurisdiction over us. We have reminded them of the circumstances of our emigration and settlement here. We have appealed to their native justice and magnanimity; and we have conjured them, by the ties of our common kindred, to disavow these usurpations, which would inevitably interrupt our connections and correspondence. They, too, have been deaf to the voice of justice and consanguinity. We must, therefore, acquiesce in the necessity which denounces our separation, and hold them, as we hold the rest of mankind, enemies in war; in peace, friends.

We, therefore, the representatives of the United States of America, in General Congress assembled, appealing to the Supreme Judge of the world for the rectitude of our intentions, do, in the name and by the authority of the good people of these colonies, solemnly publish and declare that these United Colonies are, and of right ought to be, free and independent states; that they are absolved from all allegiance to the British crown, and that all political connection between them and the state of Great Britain is, and ought to be, totally dissolved; and that, as free and independent states, they have full power to levy war, conclude peace, contract alliances, establish commerce, and do all other acts and things which independent states may of right do. And, for the support of this declaration, with a firm reliance on the protection of Divine Providence, we mutually pledge to each other our lives, our fortunes, and our sacred honor.

Button Gwinnett (GA)	Benjamin Harrison (VA)	Lewis Morris (NY)
Lymann Hall (GA)	Thomas Nelson, Jr. (VA)	Richard Stockton (NJ)
George Walton (GA)	Francis Lightfoot Lee (VA)	John Witherspoon (NJ)
William Hooper (NC)	Carter Braxton (VA)	Francis Hopkinson (NJ)
Joseph Hewes (NC)	Robert Morris (PA)	John Hart (NJ)
John Penn (NC)	Benjamin Rush (PA)	Abraham Clark (NJ)
Edward Rutledge (SC)	Benjamin Franklin (PA)	Josiah Bartlett (NH)
Thomas Heyward, Jr. (SC)	John Morton (PA)	William Whipple (NH)
Thomas Lynch, Jr. (SC)	George Clymer (PA)	Samuel Adams (MA)
Arthur Middleton (SC)	James Smith (PA)	John Adams (MA)
John Hancock (MA)	George Taylor (PA)	Robert Treat Paine (MA)
Samuel Chase (MD)	James Wilson (PA)	Elbridge Gerry (MA)
William Paca (MD)	George Ross (PA)	Stephen Hopkins (RI)
Thomas Stone (MD)	Caesar Rodney (DE)	William Ellery (RI)
Charles Carroll of Carrollton (MD)	George Read (DE)	Roger Sherman (CT)
	Thomas McKean (DE)	Samuel Huntington (CT)
George Wythe (VA)	William Floyd (NY)	William Williams (CT)
Richard Henry Lee (VA)	Philip Livingston (NY)	Oliver Wolcott (CT)
Thomas Jefferson (VA)	Francis Lewis (NY)	Matthew Thornton (NH)

We have also asked for help from the British people. We have warned them, from time to time, of attempts by their government to extend illegal power over us. We have reminded them of why we came to America. We have appealed to their sense of justice and generosity; and we have begged them, because of all we have in common, to give up these abuses of power. They, like the king, have not listened to the voice of justice and brotherhood. We must, therefore, declare our separation. In war the British are our enemies. In peace they are our friends.

Therefore as the representatives of the people of the United States of America, in this General Congress assembled, appealing to God for the honesty of our purpose, do solemnly publish and declare that these United Colonies are, and rightly should be, free and independent states. The people of the United States are no longer subjects of the British crown. All political connections between the colonies and Great Britain, are totally ended. These free and independent states have full power to declare war, make peace, make treaties with other countries, establish trade, and do all other acts and things which independent states have the right to do. To support this declaration, with a firm trust on the protection of Divine Providence, we pledge to each other our lives, our fortunes, and our sacred honor.

"Among the natural rights of the Colonists are these: First a right to life; Secondly, to liberty; Thirdly, to property; together with the right to support and defend them in the best manner they can."

Samuel Adams, The report of the Committee of Correspondence to the Boston Town Meeting

"All, too, will bear in mind this sacred principle, that though the will of the majority is in all cases to prevail, that will to be rightful must be reasonable; that the minority possess their equal rights, which equal law must protect, and to violate would be oppression."

Thomas Jefferson, First Inaugural Address

United States Documents

The Constitution of the United States of America

We the people of the United States, in order to form a more perfect union, establish justice, insure peace in our nation, provide for our defense, promote the general welfare, and secure the blessings of liberty to ourselves and our descendants, do authorize and establish this Constitution for the United States of America.

ARTICLE 1

Legislative Branch

SECTION 1. Congress
Only the Congress of the United States has the power to make national laws. Congress is made up of a Senate and House of Representatives.

SECTION 2. House of Representatives
Members of the House of Representatives will be chosen every two years. People who are eligible to vote for state legislators are also eligible to vote for members of the House of Representatives.

To be a member of the House of Representatives, a person must be at least twenty-five years of age, and must have been a citizen of the United States for at least seven years, and live in the state the person is chosen to represent.

The number of representatives a state has is determined by the state's population. A census, or count, of the population must be taken every ten years. Each state shall have at least one representative.

We the people of the United States, in order to form a more perfect union, establish justice, insure domestic tranquility, provide for the common defense, promote the general welfare, and secure the blessings of liberty to ourselves and our posterity, do ordain and establish this Constitution for the United States of America.

ARTICLE 1

Legislative Branch

SECTION 1. Congress
All legislative powers herein granted shall be vested in a Congress of the United States, which shall consist of a Senate and House of Representatives.

SECTION 2. House of Representatives
The House of Representatives shall be composed of members chosen every second year by the people of the several states, and the electors in each state shall have the qualifications requisite for electors of the most numerous branch of the State legislature.

No person shall be a representative who shall not have attained to the age of twenty-five years, and been seven years a citizen of the United States, and who shall not, when elected, be an inhabitant of that state in which he shall be chosen.

Representatives ~~and direct taxes~~ shall be apportioned among the several states which may be included within this Union, according to their respective numbers, ~~which shall be determined by adding to the whole numbers of free persons, including those bound to service for a term of years, and excluding Indians not taxed, three fifths of all other persons.~~* The actual enumeration shall be made within three years after the first meeting of the Congress of the United States, and within every subsequent term of ten years, in such manner as they shall by law direct. The number of representatives shall not exceed one for every thirty thousand, but each State shall have at least one representative;~~and until such enumeration shall be made, the State of New Hampshire shall be entitled to choose three, Massachusetts eight, Rhode Island and Providence Plantations one, Connecticut five, New York six, New Jersey four, Pennsylvania eight, Delaware one, Maryland six, Virginia ten, North Carolina five, South Carolina five, and Georgia three.~~ (*Changed by the Fourteenth Amendment*)

When vacancies happen in the representation from any state, the executive authority thereof shall issue writs of election to fill such vacancies.

The House of Representatives shall choose their speaker and other officers, and shall have the sole power of impeachment.

SECTION 3. Senate
The Senate of the United States shall be composed of two senators from each state, ~~chosen by the legislature thereof,~~* for six years; and each senator shall have one vote.(*Changed by the Seventeenth Amendment*)

Immediately after they shall be assembled in consequence of the first election, they shall be divided as equally as may be into three classes. The seats of the senators of the first class shall be vacated at the expiration of the second year, of the second class at the expiration of the fourth year, and of the third class at the expiration of the sixth year, so that one third may be chosen every second year; ~~and if vacancies happen by resignation, or otherwise, during the recess of the legislature of any State, the executive thereof may make temporary appointments until the next meeting of the legislature, which shall then fill such vacancies.~~*
(*Changed by the Seventeenth Amendment*)

No person shall be a senator who shall not have attained to the age of thirty years, and been nine years a citizen of the United States, and who shall not, when elected, be an inhabitant of that State for which he shall be chosen.

The Vice President of the United States shall be president of the Senate, but shall have no vote, unless they be equally divided.

The Senate shall choose their other officers, and also a president pro tempore, in the absence of the Vice President, or when he shall exercise the office of President of the United States.

The Senate shall have the sole power to try all impeachments. When sitting for that purpose, they shall be an oath or affirmation. When the President of the United States is tried, the Chief Justice shall preside: and no person shall be convicted without the concurrence of two thirds of the members present.

Judgment in cases of impeachment shall not extend further than to removal from office, and disqualification to hold any office of honor, trust or profit under the United States: but the party convicted shall nevertheless be liable and subject to indictment, trial, judgment and punishment, according to law.

When vacancies happen in the representation from any state, the governor of the state will call a special election to fill the empty seat.

The House of Representatives shall choose their speaker and other officers, and only the House of Representatives may impeach, or accuse, government officials of crimes in office.

SECTION 3. Senate
The Senate of the United States shall be made up of two senators from each state. Each senator serves for six years; and each senator shall have one vote.

(*Until the Seventeenth Amendment, the senators were chosen by the legislature of the state they represented.*)

Only one-third of the senators are up for election at one time.

(*The remaining section was changed by the Seventeenth Amendment*).

A senator must be at least thirty years old, a citizen of the United States for at least nine years, and live in the state the senator is chosen to represent.

The Vice President of the United States is also the president of the Senate, but has no vote, unless there is a tie.

The Senate chooses its own officers. The Senate also chooses a senator to be the president pro tempore who serves as the temporary president of the Senate in the absence of the Vice President, or when the Vice President acts as President of the United States.

Only the Senate has the power to try all impeachments. When meeting on an impeachment, the senators shall take an oath or affirmation. When the President of the United States is tried on impeachment charges, the Chief Justice shall be in charge: and no person shall be found guilty without the agreement of two-thirds of the members present.

Impeached officials who are convicted can be removed from office, and disqualified from holding any other government office. Other courts in the country may still try, judge, and punish the impeached official.

SECTION 4. Elections and Meetings of Congress
The state legislature determines the times, places, and method of holding elections for senators and representatives. Congress may make laws that change some of the regulations.

The Congress shall meet at least once in every year.

(Until the passing of the Twentieth Amendment, Congress met on the first Monday in December.)

SECTION 5. Rules for Congress
The Senate and House of Representatives judge the fairness of the elections and the qualifications of its own members. At least half of the members must be present to do business; but a smaller number may end the meeting from day to day, and may force absent members to attend and may penalize a member for not attending.

Each house may determine the rules of its proceedings and punish its members for disorderly behavior. Each house may, with the agreement of two-thirds of its members, force a member out of office.

Each house of Congress shall keep a record of its proceedings, and from time to time publish the record, except those parts that may need to be kept secret. If one-fifth of the members want it, the votes on any matter shall be published.

During the session of Congress, neither house shall adjourn for more than three days without the permission of the other, nor can they decide to meet at any other place than where both houses agree.

SECTION 6. Rights and Restrictions of Members of Congress
The senators and representatives shall receive a payment for their services, to be decided by law, and paid out of the Treasury of the United States. Except for very serious crimes, senators and representatives are protected from arrest during their attendance at the session of Congress, and in going to and returning from Congress. Members of Congress shall not be arrested for anything they say in Congress.

No senator or representative shall be appointed to any government job while serving in Congress. No senator or representative is allowed to take a government job that is created or has its salary increased during the senator's or representative's term of office. While holding a government office, no person shall also be a member of Congress.

SECTION 4. Elections and Meetings of Congress
The times, places, and manner of holding elections for senators and representatives shall be prescribed in each State by the legislature thereof; but the Congress may at any time by law make or alter such regulations, except as to the places of choosing senators.

The Congress shall assemble at least once in every year, ~~and such meeting shall be on the first Monday in December,~~* unless they shall by law appoint a different day. (**Changed by the Twentieth Amendment*)

SECTION 5. Rules for Congress
Each house shall be the judge of the elections, returns and qualifications of its own members, and a majority of each shall constitute a quorum to do business; but a smaller number may adjourn from day to day, and may be authorized to compel the attendance of absent members, in such manner, and under such penalties as each house may provide.

Each house may determine the rules of its proceedings, punish its members for disorderly behavior, and, with the concurrence of two thirds, expel a member.

Each house shall keep a journal of its proceedings, and from time to time publish the same, excepting such parts as may in their judgment require secrecy; and the yeas and nays of the members of either house on any question shall, at the desire of one fifth of those present, be entered on the journal.

Neither house, during the session of Congress, shall, without the consent of the other, adjourn for more than three days, nor to any other place than that in which the two houses shall be sitting.

SECTION 6. Rights and Restrictions of Members of Congress
The senators and representatives shall receive a compensation for their services, to be ascertained by law, and paid out of the Treasury of the United States. They shall in all cases, except treason, felony and breach of the peace, be privileged from arrest during their attendance at the session of their respective houses, and in going to and returning from the same; and for any speech or debate in either house, they shall not be questioned in any other place.

No senator or representative shall, during the time for which he was elected, be appointed to any civil office under the authority of the United States, which shall have been created, or the emoluments thereof shall have been increased during such time; and no person holding any office under the United States shall be a member of either house during his continuance in office.

SECTION 7. How Laws Are Made
All bills for raising revenue shall originate in the House of Representatives; but the Senate may propose or concur with amendments as on other bills.

Every bill which shall have passed the House of Representatives and the Senate, shall before it become a law, be presented to the President of the United States; if he approve he shall sign it, but if not he shall return it, with his objections to that house in which it shall have originated, who shall enter the objections at large on their journal, and proceed to reconsider it. If after such reconsideration two thirds of that house shall agree to pass the bill, it shall be sent, together with the objections, to the other house, by which it shall likewise be reconsidered, and if approved by two thirds of that house, it shall become a law. But in all such cases the votes of both houses shall be determined by yeas and nays, and the names of persons voting for and against the bill shall be entered on the journal of each house respectively. If any bill shall not be returned by the President within ten days, (Sundays excepted) after it shall have been presented to him, the same shall be a law, in like manner as if he had signed it, unless the Congress by their adjournment prevent its return, in which case it shall not be a law.

Every order, resolution, or vote to which the concurrence of the Senate and House of Representatives may be necessary (except on a question of adjournment) shall be presented to the President of the United States; and before the same shall take effect, shall be approved by him, or being disapproved by him, shall be repassed by two thirds of the Senate and House of Representatives, according to the rules and limitations prescribed in the case of a bill.

SECTION 8. Powers of Congress
The Congress shall have power to lay and collect taxes, duties, imposts and excises, to pay the debts and provide for the common defense and general welfare of the United States; but all duties, imposts and excises shall be uniform throughout the United States.

To borrow money on the credit of the United States;

To regulate commerce with foreign nations, and among the several States, and with the Indian tribes;

To establish a uniform rule of naturalization, and uniform laws on the subject of bankruptcies through the United States;

To coin money, regulate the value thereof, and of foreign coin, and fix the standard of weights and measures;

To provide for the punishment of counterfeiting the securities and current coin of the United States;

To establish post offices and post roads;

SECTION 7. How Laws Are Made
All bills for raising money shall begin in the House of Representatives. The Senate may suggest or agree with amendments to these tax bills, as with other bills.

Every bill which has passed the House of Representatives and the Senate must be presented to the President of the United States before it becomes a law. If the President approves of the bill the President shall sign it. If the President does not approve, then the bill may be vetoed. The President then sends it back to the house in which it began, with an explanation of the objections. That house writes the objections on their record, and begins to reconsider it. If two-thirds of each house agrees to pass the bill, it shall become a law. But in all such cases the votes of both houses shall be determined by "yes" and "no" votes, and the names of persons voting for and against the bill shall be entered on the record of each house. If any bill is neither signed nor vetoed by the President within ten days, (except for Sundays) after it has been sent to the President, the bill shall be a law. If Congress adjourns before ten days have passed, the bill does not become a law.

Every order, resolution, or vote which passes in the Senate and House of Representatives shall be presented to the President of the United States to be signed or vetoed. A bill that is vetoed by the President can only become a law if it repassed by two-thirds of the Senate and House of Representatives.

SECTION 8. Powers of Congress
The Congress shall have power to:
- establish and collect taxes on imported and exported goods and on goods sold within the country. Congress also shall pay the debts and provide for the defense and general welfare of the United States. All federal taxes shall be the same throughout the United States.
- borrow money on the credit of the United States;
- make laws about trade with other countries, among the states, and with the American Indian tribes;
- establish one procedure by which a person from another country can become a legal citizen of the United States, and establish bankruptcy laws to deal with people and businesses who cannot pay what they owe;
- print or coin money, and regulate its value. Congress has the power to determine how much foreign money is worth in American money. Congress sets the standard of weights and measures;

- establish punishments for counterfeiting, or making fake money, stocks, and bonds;
- establish post offices and roads for mail delivery;
- promote the progress of science and useful arts by protecting, for limited times, the writings and discoveries of authors and inventors by issuing copyrights and patents;
- create courts lower than the Supreme Court;
- define and punish crimes committed on the high seas, and crimes that break international laws;
- declare war and make rules about taking enemy property on land or sea;
- set up and supply armies. Congress cannot provide funding for the armies for more than two years at a time;
- set up and supply a navy;
- make rules for the armed forces;
- provide for calling the militia to action to carry out the laws of the country, put down revolts and riots and fight off invasions;
- provide for organizing, arming, and disciplining the militia, and for governing those employed in the armed service of the United States. The states have the right to appoint the officers, and the authority of training the militia according to the rules made by Congress;
- govern the nation's capital [Washington, D.C.] and military bases in the United States;
- make all laws needed to carry out the powers mentioned earlier in the Constitution, and all other powers placed by this Constitution in the government of the United States, or in any department or officer of the government.

SECTION 9. Powers Denied to Congress
Congress does not have the power to prevent enslaved people from being brought into the country until 1808, but a tax may be placed on each imported person.

(Congress passed a law in 1808 forbidding the slave trade.)

Congress may not do away with laws that protect an individual from being jailed unless the person goes to trial or unless specific criminal charges are filed, unless the public safety requires it during a rebellion or invasion.

No law shall be passed that penalizes a person or group without the benefit of a trial or makes an action illegal after the action was taken.

To promote the progress of science and useful arts by securing for limited times to authors and inventors the exclusive right to their respective writings and discoveries;

To constitute tribunals inferior to the Supreme Court;

To define and punish piracies and felonies committed on the high seas, and offenses against the law of nations;

To declare war, ~~grant letters of marque and reprisal~~, and make rules concerning captures on land and water;

To raise and support armies, but no appropriation of money to that use shall be for a longer term than two years;

To provide and maintain a navy;

To make rules for the government and regulations of the land and naval forces;

To provide for calling forth the militia to execute the laws of the Union, suppress insurrections and repel invasions;

To provide for organizing, arming, and disciplining the militia, and for governing such part of them as may be employed in the service of the United States, reserving to the States respectively the appointment of the officers, and the authority of training the militia according to the discipline prescribed by Congress;

To exercise exclusive legislation in all cases whatsoever, over such district (not exceeding ten miles square) as may, by cession of particular States and the acceptance of Congress, become the seat of the government of the United States, and to exercise like authority over all places purchased by the consent of the legislature of the State in which the same shall be, for the erection of forts, magazines, arsenals, dockyards, and other needful buildings; and

To make all laws which shall be necessary and proper for carrying into execution the foregoing powers, and all other powers vested by this Constitution in the government of the United States, or in any department or officer thereof.

SECTION 9. Powers Denied to Congress
~~The migration or importation of such persons as any of the States now existing shall think proper to admit, shall not be prohibited by the Congress prior to the year one thousand eight hundred and eight, but a tax or duty may be imposed on such importation, not exceeding ten dollars for each person.~~

The privilege of the writ of habeas corpus shall not be suspended, unless when in cases of rebellion or invasion the public safety may require it.

No bill of attainder or ex post facto law shall be passed.

No capitation, or other direct,* tax shall be laid, ~~unless in proportion to the census or enumeration herein before directed to be taken~~. (**Changed by the Sixteenth Amendment*)

No tax or duty shall be laid on articles exported from any State.

No preference shall be given by any regulation of commerce or revenue to the ports of one State over those of another; nor shall vessels bound to, or from, one State be obliged to enter, clear, or pay duties in another.

No money shall be drawn from the Treasury, but in consequence of appropriations made by law; and a regular statement and account of the receipts and expenditures of all public money shall be published from time to time.

No title of nobility shall be granted by the United States: and no person holding any office of profit or trust under them, shall, without the consent of the Congress, accept any present, emolument, office, or title of any kind whatever, from any king, prince, or foreign State.

SECTION 10. Powers Denied to the States
No State shall enter into any treaty, alliance, or confederation; grant letters of marque and reprisal; coin money; emit bills of credit; make anything but gold and silver coin a tender in payment of debts; pass any bill of attainder, ex post facto law, or law impairing the obligation of contracts, or grant any title of nobility.

No State shall, without the consent of the Congress, lay any imposts or duties on imports or exports, except what may be absolutely necessary for executing its inspection laws: and the net produce of all duties and imposts laid by any State on imports or exports, shall be for the use of the Treasury of the United States; and all such laws shall be subject to the revision and control of the Congress.

No State shall, without the consent of Congress, lay any duty of tonnage, keep troops, or ships of war in time of peace, enter into any agreement or compact with another State, or with a foreign power, or engage in war, unless actually invaded, or in such imminent danger as will not admit of delay.

ARTICLE 2
The Executive Branch

SECTION 1. The President and Vice President
The executive power shall be vested in a President of the United States of America. He shall hold his office during the term of four years, and, together with the Vice President chosen for the same term, be elected as follows:

No person in the United States may be taxed unless everyone is taxed the same.

*(*The Sixteenth Amendment allowed an income tax.)*

No tax shall put on articles exported from any state.

No laws shall be passed that give special treatment to one state over those of another in trade. Ships shall not be required to pay a tax to enter another state.

No money shall be taken from the Treasury, without passing a law. A public record must be kept of money raised and money spent.

The United States shall not give any titles of nobility, such as king or queen. No person holding any government office shall accept any present, payment, office, or title of any kind, from another country, without the consent of the Congress.

SECTION 10. Powers Denied to the States
No state can make treaties or alliances with other nations or issue official documents permitting private citizens to capture the merchant ships or engage warships of another nation. No state can issue its own money or make anything, other than gold or silver, legal as currency. No state can pass laws that apply to actions before the law was passed. No state may allow a person to be punished without a fair trial. No state can pass laws that excuse anyone from a contract. No state can give anyone a title of nobility.

Without approval from Congress, no state can collect taxes on goods coming in or going out of the state, except those small fees needed for customs inspections. Any taxes from trade become the property of the United States government.

Without approval from Congress, states are forbidden to tax ships or keep troops or warships in peacetime, unless endangered by actual invasion. States may not enter into an agreement with another state or foreign nation.

ARTICLE 2
The Executive Branch

SECTION 1. The President and Vice President
The President has the power to carry out the laws of Congress, and the President and Vice President serve a four-year term.

The legislature of each state determines the process for electing its representatives in the Electoral College, which officially elects the President and the Vice President. Each state's total number of electors is determined by the state's total number of members in Congress. No person holding any office in the federal government can become an elector.

(Until this was changed by the Twelfth Amendment, the person who received the most electoral votes became the President and the person with the next highest number became the Vice President. The Twelfth Amendment overruled this clause and changed the way the election process worked.)

Each State shall appoint, in such manner as the legislature thereof may direct, a number of electors, equal to the whole number of senators and representatives to which the State may be entitled in the Congress: but no senator or representative, or person holding an office of trust or profit under the United States, shall be appointed an elector.

~~The electors shall meet in their respective States, and vote by ballot for two persons, of whom one at least shall not be an inhabitant of the same State with themselves. And they shall make a list of all the persons voted for, and of the number of votes for each; which they shall sign and certify, and transmit sealed to the seat of the government of the United States, directed to the president of the Senate. The president of the Senate shall, in the presence of the Senate and House of Representatives, open all the certificates, and the votes shall then be counted. The person having the greatest number of votes shall be the President, if such number be a majority of the whole number of electors appointed; and if there be more than one who have such majority, and have an equal number of votes, then the House of Representatives shall immediately choose by ballot one of them for President; and if no person have a majority, then from the five highest on the list the said house shall in like manner choose the President. But in choosing the President, the votes shall be taken by States, the representation from each State having one vote; a quorum for this purpose shall consist of a member or members from two thirds of the States, and a majority of all the States shall be necessary to a choice. In every case, after the choice of the President, the person having the greatest number of votes of the electors shall be the Vice President. But if there should remain two or more who have equal votes, the Senate shall choose from them by ballot the Vice President.~~* (**Changed by the Twelfth Amendment*)

Congress determines the date and time when each state's electors are to cast their votes for President and Vice President.

To become President a person must be born a citizen of the United States, be at least thirty-five years old, and have lived in the United States for at least fourteen years.

If a President dies, is disabled or is removed from office, the Vice President becomes President.

(The Twenty Fifth Amendment changed the method for filling these offices if they become vacant.)

The Congress may determine the time of choosing the electors, and the day on which they shall give their votes; which day shall be the same throughout the United States.

No person except a natural-born citizen, or a citizen of the United States, at the time of the adoption of this Constitution, shall be eligible to the office of President; neither shall any person be eligible to that office who shall not have attained to the age of thirty-five years, and been fourteen years a resident within the United States.

In case of the removal of the President from office, or of his death, resignation, or inability to discharge the powers and duties of the said office, the same shall devolve on the Vice President, ~~and the Congress may by law provide for the case of removal, death, resignation, or inability, both of the President and Vice President, declaring what officer shall then act as President, and such officer shall act accordingly, until the disability be removed, or a President shall be elected.~~

The President shall, at stated times, receive for his services a compensation, which shall neither be increased nor diminished during the period for which he shall have been elected, and he shall not receive within that period any other emolument from the United States, or any of them.

Before he enter on the execution of his office, he shall take the following oath or affirmation: — " I do solemnly swear (or affirm) that I will faithfully execute the office of President of the United States, and will to the best of my ability, preserve, protect and defend the Constitution of the United States."

SECTION 2. Powers of the President

The President shall be commander in chief of the army and navy of the United States, and of the militia of the several States, when called into the actual service of the United States; he may require the opinion, in writing, of the principal officer in each of the executive departments, upon any subject relating to the duties of their respective offices, and he shall have power to grant reprieves and pardons for offenses against the United States, except in cases of impeachment.

He shall have power, by and with the advice and consent of the Senate, to make treaties, provided two thirds of the senators present concur; and he shall nominate, and by and with the advice and consent of the Senate, shall appoint ambassadors, other public ministers and consuls, judges of the Supreme Court, and all other officers of the United States, whose appointments are not herein otherwise provided for, and which shall be established by law: but the Congress may by law vest the appointment of such inferior officers, as they think proper, in the President alone, in the courts of law, or in the heads of departments.

The President shall have power to fill up all vacancies that may happen during the recess of the Senate, by granting commissions which shall expire at the end of their next session.

SECTION 3. Duties of the President

He shall from time to time give to the Congress information of the state of the Union, and recommend to their consideration such measures as he shall judge necessary and expedient; he may, on extraordinary occasions, convene both houses, or either of them, and in case of disagreement between them with respect to the time of adjournment, he may adjourn them to such time as he shall think proper; he shall receive ambassadors and other public ministers; he shall take care that the laws be faithfully executed, and shall commission all the officers of the United States.

The President will receive a salary, but it cannot be increased or decreased during the term(s) of office. The President cannot have another occupation or receive outside compensation while in office.

Before assuming the duties of the office, the President must take the following oath or affirmation: "I do solemnly swear (or affirm) that I will faithfully execute the office of President of the United States, and will to the best of my ability, preserve, protect and defend the Constitution of the United States."

SECTION 2. Powers of the President

The President is the leader of the armed forces of the United States and of the state militias during times of war. The President may require the principal officer in each of the executive departments to write a report about any subject relating to their duties, and can grant delays of punishments or pardons for criminals, except in cases of impeachment.

With the advice and consent of two-thirds of the members of the Senate, the President can make treaties with foreign nations and can appoint ambassadors and other officials as necessary to handle our diplomatic affairs with other countries. The President can appoint federal judges and other key officers in the executive branch of government, with the consent of two-thirds of the Senate. Congress may give power to the President to appoint minor government officials and heads of departments.

When the Senate is not in session, the President can make temporary appointments to offices which require Senate approval. These appointments expire when the next session has ended.

SECTION 3. Duties of the President

The President must make a report to Congress on a regular basis providing information concerning important national developments and goals. Law-making requests for Congress should be given as well. The President can call for special sessions of one or both houses of Congress for special reasons. If the houses of Congress cannot agree on a common date for adjournment, the President has the power to make that decision. The President is to officially receive foreign ambassadors and other public ministers. The President is to fully and faithfully carry out the laws of Congress and sign the documents required to give officers the rights to perform their duties.

United States Documents
The Constitution of the United States of America

SECTION 4. Removal from Office

The President, Vice President, and all civil officers can be removed from office if convicted on impeachment charges for treason, bribery, or other high crimes and misdemeanors.

ARTICLE 3

The Judicial Branch

SECTION 1. Federal Courts

The Supreme Court is the highest court in the land. Congress has the power to create all other federal courts. Federal judges may hold office for life as long as they act properly and shall receive a salary that cannot be lowered during the judge's time of service.

SECTION 2. Powers of Federal Courts The power of the federal courts covers two types of cases: (1) those involving the interpretation of the Constitution, federal laws, treaties and laws relating to ships on the high seas; and (2) those involving the United States government itself, foreign diplomats, two or more state governments, citizens of different states, and a state or its citizens versus foreign countries or their citizens.

Cases involving foreign diplomats and any state in the United States will be tried by the Supreme Court. Other cases tried by the Supreme Court are those appealed or brought forward from lower federal courts or from state courts. Congress can decide to make exceptions to these regulations.

Except for those trials involving impeachment, all persons accused of crimes are guaranteed a jury trial in the same state where the crime was committed. When a crime is committed outside of any state, such as a ship at sea, Congress will decide where the trial will take place.

SECTION 3. Treason

Anyone who makes war against the United States or gives help to the nation's enemies, can be charged with treason. No one can be convicted of treason unless two witnesses support the charge or unless the person confesses to the charge in open court.

SECTION 4. Removal from Office

The President, Vice President, and all civil officers of the United States, shall be removed from office on impeachment for, and conviction of, treason, bribery, or other high crimes and misdemeanors.

ARTICLE 3

The Judicial Branch

SECTION 1. Federal Courts

The judicial power of the United States shall be vested in one Supreme Court, and in such inferior courts as the Congress may from time to time ordain and establish. The judges, both of the Supreme and inferior courts, shall hold their offices during good behavior, and shall, at stated times, receive for their services, a compensation which shall not be diminished during their continuance in office.

SECTION 2. Powers of Federal Courts

The judicial power shall extend to all cases, in law and equity, arising under this Constitution, the laws of the United States, and treaties made, or which shall be made, under their authority; — to all cases affecting ambassadors, other public ministers and consuls; — to all cases of admiralty and maritime jurisdiction; — to controversies to which the United States shall be a party; — to controversies between two or more States; — between a State and citizens of another State; —between citizens of different states — between citizens of the same State claiming lands under grants of different States, and between a State, or the citizens thereof, and foreign States, citizens or subjects.

In all cases affecting ambassadors, other public ministers and consuls, and those in which a State shall be party, the Supreme Court shall have original jurisdiction. In all the other cases before mentioned, the Supreme Court shall have appellate jurisdiction, both as to law and fact, with such exceptions, and under such regulations as the Congress shall make.

The trial of all crimes, except in cases of impeachment, shall be by jury; and such trial shall be held in the State where the said crimes shall have been committed; but when not committed within any State, the trial shall be at such place or places as the Congress may by law have directed.

SECTION 3. Treason

Treason against the United States shall consist only in levying war against them, or in adhering to their enemies, giving them aid and comfort. No person shall be convicted of treason unless on the testimony of two witnesses to the same overt act, or on confession in open court.

The Congress shall have power to declare the punishment of treason, but no attainder of treason shall work corruption of blood, or forfeiture except during the life of the person attained.

ARTICLE 4

Relations Among the States

SECTION 1. Recognition by Each State

Full faith and credit shall be given in each State to the public acts, records, and judicial proceedings of every other State. And the Congress may by general laws prescribe the manner in which such acts, records, and proceedings shall be proved, and the effect thereof.

SECTION 2. Rights of Citizens in States

The citizens of each State shall be entitled to all privileges and immunities of citizens in the several States.

A person charged in any State with treason, felony, or other crime, who shall flee from justice, and be found in another State, shall on demand of the executive authority of the State from, which he fled, be delivered up to be removed to the State having jurisdiction of the crime.

~~No person held to service or labor in the State, under the laws thereof, escaping into another, shall, in consequence of any law or regulation therein, be discharged from such service or labor, but shall be delivered up on claim of the party to whom such service or labor may be due.~~ * (**Changed by the Thirteenth Amendment*)

SECTION 3. New States

New States may be admitted by the Congress into this *Union*; but no new State shall be formed or erected within the jurisdiction of any other State; nor any State be formed by the junction of two or more States, or parts of States, without the consent of the legislatures of the States concerned as well as of the Congress.

The Congress shall have power to dispose of and make all needful rules and regulations respecting the territory or other property belonging to the United States; and nothing in this Constitution shall be so construed as to prejudice any claims of the United States, or of any particular State.

SECTION 4. Guarantees to the States

The United States shall guarantee to every State in this Union a republican form of government, and shall protect each of them against invasion; and on application of the legislature, or of the executive (when the legislature cannot be convened) against domestic violence.

Congress has the power to decide punishments for acts of treason. The family of the traitor does not share in the guilt.

ARTICLE 4

Relations Among the States

SECTION 1. Recognition by Each State

Each state must recognize the laws, records, and legal decisions made by all the other states. Congress has the power to make laws to determine how these laws, records, and legal decisions can be proved.

SECTION 2. Rights of Citizens in States

States must give the same rights to citizens from other states that they give their own citizens.

If a person charged with a crime runs away to another state, the person must be returned to the original state for a trial.

No person who was a slave in one state may become free by escaping to a different state.

(This was changed by the 13th Amendment which made slavery illegal in all states.)

SECTION 3. New States

New states may become part of the United States with the permission of Congress. New states cannot be formed from land in an existing state, nor can two or more states or their parts join to create a new state without the consent of the states involved and of Congress.

Congress may sell or give away land or property belonging to the United States. Congress has the power to make all laws related to territories or other property owned by the United States and to make laws to govern federal territories and possessions.

SECTION 4. Guarantees to the States

The United States government is required to guarantee that each state has a republican form of government, a government that is responsible to the will of its people through their elected representatives. The federal government also must protect the states if they are invaded by foreign nations and to do the same in case of riots, if requested by the governor or legislature of the state.

ARTICLE 5
Amending the Constitution

Amendments may be proposed by a two-thirds vote of each house of Congress or by a national convention called by Congress at the request of two-thirds of the states. To add an amendment to the Constitution, the legislatures or special conventions of three-fourths of the states must give approval or ratify it. However, no amendment can be added that keeps a state from having an equal vote in the United States Senate. No amendment may be added before 1808 that affects the slave trade or certain taxes.

ARTICLE 5
Amending the Constitution

The Congress, whenever two thirds of both houses shall deem it necessary, shall propose amendments to this Constitution, or, on the application of the legislatures of two thirds of the several States, shall call a convention for proposing amendments, which, in either case, shall be valid to all intents and purposes, as part of this Constitution, when ratified by the legislatures of three fourths of the several States, or by conventions in three fourths thereof, as the one or the other mode of ratification may be proposed by the Congress; provided ~~that no amendment which may be made prior to the year one thousand eight hundred and eight shall in any manner affect the first and fourth clauses in the ninth section of the first article, and~~ that no State, without its consent, shall be deprived of its equal suffrage in the Senate.

ARTICLE 6
Debts, Federal Supremacy, Oaths of Office

The federal government must pay all debts owed by the United States, including those debts which were taken on under the Articles of Confederation.

The Constitution and the laws of the United States are the supreme, or highest, laws of the land. All public officials in the federal government or within the states, regardless of other laws to the contrary, are bound by the Constitution and the national laws.

All officials in both federal and state governments must promise to obey and support the Constitution. No religious qualifications can be required as a condition for holding public office.

ARTICLE 6
Debts, Federal Supremacy, Oaths of Office

All debts contracted and engagements entered into, before the adoption of this Constitution, shall be as valid against the United States under this Constitution, as under the Confederation.

This Constitution, and the laws of the United States which shall be made in pursuance thereof; and all treaties made, or which shall be made, under the authority of the United States, shall be the supreme law of the land; and the judges in every State shall be bound thereby, anything in the Constitution or laws of any State to the contrary notwithstanding.

The senators and representatives before mentioned, and the members of the several State legislatures, and all executive and judicial officers, both of the United States, and of the several States, shall be bound by oath or affirmation to support this Constitution; but no religious test shall ever be required as a qualification to any office or public trust under the United States.

ARTICLE 7
Ratifying the Constitution

The Constitution will take effect when it is approved by at least nine of the thirteen states.

On September 17, 1787, all twelve state delegations present have given approval for adopting the Constitution. As proof, the delegates have each placed their signatures on the document.

ARTICLE 7
Ratifying the Constitution

The ratification of the conventions of nine States shall be sufficient for the establishment of this Constitution between the States so ratifying the same.

Done in Convention by the unanimous consent of the States present the seventeenth day of September in the year of our Lord one thousand seven hundred and eighty-seven, and of the independence of the United States of America the twelfth. In witness whereof we have hereunto subscribed our names.

George Washington, *President* (Virginia)

Massachusetts
Nathaniel Gorham
Rufus King

New York
Alexander Hamilton

Georgia
William Few
Abraham Baldwin

Delaware
George Read
Gunning Bedford, Jr.
John Dickinson
Richard Bassett
Jacob Broom

Virginia
John Blair
James Madison, Jr.

Pennsylvania
Benjamin Franklin
Thomas Mifflin
Robert Morris
George Clymer
Thomas FitzSimons
Jared Ingersoll
James Wilson
Gouverneur Morris

New Hampshire
John Langdon
Nicholas Gilman

New Jersey
William Livingston
David Brearley
William Paterson
Jonathan Dayton

Connecticut
William Samuel Johnson
Roger Sherman

North Carolina
William Blount
Richard Dobbs Spaight
Hugh Williamson

South Carolina
John Rutledge
Charles Cotesworth Pinckney
Charles Pinckney
Pierce Butler

Maryland
James McHenry
Daniel of St. Thomas Jenifer
Daniel Carroll

"Let virtue, honor, and love of liberty and of science be and remain the soul of this constitution, and it will become the source of great and extensive happiness to this and future generations."

From Jay's charge to the Grand Jury of Ulster County. The Correspondence and Public Papers of John Jay, Henry P. Johnston, editor (New York: Burt Franklin, 1970), Vol. I, pp, 158-165, September 9, 1777.

"The power under the Constitution will always be in the people."

George Washington, The Writings of George Washington, Jared Sparks, editor (Boston: Russell, Odiorne and Metcalf, 1835), Vol. IX, p. 279, to Bushrod Washington on November 10, 1787.

FIRST AMENDMENT—1791
Freedom of Religion, Speech, Press, Assembly, and Petition

Congress shall not make any laws that set up an official national religion or that keeps people from worshiping according to their conscience. Congress may not limit the freedom of speech, the press, or the freedom to meet peaceably. People must have the right to ask the government to correct a problem.

FIRST AMENDMENT—1791
Freedom of Religion, Speech, Press, Assembly, and Petition

Congress shall make no law respecting an establishment of religion, or prohibiting the free exercise thereof; or abridging the freedom of speech, or of the press; or the right of the people peaceably to assemble, and to petition the government for a redress of grievances.

SECOND AMENDMENT—1791
Right to Have Firearms

Because an organized militia is needed to protect the states, the right of people to keep and bear firearms shall not be violated.

SECOND AMENDMENT—1791
Right to Have Firearms

A well-regulated militia, being necessary to the security of a free state, the right of the people to keep and bear arms, shall not be infringed.

THIRD AMENDMENT—1791
Right Not to House Soldiers

Soldiers may not be housed in private homes, without the consent of the owner, unless a law for that purpose is passed during a time of war.

THIRD AMENDMENT—1791
Right Not to House Soldiers

No soldier shall, in time of peace, be quartered in any house, without the consent of the owner, nor in time of war, but in a manner to be prescribed by law.

FOURTH AMENDMENT—1791
Freedom from Unreasonable Search and Seizure

People and their property are to be protected from unreasonable search and seizure. Government authorities must have good cause and have a written order from a judge describing the place to be searched and the person or things to be seized.

FOURTH AMENDMENT—1791
Freedom from Unreasonable Search and Seizure

The right of the people to be secure in their persons, houses, papers, and effects, against unreasonable searches and seizures, shall not be violated, and no warrants shall issue, but upon probable cause, supported by oath or affirmation, and particularly describing the place to be searched, and the persons or things to be seized.

FIFTH AMENDMENT—1791
Rights of People Accused of Crimes

A person may not be put on trial for a crime that is punishable by death or imprisonment without first being accused by a grand jury. [A grand jury is a group of citizens selected to decide whether there is enough evidence against a person to hold a trial.] However, during war time or a time of public danger, people in military service may not have that right.

A person may not be put on trial twice for the same crime.

FIFTH AMENDMENT—1791
Rights of People Accused of Crimes

No person shall be held to answer for a capital or otherwise infamous crime, unless on a presentment or indictment of a grand jury, except in cases arising in the land or naval forces, or in the militia, when in actual service in time of war or public danger; nor shall any person be subject for the same offense to be twice put in jeopardy of life or limb; nor shall be compelled in any criminal case to be a witness against himself, nor be deprived of life, liberty, or property, without due process of law; nor shall private property be taken for public use without just compensation.

People can not be required to give evidence against themselves.

People may not have their lives, liberty, or property taken away without fair and equal treatment under the laws of the land.

People may not have their property taken for public use without receiving access to the lawful judicial processes.

SIXTH AMENDMENT—1791
Right to a Jury Trial in a Criminal Case

In all criminal prosecutions, the accused shall enjoy the right to a speedy and public trial, by an impartial jury of the state and district wherein the crime shall have been committed, which district shall have been previously ascertained by law, and to be informed of the nature and cause of the accusation; to be confronted with the witnesses against him; to have compulsory process for obtaining witnesses in his favor, and to have the assistance of counsel for his defense.

SIXTH AMENDMENT—1791
Right to a Jury Trial in a Criminal Case

A person accused of a crime must have a speedy, public trial held before an open-minded jury made up of citizens living in the community where the crime occurred. The accused person must also be told about the nature of the charge of wrongdoing. Accused people are allowed to meet and question witnesses against them, to have witnesses testify in their favor, and to have the services of a lawyer.

SEVENTH AMENDMENT—1791
Right to a Jury Trial in a Civil Case

In suits at common law, where the value in controversy shall exceed twenty dollars, the right of trial by jury shall be preserved, and no fact tried by a jury shall be otherwise reexamined in any court of the United States, than according to the rules of the common law.

SEVENTH AMENDMENT—1791
Right to a Jury Trial in a Civil Case

In civil cases, where the value of the property in question is over $20, the right of a jury trial is guaranteed. The decision of the jury is final and cannot be changed by a judge but only by a new trial.

EIGHTH AMENDMENT—1791
Protection from Unfair Bail and Punishment

Excessive bail shall not be required, nor excessive fines imposed, nor cruel and unusual punishments inflicted.

EIGHTH AMENDMENT—1791
Protection from Unfair Bail and Punishment

Bails and fines must not be too large, and punishments may not be cruel and unusual.

NINTH AMENDMENT—1791
Other Rights

The enumeration in the Constitution of certain rights shall not be construed to deny or disparage others retained by the people.

NINTH AMENDMENT—1791
Other Rights

Fundamental rights not listed in the Constitution remain guaranteed to all citizens.

TENTH AMENDMENT—1791
Powers of the States and People

The powers not delegated to the United States by the Constitution, nor prohibited by it to the States are reserved to the states respectively, or to the people.

TENTH AMENDMENT—1791
Powers of the States and People

The states or the people keep all powers not granted to the federal government and not denied to the states by the Constitution.

ELEVENTH AMENDMENT—1795
Limits on Right to Sue States

A state government cannot be sued in a federal court by people from a different state or from a foreign country.

TWELFTH AMENDMENT—1804
Election of President and Vice President

In each state, members of the Electoral College vote on separate ballots for one person as President and another person as Vice President. At least one of these choices may not live in the same state as the electors. Each person, on the ballot, receiving votes in a given state must be listed by the total numbers of votes. Final counts of votes from each state must be signed and officially recognized as accurate and complete. These results must be delivered to the national capital to be opened and read aloud by the president of the Senate at a joint session of Congress.

If a person receives a majority of votes for President, that person shall be the President. If no person has a majority, then from the three who received the largest number of votes, the House of Representatives will immediately choose the President by ballot. But in choosing the President, the votes shall be taken by states with each state having one vote. Two-thirds of the states must participate in this choice. *(Until changed by the Twentieth Amendment, if the House of Representatives failed to elect a President by March 4, the Vice President served as President.)*

If a person receives a majority of votes as Vice President, that person shall be the Vice President. If no person has a majority, then from the two highest numbers on the list, the Senate will choose the Vice President, provided that two-thirds of the senators are present to vote. A simple majority, with each senator voting individually, is necessary to make a final choice. A person who is not eligible to be President can not be eligible for the office of Vice President.

ELEVENTH AMENDMENT—1795
Limits on Right to Sue States

The judicial power of the United States shall not be construed to extend to any suit in law or equity, commenced or prosecuted against one of the United States, by citizens of another State, or by citizens or subjects of any foreign State.

TWELFTH AMENDMENT—1804
Election of President and Vice President

The electors shall meet in their respective States, and vote by ballot for President and Vice President, one of whom, at least, shall not be an inhabitant of the same State with themselves; they shall name in their ballots the person voted for as Vice President, and they shall make distinct lists of all persons voted for as President and of all persons voted for as Vice President, and of the number of votes for each, which lists they shall sign and certify, and transmit sealed to the seat of government of the United States, directed to the president of the Senate;—The president of the Senate shall, in the presence of the Senate and House of Representatives, open all the certificates and the votes shall then be counted;—The person having the greatest number of votes for President shall be the President, if such number be a majority of the whole number of electors appointed; and if no person have such majority, then from the persons having the highest numbers not exceeding three on the list of those voted for as President, the House of Representatives shall choose immediately, by ballot, the President. But in choosing the President, the votes shall be taken by States, the representation from each State having one vote; a quorum for this purpose shall consist of a member or members from two thirds of the States, and a majority of all the States shall be necessary to a choice. ~~And if the House of Representatives shall not choose a President whenever the right of choice shall devolve upon them, before the fourth day of March next following,~~* then the Vice President shall act as President, as in the case of the death or other constitutional disability of the President. The person having the greatest number of votes as Vice President shall be the Vice President, if such number be a majority of the whole number of electors appointed, and if no person have a majority, then from the two highest numbers on the list, the Senate shall choose the Vice President; a quorum for the purpose shall consist of two thirds of the whole number of senators and a majority of the whole number shall be necessary to a choice. But no person constitutionally ineligible to the office of President shall be eligible to that of Vice President of the United States. *(*Changed by the Twentieth Amendment)*

THIRTEENTH AMENDMENT—1865
Abolition of Slavery

SECTION 1. Slavery Outlawed
Neither slavery nor involuntary servitude, except as a punishment for crime whereof the party shall have been duly convicted, shall exist within the United States, or any place subject to their jurisdiction.

SECTION 2. Enforcement
Congress shall have power to enforce this article by appropriate legislation.

FOURTEENTH AMENDMENT—1868
Rights of Citizens

SECTION 1. Citizenship
All persons born or naturalized in the United States, and subject to the jurisdiction thereof, are citizens of the United States and of the State wherein they reside. No State shall make or enforce any law which shall abridge the privileges or immunities of citizens of the United States; nor shall any State deprive any person of life, liberty, or property, without due process of law; nor deny to any person within its jurisdiction the equal protection of the laws.

SECTION 2. Representation in Congress
Representatives shall be apportioned among the several States according to their respective numbers, counting the whole number of persons in each State, ~~excluding Indians not taxed~~. But when the right to vote at any election for the choice of electors for President and Vice President of the United States, representatives in Congress, the executive and judicial officers of a State, or the members of the legislature thereof, is denied to any of the ~~male~~ inhabitants of such State, being ~~twenty-one years of age, and~~ citizens of the United States, or in any way abridged, except for participation in rebellion, or other crime, the basis of representation therein shall be reduced in the proportion which the number of such citizens shall bear to the whole number of ~~male~~ citizens ~~twenty-one years of age~~ in such State.

SECTION 3. Penalties for Leaders of the Confederacy
No person shall be a senator or representative in Congress, or elector of President and Vice President, or hold any office, civil or military, under the United States, or under any State, who, having previously taken an oath, as

THIRTEENTH AMENDMENT—1865
Abolition of Slavery

Slavery shall not exist anywhere in the United Sates or anyplace governed by the United States. Forced labor may only be required after being fairly convicted of a crime.

Congress may make laws to enforce this article.

FOURTEENTH AMENDMENT—1868
Rights of Citizens

All persons born in the United States or granted citizenship are citizens of both the United States and of the states in which they live.

No state may pass laws which take away or limit the freedoms or privileges of any of its citizens. Citizens may not have their lives, liberties, or property taken away without access to a regular judicial process conducted according to the laws. All people must be protected equally by the laws.

A state's representation in Congress is determined by the state's population. A state which does not allow qualified voters to vote may have its representation in Congress reduced. *(Other provisions of this section were changed by the Fifteenth, Nineteenth, Twenty-fourth and Twenty-sixth Amendments.)*

No person may hold a civil or military office in the federal or a state government who had previously taken an oath to uphold the Constitution and then aided or helped the confederacy during the Civil War or other rebellions against the United States.

Congress may remove this provision by a two-thirds vote of both houses.

Any federal debts resulting from fighting to end a civil war or put down a rebellion must be paid in full. However, the federal or state government shall not pay debts made by those who participate in a rebellion against the United States.

Former owners of slaves shall not be paid for the financial losses caused by the freeing of slaves.

Congress has the power to pass laws to enforce the provisions of this article.

FIFTEENTH AMENDMENT—1870
Voting Rights

A citizen's right to vote in any election cannot be denied based on the person's race, color, or because they were once enslaved.

Congress has the power to pass laws to enforce the provisions of this article.

SIXTEENTH AMENDMENT—1913
Income Tax

Congress has the power to directly tax all individuals based on their personal incomes, without collecting taxes based on a division among the States or in consideration of a State's population.

a member of Congress, or as an officer of the United States, or as a member of any State legislature, or as an executive or judicial officer of any State, to support the Constitution of the United States, shall have engaged in insurrection or rebellion against the same, or given aid or comfort to the enemies thereof. But Congress may by a vote of two thirds of each house, remove such disability.

SECTION 4. Responsibility for the Public Debt
The validity of the public debt of the United States, authorized by law including debts incurred for payment of pensions and bounties for services in suppressing insurrection or rebellion, shall not be questioned. But neither the United States nor any State shall assume or pay any debt or obligation incurred in aid of insurrection or rebellion against the United States, or any claim for the loss or emancipation of any slave; but all such debts, obligations and claims shall be held illegal and void.

SECTION 5. Enforcement
The Congress shall have power to enforce, by appropriate legislation, the provisions of this article.

FIFTEENTH AMENDMENT—1870
Voting Rights

SECTION 1. Suffrage for African Americans
The right of citizens of the United States to vote shall not be denied or abridged by the United States or by any State on account of race, color, or previous condition of servitude.

SECTION 2. Enforcement
The Congress shall have power to enforce this article by appropriate legislation.

SIXTEENTH AMENDMENT—1913
Income Tax

The Congress shall have power to lay and collect taxes on incomes, from whatever source derived, without apportionment among the several States, and without regard to any census or enumeration.

SEVENTEENTH AMENDMENT—1913
Direct Election of Senators

The Senate of the United States shall be composed of two senators from each State, elected by the people thereof, for six years; and each senator shall have one vote. The electors in each State shall have the qualifications requisite for electors of the most numerous branch of the State legislatures.

When vacancies happen in the representation of any State in the Senate, the executive authority of such State shall issue writs of election to fill such vacancies: Provided, that the legislature of any State may empower the executive thereof to make temporary appointments until the people fill the vacancies by election as the legislature may direct.

This amendment shall not be so construed as to affect the election or term of any Senator chosen before it becomes valid as part of the Constitution.

EIGHTEENTH AMENDMENT*—1919
Prohibition

SECTION 1.
~~After one year from the ratification of this article the manufacture, sale, or transportation of intoxicating liquors within, the importation thereof into, or the exportation thereof from the United States and all territory subject to the jurisdiction thereof for beverage purposes is hereby prohibited.~~

SECTION 2. Enforcement
~~The Congress and the several States shall have concurrent power to enforce this article by appropriate legislation~~.

SECTION 3. Time Limit for Ratification
~~This article shall be inoperative unless it shall have been ratified as an amendment to the Constitution by the legislatures of the several States, as provided in the Constitution, within seven years from the date of the submission hereof to the States by the Congress~~. *(*Repealed by the Twenty-First Amendment)*

SEVENTEENTH AMENDMENT—1913
Direct Election of Senators

Two senators will represent each state in Congress, each elected for six-year terms and having one vote in the Senate. They will be elected directly by the qualified voters in the states. *(not by state legislatures, which was originally provided for in Article I, Section 3, Clause 1)*

When vacancies occur in the Senate, the governor of the state will call for an election to fill the vacancy. In the meantime the state legislature will permit the governor to make a temporary appointment until the election occurs. The legislature organizes the election.

This amendment shall not affect the election or term of any Senator chosen before it becomes part of the Constitution.

EIGHTEENTH AMENDMENT*—1919
Prohibition

The making, sale, and transporting of alcoholic beverages anywhere in the United States and its territories is outlawed. This amendment takes effect one year after the amendment is passed.

Congress and the states will share lawmaking powers to enforce this article.

This amendment will become part of the Constitution only if it is ratified within seven years after Congress has sent it to the States.

(This amendment was repealed by the Twenty-First Amendment).

NINETEENTH AMENDMENT—1920
Women's Right to Vote

A citizen's right to vote in any election cannot be denied based on the person's sex.

Congress shall have power to pass laws to enforce the provisions of this article.

TWENTIETH AMENDMENT—1933
Terms of Office

The terms of the President and Vice President end at noon on January 20th, and the terms of senators and representatives end at noon on January 3rd, following the federal elections held the previous November. The terms of their successors begin at that time.

Congress must meet at least once a year, and the session will begin at noon on January 3rd unless a law is passed to change the day.

If the President-elect dies before taking office, the Vice President- elect becomes President. If a President has not been chosen before January 20, or if the President-elect has not qualified, then the Vice President-elect acts as President until a President becomes qualified. If neither the President-elect or Vice President-elect is able to take office on the designated date, then Congress will decide who will act as President until a President or Vice President has been qualified.

If a candidate fails to win a majority in the Electoral College, and then dies while the election is being decided in the House of Representatives, Congress will have the power to pass laws to resolve the problem. Congress has similar power in the event that a candidate for Vice President dies while the election is in the Senate.

NINETEENTH AMENDMENT—1920
Women's Right to Vote

SECTION 1. Suffrage for Women
The right of citizens of the United States to vote shall not be denied or abridged by the United States or by any State on account of sex.

SECTION 2. Enforcement
Congress shall have power, by appropriate legislation, to enforce the provisions of this article.

TWENTIETH AMENDMENT—1933
Terms of Office

SECTION 1. Start and End of Terms
The terms of the President and Vice President shall end at noon on the 20th day of January, and the terms of senators and representatives at noon on the 3d day of January, of the years in which such terms would have ended if this article had not been ratified; and the terms of their successors shall then begin.

SECTION 2. Congressional Meeting
The Congress shall assemble at least once in every year, and such meeting shall begin at noon on the 3d day in January, unless they shall by law appoint a different day.

SECTION 3. Successor for the President-Elect
If, at the time fixed for the beginning of the term of the President, the President-elect shall have died, the Vice President-elect shall become President. If a President shall not have been chosen before the time fixed for the beginning of his term, or if the President-elect shall have failed to qualify, then the Vice President-elect shall act as President until a President shall have qualified; and the Congress may by law provide for the case wherein neither a President-elect nor a Vice President-elect shall have qualified, declaring who shall then act as President, or the manner in which one who is to act shall be selected, and such persons shall act accordingly until a President or Vice President shall have qualified.

SECTION 4. Elections Decided by Congress
The Congress may by law provide for the case of the death of any of the persons from whom the House of Representatives may choose a President

whenever the right of choice shall have devolved upon them, and for the case of the death of any of the persons from whom the Senate may choose a Vice President whenever the right of choice shall have devolved upon them.

SECTION 5. Effective Date
Sections 1 and 2 shall take effect on the 15th day of October following the ratification of this article.

SECTION 6. Time Limit for Ratification
This article shall be inoperative unless it shall have been ratified as an amendment to the Constitution by the legislatures of three fourths of the several States within seven years from the date of its submission.

TWENTY-FIRST AMENDMENT—1933
Repeal of Prohibition Amendment

SECTION 1. End of Prohibition
The eighteenth article of amendment to the Constitution of the United States is hereby repealed.

SECTION 2. Protection of State Prohibition Laws
The transportation or importation into any State, territory, or possession of the United States for delivery or use therein of intoxicating liquors, in violation of the laws thereof, is hereby prohibited.

SECTION 3. Time Limit for Ratification
This article shall be inoperative unless it shall have been ratified as an amendment to the Constitution by conventions in the several States, as provided in the Constitution, within seven years from the date of submission hereof to the States by the Congress.

TWENTY-SECOND AMENDMENT—1951
Limit on Terms of the President

Section 1. Two-Term Limit
No person shall be elected to the office of the President more than twice, and no person who has held the office of President, or acted as President, for more than two years of a term to which some other person was elected President shall be elected to the office of the President more than once.

Sections 1 and 2 of this amendment shall take effect on October 15, after this amendment is ratified.

This amendment will become part of the Constitution only if it is ratified within seven years after Congress has sent it to the States.

TWENTY-FIRST AMENDMENT—1933
Repeal of Prohibition Amendment

The Eighteenth Amendment prohibiting the making, sale, and transportation of alcoholic beverages in the United States and its possessions is repealed.

Individual states may prohibit the transporting or importing of alcoholic beverages.

This amendment will become part of the Constitution only if it is ratified in seven years.

TWENTY-SECOND AMENDMENT—1951
Limit on Terms of the President

No person can be elected to the office of the President more than twice. If a President has served two or more years of a previous President's term, then the President may be re-elected for one additional term.

The current President in office at the time of this amendment's ratification process is not limited to term restrictions.

This amendment will become part of the Constitution only if it is ratified by three-fourths of the States within seven years after Congress has sent it to the States.

TWENTY-THIRD AMENDMENT—1961
Presidential Elections for District of Columbia

Citizens living in the District of Columbia may elect members to the Electoral College to vote in federal elections for President and Vice President. The number of electors is limited to the number of votes of the least populated state. The voters must live in the district and follow all duties and procedures outlined in the Twelfth Amendment.

Congress has the power to make laws necessary to enforce this amendment.

TWENTY-FOURTH AMENDMENT—1964
Outlawing of Poll Tax

United States citizens may not have their voting rights restricted in federal elections by the establishment of a poll tax or other tax.

But this Article shall not apply to any person holding the office of President when this Article was proposed by the Congress, and shall not prevent any person who may be holding the office of President, or acting as President, during the term within which this Article becomes operative from holding the office of President or acting as President during the remainder of such term.

SECTION 2. Time Limit on Ratification
This article shall be inoperative unless it shall have been ratified as an amendment to the Constitution by the legislatures of three-fourths of the several States within seven years from the date of its submission to the States by the Congress.

TWENTY-THIRD AMENDMENT—1961
Presidential Elections for District of Columbia

SECTION 1. Presidential Electors
The District constituting the seat of government of the United States shall appoint in such manner as the Congress may direct:

A number of electors of President and Vice President equal to the whole number of senators and representatives in Congress to which the District would be entitled if it were a State, but in no event more than the least populous state; they shall be in addition to those appointed by the States, but they shall be considered, for the purposes of the election of President and Vice President, to be electors appointed by a State; and they shall meet in the District and perform such duties as provided by the twelfth article of amendment.

SECTION 2. Enforcement
The Congress shall have power to enforce this article by appropriate legislation.

TWENTY-FOURTH AMENDMENT—1964
Outlawing of Poll Tax

SECTION 1. Ban on Poll Tax in Federal Elections
The right of citizens of the United States to vote in any primary or other election for President or Vice President, for electors for President or Vice President, or for senator or representative in Congress, shall not be denied or abridged by the United States or any State by reason of failure to pay any poll tax or other tax.

SECTION 2. Enforcement
The Congress shall have power to enforce this article by appropriate legislation.

TWENTY-FIFTH AMENDMENT—1967
Presidential Succession

SECTION 1. Filling Vacant Office of President
In case of the removal of the President from office or his death or resignation, the Vice President shall become President.

SECTION 2. Filling Vacant Office of Vice President
Whenever there is a vacancy in the office of the Vice President, the President shall nominate a Vice President who shall take the office upon confirmation by a majority vote of both houses of Congress.

SECTION 3. Disability of the President
Whenever the President transmits to the president pro tempore of the Senate and the speaker of the House of Representatives his written declaration that he is unable to discharge the powers and duties of his office, and until he transmits to them a written declaration to the contrary, such powers and duties shall be discharged by the Vice President as Acting President.

SECTION 4. When Congress Names an Acting President
Whenever the Vice President and a majority of either the principal officers of the executive departments or of such other body as Congress may by law provide, transmit to the president pro tempore of the Senate and the speaker of the House of Representatives their written declaration that the President is unable to discharge the powers and duties of his office, the Vice President shall immediately assume the powers and duties of the office as Acting President.

Thereafter, when the President transmits to the president pro tempore of the Senate and the speaker of the House of Representatives his written declaration that no inability exists, he shall resume the powers and duties of his office unless the Vice President and a majority of either the principal officers of the executive department or of such other body as Congress may by law provide, transmit within four days to the president pro tempore of the Senate and the speaker of the House of Representatives their written declaration that the President is unable to discharge the powers and duties of his office. Thereupon Congress shall decide the issue, assembling within 48 hours for that purpose if not in session. If the

Congress has the power to make laws necessary to enforce this amendment.

TWENTY-FIFTH AMENDMENT—1967
Presidential Succession

If a President dies or is removed from office, then the Vice President will become President.

If the office of Vice President becomes vacant, the President may nominate a new Vice President. The person nominated must be approved by a majority vote in both houses of Congress.

If the President sends a written notice to officers of both houses of Congress that the President is unable to perform the duties of the office, then the Vice President will become Acting President. The Vice-President will act as the President until the President informs Congress that the President is again ready to take over the presidential responsibilities.

If the President is unconscious or refuses to admit a disabling illness, the Vice President and a majority of the Cabinet have the right to inform Congress in writing that the President is unable to carry out the duties of being President. The Vice President then becomes Acting President until the President can return to work.

When the President informs the leaders of Congress in writing that the disability no longer exists, the President shall resume the office. But if there is a disagreement between the President and the Vice President and a majority of the Cabinet about the President's ability to carry out the duties of being President, the Vice President, or other appropriate authority, has four days to notify Congress, and Congress has the power to decide the issue. If not in session, both houses of Congress must meet within 48 hours for that purpose and will have 21 days to make a decision. A two-thirds vote in both houses of Congress is required to find the President unfit to perform the duties of the office.

Congress, within 21 days after receipt of the latter written declaration, or, if Congress is not in session, within 21 days after Congress is required to assemble, determines by two-thirds vote of both houses that the President is unable to discharge the powers and duties of his office, the Vice President shall continue to discharge the same as Acting President; otherwise, the President shall resume the powers and duties of his office.

TWENTY-SIXTH AMENDMENT—1971
Voting Rights for Eighteen-Year-Olds

SECTION 1. New Voting Age
The right of citizens in the United States, who are eighteen years of age or older, to vote shall not be denied or abridged by the United States or by any State on account of age.

SECTION 2. Enforcement
The Congress shall have power to enforce this article by appropriate legislation.

TWENTY-SEVENTH AMENDMENT—1992
Limits on Congressional Salary Changes

No law varying the compensation for the services of the Senators and Representatives shall take effect, until an election of Representatives shall have intervened.

R52 Social Studies Reference Guide

Gazetteer

This Gazetteer is a geographic dictionary that will help you locate and pronounce the names of the places in this book. Latitude and longitude are given for cities. The page numbers tell you where each place appears on a map (m) or in the text (t).

Abilene (ab′ ə lēn′) City in Kansas that was a cowtown in the 1860s; 39°N, 97°W. (m. 546, t. 550)

Afghanistan (af gan′ ə stan) country in Central Asia, between Pakistan and Iran. (m. 665, t. 664)

Africa (af′ rə kə) Second largest of Earth's seven continents. (m. R4–R5, t. 107)

Alamo (al′ ə mō) Mission in San Antonio, Texas, which was used by Texans as a fort during the Texas Revolution. (t. 432)

Amazon River (am′ə zon riv′ər) Longest river in South America, flowing from the Andes Mountains to the Atlantic Ocean. (m. 689)

American River (ə mâr′ə kən riv′ər) River in California, where gold was discovered in 1848. (t. 443)

Andes Mountains (an′ dēz moun′tənz) Mountain range on the west coast of South America, the longest mountain chain in the world. (m. 691)

Angel Island (ān′jəl i′lənd) Island in San Francisco Bay, California, which was the entry point for immigrants from Asia from 1910 to 1940. (m. 568, t. 569)

Antarctica (ant ärk′tə kə) One of Earth's seven continents, around the South Pole. (R4–R5)

Antietam (an tē′təm) Creek near Sharpsburg, Maryland, site of a major Civil War battle in 1862. (t. 495)

Appalachian Mountains (ap′ə lā′chən moun′tənz) Chain of mountains in eastern North America, extending from Canada to Alabama. (m. 27)

Appomattox Court House (ap′ə mat′əks kôrt′hous) Town in central Virginia, site of Confederate General Lee's surrender to Union General Grant on April 9, 1865, ending the Civil War. (m. 506, 509; t. 511)

Arctic Ocean (ärk′tik ō′shən) Smallest of Earth's four oceans. (R4–R5)

Asia (ā′zhə) Largest of Earth's seven continents. (m. R4–R5, t. 103)

Atlanta (at lan′tə) Capital and largest city of Georgia, site of Union victory in a Civil War battle on September 2, 1864; 33°N, 84°W. (m. 506, 509; t. 510)

Atlantic Ocean (at lan′tik ō′shən) One of Earth's four oceans. (m. R4–R5)

Australia (ô strā′lyə) Smallest of Earth's seven continents. (m. R4–R5)

Bahama Islands (bə hä′mə i′ləndz) Island group in the West Indies, southeast of Florida. (m. 134, t. 135)

Pronunciation Key

a in hat	ō in open	sh in she
ā in age	ô in all	th in thin
â in care	ô in order	TH in then
ä in far	oi in oil	zh in measure
e in let	ou in out	ə = a in about
ē in equal	u in cup	ə = e in taken
ėr in term	ù in put	ə = i in pencil
i in it	ü in rule	ə = o in lemon
ī in ice	ch in child	ə = u in circus
o in hot	ng in long	

Social Studies Reference Guide **R53**

Gazetteer

Baltimore (bôl′tə môr) Seaport and largest city in Maryland; 39°N, 76°W. (m. 380, t. 383)

Bering Strait (bir′ing strāt) Narrow body of water that separates Asia from North America. (m. 54, 55; t. 55)

Berlin (bər lin′) Capital of Germany, was divided from 1945 to 1989; 52°N, 13°E. (t. 658)

Black Hills (blak hilz) Mountain range in South Dakota and Wyoming, where gold was discovered in 1874. (m. 554, t. 554–555)

Boston (bô′stən) Capital and largest city of Massachusetts; 42°N, 71°W. (m. 168, 216, 268, 276; t. 172, 217, 271, 277–280)

Bull Run (bùl run) Stream in northeastern Virginia, site of major Civil War battles in 1861 and 1862. (m. 491, t. 495)

Cahokia (kə hō′kē ə) Town in present-day Illinois, site of a 100-foot-high mound built by people called the Mound Builders; 39°N, 90°W. (m. 60, 62; t. 61)

California Trail (kal′ə fôr′nyə trāl) Trail from Independence, Missouri, to the Central Valley of California, used by gold seekers in 1849. (m. 440, 442; t. 443)

Canada (kan′ə də) Country in the northern part of North America, north of the United States. (m. 678–679, t. 680–681)

Canadian Shield (kə nā′dē ən shēld) Large area of ancient rocks that covers about half of Canada's land. (m. 678–679)

Canary Islands (kə nâr′ē i′ləndz) Island group in the Atlantic Ocean off the northwest coast of Africa. (m. 141)

Cape of Good Hope (kāp əv gùd hōp) Southwestern tip of Africa. (m. 110, 114; t. 114)

Caribbean Region (kâr′ə bē′ən rē′jən) Islands in the Caribbean Sea. (m. 689, t. 688)

Caribbean Sea (kâr′ə bē′ən sē) Part of the Atlantic Ocean, bordered by the West Indies and Central and South America. (m. 141)

Central America (sen′trəl ə mâr′ə kə) Region of North America, between Mexico and South America, area of seven countries. (m. 686–687, t. 686)

Charleston (chärlz′tən) Port city in southeastern South Carolina; 32°N, 79°W. (m. 202, t. 206)

Charlestown (chärlz′ toun) Oldest part of Boston, near where the battle of Bunker Hill was fought in 1775. (m. 286, 290; t. 290)

Chesapeake Bay (ches′ ə pēk′ bā) Inlet of the Atlantic Ocean, surrounded by Maryland and Virginia. (m. 159)

Chicago (shə kô′gō) Largest city in Illinois, located on Lake Michigan; 41°N, 87°W. (m. 550, t. 567)

China (chī′nə) Country in eastern Asia, with the world's largest population. (m. 103, t. 103)

Cleveland (klēv′lənd) Port city in Ohio, on Lake Erie; 41°N, 81°W. (m. 562, t. 566)

Coast Ranges (kōst rān′jəz) Mountains extending along the Pacific coast of North America. (m. R9, R14)

Colorado River (kol′ə rad′ō riv′ər) River in the southwestern United States, flowing from the Rocky Mountains to the Gulf of California. (m. 26)

Columbia River (kə lum′bē ə riv′ər) River in northwestern North America, which begins in Canada, forms part of the border between Washington and Oregon, and flows into the Pacific Ocean. (m. 26)

Concord (kong′kərd) Town in eastern Massachusetts, site of one of the first battles of the American Revolution, on April 19, 1775; 42°N, 71°W. (m. 286, t. 287)

R54 Social Studies Reference Guide

Copán (kō pän′) Ancient city of the Maya, located in present-day Honduras; 15°N, 88°W. (m. 66, 68; t. 67)

Cuba (kyü′ bə) Largest country in the West Indies. (m. 578, t. 580)

Cumberland Gap (kum′bər lənd gap) Pass through the Appalachian Mountains, in northeastern Tennessee. (m. 370, t. 372)

Cuzco (küz′ kō) Capital of the Inca Empire, located in present-day Peru; 13°N, 72°W. (m. 66, 68; t. 69, 145)

Dallas (dal′əs) City in northeastern Texas; 33°N, 97°W. (m. R12–R13)

Death Valley (deth val′ē) Lowest point in North America, located in the Mojave Desert in California. (m. R12–R13)

Denver (den′vər) Capital and largest city in Colorado; 40°N, 105°W. (m. 26)

Detroit (di troit′) Largest city in Michigan; 42°N, 83°W. (m. 27)

Eastern Hemisphere (ē′stərn hem′ə sfir) Half of Earth east of the prime meridian, including the continents of Africa, Asia, Europe, and Australia. (m. H14, t. H14)

Eastern Woodlands cultural region (ē′stərn wüd′ləndz kul′chər əl rē′jən) Area in eastern North America that was home to many Native Americans such as the Iroquois. (m. 76, 77; t. 77)

Ellis Island (el′is i′lənd) Island in New York Harbor, which was the entry point for immigrants from Europe from 1892 to 1954. (m. 568, t. 569)

England (ing′ glənd) Part of the United Kingdom of Great Britain and Northern Ireland. England occupies the southern part of the island of Great Britain. (m. 206, t. 248)

Erie Canal (ir′ē kə nal′) Human-made waterway in New York State, connecting Lake Erie and the Hudson River. (m. 408, t. 411)

Europe (yùr′əp) One of Earth's seven continents. (m. R4–R5, t. 103)

Everglades National Park (ev′ər glādz′ nash′ə nəl pärk) National park located in southern Florida. (m. 34, t. 37)

Florida (flôr′ə də) State located in the southeastern United States, settled by the Spanish in the middle 1500s. (m. 232, t. 233)

Fort Duquesne (fôrt dü kān′) Fort built by the French in 1754 in western Pennsylvania, site of present-day Pittsburgh. (m. 246, 248; t. 248)

Fort McHenry (fôrt mək hen′rē) Fort protecting the harbor of Baltimore, Maryland, site of a major battle in the War of 1812. (m. 380, t. 383)

Fort Necessity (fôrt nə ses′ə tē) Fort built by George Washington's soldiers in western Pennsylvania in 1754. (m. 246, t. 246–247)

Pronunciation Key

a in hat	ō in open	sh in she
ā in age	ô in all	th in thin
â in care	ô in order	TH in then
ä in far	oi in oil	zh in measure
e in let	ou in out	ə = a in about
ē in equal	u in cup	ə = e in taken
ėr in term	ù in put	ə = i in pencil
i in it	ü in rule	ə = o in lemon
ī in ice	ch in child	ə = u in circus
o in hot	ng in long	

Social Studies Reference Guide **R55**

Gazetteer

Fort Sumter (fôrt sump′tər) Fort in Charleston Harbor, South Carolina, site of the first battle of the Civil War in 1861. (m. 484, t. 485)

Fort Ticonderoga (fôrt ti′kon də rō′gə) Fort on Lake Champlain in northeastern New York, site of major battles in the American Revolution. (m. 302, t. 303)

Fort Vincennes (fôrt vin senz′) Fort on the site of present-day Vincennes, Indiana. (m. 314, 317; t. 316)

Fort Wagner (fôrt wag′nər) Fort that protected the harbor of Charleston, South Carolina, attacked by the African American 54th Regiment in the Civil War in July, 1863. (m. 498, t. 501)

Four Corners (fôr kôr′nərz) Place where four states—New Mexico, Arizona, Colorado, and Utah—come together; was the home of the Anasazi people. (m. 60, 62; t. 62)

France (frans) Country in Western Europe. (m. R4–R5, t. 305)

Gettysburg (get′ ēz bėrg′) Town in southern Pennsylvania, site of a major Union victory during the Civil War in 1863; 40°N, 77°W. (m. 506, t. 507)

Ghana (gä′nə) Country in Africa, named for early kingdom in West Africa. (m. 106–107, t. 107)

Grand Canyon (grand kan′ yən) Large canyon on the Colorado River in northwestern Arizona. (m. 26, t. 26)

Great Lakes (grāt lāks) Group of five, large, freshwater lakes on the border between the United States and Canada. (m. 29, t. 27)

Great Plains (grāt plānz) Region in central North America, east of the Rocky Mountains and extending from Canada to Texas. (m. 546, t. 547)

Great Plains cultural region (grāt plānz kul′chər əl rē′jən) Area in central North America that was home to many Native Americans such as the Lakota and Cheyenne. (m. 82, 84; t. 83)

Great Salt Lake (grāt sòlt lāk) Lake in northwestern Utah, largest salt lake in North America. (m. 440, R14–R15; t. 441)

Greenland (grēn′ lənd) Island in the northern Atlantic Ocean, largest island on Earth. (m. 110–111, t. 111)

Guam (gwäm) Island in the western Pacific Ocean. (m. 581, t. 581)

Gulf of California (gulf əv kal′ ə fôr′ nyə) Inlet of the Pacific Ocean, between Baja, California, and the western coast of Mexico. (m. 148)

Gulf of Mexico (gulf əv mek′sə kō) Inlet of the Atlantic Ocean, between the United States and Mexico. (m. 29)

Haiti (hā′tē) Country in the West Indies, occupying the western part of the island of Hispaniola. (m. 689, t. 688)

Harlem (här′ ləm) part of New York City. (t. 618)

Harpers Ferry (här′pərz fār′ē) Town in northeastern West Virginia, site of federal arsenal raided by abolitionist John Brown in 1859; 39°N, 78°W. (m. 476, t. 480)

Havana (hə van′ə) Capital of Cuba, located on the northwest coast; 23°N, 82°W. (m. 581, t. 580)

Hiroshima (hir′ō shē′mə) City in southwestern Japan; the first city where an atomic bomb was dropped; 35°N, 132°E. (m. 624, 629; t. 629)

Hispaniola (his′ pə nyō′lə) Island in the Caribbean Sea, made up of Haiti and the Dominican Republic. (m. 146, 148; t. 150)

Hudson Bay (hud′sən bā) Inland sea in northern Canada. (m. 678–679, R6–R9)

R56 Social Studies Reference Guide

Hudson River (hud′ sən riv′ ər) River in eastern New York that flows into the Atlantic Ocean. (m. 164, 166; t. 165–166)

Indian Ocean (in′dē ən ō′shən) One of Earth's four oceans. (m. 114, t. 114)

Indian Territory (in′ dē ən tār′ ə tôr′ ē) Land set aside by the Indian Removal Act of 1830 for the Native Americans who were forced to move from the southeastern United States; now forms most of Oklahoma. (m. 402, t. 405)

Iraq (i rak′) country in southwest Asia, west of Iran. (m. 665, t. 664)

Iroquois Trail (ir′ ə kwoi trāl) Trail that linked the lands of the Iroquois League, extended from present-day Albany to Buffalo. (m. 76–77, t. 77)

Isthmus of Panama (is′ məs əv pan′ ə mä) Narrow strip of land connecting North and South America. (t. 604)

Jamaica (jə mā′ kə) Island country in the West Indies. (m. 689)

Jamestown (jāmz′ toun) First permanent English colony in North America, founded in 1607; located in eastern Virginia; 37°N, 77°W. (m. 156, t. 159)

Kansas Territory (kan′ zəs tār′ ə tôr′ē) Territory created in 1854 by the Kansas-Nebraska Act; became the state of Kansas. (m. 476, 479; t. 479)

Kitty Hawk (kit′ē hòk) Village in North Carolina where the Wright Brothers flew the first powered airplane in 1903; 36°N, 76°W. (m. 616, t. 617)

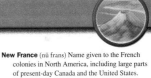

Lake Champlain (lāk sham plān′) Lake between New York and Vermont. (m. 305, t. 305)

Lake Erie (lāk ir′ ē) Most southern of the Great Lakes, bordering the United States and Canada. (m. 29)

Lake Huron (lāk hyür′ ən) Second largest of the Great Lakes, bordering the United States and Canada. (m. 29)

Lake Michigan (lāk mish′ə gən) Third largest of the Great Lakes, only one completely in the United States. (m. 27)

Lake Ontario (lāk on tär′ē ō) Smallest of the Great Lakes, bordering the United States and Canada. (m. 29)

Lake Superior (lāk sə pir′ ē ər) Largest of the Great Lakes, bordering the United States and Canada. (m. 29)

Lake Texcoco (lāk tes kō′ kō) Lake that was the site of the ancient Aztec city of Tenochtitlan in Mexico. (t. 68)

Lame Deer (lām dir) City in Montana where an annual Northern Cheyenne Powwow is held; 46°N, 107°W. (m. 82, t. 85)

Pronunciation Key

a in hat	ō in open	sh in she
ā in age	ò in all	th in thin
â in care	ô in order	ŦH in then
ä in far	oi in oil	zh in measure
e in let	ou in out	ə = a in about
ē in equal	u in cup	ə = e in taken
ėr in term	ú in put	ə = i in pencil
i in it	ü in rule	ə = o in lemon
ī in ice	ch in child	ə = u in circus
o in hot	ng in long	

Social Studies Reference Guide **R57**

Gazetteer

Lexington (lek′ sing tən) Town in eastern Massachusetts, site of the first battle of the American Revolution in 1775; 42°N, 71°W. (m. 286, t. 287)

Lima (lē′ mə) Capital of Peru, founded by Spanish conquistador Francisco Pizarro; 12°S, 77°W. (m. 142, t. 145)

Little Bighorn River (lit′l big′hôrn riv′ər) River in Wyoming and Montana, where General George Custer was defeated by the Sioux and Cheyenne. (t. 556)

Los Angeles (lòs an′jə ləs) Largest city in California, located in the southern part of the state; 34°N, 118°W. (m. 26)

Louisiana (lù ē′ zē an′ ə) State in the southeastern United States, originally the name given to the entire Mississippi Valley. (m. 240, 242; t. 242)

Louisiana Territory (lù ē′ zē an′ ə tär′ ə tôr′ ē) The land included in the Louisiana Purchase in 1803 soon became the Louisiana Territory. (m. 370, t. 374)

Lowell (lō′ əl) City in northeastern Massachusetts; 42°N, 71°W. (m. 408, t. 408–409)

Mali (mä′ lē) Kingdom in Africa in the early 1300s; present-day country in West Africa. (m. 106, t. 108)

Manassas Junction (mə nas′əs jungk′shən) Town in Virginia near a major Civil War battle in the 1860s; 39°N, 78°W. (m. 492, t. 495)

Maryland (mâr′ ə lənd) Colony founded by Lord Baltimore, a Catholic, in 1632. Baltimore declared that his colony would be a safe place for Catholics. Maryland was also a proprietary colony, meaning that its land was controlled by landowners. (m. 177, t. 180)

Massachusetts Bay Colony (mas′ ə chü′ sits bā kol′ ə nē) Colony founded by the Puritans in New England in 1630. (m. 168, t. 172)

Mecca (mek′ə) City in Saudi Arabia, pilgrimage site for Muslims; 22°N, 40°E. (m. 106, t. 108)

Menlo Park (men′ lō pärk) Town in central New Jersey, site of Thomas Edison's laboratory. (m. 562, t. 563)

Mesa Verde (mā′ sə vâr′ dē) Anasazi community located in present-day Colorado; 37°N, 108°W. (m. 60, 62; t. 62)

Mexico (mek′sə kō) Country in North America, on the southern border of the United States. (m. 430, 682–683, t. 431, 684–685)

Mexico City (mek′ sə kō sit′ ē) Capital and largest city of Mexico, built as the capital of New Spain; 19°N, 99°W. (m. 142, t. 144)

Middle Colonies (mid′ l kol′ ə nēz) Region of the 13 Colonies, located between the New England and Southern Colonies. (m. 176, t. 179)

Midwest (mid′ west) Region of the north-central United States. (m. 27, t. 27)

Mississippi River (mis′ə sip′ ē riv′ ər) River in the central United States, flowing from Minnesota to the Gulf of Mexico. (m. 27, 240; t. 241)

Missouri (mə zúr′ē) The twenty-third state to join the United States, it was admitted in 1820. (m. 477, t. 477)

Missouri River (mə zúr′ē riv′ ər) Major tributary of the Mississippi River, flowing from Montana to Missouri. (m. 26, t. 374)

Montgomery (mont gum′ ər ē) Capital of Alabama, site of bus boycott in 1955–1956; 32°N, 86°W. (m. 642, t. 644)

Montreal (mon′ trē òl′) Largest city in Canada; 46°N, 74°W. (m. 242)

R58 Social Studies Reference Guide

Mormon Trail (môr′ mən trāl) Route west, named for the Mormons who traveled on it from Nauvoo, Illinois, to Salt Lake City, Utah, in the 1840s. (m. 438, 440; t. 441)

Mount Katahdin (mount kə täd′ən) Mountain in north central Maine. (m. 27, t. 25)

Mount McKinley (mount mə kin′ lē) Highest peak in North America, located in Alaska's Denali National Park. (m. 34, t. 37)

Mount St. Helens (mount sānt hel′ ənz) Active volcano in the Cascade Range in southwestern Washington. (m. 26, t. 25)

Mount Whitney (mount hwit′ nē) Highest mountain in the contiguous states, located in southeastern California. (m. R14–R15)

Nagasaki (nä′ gə sä′kē) City in Japan, second city on which an atomic bomb was dropped; 32°N, 129°E. (t. 629)

National Road (nash′ə nəl rōd) Road built in the early 1800s; extended from Cumberland, Maryland, to St. Louis, Missouri. (m. 412, t. 411)

Nebraska Territory (nə bras′ kə tär′ ə tôr′ē) Territory created in 1854 as a result of the Kansas-Nebraska Act. (m. 479, t. 479)

New Amsterdam (nü am′ stər dam) Settlement founded by the Dutch on Manhattan Island; became present-day New York City. (m. 164, 166; t. 165)

New England (nü ing′ glənd) Name given by John Smith to the northeastern region of North America; present-day name for part of the Northeast region of the United States. (m. 27, t. 27)

New England Colonies (nü ing′ glənd kol′ ə nēz) Region of the 13 Colonies that was located north of the Middle Colonies. (m. 176–177, t. 177–178)

New France (nü frans) Name given to the French colonies in North America, including large parts of present-day Canada and the United States. (m. 164, 166; t. 165)

New Haven (nü hā′ vən) City in southern Connecticut, site of the trial of Africans who took control of the Spanish slave ship *Amistad*; 41°N, 72°W. (m. 470, t. 472)

New Mexico (nü mek′ sə kō) State in the southwestern United States, originally the name given by the Spanish to what is now the entire Southwest region of the United States. (m. 234, t. 234)

New Netherland (nü neᴛʜ′ ər lənd) Dutch colony in North America, included parts of present-day New York, New Jersey, and Connecticut. (m. 164, 166; t. 165)

New Orleans (nü ôr′ lē ənz) Port city in Louisiana, largest city in the state; 29°N, 90°W. (m. 240, t. 243)

New Spain (nü spān) Colony established mostly in North America by Spain in 1535, included parts of what are today the United States, Mexico, Central America, and the West Indies. (m. 142, t. 144)

New Sweden (nü swēd′n) Swedish colony in North America, along the Delaware River. (m. 166)

Pronunciation Key

a in hat	ō in open	sh in she
ā in age	ò in all	th in thin
â in care	ô in order	ŦH in then
ä in far	oi in oil	zh in measure
e in let	ou in out	ə = a in about
ē in equal	u in cup	ə = e in taken
ėr in term	ú in put	ə = i in pencil
i in it	ü in rule	ə = o in lemon
ī in ice	ch in child	ə = u in circus
o in hot	ng in long	

Social Studies Reference Guide **R59**

New York City (nü yôrk sit′ ē) Largest city in the United States, located in southeastern New York; 40°N, 73°W. (m. 268, t. 270)

Newport (nü pôrt) City in southern Rhode Island; 41°N, 71°W. (m. 216, t. 218)

Nicodemus (nik ə dē′ məs) Town in Kansas that was founded in 1877 by African American pioneers; 39°N, 100°W. (m. 546, 549; t. 549)

Normandy (nôr′ mən dē) Region in northern France; 49°N, 2°E. (m. 624, 628; t. 628)

North America (nôrth ə mâr′ ə kə) One of Earth's seven continents. (m. R8, R9, H8)

North Korea (nôrth kô rē′ ə) Country occupying the northern part of the Korean Peninsula. (m. 636, t. 639)

North Pole (nôrth pōl) Northernmost point on Earth; 90°N. (m. H13, t. H13)

North Vietnam (nôrth vē et′ näm′) Country in southeast Asia from 1954 to 1975, now part of the united country of Vietnam. (m. 650, 652; t. 652)

Northeast (nôrth′ ēst′) Region in the northeastern United States. (m. 27, t. 27)

Northern Hemisphere (nôr′ ᴛʜərn hem′ə sfir) Half the Earth north of the Equator. (m. H13)

Northwest Coast cultural region (nôrth′ west′ kōst kul′ chər əl rē′ jən) Area in northwestern North America that was home to many Native Americans such as the Kwakiutl, Tlingit, and Nootka. (m. 94–95, t. 95)

Northwest Territory (nôrth′ west′ târ′ ə tôr′ ē) Part of the lands that became part of the United States after the American Revolution. (m. 338, 342; t. 342)

O

Ohio River (ō hi′ ō riv′ ər) River in the east-central United States, which flows from Pittsburgh, Pennsylvania, to the Mississippi River at Cairo, Illinois. (m. 27, t. 248)

Ohio River Valley (ō hi′ ō riv′ ər val′ ē) Region of fertile land along the Ohio River. (m. 246, t. 247)

Omaha (ō′ mə hô) Largest city in Nebraska, located in the eastern part of the state; 41°N, 95°W. (m. 538, t. 539)

Oraibi (ôr i′bē) Hopi village built about 1050, probably the oldest town in the United States; 36°N, 111°W. (m. 88, t. 91)

Oregon Country (ôr′ ə gən kun′ trē) Former region that makes up the present-day northwestern United States. (m. 438, t. 439)

Oregon Trail (ôr′ ə gən trāl) Route west used by the pioneers that extended from Independence, Missouri, to Oregon. (m. 438, t. 439)

P

Pacific Ocean (pə sif′ ik ō′ shən) Largest of Earth's four oceans. (m. R4–R5)

Panama (pan′ ə mä) Southernmost country in Central America. (m. 602, 604; t. 604)

Panama Canal (pan′ ə mä kə nal′) Canal through the Isthmus of Panama, connecting the Atlantic and Pacific oceans. (m. 602, 604; t. 604)

Pearl Harbor (pėrl här′ bər) Harbor in Hawaii. Japanese planes bombed United States naval base there in a surprise attack on December 7, 1941; 21°N, 159°W. (m. 624, 626; t. 626)

Peru (pə rü′) Country in western South America; founded as a Spanish colony in the 1500s. (m. 689, t. 688)

Philadelphia (fil′ə del′ fē ə) City in southeastern Pennsylvania, was the capital of the United States from 1790 to 1800; 39°N, 75°W. (m. 210, t. 211)

Philippines (fil′ ə pēnz′) Group of islands in the Pacific Ocean, making up the country of the Philippines. (m. 581, t. 581)

Pittsburgh (pits′bėrg′) City in southwestern Pennsylvania; 40°N, 79°W. (m. 562, t. 564)

Plymouth (plim′əth) Town in southeastern Massachusetts, founded by the Pilgrims in 1620; 42°N, 71°W. (m. 168, t. 170)

Portugal (pôr′chə gəl) Country in southwestern Europe. (m. 110, t. 113)

Promontory Point (prom′ən tôr′ē point) Place in northwestern Utah where tracks of the Union Pacific and Central Pacific railroads met in 1869 to complete the transcontinental railroad; 41°N, 112°W. (m. 538, 540; t. 541)

Providence (prov′ə dəns) Capital and largest city of Rhode Island; 41°N, 71°W. (m. R12–R13, t. 178)

Puerto Rico (pwâr′tō rē′kō) Island in the West Indies, a commonwealth of the United States. (m. 578, t. 580)

Q

Quebec (kwi bek′) Capital of the Canadian province of Quebec, the first French colony in the Americas; 46°N, 71°W. (m. 164, t. 165)

R

Richmond (rich′mənd) Capital of Virginia, was capital of the Confederacy during the Civil War; 37°N, 77°W. (m. 492, t. 495)

Rio Grande (rē′ō grand′) River in southwestern North America, flowing from Colorado into the Gulf of Mexico; forms part of the border between the United States and Mexico. (m. 62)

Roanoke Island (rō′ə nōk i′lənd) Island off the coast of North Carolina, site of England's first attempt at a permanent settlement in the Americas, known as the "Lost Colony." (m. 156, t. 157)

Rocky Mountains (rok′ē moun′tənz) High, rugged chain of mountains in western North America, extending from Alaska to Mexico. (m. 26)

S

Sacramento (sak′ rə men′tō) Capital of California; 38°N, 121°W. (m. 538, t. 539)

Sahara (sə hâr′ə) Largest desert in the world, located in North Africa. (m. 106–107, t. 107)

Salt Lake City (sôlt lāk sit′ē) Capital and largest city of Utah; 40°N, 111°W. (m. 438, 440; t. 441)

San Antonio (san an tō′nē ō) City in south central Texas, site of the Alamo; 29°N, 98°W. (m. 430, t. 432)

San Diego (san dē ā′gō) Port city in southern California; 32°N, 117°W. (m. R12–R13)

San Francisco (san frən sis′kō) City in northern California; 37°N, 122°W. (m. 442, t. 443)

Santa Fe (san′tə fā) Capital of New Mexico; 35°N, 105°W. (m. 232, t. 234)

Saratoga (sâr′ə tō′gə) Village in northeastern New York, site of a major Patriot victory in 1777 during the American Revolution; 43°N, 74°W. (m. 302, t. 305)

Pronunciation Key

a in hat	ō in open	sh in she
ā in age	ò in all	th in thin
â in care	ô in order	ᴛʜ in then
ä in far	oi in oil	zh in measure
e in let	ou in out	ə = a in about
ē in equal	u in cup	ə = e in taken
ėr in term	ů in put	ə = i in pencil
i in it	ü in rule	ə = o in lemon
ī in ice	ch in child	ə = u in circus
o in hot	ng in long	

Savannah (sə van′ə) Port city on the coast of Georgia; 32°N, 81°W. (m. 314, t. 316)

Scandinavia (skan′də nā′vē ə) Region of northern Europe, includes the countries of Norway, Sweden, and Denmark. (t. 111)

Seneca Falls (sen′ə kə fôlz) Town in west central New York, site of the first women's rights convention in the United States, 1848; 43°N, 77°W. (m. 416, t. 419)

Shangdu (shang dü′) Town in China; 42°N, 114°E. (m. 102, t. 103)

Sierra Nevada (sē âr′ə nə vad′ə) Mountain range in eastern California. (m. 33)

Silk Road (silk rōd) Network of overland trade routes between China and Europe. (m. 102–103, t. 103)

Songhai (song gi′) Kingdom in Africa that flourished from the middle 1300s through the 1500s. (m. 106, t. 108)

South America (south ə mâr′ə kə) One of Earth's seven continents. (m. 691, t. 690)

South Korea (south kô rē′ə) Country occupying the southern part of the Korean Peninsula. (m. 636, t. 639)

South Pole (south pōl) Southernmost point on Earth; 90°S. (m. H13, t. H13)

South Vietnam (south vē et′näm′) Country in southeast Asia from 1954 to 1975, now part of the united country of Vietnam. (m. 650, 652; t. 652)

Southampton County (south amp′tən koun′tē) County in southeastern Virginia, location of Nat Turner's slave revolt in 1831. (m. 470, t. 472)

Southeast (south′ ēst′) Region in the southeastern United States. (m. 27, t. 27)

Southern Colonies (suᴛʜ′ərn kol′ə nēz) Southernmost region of the 13 Colonies. (m. 176, t. 179–180)

Southern Hemisphere (suᴛʜ′ərn hem′ə sfir) Half the Earth south of the Equator. (m. H13, t. H13)

Southwest (south′west′) Region in the southwestern United States. (m. 26, t. 26)

Southwest Desert cultural region (south′ west′ dez′ėrt kul′chər əl rē′jən) Area in southwestern North America that was home to many Native Americans such as the Hopi, Zuni, and Pima. (m. 88–89, t. 89)

Spain (spān) Country in southwestern Europe. (m. 141, t. 135)

Springfield (spring′fēld) City in southwestern Massachusetts, site of Shays' Rebellion. (m. 338, t. 341)

St. Augustine (sānt ô′ gə stēn) City on the northeast coast of Florida, founded by the Spanish in 1565; was the first permanent European settlement in the United States; 29°N, 81°W. (m. 232, t. 233)

St. Lawrence River (sānt lôr′əns riv′ər) River in northeastern North America, forms part of the border between the United States and Canada. (m. 164, t. 165)

St. Louis (sānt lü′is) Port city in east central Missouri, was known as the "Gateway to the West"; 38°N, 90°W. (m. 370, t. 374)

Strait of Magellan (strāt əv mə jel′ən) Narrow waterway between the southern tip of South America and Tierra del Fuego, links the Atlantic and Pacific Oceans. (m. 137)

T

Tenochtitlan (tā nòch′tē tlän′) Capital of the Aztec Empire in the Valley of Mexico, on the site of present-day Mexico City; 19°N, 99°W. (m. 66, 68; t. 68)

Texas (tek′səs) State in the southwestern United States, part of Mexico until 1836. (m. 430, t. 431)

Timbuktu (tim′ buk tü′) Town in West African kingdom of Mali, was one of the important stops along the caravan routes; 17°N, 3°E. (m. 106, 107)

Trenton (trent′n) Capital of New Jersey, site of an important battle in the American Revolution in 1776; 40°N, 74°W. (m. 302, t. 304)

V

Valley Forge (val′ē fôrj) Site in southeastern Pennsylvania where George Washington and the Continental Army camped during the winter of 1777 to 1778; 40°N, 75°W. (m. 302, t. 308)

Valley of Mexico (val′ē əv mek′sə kō) Region in central Mexico, location of the Aztec city of Tenochtitlan. (t. 68)

Vancouver Island (van kü′vər i′lənd) Island off the southwest coast of Canada. (m. 94, t. 95)

Venice (ven′is) Port city in northeastern Italy, built on 118 small islands in a lagoon in the Gulf of Venice; 45°N, 12°E. (m. 102–103, t. 103)

Versailles (vər si′) City in north central France, where treaty was signed ending World War I; 49°N, 2°E. (m. 608, t. 611)

Vicksburg (viks′bərg) City in western Mississippi on the Mississippi River, site of a major Union victory during the Civil War in 1863; 32°N, 90°W. (m. 509, t. 509)

Vinland (vin′ land) Name meaning "Land of Wine," given by Leif Ericsson to the present-day Canadian province of Newfoundland. (m. 110, t. 111)

W

Washington, D.C. (wäsh′ing tən dē cē) Capital of the United States; 38°N, 77°W. (m. 362, t. 365)

West (west) Region in the western United States. (m. 26, t. 26)

West Africa (west af′rə kə) Western region of Africa. (m. 202, 206; t. 206)

West Indies (west in′dēz) Islands between the Atlantic Ocean and the Caribbean Sea, extending from Florida in North America to Venezuela in South America. (m. 134, t. 135)

Western Hemisphere (west′ərn hem′ ə sfir) Half of Earth west of the prime meridian; includes South America and North America. (m. H14, R6–R7; t. H10)

Wilderness Road (wil′dər nis rōd) Trail used by pioneers through the Appalachian Mountains from Virginia to Kentucky, established by Daniel Boone in 1775. (m. 370, t. 372)

Williamsburg (wil′yəmz bėrg) City in southeastern Virginia, capital of the colony of Virginia from 1699 to 1779; 37°N, 77°W. (m. 216, t. 217)

Y

Yellowstone National Park (yel′ə stōn nash′ə nəl pärk) First national park in the United States, established in Wyoming in 1872. (m. 34, t. 37)

Yorktown (yôrk′toun) Town in southeastern Virginia near Chesapeake Bay, site of the last major battle of the American Revolution; 37°N, 76°W. (m. 317, t. 318)

Pronunciation Key

a in hat	ō in open	sh in she
ā in age	ò in all	th in thin
â in care	ô in order	ᴛʜ in then
ä in far	oi in oil	zh in measure
e in let	ou in out	ə = a in about
ē in equal	u in cup	ə = e in taken
ėr in term	ů in put	ə = i in pencil
i in it	ü in rule	ə = o in lemon
ī in ice	ch in child	ə = u in circus
o in hot	ng in long	

Biographical Dictionary

This Biographical Dictionary tells you about the people in this book and how to pronounce their names. The page numbers tell you where the person first appears in the text.

A

Adams, Abigail (ad′əmz) 1744–1818 Writer and wife of President John Adams, she was the first First Lady to live in what later became known as the White House. (p. 366)

Adams, John (ad′əmz) 1735–1826 Patriot leader during the American Revolution and second President of the United States. (p. 277)

Adams, Samuel (ad′əmz) 1722–1803 Boston Patriot and organizer of the Sons of Liberty. (p. 270)

Addams, Jane (ad′əmz) 1860–1935 American social worker who opened Hull House, a Chicago settlement house, in 1889. (p. 571)

Albright, Madeleine (al′brit) 1937– First woman to serve as United States secretary of state, appointed in 1997. (p. 660)

Allen, Ethan (al′ən) 1738–1789 Leader of the Green Mountain Boys, Vermont soldiers who captured Fort Ticonderoga in May, 1775. (p. 303)

Anthony, Susan B. (an′thə nē) 1820–1906 Key leader of the women's suffrage movement. (p. 612)

Antin, Mary (an′tin) 1881–1949 Immigrant from Russia who published a popular autobiography called *The Promised Land.* (p. 569)

Armistead, James (är′mə sted) 1759?–1830 African American Patriot who spied for the Americans during the American Revolution. (p. 306)

Armstrong, Neil (ärm′strông) 1930– Astronaut who became the first person to walk on the moon in 1969. (p. 651)

Arnold, Benedict (är′nəld) 1741–1801 Successful American general during the Revolution who turned traitor in 1780 and joined the British cause. (p. 305)

Atahualpa (ä′tə wäl′pə) 1502?–1533 Ruler of the Incas when the empire was invaded by the Spanish in 1531. (p. 145)

Attucks, Crispus (at′əks) 1723?–1770 African American Patriot and former slave who was killed in the Boston Massacre in 1770. (p. 277)

Austin, Stephen F. (ô′stən) 1793–1836 Pioneer who founded the first settlement for people from the United States in Texas in the 1820s. (p. 432)

B

Balboa, Vasco Núñez de (bal bō′ə, väs′kō nü′nyes dē) 1475?–1519 Spanish explorer who was the first European to reach the eastern shore of the Pacific Ocean. (p. 137)

Banneker, Benjamin (ban′ə kər) 1731–1806 Astronomer, inventor, mathematician, and son of a freed slave, he surveyed the land on which Washington, D.C., was built. (p. 365)

Barton, Clara (bärt′ən) 1821–1912 Civil War nurse and founder of the American Red Cross. (p. 502)

Bell, Alexander Graham (bel) 1847–1922 Inventor who built the first telephone in 1876. (p. 563)

Boone, Daniel (bün) 1734–1820 American pioneer who led many early settlers to lands west of the Appalachian Mountains. (p. 372)

Boyd, Belle (boid) 1844–1900 Confederate spy during the Civil War. (p. 502)

Bradford, William (brad′fərd) 1590–1657 Leader of the Pilgrims who came to North America on the *Mayflower* and founded Plymouth colony in 1620. (p. 169)

Brady, Mathew (brā′dē) 1823?–1896 Civil War photographer. (p. 499)

Brown, John (broun) 1800–1859 Abolitionist who believed in the use of force to oppose slavery. He was hanged for leading a raid on Harpers Ferry, Virginia, in 1859. (p. 480)

Bruce, Blanche K. (brüs) 1841–1898 Former slave elected to United States Senate in 1874. (p. 518)

Burgoyne, John (bər goin′) 1722–1792 British general defeated by American forces at the Battle of Saratoga in 1777. (p. 305)

Bush, George H. (bu̇sh) 1924– Forty-first President of the United States, 1989–1993. (p. 659)

Bush, George W. (bu̇sh) 1946– Became forty-third President of the United States in 2001; son of President George H. Bush. (p. 661)

C

Cabeza de Vaca, Álvar Núñez (kä bä′sä de vä′kä) about 1490–1557 Spanish explorer who explored what is now Texas in 1528. (p. 147)

Calhoun, John C. (kal hün′) 1782–1850 United States senator from South Carolina who believed in states' rights. (p. 477)

Carnegie, Andrew (kär′ nə gē) 1835–1919 Industrialist who made steel a major industry in the United States. (p. 564)

Carney, William (kär′nē) 1840–1908 A hero of the Civil War battle at Fort Wagner in 1863; one of sixteen African Americans to win the Congressional Medal of Honor for heroism in the Civil War. (p. 501)

Carter, Jimmy (kär′tər) 1924– Thirty-ninth President of the United States, 1977–1981. (p. 655)

Carver, George Washington (kär′vər) 1861–1943 Scientist who discovered hundreds of new uses for peanuts, sweet potatoes, and other crops. (p. 28)

Catt, Carrie Chapman (kat) 1859–1947 Key leader of the women's suffrage movement; helped win passage of the Nineteenth Amendment. (p. 612)

Champlain, Samuel de (sham plān′) 1567–1635 French explorer who founded Quebec, the first permanent French settlement in North America. (p. 165)

Chávez, César (shä′vez, sä sär′) 1927–1993 Leader of the struggle to improve life for migrant farm workers. (p. 648)

Cinque, Joseph (sin′kā) 1813?–1879? West African captive who led the 1839 slave revolt on the Spanish slave ship *Amistad.* (p. 472)

Clark, George Rogers (klärk) 1752–1818 Leader of a small Patriot force that captured British-controlled Fort Vincennes in the Ohio Valley in 1779. (p. 316)

Clark, William (klärk) 1770–1838 Shared command of the Lewis and Clark expedition with Meriwether Lewis. (p. 374)

Clay, Henry (klā) 1777–1852 United States senator who was nicknamed "The Great Compromiser" for helping to work out important compromises such as the Missouri Compromise in 1820 and the Compromise of 1850. (p. 382)

Clinton, Bill (klin′tən) 1946– Forty-second President of the United States, 1993–2001. (p. 660)

Coffin, Catherine (ko′fin) 1803–1881 Conductor on the Underground Railroad, she helped more than 2,000 people escape from slavery to freedom. (p. 473)

Pronunciation Key

a in hat	ō in open	sh in she
ā in age	ô in order	th in thin
ä in far	oi in oil	ᴛʜ in then
e in let	ou in out	zh in measure
ē in equal	u in cup	ə = a in about
ėr in term	u̇ in put	ə = e in taken
i in it	ü in rule	ə = i in pencil
ī in ice	ch in child	ə = o in lemon
o in hot	ng in long	ə = u in circus

Biographical Dictionary

Coffin, Levi (ko′fin) 1798–1877 Conductor on the Underground Railroad; married to Catherine Coffin. (p. 473)

Columbus, Christopher (kə lum′bəs) 1451?–1506 Italian-born explorer who sailed to the Americas in 1492. He was the first European to establish lasting contact between Europe and the Americas. (p. 135)

Cooper, Peter (kü′ pər) 1791–1883 Inventor of a steam-powered train, the *Tom Thumb,* in 1830. (p. 412)

Cornwallis, Charles (kôrn wä′lis) 1738–1805 Commanding general of the British forces that were defeated at Yorktown in 1781, ending the American Revolution. (p. 318)

Coronado, Francisco Vásquez de (kôr′ ə nä′dō, frän sēs′ kō väs′kes dā) 1510–1554 Spanish explorer of the American Southwest; searched for Cíbola, the legendary kingdom of gold. (p. 147)

Cortés, Hernando (kôr tez′) 1485–1547 Spanish conqueror of the Aztec empire. (p. 143)

Crazy Horse (krā′zē hôrs) 1842?–1877 Lakota leader who helped defeat General George Custer at the Battle of Little Bighorn in 1876. (p. 556)

Crockett, David (krok′it) 1786–1836 Frontiersman and member of Congress from Tennessee who died defending the Alamo. (p. 432)

Custer, George (kus′tər) 1839–1876 United States military leader defeated by the Lakota at the Battle of Little Bighorn in 1876. (p. 556)

D

da Gama, Vasco (də gä′mə, väs′kō) 1469?–1524 Portuguese explorer who sailed to India in 1497. (p. 114)

Davis, Jefferson (dā′vis) 1808–1889 President of the Confederacy during the Civil War and former United States senator from Mississippi. (p. 485)

Dawes, William (dȯz) 1744–1799 Patriot who rode with Paul Revere on the night of April 18, 1775, to warn colonists that British troops were coming. (p. 287)

Deere, John (dir) 1804–1886 Blacksmith who invented the steel plow. (p. 410)

Deganawidah (dā gän ə wē′də) 1500s Iroquois leader who told warring Iroquois groups to stop fighting. (p. 77)

De Soto, Hernando (di sō′tō) 1500?–1542 Spanish explorer who became the first European to reach the Mississippi River in 1541. (p. 147)

Dias, Bartolomeu (dē ′əs) 1450?–1500 Portuguese explorer who sailed around the Cape of Good Hope, the southwestern tip of Africa. (p. 114)

Douglas, Marjory Stoneman (dug′ləs) 1890–1998 Writer who dedicated many years of her life to protecting the Everglades. (p. 37)

Douglas, Stephen (dug′ləs) 1813–1861 United States senator from Illinois who was defeated for the presidency by Abraham Lincoln in 1860. (p. 479)

Douglass, Frederick (dug′ləs) 1817–1895 Former slave who was a writer, editor, and leading abolitionist. (p. 418)

Drake, Francis (drāk) 1540?–1596 First English sea captain to sail around the world in 1577. (p. 158)

Du Bois, W.E.B. (dü bois′) 1868–1963 African American leader who helped start the National Association for the Advancement of Colored People (NAACP). (p. 613)

E

Earhart, Amelia (âr′härt, ə mē′lyə) 1897–1937? First woman to fly solo across the Atlantic Ocean in 1932. (p. 617)

Edison, Thomas (ed′ə sən) 1847–1931 Inventor whose many inventions included the light bulb and the phonograph. (p. 21)

Eisenhower, Dwight D. (ī′zn hou′ ər) 1890–1969 Thirty-fourth President of the United States, 1953–1961. Commander of Allied forces in Europe during World War II. (p. 628)

Elizabeth I (i liz′ə bəth) 1533–1603 Queen of England during the English defeat of the Spanish Armada and the founding of Roanoke, England's first colony in the Americas. (p. 157)

Equiano, Olaudah (i kwē ä′nō) 1750–1797 African who was enslaved and brought to North America in 1756. He later wrote a book about the journey from West Africa to the colonies. (p. 227)

Eric the Red (âr′ik) 900s Viking explorer who sailed to Iceland in about 965 and Greenland in about 982. (p. 111)

Ericsson, Leif (âr′ik sən, lēf) late 900s–early 1000s Son of Eric the Red; sailed to North America in about 1000 and explored what is today known as Newfoundland. (p. 111)

Estéban (es te′bän) 1500s African sailor who traveled throughout the Southwest region of the United States. His stories led to the search for Cíbola. (p. 147)

F

Ferdinand (fėr′də nand) 1452–1516 King of Spain who agreed to finance Christopher Columbus's expedition to the Americas in 1492. (p. 135)

Fitzgerald, F. Scott (fits jâr′əld) 1896–1940 Writer of novels and stories depicting the Jazz Age. (p. 618)

Ford, Gerald (fôrd) 1913–2006 Thirty-eighth President of the United States, 1974–1977; took over as President when Richard Nixon resigned in 1974. (p. 654)

Ford, Henry (fôrd) 1863–1947 Automobile maker who introduced the assembly line as a way to produce cars more quickly and easily. (p. 617)

Franklin, Benjamin (frang′klən) 1706–1790 Writer, scientist, inventor, and diplomat. He helped write the Declaration of Independence and the Constitution. (p. 211, 221)

Fulton, Robert (fu̇lt′n) 1765–1815 Engineer who built the first successful steamboat, the *Clermont,* in 1807. (p. 411)

G

Gage, Thomas (gāj) 1721–1787 British general who controlled Boston following the Boston Tea Party. (p. 280)

Gálvez, Bernardo de (gal′vəz) 1746–1786 Governor of Spanish Louisiana and ally of the Patriots, he led Spanish troops against the British during the American Revolution. (p. 315)

Garrison, William Lloyd (gâr′ə sən) 1805–1879 Journalist and reformer, founder of the anti-slavery newspaper *The Liberator.* (p. 418)

George III (jôrj) 1738–1820 King of Britain during the time of the American Revolution. (p. 251)

Glenn, John (glen) 1921– Astronaut who became the first American to orbit Earth in 1962. (p. 651)

Gompers, Samuel (gom′pərz) 1850–1924 Labor leader; founded the American Federation of Labor in 1886. (p. 573)

Goodnight, Charles (gu̇d nit) 1836–1929 Rancher who established a major cattle drive trail known as the Goodnight-Loving Trail. (p. 551)

Pronunciation Key

a in hat	ō in open	sh in she
ā in age	ô in order	th in thin
ä in far	oi in oil	ᴛʜ in then
e in let	ou in out	zh in measure
ē in equal	u in cup	ə = a in about
ėr in term	u̇ in put	ə = e in taken
i in it	ü in rule	ə = i in pencil
ī in ice	ch in child	ə = o in lemon
o in hot	ng in long	ə = u in circus

Biographical Dictionary

Gorbachev, Mikhail (gôr′bə chôf) 1931– Leader of the Soviet Union in the 1980s; began reforming the country to give people more political and economic freedom. (p. 659)

Grant, Ulysses S. (grant) 1822–1885 Eighteenth President of the United States, 1869–1877. Commander of Union forces in the Civil War. (p. 509)

Greene, Nathanael (grēn) 1742–1786 Patriot general during the American Revolution. (p. 318)

Gutenberg, Johann (güt′n bėrg) 1395?–1468 German inventor of the printing press about 1450. (p. 112)

H

Hale, Nathan (hāl) 1755–1776 Patriot hanged as a spy by the British in 1776. (p. 304)

Hall, Prince (hôl) 1745?–1807 Minister who fought in the Continental Army and became an early leader in the struggle to end slavery in the United States. (p. 306)

Hamilton, Alexander (ham′əl tən) 1755?–1804 Delegate to the Constitutional Convention and leader of the Federalists; first secretary of the treasury. (p. 345)

Hancock, John (han′kok) 1737–1793 Patriot leader and president of the Second Continental Congress; first person to sign the Declaration of Independence. (p. 287)

Hays, Mary Ludwig (hāz) 1744–1832 Patriot known for her brave service on the battlefield; nicknamed "Molly Pitcher." (p. 307)

Hemingway, Ernest (hem′ing wā) 1899–1961 Writer of novels and stories depicting life in the 1920s and 1930s. (p. 618)

Hendrick (hen′drik) 1680?–1755? Iroquois leader during the French and Indian War. (p. 249)

Henry, Patrick (hen′rē) 1736–1799 Virginia Patriot and lawyer known for his bold speeches in support of American independence. (p. 270)

Henry, Prince (hen′rē) 1394–1460 Prince of Portugal who established a school for sailors and navigators. (p. 113)

Hiawatha (hī′ə wäth′ə) 1500s Helped found the Iroquois League in the late 1500s. (p. 77)

Hitler, Adolf (hit′lər) 1889–1945 Nazi dictator of Germany during World War II. (p. 625)

Hooker, Thomas (hu̇k′ər) 1586–1647 Puritan minister who founded the colony of Connecticut in 1636. (p. 178)

Houston, Sam (hyü′stən) 1793–1863 Commander of victorious forces during the Texas Revolution; elected first president of the Republic of Texas in 1836. (p. 432)

Hudson, Henry (hud′sən) 1565–1611 English sea captain who explored North America in search of a Northwest Passage in the early 1600s. (p. 165)

Huerta, Dolores (wâr′tä) 1930– Mexican American leader who worked to improve life for migrant farm workers. (p. 648)

Hughes, Langston (hyüz) 1902–1967 Writer who was a key figure of the Harlem Renaissance. (p. 618)

Hurston, Zora Neale (hėr′stən) 1901?–1960 Writer who was a key figure of the Harlem Renaissance. (p. 618)

Hutchinson, Anne (huch′ən sən) 1591–1643 Puritan leader banished from Massachusetts for her religious views. (p. 178)

I

Isabella (iz′ə bel′ə) 1451–1504 Queen of Spain who agreed to finance Christopher Columbus's expedition to the Americas in 1492. (p. 135)

J

Jackson, Andrew (jak′sən) 1767–1845 Seventh President of the United States, 1829–1837. Army general who led American troops to victory at the Battle of New Orleans during the War of 1812. (p. 384)

Jackson, Thomas "Stonewall" (jak′sən) 1824–1863 Confederate general who helped the Confederates win several early victories in the Civil War. (p. 495)

James I (jāmz) 1566–1625 King of England who, in 1606, gave the Virginia Company of London a charter to set up a colony in Virginia. (p. 159)

Jefferson, Thomas (jef′ər sən) 1743–1826 Third President of the United States, 1801–1809. Member of the Continental Congress and main writer of the Declaration of Independence. (p. 298)

Johnson, Andrew (jon′sən) 1808–1875 Seventeenth President of the United States, 1865–1869. Took office following Abraham Lincoln's assassination. (p. 517)

Johnson, Lyndon B. (jon′sən) 1908–1973 Thirty-sixth President of the United States, 1963–1969. Took office after President John Kennedy was assassinated. (p. 640)

Jolliet, Louis (jō′lē et) 1645–1700 French fur trader and explorer who accompanied Jacques Marquette on an exploration of the Mississippi River in 1673. (p. 241)

Jones, John Paul (jōnz) 1747–1792 Patriot naval leader who commanded the American ship *Bonhomme Richard,* which defeated the British ship *Serapis* in 1779. (p. 316)

Jones, Mary Harris (jōnz) 1830–1930 Labor leader who helped organize unions and was nicknamed "Mother Jones." (p. 573)

Joseph, Chief (jō′zəf) 1840?–1904 Nez Percé leader who led his people in their effort to escape to Canada to avoid being forced onto a reservation. (p. 556)

K

Kennedy, John F. (ken′ə dē) 1917–1963 Thirty-fifth President of the United States, 1961–1963; youngest person and first Catholic elected President. (p. 16)

Key, Francis Scott (kē) 1779–1843 Writer of the poem "The Star-Spangled Banner" during the War of 1812. This poem later became the national anthem of the United States. (p. 383)

King, Martin Luther, Jr, (king) 1929–1968 Minister and civil rights leader during the 1950s and 1960s; believed in peaceful protests. (p. 644)

Knox, Henry (noks) 1750–1806 Continental army leader who brought captured British cannons from Fort Ticonderoga to Boston in 1775. (p. 303)

Kosciusko, Thaddeus (kos ē us′kō) 1746–1817 Polish engineer who served in the Continental Army; designed a fort near Saratoga, where Americans won a key victory. (p. 305)

Kublai Khan (kü′blī kän′) 1216–1294 Emperor of China who met with Marco Polo in the late 1200s. (p. 103)

L

Lafayette, Marquis de (lä fē et′, mar kē′ də) 1757–1834 French soldier who joined General Washington's staff and became a general in the Continental Army. (p. 315)

La Salle, Robert (lə sal′) 1643–1687 French explorer who explored the Mississippi River in 1681 and 1682. He claimed the entire Mississippi River valley for France, naming this territory Louisiana. (p. 242)

Las Casas, Bartolomé de (läs kä′säs) 1474–1566 Spanish priest who spoke out against the mistreatment of Indians in New Spain. (p. 149)

Latimer, Lewis (lat′ə mėr) 1848–1929 Inventor who improved Thomas Edison's light bulb, making electric lighting more practical. (p. 563)

Biographical Dictionary

Lee, Richard Henry (lē) 1732–1794 Member of the Second Continental Congress who urged Congress to support independence; signer of the Declaration of Independence. (p. 298)

Lee, Robert E. (lē) 1807–1870 Commander of the Confederate forces in the Civil War. (p. 495)

L'Enfant, Pierre (län fän′) 1754–1825 French artist and engineer who designed Washington, D.C. (p. 365)

Lewis, Meriwether (lü′is) 1774–1809 Army captain appointed by Thomas Jefferson to lead the Lewis and Clark expedition to explore the lands gained in the Louisiana Purchase. (p. 374)

Liliuokalani (lē lē′ ə ō kä lä′nē) 1838–1917 Last queen of the Hawaiian Islands, she protested the American takeover of Hawaii in the 1890s. (p. 579)

Lin, Maya Ying (lin) 1959– Architect and artist who designed the Vietnam Veterans Memorial in Washington, D.C. (p. 653)

Lincoln, Abraham (ling′kən) 1809–1865 Sixteenth President of the United States, 1861–1865, who led the United States during the Civil War. (p. 16)

Lindbergh, Charles (lind′bėrg) 1902–1974 Pilot who made the first solo nonstop flight across the Atlantic Ocean in 1927. (p. 617)

Love, Nat (luv) 1854–1921 Cowboy and author of a popular autobiography. (p. 551)

Lowell, Francis Cabot (lō′əl) 1775–1817 Boston merchant who built the first textile mill in the United States. (p. 409)

M

MacArthur, Douglas (mak är′thər) 1880–1964 Allied supreme commander in the Pacific and general of the U.S. Army during World War II; supreme commander of UN forces during Korean War. (p. 639)

Madison, Dolley (mad′ə sən) 1768–1849 Wife of President James Madison, she rescued a famous portrait of George Washington from the White House when the British invaded Washington, D.C., during the War of 1812. (p. 383)

Madison, James (mad′ə sən) 1751–1836 Fourth President of United States, 1809–1817. One of the main authors of the Constitution. (p. 345)

Magellan, Ferdinand (mə jel′ən) 1480?–1521 Portuguese explorer who led the first expedition around the world. (p. 137)

Malcolm X (mal′kəm eks) 1925–1965 Civil rights leader in the 1960s; believed African Americans should rely on themselves. (p. 646)

Mansa Musa (män′sä mü′sä) 1312?–1337 King of the African kingdom of Mali in the early 1300s. (p. 108)

Marina, Doña (mə rē nə) 1501–1550 Aztec woman who became an interpreter for Hernando Cortés during his conquest of the Aztec empire. (p. 143)

Marion, Francis (mâr′ē ən) 1732–1795 South Carolina militia leader nicknamed the "Swamp Fox" for his hit-and-run attacks on the British during the American Revolution. (p. 316)

Marquette, Jacques (mär ket′, zhäk) 1637–1675 French missionary who explored the Mississippi River with Louis Jolliet in 1673. (p. 241)

Marshall, James (mär′shəl) 1810–1885 Discovered gold in California in 1848, leading to the Gold Rush. (p. 443)

Marshall, John (mär′shəl) 1755–1835 Chief Justice of the Supreme Court from 1831 to 1835. (p. 405)

Marshall, Thurgood (mär′shəl) 1908–1993 First African American Supreme Court justice, served from 1967 to 1991. (p. 643)

Massasoit (mas′ə soit) 1580?–1661 Leader of the Wampanoag who signed a peace treaty with the Pilgrims at Plymouth. (p. 171)

McCarthy, Joseph (mə kär′ thē) 1908–1957 United States senator who in the 1950s claimed that communists were working inside the United States government. (p. 639)

McCormick, Cyrus (mə kôr′mik) 1809–1884 Inventor of a mechanical reaper in 1831. (p. 410)

Menendez de Avilés, Pedro (me nen′dez dā ä vē′läs) 1519–1574 Commander of the Spanish fleet that defeated the French and took control of Florida, claiming it for New Spain in 1565. (p. 233)

Metacom (met ə käm′) 1640–1676 Massasoit chief called "King Philip" by the English. Led several Native American groups against the British during King Philip's War in the 1670s. (p. 247)

Moctezuma (mäk tə zü′mə) 1480–1520 Leader of the Aztecs when Hernando Cortés conquered the Aztec empire. (p. 143)

Monroe, James (mən rō′) 1758–1831 Fifth President of the United States, 1817–1825. (p. 373)

Morse, Samuel (môrs) 1791–1872 Inventor of Morse Code, a code used to send messages by telegraph. (p. 539)

Mott, Lucretia (mot, lü krē′shə) 1793–1880 American abolitionist and supporter of women's rights. (p. 419)

Mussolini, Benito (mü′ sə lē′nē) 1883–1945 Italian dictator who came to power in 1922 and led Italy during World War II. (p. 625)

N

Nampeyo (nam pä′yō) 1860?–1942 Pueblo woman who worked to re-create the Anasazi way of making pottery. (p. 65)

Nixon, Richard (nik′sən) 1913–1994 Thirty-seventh President of the United States, 1969–1974. First President to resign from office. (p. 653)

O

O'Connor, Sandra Day (ō kon′ər) 1930– First woman to serve on the Supreme Court, appointed in 1981. (p. 647)

Oglethorpe, James (ō′gəl thôrp) 1696–1785 English leader who founded the colony of Georgia as a place where debtors from England could begin new lives. (p. 180)

Oñate, Don Juan de (ō nyä′te) 1550?–1630 Spanish leader who claimed the Southwest region of what is now the United States for the Spanish in 1598. (p. 234)

Osceola (os′ ē ō′ lə) 1803?–1838 Leader of the Seminole in Florida. (p. 431)

P

Paine, Thomas (pān) 1737–1809 Patriot and writer whose pamphlet *Common Sense,* published in 1776, convinced many Americans that it was time to declare independence from Britain. (p. 298)

Parker, John (pär′kər) 1729–1775 Captain of the Lexington minutemen; leader at the Battle of Lexington in April 1775, where the first shots of the American Revolution were fired. (p. 288)

Pronunciation Key

a	in hat	ō	in open	sh	in she
ā	in age	ô	in order	th	in thin
ä	in far	oi	in oil	ᴛʜ	in then
e	in let	ou	in out	zh	in measure
ē	in equal	u	in cup	ə	= a in about
ėr	in term	u̇	in put	ə	= e in taken
i	in it	ü	in rule	ə	= i in pencil
ī	in ice	ch	in child	ə	= o in lemon
o	in hot	ng	in long	ə	= u in circus

Parks, Rosa (pärks) 1913–2005 Civil rights leader arrested for protesting bus segregation in Montgomery, Alabama, in 1955. Her actions helped end the segregation of public buses. (p. 644)

Penn, William (pen) 1644–1718 Quaker who founded the colony of Pennsylvania in 1681. (p. 179)

Perry, Oliver Hazard (pâr′ē) 1785–1819 Commander of United States naval fleet that defeated the British in the Battle of Lake Erie during the War of 1812. (p. 382)

Pinckney, Eliza Lucas (pingk′nē) 1722–1793 South Carolina plantation owner who became the first person in the colonies to successfully raise a crop of indigo. (p. 213)

Pizarro, Francisco (pi zär′ō) 1478?–1541 Spanish conquistador who defeated the Inca empire in 1533. (p. 145)

Pocahontas (pō′ kə hon′təs) 1595?–1617 Daughter of Chief Powhatan, she helped establish a time of peace between the Powhatan and the English colonists in Jamestown. (p. 160)

Polk, James K. (pōk) 1795–1849 Eleventh President of the United States, 1845–1849. (p. 433)

Polo, Marco (pō′lō) 1254?–1324? Italian explorer who traveled through China in the late 1200s. (p. 103)

Ponce de Léon, Juan (pons′ də lē′ ən) 1460?–1521 Spanish explorer who reached the Florida peninsula in 1513. (p. 147)

Pontiac (pon′tē ak) 1720–1769 Ottawa leader who led Pontiac's Rebellion, a revolt against the British in 1763. (p. 251)

Popé (pō pā′) Pueblo leader who led the Pueblo Revolt against the Spanish in New Mexico in 1680. (p. 235)

Powell, Colin (pou′el) 1937– Highest-ranking American military leader during the Persian Gulf War. In 2001, became first African American secretary of state. (p. 660)

Powhatan (pou′ ə tan′) 1550?–1618 Leader of the Powhatan people and father of Pocahontas. (p. 160)

Prescott, Samuel (pres′kot) 1751–1777 Doctor who helped William Dawes and Paul Revere warn Patriots about the arrival of the British on the night of April 18, 1775. (p. 287)

Prescott, William (pres′kot) 1726–1795 Patriot leader at the Battle of Bunker Hill in 1775. (p. 290)

R

Raleigh, Walter (rò′lē) 1552?–1618 English explorer and soldier who explored North America in the 1580s and founded the "Lost Colony" of Roanoke in 1587. (p. 157)

Reagan, Ronald (rā′gən) 1911–2004 Fortieth President of the United States, 1981–1989. (p. 659)

Red Cloud (red kloud) 1822–1909 Lakota chief who objected to the railroad crossing Lakota lands. (p. 540)

Revels, Hiram R. (rev′əlz) 1822–1901 First African American elected to the United States senate in 1870. (p. 518)

Revere, Paul (ri vir′) 1735–1818 Patriot express rider and silversmith; rode from Boston to Lexington on the night of April 18, 1775, warning people that British soldiers were coming. (p. 278)

Rockefeller, John D. (rok′ə fel ər) 1839–1937 Industrialist who built the Standard Oil Company into a monopoly. (p. 566)

Rolfe, John (rälf) 1585–1622 Jamestown colony leader who showed that tobacco could be grown successfully in Virginia. (p. 161)

Roosevelt, Eleanor (rō′zə velt) 1884–1962 First Lady who worked to help people during the Great Depression and World War II. (p. 620)

Roosevelt, Franklin D. (rō′zə velt) 1882–1945 Thirty-second President of the United States, 1933–1945. (p. 620)

Roosevelt, Theodore (rō′zə velt) 1858–1919 Twenty-sixth President of the United States, 1901–1909. Led the Rough Riders during the Spanish-American War in 1898. (p. 37)

Ross, John (rós) 1790–1866 Cherokee leader who argued that it was illegal for the United States to remove the Cherokee from their land. (p. 405)

Rush, Benjamin (rush) 1745?–1813 Patriot and doctor; signer of the Declaration of Independence and strong supporter of the Constitution. (p. 354)

S

Sacagawea (sə kä′ ga wä′ yə) 1787?–1812 Shoshone woman who acted as guide and translator on the Lewis and Clark expedition. (p. 374)

Salem, Peter (sā′ləm) 1750?–1816 Patriot who fought at the Battle of Bunker Hill and the Battle of Saratoga. (p. 306)

Samoset (sam′ə set) 1590?–1655? Wampanoag man who helped the Pilgrims in 1620. (p. 170)

Sampson, Deborah (samp′sən) 1760–1827 Patriot who disguised herself as a man and served in the Continental Army. (p. 307)

Santa Anna, Antonio López de (sän′tä än′ä) 1795–1876 President of Mexico who led Mexican forces against Texas in the Texas Revolution of 1835–1836. (p. 432)

Scott, Dred (skot) 1795–1858 Enslaved African American who claimed he was free because he had lived in free states. His claim led to a key Supreme Court case. (p. 480)

Scott, Winfield (skot) 1771–1832 Hero of the Mexican War and leading Union general in the Civil War; architect of the Anaconda Plan. (p. 494)

Seguín, Juan (se gēn′) 1806–1889 Tejano leader who fought in the Texas Revolution. (p. 432)

Sequoyah (si kwoi′ə) 1770?–1843 Cherokee leader who developed a written alphabet for the Cherokee language. (p. 405)

Serra, Junípero (sâr′ä) 1713–1784 Spanish missionary who founded the first Spanish missions in California. (p. 236, 237)

Shays, Daniel (shāz) 1747–1825 Revolutionary War veteran and farmer who led Shays' Rebellion in 1786. (p. 341)

Sherman, William Tecumseh (shėr′mən) 1820–1891 Union general in the Civil War whose "March to the Sea" in 1864 helped defeat the Confederacy. (p. 510)

Shima, George (shē′mä) 1863?–1926 Immigrant from Japan who became known as the "Potato King" for his successful farming of potatoes in California. (p. 552)

Sinclair, Upton (sin klâr′) 1878–1968 Author of *The Jungle,* a book describing the unhealthy conditions in the meatpacking plants of Chicago. (p. 603)

Singleton, Benjamin (sin′gel ton) 1809–1892 Leader of African American homesteaders known as Exodusters. (p. 549)

Sitting Bull (sit′ing bůl) 1834?–1890 Lakota leader who defeated American forces at the Battle of Little Bighorn in 1876. (p. 555)

Pronunciation Key

a in hat	ō in open	sh in she
ā in age	ô in order	th in thin
â in far	oi in oil	ŦH in then
e in let	ou in out	zh in measure
ē in equal	u in cup	ə = a in about
ėr in term	ů in put	ə = e in taken
i in it	ü in rule	ə = i in pencil
ī in ice	ch in child	ə = o in lemon
o in hot	ng in long	ə = u in circus

Slater, Samuel (slāt′ər) 1768–1835 Brought plans for cotton-spinning machine to the United States from Britain and started the first cotton-spinning factory in the United States in 1790. (p. 409)

Smith, John (smith) 1580–1631 Leader of the Jamestown Colony. (p. 159)

Smith, Joseph (smith) 1805–1844 Founder of the Mormons in 1830. (p. 441)

Smith, Venture (smith) 1729–1805 African enslaved in New England who purchased his freedom and wrote a book telling the story of his life. (p. 225)

Squanto (skwon′tō) 1590–1622 Pawtuxet Native American who helped English settlers at Plymouth by teaching them key survival skills, such as how to grow corn. (p. 171)

Stalin, Joseph (stä′lin) 1879–1953 Dictator of the Soviet Union from 1929 to 1953. (p. 626)

Stanton, Elizabeth Cady (stan′tən) 1815–1902 Women's suffrage leader who helped organize the first women's rights convention in 1848. (p. 419)

Steuben, Friedrich von (stü′ben) 1730–1794 Military officer from Germany who trained American soldiers during the American Revolution. (p. 315)

Stowe, Harriet Beecher (stō) 1811–1896 Author of *Uncle Tom's Cabin,* which exposed the cruelties of slavery to a wide audience before the Civil War. (p. 480)

Strauss, Levi (strous) 1829–1902 Immigrant to San Francisco who manufactured the first denim pants during the California Gold Rush. (p. 444)

Sutter, John (sut′er) 1803–1880 Pioneer on whose land gold was discovered in 1848, leading to the California Gold Rush. (p. 443)

T

Tarbell, Ida (tär′bəl) 1857–1944 Muckraker and writer who wrote about unfair practices by large corporations. (p. 603)

Tecumseh (tə kum′sə) 1768?–1813 Shawnee leader who organized Native Americans in the Northwest Territory to resist pioneer settlement. (p. 381)

Tomochichi (tō mä chē′chē) 1650?–1739 Yamacraw chief who agreed to give James Oglethorpe land to found the new colony of Georgia. (p. 180)

Truman, Harry S. (trü′mən) 1884–1972 Thirty-third President of the United States, 1945–1953. (p. 629)

Truth, Sojourner (trüth) 1797?–1883 Abolitionist and women's rights leader who escaped from slavery in 1827. (p. 418)

Tubman, Harriet (tub′mən) 1820?–1913 Abolitionist who escaped from slavery in 1849 and became a conductor on the Underground Railroad. She led more than 300 slaves to freedom. (p. 473)

Turner, Nat (tėr′nər) 1800–1831 Leader of a slave rebellion in Southampton County, Virginia, in 1831. (p. 472)

V

Vespucci, Amerigo (ve spü′chē) 1454–1512 Italian navigator who sailed along the eastern coast of South America in 1501. (p. 137)

W

Walker, David (wó′kər) 1785–1830 Abolitionist who urged enslaved people to fight for their freedom. (p. 467)

Walker, Madam C. J. (wó′kər) 1867–1919 Entrepreneur who was the first African American woman to become a millionaire. (p. 21)

Warren, Mercy Otis (wôr′ən) 1728–1814 Patriot writer who wrote articles and plays in support of American independence. (p. 272)

Washington, Booker T. (wäsh′ing tən) 1856–1915 Educator and founder of Tuskegee Institute, a college for African Americans. (p. 613)

Washington, George (wäsh′ing tən) 1732–1799 First President of the United States, 1789–1797. Commander-in-Chief of the Continental Army during the American Revolution and President of the Constitutional Convention. (p. 217)

Washington, Martha (wäsh′ing tən) 1731–1802 Wife of President George Washington who assisted the Continental Army during the American Revolution. (p. 307)

Webster, Daniel (web′stər) 1782–1852 Senator from Massachusetts and opponent of slavery who supported the Compromise of 1850. (p. 478)

Wells-Barnett, Ida (welz′bär net′) 1862–1931 Fought against segregation and helped found the National Association for the Advancement of Colored People (NAACP). (p. 614)

Wheatley, Phillis (hwēt′lē) 1753?–1784 Poet who was the first African American woman to have a book of poetry published. (p. 307)

White, John (hwit) 1540?–1593 Leader of the English colony of Roanoke in 1587. (p. 157)

Whitefield, George (hwit′fēld) 1714–1770 Minister during the Great Awakening who traveled throughout the American colonies. (p. 218)

Whitman, Marcus (hwit′mən) 1802–1847 Missionary to Native Americans in the Oregon Territory beginning in 1836. (p. 439)

Whitman, Narcissa (hwit′mən) 1808–1847 Missionary to Native Americans in the Oregon Territory beginning in 1836. (p. 439)

Whitney, Eli (hwit′nē) 1765–1825 Inventor of the cotton gin in 1793. (p. 410)

Williams, Roger (wil′yəmz) 1604?–1683 Puritan minister who founded Rhode Island as a place of religious freedom in 1636. (p. 178)

Wilson, Luzena Stanley (wil′sən) 1821?–1890? Entrepreneur who ran hotels and restaurants during the California Gold Rush. (p. 444)

Wilson, Woodrow (wil′sən) 1856–1924 Twenty-eighth President of the United States, 1913–1921. (p. 610)

Winthrop, John (win′thrəp) 1588–1649 Puritan leader and first governor of the Massachusetts Bay Colony in 1630. (p. 172)

Wolfe, James (wůlf) 1727–1759 British General who captured Quebec in 1759, helping Great Britain win the French and Indian War. (p. 250)

Wright, Orville (rit) 1871–1948 Inventor who, with his brother Wilbur, developed the first successful airplane in 1903. (p. 617)

Wright, Wilbur (rit) 1867–1912 Inventor who, with his brother Orville, developed the first successful airplane in 1903. (p. 617)

Y

York (yôrk) 1770–1832? African American member of the Lewis and Clark expedition. (p. 374)

Young, Brigham (yung) 1801–1877 Mormon leader who founded Salt Lake City, Utah, and was first governor of the Utah Territory. (p. 441)

Z

Zenger, John Peter (zeng′ər) 1697–1746 Printer who was arrested for libel in 1734. His trial helped establish the principle of freedom of the press. (p. 219)

Zheng He (zheng hu) 1371–1433 Chinese explorer who made seven major voyages to different parts of the world. (p. 104–105)

Pronunciation Key

a in hat	ō in open	sh in she
ā in age	ô in order	th in thin
â in far	oi in oil	ŦH in then
e in let	ou in out	zh in measure
ē in equal	u in cup	ə = a in about
ėr in term	ů in put	ə = e in taken
i in it	ü in rule	ə = i in pencil
ī in ice	ch in child	ə = o in lemon
o in hot	ng in long	ə = u in circus

Glossary

This Glossary will help you understand the meanings and pronounce the vocabulary words in this book. The page number tells you where the word first appears.

A

abolitionist (ab′ə lish′ə nist) Person who wants to abolish, or end, slavery. (p. 418)

advertisement (ad′vər tiz′mənt) Tries to sell people goods, services, or ideas. (p. 446)

agriculture (ag′rə kul ′chər) Business of growing crops and raising animals. (p. 28)

alliance (ə lī′əns) Agreement between nations to defend one another. (p. 609)

ally (al′ī) A friend who will help in a fight. (p. 143)

almanac (ôl′mə nak) Reference book with helpful facts and figures. (p. H6)

amendment (ə mend′mənt) A change, or addition, to the Constitution. (p. 354)

American Revolution (ə mâr′ə kən rev′ə lü′shen) The war between the 13 Colonies and Great Britain from 1775 to 1783 in which the 13 Colonies won their independence and became the United States. (p. 289)

Anaconda Plan (an′ə kon′də plan) Union strategy for defeating the Confederacy. (p. 494)

annex (ə neks′) To add or attach. (p. 433)

Antifederalist (an′ti fed′ər ə list) Person opposed to the new U.S. Constitution and its emphasis on a strong national government. (p. 353)

apprentice (ə pren′tis) Young person who learns a skill from a more experienced worker. (p. 203)

archaeologist (är kē ol′ə jist) Scientist who studies the artifacts of people who lived long ago and draws conclusions from them. (p. 56)

arms control (ärmz kən trōl′) Agreement to limit the production of weapons. (p. 654)

arms race (ärmz rās) Countries hurrying to build more powerful weapons. (p. 641)

Articles of Confederation (är′tə kəlz əv kən fed′ə rā′shən) First plan of government for the United States, in effect from 1781 to 1789. It gave more power to the states than to the central government. (p. 339)

artifact (är′tə fakt) Object made by people in the past. (p. 56)

artisan (är′tə zən) Skilled worker who makes things by hand. (p. 203)

assassination (ə sas ə nā′shən) The killing of a high-ranking official or leader. (p. 517)

assembly line (ə sem′blē lin) Method of mass production in which the product is put together as it moves past a line of workers. (p. 617)

astrolabe (as′trə lāb) Navigational tool that helped sailors use the sun and stars to find their way. (p. 109)

atlas (at′ləs) Book of maps. (p. R2)

atomic bomb (ə tom′ik bom) Powerful type of bomb with destructive force of 20,000 tons of ordinary explosives . (p. 629)

B

back country (bak kun′trē) In the 13 Colonies the rugged stretch of land near the Appalachian Mountains. (p. 247)

barbed wire (bärbd wir) Wire with sharp points used by farmers for fences. (p. 551)

Battle of Antietam (bat′l əv an tē′təm) Union victory over Confederate forces in the Civil War in 1862 that was fought near Sharpsburg, Maryland. (p. 495)

Battle of Bunker Hill (bat′l əv bung′kər hil) Costly victory for British troops over the Patriots in Charlestown, Massachusetts, in the American Revolution on June 17, 1775. (p. 291)

Battle of Gettysburg (bat′l əv get′ēz bėrg) Union victory over Confederate forces in 1863 near Gettysburg, Pennsylvania, that marked a turning point of the Civil War. (p. 507)

Battle of Little Bighorn (bat′l əv lit′l big′hôrn′) Lakota victory over United States soldiers on June 25, 1876. (p. 556)

Battle of New Orleans (bat′l əv nü ôr′lē ənz) Victory of United States forces commanded by Andrew Jackson over the British in the War of 1812. (p. 384)

Battle of Saratoga (bat′l əv sâr′ə tō′gə) American victory over British troops in 1777 that was a turning point in the American Revolution. (p. 305)

Battle of Tippecanoe (bat′l əv tip ē kə nü′) Battle between United States soldiers and the Shawnee in 1811 that neither side won. (p. 381)

Battle of Vicksburg (bat′l əv viks′bėrg) Union victory over Confederate forces in 1863 at Vicksburg, Mississippi, that split the Confederacy in two. (p. 509)

Bear Flag Revolt (bâr flag ri vōlt′) Rebellion of California settlers against Mexican rule in 1846. (p. 434)

Bill of Rights (bil əv rits) First ten amendments to the Constitution, ratified in 1791. (p. 354)

black codes (blak kōdz) Laws passed by Southern state governments after the Civil War that denied African Americans many civil rights. (p. 517)

blockade (blo kād′) Shutting off an area by troops or ships to keep people and supplies from moving in or out. (p. 494)

border state (bôr′dər stāt) During the Civil War, a state between the Union and the Confederacy that allowed slavery but remained in the Union. (p. 486)

Boston Massacre (bô′stən mas′ə kər) Event in 1770 in Boston in which British soldiers killed five colonists who were part of an angry group that had surrounded them. (p. 277)

Boston Tea Party (bô′stən tē pär′tē) Protest against British taxes in which the Sons of Liberty boarded British ships and dumped tea into Boston Harbor in 1773. (p. 279)

boycott (boi′kot) Organized refusal to buy goods. (p. 272)

Buffalo Soldiers (buf′ ə lō sōl′jərz) Nickname for African American soldiers who fought in the wars in the plains against Native Americans in the 1870s. (p. 581)

C

Cabinet (kab′ə nit) Officials appointed by the President as advisers and to head the departments in the executive branch. (p. 363)

canal (kə nal′) Human-made waterway. (p. 411)

caravan (kâr′ə van) Group of traders traveling together, especially in the desert. (p. 107)

cardinal direction (kärd′n əl də rek′shən) One of the four main directions on Earth: north, south, east, and west. (p. H17)

caring (kâr′ing) Being interested in the needs of others. (p. H2)

Pronunciation Key

a in hat	ō in open	sh in she
ā in age	ô in order	th in thin
â in far	oi in oil	ᴛʜ in then
e in let	ou in out	zh in measure
ē in equal	u in cup	ə = a in about
ėr in term	ů in put	ə = e in taken
i in it	ü in rule	ə = i in pencil
ī in ice	ch in child	ə = o in lemon
o in hot	ng in long	ə = u in circus

Glossary

cash crop (kash krop) Crop grown to be sold for profit. (p. 161)

cattle drive (kat′l driv) Way cowboys moved huge herds of cattle from ranches in Texas to railroads in the late 1800s. (p. 550)

cause (kôz) Action that makes something happen. (p. 264)

census (sen′səs) Count of the population. (p. 8)

ceremony (sâr′ə mō′ nē) Activity done for a special purpose. (p. 61)

charter (chär′tər) Official document giving a person or group permission to do something. (p. 159)

checks and balances (cheks and bal′ən səz) System set up by the Constitution that gives each branch of government the power to check, or limit, the power of the other branches. (p. 348)

citizen (sit′ə zən) Member of a country. (p. 16)

civil rights (siv′əl ritz) Rights guaranteed to all citizens by the Constitution. (p. 643)

civil war (siv′əl wôr) War between people of the same country. (p. 487)

civilization (siv′ ə lə zā′shən) Culture with organized systems of government, religion, and learning. (p. 67)

climate (klī′mit) Weather in an area over a long period of time. (p. 29)

climograph (klī′mə graf) Graph that shows the average temperature and average precipitation for a place over time. (p. 58)

Cold War (kōld wôr) Struggle between the United States and the Soviet Union that was fought with ideas, words, and money instead of soldiers. (p. 637)

colonist (kol′ə nist) Person who lives in a colony. (p. 144)

colony (kol′ə nē) Settlement far from the country that rules it. (p. 136)

Columbian Exchange (kə lum′bē ən eks chānj′) Movement of people, animals, plants, diseases, and ways of life between the Eastern Hemisphere and Western Hemisphere following the voyages of Columbus. (p. 136)

Committees of Correspondence (kə mit′ēz əv kôr ə spon′dəns) Groups of colonists formed in the 1770s to spread news quickly about protests against the British. (p. 278)

communism (kom′yə niz′əm) Political and economic system in which the government owns all businesses and land. (p. 637)

compass rose (kum′pəs rōz) Pointer that shows directions on a map. (p. H17)

compromise (kom′prə miz) Settlement of a disagreement in which each side agrees to give up part of its demands. (p. 347)

Compromise of 1850 (kom′prə miz əv) Law passed by Congress under which California was admitted to the Union as a free state and the Fugitive Slave Law was passed. (p. 478)

concentration camp (kon′ sən trā′shən kamp) Prison in which the Nazis enslaved and murdered millions of people during World War II. (p. 628)

conclusion (kən klü′ zhən) Opinion that is formed based on facts. (p. 334)

Confederacy (kən fed′ər ə sē) Confederate States of America formed by the 11 Southern states that seceded from the Union. (p. 485)

conquest (kon′kwest) Capture or taking of something by force. (p. 144)

conquistador (kon kē′stə dôr) Spanish word for conquerors who came to the Americas in the 1500s. (p. 143)

conservation (kon′ sər vā′shən) Protection and careful use of natural resources. (p. 36)

constitution (kon′ stə tü′shən) Written plan of government. The United States Constitution, adopted in 1789, is the plan for the national government. (p. 15)

Constitutional Convention (kon′stə tü′shə nəl kən ven′shən) Meeting of delegates who met in Philadelphia, Pennsylvania, in 1787 and replaced the Articles of Confederation with the Constitution. (p. 345)

consumer (kən sü′mər) Person who buys or uses goods and services. (p. 21)

Continental Army (kon′ tə nen′ tl är′mē) Army formed in 1775 by the Second Continental Congress and led by General George Washington. (p. 297)

convert (kən vėrt′) To change from one belief to another. (p. 144)

corporation (kôr′ pə rā′shən) Business owned by investors. (p. 566)

cotton gin (kot′n jin) Machine invented by Eli Whitney that cleaned the seeds from cotton. (p. 410)

courage (kėr′ij) Doing what is right even when it is frightening or dangerous. (p. H2)

cross-section diagram (krôs sek′shən dī′ə gram) Drawing that shows a view of something as if you could slice through it. (p. 414)

Cuban Missile Crisis (kyü′bən mis′əl krī′sis) Conflict between the United States and the Soviet Union over nuclear missiles in Cuba. (p. 640)

cultural region (kul′chər əl rē′jən) Area in which people with similar cultures live. (p. 77)

culture (kul′chər) Way of life of a group of people. (p. 7)

D

dateline (dāt′lin) Line at the beginning of a newspaper article that tells where and when the story was written. (p. 209)

Daughters of Liberty (dô′tərz əv lib′ər tē) Groups of American women Patriots who wove cloth to replace boycotted British goods. (p. 272)

debtor (det′ər) Person who owes money. (p. 180)

Declaration of Independence (dek′lə rā′shən əv in′di pen′dəns) Document declaring the 13 American colonies independent of Great Britain, written mainly by Thomas Jefferson and adopted on July 4, 1776, by the Second Continental Congress. (p. 298)

degree (di grē′) Unit of measuring, used in latitude and longitude. (p. H15)

delegate (del′ə git) Person chosen to represent others. (p. 345)

demand (di mand′) Amount of a product that people are willing to buy. (p. 19)

democracy (di mok′rə sē) Government that is run by the people. (p. 15)

dictator (dik′tā tər) Leader with total power. (p. 625)

dictionary (dik′shə nâr′ē) Alphabetical collection of words that includes the meaning and pronunciation of each word. (p. H6)

discrimination (dis krim′ə nā′shən) Unfair treatment of a group or individual. (p. 445)

dissenter (di sent′ər) Person whose views differ from those of his or her leaders. (p. 178)

distribution maps (dis′ trə byü′shən maps) Maps that show how people or resources are spread out over an area. (p. 378)

draft (draft) Law that requires men of a certain age to serve in the military, if called. (p. 499)

drought (drout) Long period without rain. (p. 63)

Pronunciation Key

a in hat	ō in open	sh in she
ā in age	ô in order	th in thin
â in far	oi in oil	ᴛʜ in then
e in let	ou in out	zh in measure
ē in equal	u in cup	ə = a in about
ėr in term	ů in put	ə = e in taken
i in it	ü in rule	ə = i in pencil
ī in ice	ch in child	ə = o in lemon
o in hot	ng in long	ə = u in circus

Glossary

Dust Bowl (dust bōl) Period of severe drought in the 1930s that destroyed many farms on the Great Plains. (p. 621)

E

economy (i kon′ə mē) System for producing and distributing goods and services. (p. 19)

effect (ə fekt′) What happens as a result of an action. (p. 264)

El Camino Real (el kä mē′nō rē′əl) Spanish for "the royal road," a route that linked Spain's colonies in the American Southwest with Mexico. (p. 234)

electoral college (i lek′tər əl kol′ij) Group of people chosen by the people of each state who vote for President. (p. 363)

elevation (el′ ə vā′shən) Height of the land above sea level. (p. H21)

elevation map (el′ ə vā′ shən map) Physical map that uses color to show elevation. (pp. H21, H32)

Emancipation Proclamation (i man′ sə pā′shən prok′lə mā′shən) Statement issued by President Abraham Lincoln on January 1, 1863, freeing all slaves in Confederate states still at war with the Union. (p. 500)

emperor (em′pər ər) Ruler of an empire. (p. 103)

empire (em′pir) Large group of lands and peoples ruled by one leader. (p. 68)

encomienda (en kō mē en′də) Grant given by the King of Spain to wealthy settlers in New Spain. Gave settlers control of all the Native Americans living on an area of land. (p. 148)

encyclopedia (en sī′ klə pē′dē ə) Book or set of books with articles, alphabetically listed, on various topics. (p. H6)

entrepreneur (än′ trə prə nėr′) Person who starts a new business, hoping to make a profit. (p. 21)

environment (en vī′ rən mənt) All things that surround us, such as land, water, air, and trees. (p. 36)

equator (i kwā′tər) Imaginary line around the middle of Earth, halfway between the North Pole and the South Pole; 0° latitude. (p. H12)

Era of Good Feelings (ir′ə əv gu̇d fē′lingz) Name given to the period after the War of 1812 marked by optimism, a geographically expanding country, and a growing economy. (p. 403)

ethnic group (eth′nik grüp) Group of people who share the same customs and language. (p. 8)

evaluate (i val′yü āt) To make judgments about. (p. 447)

executive branch (eg zek′yə tiv branch) Part of the government, headed by the President, that carries out the laws. (p. 339)

exoduster (ek′sə dəs tər) Name for African American pioneers who moved to the Great Plains after the Civil War. (p. 549)

expedition (ek′ spə dish′ən) Journey made for a special purpose. (p. 135)

export (ek′spôrt) Good that one country sells to another country. (p. 20)

F

fact (fakt) Statement that can be proven to be true. (p. 174)

fairness (fer′ness) Not favoring one more than others. (p. H2)

feature article (fē′chər är′tə kəl) Newspaper article about people, places, or events. (p. 208)

federal (fed′ər əl) Refers to the national government. (p. 353)

Federalist (fed′ər ə list) Supporter of a strong national government and in favor of adopting of the Constitution. (p. 353)

Federalist, The (fed′ər ə list) Series of essays in 1787 and 1788 by James Madison, Alexander Hamilton, and John Jay that urged support of the new Constitution. (p. 353)

Fifteenth Amendment (fif′tēnth′ ə mend′mənt) Amendment to the Constitution, ratified in 1870, that gave the right to vote to male citizens of all races. (p. 519)

First Battle of Bull Run (fėrst bat′l əv bu̇l run) First major battle of the Civil War, on July 16, 1861. (p. 495)

First Continental Congress (fėrst kon′ tə nen′tl kong′gris) Meeting of representatives from every colony except Georgia held in Philadelphia in 1774 to discuss actions to take in response to the Intolerable Acts. (p. 281)

forty-niner (fôr′tē nī′ nər) Nickname for a person who arrived in California in 1849 to look for gold. (p. 443)

fossil fuel (fos′əl fyü′əl) Fuel, such as coal, oil, or natural gas, that is formed from the remains of plants and animals that lived thousands of years ago. (p. 35)

Fourteenth Amendment (fôr′tēnth′ ə mend′mənt) Amendment to the Constitution, ratified in 1868, that said that no state could deny any citizen the equal protection of the law. (p. 519)

free enterprise (frē en′tər prīz) Economic system in which people are free to start their own businesses and own their own property. (p. 19)

free state (frē stāt) State that did not allow slavery. (p. 477)

Freedmen's Bureau (frēd′mənz byu̇r′ō) Federal agency set up in 1865 to provide food, schools, and medical care to freed slaves in the South. (p. 518)

French and Indian War (french and in′dē ən wôr) War fought by the British against the French and their Native American allies in North America, which was won by the British in 1763. (p. 249)

frontier (frun tir′) Outer edge of a settled area. (p. 372)

Fugitive Slave Law (fyü′jə tiv slāv lô) Law passed by Congress in 1850 that said escaped slaves had to be returned to their owners. (p. 478)

G

generalization (jen′ ər ə lə zā′shən) Broad statement or idea about a subject. (p. 320)

geography (jē og′rə fē) Study of Earth and how people use it. (p. 25)

Gettysburg Address (get′ēz bėrg′ ə dres′) Famous Civil War speech given by President Lincoln in 1863 at the site of the Battle of Gettysburg. (p. 508)

glacier (glā′shər) Thick sheets of ice that covered Earth's surface during the Ice Age. (p. 55)

globe (glōb) Round model of Earth. (p. H12)

gold rush (gōld rush) Sudden movement of many people to an area where gold has been found. (p. 443)

Great Awakening (grāt ə wā′kə ning) Important religious movement among Christians that began in the colonies in the 1730s. This movement revived many colonists' interest in religion. (p. 218)

Great Compromise (grāt kom′prə mīz) Agreement at the Constitutional Convention to create a Congress with two houses. First proposed by Roger Sherman of Connecticut. (p. 347)

Pronunciation Key

a in hat	ō in open	sh in she
ā in age	ô in order	th in thin
ä in far	oi in oil	ᴛʜ in then
e in let	ou in out	zh in measure
ē in equal	u in cup	ə = a in about
ėr in term	u̇ in put	ə = e in taken
i in it	ü in rule	ə = i in pencil
ī in ice	ch in child	ə = o in lemon
o in hot	ng in long	ə = u in circus

Glossary

Great Depression (grāt di presh′ən) Period of severe economic depression that began in 1929. (p. 619)

Great Migration (grāt mī grā′shən) Movement between 1915 and 1940s of millions of African Americans to the North in search of work and fair treatment. (p. 613)

Green Mountain Boys (grēn moun′tən boiz) Group of Vermont soldiers who captured Fort Ticonderoga in 1775. (p. 303)

grid (grid) Pattern of criss-crossing lines that can help you find locations on a map. (p. 140)

H

haciendas (hä′sē en′dəz) Large estates built by wealthy Spanish ranchers in North America. (p. 234)

Harlem Renaissance (här′ləm ren′ ə säns′) Cultural movement centered in Harlem, an African American section of New York City. (p. 618)

headline (hed′līn) Words printed in large type at the head, or beginning, of an article. Often includes the main idea of the article. (p. 209)

hemisphere (hem′ə sfir) Half of a sphere or globe. Earth can be divided into hemispheres. (p. H13)

hijack (hī′jak) Take over by force. (p. 662)

Holocaust (hol′ə kôst) Murder of six million Jews during World War II. (p. 628)

Homestead Act (hōm′sted′ akt) 1862 law offering free land to pioneers willing to start farms on the Great Plains. (p. 547)

homesteaders (hōm′sted′ ərz) Settlers who claimed land in the Great Plains under the Homestead Act. (p. 547)

honesty (on′ə stē) Truthfulness. (p. H2)

House of Burgesses (hous əv bėr′jis ez) Law-making assembly in colonial Virginia. (p. 162)

I

Ice Age (īs āj) Period during which low temperatures caused large areas of Earth's water to freeze. (p. 55)

ideals (ī dē′əlz) Important beliefs. (p. 7)

immigrants (im′ə grənts) People who leave one country to go live in another country. (p. 10)

impeachment (im pēch′mənt) Bringing of charges of wrongdoing against an elected official. (p. 519)

import (im′pôrt) Good that one country buys from another country. (p. 20)

inauguration (in ȯ′ gyə rā′shən) Ceremony in which a newly-elected President takes office. (p. 363)

indentured servant (in den′chərd sėr′vənt) Person who agreed to work for someone for a certain amount of time in exchange for the cost of the voyage to North America. (p. 161)

Indian Removal Act (in′dē ən ri mü′vəl akt) Law passed in 1830 forcing American Indians living in the Southeast to be moved west of the Mississippi. (p. 405)

Industrial Revolution (in dus′trē əl rev′ ə lü′shən) Period of important change from making goods by hand to making goods by machine in factories. (p. 409)

inflation (in flā′shən) Economic condition in which prices rise very quickly. (p. 340)

inset map (in′ set′ map) Small map within a larger map. Shows areas outside of or in greater detail than the larger map. (p. H18)

interdependent (in′tər di pen′dənt) Needing each other. (p. 30)

intermediate direction (in′ tər mē′dē it də rek′shən) Pointers halfway between the main directions: northeast, northwest, southeast, southwest. (p. H17)

Internet (in′tər net′) Worldwide network of computers; became popular in the 1990s. (p. 86)

interstate highway (in′tər stāt hī′wā′) Road that connects cities in different states. (p. 512)

Intolerable Acts (in tol′ər ə bəl akts) Laws passed by British Parliament to punish the people of Boston following the Boston Tea Party. (p. 280)

Iron Curtain (ī′ərn kėrt′n) Imaginary border dividing Europe into communist and noncommunist countries after World War II. (p. 638)

irrigation (ir ə gā′ shən) Method of bringing water to dry land. (p. 28)

isolationism (ī′ sə lā′ shə niz′ əm) Policy of avoiding political involvement with other nations. (p. 611)

isthmus (is′məs) Narrow strip of land that connects two larger areas. (p. 604)

J

Jim Crow laws (jim′ krō lôz) Laws passed in the South after Reconstruction establishing segregation of whites and blacks. (p. 520)

judicial branch (jü dish′əl branch) Part of the government that decides the meaning of laws. (p. 339)

K

Kansas-Nebraska Act (kan′zəs nə bras′kə akt) Law passed in 1854 allowing these two territories to decide for themselves whether or not to allow slavery. (p. 479)

key (kē) Box explaining the symbols on a map. It is also known as a legend. (p. H16)

King Philip's War (king fil′əps wôr) War in 1670s between Native Americans and English settlers living in New England. (p. 247)

Korean War (kô rē′ən wôr) War between North Korea and South Korea lasting from 1950 to 1953. United States fought with South Korea to stop the spread of communism. (p. 639)

L

labor unions (lā′bər yü′nyənz) Groups of workers joined together to gain improved working conditions and better wages. (p. 572)

large-scale map (lärj′ skāl map) Map showing a small area in detail. (p. 244)

latitude (lat′ə tüd) Distance north or south of the equator, measured in degrees. (p. H15)

league (lēg) Union of people or groups. (p. 77)

League of Nations (lēg əv nā′shənz) Organization of nations formed after World War I. (p. 611)

legislative branch (lej′ə slā′tiv branch) Part of the government that passes laws. (p. 339)

locator (lō′kāt′ər) Small map that appears with a larger map. A locator shows where the subject area of the larger map is located on Earth. (p. H16)

lodge (loj) Large, round hut built by Plains Indians. (p. 83)

longhouse (lông′ hous′) Building used for shelter by Iroquois. (p. 78)

longitude (lon′jə tüd) Distance east or west of the prime meridian, measured in degrees. (p. H15)

Louisiana Purchase (lü ē′ zē an′ ə pėr′ chəs) Territory purchased by the United States from France in 1803, extending from the Mississippi River to the Rocky Mountains and from the Gulf of Mexico to Canada. (p. 373)

Pronunciation Key

a in hat	ō in open	sh in she
ā in age	ô in order	th in thin
ä in far	oi in oil	ᴛʜ in then
e in let	ou in out	zh in measure
ē in equal	u in cup	ə = a in about
ėr in term	u̇ in put	ə = e in taken
i in it	ü in rule	ə = i in pencil
ī in ice	ch in child	ə = o in lemon
o in hot	ng in long	ə = u in circus

Glossary

Loyalists (loi′ə lists) Colonists who remained loyal to the British during the American Revolution. (p. 280)

M

magnetic compass (mag net′ik kum′pəs) Chinese invention that aided navigation by showing which direction was north. (p. 104)

manifest destiny (man′ə fest des′tə nē) Belief that the United States should expand west to the Pacific Ocean. (p. 433)

manufacture (man′yə fak′chər) To make goods from raw materials. (p. 409)

map projection (map prə jek′shən) Shows Earth as a flat surface. (p. 656)

Mayflower Compact (mā′flou′ ər kom′pakt) Plan of government written by the Pilgrims who sailed on the *Mayflower.* (p. 170)

mechanical reaper (mə kan′ə kəl rē′pər) Machine invented by Cyrus McCormick that could harvest wheat quickly. (p. 410)

mercenaries (mėr′sə nâr′ ēz) Soldiers from one country who are paid to fight for another country. (p. 303)

meridian (mə rid′ē ən) Imaginary line extending from the North Pole to the South Pole, also called longitude line. (p. H15)

mesa (mā′sə) High, flat landform that rises steeply from the land around it. (p. 62)

Mexican War (mek′sə kən wôr) War lasting from 1846 to 1848 in which the United States defeated Mexico and gained Mexican territory. (p. 434)

Middle Passage (mid′l pas′ij) Name given to the second leg of the triangular trade routes; extended from West Africa to the West Indies. (p. 206)

migrate (mī′grāt) To move from one area to another. (p. 55)

militias (mə lish′əz) Volunteer armies. (p. 281)

mineral (min′ər əl) Substance such as gold, copper, or salt that is found in the earth and is not a plant or animal. (p. 35)

minutemen (min′it men′) Colonial militia groups that could be ready to fight at a minute's notice. (p. 281)

mission (mish′ən) Religious settlement where missionaries live and work. (p. 149)

missionary (mish′ə nâr′ē) Person who teaches his or her religion to others who have different beliefs. (p. 149)

Missouri Compromise (mə zůr′ē kom′prə mīz) Law passed in 1820 dividing the Louisiana Territory into areas prohibiting slavery and areas allowing slavery. (p. 477)

monopoly (mə nop′ə lē) Company that has control of an entire industry and stops competition. (p. 566)

Monroe Doctrine (mən rō′ dok′trən) Policy declared by President James Monroe warning European nations not to interfere in the Western Hemisphere. (p. 403)

mountain men (moun′tən men) Fur trappers who helped explore and settle the Oregon Country. (p. 439)

muckraker (muk′rā′kər) Writers and journalists who exposed shameful conditions in business and other areas of American life. (p. 603)

N

national anthem (nash′ə nəl an′thəm) Official song of a country. "The Star-Spangled Banner" is the national anthem of the United States. (p. 383)

nationalism (nash′ə nə liz′ əm) Strong feeling of pride in one's country. (p. 403)

natural resource (nach′ər əl ri sôrs′) Something found in nature that people can use. (p. 35)

navigation (nav′ ə gā′shən) Science used by sailors to plot their course and determine their location. (p. 113)

neutral (nü′trəl) Not taking sides. (p. 381)

New Deal (nü dēl) Series of programs started by President Franklin D. Roosevelt to help the nation recover from the Great Depression. (p. 620)

New Jersey Plan (nü jėr′zē plan) Proposal during the Constitutional Convention that each state should have the same number of representatives in Congress. (p. 346)

news article (nüz är′tə kəl) News story based on facts about recent events. (p. 208)

Nineteenth Amendment (nīn′tēnth′ ə mend′mənt) Amendment to the Constitution giving women the right to vote; ratified in 1920. (p. 612)

nonfiction book (non fik′shən bůk) Book that is based on fact. (p. H6)

nonrenewable resource (non′ ri nü′ə bəl ri sôrs′) Resource that cannot be easily replaced, such as a fossil fuel. (p. 36)

Northwest Ordinance of 1787 (nôrth′ west′ ôrd′n əns əv) Federal order that divided the Northwest Territory into smaller territories and created a plan for how the territories could become states. (p. 342)

Northwest Passage (nôrth′ west′ pas′ij) Water route that explorers hoped would flow through North America, connecting the Atlantic and Pacific oceans. (p. 165)

O

Olive Branch Petition (ol′iv branch pə tish′ən) Letter sent by the Second Continental Congress to King George III in 1775 in an attempt to avoid war. (p. 297)

opinion (ə pin′yən) Personal view about an issue. (p. 174)

P

parallel time lines (pâr′ə lel tīm līnz) Two or more time lines grouped together. (p. 116)

Parliament (pär′lə mənt) Britain's law-making assembly. (p. 269)

Patriots (pā′trē əts) American colonists who opposed British rule. (p. 280)

periodical (pir′ ē od′ə kəl) Newspaper or magazine that is published on a regular basis. (p. H6)

persecution (pėr′sə kyü′ shən) Unjust treatment because of one's beliefs. (p. 169)

Persian Gulf War (pėr′zhən gulf wôr) War involving the United States and its allies against Iraq in 1991. (p. 660)

physical map (fiz′ ə kəl map) Map showing geographic features such as mountains and rivers. (p. H17)

pilgrim (pil′grəm) Person who travels to a new place for religious reasons. (p. 169)

pilgrimage (pil′grə mij) Journey taken for religious reasons. (p.108)

pioneer (pī′ə nir′) Early settler of a region. (p. 372)

plantation (plan tā′shən) Large farm with many workers who live on the land they work. (p. 148)

point of view (point əv vyü) A person's own opinion of an issue or event. (p. 468)

Pronunciation Key

a	in hat	ō	in open	sh	in she
ā	in age	ô	in order	th	in thin
ä	in far	oi	in oil	ᴛʜ	in then
e	in let	ou	in out	zh	in measure
ē	in equal	u	in cup	ə	= a in about
ėr	in term	ů	in put	ə	= e in taken
i	in it	ü	in rule	ə	= i in pencil
ī	in ice	ch	in child	ə	= o in lemon
o	in hot	ng	in long	ə	= u in circus

Glossary

political cartoon (pə lit′ə kəl kär tün′) Drawing that shows people or events in the news in a funny way. (p. 606)

political map (pə lit′ə kəl map) Map that shows borders between states or countries. (p. H16)

political party (pə lit′ə kəl pär′tē) Organized group of people who share similar views of what government should do. (p. 364)

pollution (pə lü′shən) Something that dirties the water, air, or soil. (p. 38)

Pontiac's Rebellion (pon′tē aks ri bel′yən) Native American rebellion led by the Ottawa leader Pontiac in 1763. (p. 251)

Pony Express (pō′nē ek spres′) Mail delivery service begun in 1860 that used a relay of riders on horses to carry mail from Missouri to California in ten days. (p. 539)

population density map (pop′ yə lā′shən den′sə tē map) Map that shows the number of people living in a certain amount of space, such as a square mile. (p. 378)

potlatch (pot′ lach′) Native American celebration in which the hosts give gifts to their guests. (p. 95)

powwow (pou′wou) Native American ceremony that often includes traditional dancing and games. (p. 85)

Preamble (prē′am′ bəl) Introduction to the Constitution, beginning, "We the People of the United States . . ." (p. 348)

precipitation (pri sip′ ə tā′ shən) Moisture that falls to Earth in the form of rain, snow, or sleet. (p. 29)

prejudice (prej′ə dis) Unfair negative opinion about a group of people. (p. 571)

presidio (pri sid′ē ō) Military fort built by the Spanish. (p. 234)

primary source (prī′mâr′ ē sôrs) Eyewitness account of a historical event. (p. H6)

prime meridian (prīm mə rid′ē ən) Line of longitude marked 0 degrees. Other lines of longitude are measured in degrees east or west of the prime meridian. (p. H15)

private property (prī′ vit prop′ər tē) Something owned by individual people. (p. 19)

Proclamation of 1763 (prok′lə mā′shən əv) Law issued by King George III stating that colonists were no longer allowed to settle on land west of the Appalachian Mountains. (p. 251)

profit (prof′it) Money a business has left over after it has paid all its costs. (p. 19)

Progressives (prə gres′ivz) Reformers who wanted to improve government. (p. 603)

proprietor (prə prī′ə tər) Owner. (p. 180)

pueblo (pweb′lō) Spanish word for "village." (p. 89)

Pueblo Revolt (pweb′lō ri vōlt′) Native American revolt in the late 1600s in which the Pueblo temporarily drove the Spanish out of New Mexico. (p. 235)

Puritans (pyůr′ə tənz) Group of people who wanted to "purify" the Church of England. They established the Massachusetts Bay Colony in 1630. (p. 172)

pyramid (pir′ə mid) Building with three or more sides shaped like triangles that slant toward a point at the top. (p. 67)

R

ratify (rat′ə fī) To officially approve (p. 339)

Reconstruction (rē′ kən struk′shən) Period of rebuilding after the Civil War during which the Southern states rejoined the Union. (p. 517)

reform (ri fôrm′) Change. (p. 417)

region (rē′jən) Large area that has common features that set it apart from other areas. (p. 25)

Renaissance (ren′ ə säns′) Period in Europe beginning in about 1350 during which there was a new desire to learn more about the arts, sciences, and other parts of the world. (p. 112)

renewable resource (ri nü′ə bəl ri sôrs′) Resource that can be renewed or replaced, such as a tree. (p. 36)

repeal (ri pēl′) To cancel. (p. 270)

republic (ri pub′ lik) Form of government in which the people elect representatives to make laws and run the government. (p. 15)

reservation (rez′ ər vā′shən) Land set aside by the United States government for Native Americans. (p. 80)

reserved powers (ri zėrvd′ pou′ərz) Powers in the Constitution that are left to the individual states. (p. 348)

respect (ri spekt′) Consideration for others. (p. H2)

responsibility (ri spon′ sə bil′ə tē) Doing what you are supposed to do. (p. H2)

revival (ri vī′vəl) Act of awakening or strengthening people's religious feelings. (p. 419)

road map (rōd map) Map showing roads; can be used to plan driving trips to cities or other places of interest. (p. H22)

Rough Riders (ruf rī′dərz) Group of American volunteer soldiers during the Spanish-American War organized by Theodore Roosevelt. (p. 580)

S

saga (sä′gə) Long, spoken tale repeated from one generation to the next. (p. 111)

scale (skāl) Tool that helps you measure distances on a map. (p. H18)

sea level (sē lev′əl) An ocean's surface, compared to which the height of land is measured either above or below. (p. 32)

search engine (sėrch en′jən) Computer site that searches for information from numerous Internet Web sites. (p. H7)

secede (si sēd′) To break away from a group, as the Southern states broke away from the United States in 1861. (p. 485)

Second Continental Congress (sek′ənd kon′ tə nen′tl kong′gris) Congress of American leaders that first met in 1775, declared independence in 1776, and helped lead the United States during the Revolution. (p. 297)

secondary source (sek′ən dâr′ ē sôrs) Description of events written by people who did not witness the event. (p. H6)

sectionalism (sek′shə nə liz′ əm) Loyalty to one section of a country rather than to the whole country. (p. 465)

segregation (seg′ rə gā′shən) Separation of people of different races. (p. 520)

self-sufficient (self′ sə fish′ənt) Ability to rely on oneself for most of what one needs. (p. 212)

Seneca Falls Convention (sen′ə kə fôlz kən ven′shən) First national convention on women's rights, organized in 1848 by Lucretia Mott and Elizabeth Cady Stanton. (p. 419)

separation of powers (sep′ ə rā′shən əv pou′ərz) Division of power among the three branches of the federal government under the Constitution. (p. 348)

Pronunciation Key

a	in hat	ō	in open	sh	in she
ā	in age	ô	in order	th	in thin
ä	in far	oi	in oil	ᴛʜ	in then
e	in let	ou	in out	zh	in measure
ē	in equal	u	in cup	ə	= a in about
ėr	in term	ů	in put	ə	= e in taken
i	in it	ü	in rule	ə	= i in pencil
ī	in ice	ch	in child	ə	= o in lemon
o	in hot	ng	in long	ə	= u in circus

Glossary

Separatists (sep′ər ə tists) Group of people from England who wanted to separate themselves from the church of England. Some traveled to North America in search of religious freedom. (p. 169)

settlement house (set′l mənt hous) Center that provides help for immigrants or the poor. (p. 571)

shaman (shä′mən) Native American doctor or healer. (p. 96)

sharecropping (shâr′krop′ ing) System of farming in which farmers rented land and paid the landowner with a share of the crops they raised. (p. 520)

Shays' Rebellion (shāz ri bel′yən) Revolt of Massachusetts farmers against high state taxes, led by Daniel Shays. (p. 341)

slave codes (slāv kōdz) Laws designed to control the behavior of slaves. (p. 471)

slave state (slāv stāt) State in which slavery was legally allowed. (p. 477)

slave trade (slāv trād) Buying and selling of human beings. (p. 113)

slavery (slā′vər ē) Practice of owning people and forcing them to work. (p. 68)

small-scale map (smôl skāl map) Map showing a large area of land but not much detail. (p. 244)

society (sə sī′ə tē) Group of people forming a community. (p. 148)

sodbusters (sod′bus tərz) Great Plains farmers of the late 1800s who had to cut through the sod, or thick grass, before planting crops. (p. 547)

Sons of Liberty (sunz ov lib′ər tē) Groups of Patriots who worked to oppose British rule before the American Revolution. (p. 271)

source (sôrs) Written or oral account that may provide information. (p. 584)

space race (spās rās) Race between the United States and the Soviet Union to explore outer space during the Cold War. (p. 651)

Spanish-American War (span′ish ə mâr′ə kən wôr) War in which the United States defeated Spain in 1898 and gained Spanish territory. (p. 580)

specialize (spesh′ə līz) Focus on one particular product, activity, or job. (p. 67)

Stamp Act (stamp akt) Law passed by Parliament in 1765 that taxed printed materials in the 13 Colonies. (p. 269)

standard time (stan′dərd tim) Official time used in a country or region. (p. 542)

states' rights (stāts rits) Idea that states have the right to make decisions about issues that concern them. (p. 477)

stock (stok) Share in a company. (p. 159)

stock market (stok mär′kit) Organized meeting where stocks are bought and sold. (p. 619)

Stono Rebellion (stō′nō ri bel′yən) Slave rebellion in South Carolina in 1739. (p. 227)

strike (strik) Refusal of workers to work until business owners meet their demands. (p. 573)

suffrage (suf′rij) Right to vote. (p. 404)

supply (sə plī′) Amount of a product that is available. (p. 19)

surplus (sèr′pləs) More than is needed. (p. 67)

symbol (sim′bəl) Something that stands for something else. (p. H16)

tariff (târ′if) Tax on imported goods. (p. 272)

tax (taks) Money or goods people pay to a government. (p. 107)

Tea Act (tē akt) Law passed by Parliament in the early 1770s stating that only the East India Company, a British business, could sell tea to the 13 Colonies. (p. 279)

---

technology (tek nol′ə jē) Use of scientific knowledge or new tools to make or do something. (p. 409)

telegraph (tel′ə graf) Machine used to send messages along wires using electricity. (p. 539)

temperance (tem′pər əns) Moderation, usually in drinking of alcohol. (p. 417)

tenement (ten′ə mənt) Building that is divided into very small apartments. (p. 571)

tepee (tē′pē) Dwelling built by Plains Indians, made of poles arranged in a circle covered by buffalo hides. (p. 83)

terrorist (târ′ər ist) Person who uses violence and fear to try to achieve goals. (p. 662)

Texas Revolution (tek′səs rev′ ə lü′shən) War between Texas settlers and Mexico from 1835 to 1836 resulting in the formation of the Republic of Texas. (p. 432)

theory (thē′ər ē) One possible explanation for something. (p. 55)

Thirteenth Amendment (thèr′ tēnth′ ə mend′mənt) Amendment to the Constitution in 1865 that ended slavery. (p. 517)

Three-Fifths Compromise (thrē′ fifths′kom′prə miz) Agreement made at the Constitutional Convention that only three-fifths of the slaves in a state would be counted for representation and tax purposes. (p. 347)

time zone (tim zōn) Region in which one standard time is used. There are total of 24 around the world. (p. 542)

time zone map (tim zōn map) Map showing the world's or any country's time zones. (p. H20)

title (ti′təl) Name of something, such as a book or map. (p. H16)

total war (tō′tl wôr) Method of warfare used by Union General William Sherman in which both the opposing army and an enemy's civilian population are targets. (p. 510)

totem pole (tō′təm pōl) Wooden post carved with animals or other images; often made by Native Americans of the Pacific Northwest to honor ancestors or special events. (p. 95)

town common (toun kom′ən) Open space in the center of many New England and Middle Colony towns where cattle and sheep could graze. (p. 212)

Townshend Acts (toun′zend akts) Laws passed by Parliament in 1767 that taxed goods imported from the 13 Colonies from Britain. (p. 272)

trading post (trād′ing pōst) Place in colonial North America where settlers and Native Americans met to trade goods. (p. 241)

Trail of Tears (trāl ov tirz) Forced march of 15,000 Cherokee from the southeastern United States to Indian Territory in present-day Oklahoma in 1838. (p. 406)

traitor (trā′tər) Person who works against his or her country. (p. 300)

transcontinental railroad (tran′ skon tə nen′tl rāl′rōd) Railroad that crosses an entire continent. The United States completed its first transcontinental railroad in 1869. (p. 539)

travois (trə voi′) Sled made of poles tied together; used by Native Americans to transport goods across the plains. (p. 83)

Treaty of Guadalupe Hidalgo (trē′tē ov gwä′ dl üp′ hi dal′gō) Treaty ending the Mexican War in 1848. Mexico gave up most of its northern territory to the United States in return for $15 million. (p. 435)

Pronunciation Key		
a in hat	ō in open	sh in she
ā in age	ô in order	th in thin
ä in far	oi in oil	ᴛᴴ in then
e in let	ou in out	zh in measure
ē in equal	u in cup	ə = a in about
ėr in term	ú in put	ə = e in taken
i in it	ü in rule	ə = i in pencil
ī in ice	ch in child	ə = o in lemon
o in hot	ng in long	ə = u in circus

Glossary

Treaty of Paris (trē′tē ov pâr′is) Treaty signed in 1783 that officially ended the American Revolution. Great Britain recognized the United States as an independent country. (p. 319)

Treaty of Versailles (trē′tē ov ver si′) Treaty signed in 1919 that officially ended World War I. (p. 611)

triangular trade route (tri ang′gyə lər trād rout) Three-sided trade route between the 13 Colonies, the West Indies, and Africa; included the slave trade. (p. 206)

tribe (trib) Group of families bound together under a single leadership. (p. 77)

tributary (trib′yə târ′ē) Stream or river that flows into a larger river. (p. 242)

tribute (trib′yüt) Payment a ruler demands from people he or she rules. (p. 68)

Underground Railroad (un′ dər ground′ rāl′rōd) System of secret routes used by escaping slaves that led from the South to the North or Canada. (p. 473)

unemployment (un′ em ploi′mənt) Number of workers who are without jobs. (p. 619)

Union (yü′nyən) United States of America. (p. 485)

United Nations (yü ni′tid nā′shənz) International organization formed in 1945 to promote peace and end conflicts. (p. 637)

veto (vē′tō) Power of the President to reject a bill passed by Congress. (p. 348)

Vietnam War (vē et′ näm′ wôr) War in the 1960s and 1970s in which the United States sent soldiers to South Vietnam to try to prevent communist forces from taking over the nation. (p. 653)

Virginia Plan (vər jin′yə plan) Proposal during the Constitutional Convention that Congress be given greater power over the states and that large states have more representatives in Congress than small states. (p. 346)

wagon train (wag′ən trān) Common method of transportation to the West, in which wagons traveled in groups for safety. (p. 439)

wampum (wäm′pəm) Belts or strings of polished seashells that were used for trading and gift-giving by Iroquois and other Native Americans. (p. 79)

War Hawks (wôr hôkz) Members of Congress who supported war with Britain in 1812. (p. 382)

War of 1812 (wôr əv) Conflict between the United States and Britain that lasted from 1812 to 1815. (p. 382)

Watergate scandal (wô′tər gāt skan′dl) Scandal that forced President Richard Nixon to resign from office in 1974. (p. 654)

Web site (web sit) Place on the World Wide Web where information can be found. (p. 86)

World War I (wèrld wôr wun) War between the Allies and the Central Powers that lasted from 1914 to 1918. The United States joined the Allies in 1917, helping the Allies to win the war. (p. 609)

World War II (wèrld wôr tü) War fought from 1939 to 1945 between the Allies and the Axis, and involving most of the countries in the world. The United States joined the Allies in 1941, helping the Allies gain victory. (p. 625)

Index

This Index lists the pages on which topics appear in this book. Page numbers after an *m* refer to a map. Page numbers after a *p* refer to a photograph. Page numbers after a *c* refer to a chart or graph.

Index

- **Britain.** *See* England, Great Britain
- **Brown, John,** 480
- **Brown, Linda,** 643, *p643*
- **Bruce, Blanche K.,** 518
- **Bruchac, Joseph,** 120–121
- **Buchanan, James,** R22
- **Buddhists,** 63
- **buffalo,** 83–84, 377, 555
- **Buffalo Soldiers,** 581
- **Bunker Hill, Battle of,** 290–291, 306, 310, *m290, p306*
- **Burgoyne, John,** 305
- **Bush, George H.W.,** 15, 659–660, R25
- **Bush, George W.,** 661, 662, 664, R25, *p661*

C

- **Cabinet,** 335, 363–364
- **Cabot, John,** 166
- **Cahokia,** 61, *p61*
- **Calhoun, John C.,** 477–478
- **California,** 399, 442–445, 478, 537, 553, R18, *p434*
- **California Trail,** 443, *m440*
- **Canada**
  - facts about, 678–679, 681, *p678–679, 681, m678–679*
  - history of, 241, 680, *c680*
- **canal,** 411, *c414–415*
- **Cape of Good Hope,** 114
- **caravan,** 107
- **cardinal directions,** H17
- **careers,** 22
- **Caribbean region, countries of,** 688–689, *c688, m689*
- **Carnegie, Andrew,** 532, 564, *p532, p564*
- **Carney, William,** 501
- **Carter, James E.,** 15, 655, R24, *p655*
- **Cartier, Jacques,** 166
- **Carver, George Washington,** 28, 31, *p31*
- **cash crop,** 161
- **Castro, Fidel,** 640
- **Catholics.** *See* Roman Catholic Church, Roman Catholics
- **Catt, Carrie Chapman,** 612
- **cattle drives,** 550–551, *m550*
- **cause and effect,** 85, 167, 251, 264–265, 273, 282, 291, 292, 300, 322, 384, 582, 648
- **census,** 8–9
- **Central America, countries of,** 686–687, *c686, m687, R4*
- **Central Powers,** 609–611
- **Champlain, Samuel de,** 128, 165–166, *p128*
- **character traits,**
  - caring, H2, 504–505
  - courage, H2, 92–93, 666–667
  - fairness, H2, 422–423
  - honesty, H2, 274–275
  - respect, H2, 184–185
  - responsibility, H2, 40–41
- **Charles I, King of England,** 180
- **Charles II, King of England,** 179
- **Charleston, South Carolina,** 206, 464, 484–485
- **Charlestown, Massachusetts,** 290
- **charter,** 159
- **Chávez, César,** 648. *p648*
- **checks and balances,** 349, *c349*
- **Cherokee,** 405–406, *m77, m405, p406*
- **Chestnut, Mary Boykin,** 484
- **Cheyenne,** 84–85, *m84, p84, p85*
- **Chicago, Illinois,** 28, 567, 571
- **Chickasaw,** 405, *m405*
- **child labor,** 572, 576–577, 583
- **China,** 63, 102–105, 639, 652, 654
- **Chisholm, Shirley,** 647
- **Choctaw,** 405, *m405*
- **Christianity,** 136, 148, 218, 234, 238, 417. *See also* Great Awakening, missionary, Pilgrims, Protestants, Puritans, Quakers, Roman Catholics, Second Great Awakening
- **Church of England,** 169, 172
- **Church of Jesus Christ of Latter-day Saints,** 441
- **Churchill, Winston,** 638
- **Cíbola,** 147
- **Cinque, Joseph,** 459, 472, *p459*
- **circle graphs, reading,** 12–13, *c13*
- **cities, colonial,** 211, *c211*
- **Cities of Gold,** 147, 238
- **citizen,** 16
- **citizenship**
  - caring, H2, 504–505
  - courage, H2, 92–93, 666–667
  - decision-making, H3
  - fairness, H2, 422–423
  - honesty, H2, 274–275
  - problem-solving, H3
  - respect, H2, 184–185
  - responsibility, H2, 40–41
- **civil rights,** 643
- **Civil Rights Act of 1964,** 646
- **Civil War**
  - African Americans and, 501, *p501*
  - attack on Fort Sumter, 484, 486
  - battles of, 495, 507, 509, *m509*
  - communications during, 514–515, *p514, 515*
  - definition of, 487
  - life during, 498–503
  - secession of Southern states, 485
  - slavery and, 10
  - strategies of, 494
  - technology, 496
  - women and, 502
- **Civilian Conservation Corps,** 620
- **civilization,** 67
- **Clark, George Rogers,** 316, *p316*
- **Clark, William,** 36, 374–375, 377, *p374*
- **Clay, Henry,** 382, 458, 477–478, *p458*
- **Cleveland, Grover,** R23
- **Cleveland, Ohio,** 566
- **climate,** 19, *m29*
- **Clinton, William J.,** 660–661, R25
- **Code Talkers,** 92–93, *p92*
- **Coffin, Catherine,** 473
- **Coffin, Levi,** 473
- **Cold War,** 637–641, 650–653, 658–659
- **Colombia,** 403, 690, *m403, 691*
- **colonial America**
  - cities of, 211, *c211*
  - economies of, 205, *m205*
  - families in, 214
  - life in, 216–220, 254–255
  - towns of, 212, *p212*
  - trade in, 206–207
  - working in, 202–204, 254, *c204*
  - colonist, 144
- **colony,** 136
- **Colorado,** R18
- **Columbian Exchange,** 136, *c136*
- **Columbus, Christopher,** 128, 131, 133, 135–139, *p128, 135, 137, m141*

- **Columbus Day,** 133
- **Committees of Correspondence,** 278–280
- ***Common Sense,*** 298, *p298*
- **Communism,** 637–640, 652–653
- **compare and contrast,** 162, 173, 182, 198–199, 207, 214, 220, 227, 228, 236, 252, 398–399, 406, 413, 426, 436, 445, 448, 664
- **compass rose,** H17
- **compromise,** 347
- **Compromise of 1850,** 478
- **computers,** 661, 666, *p666*
- **concentration camps,** 628
- **conclusions, draw,** 97, 115, 319, 334–335, 343, 350, 355, 358, 366, 386
- **Concord, Battle of,** 289, *m288*
- **Concord, Massachusetts,** 287, 289
- **Confederacy,** 485, 493–494, *m486, c493*
- **Congress,** 15, 347–349, 517–520
- **Connecticut,** 178, R19, *c181*
- **conquest,** 144
- **conquistador,** 143–144, 146–148
- **conservation,** 36, 602–603
- **constitution,** 15
- **Constitution, United States**
  - as basis of government, 15
  - creation of, 337, 345–347
  - Preamble of, 3, 17, 331, 348, *p348*
  - principles of, 348, *c349*
  - ratification of, 352–354
  - text of, R30–R52
- ***Constitution,* USS,** 382, *p382*
- **Constitutional Convention,** 345–347, *p346*
- **consumer,** 21
- **Continental Army,** 297, 303–306
- **convert,** 144
- **Coolidge, Calvin,** R25
- **Cooper, Peter,** 412–413
- **Copán,** 66–67
- **Cornwallis, Charles,** 318
- **Coronado, Francisco Vásquez de,** 147, *m147*
- **corporation,** 566
- **Cortés, Hernando,** 142–143
- **cotton gin,** 410, 431, *p410*
- **cotton production,** 410, *c410*
- **cowboys,** 551, *p551*
- **Creek,** 405
- **Croatoan,** 157
- **Crockett, David,** 432, *p432*
- **cross-section diagram, reading,** 414–415, *c414, 415*
- **Cuba,** 580–581, 640, *m581, 640*
- **Cuban Missile Crisis,** 640
- **cultural region,** 77
- **culture,** 7
- **Cumberland Gap,** 372
- **Custer, George,** 556
- **Cuzco,** 69, 145

D

- **Da Gama, Vasco,** 114, *m114*
- **dateline,** 209
- **Daughters of Liberty,** 272
- **Davis, Jefferson,** 458, 485–486, *p458, 485*
- **Dawes, William,** 287
- **D-Day,** 628, 631, *p628*
- **debtors,** 180
- **decision-making,** H3
- **Declaration of Independence,** 295, 298–301, 339, R26–R29, *p299*
- **Deere, John,** 410
- **Deganawidah,** 49, 76–77, *p49*
- **degrees,** H15
- **Delaware,** 179, 354, R19, *c181*
- **Delaware River,** 304
- **De la Warre, Lord,** 160
- **delegates,** 345
- **demand,** 19
- **democracy,** 15
- **Democratic Party,** 404, 481–482, *p606*
- **Democratic-Republicans,** 364, 368
- **De Soto, Hernando,** 146–147, *m147*
- **details.** *See* main idea and details
- **De Vaca, Álvar Núñez Cabeza,** 147, *m147*
- **Dewey, George,** 580
- **Dias, Bartolomeu,** 114
- **dictators,** 625
- **dictionary,** H6
- **discrimination,** 445, 466, 553, 613–614
- **dissenter,** 178
- **distribution maps,** 378
- **diversity,** 5, 7–8, 10–11
- **Dix, Dorothea,** 420
- **Dominican Republic,** 688, *m689*
- **Douglas, Marjory Stoneman,** 37, 39, *p39*
- **Douglas, Stephen,** 479, 481–482, *p481*
- **Douglass, Frederick,** 397, 418–419, 422–423, 500, *p397, 424*
- **draft,** 499
- **Drake, Francis,** 158, *p158*
- **drought,** 63
- **Du Bois, W.E.B.,** 613
- **Dust Bowl,** 621, *m621*

E

- ***Eagle*** (spacecraft), 650, *p650*
- **Earhart, Amelia,** 617
- **Eastern Hemisphere,** H14
- **Eastern Woodlands cultural region,** 77, *m77*
- **economic freedoms,** 19
- **economy,** 19. *See also* colonial America, economies of
- **Edison, Thomas,** 21, 23, 563, *p21*
- **education**
  - colonial, 216–217
  - public, 342, 420, 518, 521
  - Puritans and, 173
  - during Reconstruction, 518
  - segregation and, 643
- **Egypt,** 655
- **Eisenhower, Dwight D.,** 596, 628, 631, 639, 652, R25, *p596, 631, 639*
- **El Camino Real,** 234, *m234*
- **electoral college,** 363
- **elevation,** 32
- **elevation maps, reading,** H21, 32–33, *m33*
- **Elfreth's Alley, Philadelphia,** 211, *p211*
- **Elizabeth I, Queen of England,** 157, *p157*
- **Ellis Island,** 10, 569
- **Emancipation Proclamation,** 500
- **emperor,** 103
- **empire,** 68
- **encomienda,** 148–151
- **encyclopedia,** H6
- **England.** *See also* Great Britain
  - colonies of, 168–173, 176–182, *m177, c181*
  - exploration and, 138,

  - 166
  - Pilgrims and, 169
  - Spain and, 157–158
- **entrepreneur,** 21
- **environment,** 36, 38
- ***E Pluribus Unum,*** 7
- **equator,** H13, H15
- **Equiano, Olaudah,** 197, 206, 227, *p197*
- **Era of Good Feelings,** 403
- **Eric the Red,** 110–111
- **Ericsson, Leif,** 48, 111, *p48*
- **Erie Canal,** 411, 414–415, *c414–415, p414*
- **Estéban,** 147
- **ethnic group,** 8, *c8*
- **Everglades,** 39
- **Everglades National Park,** 37
- **executive branch,** 339, 346, 348, *c349*
- **exodusters,** 549
- **expedition,** 135
- **export,** 20, 161, *c20, 161*
- **express riders,** 278, *m278*

F

- **fact and opinion,** 174–175
- **fair trial, right to,** 16
- **families**
  - colonial American, 214
  - slave, 471, *p471*
- **feature article,** 208
- **federal,** 353
- ***Federalist, The,*** 351, 353, *p353*
- **Federalists,** 353–354
- **Federalists (political party),** 364, 368
- **Ferdinand, King of Spain,** 135
- **Fifteenth Amendment,** 519, *c519*
- **Fillmore, Millard,** R22
- **First Amendment,** 351
- **First Battle of Bull Run,** 495, *m509*
- **First Continental Congress,** 265, 281, 297
- **"First Flute, The,"** 120–121
- **Fitzgerald, F. Scott,** 618
- **Fitzhugh, George,** 468–469, *p468*
- **Florida,** 180, 232–233, 399, 403, 431, 640, R19
- **Ford, Gerald,** 654, R24
- **Ford, Henry,** 617
- **Fort Duquesne,** 248–249
- **Fort McHenry,** 383
- **Fort Necessity,** 246–247, 249
- **Fort Sumter,** 484–486
- **Fort Ticonderoga,** 302–303
- **Fort Vincennes,** 316
- **Fort Wagner,** 501
- **Forty-niners,** 443–444
- **fossil fuels,** 35
- **Four Corners,** 62–63, 89
- **Fourteenth Amendment,** 519, *c519*
- **Fourth of July,** 295
- **France**
  - American Revolution and, 305, 315
  - exploration and, 240–243
  - French and Indian War and, 249–250
  - Louisiana Purchase and, 373
  - revolution in, 341, *p341*
  - settlements of, 165, 243
  - World War I and, 609
  - World War II and, 625–626, 628
- **Franklin, Benjamin,** 6, 196, 210–211, 218–219, 298, 305, 344, 350, 355, *p6,196, 299, 349*
- **free enterprise,** 18–19, 21–22, 637
- **free states,** 477, *m479*
- **Freedman's Bureau,** 461, 518
- **freedom, economic,** 19
- **freedom, political.** *See* specific freedoms
- **French and Indian War,** 199, 246, 249–250, *m250*
- **French Revolution,** 341, *p341*
- **Friedan, Betty,** 647
- **frontier,** 372
- **Fugitive Slave Act,** 478, *p478*
- **Fulton, Robert,** 411
- **Fur Trade,** 165

G

- **Gadsden Purchase,** 435, *m435*
- **Gage, Thomas,** 280, 287
- **Gálvez, Bernardo de,** 263, 315, *p263, 315*
- **Gandhi, Mohandas,** 311, *p311*
- **Garfield, James A.,** R23
- **Garrison, William Lloyd,** 418
- **generalizations, make,** 320–321
- **geography**
  - definition of, 25
  - of United States, 24–30
  - themes of, H10–H11. *See also* specific themes
- **George III, King of England,** 251, 269–270, 272, 274–275, 279, 282, 297, 303, 316, *p269*
- **Georgia,** 180–181, R19, *c181*
- **Germany,** 599, 609–611, 625–626, 628, 631
- **Gettysburg Address,** 457, 491, 506, 508
- **Gettysburg, Battle of,** 507, 509, *m507*
- **Gettysburg, Pennsylvania,** 491, 506–508, *p512*
- **Ghana,** 107, *m107*
- **Gilmore, Patrick S.,** 524
- **Giuliani, Rudolph,** 665
- **glacier,** 55
- **Glenn, John,** 651
- **globe,** H8
- **gold rush,** 443–445
- **Gompers, Samuel,** 573
- **Goodnight, Charles,** 551
- **Gorbachev, Mikhail,** 659
- **Gordimer, Nadine,** 223
- **Gorgas, W.C.,** 604
- **Grant, Ulysses S.,** 459, 509–511, R23, *p459, 510*
- **graphs, reading**
  - circle, 12–13, *c13*
  - line, 12–13, *c12*
- **Great Awakening,** 218. *See also* Second Great Awakening
- **Great Britain.** *See also* England
  - American Revolution and, 295, 303, 305, 315, 319
  - Civil War and, 494
  - colonists and, 268–273, 280, 282, 298
  - French and Indian War and, 249–250
  - Industrial Revolution and, 409
  - Oregon Country and, 439
  - War of 1812 and, 382–384
  - World War I and, 609
  - World War II and, 625–626, 628
- **Great Compromise,** 347
- **Great Depression,** 619–620, 622
- **Great Migration,** 613, *p613*
- **Great Plains,** 28, 441, 547–549, 555, *m26–27, p27, p546*
- **Great Plains cultural region,** 83, *m84*

- **Great Salt Lake,** 441
- **Great Seal of the United States,** 6–7, *p7*
- **Great Serpent Mound,** 60–61, *p60*
- **Green Mountain Boys,** 303
- **Greene, Nathanael,** 318
- **Greenland,** 111
- **Grenville, George,** 268–269, *p268*
- **grid,** 140
- **Guatemala,** 686, *m686*
- **Gutenberg, Johann,** 112

H

- **haciendas,** 234, 238, *p239*
- **Haiti,** 688, *m689*
- **Hale, Nathan,** 304
- **Hall, Prince,** 306, 310, *p310*
- **Hamilton, Alexander,** 333, 345, 353, 363–364, 368, *p333, 353, 364, 369*
- **Hancock, John,** 287, 297, 300, 353, *p297*
- **Harding, Warren G.,** R25
- **Harlem Renaissance,** 618
- **Harpers Ferry, Virginia,** 480
- **Harris, Mike,** 40–41, *p40*
- **Harrison, Benjamin,** R24
- **Harrison, William H.,** R23
- **Harvard University,** 217, *p217*
- **Hawaii,** 535, 579, R19
- **Hayes, Rutherford,** R23
- **Hays, Mary Ludwig,** 307, *p307*
- **headline,** 209
- **Hemingway, Ernest,** 618
- **hemisphere,** H13–H14
- **Hendrick,** 249
- **Henry, Patrick,** 270, 274–275, 282, 353, *p274*
- **Henry, Prince of Portugal,** 49, 113, *p49, 113*
- **Henry VIII, King of England,** 169
- **Hessians,** 304
- **Hiawatha,** 49, 76–77, *p49, 76*
- **hijack,** 662
- **Hiroshima, Japan,** 629
- **Hispanics,** 8, *c8*
- **Hispaniola,** 150
- **Hitler, Adolf,** 625, *p625*
- **Holocaust,** 628
- **Homestead Act,** 547, 549
- **homesteaders,** 547–548
- **Hooker, Thomas,** 178, *c181*
- **Hoover, Herbert,** R25
- **Hoovervilles,** 619
- **Hopi,** 63, 88–89, *p90, 91*
- **House of Burgesses,** 162, 270, 274
- **House of Representatives, U.S.,** 347. *See also* Congress
- **Houston, Sam,** 432–433
- **Houston, Texas,** 28
- **Hudson, Henry,** 165–166, *p165*
- **Hudson River,** 165
- **Huerta, Dolores,** 597, 648–649, *p597, 649*
- **Hughes, Langston,** 618, *p618*
- **Hull House,** 571, *p571*
- **human-environment interaction (as geographical theme),** H10–H11, 62
- **Hurston, Zora Neale,** 618
- **Hussein, Saddam,** 660, 664
- **Hutchinson, Anne,** 129, 178, 184–185, *p129, 185*
- **hydrogen bomb,** 641

I

- **"I, Too, Am America"** 618
- **Ice Age,** 55, 57
- **Idaho,** R19
- **ideals,** 7, 11, 17, 663
- **Illinois,** 376, R19
- **immigrants**
  - Africans, 10, *c570*
  - Asian, 10, 569, *c570, p10*
  - Chinese, 540, *p540*
  - European, 10, 535, 549, 569, *c570, p10, 535*
  - Irish, 569
  - Japanese, 552, 553
  - Jewish, 568–569
  - Latin America, 10, *c570*
  - life of, 570–571
  - twentieth century, 570, *c570*
- **impeachment,** 519, 654, 661
- **import,** 20, *c20*
- **inauguration,** 363
- **Inca,** 69, 70, 145, *m68*
- **indentured servant,** 161
- **India,** 114
- **Indian Removal Act,** 405
- **Indian Territory,** 405
- **Indiana,** 376, R18
- **Indians.** *See* Native Americans
- **indigo,** 205, 213, 215
- **Industrial Revolution,** 401, 409
- **industry,** 564, 566
- **inflation,** 340
- **information, gathering and reporting,** 356–357
- **inset map,** H18
- **interdependence,** 30
- **intermediate directions,** H17
- **Internet,** H7, 86–87, 661
- **interstate highway,** 512
- **interview,** H8
- **Intolerable Acts,** 280
- **Inuit,** 64
- **inventions,** *See also* Technology 21, 23, 31, 410, 563–566, *c565*
- **Iowa,** R18
- **Iqaluit, Canada,** 681, *p681*
- **Iraq,** 660, 664
- **Ireland,** 569, *m569*
- **Irish potato famine,** 569
- **Iron Curtain,** 638, *m638*
- **Iroquois,** 77–80, 249–250
- **Iroquois League,** 77, 80, 249
- **Iroquois Trail,** 77
- **irrigation,** 28, *p28*
- **Isabella, Queen of Spain,** 135
- **Islam,** 107
- **Israel,** 655
- **isthmus,** 604
- **Italy,** 599, 625
- **Iwo Jima,** 92, *p632*

J

- **Jackson, Andrew,** 384, 396, 403–405, 407, 431, 433, R23, *p396, 404, 407*
- **Jackson, Thomas "Stonewall,"** 495
- **Jamaica,** 688, *m689*
- **James I, King of England,** 159, 161
- **Jamestown, Virginia,** 131, 159–161, 163, *m159, p161*
- **Japan,** 599, 625, 626, 629
- **Japanese Americans,** 627
- **Jay, John,** 353
- **Jefferson, Thomas,** 6, 263, 298–299, 301, 351, 353, 363–364, 368–376, 381, 402, R22, *p263, 299, 301, 364, 369*
- **Jews,** 218, 625, 628, *c8*
- **Jim Crow laws,** 461, 520

Index

Santa Fe, New Mexico, 234–235
Santa Fe Trail, 440, *m440*
Santa Maria, 135, 139, *p139*
Saratoga, Battle of, 305–306, *m305*
Saratoga, New York, 305
Savannah, Georgia, 510
scales, map, H18, 244–245, *m244, 245*
scarcity, 22
Schlafly, Phyllis, 647
Scott, Dred, 480
Scott, Winfield, 494
sea level, 32
search engine, H7, 87
Seattle, Washington, 552
secede, 485
Second Continental Congress, 265, 296–298, 300, 339, *p339*
Second Great Awakening, 417. *See also* Great Awakening
sectionalism, 465
segregation, 520, 642–644, 646
Seguin, Juan, 432, 450–451
self-government, 162, 170, 269
self-sufficient, 212–213
Seminole, 403, 405
Senate, U.S., 347. *See also* Congress
Seneca Falls Convention, 419, 612
Seneca Falls, New York, 419
separation of powers, 348, *c349*
Separatists, 169
sequence, 109, 130–131, 138, 145, 150, 243, 308, 534–535, 541, 552, 557, 558, 567, 586
Sequoyah, 405
serfs, 500, *p500*
Serra, Junipero, 197, 236–237, 271, *p197, 237*
settlement house, 571
Seward, William, 579
shaman, 96–97
Shangdu, China, 103
sharecropping, 520
Shawnee, 381, 385
Shays, Daniel, 341
Shays' Rebellion, 335, 341
Sherman Antitrust Act, 603
Sherman, Roger, 298
Sherman, William Tecumseh, 510
Shima, George, 533, 552–553, *p533, 553*
ship-building, 19, *p19*
Silk Road, 102–103, 113, 135, *m103*
Sinclair, Upton, 603
Sitting Bull, 554–556, *p554*
Slater, Samuel, 409
slave codes, 471
slave states, 477, *m479*
slave trade, 113, 206–207, *m206*
slavery
American Revolution and, 306, 310
Aztec, 68–69
colonial, 206–207, 213, 224–227, *c225*
Compromise of 1850 and, 478
Constitution and, 347
definition of, 68
Emancipation Proclamation and, 500
end of, 10, 516–521
Missouri Compromise and, 477
Native Americans and, 149–151, 235
Northwest Territory and, 342
protests against, 367, 418, 421–423, 467
resisting, 227, 470–475
Southern states and, 466–467
Spanish colonies and, 150
trade and, 113, 206–207
West Africa and, 206–207
smallpox, 136, 143
small-scale map, 244–245, *m244*
Smith, John, 128, 159–160, 163, 170, *p128, 160, 163, c181*
Smith, Joseph, 441, *p441*
Smith, Venture, 224–225
Social Security Act, 620, 622
society, 148
sodbusters, 547
Songhai, 108, *m107*
songs
"Red River Valley," 588–589
"Star-Spangled Banner, The," 388–389
"When Johnny Comes Marching Home," 524–525
"Yankee Doodle," 324–325
"You're a Grand Old Flag," 670–671
Sons of Liberty, 271, 279
source, credibility of, 584–585
South Africa, 661, *m661*
South America, countries of, 690–691, *c690, m691*
South Carolina, 180, 213, 227, 485, R20, *c181*
South Dakota, R20
South Korea, 639
South Vietnam, 652–653, *m652*
Southampton County, Virginia, 472
Southeast region, 25–27, *m27*
Southern Colonies, 177, 180, 199, 205, 226, *m177, c181*
Southern Hemisphere, H13
Southwest Desert cultural region, 89, *m89*
Southwest region, 25–27, 238–239, *m26–27*
Soviet Union, 599, 626, 628, 635, 636–641, 651–655, 659. *See also* Russia
space race, 651
Spain
colonies of, 231–236, 238–239
England and, 157–158
exploration and, 131, 135, 137–138, 146–147, *m137, 147*
Florida and, 403
in the Southwest, 238–239
New Spain and, 144–145, 148–150
Spanish-American War and, 580–582
Spanish-American War, 580–582
Spanish Armada, 158, *p158*
specialization, 20, 617
specialize, 67
speech, freedom of, 7, 16
Sputnik, 651, *p651*
Squanto, 129, 171, *p129*
stage coach, 538–539, *p538*
Stalin, Joseph, 626, 637
Stamp Act, 265, 269, 274
Standard Oil Company, 566, 603
standard time, 542
Stanton, Elizabeth Cady, 397, 416, 419, 612, *p397, 418, 421*
"Star-Spangled Banner, The," 383, 388–389

State, Department of, 363
states' rights, 477, 485, 487
Statue of Liberty, 561, *p531*
steam engine, 411–412
steel industry, 564–565
stock, 159
stock market, 619
Stono Rebellion, 227
Stowe, Harriet Beecher, 425, 480, *p425*
Strauss, Levi, 397, 444, *p397, 444*
strike, 573
submarines, 496
suffrage, 404, 616
summarize, 50–51, 57, 64, 69, 72, 80, 98, 104, 118, 176, 441, 598–599, 605, 614, 622, 630, 632, 641, 655, 670
supply, 19
Supreme Court, U.S., 348, 642–643, 647, *c349, p647*
surplus, 67
survey, H8
Sutter, John, 443
Sutter's Mill, 442–443
sweatshop, 572
symbol, map, H16

T

Taft, William H., R24
Taino, 135–136
Taj Mahal, 235, *p235*
Taney, Roger, 480
Tarbell, Ida, 603
tariff, 272, 465
taxes
Articles of Confederation and, 339–340
British colonies and, 268–270, 272
in ancient Ghana, 107
Taylor, Zachary, 434, R22, *p434*
Tea Act, 279
technology, *See also* inventions
Civil War, 496, 499
definition of, 409
farming, 548, 551
twenty-first century, 661, 666–667
World War I, 609, 615
Tecumseh, 333, 381, 385, *p333, 385*
Tejanos, 432
telegraph, 514–515, 539, *p514, 515*
telephone, 563, 565, *p562, 565*
temperance, 417
tenement, 571, *p571*
Tennessee, 376, R20
Tennessee Valley Authority (TVA), 621
Tenochtitlan, 68, 71, 142–144, *p69*
tepee, 83, *p83*
territories, 581, *m581*
terrorism, 662–665
terrorists, 662–664
Texas, 147, 238, 399, 430, 432–435, 485, 621, R20, *p25, 238, 433, m171*
Texas Revolution, 432
Thanksgiving, 155, 168, 171, *m171, p125–126*
theory, 55
Thirteenth Amendment, 517, *c519*
Three-Fifths Compromise, 347
Timbuktu, 107–108
time lines, parallel, 116–117, *c116–117*
time zone, 542
time zone maps, reading, H20, 542–543, *m542*
Tippecanoe, Battle of, 381, *p381*
title, map, H16
"To Build a Fire," 579
tobacco, 161, *c161*
Tom Thumb, 412–413, *p412*
Tomochichi, 180, *p180*
total war, 510
totem pole, 95, *p95*
Touro Synagogue, 218, *p218*
town common, 212
towns, colonial, 212, *p212*
Townshend Acts, 272, 278
trade
Africa and, 106–108, *m107*
China and, 102–104
European, 115
Italy and, 112
Portugal and, 113–114
slave, 113, 206–207
triangular, 206, *m206*
world, 20, *c20*
trading posts, 241
Trail of Tears, 406, *m405, p406*
trails, Western, 438–441, *m440*
traitor, 300, 305
transcontinental railroad, 539–541, 547, *m540*
Travis, William, 432
travois, 83–84, *p84*
treason, 275
Treasury, Department of, 363
Treaty of Guadalupe Hidalgo, 435–436
Treaty of Paris, 319, 342
Treaty of Versailles, 611
Trenton, New Jersey, 304
Triangle Shirtwaist Company, 572
triangular trade, 206, *m206*
tribe, 77
tributary, 242
tribute, 68
Truman, Harry S., 629, 638–639, 643, R25, *p638*
Truth, Sojourner, 397, 418–419, 421, 519, *p397, 421*
Tubman, Harriet, 459, 473, 475, *p459, 475*
Turkey, 609
Turner, Nat, 472
Tyler, John, R23
typewriter, 565, *p565*

U

Uncle Tom's Cabin, 480, *p480*
Underground Railroad, 473, 475, *m473*
unemployment, 619
union, 485, 493–495, 649, *m486, c493*
United Nations (UN), 637, 639, 660
United States, maps of the, *mH16, H17, H20, R10–R11, R12–R13, R14–R15*
Utah, 441, R20

V

Valley Forge, Pennsylvania, 308, 314–315, *p314, 315*
Valley of Mexico, 68
Values. *See* ideals
Van Buren, Martin, R23
Vancouver Island, 95
Vaqueros, 436
Venice, Italy, 103, 112
Vermont, 376, R20
Verrazano, Giovanni da, 166
Versailles, France, 611
Vespucci, Amerigo, 137–139, *p137*
Veterans Day, 611
veto, 348
Vicksburg, Battle of, 509

Index

Vicksburg, Mississippi, 509
Vietnam, 652–653, *m652*
Vietnam Veterans Memorial, 653, *p653*
Vietnam War, 599, 652–653
Vikings, 110–111
Vinland, 111
Virginia, 159–163, 169, 497, R21, *c181*
Virginia, 496
Virginia Company, 159, 162–163, 169
Virginia Plan, 346
Virginia Statute of Religious Freedom, 351
Von Steuben, Friedrich, 314–315, *p314*
vote, right to, 404
African Americans and, 466, 517–520, 646
18-year olds and, 16
women and, 17, 612
Voting Rights Act of 1965, 646

W

wagon train, 439, *p439*
Walker, David, 467
Walker, Madam C. J., 21, *p21*
Wampanoag, 170–171, 184, 247
wampum, 79, *p79*
War Hawks, 382
War of 1812, 335, 382–385
Warren, Mercy Otis, 272, 307, 369, *p272, 369*
Washington, Booker T., 613
Washington, D.C., 335, 365–366, 383, 495, 517, 646, 662, *m365*
Washington, George, 217, 246–249, 262, 281, 283, 296–297, 303–304, 307–309, 315, 318–319, 335, 340, 343, 344–345, 355, 362–365, 368, R22, *p248, 249, 262, 283, 296, 304, 320, 330–331, 349, 363, 364*
Washington, Martha, 307, *p307*
Washington State, R21
Watergate scandal, 654
weather, 29
Web site, 86–87
Webster, Daniel, 478
Wells-Barnett, Ida, 596, 614, *p596, 614*
West Africa, 206, 226, *m226*
West Indies, 135–136, 206–207
West region, 25–26, *m26*
West Virginia, R21
Western Hemisphere, H14, *mR6, R7*
Wheatley, Phillis, 263, 307, 309, *p263, 309*
"When Johnny Comes Marching Home," 524–525
White House, 366
White, John, 156–157
Whitefield, George, 218, *p218*
Whitman, Marcus, 439
Whitman, Narcissa, 439
Whitney, Eli, 410
Wilderness Road, 372
Williams, Jody, 504–505, *p504*
Williams, Roger, 178, 184–185, *p184, c181*
Williamsburg, Virginia, 217, 270
Wilson, Luzena Stanley, 444
Wilson, Woodrow, 610–611, R24
Winthrop, John, 172, *c181*
Wisconsin, R21
women
in American Revolution, 307
in Civil War, 502
employment of, 567, 572, 612, 627
Industrial Revolution and, 409
rights of, 419, 519, 612, 647
salaries of, *c647*
in World War I, 612
in World War II, 627, *p627*
World Trade Center, 662–663, 665, *p662*
World War I, 599, 608–613, 615, *p609, 610, 611, 615*
World War II, 92, 599, 624–630, *p599, 625, 628, 630, m629*
Wright, Orville, 565, 617
Wright, Wilbur, 565, 617
Wyoming, R21

Y

Yamacraw, 180
"Yankee Doodle," 324–325
yellow fever, 604
Yellowstone National Park, 37, *p37*
York, 374
Yorktown, Battle of, 318
Yorktown, Virginia, 318
Young, Brigham, 441
"You're a Grand Old Flag," 670–671

Z

Zenger, John Peter, 196, 219, 222, *p196, 219*
Zheng He, 48, 104–105, *p48, 105*

Credits

TEXT: **Dorling Kindersley (DK)** is an international publishing company specializing in the creation of high quality reference content for books, CD-ROMs, online and video. The hallmark of DK content is its unique combination of educational value and strong visual style. This combination allows DK to deliver appealing, accessible and engaging educational content that delights children, parents and teachers around the world. Scott Foresman is delighted to have been able to use selected extracts of DK content within this Social Studies program.

70–71 from Eyewitness: Aztec, Inca & Maya by Elizabeth Baquedano. Copyright ©2000 by Dorling Kindersley Limited.

139 from Eyewitness: Explorer by Rupert Matthews. Copyright ©2000 by Dorling Kindersley Limited.

238–239 from Eyewitness: Wild West by Stuart Murray. Copyright ©2001 by Dorling Kindersley Limited.

312–313 from The Visual Dictionary of Military Uniforms. Copyright ©1992 by Dorling Kindersley Limited.

377 from Eyewitness: Explorer by Rupert Mattews. Copyright ©2000 by Dorling Kindersley Limited.

514–515 from The Visual Dictionary of the Civil War by John Stanchak. Copyright ©2000 by Dorling Kindersley Limited.

Excerpts from *Juan Seguin –A Hero of Texas by Rita Kerr.* Copyright © 1985 by Rita Kerr. Used by permission of Eakin Press. 432

Excerpt from *The Log of Christopher Columbus,* translated by Robert H. Fuson. Copyright © 1987 by Robert H. Fuson. Reprinted by permission. 135

Excerpt from *Friends of the Everglades—Marjory Stoneman Douglas* by Tricia Andryszewski. Reprinted by permission of The Millbrook Press. 37

Excerpts from ballad in *The English Literature of America 1500-1800* edited by Myra Jehlen and Michael Warner. Copyright © 1997 by Routledge. Reprinted by permission. 188–189

"I, Too" from *The Collected Poems of Langston Hughes* by Langston Hughes, copyright © 1994 by the Estate of Langston Hughes. Used by permission of Alfred A. Knopf, a division of Random House, Inc. 618

Excerpt from "I Have a Dream" speech by Martin Luther King, Jr. Reprinted by permission. 646

Song "Let There Be Peace on Earth" words and music by Sy Miller and Jill Jackson. Used by permission of Jan-Lee Music.

Excerpt from *When China Rules the Seas, The Treasure Fleet of The Dragon Throne 1405-1433* by Louise Levathes. Copyright © 1994 by Louise E. Levathes. Reprinted by permission. 105

Excerpts from *Native American Animal Stories* told by Joseph Bruchac. Copyright © 1992 by Joseph Bruchac. Used by permission of Fulcrum Publishing. 120–121

"Did people work hard in colonial days?" from *If You Lived in Colonial Times* . . . by Ann McGovern. Copyright © 1964 by Ann McGovern. Reprinted by permission of the author. 254–255

Excerpt from Island. *Poetry and History of Chinese Immigrants on Angel Island* by Him M. Lai, Genny Lim and Judy Yung. Reprinted by permission. 569

Fair Use

From *The March on Washington Address* by Martin Luther King, Jr. Reprinted by arrangement with the Estate of Martin Luther King, Jr. c/o Writers House as agent for the proprietor. Copyright Martin Luther King 1963, copyright renewed 1991 Coretta Scott King.

From "George Percy's Relation." Copyright © 1997, 2000 by The Association for the Preservation of Virginia Antiquities. Found on http://www.apva.org/findingpercy.html.

From *Smithsonian Visual Timeline of Inventions* by Richard Platt. New York, New York: Dorling Kindersley, 1994.

From *The Annals of America, Vol. 1, Encyclopedia Britannica,* pages 97, 98, 115, and 329.

From *In Defense of the Indians,* translated and edited by Stafford Poole, C.M. Dekalb Illinois: Northern Illinois University Press.

From *History of the Indies,* translated and edited by Andree Collard. New York, New York: Harper & Row, 1971.

From *Witnessing America,* compiled and edited by Noel Rae. New York, New York: First published in 1996 by Penguin Reference, an imprint of Penguin Books, USA.

From *Edison His Life and Inventions,* by Frank Lewis Dyer, et al. New York, New York: Harper Brothers, 1929.

From *The English Literatures of America,* by Frank Lewis Dyer and Thomas Commerford Martin. New York, New York: Routledge, 1997

From George Washington Carver. Tuskegee Institute National Historical Site, http://www.nps.vov/bowa/tuskin.html.

From *Madam C.J. Walker* by A'Lelia Perry Bundles. Pittsburgh, Pennsylvania: Chelsea House Publishers, a division of Main Line Book Co., 1991.

From *A History of English Speaking Peoples,* Volume 2, The New World. New York, New York: Dodd, Mead & Company, Inc.

From *In Their Own Words THE COLONIZERS,* collected and edited by T.J. Stiles, pages 68 & 91. New York, New York, The Berkley Publishing Group, a member of Penguin Putnam, Inc.

From *Settlements to Society,* 1607-1763, edited by Jack P. Greene. New York, New York: W.W. Norton & Company, Inc.

From *Modern History Sourcebook: William Bradford: from History of Plymouth Plantation, c1650.* http://www.fordham.edu/halsall/mod/1650bradford.html.

From *The Alleged Gov. Bradford First Thanksgiving Proclamation, Who Attended the 1621 "First Thanksgiving."* http://www.plimoth.org/library/Thanksgiving/thnksref.html.

From *Of Plymouth PLANTATION 1620-1647,* pages 85, 87 and 88, by William Bradford. New York, New York: Random House, Inc. 1981.

From *William Penn* by Rebecca Stefoff. Pittsburgh, Pennsylvania: Chelsea House Publishers, a division of Main Line Book Co., 1998.

From *Women's Rights on Trial* by Elizabeth Frost-Knappman and Kathryn Cullen-DuPont. Detroit, MI: Gale Research, 1997.

From *Time-Life Books 1930-1940,* Volume IV by the editors of Time-Life Books. Alexandria, VA: Time Life, Inc., 1969.

From *Time-Life Books 1940-1950,* Volume V by the editors of Time-Life Books, Alexandria, VA: Time Life, Inc., 1969.

From *The Report from the Dachau Liberation,* 1st Lt. William Cowling. Found on http://remember.org/witness/cowling.html.

From *Stride Toward Freedom, The Montgomery Story* by Martin Luther King, Jr. New York, New York: Harper&Row Publishers.

From *The Autobiography of Malcolm X* with the assistance of Alex Haley, introduction by M.S. Handler, epilogue by Alex Haley. New York, New York: Grove Press, Inc.

From *American Women of Achievement: Sandra Day O'Connor* by Peter Huber. New York, New York: Chelsea House Publishers, 1990.

From *Dolores Huerta Biography.* Found on http://www.ufw.org/ufw/dh.htm.

From *CNN Cold War, Interviews: George Bush.* Found on http://cnn.net/SPECIALS/cold.war/episodes/23/interviews/bush.

From *The Autobiography of Martin Luther King, Jr.,* edited by Clayborne Carson. New York, New York: Warner Books, 1998.

From *Life in a Japan American Internment Camp* by Diane Yancey. San Diego, CA: Lucent Books, 1998.

From *The Quotable Woman: Volume One* compiled and edited by Elaine Partnow. Los Angeles, CA: Pinnacle Books, Inc., 1980.

From *"Back to Hell"* by Samuel Cranston Benson. Chicago, IL: A.C. McClurg & Company, 1918.

From *Out of the Sweatshop: The Struggle for Industrial Democracy.* New York, New York: Quadrangle/New Times Book Company, 1977.

From *The Globe and Mail,* Friday, March 7, 1997. Found on http://www.freethe children.org/info/mediacanada08.htm.

From *Florence Kelley Speaks Out on Child Labor and Woman Suffrage,* Philadelphia, PA, July 22, 1905 found on http://www.pbs.org/greatspeeches/timeline/f_kelley_s.html.

From *The West: An Illustrated History* by Geoffrey C. Ward. The West Book Project, 1996.

From *Bury My Heart at Wounded Knee: An Indian History of the American West* by Dee Brown. New York, New York: Holt, Rinehart & Winston, 1971

From *The Importance of Alexander Graham Bell* by Robyn M. Weaver. San Diego, CA: Lucent Books, 2000.

From *The Promised Land* by Mary Antin, 1881-1949. New York, New York: Arno Press, A New York Times Co., 1980.

From *Northland Stories* by Jack London. New York, New York: Penguin Books, 1997.

From *The Spirit of Seventy-Six: The Story of the American Revolution* as told by the Participants edited by Henry Steele Commager and Richard B. Norris. New York, New York: Da Capo Press, 1995.

From *PATRIOTS The Men Who Started the American Revolution* by A.J. Langguth. New York, New York: Simon & Schuster, 1989.

From *Voyages of Marquette in The Jesuit Relations,* 59 by Jacques Marquette. University Microfilms, Inc., 1966.

From *The Life and Times of Fray Junipero Serra, O.F.M. or The Man Who Never Turned Back (1713-1784),* a biography by Maynard J. Geiger, O.F.M., Ph.D. VOLUME 1. Washington, DC: Academy of American Franciscan History, 1959.

Quote by Mohandas Gandhi, January 4, 1932 from *Messages to the United States* found on http://www.mkgandhi.org/letters/index.htm.

Quote by Nelson Mandela, March 27, 1993 from *Keynote Address by Nelson Mandela, President of the African National Congress,* to the conference of the broad patriotic front found on http://www.anc.org.za/ancdocs/history/mandela/1993/sp930327.html.

Quote by Joan of Arc, 1429, found on http://dc/smu.edu/ijasdelteil.html.

Quote by Venture Smith from Venture Smith's Narrative found on http://www.pbs.org/wgbh/aia/part2/2h5t.html.

From *The Courage to Stand Alone, Letters from Prison and Other Writings* by Wei Jingsheng. New York, New York: Viking Penguin, a division of Penguin Books USA Inc., 1997

From *A Brief Narrative of the Cage and Trial of John Peter Zenger* by James Alexander. Cambridge, Massachusetts: Harvard University Press, 1972.

From *Equiano's Travels, The Interesting Narrative of The Life of Olaudah Equiano or Gustavus Vassa the African* abridged and edited by Paul Edwards. New York, New York: Frederick A. Prager, Inc., 1966.

From *The Encyclopedia of Native America* by Trudy Griffin-Pierce.

Quote by Nadine Gordimer from *"Censorship and its Aftermath,"* address, 1990, found on http://informatics.buffalo.edu/faculty/ellison/quotes/ifquotesg.html

"Thomas Jefferson Survives": Susan Boylston Adams Clark to Abigail Louisa Smith Adams Johnson, July 9, 1826, A.B. Johnson Papers, MHS.

From *Cherokee Legends and the Trail of Tears* adapted by Thomas Bryan Underwood. Cherokee, NC: Cherokee Publications.

From *The Shaping of America* by Richard O. Curry, John G. Sproat, Kenyon C. Cramer. New York, New York: Holt, Rinehart and Winston.

From *Frederick Douglass, Selected Speeches and Writings* edited by Philip S. Foner, abridged and adapted by Yuval Taylor. Chicago, IL: Laurence Hill Books, 1999.

From *Narrative of the Life of Frederick Douglass, An American Slave,* written by Himself edited with an introduction by David W. Blight. Boston, MA: Bedford Books of St. Martin's Press, 1993.

From TEXAS *From the Frontier to Spindletop* by James L. Haley. New York, NY: St. Martin's Press, 1985.

From *STEPHEN F. AUSTIN, Empresario of Texas* by Gregg Cantrell. New Haven, CT: Yale University Press.

From *STEPHEN F. AUSTIN, Founder of Texas, 1793-1836* by Eugene C. Barker. Dallas, TX: Cokesbury Press, 1925.

From *The Gold Rush* by Liza Ketchum. The West Project, Inc., 1996.

From *Harriet Tubman, Conductor on the Underground Railroad* by Ann Petry. New York, NY: HarperCollins Publisher, Inc, 1996.

From *The Oxford History of the American People, Volume Two, 1789 Through Reconstruction* by Samuel Eliot Morison. New York, NY: Meridian, an imprint of Dutton Signet, a division of Penguin Books USA Inc., 1994.

From *The Civil War, A Narrative* by Shelby Foote. New York, NY: Random House, 1994.

Quote by Jody Williams from *Jody Williams: The woman who waged war on land minds* found on http://www.cnn.com/SPECIALS/1997/nobel.prize/stories/williams.profile/.

From *Uncle Tom's Cabin or Life Among the Lowly* by Harriet Beecher Stowe. New York, NY: Signet Classic , an imprint of New American Library, a division of Penguin Putnam, Inc., 1998.

From *Nobel Lecture* by Jody Williams found on www.icbl.org/resources/jodynobel.html.

From *The Negro People in the United States* edited by Herbert Aptheker. New York, NY: Citadel Press, Inc., 1969.

From *Cannibals All!, or Slaves Without Masters* by George Fitzhugh found on http://docsouth.unc.edu/fitzhughcan/fitcan.html.

From *The Underground Railroad* by William Still. Chicago, IL: Johnson Publishing Company, Inc., 1970.

MAPS:

MapQuest.com, Inc.

ILLUSTRATIONS:

114 Mike Reagan
120 Marcela Cabrera
136 Albert Lorenz
159 John Sandford
163, 188, 189, 310, 311 Troy Howell
184, 185 Gregory M. Dearth
212 Robert LoGrippo
230 Guy Porfirio
274, 275 Stephen Snider
278 Barbara Emmons
365 John Sandford
367, 548 Troy Howell
388 Domenick D'Andrea
412 Kate Thomssen
417 Robert Van Nutt
450 Edward Martinez
507 Barbara Emmons
577 David Cunningham
588, 589 Shelly Hehenberger
606 Tom Herzberg

PHOTOGRAPHS:

Every effort has been made to secure permission and provide appropriate credit for photographic material. The publisher deeply regrets any omission and pledges to correct errors called to their attention in subsequent editions.

Unless otherwise acknowledged, all photographs are the property of Scott Foresman, a division of Pearson Education.

Photo locators are denoted as follows: Top (T), Center (C), Bottom (B), Left (L), Right (R), Background (Bkgd).

Cover: ©Mitchell Funk/Getty Images, Steve Allen
Endsheets: (R) ©Mitchell Funk/Getty Images, (L) Steve Allen
Front Matter:
iii Superstock iv David David Gallery, Philadelphia/Superstock v ©Bettmann/Corbis vi The Granger Collection vii Photo from the collection of the Lexington, Massachusetts Historical Society viii The Granger Collection ix The Granger Collection x The Granger Collection xi From the Original painting by Mort Künstler, "First View of the Lady" ©1986 Mort Künstler, Inc. xii Identikal/Artville H4 Colonial Williamsburg Foundation H5 Colonial Williamsburg Foundation H6 (BR), (BC) ©Dave Bartruff/Corbis, (Bkgd) Joel Sartore/Grant Heilman Photography H7 (BR) ©Phil Schermeister/Corbis, (L) Joel Sartore/Grant Heilman Photography H8 Earth Imaging/Getty Images H15 Michael Newman/PhotoEdit H19 PhotoDisc
Overview:
1, 2, 3 SuperStock 5 PhotoDisc 6 Historical Society of Pennsylvania 8 (TL) ©Joseph Sohm; ChromoSohm Inc/Corbis 9 PhotoDisc 10 (R) Brown Brothers, (L) Courtesy National Archives of the United States (from The National Archives of the United States by Herman J. Viola, ©1984 Harry N. Abrams, Inc. New York) 13 Ramey/PhotoEdit 15 (B) ©Dennis Degnan/Corbis 16 (B) Bob Daemmrich Photography, (T) ©Bettmann/Corbis 19 New York Public Library Picture Collection 21 (BL) The Granger Collection, (T) Bettmann/Corbis, (BR) The Madam Walker Urban Life Center, photographed by William Russell/From the Walker Collection of A'Lelia Bundles 22 (LCL), (R), (CL), (RCR) PhotoDisc, (BC) ©Scott T. Baxter, PhotoDisc, (CR) ©Dave Buffington, PhotoDisc, (L) ©Bob Daemmrich/Image Works 23 (BR) Library of Congress/Corbis, (T) Hulton-Deutsch Collection/Corbis, (Bkgd) Douglas C. Jones/Edison National Historic Site/National Park Service/U.S. Department of the Interior 24 ©David Muench/Corbis 25 (BR) ©David Muench/Corbis, (BL)

Notes

Facing Fear: Helping Students Cope with Tragic Events

American Red Cross

Together, we can save a life

As much as we would like to protect our children, we cannot shield them from personal or community tragedies. We can, however, help them to be prepared for unforeseen dangerous events and to learn about facing and moving beyond their fears and related concerns.

Common Responses to Trauma and Disaster

Young people experience many common reactions after a trauma. These include reexperiencing the event (for example, flashbacks), avoidance and numbing of feelings, increased agitation, and changes in functioning. These reactions may be manifested in clingy behaviors, mood changes, increased anxieties, increased startle responses (for example, more jumpy with noises), physical complaints, and regressive behavior. Increased aggressive behaviors may also be seen. When the trauma or disaster is human-made, such as a terrorist event, young people may react with hurtful talk, behaviors, or play. All of these reactions are normal responses and will, in general, dissipate with time. However, should these persist or increase over time, a referral to a mental health professional might be considered. Similarly, should these reactions result in a danger to self or others, immediate action is warranted.

Issues of Safety, Security, and Trust

In the aftermath of terrorism or other tragic events, students can feel overwhelmed with concerns of safety, security, and trust. Worries about their own safety as well as the safety of those important in their lives are likely heightened. Although they have developed a sense of empathy and are concerned about others, their immediate needs for personal reassurance will take priority. They will need repeated reassurances about their safety and the safety of those around them. They may have concerns about the event reoccurring; this concern may be exacerbated by repeated exposure to media images. At times students may feel as if they are reexperiencing the event. They may have triggers for memories, such as noises, sights, or smells. These "flashbacks" may also occur without an obvious reminder. Reexperiencing can be very frightening for students this age. They may try (without success) to NOT think about the event. Their inability to block the thoughts may produce increased levels of stress. Although students will continue to process recent events, a return to a classroom routine is one of the best ways to reinforce a sense of security and safety.

Expressing Thoughts and Feelings

Young people seven to twelve years old have the ability to understand the permanence of loss from trauma. They may become preoccupied with details of it and want to talk about it continually. The questions and the details discussed are often disturbing to adults (for example, talk of gore and dismemberment). Such discussions are not meant to be uncaring or insensitive but rather are the way that many students attempt to make sense of a tragedy. Since their thinking is generally more mature than that of students under seven, their understanding of the disaster is more complete. They understand the irreversibility of death but may continue to ask questions about death and dying as they try to understand the repercussions of the event.

Students this age will attempt to create the "story" of the terrorist action or tragic event. Unfortunately, their attempts will contain misinformation as well as misperceptions. Unless addressed directly, the misunderstanding may be perpetuated and lead to increased levels of stress. Students are trying to make the story "fit" into their concept of the world around them. Questions related to the trauma may be equally repetitive. Teachers may answer students' questions only to have the same questions repeated within a few minutes. Having the same answer will increase the students' sense of security and help them process the trauma.

One result of a human-made tragedy may be intense feelings of anger and a sense of revenge. With an inaccurate understanding of events, these feelings may develop into hateful/hurtful talk or play. It may be directed toward classmates or groups of people. This behavior should be immediately addressed. Open discussions with these young students may improve their understanding of the event as well as reduce inappropriate direction of anger toward others.

Identifying Factors to Predict Students at Greatest Risk

Feelings accompanying the event may overwhelm elementary-aged students. In addition to the anger, they may also have feelings of guilt and intense sadness; nervousness is also seen. As they attempt to process these feelings, a change in school performance may be seen. Some students will have a drop in school performance as attention to and concentration on their work are diminished. They may not be able to grasp new concepts as easily as before the event, and grades may show a decline. Students may become more active in their behaviors as well as more impulsive and reckless. These behaviors often appear similar to attention deficit hyperactivity disorder and/or learning disabilities. Although either may be present, the impact of the event as a reason for the behavior changes should be considered. Students may develop problems in sleep and appetite after a traumatic event or disaster. These changes may contribute to a decrease in school performance.

It is important to note that some students may try to handle feelings of guilt and worry by an intense attention to schoolwork. These students may be worried about disappointing teachers and parents. Through their intense focus on school, they may be attempting to avoid activities and thoughts that are disturbing.

Students' anxiety and fear may be seen in an increased number of physical complaints. These may include headaches, stomachaches, feelings of nausea, or vague aches and pains. Expression of these emotions may also be seen in mood changes. *(continued on the following page)*

TR1

(continued from p. TR1)

Students may become more irritable and quarrelsome. They may become more aggressive at recess. Although some students may act out more, others may become more withdrawn and detached from activities and friends around them. They may be having an equally hard time processing the events, but because of their quietness, they are often overlooked as having any difficulties.

In the face of tragic events, students of this age will be seeking ways to help others. By finding positive avenues for expressing their concerns and need for involvement, initial negative reactions to the event may begin to diminish. Working to guide students in positive directions can be an important aspect of the healing process.

It is important to remember that all of these reactions are normal and, generally, will begin to diminish with time.

Moving Forward in Spite of Life-Affecting Events

Frightening events, such as the terrorist attacks in the United States on September 11, 2001, the Oklahoma City bombing in 1995, earthquakes, tornadoes, and hurricanes here and in other countries, massive transportation accidents, and war or armed conflict or other military action, impact us all. Events that are caused by human beings can be particularly frightening and raise unique concerns.

Terrorist actions and other violent acts are designed to instill fear in individuals and communities, if not countries. Because they happen without warning, there is no time to prepare. This unpredictability leaves us with a heightened sense of vulnerability and anxiety that the event could be repeated again, anywhere. With increased media coverage, even those not directly impacted can be significantly affected by an event. Images make us feel closer to the victims, and we may perceive ourselves as victims of the actions as well. The questions that arise from disasters of human design are difficult, if not impossible, to answer. We want answers to "Why?" and "How could they?" and are often left frustrated by the lack of satisfying responses. This frustration also gives rise to intense feelings of anger. The anger toward the perpetrators may be uncomfortable and difficult to express in productive ways. As adults struggle with reactions and feelings in the aftermath of a terrorist action or tragic event, young people are similarly searching for how to best handle their feelings. At all ages, they take cues from adults around them (parents, teachers, and community and national leaders).

Students need to know that their reactions to and feelings about such events are normal. They need to recognize that others feel very similarly. Most important, young people need to know that they will begin to feel better with time and that it is acceptable to enjoy friends, family, and activities. They need to know that there are things they can do to help themselves move forward in a positive way.

Activities to Help Students Address Fears

The following activities are designed to help you help your students address their fears and move beyond them.

- **What Happened**—Have students tell what they remember about the trauma/ disaster. Validate their experiences, but be sure to correct any misperceptions and misunderstandings.

- **Searching for a Sense of Safety**—Review with students school and family emergency procedures for natural or human-made disasters. Have students list people to contact in an emergency as well as identifying a "buddy family" that will be available to check on their safety.

- **Dealing with Feelings**—Make a chart with *Uncomfortable Feelings* and *What We Can Do About Them* as heads. List feelings students may have following a traumatic event. Then work together to come up with things to do to feel better (examples may include talking to adults, writing letters, helping in the relief effort, relaxation exercises, activities with friends, and watching a funny movie together).

- **Redirecting Thoughts**—Have students make an activity wheel by writing or drawing an activity that they enjoy doing (playing with a pet, singing a song, reading a book, riding a bike, shooting baskets, kicking soccer balls, stringing beads, watching a favorite show or video). Show them how to put a paper arrow and a paper fastener through the middle of the wheel loosely enough to spin the arrow. Suggest that when an unwanted thought or picture pops into their mind, they can spin to choose an activity to help get rid of the thought or picture.

- **Looking Ahead and Setting Goals**—Help students identify and write short-range goals as well as long-range ones. Discuss setting realistic goals and how they can be achieved. Also discuss ways of keeping track of the goals and the progress toward meeting them, reminding students of the importance of sharing thoughts and feelings while working toward the goals.

Books for Young Readers

Molly's Pilgrim Cohen, Barbara. Illus. by Daniel M. Duffy. Beech Tree Books, 1998. A recent Jewish Russian immigrant teaches her third-grade class about all kinds of pilgrims.

Number the Stars Lowry, Lois. Laureleaf, 1998. In 1943, Jews in Denmark are hidden and smuggled to safety in Sweden.

Heroes Mochizuki, Ken. Illus. by Dom Lee. Lee and Low Books, 1997. A Japanese American child, treated as an outsider by classmates during the Vietnam War, begs his father and uncle to tell how they fought in the U.S. Army during World War II.

The Tenth Good Thing About Barney Viorst, Judith. Illus. by Eric Blegvad. Aladdin, 1976. After the death of a pet cat, a young child tries to think of ten good things about him.

Jumping into Nothing Willner-Pardo, Gina. Illus. by Heidi Chang. Houghton Mifflin, 1999. Sophie devises a plan to overcome her fear of jumping off the high dive.

 American Red Cross Information on American Red Cross *Facing Fear: Helping Young People Deal with Terrorism and Tragic Events*

The American Red Cross *Facing Fear* curriculum contains lesson plans for teachers and includes hands-on or interactive activities for the classroom that will help students and their families prepare for disastrous situations and equip them with tools to sort out their feelings and fears.

For further information or to obtain copies of the *Facing Fear* curriculum materials, or the curriculum materials that focus on natural disaster preparedness, called *Masters of Disaster*™, contact your local American Red Cross chapter. Visit **http://www.redcross.org** to find your nearest Red Cross chapter, and visit **www.redcross.org/disaster/masters** for specific information on the curriculum. American Red Cross products are available exclusively from local Red Cross chapters in the United States.

With permission, parts above were adapted from Healing After Trauma Skills, *Robin H. Gurwitch and Anne K. Messenbaugh, University of Oklahoma Health Sciences Center.*

School to Home

Overview

Newsletter

Here are the main ideas that we are learning:

★ The United States has a varied population that shares many ideals.

★ The United States is a republic in which citizens elect their leaders.

★ The free enterprise system gives Americans many economic freedoms.

★ Dividing the United States into regions makes it easier to study our country's geography.

★ Americans rely on natural resources for food, energy, and building materials.

Fast Facts

• A proclamation by President Reagan in 1988 said that the United States claims the 12 nautical miles of sea that border the country.

• The total length of the Atlantic coastline of the United States is 2,069 miles. The total length of the Pacific coastline of the United States is 7,623 miles. The Gulf coast is 1,631 miles long and the Arctic coast is 1,060 miles long.

Family Activities

Talk Together

Ask your child to tell you what he or she knows about the geography, people, and natural resources of the United States. Discuss the differences that can be found among different parts of the country. Ask how your child thinks these differences help make the nation successful.

Learn Together

Help your child learn about the similarities and differences among different parts of the United States.

✔ With your child look at the map of the United States on pages 26 and 27 of the student text. Help your child locate your state on the map.

✔ Together make a list of things about your state that make it special.

✔ If you or your child are familiar with other states, talk about what makes your state different from them. Then discuss how all the states are alike.

Read Together

This Land Is Your Land, by Woody Guthrie (Little, Brown, ISBN 0-316-39215-4, 2000) NCSS Notable Book

Legends of Landforms: Native American Lore and the Geology of the Land, by Carole G. Vogel (Millbrook, ISBN 0-761-30272-7, 1999) NCSS Notable Book

The Kids' Business Book, by Arlene Erlbach (Lerner, ISBN, 0-822-52413-9, 1998) NCSS Notable Book

 Go online to find more activities at **www.sfsocialstudies.com**

Thank you for supporting your child's Social Studies education!

De la escuela al hogar

Panorama general   Boletín

Estas son las ideas principales que estamos estudiando:

★ Los Estados Unidos tienen una población diversa que comparte muchos ideales.

★ Los Estados Unidos son una república en la que los ciudadanos eligen a sus líderes.

★ El sistema de libre empresa da a los estadounidenses muchas libertades económicas.

★ Es más fácil estudiar la geografía del país si se dividen los Estados Unidos en regiones.

★ Los estadounidenses cuentan con recursos naturales para obtener alimentos, energía y materiales de construcción.

Datos curiosos

• Según una proclamación del Presidente Ronald Reagan de 1988, los Estados Unidos reclaman 12 millas náuticas de las aguas que rodean el país.

• La longitud total de la costa atlántica de los Estados Unidos es de 2,069 millas. La longitud de la costa del Pacífico es de 7,623 millas. La costa del Golfo tiene 1,631 millas de longitud, y la costa ártica tiene 1,060 millas.

Actividades en familia

Para conversar

Pida a su niño o niña que le diga lo que sabe sobre la geografía, habitantes y recursos naturales de los Estados Unidos. Hablen de las diferencias que se pueden encontrar entre las distintas partes del país. Pregunte a su niño o niña si cree que estas diferencias contribuyen a que el país sea exitoso.

Para aprender juntos

Ayude a su niño o niña a darse cuenta de las semejanzas y diferencias entre las distintas partes de los Estados Unidos.

✔ Fíjese con su niño o niña en el mapa de los Estados Unidos de las páginas 26 y 27 del libro de texto del estudiante. Ayude a su niño o niña a localizar en el mapa el estado en que viven.

✔ Preparen juntos una lista de las cosas que hacen a su estado especial.

✔ Si usted o su niño o niña está familiarizado con otros estados, comenten lo que hace que su estado sea diferente. Luego hablen de las semejanzas entre todos los estados.

Para leer juntos

Cuando Jessie cruzó el océano, por Amy Hest y P.J. Lynch (ilustrador), Lectorum, ISBN 1-880507-46-3, 1998) Kate Greenaway Medal

El paisaje, por Miguel Ángel Gibert y Lidia di Blasi (ilustradora), (Parramón, ISBN 84-342-1048-4, 1996)

Hijos de la primavera: Vida y palabras de los indios de América, por Daniel Goldin (Fondo de Cultura Económica, ISBN 968-16-4434-4, 1998)

 Para encontrar más actividades, visite **www.estudiosocialessf.com**

¡Gracias por apoyar la educación de sus hijos en Estudios sociales!

School to Home

Unit 1

Newsletter

Here are the main ideas that we are learning:

★ People reached the Americas from Asia and began to settle throughout North and South America.

★ Early cultures developed in different parts of North America.

★ Powerful civilizations developed and spread in Mexico, Central America, and South America.

★ People of the Eastern Woodlands developed a variety of cultures based on hunting and farming.

★ People of the Great Plains adapted their cultures to the introduction of the horse.

★ The need for water affected the cultures developed by the people of the Southwest.

★ People of the Northwest Coast developed cultures based on the region's rich natural resources.

★ The desire for trade led people of Asia and Europe to travel and build stronger ties to people of other continents.

★ Beginning more than one thousand years ago, rich trading kingdoms developed in West Africa.

★ In the 1400s European explorers developed sea routes to Africa and Asia.

Fast Facts

• Mammoths lived in North America before and during the Ice Age.

• Some mammoths were 14 feet high at the shoulders, with tusks up to 13 feet long.

Family Activities

Talk Together

Discuss with your child what it is like to visit an unknown place. What would make the visit exciting? How might it be scary? Have your child tell you how he or she thinks people from early cultures felt when they traveled to new lands.

Learn Together

Help your child learn about early cultures.

✔ Provide your child with index cards or pieces of paper.

✔ On separate cards or pieces of paper, have your child write facts about the different cultures he or she learned about in Unit 1.

✔ Ask your child to compare and contrast the cultures they learned about. Your child should use the facts he or she wrote to describe similarities and differences.

Read Together

Machu Picchu: The Story of the Amazing Inkas and Their City in the Clouds, by Elizabeth Mann (Mikaya Press, ISBN 0-965-04939-6, 2000)

The Navajo, by Raymond Bial (Marshall Cavendish, ISBN 0-761-40803-7, 1998) NCSS Notable Book

Around the World in a Hundred Years: From Henry the Navigator to Magellan, by Jean Fritz (Penguin Putnam Books for Young Readers, ISBN 0-698-11638-0, 1998) INA Teacher's Choice Award

 Go online to find more activities at **www.sfsocialstudies.com**

Thank you for supporting your child's Social Studies education!

De la escuela al hogar

Unidad 1

Boletín

Estas son las ideas principales que estamos estudiando:

★ Los primeros pobladores de las Américas llegaron de Asia y empezaron a establecerse en toda América del Norte y América del Sur.

★ Las primeras culturas se desarrollaron en distintas partes de América del Norte.

★ Hubo grandes y poderosas civilizaciones que se desarrollaron y esparcieron por México, América Central y América del Sur.

★ Los habitantes de las zonas boscosas del Este desarrollaron una variedad de culturas basadas en la caza y la agricultura.

★ Los pueblos de las Grandes Llanuras adaptaron sus culturas a la introducción del caballo.

★ La falta de agua afectó a las culturas desarrolladas por los habitantes del Suroeste.

★ Los habitantes de la costa del Noroeste desarrollaron culturas basadas en los ricos recursos naturales de la región.

★ El deseo de comerciar hizo que los habitantes de Asia y Europa viajaran y establecieran fuertes lazos con los habitantes de otros continentes.

★ Hace más de mil años, ricos reinos comerciales florecieron en África occidental.

★ En el siglo XV los exploradores europeos establecieron rutas marítimas hacia África y Asia.

Datos curiosos

- Los mamuts vivieron en América del Norte antes de y durante el periodo glacial.

- Algunos mamuts medían 14 pies de alto hasta el lomo y tenían colmillos de hasta 13 pies de largo.

Actividades en familia

Para conversar

Comente con su niño o niña sobre cómo debe ser ir a un lugar desconocido. ¿Qué haría la visita más interesante? ¿Qué podría causar miedo? Pida a su niño o niña que le diga lo que cree que sintieron los habitantes de las primeras culturas cuando viajaron a nuevas tierras.

Para aprender juntos

Ayude a su niño o niña a aprender cosas sobre estas primeras culturas.

✔ Proporcione fichas u hojas de papel a su niño o niña.

✔ Pídale que escriba datos sobre las distintas culturas que estudiaron en la Unidad 1 en fichas y hojas de papel separadas.

✔ Pida a su niño o niña que compare y contraste las culturas que estudiaron. Su niño o niña debe usar los datos que escribió para describir semejanzas y diferencias.

Para leer juntos

Ani y la anciana, por Miska Miles y Peter Parnall (ilustrador), (Lectorum, ISBN 9-6816374-8-8, 1992) Newbery Honor Book

Flecha al sol, por Gerald McDermot (Live Oak Media, ISBN 0-87499-411-X, 1997) Caldecott Medal

Los grandes descubrimientos, por Jean Favier (Fondo de Cultura Económica, ISBN 968-16-4015-2, 1995)

Para encontrar más actividades, visite **www.estudiosocialessf.com**

¡Gracias por apoyar la educación de sus hijos en Estudios sociales!

School to Home

Unit 2

Newsletter

Here are the main ideas that we are learning:

★ Columbus's voyages led to European settlement of the Americas and an exchange of people, animals, goods, and ways of life between East and West.

★ Spanish conquistadors established new colonies in North America and South America.

★ Spain gained great wealth from the settlement and growth of New Spain.

★ England founded Jamestown, the first permanent English settlement in North America, in 1607.

★ The search for a Northwest Passage led to the founding of French and Dutch colonies in North America.

★ In search of religious freedom, English settlers established colonies in New England.

★ By 1733 the English had established 13 colonies along the east coast of North America.

Fast Facts

• In colonial times, Jamestown sat on a peninsula. Today its site is located on an island. Over time water has separated the peninsula from the mainland.

Family Activities

Talk Together

Talk with your child about the hardships settlers faced when they arrived in new lands. What were the problems? How did they solve them? Ask your child what he or she thinks the settlers should have done differently.

Learn Together

Help your child learn about what it is like to move to a new land.

✔ Suppose that you and your child are moving to a new place. You, your child, and a few other people will be colonists in this land.

✔ Brainstorm with your child to decide what the place is like. Is the climate hot or cold? Is the soil good for farming? Is water plentiful?

✔ What would you take with you? Together make a list. Because space is limited, suppose that you are only allowed to take one large trunk.

Read Together

Columbus and the Renaissance, by Colin Hynson (Barrons Juveniles, ISBN 0-764-10530-2, 1998)

Where Do You Think You're Going, Christopher Columbus?, by Jean Fritz (Paper Star, ISBN 0-698-11580-5, 1997) ALA Notable Book

William Bradford: Rock of Plymouth, by Kieran Doherty (Millbrook, ISBN 0-761-31304-4) NCSS Notable Book

 Go online to find more activities at **www.sfsocialstudies.com**

Thank you for supporting your child's Social Studies education!

De la escuela al hogar

Unidad 2   Boletín

Estas son las ideas principales que estamos estudiando:

★ Los viajes de Colón culminaron en la colonización europea de las Américas y en un intercambio de personas, animales, bienes y estilos de vida entre el Oriente y el Occidente.

★ Los conquistadores españoles establecieron nuevas colonias en América del Norte y América del Sur.

★ España generó una gran fortuna como resultado de la colonización y el crecimiento de Nueva España.

★ Inglaterra fundó Jamestown, el primer asentamiento inglés permanente de América del Norte, en 1607.

★ La búsqueda del paso del noroeste trajo como consecuencia la fundación de colonias francesas y holandesas en América del Norte.

★ Los colonos ingleses establecieron colonias en Nueva Inglaterra en búsqueda de libertad de religión.

★ Para 1733 los ingleses habían establecido 13 colonias a lo largo de la costa este de América del Norte.

Datos curiosos

• En la época colonial, Jamestown quedaba en una península. Hoy es una isla. Con el tiempo el agua separó la península del continente.

Actividades en familia

Para conversar

Hable con su niño o niña sobre las dificultades que enfrentaron los colonos cuando llegaron a las nuevas tierras. ¿Qué problemas tenían? ¿Cómo los resolvieron? Pregunte a su niño o niña lo que cree que los colonos pudieron haber hecho diferente.

Para aprender juntos

Ayude a su niño o niña a aprender cómo se debe sentir mudarse a una nueva tierra.

✔ Suponga que usted y su niño o niña se mudan a un nuevo lugar. Usted, su niño o niña y algunos acompañantes serán los colonos de esta tierra.

✔ Imagínense cómo sería el lugar. ¿Cómo es el clima, frío o caliente? ¿Es el suelo bueno para la agricultura? ¿Hay agua en abundancia?

✔ ¿Qué llevarían consigo? Hagan una lista juntos. Supongan que el espacio es limitado y que sólo pueden llevar un baúl grande.

Para leer juntos

1492 El año del Nuevo Mundo, por Piero Ventura (Everest, ISBN 842-4158-784, 1992)

El oro de los sueños, por José María Merino (Alfaguara, ISBN 84-2044-794-3, 2001)

 Taínos, por Michael Dorris (Alfaguara, ISBN 84-204-4757-9) Scott O'Dell Award

Para encontrar más actividades, visite **www.estudiossocialessf.com**

¡Gracias por apoyar la educación de sus hijos en Estudios sociales!

School to Home

Unit 3

Newsletter

Here are the main ideas that we are learning:

★ The people in the 13 colonies produced a wide variety of goods and developed thriving trade routes.

★ The 13 colonies had big cities, small towns, and farms of all sizes.

★ Going to school, attending religious services, and reading for news and entertainment were important parts of everyday life in the colonies.

★ Slavery expanded rapidly in the English colonies during the 1700s, especially in the Southern colonies.

★ During the 1500s and 1600s, New Spain expanded by establishing colonies in Florida and New Mexico.

★ French exploration of the Mississippi River led to new French colonies in North America.

★ In the French and Indian War, the British, French, and Native Americans fought for control of a large part of North America.

Fast Facts

• Money was scarce in the colonies, so colonists often used barter for transactions.

• In the winter, milk was scarce for the colonists. Instead they drank sweetened cider thinned with water, into which they might soak bread to make it more substantial.

Family Activities

Talk Together

Ask your child to tell you about life in the 13 colonies. Discuss what a typical day might have been like. What part of the day was similar to what we do today? How were things different?

Learn Together

Help your child learn about working in colonial times.

✔ With your child look at the list of colonial jobs on page 204 of the student text.

✔ Talk about which jobs you and your child would have liked to do.

✔ Have your child choose one job and together write a letter explaining why your child is well-suited for the position.

Read Together

Molly Bannaky, by Alice McGill (Houghton Mifflin, ISBN 0-395-72287-X, 1999) Jane Addams Book Award; ALA Notable Book

Calico Bush, by Rachel Field (Simon & Schuster Children's Publishing, ISBN 0-689-82968-X, 1999) Newbery Honor Book

Black Hands, White Sails: The Story of African-American Whalers, by Patricia C. and Fredrick L. McKissack (Scholastic, ISBN 0-590-48313-7, 1999) Coretta Scott King Honor Book

 Go online to find more activities at **www.sfsocialstudies.com**

Thank you for supporting your child's Social Studies education!

De la escuela al hogar

Unidad 3

Boletín

Estas son las ideas principales que estamos estudiando:

★ Los habitantes de las 13 colonias produjeron una gran variedad de mercancías y desarrollaron rutas comerciales prósperas.

★ Las 13 colonias tenían grandes ciudades, pequeñas poblaciones y granjas de todos los tamaños.

★ La escuela, los servicios religiosos y la lectura, ya fuera para entretenerse o para informarse de las noticias, formaban parte importante de la vida diaria de las colonias.

★ La esclavitud se expandió rápidamente en las colonias inglesas durante el siglo XVIII, especialmente en las colonias del Sur.

★ Durante los siglos XVI y XVII, Nueva España se expandió y estableció colonias en la Florida y Nuevo México.

★ La exploración del río Mississippi por parte de los franceses condujo a nuevas colonias francesas en América del Norte.

★ En la Guerra Franco-Indígena, los británicos, franceses e indígenas norteamericanos lucharon por controlar una gran parte de América del Norte.

Datos curiosos

• Como el dinero era escaso en las colonias, los colonos con frecuencia hacían intercambios para realizar transacciones.

• En el invierno, la leche escaseaba para los colonos. En lugar de leche bebían sidra endulzada y adelgazada con agua, en la cual a veces remojaban pan para hacerla más sustanciosa.

Actividades en familia

Para conversar

Pida a su niño o niña que le cuente cómo era la vida en las 13 colonias. Hablen de cómo pudo haber sido un día típico. ¿Qué parte del día se parecía a lo que hacemos hoy? ¿Cuán diferentes eran las cosas?

Para aprender juntos

Ayude a su niño o niña a aprender sobre los trabajos de la época colonial.

✔ Fíjese con su niño o niña en la lista de trabajos coloniales en la página 204 del libro de texto del estudiante.

✔ Hablen sobre los trabajos que a usted y a su niño o niña les hubiera gustado hacer.

✔ Pida a su niño o niña que escoja un trabajo y juntos escriban una carta a un empleador, explicando por qué su niño o niña es un buen candidato.

Para leer juntos

Molly y los peregrinos, por Barbara Cohen y Michael J. Deraney (ilustrador), (Lectorum, ISBN 1-880507-34-X, 1995)

Benjamin Franklin, por Ricardo García (Limusa, ISBN 968-18-5367-9, 1994)

Nightjohn: El esclavo que me enseñó a leer, por Gary Paulsen (Bronce, ISBN 84-8453-003-5, 2000)

 Para encontrar más actividades, visite **www.estudiosocialessf.com**

¡Gracias por apoyar la educación de sus hijos en Estudios sociales!

School to Home

Here are the main ideas that we are learning:

★ British taxes led to greater cooperation among colonies.

★ Events in Boston brought Britain and the colonies closer to war.

★ The American Revolution began with the battles at Lexington and Concord.

★ The American colonies declared independence from Britain in July 1776.

★ The contributions of a wide variety of people helped the Continental Army win important battles.

★ With help from France and Spain, the Continental Army won the American Revolution.

Fast Facts

• The king and Parliament of Britain feared the Revolutionary War would bankrupt their country. Ironically, greatly expanded trade with the United States after the war helped Britain's economy recover.

• Women fought in the Revolutionary War too. Deborah Samson of Plymouth volunteered for the American army in 1778. She spent three years disguised as a man, taking the name Robert Shirtliffe.

Family Activities

Talk Together

Ask your child how he or she might have felt as a colonist who had to pay taxes to Britain. Explain that although we pay taxes in the United States today, citizens elect officials who decide what is taxed. Discuss how having the freedom to elect those who make the taxes might affect how a person feels about taxation.

Learn Together

Help your child learn about opposing views in a conflict.

✔ With your child look through newspapers for articles about countries that are involved in conflicts with other countries.

✔ Make a list of these conflicts. Talk about the reasons for each.

✔ Help your child identify the viewpoints of people on opposing sides of each conflict. Choose a few examples and discuss how you and your child would feel if you were on either side of the conflict.

Read Together

Can't You Make Them Behave, King George?, by Jean Fritz (PaperStar, ISBN 0-698-11402-7, 1996) Newbery Honor Book

Hannah's Winter of Hope, by Jean Van Leeuwen (Penguin Putnam Books for Young Readers, ISBN 0-141-30950-4, 2001) Young Reader's Choice Award

The Fifth of March: A Story of the Boston Massacre, by Ann Rinaldi (Gulliver Books, ISBN 0-152-27517-7, 1993)

 Go online to find more activities at **www.sfsocialstudies.com**

Thank you for supporting your child's Social Studies education!

De la escuela al hogar

Unidad 4 | Boletín

Estas son las ideas principales que estamos estudiando:

★ Los impuestos británicos hicieron que aumentara la cooperación entre las colonias.

★ Ciertos acontecimientos que ocurrieron en Boston hicieron que Gran Bretaña y las colonias se acercaran a la guerra.

★ La Guerra de Independencia empezó con las batallas de Lexington y Concord.

★ Los colonos americanos declararon su independencia de Gran Bretaña en julio de 1776.

★ Las contribuciones de una gran cantidad de personas ayudaron al Ejército Continental a ganar batallas importantes.

★ El Ejército Continental, con la ayuda de Francia y España, ganó la Guerra de Independencia.

Datos curiosos

• El rey y el Parlamento de Gran Bretaña temían que la Guerra de Independencia llevara a su país a la bancarrota. Irónicamente, el aumento de comercio con los Estados Unidos después de la guerra contribuyó a la recuperación de la economía británica.

• Las mujeres también pelearon en la Guerra de Independencia. Deborah Samson, de Plymouth, se presentó voluntaria al ejército estadounidense en 1778. Vivió tres años disfrazada de hombre, bajo el nombre de Robert Shirtliffe.

Actividades en familia

Para conversar

Pregunte a su niño o niña cómo se hubiera sentido si hubiera sido un colono obligado a pagar impuestos a Gran Bretaña. Explique que aunque hoy pagamos impuestos en los Estados Unidos, los ciudadanos eligen a las personas que deciden por qué hay que pagarlos. Comenten que tener la libertad para elegir a las personas que establecen los impuestos puede afectar nuestra opinión sobre los impuestos.

Para aprender juntos

Ayude a su niño o niña a estudiar opiniones opuestas de un conflicto.

✔ Junto con su niño o niña busque artículos en periódicos sobre países que están involucrados en conflictos con otros países.

✔ Hagan una lista de estos conflictos. Comenten las razones por las que se da cada uno de ellos.

✔ Ayude a su niño o niña a identificar los puntos de vista de personas en bandos opuestos de un conflicto. Escoja unos cuantos ejemplos y hablen sobre cómo se sentirían si formaran parte de cualquiera de los bandos del conflicto.

Para leer juntos

Washington, por T. M. Usel (Capstone Press, ISBN 1-56065-805-3, 1999)

Estampas de la colonia, por Solange Alberró (Patria, ISBN 968-39-1084-X, 1994)

 Para encontrar más actividades, visite **www.estudiosocialessf.com**

¡Gracias por apoyar la educación de sus hijos en Estudios sociales!

Here are the main ideas that we are learning:

★ The new nation struggled to govern itself under the Articles of Confederation.

★ At the Constitutional Convention, a group of leaders wrote the Constitution, a new plan for a stronger national government.

★ After a long debate, the states ratified the United States Constitution.

★ George Washington became the nation's first President and organized the new government.

★ The new nation doubled its size and expanded settlement westward.

★ The United States fought Britain in the War of 1812 to gain freedom of the seas and to end British interference with the westward expansion of the United States.

Fast Facts

• George Washington's great-grandfather, John Washington, did not intend to settle in America. He was a mate on a small British ship that ran aground in the Potomac River. While waiting for the ship to be repaired, he decided to stay.

• John Washington was in Westmoreland County, Virginia, by 1657, and settled on land near Bridge Creek. By 1674, he had acquired the land that would become Mount Vernon, where our future first president was born.

Family Activities

Talk Together

Ask your child to tell you how the first political parties formed in the United States. Discuss the differences among political parties in the United States today. Help your child understand that by uniting into an organized group, people are better able to accomplish their goals.

Learn Together

Help your child understand the viewpoints of political parties.

✔ Look through newspapers or listen to news programs with your child. Look for information about the issues and viewpoints of different political parties. Note how they agree of disagree on certain issues.

✔ Create a chart that shows what political parties think about different issues. In the first column, help your child list issues.

✔ Add an additional column for each political party you gathered information about. Help your child fill in the chart by writing each political party's viewpoint about the issues.

Read Together

The Star Spangled Banner, by Francis Scott Key (Random House Children's Books, ISBN 0-375-81596-1, 2002) Children's Book of the Year

A More Perfect Union: The Story of Our Constitution, by Betsy Maestro (HarperCollins, ISBN 0-688-10192-5, 1990) ALA Notable Book

A Kids' Guide to America's Bill of Rights: Curfews, Censorship, and the 100-Pound Giant, by Kathleen Krull (Avon Books, ISBN 0-380-97497-5, 1999)

 Go online to find more activities at **www.sfsocialstudies.com**

Thank you for supporting your child's Social Studies education!

De la escuela al hogar

Unidad 5

Boletín

Estas son las ideas principales que estamos estudiando:

★ A la nueva nación le dio trabajo gobernarse según los Artículos de Confederación.

★ En la Convención Constitucional, un grupo de líderes redactó la Constitución para disponer de un gobierno nacional más fuerte.

★ Tras un largo debate, los estados ratificaron la Constitución de los Estados Unidos.

★ George Washington, el primer presidente de la nación, organizó el nuevo gobierno.

★ La nueva nación duplicó su tamaño y expandió la colonización hacia el oeste.

★ Los EE. UU. lucharon contra Gran Bretaña en la Guerra de 1812 para obtener libre acceso a los mares y terminar con la interferencia británica en la expansión de los EE. UU. hacia el oeste.

Datos curiosos

- El bisabuelo de George Washington no tenía intenciones de establecerse en América. Era marinero de un pequeño barco británico que quedó varado en el río Potomac. Mientras esperaba a que lo repararan, decidió quedarse.

- John Washington llegó a Westmoreland County, Virginia, en 1657, y se estableció en tierras cercanas a Bridge Creek. Para 1674, había adquirido las tierras que se convertirían en Mount Vernon, donde nació nuestro futuro presidente.

VA

Actividades en familia

Para conversar

Pida a su niño o niña que le diga cómo se formaron los primeros partidos políticos de los EE. UU. Hablen de las diferencias entre los partidos políticos actuales. Ayude a su niño o niña a entender que cuando las personas se organizan en grupo, logran cumplir sus objetivos con mayor facilidad.

Para aprender juntos

Ayude a su niño o niña a entender los puntos de vista de los partidos políticos.

✔ Lea periódicos o escuche noticias con su niño o niña. Busquen información sobre los asuntos y puntos de vista de los distintos partidos políticos. Fíjense en la forma en que están de acuerdo o en desacuerdo sobre ciertos asuntos.

✔ Hagan una tabla que muestre lo que opinan los partidos políticos sobre distintos asuntos. En la primera columna, ayude a su niño o niña a escribir los asuntos.

✔ Luego añada una columna por cada partido político sobre el que haya conseguido información. Ayude a su niño o niña a rellenar la tabla escribiendo el punto de vista de cada partido político sobre los distintos asuntos.

Para leer juntos

Una unión más perfecta: La historia de nuestra Constitución, por Betsy y Giulio Maestro (Lectorum, ISBN 0-962516-28-7, 1993) ALA Notable Book

La historia de la Casa Blanca, por Kate Waters (Scholastic, ISBN 0-590-47397-2, 1993)

Para encontrar más actividades, visite **www.estudiosocialessf.com**

¡Gracias por apoyar la educación de sus hijos en Estudios sociales!

School to Home

Unit 6

Newsletter

Here are the main ideas that we are learning:

★ In the 1820s and 1830s, the United States expanded its territory in North America and its power in the Western Hemisphere.

★ The Industrial Revolution dramatically changed the way Americans lived and worked.

★ Beginning in the 1830s, a spirit of reform changed life in the United States.

★ The United States expanded as Americans settled the South, revolted in Texas, and fought a war with Mexico.

★ Using a network of trails, people moved west to make better lives for themselves.

★ The discovery of gold in California led to rapid settlement of the region.

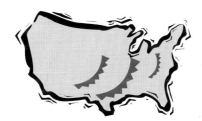

Fast Facts

• Inventors apply for a patent on their invention with the United States Patent Office, founded in 1790.

• From 1790 to 2000, the United States Patent Office granted more than 6 million patents!

Family Activities

Talk Together

Talk with your child about the changes you have witnessed as a result of new technology. Ask your child what changes he or she has noticed. Help your child recognize that some technology, such as the computer, can cause many changes that affect the way society operates.

Learn Together

Help your child learn how technology causes changes in society.

✔ With your child, walk through your home, noting any technology, such as a television, toaster, electric light, and so on. List each item you identify on a sheet of paper.

✔ Talk about how things have changed as a result of the use of each item. For example, what did people do before television became a common source of entertainment in the home?

✔ Choose several items, and have your child tell how his or her life might change if the item was no longer available.

Read Together

Only Passing Through: The Story of Sojourner Truth, by Anne Rockwell (Random House Children's Books, ISBN 0-440-41766-X, 2002) Coretta Scott King Honor Book

The Amazing Impossible Erie Canal, by Cheryl Harness (Aladdin, ISBN 0-689-82584-6, 1999)

Frederick Douglass and the Fight for Freedom, by Douglas Miller (Facts on File, ISBN 0-816-01617-8, 1998)

 Go online to find more activities at **www.sfsocialstudies.com**

Thank you for supporting your child's Social Studies education!

De la escuela al hogar

Unidad 6

Boletín

Estas son las ideas principales que estamos estudiando:

★ De 1820 a 1840, los Estados Unidos ampliaron su territorio en América del Norte y su poderío en el hemisferio occidental.

★ La Revolución Industrial cambió drásticamente la forma en que los estadounidenses vivían y trabajaban.

★ A principios de la década de 1830, un espíritu de reforma cambió la vida en los Estados Unidos.

★ Los Estados Unidos se expandieron cuando los estadounidenses se establecieron en el Sur, se rebelaron en Texas y pelearon una guerra contra México.

★ Las personas se trasladaban hacia el oeste en busca de una mejor vida haciendo uso de una red de caminos.

★ El descubrimiento de oro en California condujo a una colonización rápida de la región.

Datos curiosos

- Los inventores solcitan una patente para su invento en la Oficina de Patentes de los Estados Unidos, fundada en 1790.

- Entre 1790 y el año 2000, la Oficina de Patentes de los Etados Unidos otorgó más de 6 millones de patentes.

Actividades en familia

Para conversar

Hable con su niño o niña sobre los cambios que ha presenciado como resultado de nueva tecnología. Pregunte a su niño o niña qué cambios ha observado. Ayude a su niño o niña a reconocer que cierta tecnología, como la computadora, puede producir muchos cambios en la sociedad.

Para aprender juntos

Ayude a su niño o niña a aprender cómo la tecnología produce cambios en la sociedad.

✔ Caminen por la casa observando cualquier uso de tecnología, como un televisor, una tostadora, la luz eléctrica y así sucesivamente. En una hoja de papel hagan una lista de los usos de tecnología que identifiquen.

✔ Hablen sobre cómo cambiaron las cosas como consecuencia de cada uso de tecnología. Por ejemplo, ¿qué hacía la gente antes de que la televisión se convirtiera en una fuente común de entretenimiento en el hogar?

✔ Escoja varios usos de tecnología y pida a su niño o niña que le diga cómo cambiaría su vida si no los tuvieran.

Para leer juntos

La Osa Menor: Una historia del ferrocarril subterráneo, por F.N. Monjo y Fred Brenned (ilustrador), (HarperCollins, ISBN 0-06-444217-9, 1997)

Un granjero de diez años, por Laura Ingalls Wilder y Garth Williams (ilustrador), (Noguer y Caralt, ISBN 84-279-3224-3, 1994)

 Para encontrar más actividades, visite **www.estudiosocialessf.com**

¡Gracias por apoyar la educación de sus hijos en Estudios sociales!

School to Home

Unit 7 — Newsletter

Here are the main ideas that we are learning:

★ Differences between North and South led to growing tensions between the two regions.

★ Enslaved African Americans resisted slavery in many different ways.

★ Despite attempts to compromise, the struggle over slavery threatened to tear the United States apart.

★ Eventually 11 Southern states seceded from the United States, leading to the outbreak of the Civil War.

★ In the early years of the Civil War, the North and the South formed strategies in hopes of gaining a quick victory.

★ As the Civil War continued, people in the North and the South suffered many hardships, including the growing loss of life.

★ A series of Northern victories led to the end of the Civil War by 1865.

★ The country faced many difficult challenges after the Civil War ended, including rebuilding the South and protecting the rights of newly freed African Americans.

Fast Facts

- During the Civil War, drummers transmitted messages on the battlefield.

- Photography, a new invention, helped Americans at home see what the battlefield looked like for the first time. Photographers used giant cameras and traveled by horse and wagon to different battles.

Family Activities

Talk Together

Discuss with your child the importance of freedom. Talk about the freedoms your child has, as well as the limits of these freedoms. Ask what your child thinks having most of the freedoms taken away would be like.

Learn Together

Help your child learn about the conflict between the North and the South during the Civil War.

✔ Have your child describe the problems that existed between the North and the South before the Civil War.

✔ Ask your child how each of the problems might have been solved without fighting a war.

✔ Discuss the solutions that your child proposes.

Read Together

A Freedom River, by Doreen Rappaport (Jump at the Sun Books, ISBN 0-786-80350-9, 2000) Coretta Scott King Honor Book

Steal Away, by Jennifer Armstrong (Scholastic Paperbacks, ISBN 0-590-46921-5, 1993) ALA Notable Book

Anthony Burns: The Defeat and Triumph of a Fugitive Slave, by Virginia Hamilton (Laureleaf, ISBN 0-679-83997-6, 1993) ALA Notable Book, Boston Globe Horn Book Award, Jane Addams Book Award

 Go online to find more activities at **www.sfsocialstudies.com**

Thank you for supporting your child's Social Studies education!

De la escuela al hogar

Unidad 7

Boletín

Estas son las ideas principales que estamos estudiando:

★ Las diferencias entre el Norte y el Sur aumentaron las tensiones entre las dos regiones.

★ Los afroamericanos esclavizados se resistieron a la esclavitud de muchas formas diferentes.

★ A pesar de los intentos para llegar a un compromiso, la lucha por la esclavitud amenazó con separar al país.

★ Con el tiempo, 11 estados sureños se separaron de los Estados Unidos, y estalló la Guerra Civil.

★ Durante los primeros años de la Guerra Civil, el Norte y el Sur implementaron estrategias con la esperanza de obtener una victoria rápida.

★ A medida que la Guerra Civil continuaba, los habitantes del Norte y del Sur sufrieron muchas dificultades, entre ellas la creciente pérdida de vidas.

★ Una serie de victorias del Norte puso fin a la Guerra Civil en 1865.

★ Después de que concluyó la Guerra Civil el país se enfrentó a muchos retos difíciles, como lo fueron la reconstrucción del Sur y la protección de los derechos de los afroamericanos recién liberados.

Datos curiosos

• Durante la Guerra Civil se usaban tambores para transmitir mensajes en el campo de batalla.

• La fotografía, un nuevo invento, hizo posible que muchos estadounidenses vieran por primera vez un campo de batalla. Los fotógrafos usaban cámaras gigantes y viajaban a las diferentes batallas a caballo o en carretas.

Actividades en familia

Para conversar

Hable con su niño o niña sobre la importancia de la libertad. Hablen sobre las libertades que tiene su niño o niña y las cosas que no puede hacer. Pregunte a su niño o niña cómo se sentiría si le quitaran la mayoría de las libertades que tiene.

Para aprender juntos

Ayude a su niño o niña a aprender sobre el conflicto entre el Norte y el Sur durante la Guerra Civil.

✔ Pida a su niño o niña que describa los problemas que existían entre el Norte y el Sur antes de la Guerra Civil.

✔ Pregunte a su niño o niña de qué forma se pudieron haber resuelto los problemas sin recurrir a la guerra.

✔ Hablen sobre las soluciones que proponga su niño o niña.

Para leer juntos

La guerra de secesión, por Steve Perry (Timun Mas, ISBN 84-7176-745-7, 1992)

Azules contra grises, por William Camus (Ediciones SM, ISBN 84-3481-455-2, 1985)

Abraham Lincoln (Hombres famosos), por A. Guerrero (Ediciones Toray, ISBN 84-3101-740-6, 1990)

 Para encontrar más actividades, visite **www.estudiosocialessf.com**

¡Gracias por apoyar la educación de sus hijos en Estudios sociales!

School to Home

Unit 8   Newsletter

Here are the main ideas that we are learning:

★ After years of hard work, the first railroad across the United States was completed in 1869.

★ Following the Civil War, farmers and cowboys helped the Great Plains become an important farming and ranching region.

★ In the 1860s and 1870s, many Native American groups fought to maintain control of their traditional lands.

★ In the late 1800s, new inventions powered the growth of American industry and changed the way people lived.

★ During the late 1800s and early 1900s, millions of immigrants moved to American cities and workers struggled for better conditions.

★ By the end of the 1800s, the United States had gained new territory and become a world power.

Fast Facts

• Between 1820 and 2000, more than 65 million people immigrated to the United States from all over the world.

• There are more than 550 federally recognized Native American groups in the United States today.

Family Activities

Talk Together

Ask your child to tell you about how each of the following contributed to the growth of the nation in the late 1800s: railroad, telephone, electric light bulb, and the Bessemer process.

Learn Together

Help your child learn about how one invention—the light bulb—helped change life in the late 1800s.

✔ Plan to spend an evening with your child without using electricity. Plan different activities you can do without electricity.

✔ Plans might include reading by candlelight or making a meal without the use of electricity.

✔ After your evening without the use of electricity, talk about what you liked about it and what you found difficult.

Read Together

Pony Express!, by Steve Kroll (Scholastic, ISBN 0-590-20240-5, 2000)

Industry & Business (Life in America 100 Years Ago), by Linda Leuzzi (Chelsea House Publishers, ISBN 0-791-02846-1, 1997)

Sitting Bull and His World, by Albert Marrin (Dutton, ISBN 0-525-45944-8, 2000) NCSS Notable Book

 Go online to find more activities at **www.sfsocialstudies.com**

Thank you for supporting your child's Social Studies education!

De la escuela al hogar

Unidad 8   Boletín

Estas son las ideas principales que estamos estudiando:

★ Después de años de trabajo, en 1869 se completó el primer ferrocarril a través de los Estados Unidos.

★ Después de la Guerra Civil, los agricultores y los vaqueros contribuyeron a convertir las Grandes Llanuras en una región agrícola y ganadera importante.

★ De 1860 a 1880, muchos grupos indígenas norteamericanos lucharon para mantener el control de sus tierras.

★ A finales del siglo XIX, nuevos inventos impulsaron el crecimiento de la industria en los Estados Unidos y cambiaron el estilo de vida de la gente.

★ Durante los últimos años del siglo XIX y primeros del XX, millones de inmigrantes se trasladaron a las ciudades de los Estados Unidos y los trabajadores lucharon por mejorar sus condiciones de trabajo.

★ A finales del siglo XIX, los Estados Unidos habían obtenido nuevos territorios y se habían convertido en una potencia mundial.

Datos curiosos

• Entre 1820 y el año 2000, más de 40 millones de personas de todo el mundo emigraron a los Estados Unidos.

• En la actualidad existen más de 550 grupos indígenas norteamericanos con reconocimiento federal.

Actividades en familia

Para conversar

Pida a su niño o niña que le explique la forma en que cada una de las siguientes cosas contribuyó al crecimiento de la nación a fines del siglo XIX: el ferrocarril, el teléfono, la bombilla eléctrica y el proceso de Bessemer.

Para aprender juntos

Ayude a su niño o niña a aprender cómo un invento (la bombilla eléctrica) contribuyó a cambiar la vida a finales del siglo XIX.

✔ Prepárese para pasar una noche con su niño o niña sin usar electricidad. Planee diferentes actividades que se puedan hacer sin el uso de electricidad.

✔ Sus planes pueden incluir leer a la luz de una vela o preparar una comida sin usar electricidad.

✔ Después de pasar la noche sin el uso de electricidad, hablen de lo que les gustó y de lo que encontraron difícil.

Para leer juntos

¿Quién es de aquí?, por Margy Burns Knight y Anne Sibley (ilustradora), 9Tilbury House, ISBN 0-88448-159-X)

La estatua de la libertad, por Lynda Sorensen (Rourke, ISBN 1-55916-067-5, 1994)

Los inventos, por Lionel Bender 9Altea, ISBN 84-372-3706-2)

 Para encontrar más actividades, visite **www.estudiosocialessf.com**

¡Gracias por apoyar la educación de sus hijos en Estudios sociales!

Here are the main ideas that we are learning:

★ As President, Theodore Roosevelt promoted reform at home and expanded United States power overseas.

★ The United States fought in World War I, leading to important and long-lasting changes in American life.

★ After World War I, the United States went through the boom of the 1920s and the Great Depression in the 1930s.

★ The United States and its allies fought and won World War II, the most widespread and costliest war in human history.

★ The Cold War was a worldwide struggle between the United States and the Soviet Union, two countries with very different governments, economies, and ways of life.

★ In the 1950s and 1960s, African Americans, women, and other groups struggled to gain civil rights and equal opportunities.

★ The United States continued to oppose the spread of communism and Soviet power in the 1960s and 1970s.

★ The Cold War ended in the late 1980s, leaving the United States as the world's only superpower.

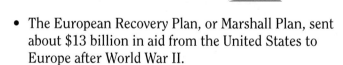
Fast Facts

• The European Recovery Plan, or Marshall Plan, sent about $13 billion in aid from the United States to Europe after World War II.

• Approximately 6 million Jews died in concentration camps in WWII, out of a total of 12 million people.

Family Activities

Talk Together

Discuss with your child the role of the United States as the world's only superpower. What responsibilities does your child think come with this role? What does the nation do well as a world leader? What might it be doing better?

Learn Together

Help your child learn about the role of the United States in the world today.

✔ With your child look through current newspapers and magazines for news items about things the United States is doing with and for other countries.

✔ Help your child make a list of the news items you find.

✔ Look over the list and talk about the many roles the United States plays. Discuss reasons why other countries look to the United States for help.

Read Together

Pearl Harbor Is Burning!: A Story of World War II, by Kathleen V. Kudlinski (Puffin Books, ISBN 0-140-34509-4, 1993)

The Fall of the Soviet Union, by Miles Harvey (Children's Press, ISBN 0-516-46694-1, 1995)

 Rosie the Riveter: Women Working on the Home Front in World War II, by Penny Coleman (Crown Publishers, Inc., ISBN 0-517-88567-0, 1998) ALA Notable Book

Go online to find more activities at **www.sfsocialstudies.com**

Thank you for supporting your child's Social Studies education!

De la escuela al hogar

Unidad 9

Boletín

Estas son las ideas principales que estamos estudiando:

★ Como presidente, Theodore Roosevelt fomentó la reforma en el país y expandió el poderío de Estados Unidos en el exterior.

★ Los EE. UU. lucharon en la Primera Guerra Mundial, lo que produjo cambios importantes y duraderos en la vida de los EE. UU.

★ Después de la Primera Guerra Mundial, los EE. UU. experimentaron un auge económico en los años veinte y luego la Gran Depresión en los años treinta.

★ Los EE. UU. y sus aliados lucharon y ganaron la Segunda Guerra Mundial, la guerra más extendida y costosa de la historia humana.

★ La Guerra Fría fue un conflicto a escala mundial entre los EE. UU. y la Unión Soviética, dos países con gobiernos, economías y estilos de vida muy diferentes.

★ En los años cincuenta y sesenta, los afroamericanos, las mujeres y otros grupos lucharon para obtener derechos civiles e igualdad de oportunidades.

★ En los años sesenta y setenta, los EE. UU. siguieron oponiéndose a la expansión del comunismo y la influencia de la Unión Soviética.

★ La Guerra Fría terminó a finales de los ochenta, y los EE. UU. permanecieron como la única superpotencia mundial.

Datos curiosos

- El Plan de Recuperación Europea, o Plan Marshall, envió unos trece mil millones de dólares de los Estados Unidos a Europa después de la Segunda Guerra Mundial.

- Aproximadamente seis millones de judíos murieron en campos de concentración durante la Segunda Guerra Mundial, de un total de 12 millones de personas.

Actividades en familia

Para conversar

Hable con su niño o niña sobre el papel que desempeñan los EE. UU. como la única superpotencia mundial. ¿Qué responsabilidades cree su niño o niña que acompañan a este papel? ¿Qué hace bien la nación como líder mundial? ¿Qué podría hacer mejor?

Para aprender juntos

Ayude a su niño o niña a aprender cuál es la función de los EE. UU. en el mundo actual.

✔ Lea con su niño o niña periódicos y revistas actuales para encontrar noticias sobre las cosas que están haciendo los EE. UU. junto con otros países o para otros países.

✔ Ayude a su niño o niña a hacer una lista de las noticias que encuentre.

✔ Fíjense en la lista y hablen de los múltiples papeles que desempeñan los EE. UU. Comenten las razones por las que otros países solicitan ayuda de los EE. UU.

Para leer juntos

El béisbol nos salvó, por Ken Mochizuki y Dom Lee (ilustrador), (Lee & Low Books, Inc., ISBN 1-880000-22-9, 1995)

Pasaje a la libertad: la historia de Chiune Sugihara, por Ken Mochizuki y Dom Lee (ilustrador), (Lee & Low Books, Inc., ISBN 1-880000-82-2, 1999) ALA Notable Book

César Chávez, por Consuelo Rodríguez (Chelsea House, ISBN 0-79103-102-0, 1994)

 Para encontrar más actividades, visite **www.estudiossocialessf.com**

¡Gracias por apoyar la educación de sus hijos en Estudios sociales!

Calendar Pages

Each month of the year provides new opportunities for students to learn about history, geography, government, good citizenship, economics, culture, and technology through holidays, "firsts," and important birthdays and anniversaries. The 12-month format is ideal for year-round schools and summer schools but also provides a wealth of information for students who attend a standard 9-month school.

The following pages offer an entire year of calendar activities, including:

- A list of facts about the month: birthdays, holidays, and other red-letter days
- Detailed instructions for constructing a bulletin board for each month
- At least one additional activity per month
- A selection of books for students to read about a monthly subject
- A Web link for *This Day in History,* part of the Scott Foresman Social Studies Web site

An extra page is given for you to note state or community celebrations.

▶ **Have a class census on page TR25.**

OUR FAVORITE SPORTS

25% Baseball
15% Soccer
35% Basketball
25% Football

▲ **Have children create their own "John Hancock" on page TR36.**

moon festival in China

Jim Henson's Birthday

Labor Day

Our Class Play September 20th

▼ **Learn about Patrick Henry on page TR32.**

"Give me liberty…"

▲ **"Fall" into September on page TR26.**

Notes

August _____

_____

September _____

_____

October _____

_____

November _____

_____

December _____

_____

January _____

_____

February _____

_____

March _____

_____

April _____

_____

May _____

_____

June _____

_____

July _____

_____

August

OUR CLASS CENSUS

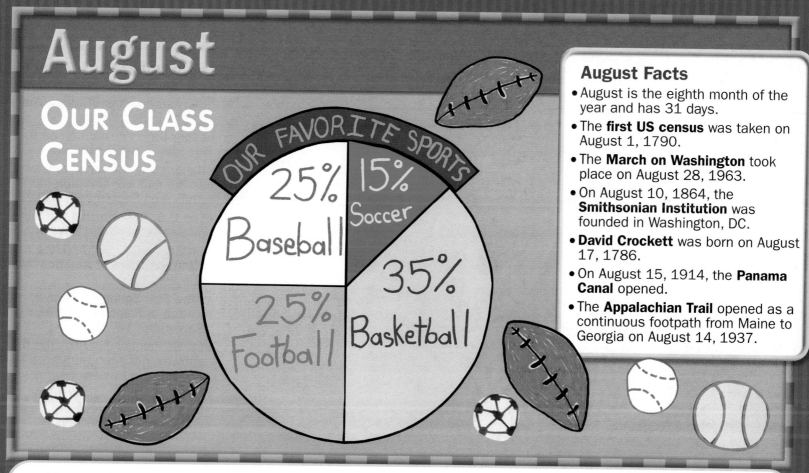

OUR FAVORITE SPORTS

25% Baseball

15% Soccer

25% Football

35% Basketball

Activities

Our Class Census

In honor of the first United States census, taken August 1, 1790 and taken every ten years since then, have students design their own classroom census and make an "Our Class Census" bulletin board. A census does not only count the number of people in an area, but it also collects information such as occupation and income. The Web site **www.census.gov** has excellent information about categories covered in a census. Since most students don't have occupations or incomes, let them choose categories they would like to use for a survey about themselves and their classmates. These can include family size, pet ownership, or favorite sports. Create a survey sheet and have each student fill it out. Have students compile data into color-coded and labeled circle graphs, showing the percent for each answer. Each graph should also be titled, such as "Family Size," "Pets We Own," and "Our Favorite Sports." Place the graphs on a bulletin board titled "Our Class Census."

This Day in History

For additional August events or project ideas, go to *This Day in History* at **www.sfsocialstudies.com.** Select a birthday or historic event for any day in August and base an activity on it.

Smithsonian Institution

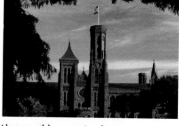

Ask if any students have ever visited the Smithsonian Institution in Washington, DC. Find out what they already know about the museums there. Have students gather information about the different types of collections in each museum.

Have students discuss how to set up their own classroom museum with their own interesting collections. Find out if any students collect the same kinds of things. Have students bring in personal collections to share or start a unique classroom collection to put on display.

March on Washington

For more information on the **March on Washington,** look for books such as these.

Civil Rights Marches by Linda George, (Children's Press, ISBN 0-516-26516-4, 1999)

The March on Washington by L. S. Summer, (Child's World, ISBN 1-56766-718-X, 2001)

September

FALL INTO SEPTEMBER

Activities

Falling Leaves

Autumn begins in September, so take advantage of the change in season to create a colorful bulletin board. Have students find out the different types of trees in their local region and the type of leaf each tree has. Have students cut out leaf shapes that represent the different trees in your area. Do the leaves change color in your area? Do they stay green? Students should make the colors of the leaves match what they see in the fall.

Now have students research special holidays, celebrations, and activities for the month of September, including school and community events. Ask them to write one special event on each leaf, then cover the bulletin board with all this September information.

"The Star Spangled Banner"

Sing some patriotic songs, including "The Star Spangled Banner" (pages 388–389) with your class. Ask students to find out more about our national anthem and the man who wrote the words, Francis Scott Key.

Now ask student to write some new patriotic songs. They can write the words and the tune or just write words to the tune of familiar song. Set a special time on September 14 for students to present their new songs.

The United States Constitution

For more information on the **U.S. Constitution,** look for books such as these.

The Constitution by Patricia Ryon Quiri, (Children's Press, ISBN 0-516-20663-X, 1998)

The United States Constitution by Kristal Leebrick, (Bridgestone Books, ISBN 0-7368-1094-3, 2002)

This Day in History

For additional September events or project ideas, go to *This Day in History* at **www.sfsocialstudies.com.** Select a birthday or historic event for any day in September and base an activity on it.

Alternatively, have students go to this Web Site and choose an event in September on which to do a project or report.

October

UNITED NATIONS COUNTRY QUILT

October Facts

- October is the tenth month of the year and has 31 days.
- In October, we set our clocks to **Standard Time** by turing them back an hour.
- October 24 is **United Nations Day.**
- The **Statue of Liberty** was dedicated on October 28, 1886.
- **Columbus Day** is celebrated on the second Monday in October.
- The comic strip **"Peanuts"** debuted on October 2, 1950.
- **Fire Prevention Week** is the second week in October.

Activities

United Nations Day

Ask student what they know about the United Nations. Have students research information about the organization, including its member countries. Have individual students or partners choose and research one of these countries. Once students have gathered information, ask each student to choose a specific symbol or design to represent his or her country. Ask them to draw this design on a 9" X 9" square piece of construction paper. Put the squares together to form a "Country quilt" on the bulletin board.

Statue of Liberty Collages

In honor of the Statue of Liberty, which was dedicated October 28, 1886, have students create "Statue of Liberty Collages." Have students research the history of the statue and discuss what the statue means to Americans. Have students find pictures of the statue in encyclopaedias or on the Internet. Have them copy the outline of the statue's head, shoulders, and raised arm on large white drawing paper. You might also use an opaque projector to make the outlines. Have students cut out pictures of all kinds of people from magazines and glue them onto the paper, filling in the statue, to represent those who enjoy freedom in the United States. Cut out collages to remove rough edges made by glued pictures. Display collages.

Columbus Day

For more information on **Christopher Columbus** and **Columbus Day,** look for books such as these.

Christopher Columbus: Explorer of the New World by Peter Chrisp, (DK, ISBN 0-7894-7936-2, 2001)

Where Do You Think You're Going, Christopher Columbus? by Jean Fritz, (PaperStar, ISBN 0-698-11580-5, 1997)

This Day in History

For additional October events or project ideas, go to *This Day in History* at **www.sfsocialstudies.com.** Select a birthday or historic event for any day in October and then base an activity on it.

Alternatively, have students go to this Web site and choose an event in October on which to do a project or report.

November

LET'S VOTE!

Margonia - pizza
Freelon - pizza
Brickalee - cookies
North Rivener - chips and salsa
West Calinar - pizza

Winner - pizza

Margonia - kickball
Freelon - kickball
Brickalee - softball
North Rivener - freeze tag
West Calinar - kickball

Winner - kickball

November Facts

- November is the eleventh month of the year and has 30 days.
- **Election Day** is the first Tuesday after the first Monday in November. Every four years there is a Presidential Election.
- November 11 is **Veterans Day.**
- **Thanksgiving** is the fourth Thursday in November.
- The **Berlin Wall** was opened on November 9, 1989.
- On November 19, 1863, President Lincoln delivered the **Gettysburg Address.**

Activities

Let's Vote!

In honor of Election Day, have students vote on a number of classroom issues throughout November. They can record the results on a "Let's Vote!" bulletin board. Discuss the kinds of issues decided on Election Day: city council members, tax referendums, mayor and sheriffs, senators and representatives, President and Vice-President. Presidential elections are held every four years. Presidential and vice-presidential elections are decided by the Electoral College. To give students a very simple demonstration of the Electoral College process, divide the class into 4 or 5 groups, or "states." Let them name their states. Each state will pick an **elector,** a representative who will cast a vote for the whole state. Throughout the month have the "states" vote on class issues, such as an outdoor game to play, what food to serve during a party, a book to read as a class. Everyone will discuss their choices within their "state" but only the electors will vote. Post the issues and how each state elector voted on the bulletin board.

Design a Presidential House

On November 1, 1800, President John Adams moved into the newly completed White House in Washington, DC. In honor of this event, have students design their own presidential house. This can be done in one or two stages. First, have students draw a floor plan for each floor of their presidential home. Have them include important rooms for meeting with diplomats, sleeping, dining, entertaining, studying or reading, as well as private office space and any

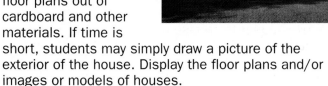

other areas students feel a president might need. Second, have students construct three-dimensional houses based on their floor plans out of cardboard and other materials. If time is short, students may simply draw a picture of the exterior of the house. Display the floor plans and/or images or models of houses.

Veterans Day

For more information on **Veterans Day,** look for books such as these.

Veterans Day by Jacqueline Cotton, (Children's Press, ISBN 0-516-27499-6, 2002)

Veterans Day: Remembering Our War Heroes by Elaine Landau, (Enslow, ISBN 0-7660-1775-3, 2002)

This Day in History

For additional November events or project ideas, go to *This Day in History* at **www.sfsocialstudies.com.** Select a birthday or historic event for any day in November and base an activity on it.

December

CELEBRATE DECEMBER

1 — Basketball

2 — James Monroe

3 — Illinois

4

5

Activities

December Holidays and Celebrations

To celebrate the many December holidays and special events, have students create a gift-filled bulletin board, where one gift is opened each day. Hand out 31 colorful pieces of paper in a variety of sizes. Ask students to fold the papers in half, so the paper looks like a greeting card. Students can now decorate the front of the card to make it look like a gift package. Ribbons, glitter, and sequins can be added to brighten up the "packages." For inside the card, assign a different day of the month for each gift. Students should research to find special happenings, holidays, famous birthdays, and historical events for each day in December. Don't forget to include school dates and community events.

Have students find photos or make drawings to represent each event in December. Display the packages on the bulletin board and open one each day of the month.

Washington Crossing the Delaware

Have students gather information about Washington crossing the Delaware on December 25, 1776. Discuss where it took place, what time of day (or night) it was, who was there, and why this happened. Ask students to work in small groups to create short skits about this historic event. Tell students to keep the setting, characters, costumes, and props in mind as they write the dialog.

Boston Tea Party

For more information on the **Boston Tea Party,** look for books such as these.

The Boston Tea Party by Michael Burgan, (Compass Point Books, ISBN 0-7565-0040-0, 2000)

The Boston Tea Party by Nancy Furstinger, (Bridgestone Books, ISBN 0-7368-1093-5, 2002)

This Day in History

For additional December events or project ideas, go to *This Day in History* at **www.sfsocialstudies.com.** Select a birthday or historic event for any day in December and base an activity on it.

Alternatively, have students go to this Web site and choose an event in December on which to do a project or report.

January

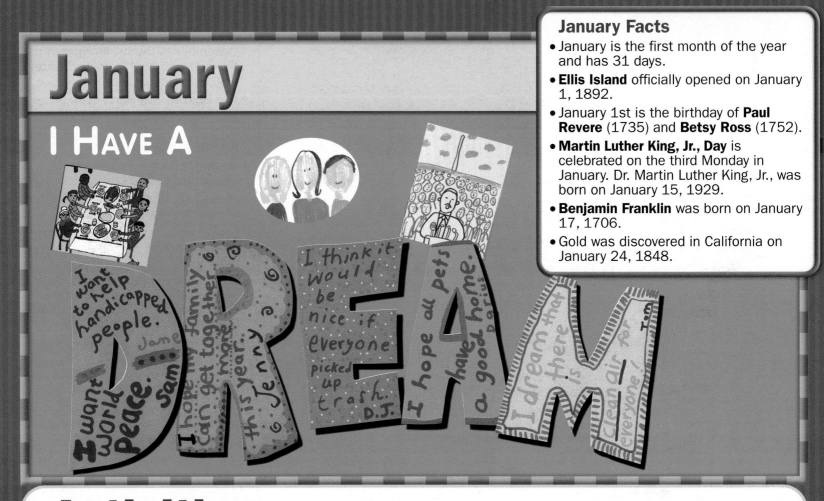

I HAVE A DREAM

Activities

Martin Luther King, Jr., Day

In honor of this special day, have students create a bulletin board that illustrates their own dreams. Ask students to brainstorm things they would like to help change in their community, their country, or the world.

Volunteers can draw and cut out large, colorful letters that spell out Martin Luther King's famous words, 'I HAVE A DREAM." Before putting these words up on the bulletin board, ask each student to write down his or her "dreams" inside the different letters. Display these famous words, which now carry new dreams for the future, beside a January calendar that highlights Martin Luther King, Jr., Day. During the month, students can add drawings and pictures to illustrate some of their dreams.

A Closer Look at Benjamin Franklin

One of Franklin's many inventions was bifocal glasses. The glasses contained two different types of lenses, with the bottom lenses acting as magnifying glasses. Have students research Franklin's other inventions and contributions to our nation. Then, using large construction paper, have students cut out oversized glasses frames, and glue white paper "lenses" onto the frames. Ask students to draw

horizontal lines to give the glasses the "bifocals" look, and draw pictures to illustrate some of Franklin's inventions and contributions on the lenses. Students should draw smaller pictures above the lines and magnified pictures below the lines.

Paul Revere

For more information on **Paul Revere,** look for books such as these.

Paul Revere by George Sullivan, (Scholastic Reference, ISBN 0-439-14748-4, 2000)

Paul Revere : American Patriot by JoAnn A. Grote, (Chelsea House Publishers, ISBN 0-7910-5698-8, 1999)

This Day in History

For additional January events or project ideas, go to *This Day in History* at **www.sfsocialstudies.com.** Select a birthday or historic event for any day in January and base an activity on it.

Alternatively, have students go to this Web site and choose an event in January on which to do a project or report.

February

TWO PRESIDENTS

Venn diagram bulletin board display:

George Washington
- 1st president
- Born in Virginia
- Born in the 1700's
- Lived during revolutionary War

How are they alike?
- president of USA
- born in month of February
- both were married

Abraham Lincoln
- 16th president
- Born in Kentucky
- Born in the 1800's
- Lived during civil War

Activities

Presidents' Day

Presidents' Day is a time to honor George Washington and Abraham Lincoln. Have students research these two men. Ask students to compare and contrast Washington and Lincoln using Venn diagrams. Challenge students to find a wide variety of ways to compare the men, including places of birth, physical traits, political views, and personal interests.

As a class, make a large Venn diagram to display on the bulletin board for February. Students can write down information in the corresponding section of the diagram, then add illustrations to brighten the display.

February is the Shortest Month

Since February is the shortest month of the year (even during Leap Year), see which student or group of students can complete simple tasks in the shortest amount of time. Time small groups as they put together 50-piece puzzles or complete a simple obstacle course. Make a graph of how long it took each individual or group to complete each assignment. Who did each task in the shortest amount of time?

Black History Month

For more information on **Black History Month,** look for books such as these.

Through My Eyes by Ruby Bridges, (Scholastic, ISBN 0-590-18923-9, 1999)

Words With Wings: A Treasury of African-American Poetry and Art selected by Belinda Rochelle, (HarperCollins, ISBN 0-06-029363-2, 2001)

This Day in History

For additional February events or project ideas, go to *This Day in History* at **www.sfsocialstudies.com.** Select a birthday or historic event for any day in February and base an activity on it.

Alternatively, have students go to this Web site and choose an event in February on which to do a project or report.

March

MARCH IS NOTEWORTHY

March Facts
- March is the third month of the year and has 31 days. **Spring** begins in March.
- March is **Music in our Schools Month.**
- The **Peace Corps** was established on March 1, 1961.
- Theodor **"Dr. Seuss"** Geisel was born on March 2, 1904.
- March is **Women's History Month.**
- The **telephone was invented** in March 1876.

Activities

March Is Noteworthy

Create a musical bulletin board in recognition of Music in our Schools Month that also includes other special events in March. Have students draw a musical staff on the bulletin board. Include the musical symbols such as the G clef and the time signature. Ask students to cut out large, colorful musical notes out of construction paper. Working with a partner or in small groups, have students research special events or dates in March. Ask students to write down one special date on each musical note. They may also add one interesting fact about that event. Notes can be placed on the bulletin board, if they wish. More notes can be added for school and community events.

Write an Editorial

After reading and discussing Patrick Henry's famous speech in which he said "Give me liberty or give me death," tell students that they are going to write editorials about the speech. Explain that an editorial is an article that expresses an editor's opinion on a certain subject. Ask each "editor" to write an article expressing his or her feelings about Patrick Henry's words. Do the young editors support or reject Patrick Henry's point of view?

Women's History Month

For more information on **Women's History Month,** look for books such as these.

Clara Barton: Founder of the American Red Cross by Cynthia Fitterer Klingel, (Child's World, ISBN 1-56766-172-6, 2002)

Vision of Beauty: the Story of Sarah Breedlove Walker by Kathryn Lasky, (Candlewick Press, ISBN 0-7636-1834-9, 2003)

This Day in History

For additional March events or project ideas, go to *This Day in History* at **www.sfsocialstudies.com.** Select a birthday or historic event for any day in March and base an activity on it.

Alternatively, have students go to this Web site and choose an event in March on which to do a project or report.

April

HAPPY BIRTHDAY, MR. JEFFERSON

Activities

Thomas Jefferson's Birthday

Ask students what they know about Thomas Jefferson. Tell them that Jefferson was an inventor and a writer who had many interests, as well as being our third President.

Have students research one major interest of Jefferson's such as politics, freedom, education, gardening, cooking, and architecture. Have each student write a report, decorate a cover sheet to look like a birthday package, and attach it to his or her report. Display the packages on the bulletin board and have students take turns "opening" the birthday gifts and sharing their reports.

Pony Express

The Pony Express began April 3, 1860. It was like a cross-country relay race. Ask students to find out more about how the Pony Express operated, what route was taken by the riders, and how much it cost to send a letter.

Now, ask students to write letters to each other, then deliver the letters by their own "Pony Express." Put all the letters in a sack or bookbag. Have students run a relay race around the track or across the playground, handing off the sack of letters to the next runner after each lap or leg of the journey. Time the first round, then try to see if the students can beat their own time.

Earth Day

For more information on **Earth Day,** look for books such as these.

Earth Day by Amy Margaret, (PowerKids Press, ISBN 0-8239-5787-X, 2002)

Earth Day by Jason Cooper, (Rourke Pub., ISBN 1-58952-218-4, 2002)

This Day in History

For additional April events or project ideas, go to *This Day in History* at **www.sfsocialstudies.com.** Select a birthday or historic event for any day in April and base an activity on it.

Alternatively, have students go to this Web site and choose an event in April on which to do a project or report.

May

MORSE CODE MESSAGES

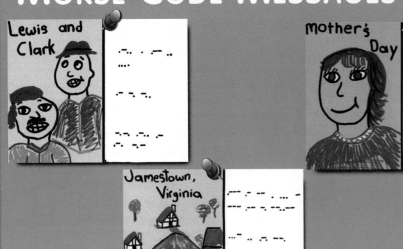

May Facts

- **Memorial Day** is the last Monday in May.
- The second Sunday in May is **Mother's Day.**
- On May 14, 1607, **Jamestown, Virginia,** was founded.
- The **Lewis and Clark Expedition** began on May 14, 1804.
- On May 24, 1844, the **first telegraph message** was transmitted by Samuel Morse.
- **The Transcontinental Railroad** was completed on May 10, 1869.

Activities

May Morse Code Messages

Have students research information about Samuel Morse, Morse Code, the first telegraph message sent on May 24, 1844, and the importance of this event. Provide each student with a Morse Code chart. Ask students to write their names using Morse Code.

Now, have students write down special events and holidays that occur in May, then translate them into Morse Code. Morse Code messages can be placed on the bulletin board along with photos or illustrations to help decode each event.

Map It Out

Display a map of the United States. As a class, track Lewis and Clark's expedition on the map. Research and discuss the trip. Ask students how Lewis and Clark knew where they were going when there was no map to follow. How do mapmakers make maps of new, unexplored territory? Ask student to make a map of the school ground or neighborhood as if the place were a new, unexplored area. Tell them to note any landmarks and outstanding physical features they encounter.

Memorial Day

For more information on **Memorial Day,** look for books such as these.

Memorial Day by Amy Margaret, (PowerKids Press, ISBN 0-8239-5784-5, 2002)

Memorial Day by Jacqueline S. Cotton, (Children's Press, ISBN 0-516-27369-8, 2002)

This Day in History

For additional May events or project ideas, go to *This Day in History* at **www.sfsocialstudies.com.** Select a birthday or historic event for any day in May and base an activity on it.

Alternatively, have students go to this Web site and choose an event in May on which to do a project or report.

June

OUR FLAG GROWS UP

1776

1795

1818

1846

today

Activities

Flag Day

Celebrate Flag Day by creating a time line of the "Stars and Stripes" on the bulletin board. Have students research our flag's history from 1776 through today. Discuss the possible decisions behind the design changes. Assign different flags to small groups and ask each group to construct their flag using red, white, and blue construction paper. Play a flag game to see if students can put the flags in chronological order on the time line.

Great Seal of the United States

On July 4, 1776, a committee of the Continental Congress started to work on a design for a national seal. It was finally completed and adopted on June 20, 1782. Display a picture of the Great Seal and ask students why they think each item was chosen by our Founders.

Students can research the meanings behind each design on the seal. Challenge students to design their own versions of the Great Seal of the United States. What symbols, colors, and designs would they choose? Ask students to explain their choices.

Helen Keller

For more information on **Helen Keller,** look for books such as these.

Helen Keller by George Sullivan, (Scholastic Reference, ISBN 0-439-14751-4, 2002)

Helen Keller: a Photo-Illustrated Biography by Muriel Dubois, (Bridgestone Books, ISBN 0-7368-1605-4, 2003)

This Day in History

For additional June events or project ideas, go to *This Day in History* at **www.sfsocialstudies.com.** Select a birthday or historic event for any day in June and base an activity on it.

Alternatively, have students go to this Web site and choose an event in June on which to do a project or report.

July

PUT YOUR JOHN HANCOCK HERE

July Facts

- July is the seventh month of the year and has 31 days.
- **Independence Day** is July 4.
- **The Declaration of Independence was adopted** on July 4, 1776.
- The **first moon landing** was on July 20, 1969.
- July is **National Hot Dog Month**.
- **Disneyland** opened in California on July 18, 1955.
- July is **Recreation and Parks Month**.
- Ford Motor Company sold its first car (a Model A) on July 23, 1903.

Activities

The Declaration of Independence

Make a bulletin board titled, "Put your 'John Hancock' Here." Explain that the Declaration of Independence was adopted on July 4, 1776 and was signed by John Hancock, the president of the Continental Congress. He used big, bold letters to sign his name so that King George was sure to see it. Tell students that today the term "Put your 'John Hancock' here," means to write your signature on something.

Ask students to make a statement with their own signatures. Give out large white construction paper and tell students to sign their names in letters large enough to take up all the space on the paper. Students can decorate their signatures with bright designs and glitter. Then display the signatures on the bulletin board. John Hancock would be proud!

Hot Dog Month

July is National Hot Dog Month, so have student create a giant hot dog-shaped book filled with facts about this summer month. Ask students to do an Internet search for the month of July. Have them fill the ... with July holidays, activities, and special events. A ... of summertime activities that can be enjoyed ... an also be added to the book. Students can draw pictures or find photos to illustrate each page. Add a hot dog cover to finish the book, then share it with other classes in the school.

First Moon Landing

For more information on the **first moon landing,** look for books such as these.

The Apollo 11 Mission: The First Man to Walk on the Moon by Helen Zelon, (PowerKids Press, ISBN 0-8239-5772-1, 2001)

Neil Armstrong by Shannon Zemlicka, (Lerner, ISBN 0-8225-1563-6, 2002)

This Day in History

For additional July events or project ideas, go to *This Day in History* at **www.sfsocialstudies.com.** Select a birthday or historic event for any day in July and base an activity on it.

Alternatively, have students go to this Web site and choose an event in July on which to do a project or report.

Writing Rubrics

Rubric for Narrative Writing

	6	**5**	**4**
Content Quality and Idea Development	• well-focused on topic and purposeful • ideas thoroughly developed • reflects insight into writing situation • conveys sense of completeness	• focused on topic • ideas developed • reflects firm grasp of writing situation • conveys sense of completeness	• fairly focused on topic • moderately developed ideas • may include extraneous or loosely related material • conveys some sense of completeness
Voice	• clear and fitting for topic • expressive and engaging • well-suited for audience and purpose	• clear and fitting for topic • engaging • suited for audience and purpose	• fairly clear and seems to fit topic • fairly engaging style • suited for audience and purpose
Organization	• logical progression of ideas • sequence very clear	• logical progression of ideas • sequence clear	• organizational pattern apparent • some lapses may occur in organization • sequence fairly clear
Word Precision	• demonstrates mature command of language • precise and interesting word choice • wide variety of word choice	• demonstrates command of language • interesting word choice • variety of word choice	• adequate word choice • some variety of word choice
Sentence Fluency	• uses complete sentences • varied sentence structures and lengths	• uses complete sentences • varied sentence structures	• uses complete sentences • varied sentence structures attempted • some simple sentence structures
Mechanics	• correct spelling, punctuation, and capitalization • proper grammar and usage • errors do not prevent understanding	• few errors in spelling, punctuation, and capitalization • proper grammar and usage • errors do not prevent understanding	• mostly correct spelling, punctuation, and capitalization • few errors in grammar and usage • errors do not prevent understanding
If using a four-point rubric	**4**	**4**	**3**

3	2	1	Cannot be scored
generally focused on topic ideas may be vague erratic development of ideas some loosely related material conveys some sense of completeness	• somewhat related to topic • insufficient development of ideas • includes extraneous or loosely related material • may lack sense of completeness	• minimally focused on topic • little, if any, development of ideas • lacks sense of completeness	• no focus on topic • no development of ideas • incomplete
generally clear and seems to fit topic engaging at times generally suited for audience and purpose	• rarely comes through • basic attempt to engage reader • ill-suited for audience and purpose	• weak • basic attempt to engage reader • not suited for audience or purpose	• no attempt to engage reader • unaware of audience or purpose
organizational pattern attempted sequence generally clear	• little evidence of organizational pattern • sequence may be unclear	• no organizational pattern evident • sequence unclear	• no attempt at organization present • no sequence • cannot follow
adequate word choice limited, predictable, or occasionally vague word choice some variety of word choice	• word choice limited, inappropriate, or vague • little variety of word choice	• limited or inappropriate word choice may obscure meaning • words/phrases repetitive and show minimal variety	• incorrect word choice • word choice shows no variety
uses complete sentences varied sentence structure attempted generally simple sentence structures	• occasional sentence fragment or run-on sentence • limited to simple sentence structure	• excessive use of sentence fragments or run-on sentences • limited to simple sentence structure • sentences difficult to understand	• no complete sentences • sentence structure basic/below grade level
generally correct spelling, punctuation, and capitalization some errors in grammar and usage errors do not prevent understanding	• some errors in spelling, punctuation, and capitalization • errors in grammar and usage • errors may prevent understanding	• errors in spelling, punctuation, and capitalization • frequent errors in grammar and usage • errors prevent understanding	• critical errors in spelling, punctuation, and capitalization/below grade level • critical errors in grammar and usage/below grade level • errors prevent understanding
3	**2**	**1**	

	6	**5**	**4**
Content Quality and Idea Development	• well-focused on topic • clear position stated • many facts and opinions to support position • convincing argument • conveys sense of completeness	• focused on topic • clear position stated • ample support • presents convincing argument • conveys sense of completeness	• fairly focused on topic • position apparent • adequate support, though perhaps uneven • may include extraneous or loosely related material • presents reasonable argumen • conveys some sense of completeness
Voice	• clear and fitting for topic • confident, engaging, and credible • well-suited for audience and purpose	• clear and fitting for topic • engaging and credible • suited for audience and purpose	• fairly clear and seems to fit topic • fairly engaging • suited for audience and purpose
Organization	• logical organization with reasons presented in clear order • clearly contains beginning, middle, and end • easy to follow argument	• logical organization with reasons presented in order • contains beginning, middle, and end • easy to follow argument	• organizational pattern appar • some lapses may occur in organization • vaguely contains beginning, middle, and end • fairly easy to follow argumen
Word Precision	• demonstrates mature command of language • precise, persuasive, and interesting word choice • wide variety of word choice	• demonstrates command of language • interesting word choice • variety of word choice	• adequate word choice • some variety of word choice
Sentence Fluency	• uses complete sentences • varied sentence structures and lengths	• uses complete sentences • varied sentence structures	• uses complete sentences • varied sentence structure attempted • some simple sentence structures
Mechanics	• correct spelling, punctuation, and capitalization • proper grammar and usage • errors do not prevent understanding	• few errors in spelling, punctuation, and capitalization • proper grammar and usage • errors do not prevent understanding	• mostly correct spelling, punctuation, and capitalization • few errors in grammar and usage • errors do not prevent understanding
If using a four-point rubric	**4**	**4**	**3**

③	②	①	Cannot be scored
• generally focused on topic • position may be present • some support included, but erratic development • includes loosely related material • presents mediocre argument • conveys some sense of completeness	• somewhat related to topic • position may be unclear • inadequate support • includes extraneous or unrelated material • may lack sense of completeness	• minimally focused on topic • position unclear • little, if any, development of support • lacks sense of completeness	• no focus on topic • no position • no development of support • incomplete
• generally clear and seems to fit topic • engaging at times • generally suited for audience and purpose	• rarely comes through • basic attempt to engage reader • ill-suited for audience and purpose	• weak • basic attempt to engage reader • not suited for audience or purpose	• no attempt to engage reader • unaware of audience or purpose
• organizational pattern attempted attempts to contain beginning, middle, and end generally easy to follow argument	• little evidence of organizational pattern • somewhat difficult to follow argument	• no organizational pattern evident • difficult to follow argument	• no attempt at organization present • cannot follow argument
adequate word choice limited, predictable, or occasionally vague word choice some variety of word choice	• word choice limited, inappropriate, or vague • little variety of word choice	• limited or inappropriate word choice may obscure meaning • words/phrases repetitive and show minimal variety	• incorrect word choice • word choice shows no variety
uses complete sentences varied sentence structure attempted generally simple sentence structures	• occasional sentence fragment or run-on sentence • limited to simple sentence structure	• excessive use of sentence fragments or run-on sentences • limited to simple sentence structure • sentences difficult to understand	• no complete sentences • sentence structure basic/below grade level
generally correct spelling, punctuation, and capitalization some errors in grammar and usage errors do not prevent understanding	• some errors in spelling, punctuation, and capitalization • errors in grammar and usage • errors may prevent understanding	• errors in spelling, punctuation, and capitalization • frequent errors in grammar and usage • errors prevent understanding	• critical errors in spelling, punctuation, and capitalization/below grade level • critical errors in grammar and usage/below grade level • errors prevent understanding
3	**2**	**1**	

Rubric for Expressive/Descriptive Writing

	6	**5**	**4**
Content Quality and Idea Development	• well-focused on topic • ideas supported with interesting and vivid details • "paints a picture" for reader • conveys sense of completeness	• focused on topic • ideas supported with details • sustains interest of reader • conveys sense of completeness	• fairly focused on topic • ideas supported with adequate detail, but development may be uneven • may include extraneous or loosely related material • conveys some sense of completeness
Voice	• clear and fitting for topic • thoughtful, expressive, and engaging • well-suited for audience and purpose	• clear and fitting for topic • expressive and engaging • suited for audience and purpose	• fairly clear and seems to fit topic • fairly engaging with some expression • suited for audience and purpose
Organization	• logical progression of ideas • easy to follow	• logical progression of ideas • easy to follow	• organizational pattern apparent • some lapses may occur in organization • fairly easy to follow
Word Precision	• demonstrates mature command of language • precise, vivid, and interesting word choice • wide variety of word choice	• demonstrates command of language • interesting word choice • variety of word choice	• adequate word choice • some variety of word choice
Sentence Fluency	• uses complete sentences • varied sentence structures and lengths	• uses complete sentences • varied sentence structures	• uses complete sentences • varied sentence structure attempted • some simple sentence structures
Mechanics	• correct spelling, punctuation, and capitalization • proper grammar and usage • errors do not prevent understanding	• few errors in spelling, punctuation, and capitalization • proper grammar and usage • errors do not prevent understanding	• mostly correct spelling, punctuation, and capitalization • few errors in grammar and usage • errors do not prevent understanding
If using a four-point rubric	**4**	**4**	**3**

③	②	①	Cannot be scored
• enerally focused on topic • deas may be vague • ome details included, but rratic development • ome loosely related material • onveys some sense of ompleteness	• somewhat related to topic • inadequate details • includes extraneous or unrelated material • may lack sense of completeness	• minimally focused on topic • little, if any, development of ideas • lacks sense of completeness	• no focus on topic • no development of ideas • incomplete
• enerally clear and seems to t topic • ngaging at times • enerally suited for audience nd purpose	• rarely comes through • basic attempt to engage reader • ill-suited for audience and purpose	• weak • basic attempt to engage reader • not suited for audience or purpose	• no attempt to engage reader • unaware of audience or purpose
• rganizational pattern ttempted • enerally easy to follow	• little evidence of organizational pattern • somewhat difficult to follow	• no organizational pattern evident • difficult to follow	• no attempt at organization present • cannot follow
• dequate word choice • mited, predictable, or ccasionally vague word hoice • ome variety of word choice	• word choice limited, inappropriate, or vague • little variety of word choice	• limited or inappropriate word choice may obscure meaning • words/phrases repetitive and show minimal variety	• incorrect word choice • word choice shows no variety
• ses complete sentences • aried sentence structure ttempted • enerally simple sentence tructures	• occasional sentence fragment or run-on sentence • limited to simple sentence structure	• excessive use of sentence fragments or run-on sentences • limited to simple sentence structure • sentences difficult to understand	• no complete sentences • sentence structure basic/below grade level
• enerally correct spelling, unctuation, and apitalization • ome errors in grammar and sage • rors do not prevent nderstanding	• some errors in spelling, punctuation, and capitalization • errors in grammar and usage • errors may prevent understanding	• errors in spelling, punctuation, and capitalization • frequent errors in grammar and usage • errors prevent understanding	• critical errors in spelling, punctuation, and capitalization/below grade level • critical errors in grammar and usage/below grade level • errors prevent understanding
3	**2**	**1**	

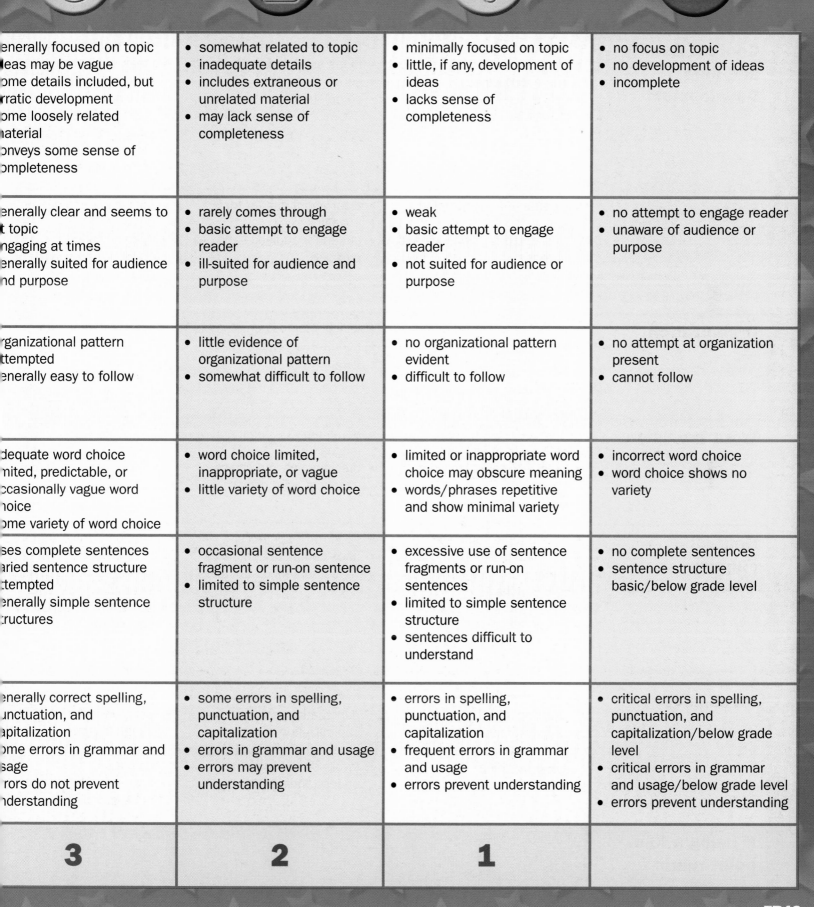

	6	**5**	**4**
Content Quality and Idea Development	• well-focused on topic • ideas supported with interesting details • conveys sense of completeness	• focused on topic • ideas supported with details • conveys sense of completeness	• fairly focused on topic • ideas supported with adequate detail, but development may be unev • may include extraneous o loosely related material • conveys some sense of completeness
Voice	• clear and fitting for topic • engaging • well-suited for audience and purpose	• clear and fitting for topic • engaging • suited for audience and purpose	• fairly clear and seems to f topic • fairly engaging • suited for audience and purpose
Organization	• logical progression of ideas • excellent transitions • easy to follow	• logical progression of ideas • good transitions • easy to follow	• organizational pattern app • some lapses may occur in organization • some transitions • fairly easy to follow
Word Precision	• demonstrates mature command of language • precise, interesting word choice • wide variety of word choice	• demonstrates command of language • precision in word choice • variety of word choice	• adequate word choice • some variety of word choi
Sentence Fluency	• strong topic sentence • uses complete sentences • varied sentence structures and lengths	• good topic sentence • uses complete sentences • varied sentence structures	• adequate topic sentence • uses complete sentences • varied sentence structure attempted • some simple sentence structures
Mechanics	• correct spelling, punctuation, and capitalization • proper grammar and usage • errors do not prevent understanding	• few errors in spelling, punctuation, and capitalization • proper grammar and usage • errors do not prevent understanding	• mostly correct spelling, punctuation, and capitalization • few errors in grammar and usage • errors do not prevent understanding
If using a four-point rubric	**4**	**4**	**3**

③	②	①	Cannot be scored
generally focused on topic some loosely related material some details included, but erratic development	• somewhat related to topic • inadequate details • includes extraneous or unrelated material • may lack sense of completeness	• minimally focused on topic • little, if any, development of ideas • lacks sense of completeness	• no focus on topic • no development of ideas • incomplete
generally clear and seems to fit topic engaging at times generally suited for audience and purpose	• rarely comes through • basic attempt to engage reader • ill-suited for audience and purpose	• weak • basic attempt to engage reader • not suited for audience or purpose	• no attempt to engage reader • unaware of audience or purpose
organizational pattern attempted few transitions generally easy to follow	• little evidence of organizational pattern • no transitions • somewhat difficult to follow	• no organizational pattern evident • difficult to follow	• no attempt at organization present • cannot follow
adequate word choice limited, predictable, or occasionally vague word choice some variety of word choice	• word choice limited, inappropriate, or vague • little variety of word choice	• limited or inappropriate word choice may obscure meaning • words/phrases repetitive and show minimal variety	• incorrect word choice • word choice shows no variety
adequate topic sentence uses complete sentences varied sentence structure attempted generally simple sentence structures	• weak topic sentence • occasional sentence fragment or run-on sentence • limited to simple sentence structure	• topic sentence not evident • excessive use of sentence fragments or run-on sentences • limited to simple sentence structure • sentences difficult to understand	• no topic sentence • no complete sentences • sentence structure basic/below grade level
generally correct spelling, punctuation, and capitalization some errors in grammar and usage errors do not prevent understanding	• some errors in spelling, punctuation, and capitalization • errors in grammar and usage • errors may prevent understanding	• errors in spelling, punctuation, and capitalization • frequent errors in grammar and usage • errors prevent understanding	• critical errors in spelling, punctuation, and capitalization/below grade level • critical errors in grammar and usage/below grade level • errors prevent understanding
3	**2**	**1**	

Notes

Overview Bibliography

Come Back, Salmon: How a Group of Dedicated Kids Adopted Pigeon Creek and Brought It Back to Life, by Molly Cone (Sierra Club Juveniles, ISBN 0-871-56489-0, 1992) **Easy**

George Washington Carver: A Photo-Illustrated Biography, by Margo McLoone (Bridgestone, ISBN 1-560-65516-X, 1997) **Easy**

Kids Learn America! Bringing Geography to Life With People, Places & History, by Patricia Gordon and Reed C. Snow (Williamson Publishing, ISBN 1-885-59331-7, 1999) **Easy**

Once Upon a Company: A True Story, by Wendy Anderson Halperin (Orchard, ISBN 0-531-30089-7, 1998) **Easy** *NCSS Notable Book*

This Land Is Your Land, by Woody Guthrie (Little, Brown, ISBN 0-316-39215-4, 1998) **Easy** *NCSS Notable Book*

Thomas A. Edison: Young Inventor, by Sue Guthridge (Aladdin Paperbacks, ISBN 0-020-41850-7, 1990) **Easy**

Counting Heads and More: The Work of the U.S. Census Bureau, by Marta McCave (Twenty-First Century Books, Inc., ISBN 0-761-33017-8, 1998) **On-Level**

If You Were There When They Signed the Constitution, by Elizabeth Levy (Scholastic Trade, ISBN 0-590-45159-6, 1992) **On-Level**

Legends of Landforms: Native American Lore and the Geology of the Land, by Carole G. Vogel (Millbrook, ISBN 0-761-30272-7, 1999) **On-Level** *NCSS Notable Book*

So You Want to Be President? by Judith St. George (Philomel Books, ISBN 0-399-23407-1, 2001) **On-Level** *Caldecott Medal*

The Story of George Washington Carver, by Eva Moore (Scholastic, ISBN 0-590-42660-5, 1995) **On-Level**

Thomas Alva Edison: Young Inventor, by Louis Sabin (Troll Communications, ISBN 0-893-75842-6, 1988) **On-Level**

Coming to America: The Story of Immigration, by Betsy C. Maestro (Scholastic, ISBN 0-590-44151-5, 1996) **Challenge**

George Washington Carver, by Gene Adair (Chelsea House, ISBN 1-555-46577-3, 1989) **Challenge**

The Kids' Business Book, by Arlene Erlbach (Lerner, ISBN 0-822-52413-9, 1998) **Challenge** *NCSS Notable Book*

Neal S. Godfrey's Ultimate Kids' Money Book, by Neal S. Godfrey (Simon & Schuster, ISBN 0-689-81717-7, 1998) **Challenge** *NCSS Notable Book*

The Orphan of Ellis Island: A Time-Travel Adventure, by Elvira Woodruff (Scholastic Trade, ISBN 0-590-48245-9, 1997) **Challenge**

The Story of Thomas Alva Edison, by Margaret Cousins (Random House, ISBN 0-394-84883-7, 1997) **Challenge**

A People's History of the United States: 1492–Present, by Howard Zinn (Harperperennial Library, ISBN 0-060-92643-0, 1995) **Teacher reference**

The U.S. Constitution and Fascinating Facts About It, by Terry L. Jordan (Oak Hill Publishers, ISBN 1-891-74300-7, 1999) **Teacher reference**

Look for this symbol throughout the Teacher's Edition to find **Award-Winning Selections**.

Unit 1 Bibliography

Incas, by Tim Wood (Viking Penguin, ISBN 0-670-87037-4, 1996) **Easy**

Machu Picchu: The Story of the Amazing Inkas and Their City in the Clouds, by Elizabeth Mann (Mikaya Press, ISBN 0-965-04939-6, 2000) **Easy**

Marco Polo, by Charles P. Graves (Chelsea House, ISBN 0-791-01505-X, 1991) **Easy**

Marco Polo: A Journey Through China, by Fiona MacDonald (Franklin Watts, ISBN 0-531-15340-1, 1998) **Easy**

People of the Longhouse: How the Iroquoian Tribes Lived, by Jillian and Robin Ridington (Firefly Books, ISBN 1-550-54221-4, 1992) **Easy**

Thirteen Moons on Turtle's Back, by Joseph Bruchac (Philomel Books, ISBN 0-399-22141-7, 1992) **Easy** *NCSS Notable Book/NSTA Outstanding Book*

The Turkey Girl: A Zuni Cinderella Story, by Penny Pollock (Little, Brown, ISBN 0-316-71314-7, 1996) **Easy**

American Indian Mythology, by Evelyn Wolfson (Enslow Publishers, ISBN 0-766-01411-8, 2000) **On-Level**

Daily Life in a Plains Indian Village, 1868, by Michael Bad Hand Terry (Houghton Mifflin, ISBN 0-395-97499-2, 1999) **On-Level** *NCSS Notable Book*

Daily Life in Ancient and Modern Timbuktu, by Larry Brook (Runestone Press, ISBN 0-822-53215-8, 1999) **On-Level**

A Day with the Chumash, by Georgia Lee (Lerner, ISBN 0-822-51918-6, 1999) **On-Level**

Earthmaker's Tales: North American Indian Stories About Earth Happenings, by Gretchen Will Mayo (Walker and Company, ISBN 0-8027-7343-5, 1990) **On-Level**

The Magic of Spider Woman, by Lois Duncan (Scholastic, ISBN 0-590-46155-9, 1996) **On-Level**

Maya, by Peter Chrisp (Raintree, ISBN 0-739-81410-9, 1994) **On-Level**

The Navajo, by Raymond Bial (Marshall Cavendish, ISBN 0-761-40803-7, 1998) **On-Level** *NCSS Notable Book*

What Do We Know About the Vikings? by Helen Mary Martell (Peter Bedrick Books, ISBN 0-872-26355-X, 1992) **On-Level**

Around the World in a Hundred Years: From Henry the Navigator to Magellan, by Jean Fritz (G.P. Putnam's Sons, ISBN 0-698-11638-0, 1993) **Challenge** *INA Teacher's Choice Award*

Empire of Mali, by Carol Thompson (Franklin Watts, ISBN 0-531-20277-1, 1998) **Challenge**

Heetunka's Harvest: A Tale of the Plains Indians, by Jennifer Jones (Rinehart, ISBN 1-879-37317-3, 1994) **Challenge**

Indians of the Four Corners: The Anasazi and Their Pueblo Descendants, by Alice Marriott (Ancient City Press, ISBN 0-941-27091-2, 1996) **Challenge**

Marco Polo and the Medieval Explorers, by Rebecca Stefoff (Chelsea House, ISBN 0-791-01294-8, 1992) **Challenge**

Montezuma and the Fall of the Aztecs, by Eric A. Kimmel (Holiday House, ISBN 0-823-41452-3, 2000) **Challenge**

Pushing Up the Sky: Seven Native American Plays for Children, by Joseph Bruchac (Dial Books for Young Readers, ISBN 0-803-72168-4, 2000) **Challenge**

The Royal Kingdoms of Ghana, Mali and Songhay: Life in Medieval Africa, by Patricia and Fredrick McKissack (Henry Holt, ISBN 0-805-04259-8, 1995) **Challenge**

Turtle Island: Tales of the Algonquian Nations, by Jane Louise Curry (Simon & Schuster, ISBN 0-689-82233-2, 1999) **Challenge** *NCSS Notable Book*

Aztec, Inca, and Maya, by Elizabeth Baquedano (Dorling Kindersley, ISBN 0-789-46115-3, 2000) **Teacher reference**

Early Explorers of North America, by C. Keith Wilbur (Chelsea Juniors, ISBN 0-7910-4531-5, 1996) **Teacher reference**

 Look for this symbol throughout the Teacher's Edition to find **Award-Winning Selections**.

Unit 2 Bibliography

Bartolomé de Las Casas: Champion of Indian Rights, by Fred Stopsky (Discovery Enterprises Ltd., ISBN 1-878-66812-9, 1992) **Easy**

Columbus and the Renaissance Explorers, by Colin Hynson (Barron's Educational Series, ISBN 0-764-10530-2, 1998) **Easy**

Exploration and Conquest: The Americas After Columbus: 1500–1620, by Betsy Maestro (Harper Trophy, ISBN 0-688-15474-3, 1997) **Easy**

Jamestown: New World Adventure, by James E. Knight (Troll Associates, ISBN 0-816-74554-4, 1998) **Easy**

Magellan: A Voyage Around the World, by Fiona MacDonald (Franklin Watts, ISBN 0-531-15341-X, 1998) **Easy**

The Spinner's Daughter, by Amy Littlesugar (Pippin Press, ISBN 0-945-91222-6, 1994) **Easy**

Stranded at Plimoth Plantation 1626, by Gary Bowen (HarperCollins, ISBN 0-064-40719-5, 1998) **Easy**

Explorers Who Got Lost, by Diane Sansevere-Dreher (Tor Books, ISBN 0-812-52038-6, 1994) **On-Level**

Increase Mather: Clergyman and Scholar, by Norma Jean Lutz (Chelsea House Publishers, ISBN 0-791-06119-1, 2000) **On-Level**

A Journey to the New World: The Diary of Remember Patience Whipple, Mayflower, 1620, by Kathryn Lasky and Kristiana Gregory (Scholastic, ISBN 0-590-50214-X, 1996) **On-Level**

Juan Ponce de León and the Search for the Fountain of Youth, by Dan Harmon (Chelsea House Publishers, ISBN 0-791-05517-5, 1999) **On-Level**

Pocahontas: The True Story of the Powhatan Princess, by Catherine Iannone (Chelsea House Publishers, ISBN 0-791-02497-0, 1995) **On-Level**

The Travels of Samuel de Champlain, by Joanne Mattern (Raintree, ISBN 0-739-81494-X, 1999) **On-Level**

🎖 ***Where Do You Think You're Going, Christopher Columbus?*** by Jean Fritz (Paper Star, ISBN 0-698-11580-5, 1997) **On-Level ALA Notable Book**

🎖 ***Around the World in a Hundred Years: From Henry the Navigator to Magellan,*** by Jean Fritz (PaperStar, ISBN 0-698-11638-0, 1998) **Challenge INA Teacher's Choice Award**

Empires Lost and Won: The Spanish Heritage in the Southwest, by Albert Marrin (Atheneum, ISBN 0-689-80414-8, 1997) **Challenge**

The Paradox of Jamestown: 1585–1700, by Christopher Collier and James Lincoln Collier (Benchmark Books, ISBN 0-761-40437-6, 1997) **Challenge**

Pilgrims and Puritans: 1620–1676, by Christopher Collier and James Lincoln Collier (Benchmark Books, ISBN 0-761-40438-4, 1997) **Challenge**

Pocahontas: The Life and the Legend, by Frances Mossiker (Da Capo, ISBN 0-306-80699-1, 1996) **Challenge**

Seeds of Change: The Story of Cultural Exchange after 1492, by J. Davis Hawke and Sharryl Hawke (Addison Wesley Longman, ISBN 0-201-29419-2, 1993) **Challenge**

🎖 ***William Bradford: Rock of Plymouth,*** by Kieran Doherty (Millbrook, ISBN 0-761-31304-4, 1999) **Challenge NCSS Notable Book**

Age of Discovery: 1492 to 1815 (World Atlas of the Past, Vol. 3), by John Haywood (Oxford University Press, ISBN 0-195-21691-1, 2000) **Teacher reference**

History of the Conquest of Peru, by William Hickling Prescott (Modern Library, ISBN 0-679-60304-2, 1998) **Teacher reference**

🎖 Look for this symbol throughout the Teacher's Edition to find **Award-Winning Selections**.

Unit 3 Bibliography

The Amazing Life of Benjamin Franklin, by James Cross Giblin (Scholastic Press, ISBN 0-590-48534-2, 2000) **Easy**

Benjamin Franklin, by Steve Parker (Chelsea House, ISBN 0-791-03006-7, 1995) **Easy**

Daily Life: A Sourcebook on Colonial America, by Carter Smith, ed. (Millbrook Press, ISBN 1-562-94038-4, 1991) **Easy**

Historic St. Augustine, by Sandra and Susan Steen (Silver Burdett Press, ISBN 0-382-39331-7, 1996) **Easy**

Journey to Monticello: Traveling in Colonial Times, by James E. Knight (Troll Associates, ISBN 0-816-74973-6, 1999) **Easy**

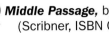 **Molly Bannaky,** by Alice McGill (Houghton Mifflin, ISBN 0-395-72287-X, 1999) **Easy Jane Addams Book Award; ALA Notable Book**

Never Turn Back: Father Serra's Mission, by George Guzzi (Raintree/Steck-Vaughn, ISBN 0-811-48061-5, 1996) **Easy**

The Village: Life in Colonial Times, by James E. Knight (Troll Associates, ISBN 0-816-74800-4, 1998) **Easy**

Ben and Me, by Robert Lawson (Little, Brown and Co., ISBN 0-316-51730-5, 1988) **On-Level**

Calico Bush, by Rachel Field (Macmillan, ISBN 0-689-82285-5, 1987) **On-Level Newbery Honor Book**

Exploration & Conquest: The Americas After Columbus, 1500–1620, by Betsy Maestro (Lothrop, ISBN 0-688-09267-5, 1994) **On-Level**

George-Isms: The 110 Rules George Washington Wrote When He Was 14 and Lived by All His Life, by George Washington (Atheneum Books for Young Readers, ISBN 0-689-84082-9, 2000) **On-Level**

Growing Up in Colonial America, by Tracy Barrett (Millbrook Press, ISBN 1-562-94578-5, 1995) **On-Level**

Junípero Serra, by Sean Dolan (Chelsea House Publishing, ISBN 0-791-01282-4, 1992) **On-Level**

The Kidnapped Prince: The Life of Olaudah Equiano, adapted by Ann Cameron (Random House, ISBN 0-375-80346-7, 2000) **On-Level**

Pontiac: Ottawa Rebel, by Celia Bland (Chelsea House, ISBN 0-791-01717-6, 1994) **On-Level**

American Sisters: Voyage to a Free Land, 1630, by Laurie Lawlor (Simon & Schuster, ISBN 0-671-77562-6, 2001) **Challenge**

Benjamin Banneker, by Kevin Conley (Chelsea House, ISBN 1-555-46573-0, 1989) **Challenge**

Benjamin Franklin: Founding Father and Inventor, by Leila Merrell Foster (Enslow Publishers, Inc., ISBN 0-894-90784-0, 1997) **Challenge**

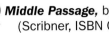 **Black Hands, White Sails: The Story of African-American Whalers,** by Patricia C. and Fredrick L. McKissack (Scholastic, ISBN 0-590-48313-7, 1999) **Challenge Coretta Scott King Honor Book**

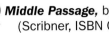 **The Captive,** by Joyce Hansen (Apple, ISBN 0-590-41624-3, 1995) **Challenge Coretta Scott King Honor Book**

Father Junípero Serra: Founder of California Missions, by Donna Genet (Enslow Publishers, Inc., ISBN 0-894-90762-X, 1996) **Challenge**

John Peter Zenger: Free Press Advocate, by Karen Westermann (Chelsea House, ISBN 0-791-05966-9, 2000) **Challenge**

Making Thirteen Colonies (History of U.S., Book 2), by Joy Hakim (Oxford University Press Children's Books, ISBN 0-195-15322-7, 1999) **Challenge**

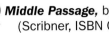 **Middle Passage,** by Charles R. Johnson (Scribner, ISBN 0-684-85588-7, 1998) **Teacher reference National Book Award**

Rearing Wolves to Our Own Destruction: Slavery in Richmond, Virginia, 1782–1865, by Midori Takagi (University of Virginia Press, ISBN 0-813-92099-X, 2002) **Teacher reference**

Discovery Channel School Videos

George Washington: The Unknown Years Learn about George Washington's colonial life and what prepared him to become one of the country's founding fathers. (Item #716530, 26 minutes)

The Real Ben Franklin This video biography reveals Franklin's many accomplishments, including being a builder of the new American nation. (Item #716712, 26 minutes)

The Real Thomas Jefferson Discover the complexities and contradictions of a great American. (Item #716720, 26 minutes)

 Look for this symbol throughout the Teacher's Edition to find **Award-Winning Selections**.

Unit 4 Bibliography

 Can't You Make Them Behave, King George? by Jean Fritz (PaperStar, ISBN 0-698-11402-7, 1996) **Easy** *Newbery Honor Book*

Crossing the Delaware: A History in Many Voices, by Louise Peacock (Atheneum, ISBN 0-689-80994-8, 1998) **Easy**

The Declaration of Independence (Cornerstones of Freedom), by R. Conrad Stein (Children's Press, ISBN 0-516-46693-3, 1995) **Easy**

George Washington, by Cheryl Harness (National Geographic Society, ISBN 0-792-26906-3, 2000) **Easy**

Phoebe the Spy, by Judith Berry Griffin (Scholastic Paperbacks, ISBN 0-590-42432-7, 1991) **Easy**

A Picture Book of Patrick Henry, by David A. Adler (Holiday House, ISBN 0-823-41678-X, 2001) **Easy**

A Picture Book of Thomas Jefferson, by David A. Adler (Holiday House, ISBN 0-823-40881-7, 1991) **Easy**

 Sybil Ludington's Midnight Ride, by Marsha Amstel (Carolrhoda, ISBN 1-575-05456-6, 2000) **Easy** *Horn Book Award*

Thomas Jefferson: Voice of Liberty (Community Builders), by Andrew Santella (Children's Press, ISBN 0-516-26514-8, 2000) **Easy**

Where Was Patrick Henry on the 29th of May? by Jean Fritz (PaperStar, ISBN 0-698-11439-6, 1997) **Easy**

George Washington, by Tara Baukus Mello (Chelsea House Publishing, ISBN 0-791-05695-3, 1999) **On-Level**

George Washington's Socks, by Elvira Woodruff (Scholastic, Inc., ISBN 0-590-44036-5, 1993) **On-Level**

Hannah's Winter of Hope, by Jean Van Leeuwen (Puffin, ISBN 0-141-30950-4, 2001) **On-Level** *Young Reader's Choice Award*

If You Lived at the Time of the American Revolution, by Kay Moore (Scholastic Trade, ISBN 0-590-67444-7, 1998) **On-Level**

Lexington and Concord, by Deborah Kent (Scholastic, Inc., ISBN 0-516-26229-7, 1998) **On-Level**

Meet Thomas Jefferson, by Marvin Barrett (Random House, ISBN 0-394-81964-0, 1989) **On-Level**

The Midnight Ride of Paul Revere, by Henry Wadsworth Longfellow (National Geographic Society, ISBN 0-792-26558-0, 2000) **On-Level**

Patrick Henry: Voice of the American Revolution, by Louis Sabin (Troll Communications, ISBN 0-893-75765-9, 1996) **On-Level**

The Secret Soldier: The Story of Deborah Sampson, by Ann McGovern (Scholastic, ISBN 0-590-43052-1, 1990) **On-Level**

Crispus Attucks: Black Leader of Colonial Patriots (Childhood of Famous Americans Series), by Dharathula H. Millender (Aladdin Paperbacks, ISBN 0-020-41810-8, 1986) **Challenge**

The Fifth of March: A Story of the Boston Massacre, by Ann Rinaldi (Gulliver Books, ISBN 0-152-27517-7, 1993) **Challenge**

George Washington, by Wendie C. Old (Enslow Publishers, ISBN 0-894-90832-4, 1997) **Challenge**

Give Me Liberty! The Story of the Declaration of Independence, by Russell Freedman (Holiday House, ISBN 0-823-41753-0, 2002) **Challenge**

If You Were There in 1776, by Barbara Brenner (Simon & Schuster, ISBN 0-027-12322-7, 1994) **Challenge**

Patrick Henry, by Stuart Kallen (ABDO Publishing, ISBN 1-577-65012-3, 2001) **Challenge**

Thomas Jefferson (World Leaders Past and Present), by Roger Bruns (Chelsea House, ISBN 0-791-00644-1, 1986) **Challenge**

A Young Patriot: The American Revolution as Experienced by One Boy, by Jim Murphy (Houghton Mifflin Co., ISBN 0-395-90019-0, 1998) **Challenge**

A Battlefield Atlas of the American Revolution, by Craig L. Symonds (Nautical & Aviation Pub. Co. of America, ISBN 0-933-85253-3, 1986) **Teacher reference**

Encyclopedia of the American Revolution, by Mark Mayo Boatner (Stackpole Books, ISBN 0-811-70578-1, 1994) **Teacher reference**

Discovery Channel School Videos

George Washington: The Unknown Years Learn what prepared Washington to be a founding father. (Item #716530, 26 minutes)

The Real Thomas Jefferson Explore the complexities and contradictions of a great American. (Item #716720, 26 minutes)

 Look for this symbol throughout the Teacher's Edition to find **Award-Winning Selections**.

Grade 5 • Unit 4 Bibliography **TR51**

Unit 5 Bibliography

Dear Benjamin Banneker, by Andrea Davis Pinkney (Harcourt Paperbacks, ISBN 0-152-01892-1, 1998) **Easy**

The Inside-Out Book of Washington, D.C., by Roxie Munro (Seastar Publishing Co., ISBN 1-587-17078-7, 2001) **Easy**

Shh! We're Writing the Constitution, by Jean Fritz (Penguin Putnam Books for Young Readers, ISBN 0-698-11624-0, 1997) **Easy**

The Star-Spangled Banner, by Francis Scott Key (Random House Children's Books, ISBN 0-375-81596-1, 2002) **Easy Children's Book of the Year**

The U.S. Constitution and You, by Syl Sobel (Barron's Educational Series, ISBN 0-764-11707-6, 2001) **Easy**

The Voice of the People: American Democracy in Action, by Betsy Maestro (Harper Trophy, ISBN 0-688-16157-X, 1998) **Easy**

Across America: The Story of Lewis and Clark, by Jacqueline Morley and David Antram (Franklin Watts, ISBN 0-531-15342-8, 1999) **On-Level**

Francis Scott Key: Poet and Patriot (Discovery Biographies), by Lillie Patterson and Victor Dowd (Chelsea House Publishing, ISBN 0-791-01461-4, 1991) **On-Level**

More Perfect Union: The Story of Our Constitution, by Betsy Maestro (Harper Trophy, ISBN 0-688-10192-5, 1990) **On-Level ALA Notable Book**

Off the Map: The Journals of Lewis and Clark, edited by Connie Roop and Peter Geiger Roop (Walker and Co., ISBN 0-802-77546-2, 1998) **On-Level**

The U.S. Constitution and Fascinating Facts About It, by Terry L. Jordan (Oak Hill Publishing, ISBN 1-891-74300-7, 1999) **On-Level**

The U.S. Constitution (Your Government: How It Works), by Joan Banks (Chelsea House Publishing, ISBN 0-791-05991-X, 2000) **On-Level**

The Captain's Dog: My Journey with Lewis and Clark, by Roland Smith (Harcourt Brace, ISBN 0-152-02696-7, 2000) **Challenge**

The Constitution of the United States (American Government in Action), by Karen Judson (Enslow Publishing, ISBN 0-894-90586-4, 1996) **Challenge**

Creating the Constitution: 1787 (Drama of American History), by Christopher Collier and James Lincoln Collier (Benchmark Books, ISBN 0-761-40776-6, 1998) **Challenge**

The Dictionary of the U.S. Constitution, by Barbara Feinberg (Franklin Watts, ISBN 0-531-11570-4, 1999) **Challenge**

How the U.S. Government Works, by Syl Sobel and Pam Tanzey (Barron's Educational Series, ISBN 0-764-11111-6, 1999) **Challenge**

A Kids' Guide to America's Bill of Rights: Curfews, Censorship, and the 100-Pound Giant, by Kathleen Krull (Avon Books, ISBN 0-380-97497-5, 1999) **Challenge**

Woman of Independence: The Life of Abigail Adams, by Susan Provost Beller (iUniverse.com, ISBN 0-595-00789-9, 2000) **Challenge**

The Debate on the Constitution, by Bernard Bailyn, ed. (Library of America, ISBN 0-940-45042-9, 1993) **Teacher reference**

Decision in Philadelphia: The Constitutional Convention of 1787, by Christopher Collier and James Lincoln Collier (Ballantine Books, ISBN 0-345-34652-1, 1987) **Teacher reference**

Founding Fathers: Brief Lives of the Framers of the United States Constitution, by M. E. Bradford (University Press of Kansas, ISBN 0-700-60657-2, 1994) **Teacher reference**

 Look for this symbol throughout the Teacher's Edition to find **Award-Winning Selections**.

65455-4, 1996) **Easy**

Eli Whitney: Great Inventor, by Jean Lee Latham (Chelsea House, ISBN 0-791-01453-3, 1991) **Easy**

Frederick Douglass, by John Passaro (Child's World, ISBN 1-567-66621-3, 1999) **Easy**

Kids During the Industrial Revolution, by Lisa A. Wroble (Rosen Publishing Group, ISBN 0-823-95254-1, 1999) **Easy**

 **Only Passing Through: The Story of Sojourner Truth,** by Anne Rockwell (Dragonfly Books, ISBN 0-440-41766-X, 2002) **Easy Coretta Scott King Honor Book**

Sojourner Truth, by Laura Spinale (Child's World, ISBN 1-567-66623-X, 1999) **Easy**

Voices of the Alamo, by Sherry Garland (Scholastic Trade, ISBN 0-590-98833-6, 2000) **Easy**

Cheryl Harness (Aladdin, ISBN 0-689-82584-6, 1999) **On-Level**

Andrew Jackson, by Anne Welsbacher (ABDO Publishing, ISBN 1-562-39811-3, 1999) **On-Level**

The Ballad of Lucy Whipple, by Karen Cushman (HarperCollins Children's Books, ISBN 0-064-40684-9, 1998) **On-Level**

Escape to Freedom: A Play About Young Frederick Douglass, by Ossie Davis (Penguin Putnam, ISBN 0-140-34355-5, 1990) **On-Level**

Railroad, by Bobbie Kalman (Crabtree Publishing Co., ISBN 0-778-70108-5, 1999) **On-Level**

Sojourner Truth: Abolitionist and Women's Rights Activist, by Catherine Bernard (Enslow Publishers, ISBN 0-766-01257-3, 2001) **On-Level**

Sojourner Truth and the Struggle for Freedom, by Edward Beecher Claflin (Barron's Educational Series, ISBN 0-812-03919-X, 1987) **On-Level**

They Shall Be Heard: Susan B. Anthony and Elizabeth Cady Stanton, by Kate Connell (Raintree, ISBN 0-811-48068-2, 1993) **On-Level**

(Children's Press, ISBN 0-516-01387-4, 1987) **Challenge**

Frederick Douglass and the Fight for Freedom, by Douglas Miller (Facts on File, ISBN 0-816-01617-8, 1998) **Challenge**

Frederick Douglass: Freedom's Force, by Melva Lawson Ware (Time-Life, ISBN 0-783-55437-0, 1999) **Challenge**

Industrial Revolution, by Mary Collins (Children's Press, ISBN 0-516-27036-2, 2000) **Challenge**

Mr. Blue Jeans: A Story About Levi Strauss, by Maryann Weidt (Lerner Publications, ISBN 0-876-14588-8, 1992) **Challenge**

Sojourner Truth: Antislavery Leader, Early Feminist, by Peter Krass (Holloway House, ISBN 0-870-67559-1, 1990) **Challenge**

Sojourner Truth: Ain't I a Woman? by Patricia C. McKissack (Scholastic, ISBN 0-590-44691-6, 1994) **Challenge Coretta Scott King Honor Book**

Trail of Tears: The Cherokee Journey from Home, by Marlene Targ Brill (Millbrook Press, ISBN 1-562-94486-X, 1995) **Challenge**

The Industrial Revolution, by William Dudley, ed. (Greenhaven Press, Inc., ISBN 1-565-10706-3, 1997) **Teacher reference**

Let It Shine: Stories of Black Women Freedom Fighters, by Andrea Davis Pinkney (Harcourt Brace, ISBN 0-152-01005-X, 2000) **Teacher reference Coretta Scott King Honor Book**

Pushing the Bear: A Novel of the Trail of Tears, by Diane Glancy (Harcourt Trade, ISBN 0-156-00544-1, 1998) **Teacher reference**

Look for this symbol throughout the Teacher's Edition to find **Award-Winning Selections**.

Turner (HarperCollins Juvenile Books, ISBN 0-060-27577-4, 2000) **Easy**

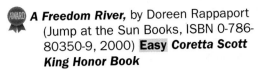 **A Freedom River,** by Doreen Rappaport (Jump at the Sun Books, ISBN 0-786-80350-9, 2000) **Easy** *Coretta Scott King Honor Book*

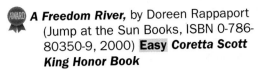 **Harriet and the Promised Land,** by Jacob Lawrence (Aladdin Paperbacks, ISBN 0-689-80965-4, 1997) **Easy** *New York Times Best Illustrated Book*

I Thought My Soul Would Rise and Fly: The Diary of Patsy, a Freed Girl, by Joyce Hansen (Scholastic, Inc., ISBN 0-590-84913-1, 1997) **Easy**

Robert E. Lee, Brave Leader, by Rae Bains (Troll Associates, ISBN 0-816-70546-1, 2003) **Easy**

Sweet Clara and the Freedom Quilt, by Deborah Hopkinson (Random House, ISBN 0-679-87472-0, 1995) **Easy**

Voice of Freedom: A Story About Frederick Douglass, by Maryann N. Weidt (Lerner Publishing Group, ISBN 1-575-05553-8, 2001) **Easy**

of His Greatest Speeches and Letters, by Harold Holzer, ed. (Boyds Mills Press, ISBN 1-563-97772-9, 2000) **On-Level**

The Africans (We Came to North America), by Jen Green (Crabtree Publishing, ISBN 0-778-70198-0, 2000) **On-Level**

Harriet Tubman: Conductor on the Underground Railroad, by Ann Petry (Harper Trophy, ISBN 0-064-46181-5, 1996) **On-Level**

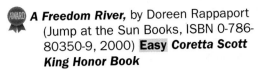 *Lincoln: A Photobiography,* by Russell Freedman (Clarion Books, ISBN 0-899-19380-3, 1987) **On-Level** *Newbery Medal*

My Brother's Keeper: Virginia's Diary— Gettysburg, Pennsylvania, by Mary Pope Osborne (Scholastic, Inc., ISBN 0-439-15307-7, 2000) **On-Level**

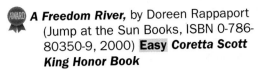 *Steal Away,* by Jennifer Armstrong (Scholastic Paperbacks, ISBN 0-590-46921-5, 1993) **On-Level** *ALA Notable Book*

The World in the Time of Abraham Lincoln, by Fiona MacDonald (Chelsea House Publishers, ISBN 0-791-06028-4, 2000) **On-Level**

Veronica Chambers (Harcourt Brace, ISBN 0-152-01803-4, 1998) **Challenge**

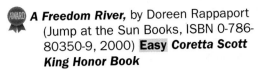 *Anthony Burns: The Defeat and Triumph of a Fugitive Slave,* by Virginia Hamilton (Laurel-Leaf, ISBN 0-679-83997-6, 1988) **Challenge** *ALA Notable Book, Boston Globe Horn Book Award, Jane Addams Book Award*

Clara Barton: Civil War Nurse, by Nancy Whitelaw (Enslow Publishers, ISBN 0-894-90778-6, 1997) **Challenge**

Dear Ellen Bee: A Civil War Scrapbook of Two Union Spies, by Mary E. Lyons and Muriel M. Branch (Atheneum, ISBN 0-689-82379-7, 2000) **Challenge**

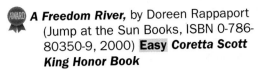 *House of Dies Drear,* by Virginia Hamilton (Aladdin Paperbacks, ISBN 0-020-43520-7, 1984) **Challenge** *Edgar Allen Poe Juvenile Book*

Lincoln: In His Own Words, by Milton Melzer, ed. (Harcourt Brace & Company, ISBN 0-152-45437-3, 1993) **Challenge**

Nightjohn, by Gary Paulsen (Delacorte Press, ISBN 0-385-30838-8, 1993) **Challenge**

Battle Cry of Freedom: The Civil War Era, by James M. McPherson (Oxford University Press, ISBN 0-19-516895-X, 2003) **Teacher reference**

With Malice Toward None: A Life of Abraham Lincoln, by Stephen B. Oates (HarperPerennial Library, ISBN 0-060-92471-3, 1994) **Teacher reference**

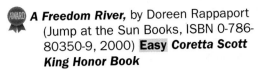 Look for this symbol throughout the Teacher Edition to find **Award-Winning Selections.**

Unit 8 Bibliography

Eyewitness: Cowboy, by David H. Murdoch (Dorling Kindersley Publishing, ISBN 0-789-45854-3, 2000) **Easy**

New Land: A First Year on the Prairie, by Marilynn Reynolds (Orca Books, ISBN 1-551-43071-1, 1999) **Easy**

Pony Express!, by Steven Kroll (Scholastic Incorporated, ISBN 0-590-20240-5, 2000) **Easy**

Streets of Gold, by Rosemary Wells (Dial Books for Young Readers, ISBN 0-803-72149-8, 1999) **Easy**

Teddy Roosevelt: Young Rough Rider, by Edd Winfield Parks (Aladdin, ISBN 0-689-71349-5, 1989) **Easy**

Ten Mile Day and the Building of the Transcontinental Railroad, by Mary Ann Fraser (Henry Holt & Co., ISBN 0-805-04703-4, 1996) **Easy**

Theodore Roosevelt, by Michael A. Schuman (Enslow, ISBN 0-894-90836-7, 1997) **Easy**

Thomas A. Edison: Young Inventor, by Sue Guthridge (Alladin, ISBN 0-020-41850-7, 1986) **Easy**

When Jesse Came Across the Sea, by Amy Hest (Candlewick, ISBN 0-763-60094-6, 1997) **Easy**

Andrew Carnegie: Builder of Libraries, by Charnan Simon (Children's Press, ISBN 0-516-20289-8, 1997) **On-Level**

Bully for You, Teddy Roosevelt, by Jean Fritz (PaperStar, ISBN 0-698-11609-7, 1997) **On-Level** **ALA Notable Book**

Ellis Island: A True Book, by Patricia R. Quiri (Children's Press, ISBN 0-516-20622-2, 1998) **On-Level**

Immigrant Kids, by Russell Freedman (Puffin, ISBN 0-140-37594-5, 1995) **On-Level**

Industry & Business (Life in America 100 Years Ago), by Linda Leuzzi (Chelsea House Publishers, ISBN 0-791-02846-1, 1997) **On-Level**

The Story of Alexander Graham Bell: Inventor of the Telephone, by Margaret Davidson (Gareth Stevens Publishing, ISBN 0-836-81483-5, 1997) **On-Level**

Thomas Edison & Electricity, by Steve Parker (Chelsea House, ISBN 0-791-03012-1, 1995) **On-Level**

Yang the Second and Her Secret Admirers, by Lensey Namioka (Bantam Doubleday Books, ISBN 0-440-41641-8, 2000) **On-Level**

Alexander Graham Bell: An Inventive Life, by Elizabeth MacLeod (Kids Can Press, ISBN 1-550-74456-9, 1999) **Challenge**

Chief Joseph: Nez Perce Leader, by Marian W. Taylor (Chelsea House, ISBN 0-791-01708-7, 1993) **Challenge**

James K. Polk, Abraham Lincoln, Theodore Roosevelt (Presidents Who Dared), by Edmund Lindop (Twenty-First Century, ISBN 0-805-03402-7, 1995) **Challenge**

Legendary Labor Leaders, by Thomas Streissguth (Oliver Press, ISBN 1-881-50844-7, 1998) **Challenge**

The Orphan of Ellis Island: A Time-Travel Adventure, by Elvira Woodruff (Scholastic, ISBN 0-590-48246-7, 2000) **Challenge**

Sitting Bull and His World, by Albert Marrin (Dutton, ISBN 0-525-45944-8, 2000) **Challenge** **NCSS Notable Book**

Soldier Boy, by Brian Burks (Harcourt Brace, ISBN 0-152-01219-2, 1997) **Challenge**

The Story of Thomas Alva Edison, by Margaret Cousins (Random House, ISBN 0-394-84883-7, 1997) **Challenge**

The Great Migrations: 1880s–1912, by William L. Katz (Steck-Vaughn Company, ISBN 0-811-42915-6, 1996) **Teacher reference**

Nothing Like It in the World: The Men Who Built the Transcontinental Railroad, 1863–1869, by Stephen E. Ambrose (Simon & Schuster, ISBN 0-684-84609-8, 2000) **Teacher reference**

The Prairies & Their People, by David Flint (Raintree, ISBN 0-817-24673-8, 1994) **Teacher reference**

The Promised Land, by Mary Antin (Modern Library, ISBN 0-375-75739-2, 2001) **Teacher reference**

Look for this symbol throughout the Teacher's Edition to find **Award-Winning Selections**.

Unit 9 Bibliography

Eleanor Roosevelt: A Life of Discovery, by Russell Freedman (Houghton Mifflin, ISBN 0-395-84520-3, 1997) **Easy**

Fire! by Joy Masoff (Scholastic, Inc., ISBN 0-590-97585-4, 1998) **Easy**

Franklin D. Roosevelt, by Steve Potts (Capstone, ISBN 1-560-65453-8, 1996) **Easy**

Free at Last: The Story of Martin Luther King, Jr., by Angela Bull (Dorling Kindersley, ISBN 0-789-45717-2, 2000) **Easy**

 I Am Rosa Parks, by Rosa Parks and James Haskins (Puffin, ISBN 0-141-30710-2, 1999) **Easy Horn Book Award, NCSS Notable Book**

John Glenn: A Space Biography, by Barbara Kramer (Enslow Publishers, Inc., ISBN 0-894-90964-9, 1998) **Easy**

Learning about Justice from the Life of César Chávez, by Jeanne M. Strazzabosco (Rosen Publishing Group, ISBN 0-823-92417-3, 1996) **Easy**

The Little Ships: The Heroic Rescue at Dunkirk in World War II, by Louise Borden (Simon & Schuster Children's, ISBN 0-689-85396-3, 2003) **Easy**

Pearl Harbor Is Burning: A Story of World War II, by Kathleen V. Kudlinski (Viking Penguin, ISBN 0-140-34509-4, 1993) **Easy**

Princess of the Press: The Story of Ida B. Wells-Barnett, by Angela Shelf Medearis (Lodestar Books, ISBN 0-525-67493-4, 1997) **Easy**

Rose Blanche, by Roberto Innocenti (Stewart, Tabori & Chang, ISBN 1-556-70207-8, 1990) **Easy**

Young Martin's Promise, by Walter Dean Myers (Raintree, ISBN 0-811-48050-X, 1996) **Easy**

Airplanes of World War II, by Nancy Robinson Masters (Capstone, ISBN 1-560-65531-3, 1998) **On-Level**

Attack on Pearl Harbor: The True Story of the Day America Entered World War II, by Shelley Tanaka (Hyperion Books for Children, ISBN 0-786-80736-9, 2001) **On-Level**

César Chávez: Mexican American Labor Leader, by Consuelo Rodriguez (Chelsea House, ISBN 0-791-01259-X, 1995) **On-Level**

Dwight D. Eisenhower, by Paul Joseph (ABDO Publishing, ISBN 1-562-39744-3, 1999) **On-Level**

The Fall of the Soviet Union, by Miles Harvey (Children's Press, ISBN 0-516-46694-1, 1995) **On-Level**

Fighting for Honor: Japanese Americans and World War II, by Michael L. Cooper (Houghton Mifflin, ISBN 0-395-91375-6, 2000) **On-Level**

Firefighting: Behind the Scenes, by Maria Mudd-Ruth (Houghton Mifflin, ISBN 0-395-70129-5, 1998) **On-Level**

Franklin D. Roosevelt, by Paul Joseph (ABDO Publishing, ISBN 1-562-39813-X, 2000) **On-Level**

 Mae Jemison, by Sonia W. Black (Mondo Publishers, ISBN 1-572-55801-6, 2000) **On-Level NCSS Notable Book**

Martin Luther King, by Rosemary Bray (Mulberry Books, ISBN 0-688-15219-8, 1997) **On-Level**

 Number the Stars, by Lois Lowry (Dell Books for Young Readers, ISBN 0-440-80291-1, 1989) **On-Level Newbery Medal**

Dare to Dream: Coretta Scott King and the Civil Rights Movement, by Angela Shelf Medearis (Puffin, ISBN 0-141-30202-X, 1999) **Challenge**

An Elegy on the Death of César Chávez: A Poem, by Rudolfo A. Anaya (Cinco Puntos Press, ISBN 0-938-31751-2, 2000) **Challenge**

Fire in Their Eyes: Wildfires and the People Who Fight Them, by Karen Magnuson Beil (Harcourt, ISBN 0-152-01042-4, 1999) **Challenge**

Footprints on the Moon, by Alexandra Siy (Charlesbridge Publishing, ISBN 1-570-91409-5, 2001) **Challenge**

Franklin D. Roosevelt, by Karen Bornemann Spies (Enslow Publishers, ISBN 0-766-01038-4, 1999) **Challenge**

Franklin D. Roosevelt: The Four-Term President, by Michael A. Schuman (Enslow Publishers, ISBN 0-894-90696-8, 1996) **Challenge**

A Garden of Thorns: My Memoir of Surviving World War II in France, by Roger De Anfrasio (Silk City Press, ISBN 0-965-44522-4, 2000) **Challenge**

The Good Fight: How World War II Was Won, by Stephen Ambrose (Atheneum Books for Young Readers, ISBN 0-689-84361-5, 2001) **Challenge**

The Great Depression in American History, by David K. Fremon (Enslow Publishers, ISBN 0-894-90881-2, 1997) **Challenge**

 Rosie the Riveter: Women Working on the Home Front in World War II, by Penny Coleman (Crown Publishers, Inc., ISBN 0-517-88567-0, 1998) **Challenge ALA Notable Book**

Sally Ride: Shooting for the Stars, by Jane Hurwitz (Ballantine Books, ISBN 0-449-90394-0, 1989) **Challenge**

Cold War: The American Crusade Against the Sovient Union and World Communism, 1945–1990, by James A. Warren (HarperCollins Children's, ISBN 0-688-10596-3, 1996) **Teacher reference**

Great Society to the Reagan Era: 1964–1993, by William Loren Katz (Raintree, ISBN 0-811-42919-9, 1993) **Teacher reference**

Last Days of Innocence: America at War, 1917–1918, by Meirion and Susie Harries (Vintage Books, ISBN 0-679-74376-6, 1998) **Teacher reference**

 Look for this symbol throughout the Teacher Edition to find **Award-Winning Selections.**

Main Idea and Details

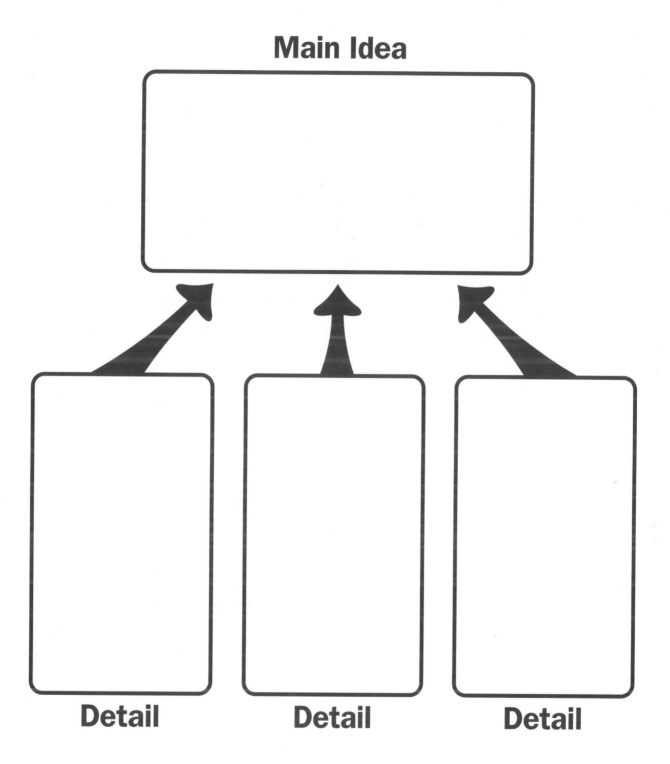

Main Idea

Detail   Detail   Detail

Sequence

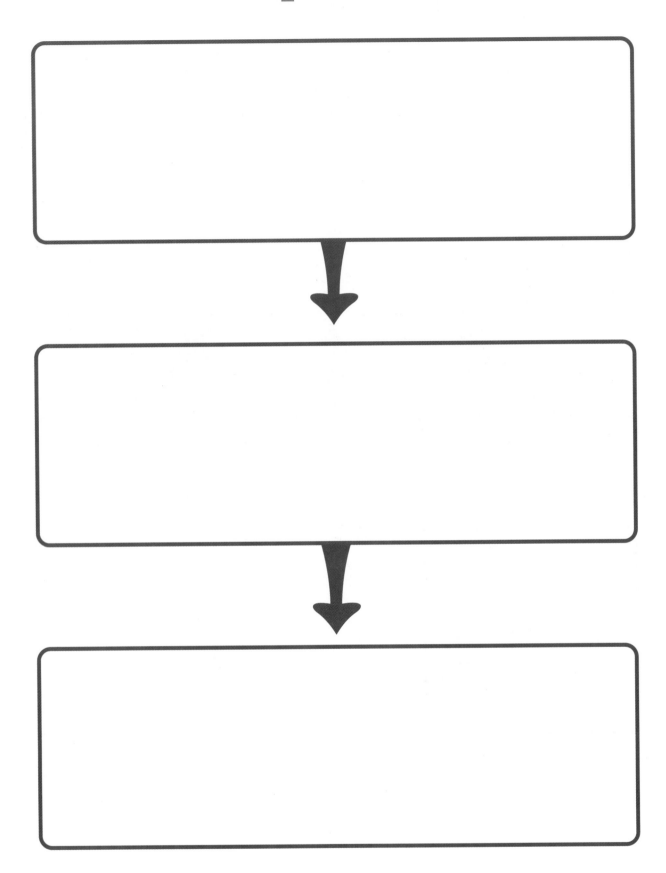

Cause and Effect

Cause   **Effect**

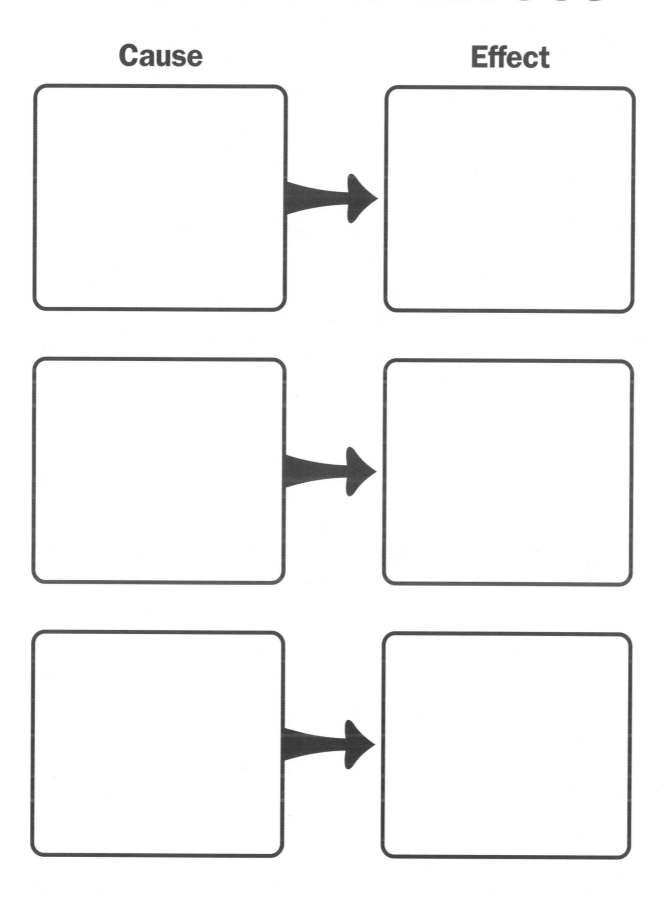

Compare and Contrast

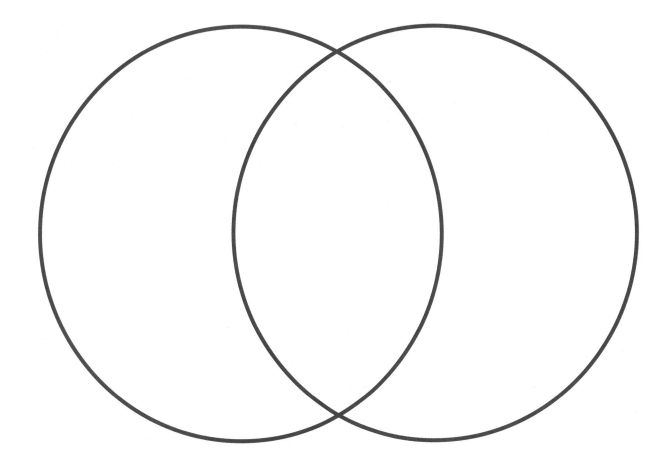

Compare and Contrast

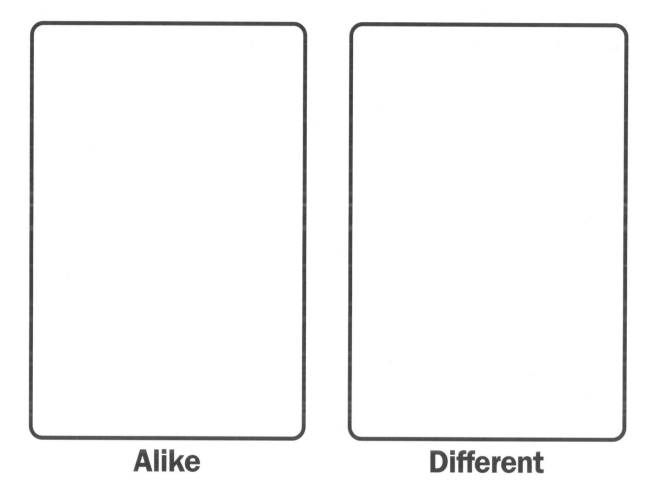

Alike

Different

kidspiration Find a 30-day Kidspiration trial at www.inspiration.com/sf.

Grade 5 • Graphic Organizers **TR61**

Summarize

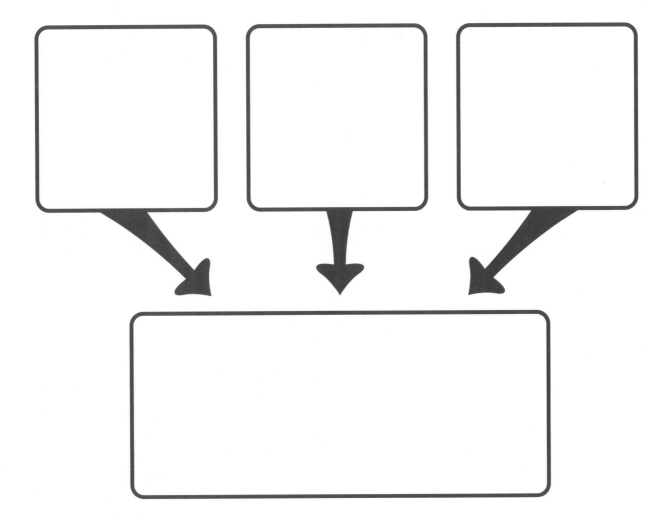

Draw Conclusions

Facts

Conclusion

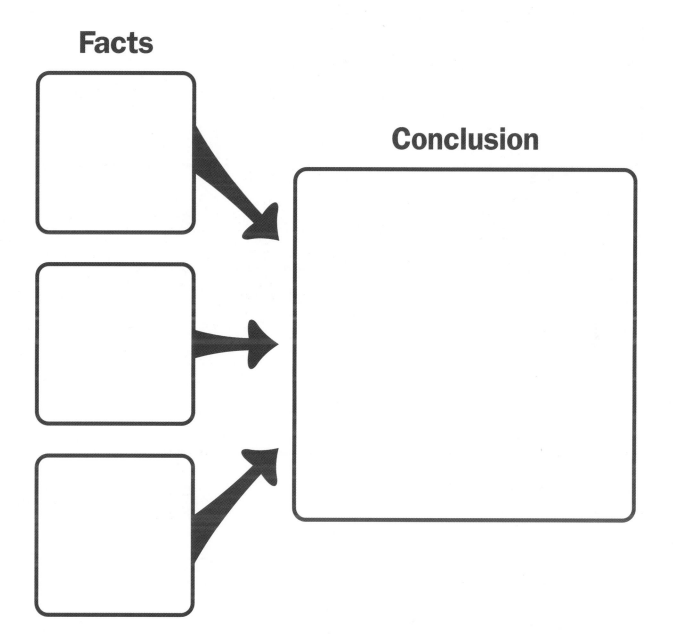

Make Generalizations

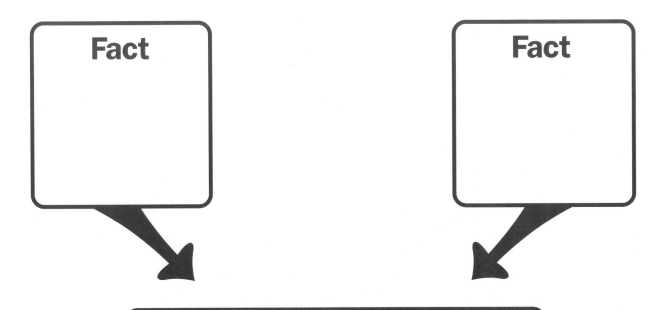

Fact

Fact

Generalization

Fact

Fact

K-W-L Chart

Topic _____

What We **K**now	What We **W**ant to Know	What We **L**earned

K-W-L Interactive Reading Strategy was developed and is reprinted by permission of Donna Ogle, National-Louis University, Evanston, Illinois.

Event Summary

Name of event _____

WHO? | Who was part of this event?

WHAT? | What happened?

WHEN? | When did this happen?

WHERE? | Where did this happen?

WHY? | Why did this happen?

Lesson Summary

Chapter_____ Lesson_____ Title_____

Section Title	Notes
Summary	

Section Title	Notes
Summary	

Section Title	Notes
Summary	

Section Title	Notes
Summary	

Categorize

Topic	Category 1	Category 2	Category 3	Category 4

Social Studies Daily Journal

Today I learned…

Some new words I learned…

One way this relates to me…

I would like to learn more about…

Current Event Organizer

Article Title _____

Article Source _____ Article Date _____
(magazine/newspaper title)

WHAT?

What is the issue or event?

TOPIC?

What is the article about?

WHY?

Why is the event taking place? Why is it important?

WHERE?

Where is the event taking place?

WHEN?

When did the event take place? Is it still going on?

WHO?

Who are the people involved?

My reaction to this issue/event:

kidspiration Find a 30-day Kidspiration trial at www.inspiration.com/sf.

Solve a Problem

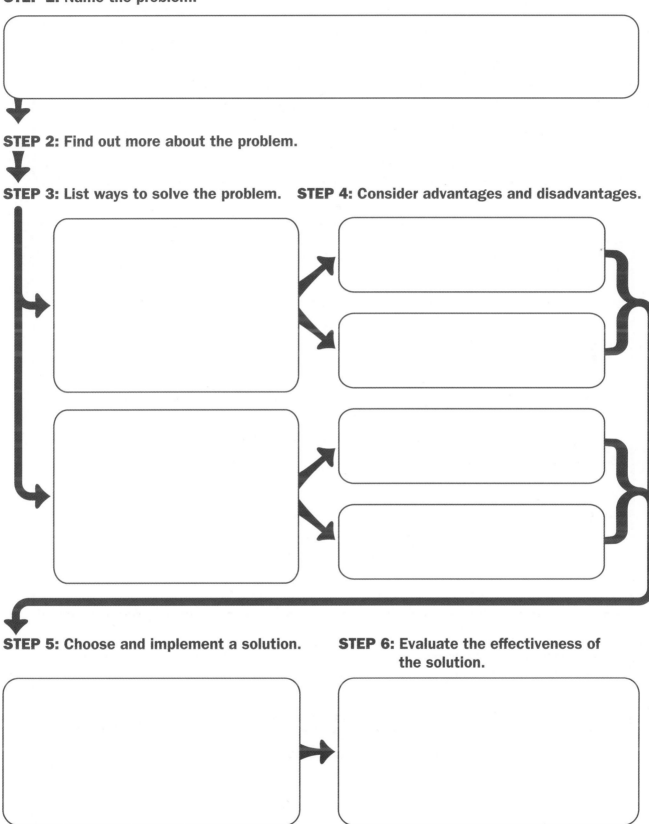

STEP 1: Name the problem.

STEP 2: Find out more about the problem.

STEP 3: List ways to solve the problem.   **STEP 4:** Consider advantages and disadvantages.

STEP 5: Choose and implement a solution.   **STEP 6:** Evaluate the effectiveness of
the solution.

© Scott Foresman

Vocabulary Organizer

Word	Definition

One thing I learned about this word…

Word	Definition

One thing I learned about this word…

Word	Definition

One thing I learned about this word…

Word	Definition

One thing I learned about this word…

Writing Organizer

Topic of Writing Piece	Audience	Purpose

Main Idea	Supporting Details

Transition Sentence

Main Idea	Supporting Details

Transition Sentence

Main Idea	Supporting Details

© Scott Foresman

kidspiration Find a 30-day Kidspiration trial at www.inspiration.com/sf.

Grade 5 ● Graphic Organizers **TR73**

Artifact Analysis

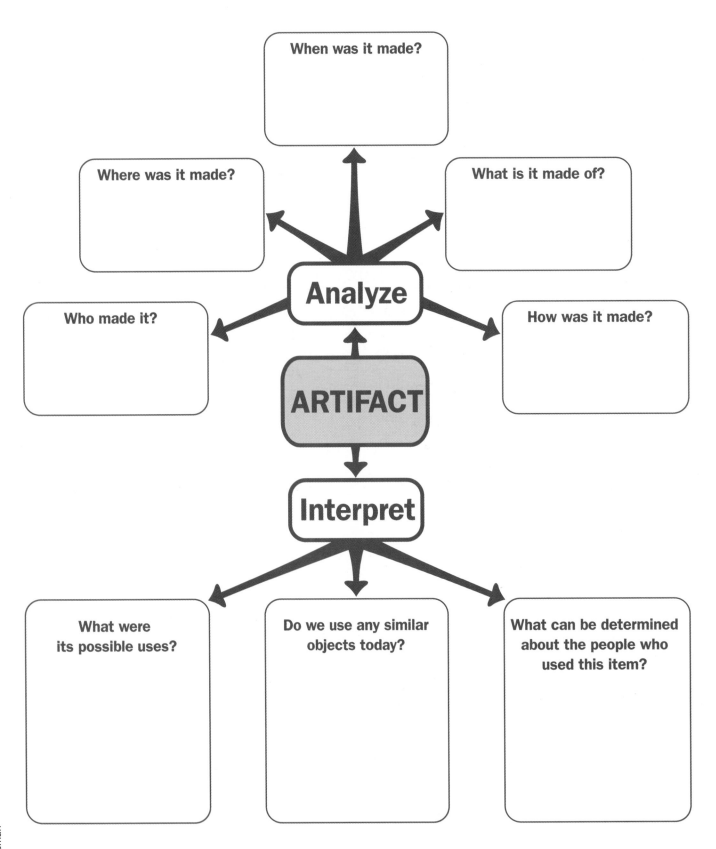

When was it made?

Where was it made?

What is it made of?

Analyze

Who made it?

How was it made?

ARTIFACT

Interpret

What were its possible uses?

Do we use any similar objects today?

What can be determined about the people who used this item?

kidspiration Find a 30-day Kidspiration trial at www.inspiration.com/sf.

Document Analysis

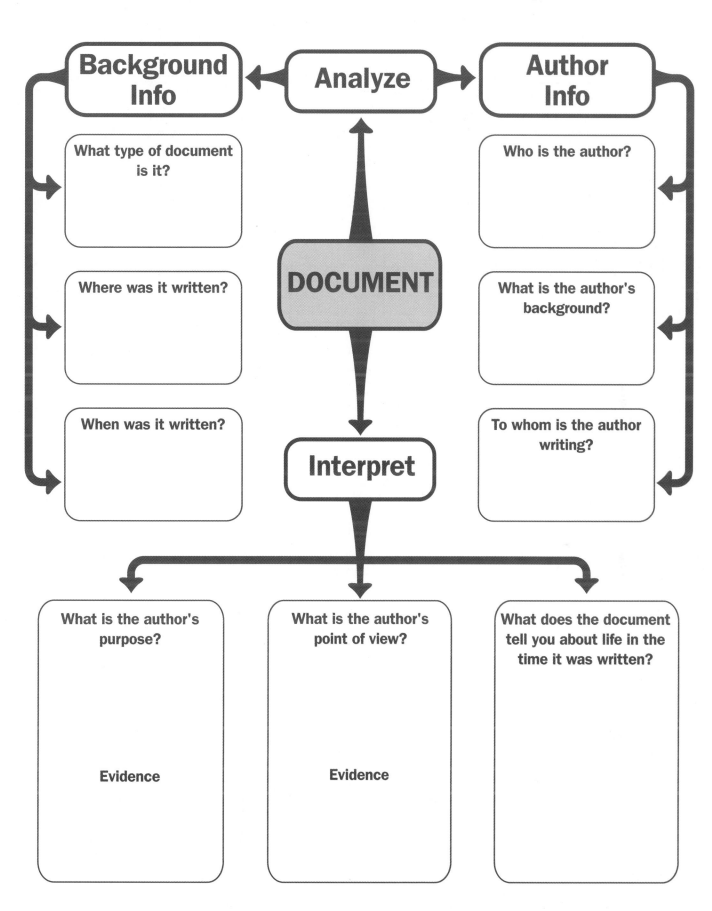

Background Info

Analyze

Author Info

What type of document is it?

Who is the author?

Where was it written?

DOCUMENT

What is the author's background?

When was it written?

Interpret

To whom is the author writing?

What is the author's purpose?

What is the author's point of view?

What does the document tell you about life in the time it was written?

Evidence

Evidence

Graph Paper

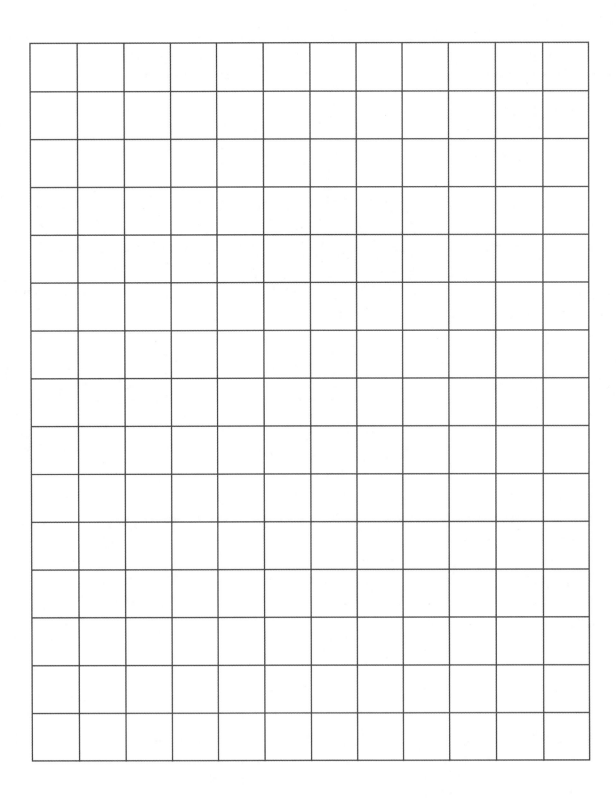

Time Line

kidspiration Find a 30-day Kidspiration trial at www.inspiration.com/sf.

Grade 5 • Graphic Organizers **TR77**

Grid

Name _____ Date _____

The World

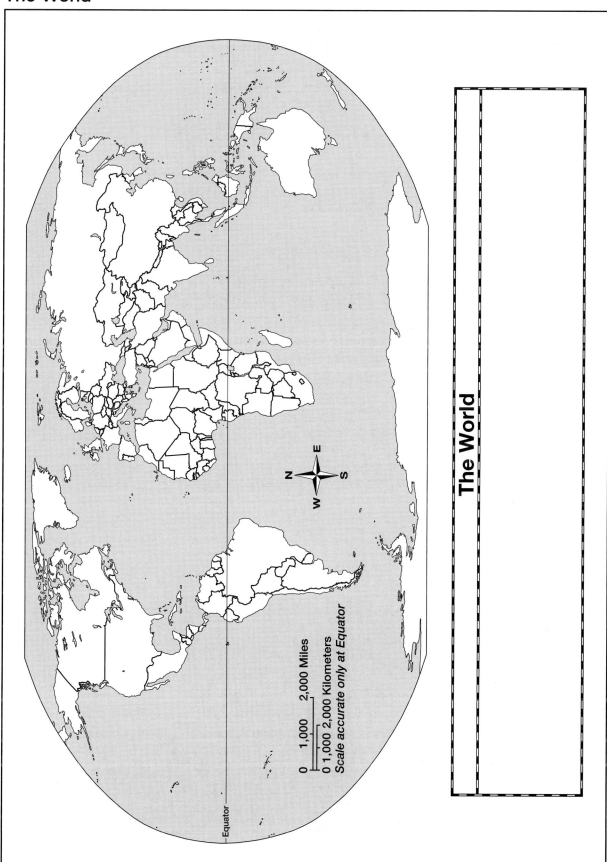

Name _____   Date _____

North America

0   250   500 Miles

0   250 500 Kilometers

North America

Name _____ Date _____

The United States

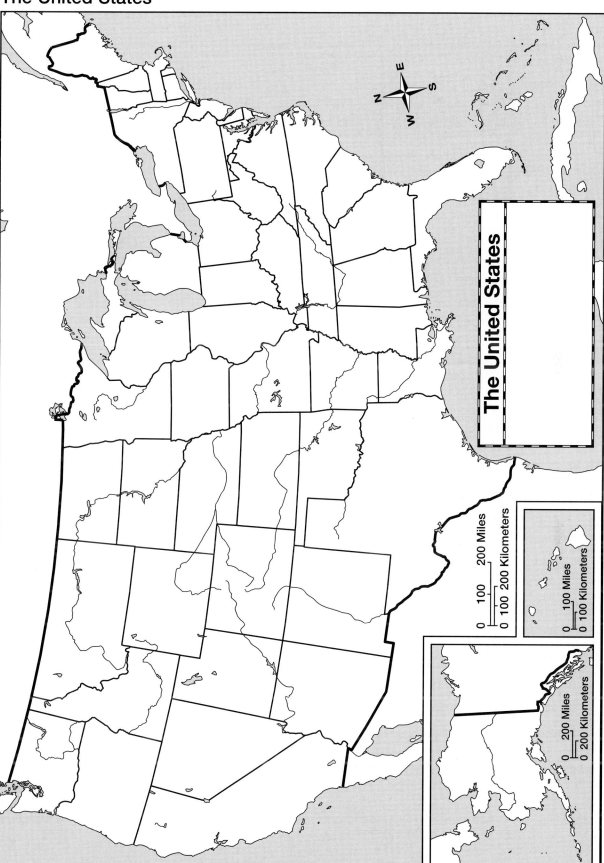

The United States

200 Miles

100

0   100   200 Kilometers

100 Miles

0   100 Kilometers

200 Miles

0   200 Kilometers

Calendar

Sunday	Monday	Tuesday	Wednesday	Thursday	Friday	Saturday

kidspiration Find a 30-day Kidspiration trial at www.inspiration.com/sf.

Index

Index

Index

Index

Index

Workbook

Writing

Credits

Maps:

MapQuest.com, Inc.

Illustrations:

193H Matt Straub

Photographs:

Every effort has been made to secure permission and provide appropriate credit for photographic material. The publisher deeply regrets any omission and pledges to correct errors called to its attention in subsequent editions.

Unless otherwise acknowledged, all photographs are the property of Scott Foresman, a division of Pearson Education.

Photo locators denoted as follows: Top (T), Center (C), Bottom (B), Left (L), Right (R), Background (Bkgd)

Cover: ©Mitchell Funk/Getty Images, ©Steve Allen/Getty Images, ©Jeff Hunter/Getty Images, Todd Gipstein/NGS Image Collection, ©Cameron Heryet/Getty Images; **Endsheets:** ©Mitchell Funk/Getty Images, Steve Allen/Getty Images; **Front Matter:** SF4 Smithsonian Institution; SF6 Lexington Historical Society; SF12 ©Everett Johnson/Getty Images; **Overview:** 1A SuperStock; 1C The Madam Walker Urban Life Center/photographed by William Russell/From the Walker Collection of A'Lelia Bundles; 1H Getty Images; **Unit 1:** 45A David David Gallery, Philadelphia/SuperStock; 45B North Wind Picture Archives; 45C Scott Polar Institute/©Dorling Kindersley; 45D Reinhard Brucker/Westwind Enterprises; 45H

The Granger Collection; 52A The Lowe Art Museum, The University of Miami/SuperStock; 52B Robert Frerck/Odyssey Productions ; 74A Marine Corps/Department of Defense; 74B ©2001, Mashantucket Pequot Museum & Research Center, All rights reserved; 100A ©Ira Rubin/Getty Images ; 100B Archive Photos; **Unit 2:** 125A ©Bettmann/Corbis; 125B ©Hulton/Getty Images; 125C ©Dorling Kindersley; 125D British Museum/©Dorling Kindersley; 125H Pilgrim Society; 132A The Granger Collection; 132B Royal Museum of Scotland/©Dorling Kindersley; 154A Pilgrim Society; 154B Courtesy of the Edward E. Ayer Collection/Newberry Library, Chicago; **Unit 3:** 193A The Granger Collection; 193B North Wind Picture Archives; 193C North Wind Picture Archives; 193D British Museum; 200A IT Stock International/Index Stock Imagery; 200B South Carolina Historical Society; 230A Stock Montage; 230B North Wind Picture Archives; **Unit 4:** 259A Lexington Historical Society; 259B SuperStock; 259C Manuscripts & Archives Division/New York Public Library, Astor, Lenox and Tilden Foundations; 259D The Granger Collection; 259H Bedford Free Public Library; 266A Collection of Guilford Courthouse National Military Park, NC; 266B Library of Congress; 294A SuperStock; 294B North Wind Picture Archives; **Unit 5:** 329A The Granger Collection; 329B Smithsonian Institution; 329C SuperStock; 329D ©Bettmann/Corbis; 329H SuperStock; 336A SuperStock; 336B R. Kord/H. Armstrong Roberts; 360A Culver Pictures, Inc.; 360B The Granger Collection; **Unit 6:** 393A The Granger Collection; 393B North Wind Picture Archives; 393D SuperStock; 400A Archive Photos; 400B Culver Pictures

Inc.; 428A ©C Squared Studios/Getty Images; 428B Corbis; **Unit 7:** 455A The Granger Collection; 455C Corbis; 455D North Wind Picture Archives; 455H Library of Congress; 462A The Granger Collection; 462B ©Richard Hamilton Smith/Corbis; 490A Harper's Weekly, November 16, 1867; 490B Corbis; **Unit 8:** 529A From the Original painting by Mort Künstler, "First View of the Lady" ©1986 Mort Künstler, Inc.; 529B ©E.O. Hoppé/Corbis; 529C The Granger Collection; 529D The Granger Collection; 536A The Granger Collection; 560A The Granger Collection; 560B Smithsonian Institution; **Unit 9:** 593A Identikal/Artville; 593B Charles Bonnay/Black Star; 593C ©Hulton Archive/Getty Images; 593D Chris Niedenthal/Black Star; 600A ©Bettmann/Corbis; 600B The Granger Collection; 634A AP/Wide World; 634B ©Hulton Archive/Getty Images; End Matter; TR1 Getty Images; TR19 Corbis; TR22 Getty Images; TR23 ©Bettmann/Corbis; TR27 ©Bettmann/Corbis; TR28 Corbis; TR30 Getty Images; TR61 Hallogram Publishing ; TR63 Hallogram Publishing; TR65 Hallogram Publishing; TR47 Courtesy Lehmann's Antique Advertising & Collectibles; TR48 Werner Forman/Art Resource, NY; TR49 Steven Lunetta/PhotoEdit; TR50 The Granger Collection; TR51 Colonial Williamsburg Foundation; TR52 North Wind Picture Archives; TR53 ©Bettmann/Corbis; TR54 ©Tria Giovan/Corbis; TR55 The Granger Collection; **End Matter:** T25 Corbis; T28 Getty Images; T29 ©Bettmann/Corbis; T33 ©Bettmann/Corbis; T34 Corbis; T36 Getty Images

Notes

Notes

Notes

Notes

Notes

Notes

Notes

Notes

Notes

Notes

Notes